Fodor

Great Britain

PRAISE FOR FODOR'S GUIDES

"Fodor's guides . . . are an admirable blend of the cultural and the practical."
—The Washington Post

"Researched by people chosen because they lived or have lived in the country, well-written, and with good historical sections . . . Obligatory reading for millions of tourists."
—The Independent, *London*

"Usable, sophisticated restaurant coverage, with an emphasis on good value."
—Andy Birsh, Gourmet restaurant columnist, quoted by Gannett News Service

"Packed with dependable information."
—Atlanta Journal Constitution

"Fodor's always delivers high quality . . . thoughtfully presented . . . thorough."
—Houston Post

"Valuable because of their comprehensiveness."
—Minneapolis Star-Tribune

Fodor's Travel Publications, Inc.
New York • Toronto • London • Sydney • Auckland

Fodor's Great Britain

Editor: David Low
Area Editor: Richard Moore
Contributors: Robert Blake, Jules Brown, Samantha Cook, Janet Foley, Echo Garrett, Bevin McLaughlin, Mary Ellen Schultz, Kate Sekules, Gilbert Summers, Roger Thomas, Nancy van Itallie
Creative Director: Fabrizio La Rocca
Cartographers: David Lindroth, Maryland Cartographics
Illustrator: Karl Tanner
Cover Photograph: Bob Krist

Design: Vignelli Associates

Special Sales

Contents

Foreword *vii*

Highlights '95 *x*

Fodor's Choice *xiii*

Introduction *xxiv*

1 Essential Information *1*

Before You Go *2*

Government Tourist Offices *2*
Tours and Packages *2*
When to Go *5*
Festivals and Seasonal Events *6*
What to Pack *8*
Taking Money Abroad *9*
Getting Money from Home *9*
British Currency *10*
What It Will Cost *10*
Long-Distance Calling *11*
Passports and Visas *11*
Customs and Duties *11*
Traveling with Cameras, Camcorders, and Laptops *13*
Insurance *14*
Car Rentals *15*
Rail Passes *16*
Student and Youth Travel *17*
Traveling with Children *18*
Hints for Travelers with Disabilities *19*
Hints for Older Travelers *20*
Hints for Gay and Lesbian Travelers *21*
Further Reading *22*

Arriving and Departing *23*

From North America by Plane *23*
From North America by Ship *25*

Staying in Britain *26*

Getting Around *26*
Telephones *30*
Mail *31*
Tipping *31*
Opening and Closing Times *31*
Museums, Stately Homes, and Castles *32*
Guides *33*
Shopping *33*
Sports and the Outdoors *34*
Dining *35*
Lodging *36*

Credit Cards *37*
The Performing Arts *37*

Great Itineraries *41*

2 Portraits of Great Britain *45*

Great Britain at a Glance: A Chronology *46*
Kings and Queens *50*
The Basics of British Architecture *52*

3 London *57*

4 The Southeast *124*
Canterbury, Dover, Brighton, Tunbridge Wells

5 The South *156*
Winchester, Salisbury, Stonehenge

6 The Southwest *186*
Somerset, Devon, Cornwall

7 The Channel Islands *216*
Guernsey, Jersey

8 The Thames Valley *232*
Windsor, Henley-on-Thames, Oxford

9 The Heart of England *257*
Stratford-upon-Avon, the Cotswolds, the Forest of Dean,
Bath, Bristol, Birmingham

10 East Anglia *294*
Bury St. Edmunds, Cambridge, Norwich, Lincoln

11 The Welsh Borders *334*
Worcester, Hereford, Shrewsbury, Chester

12 Wales *358*

13 The Northwest and Lake District *392*
Manchester, Liverpool, Blackpool,
and Lake District National Park

14 The Peaks and Yorkshire Moors *431*
Buxton, Bradford, Haworth, York, Scarborough, and Leeds

15 The Northeast *462*
Durham, Hexham, Berwick-upon-Tweed

16 Scotland: Edinburgh and the Borders *488*

17 Scotland: Southwest and Highlands *513*

Index *548*

Maps

Great Britain *xviii–xix*
Europe *xx–xxi*
World Time Zones *xxii–xxiii*
London Underground *60*
London *66–67*
London Shopping *96–97*
London Dining *104–105*
London Lodging *114–115*
The Southeast *128–129*
Canterbury *131*
Brighton *138*
The South *160–161*
Winchester *162*
Salisbury *168*
The Southwest *190–191*
Plymouth *202*
The Channel Islands *221*
St. Helier *222*
St. Peter Port *225*
Thames Valley *236–237*
Windsor Castle *238*
Oxford *244*
The Shakespeare Zone and the Cotswolds *261*
Stratford-upon-Avon *263*
Birmingham *268*
The Forest of Dean and Bath Environs *274–275*
Bath *278*
East Anglia *298–299*
Cambridge *301*
Norwich *310*
Lincoln Region *317*
The Welsh Borders *338*
Shrewsbury *344*
Wales *364–365*
Aberystwyth *373*
The Northwest *399*
Manchester *400*
The Lake District *404–405*
Buxton and the Peak District *436*
Yorkshire and the Dales *440–441*
York *444*
Scarborough and the North York Moors *451*
The Northeast *467*

Durham *468*
The Scottish Borders *493*
Edinburgh *494*
Southwest Scotland and the Western Highlands *518–519*
Glasgow *521*
The Inverness Area *531*

Foreword

While every care has been taken to ensure the accuracy of the information in this guide, the passage of time will always bring change, and consequently, the publisher cannot accept responsibility for errors that may occur.

All prices and opening times quoted here are based on information supplied to us at press time. Hours and admission fees may change, however, and the prudent traveler will avoid inconvenience by calling ahead.

Fodor's wants to hear about your travel experiences, both pleasant and unpleasant. When a hotel or restaurant fails to live up to its billing, let us know and we will investigate the complaint and revise our entries where the facts warrant it.

Send your letters to the editors of Fodor's Travel Publications, 201 East 50th Street, New York, NY 10022.

For Richard Moore

In fond appreciation of your 20 years of contributions to Fodor's guides, your grace in the face of deadlines, and your abundant good humor.

Highlights'95 and Fodor's Choice

Highlights '95

The often-delayed **Channel Tunnel** opened for cars, trucks, buses, and motorcycles in May 1994, ending Britain's age-old isolation from the Continent. Passenger train service began in 1994 between London and Paris and London and Brussels. For more details, *see* Getting Around in Chapter 1.

The **British telephone system** is constantly in a state of flux, as it is modernized and brought into line with international practice. Only a few years ago the area code in London was changed to 071 and 081. **The latest big development is scheduled to happen in April 1995, when all the numbers in the country will change their area codes,** including London all over again. The new change will consist of the insertion of a "1" after the initial "0." London's area code will therefore become 0171 and 0181. The only exceptions to this countrywide system are scheduled to occur in the five cities of Bristol, Leicester, Leeds, Nottingham, and Sheffield, whose area codes will change according to a different system. British Telecom plans to have messages telling you how the new system works, and how these five cities' telephone numbers differ from the rest of the country.

The number of tourists visiting **historic properties in Britain** is still on the rise, despite the recession. Seven historic properties had visitor increases of more than 20%, with Penshurst Place in Kent and Little Moreton Hall in Cheshire both up 34%, and the Cabinet War Rooms in London 21% more. The top 10 historic properties charging admission were: the Tower of London; St. Paul's, London; Roman Baths and Pump Room, Bath; Windsor Castle; Warwick Castle; Stonehenge; Hampton Court Palace; Shakespeare's Birthplace, Stratford; Blenheim Palace; and Leeds Castle, Kent. London's Savoy Hotel, a great favorite with U.S. guests, counts its ever-increasing popularity with stateside tourists in turkeys. It had to provide guests with 743 such birds for Christmas 1993, 129 more than the year before.

The National Trust celebrates its centenary in 1995. It was founded in 1895 to work for the preservation of places of historic interest or natural beauty in England, Wales, and Northern Ireland. Today the Trust is the largest private landowner and conservation society in Britain. Apart from its dozens of stately homes, more than 570,000 acres belong to the Trust—140,000 acres of fell, dale, lake, and forest are managed by the establishment in the Lake District alone. Many celebratory events will be staged in 1995 at the Trust's properties.

The **Promenade Concerts** program had its 100th season in 1994. Organized for many years by the BBC, the concerts are broadcast all over the world, and the rumbustious "Last Night of the Proms" has become one of the major events in the British artistic calendar. The concerts are staged every night for six summer weeks, mostly at London's Royal Albert Hall, with international orchestras and soloists taking part.

Since 1967, the Crown Jewels had been displayed in the cramped conditions of the old subterranean Jewel House in the **Tower of London.** The Tower has always been one of the most popular tourist venues in Britain, currently attracting more than 2 million visitors a year. The old Jewel House was originally designed to handle 5,000 visitors a day, but had to cope recently with more than three times that number at peak periods. Visitors often had to wait patiently in line for more than two hours to see the regalia. By moving part of the Armouries Collection from the Tower to Leeds, space was freed to create a new Jewel House at a cost of more than £10 million. It was opened to the public in March 1994.

Visitors are now carried past the more important pieces on moving walkways and those wishing to linger can do so on a raised platform. (The planners studied the control of crowd flow in, among other places, Disney World.) The new exhibition space employs the latest display techniques—the rooms are dimly lit; wafer-thin, bullet-proof glass creates the illusion that there is no glass at all; and fiber optics carry pencils of light to key parts of each item. The jewels are more spread out than before, and many of them are now shown in separate cases, so they are much more easily viewed than in the higgledy-piggledy conditions of their former, cramped space. To prove that it is the regalia of a working monarchy that is on display, every so often a crown will be missing, replaced by a card that says "in use."

Near Bankside Power Station, the **Shakespeare Globe Theater,** ambitious dream scheme of the late lamented American movie director and entrepreneur Sam Wanamaker, is slated to open in April 1995, although funds are still needed. You can purchase a permanent London home for your name by donating £300 to the project, for which you will be thanked with an inscribed flagstone in the surrounding piazza.

On the Thames, riverfront excitement is imminent on the South Bank, east of Westminster Bridge, at **County Hall,** the former home of the much missed Greater London Council. The structure is now halfway through its conversion into something London needs desperately—a grand hotel on the Thames. The city may take no credit for this development, however, since the project is Japanese. Not only will the giant 570-bedroom hotel have the finest views in town—overlooking Westminster Bridge and the Houses of Parliament (with which even the Savoy's beautiful-but-pricey Riverview Suites cannot compete)—but the developers, Shirayama, are proposing a bargain £90/night rack rate, for which you get a health club with pool, a children's center, conference facilities, and no fewer than six restaurants thrown in. The opening is slated for 1996, by which time **Westminster Bridge** should be about halfway through its £8 million restoration. The construction, of course, will play havoc with one of London's favorite sights, not to mention its traffic flow.

May 1994 saw the opening of **Glyndebourne's new opera house.** The first work to be staged was Mozart's *Marriage of Figaro*, the same opera that opened the old theater in 1934. But there the echoes of the past ended. The new house is much bigger. Gone is the genteel "let's stage an opera in the village hall" atmosphere of the former theater. In its place, there is now a large, modern house with 1,200 seats, instead of 830. Gone, too, is the pokey little stage with its totally inadequate backstage area. Now a large main stage has two side stages and a huge backstage area that can house all the season's scenery. A full-size rehearsal stage lies at the back of the building. The horse-shoe-shaped auditorium is clad in seasoned wood—pitch pine rescued from Victorian warehouses—with wooden floors and seat frames. The upholstery is charcoal, the stage curtain and proscenium arch are black, and the lighting is subtle and luminous as candlelight. Even though the design is thoroughly modern, the new hall gives the impression of being a mellow old theater, stripped of any red plush or golden glitter, whose quiet color scheme allows the eye to concentrate on the stage.

The rebuilding has cost £33 million, all of it raised from corporate and private donations, not a penny from the state, and the work was completed on time, a thing almost unheard of in today's Britain. The considerable increase in audience capacity has resulted in a restructure of seat prices. Top price is now £100, but there are seats as low as £15 (restricted view), with standing room available for the first time at £10. For the first few seasons, though, seats are going to be hard to get, as British music lovers flock to see the new theater. Glyndebourne, with it's much larger facilities, should now be able to present works that were simply not possible in the confined spaces of the old theater.

Queens Moat Houses is currently Britain's third biggest hotel chain. It has 189 prestigious hotels in Britain and Europe, among them **The Royal Crescent** in **Bath,** and the five-star **Caledonian** in **Edinburgh.** In 1993 and 1994 it found itself with a £1.3 billion debt, partly caused by a valuation farce on its noted properties. Not only had the holdings of the chain been grossly overvalued, but the shareholders in the company were furious at the size of the incentive arrangements certain executives of the group were being awarded. Most of the directors resigned and a trade department investigation was underway. While the battle raged, the Caledonian serenely celebrated its 90th birthday. When it opened its doors in 1903 its telegraphic address was *Luxury, Edinburgh.*

Manchester's failure to capture the Olympic Games for 2000 (it lost out to Sydney, Australia) didn't dampen the city's enthusiasm for regeneration. The new transportation links, sports, and leisure facilities that formed part of the city's Olympic bid are all up and running, making the city an even more pleasant place to visit. In addition, the city should be proud of its new first-class hotel—the Victoria and Albert—which has already garnered numerous awards.

Fodor's Choice

Although no two people ever agree on what makes a perfect vacation, it's always fun to find out what others think. Here are a few choice ideas to enhance your visit to Britain. For more details, refer to the appropriate chapter.

Scenery

Aira Force Waterfalls (*see* Northwest and Lake District)

Bwlch y Groes—Pass of the Cross (*see* Wales)

Ceiriog Valley (*see* Wales)

Countryside seen from the Fort William–Mallaig railroad (*see* Scotland: Southwest and Highlands)

Forest of Dean (*see* Heart of England)

Trossachs (*see* Scotland: Southwest and Highlands)

Stately Homes

Blenheim Palace (*see* Thames Valley)

Castle Howard (*see* Peaks and Yorkshire Moors)

Chatsworth (*see* Peaks and Yorkshire Moors)

Cragside (*see* Northeast)

Holkham Hall (*see* East Anglia)

Ightham Mote (*see* Southeast)

Petworth (*see* Southeast)

Powis Castle (*see* Wales)

Restaurants

Bibendum—London (*$$$$*)

Café du Moulin—Guernsey, *see* Channel Islands (*$$*)

The Carved Angel—Dartmouth, *see* Southwest (*$$$*)

Chewton Glen—New Milton, *see* South (*$$$*)

Croque en Bouche—Malvern, *see* Welsh Borders (*$$$*)

Horn of Plenty—Tavistock, *see* Southwest (*$$*)

The Ivy—London (*$$$*)

Landgate Bistro—Rye, *see* Southeast (*$$*)

Le Manoir aux Quat' Saisons—Great Milton,
see Thames Valley (*$$$$*)

Lock 16 (Crinan Hotel)—Crinan, *see* Scotland: Southwest and Highlands (*$$$*)

Longueville Manor—Jersey, *see* Channel Islands (*$$$$*)

L'Ortolan—Shinfield, *see* Thames Valley (*$$$*)

Lou Pescadou—London (*$$*)

Martin's Restaurant—Edinburgh, *see* Scotland: Edinburgh and the Borders (*$$*)

Miller Howe—Windermere, *see* Northwest and Lake District (*$$$$*)

Penrhos Court—Kington, *see* Welsh Borders (*$$–$$$*)

Plas Bodegroes—Pwllheli, *see* Wales (*$$–$$$*)

Le Talbooth—Dedham, *see* East Anglia (*$$$*)

Thornbury Castle—Thornbury, *see* Heart of England (*$$$$*)

The Yew Tree—Seatoller, *see* Northwest and Lake District (*$*)

Hotels

Bodysgallen Hall—Llandudno, *see* Wales (*$$$$*)

Buckland Manor—Buckland, *see* Heart of England (*$$$$*)

Caledonian Hotel—Edinburgh, *see* Scotland: Edinburgh and the Borders (*$$$*)

Castle Coombe Manor House—Charingworth, *see* Heart of England (*$$$$*)

Castle Hotel—Taunton, *see* Southwest (*$$$*)

Crabwall Manor—Chester, *see* Welsh Borders (*$$$*)

Dorset Square—London (*$$$*)

—The Dorchester—London (*$$$$*)

Ettington Park—Stratford-upon-Avon, *see* Heart of England (*$$$$*)

The Gore—London (*$$$*)

Greywalls—Gullane, *see* Scotland: Edinburgh and the Borders (*$$$*)

Hazlitt's—London (*$$*)

Horsted Place—Uckfield, *see* Southeast (*$$$$*)

Lamperts Cottage—Dorchester, *see* South (*$*)

Langley Castle Hotel—Hexham, *see* Northeast (*$$–$$$*)

Middlethorpe Hall—York, *see* Peaks and Yorkshire Moors (*$$$$*)

Portledge Hotel—Fairy Cross, *see* Southwest (*$$*)

Portobello—London (*$$*)

Queensberry Hotel—Bath (*$$$*)

Regency House—Cheltenham, *see* Heart of England (*$–$$*)

Rising Sun—Lynmouth, *see* Southwest (*$$*)

— The Savoy—London (*$$$$*)

Ty Mawr Country Hotel—Brechfa, *see* Wales (*$$*)

Cathedrals and Churches

Canterbury Cathedral (*see* Southeast)

Durham Cathedral (*see* Northeast)

Gloucester Cathedral (*see* Heart of England)

King's College Chapel (*see* East Anglia)

St. David's Cathedral (*see* Wales)

Salisbury Cathedral (*see* South)

Westminster Abbey (*see* London)

York Minster (*see* Peaks and Yorkshire Moors)

Castles

Berkeley (*see* Heart of England)

Caernarfon (*see* Wales)

Cardiff (*see* Wales)

Dunstanburgh (*see* Northeast)

Edinburgh (*see* Scotland: Edinburgh and the Borders)

Harlech (*see* Wales)

Stirling (*see* Scotland: Southwest and Highlands)

Tower of London (*see* London)

Warwick (*see* Heart of England)

Gardens

Bodnant (*see* Wales)

Hidcote Manor (*see* Heart of England)

Kew (*see* London)

Levens Hall (*see* Northwest and Lake District)

Stourhead (*see* South)

Threave (*see* Scotland: Southwest and Highlands)

Ancient Stones

Avebury (*see* South)

Barrow-in-Furness Abbey (*see* Northwest and Lake District)

Fountains Abbey (*see* Peaks and Yorkshire Moors)

Jedburgh Abbey (*see* Scotland: Edinburgh and the Borders)

Rievaulx Abbey (*see* Peaks and Yorkshire Moors)

Stanton Drew Circles (*see* Heart of England)

Stonehenge (*see* South)

Whitby Abbey (*see* Peaks and Yorkshire Moors)

Towns and Villages

Bath (*see* Heart of England)

Cambridge (*see* East Anglia)

Ewelme (*see* Thames Valley)

Knutsford (*see* Welsh Borders)

Lavenham (*see* East Anglia)

Portmeirion (*see* Wales)

Rye (*see* Southeast)

York (*see* Peaks and Yorkshire Moors)

Museums and Galleries

British Museum (*see* London)

Burrell Collection, Glasgow
(*see* Scotland: Southwest and Highlands)

Corinium Museum, Cirencester (*see* Heart of England)

Fitzwilliam Museum, Cambridge (*see* East Anglia)

Ironbridge Gorge Museum, Ironbridge (*see* Welsh Borders)

Jorvik Viking Centre, York (*see* Peaks and Yorkshire Moors)

Montacute House (*see* Southwest)

Museum of the Moving Image (*see* London)

National Gallery of Scotland
(*see* Scotland: Edinburgh and the Borders)

Queen's Gallery (*see* London)

Welsh Folk Museum (*see* Wales)

Times to Treasure

Sunset from the Mull of Kintyre

A boat ride on Lake Windermere

Champagne at the Henley Regatta

The Edinburgh Tattoo on a fine night

The view of Stonehenge on a stormy evening

Searching for a bargain in London's Portobello market—and finding one!

Going to a Prom Concert at the Royal Albert Hall on a very popular night

A summer trip on the Fort William–Mallaig railroad

A walk along the battlements of Harlech Castle

Great Britain

N

SHETLAND ISLANDS
Unst
Yell
Mainland
Lerwick

ORKNEY ISLANDS
Mainland
Kirkwall
Hoy

North Sea

ATLANTIC OCEAN

ORKNEY ISLANDS
Thurso
John O'Groats
Wick
Dornoch
Ullapool
Stornoway
Lewis
Harris
OUTER HEBRIDES
North Uist
South Uist
Portree
Skye
Kyle of Lochalsh
Loch Ness
Inverness
Aviemore
Braemar
Fort William
Oban
Callander
Coll
Tiree
Mull
INNER HEBRIDES
Islay
Arran
Campbeltown
Stranraer
Bangor
Belfast
Londonderry
NORTHERN IRELAND
Portadown

SCOTLAND
Banff
Peterhead
Aberdeen
Montrose
Dundee
Firth of Tay
St. Andrew's
Firth of Forth
Perth
Stirling
Dunfermline
Edinburgh
Glasgow
Greenock
Lanark
Kilmarnock
Ayr
Dumfries
Kirkcudbright

Berwick-on-Tweed
Newcastle
Sunderland
Middlesbrough
Whitby
Durham
Carlisle
Keswick

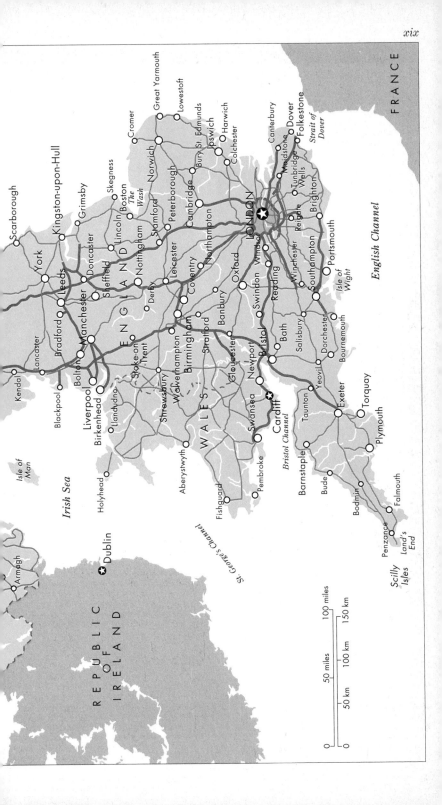

World Time Zones

Numbers below vertical bands relate each zone to Greenwich Mean Time (0 hrs.).
Local times frequently differ from these general indications,
as indicated by light-face numbers on map.

Algiers, **29**	Berlin, **34**	Delhi, **48**	Istanbul, **40**
Anchorage, **3**	Bogotá, **19**	Denver, **8**	Jerusalem, **42**
Athens, **41**	Budapest, **37**	Djakarta, **53**	Johannesburg, **44**
Auckland, **1**	Buenos Aires, **24**	Dublin, **26**	Lima, **20**
Baghdad, **46**	Caracas, **22**	Edmonton, **7**	Lisbon, **28**
Bangkok, **50**	Chicago, **9**	Hong Kong, **56**	London (Greenwich), **27**
Beijing, **54**	Copenhagen, **33**	Honolulu, **2**	Los Angeles, **6**
	Dallas, **10**		Madrid, **38**
			Manila, **57**

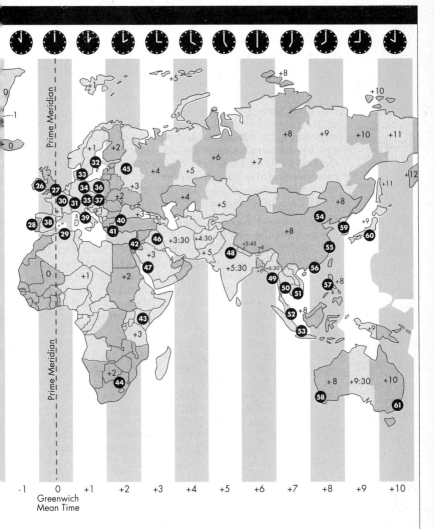

Mecca, **47**
Mexico City, **12**
Miami, **18**
Montréal, **15**
Moscow, **45**
Nairobi, **43**
New Orleans, **11**
New York City, **16**

Ottawa, **14**
Paris, **30**
Perth, **58**
Reykjavík, **25**
Rio de Janeiro, **23**
Rome, **39**
Saigon (Ho Chi Minh City), **51**

San Francisco, **5**
Santiago, **21**
Seoul, **59**
Shanghai, **55**
Singapore, **52**
Stockholm, **32**
Sydney, **61**
Tokyo, **60**

Toronto, **13**
Vancouver, **4**
Vienna, **35**
Warsaw, **36**
Washington, D.C., **17**
Yangon, **49**
Zürich, **31**

Introduction

The British are different, and proud of it. They still have odd customs, like driving on the left and playing cricket. Only reluctantly have they decimalized, turning their cherished pints into liters (except when ordering beer) and inches into centimeters. Until 1971 they still had a bizarre three-tier nondecimal coinage, whereby a meal check might add up, say, to four pounds six shillings and sevenpence halfpenny (today that would translate as £4.33). And although the rest of Europe counts distances in kilometers, the British still cling to their miles—though they now buy material in meters, not yards. Logic is not a prominent feature of the British character.

These are symptoms of a certain psychological gulf still existing between Britain and the rest of Europe, a gulf not greatly narrowed by its membership in the European Union since 1973. The English Channel, a mere 22 miles of water between Dover and Calais, has played a crucial role in British history, acting as a kind of moat to protect the "island fortress" from invaders (witness 1940), and preserving a separate mentality. Many Britons want to keep that moat, hence their wariness—more emotional than economic—of the Channel Tunnel. It is difficult to estimate just how the opening of the tunnel will eventually affect the British psyche. They have resisted integration into Europe for so many centuries, that the reality of a link open for 24 hours a day, whatever the weather, may well be traumatic. Even today, that oft-quoted old newspaper headline, "Fog in Channel, Continent isolated," retains some validity. But this proud and insular nation is not unwelcoming to visitors. On its own terms, it is glad to show them the delights and virtues of what it believes to be one of the most genuinely civilized societies in the world.

There is still some truth in the popular foreign perception that the British are reserved. They are given to understatement— "It's not bad" is the nearest a Briton may get to showing enthusiasm—and may look a little solemn and stiff-upper-lipped, because they don't easily show their emotions. But they are not on the whole unhappy, even in today's anxious times. (In fact, an international Gallup survey showed that far more people in Britain than in neighboring countries thought of themselves as leading happy lives.) The British are easygoing, accepting of nonconformity and eccentricity, and their strong sense of humor and love of the absurd keeps them on an even keel. They have a strange habit of poking good-humored fun at what they love without meaning disrespect, not least at royalty and religion, although the recent undignified capers of the royal family have honed an edge to the good humor. This kind of humor often disconcerts foreigners.

It is a densely populated land. Scotland and Wales have wide open spaces but in England people are crammed 940 to the square mile, more thickly than in any European country save Holland. But it is also a green and fertile land, and because the countryside is a limited commodity, the English tend it with special loving care. Everywhere are trim hedgerows, tidy flower beds, and lawns mown smooth as billiard tables—one Oxford don, asked by an American visitor how the college lawn came to be so perfect, said casually, "Oh, it's been mown every Tuesday for the past 500 years." The English love gardens but are also at ease in untamed surroundings. They relish hiking over moors where the westerly gales blow, or splashing rubber-booted through streams, or bird-watching in a quiet copse. A few people, in their black or scarlet coats and riding caps, still go fox hunting with hounds—"the unspeakable in full pursuit of the uneatable," as Oscar Wilde put it. Others are violent in their condemnation of this blood sport.

This smallish island contains great scenic variety. The Midlands and much of eastern England tend to be flat and dull. But the watery fenlands, between Cambridge and the sea, the low horizons, broken by rows of poplars or by a distant windmill or tall church spire, have a misty poetic quality, and the sunsets and swirling clouds evoke Turner skyscapes. Kent, southeast of London, with its cherry and apple orchards, is known as the garden of England; west of here are the wooded hills of Surrey, and to the southwest the bold, bare ridge of the South Downs, beloved of Kipling. While the east coast of Britain is mainly smooth, with long sandy beaches and an occasional chalky cliff, the west coast is far more rugged: Here the Atlantic gales set the seas lashing against the rocky headlands of Cornwall and south Wales.

The spine of northern England is a line of high hills, the Pennines, where sheep graze on lonely moors, and just to the west is the beautiful mountainous Lake District, where Wordsworth lived. Scotland is even more lonely and mountainous. Beyond the urban belt of the lowlands around Glasgow and Edinburgh, you enter the romantic realm of the Highlands, a thinly populated region where heather and gorse cover the hillsides above silent fjordlike lochs and verdant glens. Roads here are few, but they all seem to lead westward to the Isles, blue-gray jewels in a silver Atlantic sea, with their strange Celtic names: Barra, Eigg, Benbecula, Skye. . . .

Western Britain is washed by the warm waters of the Gulf Stream, and therefore its climate is mild and damp. Indeed, Britain's weather is something of a stock joke, and some foreigners imagine the whole country permanently shrouded in fog. This has not been true for years, since the use of smokeless fuel has cleared polluted mists from urban skies. Yet the weather *is* very changeable, by south European standards, with shower and shine often following each other in swift succession. At least it provides the thrill of the unexpected.

The people are as varied as the landscape, coming as they do from a variety of origins: Celtic, Viking, Saxon, Norman, not to mention later immigrations. Modern mobility and the drift toward cities and to the warmer and wealthier South has tended to mix them up in the urban centers. But the countryside populations have remained much the same. The gap between the two has widened enormously, so that now those in the country simply cannot understand the problems that bedevil the cities. Regional differences remain distinct, and local loyalties are fierce, even parochial. A London politician newly settled in north Yorkshire was warned by his constituents, "Take no notice o' folk t'oother side o' water!" He feared, as well he might, that this was some anti-EU or anti-American hostility—but discovered they were referring to the people just 10 miles away across the river Tees, in County Durham.

The millions of foreigners who have come to live in Britain during the last few decades have had a generally positive influence. They have widened the horizons of an insular—in every sense of the word—people, even in such matters as cuisine. Until the '50s almost all restaurants served dull British fare, but today in even the smallest provincial town you will find Indians, Chinese, Greeks, Italians, French and others all serving their national dishes—and they are very popular indeed.

The same can't always be said of the immigrants themselves, especially those from what is euphemistically dubbed the "New Commonwealth"—meaning the Asians and Afro-Caribbeans brought into Britain in the '50s and '60s to provide essential services and fill a chronic labor shortage. Most middle-class British people will profess themselves broadminded, of course, but their day-to-day attitudes still suggest that their commitment to a truly racially egalitarian society is only skin deep (if that). The debate over assimilation—to what extent the immigrant communities should be asked to surrender their own identities—still rages. Should schools in Bradford, where a majority of pupils are Muslims, base their moral precepts on the Koran rather than the Bible? Should the history of the Caribbean islands or of Africa be taught to young blacks in south London as part of their culture?

The British are clearly torn between their traditions of tolerance on one hand and their belief on the other hand that even a somewhat anachronistic law must be upheld. Never has this situation been more clear-cut than in the confrontation over Rushdie's *Satanic Verses*, when British Muslims saw themselves discriminated against under Britain's ancient blasphemy laws, which applied only to the God of the Christians. Until a clear line is drawn—either rigorous assimilation, or multiculturalism that implies a new respect for alien cultures taking root in their towns and cities—the British will be constantly wrongfooted, embarrassed, and occasionally very frightened by the newcomers erupting in their midst.

Britain is a land where the arts flourish. It is true that the artist, writer or philosopher is not held in the same public esteem as, say, in France. The average Briton affects a certain philistinism, and "intellectual" and "arty" are common terms of reproach. And yet sales of books and of theater and concert tickets are amazingly high. Helped by the worldwide spread of the English language, the British publishing industry produces around 50,000 new titles a year—too many for profitability. A passion for classical music developed during the last war and has continued ever since, so that even the smallest town has its choral society performing Bach or Handel, and its season of concerts by visiting artists. London theater is regarded by many as the best in the world, for its standards of production and acting and for its new writing. This richness is reflected in the provinces, where hundreds of theaters, some of them small fringe groups in makeshift premises, attract ready audiences.

Culture thrives also in a classical mode—for example, through the Royal Shakespeare Company with its base in the bard's hometown of Stratford-upon-Avon. Like Shakespeare, many leading British writers and other creative artists are closely associated with some particular place, in a land where literature and the other arts have always been nourished by strong local roots, by some *genius loci*. A tour around Britain can thus become a series of cultural pilgrimages: to the Dorset that inspired the novels of Thomas Hardy, to the wild Yorkshire moors where the Brontë sisters lived and wrote, to Wordsworth's beloved Lake District, to the Scottish Border landscapes that pervade the novels of Walter Scott, to Laugharne on the south Wales coast that Dylan Thomas's *Under Milk Wood* has immortalized, to Dickensian London, to the Constable country on the Suffolk/Essex border, or to nearby Aldeburgh where composer Benjamin Britten lived.

These personalities are significant parts of a long national history that lies buried deep in the British psyche. The history began centuries before Christ, when huge stone circles were raised at Stonehenge and Avebury, on the Wiltshire downs. Then came the Romans, who left their imprint across the land up to Hadrian's Wall in the north. Great feudal castles survive as reminders of the dark days when barons and kings were in constant conflict, and peaceful fields the length and breadth of the land became nightmarish landscapes of blood and death. Stately redbrick Elizabethan manors bear witness to the more settled and civilized age of Good Queen Bess.

Britain is rich in old towns and villages whose streets are lined with buildings dating back for centuries, with old half-timbered houses where black beams crisscross the white plasterwork, or with carefully proportioned facades that bring a measured classical elegance to the townscape. In many areas, buildings are of local stone—most strikingly in the mellow golden-brown Cotswold villages—and often a simple cottage is topped with a neat thatch roof. Above all, British architecture is famed for its cathedrals dating mostly from the Middle Ages, with Wells, Ely, and Durham among the finest. Local churches, too, are often of great beauty, especially in East Anglia where the wealth of the

15th-century wool trade led to the building of majestic churches on the edge of quite modest villages. Church builders of the past were profligate in their service to God, and modern Britain is deeply in their debt. Unfortunately, the Church is just as deeply in debt, because it has these mammoth edifices to maintain with dwindling congregations to help with its finances.

Despite constant social upheavals, the British maintain many of their special traditions. On a village green in summer, you may see a cricket match in progress between two white-clad teams. It is a slow and stately game that will seem boring to the uninitiated, yet is full of its own skills and subtleties. In village pubs people frequently play darts, or perhaps backgammon, checkers, or chess. The English pub is a venerable institution, as popular as ever and endlessly diverse. With some exceptions, pubs in towns tend to be dull, and many have been modernized in dubious taste, with too much chrome, plush, and plastic. But the country pub can be a real joy. It will often be called by the name of the local landed family—*The Bath Arms*, or *Lord Crewe's Arms*, "arms" meaning the family coat of heraldic arms on the inn sign—and very possibly it will have old beams and inglenooks, and a blazing log fire in winter. If you sit at a table in the corner, you can have privacy of a sort; but between those who prop up the bar, conversation is general, no introductions are needed, and new acquaintances are quickly made.

British society, while troubled by doubts and uncertainties, and constantly challenged to resolve key social problems, is certainly not in terminal decline, or even slowly fading away. But it is deeply troubled and seriously questioning many of its traditional, long-accepted institutions. As an American observer remarked during the Falklands War, "The British can be relied upon to fall at every hurdle—except the last." When the chips are down, the British come up trumps. This can't be explained rationally. What was it that sank the Spanish Armada or defeated Goering's Luftwaffe? It certainly wasn't superior economic resources or disciplined social organization. Maybe there is more in the souls of a free people united in a common purpose than generations of economists and sociologists could ever hope to understand. The British are such a people; and their quirkiness, their social "distance," and their habit of driving on the left are inseparable parts of a greater whole. Without Britain, even a changed Britain, the world would be a poorer place.

1 Essential Information

Before You Go

Government Tourist Offices

Contact the **British Tourist Authority** (BTA).

In the U.S. 551 5th Ave., New York, NY 10176, tel. 212/986–2200; 625 N. Michigan Ave., Chicago, IL 60611, tel. 312/787–0490; World Trade Center, 350 S. Figueroa St., Suite 450, Los Angeles, CA 90071, tel. 213/628–3525; 2580 Cumberland Pkwy., Suite 470, Atlanta, GA 30339-3909, tel. 404/432–9635.

U.S. Government Travel Briefings The U.S. Department of State's **Overseas Citizens Emergency Center** (Room 4811, Washington, DC 20520; enclose S.A.S.E.) issues Consular Information Sheets, which cover crime, security, political climate, and health risks as well as embassy locations, entry requirements, currency regulations, and other routine matters. For the latest information, stop in at any U.S. passport office, consulate, or embassy; call the interactive hotline (tel. 202/647–5225; fax 202/647–3000); or, with your PC's modem, tap into the Bureau of Consular Affairs' computer bulletin board (tel. 202/647–9225).

In Canada 94 Cumberland St., Suite 600, Toronto, Ont. M5R 3N3, tel. 416/925–6326.

In Britain Thames Tower, Black's Rd., London W6 9EL; written inquiries only.

Tours and Packages

Should you buy your travel arrangements to Great Britain packaged or do it yourself? There are advantages either way. Buying packaged arrangements—and there are more options to Great Britain than to any other European destination—saves you money, particularly if you can find a program that includes exactly the features you want. You also get a pretty good idea of what your trip will cost from the outset. Generally, you have two options: fully escorted tours and independent packages.

Escorted tours are most often via motorcoach, with a tour director in charge. They're ideal if you don't mind having limited free time and traveling with strangers. Your baggage is handled, your time rigorously scheduled, and most meals planned. Escorted tours are therefore the most hassle-free way to see a destination, as well as generally the least expensive. Independent packages allow plenty of flexibility. They generally include airline travel and hotels, with certain options available, such as sightseeing, car rental, and excursions. Independent packages are usually more expensive than escorted tours, but your time is your own.

Travel agents are your best source of recommendations for both tours and packages. They will have the largest selection, and the cost to you is the same as buying direct. Whatever program you ultimately choose, be sure to find out exactly what is included: taxes, tips, transfers, meals, baggage handling, ground transportation, entertainment, excursions, sports or recreation (and rental equipment if necessary). Ask about the level of hotel used, its location, the size of its rooms, the kind of beds, and its amenities, such as pool, room service, or programs for children, if they're important to you. Find out the operator's cancellation penalties. Nearly everyone charges them, and the only way to avoid them is to buy trip-cancellation insurance (*see* Trip Insurance, *below*). Also ask about the single supplement, a surcharge assessed to solo travelers. Some operators do not make you pay it if you agree to be matched up with a room-mate of the same sex, even if one is not found by departure time. Remember that a program that has features you won't use, whether for rental sporting equipment or discounted museum admissions, may not be the most cost-wise choice for you.

Fully Escorted Tours Escorted tours are usually sold in three categories: deluxe, first-class, and tourist or budget class. The most important difference is the level of accommodations. Among operators offering programs in the deluxe category are **Tauck Tours** (11 Wilton Rd., Westport, CT 06881, tel. 203/226–6911 or 800/468–2825) and **Maupintour** (Box 807, Lawrence, KS 66044, tel. 913/843–1211 or 800/255–4266). Most escorted tours to Great Britain fall into the first-class category, including those offered by **American Airlines Fly AAway Vacations** (tel. 800/321–2121); **British Airways** (tel. 800/247–9297); **Certified Vacations** (Box 1525, Ft. Lauderdale, FL 33302, tel. 305/522–1414 or 800/233–7260); **CIE Tours** (108 Ridgedale Ave., Morristown, NJ 07960, tel. 201/292–3438 or 800/243–8687), which specializes in the United Kingdom and Ireland; **Continental's Grand Destinations** (tel. 800/634–5555); **Globus** (5301 S. Federal Circle, Littleton, CO 80123, tel. 303/797–2800 or 800/221–0090); **Olson-Travelworld** (Box 10066, Manhattan Beach, CA 90226, tel. 310/546–8400 or 800/421–5785); **Trafalgar Tours** (21 E. 26th St., New York, NY 10010, tel. 212/689–8977 or 800/854–0103); and **V E Tours** (1150 N.W. 72nd Ave., Suite 450, Miami, FL 33126, tel. 800/222–8383).

Budget offerings include programs by **AESU Travel** (2 Hamill Rd., Suite 248, Baltimore, MD 21210, tel. 410/323–4416 or 800/638–7640), **Cosmos Tourama,** a sister company of **Globus** (*see above*), and the "CostSavers" of **Trafalgar Tours** (*see above*).

Most itineraries are jam-packed with sightseeing, so you see a lot in a short amount of time (usually one place per day). To judge just how fast-paced the tour is, review the itinerary carefully. If you are in a different hotel each night, you will be getting up early each day to head out, travel to your next destination, do some sightseeing, have dinner, and go to bed, then you'll start all over again. If you want some free time, make sure it's mentioned in the tour brochure; if you want to be escorted to every meal, confirm that any tour you consider does that. Also, when comparing programs, be sure to find out if the motorcoach is air-conditioned and has a rest room on board. Make your selection based on price and stops on the itinerary.

Independent Packages Independent packages, which travel agents call FITs (for Foreign Independent Travel), are offered by airlines, tour operators who may also do escorted programs, and any number of other companies from large, established firms to small, new entrepreneurs.

Independent programs to Britain range from a week of theater and the arts in London to a visit to country inns and manor houses throughout the countryside. Levels of luxury vary as well; they may include sightseeing, car rental, transfers, admission to local attractions, and other extras. **American Airlines Fly AAway Vacations, British Airways, CIE Tours, Continental's Grand Destinations, Globus, Trafalgar Tours** (*see above*), and **TWA Getaway Vacations** (tel. 800/438–2929) all offer independent packages as well as fully escorted tours. For additional options, consult **United Airlines' Vacation Planning Center** (tel. 800/328–6877) and **Abercrombie & Kent** (1420 Kensington Rd., Oak Brook, IL 60521, tel. 708/954–2944 or 800/323–7308), which operates a variety of deluxe programs.

Note that when pricing different packages, it sometimes pays to purchase the same arrangements separately, as when a rock-bottom promotional airfare is being offered, for example. Again, base your choice on what's available at your budget for the destinations you want to visit.

Special-Interest Travel Britain has just about everything for travelers with special interests, particularly golfers and gardeners. Such programs may be fully escorted or independent. Some require a certain amount of expertise, but most are for the average traveler with an interest and are usually hosted by experts in the subject matter. Because your fellow travelers are apt to be passionate or knowledgeable about the subject, they can prove as enjoyable a part of your travel experience as the destination itself. The price range is wide, but in general they cost more than independent packages because of the expert guide and the special activities.

Barge Cruises **The Barge Lady** (225 N. Michigan Ave., Chicago, IL 60601, tel. 312/540–5500 or 800/880–0071) combines barging and golfing cruises. **Le Boat** (Box E, Maywood, NJ 07607, tel. 201/342–1838 or 800/922–0291) is the U.S. representatives for U.K. Waterway Holidays, which cruises on Britain's rivers and canals. Also contact **Skipper Travel Services** (9029 Soquel Ave., Suite G, Santa Cruz, CA 95062, tel. 408/462–5333).

Biking **Backroads** (1516 5th St., Suite Q333, Berkeley, CA 94710-1740, tel. 510/527–1555 or 800/BIKE–TRIP) offers biking tours for all levels of endurance, with a sag wagon bringing up the rear in case the rolling terrain gets to be too much. **Classic Adventures** (Box 153, Hamlin, NY 14464, tel. 716/964–8488 or 800/777–8090) has a 14-day tour through England and Scotland.

Castles **Smithsonian Institution**'s Study Tours and Seminars (1100 Jefferson Dr. SW, Room 3045, Washington, DC 20560, tel. 202/357–4700) sail the less accessible islands and inlets of the British Isles, observing the development of the English country house, from castles to mansions.

Culture **Polly Stewart Fritch** (1 Scott La., Greenwich, CT 06831, tel. 203/661–7742) offers "cultural-culinary" tours with cooking demonstrations and behind-the-scenes visits to unique markets. Thanks to some well-placed friends, Fritch's tour occasionally features such extras as an insider's tour of Parliament with time to sip sherry in a private room in the House of Lords. **Smithsonian Institution**'s Study Tours and Seminars (*see above*) explore the culture of the Wessex, Cotswold, and Yorkshire countrysides. **Earthwatch** (680 Mount Auburn St., Watertown, MA 02272, tel. 617/926–8000) recruits volunteers to serve in its EarthCorps as short-term assistants to scientists excavating, surveying, and mapping the site of a 1st-century Roman fort in northeastern England.

English Homes and Gardens **Rolfes Travel Inc.** (1744 E. Joppa Rd., Baltimore, MD 21234, tel. 410/668–0077) and **Travel Etcetera Inc.** (1730 Huntington Dr., South Pasadena, CA 91030, tel. 818/441–3184) have personalized tours that include, among other features, visits to stately homes not open to the general public. For garden tours, look into **Heritage World Tours** (16903 Lilly Crest, San Antonio, TX 78232, tel. 800/622–1663, fax 210/490–7490), for deluxe programs, with stays in stately homes converted to luxury hotels; **Expo Garden Tours** (145 4th Ave., Suite 4A, New York, NY 10003, tel. 212/677–6704 or 800/448–2685); and **Coopersmith's England** (6441 Valley View Rd., Oakland, CA 94611, tel. 510/339–2499). Some programs include admission to the Chelsea Flower Show.

Fishing **Trac International** (2075 S. University Blvd., Suite 300, Denver, CO 80210, tel. 303/871–9797) will help you find the stream or lake of your dreams to either land a big one or just enjoy the water.

Golf **Adventure Holidays** (815 North Rd., Westfield, MA 01085, tel. 413/568–2855 or 800/628–9655) and **Golf International** (275 Madison Ave., New York, NY 10016, tel. 212/986–9176 or 800/833–1389, fax 212/986–3720) offer independent golf programs to the United Kingdom. **ITC Golf Tours** (4134 Atlantic Ave., Suite 205, Long Beach, CA 90807, tel. 310/595–6905 or 800/257–4981) has packages to the land where golf began.

Music **Dailey-Thorp Travel** (330 W. 58th St., New York, NY 10019, tel. 800/99–THORP) specializes in music and opera programs, and offers a "London Theater Week," while **Keith Prowse & Co.** (234 W. 44th St., New York, NY 10036, tel. 212/398–1430 or 800/669–8687) does all kinds of music, from rock to opera.

Rail **Abercrombie & Kent** (1520 Kensington Rd., Oak Brook, IL 60521, tel. 708/954–2944 or 800/323–7308) takes you on an oh-so-civilized train ride around the country on The Great Rail Express from London to Inverness and back, in seven or 11 days.

Riding Tours **FITS Equestrian** (2011 Alamo Pintado Rd., Solvang, CA 93463, tel. 805/688–9494 or 800/660–3487, fax 805/688–2943) plans and runs escorted tours on horseback throughout Britain.

Sports **Steve Furgal's International Tennis Tours** (11828 Rancho Bernardo Rd., San Diego, CA 92128, tel. 619/487–7777 or 800/258–3664) has tours to Wimbledon; one of them combines passage on the *QE2* to England and the *Concorde* back home. **Keith Prowse & Co.** (*see above*), also a sports specialist, has programs to the British Open, Royal Ascot, and Wimbledon. **Sportsworld Travel** (1730 Northeast Expressway, Atlanta, GA 30329, tel. 404/329–9902 or 800/338–0155) also handles Wimbledon.

Walking Tours Dozens of organizations sponsor walking tours on Britain's huge network of trails, among them the American-based **British Coastal Trails** (California Plaza, 1001 B Ave., Suite 302, Coronado, CA 92118, tel. 619/437–1211) and **English Lakeland Ramblers** (18 Stuyvesant Oval, Suite 1A, New York, NY 10009, tel. 212/505–1020 or 800/724–8801).

In the UK: Countrywide Holidays (Birch Heys, Cromwell Range, Manchester M14 6HU, tel. 061/225–1000), have a wide range of walks, in many parts of the country for both beginners and experienced walkers, with lodging in country houses and hotels. **Greenscape UK** (Milkway Lane Croyde, North Devon EX33 1NG, tel. 0271/890677) run relaxed walking tours of the West Country and the Yorkshire Dales, aimed mainly at overseas visitors. **Mountain Goat Holidays and Tours** (Victoria St., Windermere, Cumbria LA23 1AD, tel. 05394/45161) has guided weekly walks and tours around the Lake District.

When to Go

The British tourist season is year-round—with short lulls. It peaks mid-April to mid-October, with another burst at Christmas (although most historic houses are closed from October to Easter). Spring is the time to see the countryside at its freshest and greenest, while in fall the northern moorlands and Scottish Highlands are at their most colorful. June is a good month to visit Wales and the Lake District. During July and August, when most of the British take their vacations, accommodations in the most popular resorts and areas are in high demand and at their most expensive. The winter season in London is lively with the opera, ballet, and West End theater among the prime attractions.

Climate   In the main, the climate is mild, although the weather has been extremely volatile in recent years. Summer temperatures can reach the 90s and the atmosphere can be humid, while in winter there can be heavy frost, snow, thick fog, and, of course, rain.

What follows are the average daily maximum and minimum temperatures for three major cities in Britain—but note that they are based on long-term averages and do not necessarily reflect the climatic swings of the last few years:

Aberystwyth									
(Wales)	Jan.	44F	7C	May	58F	15C	Sept.	62F	16C
		36	2		45	7		51	11
	Feb.	44F	7C	June	62F	16C	Oct.	56F	13C
		35	2		50	10		46	8
	Mar.	49F	9C	July	64F	18C	Nov.	50F	10C
		38	4		54	12		41	5
	Apr.	52F	11C	Aug.	65F	18C	Dec.	47F	8C
		41	5		54	12		38	4

Edinburgh									
(Scotland)	Jan.	42F	5C	May	56F	14C	Sept.	60F	18C
		34	1		43	6		49	9
	Feb.	43F	6C	June	62F	17C	Oct.	54F	12C
		34	1		49	9		44	7
	Mar.	46F	8C	July	65F	18C	Nov.	48F	9C
		36	2		52	11		39	4
	Apr.	51F	11C	Aug.	64F	18C	Dec.	44F	7C
		39	4		52	11		36	2

London									
	Jan.	43F	6C	May	62F	17C	Sept.	65F	19C
		36	2		47	8		52	11
	Feb.	44F	7C	June	69F	20C	Oct.	58F	14C
		36	2		53	12		46	8
	Mar.	50F	10C	July	71F	22C	Nov.	50F	10C
		38	3		56	14		42	5
	Apr.	56F	13C	Aug.	71F	21C	Dec.	45F	7C
		42	6		56	13		38	4

Information   Sources   For current weather conditions and forecasts for cities in the United States and abroad, plus the local time and helpful travel tips, call the **Weather Channel Connection** (tel. 900/932–8437; 95¢ per minute) from a touch-tone phone.

Festivals and Seasonal Events

Tickets for popular sporting events must be obtained months in advance—check first to see if your travel agent can get them. There is a complete list of ticket agencies in *Britain Events*, free from the British Tourist Authority.

Jan. (first two weeks). London International Boat Show is the largest boat show in Europe. *Earls Court Exhibition Centre, Warwick Rd., London SW5 9TA, tel. 0784/473377.*
Apr.–Jan. Shakespeare Season is held by the world-renowned Royal

Shakespeare Company. *Stratford-upon-Avon, Warwickshire CV37 6BB, box office, tel. 0789/295623.*

Mid-Apr. London Marathon. *Information from Box 262, Richmond, Surrey TW10 5JB, tel. 081/948–7935.*

May. Glasgow Mayfest is a citywide international festival of theater, dance, music, and street events—Glasgow's answer to the Edinburgh Festival. *Festival Dir., 18 Albion St., Glasgow G1 1LH, tel. 041/552–8000.*

Late May. Chelsea Flower Show is Britain's major flower show, covering 22 acres. *Royal Hospital, Chelsea, London SW3, tel. 071/834–4333.*

Late May–early June. Glyndebourne Opera opened last year in its brand new auditorium. *Glyndebourne Festival Opera, Glyndebourne, Lewes, East Sussex BN8 5UU, tel. 0273/812321.*

Early June. Derby Day is the world-renowned horse-racing event, at Epsom Racecourse, Epsom, Surrey. *Information from United Racecourses Ltd., Racecourse Paddock, Epsom, Surrey KT18 5NJ, tel. 0372/463072.*

Mid-June. Trooping the Colour is Queen Elizabeth's colorful official birthday show at Horse Guards Parade, Whitehall, London. (Her actual birthdate is in April.) *Write for tickets early in the year to The Brigade Major, H.Q. Household Division, Chelsea Barracks, London SW1 8RF.*

Late June–early July. Wimbledon Lawn Tennis Championships is a big draw, so write early for Center and No. One court tickets. *All-England Lawn Tennis and Croquet Club, Church Rd., Wimbledon, London SW19 5AE, tel. 081/946–2244.*

Early–mid-July. Llangollen International Musical Eisteddfod sees the little Welsh town of Llangollen overflow with music, costumes, and color. *Musical Eisteddfod Office, Llangollen, Clwyd LL20 8NG, tel. 0978/860236.*

Mid-July. Royal Tournament features military displays and pageantry by the Royal Navy, Royal Marines, Army, and Royal Air Force. *Earls Court Exhibition Centre, Warwick Rd., London SW5 9TA, tel. 071/373–8141.*

Mid-July. British Open Championship is played at a different course each year. It will be held in St. Andrews in 1995, July 20–23. *Royal and Ancient Golf Club, St. Andrews, Fife KY16 9JD, tel. 0334/72112.*

Mid-July–mid-Sept. Henry Wood Promenade Concerts is a celebrated series of concerts, founded in 1895. *Royal Albert Hall, Kensington Gore, London SW7 2AP, tel. 071/589–8212.*

Mid-Aug. Three Choirs Festival is an ancient choral and orchestral music festival, to be held in Hereford in 1994. *John Harris, The Gable, South St., Leominster, Hereford HR6 8JN, tel. 0568/615223.*

Mid-Aug.–early Sept. Edinburgh International Festival, the world's largest festival of the arts, includes the nighttime Edinburgh Military Tattoo. *Edinburgh Festival Society, 21 Market St., Edinburgh EH1 1BW, tel. 031/226–4001.*

Early Nov. Lord Mayor's Procession and Show coincides with the Lord Mayor's inauguration, with a procession from the Guildhall to the Royal Courts of Justice. No tickets. *The City of London, tel. 071/606–3030.*

Mid–late Dec. Olympia International Show Jumping Championships is an international equestrian competition. *Earls Court Exhibition Centre, Warwick Rd., London SW5 9TA, tel. 071/370–8189.*

What to Pack

Clothing   Britain can be cool, damp, and overcast, even in summer. You'll want a heavy coat for winter and a lightweight coat or warm jacket for summer. There's no time of year when a raincoat or umbrella won't come in handy. For the cities, pack as you would for an American city: coats and ties for expensive restaurants and night spots, casual clothes elsewhere. Jeans are popular in Britain and are perfectly acceptable for sightseeing and informal dining. Tweeds and sports jackets are popular here with men. For women, ordinary street dress is acceptable everywhere.

Miscellaneous   If you plan to stay in budget hotels, take your own soap. Many do not provide soap and some give guests only one tiny bar per room. Bring an extra pair of eyeglasses or contact lenses in your carry-on luggage. If you have a health problem that requires a prescription drug, pack enough to last the duration of the trip or have your doctor write a prescription using the drug's generic name, because brand names vary from country to country. Always carry prescription drugs in their original packaging to avoid problems with customs officials. Don't pack them in luggage that you plan to check in case your bags go astray. Also, pack a list of the offices that supply refunds for lost or stolen traveler's checks.

Electricity   The electrical current in Great Britain is 220 volts, 50 cycles alternating current (AC); the United States runs on 110-volt, 60-cycle AC current. Unlike wall outlets in the United States, which accept plugs with two flat prongs, outlets in Great Britain take plugs with three prongs.

Adapters,   To use U.S.-made electric appliances abroad, you'll need an adapter
Converters,   plug. Unless the appliance is dual-voltage and made for travel, you'll
Transformers   also need a converter. Hotels sometimes have 110-volt outlets for low-wattage appliances marked "For Shavers Only" near the sink; don't use them for a high-wattage appliance like a blow-dryer. If you're traveling with an older laptop computer, carry a transformer. New laptop computers are auto-sensing, operating equally well on 110 and 220 volts, so you need only the appropriate adapter plug. For a copy of the free brochure "Foreign Electricity is No Deep Dark Secret," send a stamped, self-addressed envelope to adapter-converter manufacturer Franzus Company (Customer Service, Dept. B50, Murtha Industrial Park, Box 142, Beacon Falls, CT 06403, tel. 203/723–6664).

Luggage   Free-baggage airline allowances depend on the airline, the route,
Regulations   and the class of your ticket; ask in advance. In general, on domestic flights and on international flights between the United States and foreign destinations, you are entitled to check two bags—neither exceeding 62 inches, or 158 centimeters (length + width + height), or weighing more than 70 pounds (32 kilograms). A third piece may be brought aboard as a carryon; its total dimensions are generally limited to less than 45 inches (114 centimeters), so it will fit easily under the seat in front of you or in the overhead compartment. In the United States, the Federal Aviation Administration (FAA) gives airlines broad latitude to limit carry-on allowances and tailor them to different aircraft and operational conditions. Charges for excess, oversize, or overweight pieces vary, so inquire before you pack.

If you are flying between two foreign destinations, note that baggage allowances may be determined not by piece but by weight, which generally allows 88 pounds (40 kilograms) of luggage in first class, 66 pounds (30 kilograms) in business class, and 44 pounds (20 kilograms) in economy. If your flight between two cities abroad *connects* with your transatlantic or transpacific flight, the piece method still applies.

Safeguarding Your Luggage   Before leaving home, itemize your bags' contents and their worth in case they go astray. To minimize that risk, tag them inside and out with your name, address, and phone number. (If you use your home address, cover it so that potential thieves can't see it.) Put a copy of your itinerary inside each bag, so that you can easily be tracked. At check-in, make sure that the tag attached by baggage handlers bears the correct three-letter code for your destination. If your bags do not arrive with you, or if you detect damage, immediately file a written report with the airline before you leave the airport.

Taking Money Abroad

Traveler's Checks   Although you'll need cash in rural areas and small towns, traveler's checks are preferable in metropolitan centers. The most widely recognized are **American Express, Citicorp, Diners Club, Thomas Cook,** and **Visa,** which are sold by major commercial banks. Both American Express and Thomas Cook issue checks that can be countersigned and used by you or your traveling companion. Typically the issuing company or the bank at which you make your purchase charges 1% to 3% of the checks' face value as a fee. Some foreign banks charge as much as 20% of the face value as the fee for cashing traveler's checks in a foreign currency. Buy a few checks in small denominations to cash toward the end of your trip, so you won't be left with excess foreign currency. Record the numbers of checks as you spend them, and keep this list separate from the checks.

Currency Exchange   Banks offer the most favorable exchange rates. If you use currency exchange booths at airports, rail and bus stations, hotels, stores, and privately run exchange firms, you'll typically get less favorable rates, but you may find the hours more convenient.

You can get good rates and avoid long lines at airport currency-exchange booths by getting a small amount of currency at **Thomas Cook Currency Services** (630 5th Ave., New York, NY 10111, tel. 212/757–6915 or 800/223–7373 for locations in major metropolitan areas throughout the United States) or **Ruesch International** (tel. 800/424–2923 for locations) before you depart. Check with your travel agent to be sure that the currency of the country you will be visiting can be imported.

Getting Money from Home

Cash Machines   Many automated-teller machines (ATMs) are tied to international networks such as **Cirrus** and **Plus.** You can use your bank card at ATMs away from home to withdraw money from your checking account and to get cash advances on a credit-card account if your card has been programmed with a personal identification number, or PIN. Check in advance on limits on withdrawals and cash advances within specified periods. Ask whether your bank-card or credit-card PIN will need to be reprogrammed for use in the area you'll be visiting. Four digits are commonly used overseas. Note that Discover is accepted only in the United States. On cash advances you are charged interest from the day you receive the money from ATMs as well as from tellers. Although transaction fees for ATM withdrawals abroad may be higher than fees for withdrawals at home, Cirrus and Plus exchange rates are excellent, because they are based on wholesale rates only offered by major banks.

Be sure to plan ahead: Obtain ATM locations and the names of affiliated cash-machine networks before departure. For specific foreign Cirrus locations, call 800/424-7787; for foreign Plus locations, consult the Plus directory at your local bank.

Wiring Money You don't have to be a cardholder to send or receive a **MoneyGram from American Express** for up to $10,000. Go to a MoneyGram agent in retail and convenience stores and American Express travel offices, pay up to $1,000 with a credit card and anything over that in cash. You are allowed a free long-distance call to give the transaction code to your intended recipient, who needs only present identification and the reference number to the nearest MoneyGram agent to pick up the cash. MoneyGram agents are in more than 70 countries (call 800/926-9400 for locations). Fees range from 3% to 10%, depending on the amount and how you pay.

You can also use **Western Union.** To wire money, take either cash or a cashier's check to the nearest office or call and use your MasterCard or Visa. Money sent from the United States or Canada will be available for pick up at agent locations in Great Britain within minutes. Once the money is in the system it can be picked up at *any* one of 22,000 locations (call 800/325-6000 for the one nearest you).

British Currency

The unit of currency in Britain is the pound sterling, divided into 100 pence (p). The bills are 50, 20, 10, and 5 pounds (Scotland and the Channel Islands have their own £1 bills). Newly designed, smaller bills are being issued over the next three years. The new £5 and £10 notes are already in circulation. Coins are £1, 50, 20, 10, 5, 2, and 1p. New small 5p and 10p coins already make the change in your pocket much lighter. At press time, the exchange rate was about U.S. $1.57 and Canadian $2.08 to the pound sterling.

What It Will Cost

Sample Costs A man's haircut will cost £7.50 and up (around £12 at a central London barber); a woman's anywhere from £15 to £30. It costs about £2 to have a shirt laundered, from £4 to dry-clean a dress, or £4.50 for dry-cleaning a man's suit. A local paper will cost you about 35p and a national daily 50p (up to £1 on Sundays). A pint of beer is around £1.40, and a gin and tonic £1.60 (mixers are pricey in pubs, and remember that British measures for spirits are on the mean side). A cup of coffee will run from 60p to £1, depending on where you drink it; a ham sandwich £1.75; lunch in a pub, £2 and up (plus your drink).

A theater seat will cost from £7.50 to £40 in London, less elsewhere, while an evening at Covent Garden could set you back £113 each for the best seats. Movie theater prices vary widely—from £2.50 in the daytime in the provinces (more in the evening) to anything up to £8 in central London. Nightclubs will take all they can get from you—even the membership fees are variable.

Sales Tax The British sales tax (VAT, Value Added Tax) is 17½%. The tax is almost always included in quoted prices in shops, hotels, and restaurants. See Shopping, later in this chapter, for the ways to recover VAT when you leave the country. There is no VAT in the Channel Islands.

Long-Distance Calling

AT&T, MCI, and Sprint have several services that make calling home or the office more affordable and convenient when you're on the road. Use one of them to avoid pricey hotel surcharges. **AT&T Calling Card** (tel. 800/225–5288) and the **AT&T Universal Card** (tel. 800/662–7759) give you access to the service. With **AT&T's USADirect** (tel. 800/874–4000 for codes in the countries you'll be visiting) you can reach an AT&T operator with a local or toll-free call. **MCI's Call USA** (MCI Customer Service, tel. 800/444–4444) allows that service from 85 countries or from country to country via **MCI WorldReach. Sprint Express** (tel. 800/793–1153) has a toll-free number travelers abroad can dial to reach a Sprint operator in the United States.

Passports and Visas

If your passport is lost or stolen abroad, report it immediately to the nearest embassy or consulate and to the local police. If you can provide the consular officer with the information contained in the passport, he or she will usually be able to issue you a new passport. For this reason, keep a photocopy of the data page of your passport separate from your money and traveler's checks. Also leave a photocopy with a relative or friend at home.

U.S. Citizens All U.S. citizens, even infants, need a valid passport to enter Great Britain for stays of up to three months. You can pick up new and renewal application forms at any of the 13 U.S. Passport Agency offices and at some post offices and courthouses. Although passports are usually mailed within four weeks of your application's receipt, allow five weeks or more from April through summer. Call the Department of State Office of Passport Services' information line (tel. 202/647–0518) for fees, documentation requirements, and other details.

Canadian Citizens Canadian citizens need a valid passport to enter Great Britain for stays of up to three months. Application forms are available at 23 regional passport offices as well as post offices and travel agencies. Whether for a first or subsequent passport, you must apply in person. Children under 16 may be included on a parent's passport but must have their own to travel alone. Passports are valid for five years and are usually mailed within two weeks of an applications' receipt. For fees, documentation requirements, and other information in English or French, call the passport office (tel. 514/283–2152 or 800/567–6868).

Customs and Duties

On Arrival In January 1992, the customs regulations of the EU (European Union) were loosened and everything turned into a free-for-all. Now there are two levels of duty-free allowance for travelers entering Great Britain: one for goods bought outside the EU and the other, for goods bought in the EU.

In the first category, you may import duty-free: (1) 200 cigarettes or 100 cigarillos or 50 cigars or 250 grams of tobacco (these allowances are doubled if you live outside Europe); (2) two liters of table wine and, in addition, (a) one liter of alcohol over 22% by volume (most spirits), (b) two liters of alcohol under 22% by volume (fortified or sparkling wine), or (c) two more liters of table wine; (3) 60 cc/ml of perfume and 250 cc/ml of toilet water; and (4) other goods up to a value of £36.

In the second category, you may import duty-free a considerable amount of liquor and tobacco—800 cigarettes, 400 cigarillos, 200 cigars, 1 kg of pipe tobacco, 10 liters of spirits, 90 liters of wine, and 100 liters of beer. You'll need a truck!

No animals or pets of any kind can be brought into the United Kingdom without a six-month quarantine. The penalties are severe and strictly enforced. However, with the opening of the Channel Tunnel, it is unlikely that this particularly strict regulation can be maintained for very long. Similarly, fresh meats, plants and vegetables, controlled drugs, and firearms and ammunition may not be brought into Britain. There are no restrictions on the import or export of British and foreign currencies. You will face no customs formalities if you enter Scotland or Wales from any other part of the United Kingdom, though anyone coming from Northern Ireland should expect a security check.

Returning Home
U.S. Customs If you've been out of the country for at least 48 hours and haven't already used the exemption, or any part of it, in the past 30 days, you may bring home $400 worth of foreign goods duty-free. So can each member of your family, regardless of age; and your exemptions may be pooled, so one of you can bring in more if another brings in less. A flat 10% duty applies to the next $1,000 of goods; above $1,400, the rate varies with the merchandise. (If the 48-hour or 30-day limits apply, your duty-free allowance drops to $25, which may not be pooled.) Please note that these are the *general* rules, applicable to most countries, including Great Britain.

Travelers 21 or older may bring back 1 liter of alcohol duty-free, provided the beverage laws of the state through which they reenter the United States allow it. In addition, 100 non-Cuban cigars and 200 cigarettes are allowed, regardless of your age. Antiques and works of art more than 100 years old are duty-free.

Gifts valued at less than $50 may be mailed to the United States duty-free, with a limit of one package per day per addressee, and do not count as part of your exemption (do not send alcohol or tobacco products or perfume valued at more than $5); mark the package "Unsolicited Gift," and write the nature of the gift and its retail value on the outside. Most reputable stores will handle the mailing for you.

For a copy of "Know Before You Go," a free brochure detailing what you may and may not bring back to the United States, rates of duty, and other pointers, contact the **U.S. Customs Service** (Box 7407, Washington, DC 20044, tel. 202/927–6724).

Canadian Customs Once per calendar year, when you've been out of Canada for at least seven days, you may bring in C$300 worth of goods duty-free. If you've been away less than seven days but more than 48 hours, the duty-free exemption drops to C$100 but can be claimed any number of times (as can a C$20 duty-free exemption for absences of 24 hours or more). You cannot combine the yearly and 48-hour exemptions, use the C$300 exemption only partially (to save the balance for a later trip), or pool exemptions with family members. Goods claimed under the C$300 exemption may follow you by mail; those claimed under the lesser exemptions must accompany you on your return.

Alcohol and tobacco products may be included in the yearly and 48-hour exemptions but not in the 24-hour exemption. If you meet the age requirements of the province through which you reenter Canada, you may bring in, duty-free, 1.14 liters (40 imperial ounces) of wine or liquor *or* two dozen 12-ounce cans or bottles of beer or ale. If you are 16 or older, you may bring in, duty-free, 200 cigarettes, 50 cigars or cigarillos, and 400 tobacco sticks or 400 grams of manufactured tobacco. Alcohol and tobacco must accompany you on your return.

An unlimited number of gifts valued up to C$60 each may be mailed to Canada duty-free. These do not count as part of your exemption. Label the package "Unsolicited Gift—Value under $60." Alcohol and tobacco are excluded.

For more information, including details of duties on items that exceed your duty-free limit, ask the Revenue Canada Customs and Excise Department (2265 St. Laurent Blvd. South, Ottawa, Ont., K1G 4K3, tel. 613/957–0275) for a copy of the free brochure "I Declare/Je Déclare."

Traveling with Cameras, Camcorders, and Laptops

About Film and Cameras   If your camera is new or if you haven't used it for a while, shoot and develop a few rolls of film before leaving home. Store film in a cool, dry place—never in the car's glove compartment or on the shelf under the rear window.

Airport security X-rays generally aren't harmful to film with ISO below 400. To protect your film, carry it with you in a clear plastic bag and ask for a hand inspection. Such requests are honored at U.S. airports; it's up to the inspector abroad. Don't depend on a lead-lined bag to protect film in checked luggage—the airline may increase the radiation to see what's inside. Call the Kodak Information Center (tel. 800/242–2424) for details.

About Camcorders   Before your trip, put camcorders through their paces, invest in a skylight filter to protect the lens, and check all the batteries. Most newer camcorders are equipped with batteries that can be recharged with a universal or worldwide AC adapter charger (or multivoltage converter) that is usable whether the voltage is 110 or 220. All that's needed is the appropriate plug.

About Videotape   Videotape is not damaged by X-rays, but it may be harmed by the magnetic field of a walk-through metal detector, so ask for a hand-check. Airport security personnel may ask you to turn on the camcorder to prove that it's what it appears to be, so make sure the battery is charged. Note that rather than the National Television System Committee video standard (NTSC) used in the United States and Canada, Great Britain uses SECAM technology. You will not be able to view your tapes through the local TV set or view movies bought there in your home VCR. Blank tapes bought in Great Britain can be used for NTSC camcorder taping, but they are pricey.

About Laptops   Security X-rays do not harm hard-disk or floppy-disk storage, but you may request a hand-check, at which point you may be asked to turn on the computer to prove that it is what it appears to be. (Check your battery before departure.) Most airlines allow you to use your laptop aloft except during takeoff and landing (so as not to interfere with navigation equipment). For international travel, register your foreign-made laptop with U.S. Customs as you leave the country. If your laptop is U.S.-made, call the consulate of the country you'll be visiting to find out whether it should be registered with customs upon arrival. Before departure, find out about repair facilities at your destination, and don't forget any transformer or adapter plug you may need (*see* Electricity, *above*).

Insurance

U.S. Residents Most tour operators, travel agents, and insurance agents sell specialized health-and-accident, flight, trip-cancellation, and luggage insurance as well as comprehensive policies with some or all of these features. But before you make any purchase, review your existing health and homeowner policies to find out whether they cover expenses incurred while traveling.

Health-and-Accident Insurance Specific policy provisions of supplemental health-and-accident insurance for travelers include reimbursement for $1,000 to $150,000 worth of medical and/or dental expenses caused by an accident or illness during a trip. The personal-accident, or death-and-dismemberment, provision pays a lump sum to your beneficiaries if you die or to you if you lose one or more limbs or your eyesight; the lump sum awarded can range from $15,000 to $500,000. The medical-assistance provision may reimburse you for the cost of referrals, evacuation, or repatriation and other services, or it may automatically enroll you as a member of a particular medical-assistance company.

Flight Insurance Often bought as a last-minute impulse at the airport, flight insurance pays a lump sum when a plane crashes either to a beneficiary if the insured dies or sometimes to a surviving passenger who loses eyesight or a limb. Like most impulse buys, flight insurance is expensive and basically unnecessary. It supplements the airlines' coverage described in the limits-of-liability paragraphs on your ticket. Charging an airline ticket to a major credit card often automatically entitles you to coverage and may also embrace travel by bus, train, and ship.

Baggage Insurance In the event of loss, damage, or theft on international flights, airlines' liability is $20 per kilogram for checked baggage (roughly about $640 per 70-pound bag) and $400 per passenger for unchecked baggage. On domestic flights, the ceiling is $1,250 per passenger. Excess-valuation insurance can be bought directly from the airline at check-in for about $10 per $1,000 worth of coverage. However, you cannot buy it at any price for the rather extensive list of excluded items shown on your airline ticket.

Trip Insurance **Trip-cancellation-and-interruption insurance** protects you in the event you are unable to undertake or finish your trip, especially if your airline ticket, cruise, or package tour does not allow changes or cancellations. The amount of coverage you purchase should equal the cost of your trip should you, a traveling companion, or a family member fall ill, forcing you to stay home, plus the nondiscounted one-way airline ticket you would need to buy if you had to return home early. Read the fine print carefully, especially sections defining "family member" and "preexisting medical conditions." **Default** or **bankruptcy insurance** protects you against a supplier's failure to deliver. Such policies often do not cover default by a travel agency, tour operator, airline, or cruise line if you bought your tour and the coverage directly from the firm in question. Tours packaged by one of the 33 members of the United States Tour Operators Association (USTOA, 211 E. 51st. St., Suite 12B, New York, NY 10022; tel. 212/750–7371), which requires members to maintain $1 million each in an account to reimburse clients in case of default, are likely to present the fewest difficulties. Even better, pay for travel arrangements with a major credit card, so that you can refuse to pay the bill if services have not been rendered—and let the card company fight your battles.

Comprehensive Companies supplying comprehensive policies with some or all of the
Policies above features include **Access America, Inc.,** (Box 90315, Richmond,
VA 23230, tel. 800/284–8300); **Carefree Travel Insurance,** (Box 310,
120 Mineola Blvd., Mineola, NY 11501, tel. 516/294–0220 or 800/
323–3149); **Tele-Trip** (Mutual of Omaha Plaza, Box 31762, Omaha,
NE 68131, tel. 800/228–9792); **The Travelers Companies** (1 Tower
Sq., Hartford, CT 06183, tel. 203/277–0111 or 800/243–3174); **Travel
Guard International,** (1145 Clark St., Stevens Point, WI 54481, tel.
715/345–0505 or 800/782–5151); and **Wallach and Company, Inc.** (107
W. Federal St., Box 480, Middleburg, VA 22117, tel. 703/687–3166 or
800/237–6615).

Car Rentals

All major car-rental companies are represented in Great Britain, including **Alamo** (tel. 800/327–9633); **Avis** (tel. 800/331–1084 or 800/
879–2847 in Canada); **Budget** (tel. 800/472–3325); **Eurodollar Rent A
Car Ltd.** (tel. 800/800–6000); **Hertz** (tel. 800/654–3001 or 800/263–
0600 in Canada); **National** (tel. 800/227–3876), known internationally as InterRent and Europcar. Weekly unlimited-mileage rates
range from about $110 for an economy car to about $250 for a mid-
size four-door sedan, not including insurance and the 17.5% VAT.

Remember, however, that Britain drives on the left, and the rest of
Europe on the right. Therefore, you may want to leave your rented
car in Britain and pick up a left-side drive when you cross the Channel.

Requirements Your own U.S. or Canadian driver's license is acceptable. An International Driver's Permit, available from the American Automobile
Association, may be a good idea.

Extra Charges Picking up the car in one city or country and leaving it in another
may entail substantial drop-off charges or one-way service fees. The
cost of a collision or loss damage waiver (*see below*) can be high, also.
Some rental agencies will charge you extra if you return the car before the time specified on your contract. Ask before making un-
scheduled drop-offs. Fill the tank when you turn in the vehicle to
avoid being charged for refueling at what you'll swear is the most
expensive pump in town. Automatic transmissions and air-conditioning are not universally available abroad; ask for them when you
book if you want them, and check the cost before you commit yourself to the rental.

Cutting Costs If you know you will want a car for more than a day or two, you can
save by planning ahead. Major international companies have pro-
grams that discount their standard rates by 15%–30% if you make
the reservation before departure (anywhere from 24 hours to 14
days), rent for a minimum number of days (typically three or four),
and prepay the rental. Ask about these advance-purchase schemes
when you call for information. More economical rentals may come as
part of fly/drive or other packages, even bare-bones deals that combine only the rental plus an airline ticket (*see* Tours and Packages,
above). If you're flying into Britain and plan to spend some time first
in London, save money by arranging to pick up your car in the city
the day you depart; otherwise, arrange to pick up and return your
car at the airport.

Several companies operate as wholesalers—they do not own their
own fleets but rent in bulk from those that do and offer advanta-
geous rates to their customers. Rentals through such companies
must be arranged and paid for before you leave the United States.

Among them are **Auto Europe** (Box 1097, Camden, ME 04843, tel. 207/236–8235 or 800/223–5555, 800/458–9503 in Canada), **Connex International** (23 N. Division St., Peekskill, NY 10566, tel. 914/739–0066, 800/333–3949, or 800/843–5416 in Canada), **Europe by Car** (mailing address, 1 Rockefeller Plaza, New York, NY 10020; walk-in address, 14 W. 49th St., New York, NY 10020, tel. 212/581–3040 or 212/245–1713; 9000 Sunset Blvd., Los Angeles, CA 90069, tel. 213/252–9401 or 800/223–1516 in CA), **Foremost Euro-Car** (5430 Van Nuys Blvd., Suite 306, Van Nuys, CA 91401, tel. 818/786–1960 or 800/272–3299), and **The Kemwel Group** (106 Calvert St., Harrison, NY 10528, tel. 914/835–5555 or 800/678–0678). You won't see wholesalers' deals advertised: they're even better in summer, when business is down. Always ask whether the prices are guaranteed in U.S. dollars or foreign currency and if unlimited mileage is available. Find out about any required deposits, cancellation penalties, and drop-off charges, and confirm the cost of any required insurance coverage.

Insurance and Collision Damage Waivers
Before you rent a car, find out exactly what coverage, if any, is provided by your personal auto insurer and the rental company. Don't assume that you are covered. If you do want insurance from the rental company, secondary coverage may be the only type offered. You may already have secondary coverage if you charge the rental to a credit card.

In general if you have an accident, you are responsible for the automobile. Car rental companies may offer a collision damage waiver (CDW), which ranges in cost from $4 to $14 a day. You should decline the CDW only if you are certain you are covered through your personal insurer or credit card company.

Leasing
For trips of 21 days or more, you may save money by leasing a car. With the leasing arrangement, you are technically buying a car and then selling it back to the manufacturer after you've used it. You receive a factory-new car, tax free, with international registration and extensive insurance coverage. Rates vary with the make and model of car and length of time used. Before you go, compare long-term rental rates with leasing rates. Remember to add taxes and insurance costs to the car rentals, something you don't have to worry about with leasing. Companies that offer leasing arrangements include **The Kemwel Group, Europe by Car,** and **Auto Europe,** all listed above.

Rail Passes

If you plan on doing a lot of traveling while in Britain, consider purchasing a **BritRail Pass,** which gives unlimited travel over the entire British Rail Network and will save you a great deal of money. A variety of passes are offered. The adult first-class pass costs $299 for eight days, $489 for 15 days, $615 for 22 days, and $715 for one month. The adult standard pass costs $219 for eight days, $339 for 15 days, $425 for 22 days, and $495 for one month. Those over 60 can obtain a **Senior Citizen Pass,** which entitles the bearer to unlimited first-class travel. It costs $279 for eight days, $455 for 15 days, $555 for 22 days, and $645 for one month. There is also a standard pass. Young travelers (aged 16–25) can buy the **BritRail Youth Pass,** which allows unlimited standard travel. It costs $179 for eight days, $269 for 15 days, $339 for 22 days, and $395 for one month. (These are U.S. dollar figures; Canadian ones will be a little higher.) There are also **Flexi Passes,** which allow four, eight, or 15 days' travel in one month. All BritRail Pass holders also get useful discounts on

Britainshrinkers, escorted rail and coach tours of one–three days
out of London to various heritage attractions. Another option is the
England/Wales Flexipass, good for four day's unlimited travel within
an eight-day period. The adult first-class ticket costs $219, standard
class is $149. The **BritIreland Pass** allows five days out of 15 unlim-
ited travel for $399 and $269; any 10 days within a month will cost
$629 in first, $419 in standard.

If you want the flexibility of a car combined with the speed and comfort of the train, try **BritRail/Drive** (from around $280 per person,
based on two adults sharing a car, more for automatic transmission);
this gives you a three-day BritRail FlexiPass and three vouchers
valid for Hertz car hire from more than 100 locations throughout
Great Britain. If you call your travel agency or Hertz's international
desk (tel. 800/654–3131), the car of your choice will be waiting for
you at the station as you alight from your train.

You *must* purchase your BritRail Pass before you leave home. They
are available from most travel agents or from the BritRail Travel International office (1500 Broadway, New York, NY 10036, tel. 212/
575–2667 or 800/677–8585). Note that the **Eurail Pass** is not valid in
Britain.

Many travelers assume that rail passes guarantee them seats on the
trains they wish to ride. Not so. Seat reservations are required on
some European trains, particularly high-speed trains, and are a
good idea on trains that may be crowded—in Great Britain, particularly in summer on popular routes such as London–Edinburgh. You
will also need a reservation if you purchase overnight sleeping accommodations. BritRail can help you determine if you need reservations and can make them for you. They cost about $6 each, less if you
purchase them in Europe at the time of travel.

Student and Youth Travel

Travel Agencies **Council Travel Services (CTS),** a subsidiary of the nonprofit Council
on International Educational Exchange, specializes in low-cost
travel arrangements abroad for students and is the exclusive U.S.
agent for several discount cards. Also newly available from CTS are
domestic air passes for bargain travel within the United States.
CIEE's twice-yearly *Student Travels* magazine is available at the
CTS office at CIEE headquarters (205 E. 42nd St., 16th Floor, New
York, NY 10017, tel. 212/661–1450) and in Boston (tel. 617/266–
1926), Miami (tel. 305/670–9261), Los Angeles (tel. 310/208–3551)
and at 43 branches in college towns nationwide (free in person, $1 by
mail). **Campus Connections** (1100 E. Marlton Pike, Cherry Hill, NJ
08034, tel. 800/428–3235) specializes in discounted accommodations
and airline fares for students. The **Educational Travel Centre** (438 N.
Frances St., Madison, WI 53703, tel. 608/256–5551) offers low-cost
domestic and international airline tickets, mostly for flights departing from Chicago, and rail passes. Other travel agencies catering to
students include **TMI Student Travel** (1146 Pleasant St., Watertown,
MA 02172, tel. 617/661–8187 or 800/245–3672), and **Travel Cuts** (187
College St., Toronto, Ont. M5T 1P7, tel. 416/979–2406).

Discount Cards For discounts on transportation and on museum and attractions admissions, buy the **International Student Identity Card** (ISIC) if
you're a bona fide student, or the **International Youth Card** (IYC) if
you're under 26. In the United States the ISIC and IYC cards cost
$16 each and include basic travel accident and sickness coverage.
Apply to **CIEE** (*see above,* tel. 212/661–1414; the application is in
Student Travels). In Canada the cards are available for $15 each

from **Travel Cuts** (*see above*). In the United Kingdom they cost £5 and £4 respectively at student unions and student travel companies, including Council Travel's London office (28A Poland St., London W1V 3DB, tel. 071/437–7767).

Hosteling A **Hostelling International** (HI) membership card is the key to more than 6,000 hostels in 70 countries; the sex-segregated, dormitory-style sleeping quarters, including some for families, go for $7 to $20 a night per person. Membership is available in the United States through **Hostelling International/American Youth Hostels** (HI/AYH, 733 15th St. NW, Washington, DC 20005, tel. 202/783-6161), the American link in the worldwide chain, and costs $25 for adults 18–54, $10 for those under 18, $15 for those 55 and over, and $35 for families. Volume 1 of the two-volume *Guide to Budget Accommodation* lists hostels in Europe and the Mediterranean ($13.95, including postage). HI membership is available in Canada through **Hostelling International-Canada** (205 Catherine St., Suite 400, Ottawa, Ont. K2P 1C3, tel. 613/748–5638) for $26.75, and in the United Kingdom through the **Youth Hostel Association of England and Wales** (Trevelyan House, 8 St. Stephen's Hill, St. Albans, Herts. AL1 2DY, tel. 0727/55215) for £9.

Traveling with Children

For information and advice when in London, call **Kidsline** (tel. 071/222–8070).

Publications Helpful local publications include *Capital Radio's London for Kids*
Local Guides magazine (available at newsstands, £2.50) and *Children's London*, a free booklet from the London Visitor and Convention Bureau (Tourist Information Centre, Victoria Station Forecourt, London SW1V 1JT, tel. 071/730–3488).

Newsletter *Family Travel Times*, published 10 times a year by **Travel With Your Children** (TWYCH, 45 W. 18th St., 7th Floor Tower, New York, NY 10011, tel. 212/206–0688; annual subscription $55), covers destinations, types of vacations, and modes of travel.

Books *Traveling with Children—And Enjoying It*, by Arlene K. Butler ($11.95 plus $3 shipping per book; Globe Pequot Press, Box 833, Old Saybrook, CT 06475, tel. 800/243–0495 or 800/962–0973 in CT), helps you plan your trip with children, from toddlers to teens. *Innocents Abroad: Traveling with Kids in Europe*, by Valerie Wolf Deutsch and Laura Sutherland ($15.95 or $4.95 paperback, Penguin USA, 120 Woodbine St., Bergenfield, NJ 07621, tel. 800/253–6476), covers child- and teen-friendly activities, food, and transportation.

Tour **Grandtravel** (6900 Wisconsin Ave., Suite 706, Chevy Chase, MD
Operators 20815, tel. 301/986–0790 or 800/247–7651) offers international and domestic tours for people traveling with their grandchildren. The catalogue, as charmingly written and illustrated as a children's book, positively invites armchair traveling with lap-sitters aboard. **Families Welcome!** (21 W. Colony Pl., Suite 140, Durham, NC 27705, tel. 919/489–2555 or 800/326–0724) packages and sells family tours to Europe.

American Institute for Foreign Study (AIFS, 102 Greenwich Ave., Greenwich, CT 06830, tel. 203/869–9090) offers a family-vacation program in Britain specifically designed for parents and children.

Getting There On international flights, the fare for infants under age two not occu-
Airfares pying a seat is generally either free or 10% of the accompanying adult's fare; children ages 2–11 usually pay half to two-thirds of the

adult fare. On domestic flights, children under two not occupying a seat travel free, and older children currently travel on the "lowest applicable" adult fare.

Baggage In general, infants paying 10% of the adult fare are allowed one carry-on bag, not to exceed 70 pounds or 45 inches (length + width + height) and a collapsible stroller; check with the airline before departure, because you may be allowed less if the flight is full. The adult baggage allowance applies for children paying half or more of the adult fare.

Safety Seats The FAA recommends their use and details approved models in the free leaflet "**Child/Infant Safety Seats Recommended for Use in Aircraft**" (available from the Federal Aviation Administration, APA–200, 800 Independence Ave. SW, Washington, DC 20591, tel. 202/267–3479). Airline policy varies. U.S. carriers allow FAA-approved models bearing a sticker declaring their FAA approval. Because these seats are strapped into a regular passenger seat they may require that parents buy a ticket even for an infant under two who would otherwise ride free. Foreign carriers may not allow infant seats, may charge the children' rather than the infant's fare for their use, or may require you to hold your baby during takeoff and landing, thus defeating the seat's purpose.

Facilities Aloft Some airlines provide other services for children, such as children's meals and freestanding bassinets (only to those with seats at the bulkhead, where there's enough legroom). Make your request when reserving. The annual February/March issue of *Family Travel Times* gives details of the children's services of dozens of airlines (*see below*). "Kids and Teens in Flight" (free from the U.S. Department of Transportation, tel. 202/366–2220) offers tips for children flying alone.

Lodging Novotel (tel. 800/221–4542) hotels allow up to two children to stay free in their parents' room. **Trusthouse Forte Hotels** in Britain have special Babycare Kits and children's menus; children under five are free and ages 6–13 in parents' room enjoy reduced rates. (Keep in mind that in Britain, hotels will often allow only three people in a room.)

Baby-sitting Services First check with the hotel desk for recommended local child-care arrangements. Also try **Nanny Service** (9 Paddington St., London WIM 3LA, tel. 071/935–3515) and **Universal Aunts** (Box 304, London SW4 ONN, tel. 071/738–8937).

Hints for Travelers with Disabilities

Organizations Several organizations provide travel information for people with disabilities, usually for a membership fee, and some publish newsletters and bulletins. Among them are the **Information Center for Individuals with Disabilities** (Fort Point Pl., 27–43 Wormwood St., Boston, MA 02210, tel. 617/727–5540 or 800/462–5015 in MA between 11 and 4, or leave message; TDD 617/345–9743); **Mobility International USA** (Box 10767, Eugene, OR 97440, tel. and TDD 503/343–1284, fax 503/343–6812), the U.S. branch of an international organization based in Britain (*see below*) and present in 30 countries; **MossRehab Hospital Travel Information Service** (1200 W. Tabor Rd., Philadelphia, PA 19141, tel. 215/456–9603, TDD 215/456–9602); the **Travel Industry and Disabled Exchange** (TIDE, 5435 Donna Ave., Tarzana, CA 91356, tel. 818/368–5648, fax 818/344–0078); and **Travelin' Talk** (Box 3534, Clarksville, TN 37043, tel. 615/552–6670, fax 615/552–1182).

In the United Kingdom Main information sources include the **Royal Association for Disability and Rehabilitation** (RADAR, 25 Mortimer St., London W1N 8AB, tel. 071/637–5400), which publishes travel information for the disabled in Britain, and **Mobility International** (228 Borough High St., London SE1 1JX, tel. 071/403–5688), the headquarters of an international membership organization that serves as a clearinghouse of travel information for people with disabilities.

Travel Agencies and Tour Operators **Flying Wheels Travel** (143 W. Bridge St., Box 382, Owatonna, MN 55060, tel. 507/451–5005 or 800/535–6790) is a travel agency specializing in domestic and worldwide cruises, tours, and independent travel itineraries for people with mobility impairments. Adventurers should contact **Wilderness Inquiry** (1313 5th St. SE, Minneapolis, MN 55414, tel. and TDD 612/379–3838), which orchestrates action-packed trips like white-water rafting, sea kayaking, and dog sledding for those challenged with disabilities. Tours are designed to bring together people who are physically challenged with those who aren't.

Publications In addition to the fact sheets, newsletters, and books mentioned above are several free publications available from the Consumer Information Center (Pueblo, CO 81009): "New Horizons for the Air Traveler with a Disability," a U.S. Department of Transportation booklet describing changes resulting from the 1986 Air Carrier Access Act and those still to come from the 1990 Americans with Disabilities Act (include Dept. 608Y in the address), and the Airport Operators Council's *Access Travel: Airports* (Dept. 5804), which describes facilities and services for the disabled at more than 500 airports worldwide.

Travelin' Talk Directory (*see* Organizations, *above*) was published in 1993. This 500-page resource book ($35) is packed with information for travelers with disabilities. Twin Peaks Press (Box 129, Vancouver, WA 98666, tel. 206/694–2462 or 800/637–2256) publishes the *Directory of Travel Agencies for the Disabled* ($19.95), listing more than 370 agencies worldwide and *Wheelchair Vagabond* ($14.95), a collection of personal travel tips. Add $2 per book for shipping.

Hints for Older Travelers

Organizations The **American Association of Retired Persons** (AARP, 601 E St. NW, Washington, DC 20049, tel. 202/434–2277) provides independent travelers who are members of the AARP (open to those age 50 or older; $8 per person or couple annually) with the Purchase Privilege Program, which offers discounts on hotels, car rentals, and sightseeing, and also arranges group tours, cruises, and apartment living through AARP Travel Experience from American Express (400 Pinnacle Way, Suite 450, Norcross, GA 30071, tel. 800/927–0111 or 800/745–4567).

Two other organizations offer discounts on lodgings, car rentals, and other travel products, along with such nontravel perks as magazines and newsletters; the **National Council of Senior Citizens** (1331 F St. NW, Washington, DC 20004, tel. 202/347–8800; membership $12 annually) and **Mature Outlook** (6001 N. Clark St., Chicago, IL 60660, tel. 800/336–6330; $9.95 annually).

Note: Mention your senior-citizen identification card when booking hotel reservations for reduced rates, not when checking out. At restaurants, show your card before you're seated; discounts may be limited to certain menus, days, or hours. If you are renting a car, ask about promotional rates that might improve on your senior-citizen discount.

Educational Travel The nonprofit **Elderhostel** (75 Federal St., 3rd Floor, Boston, MA 02110, tel. 617/426–7788) has offered inexpensive study programs for people 60 and older since 1975. Held at more than 1,800 educational institutions, courses cover everything from marine science to Greek myths and cowboy poetry. Participants usually attend lectures in the morning and spend the afternoon sightseeing or on field trips; they live in dorms on the host campuses. Fees for two- to three-week international trips—including room, board, and transportation from the United States—range from $1,800 to $4,500.

Interhostel (University of New Hampshire, 6 Garrison Ave., Durham, NH 03824, tel. 800/733–9753), a slightly younger enterprise than Elderhostel, caters to a slightly younger clientele—50 and over—and runs programs overseas in some 25 countries. The idea is similar: Lectures and field trips mix with sightseeing, and participants stay in dormitories at cooperating educational institutions or in modest hotels. Programs are usually two weeks in length and cost $1,500–$2,100 excluding airfare.

Tour Operators The following tour operators specialize in older travelers: **Evergreen Travel Service** (4114 198th St. SW, Suite 3, Lynnwood, WA 98036, tel. 206/776–1184 or 800/435–2288) has introduced the "Lazy Bones" tours for those who like a slower pace. If you want to take your grandchildren, look into **Grandtravel** (*see* Traveling with Children, *above*). **Saga International Holidays** (222 Berkeley St., Boston, MA 02116, tel. 800/343–0273) caters to those over age 60 who like to travel in groups.

Publications *The 50+ Traveler's Guidebook: Where to Go, Where to Stay, What to Do* by Anita Williams and Merrimac Dillon ($12.95; St. Martin's Press, 175 5th Ave., New York, NY 10010) is available in bookstores and offers many useful tips. "The Mature Traveler" (Box 50820, Reno, NV 89513, tel. 702/786–7419; $29.95 per year), a monthly newsletter, contains many travel deals for older travelers.

Hints for Gay and Lesbian Travelers

Organizations The **International Gay Travel Association** (Box 4974, Key West, FL 33041, tel. 305/292–0217, 800/999–7925, or 800/448–8550), which has 700 members, will provide you with names of travel agents and tour operators who specialize in gay travel. The **Gay & Lesbian Visitors Center of New York Inc.** (135 W. 20th St., 3rd Floor, New York, NY 10011, tel. 212/463–9030 or 800/395–2315; $100 annually) mails a monthly newsletter, valuable coupons, and more to its members.

Tour Operators and Travel Agencies The dominant travel agency in the market is **Above and Beyond** (3568 Sacramento St., San Francisco, CA 94118, tel. 415/922–2683 or 800/397–2681). Tour operator **Olympus Vacations** (8424 Santa Monica Blvd., Suite 721, West Hollywood, CA 90069; tel. 310/657–2220 or 800/965–9678) offers all-gay and lesbian resort holidays. **Skylink Women's Travel** (746 Ashland Ave., Santa Monica, CA 90405, tel. 310/452–0506 or 800/225–5759) handles individual travel for lesbians all over the world and conducts two international and five domestic group trips annually.

Publications The premiere international travel magazine for gays and lesbians is *Our World* (1104 North Nova Rd., Suite 251, Daytona Beach, FL 32117, tel. 904/441–5367; $35 for 10 issues). "Out & About" (tel. 203/789–8518 or 800/929–2268; $49 for 10 issues) is a 16-page monthly newsletter with extensive information on resorts, hotels, and airlines that are gay-friendly.

Further Reading

Many writers' names have become inextricably linked with the regions in which they set their books or plays. Hardy's Wessex, Daphne Du Maurier's Cornwall, Wordsworth's Lake District, Shakespeare's Arden, or Brontë Country, are now evocative catch phrases, treasured by local tourist boards. But however hackneyed the tags may now be, you *can* still get a heightened insight to an area through the eyes of authors of genius, even though they may have been writing a century or more ago. Here are just a few works that may provide you with an understanding of their authors' loved territory.

Thomas Hardy's *Mayor of Casterbridge, Tess of the D'Urbervilles, Far from the Madding Crowd*, and indeed almost everything he wrote is solidly based on his Wessex (Dorset) homeland. Daphne Du Maurier had a deep love of Cornwall from her childhood; *Frenchman's Creek, Jamaica Inn*, and *The King's General* all capture the county's Celtic atmosphere. The Brontë sisters' *Wuthering Heights, The Tennant of Wildfell Hall*, and *Jane Eyre* all breathe the sharp air of the high Fells around their Haworth home. William Wordsworth, who was born at Cockermouth in the Lake District, depicts the area's rugged beauty in many of his poems, especially the *Lyrical Ballads*.

Virginia Woolf's visits to Vita Sackville-West at her ancestral home of Knole, in Sevenoaks, resulted in the novel *Orlando*. The stately home is now a National Trust property. The country around Batemans, near Burwash in East Sussex, the home where Rudyard Kipling lived for more than 30 years, was the inspiration for *Puck of Pook's Hill* and *Rewards and Fairies*. Lamb House in Rye, also in East Sussex, was home to the American writer, Henry James, and after him E. F. Benson, whose delicious Lucia books are set in a thinly disguised version of the town. Both Batemans and Lamb House are National Trust buildings.

A highly irreverent—and very funny—version of academic life, *Porterhouse Blue*, by Tom Sharpe, will guarantee that you look at Oxford and Cambridge with a totally different eye. John Fowles's *The French Lieutenant's Woman*, largely set in Lyme Regis, is full of local color for visitors to Dorset.

James Herriot's successfully televised veterinary surgeon books, among them *All Creatures Great and Small*, give evocative accounts of life in the Yorkshire dales.

Mysteries are almost a way of life in Britain, partly because many of the best English mystery writers set their plots in their home territory. Modern whodunits by P. D. James and Ruth Rendell can be relied on to convey a fine sense of place, while Ellis Peters's Brother Cadfael stories re-create life in medieval Shrewsbury with a wealth of telling detail. There are always, of course, the villages, vicarages, and scandals of Agatha Christie's "Miss Marple" books.

For the many fans of the Arthurian legends, there are some excellent, imaginative novels, which not only tell the stories, but give fine descriptions of the British countryside. Among them are *Sword at Sunset*, by Rosemary Sutcliffe; *The Once and Future King*, by T. H. White; and the four Merlin novels by Mary Stewart, *The Crystal*

Cave, The Hollow Hills, The Last Enchantment, and *The Wicked Day.*

An animal's close-to-the-earth viewpoint can reveal all kinds of countryside insights about Britain. *Watership Down,* by Richard Adam, was a runaway best seller about rabbits in the early '70s, and *Wind in the Willows,* by Kenneth Grahame, gives a vivid impression of the Thames Valley 80 years ago which still holds largely true today.

Anyone interested in writers and the surroundings that may have influenced their works should get *The Oxford Literary Guide to the British Isles,* edited by Dorothy Eagle and Hilary Carnell, and *Literary Britain,* by Frank Morley.

Two good background books on England are *The English World,* edited by Robert Blake, and Godfrey Smith's *The English Companion. The London Encyclopaedia,* by Ben Weinreb and Christopher Hibbert, is invaluable as a source of information on the capital.

The Buildings of England and *The Buildings of Scotland,* originally by Nicholas Pevsner, but much updated since his death, are a multivolume series, organized by county, which sets out to chronicle every building of any importance. The series contains an astonishing amount of information.

Arriving and Departing

From North America by Plane

Flights are either nonstop, direct, or connecting. A **nonstop** flight requires no change of plane and makes no stops. A **direct** flight stops at least once and can involve a change of plane, although the flight number remains the same; if the first leg is late, the second waits. This is not the case with a **connecting** flight, which involves a different plane and a different flight number.

The Airlines   Airlines serving London and other major cities in Britain include **American Airlines** (tel. 800/433–7300); **British Airways** (tel. 800/247–9297); **Continental** (tel. 800/231–0856); **Delta** (tel. 800/241–4141); **Northwest Airlines** (tel. 800/447–4747); **TWA** (tel. 800/892–4141); and **United** (tel. 800/538–2929).

Flying Time   The flight time to London from New York is about 6½ hours, from Chicago 7½ hours, and from Los Angeles 10 hours.

Cutting Flight   The Sunday travel section of most newspapers is a good source of
Costs   deals. When booking, particularly through an unfamiliar company, call the Better Business Bureau and your local or state Consumer Protection Bureau to find out whether any complaints have been registered against it, pay with a credit card if you can, and consider trip-cancellation and default insurance (*see* Insurance, *above*).

Promotional   Less expensive fares, called promotional or discount fares, are
Airfares   round-trip and involve restrictions, which vary according to the route and season. You must usually buy the ticket—commonly called an APEX (advance purchase excursion) when it's for international travel—in advance (seven, 14, or 21 days are usual), although some of the major airlines have added no-frills, cheap flights to compete with new bargain airlines on certain routes.

With the major airlines the cheaper fares generally require minimum and maximum stays (for instance, over a Saturday night or at least seven and no more than 30 days). Airlines generally allow some return date changes for a $25 to $50 fee, but most low-fare tickets are nonrefundable. Only a death in the family would prompt the airline to return any of your money if you cancel a nonrefundable ticket. However, you can apply an unused nonrefundable ticket toward a new ticket, again with a small fee. The lowest fare is subject to availability, and only a small percentage of the plane's total seats will be sold at that price. Contact the U.S. Department of Transportation's Office of Consumer Affairs (I–25, Washington, DC 20590, tel. 202/366–2220) for a copy of "Fly-Rights: A Guide to Air Travel in the U.S." *The Official Frequent Flyer Guidebook* by Randy Petersen ($14.99 plus $3 shipping; 4715-C Town Center Dr., Colorado Springs, CO 80916, tel. 719/597–8899, 800/487–8893, or 800/485–8893) yields valuable hints on getting the most for your air travel dollars.

Consolidators   Consolidators or bulk-fare operators—"bucket shops"—buy blocks of seats on scheduled flights that airlines anticipate they won't be able to sell. They pay wholesale prices, add a markup, and resell the seats to travel agents or directly to the public at prices that still undercut the airline's promotional or discount fares (higher than a charter ticket but lower than an APEX ticket, and usually without the advance-purchase restriction). Moreover, some consolidators sometimes give you your money back. Carefully read the fine print detailing penalties for changes and cancellations. If you doubt the reliability of a company, call the airline once you've made your booking and confirm that you do, indeed, have a reservation on the flight.

The biggest U.S. consolidator, C.L. Thomson Express, sells only to travel agents. Well-established consolidators selling to the public include **UniTravel** (Box 12485, St. Louis, MO 63132, tel. 314/569–0900 or 800/325–2222), **Council Charter** (205 E. 42nd St., New York, NY 10017, tel. 212/661–0311 or 800/800–8222), and **Travac** (989 6th Ave., New York, NY 10018, tel. 212/563–3303 or 800/872–8800).

Charter Flights   Charters usually have the lowest fares and the most restrictions. Departures are limited and seldom on time, and you can lose all or most of your money if you cancel. (The closer to departure you cancel, the more you lose, although sometimes you will be charged only a small fee if you supply a substitute passenger.) The charterer, on the other hand, may legally cancel the flight for any reason up to 10 days before departure; within 10 days of departure, the flight may be canceled only if it becomes physically impossible to operate it. The charterer may also revise the itinerary or increase the price after you have bought the ticket, but if the new arrangement constitutes a "major change" you have the right to a refund. Before buying a charter ticket, read the fine print for the company's refund policy and details on major changes. Money for charter flights is usually paid into a bank escrow account, the name of which should be on the contract. If you don't pay by credit card, make your check payable to the escrow account (unless you're dealing with a travel agent, in which case, his or her check should be payable to the escrow account). The U.S. Department of Transportation's Office of Consumer Affairs (I–25, Washington, DC 20590, tel. 202/366–2220) can answer questions on charters and send you its "Plane Talk: Public Charter Flights" information sheet.

Charter operators may offer flights alone or with ground arrangements that constitute a charter package. You typically must book charters through your travel agent. One good source is **Charterlink** (988 Sing Sing Rd., Horseheads, NY 14845, tel. 607/739–7148 or 800/221–1802), a no-fee charter broker that operates 24 hours a day.

Discount
Travel Clubs
Travel clubs offer members unsold space on airplanes, cruise ships, and package tours at as much as 50% below regular prices. Membership may include a regular bulletin or access to a toll-free hot line giving details of available trips departing from three or four days to several months in the future. Most also offer 50% discounts off hotel rack rates, but double check with the hotel to make sure it isn't offering a better promotional rate independent of the club. Clubs include **Discount Travel International** (114 Forrest Ave., Suite 203, Narberth, PA 19072, tel. 215/668–7184; $45 annually, single or family), **Entertainment Travel Editions** (Box 1014, Trumbull, CT 06611, tel. 800/445–4137; $28–$48 annually), **Great American Traveler** (Box 27965, Salt Lake City, UT 84127, tel. 800/548–2812; $29.95 annually), **Moment's Notice Discount Travel Club** (425 Madison Ave., New York, NY 10017, tel. 212/486–0503; $45 annually, single or family), **Privilege Card** (3391 Peachtree Rd. NE, Suite 110, Atlanta, GA 30326, tel. 404/262–0222 or 800/236–9732; domestic annual membership $49.95, international, $74.95), **Travelers Advantage** (CUC Travel Service, 49 Music Sq. W, Nashville, TN 37203, tel. 800/548–1116; $49 annually, single or family), and **Worldwide Discount Travel Club** (1674 Meridian Ave., Miami Beach, FL 33139, tel. 305/534–2082; $50 annually for family, $40 single).

Enjoying the
Flight
Many experienced travelers prefer to take a morning flight to Great Britain and arrive in the evening, just in time for a good night's sleep. Others prefer to have the extra day at their destination, and fly at night, arriving in the morning.

Fly at night if you're able to sleep on a plane. Because the air aloft is dry, drink plenty of beverages while on board; remember that drinking alcohol contributes to jet lag, as do heavy meals. Since feet swell at high altitudes, remove your shoes before take off. Sleepers usually prefer window seats to curl up against; restless passengers ask to be on the aisle. Bulkhead seats, in the front row of each cabin, have more legroom, but since there's no seat ahead, trays attach awkwardly to the arms of your seat, and you must stow all possessions overhead. Bulkhead seats are usually reserved for the disabled, the elderly, and people traveling with babies.

Smoking
Since February 1990, smoking has been banned on all domestic flights of less than six hours duration; the ban also applies to domestic segments of international flights aboard U.S. and foreign carriers. On U.S. carriers flying to Great Britain and other destinations abroad, a seat in a no-smoking section must be provided for every passenger who requests one, and the section must be enlarged to accommodate such passengers if necessary as long as they have complied with the airline's deadline for check-in and seat assignment. If smoking bothers you, request a seat far from the smoking section.

Foreign airlines are exempt from these rules but do provide no-smoking sections, and some nations, including Canada as of July 1, 1993, have banned smoking on all domestic flights; other countries may ban smoking on flights of less than a specified duration. The International Civil Aviation Organization has set July 1, 1996, as the date to ban smoking aboard airlines worldwide, but the body has no power to enforce its decisions.

From North America by Ship

Cunard Line (555 5th Ave., New York, NY 10017, tel. 800/221–4770) operates four ships that make transatlantic crossings. The *Queen Elizabeth 2* (*QE2*) makes regular crossings April–December, between Southampton, England, and Baltimore, Boston, and New

York City. Arrangements for the *QE2* can include one-way airfare. Cunard Line also offers fly/cruise packages and pre- and post-land packages. Check the travel pages of your Sunday newspaper for other cruise ships that sail to Britain.

Staying in Britain

Getting Around

By Plane Because Britain is such a small country, internal air travel is much less important there than in the United States. Broadly speaking, for trips of less than 200 miles, the train is quicker given the time required to get to and from city centers and airports, compared with the centrally based rail stations. Flying tends to cost more, and many internal U.K. flights exist primarily as feeders from provincial airports into Heathrow and Gatwick for international flights. For trips of more than 200 miles—for example, between London and Glasgow or Edinburgh—or where a sea crossing is involved, to places such as the Isle of Man, Belfast, the Channel Islands, or the Scottish islands, air travel has a considerable time advantage.

British Airways operates shuttle services between London/ Heathrow and Edinburgh, Glasgow, Belfast, and Manchester. Passengers can simply turn up and get a flight (usually hourly) without booking. There are also shuttle services from Gatwick. **British Midlands** operates from Heathrow to Teesside, Belfast, Glasgow, Liverpool, and the Isle of Man. The Scottish islands are served by **Loganair** from Glasgow and Edinburgh, while in the Southwest of England **Brymon Airways** flies from Plymouth and Exeter to the Scilly Isles. For services to the Channel Islands, see Chapter 7.

An airport tax has been introduced in Britain, which has never had one, to bring it into line with most other countries. For departures to the United Kingdom and European destinations, the tax is £5, or £10 when your flight travels to anywhere else in the world.

You can book all flights through **British Airways** (Bulova Center, 75–20 Astoria Blvd., Jackson Heights, New York, NY 11370, tel. 800/247–9297) or through local travel agents in Britain.

By Train Britain's state-owned rail system, has offered, for many years, an excellent way of exploring Britain without the stress and hassle of driving yourself around. But the long-awaited reprivatization raises many questions about the future. By the time you read this, everything we say about train travel in Britain may have changed.

British Rail, the basic BritRail network, has been one of the densest in the world, with frequent main-line service, especially on the InterCity network (*see below*). On main routes (but not on Sundays or in remote rural areas), you can expect to find a train departing within the hour. And there has been a reintroduction of vintage steam locomotives on scenic tourist routes. The semiannual *British Rail Passenger Timetable* (about £6.75) covers all BritRail services, including private, narrow-gauge, and steam lines, as well as special services and rail-based tourist facilities.

You can also find detailed timetables of most rail services in Britain and some ferry services in the *Thomas Cook European Timetable*, issued monthly and on sale in the United States at **Forsyth Travel Library** (9154 W. 57th St., Dept. TCT, Shawnee Mission, KS, 66201). You can order a timetable with Discover, Visa, or MasterCard Monday–Saturday 9:30–4:30 Central Time (tel. 913/384–3440 or 800/ 367–7984, fax 913/384–3553).

BritRail offers high-speed modern service on the **InterCity** passenger network between large cities, either on electric trains or streamlined InterCity 125 diesels (which can go 125 mph). The new 140-mph electrified route between London and Yorkshire is being extended to Newcastle and Edinburgh. London's suburban **Network SouthEast** is a largely electrified commuter service that extends to Brighton, northwest to Oxford, and northeast to Cambridge. Seat reservations are strongly advised on the major express routes out of London, and mandatory on some trains. You can reserve a seat (smoking or non-smoking) on any InterCity train from any main-line station or BR travel agent, at £1 for standard class, £2 for first class.

The London area has 13 major terminals all serving both main and suburban lines, so be sure you know which station you're arriving at or leaving from. All are linked by London's Underground network.

Rail Passes   If you'd rather explore a specific part of Britain in greater detail, the series of **Regional Rail Rover** unlimited travel tickets offers excellent value. **All Line** tickets, covering the whole of Britain, cost £215 for seven days and £350 for 14. The country is also divided up into areas, for which Rover tickets are sold at different prices, depending on the size of the area covered. Details can be obtained from the **British Rail Travel Centre** (Euston Station, London NW1 1DF, tel. 071/387–7070). (*See also* Rail Passes in Before You Go, *above*.)

By Bus   Britain has a comprehensive bus (short-haul) and coach (long-distance) network, which offers an inexpensive way of seeing the country. Coaches are much cheaper than trains, usually about half the price or even less, but are generally slower, although some motorway services with the modern **Rapide** coaches reduce the margin considerably. Seats are comfortable, with meal and rest stops usually arranged on longer trips. (Some coaches have toilet facilities on board.) Information about coach services throughout Britain can be obtained from **Victoria Coach Station** (Buckingham Palace Rd., London SW1W 9TP, tel. 071/730–0202) or from **Eastern Scottish** (St. Andrew's Sq., Edinburgh).

The British equivalent to Greyhound coaches is **National Express**, which with its Scottish associate, **Caledonian Express,** is by far the largest British operator. Victoria Coach Station in London is the hub of the National Express network, serving around 1,500 destinations. Information is available from any of the company's 2,500 agents nationwide. There are also National Express sales offices at London's Heathrow and Gatwick airport coach stations.

National Express's **Tourist Trail Pass** costs £49 for three consecutive days of travel, £79 for five days travel out of 10 consecutive days, £119 for eight days out of 16, and £179 for 15 days out of 30. They can be bought for U.S. dollars from **British Travel Associates** (Box 299, Elkton, VA 22827, tel. 703/298–2232 or 800/327–6097).

The classic British double-decker buses still operate on many of the routes of Britain's extensive network of local bus services. It's difficult to plan a journey by country bus, because privatization of lines has led to the development of many small companies and schedules are constantly changing. But the local bus station wherever you're staying, and maybe the local tourist information center, will have precise information. Most companies offer day or week "Explorer" or "Rover" unlimited-travel tickets, and those in popular tourist areas invariably operate special scenic tours in summer. The top deck of a stately double-decker bus is a great place from which to view the surrounding countryside.

By Car With well over 55 million inhabitants in a country about the size of California, Britain's roads are among the most crowded in the world. And yet, away from the towns and cities, you can find miles of little-used roads and lanes where driving can be a real pleasure—and adventure.

If you are a member of a motoring organization, there may be reciprocal membership benefits with the Automobile Association (AA) in Britain, including breakdown assistance. Check with your club; they will also be able to advise you about procedures, insurance, and necessary documentation. Both the **AA** (Fanum House, Basingstoke, Hampshire, RQ21 2 EA, tel. 0256/20123) and the **Royal Automobile Club** (RAC House, Bartlett St., Box 10, Croydon, Surrey CR2 6XW, tel. 081/686–2525) offer associate membership for overseas visitors and a wealth of detailed information about motoring in Britain.

Rules of the Road The most noticeable difference for the visitor is that when in Britain you drive on the left. This takes a bit of getting used to, but it's easier if you're driving a British car where the steering and mirrors are designed for U.K. conditions. Study your map before leaving the airport, and be sure to give yourself plenty of time to adjust. And don't forget that jet lag can seriously affect your reaction time. The use of seat belts is obligatory in the front seat and in the backseat where they exist.

Speed limits are complicated, and traffic police can be hard on speeders, especially in urban areas. In those areas, the limit (shown on circular red signs) is generally 30 mph, but 40 mph on some main roads. In rural areas the limit is 60 mph on ordinary roads and 70 mph on motorways (*see below*). At traffic circles ("roundabouts" here) circulation is clockwise, and entering motorists must give way to cars coming from their right.

Types of Roads There's now a very good network of superhighways (motorways) and divided highways (dual carriageways) throughout most of Britain, though in remoter parts, especially of Wales and Scotland, travel is noticeably slower. Motorways (with the prefix *M*), shown in blue on most maps and road signs, are mainly two or three lanes in each direction, without any right-hand turns. Service areas are about an hour's travel time apart (or less). Dual carriageways with the prefix *A*, shown on maps as thick red lines, often with a black line in the center, have both traffic lights and traffic circles, and right turns are sometimes permitted. Roads whose numbers have a *T* suffix are toll roads, but these are very few.

The vast network of lesser roads (single red *A* and narrower brown *B* lines), for the most part old coach and turnpike roads, might make your trip take twice the time and show you twice as much. Minor roads drawn in yellow or white, unlettered and unnumbered, are the ancient lanes and byways, a superb way of discovering the real Britain. Sometimes there isn't even room for two vehicles, and you must reverse into a passing place if you meet an oncoming car or tractor.

Good planning maps are available from the **AA** and the **RAC** (*see above*); for in-depth exploring, try the **Ordnance Survey** 1:50,000 series maps, which show every road, track, and footpath in the country. For ordinary motoring, the less detailed Ordnance Survey **Motoring Atlas,** which costs £6.99, will suffice.

Gasoline Expect to pay a good deal more for gasoline than you would in the United States; it costs about £2.60 a gallon (57p a liter) for four star—and up to 10p a gallon higher in remote locations—but remember that the British Imperial gallon (4½ liters) is about 20% more in volume than the U.S. gallon. Most gas stations stock two-, three-, and four-star (91, 94, and 97 octane ratings) plus diesel fuels; lead-free gas is increasingly common and cheaper than leaded. Service stations on motorways are located at regular intervals and are usually open 24 hours a day; elsewhere they usually close overnight, and by 6 PM and all day Sunday in country areas.

Car Rental If you have a current driver's license, you can rent a car with ease at most towns and cities. On average, a medium-size sedan is around £250 per week (unlimited mileage) or around £50 per day, including insurance and temporary AA membership. If you use one of the major credit cards as security, a cash deposit isn't required and full payment for the rental (cash or credit) can be made at the end of the trip. (*See also* Car Rentals in Before You Go, *above.*)

These are just a sample of the car-rental agencies operating in Britain: **Avis Rent-a-Car** (International Reservations, Trident House, Station Rd., Hayes, Middlesex UB3 4DJ, tel. 081/848–8765); **Hertz Rent-a-Car** (Radnor House, 1272 London Rd., London SW16 4XW, tel. 081/679–1777), with whom reservations can also be made in conjunction with the BritRail Pass from the United States (*see* Rail Passes, *above*); **Kenning Car Hire** (Manor House, Old Rd., Chesterfield, Derbyshire S40 3RW, tel. 0246/208888 or 800/227–8990 to reserve in the United States).

Motorail One way to combine the convenience of the car with the speed of the train is by **Motorail.** The car is put on a specially designed rail car while passengers relax in comfortable coaches or, in some cases, overnight sleeping compartments. Check for the latest services available. You have to book in advance through British Rail agencies.

By Boat Most of the islands off the coast of Britain are served by regular car ferries, usually linked to train and coach services on the mainland. For shorter crossings, reservations are not needed, but you should reserve for the longer crossings to Ireland, the Isle of Man, the Channel Islands, and the Continent. Details of most crossings will be found in either the *Thomas Cook European Timetable*, or in the British Rail timetables.

Only a few rivers and lakes in Britain are big enough to maintain regular boat or waterbus systems. The Scottish Highlands offer tourist services on Loch Lomond, Loch Etive, and Loch Katrine; details of rail tours (about 200 a year) using ferries and boat services can be obtained from **Chiltern Trains** (Box 10, Chinnor, Oxford OX9 4GW, tel. 0844/353500). The Lake District has regularly scheduled boat service from April until October on the larger lakes—Windermere, Coniston, Ullswater, and Dertwentwater. Passengers are allowed to alight and return on foot along the shore or by a later boat.

The British Tourist Authority's booklet *U.K. Waterway Holidays* is a good source of information. You can also contact the **Inland Waterways Association** (114 Regents Park Rd., London NW1 8UQ, tel. 071/586–2510) or the **British Waterways Board** (Willow Grange, Church Rd., Watford WD1 3QA, tel. 0923/226422). **U.K. Waterway Holidays** (1 Port Hill, Hertford SG14 1PJ, tel. 0992/550616) is a knowledgeable company in contact with several U.S. firms. It runs the *Merganser*, the only luxury barge that cruises the length of the Thames, and also cruises on waterways all over England and Wales.

The Channel Tunnel The **Channel Tunnel** opened officially in May 1994, providing the fastest route across the Channel—35 minutes from Folkestone to Calais, or 60 minutes from motorway to motorway. It consists of two large 50-kilometer (31-mile)-long tunnels for trains, one in each direction, linked by a smaller service tunnel running between them. **Le Shuttle** (tel. 0345/353535 in Great Britain, 800/388–3876 in the United States), a special car, bus, and truck train, was scheduled to begin running in 1994 operating a continuous loop, with services departing every 15 minutes at peak times and at least once an hour through the night. No reservations are necessary, although tickets may be purchased in advance from travel agents. Most passengers stay in their own car throughout the "crossing"; progress updates are provided on display screens and radio. Motorcyclists park their bikes in a separate section with its own passenger compartment, while foot passengers must book passage by coach (*see* By Train, *above*).

The Tunnel is reached from exit 11a of the M20/A20. Drivers purchase tickets from tollbooths, then pass through frontier control before loading onto the next available service. Unloading at Calais takes eight minutes. Ticket prices start at £130 for a low-season five-day round-trip in a small car and are based on season, time of day, length of stay, and car size regardless of the number of passengers. Peak season fares are not always competitive with ferry prices.

Eurostar (for information, tel. 071/922–4486 in the U.K., 800/942–4866 in the U.S.) high-speed train service was also scheduled to begin in 1994, with passenger-only trains whisking riders between new stations in Paris (Gare du Nord) and London (Waterloo) in three hours and between London and Brussels (Midi) in 3¼ hours. The service of five trains daily each way was scheduled to increase in 1995 to 15 trains daily in each direction. At press time, ticket prices had not been set. Tickets are available in the United Kingdom through **InterCity Europe,** the international wing of BritRail (London/Victoria Station, tel. 071/834–2345 or 071/828–8092 for credit-card bookings), and in the United States through **Rail Europe** (tel. 800/942–4866) and **BritRail Travel** (1500 Broadway, New York, NY 10036, tel. 800/677–8585).

Telephones

For years, both foreign visitors and the British themselves have cursed the country's inefficient and antiquated phone system. The privatization of British Telecom has brought little improvement, although changes are slowly being introduced and central equipment modernized. This has meant that numbers are changing all over the country, all the time.

Important note: There will be **a nationwide change to all telephone numbers on April 5, 1995,** when an extra digit will be added to area codes. In most areas this will consist of a "1" after the initial "0."

Local Calls Public telephones are plentiful, particularly in London, although you may find many of them vandalized and broken. Other than on the street, the best place to find a bank of pay phones is in a rail station, hotel, or large post office. The distinctive red boxes are gradually being replaced by generic glass and steel cubicles, but they remain in more remote areas of the country. The workings of coin-operated telephones vary, but there are usually instructions in each unit. The oldest kind takes only 10p coins; the new ones take 10p, 20p, 50p, and £1 coins. But the most modern system (which also discourages vandals) is the Phonecard, which comes in denominations of 10, 20, 40, and 100 units of 10p each, and can be bought at a number of post offices and newsstands. Cardphones are clearly marked with a special green insignia, and they will not accept coins.

A short local call during the peak period (9 AM–1 PM) costs about 20p, or two units. Each large city or region in Britain has its own numerical prefix, which is used only when you are dialing from outside the city. In provincial areas, the dialing codes for nearby towns are often posted in the booth, and some even list international codes.

International Calls The cheapest way to make an overseas call is to dial it yourself, but be sure to have plenty of coins or Phonecards on hand. After you have inserted the coins or card, dial 101 (the international code), then the country code—for the United States this is 1—followed by the area code and local number. To make a collect or other operator-assisted call, dial 155. *Never make a call home from your hotel—the surcharge can be as much as 300%.*

See also Long-Distance Calling in Before You Go, *above.*

Operators and Information For information anywhere in Britain, dial either 142 or 192. For help in making a U.K. call, dial 100; in making an international one, dial 155.

Mail

Postal Rates Airmail letters to the United States and Canada cost 41p for 10 grams; postcards 35p; aerogrammes 36p. Letters and postcards to Europe not over 20 grams, 30p (25p to EU member countries). Letters within the United Kingdom, first class 25p, second class and postcards 19p. These rates may have increased by early 1995.

Receiving Mail If you're uncertain where you'll be staying, you can arrange to have your mail sent to American Express (6 Haymarket, London SW1Y 4BS). The service is free to cardholders; all others pay a small fee. You can also collect letters at London's main post office. Ask to have them sent to Poste Restante, Main Post Office, London. The point of collection is the King Edward Building (King Edward St., London EC1A 1AA, tel. 071/239–5047). Hours are Monday, Tuesday, Thursday, and Friday 8:30 AM–6:30 PM; Wednesday 9 AM–6:30 PM. You'll need your passport or other official form of identification.

Tipping

Some restaurants and most hotels add a service charge of 10%–15% to the bill. In this case, do not tip. If no service charge is indicated, add 10% to your total bill. Taxi drivers should also get 10%. You are not expected to tip theater or cinema ushers, elevator operators, or bartenders in pubs. Hairdressers and barbers should receive 10%–15%.

Opening and Closing Times

Banks Most banks are open weekdays 9:30–4:30. Some have Thursday evening hours, and a few are open on Saturday mornings.

Shops Usual business hours are Monday–Saturday 9–5:30; on Sunday, small shops stay open all day if they wish to, and supermarkets remain open just six hours. Outside the main centers, most shops close at 1 PM one day a week, often Wednesday or Thursday. In small villages, many also close for lunch. In large cities—especially London—department stores stay open late (usually until 7:30 or 8) one day a week.

National Holidays April 14 (Good Friday); April 17 (Easter Monday); May 1 (May Day); May 29 (Bank Holiday); August 28 (Bank Holiday, except in Scotland); December 25 and 26 (Christmas).

Museums, Stately Homes, and Castles

Museum and gallery hours vary considerably from one part of the country to another, and holiday closings vary, so be sure to check. In large cities, most are open Tuesday–Saturday; many are also open on Sunday afternoons. The majority close on Monday. Many museums admit children under 6 free.

Most stately homes change their opening times at Easter and in October—or when Britain changes its clocks for summertime. Many of them close down completely from October to Easter, or to April 1, whichever is earlier. Opening and closing times can change at a moment's notice, especially if staff is suddenly not available, so always phone first. Many stately homes close their doors a half-hour to an hour before the stated time, to allow the last parties time to complete their tour.

Admission Fees Admission to museums is often free, though some have started to charge. Stately homes, if still in private hands, can survive only by charging entry fees, which have rocketed over the last few years together with the owners' expenses. Many attractions now offer family tickets that cover two parents and two or three children. Luckily, most stately homes and nearly all castles belong to either the **National Trust** or to **English Heritage.** If you are visiting lots of castles or stately homes, buying an annual membership in both organizations before you start out would mean huge savings.

The National Trust **Royal Oak Membership** is available in the United States at $40 for individuals, $60 for families (tax deductible). Besides entry to all National Trust properties, this also covers thrice-yearly literature and admission to lectures and other events in both the United Kingdom and the United States. Contact: Damaris Horan, Executive Director, Royal Oak Foundation (285 West Broadway, Suite 400, New York, NY 10013, tel. 212/966–6565). English Heritage annual membership has no U.S. version, but its British membership is £17.50 for an adult, £30 for two adults at the same address. Contact: English Heritage Membership Department (Box 1BB, London W1A 1BB).

For Scotland and Wales: Contact **Friends of Scottish Monuments** (Historic Scotland, SDD Room 306, 20 Brandon St., Edinburgh EH3 5RA, tel. 031/244–3101), membership £14 adult, £28 family. **Heritage in Wales** (Dept. EH, Cadw, Brunel House, 2 Fitzalan Rd., Cardiff CF2 1UY, tel. 022/246–5511), membership £15 (adult) and £30 (family).

Also available is a **Great British Heritage Pass,** which will admit you to Hampton Court, Stonehenge, the Shakespeare Birthplace Trust properties, Tower Bridge, and others. It costs $45 (£27) for a 15-day version, $67 (£41) for a month-long pass. It can be obtained in the United States from British Airways or the British Travel Bookshop (tel. 800/448–3039).

Guides

In several chapters of this guide, we mention the availability of **Blue Badge Guides.** These are fully qualified guides, whose badges are awarded by the Regional Tourist Boards after rigorous training and examination. Lists of them are obtainable from the Regional Tourist Offices listed in each chapter under *Essential Information.* Many of these guides are also members of the **Guild of Guide Lecturers** (Guild House, 52D Borough High St., London SE1 1XN, tel. 071/403–1115). The Guild has over 1,200 members, who come from all walks of life and are extensively trained in the needs of visitors to Britain. They can not only organize tailor-made sightseeing tours and specialized walking trips, but can help with theater tickets, or arrange shopping trips. Contact the Guild for further details.

British Tours Ltd. (6 South Molton St., London W1Y 1DH, tel. 071/629–5267) has been offering personalized tours of Britain by car and chauffeur-guide since 1958. This is a luxurious way of seeing the country. Their prices include hotels, breakfast, and dinner, and such extras as theater tickets for the Royal Shakespeare Company in Stratford. Although they do have many tried and tested regular tours, they also customize trips to fit your special needs and preferred pace.

Shopping

Throughout Britain, souvenir and gift shops abound, and museum and gallery shops offer high-quality posters, books, art prints, and crafts. Both Wales and Scotland are famous for woolen products, and retail outlets sell sweaters, tartans, tweeds, scarves, skirts, and hats at reasonable prices. Traditional Celtic jewelry is also popular. The Midlands offers world-renowned china and pottery, including Wedgwood, Royal Doulton, and Royal Worcester. The factory outlet shops, where you can buy seconds, are well worth a detour. The Southwest, especially Devon and Cornwall, is known for its edibles—"scrumpy" (strong local cider), homemade toffees, rich fudge, and heavenly clotted cream.

Little-known even to most Brits are the factory shops that sell directly to the public, where the saving can be as much as 50% on the normal store price. *Factory Shop Guides* are published by Gillian Cutress and Rolf Stricker (1 Rosebery Mews, Rosebery Rd., London SW2 4DQ, tel. 081/678–0593) and cost between £3.50 and £4.50. There is also a national version. *The Great Britain Factory Shop Guide,* costing £14.95.

We should point out that shops in Britain have been hit just as hard by the recession as those in the United States. You will find many High Streets with empty premises, and some of the shops we list may have been forced to close.

VAT Refunds Foreign visitors can get a refund of Britain's 17½% Value Added Tax (VAT) by the Over the Counter and the Direct Export method. Most larger stores provide these services, but only if you request them, and will handle the paperwork. For the **Over the Counter** method, you must spend more than £75 in one store. Ask the store for Form VAT 407 (you must have identification—passports are best), to be given to Customs when you leave the country. (Lines at major airports are usually long, so allow plenty of time.) The refund will be forwarded to you in about eight weeks, minus a small service charge, either in the form of a British check or as a credit to your charge card. (American banks will tag on a conversion fee for cashing the check, however). The **Direct Export** method, where the goods go directly to your home, is more cumbersome. VAT Form 407 must be certified by Customs, police, or a notary public when you get home and then sent back to the store, which will refund your money.

Sports and the Outdoors

Biking Bikes are banned from motorways and most dual carriageways or main trunk roads, but on side roads and country lanes, the bike is one of the best ways to explore Britain. You will find the Ordnance Survey 1:50,000 maps invaluable. Some parts of Britain have bicycle routes in towns and through parts of the countryside; for example, in the Peak District National Parks, bikes can be hired by the day for use on special traffic-free trails. Cyclists can legally use public bridleways—green, unsurfaced tracks reserved for horses, walkers, and cyclists.

If you're considering a cycling holiday in Britain, it is well worth joining the **Cyclists' Touring Club** (69 Meadrow, Godalming, Surrey GU7 3HS, tel. 0483/417217), the national body in Britain that promotes the interests of cycle tourists. Membership is £24 a year (£12 for students and those under 18, £16 for those over 65, £40 for a family of more than three). Members receive free advice and information, including a detailed route-planning service for any region of Britain, a handbook of recommended bed-and-breakfasts, and a magazine, *Cycle Touring and Campaigning.*

Boating and Sailing If you feel like taking a boat out on Britain's several hundred miles of historic canals and waterways, the **Association of Pleasure Craft Operators** (35a High St., Newport, Shropshire TF10 8JW, tel. 0952/813572) provides a complete list of all its boat-rental operators in Britain. (*See also* Getting Around by Boat, *above.*) One of the best areas for boating is the Broads, in Norfolk, where the local TIC can help you with up-to-date information. You'll also find regular short river and canal cruises in the major tourist centers such as York, Bristol, Bath, and Stratford-upon-Avon during the season.

Camping Britain offers an abundance of campsites. Some are large and well equipped; others are merely farmers' fields, offering primitive facilities. For information, contact the British Tourist Authority in the United States or the **Camping and Caravanning Club** (Greenfields House, Westwood Way, Coventry, West Midlands CV4 8JH, tel. 0492/531066).

Golf There are hundreds of fine courses all over the country, especially in Scotland, the birthplace of the sport, and visiting golfers are welcome at many private clubs. If you plan to play a great deal, a book you'll find useful is *The Golf Guide* (FHG Publications, Abbey Mill Business Centre, Seed Hill, Paisley, PA1 1TJ Scotland, tel. 041/887–0428, £7.99).

Tennis Tennis is a favorite recreation in Britain, and most towns have municipal courts where you can play for a small fee. Country hotels, too, often have courts. The hotel service information in each chapter lists tennis availability.

Walking The whole country is crisscrossed by meandering trails—there are more than 100,000 miles of footpaths in England and Wales—some tiny and local, some very long and of historic significance, such as Peddar's Way in East Anglia, or the Pennine Way in Yorkshire. For £15 (£19 joint membership) you can join **The Ramblers Association** (1–5 Wandsworth Rd., London SW8 2XX, tel. 071/582–6878), which issues a magazine every two months and a yearbook with many addresses useful to the walker, and a list of more than 2,000 bed-and-breakfast accommodations within 2 miles of selected long-distance paths.

Other organizations active in the field, and which can provide much background information, are the delightfully named **Byways and Bridleways Trust** (The Granary, Charlcutt, Calne, Wiltshire SN11 9HL, tel. 024/974–273); **Long Distance Walkers Association** (c/o Kevin Uzzell, 7 Ford Dr., Yarnfield, Stone, Staffordshire ST15 0RP, tel. 0785/760684); and the information centers of the National Parks, which all have books, maps, and walking information. You may also wish to contact **The Farm Holiday Bureau,** (National Agricultural Centre, Stoneleigh, Kenilworth, Warwickshire CV8 2LZ, tel. 0203/696909), a national network of farming families offering country holidays.

Water Sports Britain brims with rivers and lakes, and it is possible to swim and fish on many of them. One drawback is that pollution is a major problem here, so check carefully beforehand. The other problem is that the water can be icy cold! Most local authorities operate indoor pools, and a few have outdoor ones; entrance fees are minimal. Nearly all large hotels now have pools, as indicated in the hotel entries.

In some areas, like Cornwall and the coast of Wales, there are excellent sandy beaches with good swimming, but generally, the sea around Britain is very cold most of the year and much of the coast is fringed with pebbled beaches. Many seaside towns have windsurfing boards available. Some beaches are awarded a European Blue Flag, granted to beaches with a high standard of water quality (they should be cleaned daily during high season), and good facilities. Britain wins very few each year, usually only a couple of dozen, mostly in Wales and the Southwest. To counter the disturbing picture created by winning so few European Blue Flags, Britain has instituted its own awards, the Seaside Awards—which, coincidentally, are also blue! Always ask if a beach has been given either a Flag or a Seaside Award before deciding to use it.

Dining

Until relatively recently, British food was condemned the world over for its plainness and mediocrity, but an influx of foreign restaurants and the birth of the New British Cuisine have had a noticeable effect on quality. It is now possible to eat interesting food all over the country. And most restaurants in Britain now offer vegetarian selections.

The limiting factor is now not so much the quality and variety of the food, as the price of the meal. Restaurants in Britain can be outrageously expensive for what they offer. Be very sure to check the menu posted outside almost all establishments before venturing in. As a general rule of thumb, wine bars and bistros offer reasonably priced meals in interesting surroundings, and you will find excellent budget food at lunchtime in good pubs and inns. Be careful of the prices of drinks in a restaurant. They can double your final check. Remember, the owner puts a profitable markup on wine—and mineral water. Many restaurants will charge you as much for a glass of mineral water as a whole 2-liter bottle would cost you in a supermarket.

Mealtimes Breakfast is generally served between 7:30 and 9, and lunch between noon and 2. Tea—often a meal in itself—is eaten between 4:30 and 5:30, dinner or supper between 7:30 and 9:30, sometimes earlier, seldom later except in large cities. High tea, at about 6, replaces dinner in some areas.

Lodging

Hotels   Most hotels have rooms with private bathrooms, although some older ones may have only washbasins; in this case, showers and bathtubs (and toilets) are usually just down the hall. Generally, hotel prices include breakfast, but it's often only a Continental breakfast. Prices in London are significantly higher than in the rest of the country, they usually do *not* include breakfast, and often the quality and service are not as good. TICs will reserve rooms for you, usually for a small fee. A great many hotels offer special weekend and off-season bargain packages.

Bed-and-Breakfasts   These are a special British tradition, and the backbone of budget travel. They are usually in a family home, few have private bathrooms, and most offer only breakfast. Guest houses are a slightly larger, somewhat more luxurious, version. Both provide a glimpse of everyday British life. The famous *Cottages, B&Bs and Country Inns of England and Wales*, by Elizabeth H. Gundrey, covers the waterfront and has given its author's name to the language, as in "Let's go Gundreying."

Farmhouses   These have become increasingly popular in recent years; their special appeal is the rustic, rural experience. Consider this option only if you are touring by car. Prices are generally very reasonable. Ask for the British Tourist Authority booklet *Farmhouse Vacations*. Farming and country people who offer B&B accommodation, usually on working farms, have joined together in a network that calls itself **The Farm Holiday Bureau** (National Agricultural Centre, Stoneleigh, Kenilworth, Warwickshire CV8 2LZ, tel. 0203/696909). Members are endorsed by their Regional Tourist Board, who inspect all FHB properties.

Historic Buildings   Want to spend your vacation in a gothic banqueting house, an old lighthouse, or maybe in a gatehouse that sheltered Mary, Queen of Scots in 1586? Several organizations have specially adapted historic buildings to rent. Most of them are self-catering, so for a short while you can pretend you live there. Try **The Landmark Trust** (Shottesbrooke, Maidenhead, Berkshire SL6 3SW, tel. 0628/825925) and the **National Trust** (Box 101, Western Way, Melksham, Wiltshire SN12 8EA, tel. 0225/705676). All the buildings have been modernized, with due respect to their historic status, (but there are no TVs in the Landmark Trust properties). Other organizations are **Portmeirion Cottages** (Portmeirion, Gwynedd, Wales LL48 6ER, tel. 0766/770228) and the rather upscale **Rural Retreats** (Retreat House, Station Rd., Blockley, Moreton-in-Marsh, Gloucestershire GL56 9DZ, tel. 0386/701177).

Holiday Cottages   Furnished apartments, houses, cottages, and trailers are available for weekly rental in all areas of the country. These vary from quaint, cleverly converted farmhouses to brand-new buildings set in scenic surroundings. For families and large groups, they offer the best value-for-money accommodations, but as they are often in isolated locations, a car is vital. Lists of rental properties are available free of charge from the **British Tourist Authority**. Discounts of up to 50% apply during the off-season (October–March). A good publication on the subject is the *Good Holiday Cottage Guide* (Swallow Press, tel. 0438/869489; £3.50).

University Housing In larger cities and in some towns, certain universities offer their residence halls to paying vacationers out of term time. The facilities available are usually compact single sleeping units, and they can be rented on a nightly basis. Contact the **British Universities Accommodation Consortium** (Box 907, University Park, Nottingham NG7 2RD, tel. 0602/504571).

Youth Hostels There are more than 350 youth hostels throughout Britain, ranging from very basic to almost luxurious. Many are in remote and beautiful areas; others on the outskirts of large cities. Despite the name, there is no age restriction. They are inexpensive, generally reliable, and usually contain cooking facilities. Contact the **YHA Headquarters** (Trevelyan House, 8 St. Stephens's Hill, St. Albans, Hertfordshire AL1 2DY, tel. 0727/55215).

Home Exchange You can find a house, apartment, or other vacation property to exchange for your own by becoming a member of a home-exchange organization, which then sends you its annual directories listing available exchanges and includes your own listing in at least one of them. Arrangements for the actual exchange are made by the two parties to it, not by the organization. For more information contact the **International Home Exchange Association** (IHEA, 41 Sutter St., Suite 1090, San Francisco, CA 94104, tel. 415/673-0347 or 800/788-2489). Principal clearinghouses include: **Intervac International** (Box 590504, San Francisco, CA 94159, tel. 415/435-3497), which publishes three annual directories; membership is $62, or $72 if you want to receive the directories but remain unlisted. **Loan-a-Home** (2 Park La., Apt. 6E, Mount Vernon, NY 10552, tel. 914/664-7640) specializes in long-term exchanges; there is no charge to list your home, but the directories cost $35 or $45 depending on the number you receive. **Villa Leisure** (Box 209, Westport, CT 06881, tel. 407/624-9000 or 800/526-4244) facilitates swaps.

Apartment and Villa Rentals **Heritage of England** (Box 297, Falls Village, CT 06031, tel. 203/824-5155 or 800/533-5405) specializes in British rentals. Other companies include **At Home Abroad** (405 E. 56th St., Suite 6H, New York, NY 10022, tel. 212/421-9165); **Europa-Let** (92 N. Main St., Ashland, Oregon 97520, tel. 503/482-5806 or 800/462-4486); **Interhome Inc.** (124 Little Falls Rd., Fairfield, NJ 07004, tel. 201/882-6864); **Property Rentals International** (1 Park West Circle, Suite 108, Midlothian, VA 23113, tel. 804/378-6054 or 800/220-3332); **Rent a Home International** (7200 34th Ave. NW, Seattle, WA 98117, tel. 206/789-9377 or 800/488-7368); and **Vacation Home Rentals Worldwide** (235 Kensington Ave., Norwood, NJ 07648, tel. 201/767-9393 or 800/633-3284). **Hideaways International** (15 Goldsmith St., Box 1270, Littleton, MA 01460, tel. 508/486-8955 or 800/843-4433) functions as a travel club; membership ($99 yearly per person or family at the same address) includes two annual guides plus quarterly newsletters, and rentals are arranged directly between members, not by the club staff.

Credit Cards

The following credit-card abbreviations are used: AE, American Express; DC, Diners Club; MC, MasterCard; and V, Visa.

The Performing Arts

Britain may be a comparatively small country, but its arts, especially its performing arts, are as varied as its landscape, and have become famous all over the world. Drama, ballet, opera, and music all are still surprisingly healthy, despite the difficulties under which they struggle. The days of state subsidy are seriously threatened. The political dogmas of Thatcherism and the restraints of the recession have hit the bank accounts of arts organizations badly. Private sponsorship, long a feature of the American arts scene, is now looming large in Britain.

The British arts scene is not only rich and colorful, but incredibly complex. We can only do justice to a fraction of it here, just enough, we hope, to whet your appetite.

Drama An evening taking in a play is a vital element of any visitor's trip to Britain. And not just in London's West End. There are provincial theaters in most of the cities and large towns up and down the land. Several of the most interesting ones were built soon after World War II, and are often impressive pieces of civic architecture. The Birmingham Rep's modern building, with its great glass wall, dominated the city center for years before it was joined by the new Symphony Hall. The theaters in Sheffield, Derby, Nottingham, and Leicester all dramatically expressed the role that the arts were expected to play in their cities' postwar lives. In Coventry it was as important to build a new theater as a new cathedral.

But not all theaters are in recent buildings. The Bristol Old Vic has modern theatrical quarters that surround a delightful Georgian auditorium, lovingly preserved. In Manchester, the Royal Exchange Theatre is a space-capsule theater-in-the-round constructed inside an 1840s Victorian stock exchange, like a giant metal spider trapped in an ornate teapot. The productions here are some of the most exciting in the country.

Many of the provincial theaters have developed their own national and international reputations. The Haymarket in Leicester is renowned for musicals, many of which have transferred to London. Theatre Clwyd in Mold, North Wales, is almost a national theater for Wales, with brilliantly cast revivals of the classics, which travel far afield. In Scarborough, a seaside town in Yorkshire, the dramatist-director, Alan Ayckbourn, has run for many years the Stephen Joseph Theatre, where he tries out his own plays, most of which are regularly transferred to London, appearing as often as not at the National Theatre.

But the delight of British regional theaters lies in their great diversity and local panache. In the little town of Richmond, in Yorkshire, is a charming little Georgian theater, seating about 200 in rows and balconies that still reflect the 18th-century class divisions. In Bagnor, near Newbury, Berkshire, a water mill has been converted into a lovely little theater overlooking a lake. Porthcurno, near Penzance, Cornwall, has the Minack Theatre, which is situated on a cliff top, overlooking the sea. The lovely 1819 Theatre Royal in Bury St. Edmunds is owned and run by the National Trust and is still fully functioning. There are woodland theaters, theaters in barns, and several in grand old country houses.

Of course, the pinnacle of the dramatic scene consists of two great national companies, the National Theatre and the Royal Shakespeare Company (RSC). They do have separate identities, though it is not always easy to pin down the way in which they differ. The RSC (as it is always known) is the more prolific, performing in five auditoriums, including two at the Barbican in London—one a large house built to their own specifications, the other called The Pit, a small studio space. RSC has three stages at Stratford-upon-Avon—the large Memorial Theatre, the Swan, and The Other Place. Thanks to the financial help of an American philanthropist, the Swan was constructed inside the only part left of a Victorian theater, which burnt down in 1936. Constructed on the lines of Shakespeare's Globe, it is one of the most exciting acting spaces anywhere in the country. The Other Place is a newer venue used for experimental staging. The RSC has also been keen on touring, but unfortunately, at press time, the Company announced that it had to cancel its tours, yet another victim of the recession.

The National Theatre plays in the three auditoriums in its concrete fortress on the South Bank—the Olivier, the Lyttleton, and the Cottesloe, in descending order of size, the Olivier being huge and the Cottesloe quite small. Of the two companies, the RSC is the more cohesive, with a very impressive volume of work, and a steadily developing style, though it also suffers from serious lapses of taste and concentration in its productions. The great majority of its offerings are works of Shakespeare and the English classics, with the occasional ventures into musicals. The National, on the other hand, ransacks world drama for its fare, having notable successes with Greek classics and French tragedy, as well as mounting some of the best stagings of American musicals anywhere outside Broadway. It also attracts star performers more than the RSC, which relies largely on teamwork, and creates stars from its own ranks. Both companies suffer from serious financial problems, even though some of their best productions are transferred to the commercial sector, and often develop into considerable hits.

Opera   Opera, like drama, is well represented around the country. Apart from the two major companies in London, the English National Opera, and the Royal Opera at Covent Garden, there are two other national companies, the Welsh National at Cardiff, and the Scottish National in Glasgow. They both have adventurous artistic policies, attacking such blockbusters as Wagner's *Ring* and *The Trojans* of Berlioz. They also tour, the Welsh National especially, appearing in small towns around the principality, even performing in movie houses when no other stage is available. There is also a northern England company, originally a spin-off from the English National, called Opera North, based in Leeds, and is as venturesome as its begetter.

Opera has always been an extravagant art form, and the recession has hit it severely. But one company has managed to build itself a new home. Glyndeboure, in deepest Sussex, relies entirely on sponsors and its ticket sales, having no state subsidy. It opened a new theater last year, ending 50 years of its "let's-do-an-opera-in-the-barn" image. A visit there will cost you an arm and a leg, but you'll feel like a guest at a very superior house party.

The two London companies are poles apart. The Royal Opera at Covent Garden is socially the most prestigious. It is housed in an atmospheric, plush, and gilt, 1812 theater. But it suffers from the problems that bedevil all companies that rely largely on international stars—not enough rehearsal time, a wobbly artistic policy, and stratospherically expensive seat prices. The English National Opera (ENO) was originally a *volksoper*, based at the small Sadler's Wells Theater in north London, and moved to the Coliseum, beside Trafalgar Square, 30 years ago. It is still a peoples' opera, though now housed in a huge theater. For the last decade it has had a brilliantly innovative directoral team, though they have now changed and their replacements have not yet settled in. Seat prices here are half those at Covent Garden, and the productions are excitingly inventive. The company, like the RSC, is a team, mostly of British singers, who act as well as they sing. The one drawback is that the auditorium sometimes dwarfs the voices.

Festivals   Britain is a land of festivals, mostly, though not exclusively, in the summer. Whatever the size of the town, it'll have a festival some time. Some are of international scope, while others are small local wingdings. Leading the parade is the Edinburgh Festival (mid-August–early September), born in the dark days after World War II, when people needed cheering up. Today it is still going strong, with opera, drama, recitals, and ballet by artists from all over the world. The festival now has the added attraction of the Fringe, a concurrent event, with as many as 800 performances crammed into three weeks, small-scale productions from the classic to the bizarre, held in everything from telephone kiosks to church halls. Not to be outdone, Edinburgh's rival city, Glasgow, now stages the Mayfest (May), a city-wide festival of theater, dance, rock and pop, and street entertainment.

Smaller than Edinburgh and Glasgow's events, but still notable, are the dozens of festivals up and down the country. In Bath, the International Festival (late May–mid-June) is noted for its music especially. In Aldeburgh, the Festival of Music and the Arts (mid–late June) in a windswept East Anglian seaside town, is dedicated to the memory of Benjamin Britten, and again is mainly a music festival. In Cheltenham, there are two festivals, one musical (July), the other (early–mid-October) dedicated to literature, with readings, seminars, and lectures. York has both an early music festival (summer), and a Viking one (February). Llandrindod Wells, in Wales, goes Victorian and dresses up (late August). Worcester, Hereford, and Gloucester, take turns to mount the annual Three Choirs Festival (mid-August), the oldest in the world, which has seen premieres of some notable music. Truro stages a Three Spires Festival (June) in imitation. Wales has an annual feast of song and poetry (late July–early August) called the Royal National Eisteddfod. At Pitlochry in Scotland and Chichester in Sussex, there are summer drama festivals which have been so popular that the towns have managed to build theaters specially for them. At Ludlow, Shakespeare is performed during the summer in the open air, with the dramatic castle as backdrop. All these festivals have the advantage of focusing a visit to a town and helping you to meet the locals, but be sure to book well in advance, as they are extremely popular.

Ballet   Ballet is a surprising art to flourish in Britain, and it must be admitted that it only does so with a struggle. The premier company is, again, located at the Theatre Royal, Covent Garden, sharing it with the Royal Opera company. The Royal Ballet is going through a rather bad patch, suffering as it does from artistic arteriosclerosis. It is no longer adventurous enough in its choice of repertoire, having to dance endless performances of favorite three-act classics, just to make ends meet. But on a good night, as with the Royal Opera, a ballet performance in that lovely theater can be memorable.

The sibling Birmingham Royal Ballet is just the reverse. Young, zesty, with an adventurous director in Peter Wright, it is yet another excellent reason for visiting Birmingham. The Festival Ballet which renamed itself the English National Ballet, with very little cause, is Britain's only major dance company without a permanent home. It regularly tours its repertoire of classics countrywide. The Scottish Ballet is housed in Glasgow, and is as up-to-date as its sister opera company. There are several other smaller companies that tour the country, but that have suffered serious cutbacks from the financial restrictions of recent years.

Music Music performance, too, has seen a tremendous surge in popularity in the last 50 years. Recently, this popularity has been made concrete, as it were, with the opening of two major new concert halls, both with notable acoustics. Symphony Hall in Birmingham is the new home of the Birmingham Symphony, under its phenomenal young conductor, Simon Rattle. Glasgow has yet again stolen a march on its rival, Edinburgh, by opening its splendid new Royal Concert Hall. Apart from Birmingham, other cities have fine resident orchestras, including Liverpool, Manchester, and even the seaside town of Bournemouth.

In London, the three concert halls on the South Bank, together with the Barbican, the Albert Hall, and the Wigmore Hall, all provide the capital with venues for a rich and varied musical fare. For example, every night for six weeks in the summer, sponsored by the BBC, the Albert Hall hosts the biggest series of concerts in the world, involving 10 or more orchestras and dozens of other artists.

Musical life around the country flourishes, even outside the festival season. One particularly interesting aspect is the increasing number of empty churches that are being turned into community concert halls, and excellent ones they make, too. The prime example is London's lovely Baroque church of St. John's, Smith Square.

Great Itineraries

Writers at Home: Southwest England

All of Britain contains a wealth of fictional and real literary figures and places; there are several literary walking tours of London alone. For those who like to venture out on their own and explore more than just isolated plaques commemorating who slept (or was born or died) where, the following excursion takes in some lovely settings as well as enough artistic associations to keep any literature buff happy. For a free copy of the new pamphlet "Literary Britain," send a SASE (business size, 52¢) to any office of the British Tourist Authority (*see* Government Tourist Offices, *above*).

Duration Four days

Getting Around **By Car.** It is 220 miles round-trip from London (southwest).

By Public Transportation. Trains and buses depart regularly from London to Dorchester and Bath. Local services are available within the region, but plan carefully.

Two days: Hardy's Wessex

The environs of Dorchester are Hardy country. The early years of his life were spent in **Higher Brockhampton** (2 mi west of Dorchester on A31), part of the parish of Stinsford, or "Mellstock." Leave at least a day to visit Sherborne, Cranborne, and Bridport, and to travel to Lullworth Cove, to get a true sense of the countryside that inspired so much of his work. All the sights are within 25 miles of Dorchester. You can also include Salisbury and Stonehenge, which figure prominently in *Jude the Obscure* and *Tess of the D'Urbervilles*, respectively, by going northwest 30 miles on A31/A350/A30.

Two days: The Homes of Jane Austen

From rural delights we head for the civilized society of Jane Austen's world and novels. *Persuasion* and *Northanger Abbey* are especially associated with the city of **Bath** (105 miles west of London on

A4). She visited Bath frequently in her youth, and lived here between the ages of 26 and 31 (1801–1806). In 1809, Austen moved with her mother and sister Cassandra to **Chawton,** 50 miles south and 30 miles east of Bath on A36/A31. You will pass through Southampton, where she lived for three years, although all records of precisely where have been lost. She lived in Chawton until 1817, and her home there is now a museum. In the last year of her life she moved to lodgings in **Winchester,** 10 miles south on A31. She lived here at 8 College Street, and she is buried at Winchester Cathedral.

Aristocratic Houses of West Yorkshire and Derbyshire

Set between the industrial cities of England's east Midlands and Yorkshire are some of the finest mansions and grounds in the country. Many are within easy reach of one another, making a few days' manor-house spotting easy as well as fun. These two outings start from York and Nottingham, but you can just as easily start out from a base in Derby, Leeds, or Sheffield.

Duration Four–five days

Getting Around **By Car.** It is 60 miles round-trip from York; 80 miles round-trip from Nottingham.

Two days: Stately Houses in West Yorkshire

There are three houses to visit on this itinerary, which traces an ellipse southeast of York. The first stop is **Harewood House,** home of the earl and countess of Harewood and designed in 1759 with grounds landscaped by Capability Brown. It is on A64/A659, 25 miles west of York. **Oakwell Hall,** 12 miles south through Leeds, is an Elizabethan manor house complete with moat. **Lotherton Hall,** east on M62 and north on A642, is a country-house museum, with an Edwardian garden, bird garden, and deer park.

Two–three days: Stately Houses in Derbyshire

From Nottingham, follow A453/B587 to Melbourne, and **Melbourne Hall.** Ten miles northwest via the road to Derby and A52 brings you to **Kedleston Hall,** a magnificent mansion designed by the Adam brothers. Head due north for 20 miles to reach **Haddon Hall,** and 3 miles farther, **Chatsworth.** The first is medieval; the second dates from the 17th century. Finally, turning back toward Nottingham for 10 miles on A617, you will come to **Hardwick Hall,** built in 1597.

The Malt Whisky Trail of Scotland

Speyside, the valley of the River Spey, is arguably the most important whisky-producing area of Scotland. On the banks of the river itself, which runs from the Grampian Hills down to the Moray Firth, are many of Scotland's most famous malt-whisky distilleries. The route map reads like a list of the whisky bottles on the shelves of any well-stocked Scottish pub or hotel: Glenfarclas, Glenfiddich, Glen Grant, Cardhu, The Glenlivet, Strathisla, Tamdhu, and Tamnavulin. These eight whisky distilleries are linked by the signposted Malt Whisky Trail. The circular car trail, within two to three hours of Edinburgh or Glasgow, takes you on quiet roads through some of Scotland's most varied scenery of hill, woodland, and river valley—besides giving you insight into one of Scotland's most important exports. All the distilleries mentioned have visitor centers, give tours, and usually offer a wee dram (a free tasting!) at the end of the visit.

Duration It can be driven in one day, but a distillery visit could mean you will want two days.

Getting Around **By Car.** It will be at least a 50-mile round-trip, more if you spend the night in the Tomintoul area.

By Public Transport. Not recommended. You can reach Keith by rail and visit at least one distillery (Strathisla) on the trail, but bus service "upcountry" in this very rural area is not easy to plan around. The Keith (tel. 05422/2634; open May–Sept.) or Elgin (tel. 0343/542666 or 0343/543388) Tourist Information Centre can advise you on your itinerary.

Day one: Keith to Glenlivet

From Keith, take the B9014, which twists through pleasant, hilly farmlands, to Dufftown. Here, more than 30 years ago, the **Glenfiddich** Distillery pioneered the "open door" approach with extensive visitor facilities, and it still has one of the best presentations offered. If you have time for only one visit, make it Glenfiddich. It has as its backdrop the ruins of 13th-century Balvenie Castle. Southwest on the B9009/9008 is an attractive route toward the higher hills, with purple moorlands and birch woods giving a more upland air to the journey. Along the way, if the **Glenlivet** and **Tamnavulin** distilleries tempt you, you can find a bed here, or go on a little way to the village of Tomintoul.

Day Two

Reach Bridge of Avon (pronounced "Aan" with a long "a") by the B9008. This in turn leads to the main valley of the River Spey, with fine vistas of its glittering and fast-flowing course from the B9102, which has **Tamdhu** and **Cardhu** distilleries on the way. Alternatively, take the A95 to Aberlour (often marked on maps as Charlestown of Aberlour), an appealing community on the banks of the Spey. Buy some locally made shortbread here. Return to Keith via the A941 to Rothes (**Glen Grant**) and the B9015—or exit northward on A941 for the attractive town of Elgin and the delights of the Moray coast.

The Best of Roman Britain

The Romans occupied much of Britain from the Cornish coast up into Scotland. Ruins dot the landscape, and a few of Britain's major highways (as well as many minor ones) lie over Roman roads. The following two journeys present some highlights. The first excursion covers parts of western Britain not far north of London, an area that seems to have been particularly prosperous in Roman times; the second takes us north to explore that feat of engineering, Hadrian's Wall.

Duration Four–five days

Getting Around **By Car.** It is 150 miles round-trip from London (St. Albans and westward); 150 miles round-trip from Newcastle (Hadrian's Wall).

By Public Transportation. This might prove a bit difficult, although you can cover the route by train and bus if you are willing to risk possible delays. The British Tourist Association sometimes offers organized tours to these regions.

Two–three days: St. Albans and Westward

This excursion begins in **St. Albans** (known in Roman times as Verulamium), 20 miles northwest of London on A1, and continues due west to the Roman "villas" of **North Leigh, Chedworth,** and **Gloucester** before heading back south through **Cirencester** to **Bath.**

Along the way you will see some fantastic artifacts, tombs, forts, and amphitheaters, as well as the world-famous baths in, naturally, Bath. If you do some research beforehand (or even afterward) in London's **British Museum,** you will discover a wealth of archaeological finds.

One–two days: Hadrian's Wall

Following the 72-mile-long wall, built in AD 122–126, from east to west, this journey offers several museum stopping points along the way, the first in **Newcastle-upon-Tyne** and continuing through **Corbridge, Chester, Chesterholm,** and on to **Carlisle** (a city that recently celebrated its 1,000th anniversary.)

Castles and Strongholds

This itinerary, based in northeastern Kent, offers a quick history of castle architecture and the opportunity to visit some of the best examples Britain has to offer.

Duration Two–three days

Getting Around **By Car.** It is 150 miles round-trip from London.

By Public Transportation. Check with British Rail information centers and National Express or other bus companies.

One–two days: Down to Dover

Heading southeast from London on A2/A257 for Sandwich brings you to **Richborough Castle,** a 4th-century Saxon fort. From here take A258 to Deal, where you will find both **Deal Castle,** dating from 1540, and **Walmer Castle,** another Renaissance fortification, converted in the 18th century. Next comes **Dover Castle,** one of England's most impressive castles, which was still in military use as late as World War II.

One day: The Coast and Leeds

South down the coast is the town of Hythe and **Lympne Castle,** a 14th- to 15th-century building with a 13th-century Norman east tower. Leaving the best for last, M20 northwest will take you to **Leeds Castle,** a magnificent Norman fortress with 19th-century additions, set on two islands in a lake, surrounded by landscaped parkland.

2 Portraits of Great Britain

Great Britain at a Glance: A Chronology

2800 BC	First building of Stonehenge (later building 2100–1900)
54 BC	Julius Caesar's exploratory invasion of England
AD 43	Romans conquer England, led by Emperor Claudius
60	Boudicca, a native British queen, razes the first Roman London (Londinium) to the ground
122–27	Emperor Hadrian completes the Roman conquest and builds a wall across the north to keep back the Scottish Picts
145	The Antonine Wall built, north of Hadrian's, running from the Firth of Forth to the Firth of Clyde
300–50	Height of Roman colonization, administered from such towns as Verulamium (St. Albans), Colchester, Lincoln, and York
383–410	Romans begin to withdraw from Britain; waves of Germanic invaders—Jutes, Angles, and Saxons
c. 490	Possible period for the legendary King Arthur, who may have led resistance to Anglo-Saxon invaders; in 500 the Battle of Badon is fought
563	St. Columba, an Irish monk, founds monastery on the Scottish island of Iona; begins to convert Picts and Scots to Christianity
597	St. Augustine arrives in Canterbury to Christianize Britain
550–700	Seven Anglo-Saxon kingdoms emerge—Essex, Wessex, Sussex, Kent, Anglia, Mercia, and Northumbria—to become the core of English social and political organization for centuries
731	Bede completes the *Ecclesiastical History*
800s	Danish Viking raids solidify into widespread colonization
871–99	Alfred the Great, king of Wessex, unifies the English against Viking invaders, who are then confined to the northeast
919–54	Short-lived Norse kingdom of York

1040	Edward the Confessor moves his court to Westminster and founds Westminster Abbey
1066	William, duke of Normandy, invades; defeats Harold at the Battle of Hastings; is crowned at Westminster in December
1086	Domesday Book completed, a survey of all taxpayers in England, drawn up to assist administration of the new realm
1167	Oxford University founded
1170	Thomas à Becket murdered in Canterbury; his shrine becomes center for international pilgrimage
1189	Richard the Lionheart embarks on the Third Crusade
1209	Cambridge University founded

1215 King John forced to sign Magna Carta at Runnymede; it promulgates basic principles of English law: no taxation except through Parliament, trial by jury, and property guarantees

1272–1307 Edward I, a great legislator; in 1282–83 he conquers Wales and reinforces his rule with a chain of massive castles

1295 The Model Parliament sets future parliamentary pattern, with membership of knights from the shires, lower clergy, and civic representatives

1296 Edward I invades Scotland

1314 Robert the Bruce routs the English at Bannockburn

1337–1453 Edward III claims the French throne, starting the Hundred Years War. In spite of dramatic English victories—1346 at Crécy, 1356 at Poitiers, 1415 at Agincourt—the long war of attrition ends with the French driving the English out from all but Calais, which finally fell in 1558

1348–49 The Black Death (bubonic plague) reduces the population of Britain to around 2½ million; decades of social unrest follow

1381 The Peasants Revolt is defused by the 14-year-old Richard II

1399 Henry Bolingbroke (Henry IV) deposes and murders his cousin Richard II; beginning of the rivalry between houses of York and Lancaster

---

1402–10 The Welsh, led by Owen Glendower, rebel against English rule

1455–85 The Wars of the Roses—the York/Lancaster struggle erupts in civil war

1477 William Caxton prints first book in England

1485 Henry Tudor (Henry VII) defeats Richard III at the Battle of Bosworth, and founds the Tudor dynasty; he suppresses private armies, develops administrative efficiency and royal absolutism

---

1530s Under Henry VIII the Reformation takes hold; he dissolves the monasteries, finally demolishes medieval England and replaces it with a new society

Henry's marital history—in 1534 he divorces Katherine of Aragon after 25 years of marriage; in 1536 Anne Boleyn (mother of Elizabeth I) is executed in the Tower of London; in 1537 Jane Seymour dies giving birth to Edward VI; in 1540 Henry marries Anne of Cleves (divorced same year); in 1542 Katherine Howard is executed in the Tower; in 1542 he marries Katherine Parr, who outlives him

1554 Mary I marries Philip II of Spain; tries to restore Catholicism to England

1555 Protestant Bishops Ridley and Latimer are burned in Oxford; in 1556 Archbishop Cranmer is burned

1558–1603 Reign of Elizabeth I—Protestantism re-established; Drake, Raleigh, and other freebooters establish English claims in the West Indies and North America

1568 Mary, Queen of Scots, flees to England; in 1587 she is executed

1588 Spanish Armada fails to invade England

1603 James VI of Scotland becomes James I of England

1605 Guy Fawkes and friends in Catholic plot to blow up Parliament

1611 King James Authorized Version of the Bible published

1620 Pilgrims sail from Plymouth on the *Mayflower* and settle in New England

1629 Charles I dissolves Parliament, decides to rule alone

1642–49 Civil War between the Royalists and Parliamentarians (Cavaliers and Roundheads); the Parliamentarians win

1649 Charles I executed; England is a republic

1653 Cromwell becomes Lord Protector, England's only dictatorship

1660 Charles II restored to the throne; accepts limits to royal power

1665 The Great Fire of London, accession of William III (of Orange) and his wife, Mary II, as joint monarchs; royal power limited still further

1694 Bank of England founded

1706–09 Marlborough's victories over the French under Louis XIV

1707 The Act of Union: England, Scotland, and Wales join in the United Kingdom of Great Britain (as against the countries being united in the person of the king)

1714 The German Hanoverians succeed to the throne; George I's lack of English leads to a council of ministers, the beginning of the Cabinet system of government

1700s Under the first four Georges, the Industrial Revolution develops and with it Britain's domination of world trade

1715/1745 Two Jacobite rebellions fail to restore the House of Stuart to the throne; in 1746 final defeat takes place at Culloden Moor

1756–63 Seven Years War; Britain wins colonial supremacy from the French in Canada and India

1775–83 Britain loses its American colonies

1795–1815 Britain and its allies defeat French in the Napoleonic Wars; in 1805 Nelson is killed at Trafalgar; in 1815 Battle of Waterloo is fought

---

1801 Union with Ireland

1811–20 Prince Regent rules during his father's (George III) madness—the Regency period

1825 The Stockton to Darlington railway, the world's first passenger line with regular service, is established

1832 The Reform Bill extends the franchise, limiting the power of the great landowners

1834 Parliament outlaws slavery

1837–1901 The long reign of Victoria—Britain becomes the world's richest country, and the British Empire reaches its height; railways, canals, and telegraph lines draw Britain into one vast manufacturing net

1851 The Great Exhibition, Prince Albert's brainchild, is held in Crystal Palace, Hyde Park

1861 Prince Albert dies

1887 Victoria celebrates her Golden Jubilee; in 1901 she dies, marking the end of an era

---

1911–12 Rail, mining, and coal strikes

1914–18 World War I: Fighting against Germany, Britain loses a whole generation, with 750,000 men killed in trench warfare alone; enormous debts and inept diplomacy in the postwar years undermine Britain's position as a world power

1919 Ireland declares independence from England; bloody Black-and-Tan struggle results

1926 General Strike in sympathy with striking coal miners

1936 Edward VIII abdicates to marry American divorcée, Mrs. Wallis Simpson

1939–45 World War II—Britain faces Hitler alone until Pearl Harbor; London badly damaged during the Blitz, September '40–May '41; Britain's economy shattered by the war

1945 Labour wins a landslide victory; stays in power for six years, transforming Britain into a welfare state

1952 Queen Elizabeth accedes to the throne

1969 Serious violence breaks out in Northern Ireland

1972 National miners' strike

1973 Britain joins the European Economic Community after referendum

1975 Britain begins to pump North Sea oil

1981 Marriage of Prince Charles and Lady Diana Spencer

1982 Falklands regained

1987 Conservatives under Margaret Thatcher win a third term in office

1990 Glasgow is European Cultural Capital for the year

1990 John Major takes over as prime minister, ending Margaret Thatcher's illustrious, if controversial, career in office

1991 The Persian Gulf War

1992 Great Britain and the European countries join to form one European Community (EC), whose name was officially changed to European Union in 1993.

1994 Official opening of the Channel Tunnel by Queen Elizabeth II and President Mitterand

Kings and Queens

To help you sort out Britain's monarchs, we give here a list of those who have sat on the throne (before 1603 the throne of England, after that the joint throne of England, Scotland, and Wales). The dates are those of the reign, not of the monarch's life.

	1042–66	Edward the Confessor
	1066	Harold
House of Normandy	1066–87	William I—The Conqueror
	1087–1100	William II—Rufus (murdered)
	1100–35	Henry I
	1135–54	Stephen
House of Plantagenet	1154–89	Henry II
	1189–99	Richard I—Lionheart (killed in battle)
	1199–1216	John
	1216–72	Henry III
	1272–1307	Edward I
	1307–27	Edward II (murdered)
	1327–77	Edward III
	1377–99	Richard II (deposed, then murdered)
	1399–1413	Henry IV
	1413–22	Henry V
	1422–61	Henry VI (deposed)
House of York	1461–83	Edward IV
	1483	Edward V (probably murdered)
	1483–85	Richard III (killed in battle)
House of Tudor	1485–1509	Henry VII
	1509–47	Henry VIII
	1547–53	Edward VI
	1553	Jane (beheaded)
	1553–58	Mary I
	1558–1603	Elizabeth I
House of Stuart	1603–25	James I (VI of Scotland)
	1625–49	Charles I (beheaded)
Commonwealth	1653–58	Oliver Cromwell (Protector)
	1658–59	Richard Cromwell
House of Stuart (Restored)	1660–85	Charles II
	1685–88	James II (deposed and exiled)
	1689–95	William III and Mary II (joint monarchs)
	1695–1702	William III (reigned alone)
	1702–14	Anne
House of Hanover	1714–27	George I
	1727–60	George II
	1760–1820	George III
	1820–30	George IV (Regent from 1811)
	1830–37	William IV

House of Saxe-Coburg	1837–1901	Victoria
	1901–10	Edward VII

House of Windsor	1910–36	George V
	1936	Edward VIII (abdicated)
	1936–52	George VI
	1952–	Elizabeth II

The Basics of British Architecture

In Britain, you can see structures that go back to the dawn of history, in the hauntingly mysterious circles of monoliths at Stonehenge or Avebury, for example; or the resurrected remains of Roman empire builders preserved in towns such as St. Albans or Cirencester. On the other hand, you can startle your eyes with the very current, very controversial designs of contemporary architects in new developments, including London's Docklands area. Appreciating the wealth of Britain's architectural heritage does not require a degree in art history, but knowing a few hallmarks of various styles can enhance your enjoyment of what you see. Here, then, is a primer of nearly a millennium of various architectural styles.

Norman The solid Norman style, ideal for castle building, arrived in England slightly before the Conquest, with the building of Westminster Abbey in 1040. From 1066 to around 1200, it was clearly the style of choice for buildings of any importance. Norman towers tended to be hefty and square, arches always round-topped, and the vaulting barrel-shaped. Decoration was mostly geometrical, but within those limits, ornate. *Best seen in the Tower of London, St. Bartholomew's and Temple Churches, London; and in the cathedrals of St. Albans, Ely, Gloucester, Durham, and Norwich, and at Tewkesbury Abbey.*

Gothic Early English From 1130–1300, pointed arches began to supplant the rounded ones, buttresses became heavier than the Norman variety, and the windows lost their rounded tops to become "lancet" shaped. Buildings climbed skyward, less squat and heavy, with the soaring effect accentuated by steep roofs and spires. *Best seen in the cathedrals of York, Salisbury, Ely, Worcester, Canterbury (east end), and Westminster Abbey's chapter house.*

Decorated From the late 1100s until around 1400, elegance and ornament became fully integrated into architectural design, rather than applied onto the surface of a solid basic form. Windows filled more of the walls and were divided into sections by carved mullions. Vaulting grew increasingly complex, with ribs and ornamented bosses proliferating; spires became even pointier; arches took on the "ogee" shape, with its unique double curve. This style was one of England's greatest gifts to world architecture. *Best seen at the cathedrals of Wells, Lincoln, Durham (east transept), and Ely (Lady Chapel and Octagon).*

Perpendicular In later Gothic architecture, the emphasis on the vertical grew even more pronounced, featuring slender pillars, huge expanses of glass, and superb fan vaulting resembling the formalized branches of frozen trees. Walls were divided by panels. One of the chief areas in which to see Perpendicular architecture is East Anglia, where the rich wool towns built magnificent churches in the new style. Houses, too, began to reflect prevailing taste. Perpendicular Gothic lasted for well over two centuries from its advent around 1330. *Best seen at St. George's Chapel, Windsor; the cathedrals of Gloucester (cloister), and Hereford (chapter house); Henry VII's Chapel, Westminster Abbey; and King's College Chapel, Cambridge.*

Tudor With the great period of cathedral building over, from 1500 to 1560 the nation's attention turned to the construction of spacious homes, characterized by this new architectural style. The rapidly expanding *nouveau riche* class—created by the first two Tudor Henrys (VII and VIII) to challenge the power of the aristocracy—built spacious manor houses, often on the foundations of pillaged monasteries, thus beginning the era of the great stately homes. Brick replaced stone as the most popular medium, with plasterwork and carved wood to carry the elaborate motifs of the age. Another way the new rich could make their mark—and ensure their place in the next world—was by building churches. This was the age of the splendid parish churches built on fortunes made in the wool trade. Some of the most magnificent are in Suffolk, Norfolk, and the Cotswolds. *Domestic architecture is best seen at Hampton Court and St. James's Palace, London; for wool churches, Lavenham, and Long Melford, though its tower is much later, both in Suffolk.*

Renaissance For a short period under Elizabeth I, 1560–1600, this develop-
Elizabethan ment of Tudor flourished as Italian influences began to seep into England, seen especially in symmetrical facades. The most notable example was Hardwick Hall in Derbyshire, built in the 1590s by Bess of Hardwick—the jingle that describes it goes "Hardwick Hall, more glass than wall." But, however grand the houses were, they were still on a human scale, warm and livable, built of a mellow amalgam of brick and stone. *Other great Elizabethan houses are Montacute, Somerset; Longleat, Wiltshire; and Burghley House, Cambridgeshire.*

Jacobean For the first 15 years of the reign of James I (the name Jacobean is taken from the Latin word for James, Jacobus) there was little noticeable change. Windows were still large in proportion to the wall surfaces. Gables, in the style of the Netherlands, were popular. Carved decoration in wood and plaster (especially the geometrical patterning called "strapwork," like intertwined leather belts, also of Dutch origin) was still exuberant, now even more so. But a change was on the way. Inigo Jones (1573–1652), the first great modern British architect, was attempting to synthesize the architectural heritage of England with the current Italian theories. Two of his finest remaining buildings—the Banqueting Hall, Whitehall, and the Queen's House at Greenwich—epitomize his genius, which was to introduce the Palladian style that dominated British architecture for centuries. It uses the classical Greek orders—Doric, Ionic, and Corinthian. This was grandeur. But the classical style that was so monumentally effective under a hot Mediterranean sun was somehow transformed in Britain, domesticated and tamed. Columns and pediments were used to decorate the façades, and huge frescoes provided acres of color to interior walls and ceilings, all in the Italian manner. But these architectural elements had not yet been totally naturalized. There were in fact two quite distinct styles running concurrently, the comfortably domestic and the purer classical in public buildings. They were finally fused together by the talent of Christopher Wren (1632–1723). *Jacobean is best seen at the Bodleian Library, Oxford; Hatfield House, Herefordshire; Audley End, Essex; and Clare College, Cambridge.*

Wren Sir Christopher Wren's work constituted an era all by itself. Not only was he naturally one of the world's greatest architects, but he was also given an unparalleled opportunity when the disastrous Great Fire of London in 1666 wiped out the center of the capital, destroying no fewer than 89 churches and 13,200 houses. Although Wren's great scheme for a totally new city center was rejected, he did build 51 churches, the greatest of which was St. Paul's, completed in just 35 years. The range of Wren's designs is extremely wide, from simple classical shapes to the extravagantly dramatic baroque. He was also at home with domestic architecture, where his combinations of brick and stone produced a warm, homey effect. *Wren's ecclesiastical architecture is best seen at St. Paul's Cathedral and the other remaining city churches, his domestic style at Hampton Court Palace, Kensington Palace, and the Royal Hospital in Chelsea.*

Palladian This style is often referred to as Georgian, so-called from the Hanoverian kings George I through IV, although it was introduced as early as Inigo Jones's time. Classical inspiration has now been thoroughly acclimatized. Though they were completely at home among the hills, lakes, and trees of the British countryside, Palladian buildings were derived from the designs of the Italian architectural theorist Palladio, with pillared porticoes, triangular pediments, and strictly balanced windows. In domestic architecture, this large-scale classicism was usually modified to quiet simplicity, preserving mathematical proportions of windows, doors, and the exactly calculated volume of room space, to create a feeling of balance and harmony. There were some outrageous departures from the classical manner at this time, most notably with the Brighton Pavilion, built for the Prince Regent (later George IV). The Regency style comes under the Palladian heading, though strictly speaking it lasted only for the few years of the actual Regency. In Britain, the Palladian style was handled with more freedom than elsewhere in Europe, and America took its cue from the British architects. *Among the best Palladian examples are Regent's Park Terraces (London); the library at Kenwood (London); Royal Crescent and other streets in Bath; Holkham Hall, Blenheim Palace, and Castle Howard.*

Victorian Elements of imaginative fantasy, already seen in the Palladian era, came to the fore during the long reign of Victoria. The country's vast profits made from the Industrial Revolution were spent lavishly. Civic building accelerated in all the major cities with town halls modeled after medieval castles or French châteaus. The Victorians plundered the past for styles, with Gothic—about which the scholarly Victorians were very knowledgeable—leading the field. The supreme example here is the Houses of Parliament in London. (To distinguish between the Victorian variety and an earlier version, which flourished in the late 1700s, the earlier one is commonly spelled "Gothick.") But there were many other styles in the running, including the attractively named—and self-explanatory—"Wrenaissance." *Among the most striking examples are Truro Cathedral, the Albert Memorial (London), Manchester Town Hall, the Foreign Office (London), Ironbridge, and Cragside (Northumberland).*

Edwardian   Toward the end of the Victorian era, in the late 1800s, architecture calmed down considerably, with a return to a solid sort of classicism, and to even a muted baroque. The Arts and Crafts movement, especially the work and inspiration of William Morris, produced simpler designs, returning often to medieval models. *Best seen in Buckingham Palace and the Admiralty Arch in London.*

Modern   A furious public debate has raged in Britain for many years between traditionalists and the adherents of modernistic architecture. Britons are strongly conservative when it comes to their environment. These arguments have been highlighted and made even more bitter by the intervention of such notable figures as Prince Charles, who derides excessive modernism, and said, for instance, that an advanced design for the new wing of the National Gallery in Trafalgar Square would be like "a carbuncle on a much-loved face." One reason for the strength of the British attitude is that the country suffered from far too much ill-conceived building development after World War II, when large areas of city centers had to be rebuilt after the devastation of German bombs, and there was a pressing need for housing. Town planners and architects at this time encumbered the country with endless badly built and worse-designed tower blocks and shopping areas.

The situation that was thus created in the '50s and '60s is gradually being reversed. High-rise apartment blocks are being blown up and replaced by more user-friendly housing. Large-scale commercial areas, such as the Bull Ring in Birmingham, are being rethought and slowly rebuilt, although so much ill-considered building went on in the past that Britain can never be completely free of it. The emphasis is gradually, far too gradually, moving to a type of planning, designing, and construction that pays more attention to the needs of the inhabitants of buildings. At last, the lessons of crime statistics and the sheer human misery caused by unacceptable living conditions are being learned. There is, too, a healthier attitude now to the conservation of old buildings. As part of the post-war building splurge, houses that should have been treasured for posterity were torn down wholesale. Happily many of those that survived the wreckers' ball are now being restored and put back to use.

The architecture styles employed nowadays are very eclectic. A predominant one, favored incidentally by Prince Charles, draws largely on the past, with nostalgic echoes of the country cottage, and leans heavily on variegated brickwork and on close attention to decorative detail. Supermarkets are going up in every town designed on a debased form of this style. Stark modernism does crop up every now and again. The Lloyd's Tower in the City of London, by Sir Richard Rogers, designer of the Pompidou Center in Paris, is perhaps the leading, and most flamboyantly extreme, example. Another, gentler one is the Queen's Stand at the Epsom Racecourse. This elegant building by Richard Horden is rather like an elegant, white ocean liner, berthed beside the racetrack, with sweeping, curved staircases inside, and viewing balconies outside. But England generally is still light years behind the States in experimentation with design. The skyscrapers of the City of London are the exception in Britain rather than the rule.

However, public buildings are being built on a smaller scale; schools and libraries, designed in a muted modernism, use traditional, natural materials, such as wood, stone, and brick. A slightly special case, though representative of what can be achieved, is the new Visitors' Centre at the National Trust's most popular venue, Fountains Abbey in Yorkshire. Designed by Edward Cullinan, it is a fusion of dry stone walls, lead and wooden-shingle roofs outside, white-painted steel pillars and flowing ceilings inside. It is perfectly conceived for the needs of such a historically important site. Unfortunately, the recession has stopped most commercial building dead in its tracks, so the architectural debate will be largely a theoretical one for years to come. *Among the new buildings to see are the Lloyd's Tower, some of the Docklands development, Richmond House (79 Whitehall), and the Clore Building at the Tate Gallery (all in London); the campus of Sussex University (outside Brighton), the Royal Regatta Building (Henley), the Sainsbury Centre (Norwich), the Burrell Collection (Glasgow); the Queen's Stand at Epsom, Surrey; The Visitors' Centre, Fountains Abbey, Yorkshire.*

3 London

London is an ancient city and its history greets you at every corner. To gain a sense of its continuity, stand on Waterloo Bridge at sunset. To the east, the great globe of St. Paul's Cathedral glows golden in the dying sunlight as it has since the 17th century: still majestic amid the towers of glass and steel that hem it in. To the west stand the mock-medieval ramparts of Westminster, home to the "Mother of Parliaments," which has met here or hereabouts since the 1250s. And past them both snakes the swift, dark Thames, as it flowed past the first Roman settlement nearly 2,000 years ago.

Unlike most European capitals, London has almost no grand boulevards, planned for display. The exception is the Mall, running from Admiralty Arch on Trafalgar Square to Buckingham Palace. It was specifically designed for heraldic processions and stately occasions and, in a typically British way, is surrounded by gardens and lined with spreading trees. Apart from this one extravagance, present-day London still largely reflects its medieval layout, a bewildering tangle of streets.

Even when the City was devastated in the Great Fire of 1666, and again in the Blitz of the 1940s, it was rebuilt on its old street plan. (Visitors will learn that the City, spelled with a capital "C," refers to just the square mile beside the Tower, where London originated, while Greater London as a whole is the city, without a capital letter.) Sir Christopher Wren's 17th-century master concept for a classical site, with vistas and crossing avenues, was turned down; and the plans for rebuilding in the 1950s again followed the ancient disposition of streets, and a wonderful opportunity for imaginative replanning was lost. In fact, this is all gain for the visitor who wants to experience that indefinable historic atmosphere. London is a walking city, and will repay every moment you spend exploring on foot. Its contrasts can best be savored as you walk from one neighborhood to another, wandering thoroughfares of stately houses which lie next to a muddle of mean streets, seeking out winding lanes and narrow courts and finding they suddenly give onto the grass, trees, and flowerbeds of well-kept squares.

Close-up exploration will also reveal that London, like all great cities, has its darker side: the squalor and crowds that are as much a part of every modern city as they were of medieval ones. Squalor will be near at hand as you stand on Waterloo Bridge. On an icy winter's evening, when you are coming out of the warm Queen Elizabeth Hall at the southern end of the bridge. After a concert, you will pass down-and-outs sheltering in cardboard lean-tos in the open spaces underneath the building, grateful for the mobile soup kitchen that rolls up every night at 10:30. Both Shakespeare and Dickens would have recognized the scene.

And where crowds are concerned, London definitely has the edge on any city in western Europe. It starts with the largest population—nearly seven million live here—and has well over the same number of visitors every year. Indeed, in one busy year the tourists numbered 24 million!

But in the midst of all those millions, life goes on as it has for centuries. Whether your interests center on the past or the present, on the arts, on shopping, theater or architecture, London has it all. The city fully justifies Dr. Johnson's famous dictum that "When a man is tired of London he is tired of life."

Essential Information

Arriving and Departing by Plane

Airports and Airlines
London is admirably served by two major airports—Gatwick, 28 miles to the south, and Heathrow, 15 miles to the west—and three smaller ones, Luton, 35 miles northwest, Stansted, 34 miles northeast, and London City, in the Docklands.

U.S. airlines flying to London include **Delta** (tel. 800/241–4141); **TWA** (tel. 800/892–4141); **United Airlines** (tel. 800/241–6522); **USAir** (tel. 800/428–4322); **American Airlines** (tel. 800/433–7300), which also serves Manchester, England; and **Northwest Airlines** (tel. 800/447–4747), which also serves Glasgow, Scotland. Flying time is about 6½ hours from New York, 7½ hours from Chicago, and 10 hours from Los Angeles.

From the Airports to Downtown
Heathrow
The quickest and least expensive route into London is via the **Piccadilly Line** of the **Underground.** Trains run every four to eight minutes from all terminals; the 40-minute trip costs £3 one-way.

London Transport (tel. 071/222–1234) runs two bus services from the airport; each costs £5 one-way and travel time is about one hour. The A1 leaves for Victoria Station, with stops along Cromwell Road and Sloane Street, every 30 minutes 6:40 AM–8:15 PM. The A2 leaves for Russell Square, with stops at Marble Arch, every 30 minutes 6 AM–9:30 PM. The Thames Transit No. 390 bus departs Bay C, Heathrow Central Bus Station, for Victoria Coach Station at 6:30, 9:35, and 11:45 AM; 1:45, 3:15, 5:15, and 7:45 PM (times vary slightly on weekends). The journey takes about one hour and the fare is £4 one-way.

Gatwick
Fast, nonstop **Gatwick Express** trains leave for Victoria Station every 15 minutes 5:30 AM–9:45 PM; hourly 10 PM–5 AM. The 40-minute trip costs £8.60 one-way. An hourly local train also runs all night.

Speedlink's Flightline 777 bus leaves for Victoria Coach Station every 30 minutes; travel time is about 70 minutes and the cost is £7.50 one-way. A round-trip ticket valid for three months costs £11.

Stansted. London's newest airport, opened in 1991, serves mainly European destinations with no direct flights to the United States at press time.

Arriving and Departing

By Car
The major approach roads to London are motorways (six-lane highways; look for an "M" followed by a number) or "A" roads; the latter may be "dual carriageways" (divided highways), or two-lane highways. Motorways are usually the faster option for getting in and out of town, although rush-hour traffic is horrendous. Stay tuned to local radio stations for regular traffic updates.

By Train
London has 15 major train stations, each serving a different area of the country, all accessible by Underground or bus. Since April 1994, **Railtrack** has been operating all these stations, as well as the tracks countrywide, while **British Rail** still controls all train services, until they are sold off as franchises. These major changes in the structure of Britain's railways should not affect the traveler unduly, although nobody can predict exactly what will happen to the fares.

By Bus
National Express buses operate from Victoria Coach Station to over 1,000 major towns and cities. It's less expensive than the train but trips usually take longer. **Green Line** buses (tel. 081/668–7261) cover

London Underground

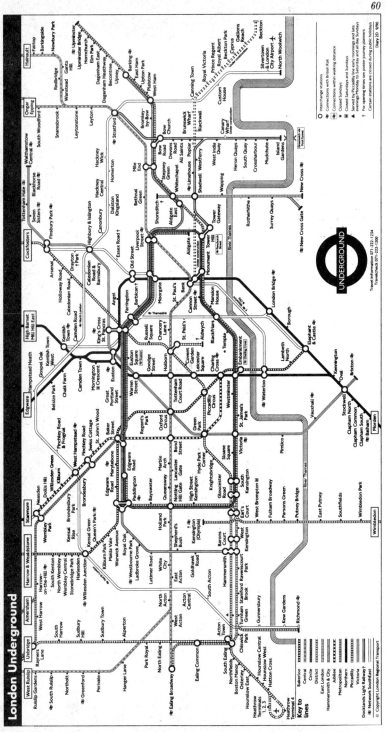

Diary 2D 9/90

UNDERGROUND

Travel Information 071-222-1234
Travelcheck 071-222-1200

○ Interchange stations
⊖ Connections with British Rail
⊖ Connections within walking distance
✦ Closed Saturdays and Sundays
✦ Closed Sundays
▲ Served by Piccadilly line early mornings and late evenings Monday to Saturday and all day Sundays
† Certain stations are closed during public holidays

For opening times see poster journey planners

Key to lines

Bakerloo
Central
Circle
District
East London
Hammersmith & City
Jubilee
Metropolitan
Northern
Piccadilly
Victoria
Docklands Light Railway †
Network SouthEast

© Copyright London Regional Transport

a 30- to 40-mile radius of London, ideal for excursions. Their **Golden Rover** ticket allows unlimited travel for either a day or a week.

Getting Around

By Underground Known colloquially as "the tube," London's extensive Underground system is by far the most widely used form of city transport. (In Britain, the word "subway" means "pedestrian underpass.") Trains run both beneath and above ground out into the suburbs, and are all one class; smoking is *not* allowed on board or in the stations.

There are 10 basic lines—all named—plus the Docklands Light Railway and the East London line, which runs from Shoreditch and Whitechapel across the Thames and south to New Cross.

From Monday to Saturday, trains start just after 5 AM and run until midnight or 12:30. On Sunday trains start two hours later and finish about an hour earlier. The maximum wait should be no more than about 10 minutes in central areas. A pocket map is available free from most ticket counters, and there are large maps on the platforms.

By Bus In central London, buses are traditionally bright red double- and single-deckers, though there are now many privately owned buses of different colors. Not all buses run the full length of their route at all times; check with the driver or conductor. On some buses you pay the conductor after finding a seat, on others you pay the driver upon boarding. Bus stops are clearly indicated; the main stops have a red LT symbol on a plain white background. When the word "Request" is written across the sign, you must flag the bus down. Buses are a good way of seeing the town, but don't take one if you are in a hurry. Fares start at 50p for short distances.

Fares London is divided into six concentric zones for both bus and tube fares: the more zones you cross, the higher the fare. Regular single-journey or round-trip **One Day Travelcards** (£2.70–£3.70) allow unrestricted travel on bus and tube after 9:30 AM and all day on weekends and national holidays. **Visitor Travelcards** (£3.70) are the same as the One Day Travelcards, but with the bonus of a booklet of money-off vouchers to major attractions. **One Day LT Cards** (£3.90–£6.30) are similar to Travelcards, but without time restrictions. Visitor Travelcards (for three, four, and seven days) are also available in the United States, complete with voucher booklet at $25, $32, and $49, from BritRail Travel International (1500 Broadway, New York, NY 10036, tel. 212/382–3737). For more information, stop at an LT Travel Information Centre at the following tube stations: Heathrow, Oxford Circus, Piccadilly Circus, St. James's Park, and Victoria, or call 071/222–1234.

By Taxi Hotels and main tourist areas have taxi ranks; you can also flag taxis down on the street. If the yellow "for hire" sign is lit on top, the taxi is available. But drivers often cruise at night with their signs unlit to avoid unsavory characters, so if you see an unlit cab, keep your hand up and you might be lucky. Fares are £1 for the first 582 yards, increasing by units of 20p per 291 yards or 60 seconds. Surcharges are added after 8 PM and on weekends and public holidays. Fares increase annually.

By Car The simple advice about driving in London is: don't. Because the city grew as a series of villages, there was never a central street plan, and the result is a chaotic winding mass, made no easier by the one-way street systems. If you must drive in London, remember to drive on the left, and stick to the speed limit.

Important Addresses and Numbers

Tourist Information The main **London Tourist Information Centre** at Victoria Station also provides information on the rest of Britain and is open weekdays and Saturday 8–7, Sunday 8–5. There are other TICs in **Harrods** (Brompton Rd.) and **Selfridges** (Oxford St.), which are open store hours only; and there are offices also at **Heathrow Airport** (Terminals 1, 2, and 3). The **British Travel Centre** (12 Regent St.) provides details about travel, accommodations, and entertainment for the whole of Britain. You need to visit the Centre in person to get information. Open weekdays 9–6:30 and Saturday 10–4. **Visitorcall** is the London Tourist Board's phone service—it's a premium-rate (48p per minute; 36p off-peak) recorded information line, with different numbers for theater, events, museums, sports, getting around, etc. To access the list of options, call 0839/123456, or see the display advertisement in the city phone book. A faxed events calendar is also available (tel. 0839/401278).

Embassies and Consulates **American Embassy** (24 Grosvenor Sq., W1A 1AE, tel. 071/499–9000). Inside the embassy is the American Aid Society, a charity that helps Americans in distress. Dial the embassy number and ask for extension 570 or 571.

Canadian High Commission (Canada House, Trafalgar Sq., SW1Y 5BJ, tel. 071/629–9492).

Emergencies For police, fire department, or ambulance, dial 999.

The following hospitals have 24-hour emergency sections: **Charing Cross,** tel. 081/846–1234; **Guys,** St. Thomas St., tel. 071/407–7600; **Royal Free,** Pond St., Hampstead, tel. 071/794–0500; **St. Bartholomew's,** West Smithfield, tel. 071/600–9000; **St. Thomas's,** Lambeth Palace Rd., tel. 071/928–9292; **Westminster,** Horseferry Rd. at Dean Ryle St., tel. 071/828–9811.

Pharmacies **Bliss Chemist,** at 5 Marble Arch, tel. 071/723–6116, is open daily 9 AM–midnight; and at 50 Willesden La., tel. 071/624–8000, is open daily 9 AM–2 AM.

Travel Agencies **American Express,** at 6 Haymarket, tel. 071/930–4411, and at 89 Mount St., tel. 071/499–4436; **Thomas Cook,** 4 Henrietta St., WC2, tel. 071/240–4872; 1 Marble Arch, W1, tel. 071/706–4188; and other branches.

Guided Tours

Orientation Tours
By Bus **London Plus** tours, run by London Transport (tel. 071/828–6449) offer passengers a good introduction to the city from double-decker buses. These tours run daily every half hour, or more during summer, 10–5, from Marble Arch, Victoria, Piccadilly, Harrods, Trafalgar Square, and some 30 more places of interest. You may board or alight at any stop to view the sights, and then get back on the next bus. Tickets (£12 adults, £6 children) may be bought from the driver. Other agencies offering half- and full-day bus tours include **Evan Evans** (tel. 071/930–2377), **Frames Rickards** (tel. 071/837–3111), **Travellers Check-In** (tel. 071/580–8284), and **The Big Bus Company** (tel. 081/944–7810).

By River From April to October boats cruise the Thames. Most leave from Westminster Pier (tel. 071/930–4097), Charing Cross Pier (Victoria Embankment, tel. 071/839–3312), and Tower Pier (tel. 071/488–0344). Downstream routes go to the Tower of London, Greenwich, and the Thames Barrier; upstream destinations include Kew, Richmond, and Hampton Court. Depending upon destination, river trips may last from one to four hours.

By Canal During summer, narrow boats and barges cruise London's two canals, the Grand Union and Regent's Canal. Companies include **Jason's Trip** (tel. 071/286–3428), **London Waterbus Co.** (tel. 071/482–2550), and **Canal Cruises** (tel. 071/485–4433).

Walking Tours One of the best ways to get to know London is on foot, and there are many guided walking tours from which to choose. **Original London Walks** (tel. 071/624–3978) has a very wide selection and takes great pride in the infectious enthusiasm of its guides. Other firms include **City Walks** (tel. 071/700–6931), **Streets of London** (tel. 081/346–9255), and **Citisights** (tel. 081/806–4325).

Excursions London Regional Transport, **Evan Evans, Frames Rickards,** and **Travellers Check-In** all offer day excursions by bus to places within easy reach of London, such as Hampton Court, Oxford, Stratford, and Bath.

Exploring London

Traditionally, central London has been divided between the City to the east, where its banking and commercial interests lie; Westminster to the west, the seat of the royal court and the government; and the mainly residential areas that surround them both. That distinction still holds, as our itineraries show.

The City route covers London's equivalent of New York's Wall Street, while the **Westminster and Royal London** exploration roves past royal palaces and surveys the government area in and around Parliament Square. Part of another walk, **Legal London, Covent Garden, and Bloomsbury,** explores the capital's legal center, a lively, rejuvenated shopping district, and its university and literary quarter.

London expanded from Westminster during the 17th and 18th centuries. Elegant town houses sprang up in St. James's and Mayfair, and later in Bloomsbury, Chelsea, Knightsbridge, and Kensington. These are today pleasant residential districts, and elegant, if pricey, shopping areas. London also enjoys unique "lungs"—its stupendous parks—thanks to past royalty who reserved these great tracts of land for their own hunting and relaxation. The two largest of them, now administered by the government, feature in the **Two Royal Parks—Knightsbridge and Kensington** walk.

The area along the Thames, once London's most important highway, is currently enjoying a renaissance. The **South Bank** takes you along the river's traditionally less fashionable south side, while the last exploring section, **Up and Down the Thames,** covers out-of-town riverside attractions, old and new.

Highlights for First-time Visitors

British Museum: Tour 2
Covent Garden: Tour 2
Hampton Court Palace: Tour 6
Museum of London: Tour 4
National Gallery: Tour 1
St. James's Park: Tour 1
South Kensington Museums: Tour 3
Tate Gallery: Tour 1

Tower of London: Tour 4
Westminster Abbey: Tour 1

Tour 1: Westminster and Royal London

Numbers in the margin correspond to points of interest on the London map.

Westminster could be called the royal backyard. Generations of monarchs have lived here since King Edward the Confessor moved his court from the City in the 11th century. All the medieval sovereigns occupied the Palace of Westminster until 1512, when Henry VIII vacated it for nearby Whitehall Palace. Except for one building, Whitehall Palace no longer exists; it was destroyed by a series of fires culminating in the most disastrous one in 1698. The court then moved to St. James's Palace, across the park. Buckingham Palace, the residence and administrative headquarters of the present royal family, was first occupied by Queen Victoria after her coronation in 1837.

❶ Start in **Trafalgar Square,** the point from which all distances from London are officially measured. It is also the focal point of New Year's Eve and election night celebrations, and political rallies. Trafalgar Square's present shape and name date only from 1830, when the central portion was leveled to accommodate **Nelson's Column** (185 feet high). Admiral Horatio Nelson is remembered for his victory over Napoleon's navy in 1805 at Trafalgar in Spain, where he lost his life. Lions guard the column's base, and four huge bronze panels depict naval battles against the French. The equestrian statue to the south is of **Charles I,** looking down Whitehall toward the spot where he was executed in 1649.

❷ The **National Gallery** occupies the classical building which fills the square's north side. It houses one of the world's great European art collections, whose strengths are Flemish and Dutch masters such as Rubens and Rembrandt, Italian Renaissance works, English 18th- and 19th-century paintings, and French Impressionists. The Sainsbury Wing now houses the early Renaissance collection. *Trafalgar Sq., tel. 071/839–3321 or 071/839–3526 (recording). Admission free except special exhibitions (tel. 071/389–1773). Open Mon.– Sat. 10–6, Sun. 2–6.*

❸ Around the corner, at the foot of Charing Cross Road, is the **National Portrait Gallery,** containing likenesses of celebrated (and not so well known) monarchs, statesmen, and writers, in the form of painted portraits, busts, photographs, and even cartoons. You can supplement your knowledge of British history at the recently opened Heinz Archive and Library. *2 St. Martin's Pl., tel. 071/930– 1552. Admission free. Open weekdays 10–5, Sat. 10–6, Sun. 2–6.*

❹ Across from the entrance to the portrait gallery is the church of **St. Martin-in-the-Fields,** built in 1724, set off by its elegant spire. The church still carries on its traditional role of caring for the destitute. The celebrated Academy of St. Martin-in-the-Fields, which performed the music for the movie *Amadeus,* was founded here. At the **London Brass Rubbing Centre** in the crypt, you can make your own copies from replica tomb brasses (memorial plates), some from churches throughout Britain. Wax, paper, and instructions are provided. *St. Martin-in-the-Fields, Trafalgar Sq., tel. 071/437– 6023. Rubbing fee from £1 according to size of brass selected. Open Mon.–Sat. 10–6, Sun. noon–6, closed Good Friday, Dec. 24–26, Jan 1.*

Time Out | **The Brasserie** in the National Gallery's Sainsbury Wing serves a fashionable lunch, such as charcuterie, plus coffee, pastries, and baguette sandwiches, the rest of the day.

❺ **Admiralty Arch,** near the Royal Navy headquarters in the Admiralty Building, marks the entrance to **The Mall,** the great promenade leading from one corner of Trafalgar Square past St. James's Park to Buckingham Palace. The present Mall was laid out in 1904 to provide a stately approach to Buckingham Palace, replacing a more modest avenue dating from 1660. The name Mall (pronounced to rhyme with "pal") comes from a version of croquet called "pell mell" that Charles II and his courtiers used to play here in the late 1600s.

St. James's Park is small but handsome, and like most of London's parks, has royal origins. In ancient times the Thames spread far and wide, and the marshes here were drained by Henry VIII to be used as a playground for his deer. Charles II employed the famous French landscape gardener, Le Nôtre, to reshape it, and in 1829 it was given its present look by John Nash, the prolific architect and friend of George IV. Meticulously maintained flowerbeds and many varieties of waterfowl make the park a beautiful place for a stroll, especially on a summer's evening, when illuminated fountains cascade and, beyond the trees, Westminster Abbey and the Houses of Parliament are floodlit.

❻ On the other side of the Mall, you'll pass the imposing **Carlton House Terrace,** built in 1827–32 (also by Nash), with a gleaming white stucco facade and massive Corinthian columns. The column at the head of the steps is topped by a statue of the Duke of York, George III's second son and commander-in-chief of the British forces during the French Revolution.

❼ To the right up Marlborough Road is **St. James's Palace,** the earliest parts of which date from the 1530s. The palace has declined in importance since 1837, when Queen Victoria moved to Buckingham Palace, but some royal officials still work here, and court functions are occasionally held in the state rooms. All foreign ambassadors to Britain are officially accredited to the Court of St. James's.

Inside the palace is the **Chapel Royal,** said to have been designed for Henry VIII by the painter Holbein. Although redecorated in the mid-19th century, the ceiling still displays the intertwined initials H and A, for Henry VIII and his second wife, Anne Boleyn, the mother of Elizabeth I and the first of Henry's wives to lose her head. *The chapel is only open for Sunday morning services from early October to Good Friday.*

Across from the palace on Marlborough Road is the exquisite **Queen's Chapel.** It was built by Inigo Jones in the 1620s for Henrietta Maria, wife of Charles I, and was one of the first purely classical buildings in the country. *Open for services Sunday mornings at 8:30 and 11:15 from Easter to the end of July.*

Turn left at the end of Marlborough Road along Cleveland Row, past ❽ **York House,** the London home of the duke and duchess of Kent. Another ❾ left turn onto Stable Yard Road brings you to **Lancaster House,** built for the duke of York by Nash in the 1820s and now used for government receptions and conferences. On the other side of Stable Yard is **Clarence House,** built by Nash in 1825 for the duke of ❿ Clarence, who later became King William IV. Restored in 1949, it is now the home of the Queen Mother (i.e., Queen Elizabeth's mother).

London

Admiralty Arch, **5**

Albert Memorial, **42**

Bank of England, **53**

Bankside Gallery, **70**

Banqueting House, **17**

Barbican, **50**

British Museum, **33**

Buckingham Palace, **11**

Butler's Wharf, **62**

Cabinet War Rooms, **15**

Carlton House Terrace, **6**

Clarence House, **10**

Commonwealth Institute, **44**

Courtauld Institute Galleries, **32**

Covent Garden, **30**

Dickens House, **35**

Dr. Johnson's House, **25**

Gabriel's Wharf, **69**

Guildhall, **51**

H.M.S. *Belfast*, **63**

Hay's Galleria, **64**

Horse Guards Parade, **16**

Hyde Park Corner, **36**

Imperial War Museum, **73**

Inner and Middle Temples, **26**

Kensington Palace, **43**

Lambeth Palace, **72**

Lancaster House, **9**

Leadenhall Market, **56**

Leighton House, **46**

Lincoln's Inn, **28**

Linley Sambourne House, **45**

Lloyd's of London, **57**

London Dungeon, **65**

Ludgate Circus, **23**

Mansion House, **55**

The Monument, **58**

Museum of London, **49**

National Gallery, **2**

National Portrait Gallery, **3**

National Postal Museum, **48**

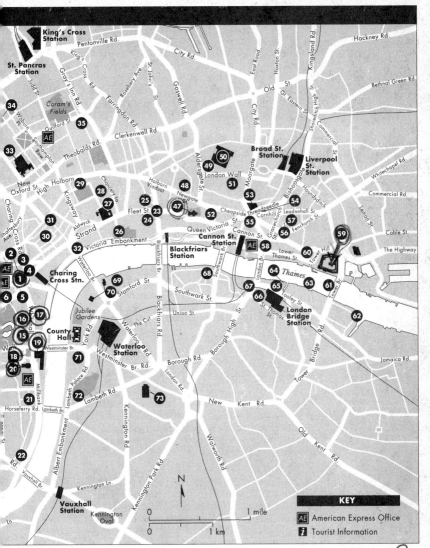

KEY	
AE	American Express Office
𝒊	Tourist Information

Natural History Museum, **39**

Old St. Thomas's Hospital, **66**

Palace of Westminster, (Houses of Parliament), **19**

Parliament Square, **18**

Percival David Foundation of Chinese Art, **34**

Queen's Gallery, **12**

Royal Albert Hall, **41**

Royal Courts of Justice, **27**

Royal Exchange, **54**

Royal Mews, **13**

Royal Opera House, **31**

Science Museum, **40**

Shakespeare Globe Museum, **68**

Sir John Soane's Museum, **29**

South Bank Arts Complex, **70**

Southwark Cathedral, **67**

St. Bride's Church, **24**

St. James's Palace, **7**

St. John's, **21**

St. Mary-le-Bow, **52**

St. Martin-in-the-Fields, **4**

St. Paul's Cathedral **47**

St. Thomas's Hospital, **71**

Tate Gallery, **22**

Tower Bridge, **61**

Tower Hill Pageant, **60**

Tower of London, **59**

Trafalgar Square, **1**

Victoria and Albert Museum, **38**

Wellington Barracks, **14**

Wellington Museum (Apsley House), **37**

Westminster Abbey, **20**

York House, **8**

⑪ Buckingham Palace stands at the end of the Mall, behind a huge traffic circle edged with flowerbeds. When the queen is in residence (generally on weekdays except in January, August, September, and part of June), the royal standard flies over the east front. Inside, there are dozens of splendid state rooms used on formal occasions; offices for the royal staff; and, in the north wing, the private apartments of the queen and Prince Philip. Behind the palace lie 40 acres of secluded garden. The palace is now being opened to tourists for eight weeks in August and September, when the royal family is away. *Buckingham Palace Rd., tel. 071/799–2331. Admission: £8 adults, £5.50 senior citizens, £3.50 children under 17. Telephone for hours, which had not been set at press time.*

Despite cuts to the Armed Forces announced in early 1993, that most celebrated of all London ceremonies, the **Changing of the Guard,** still takes place in front of the palace daily from April through July, and on alternate days the rest of the year. The guard marches from Wellington Barracks (*see below*) at 11 AM to the palace. The ceremony itself begins promptly at 11:30, but arrive early for a good view; the Queen Victoria Memorial in the traffic circle provides a convenient grandstand.

The palace was orginally Buckingham House, built in the early 18th century for the duke of Buckingham. George III bought it in 1762. In 1824, Nash remodeled it for George IV, at which time it acquired palace status. The east end, which faces the public, is the result of a 1913 remodeling, which rendered it dull and heavy.

⑫ The former palace chapel, bombed during World War II and rebuilt in 1961, has been converted into the **Queen's Gallery,** where exhibitions from the royal art collections are held. *Admission: £2.50 adults, £1.20 children, £1.80 senior citizens. Open Tues.–Sat. 10–5, Sun. 2–5.*

⑬ The Royal Mews, farther along the road, houses the queen's horses and the gilded state coaches. *Buckingham Palace Rd. Admission: £2.50 adults, £1.20 children under 16, £1.80 senior citizens. Open Wed.–Thurs. 2–4; closed before state occasions, and Ascot week (mid-June). Combined ticket with Queen's Gallery: £4.50 adults, £1.90 children, £3.10 senior citizens.*

Birdcage Walk, once the site of the royal aviaries, runs along the **⑭** south side of St. James's Park past **Wellington Barracks,** the regimental headquarters of the Guards Division. The elite troops that guard the sovereign and mount the guard at Buckingham Palace live here. The **Guards Museum** relates their history; many conflicts, including the Falklands campaign, are represented. Battle paintings, uniforms, and a cat o' nine tails are among the displays. *Wellington Barracks, Birdcage Walk, tel. 071/930–4466, extension 3430. Admission: £2 adults, £1 children under 16 and senior citizens. Open Sat.–Thurs. 10–4.*

Next to the museum stands the **Guards Chapel,** rebuilt in the early '60s after it was bombed in 1944. Off Birdcage Walk to the south is **Queen Anne's Gate,** lined with handsome 18th-century town houses, now mostly used as offices. A very formal statue of Queen Anne is hidden among them.

Back on Birdcage Walk and still following the perimeter of St. James's Park, turn left on to Horse Guards Road. Between the mas**⑮** sive bulks of the Home Office and the Foreign Office nestles the **Cabinet War Rooms,** a labyrinth of underground offices used by the British high command during World War II. Many strategic decisions were made here. You can see the Prime Minister's Room, where Winston Churchill made some of his inspiring broadcasts, and the Transatlantic Telephone Room, where he spoke to President Roosevelt. *Clive Steps, King Charles St., tel. 071/930–6961. Admission: £3.80 adults, £1.90 children under 16, £2.80 senior citizens. Open daily 10–5:15.*

16 Continue along Horse Guards Road to the mid-18th-century Horse Guards Building, overlooking **Horse Guards Parade.** Originally the tilt yard (a place for jousting) of Whitehall Palace, the square is now the site of the **Trooping the Colour** each June, the great military parade marking the queen's official birthday. (Her real birthday is April 21.) The "Colour" (or flag) displayed identifies the battalion selected to provide the monarch's escort for that year. Cross the parade ground and walk through the arch.

The queen's Life Guards—cavalrymen in magnificent uniforms—stand duty on the facade overlooking Whitehall. The guard changes here at 11 AM Monday through Saturday and at 10 AM on Sunday.

17 The **Banqueting House,** across Whitehall, survived the Whitehall Palace fire; Charles I was beheaded here in 1649. The Banqueting House was built by Inigo Jones in 1625; the main hall's magnificent ceiling frescoes, painted by Rubens for Charles I in 1630, honor the house of Stuart. Charles and his father, James I, assume a god-like stance—typical of the attitude that led to Charles's downfall at the hands of Cromwell and the Parliamentarians. *Whitehall, tel. 071/ 930–4179. Admission: £2.75 adults, £1.90 children under 15, £2.10 senior citizens. Open Mon.–Sat. 10–5.*

Walking south, you pass on the right the entrance to **Downing Street,** a terrace of three unassuming 18th-century houses. No. 10 has been the official residence of the prime minister since 1732. The cabinet office, the hub of the British system of government, is on the ground floor; the prime minister's private apartment is on the top floor. The chancellor of the exchequer, the chief finance minister, occupies No. 11. Downing Street is cordoned off, but you should be able to catch a glimpse of it from Whitehall.

The **Cenotaph,** in the center of Whitehall, commemorates the dead of both world wars. On Remembrance Day in November the sovereign lays a tribute of silken Flanders poppies here, symbolic of the blood-red flowers that grew on the killing fields of World War I. A statue of **18** Winston Churchill dominates traffic-beleaguered **Parliament Square,** at the foot of Whitehall. Other statues in the square are mostly of 19th-century prime ministers, but Abraham Lincoln is here, too, and outside the Houses of Parliament are Richard I (Richard the Lionheart) and Oliver Cromwell, Lord Protector of England during the country's sole, brief republican period in the 1650s.

19 The only remains of the original **Palace of Westminster** (still the official name of the complex) is the 240-foot-long **Westminster Hall,** built at the end of the 11th century; the fine hammer-beam roof was added by Richard II in 1397. The hall, where the country's early parliaments met and which once housed the law courts, is now used only on ceremonial occasions. The rest of the palace, extended and altered over the centuries, was destroyed by fire in 1834. It was rebuilt in mock-medieval Gothic style with an ornate interior by architect Augustus Pugin, whose many delightful touches include Gothic umbrella stands.

The palace contains the debating chambers and committee rooms of the two Houses of Parliament, the Commons (whose members are elected) and the Lords (which contains a mixture of appointed and hereditary members), plus offices and libraries. The public is admitted only to the public gallery of each.

The most famous features of the palace are the towers at each end. At the south end is the 336-foot **Victoria Tower** (currently undergoing restoration). **St. Stephen's Tower,** better known as **Big Ben,** after the clock and its 13-ton bell that strikes the hours, is thought to have been named after Sir Benjamin Hall, Commissioner of Works when the bells were installed in the 1850s. A light shines from the top of the tower when Parliament meets at night.

✓ ➋ **Westminster Abbey** is the most ancient of London's great churches. Britain's monarchs have been crowned here since the coronation of William the Conqueror on Christmas Day 1066. There has almost certainly been a church here since the 6th century, and some historians believe the site was a place of pagan worship long before Christianity reached Britain. The present abbey is a largely 13th- and 14th-century rebuilding of the 11th-century church founded by Edward the Confessor. Two notable later additions are the Henry VII Chapel, built in the early 1500s, and the 18th-century twin towers over the west entrance. Early morning is a good time to catch something of the abbey's sacred atmosphere and to avoid the hordes of visitors; better still, attend a service here.

There is space here to mention only a few of the abbey's many memorials. **Winston Churchill's** is just inside the west door (he is buried near Blenheim Palace, where he was born). The **Tomb of the Unknown Warrior** contains the body of a nameless World War I soldier buried in earth brought from France with his corpse; nearby hangs the **U.S. Congressional Medal** awarded to him symbolically. Among the many other nonroyal people commemorated in the abbey are Robert Baden-Powell, founder of the Boy Scout movement, and the Wesleys, pioneers of Methodism. **Poets' Corner** memorializes an idiosyncratic collection of British writers.

Behind the high altar, the **Chapel of Edward the Confessor** contains Edward I's primitive oak Coronation Chair, and just beyond lies the **Henry VII Chapel,** an exquisite example of the rich Late Gothic style—the last riot of medieval design in England. Binoculars will help you spot the statues high up on the walls and the details of the abbey's stained glass. Striking effigies adorn the royal tombs of Elizabeth I and her half-sister "Bloody" Mary; Mary, Queen of Scots; Henry V; Richard II and his wife Anne of Bohemia; and many more. *Broad Sanctuary, tel. 071/222–5152. Admission to nave free; to Poets' Corner and Royal Chapels: £3 adults, £1 children, £1.50 senior citizens (Royal Chapels free Wed. 6–8 PM). Open Mon., Tues., Thurs., Fri. 9–4:45; Wed. 9–7:45; Sat. 9–2, 3:45–5:45; Sun. for services only; closed to visitors during weekday services.*

Medieval monks strolled in the **Cloisters,** discussing the state of government and of their souls. There is also a **Brass Rubbing Centre,** where you can take impressions from facsimiles of old tombs. *Tel. 071/222–2085. Admission free. Fee for rubbings £2.50–£10. Open late Mar.–late Oct., Mon.–Sat. 9–5:30.*

The Norman **Undercroft,** just off the cloisters, houses a museum on the abbey's history; among its exhibits are lifelike royal effigies that used to be carried in funeral processions. The **Pyx Chamber** next door displays silver vessels and other treasures. The **Chapter House,** where Parliament first met, was built in the 1240s and is remarkable for its feeling of space and its daring design. A single column, like a frozen fountain, supports the roof. *Tel. 071/222–5152. Joint admis-*

sion: £2 adults, £1 children under 16, £1.60 senior citizens. Open daily 10:30–1:45.

Outside the abbey's west front an archway leads to **Dean's Yard,** a quiet, green courtyard. This side of the abbey was once the monks' living quarters; it's now used by **Westminster School,** a prestigious private ("public") school on the abbey grounds.

Continue through the courtyard, turn immediately left, then first right into Barton Street which leads via Cowley Street and Lord North Street to Smith Square, one of London's most attractive

㉑ Georgian residential areas. The splendidly classical church of **St. John's** (1729) has been deconsecrated and now functions as one of London's favorite small concert halls. Turn left back onto Millbank, then right to follow the river to the Tate.

㉒ The **Tate Gallery,** Britain's most important museum of British and modern art, has an innovative policy of rehanging the whole gallery every nine months. While this lets the whole collection be seen, favorite pieces may not be on view when you are visiting. The Clore Gallery has a permanent exhibition of the magnificent (J.M.W.) Turner Bequest, including one hundred of his paintings. At press time, it was not yet known where the major, South Bank **Tate Gallery of Modern Art** is to be situated, though work should be in progress this year. *Millbank, tel. 071/821–1313 or 071/821–7128 (recording). Admission free; fee for special exhibitions. Open Mon.–Sat. 10–5:50, Sun. 2–5:50; closed Good Friday, May Day holiday, Dec. 24–26, Jan. 1.*

Tour 2: Legal London, Covent Garden, and Bloomsbury

This walk explores three diverse areas that exemplify London's rich history: the Inns of Court, where the country's top solicitors and barristers have had their chambers for centuries; Covent Garden, the former monastery turned garden; and literary Bloomsbury.

㉓ Start at **Ludgate Circus,** a drab traffic circle west of St. Paul's Cathedral, where **Fleet Street,** traditional home of Britain's newspapers, begins. High operating costs have driven the papers to other parts of London, and none is now left here.

㉔ Walk west along Fleet Street. On the left stands **St. Bride's Church,** rebuilt by Christopher Wren following the Great Fire of 1666 and restored again after it was bombed in 1940. The spire was added in 1703, and became the model for multi-tiered wedding cakes. The crypt's small museum contains Roman and later antiquities found in the area. *Tel. 071/353–1301. Admission free. Open daily 9–5.*

Time Out Try a pint of real ale and a slab of cheese at **Ye Olde Cheshire Cheese** on Wine Office Court. This 17th-century inn was a favorite watering hole of Dr. Samuel Johnson, the 18th-century lexicographer and pundit, and his biographer, James Boswell.

㉕ Around the corner, on Gough Square, is **Dr. Johnson's House,** where he compiled his dictionary. *17 Gough Sq., tel. 071/353–3745. Admission: £2.50 adults, £1.50 children under 16 and senior citizens. Open May–Sept., Mon.–Sat. 11–5:30, Oct.–Apr., Mon.–Sat. 11–5.*

The Inns of Court—there are four in all, and this walk visits three— were founded at different times during the Middle Ages to provide food and lodging for lawyers; as the centuries passed, they became more or less permanent residences and offices combined. Their atmosphere is reminiscent of Oxford or Cambridge colleges, hardly surprising, since they were founded in the same era as places for serious study. The Inns of Court retain an important educational role: Aspiring barristers must pass a series of examinations held here. More quirkily, they must establish their attendance by eating a certain number of dinners in the Hall of the Inn to which they are attached.

26 The **Inner** and **Middle Temples** (there never was an Outer Temple) lie immediately south of Fleet Street. Enter through the **Old Mitre Court** passageway to see one of the finest groupings of unspoiled historic buildings in London. The two Temples derive their names from the land on which they stand, once owned by the Knights Templar, the chivalric order founded during the first Crusade in the 11th century. In the 12th century the Knights built the **Temple Church** here, one of only three round churches in Britain. Their worn tombs can still be seen on the floor. About 1250, the choir was extended in Early English style, a particularly pure form of Gothic; this is probably the country's finest example. *The Temple, tel. 071/797–8250. Admission free. Open daily 10–4.*

The **Inner Temple Hall** is not open to the public, but the superb Elizabethan **Middle Temple Hall** may be freely visited (unless in use by the Inn). *Tel. 071/353–4355. Admission free. Open weekdays 10–noon, 3–4.*

Return to Fleet Street through the **Inner Temple Gateway.** At the entrance is an early Jacobean half-timbered building inside which is **Prince Henry's Room,** with oak paneling and an elaborate plasterwork ceiling. It is named after the eldest son of James I, who became Prince of Wales in 1610, but died before he could succeed his father. *17 Fleet St. Admission: 10p. Open weekdays 1:45–5, Sat. 1:45–4.*

27 Across the way, on the left, stand the **Royal Courts of Justice,** where important civil cases are heard. Though it looks medieval, the building dates from the 1870s. The magnificent main hall—238 feet long and 80 feet high—dwarfs the bewigged and gowned figures that scurry through it. *Strand, tel. 071/936–6000. Admission free. Open weekdays 9–4:30; closed national holidays.*

Now walk up **Chancery Lane,** past the **Public Record Office** on the right, where a small museum displays historic documents, such as the Domesday Book of 1085, the earliest surviving land record. *Tel. 081/878–3666. Admission free. Open weekdays 10–5.*

28 **Lincoln's Inn,** probably the most beautiful of the Inns and the one least damaged during World War II, lies left of Chancery Lane. The buildings date from various periods beginning with the late 15th-century **Old Hall** and **Old Buildings. Stone Buildings, New Square,** is the only intact 17th-century square in London. The chapel was remodeled by Inigo Jones in 1619–23. *Chancery La., tel. 071/405–1393. Gardens open daily noon–2:30, chapel open weekdays 12:30–2:30; the public may also attend 11:30 Sunday service in the Chapel during legal terms. Guided tours are available in summer for prebooked groups.*

The adjoining **Lincoln's Inn Fields** is the capital's largest and oldest square—more like a small park—surrounded by handsome buildings. The magnificent 1806 portico on the south side faces the Royal
29 College of Surgeons. The square's great attraction, however, is **Sir John Soane's Museum,** one of the most idiosyncratic and fascinating in London. Sir John, who lived here from 1790 to 1831, was a gifted architect and an avid collector. The exhibits include Hogarth's se-

ries of paintings, *The Rake's Progress*, and the sarcophagus of the Egyptian Emperor Seti I, which Soane bought for £2,000 after the British Museum refused it. *13 Lincoln's Inn Fields, tel. 071/405–2107. Admission free. Open Tues.–Sat. 10–5.*

Southwest of Lincoln's Inn Fields on Portsmouth Street is the 16th-century antique shop (tel. 071/405–9891) that Dickens reputedly used as the model for his *Old Curiosity Shop.*

30 **Covent Garden** lies about half a mile to the west. The original "convent garden" produced fruit and vegetables for the 13th-century Abbey of St. Peter at Westminster. Later, it passed into the hands of the earls (later the dukes) of Bedford. In 1630, the fourth earl commissioned Inigo Jones to lay out a square, with St. Paul's Church at one end and colonnaded houses on two sides. Only the church now remains. The fruit, flower, and vegetable market established in the later 1700s flourished until 1974, when its traffic grew to be too much for the narrow surrounding streets and it was moved south of the Thames.

Since then, the area has been transformed through small-scale projects rather than massive redevelopment, making Covent Garden one of the most appealing areas of London for adults and children alike. The 19th-century **Market Building** is now an elegant shopping arcade. On the south side is the lively **Jubilee Market Hall** where crafts, clothes, and flea-market goods are sold. Open-air entertainers perform under the portico of **St. Paul's Church,** where George Bernard Shaw set the first scene of *Pygmalion* (reshaped as the musical *My Fair Lady*). The church, entered from Bedford Street, is known as the actors' church; inside are numerous memorials to theater people.

On the east side of the market area are two of London's newer museums. The **London Transport Museum** houses a steam locomotive, a tram, and a modern underground car, with much hands-on fun. The museum was recently expanded. *39 Wellington St., tel. 071/379–6344. Admission: £3.95 adults, £2.50 children 5–16 and senior citizens, children under 5 free. Open daily 10–6.*

The **Theatre Museum** holds a comprehensive collection on the history of English theater—not just drama, but also opera, music hall (vaudeville), pantomime, and musical comedy. Scripts, playbills, costumes, props, and memorabilia of stars are displayed. *1E Tavistock St., tel. 071/836–7891. Admission: £3 adults, £1.50 children 5–14 and senior citizens. Open Tues.–Sun. 11–7.*

Time Out There's a good selection of eating places in and around the market building. The **Theatre Museum Café** does cream teas plus muffins, open sandwiches, salads, and pastries; it's open to passers-by, too.

The streets around the central market are packed with history. Garrick Street is home to the **Garrick Club,** London's equivalent of New York's Players Club. Actors and publishers are among today's members; in the 19th century, Dickens, Thackeray, and Trollope were on the club's roster. Opposite, at the end of tiny Rose Street, is the **Lamb and Flag,** a highly atmospheric pub that Dickens used to visit when he worked in nearby Catherine Street. Shops on Long Acre specialize in maps and art books; at the **Glasshouse** you can watch the glassblowers practicing their craft.

31 Bow Street is famous for the **Royal Opera House,** home of both the Royal Ballet and the Royal Opera Company. The theater is the third on this site, its interior all rich Victorian gilt and plush seats, with excellent acoustics. The **Magistrates Court,** opposite the theater, was established in 1749 by Henry Fielding, magistrate, journalist, and novelist. He employed a band of private detectives, the "Bow Street Runners," and paid them out of the fines imposed in the court. They were the forefathers of the modern police force.

To the north, Neal Street and the surrounding lanes make for out-of-the-ordinary shopping: Eastern goods, clothes, pottery, and jewelry.

South of Bow Street, by the end of Waterloo Bridge and on the Strand, is the new home of the **Courtauld Institute Galleries.** This collection of paintings has moved from its former hidden galleries in Woburn Square into the majestic rooms of Somerset House. Here you can see some of the best French Impressionist work anywhere, with Manets, Van Goghs, and Gauguins supported by dozens of old masters. But the more convenient location means that there may be long lines. *Somerset House, The Strand, tel. 071/873–2526. Admission: £3 adults, £1.50 children. Open Mon., Wed–Sat. 10–6; Tues. 10–8; Sun. 2–6.*

Bloomsbury is a semiresidential district north of Covent Garden that contains a number of elegant 17th- and 18th-century squares; it is home to the British Museum and the University of London. The Bloomsbury Group was a coterie of writers and painters that included the novelists E. M. Forster and Virginia Woolf; her husband, Leonard; the poet Rupert Brooke; Bertrand Russell, the philosopher; and J. M. Keynes, the economist.

Museum Street, lined with print- and secondhand-book shops, leads to the **British Museum** on Great Russell Street, a monumental, severely Greek edifice built in the first half of the 19th century. The vast collection of treasures here includes Egyptian, Greek, and Roman antiquities; Renaissance jewelry, pottery, coins, glass; and drawings from virtually every European school since the 15th century. It's best to concentrate on one area that particularly interests you or, alternatively, take one of the Museum's guided tours, which cost £6 per person and last 90 minutes (tel. 071/636–1555, ext. 8299). Some of the highlights are the Elgin Marbles, sculptures from the Parthenon in Athens; the Rosetta Stone, which helped archaeologists decipher Egyptian hieroglyphics; a newly opened gallery of Oriental Antiquities; and the Mildenhall Treasure, a cache of Roman silver found in East Anglia in 1842. The King's Library, part of the **British Library,** contains illuminated and printed books, including many from the earliest days of printing. Housed here since 1759, the British Library planned at press time to move in 1995 to its controversial new home (is it ugly? is it art?) in St. Pancras. *Great Russell St., tel. 071/636–1555 or 071/580–1788 (recorded information). Admission free. Open Mon.–Sat. 10–5, Sun. 2:30–6.*

The University of London lies to the north of the British Museum. Inside the **Senate House** skyscraper (1932) are administrative offices and the university library. **University College,** on Gower Street, founded in 1826, was the first college in Britain to admit Jews and Roman Catholics. Behind University College, Gordon Square contains restored 19th-century town houses and, at No. 53, the **Percival David Foundation of Chinese Art,** a collection of Chinese ceramics from the 10th to the 19th century. *53 Gordon Sq., tel. 071/387–3909. Admission free. Open weekdays 10:30–5 (sometimes closed 1–2 for lunch).*

Turn right onto Tavistock Place, second right into Woburn Place and continue until you see Guildford Street on your left. Go past

Coram Fields (on your left) and continue until you come to Doughty
❸ Street. A little way down is the **Dickens House,** where Charles Dickens lived from 1837 to 1839. During this fertile period he finished
Pickwick Papers, wrote all of *Oliver Twist*, and started *Nicholas
Nickleby*. The house now boasts a fascinating collection of Dickens
memorabilia relating in particular to his early life and novels. *48
Doughty St., tel. 071/405–2127. Admission: £3 adults, £1 children
under 15. Open Mon.–Sat. 10–5; closed Sun.*

Tour 3: Around Two Royal Parks—
Knightsbridge and Kensington

❸ Start at traffic-clogged **Hyde Park Corner.** On the central island is
the triumphal **Wellington Arch,** originally intended to adorn the
back gate of Buckingham Palace. The original statue of the first
duke of Wellington, victor at the Battle of Waterloo in 1815 and later
prime minister, was moved to Aldershot and replaced by *Peace in
Her Chariot* in 1912. **Apsley House,** the mansion by the park entrance, built in the 1770s by celebrated Scottish architect Robert
Adam, was Wellington's London home for some 30 years and is now
❸ the **Wellington Museum.** The interior is much as it was in the Iron
Duke's day, full of heavy, ornate pieces; there's also a fine equestrian portrait of Wellington by Goya. *149 Piccadilly, tel. 071/499–5676.
Closed for major refurbishment; call for an update on its reopening.*

Hyde Park (361 acres) was originally a royal hunting ground, while
Kensington Gardens (273 acres) was once the park of Kensington
Palace. Both contain fine trees—though many were lost during the
1987 windstorm—and a surprisingly large variety of birdlife; almost 100 species have been recorded, including cormorant, heron,
and little grebe.

Enter the park through the brightly colored **Queen Mother's Gate**
beside Apsley House. Almost immediately you reach **Rotten Row,**
the long sandy avenue used for horseback riding that runs near the
bottom of the park. The odd name derives from *route du roi* ("the
King's Way"), a route William III and Queen Mary took from Kensington Palace to the court at St. James's.

North of the Row is an artificial, crescent-shaped lake called the **Serpentine** in Hyde Park and **Long Water** in Kensington Gardens,
formed in 1730 by damming a river that used to flow here. The Serpentine has its own atmosphere: festive in the summer, with its
deck chairs, rowboats, and swimmers; melancholy on windy winter
days.

Leave the park on the south side via **Park Close** for **Knightsbridge.**
The high rise to the right is the Hyde Park Barracks, headquarters
of the Household Cavalry; the soldiers often exercise their horses in
the park. At precisely 10:28 every morning (9:28 on Sundays) you
should be able to see the mounted Guards leaving for the Changing
of the Guard ceremony at the Horseguards (*see* Tour 1).

Brompton Road takes you to **Harrods** and the museums of South
Kensington. A main point of interest at Harrods is the ground-floor
Food Hall with its fine tile work and spectacular arrangements of co-
mestibles—don't miss the fish. Harrods, being on every tourist's
list, tends to get phenomenally crowded, especially during sales and
over the two weeks before Christmas.

Time Out **Richoux** (86 Brompton Rd.) is a very fancy patisserie and chocolatier, which serves delicate lunches, afternoon teas, and pastries.

Off Brompton Road, Beauchamp (pronounced "Beecham") Place and Walton Street are good places to shop away from Harrods crowds.

㊳ Beyond **Brompton Oratory,** an Italianate, late 19th-century Catholic church, stands the massive **Victoria and Albert Museum,** crowned with cupolas. The V&A, as it is known, originated in the 19th century as a museum of ornamental art, and has extensive collections of costumes, paintings, jewelry, musical instruments, and crafts from every part of the globe. The collections from India, China, Japan, and the Islamic world are especially dazzling. *Cromwell Rd., tel. 071/938–8500 or 071/938–8349 (recording). Admission: £3.50 (£1 children) donation requested. Open Mon.–Sat. 10–5:50, Sun. 2:30– 5:50.*

Time Out The V&A café-restaurant is just the place to recharge after visiting the collections. You can enjoy fresh salads, sandwiches, hot lunches, or just coffee or tea.

㊴ Past the V&A are two museums devoted to science. The **Natural History Museum** occupies an ornate late-Victorian building with modern additions; note the little animals carved into the cathedral-like entrance. The collections—from dinosaur skeletons to earthquake simulators—are among the best in the world and (like the Earth) continually evolving. Recent additions include "Plant Power," which explores our relationship with the plant kingdom, and a touch-screen, six-language interactive computer tour around all the exhibits, called "Wonders of the Natural World." *Cromwell Rd., tel. 071/ 938–9123. Admission: £4.50 adults, £2.20 children under 15 and senior citizens. Open Mon.–Sat. 10–6, Sun. 1–6.*

㊵ The **Science Museum** concerns itself with everything from locomotives to space technology, the history of medicine to computers. Working models and "hands-on" exhibits are informative and fun (great for children). *Cromwell Rd., tel. 071/938–8000 or 071/938– 8123 (recorded information). Admission: £4 adults, £2.10 children 6–14 and senior citizens. Open Mon.–Sat. 10–6, Sun. 11–6.*

㊶ On the left off Exhibition Road stands the grandiose bulk of the **Royal Albert Hall,** named after Queen Victoria's consort. It is the venue of the summer Promenade Concerts, and choral and symphony concerts throughout the year. Note the pseudo-Greek frieze called "The Triumph of Arts and Letters" that runs round its exterior below the dome.

㊷ Across the road in **Kensington Gardens** is the **Albert Memorial,** the expression of Queen Victoria's obsessive devotion to her husband's memory, epitomizing high Victorian taste. The memorial is in a bad way physically, and is permanently shrouded in scaffolding and fencing.

㊸ From the **Flower Walk,** north of the memorial, strike out across Kensington Gardens to the **Round Pond,** a favorite place for children and adults to sail toy boats; and then head for **Kensington Palace,** a royal residence since the late 17th century. The Prince and Princess of Wales and Princess Margaret now have apartments here. It was a simple country house until William III bought it in 1689. The interior was remodeled by leading architects Wren, Hawksmoor, Vanbrugh, and William Kent during the 18th century. Eighteen-year-old Princess Victoria was living here with her dominating mother and governess when, on June 20, 1837, she learned that her uncle William IV had died, which meant her accession to the throne. Some of the state apartments (a few are open to the public) have remained unchanged since then. The **Court Dress Collection** consists of the most formal clothing and uniforms from 1750 to the 1950s. Court dress and behavior were governed by strict rules, and the exhibition reveals this curious world of rigid etiquette. *Kensington Gardens, tel. 071/937–9561. Admission: £3.90 adults, £2.60 children under 16, £2.95 senior citizens. Open Mon.–Sat. 9–5, Sun. 1–5.*

Immediately behind the palace is **Kensington Palace Gardens** (called Palace Green at the south end), a wide, leafy avenue of mid-19th century mansions. This is one of the few private roads in London with uniformed guards at each end; there are several foreign embassies here, including that of Russia. Walk south to Kensington High Street. Just west, past the towering modern Royal Garden Hotel, **Kensington Church Street** runs up to the right. **St. Mary Abbotts Church** on the corner looks medieval but was built in the 1870s. This is rich territory for antiques enthusiasts: The street's shops (all the way up to Notting Hill) carry everything from Japanese armor to Victorian commemorative china. Tucked away behind the church is **Kensington Church Walk,** a pretty lane lined with tiny shops (go down Holland Street, take the second left).

Time Out   **Muffin Man** (12 Wright's La., off Kensington High St.) provides a refuge from the crowds of shoppers; salads and sandwiches, and scones and cakes at teatime, are the specialties. They serve breakfast all day!

If you follow **Kensington High Street** (another flourishing shopping street) westward, you'll come to the **Commonwealth Institute,** recognizable by its huge, tentlike copper roof. The Institute focuses on the cultures of Commonwealth countries with frequent exhibitions, concerts, and films. *230 Kensington High St., tel. 071/603–4535. Admission: £1 adults, 50p children and senior citizens. Open Mon.– Sat. 10–5, Sun. 2–5.*

On the eastern side of the Commonwealth Institute is **Linley Sambourne House,** built and furnished in the 1870s by Mr. Sambourne, for over 30 years the political cartoonist for the satirical magazine *Punch.* Full of pictures, furniture, and ornaments, it provides a marvelous insight into the day-to-day life of a prosperous, cultured family in late Victorian times. Some of the scenes from the movie *A Room with a View* were shot here. *18 Stafford Terr., tel. 081/994–1019. Admission: £3 adults, £1.50 children under 16. Open Mar.–Oct., Wed. 10–4, Sun. 2–5.*

Time Out   Enter Holland Park by the Commonwealth Institute, cross the cricket lawn, and you reach **Café,** run by an Italian family, and serving home-cooked hot dishes (risotto, lasagna) at lunchtime, plus soup, sandwiches, and pastries. There are plenty of outdoor tables.

A little way past the Commonwealth Institute, on the right, is **Melbury Road,** which leads to **Holland Park Road.** Lord Leighton, the Victorian painter par excellence, lived at No. 12. The exotic richness of late 19th-century aesthetic tastes is captured in **Leighton House,** especially the Arab hall, which is lavishly lined with Persian tiles and pierced woodwork. Thanks to the generosity of John Paul Getty III, the somewhat neglected property is now being set to rights. This neighborhood was one of the principal artists' colonies of Victorian London. If you are interested in domestic architecture of the 19th century, wander through the surrounding streets. *12 Holland Park Rd., tel. 071/602–3316. Admission free. Open Mon.–Sat. 11–5 (Mon.–Fri. 11–6 during exhibitions).*

Tour 4: The City

The City, the traditional commercial center of London, was the site of the great Roman city of Londinium. Over the past 2,000 years the City has been continually renewed. The wooden buildings of the medieval City were destroyed in the Great Fire of 1666 and rebuilt in brick and stone. There were waves of reconstruction in the 19th century, and again after World War II. Since the '60s, modern office towers have completely changed the City's skyline, as the great financial institutions indulged in conspicuous construction.

Throughout these changes, the City has preserved its unique identity. It is governed by the Lord Mayor and the Corporation (city council) of London, as it has been for centuries. Commerce remains the City's lifeblood, but with banking now ascendant over trade. Until the first half of the 19th century, merchants and traders who worked in the City also lived there. Now, despite a huge work force, scarcely 8,000 people actually live within the City's 677 acres. Try, therefore, to explore on a weekday. On weekends, the streets are empty, and most of the shops—even some of the churches—are closed.

47 St. Paul's Cathedral was rebuilt after the Great Fire of 1666 by Sir Christopher Wren, the architect who also designed 50 other City churches to replace those lost in the Fire. St. Paul's is Wren's greatest work, and fittingly, he is buried in the crypt, his epitaph composed by his son: *Lector, si monumentum requiris, circumspice*— Reader, if you seek his monument, look around you. The cathedral has been the scene of many state pageants, including Winston Churchill's funeral in 1965 and the wedding of the Prince and Princess of Wales in 1981. Fine painting and craftsmanship abound—the choir stalls are by the great 17th-century wood carver Grinling Gibbons—but overall the atmosphere is somewhat austere and remote. Perhaps this is because Wren's design was based on Italian Renaissance style rather than the English medieval tradition. The fact that the church was built in just 35 years also helps to account for its unusually unified quality.

The cathedral contains dozens of monuments and tombs. Among those commemorated are Nelson and Wellington, who defeated the French at Trafalgar and Waterloo. Dr. Samuel Johnson and even George Washington have their places. In the ambulatory (the area behind the high altar) is the **American Chapel,** a memorial to the 28,000 Americans stationed in Britain during World War II who lost their lives in active service. Henry Moore's sculpture *Mother and Child*, donated by the artist in 1984, stands near the entrance to the ambulatory.

The cathedral's crowning glory is its dome. It consists of three distinct shells: an outer, timber-framed dome covered with lead; the interior dome, built of brick, and decorated with frescoes of the life of St. Paul by the 18th-century artist Sir James Thornhill; and, in between, a brick cone that supports and strengthens both. There is a stunning view down to the body of the church from the **Whispering Gallery,** high up in the inner dome. Words whispered at one point can be heard clearly on the opposite point 112 feet away.

Above the Whispering Gallery are the **Stone Gallery** and the **Golden Gallery,** both commanding fine views across London from the cathedral's exterior. These galleries also afford close views of the flying buttresses and western tower. The steps to the Golden Gallery just below the lantern, ball, and cross, though safe, are very steep; from them you can see the brick cone that divides the inner and outer domes. *Tel. 071/248–2705. Admission to cathedral, ambulatory (American Chapel), crypt, and treasury £2.50 adults, £1.50 children, £2 senior citizens; cathedral admission free Sun., after 4:15 Mon.–Sat.; to galleries £2.50 adults, £1.50 children, £2 senior citizens; guided 1–1½ hr. tours of the cathedral weekdays at 11, 11:30, 2, and 2:30, £4.50 adults, £2.50 children, £3.50 senior citizens. Cathedral open daily 7:30–6 except for special services; ambulatory, crypt, and galleries open Mon.–Sat. 9:30–4:15; closed Sun.*

Time Out **Balls Brothers Wine Bar** (2 Old Chance Ct., St. Paul's Churchyard) serves freshly made soup and grilled steak in French bread. Arrive early at lunchtime.

48 Walk north from the cathedral to Newgate Street and the **National Postal Museum,** housed in the General Post Office, which has one of the world's most important collections of postage stamps, philatelic archives, and an extensive reference library. *King Edward Bldg., King Edward St., tel. 071/239–5420. Admission free. Open Mon.–Thurs. 9:30–4:30, Fri. 9:30–4; closed weekends, national holidays.*

A short walk via Angel Street and St. Martins le Grand to **London Wall** (which follows the line of the wall that surrounded the Roman **49** settlement), brings you to the **Museum of London.** Its imaginative displays bring London to life from Roman times to the present. Among the highlights are the Lord Mayor's Ceremonial Coach, a re-enactment of the Great Fire, and the Cheapside Hoard—jewelry hidden during an outbreak of plague in the 17th century and never recovered by its owner. The 20th-century exhibits include a Woolworth's counter and elevators from Selfridge's; both stores (founded by Americans) had considerable impact on the lives of Londoners. *London Wall, tel. 071/600–3699. Admission £3 adults, £1.50 children under 18 and senior citizens, £7.50 family ticket; admission free 4:30–6. Open Tues.–Sat. 10–6, Sun. 2–6; closed national holidays.*

Time Out **Millburn's,** the museum's restaurant, provides basic refreshments in an area short on family eating places.

50 The **Barbican** is a vast residential complex and arts center built by the City of London that takes its name from the watch tower that stood here in the Middle Ages, just outside the City walls. The arts center contains a concert hall, where the London Symphony Orchestra is based, two theaters, an art gallery for major exhibitions, cinema, library, café, and restaurant. The Royal Shakespeare Company has its London base here. *Silk St., tel. 071/638–4141. Admission free. Open Mon.–Sat. 9 AM–11 PM, Sun. noon–11 PM. Art gallery admission varies according to exhibition. Open Mon.–Sat. 10–6:45, Sun. noon–5:45.*

The parish church of the Barbican, **St. Giles Without Cripplegate** (St. Giles being the patron saint of the disabled), stands just south of the main complex, forlornly swamped by its towering modern neighbors. Only the church tower and walls are original; the remainder was rebuilt in the 1950s.

51 South of the Barbican across London Wall stands the **Guildhall,** the home of the Corporation of London, which elects the Lord Mayor here each year with great ceremony. The building dates from 1410, with much reconstruction over the centuries. *King St., tel. 071/606–3030. Admission free. Great Hall open weekdays 9:30–5 if it is not being used. Library open weekdays 9:30–4:45.*

Now walk south to **Cheapside,** the chief market place of medieval London (the Old English word *ceap* meant market). Note the area's street names: Milk Street, Ironmonger Lane, Bread Street, etc. **52** Many of them still follow the medieval layout. The church of **St. Mary-le-Bow** on the south side of Cheapside was rebuilt (by Wren) after the Great Fire, and again after it was bombed in World War II; it is said that to be a true Cockney you must be born within the sound of Bow bells.

A short walk east along Cheapside brings you to a seven-way inter- **53** section. The **Bank of England,** Britain's treasury, is the huge building on the left. A new museum here highlights the history of the "The Old Lady of Threadneedle Street" and its role in the world economy. *Bartholomew La., tel. 071/601–5545. Admission free. Open Good Friday–Sept., Mon.–Sat. 10–6, Sun. 2–6; Oct.–Good Friday, weekdays 10–6.*

54 At right angles to the Bank is the **Royal Exchange,** originally built in the 1560s for merchants and traders to conduct business. The present building, opened in 1844 (the third on the site), is now occupied by the **London International Financial Futures Exchange.** The Visitors' Gallery is open to groups from relevant organizations. *Cornhill, tel. 071/623–0444. Admission free. Open weekdays by appointment to groups of 10 or more.*

55 The third major building at this intersection is the **Mansion House,** the official residence of the Lord Mayor (not open to the general public).

Continue east along Cornhill, site of a Roman basilica and a medieval grain market. Turn right onto Gracechurch Street and left onto **56** **Leadenhall Market.** There's been a market here since the 14th century; the glass and cast-iron building dates from 1881.

Time Out   **The Bull's Head** wine bar (80 Leadenhall St.) also has a restaurant and the **Leadenhall Wine Bar** (26 Leadenhall Market) offers a fixed-price buffet plus a daily special.

Just behind the market is one of the most striking examples of con- **57** temporary City architecture: the headquarters of **Lloyd's of London,** designed by Richard Rogers and completed in 1986. Its main feature is a 200-foot-high barrel vault of sparkling glass that looks "alive" in all weathers; it encloses a great atrium ringed with twelve tiers of galleries used largely as offices. Since its founding in the 19th century, Lloyd's has earned its fame by underwriting every kind of risk imaginable: ships, aircraft, oil rigs, even Betty Grable's and Madonna's legs! An exhibition details the history of Lloyd's; there is also an open trading area. *1 Lime St., tel. 071/623–7100, ext. 6210 or 5786. Admission free. To visit the exhibition, groups from recognized organizations must apply in writing on letterhead paper at least one week in advance.*

Time Out   Lloyd's was founded in a coffee house, so **Lloyd's Coffee House** at the foot of the modern building is an apt place for a coffee break.

58 Wander south to the **Monument,** a massive column of white stone designed by Wren and erected in 1667 to commemorate the Great Fire. It stands 202 feet high, with its base exactly 202 feet from the site of the small bakery shop in Pudding Lane where the fire started. At the summit is a gilt urn with flames leaping from it, 311 steps up from the street. *Monument St., tel. 071/626–2717. Admission: £1 adults, 25p children. Open Mon.–Sat. 9–2.*

59 The **Tower of London** is one of London's most popular (hence, crowded) sights. Visit as early in the day as possible, and join one of the excellent free one-hour tours given by the Yeoman Warders of the Tower (the "Beefeaters"), who wear a picturesque Tudor-style uniform. Tours start from the Middle Tower (near the entrance) about every 30 minutes.

The Tower served as both fortress and palace in medieval times; every British sovereign from William the Conqueror (11th century) to Henry VIII (16th century) lived here, and it is still officially a royal palace. The Tower has such a long history and its buildings have known so many uses that it can be difficult to grasp the overall story. The **History Gallery** is a useful walk-through display which answers most questions about the Tower and its inhabitants.

The **White Tower** is the oldest and most conspicuous building in the entire complex. When it was completed in about 1097, it dominated the whole settlement, forcing home the power of England's new Norman overlords. Inside, the austere **Chapel of St. John** is one of the Tower's few unaltered structures, a Norman chapel of great simplicity, almost entirely lacking in ornamentation.

The **Royal Armouries,** England's national collection of arms and armor, occupies the rest of the White Tower. Sixteenth- and 17th-century armor dominate the displays, including pieces belonging to Henry VIII and Charles I. Armor from Asia and the Islamic world is on show in the **Oriental Armoury** in the **Waterloo Barracks,** including 18th-century elephant armor, brought to England by Lord Clive. Gruesome instruments of torture and punishment lie mercifully still in the **Bowyer Tower,** while the **New Armouries** house examples of almost every weapon made in the Tower for British forces between the 17th and 19th century.

Surrounding the White Tower are structures dating from the 11th to the 19th century. Sir Walter Raleigh was held prisoner in the **Bloody Tower** (originally the Garden Tower) in relative comfort between 1603 and 1616; he passed the time writing his *History of the World.* The young princes, sons of Edward IV, supposedly murdered on the orders of their uncle Richard III, lived and probably died in the Bloody Tower. Next door stands the **Wakefield Tower,** where Henry VI was allegedly murdered in 1471 during the Wars of the Roses.

Tower Green was the site of the executioner's block. It was a rare honor to be beheaded inside the Tower in relative privacy; most people were executed outside on Tower Hill, where the crowds could get a better view. Important prisoners were held in the **Beauchamp Tower** to the west of Tower Green; its walls are covered with graffiti and inscriptions carved by prisoners.

The **Crown Jewels** are now housed in the **Duke of Wellington's Barracks,** which can accommodate 20,000 visitors per day, and should reduce the fearsome line for this most popular of exhibits. The Jewels are a breathtakingly impressive collection of regalia, precious stones, gold, and silver. The Royal Sceptre contains the largest cut diamond in the world. The Imperial State Crown, made for Queen

Victoria's coronation in 1838, is studded with 3,000 precious stones, mainly diamonds and pearls. *Tower Hill, tel. 071/709-0765. Admission: £6.70 adults, £4.40 children under 15, £5.10 senior citizens; family ticket (up to 2 adults, 3 children) £19. Small additional admission charge to the Fusiliers Museum only. Open Mar.-Oct., Mon.-Sat. 9:30-5, Sun. 10-5; Nov.-Feb., Mon.-Sat. 9:30-4, telephone for Sun. times; closed Good Friday, Dec. 24-26, Jan. 1.*

60 To the west of the Tower is a new development, where various shops and food outlets surround the entrance to **Tower Hill Pageant,** London's first dark-ride museum. Automated cars take visitors past mock-ups of scenes from the past, complete with "people," sound effects, and smells. There's also an archaeological museum with finds from the Thames. *Tower Hill Terrace, tel. 071/709-0081. Admission: £4.95 adults, £2.95 children under 16 and senior citizens. Open Apr.-Oct., daily 9:30-5:30; Nov.-Mar., daily 9:30-4:30. Closed Dec. 25.*

61 **Tower Bridge** may look medieval, but it was built in 1885-94. It is London's only drawbridge, although with the virtual extinction of London's shipping trade and the movement of big ships on the Thames, the complex lifting mechanism is used only four or five times a week. To celebrate the Bridge's 100th birthday in 1994, a new permanent exhibition opened, an audio-visual journey through the history, construction, and raison d'être of what, for many people, is the very symbol of London. The show uses compact disc interactive technology to superimpose skylines of past ages over the magnificent views from the Bridge's walkways, and includes models and dramatizations of Victorian London, and animatronic tour guides. The tour ends in the Engine Room with a re-creation of the 1894 Royal Opening ceremony. *Tel. 071/403-3761. Admission: £3.60 adults, £2.50 children under 15 and senior citizens. Open Apr.-Oct., daily 10-6:30; Nov.-Mar., daily 10-4:45.*

Tour 5: The South Bank

Southwark, on the south bank of the Thames, had been long neglected. Full of derelict 19th-century warehouses, it seemed a perfect location for Jack the Ripper movies. Now ambitious new building complexes with stylish museums and stores are turning it into a riverside center of activity again.

The first settlement here was Roman. Across the river from the City proper, and thus outside its jurisdiction, by the Middle Ages Southwark had acquired a reputation for easy living. Londoners used to go there to enjoy a night in one of the many inns—Southwark was famous for good, strong beer—or to sample the pleasures of the Southwark "stews" (brothels, not casseroles!). Bear-baiting and the theater were other forms of entertainment here. At the Elizabethan Globe Theatre, Shakespeare was both actor and shareholder, and his plays were staged regularly.

62 Start at **Butler's Wharf,** a short distance downstream (east) of the south end of Tower Bridge. This was originally a large warehouse, and has been converted into a residential and commercial complex. Until 1982 there was a brewery here; its tower is all that remains. The displays at the **Design Museum** focus on the history and current evolution of mass-produced goods: everything from furniture to cars, perfume to packaging, clothing to electrical equipment. Films, sound recordings, posters, and other advertising material are used to put the exhibits in their contemporary social and cultural context. The first floor holds special exhibitions. There are also regular lectures and films and a riverside café with panoramic views. *Butler's Wharf, tel. 071/403–6933. Admission: £3.50 adults, £2.50 children and senior citizens. Open Tues.–Sun. 11:30–6:30 (later on some nights).*

63 Upstream of Tower Bridge lies **H.M.S. *Belfast*,** the largest and one of the most powerful cruisers ever built for the Royal Navy (a ferry runs between it and the Tower of London). The *Belfast* stood off Normandy on D-Day in 1944, protecting the landing beaches, and after the war served in the Far East. When her service career ended in 1963, she was saved from the scrapyard by the Imperial War Museum. Naval and World War II enthusiasts will want to tour the *Belfast;* the armaments, mess decks, punishment cells, operations room, and engine room are open to view. Others can admire it from the riverside. *Symon's Wharf, Vine Lane, Tooley St., tel. 071/407–6434. Admission: £4 adults, £2 children under 16, £3 senior citizens. Open mid-Mar.–Oct., daily 10–5:20; Nov.–mid-Mar., daily 10–4.*

64 A little farther west is **Hay's Galleria,** a shopping mall housed beneath a dramatic 100-foot-high, 300-foot-long glass barrel-vault roof. In the center is a massive kinetic sculpture, *Navigators*, by David Kemp. Shaped like a huge comic boat, parts of which move under the water jets, it recalls the history of Hay's Wharf, one of London's oldest, dating from 1651. Planners hope that the Galleria will develop into a Covent Garden on the Thames.

Time Out   Reasonably priced lunch spots are disappointingly few in the galleria. The best bet is **Balls Brothers Wine Bar and Restaurant,** which serves traditional English meals, sandwiches, and coffee. Alternatively, you can eat a take-away snack on the river and enjoy the view across to the Custom House.

Walking westward from the Galleria, follow the riverside path past the Cottons building, with its offices overlooking a 100-foot-high atrium and water garden, to the new **London Bridge** (*see* Tour 6, *below*).

65 On **Tooley Street,** below Hay's Galleria, is **the London Dungeon,** which re-creates scenes of medieval torture, execution, disease, persecution, and—on a different level—the Great Fire of 1666. The Dungeon's appeal may be lost on the squeamish, but teenagers will probably love it! *28–34 Tooley St., tel. 071/403–0606. Admission: £6 adults, £4 children under 14, £5 senior citizens. Open daily 10–4:30.*

66 **Old St. Thomas's Hospital,** on St. Thomas Street (over the railway viaduct from Tooley Street), provides an insight into hospital life of only a few generations ago. This operating theater dates from 1821 and has been restored to its original state. Surgeons at the time worked in aprons stained with blood from previous operations, washing facilities scarcely existed, and a sawdust box underneath the table caught patients' blood; when it was saturated, the surgeon called for more sawdust. The herb garret next door, where medicinal herbs were dried and laid away, has also been restored. *St. Thomas St., tel. 081/806–4325. Admission: £2 adults, £1 children, £1.50 senior citizens. Open Mon., Wed., Fri. 12:30–4, other times by appointment.*

67 **Southwark Cathedral** is the largest Gothic church in London after Westminster Abbey—building began on it in 1220. The chief feature of interest for American visitors is the Harvard Chapel. It commemorates John Harvard, founder of the great American university, baptized here in 1608. Shakespeare's younger brother Edmund is buried here.

Just before Southwark Bridge, the large pub, **The Anchor,** serves bar snacks, and gets very crowded in fine weather, when office workers swarm over the terraces.

Now walk west along Clink Street, where one of Southwark's several prisons stood, past the Bankside pub and under Cannon Street Railway Bridge and Southwark Bridge. On the left, a narrow street (68) called Bear Gardens leads to the **Shakespeare Globe Museum,** site of a massive project started by the late American actor/director Sam Wanamaker to rebuild Shakespeare's Globe Playhouse to its original open-roof design of 1599, using authentic Elizabethan materials and techniques wherever possible. Regular Shakespeare-related events are scheduled and there is a charming, small **museum,** which fills in the background of this 300-year-old theater district. *Bear Gardens, tel. 071/928–6342. Admission: £3 adults, £2 children and senior citizens. Open Mon.–Sat. 10–5, Sun. 1:30–5.*

The riverside path passes Cardinal's Wharf and then continues along Bankside toward **Blackfriars Bridge.**

On the far side of the bridge, beyond the art deco **Oxo Tower,** named after the three letters which shine out from the summit (a sneaky advertisement installed by the eponymous stock cube manufacturers in 1928) is **Coin Street,** a residential enclave that has been pre-(69) served from development. At **Gabriel's Wharf** there are craft shops, studios, and a craft market, where you can commission one of about 20 ceramists, jewelers, textile designers, and tailors to make you a unique piece. Much is happening in this corner of London, which is truly community-oriented—including craft fairs, a Friday market, and a summer festival. *56 Upper Ground, SE1, tel. 071/620–0544. Admission free. Workshops open Tues.–Sun. 11–6. Market open Fri. 11–3.*

A short walk along the new embankment promenade—look for the display panels which identify the buildings across the river—brings you to the **Royal National Theatre,** the first of the low, gray concrete (70) buildings that make up the **South Bank Arts Complex.** The foyers, open to the public six days a week, are full of activity, with bookshops, bars, cafés, exhibitions, and free performances. The Royal National Theatre Company plays here regularly in three auditoriums, each with its distinct character. Although performances can be uneven, its best work is electrifying. *South Bank, tel. 071/928–2252 (box office). Hour-long tours of the theater backstage (tel. 071/633–0880), normally 5 times daily between 10:15 and 6; £2.50 adults, £2.25 children, Actors' Equity members, and senior citizens. Foyers open Mon.–Sat. 10 AM–11 PM.*

The Royal National Theatre's bars and snack counters are ideal places to relax any time of day.

Underneath Waterloo Bridge nearby are the **National Film Theatre** (NFT) and the **Museum of the Moving Image** (MOMI). The NFT screens art and historic films drawn mainly from its huge archives. MOMI celebrates every aspect of the moving image, from Chinese shadow plays of 2,500 BC to the latest fiber optics and satellite images; cinema and television take center stage, however. This is very much a hands-on museum, with the emphasis on participatory displays, especially of film and television-making processes. *South*

Bank, tel. 071/401–2636. Admission: £5.50 adults, £4 children, stu-
dents, and senior citizens. Open daily 10–6; last admission 5 PM.
Closed Dec. 24–26.

Time Out   Open to all, the **NFT cafeteria** serves lunch and dinner.

The rest of the arts complex, on the far side of Waterloo Bridge, consists of three concert halls and the **Hayward Gallery,** which hosts
large-scale art exhibitions. The gallery is surmounted by a tall, skel-
etal sculpture made of neon tubing. At night hectic colors run up and
down it, their speed and intensity governed by the velocity of the
wind playing through an anemometer at the top. *Belvedere Rd., tel.*
071/928–3144 or 071/261–0127 (recorded information). Admission:
varies according to exhibition. Open daily 10–6, Tues. and Wed. un-
til 8.

The three concert halls, the **Royal Festival Hall,** the **Queen Elizabeth**
Hall, and the **Purcell Room,** are used for every kind of musical event,
from major symphony and choral concerts to recitals of the latest
electronic compositions. The Festival Hall has a well-stocked bookstore, a record shop, and exhibition space.

Time Out   The Festival Hall's eateries include a salt-beef bar, pasta counter,
salad bar, coffee shop, and spacious cafeteria.

The next stretch of the embankment affords photogenic views
across the river to Big Ben and the Houses of Parliament. The path
runs in front of **County Hall,** formerly the seat of local government
for Greater London (The Greater London Council, or G.L.C., which
was disbanded in 1986). The huge 1932 building, with its chill, classical facade, was bought by a Japanese company, and is being converted into a luxury hotel.

The river frontage on the far side of **Westminster Bridge** is occupied
71 by **St. Thomas's Hospital.** In early 1989 St. Thomas's became the site
of the **Florence Nightingale Museum,** dedicated to the famous
nurse's life and work and also featuring the evolution of modern
nursing techniques. *Gassiot House, 2 Lambeth Palace Rd., tel. 071/*
620–0374. Admission: £2.50 adults, £1.50 children and senior citi-
zens. Open Tues.–Sun. 10–4.

72 Beyond St. Thomas's stands **Lambeth Palace,** the London residence
of the Archbishop of Canterbury—the senior archbishop of the
Church of England—since the early 13th century. It's rarely open to
the public, but you can admire the fine Tudor gatehouse.

Beside the palace, in the yard of the now-deconsecrated **St. Mary's**
Church, are buried the two John Tradescants, father and son, who
were royal gardeners in the 17th century. They traveled widely in
Europe and America, bringing back plant specimens not previously
known in this country; their garden in Lambeth became a pioneer
nursery. St. Mary's Church now houses the Tradescant Trust's **Mu-**
seum of Garden History. This unique collection includes a duplica-
tion of a 17th-century knot garden (the name describes its shape)
containing only plants grown in the 17th century, especially those
grown by the Tradescants. *St. Mary-at-Lambeth, Lambeth Palace*
Rd., tel. 071/261–1891. Admission free; donations welcome. Open
early Mar.–early Dec., weekdays 11–3, Sun. 10:30–5; closed Sat.

73 The **Imperial War Museum** lies a short walk inland from Lambeth
Palace, down Lambeth Road. Its holdings constitute the country's
principal collection of 20th-century war artifacts. Among the hard-

ware on display are a Battle of Britain Spitfire, a World War I tank, and a German V1 pilotless flying bomb, a type dropped on London in 1944–45. The "Blitz Experience" gives you the sights, sounds, and smells of London during the World War II bombing, and "Operation Jericho" simulates the famous Mosquito Raid over France. *Lambeth Rd., tel. 071/416–5000. Admission: £3.70 adults, £1.85 children, £2.65 senior citizens. Operation Jericho: £1.30 adults, £1 children, £1.05 senior citizens. Open daily 10–6.*

Tour 6: Up and Down the Thames

The River Thames unites the oldest and the newest areas of London. It's spanned by bridges of different design. The earliest, Richmond, dates from 1774, and the most recent, London Bridge, from 1973— the former London Bridge having been sold and rebuilt in Arizona. The river has played an important role in the history of London and from it the familiar historic buildings and sites take on a new and dramatic perspective. Points of interest such as Greenwich, the Thames Barrier, Hampton Court Palace, and Kew are serviced by BritRail. Also, boat excursions can be taken in either direction from piers at Westminster, Charing Cross, and Tower Bridge. *Tel. 0891/ 505–471 for the LTB Visitorcall Riverboat Information. Calls cost 48p/min or 36p cheap rate, plus any hotel surcharge.*

Greenwich   Downstream, a few miles past the imposing bulk of the Tower of London, lies **Greenwich.** At its heart are the late-17th-century buildings of the **Royal Naval College,** once an old sailors' home; the college has been here since 1873. The buildings are the work of Sir Christopher Wren and his two assistants, Hawksmoor and Vanbrugh, later celebrated architects in their own right. You can visit the grand **Painted Hall,** the college dining hall, dramatically decorated with huge frescoes by Sir James Thornhill, who also painted the dome in St. Paul's Cathedral. It was here that Nelson's body lay in state at Christmas of 1805, after the Battle of Trafalgar. Across from the Painted Hall is the **College Chapel.** The airy 18th-century interior is a delight of pastel shades and intricate, delicate detail. The pulpit maintains the naval theme; it's made from the top deck of a three-decker sailing ship. *King William Walk, tel. 071/858–2154. Admission free. Open Fri.–Wed. 2:30–4:45.*

Two dry-docked boats alongside the river are the ***Cutty Sark,*** the last of the 19th-century clipper ships, and the tiny ***Gipsy Moth IV,*** which Sir Francis Chichester sailed singlehandedly around the world in 1966. *Cutty Sark: King William Walk, tel. 081/858–3445. Admission: £3.25 adults, £2.25 children under 16 and senior citizens. Open Mon.–Sat. 10:30–5, Sun. noon–5. Gipsy Moth IV: King William Walk, tel. 081/853–3589. Admission: 50p adults, 30p children and senior citizens. Open Apr.–Oct., Mon.–Sat. 10–6, Sun. noon–6.*

The **National Maritime Museum** charts Britain's illustrious maritime heritage through maps, paintings, and models. Among the highlights are the original royal barges, displayed in the **Barge House.** *Romney Rd., tel. 081/858–4422. Joint admission with Old Royal Observatory: £3.75 adults, £2.75 children and senior citizens. Open Mon.–Sat. 9–6, Sun. noon–6; closed Good Friday, May Day, Dec. 24–27, Jan. 1.*

On the hill behind the museum and the Naval College, in **Greenwich Park,** is the **Old Royal Observatory,** founded in 1675 by Charles II, who was a great patron of the sciences. Many original telescopes and astronomical instruments are on display here. The world's prime meridian (zero degrees longitude) runs through the courtyard: Straddle the line and you'll have a foot in each hemisphere. *Greenwich Park, tel. 081/858–1167. Admission and times as National Maritime Museum.*

A craft market takes place on weekends in the Victorian covered market, and there's also an antiques market at the foot of Crooms Hill most weekend mornings.

Time Out	Try the **Trafalgar Tavern,** a historic pub on the river just beyond the Naval College, or the **Dolphin Coffee Shop** on the Maritime museum grounds, which is also open to the public.

Thames Barrier A major attraction just a few miles downriver is the Thames Barrier. Constructed between 1975–82, it is the world's largest moveable flood barrier, designed to prevent the Thames from overflowing its banks into extensive parts of central and south London. Boats depart frequently from Greenwich Pier to visit this awesome piece of civil engineering. An additional attraction at the barrier is Hallett's *Panorama* (an oil painting and sculpture) of the city of Bath. *Unity Way, off Woolwich Rd., tel. 081/854–1373. Admission (including the* Panorama*): £2.25 adults, £1.40 children and senior citizens. Open daily 10:30–5:30.*

Hampton Court Palace A series of royal palaces and grand houses line the Thames west of central London, built as aristocratic country residences close to the capital when the river was the primary means of travel. The most celebrated is **Hampton Court Palace,** surrounded by rolling parkland, some 20 miles upstream. It was begun in 1514 by Cardinal Wolsey, taken from him by Henry VIII, and expanded 150 years later by Sir Christopher Wren for William and Mary. Steeped in history and hung with priceless paintings and tapestries, Hampton Court provides a magical trip out of town, especially if you are able to go on a sunny day from spring through to fall, to see the gardens at their colorful best. *East Molesey, tel. 081/977–8441. Admission: state apartments, and maze £6.50 adults, £4.30 children, £4.90 senior citizens; maze only £1.50 adults, £1 children and senior citizens; grounds free. State apartments open daily 10–6 Apr.–Sept.; daily 10–4:30 Oct.–Mar. Tudor tennis court open Apr.–Sept. only; grounds open daily 8–dusk.*

Nearer London is **Ham House,** an exquisite late-17th-century riverside mansion. Rich, heavy furnishings; period portraits; and powerfully carved furniture lend a sense of opulence and luxury. *Ham St., Richmond, tel. 081/940–1950. Admission: £4 adults, £2 children and senior citizens. Phone for opening times.*

Richmond **Richmond** is an old, wealthy suburb of London with elegant 18th-century houses fronting its green; **Richmond Hill** has many good antiques shops. **Richmond Park** is one of the last vestiges of the vast medieval forests and hunting grounds that once pressed in on London; deer still roam here.

Time Out	**The Cricketers,** Richmond Green, does good pub lunches: coffee and afternoon teas are served. **Mrs. Beetons,** on Hill Rise, serves filling traditional dishes.

Kew **The Royal Botanic Gardens** at Kew are the headquarters of the country's leading botanical institute as well as a public garden of 300 acres and over 60,000 species of plants. Two 18th-century royal ladies, Queen Caroline (wife of George II) and Princess Augusta (widow of Frederick, Prince of Wales), both avid gardeners, were responsible for its founding.

Kew Palace, on the grounds, was home to George III for much of his life. Its formal garden has been redeveloped on a 17th-century pattern. The 19th-century greenhouses, notably the **Palm House** and the **Temperate House,** are among the highlights here. In the ultramodern Princess of Wales Conservatory opened in 1987, there are 10 climatic zones, their temperatures all precisely controlled by computer. *Royal Botanic Gardens, tel. 081/940–1171. Admission: £3.50 adults, £1.30 children, £1.80 senior citizens and students. Gardens open daily 9:30–6:30, greenhouses 10–6:30 (both open Sun. and national holidays until 8); in winter closing times depend on the light, usually 4 or 5. Kew Palace, tel. 081/940–3321. Admission: £1.20 adults, 80p children under 16, 90p senior citizens. Open Apr.– Sept., daily 11–5:30.*

London for Free

London is a gift to the freeloader. But first, invest in a wander-at-will tube ticket. Once you have that, the city's your oyster.

Galleries Most of the museums still have no admission fees, though there is a growing movement toward charging for entry. Among the most important ones that open their doors without charge are: the British Museum, the National Gallery, the National Portrait Gallery, and the Tate Gallery. Most churches are all, or partly, free. All of Wren's lovely City churches are free. The commercial art galleries in and around Bond Street let visitors browse for free, and some will even lend you their expensive catalogues without charge. This is also true of the great auction houses, Christie's and Sotheby's.

Parks The great parks are a summer vacation in themselves. To lie on the grass in **Hyde Park** or by the **Serpentine,** or to wander among the deer in the park of Hampton Court Palace, is to enjoy the best of country life in the middle of the city. Spend a few dollars on a picnic, and you can relax for hours. To the north lies **Hampstead Heath,** a spreading parkland with views over the city (*see also* Off the Beaten Track, *below*). **Speakers' Corner,** in Hyde Park, close to Marble Arch, has been a source of free fun for decades.

Concerts In fact, there is music all over the place that the freeloader can enjoy. Bands play in the parks, many churches have magnificent choirs, the foyers of the National Theatre, the Royal Festival Hall, and the Barbican host free musical events during the day and particularly in the early evening.

Above all, London herself is a free show. You can wander the streets, explore the tiny alleys and lanes, search out historic houses where famous people have lived—all without spending a cent.

What to See and Do with Children

On London's traditional sightseeing circuit, make for the **Royal Mews** (*see* Tour 1), where some of the Queen's horses can be seen close up; the **Whispering Gallery** in **St. Paul's Cathedral** (*see* Tour 4), where it is fun to try the echo; the many attractions of the **Tower of London** (*see* Tour 4); or take the brand-new tour of **Tower Bridge** (*see* Tour 4). Museums with hands-on activities include the **London Transport Museum** in Covent Garden (*see* Tour 2), the **Museum of the Moving Image** (*see* Tour 5), the **Science Museum,** and the **Natural History Museum** (*see* Tour 3).

The **Gardens of the Zoological Society of London,** known simply as the Zoo, were founded over 150 years ago, absorbing over the years other collections, such as the royal menagerie, which used to be housed in the Tower of London. The zoo itself is one of the busiest mazes in the world, and you can wander around for hours. Major attractions include: (1) the Mappin Terraces, a natural habitat for animals such as goats, pigs, and bears; (2) the Children's Zoo; (3) the Snowdon Aviary; (4) the Lion Terraces; (5) the Elephant and Rhino Pavilion; (6) the Small Bird House; and (7) the Tropical House, with its darting hummingbirds. In the Moonlight World, in the Charles Clore Pavilion, simulated night conditions let visitors watch nocturnal animals during the day. The process is reversed at night, when the cages are lit, and the animals take up their daytime activities. *Regent's Park, tel. 071/722–3333. Admission: £6.50 adults, £4 children under 16, £5 senior citizens. Open daily 9–6.*

The **London Toy and Model Museum** (21–23 Craven Hill, tel. 071/262–9450) has a train in the garden and a mass of manufactured toys and models on display. The free **Bethnal Green Museum of Children** (Cambridge Heath Rd., tel. 081/981–1711 or 081/980–3024) has toys, dolls, dollhouses, and puppets; and the free, educational **Horniman Museum** (100 London Rd., tel. 081/699–1872) has ethnographic and natural history collections. In the charming **Pollock's Toy Museum** (1 Scala St., tel. 071/636–3452), set in two tiny adjoining 18th-century houses, there's a treasure trove of dolls, toys, and teddy bears.

Other child-pleasers include **Guinness World of Records** in the Trocadero at Piccadilly Circus, and the **London Dungeon** (*see* Tour 5)—but note that it is not suitable for young or sensitive children. Also try the **Rock Circus,** where replicas of everyone from Elvis to Madonna go through their paces amid the odd laser and a *loud* soundtrack. *Guinness World of Records, tel. 071/439–7331. Admission: £5.75 adults, £3.75 children, £4.50 senior citizens. Open daily 10–10. Rock Circus, London Pavilion, Piccadilly Circus, tel. 071/734–7203. Admission: £6.50 adults, £4.50 children, £5.50 senior citizens. Open daily.*

If it's raining, a novel idea might be to try brass-rubbing at Westminster Abbey or at St. Martin-in-the-Fields Church in Trafalgar Square (*see* Tour 1). A fun outdoor activity is boating on the **Serpentine,** the lake in **Hyde Park** (*see* Tour 3). Places where children might actually enjoy shopping are around the **Covent Garden** area and in **Hamley's,** the huge toy shop on Regent's Street.

Off the Beaten Track

London   Beyond Regent's Park, the northern reach of central London, the city changes dramatically. You'll notice a marked "neighborhood" feel here and larger open spaces to explore.

Regent's Canal, a narrow-boat canal built in the 19th century, runs through the park. On the towpath is **Camden Lock** with its market (*see* Shopping, *below*) and the starting point for barge trips—details from the Regent's Canal Information Centre (tel. 071/482–0523) at the junction of the canal and Camden High Street. Or you can follow the canal on foot. Go east and you'll traverse urban badlands that culminate at the Thames; westbound is more refined. The houses along the canal share their backyards with the houseboats that serve as permanent residences for Londoners who can't afford (or don't want) life on dry land. Over the next two miles, both houses and boats get fancier until you reach London's **"Little Venice,"** a watery millionaire's row of elegant homes. (Pick up public transportation again at Warwick Avenue tube, Bakerloo line.)

Due north of Camden is **Hampstead** and **Hampstead Heath.** A village until the late 1800s, it still has a rural feel despite its very 20th-century High Street. Wander through the network of lanes and squares that spreads outwards from the Hampstead tube station. The **Heath** is a semiwild open space where you can walk—and see—for miles. **Kenwood House,** on its northern edge, contains the **Iveagh Bequest,** a grand collection of paintings. The spacious house is set in a large park, where summer concerts are held in the open air. *Hampstead Lane, tel. 081/348-1286. Admission free. Open Easter–Sept., daily 10–6; Oct.–Easter, daily 10–4.*

East of the Tower of London are the **Docklands.** The area became derelict after London's main port moved downstream, but is now said to be Europe's largest building site, including **Canary Wharf,** a new 80-acre district, complete with gardens and a city square. The 800-foot Tower, designed by Cesar Pelli (whose other monumental works include New York's World Trade Center), is Britain's tallest landmark. The **Docklands Light Railway,** an overhead rapid-transit railway, runs through the whole area. The central London terminus of the railway is at Tower Gateway, a few minutes' walk from the Tower of London and from Tower Hill station on the Underground. Island Gardens station, at the end of one branch, is just opposite Greenwich, to which it is connected by a pedestrian tunnel under the river.

Another way of visiting Docklands is to join one of **Citisights** walking tours accompanied by a knowledgeable guide. *Citisights of London, 213 Brooke Rd., E5, tel. 081/806-4325.*

Dulwich Village in southeast London has handsome 18th-century houses lining its main street. Most of the land here belongs to the Dulwich College Estate, founded in the 17th century by actor Edward Alleyn. Well-kept **Dulwich Park** is set ablaze each May when the rhododendrons burst into bloom. **Dulwich College Picture Gallery** is a fine small gallery designed by Sir John Soane, with works by Rembrandt, Van Dyck, Rubens, Poussin, and Gainsborough. *College Rd., tel. 081/693-5254. Admission: £2 adults, children under 16 free, £1 senior citizens. Open Tues.–Fri. 10–1 and 2–5, Sat. 11–5, Sun. 2–5.*

At the **Royal Air Force Museum** in Hendon, north London, the story of the R.A.F. is told in great detail. There are uniforms, guns, and radar equipment and sections on World War I and II. **The Battle of Britain Museum** in the same complex (no extra charge) explains how the R.A.F. fought off the German threat in 1940. The nearest Underground station is Colindale on the Northern line. *Grahame Park Way, tel. 081/205-2266. Admission: £4.90 adults, £2.45 children under 16 and senior citizens. Open daily 10–6.*

St. Albans This ancient town, 24 miles northwest of London, can be reached by train from either Kings Cross or St. Pancras stations. Called "Verulamium" by the Romans, St. Albans is now a residential suburb for commuters, but it retains its ancient market-town character. It takes its present name from Alban, Britain's first Christian martyr. The shrine erected where he died became an abbey and, later, St. Albans Cathedral.

Begin a visit to St. Albans on St. Peter's Street, where the open-air market established by the Saxons is still held each Wednesday and Saturday. Walk north to **St. Peter's Church** on the right-hand side,

or south to the medieval and now pedestrianized **French Row,** which
takes its name from the French soldiers quartered here after being
recruited by the barons to fight King John in 1215, the year of the
Magna Carta. The **Clock Tower** at the south end of French Row
(1411) was the tower from which curfew was rung. It is one of only
two remaining in the country. *Admission free. Open Good Friday–
mid-Sept., weekends and national holidays 10:30–5.*

At the end of French Row opposite the junction with High Street,
the arch of **Waxhouse Gate** is all that remains of a 15th-century gateway to the abbey. The path through the gate is the shortest pedestrian route to **St. Albans Cathedral,** founded in the 8th century by
Offa II, king of Mercia (one of the seven original Anglo-Saxon kingdoms). Built mainly with bricks taken from a nearby Roman site, it
was expanded in the 11th century and became the principal Benedictine abbey in England. Later, part of the Magna Carta was prepared here. Inside is an 1872 reconstruction of St. Alban's shrine,
made from 2,000 pieces of marble, and beside it, a 15th-century decorated timber "watching-loft" for the monk who guarded the shrine.
The Saxon pillars in the transepts were probably looted from an
earlier church. The nave is one of the longest medieval ones in
existence. *Tel. 0727/60780. Admission free. Open 10–5:45 winter,
10–6:45 summer (depending on the changing of the clocks for summertime).*

Leave the cathedral by the west door and cross to the **Abbey Gatehouse,** once part of the abbey and then the city jail. Today it is part of
St. Albans School (for boys), one of the oldest schools in Britain, possibly of Saxon origin. Nicholas Breakspear, the only English pope
(he reigned as Adrian IV, 1154–59), was a pupil here.

Down Abbey Mill Lane, right beside the river Ver, stands **Ye Olde
Fighting Cocks,** an octagonal, timber-framed inn that claims to be
the oldest inhabited pub in England. The nearby St. Albans **City
Museum and Art Gallery** offers natural-history and folk-life exhibits, and an assortment of craftsmen's tools. *Hatfield Rd., tel. 0727/
56679. Admission free. Open Mon.–Sat. 10–5, Sun. 2–5.*

The **Verulamium Museum,** just opposite St. Michael's Church, displays an extensive collection of Roman artifacts, including well-
preserved mosaic tiles, jewelry, pottery, glassware, and a large
selection of tools. Your ticket also allows you to visit the **hypocaust,**
an under-floor Roman heating system housed in its own modern annex. Very close to the museum, you can see an excavated Roman theater, unique in Britain. *Museum: St. Michael's St., tel. 0727/866100,
weekends 0727/854659. Admission: £2.40 adults, £1.40 children.
Open Mon.–Sat. 10–5:30, Sun. 2–5:30. Theater: tel. 0727/835035.
Admission: £1.50 adults, 75p children. Open daily 10–5 (10–4
Nov.–Mar.).*

Sightseeing Checklist

Historic Buildings	**Banqueting House:** Tour 1
	Buckingham Palace: Tour 1
	Clarence House: Tour 1
	Houses of Parliament: Tour 1
	Inns of Court: Tour 2
	Lambeth Palace: Tour 5
	Lancaster House: Tour 1
	Lloyd's of London: Tour 4
	Royal Albert Hall: Tour 3
	Royal Courts of Justice: Tour 2

St. James's Palace: Tour 1
York House: Tour 1

Museums and Galleries

Bank of England Museum: Tour 4
Barbican Gallery: Tour 4
H.M.S. *Belfast:* Tour 5
British Museum: Tour 2
Cabinet War Rooms: Tour 1
Commonwealth Institute: Tour 3
Courtauld Institute: Tour 2
Cutty Sark: Tour 6
The Design Museum: Tour 5
Dickens House: Tour 2
Dulwich College Picture Gallery: Off the Beaten Track
Florence Nightingale Museum: Tour 5
Geffrye Museum of Furniture and Decorative Arts. Sequence of rooms furnished with pieces dating from the 16th century to the 1930s, plus staircases, paneling, and portraits from old London houses; the museum is located in a row of 18th-century almshouses. *Kingsland Rd., E2, tel. 071/739–9893. Admission free. Open Tues.–Sat., bank holiday Mon. 10–5, Sun. 2–5.*
Guards Museum: Tour 1
Ham House: Tour 6
Hampton Court Palace: Tour 6
Hayward Gallery (South Bank): Tour 5
Imperial War Museum: Tour 5
Institute of Contemporary Arts: Tour 1
Iveagh Bequest: Off the Beaten Track
The Jewish Museum. Founded over 50 years ago, the Jewish Museum illustrates the long history of Jewry in Britain, dating back to the 13th century. There are manuscripts, embroidery, and silver—many items of great intrinsic worth, and all of them of interest. *Woburn House, Tavistock Sq., tel. 071/388–4525. Admission: £1 adults, children free. Open Sun., Tues.–Thurs. (and Fri. in summer) 10–4; Fri. in winter 10–12:45. Closed national and Jewish holidays.*
Dr. Johnson's House: Tour 2
Kensington Palace and Court Collection: Tour 3
Kenwood House: Off the Beaten Track
Leighton House: Tour 3
Linley Sambourne House: Tour 3
London Toy and Model Museum: What to See and Do with Children
London Transport Museum: Tour 2
The Monument: Tour 4
Museum of Garden History: Tour 5
Museum of London: Tour 4
Museum of the Moving Image (South Bank): Tour 5
National Gallery: Tour 1
National Maritime Museum: Tour 6
National Portrait Gallery: Tour 1
National Postal Museum: Tour 4
Natural History Museum: Tour 3
Old Royal Observatory: Tour 6
Old St. Thomas's Hospital: Tour 5
Percival David Foundation of Chinese Art: Tour 2
Pollock's Toy Museum: What to See and Do with Children
Queen's Gallery: Tour 1
Royal Academy of Arts. The academy mounts major exhibitions, often ones that are on an international tour, as well as its own Summer Exhibition of mixed amateur and professional work. *Burlington*

House, Piccadilly, tel. 071/439–7438. Admission: varies according to the exhibition. Open daily 10–6.

Royal Mews: Tour 1
Royal Naval College: Tour 6
Science Museum: Tour 3
Shakespeare Globe Museum: Tour 5
Sir John Soane's Museum: Tour 2
Tate Gallery: Tour 1
Theatre Museum: Tour 2
Tower Bridge: Tour 4
Tower Hill Pageant: Tour 4
Tower of London: Tour 4
Victoria and Albert Museum: Tour 3
Wallace Collection. London's answer to the Frick Collection in New York City, peaceful Hertford House contains a wealth of 18th-century French paintings and furniture, mostly purchased immediately after the French Revolution, as well as arms and armor, porcelain, majolica, and pictures by such masters as Rembrandt, Canaletto, and Rubens. *Hertford House, Manchester Sq., tel. 071/935–0687. Admission free. Open Mon.–Sat. 10–5, Sun. 2–5.*
Wellington Museum: Tour 3

Churches
Brompton Oratory: Tour 3
Chapel Royal, St. James's Palace: Tour 1
Guards Chapel: Tour 1
Queen's Chapel: Tour 1
St. Bride's: Tour 2
St. Giles without Cripplegate: Tour 4
St. Martin-in-the-Fields: Tour 1
St. Mary Abbotts: Tour 3
St. Mary-le-Bow: Tour 4
St. Paul's Cathedral: Tour 4
Southwark Cathedral: Tour 5
Temple Church: Tour 2
Westminster Abbey: Tour 1

Parks and Gardens
Hyde Park: Tour 3
Kensington Gardens: Tour 3
Kew Gardens: Tour 6
Hampstead Heath: Off the Beaten Track
Regent's Park: Off the Beaten Track
St. James's Park: Tour 1
Richmond Park: Tour 6

Other Places of Interest
Barbican Arts Centre: Tour 4
Gardens of the Zoological Society of London (the Zoo): What to See and Do with Children
Guinness World of Records: What to See and Do with Children
Hay's Galleria: Tour 5
London Dungeon: Tour 5
London Planetarium. This show, next door to Madame Tussaud's, brings the night sky to life. *Marylebone Rd., tel. 071/486–1121, Admission: £4 adults, £2.50 children, £2.10 senior citizens. Joint ticket with Madame Tussaud's, see below. Planetarium open daily 11–4:20 (shows every 40 min.).*
Madame Tussaud's. Despite its shockingly high entrance charge, this exhibition somehow maintains its position as one of London's most sought-after attractions, with an ever-changing parade of wax celebrities, and an ever-lengthening line outside. *Marylebone Rd., tel. 071/935–6861. Admission: £7.95 adults, £4.95 children, £5.95 senior citizens. Joint ticket with Planetarium, £9.95 adults, £6.25*

children, £7.55 senior citizens. Open Easter–Sept., daily 9:30–5:30; Oct.–Easter, daily 10–5:30.
Rock Circus: What to See and Do with Children
Thames Barrier Visitor Centre: Tour 6

Shopping

Chelsea Chelsea features the famous King's Road, a mecca of the '60s and '70s, now a happy hunting ground for the antiques lover and the discriminating home furnisher. Clothing can still be a good buy.

Covent Garden Crafts stalls and boutiques cluster around this lively restored 19th-century market and in the network of nearby streets. Strolling is as pleasant a pastime as shopping (*see* Tour 2).

Kensington Antiques abound here, especially on Kensington Church Street. Kensington High Street, not as upscale as Knightsbridge, has representatives of the better high street clothing stores.

Knightsbridge This is the area for the committed shopper. Harrods' gaudy Edwardian bulk dominates Brompton Road, but there are delights all around, on Sloane Street (for fashions and fabrics), Beauchamp Place, and Walton Street (*see* Tour 3).

Mayfair Bond Street (Old and New), Savile Row, and the Burlington Arcade are where you'll find traditional British goods for men and women, with South Molton Street adding a raffish modern accent. Prices and quality are tip-top.

Oxford Street Oxford Street itself is to be endured rather than enjoyed, although Selfridges, Marks and Spencer, and John Lewis are all good department stores; St. Christopher's Place, secreted across from the Bond Street tube, has several small, chic boutiques.

Piccadilly Though its stores are few, Piccadilly boasts some classy ones, such as Simpsons for men's clothing, Hatchards for books, and Fortnum and Mason, the Queen's grocer, for its exquisite food hall. There are also fine shopping arcades, Royal Arcade among them.

Regent Street Quality stores and broad sidewalks make Regent Street an appealing alternative to adjacent Oxford Street. Liberty, for textiles and accessories, is a perennial favorite, as is Hamleys, for toys.

St. James's Though his suits may be custom-tailored on Savile Row, for the rest of his classic wardrobe the English gent comes here, especially along Jermyn Street, where a purchase is seen as an investment.

Specialty Stores If you love to shop, London can keep you busy for many days, but there is space to include only a few stores in each category.

Antiques Three prime areas are Camden Passage, Portobello Road (*see* Street Markets, *below*), and Kensington Church Street. Also worth a visit are:

Antiquarius (131–141 King's Rd., tel. 071/351–5353), at the Sloane Square end of the King's Road, is an indoor antiques market with over 200 stalls that offers a wide variety of collectibles, including metalware, meerschaum pipes, ceramics, and art nouveau bric-a-brac. **Gray's Antique Market** and **Gray's Mews** (58 Davies St. and around the corner at 1–7 Davies Mews, tel. 071/629–7034) comprise a gaggle of smaller places all selling curios and collectibles; allow yourself plenty of time here.

Books Charing Cross Road is London's book country, with a couple of dozen stores there or thereabout. Especially large, if confusing, is **Foyle** (No. 119, tel. 071/437–5660). **Waterstone's** (No. 121–125, tel. 071/434–4291) is part of a reliable chain. **Hatchards** (187–188 Piccadilly, tel. 071/437–3924) and **Dillons** (82 Gower St., tel. 071/636–1577) both have not only a huge stock, but also a well-informed staff to help you choose.

Travel books and maps are the specialty of **Stanford** (12 Long Acre, tel. 071/836–1321); art books of **Zwemmer** (24 Lichfield St., tel. 071/379–7886), just off Charing Cross Road; and sci-fi, fantasy, horror, and comic books of **Forbidden Planet** (71 New Oxford St., tel. 071/836–4179). **Books for Cooks** (4 Blenheim Cres., tel. 071/221–1992), in Notting Hill Gate, is packed with useful volumes for the voracious.

Among the secondhand meccas are: **Quinto** (83 Marylebone High St., tel. 071/935–9303) with a fascinating galleried section at the back; **Skoob Books** (15 Sicilian Ave. and branches, tel. 071/404–3063); and **Bertram Rota** (9–11 Langley Ct., tel. 071/836–0723), a very upmarket, first-editions spot in Covent Garden.

China and **Thomas Goode** (19 South Audley St., tel. 071/499–2823) carries
Glass enormous lines of crystal and china. Their very best is very expensive, but their range is fairly wide.

Clothing Many leading international houses have major branches in London. Most department stores have fashion floors, notably Harrods and Selfridges, while Harvey Nichols is nothing but top fashion. John Lewis, Simpson, and Liberty provide more traditional, though still stylish, clothes. What is true for women's wear is even more so for men's. London is still renowned for men's clothing, especially in the more sober, traditional categories. Two stores stocking largely classic clothes for both men and women are:

Aquascutum (100 Regent St., tel. 071/734–6090), which is celebrated for its high-style, expensive rainwear, also sells a superb range of clothes for both sexes. An ideal goal for the conventional executive with plenty of moola.
Burberrys (165 Regent St., tel. 071/734–4060 and 18 Haymarket, tel. 071/930–3343), famous for its trademark tartan, is laid out like a country house filled with classic clothing and magnificent raincoats.

Women's Wear **Browns** (23–27 South Molton St., tel. 071/491–7833 and 6C Sloane St., tel. 071/493–4232) put traffic-free South Molton Street on the map for trendy shoppers. Here you'll find styles by Azzedine Alaïa, Donna Karan, Jil Sander, Jean Muir, Romeo Gigli, Katherine Hamnett, Comme des Garçons, Sonia Rykiel . . . most of the best and brightest, in fact.
Droopy & Browns (99 St. Martin's La., tel. 071/379–4514). Sumptuous, theatrical clothing for every occasion—weddings, balls, cocktails, or everyday—can be found here.
Janet Reger (2 Beauchamp Pl., tel. 071/584–9360). Janet Reger's lingerie is legendary; this is its home base.
Laura Ashley (256–258 Regent St., tel. 071/437–9760; also at 120 Kings Rd., tel. 071/823–7550, and other branches). The firm founded by the late high priestess of English traditional sells designs that have captured the nostalgic imagination of the world.
Nicole Farhi (25–26 St. Christopher's Pl., tel. 071/486–3416 and 193 Sloane St., tel. 071/235–0877, plus other locations) is a store for the career woman, stocking well-cut, timeless styles in subtle colors and expensive fabrics. The "Diversion" line is younger and less pricey.
Whistles (The Market, Covent Garden, tel. 071/379–7401; also at

London Shopping

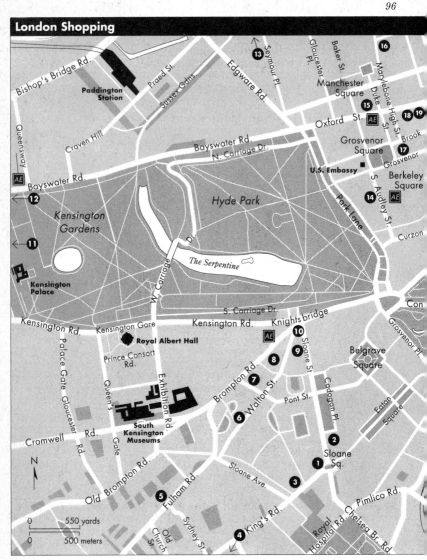

Antiquarius, **4**
Aquascutum, **27**
Asprey, **21**
Bertram Rota, **49**
Books for Cooks, **12**
Browns, **5, 18**
Burberrys, **29, 37**
Butler and
Wilson, **5, 18**
CCA Galleries, **23**
Combined Harvest, **11**
Contemporary Applied
Arts, **44**
Craftsmen Potters
Shop, **32**

Craftworks, **13**
Dillons, **41**
Droopy & Brown's, **52**
Forbidden Planet, **42**
Foyle, **39**
Garrard, **28**
General
Trading Co., **1**
Gray's Antique
Market/Gray's
Mews, **17**
Grosvenor
Prints, **50**
Hamleys, **31**
Harrods, **8**

Harvey Nichols, **10**
Hatchards, **26**
The Irish Linen
Co., **24**
Janet Reger, **7**
John Lewis, **20**
Laura Ashley, **3, 34**
Liberty, **33**
Miss Selfridge, **35**
The Monogrammed
Linen Shop, **6**
Neal Street East, **45**
Nicole Farhi, **2, 22**
The Outlaws Club, **43**

Quinto, **16**
Selfridges, **15**
Simpson, **36**
Skoob Books, **46**
Stanford, **47**
The Tea House, **48**
Thomas Goode, **14**
Tom Gilbey, **30**
Turnbull & Asser, **25**
Waterstone's, **40**
Whistles, **51**
Zwemmer, **38**

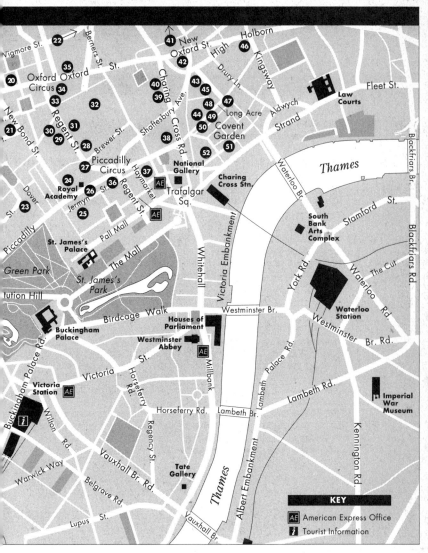

KEY

AE American Express Office

i Tourist Information

Heath St., Hampstead, tel. 071/431–2395, and other branches) is a small chain stocking its own high-fashion, mid-price label, plus several European (mostly French) designers.

Men's Wear **Tom Gilbey** (2 New Burlington Pl., tel. 071/734–4877). The exciting part of this shop is the Waistcoat Gallery, where exquisite vests, some in silk or brocades or embroidered by hand are essential accessories for the dandy.

Turnbull & Asser (71 & 72 Jermyn St., tel. 071/930–0502) is *the* custom shirt-maker. The first order must be for a minimum of six shirts, from around £100 each, but there's a range of less expensive, still exquisitely made ready-to-wear shirts, too.

Crafts **Combined Harvest** (128 Talbot Rd., just off Portobello Rd., tel. 071/221–4870) markets the work of some 50 craftsworkers at reasonable prices. Commissions are accepted.

Craftsmen Potters Shop (7 Marshall St., tel. 071/437–7605) is a cooperative carrying a wide spectrum of the potter's art.

Craftworks (31 Southend Rd., tel. 071/431–4337; tube stop: Hampstead) is packed with handmade table- and glassware, ceramics, candlesticks, wall hangings, and mirrors.

At **Contemporary Applied Arts** (43 Earlham St., tel. 071/836–6993), a mixed bag of designers and craftspeople display their wares over two floors.

Gifts **General Trading Co.** (144 Sloane St., tel. 071/730–0411) offers gifts from the world over, with an emphasis on the Far East: Indian crafts, Italian lighting fixtures, and Chinese toys.

Hamleys (188–196 Regent St., tel. 071/734–3161) has six floors of toys and games for both children and adults, ranging from teddy bears to computer games and all the latest space-age gimmickry.

Neal Street East (5 Neal St., tel. 071/240–0135). The "East" in the name refers to the Orient. This is a colorful labyrinth of Far Eastern goods.

The Tea House (15A Neal St., tel. 071/240–7539). Devoted to everything concerning the British national drink. Prettily packaged teas in scores of flavors, tea paraphernalia (strainers, infusers, tea-bag squeezers, sugar tongs—you name it), and lots of pots make great British gifts.

Jewelry and Objets d'Art **Asprey** (165–169 New Bond St., tel. 071/493–6767). If you're in the market for a six-branched Georgian candelabrum, or an emerald and diamond brooch, you won't be disappointed here.

Butler and Wilson (20 South Molton St., tel. 071/409–2955 or 189 Fulham Rd., tel. 071/352–3045). All that glitters here isn't gold—costume jewelry and fabulous window displays are their forte.

Garrard (112 Regent St., tel. 071/734–7020). Its connections with the royal family go back to 1722; this is the firm that keeps the Crown Jewels glittering. But they are also a family jeweler of enormous scope, from antique to modern. (Charles bought Diana's engagement ring here.)

The **Outlaws Club** (49 Endell St., tel. 071/379–6940) is full of wild and outlandish jewelry—dazzling yet affordable.

Linen **The Irish Linen Co.** (35–36 Burlington Arcade, tel. 071/493–8949) is a tiny store packed with crisp, embroidered linen for the table, the bed, and the nose.

The Monogrammed Linen Shop (168 Walton St., tel. 071/589–4033 and 19 S. Audley St., tel. 071/491–9595). This is the place for Italian bed linen—with matching robes and pajamas—plus christening gowns and table linens. As their name indicates, they also monogram.

Prints **CCA Galleries** (8 Dover St., tel. 071/499–6701) offers an interesting range of work by contemporary printmakers. Their prices are reasonable and their knowledgeable staff helpful.
Grosvenor Prints (28–32 Shelton St., tel. 071/836–1979). Hidden in the tangle of streets northwest of Covent Garden, Grosvenor Prints sells antiquarian prints—especially of London buildings and dogs! Its eccentricity and wide selection virtually guarantee a find.

Department Stores **Liberty** (200 Regent St., tel. 071/734–1234). Full of nooks and crannies, Liberty is like a dream of an eastern bazaar realized as a western store. Famous principally for its fabrics, it also carries Oriental goods, menswear, womenswear, fragrances, soaps, and accessories.
John Lewis (278 Oxford St., tel. 071/629–7711) claims as its motto, "Never knowingly undersold." This is a traditional English department store, with a wonderful selection of dress fabrics and curtain and upholstery materials.
Selfridges (400 Oxford St., tel. 071/629–1234). At London's mammoth upmarket version of Macy's, there are a food hall, a branch of the London Tourist Board, a theater ticket counter, and a Thomas Cook travel agency. **Miss Selfridge** is its outpost for trendy, affordable young women's clothes (also on Oxford Street, east of Oxford Circus, and other branches).
Harrods (87 Brompton Rd., tel. 071/730–1234), one of the world's most famous department stores, is currently owned by an Egyptian family. You'll either love it or wonder what the big deal is. Although it's now perhaps less exclusive than its former self, it is still a British institution. The food halls are stunning—so are the crowds!
Harvey Nichols (109 Knightsbridge, tel. 071/235–5000). Renowned for its household furnishings, jewelry, and above all, fashion, Harvey Nick's has a pleasantly glitzy atmosphere for browsing, with many designer names, and menswear in the basement.
Simpson (203 Piccadilly, tel. 071/734–2002) is a traditional department store and home of Daks classic British clothing. A barber shop, restaurant, and wine bar add to the store's appeal.

Street Markets **Bermondsey** (Tower Bridge Rd., SE1), Fri. 4 AM–2 PM. Known also as New Caledonian Market, this is one of London's largest markets, selling both junk and treasures from British attics. The real bargains start going at 4 AM, but there'll be a few left if you arrive later. Take the 15 or 25 bus to Aldgate, then a number 42 bus over Tower Bridge to Bermondsey Square; or take the tube to London Bridge and walk.
Camden Lock (NW1). Daily, 10–6 (approximately). This sprawling market in one of London's trendier quarters has undergone a major reshuffle, and much of it is now indoors in converted warehouse buildings around the canal basin. Still, it remains a good place for cheap and secondhand clothing, records, books, crafts, and jewelry. Canal trips begin here, too; check at the Regent's Canal (Camden Lock) Information Centre (tel. 071/482–0523).
Camden Passage (Islington, N1). Wed. 7–4 and Sat. 8–5. Hugged by curio stores, the passage drips with jewelry, silverware, and myriad other antiques. Saturday and Wednesday are when the stalls go up; the rest of the week, only the stores are open. Bus 19 or 38 or the tube to the Angel stop will get you there.
Petticoat Lane (Middlesex St., E1). Sun. 9–2. Petticoat Lane is the familiar name of this famous market on Middlesex Street that starts a sprawl of East End stalls stretching to Brick Lane. You'll find bargain antiques and junk, leather, electrical and household goods, clothes, cameras, bikes, books, and CDs. Liverpool Street, Aldgate, or Aldgate East tubes are closest.
Portobello Market (Portobello Rd., W11). Fruit and vegetables Mon.–Wed., Fri.–Sat. 8–5, Thurs. 8–1; antiques Sat. 6 AM–5 PM.

There are 1,500 antiques dealers trading here, so bargains are still possible. Nearer Notting Hill Gate, prices and quality are highest, with bric-à-brac appearing as you walk toward Ladbroke Grove and the flea market under the Westway and beyond. Take bus 52 or the tube to Ladbroke Grove or Notting Hill Gate.

Spitalfields (Brushfield St., E1). Weekdays 11–3, Sun. 9–3. The developers of Camden Lock have got hold of the old 3-acre indoor fruit market near Brick Lane, and for the present have set up food, crafts and clothing stalls, cafés, performance and sports facilities, and a city farm. Fun for rainy Sundays at Petticoat Lane.

Sports and the Outdoors

For information on London's sports clubs and facilities, call **Sportsline,** weekdays 10–6, tel. 071/222–8000.

Spectator Sports   Tickets for the **Wimbledon tennis championships** are costly, hard to obtain, and sell out months in advance. But you can get in by arriving early in the day and standing in line; this is especially recommended during the first week of the two-week championship, when it is not so popular and there are plenty of top stars to be seen playing on the outer courts, where there are no reserved seats and the atmosphere is pleasantly informal. Take the tube to Southfield. For tickets in advance, write to the All England Lawn Tennis and Croquet Club, Church Rd., Wimbledon, London SW19 5AE.

The annual **Boat Race** (the rowing race between Oxford and Cambridge Universities) is held on a Saturday in late March or early April, starts at Putney, and finishes at Mortlake, which is a good place to stand and watch. The **Marathon,** held on a Sunday in late April and modeled on the New York version, is a similarly pleasant occasion.

Wembley Stadium is the scene of the **FA Cup Final,** played each May at the end of the soccer season, and it is also the venue of other major soccer and rugby matches.

Golf   Visitors are often able to play at private clubs by paying a greens fee, which varies widely. It is best to telephone in advance. A letter of introduction from your home course is always useful. For a complete rundown of the area courses, as well as those throughout England, pick up the *Golf Course Guide* at larger London bookstores.

Fitness Centers   **Body Chaud Gym** (Central Club, 16–22 Great Russell St., WC1 3LR, tel. 071/636–7512, ext. 229) is a basic but well supervised facility in the basement of the YWCA.

Physique (Clare Court, Judd St., WC1H 9QW, tel. 071/837–8880) is a bright, modern gym geared toward weight training, with some cardiovascular equipment.

The Porchester Centre (Queensway, Bayswater W2, tel. 071/798–3689) has a large swimming pool, squash courts, aerobics and yoga classes, and a large suite of Turkish steam baths.

Seymour Leisure Centre (Seymour Pl., W1, tel. 071/402–5795) has squash courts, a swimming pool, martial arts courses, badminton, basketball and volleyball courts, two gyms, and an excellent program of aerobics classes, all at low cost.

Jogging   Centrally located **Green Park** and **St. James's Park** are adequate for short runs, except on summer afternoons when the many deck chairs make the going too crowded. Far better is bucolic **Hyde Park** which, with adjoining **Kensington Gardens,** measures 4 miles around. **Regent's Park** is near much of north London and its perimeter measures about 2½ miles. For longer runs, try **Hampstead Heath** (Hampstead tube) or the wilder **Richmond Park** (Richmond tube).

Dining

Be prepared for a shock: London is a great city for dining. Nearly everyone eats out regularly these days, and an increasingly knowledgeable and, therefore, demanding public has had its effect on the quality, value, and variety of the capital's restaurants. You can eat your way around the world (India, Thailand, and the Mediterranean are particularly easy to find), or hit the zenith of food fashion. Few places these days mind if you order a second appetizer instead of an entrée, and you will often find set-price menus at lunchtime, bringing even the very finest and fanciest establishments within reach. Prix-fixe dinners are beginning to proliferate, too. Note that many places are closed on Sunday or late at night, and virtually everywhere closes down for the Christmas holiday period.

The law obliges all British restaurants to display their prices, including VAT (sales tax) outside, but watch for hidden extras such as bread and vegetables charged separately, and service. Most restaurants add 10%–15% automatically to the check, or stamp "Service Not Included" along the bottom, and/or leave the total on the credit-card slip blank. Beware of paying twice for service, especially if it was less than satisfactory.

Highly recommended restaurants are indicated by a star ★.

Category	Cost*
$$$$	over £40
$$$	£25–£40
$$	£15–£25
$	under £15

per person, including first course, main course, dessert, and VAT; excluding drinks and service

St. James's

$$$$ **The Ritz.** The British menu here hasn't always lived up to its setting, but since this Louis XVI, marble, gilt, and *trompe l'oeil* treasure with its view over Green Park is known as London's most magnificent dining room, that's not such a crime. The latest chef, David Nicholls, retains the French accent and ingredients rich as the decor (foie gras terrine with fig preserve; lobster thermidor), but also offers British specialties—Irish stew, braised oxtail, steak and kidney pie, and a daily roast—which are the most enticing part of the menu. A three-course lunch at £26 and four-course dinner at £39.50 make the check more bearable, but the wine list is pricey. *Piccadilly, W1, tel. 071/493–8181. Reservations required. Jacket and tie required. AE, DC, MC, V.*

$$$ **Le Caprice.** Just behind the Ritz, the Caprice, designed by Eva Jiricna, is filled with equally sophisticated diners tucking into an eclectic selection of dishes from most world cuisines. You might try bang-bang chicken, salmon fish cakes with sorrel sauce, or a simple grill. Desserts and wines are good; the people-watching potential is excellent. *Arlington House, Arlington St., SW1, tel. 071/629–2239.*

Reservations required. Dress: casual but neat. AE, DC, MC, V. Closed Sat. lunch.

Quaglino's. Sir Terence Conran—of Bibendum, Pont de la Tour, and Conran Shop fame—lavished millions on this pre–WWII haunt of the rich, bored, and well-connected, producing a more egalitarian '90s version. The place remains very glamorous, with its sweep of staircase descending theatrically into London's most enormous dining room, the "Crustacea Altar" at one end, raised bar and dance floor at the other. The food is inevitably pan-European (*plateau de fruits de mer*, mussels with pesto, cod and chips, rabbit with prosciutto, lemon tart), and tables are inevitably hard to come by during peak hours. It is possible to spend less than this category suggests. *16 Bury St., SW1, tel. 071/930–6767. Reservations required. Dress: smart casual. AE, DC, MC, V. Closed Christmas.*

$$ Café Fish. This cheerful, bustling restaurant has a wonderful selection of fish arranged on the menu according to cooking method: chargrilled, steamed, *meunière.* There are also several *plats du jour,* some classics of fish cuisine like *bouillabaisse* and *moules marinières,* and a *plateau de fruits de mer* straight out of a Paris brasserie. Downstairs is an informal wine bar with a smaller selection of dishes. *39 Panton St., SW1, tel. 071/930–3999. Reservations advised. Dress: casual. AE, DC, MC, V. Closed Sat. lunch, Sundays, Dec. 25–26, Jan. 1.*

$ The Fountain. At the back of Fortnum and Mason's is this old-fash-
★ ioned restaurant, frumpy and popular as a boarding school matron, serving a big selection of light meals, pies, roasts and grills, sandwiches, pastries, and ice cream sodas. It's perfect for pre-theater meals and for afternoon tea or sundaes after the Royal Academy or Bond Street shopping. *181 Piccadilly, tel. 071/734–4938. Reservations accepted for dinner only. Dress: casual. AE, DC, MC, V. Closed Sun., national holidays.*

Mayfair

$$$$ Le Gavroche. Many still regard this establishment as London's top
★ temple of haute cuisine, even since Albert Roux (who is very famous around here), handed the *toque* to his son, Michel. Decor (dark, green, gentlemanly), service, and price match the food in gravity, meaning it's mostly expense-accounters who dine here, feeding on lobster (roasted, with cèpes and rosemary, or in a ginger-scented ragout), tournedos, and soufflés—classics with a Roux inflection. The set price lunch, at £36, inclusive of a half bottle of wine, and coffee, is worth it for a celebration. *43 Upper Brook St., W1, tel. 071/408–0881. Reservations advised at least 1 week in advance. Jacket and tie required. AE, DC, MC, V. Closed weekends, 10 days at Christmas, national holidays.*

★ **Nico at Ninety.** Those with refined palates and very deep pockets should not miss Nico Ladenis's exquisite gastronomy. One of the world's great chefs, and famous for knowing it, he moved to this Louis XV-plush ex-Grosvenor House hotel dining room in 1992, from Chez Nico (now Nico Central, 35 Great Portland St., tel. 071/436–8846). The menu here is still in untranslated French; vegetarians and children are still not welcome, but the set lunch is a relative bargain. *90 Park La., tel. 071/409–1290. Reservations required. Jacket and tie required. AE, DC, MC, V. Closed weekends, Christmas, Easter.*

$$$ Langan's Brasserie. Langan's, although something of a tourist trap, is still a very stylish place. A gallery of contemporary art on the walls, a hundred or so dishes on the menu (including the famous spinach soufflé with anchovy sauce), and frank, efficient waiters who'll tell you which daily specials are best make this as essential a stop as ever. *Stratton St., W1, tel. 071/491–8822. Reservations required. Dress: casual but neat. AE, DC, MC, V. Closed Sat. lunch, Sun., Christmas, national holidays.*

Mulligans. Settle in downstairs here and save the fare to Dublin—it's as comfortable and friendly as any Emerald Isle bar, but the updated Irish food is infinitely better. Black pudding or steak, Guinness and oyster pie, alongside champ or colcannon (mashed potato with scallion or cabbage) make perfect comfort food for grey London days. *13–14 Cork St., tel. 071/409–1370. Reservations advised. Dress: casual. AE, MC, V. Closed Sat. lunch, Sun., Dec. 25–26, Jan. 1.*

$$ Criterion. This wonderful, palatial neo-Byzantine mirrored marble hall, first opened in 1874, reopened in 1984, shut again, and is now back on the map under the joint aegis of Bob "irrepressible" Payton (*see below*) and hotel magnate Rocco Forte. Teatime is 3–5 PM (it's £6.50); otherwise, choose roast garlic squid, halibut with lobster oil, and pink grapefruit granita from the modish Cal-Ital brasserie menu. This is a very welcome point of light in the Piccadilly desert. *Piccadilly Circus, W1, tel. 071/925–0909. Reservations essential. Dress: smart casual. AE, DC, MC, V. Closed Christmas.*

$ The Chicago Pizza Pie Factory. A bright basement serving huge pizzas with salad and garlic bread at reasonable prices. This is one of American entrepreneur Bob Payton's places, and good gimmicks—like heart-shaped pizzas on Valentine's day—make it a popular spot. *17 Hanover Sq., tel. 071/629–2669. Reservations advised for lunch. Dress: casual. No credit cards. Closed Christmas.*

Knightsbridge

$$$$ The Capital. Chef Philip Britten ensures the Michelin star stays bright with his subtle mousses of haddock and ginger, or girolles, heartier dishes like Scotch beef stewed in red wine, and his perfect soufflés of caramel or lemon. Set-price menus make this dining room of the small and luxurious Capital Hotel more affordable. *22–24 Basil St., SW3, tel. 071/589–5171. Reservations required. Jacket and tie required. AE, DC, MC, V.*

$$ St. Quentin. A very popular slice of Paris, where the cuisine is traditional and reliable, with some more modern dishes—lime and honey marinated duck breast, for instance, or sweetbreads with a hazelnut sauce. *Tartes* for dessert come from St. Quentin's gourmet food shop, Les Specialités, as do the cheeses. *243 Brompton Rd., SW3, tel. 071/589–8005. Reservations advised. Dress: casual. AE, DC, MC, V.*

$ Luba's Bistro. ★ Hearty Russian clichés such as chicken Kiev and beef Stroganoff are served at long wooden tables; bring your own wine. *6 Yeoman's Row, tel. 071/589–2950. Reservations advised. Dress: casual. MC, V. Closed Sun., Christmas, national holidays.*

South Kensington

$$$$ Bibendum. ★ This restaurant is in the reconditioned Michelin House, with its art deco decorations, and brilliant stained glass, the Conran Shop, and an Oyster Bar. For some years now it has been home to

London Dining

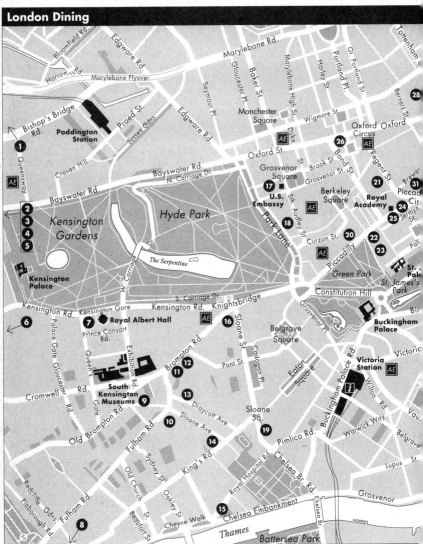

Alastair Little, **29**

Bertorelli's, **44**

Bibendum, **10**

Bistrot 190, **7**

Boulestin, **41**

Café Fish, **37**

Café Flo, **42**

Café Pacifico, **40**

The Capital, **16**

Chelsea Kitchen, **14**

Chicago Pizza Pie Factory, **26**

Chutney Mary, **8**

Clarke's, **2**

Criterion, **31**

Daquise, **9**

dell'Ugo, **34**

Food for Thought, **43**

The Fountain, **25**

Fung Shing, **30**

Gavvers, **19**

The Ivy, **38**

Joe Allen, **46**

Joe's Café, **13**

Julie's, **4**

Kensington Place, **3**

Langan's Brasserie, **20**

La Tante Claire, **15**

Le Caprice, **23**

Le Gavroche, **17**

L'Escargot, **32**

British Museum

27

Guilford St.

Gower St.

Southampton Row

Theobalds Rd.

Clerkenwell Rd.

Barbican Center

Broad St. Station

Liverpool St. Station

London Wall

35 New Oxford St. 36

High Holborn

Kingsway

Drury Ln.

Holborn Viaduct

Newgate St.

Old Bailey

St. Paul's

Moorgate

Bishopgate

Bank Of England

London Wall

48

Court Rd.

St.

34

Charing Cross Rd.

37

Covent Garden

38 43 44

40

45

Aldwych

Fleet St.

Law Courts

Strand

50

Cheapside

Cornhill

Leadenhall St.

Shaftesbury Ave.

29

33 39 41

30

42

46

47

Queen Victoria St.

Cannon St.

AE

Cannon St. Station

Lower Thames St.

Fenchurch

Victoria Embankment

Blackfriars Br.

Blackfriars Station

Southwark Br.

London Br.

Thames

National Gallery

AE

Charing Cross Stn.

Waterloo Br.

Stamford St.

Southwark St.

St. Thomas St.

Tooley St.

London Bridge Station

South Bank Arts Complex

The Mall

Haymarket

Regent St.

AE

James's

ce

Whitehall

York Rd.

The Cut

Waterloo Rd.

Blackfriars Rd.

Union St.

Borough High St.

icage

Walk

Westminster Br.

Waterloo Station

Borough Rd.

Tower Bridge Rd.

Houses of Parliament

Westminster Abbey

AE

Millbank

Lambeth Palace Rd.

Westminster Br. Rd.

London Rd.

New

Kent Rd.

Old Kent Rd.

St.

Horseferry Rd.

Horseferry Rd. Lambeth Br.

Lambeth Rd.

Kennington Rd.

Imperial War Museum

Regency St.

Tate Gallery

Albert Embankment

Kennington Park Rd.

Walworth Rd.

hall Br.

Rd.

Vauxhall Br.

Kennington Ln.

N

Vauxhall Station

Kennington Oval

0   550 yards

0   500 meters

Nine Elms Ln.

KEY

AE American Express Office

i Tourist Information

Le Poulbot, **50**
Luba's Bistro, **12**
Mulligans, **21**
Museum Street Café, **36**
New World, **33**
Nico at Ninety, **18**
The North Sea Fish Restaurant, **27**

Now & Zen, **39**
192, **1**
Orso, **45**
Quaglino's, **24**
The Ritz, **22**
Rouxl Britannia, **49**
Rudland and Stubbs, **48**

St. Quentin, **11**
Savoy Grill, **47**
Tootsies, **5**
Wagamama, **35**
White Tower, **28**
Wodka, **6**

Simon Hopkinson's enormous talent. He is famous for preparing simple dishes perfectly. Thus you can order herrings with sour cream or leeks vinaigrette followed by steak au poivre or the perfect boeuf bourgignon, or you might try brains or tripe as they ought to be cooked. The Christmas pudding ice-cream is not to be missed. The set price menu at lunchtime is money well spent. *Michelin House, 81 Fulham Rd., tel. 071/581–5817. Reservations required. Dress: casual but chic. MC, V. Closed Sun.*

$$ Bistrot 190. Chef/restauranteur and popular guy Antony Worrall-Thompson dominates this town's medium-price eating scene with his happy, hearty food from Southern Europe (liver and wild mushroom terrine; char-grilled squid with red and green salsa; lemon tart) in raucous hardwood-floor-and-art settings. This place opened in '91 and is handy for museum or Albert Hall excursions. Others in the stable are the next door fish restaurant Downstairs at 190, dell'Ugo in Soho (*see below*), and Zoe, off Oxford Street. *190 Queens Gate, SW7, tel. 071/581–5666. No reservations. Dress: casual. AE, DC, MC, V. Closed Sat. lunch, Sun., Dec. 25–26, Jan. 1.*

$ Daquise. Fill your stomach without emptying your pocketbook on Polish staples like *bigos* (sauerkraut with garlic sausage and mushrooms), stuffed cabbage, and cucumber salad, or just coffee and cakes. *20 Thurloe St., SW7, tel. 071/589–6117. Reservations advised weekend dinner. Dress: casual. No credit cards. Closed Christmas.*

Kensington and Notting Hill

$$$ Clarke's. There's no choice on the evening menu at Sally Clarke's award-winning restaurant; her set dinner features ultrafresh ingredients, plainly but perfectly cooked, accompanied by homebaked breads. *124 Kensington Church St., W8, tel. 071/221–9225. Reservations required. Dress: casual but neat. MC, V. Closed weekends, public holidays, 2 weeks in Aug.*

Julie's. Both the upstairs wine bar and downstairs restaurant, decorated with Victorian ecclesiastical furniture, have been going strong since their '60s heyday. The menu here is Anglo-French: salmon-and-halibut terrine, roast pheasant with chestnut stuffing and rowan jelly. Sunday lunch is popular, and there's a garden for outside eating. *135 Portland Rd., tel. 071/229–8331. Reservations advised for dinner, required on weekends. Jacket and tie required. AE, DC, MC, V. Closed Dec. 25 and 31, Easter.*

Kensington Place. The local glitterati make this high-tech palace a noisy and chic setting for some of London's most fashionable food— grilled foie gras with sweet corn pancake is one perennial. *201 Kensington Church St., W8, tel. 071/727–3184. Reservations advised. Dress: casual stylish. MC, V. Closed Aug. bank holiday, Christmas.*

$$ 192. Upstairs is a wine bar, which doubled its size and halved its atmosphere in late '93; downstairs is a relaxed restaurant serving flavorsome, school-of-Alastair-Little (who began here) cooking. On a menu that changes twice a day, you might find a warm salad of duck marinated in Thai spices and lime or a saffron and wild mushroom risotto. Many people order two appetizers here instead of an entrée. *192 Kensington Park Rd., W11, tel. 071/229–0482. Reservations advised. Dress: smart casual. AE, MC, V. Closed Mon., lunch, public holidays.*

Wodka. This smart, modern Polish restaurant is the only one in the world, as far as we know, to serve smart, modern Polish food. Alongside the smoked salmon, herring, caviar, and eggplant *blinis*, you might also find roast duck with spiced pear and *krupnik* (honey vodka). Try the chilled flavored vodkas. *12 St. Albans Grove, W8, tel. 071/937–6513. Reservations required for dinner. Dress: casual but neat. AE, DC, MC, V. Closed weekend lunch, public holidays.*

$ **Tootsies.** A small chain of superior burger places, all dark but cheerful, decorated with vintage advertisements and playing vintage rock. Burgers come with a choice of fixings, in two sizes, and accompanied by crinkly fries. *115 Notting Hill Gate, W11, tel. 071/727–6562, and branches. No reservations. Dress: casual. MC, V. Closed Christmas.*

Chelsea

$$$$ **La Tante Claire.** Justly famous, but cripplingly expensive. The decor
★ is light and sophisticated, the service impeccable, the French wine list impressive, but the food is the point. From the *carte*, you might choose Pierre Koffmann's famous signature dish of pig's feet stuffed with mousse of white meat with sweetbreads and wild mushrooms or the set lunch menu, which, at about £25, including coffee and service, is a genuine bargain. *68 Royal Hospital Rd., SW3, tel. 071/352–6045. Reservations advised 3–4 weeks in advance for dinner, 2–3 days for lunch. Jacket and tie required. AE, DC, MC, V. Closed weekends, 2 weeks at Christmas, Jan. 1, 10 days at Easter, 3 weeks in Aug.–Sept.*

$$$ **Chutney Mary.** London's first-and-only Anglo-Indian restaurant provides a fantasy version of the British Raj. The best choices are certainly dishes like "Country Captain" (braised chicken with almonds, raisins, chilis, and spices), re-created from the kitchens of Indian chefs cooking for English palates back in the old Raj days. *535 King's Rd., SW10, tel. 071/351–3113. Reservations advised. Dress: smart. AE, DC, MC, V. Closed Dec. 25 dinner, Dec. 26.*
Gavvers. This was the original site of Le Gavroche and is now a much simpler, less expensive *petit-Gavroche* run by people trained in the Michel and Albert Roux ways. Set dinners are composed entirely of their inventions, and include a glass of kir, three courses (with choices like a sausage of goose and foie gras, then hare in a sauce of red wine and bitter chocolate), coffee, and petits fours. Lunches are simpler and around £10 cheaper. *61–63 Lower Sloane St., SW1, tel. 071/730–5983. Reservations required. Dress: casual. AE, DC, MC, V. Closed for Sat. lunch, Sun., national holidays, Dec. 24–Jan. 1.*

$$ **Joe's Café.** A stylish brasserie just across the road from Bibendum. Light dishes at lunchtime, more choice—and expense—in the evening. *126 Draycott Ave., SW3, tel. 071/225–2217. Reservations advised. Dress: casual. AE, DC, MC, V. Closed Sun. dinner, Christmas.*

$ **Chelsea Kitchen.** This café has been crowded since the '60s with hungry people after hot, filling, and inexpensive food. Expect nothing more fancy than pasta, omelets, salads, stews, and casseroles. The menu changes every day. *98 King's Rd., SW3, tel. 071/589–1330. No reservations. Dress: casual. No credit cards. Closed Christmas.*

Soho

$$$ **Alastair Little.** Little is one of London's most original chefs, drawing
★ inspiration from practically everywhere—Thailand, Japan, Scandinavia, France—and bringing it off brilliantly. His restaurant is starkly modern, so all attention focuses on the menu, which changes not once but twice daily. Anyone truly interested in food will not be

disappointed. *49 Frith St., W1, tel. 071/734–5183. Reservations advised. Dress: casual. No credit cards. Closed weekends, national holidays, 2 weeks at Christmas, 3 weeks in Aug.*

$$ **dell'Ugo.** From the stable of Antony Worrall-Thompson (*see* Bistrot 190, *above*), this three-floor Mediterranean café-restaurant remains popular. The street-level café serves *bruschetta* loaded with marinated vegetables, mozzarella, parmesan, etc.; Tuscan soups; and country bread, while upstairs wintry, warming "one pot" ensembles and large platefuls of sunny dishes like spicy sausages, white bean casserole, and onion confit are produced. *56 Frith St., W1, tel. 071/734–8300. Reservations necessary upstairs, not taken for café. Dress: casual. AE, MC, V. Closed Sun., Christmas.*

L'Escargot. This media haunt, whose redecoration back in 1993 gave it a new lease on life, serves Anglo-French food in its ground floor brasserie and its more formal upstairs restaurant. A comprehensive, reasonably priced wine list sets off a robust ragout of spiced lamb or a simple, fresh poached or grilled fish. This place is reliable and relaxed. *48 Greek St., W1, tel. 071/437–2679. Reservations advised upstairs, not taken downstairs. Dress: casual but neat. AE, DC, MC, V. Closed Sun., public holidays.*

Fung Shing. This comfortable, cool green restaurant is a cut above the run-of-the-mill Chinatown joint. The usual options (don't miss the salt-baked chicken, served on or off the bone with an accompanying bowl of intense broth) are supplemented by dishes like intestines—deep-fried cigarette-shaped morsels, which are far more delicious than you'd think. *15 Lisle St., WC2, tel. 071/437–1539. Reservations suggested. Dress: casual. AE, DC, MC, V. Closed Dec. 25.*

$ **New World.** A large (700-seat) Cantonese restaurant in London's tiny Chinatown, New World serves the city's best-known *dim sum* from 11 AM to 6 PM in authentic fashion from trolleys. It's not a gourmet experience, but it's fun. *1 Gerrard Pl., tel. 071/734–0677. Reservations not required. Dress: casual. AE, DC, MC, V. Closed Dec. 25.*

Covent Garden

$$$$ **Boulestin.** The richest of French haute cuisine is served in this grand and comfortable basement restaurant founded in 1925. Well-known *patron* and chef Kevin Kennedy keeps up the tradition with oysters, lobster, old-fashioned *Tournedos Rossini*, and turbot with sauce *Choron*. After 10 PM, the post-opera supper is a more affordable treat. *1a Henrietta St., tel. 071/836–7061. Reservations advised 1 week in advance for dinner. Jacket and tie required. AE, DC, MC, V. Closed Sat. lunch, Sun., national holidays, last 3 weeks in Aug., 10 days at Christmas.*

★ **Savoy Grill.** The grill continues in the first rank of power dining locations, especially among politicians, newspaper barons, and tycoons. The cooking is delicious and comforting—order an omelet named after the novelist Arnold Bennett (filled with cheese and smoked fish), beef Wellington on a Tuesday, or roast Norfolk duck on Friday. *Strand, WC2, tel. 071/836–4343. Reservations required for lunch, and for Thurs.–Sat. dinner. Jacket and tie required. AE, DC, MC, V. Closed Sat. lunch, Sun.*

$$$ **The Ivy.** An unpretentious, stylish hangout with generous portions **★** of updated classic dishes from practically everywhere, which remains popular with home-grown celebs and media style-watchers. Eat anything, from scrambled eggs with smoked salmon to roast grouse, shrimp gumbo, or braised oxtail. *1 West St., W1, tel. 071/*

836–4751. Reservations essential. Dress: smart casual. AE, DC, MC, V. Closed national holidays.

Now & Zen. This spectacular restaurant, with its audacious shop-window front, glass pavement, and glass waterfall connecting the three floors would be worth patronizing for the visuals alone. The food more than matches up, since this is one of a growing group of chic Chinese restaurants which practice the creed of freshness, regional dishes, minimal sodium, and no MSG. Try the seabass (steamed, with either ginger and scallions or black bean sauce). Downstairs you can sample as many small dishes as you like for a set price. *4a Upper St. Martin's La., WC2, tel. 071/497–0376. Reservations advised. Dress: smart casual. AE, DC, MC, V. Closed Sun. lunch, Dec. 25–26, Jan. 1.*

★ **Orso.** An Italian Joe Allen's (*see below*), this basement restaurant has the same efficient staff and a clientele of glossy journalists and showbiz folk. The Southern menu changes daily, but always includes pizza and pastas, fish (grilled scallops, roast sea bass), arugula-and-shaved-parmesan-type salads, and regulars like deep fried *courgette* flowers stuffed with ricotta and calves liver with sage and lemon. *27 Wellington St., tel. 071/240–5269. Reservations required. Dress: smart. No credit cards. Closed Dec. 25–26.*

$$ ★ **Bertorelli's.** Right across from the stage door of the Royal Opera House, Bertorelli's draws many opera buffs and singers, so reserve well in advance for pre- and post-opera meals. The decor is cool, white and bright, the cooking better than ever now that Maddalena Bonino (of 192 fame) is in charge of the kitchen, offering perhaps a warm mushroom salad with polenta, then baked salmon with marinated eggplant and anchovy butter, or *roquette* and fontina risotto. *44a Floral St., tel. 071/836–3969. Reservations required. Dress: casual. AE, DC, MC, V. Closed Christmas.*

★ **Joe Allen.** This well-known basement behind the Strand Palace Hotel, twin sibling of the New York one, fills up with theater folk after the curtain falls. Ribs come with trendy wilted greens, black-eyed peas, and London's best (and only?) corn muffins; huge salads, burgers, and brownies are also some of the best in town. Loud chat ricochets off the brick walls, along with plenty of attitude. *13 Exeter St., tel. 071/836–0651. Reservations required. Dress: casual. No credit cards. Closed Dec. 25–26.*

$ **Café Flo.** This useful brasserie serves the bargain "Idée Flo"—soup or salad, *steak-frites* or *poisson-frites*, and coffee—a wide range of French café food, breakfast, wines, *tartes*, espresso, fresh orange juice, simple set-price weekend menus . . . everything for the Francophile on a budget. There are branches in Hampstead, Islington, Kensington, and Richmond. *51 St. Martin's La., WC2, tel. 071/ 836–8289. No reservations. Dress: casual. MC, V. Closed Dec. 25, Jan. 1.*

Café Pacifico. A lively atmosphere pervades this converted warehouse where reasonably priced Mexican food is served. The bar boasts a range of tequilas, cocktails, and beers, while the kitchen produces *ceviche* (marinated spiced fish, cold-cooked in lime juice) or *fajitas* (marinated beef or chicken with onions, peppers, tortillas, cheese, and guacamole) and other Tex-Mex staples that are better than most in London. *5 Langley St., tel. 071/379–7728. No reservations. Dress: casual. MC, V. Closed for lunch. Closed national holidays.*

Food for Thought. This simple, small basement café is deservedly popular for its delicious, fresh vegetarian food. Soups, stir-fries, salads, good bread, and two inventive daily specials are offered; queue downstairs to eat at one of the cramped pine tables or upstairs for take-out. There's no liquor license, and it closes early. *31 Neal St., WC1, tel. 071/836–0239. No reservations. Dress: casual. No credit cards. Closed after 8 PM Mon.–Sat.; 4:30 PM Sun., Christmas, national holidays.*

Bloomsbury

$$$ The White Tower. Barely changed since its founding in 1938, the White Tower is an elegant Greek restaurant (something of a contradiction of terms in London), though its menu isn't exclusively Greek. There are portraits on the walls, glass partitions between the tables, and a rhapsodic menu. Dishes range from the traditional— *taramosalata*—to the unique—roast duckling stuffed with crushed wheat. *1 Percy St., WC1, tel. 071/634–8141. Reservations required. Jacket and tie required. AE, DC, MC, V. Closed weekends, national holidays, 3 weeks in Aug., 1 week at Christmas.*

$$ The Museum Street Café. This tiny, uncomfortable restaurant near the British Museum serves a limited selection of impeccably fresh dishes, intelligently and plainly cooked by the two young owners. The evening menu might feature grilled, maize-fed chicken with pesto, followed by a rich chocolate cake; at lunchtime you might choose a sandwich of Stilton on walnut bread and a big bowl of soup. Bring your own wine. *47 Museum St., WC1, tel. 071/405–3211. Reservations required for dinner. Dress: casual. No credit cards. Closed weekends, public holidays.*

$ The North Sea Fish Restaurant. This popular cabbies' haunt is also known to locals and tourists for its good old British fish-and-chips— battered and deep fried fish with thick fries—cooked to a turn and always fresh. It's a bit tricky to find—head south down Judd Street three blocks from St. Pancras station. *7–8 Leigh St., tel. 071/387– 5892. Reservations advised. Dress: casual. AE, DC, MC, V. Closed Sun., Christmas, national holidays.*
Wagamama. London's gone wild for Japanese noodles, and this ultra-popular, high-tech café does them best. Ramen, in soup, topped with meat or fish, are supplemented by rice dishes, and curries, plus "raw energy" dishes for the jaded. Canteen-style, you will have to share a table, and stand on a fast-moving line to get in. *4 Streatham St., WC1, tel. 071/323–9223. No reservations. Dress: casual. No credit cards. Closed Christmas.*

City

$$$ Le Poulbot. Probably the most popular set lunch in the City. It's part of the Roux brothers' empire (*see* Le Gavroche, *above*), and specialties include smoked salmon flan and lamb cutlets with crème of sweet pepper. Beware the wine list—it will double the check if you let it. *45 Cheapside, EC2, tel. 071/236–4379. Reservations advised 2–3 days in advance. Jacket and tie required. AE, DC, MC, V. Lunch only. Closed weekends.*

$$ Rudland & Stubbs. This informal oyster bar/fresh fish restaurant adjoins Smithfield meat market. Try the *goujons* of salmon with zucchini and salmon sauce, or the John Dory in dill sauce. *35–37 Greenhill Rents, tel. 071/253–0148. Reservations advised. Dress: casual. MC, V. Closed Sat. lunch, Sun., national holidays.*

$ Rouxl Britannia. For this fairly soulless brasserie, named punningly after the Roux brothers who own it, the food is cooked in a central Roux-kitchen and transferred here *sous-vide* (under vacuum). This seems not to harm the unpretentious French/international dishes like roast wing of skate or *gravlax* with potato salad. *Triton Ct., 14 Finsbury Sq., tel. 071/256–6997. Reservations advised. Dress: casual. AE, DC, MC, V. Closed for dinner. Closed weekends, national holidays.*

Pubs

An integral part of the British way of life, public houses dispense beer "on tap," and usually a basic, inexpensive menu of sandwiches, quiche, and salads, and other snacks at lunchtime.

Admiral Codrington. This friendly, fashionable Chelsea pub has a Victorian atmosphere, complete with gaslight, antique mirrors, and Toby jugs. There's a vine-covered patio for summer drinking and barbecues. On Sunday, there's a traditional roast; on other days, shepherd's pie, sandwiches, or salads. Their malt whisky selection is impressive. *17 Mossop St., tel. 071/589–4603.*

Black Friar. You can't miss it—it's the wedge-shaped, ornate building sporting a statue of a friar outside Blackfriars tube station. It was built in 1875 and is a triumph of Victorian extravagance, with red marble pillars, a magnificent mosaic ceiling, with friars, devils, and fairies everywhere—all very art nouveau. There are six kinds of beer on tap. *174 Queen Victoria St., tel. 071/236–5650.*

The George Inn. Edging a courtyard where Shakespeare's plays were once performed, the present building dates from the late 17th century and is London's last remaining galleried inn. Dickens was a regular here. Entertainments include Shakespeare performances, jousting, and morris dancing; drinks are served at both a real ale bar and a wine bar, and there's a full restaurant. *77 Borough High St., tel. 071/407–2056.*

The Lamb. Dickens lived close by and was a regular here. This jolly, cozy pub has original cut-glass Victorian screens and home-cooked food. You can eat or drink outside on the patio (very crowded in the summer). *94 Lamb's Conduit St., tel. 071/405–0713.*

Lamb and Flag. A 17th-century pub once known as "The Bucket of Blood" because the upstairs room was used as a ring for fist-fighting, it's now a trendy, friendly place, serving food (lunchtime only) and real ale near Covent Garden, off Garrick Street. *33 Rose St., tel. 071/836–4108.*

Mayflower. An atmospheric 17th-century riverside inn, complete with exposed beams and a terrace, this is practically the very place from which the Pilgrims' ship, the *Mayflower,* set sail for America. The inn is licensed to sell American postage stamps alongside its superior pub food. *117 Rotherhithe St., SE16, tel. 071/237–4088.*

Prospect of Whitby. This historic riverside tavern dates from 1520, and is named after a ship. It was once called "The Devil's Tavern" because of the thieves and smugglers who congregated here. It's ornamented with nautical memorabilia and pewter. The à la carte menu and pub food are both recommended. *57 Wapping Wall, tel. 071/481–1095.*

Sherlock Holmes. This pub was known as the Northumberland Arms in the days when Arthur Conan Doyle frequented it. It figures in *The Hound of the Baskervilles,* and you'll see the hound's head and monstrous paws among other Holmes memorabilia in the bar. Upstairs there's a reconstruction of Holmes's study. Try the "Sherlock Holmes Chicken" or fish. *10 Northumberland St., tel. 071/930–2644.*

Wine Bars

Wine bars appeared in the '60s and '70s, and are a bit of an anachronism now that Continental-style brasseries are proliferating. These are listed for their convenient locations, and for those occasions when you want more than a pub, but less than a restaurant—plus a decent glass of wine.

Archduke. This is just about the only place convenient to the South Bank complex that isn't *in* the South Bank complex, being built into the railway arches under Hungerford Bridge beside the Festival Hall. Live jazz is played most evenings, accompanying the lackluster, but adequate, quiche and salads, pâtés, soups, and pastas. Upstairs is a separate restaurant specializing in—of all things—international sausages. *153 Concert Hall Approach, tel. 071/928–9370.*

l'Artiste Musclé. Sitting at a round, wooden table in this little '60s survivor is like visiting the *rive gauche*. Food is gallic and filling, but the best thing here is watching the Shepherd Market scene from an outside seat on a summer's evening. *1 Shepherd Market, W1Y 7HS, tel. 071/493–6150.*

Café Fish. This basement wine bar sometimes functions as overflow from the popular restaurant. The fish menu is lighter—on pocket, too—and shorter than its upstairs relation's. *39 Panton St., SW1, tel. 071/930–3999.*

Carriages. We're close to Buckingham Palace here, so it's no coincidence that the downstairs bar is called Charlie's Bar and is decorated with a polo theme. There's live jazz every night, food, and an emphasis on champagne. This is a good spot to relax in after traipsing around the royal properties. *43 Buckingham Palace Rd., tel. 071/834–0119.*

Ebury Wine Bar. This was one of England's original 1960s wine bars, and it's still popular. The food is commendable; try spring chicken and lemon tarragon cream, with plum cheesecake to finish. Port and sherry from the "wood" (barrel) is available, as are 60 kinds of wine. There's a £5 minimum charge. *139 Ebury St., tel. 071/730–5447.*

Sloane's Wine Bar. Next to the Royal Court Theater, this outfit serves coffee and snacks all day, plus lunch and dinner. It's a magnet for Sloane Rangers (British yuppies with old money). *51 Sloane Sq., tel. 071/730–4275.*

Truckles of Pied Bull Yard. There's plenty of outdoor seating, ideal for summer visitors to the British Museum nearby who want to have their lunch in the sun. *Pied Bull Yard, off Bury Pl., tel. 071/404–5334. AE, DC, MC, V. No dinner Sat. Closed Sun.*

Whittington's Wine Bar. This vaulted cellar in the City is named for its reputed owner of yore, Dick Whittington, "thrice Mayor of London." Stuffed baby squid or pot-roast guinea fowl are typical of the restaurant-style menu. The wine list is long, but the hours short: It closes at 10 PM. *21 College Hill, tel. 071/248–5855.*

Lodging

London hotels are among Europe's—indeed the world's!—most expensive. We are aware that readers feel some London hotels do not merit their inflated prices, especially when compared with their courteous Continental counterparts. Therefore, although we list hotels by price (which does not always indicate quality) we have tried to select the ones whose caliber is tried and proven. We quote the average room cost as of spring 1994; in some establishments, especially those in the "$$$$" category, you could pay considerably more—well past the £200 mark in some cases. In any case, you should confirm *exactly* what your room costs before checking in. British hotels are obliged by law to display a price chart at the reception desk; study it carefully. In January and February you'll often find reduced rates, and large hotels with a business clientele have frequent weekend packages.

The custom these days in all but the cheaper hotels is for quoted prices to cover room alone; breakfast, whether Continental or "Full English," comes as an extra. VAT (Value Added Tax—sales tax) is usually included, and service, too, in nearly all cases. Be sure to reserve, as special events can fill hotel rooms for sudden, brief periods. If you arrive in London without a room, the following organizations can help: **AAE Ltd** (1 Princess Mews, NW3 5AP, tel. 071/794–1186) offers unserviced apartments in pleasant areas of Bayswater and North London for one-week minimum; **The British Travel Centre** (12 Regent St., Piccadilly Circus, SW1Y 4PQ, personal callers only; **Central London Accommodations** (83 Addison Gardens, W14 0DT, tel. 071/602–9668) specialize in B&Bs; **Hotel Reservation Centre** (by Platform 8 at Victoria Station, tel. 071/828–1849); and **The London Tourist Board Information Centres** (Heathrow, Liverpool Street Station, and Victoria Station forecourt, no telephone reservations). Credit card bookings can be made with Visa or MasterCard on the **LTB Hotline** (tel. 071/824–8844).

Uptown Reservations (50 Christchurch St., SW3 4AR, tel. 071/351–3445, fax 071/351–9383) lists 50 host homes in fashionable areas of central London that have rooms for rent (with bath and Continental breakfast) for about £62.50 double, £35 single.

Visitors to London should be aware that certain accommodations agencies (though not the above) charge outrageous booking fees, so contact hotels directly wherever possible.

Highly recommended lodgings are indicated by a star ★ .

Category	Cost*
$$$$	over £150
$$$	£110–£150
$$	£60–£110
$	under £60

All prices are for two people sharing a double room and include service and VAT.

Mayfair and St. James's

$$$$ **Brown's.** Founded by Lord Byron's butler in 1837, this quintessential town-house hotel—one of Forte's excellent "Exclusive Hotels"—comprises no fewer than 11 interlinked Georgian buildings, bordering Piccadilly and the Bond Street shops and galleries. Brown's goes out of its way to evoke the atmosphere of an accessibly grand Victorian house party, which has pleased American Anglophiles since Teddy Roosevelt (who honeymooned here). They will like it even more, now that the smaller bedrooms have been expanded, and air-conditioning installed, without disturbing the oak paneling, grandfather clocks, and chintz. *34 Albemarle St., W1A 4SW, tel. 071/493–6020, fax 071/493–9381. 133 rooms with bath. Fa-*

Abbey Court, **2**
Basil Street, **13**
Beaufort, **11**
Berkeley, **18**
Blakes, **8**
Brown's, **26**
Capital, **12**
Claridge's, **23**
Claverley, **10**
The Dorchester, **22**
Dorset Square, **15**
Duke's, **25**
Durrants, **16**
Ebury Court, **24**
Edward Lear, **14**
Eleven Cadogan
Gardens, **19**
The Gore, **7**
Grafton, **28**
Grosvenor House, **17**
Halcyon, **3**
The Halkin, **20**
Hazlitt's, **31**
Lancaster Hall, **6**
The Lanesborough, **21**
Le Meridien, **27**
The Pelham, **9**
Portobello, **1**
Ruskin, **30**
St. Margaret's, **29**
The Savoy, **32**
Vicarage, **4**
Whites, **5**

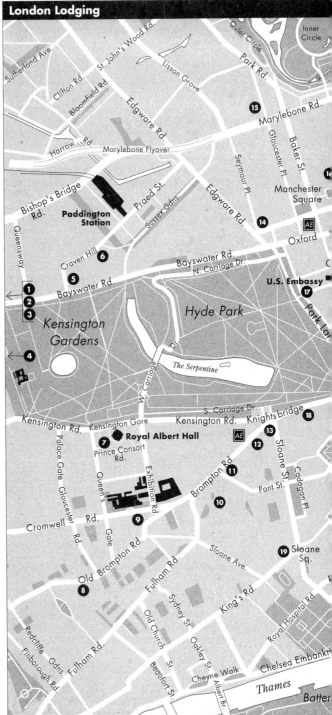

London Lodging

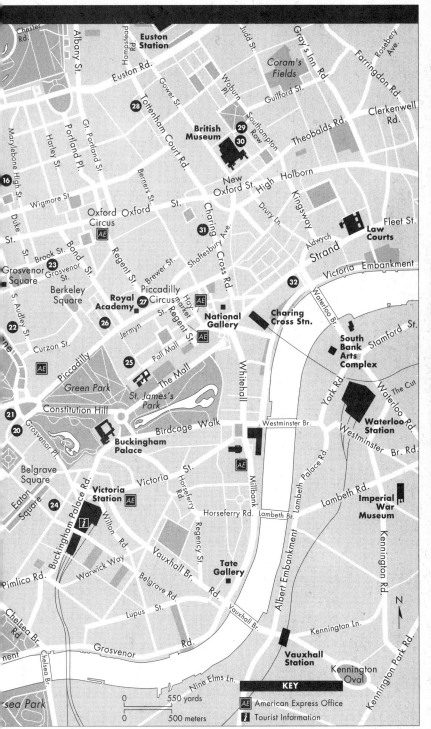

Euston Station

Chester Rd.

Albany St.

Hampstead Rd.

Euston Rd.

Gower St.

Judd St.

Coram's Fields

Gray's Inn Rd.

Rosebery Ave.

Farringdon Rd.

Woburn Pl.

Guilford St.

Clerkenwell Rd.

Marylebone High St.

Gt. Portland St.

Portland Pl.

Harley St.

Tottenham Court Rd.

28

British Museum

29
30

Southampton Row

Theobalds Rd.

16

Wigmore St.

Berners St.

New Oxford St.

High Holborn

Kingsway

Drury Ln.

Fleet St.

Law Courts

Duke St.

St.

Oxford **Oxford**
Circus

St.

St.

St.

Charing Cross Rd.

31

Shaftesbury Ave.

Aldwych

Strand

Victoria Embankment

23

Grosvenor
Square

Brook St.

Bond St.

Grosvenor St.

Regent St.

Brewer St.

Piccadilly
Circus

27

Hay market

32

Waterloo Br.

Stamford St.

Berkeley
Square

Royal
Academy

National
Gallery

Charing
Cross Stn.

South
Bank
Arts
Complex

22

S. Audley St.

26

Jermyn

St.

Regent St.

York Rd.

The Cut

Waterloo Rd.

Curzon St.

Piccadilly

25

Pall Mall

Whitehall

21

Green Park

St. James's
Park

The Mall

Waterloo
Station

20

Constitution Hill

Birdcage Walk

Westminster Br.

Westminster Br. Rd.

Grosvenor Pl.

Buckingham
Palace

Belgrave
Square

Lambeth Palace Rd.

Lambeth Rd.

Imperial
War
Museum

Eaton
Square

24

Buckingham Palace Rd.

Victoria
Station

Wilton Rd.

Victoria

St.

Horseferry Rd.

Millbank

Lambeth Br.

Albert Embankment

Kennington Rd.

Horseferry Rd.

Vauxhall Br.

Regency St.

Warwick Way

Belgrave Rd.

Tate
Gallery

Pimlico Rd.

Lupus St.

Kennington Ln.

N

Chelsea Br. Rd.

Grosvenor

Rd.

Nine Elms Ln.

Vauxhall Br.

Vauxhall
Station

Kennington
Oval

Kennington Park Rd.

Chelsea Br.

...sea Park

0   550 yards
0   500 meters

KEY

AE American Express Office

i Tourist Information

cilities: restaurant, lounge, writing room, cocktail bar. AE, DC, MC, V.

★ **Claridge's.** This famed, palatial hotel has plenty of marble and chandeliers; a Hungarian "orchestra" resident in The Foyer lounge; liveried, but friendly, staff, and luxuriously appointed, outsize rooms—or apartments, as they say here. These are decorated in art deco or English country style (with the odd maverick suite like No. 416/7, which resembles the interior of a Scottish castle), and feature windowed bathrooms with 10-inch showerheads and bells to summon "maid" or "valet." Many Claridge's guests are used to doing that. *Brook St., W1A 2JQ, tel. 071/629–8860, fax 071/499–2210. 200 rooms with bath. Facilities: 2 restaurants, lounge (with orchestra), hairdresser, valet. AE, DC, MC, V.*

★ **The Dorchester.** Five years have passed since its massive refurbishment was completed, and this London landmark still holds its place among the great hotels. Everyone rich and famous has stayed here, and they are now returning in droves to the enlarged rooms, climate control, marble bathrooms, new facilities, and sumptuous swaggering, gilded curlicues. There are three staff persons (and three phone lines) per room, and it shows. *Park La., W1A 2HJ, tel. 071/629–8888, fax 071/409–0114. 197 rooms, 55 suites, all with bath. Facilities: 3 restaurants, bar, lounge, night club, health club (no pool), business center, banqueting suites, ballroom, shopping arcade, free in-house movies, CNN, air-conditioning, valet, theater ticket desk. AE, DC, MC, V.*

Duke's. Exclusive, small, and Edwardian, with a gaslit entrance, Duke's is situated in a quiet cul-de-sac in the heart of St. James's, giving you quiet and convenience in one polished package. The rooms aim at country-style comfort, with those on the top floor being the biggest. *35 St. James's Pl., SW1A 1NY, tel. 071/491–4840, fax 071/493–1264. 62 rooms with bath. Facilities: restaurant, valet. AE, DC, MC, V.*

Grosvenor House. After major plastic surgery three years ago, "the Old Lady of Park Lane" looks youthful and gorgeous again after a frumpy period. Among the reasons to stay here are one of London's biggest hotel pools in a great health club, and one of London's best chefs next door (Nico at Ninety: *see* Dining, *above*). Spacious lounges and lobbies are antique-packed and bustling, while rooms are large, deep-carpeted, pastel-hued, and comfortable. There's often a swanky convention here, using the capacious, upmarket business facilities and public rooms. *Park La., W1A 3AA, tel. 071/499–6363, fax 071/493–3341. 360 rooms, 70 suites, with bath. Facilities: 3 restaurants, bar, lounge, library, health club, banquet suites, ballroom, valeting, satellite TV, theater ticket desk. AE, DC, MC, V.*

Le Meridien. This massive turn-of-the-century building, just off Piccadilly Circus, could hardly be more central. It boasts London's second-prettiest hotel restaurant (the Oak Room; the Ritz wins) and Champneys—the most opulent, best equipped health club. Decor is unremarkable, but comfortable. *Piccadilly, W1V 0BH, tel. 071/734–8000, fax 071/437–3574. 284 rooms with bath. Facilities: 3 restaurants, bar, health club, library, business center, shops. AE, DC, MC, V.*

$$$ **Dorset Square.** This pair of Regency town houses in Sherlock Holmes territory belongs to the welcome new breed of small, luxurious, privately run hotels. The creation of architect–interior designer husband-and-wife team, Tim and Kit Kemp (*see also* the Pelham, *below*), this is *House Beautiful* come to life, from marble and mahogany bathrooms to antique lace counterpanes, and the staff bends over backward to accommodate your wishes. *39–40 Dorset Sq., NW1*

6QN, tel. 071/723–7874, fax 071/724–3328. 37 rooms with bath. Facilities: bar/restaurant, garden, vintage Bentley limousine, 24-hr room service, air-conditioning. AE, MC, V.

$$ Durrants. A hotel since the late 18th century, Durrants offers fading olde-English charm, of the wood-paneled, leather-armchaired sort. Wan, motel-like bedrooms don't match the public areas in style, but are comfortable enough and quiet. For such a central location (by the Wallace Collection), rates are reasonable, though this isn't the bargain it used to be. *George St., W1H 6BH, tel. 071/935–8131, fax 071/487–3510. 96 rooms, 85 with bath. Facilities: restaurant, bar, private dining rooms, lounges. AE, MC, V.*

Edward Lear. Once the house of Edward Lear (of "The Owl and the Pussycat" fame), this good-value, homey hotel has spotless, styleless rooms of varying size—triple and family rooms are huge; number 14 is a closet—with peace and quiet at the back. In the brick-walled breakfast room you're served sausages and bacon from the queen's butcher. *28–30 Seymour St., W1H 5WD, tel. 071/402–5401, fax 071/706–3766. 31 rooms, 4 with bath. V.*

Kensington

$$$$ **Blakes.** This has got to be the most exotic hotel in town, the work of
★ Lady Weinberg, aka Anouska Hempel, '60s style goddess. A sober, dark green Victorian exterior belies the arty mix of Biedermeyer, bamboo, four-poster beds, and oriental screens inside, with rooms bedecked in anything from black moiré silk to dove gray or top-to-toe blush pink. Guests tend to be music or movie mavens. *33 Roland Gardens, SW7 3PF, tel. 071/370–6701, fax 071/373–0442. 52 rooms with bath. Facilities: restaurant, satellite TV. AE, DC, MC, V.*

$$$ **The Gore.** Just down the road from the Albert Hall, this small, very
★ friendly hotel, run by the same people who run Hazlitt's (*see below*), features a similar eclectic selection of prints, etchings, and antiques. Here, though, are spectacular folly-like rooms—Room 101 is a Tudor fantasy with a minstrel gallery, stained glass, and four-poster bed. Despite all that, the Gore manages to remain most elegant. *189 Queen's Gate, SW7 5EX, tel. 071/584–6601, fax 071/589–8127. 54 rooms with bath. Facilities: brasserie restaurant, lounge. AE, DC, MC, V.*

$ **Vicarage.** A family concern for nearly 30 years, the Vicarage feels
★ like a private house. It's beautifully decorated, and quiet, overlooking a garden square near Kensington's shopping streets. *10 Vicarage Gate, W8 4AG, tel. 071/229–4030. 19 rooms, none with bath. No credit cards.*

Knightsbridge, Chelsea, and Belgravia

$$$$ **Berkeley.** A remarkable mixture of the old and the new, the Berke-
★ ley stars a splendid penthouse swimming pool, open to the sky when the weather's good. The rooms are decorated in an array of sophisticated styles, each with an anteroom and palatial bathroom, and antique furniture from the old Berkeley in Mayfair. French cuisine is served in the restaurant, while the Buttery's fare is Mediterranean. *Wilton Pl., SW1X 7RL, tel. 071/235–6000, fax 071/235–4330. 160 rooms with bath. Facilities: rooftop heated indoor and outdoor pool, gymnasium, masseur, sauna, hairdresser, movie theater, florist. AE, DC, MC, V.*

Capital. Reserve way ahead if you want a room here—the same goes for the superb restaurant. Small and elegant, on a quiet street near

Harrods, it's recommended for the excellent, welcoming service it gives. Bedroom decor features specially commissioned inlaid mahogany furniture, Ralph Lauren fabrics, and paintings on the walls. In fact, everything here is *comme il faut. 22–24 Basil St., SW3 1AT, tel. 071/589–5171, U.S. 800/926–3199, fax 071/589–5171. 48 rooms with bath. Facilities: air-conditioning, bar. AE, DC, MC, V.*

★ **The Halkin.** This luxurious little place is so contemporary you worry it will be outdated in a couple of years and they'll have to redo the whole thing. Milanese designers were responsible for the clean-cut white marble lobby, and the gray-on-gray bedrooms that light up when you insert your electronic key, and contain every high-tech toy you never knew you needed. It might be like living in the Design Museum, except that this place employs some of the friendliest people around—and they look pretty good in their white Armani uniforms, too. *Halkin St., SW1X 7DJ, tel. 071/333–1000, fax 071/333–1100. 41 rooms with bath. Facilities: restaurant, cable TV, video library, personal faxes on request. Reuters news service. AE, DC, MC, V.*

The Lanesborough. London's latest grand hotel acts for all the world as though the Prince Regent (or is it Liberace?) took a ride through time and is about to resume residence. Everything coruscates with richness—gaudy brocades and Regency stripes, moiré silks and fleurs-de-lys, multiple antiques and oil paintings, handwoven £250-per-square-yard carpet. If you yearn for a bygone age and are very rich, this is for you. *1 Lanesborough Pl., SW1X 7TA, tel. 071/259–5599, fax 071/259–5606. 95 rooms with bath. Facilities: 2 restaurants, bar, satellite TV, video and CD library, personal direct-dial telephone, fax, business cards. AE, DC, MC, V.*

$$$ **Basil Street.** Female guests automatically become members of the
★ **Parrot Club** here. This serene Edwardian hotel has been family-run for nearly eight decades. Coffee, tea, and cocktails are available in the upstairs lounge. Each room is different—antiques-filled, and amazingly quiet. You can write letters home in the peaceful gallery, which has polished wood floors and fine Turkish carpets. This is a true "period" hotel. *Basil St., SW3 1AH, tel. 071/581–3311, fax 071/581–3693. 92 rooms, 72 with bath. Facilities: restaurant, winebar. AE, DC, MC, V.*

★ **Beaufort.** Actually, "hotel" is a misnomer for this elegant pair of Victorian houses. There's a sitting room instead of reception; guests have a front door key, stereos in their rooms, and the run of the drinks cabinet. The high-ceilinged rooms are decorated in muted, sophisticated shades. The rates include unlimited drinks, breakfast, plus anything, any time, from room service, and membership at a local health club. *33 Beaufort Gardens, SW3 1PP, tel. 071/584–5252, fax 071/589–2834. 29 rooms with bath. Facilities: 24-hr. complimentary bar in the sitting room, air-conditioning, video library, access to nearby health club with pool. AE, DC, MC, V.*

Eleven Cadogan Gardens. This gabled, late-Victorian town house is the perfect spot for a pampered honeymoon, though very difficult to get into. Fine period furniture and art, books, and magazines help to create the ambience of a Victorian family house; the 1990s have barely touched it. Rooms have mahogany furniture and fine bedspreads and draperies. The best rooms are at the back. There's also a private garden. *11 Cadogan Gardens, Sloane Sq., SW3 3RJ, tel. 071/730–3426, fax 071/730–5217. 60 rooms with bath. Facilities: garden, chauffeur-driven car. No credit cards.*

The Pelham. The second of architect and designer Tim and Kit Kemp's gorgeous hotels. There's 18th-century pine paneling in the drawing room, flowers galore, quite a bit of glazed chintz and antique lace bed linen, and the odd four-poster and bedroom fireplace.

Everything is exquisite, including the nearby garden with its heated pool. The Pelham stands opposite the South Kensington tube stop, by the big museums. *15 Cromwell Pl., SW7 2LA, tel. 071/589–8288, fax 071/584–8444. 37 rooms with bath. Facilities: restaurant, air-conditioning, access to garden with outdoor pool, valet. AE, MC, V.*

$$ Claverley. Sited on a quiet, tree-lined street, the Claverley offers friendly, attractive surroundings with the wealthy world of Knightsbridge shopping just around the corner. Some rooms have four-poster beds. *13–14 Beaufort Gardens, SW3 1PS, tel. 071/589–8541, fax 071/584–3410. 31 rooms with bath. AE, V.*

Ebury Court. Five 19th-century converted houses make up this Old-World-style family-run hotel near Victoria Station. The rooms are smallish and chintzy, but antique furniture—like the grandfather clock and Hepplewhite four-poster bed—lends character. Some new bedrooms were added recently, but not all of them have bathrooms. Be warned: Since the rates went up, these are the only "moderate" rooms. *26 Ebury St., SW1W 0LU, tel. 071/730–8147, fax 071/584–3410. 45 rooms, 36 with bath. Facilities: bar, restaurant. MC, V.*

Bayswater and Notting Hill Gate

$$$$ Halcyon. It certainly is expensive, but you're paying for one of London's best small hotels, converted from two enormous wedding cake town houses just off Holland Park Avenue. Elegance, space, and taste surround you, and the uniformed staff takes care of your every whim. Each room has been designed separately; some have four-poster beds, others Jacuzzis. There's a stunning patio garden and a restaurant, The Room at the Halcyon, whose young chef is making waves. *81 Holland Park, W11 3RZ, tel. 071/727–7288, fax 071/229–8516. 44 rooms with bath. Facilities: restaurant, patio. AE, DC, MC, V.*

Whites. The cream facade of this Victorian "country mansion" overlooks Kensington Gardens. Thick carpets, gilded glass, marble balustrades, silk draperies, and Louis XV-style furniture make this the most luxurious hotel in the area. Some rooms have balconies (one room has a four-poster bed) and the muted colors (powder blue, old rose, lemon yellow) are set off by crystal wall-lights. *Lancaster Gate, W2 3NR, tel. 071/262–2711, fax 071/262–2147. 55 rooms with bath. Facilities: restaurant, lounge, air-conditioning, laundry, in-house movies. AE, DC, MC, V.*

$$$ Abbey Court. You enter this 1850 building through a stately, double-fronted portico to find yourself in a luxury bed-and-breakfast filled with Empire furniture, oil portraits, and the odd four-poster bed. Kensington Gardens is close by, or you could save the walk and relax in the pretty conservatory. *20 Pembridge Gardens, W2 4DU, tel. 071/221–7518, fax 071/792–0858. 22 rooms with bath. Facilities: Jacuzzis, patio, conservatory, drawing room. AE, DC, MC, V.*

$$ ★ Portobello. Within walking distance of the Portobello antiques market, this tiny Victorian hotel (with some very tiny rooms!) overlooks a delightful private garden. Repeat guests—often from the arty end of the music biz and media—cherish its relaxed informality. The basement bar is a local hangout in this very "happening" area. *22 Stanley Gardens, W11 2NG, tel. 071/727–2777, fax 071/792–9641. 25 rooms with bath. Facilities: restaurant, bar. AE, DC, MC, V. Closed 10 days over Christmas.*

$ Lancaster Hall Hotel. The German YMCA owns this modest hotel, which guarantees efficiency and spotlessness. There's a bargain 20-

room "youth annex" with basic rooms and shared baths. *35 Craven Terr., W2, tel. 071/723–9276, fax 071/224–8343. 100 rooms, 80 with bath or shower. Facilities: restaurant, bar. MC, V.*

Bloomsbury, Soho, and Covent Garden

$$$$ ★ **The Savoy.** This historic, grand, late-Victorian hotel is beloved by the international influential, now as ever. It has its own training school, whose sought-after graduates supply all Savoy Group hotels, and it also boasts handmade beds. The spacious, elegant, bright, and comfortable rooms are furnished with antiques and serviced by valets. A room facing the Thames costs an arm and a leg, but there are few better views in London. Though the Savoy is as grand as they come, the air is tinged with a certain theatrical naughtiness, which goes down well with showbiz types. *Strand, WC2R 0EU, tel. 071/836–4343, fax 071/240–6040. 202 rooms with bath. Facilities: health club, theater, hairdressing, florist, theater ticket desk, 3 restaurants, 2 bars, valeting, free in-house movies. AE, DC, MC, V.*

$$$ **Grafton Hotel.** The bedrooms and drawing room here are done up to resemble an Edwardian country house, which is incongruous in one of London's ugliest streets. Inside, though, all is efficient and peaceful, especially in the executive wing, completed in 1990. This is a good choice if you're planning to travel on to the north of England or to Scotland: trains leave from nearby Euston or King's Cross station. *130 Tottenham Court Rd., W1P 9HP, tel. 071/388–4131, fax 071/387–7394. 236 rooms with bath. Facilities: restaurant, bar, in-house movies. AE, DC, MC, V.*

Hazlitt's. It's an open secret that Hazlitt's is a disarmingly friendly place, full of personality. Robust antiques are everywhere, assorted prints crowd every wall, and every room has a Victorian claw-foot bath in its bathroom. Book way ahead—this is the London address of media people and antiques dealers everywhere. *6 Frith St., W1V 5TZ, tel. 071/434–1771, fax 071/439–1524. 23 rooms with bath. AE, DC, MC, V.*

$ **Ruskin.** Immediately opposite the British Museum, the family-owned hotel is both pleasant and quiet—thanks to its double-glazed windows. Rooms are clean, though somewhat lacking in character; back rooms overlook a pretty garden. Notice the country-scene mural (c. 1808) in the lounge. *23–24 Montague St., WC1B 5BN, tel. 071/636–7388, fax 071/323–1662. 35 rooms, 7 with shower. AE, DC, MC, V.*

St. Margaret's. Set in a tree-lined Georgian street, this hotel has been run by a friendly Italian family for many years. Its spacious rooms, towering ceilings, and prime location by Russell Square are highlights. The back rooms have a garden view. *24 Bedford Pl., WC1B 5JL, tel. 071/636–4277. 64 rooms, 45 with bath. No credit cards.*

The Arts and Nightlife

The Arts

London is well known for its excellent theater scene, consisting, broadly, of the state-subsidized companies, the **Royal National Theatre** and the **Royal Shakespeare Company;** the commercial **West End,** equivalent to Broadway; and the **Fringe**—small, experimental companies. Another category could be added, known in the weekly listings magazine *Time Out* (the best reference guide to what's on), as **Off-West End,** shows staged at the longer-established fringe theaters. Other sources of arts information are the *Evening Standard*, the major Sunday papers, the daily *Independent* and *Guardian*, and Friday's *Times*.

Theater   Most theaters have a matinee twice a week (Wednesday or Thursday and Saturday) and nightly performances at 7:30 or 8, except Sundays. Prices vary; expect to pay from £6 for an upper balcony seat to at least £20 for the stalls (orchestra) or dress circle. Reserve tickets at the box office, over the phone by credit card (numbers in the phone book or newspaper marked "cc" are for credit card reservations), or (for a couple of quid) through ticket agents such as **First Call** (tel. 071/497–9977). To reserve before your trip use **Keith Prowse's** New York office (234 W. 44th St., Suite 902, New York, NY 10036, tel. 212/398–1430 or 800/223–4446).

Half-price, same-day tickets are sold for cash only (subject to availability) from a booth on the southwest corner of Leicester Square. Open Mon.–Sat. 12–2 for matinees, 2:30–6:30 for evening shows. There is always a long line. Larger hotels have reservation services, but add hefty service charges.

Beware the scalpers! They not only charge outrageous prices and corrupt ticket availability; they sometimes sell forged tickets. The only extra you should ever pay is a nominal booking charge.

Concerts   Ticket prices for symphony concerts range £5–£15. International guest appearances usually mean higher prices; you should reserve well in advance for such performances. Those without reservations might go to the hall half an hour before the performance for a chance at returns.

The London Symphony Orchestra is in residence at the **Barbican Arts Centre,** although the Philharmonia and the Royal Philharmonic also perform here. The **South Bank Arts Complex,** which includes the **Royal Festival Hall, Queen Elizabeth Hall,** and the small **Purcell Room,** forms another major venue. Between the Barbican and South Bank, there are concert performances every night of the year. The Barbican also features chamber music concerts with such smaller orchestras as the City of London Sinfonia.

To experience a great British institution, try for the **Royal Albert Hall** during the Promenade Concert season (July to September). Special "promenade" (standing) tickets cost about £3 and are usually available at the hall on the night. Other summer pleasures are the outdoor concerts by the lake at **Kenwood** (Hampstead Heath) or **Holland Park.**

Numerous lunchtime concerts take place across London in smaller concert halls and churches. They feature string quartets, vocalists, jazz ensembles, and gospel choirs. **St. John's,** Smith Square, and **St. Martin-in-the-Fields** are two popular locations. Performances usually begin about 1 PM and last an hour. Some are free.

Opera   The main venue for opera in London is the **Royal Opera House** (Covent Garden), which ranks with the Metropolitan Opera House in New York—in cost as well as stature. Prices range from £5 in the upper slips to about £130. Performances are sold individually or divided into series, and tickets sell out early.

English-language productions are staged at the **Coliseum** in St. Martin's Lane, home of the English National Opera Company. Prices here are generally lower than at the Royal Opera House, ranging from £4 for standing room to £43 for the best, and productions are often innovative and exciting.

Ballet The Royal Opera House is also the home of the world famous **Royal Ballet.** Prices are slightly lower for the ballet than opera, but tickets go faster; reserve ahead. The English National Ballet and visiting international companies perform at the Coliseum and the Royal Festival Hall from time to time. The **London City Ballet** is based at **Sadler's Wells Theatre,** which also hosts various other ballet companies and regional and international modern dance troupes. **The Place** is indeed the place for contemporary dance, physical theater, and the avant garde. Prices at these are much cheaper than at Covent Garden.

Opera **Coliseum,** St. Martin's La., WC2N 4ES, tel. 071/836–3161. **Royal**
and Ballet **Opera House,** Covent Garden, WC2E 9DD, tel. 071/240–1066. **The**
Box Office **Place,** 17 Duke's Rd., WC1, tel. 071/387–0031. **Sadler's Wells,**
Information Rosebery Ave., EC1R 4TN, tel. 071/278–8916.

Movies Despite the video invasion, West End movies still thrive. The largest major first-run houses (**Odeon, MGM,** etc.) are found in the Leicester Square/Piccadilly Circus area, where tickets average £7. Monday and matinees are usually half price; lines are also shorter.

Cinema clubs and repertory houses screen a wider range of movies: classics, Continental, and underground, as well as rare or underrated masterpieces. Most charge a membership fee of around £1; sometimes the membership card must be bought half an hour before the screening. The best is the **National Film Theatre** (in the South Bank Arts Complex), associated with the British Film Institute. The main events of the annual London Film Festival take place here in the fall; there are also lectures and presentations by visiting celebrities. Temporary daily membership costs 40p.

The **Institute of Contemporary Art** (ICA) presents a repertory program and various museums and galleries also have occasional screenings. Check listings for screenings at the principal repertory houses: the **Electric, Everyman, Prince Charles, Rio, Ritzy,** and **Riverside.**

Nightlife

Cabaret **Comedy Store.** The Comedy Store Players' famous improvised show is now showing at the bigger, brighter, new-look premises, with bar and food. *Haymarket House, Oxendon St., near Piccadilly Circus, tel. 0426–914433 (recording). Admission: £8–£9. Shows Tues.–Sun. 8 PM, Fri.–Sat. also at midnight.*
Madame Jo Jo's. Luxurious and civilized, this may be the most fun of any cabaret in London. The food and drinks are reasonably priced and are served by barmen wearing shorts! There are two outrageous drag shows nightly. *8 Brewer St., tel. 071/734–2473. Admission: £5–£12.50. Shows at 12:15 AM and 1:15 AM.*

Nightclubs **Camden Palace.** A young crowd still turns out at this big, multi-tiered, laser-lit cavern, which has weathered fashion. *1A Camden High St., NW1, tel. 071/387–0428. Admission: £2–£10. Open Tues., Wed., Fri., Sat. 9 PM–3 AM. Dress: casual stylish.*
Legends. This sleek club attracts a different age-range and style of clientele according to the night. Downstairs is a large, cool dance floor with a central bar. *29–30 Old Burlington St., W1, tel. 071/437–9933. Admission: £4–£15. Open Mon., Tues., Fri., Sat. 9 PM–3 AM. Dress: stylish. AE, DC, MC, V.*
Stringfellows. The ubiquitous Peter Stringfellow's first London club

has a glittery, mirrored dance floor and art deco restaurant. *16 Upper St. Martin's La., tel. 071/240–5534. Admission: £10–£15. Open Mon.–Sat. 8 PM–3:30 AM. Dress: fashionable. AE, DC, MC, V.*

Jazz   **Bass Clef.** Owned by the delightful Peter Ind (himself a jazz bass player), this Bohemian backstreet club offers some of the best live jazz in London, plus a predominantly vegetarian Anglo-French menu. Music also at the adjoining **Tenor Clef** (1 Hoxton Sq.). *35 Coronet St., N1, tel. 071/729–2440/2476. Admission: £3.50–£7 depending on the band. Open Tues.–Sat. 7:30 PM–2 AM. AE, DC, MC, V.*

Ronnie Scott's. The legendary Soho jazz club has always drawn a host of international talent—and audiences. *Frith St., tel. 071/439–0747. Admission: £10–£12 nonmembers. Open Mon.–Sat. 8:30 PM–3 AM, Sun. 8PM–11:30 PM. Reservations advised; essential some nights. AE, DC, MC, V.*

Rock   **Forum.** An ex-ballroom with balcony and dance floor that consistently attracts the best medium-to-big-name performers—and crowds. *9–17 Highgate Rd., NW5, tel. 071/284–2200. Admission: around £8. Open most nights 7–11 PM.*

The Rock Garden. Famous for the setting and for encouraging young talent to move on to bigger and better things. Talking Heads, U2, and The Smiths are just a few who made their debuts here. *6–7 The Piazza, Covent Garden, WC2, tel. 071/240–3961. Admission: £4–£7 depending on band. Open Mon.–Sat. 7:30 PM–3 AM; Sun. 8 PM–midnight. AE, DC, MC, V.*

Discos   **Hippodrome.** This features lots of sparkly black and silver, several tiers of expensive bars, a restaurant, and lots of enthusiastic lighting around a large downstairs dance floor. Very middle-of-the-road. *Hippodrome Corner, Cranbourn St., WC2, tel. 071/437–4311. Admission: £6 Wed.; £8 Mon., Tues., Thurs.; £10 Fri.; £12 Sat.*

Casinos   By law, you must apply for casino membership in person; applications usually take about two days, and in many cases clubs prefer an endorsement from a member.

Crockford's. Civilized and far removed from Las Vegas glitz, this 150-year-old club hosts an international clientele who come to play American roulette, punto banco, and blackjack. *30 Curzon St., tel. 071/493–7771. Membership £150 a year. Open daily 2 PM–4 AM. Jacket and tie required.*

Sportsman Club. This place has a dice table as well as punto banco, American roulette, and blackjack. *Tottenham Court Rd., tel. 071/637–5464. Membership £3.45 a year. Open daily 2 PM–4 AM. Jacket and tie required.*

For Singles   **The Limelight.** Owned by New York Limelighter Peter Gatien and situated, like its New York counterpart, in an old church, this offers lots of one-nighter shows and special events. *136 Shaftesbury Ave., WC2, tel. 071/434–0572. Admission: weekdays £7, Sat. £10. Open Mon.–Sat. 9:30 PM–3 AM.*

4 The Southeast

Canterbury, Dover, Brighton, Tunbridge Wells

Though it is one of the most densely populated areas of Britain—the inevitable result of its close proximity to London—the Southeast still has some of England's loveliest countryside. Its landscape is punctuated with hundreds of small farms, their tiny fields ringed by neat green hedges, with picturesque villages and gentle, rolling hills and woodlands. It is prime commuter country.

Surrey, Kent, and Sussex, East and West, make up the Southeast. The northern parts of Surrey and Kent now mainly consist of bedroom communities. Yet Kent's abundant apple orchards have earned it the title of "Garden of England." Kent is also known for its undulating chalk hills and distinctive oasthouses: tall, cylindrical brick buildings with conical tops, where hops are dried for English beer. Sussex abounds with deep, narrow lanes leading to small, quiet villages, each with its ancient church and public house. The coasts of Sussex and Kent are one long chain of seaside resorts, and the busy ports of Newhaven, Folkestone, Dover, and Ramsgate have served for centuries as gateways to continental Europe. The Channel Tunnel now runs from near Folkestone.

Much of England's history is rooted in the Southeast, not least because here the English Channel is at its narrowest. The Romans landed in this area, and stayed to rule Britain for four centuries. So did the Saxons (Sussex means "the land of the South Saxons"). William of Normandy defeated the Saxons at a battle near Hastings in 1066. Canterbury has been the seat of the Primate of All England— the archbishop of Canterbury—since Pope Gregory the Great dispatched St. Augustine to convert the heathen hordes of Britain in 597. And long before any of these invaders, the ancient Britons blazed trails that formed the routes for today's modern highways.

Essential Information

Important Addresses and Numbers

Tourist Information The **Southeast England Tourist Board** will send you a free illustrated booklet and also arrange tours and excursions. *The Old Brewhouse, 1 Warwick Park, Tunbridge Wells, Kent TN2 5TA, tel. 0892/540766, fax 0892/511008. Open Mon.–Thurs. 9–5:30, Fri. 9–5.*

Local tourist information centers (TICs) are normally open Mon.– Sat. 9:30–5:30, but vary seasonally.

Arundel: 61 High St., tel. 0903/882268.
Brighton: 10 Bartholomew Sq., tel. 0273/323755.
Canterbury: 34 St. Margaret's St., tel. 0227/766567.
Chichester: 29A South St., tel. 0243/775888.
Dover: Townwall St., tel. 0304/205108.
Eastbourne: 3 Cornfield Rd., tel. 0323/411400.
Gatwick Airport: International Arrivals Concourse, South Terminal, tel. 0293/560108.
Guildford: The Undercroft, 72 High St., tel. 0483/444007.
Hastings: 4 Robertson Terr., tel. 0424/718888.
Lewes: Lewes House, 32 High St., tel. 0273/483448.
Maidstone: The Gatehouse, Old Palace Gardens, Mill St., tel. 0622/673581.
Rye: The Heritage Centre, Strand Quay, tel. 0797/226696.
Tunbridge Wells: Monson House, Monson Way, tel. 0892/515675.

Travel Agencies **American Express:** 66 Churchill Sq., Brighton, tel. 0273/321242.
Thomas Cook: 58 North St., Brighton, tel. 0273/328154; 109 Mount

Pleasant Rd., Tunbridge Wells, tel. 0892/532372. There are other offices in Dover, Eastbourne, and Hove.

Car-Rental   **Brighton: Avis,** 6A Brighton Marina, tel. 0273/673738; **Hertz,** Mer-
    Agencies   cury Enterprises, 47 Trafalgar St., tel. 0273/738227.
          Canterbury: Avis, 130 Sturry Rd., tel. 0227/768339.
          Dover: Avis, Eastern Docks, tel. 0304/206265; **Hertz,** 173–177
          Snargate St., tel. 0304/207303.

Arriving and Departing

By Plane   **Gatwick Airport** (tel. 0293/531229) has direct flights from many U.S.
          cities and is more convenient for this region than Heathrow. The ter-
          minal for the British Rail line is in the airport buildings, and the
          train system fans out from there to feed all the major coastal towns.

By Car   Major routes radiating outward from London to the Southeast are,
          from west to east: A23/M23 to Brighton (52 mi); A21, passing by
          Tunbridge Wells to Hastings (65 mi); A20/M20 to Folkestone; and
          A2/M2 via Canterbury (56 mi) to Dover (71 mi).

By Train   **British Rail** serves the area from London's Victoria and Charing
          Cross (for eastern areas) and Waterloo (for the west). From London,
          the trip to Brighton takes about one hour by the fast train; and to
          Dover, 1½ hours.

By Bus   **National Express** (tel. 071/730–0202) serves the region from Lon-
          don's Victoria Coach Station. Trips to Brighton and Canterbury
          take about two hours; to Chichester, under three.

Getting Around

By Car   A good link route for traveling through the region, from Hampshire
          across the border into Sussex and Kent, is A272 (which becomes
          A265). It runs through the Weald (uplands), which separates the
          north downs from the more inviting south downs. Though smaller,
          less busy roads forge deeper into the downs, even the main roads
          take you through lovely countryside and villages. The main route
          south from the downs to the Channel ports and resorts of Kent is
          A27. To get to Romney Marsh (just across the Sussex border in
          Kent), take A259 from Rye. The principal roads in the Southeast are
          constantly being enlarged and upgraded to handle the ever-increas-
          ing flow of traffic to the Channel ports. One small point for the mo-
          torist to the south coast to note: You should be warned that more
          traffic tickets are issued per traffic warden in Brighton than any-
          where else in the country!

By Train   A coastal line runs west from Dover through Hastings, with connec-
          tions in Eastbourne for Lewes, and in Brighton for Chichester.

By Bus   Private companies operating within the region are linked by county
          coordinating offices: **East Sussex,** tel. 0273/481000; **West Sussex,** tel.
          0243/777556; **Surrey,** tel. 081/541–9365; and **Kent,** tel. 0622/671411.
          Maps and timetables are available at bus depots, train stations, local
          libraries, and TICs.

Guided Tours

The Southeast England Tourist Board (tel. 0892/540766) can arrange
private tours with qualified Blue Badge guides.
The Guild of Guides (tel. 0227/459779 or 0227/462017) provides
guides who have a specialized knowledge of Canterbury.
Guide Friday (head office 0789/294466) has a go-as-you-please bus

tour of Brighton lasting at least an hour. It operates between April and September, costing £6 adults, £1.50 children, £4 senior citizens.

Exploring the Southeast

The first of the southeastern tours begins in the heart of Kent, in the cathedral town of Canterbury and works its way south to Dover, England's "Continental gateway." Tour 2 heads west along the Sussex coast to Brighton, taking in the historic seaside towns along the way. Tour 3 travels west to Chichester, then swings north into Surrey, stopping in Guildford before leading to Tunbridge Wells, where Tour 4 begins a final circuit through western Kent and its many historic buildings.

Many of the towns described can easily be reached by public transportation from London for a day trip. Local buses, trains, and sometimes even steam trains provide regular service to most major tourist sites. But if you're especially interested in stately homes or quiet villages, it might be wiser to rent a car and strike out on your own.

Highlights for First-time Visitors

Brighton Pavilion: Tour 3
Canterbury Cathedral: Tour 1
Dover Castle and the White Cliffs: Tour 1
Hever Castle: Tour 4
Ightham Mote: Tour 4
Leeds Castle: Tour 4
Lewes: Tour 2
Petworth House: Tour 3
Rye: Tour 2

Tour 1: Canterbury to Dover

Numbers in the margin correspond to points of interest on the Southeast and Canterbury maps.

❶ The city of **Canterbury,** cradled in the rolling Kent countryside on the River Stour, 56 miles from London, is the undisputed star of the southeast region. Iron Age capital of the kingdom of Kent, headquarters of the Anglican Church, and center of international pilgrimage, Canterbury offers a wealth of historic treasures. It also maintains a lively atmosphere, a fact that has impressed visitors since 1388, when poet Geoffrey Chaucer wrote *The Canterbury Tales*, chronicling the journey from London to the shrine of St. Thomas à Becket. Canterbury was one of the first cities in Britain to "pedestrianize" its center, bringing a measure of tranquillity to its streets. To see it at its best, walk around early before the tourist buses arrive, or after they depart.

Canterbury is bisected by a road running northwest, beside which lie all the major tourist sites. This road begins as St. George's Street, then becomes High Street, and finally turns into St. Peter's Street. At the St. George's Street end you will see a lone church tow-
❷ er marking the site of **St. George's Church**—the rest of the building was destroyed in World War II—where playwright Christopher Marlowe was baptized in 1564. Just before you reach the modern
❸ **Longmarket** shopping center, you come to Butchery Lane and the colorful **Roman Pavement.** This ancient mosaic floor and hypocaust, the Roman version of central heating, were excavated in the 1940s,

The Southeast

GREAT BRITAIN

Thames

Hampstead

LONDON ✪

Windsor

Hounslow

Richmond

Woolwich

Thames

Staines

Merton

Sydenham

Dartfor

Egham

Bromley

Sidcup

M3

Beckenham

Leatherhead

Great Bookham

Westerham

Sevenoaks

A25

A227

West Clandon

46

A246

M25

51

52

Guildford

45

A21

Chartwell

53

44

Box Hill

A25

Hever Castle

Ightham
Mote

A31

A248

Dorking

47

M23

B2027

Penshurst Place

50

NORTH DOWNS

Reigate

49

B2176

Ton

Farnham

SURREY

A264

Penshurst

48

A287

A3

Milford

A264

Crawley

East
Grinstead

Royal
Tunbridge Wells

Wadhur

A286

Haslemere

A24

A264

Horsham

A22

TH

A283

A286

WEST

Cuckfield

Midhurst

A272

Haywards Heath

A29

SUSSEX

Uckfield

A265

Petworth

40

Burgess
Hill

Ouse

EAST

SOUTH

A283

A283

Storrington

A23

SUSSEX

Singleton

41

DOWNS

A281

Lewes

Herstn

A284

A27

29

Glyndebourne

Fishbourne
Roman Palace

39

A27

28

A27

43

42

Arundel

A259

Worthing

Wilmington

Chichester

Bognor Regis

A259

Eastbourne

Brighton

30 — 38

A259

English Channel

just one of the many long-hidden relics that were laid bare by German bombs. *Canterbury Roman Museum, Butchery La., tel. 0227/452747. Closed for redevelopment at press time. Check locally.*

Mercery Lane, with its medieval-style cottages and massive, overhanging timber roofs, runs right off the High Street and ends in the **❹ ❺** tiny **Buttermarket.** Here the immense **Christchurch Gate,** built in 1517, leads into the cathedral close.

❻ Christchurch Cathedral, focal point of the city, is the first of England's great Norman cathedrals. It is a living textbook of medieval architecture. The building was begun in 1070, demolished, begun anew in 1096, and then systematically expanded over the next three centuries. When the original choir burned to the ground in 1174, it was replaced by a new one, designed in the Gothic style, with tall, pointed arches. Don't be surprised to find a play or concert taking place in the nave; in recent years the dean and chapter (the cathedral's ruling body) have revived the medieval tradition of using the cathedral for occasional secular performances. In the Middle Ages, only the presbytery (the area around the high altar) was considered sacred, and the nave was often used as a meeting place, sometimes even as a market.

The cathedral was only a century old, and still relatively small in size, when Thomas à Becket, the archbishop of Canterbury, was murdered here in 1170. Becket, an uncompromising defender of ecclesiastical interests, had angered his friend Henry II, who was heard to exclaim, "Who will rid me of this troublesome priest?" Thinking they were carrying out the king's wishes, four knights burst in on Becket in one of the side chapels and killed him. Two years later Becket was canonized, and Henry II's subsequent submission to the authority of the Church and his penitence helped establish the cathedral as the undisputed center of English Christianity.

Becket's tomb—destroyed by Henry VIII in 1538 as part of his campaign to reduce the power of the Church and confiscate its treasures—was one of the most extravagant shrines in Christendom. It was placed in **Trinity Chapel,** where you can still see a series of 13th-century stained-glass windows illustrating Becket's miracles. So hallowed was this spot that in 1376, Edward, the Black Prince, warrior son of Edward II and a national hero, was buried near it. Over Edward's copper-gilt effigy hang replicas of his colorful surcoat, helmet, gauntlets, and a variety of other accoutrements. The faded originals are displayed in a glass case on the left.

The actual site of Becket's murder is down a flight of steps just to the left of the nave. Here you will see a modern commemorative altar, jagged and dramatic in design. A nearby plaque tells of the meeting between Pope John Paul II and Archbishop Robert Runcie, who knelt here together in 1982. In the corner, a second flight of steps leads down to the enormous Norman undercroft, or vaulted cellarage, built in the early 12th century. The room has remained virtually unchanged since then. Its roof is supported by a row of squat pillars whose capitals dance with fantastic animals and strange monsters.

If time permits, be sure to explore the **Cloisters** and other small monastic buildings to the north of the cathedral. The 12th-century octagonal water tower is still part of the cathedral's water supply. As you pass through the great gatehouse back into the city, look up at the sculpted heads of two young figures: Prince Arthur, elder brother of Henry VIII, and the young Catherine of Aragon, to whom he

Buttermarket, **4**

The Canterbury Tales Exhibition, **7**

Christchurch Cathedral, **6**

Christchurch Gate, **5**

Dane John Mound, **14**

Eastbridge Hospital, **9**

Longmarket and Roman Pavement, **3**

Medieval City Walls, **12**

Poor Priests' Hospital/Canterbury Heritage Museum, **10**

St. Augustine's Abbey, **13**

St. George's Church, **2**

Weavers' Houses, **8**

Westgate Museum of Militaria, **11**

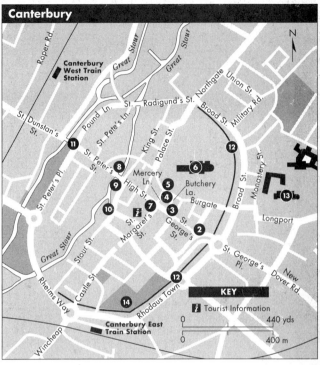

Canterbury

was betrothed. After Arthur's death, Catherine married Henry. Her failure to produce a male heir led to Henry's decision to divorce her after 25 years of marriage, creating an irrevocable breach with the Catholic Church that altered the course of English history.

The cathedral has undergone massive renovation in recent years. In 1993, the paving in most of the interior was relaid.

7 As you leave the cathedral, cross the High Street and turn onto St. Margaret's Street. Here, in a disused church, you will find a unique and vivid exhibition called **The Canterbury Tales,** which is a dramatization also of 14th-century English life. First you will encounter Chaucer's pilgrims at the Tabard Inn near London; next you will come to a series of tableaux illustrating five of the tales. Then, passing through a reconstruction of the city gate, you may enter the marketplace. Don't be surprised if one of the figures comes to life: An actor dressed in period costume often forms part of the scene. *St. Margaret's St., tel. 0227/454888. Admission: July–Aug. £4.75 adults, £3.50 children, £3.95 senior citizens, £15 family ticket; Sept.–Jun. £4.50 adults, £3.25 children, £3.75 senior citizens, £14 family ticket. Open Mar.–Oct., daily 9:30–5:30; Nov.–Feb., Sun.–Fri. 10–4:30, Sat. 9:30–5:30.*

Time Out If you are hungry on your pilgrimage, try **Il Vaticano** (35 St. Margaret's St.) for fresh pasta with a wide selection of delicious sauces.

Return to the High Street and turn left. Just past where the High Street crosses the little River Stour, you will see a distinctive group **8** of half-timbered cottages known as the **Weavers' Houses,** built in the

16th century. These were occupied by Huguenot weavers who settled in Canterbury after escaping religious persecution in France.
Before you cross the bridge over the river, stop in at the 12th-centu-

❾ ry **Eastbridge Hospital.** The hospital (which we would now call a hostel) lodged poor pilgrims who came to pray at the tomb of Thomas à
Becket. The infirmary hall, the chapel, and the crypt are open to the
public. *25 High St. Admission free. Open Mon.–Sat. 10–6, Sun.
11–6.*

Just before the High Street becomes St. Peter's Street, you will see
Stour Street running off to the left. Follow this a few blocks southwest until you arrive at the medieval **Poor Priests' Hospital,** now the

❿ site of the comprehensive and popular **Canterbury Heritage Museum,** whose exhibits provide an excellent overview of the city's history and architecture. Visit early in the day to avoid the crowds. *20
Stour St., tel. 0227/452747. Admission: £1.50 adults, 75p children,
£1 senior citizens, £3.50 family ticket. Open Mon.–Sat. 10:30–4.*

St. Peter's Street runs to Westgate, the only surviving city gate-

⓫ house. It now contains the **Westgate Museum of Militaria.** Climb to
the roof to catch a panoramic view of the city spires before walking
along the landscaped riverside gardens. *Tel. 0227/452747. Admission: 60p adults, 30p children. Open Oct.–Mar., Mon.–Sat. 2–4;
Apr.–Sept., Mon.–Sat. 2–5.*

⓬ For a panoramic view of the town, follow the circuit of the **medieval
city walls,** built on the line of the original Roman walls. Those to the
south survived intact, towering some 20 feet high. Follow the walkway along the top clockwise, along Broad Street, passing the ruins

⓭ of **St. Augustine's Abbey.** This is the burial place of Augustine,
England's first Christian missionary. The abbey was later seized by
Henry VIII, who destroyed some of the buildings and converted
others into a royal manor for his fourth wife, Anne of Cleves. Farther on, just opposite the Canterbury East train station, you will

⓮ see the **Dane John Mound,** originally part of the city defenses.

Before beginning your wide, counterclockwise tour of the region
around Canterbury, drive about 1½ miles east to the village of

⓯ **Fordwich.** This was originally the port of Canterbury, where the
Caen stone quarried in Normandy and shipped across the Channel
to be used in the construction of the cathedral was brought ashore.

A mile to the west of Canterbury, along the Roman road (now A2),

⓰ lies the village of **Harbledown** with its cluster of almshouses. Built in
the 11th century to house the poor, they provide a scenic backdrop
for this peaceful hamlet. Harbledown was customarily the spot from
which pilgrims caught their first glimpse of Canterbury.

From Harbledown, take the minor roads south through Chartham

⓱ Hatch to join A28, stopping off in the hilltop village of **Chilham.** Energetic visitors will find this a good place from which to walk the last
few miles of the traditional Pilgrim's Way, back to Canterbury. The
Chilham village square is filled with textbook examples of English
rural architecture. The 14th-century **church** contains an old school
desk covered with carved initials from the early 18th century onward. On public holidays in the summer, the **Chilham Castle Gardens** are the setting for medieval jousting and displays of falconry.
*Tel. 0227/730319. Admission: £3 adults, £1.50 children; Mon. and
Fri. (no falconry displays) £2.60 adults, £1.30 children. Open
Apr.–mid-Oct., daily 11–5.*

Time Out The **White Horse,** a 16th-century inn nestled in the shadow of the church, offers a pleasant beer garden and wholesome afternoon and evening meals; there's a log fire in winter.

⑱ A252 and A251 (11 mi) will take you northwest to **Faversham,** in Roman times a thriving seaport. Today the port is hidden from sight, and you could pass through the town without knowing it was there. The town center with its Tudor houses grouped around the market hall looks like a stage set.

Time Out The **Sun Inn** on West Street is the flagship of the Shepherde Neame Brewery chain, established in Faversham in the 17th century. The pub dates back to the 16th century. The inn follows the local tradition of hanging up hops in September; they are not only decorative, but add fragrance.

From Faversham you can either take A299 north to the seaside towns of **Whitstable, Herne Bay, Margate, Broadstairs,** and **Ramsgate**—long the playground of vacationing Londoners—or A2 through Canterbury to pick up A257 for the ancient **Cinque Ports** (pronounced "sink") lining the eastern and southern coast. The latter offer much more in the way of history and atmosphere and are generally much less crowded. The ports, originally five in number (hence *cinque,* from the Norman French), were Sandwich, Dover, Hythe, Romney, and Hastings. They were granted considerable privileges and powers of self-government in the Middle Ages in return for providing armed patrols of the English Channel against the threat of French Spanish invasion.

⑲ **Sandwich** still preserves its Tudor air. The 16th-century barbican (gatehouse) beside the toll bridge is one of the town's oldest surviving buildings. The **Guildhall,** also 16th century, has its small museum of local history, open to visitors when the court is not in session.

⑳ About 6 miles south of Sandwich is the larger seaside town of **Deal.** Caesar's legions landed here in 55 BC, and from here William Penn set sail in 1682 on his first journey to America. **Deal Castle,** erected in 1540 and built in an intricate design of concentric circles, is the largest of the coastal defenses built by Henry VIII. Cannons perched on the battlements overlook the gaping moat. The castle museum offers a range of exhibits of prehistoric, Roman, and Saxon Britain. *Victoria Rd., tel. 0304/372762. Admission: £2 adults, £1 children, £1.50 senior citizens. Open Apr.–Oct., daily 10–6; Nov.– Mar., Wed.–Sun. 10–4.*

㉑ About a mile south of Deal stands **Walmer Castle,** another of Henry VIII's fortifications. Converted in 1730 into the official residence of the Lord Warden of the Cinque Ports, it now has the atmosphere of a cozy country house. Among the famous lord wardens once in residence were the Duke of Wellington, hero of the Battle of Waterloo, who lived here from 1829 until his death here in 1852 (there's a small museum of Wellington memorabilia), and Sir Winston Churchill. The present lord warden is the Queen Mother, though she rarely stays here. After you have seen the castle chambers, take a stroll in the gardens. The moat has been converted to a grassy walk flanked by flower beds. *Tel. 0304/364288. Admission: £3 adults, £1.50 children, £2.25 senior citizens. Open Apr.–Oct., daily 10–6; Nov.– Mar., Wed.–Sun. 10–4.*

㉒ Seven miles south on A258 is **Dover,** Britain's historic gateway to Europe. Many visitors find Dover disappointing; the savage bombardments of World War II and the shortsightedness of postwar developers have left their scars on the city center. But **Dover Castle,** towering high above the chalk ramparts of the famous White Cliffs, is a spectacular sight and well worth a visit. It was one of the mightiest medieval castles in Western Europe. The first building on the site was the Roman Pharos, or lighthouse, which still remains, casting its long shadow over the encircling walls. Most of the castle dates back to Norman times. It was begun by Henry II in 1181 but incorporates additions from almost every succeeding century, and was still in use as a defense during World War II. The massive keep (central structure), with its dense walls 17 to 22 feet thick in places, is the most imposing area of the castle. A museum here offers an interesting range of exhibits, one of them a large-scale model of the Battle of Waterloo. Under the castle are the **Hellfire Caves** (included in admission fee), a network of tunnels that were until recently a military secret. They were dug when Napoleon threatened, and they were the headquarters for the evacuation of British troops from Dunkirk in 1940. *Castle Rd., tel. 0304/201628. Admission: £5.25 adults, £2.60 children, £3.95 senior citizens. Open Apr.–Oct., daily 10–6, Nov.–Mar., daily 10–4.*

Time Out | To rest your feet, stop in at the efficient, modern restaurant within the grounds. It offers tasty meals at reasonable prices.

Before you leave Dover, visit the 14th-century **Maison Dieu Hall,** in the town hall. It was founded in 1221 as a hostel for pilgrims traveling to Canterbury. A museum houses a varied collection of flags and armor, while the stained-glass windows tell the story of Dover through the ages. *Biggin St., tel. 0304/201200. Admission free. Open weekdays 10–4:30, Sat. 10–noon.*

Tour 2: Along the South Coast to Brighton

From Dover, the coast road winds through **Folkestone** (another popular seaside resort), across **Romney Marsh**—reclaimed from the sea and famous for its sheep and, at one time, its ruthless smugglers— ㉓ to the town of **Rye,** a former port now nearly 2 miles inland. Its steep hill provides dramatic views of the surrounding countryside. The medieval **Landgate,** one of three city gates, and the 13th-century **Ypres Tower**—part of the original 13th-century fortifications—remain intact. Follow Mermaid Street down to the site of the ancient port. While you are in the area, be sure to visit the **Rye Town Model,** a huge scale model of the town incorporating an imaginative and historic *son et lumière* show. *Strand Quay, tel. 0797/226696. Admission: £2 adults, £1 children, £1.50 senior citizens, £5 family ticket. Open Easter–Oct., daily 10–5 (shows on the half- hour).*

Another interesting museum is **Lamb House,** an early Georgian structure that has been home to several well-known writers. The most famous was the American Henry James, who lived here from 1898 to 1916. The ground-floor rooms contain some of his furniture and personal belongings. There is also a pretty walled garden. *West St., tel. 0892/890651. Admission: £2 adults, £1 children. Open Apr.– Oct., Wed. and Sat. 2–6.*

Leaving Rye, continue along the coast road (A259) through farmland and tiny villages. Perched atop its own small hill, like Rye, ㉔ **Winchelsea,** about 3 miles southwest, is one of the prettiest villages in the region. The town was built on a grid system devised in 1283, after the sea destroyed an earlier settlement at the foot of the hill. Some of the original town gates still stand.

Time Out The 18th-century **New Inn** in Winchelsea is an excellent place to stop for a pub lunch. It also has six inexpensive bedrooms.

㉕ **Hastings,** headquarters of the Norman invasion of 1066, is now a large, slightly run-down seaside resort. A visit to the old town provides an interesting overview of 900 years of English maritime history. Along the beach, the tall wooden **Net Shops,** unique to the town, are used for drying local fishermen's nets. And in the town hall you'll find the 250-foot **Hastings Embroidery,** made in 1966 to mark the 900th anniversary of the battle. It depicts legends and great moments from British history. *Queen's Rd., tel. 0424/722026. Admission: £1.25 adults, 75p children and senior citizens. Open Oct.–Apr., weekdays 11:30–3:30; June–Sept., Mon.–Sat. 10–5.*

All that remains of **Hastings Castle,** built by William the Conqueror in 1069, are fragments of the fortifications, some ancient walls, and a number of gloomy dungeons. Nevertheless, it is worth a visit—especially for the excellent aerial view it provides of the chalky cliffs, the coast, and the town below. *West Hill, tel. 0424/718888. Admission: £2.50 adults, £1.60 children, £1.85 senior citizens. Open mid-Mar.–Oct., daily 10–5.*

㉖ From Hastings you can either follow the coast road or take a detour about 7 miles to the town of **Battle,** the actual site of the crucial Battle of Hastings. The ruins of **Battle Abbey,** the great Benedictine abbey William erected after his victory, are worth the trip. The high altar stood on the spot where the last Saxon king, Harold II, was killed. Though the abbey was destroyed in 1539 during Henry VIII's destructive binge, you can wander across the battlefield and see the remains of many of the domestic buildings. The **Abbot's House** (closed to the public) is now a girls' school. *High St., tel. 04246/3792. Admission: £3 adults, £1.50 children, £2.25 senior citizens. Open Easter–Oct., daily 10–6; Nov.–Easter, daily 10–4.*

㉗ Leaving Battle, take B2095 and A259 to **Pevensey.** This was an important Roman settlement (called Anderida) and was where William the Conqueror landed. The town is dominated by the extensive remains of **Pevensey Castle,** once an important Norman stronghold. Its massive outer walls, built by the Romans, enclose a smaller castle built in the early 1100s by Count Robert de Mortain, half-brother of William. Inside, you will notice 20th-century machine-gun emplacements added in 1940 against a possible German invasion. *Tel. 0323/762604. Admission: £1.80 adults, 90p children, £1.35 senior citizens. Open Apr.–Oct., daily 10–6; Nov.–Mar., Wed.–Sun. 10–4.*

㉘ While passing through the pretty village of **Wilmington,** 7 miles west of Pevensey on A27, you will have no trouble identifying its most famous landmark. High on the Downs above the village a giant white figure, 226 feet tall, known as the **Long Man of Wilmington,** is carved into the chalk; he has a club in either hand. His age is a subject of great debate, but because Roman coins bearing a similar figure have been found in the neighborhood, he might originate from Roman times.

㉙ Stay on A27 and head for **Lewes,** a town so rich in architectural history that the Council for British Archaeology has named it one of the 50 most important English cities. The **High Street** is lined with old buildings of all descriptions, dating from the late Middle Ages onward, including a timber-frame house once occupied by Thomas Paine, author of *Common Sense.*

Towering over the town, high above the valley of the River Ouse, stand the majestic ruins of **Lewes Castle,** an early Norman edifice, begun in 1100. For a panoramic view of the surrounding region, climb the keep and look out from the top. The **Living History Centre** has been moved inside the castle; at Barbican House you can see the **Town Model.** *169 High St., tel. 0273/486290. Admission: £2.80 adults, £1.50 children, £2.30 senior citizens, £7.50 family ticket. Open Mon.–Sat. 10–5, Sun. 11–5; closed Christmas.*

Lewes is one of the few towns left in England that still celebrates in high style Guy Fawkes Night (November 5), the anniversary of Guy Fawkes's attempt to blow up the Houses of Parliament in 1605. It is rather like an autumnal Mardi Gras, with costumed processions and flaming tar barrels rolled down the steep High Street.

As you leave Lewes, continue west on A27 for 8 miles until you reach Brighton, one of the Southeast's liveliest seaside resorts.

Tour 3: Brighton to Royal Tunbridge Wells

Numbers in the margin correspond to points of interest on the Southeast and Brighton maps.

An article in Britain's *Independent* newspaper summed up the attractions of **Brighton** this way: "Pleasing decay is a very English taste. It is best indulged in at the seaside, especially off-season, when wind and rain enhance the melancholy romance of cracked stucco, rusting ironwork, and boarded-up shops. Brighton is a supreme example, with its faded glamour combined with raucous vulgarity." Unfortunately, with the ongoing recession. Brighton's decay has accelerated and become a lot less pleasing.

Brighton was mentioned in the *Domesday Book* as Brighthelmstone in 1086, when it paid the annual rent of 4,000 herrings to the lord of the manor; it changed its name in the 18th century. The town owes its modern fame and fortune to the supposed medicinal virtues of seawater. In 1750, physician Richard Russell published a book recommending seawater treatment for glandular diseases. The fashionable world flocked to Brighton to take Dr. Russell's "cure," and sea bathing became a popular pastime. Russell became known as "Dr. Brighton." Across from the Palace Pier, you will notice a comfortable old pub called Dr. Brighton's Tavern, where his patients used to stay.

The next windfall for the town was the arrival of the Prince of Wales (later George IV), who acted as prince regent during the madness of his father, George III. "Prinny," as he was called, created the Royal Pavilion, an extraordinary pleasure palace (*see below*) that attracted London society. The influx of visitors triggered a wave of villa building. Fortunately this was one of the greatest periods in English architecture. The elegant terraces of Regency houses are today among the town's greatest attractions.

The coming of the railroad set the seal on Brighton's popularity: One of the most luxurious trains in the country, the Pullman *Brighton Belle*, brought Londoners to the coast within an hour. They expected to find the same comforts and recreations they had in London and, as they were prepared to pay for them, Brighton obliged. This helps to explain the town's remarkable range of restaurants, hotels, and pubs. Horse racing was—and still is—another strong attraction.

Although fast rail service to London has made Brighton an important base for commuters, the town has unashamedly set itself out to be a pleasure resort. In the 1840s it featured the very first example of that peculiarly British institution, the amusement pier. Although

③ that first pier is now a rusting wreck, the restored **Palace Pier** follows the great tradition. The original mechanical amusements, including the celebrated flipcard device, "What the Butler Saw," are now exhibits in the town museum, but you can still admire the pier's handsome ironwork.

② The heart of Brighton is the **Steine** (pronounced "steen"), the large open area close to the seafront. This was a river mouth until the Prince of Wales had it drained in 1793. One of the houses here was the home of Mrs. Maria Fitzherbert, later the prince's wife. But the most remarkable building on the Steine, perhaps in all Britain, is

③ unquestionably the **Royal Pavilion,** the Prince of Wales's extravagant fairy-tale palace. First planned as a simple seaside villa and built in the fashionable classical style of 1787, the Pavilion was rebuilt between 1815 and 1822 for the prince regent, who favored an exotic, eastern design with Chinese interiors. When Queen Victoria came to the throne in 1837, she so disapproved of the palace that she stripped it of its furniture and planned to demolish it. Fortunately, the Brighton city council bought it from her, and it is now lovingly preserved and recognized as unique in Europe. After a lengthy process of restoration, the Pavilion looks much as it did in its magnificent heyday. The interior is once more filled with quantities of period furniture and ornaments, some given or lent by the present royal family. The two great set pieces are the **Music Room,** styled in the form of an oriental pavilion, and the **Banqueting Room,** with its enormous flying-dragon "gasolier," or gaslight chandelier, a revolutionary new invention in the early 19th century. The upstairs rooms (once used as bedrooms) contain a selection of cruel caricatures of the prince regent, most produced during his lifetime, and illustrations of the Pavilion at various stages of its construction. Following the decade-long renovation of the palace, attention has now turned to the gardens, which are being restored. *Old Steine, tel. 0273/ 603005. Admission: £3.75 adults, £2.10 children, £2.75 senior citizens, £5 and £9.60 family tickets. Open Oct.–May, daily 10–5; June–Sept., daily 10–6.*

Time Out One of the elegant upstairs bedrooms in the Pavilion is now a tearoom, offering a variety of snacks and light meals.

④ The grounds of the Pavilion contain the **Brighton Museum and Art Gallery,** whose buildings were designed as a stable block for the prince's horses. The museum has especially interesting Art Nouveau and Art Deco collections. *Church St., tel. 0273/603005. Admission free. Open Tues.–Sat. 10–5:45, Sun. 2–5.*

⑤ Just west of the Old Steine lies **the Lanes,** a maze of alleys and passageways that was once home to legions of fishermen and their families. It is said that the name "Lanes" refers to their fishing lines. Today the Lanes is filled with restaurants, boutiques, and, especially, antiques shops. Vehicular traffic is barred from the area, and visitors may wander at will.

The heart of the Lanes is Market Street and Square, lined with fish and seafood restaurants. The large **Pump House** pub was once an actual pumping station, bringing seawater up from the beach and distributing it to Brighton's many bathing establishments. The **Bath House Arms,** nearby, was one of these. You can spend hours wandering through the Lanes, for the architecture is as varied as the merchandise on sale.

Brighton
Museum and Art
Gallery, **34**

The Lanes, **35**

Marina, **37**

Palace Pier, **31**

Preston
Manor, **38**

Royal
Pavilion, **33**

Steine, **32**

Volk's Electric
Railway, **36**

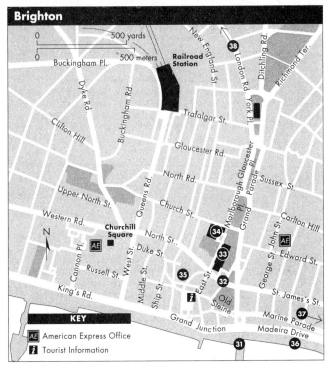

Brighton

KEY

AE American Express Office

i Tourist Information

36 **37** If you feel an urge to escape Brighton's summer crowds, take **Volk's Electric Railway** along the Marine Parade to the **Marina.** Built by inventor Magnus Volk in 1883, this was the first public electric railroad in Britain.

North of the Brighton town center, on the main London road, is **38** **Preston Manor.** This beautifully preserved gentleman's residence, with its collection of paintings, silver, porcelain, and furniture, evokes the opulence of Edwardian times. The present house was built in 1738, with additions in 1903. You can also wander through the extensive grounds. *Preston Park, tel. 0273/603005, ext. 59. Admission: £2.60 adults, £1.50 children, £2.10 senior citizens, £4.10 and £6.50 family tickets. Open Tues.–Sat., Sun. 2–5, national holidays 10–5.*

Numbers in the margin correspond to points of interest on the Southeast map.

39 Leaving Brighton, follow the coast road (A27) west to **Arundel,** about 23 miles away. This tiny hilltop town is dominated by an 11th-century castle, home of the dukes of Norfolk for more than 700 years, and an imposing **Roman Catholic cathedral**—the duke is Britain's leading Catholic peer.

The ceremonial entrance to **Arundel Castle** is at the top of the High Street, but visitors can enter at the bottom, close to the parking lot. The keep, rising from its conical mound, is as old as the original castle, while the barbican (gatehouse) and the Barons' Hall date from the 13th century. The interior of the castle was reconstructed in the then-fashionable Gothic style of the 19th century. Among the treasures on view are the rosary beads and prayer book used by Mary,

Queen of Scots, at her execution. As is so often the case with a British historic property still in private hands, Arundel Castle has a slightly shabby air about it. The spacious grounds are open to the public and there is a restaurant. *Tel. 0903/883136. Admission: £4.50 adults, £3.50 children, £4 senior citizens. Open Apr.–Oct., Sun.–Fri. 11–5.*

Time Out **The Black Rabbit.** This 18th-century pub is a find (and you must persevere along Mill Road in order *to* find it). Its location by the river, with views of the castle and the bird sanctuary, makes it ideal for a summer lunch. The bar food is good and reasonably priced, and there's a proper restaurant if you want something more substantial.

Twelve miles north of Arundel by A284, and just off A283 in the village of **Petworth,** stands **Petworth House,** built between 1688 and 1696. An extensive deer park was added later by the celebrated landscape architect Lancelot "Capability" Brown. The house holds a fine collection of English paintings, including works by Thomas Gainsborough, Sir Joshua Reynolds, J.M.W. Turner, and Sir Antony Van Dyck. Other treasures include Greek and Roman sculpture and Grinling Gibbons wood carvings. *Tel. 0798/42207. Admission: £4 adults, £2 children. Open Apr.–Oct., Tues.–Thurs., weekends 1–5:30.*

Time Out You can have either a light lunch or tea in the **Servants' Block** at Petworth House.

Leaving Petworth, follow A272 about 7 miles west to **Midhurst.** Then turn off onto A286, running south over the downs into the village of **Singleton.** Here, stop in at the **Weald and Downland Open Air Museum,** a sanctuary for endangered historical buildings. Among the "rescued" structures are a cluster of medieval houses, a working water mill, a Tudor market hall, and an ancient blacksmith's shop. The architectural styles on display span more than 400 years. *Tel. 0243/811348. Admission: £4.20 adults, £2.10 children, £3.70 senior citizens, £11 family ticket. Open Mar.–Oct., daily 11–5; Nov.–Feb., Wed., Sat., Sun. 11–4.*

From Singleton, head south on A286 for about 8 miles until you come to **Chichester,** capital city of West Sussex. The city itself, founded by the Romans, sits on the low-lying plains between the wooded south downs and the sea. Though it boasts its own giant cathedral and has all the trappings of a large, commercial city, Chichester is not much bigger than many of the provincial towns around it. The city walls and major streets follow the original Roman plan; the intersection of the four principal streets is marked by a 15th-century cross. The Norman **cathedral,** near the corner of West and South streets, also stands on Roman foundations. Inside, a glass panel reveals a group of Roman mosaics uncovered during recent restoration efforts. Other treasures include two of the most important Norman sculptures in Britain: *The Raising of Lazarus* and *Christ Arriving in Bethany*, both in the choir aisle. You will also see some outstanding modern works by artists John Piper, Marc Chagall, and Graham Sutherland. The considerable restoration work that has been going on for years is likely to be finished in the year 2010. The exterior now gleams with newly cleaned white stonework, and eroded stone columns have been replaced with new ones of Purbeck marble. There are refreshment rooms in the cloisters.

Pallant House was built in 1712 as a wine merchant's mansion for the cost of £3,000 (a huge sum in those days). It was state of the art for architecture then, with the latest in complicated brick work and superb wood carving. The rooms have been faithfully restored, and furnished with appropriate antiques and porcelain. The building also showcases a small collection of British art, as well as regularly changing exhibitions. *9 North Pallant, tel. 0234/774557. Admission: £2.50 adults, £1.50 children, £1.70 senior citizens. Open Tues.–Sat. 10–5:30.*

Time Out For a morning coffee, light lunch, or tea while seeing Chichester, try **Shepherds** (35 Little London). Most of its tables are in a modernized barnlike structure at the rear. There are six kinds of rarebit on the menu, including Hawaiian with pineapple, and oodles of fattening home-baked foods.

43 As you drive west from Chichester on A259, stop at **Fishbourne Roman Palace,** about half a mile away. This is the largest Roman villa in Britain. Probably built as a residence for Roman emperor Tiberius Claudius Cogidubnus, the villa contains a remarkable range of mosaics. Sophisticated bathing and heating systems remain, and the gardens have been laid out much as they were in the 1st century AD. *Salthill Rd., Fishbourne, tel. 0243/785859. Admission: £3.40 adults, £1.50 children, £2.60 senior citizens, £8.50 family ticket. Open mid.-Feb.–Apr. and Oct., daily 10–5; May–Sept., daily 10–6; Nov.–mid-Dec., daily 10–4; mid-Dec.–mid-Feb., Sun. 10–4.*

To continue on the northward circuit into Surrey, return to Chichester and take A286/A287/A3 to Guildford.

44 **Guildford,** the largest town in Surrey and the county's capital, lies only 28 miles from London. It is an important commuter town—and it is growing at an alarming rate—but Guildford has managed to retain a faint 18th-century air. The steep **High Street** is lined with gabled merchants' houses and preserves a pleasant, provincial appearance. **Guildford Grammar School,** at the top end, contains one of Britain's three surviving medieval chained libraries (books were so precious during the Middle Ages, they were literally chained to prevent theft). The school was founded in 1507. *Tel. 0483/502424. Open by appointment only.*

Farther along the High Street is the **Hospital of the Blessed Trinity,** with its massive Tudor facade. It was founded in 1619 as an almshouse by George Abbot, archbishop of Canterbury. Abbot, one of the translators of the King James Bible, was born in Guildford. The hospital is now an old people's home; the male residents wear Tudor hats and coats bearing Abbot's emblem. *High St., tel. 0483/62670. Chapel and common room open Sat. (call for admission times).*

Time Out **Rats Castle** (80 Sydenham Rd.), near the center of town, presents a wide range of food in a pub decorated with Edwardian tiles. There's a summer garden, a setting for barbecues.

Next you come to the **Guildhall,** its exquisite 16th-century structure concealed behind a 17th-century facade. For years this building served as the center of the town's government. Be sure to visit the **courtroom,** with its original paneling and stained-glass windows. The impressive **Guildhall Clock,** glittering with gold, reaches out over the street like a giant outstretched arm. *High St., tel. 0483/505050. Admission free. Open May–Sept., Tues., Thurs. 2–5.*

Across from the Guildhall is what appears to be a triumphal arch. This was the facade of the **Corn Exchange,** built in 1810. Turn left off the High Street onto **Quarry Street. St. Mary's Church** has a Saxon tower, while most of the building dates from the 1100s. Farther along is **Castle Arch,** complete with a slot for a portcullis, and beyond that, the remains of the castle itself. **The Guildford Museum,** in Castle Arch, contains interesting exhibits on local history, along with memorabilia of Charles Dodgson (better known by his pen name, Lewis Carroll), author of *Alice in Wonderland.* Dodgson spent the last years of his life in a house on nearby Castle Hill. *Quarry St., tel. 0483/444750. Admission free. Open Mon.–Sat. 11–5.*

The ruined shell of a Norman keep (70 feet high, with walls up to 14 feet thick) is all that survives of **Guildford Castle.** For many years the castle served as the main jail for Surrey and Sussex. Notice the giant chessboard in the grounds. *Castle St., tel. 0483/444702. Admission: 70p adults, 35p children. Open Apr.–Sept., daily 10:30–6.*

Guildford Cathedral, looming on its hilltop across the River Wey, is only the second Anglican cathedral to be built on a new site since Henry VIII's Reformation of the 1500s. It was consecrated in 1961. The redbrick exterior is severely simple, while the interior, with its stone and plaster, looks bright and cool. The Refectory Restaurant is open for light refreshments from 9:30 to 4:30 (4 in winter). *Stag Hill, tel. 0483/65287. Donation requested.*

45 Just east of Guildford at **West Clandon,** you'll want to visit **Clandon Park,** which started out as an Elizabethan manor but was transformed in the 1730s by Venetian architect Giacomo Leoni into the graceful Palladian-style residence you see today. The real glory of the house, now a National Trust property, is its interior, especially the two-story Marble Hall, one of the most imposing rooms created in the 18th century. There's a fine collection of furniture, needlework, and porcelain and, in the basement, an interesting regimental museum, full of weapons and medals. The extensive parkland (not open to the public) was another of Capability Brown's landscaping achievements. *Tel. 0483/222482. Admission: £4 adults, £2 children. Open Apr.–Oct., Sat.–Wed. 1:30–5:30.*

46 Leaving Clandon Park, follow A246 east 8 miles to **Great Bookham,** and visit **Polesden Lacey.** This handsome Regency house, built on the site of one owned by 18th-century playwright Richard Brinsley Sheridan, was from 1906 to 1942 the home of society hostess Mrs. Ronald Greville. Her many famous guests included Edward VII. Elizabeth, now the Queen Mother, and her husband, the Duke of York (later George VI), stayed here on their honeymoon. Today owned and maintained by the National Trust, Polesden Lacey contains beautiful collections of furniture, paintings, porcelain, and tapestries. In the summer, open-air theatrical performances are given on the grounds. Coffee, lunches, and teas are available in the courtyard restaurant. *Tel. 0372/458203. Admission may vary according to time of year—house £3 adults, £1.50 children; grounds £2.50 adults, £1.25 children; inclusive ticket £5.50 adults, £2.75 children. House open Apr.–Oct., Wed.–Sun. 1:30–5:30; Mar., Nov., weekends 1:30–4:30; grounds open daily 11–6 or sunset.*

47 As you start making your way southeast to Royal Tunbridge Wells via Dorking (about 28 miles), you'll pass under the shadow of **Box Hill,** named after the box trees that grow in such profusion here. It is a favorite spot for walking excursions. At Dorking, take any of the major roads and follow the signs.

Tour 4: Tunbridge Wells, Stately Homes, and Castles

48 Although the city is officially known as **Royal Tunbridge Wells,** locals ignore the prefix "royal" (it was added only in 1909, during the reign of Edward VII). The town was named after the neighboring city of Tonbridge, a few miles up the road toward London, but the spelling was changed to distinguish it. Tunbridge Wells owes its prosperity to the 17th and 18th centuries' passion for spas and mineral baths, initially as medicinal treatments and later as social gathering places. In 1606, a spring of chalybeate (mineral) water was discovered here, drawing legions of royal visitors from the court of King James I. It is still possible to drink the waters when a "dipper" (the traditional water dispenser) is in attendance, from Easter to September. Tunbridge Wells reached its zenith in the mid-18th century, when Richard "Beau" Nash presided over its social life. Today it is a pleasant town and home to many London commuters.

Start your tour at the **Pantiles,** a promenade near the spring on the other side of town, which derives its odd name from the Dutch "pan tiles" that originally paved the area. Now bordered on two sides by busy main roads, the Pantiles remains a tranquil oasis. Across the road from the Pantiles is the **Church of King Charles the Martyr,** built in 1678 and dedicated to Charles I, who was executed by Parliament in 1649 following the English Civil War. Its plain exterior belies its splendid interior; take special note of the beautifully plastered ceiling. A network of alleyways behind the church leads north back to the High Street.

Time Out **The Compasses,** a spacious, well-kept pub, in Victorian style, on a tiny, steep lane (Little Mount Sion) off the High Street, offers tasty homemade food and, in the winter, cozy open fires.

The buildings here at the lower end of the High Street are mostly 18th-century, but as the street climbs the hill north, changing its name to Mount Pleasant Road, the buildings become more modern. Here you'll find the **Tunbridge Wells Museum and Art Gallery,** which houses a permanent exhibition of interesting Tunbridge Ware pieces: small, wood-carved items inlaid with different-colored wooden fragments. *Mount Pleasant Rd., tel. 0892/26121. Admission free. Open Mon.–Sat. 9:30–5.*

Within a 15-mile radius of Tunbridge Wells lies a remarkable array of historic homes, castles, and other monuments. Moving clockwise **49** to the west, following A26 and B2176, you first arrive at **Penshurst Place,** one of England's finest medieval manor houses. The **Baron's Hall,** built in 1341, retains its original timber roof. Elizabethan poet and soldier Sir Philip Sidney was born here in 1554, and it is still the home of the Sidney family. There is a collection of tapestries and family portraits and a coffee shop. *Tel. 0892/870307. Admission: house and grounds £4.95 adults, £2.75 children, £4.50 senior citizens; grounds only £3.50 adults, £2.25 children, £3 senior citizens. Open Apr.–Sept., daily 12–5; grounds open 11–dusk.*

Time Out **The Spotted Dog,** on Smarts Hill, which first opened its doors in 1520, today tempts visitors with an inglenook fireplace, heavy beams, imaginative food, and a splendid view of Penshurst Place.

Next, follow a series of signposted minor roads about 3 miles west to **50** 13th-century **Hever Castle,** the family home of Anne Boleyn. It was here that she was courted and won by Henry VIII. He later gave

Hever to his fourth wife, Anne of Cleves. The castle was acquired in 1903 by American millionaire William Waldorf Astor, who built an entire Tudor village to house his staff and had the gardens laid out in Italianate style, with a large topiary maze. *Tel. 0732/865224. Admission: castle and grounds £5.20 adults, £2.60 children, £4.70 senior citizens, £13 family ticket; grounds only £3.80 adults, £2.20 children, £3.30 senior citizens, £9.80 family ticket. Open Easter–mid-Nov., daily noon–5; grounds: 11–6.*

⑤¹ From Hever, more minor roads, B2027 and B2026, lead you north to Sir Winston Churchill's home, **Chartwell.** He lived in this Victorian house from 1922 until his death in 1965. It was acquired by the National Trust and has been decorated to appear as it did in Churchill's lifetime—even down to a half-smoked cigar in an ash tray. In the garden you can see a wall he built himself. *Near Westerham, tel. 0732/866368. Admission: £4.20 adults, £2.10 children; garden only £2 adults, £1 children. Open Easter–Oct., Tues.–Thurs. noon–5, weekends and national holidays 11–5; Mar., Nov., weekends and Wed. 11–4.*

⑤² From Chartwell, drive north to Westerham, then pick up A25 and head east for 8 miles until you arrive in **Sevenoaks.** In the center of town you will find the entrance to **Knole,** the home of the Sackville family since 1603. Begun in the 15th century, Knole, with its vast complex of courtyards and buildings, resembles a small town. You'll need most of an afternoon to explore it thoroughly. The house is famous for its collection of tapestries and embroidered furnishings. Paintings on display include a series of portraits by 18th-century artists Thomas Gainsborough and Sir Joshua Reynolds. The decorated staircase was a novelty in its day. The house is set in a 1,000-acre deer park. *Tel. 0732/450608. Admission: £4 adults, £2 children; grounds only 50p adults, 30p children. Open Apr.–Oct., Wed. and Fri.–Sun. 11–5, Thurs. 2–5; last admission at 4.*

⑤³ Leaving Sevenoaks, follow A25 east to A227 (8 miles) until you see signs for **Ightham** (pronounced "Item") **Mote.** Finding the house itself requires careful navigation, but it is worth the effort. This is an outstanding example of a small, medieval manor house, complete with moat. (The "mote" in the name, however, refers to the role of the house as a meeting place, or "moot.") The exterior has changed little since it was built, in the 14th century, but on close inspection you'll find it does encompass styles of several different periods: The Tudor chapel, the medieval Great Hall, the hand-painted Chinese wallpaper, and the 18th-century Palladian window are just some of its incongruous features. *Ightham, tel. 0732/810378. Admission: £4 adults, £2 children. Open Easter–Oct., Mon., Wed.–Fri. noon–5:30, Sun. 11–5:30.*

⑤⁴ Next take A25 east 10 miles to **Maidstone,** Kent's county town, with its backdrop of chalky downs. The bubbling River Medway runs **⑤⁵** right through town. Only 5 miles east on A20 stands **Leeds Castle,** a fairy-tale stronghold commanding two small islands on a peaceful lake. Since the 10th century this site has held a castle, and some of the present structure is 13th-century Tudor. Leeds (not to be confused with Leeds in the North) was a favorite home of many English queens, and Henry VIII liked the place so much he had it converted from a fortress into a grand palace. The house offers a fine collection of paintings and furniture, plus an unusual **dog-collar museum.** *Tel. 0622/765400. Admission: castle and grounds, £7 adults, £4.80 children, £6 senior citizens, £19.50 family ticket; grounds only, £5.50 adults, £3.30 children, £4.50 senior citizens, £15 family ticket. Open Nov.–Mar., weekends 11–4; Easter–Oct., daily 11–5.*

From Leeds Castle, make your way south on B2163 and A274 through Headcorn until you come to another lovely fortress—or what's left of it—**Sissinghurst Castle,** nestled deep in the Kentish countryside. The gardens, laid out in the 1930s around the remains of this moated Tudor castle, were the creation of the writer Vita Sackville-West (one of the Sackvilles of Knole) and her husband, the diplomat Harold Nicolson. The grounds are at their best in June and July, when the roses are in bloom. *Cranbrook, tel. 0580/712850. Admission: Tues.–Sat. £5 adults, £2.50 children. Open Apr.–mid-Oct., Tues.–Fri. 1–6:30, weekends and Good Friday 10–5:30; as space is limited, admission is often restricted.*

Time Out **Claris's Tea Shop** (3 High St., Biddenden), near Sissinghurst Castle, serves traditional English teas in a 15th-century setting and displays attractive English craft items. There's a pretty garden for summer teas. Closed on Mondays.

As you leave Sissinghurst, continue south along A229 through **Hawkhurst,** a little village that was once the headquarters of a notorious and ruthless gang of smugglers. Turn at the Curlew pub to arrive in the tiny Sussex village of **Bodiam.** Here, surrounded by a wide moat, stands **Bodiam Castle.** Built in 1385 to withstand a threatened French invasion, it was "slighted" (partly demolished) during the English Civil War of 1642–45 and has been uninhabited ever since. You can climb some of the towers and enjoy the illusion of manning the battlements against an enemy. *Tel. 0580/830436. Admission: £2.50 adults, £1.30 children. Open Jan.–Mar., Tues.–Sun. 10–sunset; Apr.–Oct., daily 10–6; Nov. and Dec., Tues.–Sun. 10–sunset; closed Dec. 25–28.*

Follow the minor road back past the Curlew to join A21 north, then turn west onto A265. A few miles west along this road lies **Burwash,** where **Batemans,** a beautiful 17th-century house just off the main road, was the home of the writer Rudyard Kipling from 1902 to 1936. It was built for a prominent ironmaster when Sussex was the center of England's iron industry. Kipling's study looks exactly as it did when he lived here. The garden contains a water mill that still grinds flour; it is thought to be one of the oldest working water turbines. Close by, between Burwash Common and the river, is the setting for *Puck of Pook's Hill. Tel. 0435/882302. Admission: weekdays £3.50 adults, £1.80 children, Sun. and Good Friday £4 adults, £2 children. Open Apr.–Oct., Sat.–Wed. 11–5.*

Returning to A21, continue north to the town of **Lamberhurst** and England's largest vineyard. Thirty years ago, grape-growing in England was a rich man's hobby. Today it is an important rural industry, and the wines produced here are world-renowned. *Ridge Farm, tel. 0892/890844. Admission: guided tours £3 adults, £2.75 senior citizens. Tours given May–Oct.*

A visit to **Finchcocks,** an elegant Georgian mansion located between Lamberhurst and Goudhurst, is a must for music lovers. It contains a magnificent collection of historic keyboard instruments (**Finchcocks Living Museum of Music**), which are played whenever the house is open. (Demonstration recitals are included in the admission fee.) Concerts are held here during the spring and fall. *Goudhurst, tel. 0580/211702. Admission: £4.50 adults, £3 children. Open Apr.–July, Sept., Sun. and national holidays 2–6; Aug., Wed.–Sun. 2–6. Private visits by arrangement are welcomed.*

What to See and Do with Children

The seaside towns of the Southeast provide traditional entertainment for children of all ages.

The Children's Farm offers a trail through a 600-acre working farm with a variety of small tame wild animals as well as ordinary farm animals. Children can also make cream and butter to take home. A package deal with the Kent and Sussex steam railway allows you to visit the farm and ride the train. *Great Knell, Beckley, near Rye, tel. 0797/260250. Admission: £4 adults, £3 children and senior citizens. Open Mar. weekends for lambing; mid-Mar.–Sept., daily 10:30–5:30.*

Drusilla's Zoo Park has a miniature railroad and adventure playground. *Alfriston, East Sussex, tel. 0323/870234. Admission: £4.95 adults, £4.35 children, £3.35 senior citizens. Open daily 10:30–dusk.*

Howlett's Zoo Park includes tigers and gorillas, and many other animals. *Bekesbourne, near Canterbury, tel. 0227/721286. Admission: £6.50 adults, £4.50 children and senior citizens, £19 family ticket. Open Mar. 31–Dec.; summer, daily 10–5; winter, daily 10–4.*

The renovated **Sea Life Centre** in Brighton boasts the largest fish tank in Europe and the largest collection of sharks in Britain. *Marine Parade, tel. 0273/604233 or 0273/604234. Admission: £4.50 adults, £3.25 children, £3.75 senior citizens. Open Oct.–Mar., daily 10–5; Apr.–Oct., daily 10–6.*

Off the Beaten Track

Consider a visit to the Medway towns of **Rochester** and **Chatham** in north Kent. **Rochester** is closely associated with Charles Dickens; he lived at Gad's Hill Place, just outside town, for many years. The **Charles Dickens Centre** exhibits include life-size models of many of his characters. *Eastgate House, High St., tel. 0634/844176. Admission: £2.60 adults, £1.60 children and senior citizens, £6.80 family ticket. Open daily 10–5.*

You should also stop in at **Rochester Castle,** one of the finest surviving examples of Norman military architecture. The keep, built in the 1100s, partly based on the Roman city wall, is the tallest in England. *Tel. 0634/402276. Admission: £2 adults, £1 children, £1.50 senior citizens. Open Apr.–Oct., daily 10–6; Nov.–Mar., daily 10–4.*

Nearby is **Rochester Cathedral,** built in the 11th, 12th, and 14th centuries on a site consecrated in AD 604. *Tel. 0634/843366. Donation requested.*

From nearby **Chatham,** Royal Navy ships sailed to battle for hundreds of years. At the **Chatham Historic Dockyard** you can see the ancient Ropery in action, where great ship's hawsers are twisted, plus many other relics of Britain's naval heritage. *Alexandra Gate, Dock Rd., tel. 0634/812551. Admission: £5.50 adults, £2.75 children, £4.80 senior citizens, £12.75 family ticket. Open summer, Wed.–Sun., national holidays 10–6; winter, Wed., weekends 10–4:30.*

Between Dover and Folkestone, near Junction 12 of the M20 motorway, is the **Eurotunnel Exhibition Centre,** which tells the story of the building of the Channel Tunnel with all the best modern visual aids—including a full-size drilling rig. *Tel. 0303/270111. Ad-*

mission: £3.60 adults, £2.20 children and senior citizens. Open Tues.–Sun. 10–5 (6 in summer).

The Southeast also boasts three steam railroads. The **Romney, Hythe, and Dymchurch Railway** is a main-line service in miniature with locomotives one-third normal size. Some lucky children use it regularly to travel to school (New Romney Station, tel. 0679/62353). The **Bluebell Railway** is a full-size working railroad "museum" manned by enthusiastic volunteers. Steam trains run daily June to September, with reduced service at other times (Sheffield Park Station, near Uckfield, East Sussex, tel. 082572/3777). The **Kent and East Sussex Railway** is similar to the Bluebell line. Trains run daily July 16–Sept. 4, with service reduced at other times (Town Station, Tenterden, Kent, tel. 05806/2943).

The **Leonardslee Gardens** at Lower Beeding, about 15 miles north of Brighton (by A23 and A281), boast an impressive and colorful assortment of rhododendrons, azaleas, and camelias in May and an attractive display of autumn tints in the fall. There is a splendid new bonsai exhibit. The gardens celebrated their centenary in 1989. *Tel. 0403/891212. Admission: £3 adults Apr. and June–Oct., £4 May; children £2 all year. Open Apr.–Oct., daily 10–6; closed Nov.–Mar.*

For a pleasant excursion near Arundel, try the **Arun Riverside Walk,** starting from the Arundel town bridge. In about half an hour it brings you to the **Wildfowl Trust,** a preserve sheltering an assortment of England's wild birds. *Mill Rd., Arundel, West Sussex, tel. 0903/883355. Admission: £3.95 adults, £2 children, £2.95 senior citizens, £9.90 family ticket. Open Apr.–Oct., daily 9:30–6:30; Nov.–Mar., daily 9:30–5.*

Shopping

The Southeast has a wide range of sophisticated shops with London prices and is also particularly rich in crafts shops. The shops below are of outstanding quality.

Brighton   The main shopping area to head for is **The Lanes,** especially for antiques or jewelry. It also has clothing boutiques, coffee shops, and pubs. Across North Street from the Lanes lie the **North Lanes,** a network of narrow streets full of interesting little stores, less glossy than those in the Lanes, but sometimes more interesting—there are even street stalls on weekends.

The Pavilion Shop (4–5 Pavilion Bldgs., tel. 0273/603005) next door to the Pavilion not only carries well-designed souvenirs of Regency Brighton, but has high-quality fabrics, wallpapers, and ceramics based on material in the Pavilion itself.

Holleyman and Treacher (21A Duke St., at the western edge of the Lanes, tel. 0273/328007) is a book collector's dream, with a wealth of books on all subjects and a large stock of antique prints at all prices.

Pecksniff's Bespoke Perfumery (45/46 Meeting House La., tel. 0273/289404) has an original approach to the art of fragrance. In a room full of wooden drawers and brown glass bottles, Frank O'Brien will mix and match his ingredients to suit your wishes. The results are very attractive and far from expensive.

Canterbury   **National Trust Shop** (24 The Burgate, tel. 0227/457120) stocks the National Trust line of household items—ideal for gifts.

Lewes   **The Old Needle Makers** (12 Flitcroft St., tel. 0273/471582) is inside the shell of an early 19th-century candle and needle factory, just off the High Street, in a setting of huge beams and cobbled floors. Twenty small craft-based shops sell kitchenware, baskets, cosmetics, tops, and fire accessories.

Sports and the Outdoors

Golf Here are just a few of the golf courses that welcome visitors. **Brighton and Hove,** Dyke Rd., Brighton, tel. 0273/507861. **Guildford,** High Path Rd., Merrow, Guildford, tel. 0483/63941. **Leeds Castle,** Maidstone, tel. 0627/880467 (a scenically beautiful and challenging course). **Tunbridge Wells,** Langton Rd., Tunbridge Wells, tel. 0892/523034.

Walking Ardent walkers can explore both the **North Downs Way** (141 mi) and the **South Downs Way** (106 mi), following ancient paths along the tops of the downs. They both offer wide views over the countryside. The North Downs Way follows in part the ancient Pilgrims' Way to Canterbury. The South Downs Way crosses the chalk landscape of beautiful Sussex Downs, with parts of the route going through deep woodland. You can easily do short sections of both trails. Along the way, there are frequent towns and villages, mostly just off the main trail, all with handy old inns. The two routes are joined (north/south) by the 30-mile **Downs Link.** One way of seeing the Kent coast is to follow the **Saxon Shore Way,** 143 miles from Gravesend to Rye, passing through many historical sites, including four Roman forts. Section-by-section guides are available from the Southeast England Tourist Board (The Old Brew House, Warwick Park, Tunbridge Wells, Kent TN2 5TU, tel. 0892/540766.)

Water Sports **Bewl Water Activity Centre** (Lamberhurst, tel. 0892/890661) takes advantage of its location at one of England's largest reservoirs (just east of Wadhurst, 6 mi southeast of Tunbridge Wells by A267 and B2099), providing a wide range of aquatic sports. There's also an adventure playground.

Dining and Lodging

Dining Around the coast, seafood—much of it locally caught—is a specialty. You'll find not just fish-and-chips (though they are often at their best in the Southeast), but also local dishes such as Sussex smokies, and good international fish cuisine. In the larger towns, trendy restaurants tend to spring up for a time and then disappear. This is an area in which to experiment.

Highly recommended restaurants are indicated by a star ★.

Category	Cost*
$$$$	over £50
$$$	£40–£50
$$	£20–£40
$	under £20

per person, including first course, main course, dessert, and VAT; excluding drinks

Lodging The choice of accommodations runs from simple guest houses to luxury hotels. The seaside resorts can get booked up at the height of the season, especially Brighton and Eastbourne, which are also popular as conference centers.

Highly recommended lodgings are indicated by a star ★.

Category	Cost*
$$$$	over £150
$$$	£90–£150
$$	£50–£90
$	under £50

All prices are for two people sharing a double room, including service, breakfast, and VAT.

Arundel
Lodging

Avisford Park Hotel. This converted Georgian house, in 4 acres of parkland, is just 3 miles west of Arundel on B2132. It began as the home of an admiral and was a private school before its conversion into a hotel in 1974. The rooms have been carefully refurbished, with close attention to detail. The hotel is very popular for conferences. *Yapton La., Walberton BN18 0LS, tel. 0243/551215, fax 0243/552485. 126 rooms with bath. Facilities: restaurant, indoor and outdoor swimming pools, snooker room, squash court, tennis courts, sauna, solarium, fitness rooms, croquet, 9-hole golf course, horseback riding, helipad. AE, DC, MC, V. $$$*

Norfolk Arms Hotel. Like the cathedral and the castle in Arundel, this 18th-century coaching inn was also built by the dukes of Norfolk. The main body of the hotel is traditional in appearance, with lots of narrow passages and cozy little rooms. There is an annex with modern rooms in the courtyard block. *22 High St., BN18 9AD, tel. 0903/882101, fax 0903/884275. 34 rooms with bath. Facilities: restaurant, in-house movies, games room. AE, DC, MC, V. $$*

Battle
Dining

Orangery Restaurant. Located in the Powder Mills Hotel, a roadhouse just behind the abbey, the airy conservatory-style dining room makes a pleasant stop for lunch in a day of sightseeing. The food, especially the seafood, is surprisingly good; try the fish panache or the crab ravioli, with a homemade sorbet to follow. Set three-course menus are priced at £13.50 for lunch, £18.95 for dinner. Bar snacks are also available. *Powdermill La., tel. 0424/772035. Reservations advised. Dress: casual. AE, MC, V. $$*

Dining and Lodging

Netherfield Place. This is a spacious, quiet hotel, set in 30 acres of park and gardens. The large bedrooms are comfortably furnished, with plenty of cozy armchairs, and have well-equipped bathrooms (towels are especially thick). The paneled restaurant looks out at the gardens and features sensible fixed-price menus, as well as extensive table d'hôte ones. Try the pigeon breast salad, the Sussex lamb, local venison, and the home-grown vegetables. *TN33 9PP, tel. 0424/774455, fax 0424/774024. 14 rooms with bath. Facilities: restaurant, garden, tennis. Dress in restaurant: casual. AE, DC, MC, V. $$$*

Brighton
Dining
★

English's Oyster Bar. Buried in the Lanes, this is one of the few old-fashioned seafood havens left in England. It's been a family business for over 200 years. You can either eat succulent oysters and other seafood dishes at the counter or have a table in the restaurant section. It's ideal for lunch after antiques hunting. *29–31 East St., tel. 0273/327980. Reservations advised. Dress: casual. AE, DC, MC, V. $$$*

Donatello. This popular Italian restaurant in the Lanes has a brick wall and pine decor, bright with plants and checked cloths. The food is standard Italian, with an emphasis on pizzas. Donatello is a brother eatery to Pinocchio's, close to the Theatre Royal. *3 Brighton Pl., tel. 0273/774577. Reservations advised in summer. Dress: casual. AE, DC, MC, V. $$*

Brown's. Brown's, in the Lanes, is as near as Brighton gets to a brasserie. Popular with shoppers and the young, the menu on the blackboard changes daily—try the toasted goat's cheese or the scallop salads. It has recently opened a bar (with food) two doors down. *3–4 Duke St., tel. 0273/323501. Reservations not necessary. Dress: casual. AE, MC, V. $*

Deverell's. This tiny restaurant was the French Les Bouchons for years. In its new manifestation it is a welcoming and chic (wine and pink walls, pale blue tablecloths) little spot with two- and three-course, regularly changing set menus. The specialties are homemade soups, rabbit casserole, or salmon fricassee, and excellent fresh fish. *85 St. James St., tel. 0273/683152. Reservations advised. Dress: casual. AE, MC, V. Closed Tues. $*

Dining and Lodging **Brighton Thistle Hotel.** This hotel, a little east of the Grand, is built around a huge atrium, with sea views, and is very popular with conference delegates. It's smoothly designed, with an excellent color sense and ultramodern bedrooms, but on the pricey side for what it offers. The restaurant, **La Noblesse,** has delicious food, with not-too-expensive fixed menus. *King's Rd., BN1 2GS, tel. 0273/206700, fax 0273/820692. 204 rooms with bath. Facilities: restaurant, indoor pool, sauna, gym, in-house movies. AE, DC, MC, V. $$$$*

Granville Hotel. Located on hotel row, to the west of the Grand, the hotel has been converted from three former grand residences facing the sea. It is moderate in size, so service can be attentive. The bedrooms are all very comfortable; several are quite large, seven have four-poster beds, and two include Jacuzzis. The restaurant caters especially to vegetarians. *123 King's Rd., BN1 2FA, tel. 0273/326302, fax 0273/728294. 25 rooms with bath. Facilities: restaurant, bar, coffee shop, solarium. AE, DC, MC, V. $$*

★ **Topps.** Two Regency houses have been turned into this attractive hotel, run by the owners, Paul and Pauline Collins. All the rooms are attractive and well equipped, with lush bathrooms. The atmosphere is relaxed, friendly, and highly recommendable. The basement restaurant, called, appropriately, **Bottoms,** is worth a visit even if you're not staying at the hotel. The interesting fixed-price menu is prepared by Pauline Collins, and reservations are a must. *17 Regency Sq., BN1 2FG, tel. 0273/729334, fax 0273/203679. 14 rooms with bath. Facilities: restaurant. AE, DC, MC, V. Dinner only. Closed Sun. and Wed. eves., and Jan. $$*

Lodging **The Grand Hotel.** This classic old hotel, on the seafront site of a bomb attack on Prime Minister Margaret Thatcher, has recently been refurbished for the second time in a decade. The decor, especially in the public rooms, is of the spectacular chandelier-and-marble variety, but the bedrooms are traditionally comfortable. The restaurant has a good reputation. *King's Rd., BN1 2FW, tel. 0273/321188, fax 0273/202694. 163 rooms with bath. Facilities: restaurant, indoor pool, solarium, sauna. AE, DC, MC, V. $$$$*

Claremont House. The Claremont is in Hove, Brighton's twin town to the west, but still within walking distance of Brighton's attractions. Hove has the advantage of being less raffish than Brighton; the town is full of large, elegant, Victorian buildings, such as the Claremont. This B&B has comfortably sized rooms, each with a TV and facilities for making tea or coffee. There is also a reasonably priced restaurant on the premises. Room prices are less on weekends. *34 2nd Ave., Hove BN3 2LL, tel. 0273/735161, fax 0273/*

324764. 12 rooms, 9 with bath or shower. Facilities: restaurant. AE, DC, MC, V. $$

The Dove. An alternative if Topps (*see above*) is full, The Dove, next door, is another well-converted Regency house where you will receive a warm welcome from its husband-and-wife owners. Four of the rooms have a sideways sea view from their bow windows. There is no restaurant, but there is an à la carte breakfast. *18 Regency Sq., BN1 2FG, tel. 0273/779222, fax 0273/746912. 8 rooms with bath. AE, MC, V. $$*

Canterbury
Dining

George's Brasserie. This stylish bistro in a long, narrow upstairs room has predominantly French cuisine chalked on a blackboard. Try the fresh salmon, served hot and marinated with fresh herbs. There's a fine choice of cheeses, including sheep and goat cheese; the desserts are filling and old-fashioned. *72 Castle St., tel. 0227/ 765658. Reservations advised. Dress: casual. AE, DC, MC, V. Closed Sun. evening. $$*

Dining and
Lodging

County. This traditional English hotel was first licensed in the year of the Spanish Armada, 1588, and it still maintains certain links with the past—ask for a room with a four-poster bed. The bar is pleasantly traditional, and the formal **Sully's Restaurant** has a reputation as a gourmet's choice. *High St., CT1 2RX, tel. 0227/766266, fax 0227/ 451512. 74 rooms with bath. Facilities: restaurant, bar, coffee shop. Restaurant: reservations required; jacket and tie required. AE, DC, MC, V. $$$*

Slatters. The site on which this hotel is built has been occupied since Roman times, and a tiny section of Roman foundations can be seen in the cellar under the restaurant. Elsewhere there are Tudor beams and a medieval wall, but the main attraction of the hotel is its strictly 20th-century comfort, well-furnished guest rooms, restaurant, and bars. *St. Margaret's St., CT1 2DR, tel. 0227/463271, fax 0227/ 764117. 32 rooms, 28 with bath. Facilities: restaurant, bars. Restaurant: reservations required; jacket and tie required. AE, DC, MC, V. $$*

Lodging

Pointers. A friendly hotel in a Georgian building, within easy walking distance of the cathedral and city center (straight out beyond Westgate). *1 London Rd., CT2 8LR, tel. 0227/456846, fax 0227/ 831131. 14 rooms, 10 with bath or shower. Facilities: restaurant. AE, DC, MC, V. $$*

Chichester
Dining

Comme Ça. This attractively converted pub is about a five-minute walk across the park from the Festival Theatre, making it a very good spot for a meal before a performance. Plenty of dried hops, suspended from the ceiling, and antique children's toys decorate the dining room. The Norman owner, Michel Navet, also the chef, cooks authentic French dishes, and simpler fare is served in the bar at much lower prices. *67 Broyle Rd., tel. 0243/788724. Reservations advised. Dress: casual. MC, V. Closed Sun. evening, Mon. $$$*

Droveway. This restaurant was formerly Thompsons, but has been given a new name and a face-lift—softening the rather spartan surroundings. There is now, for instance, a cozy reception area on the spacious second floor. But the cuisine is still inventive; try the calves' liver with shredded celeriac and balsamic vinegar, or the honeyed magret of duck with burnt orange. *30A Southgate, tel. 0243/528832. Reservations advised. Dress: casual. AE, MC, V. Closed Sun., Mon. lunch. $$*

Micawbers. You're sure to find something tasty here. Despite its Dickensian name, this is a provincial French restaurant, especially good for local seafood. *13 South St., tel. 0243/786989. Reservations advised. Dress: casual. AE, DC, MC, V. Closed Sun. $$*

Lodging **Dolphin and Anchor Hotel.** This hotel across from the cathedral was once two separate inns, the Dolphin and the Anchor, both much older than the 18th-century facade. Locals and visitors naturally gravitate to the hotel, for it hosts everything from conferences to family occasions. The modern guest rooms are colorful and attractively decorated. *West St., PO19 1QE, tel. 0243/785121, fax 0243/533408. 49 rooms with bath. Facilities: restaurant. AE, DC, MC, V. $$$*

Ship Hotel. Staying in this hotel is something of an architectural experience. Built in 1790, it was originally the home of Admiral Sir George Murray (one of Admiral Nelson's right-hand men). Outstanding features are the classic Adam staircase and colonnade. The hotel, which has recently changed hands, is gradually being restored to its 18th-century elegance. It is close to the Festival Theatre. *North St., PO19 1NH, tel. 0243/778000, fax 0243/788000. 36 rooms with bath. Facilities: restaurant. AE, DC, MC, V. $$*

Cranbrook **Kennel Holt Hotel.** This is a quiet hotel in a redbrick Elizabethan
Dining and manor house, surrounded by beautiful, well-kept gardens. Visitors
Lodging are treated like guests in a private house. The library, for example,
★ is well stocked with books for that rainy day. The restaurant serves sole accompanied by asparagus and Mornay sauce and lamb with red currants and port. Antiques and flowers grace the restaurant as well as the rest of the hotel. There's a separate restaurant for nonresidents. *Goudhurst Rd., TN17 2PT, tel. 0580/712032, fax 0580/715495. 10 rooms, 8 with bath or shower. Facilities: 2 restaurants, croquet, in-house movies. Restaurant: reservations required; jacket and tie required. AE, DC, MC, V. $$$*

Dorking **Partners West Street.** Behind the genuine 16th-century, half-tim-
Dining bered facade is a grand, well-established restaurant, at least downstairs, where expensive fabrics are in plentiful use. Upstairs is more relaxed. Lunch is à la carte, but dinner offers a choice of set-price menus. Try the red snapper with ratatouille, breast of duck with mango, or the calf's liver with bubble and squeak. *2–4 West St., tel. 0306/882826. Reservations advised. Jacket and tie required. AE, DC, MC, V. Closed Sat. lunch, Sun. evening, Mon. $$$*

Lodging **The White Horse.** For a taste of both ancient and modern, stay at this inn. The foundations of the hotel probably go back to the 13th century, while the interior is mostly 18th-century and has been attractively—but carefully—brought up-to-date. All the rooms are cheerfully furnished and offer high standards of comfort. There is an adequate if unremarkable restaurant. *High St., RH4 1BE, tel. 0306/881138, fax 0306/887241. 68 rooms with bath. Facilities: restaurant, pool. AE, DC, MC, V. $$$*

Dover **Number One.** This popular guest house is a great bargain. A corner
Lodging terrace home built at the beginning of the 19th century, it's cozy and friendly, decorated with mural wallpapers and porcelain collections. The walled garden offers a view of the castle, and the owners are happy to give advice on local sightseeing. *1 Castle St., CT16 1QH, tel. 0304/202007. 6 rooms with bath or shower. Facilities: garden. No credit cards. $$*

Faversham **Read's.** Just outside Faversham, this restaurant is quite a find. The
Dining food, French-oriented, is magnificent, the work of chef/proprietor David Pitchford. In elegant surroundings he presents cuisine to challenge the serious eater. The menu changes every six weeks, but might include a comparison of wild and farmed salmon, for example, in the same dish. Try breast of Gressingham duck dressed with foie gras and Sauternes, or veal normande. The wine list contains some

unusual bottles. This is an excellent spot for lunch, at which there's a set menu from £14.50. *Painters Forstal (2¼ mi southwest of Faversham on A2), tel. 0795/535344. Reservations required. Dress: neat but casual. AE, DC, MC, V. Closed Sun., Mon., and 2 weeks in Aug. $$$*

Dining and Lodging
★

The White Horse Inn. Just outside Faversham on the old London to Dover road (now A2), this 15th-century coaching inn retains much of its traditional character, although it has been fully and comfortably modernized. There's a friendly bar and an excellent restaurant specializing in steak and lobster dishes. The back rooms are the most quiet. *The Street, Boughton ME13 9AX, tel. 0227/751343, fax 0227/751090. 13 rooms with bath or shower. Facilities: restaurant, bar. Restaurant: reservations required; dress: casual. AE, DC, MC, V. $$*

Guildford Dining
★

Rumwong. The elegant waitresses at this Thai restaurant wear their traditional long-skirted costumes, so at busy times the dining room looks like a swirling flower garden. On the incredibly long menu, the Thai name of each dish is given with a clear English description. Try the fisherman's soup, a mass of delicious saltwater fish in a clear broth, or *yam pla muek*, a hot salad with squid. *16–18 London Rd., tel. 0483/36092. Reservations required Fri. and Sat. Dress: casual. MC, V. Closed Mon. $$*

Lodging
★

The Angel. The Angel was the last of the old coaching inns for which Guildford was famous. The courtyard, into which coaches and horses rattled, is still open to the sky, and light lunches are served here in summer. The hotel is at least 400 years old and is even said to have a ghost. Guest rooms have attractive fabrics, reproduction antiques, and marble-lined bathrooms. There's an excellent restaurant in the medieval stone cellar and an informal coffee shop for light refreshments. The hotel, now under new management, has been redecorated. *91 High St., GU1 3DP, tel. 0483/64555, fax 0483/33770. 11 rooms with bath. Facilities: restaurant, coffee shop. AE, DC, MC, V. $$$*

Carlton Hotel. This old-fashioned Victorian house has been converted into a modern hotel with pleasant rooms. There's a restaurant and bar and adequate parking. *36–40 London Rd., GU1 2AF, tel. 0483/576539, fax 0483/34669. 36 rooms, 19 with bath. Facilities: restaurant, bar. AE, MC, V. $$*

Haslemere Dining
★

Morels. Chef Jean-Yves Morel is also the proprietor of this prize-winning restaurant, one of the best in the country. Several cottages were converted into an interesting, varied dining space, cool—white and blue—and intimate. Specialties, which change regularly, have included terrine of confit of duck and venison with a game sauce and chestnut mousse. *23 Lower St., tel. 0428/651462. Reservations required. Jacket and tie required. AE, DC, MC, V. Closed Sat. lunch, Sun., Mon. $$$$*

Hastings Dining

Rösers. This restaurant takes food very seriously. It stands opposite the pier and has dark walls with booths for dining. Chef/proprietor Röser is a German, and his cuisine is both German and French. Try the game sausages with wild boar bacon, or the chicken breasts with wild mushrooms. The desserts are scrumptious, especially the Belgian chocolate mousse. There are reasonably priced set menus. *64 Eversfield Pl., St. Leonards, tel. 0424/712218. Reservations required. Dress: casual but neat. AE, DC, MC, V. Closed Sat. lunch, Sun., Mon. $$$*

Lodging

Eagle House. This guest house, located in a large detached Victorian building, stands in its own attractive garden. In St. Leonards, the western section of Hastings, the lodging is within easy reach of the town center. The rooms are spacious and comfortable, and the dining room uses fresh produce from local farms. *12 Pevensy Rd., St. Leonards TN38 0JZ, tel. 0424/430535. 22 rooms, 19 with bath. Facilities: restaurant, garden. AE, DC, MC, V. $$*

Herstmonceux **The Sundial.** An old Sussex farmhouse, skillfully enlarged, provides
Dining the setting for this popular restaurant, which chef Giuseppe Bartoli
★ and his French wife, Laurette, have run since 1966. The menu is extensive, with some imaginative combinations. The fish dishes are particularly successful and the vegetables fresh and expertly cooked. The Dover sole flavored with thyme is recommended. *Gardner St., tel. 0323/832217. Reservations required. Dress: casual. AE, DC, MC, V. Closed Sun. evening, Mon. $$$$*

Lewes **Léonies.** This friendly restaurant-cum-bistro is in a big converted
Dining shop by the war memorial on High Street. It has old portraits, greenery, polished wood floors, and bentwood chairs. The food is hearty—try the Suffolk steak-and-ale pie, or the rabbit-and-prune stew. *197 High St., tel. 0273/487766. Reservations not necessary. Dress: casual. MC, V. Closed Sun. $*

Lodging **Shelleys.** An elegant 17th-century building in this town of attractive architecture, the hotel is on the hilly main road, and is a traditional overnight stop for visitors to the opera at Glyndebourne. Many antiques are scattered about, the wisteria on the facade is splendid in season, and the garden is a constant joy. The hotel maintains a reputation for old-fashioned, friendly service. Have lunch in either the bar or the more formal dining room. *High St., BN7 1XS, tel. 0273/472361, fax 0273/483152. 21 rooms with bath. Facilities: restaurant, bar, garden. AE, DC, MC, V. $$$*

Rye **Landgate Bistro.** Although definitely a bistro, with all its liveliness
Dining and bustle, the Landgate is serious about its food. It has won
★ awards—and deserved them. Try the scallops and brill in an orange and vermouth sauce—all the local fish is excellent—or the walnut and treacle tart. In an old, small building, in keeping with Rye's atmosphere, the restaurant attracts a steady local clientele. A fixed-price menu is available Tuesday through Thursday. *5–6 Landgate, tel. 0797/222829. Reservations required. Dress: casual. AE, MC, V. Open Tues.–Sat. evenings only. $$*

Dining and **The Mermaid.** This classic old inn has served this ancient town for
Lodging nearly six centuries; it was once the headquarters of one of the notorious smuggling gangs that ruled the Romney Marshes. Its age can be seen in every nook and cranny, with sloping, creaky floors, oak beams and low ceilings, a huge open hearth in the bar, and three four-poster beds. Every detail in this inn will make the seeker of atmosphere very happy. But be warned, the Mermaid is *very* popular with tourists. *Mermaid St., TN31 7EU, tel. 0797/223065, fax 0797/226995. 28 rooms, 25 with bath. Facilities: restaurant. AE, DC, MC, V. $$$*

Lodging **Jeake's House.** The cozy bedrooms in this lovely old house (1689), on the same cobblestoned street as the Mermaid (*see above*), are furnished with antiques, and many have views over the town. Breakfast is served in a former chapel. *Mermaid St., TN31 7ET, tel. 0797/222828, fax 0797/222623. 12 rooms, 10 with bath or shower. AE, MC, V. $$*

Tonbridge **Rose and Crown.** This was originally a 16th-century inn and it fea-
Lodging tures a distinctive portico, added later. Inside, low-beamed ceilings and Jacobean woodwork make both the bars and the restaurant snug

and inviting. Guest rooms in the main building are traditionally furnished, while in the new annex they are more modern in style; all are attractive and cozy. *125 High St., TN9 1DD, tel. 0732/357966, fax 0732/357194. 51 rooms with bath. Facilities: restaurant, bars, garden. AE, DC, MC, V. $$$*

Tunbridge Wells
Dining

Thackeray's House. Gourmets flock to this mid-17th-century house, once the home of Victorian novelist William Makepeace Thackeray. Its owner, Bruce Wass, is also the chef and tolerates none but the freshest ingredients. Everything is cooked with great flair and imagination. Specialties include warm scallop and skate salad with ginger vinaigrette and chocolate Armagnac loaf with coffee sauce. Below the main restaurant, there is a friendly little bistro, **Downstairs at Thackeray's,** with food every bit as good as upstairs, but less expensive (entrance in the courtyard). *85 London Rd., tel. 0892/ 511921. Reservations required. Jacket and tie required. MC, V. Closed Sun., Mon., and Christmas week. $$$$*

Sankey's. This double eatery features a lively basement wine bar and a more staid upstairs restaurant. The wine bar has inexpensive food—try the Moroccan lamb—while the restaurant specializes in wonderfully fresh fish. The *soupe de poissons* is excellent, and there's a good selection of British cheeses. *39 Mount Ephraim, tel. 0892/511422. Reservations advised for restaurant. Dress: casual. AE, DC, MC, V. $$*

Lodging

Spa Hotel. Carefully chosen furnishings and details help give this Georgian mansion the atmosphere of a country house, though guest rooms are equipped with many thoughtful modern extras. This hotel is run by the Goring family, who also own the Goring hotel in London. The extensive grounds give superb views across the town and into the Weald of Kent. The **Chandelier Restaurant** is very popular with locals. *Mount Ephraim, TN4 8XJ, tel. 0892/520331, fax 0892/ 510575. 75 rooms with bath. Facilities: restaurant, indoor pool, sauna, tennis, croquet, jogging track, hairdresser, Jacuzzi. AE, DC, MC, V. $$$*

The Old Parsonage. This very comfortable and friendly guest house, 2 miles south of Tunbridge Wells via the A267, stands beside the village church. Built in 1820, the place has a country house feel to it, with lovely old furniture, including two four-posters, and a big conservatory for afternoon tea. The lodging stands amid 3 acres of grounds. *Church La., Frant TN3 9DX, tel. 0892/750773. 3 rooms with bath. No credit cards. $$*

Uckfield
Dining and Lodging
★

Horsted Place. Just a few minutes' drive from Glyndebourne, this very special hotel once belonged to Prince Philip's treasurer, and it frequently accommodated the queen and other members of the royal family. It is still beautifully furnished and has such interesting features as a magnificent Victorian staircase and a Gothic library with a secret door that leads to a hidden courtyard. The dining room— Gothic like the library—offers superb haute cuisine (try the pot roast quail). *Little Horsted (2½ mi from Uckfield), TN22 5TS, tel. 0825/750581, fax 0825/750459. 17 rooms with bath. Facilities: restaurant, gardens, indoor pool, tennis, golf. AE, DC, MC, V. $$$$*

Wadhurst
Dining and Lodging

Spindlewood Hotel. This 19th-century country-house hotel, set on 5 acres of garden and woodland well off the main road (6 mi from Tunbridge Wells via A267 and B2099), has built its reputation around its restaurant. Specialties include medallions of venison marinated with juniper berries. *Wallcrouch, Wadhurst TN5 7JG, tel. 0580/ 200430, fax 0580/201132. 9 rooms with bath. Facilities: restaurant. Reservations required; dress: casual. MC, V. $$*

The Arts

Festivals The Southeast is a region of festivals, particularly for music and drama. In Kent, **Canterbury** has a three-week-long arts festival every October (tel. 0227/452853). There are **Dickens festivals** in June in two towns associated with the writer: **Rochester** (tel. 0634/843666) and **Broadstairs** (tel. 0843/63453). The **Brighton Festival** (tel. 0273/676926), an international event held every May, covers drama, music from classical to rock, dance, visual arts, and literature.

Opera **Glyndebourne Opera House** (Glyndebourne, near Lewes, East Sussex, tel. 0273/812321) is one of the world's leading opera houses. Nestled beneath the downs and surrounded by superb gardens, Glyndebourne combines excellent productions, a lovely setting, and a sense of timelessness. Seats are *very* expensive but worth every cent to the aficionado. The rebuilt auditorium opened in 1994. Seating a slightly larger audience than the original house, it is equipped with the latest in stage gadgetry and backstage facilities, and tickets are even more difficult to get than they were before.

Theater Canterbury has two main theaters. The **Gulbenkian Theatre** (Giles La., tel. 0227/769075), part of the University of Kent, mounts a full range of plays, particularly experimental works. The **Marlowe** (St. Margaret's St., tel. 0227/767246) is named after the Elizabethan playwright, atheist, and spy, who was born in Canterbury.

The Festival Theatre, Chichester (tel. 0243/781312), presents middle-of-the-road productions of classics and modern plays for the undemanding theatergoer from May to September. Like Glyndebourne (*see above*), it has an international reputation and can be the evening focus for a relaxed day out of London.

Brighton has several theaters. **The Dome** (tel. 0273/674357), beside the Pavilion, was converted into an auditorium from the prince regent's stables in the 1930s. It stages classical and pop concerts. The **Theatre Royal** (New Rd., tel. 0273/328488), close to the Pavilion, is a very attractive Regency building with a period gem of an auditorium. It is a favorite venue for shows either on their way to or fresh from London's West End. The **Gardner Centre for the Arts** (tel. 0273/685861), on the campus of Sussex University, a few miles northeast of town at Falmer, presents plays, concerts, and cabaret.

In Guildford, Surrey, the **Yvonne Arnaud Theatre** (Milbrook, tel. 0483/60191) is an unusual horseshoe-shaped building on an island in the River Wey. It frequently previews West End productions, and also has a restaurant.

5 The South

Winchester, Salisbury, Stonehenge

The South, made up of Hampshire (Hants), Dorset, and Wiltshire, offers a wide range of attractions and quiet pleasures. Two important cathedrals, Winchester and Salisbury (pronounced Sawlsbry), are here; stately homes, attractive market towns, and literally hundreds of prehistoric remains, two of which, Avebury and Stonehenge, should not be missed.

The landscape of the South incorporates the gentle, garden-like features of London's home counties, and the bleaker, harsher terrain of Salisbury Plain surrounding Stonehenge, and the Dorset heathlands. The region is spanned by rolling grass-covered chalk hills—the Downs—wooded valleys and meadows through which flow deep rivers. The dairy herds of Dorset's meadows are famous for their rich cream. The southern coast has protected harbors and sandy beaches and perilous stretches, too, such as the Fossil Coast of Lyme Regis, or Chesil Bank, where the tides and currents strike fear into the hearts of sailors.

This area has been quietly central to England's history for well over 4,000 years, occupied successively by prehistoric man, the Celts, the Romans, and the Saxons—Winchester was Alfred the Great's capital in the late 9th century, and the seat of Wessex, one of the original seven Anglo-Saxon kingdoms. History has continued to be made here, right up to the modern era. Forces sailed from ports along this coast for Normandy on D-Day, and to recover the Falklands nearly 40 years later.

Essential Information

Important Addresses and Numbers

Tourist Information

The Southern Tourist Board, 40 Chamberlayne Rd., Eastleigh, Hants S05 5JH, tel 0703/620006, fax 0703/620010. Open Mon.–Thurs. 8:30–5, Fri. 8:30–4:30. Local TICs are normally open Mon.–Sat. 9:30–5:30.

Bournemouth: Westover Rd. (overlooking the bandstand), tel. 0202/789789.

Dorchester: 1 Acland Rd., tel. 0305/267992.

Portsmouth: The Hard, tel. 0705/826722; Clarence Esplanade, Southsea, tel. 0705/832464.

Ryde: Western Esplanade (near hovercraft terminal), tel. 0983/562905.

Salisbury: Fish Row (just off Market Sq.), tel. 0722/334956.

Winchester: The Guildhall, The Broadway, tel. 0962/840500.

Travel Agencies

American Express: 99 Above Bar, Southampton, Hants SO9 1FY, tel. 0703/634722.

Thomas Cook: 7 Richmond Hill, Bournemouth, Dorset BH2 6HF, tel. 0202/299766; 19 High St., Ryde, Isle of Wight PO33 2HW, tel. 0983/567314; 18 Queen St., Salisbury, Wilts SP1 1EY, tel. 0722/412787; and 30 High St., Winchester, Hants SO23 9BL, tel. 0962/841661.

Car-Rental Agencies

Bournemouth: Avis, Hendy Lennox Ltd., 17A Christchurch Rd., Lansdowne, tel. 0202/293218; **Hertz,** Palace Parking, Hinton Rd., tel. 0202/291231.

Salisbury: EuroDollar Rent-a-Car, Lex Vauxhall, Brunel Rd., Churchfields Industrial Estate, tel. 0722/335117; **Europcar Ltd.,** Fisherton Yard, Fisherton St., tel. 0722/335625.

Arriving and Departing

By Car The South is linked to London and other major cities by a well-developed road network, which includes M3 to Winchester (59 mi); M3 and A33 to Southampton (77 mi); A3 to Portsmouth (70 mi), and M27 along the coast, from Southampton to Portsmouth. A30 (off M3) is the main route to Salisbury. A31 connects Bournemouth to Dorchester and the rest of Dorset.

By Train **British Rail** serves the South from London's Waterloo Station (tel. 071/928–5100). Travel times average an hour to Winchester; 1¼ hours to Southampton; two hours to Bournemouth; and 2½ hours to Weymouth. Portsmouth takes an hour and 40 minutes, and Salisbury about the same. There is at least one fast train every hour on all these routes.

By Bus **National Express** (tel. 071/730–0202) buses from London's Victoria Coach Station depart hourly for Southampton (2½ hrs) and Portsmouth (also 2½ hrs). Buses leave every two hours for Winchester (2 hrs), Bournemouth (2½ hrs), and Salisbury (2¾ hrs).

Getting Around

By Plane There is a small airport at Southampton, useful for flights to the Channel Islands (*see* Chapter 7). *Information tel. 0703/629600.*

By Car The area covered in this chapter involves very easy driving. In northeast Hampshire and in many parts of neighboring Wiltshire there are lanes overhung by trees and lined with thatched cottages and Georgian houses. Often the network of such lanes starts immediately as you leave a main highway. Salisbury Plain has long, straight roads surrounded by endless vistas, and the problem here is to keep to the speed limit!

By Train A "Hants (Hampshire) and Dorset Rover" ticket is valid throughout the region for seven days, or you can get a "Network SouthEast" card, valid for a year, which entitles you to one-third off particular fares. For local information, call British Rail Bournemouth, tel. 0202/292474; Salisbury, tel. 0722/27591, or Southampton and Winchester, tel. 0703/229393.

By Bus **Hampshire Bus** (tel. 0962/52352) has a comprehensive service in the Southampton, Eastleigh, Winchester, Andover, and Basingstoke areas. **Southern Vectis** (tel. 0983/62264) covers the Isle of Wight; ask about its "Rover" tickets. **Wilts (Wiltshire) & Dorset Bus Co.** (tel. 0202/673555) offers both one-day "Explorer" and seven-day "Busabout" tickets; it also conducts "Explorer Special" tours around Bournemouth.

By Ferry **Sealink British Ferries** (tel. 0304/203203) operates a car-ferry service between the mainland and the Isle of Wight. The crossing takes about 35 minutes from Lymington to Yarmouth; 40 minutes from Portsmouth to Fishbourne. **Red Funnel Ferries** (tel. 0703/330333) run a car-ferry and hydrofoil service between Southampton and Cowes. **Hovertravel** (tel. 0705/811000 and 0983/811000) has a hovercraft shuttle between Southsea and Ryde.

Guided Tours

The **Southern Tourist Board** (tel. 0703/620006) and **Wessexplore** (tel. 0722/326304) can reserve qualified Blue Badge guides who will arrange to meet you anywhere in the region for private tours of different lengths and themes.

Guide Friday (tel. 0789/294466) has a Stonehenge tour from Salisbury, Easter to early-October, costing £10.50 adults, £5.50 children, and £9.50 senior citizens, but check for availability.

Exploring the South

We begin our tour in the lovely cathedral city of Winchester, 64 miles southwest of London. From there we meander southward to the coast, stopping at the bustling ports of Southampton and Portsmouth before striking out for the restful shores of the Isle of Wight, vacation home to Queen Victoria. The island is keenly aware of tourism, and it is always worthwhile asking about the latest package tours.

Returning to the mainland, the second tour swings northwest to Salisbury, renowned for its glorious cathedral, then loops west around Salisbury Plain, up to Avebury, and back to Stonehenge, in Wiltshire. From Stonehenge we dip south to the wild, scenic expanse of the New Forest, ancient hunting preserve of William the Conqueror. Our final tour follows the Dorset coastline, immortalized by Thomas Hardy and John Fowles, taking in Bournemouth, Dorchester, Weymouth, Lyme Regis, and a host of picturesque and historic villages.

Highlights for First-time Visitors

Avebury: Tour 2
Carisbrooke Castle: Tour 1
Corfe Castle: Tour 3.
HMS *Victory* and *Mary Rose*: Tour 1
Longleat: Tour 2
Maiden Castle: Tour 3
Salisbury Cathedral: Tour 2
Stonehenge: Tour 2
Stourhead Gardens: Tour 2
Wilton House: Tour 2
Winchester Cathedral: Tour 1

Tour 1: From Winchester to the Isle of Wight

Numbers in the margin correspond to points of interest on the Winchester and South maps.

❶ **Winchester** is among the most historic of English cities, and as you walk its graceful, unspoiled streets, a sense of the past envelops you. Though it is now merely the county seat of Hampshire, for more than four centuries Winchester served as England's capital. Here, in AD 827, Egbert was crowned first king of England, and his successor, Alfred the Great, held court until his death in 899. After the Norman Conquest in 1066, William I ("the Conqueror") had himself crowned in London, but took the precaution of repeating the ceremony in Winchester. The city remained the center of ecclesiastical, commercial, and political power until the 13th century. It was renowned throughout Europe for its illuminated manuscripts, some of which you can still see in the cathedral library.

❷ Start your tour at the **Cathedral,** the city's greatest monument, begun in 1079 and consecrated in 1093. In the cathedral's tower, transepts, and crypt, as in the core of the great nave, you can see some of the world's best surviving examples of Norman architecture. Other features, such as the arcades, the clerestory (the wall dividing the

The South

Mouth of the Severn

Bristol

Avon

M5

AVON

A37

A46

Bath

M4

Calne

A4

Melksham

Devizes

WILTSHIRE

Weston-super-Mare

Trowbridge

B3098

A361

A360

Westbury

Frome

A3098

Warminster

34 Longleat House

B3092

SALISBURY PLAIN

Wells

Shepton Mallet

SOMERSET

A37

33 Stourhead House

A303

Wyly

Tisbury

Swallowcliffe

A30

Nad

B3092

B3081

32 Shaftesbury

Sherborne

Yeovil

A303

Illminster

A352

DORSET

Blandford Forum

48 Cerne Abbas

Wimbourne Minster

43

A349

Godmanstone

Tolpuddle

Bridport

A35

A35

54

A35

Lyme Regis

B3157

47 Dorchester

Frome

Piddle

A351

Poole

44

Lyme Bay

49 Maiden Castle

A352

Wareham

Brownsea Island

45

53 Abbotsbury

A353

PURBECK HILLS

A351

46

B3070

Corfe Castle

B3351

Chesil Beach

52

50 Weymouth

B3157

A354

Lulworth Cove

N

GREAT BRITAIN

51 Isle of Portland

0 ___ 10 miles

0 ___ 15 km

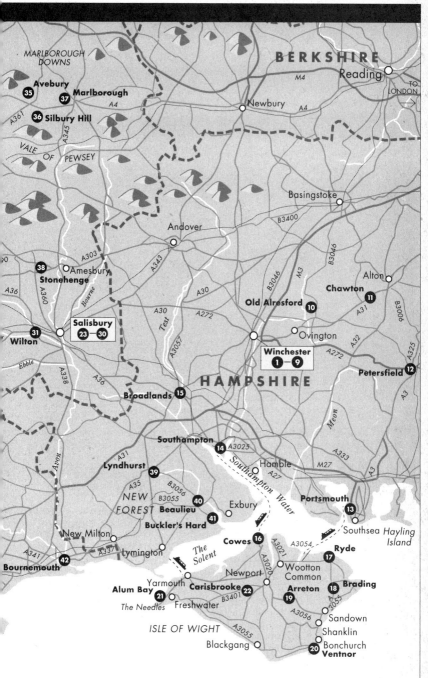

Cathedral, **2**
City Mill, **8**
City Museum, **7**
The Close, **3**
Great Hall, **6**
King's Gate/St.
Swithin's
Church, **4**
St. Giles's Hill, **9**
Winchester
College, **5**

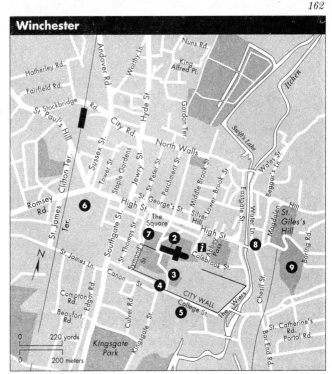

Winchester

aisles from the nave), and the windows, are Gothic alterations carried out during the 12th and 13th centuries. The remodeling of the nave in the Perpendicular style (*see* The Basics of British Architecture in Chapter 2) was not completed until the 15th century. Little of the original stained glass has survived, thanks to Cromwell's Puritan troops, who ransacked the cathedral in the 17th century, during the English Civil War.

Among the well-known people buried in the cathedral are William the Conqueror's son, William II (Rufus), mysteriously murdered in the New Forest in 1100; Izaak Walton, author of *The Compleat Angler*, whose memorial window in Silkestede's Chapel was paid for by "the fishermen of England and America"; and Jane Austen, whose memorial window can be seen in the north aisle of the nave. In the retro-choir, look for the statuette of William Walker, the diver, "who saved this cathedral with his two hands." This curious inscription refers to Walker's heroic underpinning of the building's flooded foundations (1906–12), when the medieval ones proved too shallow.

❸ Behind the cathedral is the **Close,** an area containing the Deanery, Dome Alley, and Cheyney Court. On the right, as you enter
❹ Cheyney Court, you will see the **King's Gate,** built in the 13th century, one of two gates remaining from the original city wall. **St. Swithin's Church** is built over the King's Gate. Turn left onto College Street and proceed to No. 8, the house where Jane Austen died on July 18, 1817, three days after writing a comic poem (copies are usually available in the cathedral) about the legend of St. Swithin's Day.

⑤ Continue along College Street to **Winchester College,** founded in 1382, probably England's oldest "public" school. Among the original buildings still in use is Chamber Court, center of college life for six centuries. Look out for "scholars"—students holding academic scholarships—clad in their traditional gowns. *College St., tel. 0962/ 868778. Admission: £2 adults, £1.50 children and senior citizens. Guided tours last about an hour (must be booked in advance) Apr.– Sept., Mon.–Sat. 11:15, 2:15, and 3:30, Sun. 2:15 and 3:30.*

Time Out Try a half-pint of draft bitter or dry cider at **The Royal Oak** (Royal Oak Passage, off High St.), a traditional pub which claims to have Britain's oldest bar (it has a Saxon wall). Unusually, it has a non-smoking cellar bar.

⑥ A few blocks west of the cathedral is the medieval **Great Hall,** which is all that remains of the city's castle. The English Parliament met here for the first time in 1246; Sir Walter Raleigh was tried for conspiracy against King James I and condemned to death here in 1603 (though he wasn't beheaded until 1618); and Dame Alice Lisle was sentenced here by the infamous Judge Jeffreys (*see* Dorchester in Tour 3 *below*) to be burned at the stake for sheltering a fugitive, following Monmouth's Rebellion in 1685. (King James II, in a rare act of mercy, commuted her sentence to beheading.) On the west wall of the hall hangs what is said to be King Arthur's Round Table, with places for 24 knights, and a portrait of Arthur, which bears a remarkable resemblance to King Henry VII. In fact, the table is a Tudor forgery; the real Arthur was probably a Celtic cavalry general who held off the invading Saxons following the fall of the Roman Empire. Henry VII revived the Arthurian legend for political purposes. He named his eldest son Arthur, though the boy did not live to inherit the throne. *Castle Hill, tel. 0962/846476. Admission free. Open Mar.–Oct., daily 10–5; Nov.–Feb., weekdays 10–5, weekends 10–4.*

⑦ Retrace your steps along High Street to **The Square,** across from the cathedral, and in the **City Museum** have a look at Winchester's past through Celtic pottery, Roman mosaics, and Saxon coins. *The Square, tel. 0962/848269. Admission free. Open Apr.–Sept., Mon.– Sat. 10–5, Sun. 2–5; Oct.–Mar., Tues.–Sat. 10–5, Sun. 2–4.*

⑧
⑨ For a change of scenery and era, visit the **City Mill,** an 18th-century water mill at the foot of **St. Giles's Hill,** at the east end of High Street. There are a National Trust gift shop and a café at the mill (open all year), part of the building being used as a Youth Hostel. Then climb the hill for a panoramic view of the city. *Bridge St., tel. 0962/870057. Admission: 60p adults, 30p children. Open Apr.– Sept., daily 11–4:45.*

Numbers in the margin correspond to points of interest on the South map.

⑩ Eight miles northeast of Winchester, by A31 and B3046, lies the town of **Old Alresford** (pronounced "Awlsford"), now the starting point of the **Watercress Line,** a 10-mile railroad reserved for steam locomotives. Originally named for its special deliveries of local watercress, the line takes visitors on a nostalgic tour through 19th-century England. *Tel. 0962/733810. Operates Mar.–Oct., variable hours.*

Time Out About halfway between Winchester and Old Alresford, turn north off A31 for **Ovington.** Here you will find **The Bush Inn,** an unspoilt, friendly country pub and restaurant with open log fires and a quiet riverside garden. The excellent bar food is a little pricier than the usual.

⑪ Continue east about 8 miles along A31 to **Chawton,** the village where Jane Austen lived for the last eight years of her life (she moved to Winchester only during her final illness). Here she wrote *Emma, Persuasion,* and *Mansfield Park.* The rooms of the unassuming, redbrick house retain the atmosphere of restricted gentility suitable to the unmarried daughter of a clergyman. *Tel. 0420/83262. Admission: £1.50 adults, 50p children. Open Apr.–Oct., daily 11–4:30; Nov.–Dec. and Mar., Wed.–Sun. 11–4:30; Jan. and Feb. weekends only.*

⑫ From Chawton, follow B3006, then A325 10 miles to the Georgian market town of **Petersfield,** set in a wide valley between wooded hills and open downs. Two miles south on A3 you will see signs for **Queen Elizabeth Country Park**—1,400 acres of chalk hills and shady beechwood, with scenic hiking trails you can climb to the top of Butser Hill (888 ft), to take in a splendid view of the coast. *Tel. 0705/595040. Admission free.*

⑬ Fifteen miles south of Petersfield along A3 is the city of **Portsmouth,** England's naval capital and principal port of departure for centuries. The harbor covers about 7 square miles, incorporating the world's first dry dock (built in 1495) and extensive defenses. These include **Porchester Castle,** founded more than 1,600 years ago, which has the most complete set of Roman walls in northern Europe. The keep's central tower affords a sweeping view of the harbor and coastline. *Near Fareham, tel. 0705/378291. Admission: £2 adults, £1 children under 16, £1.50 senior citizens. Open Easter–Oct., daily 10–6; Nov.–Easter, Tues.–Sun. 10–4.*

Portsmouth Naval Base has an unrivaled collection of ships: HMS *Victory,* the *Mary Rose,* HMS *Warrior,* and the Royal Naval Museum, all run by the Portsmouth Heritage Trust (tel. 0705/839766). Nelson's flagship, HMS *Victory,* has been painstakingly restored to appear as she did at the battle at Trafalgar (1805). You can inspect the cramped gun-decks, visit the cabin where Nelson entertained his officers, and stand on the spot where he was mortally wounded by a French sniper. *Admission: to each ship—HMS* Victory *includes the museum—£4.50 adult, £3.25 children, £4 senior citizens. Combination and family tickets are also available. Open Mar.–Oct., daily 10–6; Nov.–Feb., daily 10:30–5.*

In 1982, a much-publicized exercise in marine archaeology succeeded in raising the *Mary Rose,* flagship of the Tudor navy, which capsized and sank in the harbor in 1545. Described at the time as "the flower of all the ships that ever sailed," the *Mary Rose* is now housed in a fascinating, specially constructed enclosure, where her timbers are continuously sprayed with water to prevent them from drying out and breaking up. Thousands of remarkably well-preserved objects—including tools, weapons, pots, and surgical instruments—were found on board during the excavation, and a selection can be seen.

Time Out After you've visited the *Victory* and the *Mary Rose,* stop in at the refurbished **Sally Port** (High St.) for a tasty pub lunch.

HMS *Warrior,* now berthed nearby, was built in 1860 as Britain's first armored battleship—the fastest, longest (over 400 feet), and most powerful warship of her day. She spent her active life guarding the Channel. The **Royal Navy Museum** has a fine collection of painted figureheads, relics of Nelson's family, and galleries of paintings and mementos recalling different periods of naval history. In the even more popular **D-Day Museum,** near the corner of Southsea Common, exhibits vividly reconstruct the many stages of planning, the communications, and logistics involved, as well as the actual invasion. The centerpiece of the museum is the **Overlord Embroidery** ("Overlord" was the code name for the invasion), a 272-foot tapestry with 34 panels illustrating the history of World War II, from the Battle of Britain in 1940 to D-Day (June 6, 1944) and the first days of the liberation. *Clarence Esplanade, Southsea, tel. 0705/827261. Admission: £4 adults, £2.40 children, £3 senior citizens, £10.40 family ticket. Open daily 10:30–4:30.*

⓮ The maritime history of **Southampton,** 21 miles northwest, is commercial, rather than military. It boasts the best natural deepwater harbor in the country. Though the city was badly damaged during World War II, considerable parts of its castellated walls remain. They incorporate a variety of old buildings, including **God's House Tower,** originally a gunpowder factory, and now the archaeology museum. *Town Quay, tel. 0703/220007. Admission free. Open Tues.–Fri. 10–noon and 1–5, Sat. 10–noon and 1–4, Sun. 2–5.*

Mayflower Park and the **Pilgrim Fathers' Memorial** on Western Esplanade commemorate the sailing of the *Mayflower* from Southampton to the New World on August 15, 1620. (The ship was forced to stop in Plymouth for repairs.) John Alden, the hero of Longfellow's poem, *The Courtship of Miles Standish,* was a native of Southampton.

Other city attractions include a good art gallery, extensive parks, and the superb **Tudor House Museum** and garden. *St. Michael's Sq., tel. 0703/24216. Admission free. Open Tues.–Fri. 10–5, Sat. 10–4, Sun. 2–5.*

Time Out A good place to stop for lunch is **The Red Lion** (55 High St.), the city's oldest pub. While modern on the outside, its ancient inside, with a huge half-timbered bar and original minstrels' gallery, creates an intriguing Tudor ambience.

Eight miles northwest of Southampton, just off A3057, is
⓯ **Broadlands,** home of the late Lord Mountbatten, uncle of Queen Elizabeth II. This beautiful 18th-century Palladian mansion, with gardens laid out by Capability Brown, and wide lawns sweeping down to the banks of the River Test, is undoubtedly the grandest house in Hampshire. It abounds with ornate plaster moldings and paintings of British and Continental royalty, as well as personal mementos of Lord Mountbatten's distinguished career in the navy and in India. In 1947, the Queen and the Duke of Edinburgh spent their honeymoon here, and the Prince and Princess of Wales spent a few days of theirs here in 1981. *Romsey, tel. 0794/516878. Admission: £5 adults, £3.50 children, £4.25 senior citizens. Open Apr.–Sept., daily 12–4; closed Fri. except in Aug. and national holidays.*

From Southampton (and from Portsmouth, and Lymington), you can catch a ferry to the **Isle of Wight.** Since the 19th century, when Queen Victoria chose it for her vacation home, the small, diamond-shaped island has been an important resort. It has no highways or large housing complexes, and is only 23 miles long. It presents a peaceful picture of steep chalk cliffs, curving bays, sandy beaches, and quiet villages, with the occasional elegant country house.

If you embark from Southampton, your ferry will cross the Solent ⑯ and dock at **Cowes** (pronounced "cows"), internationally known for the "Cowes Week" annual yachting festival, held in July or August. At the north end of High Street, on the **Parade,** a tablet commemorates the sailing from Cowes in 1633 of two ships carrying the founders of the state of Maryland. Just to the east of town, Queen Victoria built **Osborne House** (designed by Prince Albert after an Italian villa) and spent much time here during her last years. The state rooms have scarcely been altered since her death in 1901. *Tel. 0983/200022. Admission: house and grounds—£5.50 adults, £2.75 children, £4.10 senior citizens. Open Apr.–Oct., daily 10–6.*

Leave Cowes by A3021 and follow the signs on A3054 to the town of ⑰ **Ryde,** a summer resort offering a variety of family attractions. Following the construction of **Ryde Pier** in 1814, elegant (and occasionally ostentatious) town houses sprang up along the seafront and on the slopes behind, commanding fine views of the harbor. In addition to its long, sandy beach, Ryde has a large boating lake (rowboats and pedalboats can be rented) and children's playgrounds.

Time Out A 10-minute walk along the seafront brings you to **The Solent Inn,** a small, traditional pub which serves lunches (weather permitting) in its pleasant garden. For a coffee or a quiet lunch in the heart of town, stop in at **De Luce,** on Union Street.

At **Flamingo Park,** a waterfowl reserve 2½ miles east of Ryde, many of the birds will eat from your hand. *Springvale, Seaview, tel. 0983/ 612153. Admission: £3.50 adults, £2.50 children, £3 senior citizens. Open Easter, daily 2–5:30; April–Sept., daily 10–5:30; Oct., daily 2–5.*

⑱ Three miles south of Ryde on A3055 is the village of **Brading,** whose church stands opposite a 16th-century house said to be the oldest on the island. A mile or so south, however, lie the much older remains of the substantial, 3rd-century **Brading Roman Villa,** whose splendid mosaic floors and heating system have been preserved. *Tel. 0983/ 406223. Admission: £1.50 adults, 85p children, £1 senior citizens. Open Apr.–Sept., Mon.–Sat. 10–5:30, Sun. 10:30–5:30.*

Following B3055 south from Brading brings you to the twin resorts of **Sandown** and **Shanklin,** which share the same bay. Shanklin is the quieter of the two. More interesting than the beach, however, is the ⑲ medieval village of **Arreton,** about 3 miles inland on A3056. Here a group of old farm buildings which were once part of the local manor have been restored as a **Country Crafts Village.** More than a dozen local craftspeople have studios in the village, working in wood, wool, leather, clay, metal, and other materials. You can browse and buy items direct from the makers or have a snack at the handy cafeteria. *Tel. 0983/528353. Admission free. Open daily 9:30–5.*

Leaving Arreton, rejoin the coast road and follow it south toward ⑳ **Ventnor.** The south coast resorts are the sunniest and most sheltered on the island. Ventnor itself rises from such a steep slope that the ground floors of some of its houses are level with the roofs of those across the road. The **Botanic Gardens** here laid out over 22 acres, contain more than 3,500 species of trees, plants, and shrubs. They are open all year, with no restrictions in hours and no admission charge. There's an excellent restaurant, the **Garden Tavern,** in the Gardens.

The southwestern coast is the least developed part of the shoreline, although at **Blackgang,** the deep chine (cleft in the cliffs) contains a fantasy theme park (*see* What to See and Do with Children, *below*). Farther west, stand the **Needles**, a long line of jagged chalk stacks jutting out of the sea like monstrous teeth. Take the chair lift to the

㉑ beach at **Alum Bay**, where you can catch a good view of the multicolored sands in the cliff strata. The **Alum Bay Glass Company** welcomes visitors interested in buying souvenirs or just watching glassblowing and jewelry crafting. *Tel. 0983/753473. Admission: 60p adults, 40p children, 50p senior citizens. Open daily 10:30–5, with a talk and demonstration every half-hour; no glassmaking on weekends.*

㉒ From Alum Bay, head inland about 14 miles to **Carisbrooke**, former capital of the island (the modern-day capital is **Newport**, 1 mi east). Above the village stands **Carisbrooke Castle**, built by the Normans, but enlarged in Elizabethan times. King Charles I was imprisoned here during the English Civil War. You can see the small window in the north curtain wall through which he tried to escape, and stroll along the battlements to watch the donkey-wheel, where a team of donkeys draws water from a deep well. *Tel. 0983/522107. Admission: £3.20 adults, £1.60 children, £2.40 senior citizens. Open Apr.– Oct., daily 10–6; Nov.–Mar., daily 10–4.*

Time Out For lunch, bar snacks, and local ale, visit **The Castle** (High St.), an attractive old pub in Newport.

Take the ferry back to Southampton and follow A36 north to Salisbury, about 23 miles away.

Tour 2: Salisbury, Stonehenge, and the New Forest

Numbers in the margin correspond to points of interest on the Salisbury map.

㉓ Although **Salisbury** is a historic city, and its old stone shops and houses grew up in the shadow of the great church, the city did not become important until the diocese of Old Sarum (the original settlement 2 mi to the north) was transferred here in the 13th century. The cathedral at Old Sarum was razed (today only ruins remain),

㉔ **Salisbury Cathedral** was built, and the city of Salisbury was born. In the 19th century, novelist Anthony Trollope based his tales of ecclesiastical life, notably *Barchester Towers*, on life here, although his fictional city of Barchester is really an amalgam of Salisbury and Winchester.

Salisbury continues to be dominated by its towering cathedral, a soaring hymn in stone. It is unique in that it was conceived and built as a whole, in the amazingly short span of only 38 years (1220–58). The spire, added in 1320, is a miraculous feat of medieval engineering—even though the point, 404 feet above the ground, is 2½ feet off vertical. For a fictional, keenly imaginative reconstruction of the human drama underlying such an achievement, read William Golding's novel *The Spire*.

The interior of the cathedral is remarkable for its lancet windows and sculpted tombs of crusaders and other medieval heroes. The clock in the north aisle—probably the oldest working mechanism in Europe, if not the world—was made in 1386. The spacious **cloisters** are the largest in England, and the octagonal **Chapter House** contains a marvelous 13th-century frieze showing scenes from the Old Testament. Here you can also see one of the four original copies of the **Magna Carta**, the charter of rights the English barons forced

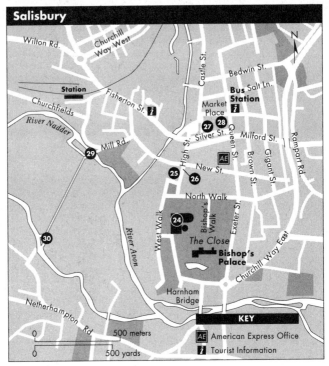

Salisbury

High Street
Gate, **26**
Long Bridge, **29**
Market
Square, **28**
Mompesson
House, **25**
Old Mill, **30**
Poultry
Cross, **27**
Salisbury
Cathedral, **24**

KEY

AE American Express Office

i Tourist Information

King John to accept in 1215; it was sent here for safekeeping in the 13th century.

The **Cathedral Close** (grounds) appears much as it did when it was first laid out. Its wide lawns are flanked by historic houses, some of which are open to the public. One of these is the impressive

25 **Mompesson House** on the north side, which boasts some fine original paneling and plasterwork, as well as a fascinating collection of 18th-century drinking glasses, and an attractive walled garden. *Tel. 0722/335659. Admission: £3 adults, £1.50 children. Open Apr.– Oct., Sat.–Wed. noon–5:30.*

26 Leaving the close on the north side will take you through **High Street Gate,** one of the four castellated stone gateways built to separate the close from the rest of the city, and into the heart of the modern town. Turn right into Silver Street, and you will find one of Salisbury's

27 best-known landmarks, the **Poultry Cross.** This little hexagonal structure is the last remaining of the four original market crosses, and dealers still set up their stalls beside it. A narrow side street

28 links it to **Market Square,** site of one of southern England's most popular markets, held on Tuesdays and Saturdays. Permission to hold an annual fair here was granted in 1221, and that right is exercised for three days every October.

Time Out Here's a historic place for lunch: The **Haunch of Venison** (1 Minster St., opposite the Poultry Cross) has been going strong for over six centuries, and is brimful with period details (like the mummified arm of an 18th-century card player still clutching his cards that was found in 1903 by workmen). It has heavy beams, an open fire, and antique, leather-covered settles. There are over 140 malt whiskies and excellent bar food, along with a proper restaurant (tel. 0722/ 322024).

Many medieval cities in England boast handsome half-timbered houses, but Salisbury has more than most. A particularly fine example can be found close to Market Square, at **No. 8 Queen Street.** This house, originally the home of a successful wool merchant, is now a store selling fine china and glassware. You can browse here and see the old staircase, the fireplaces of local Chilmark stone, and the Jacobean oak paneling.

West of High Street lies Mill Road, which leads you across Queen Elizabeth Gardens to **Long Bridge.** Cross the bridge and continue on the town path; the view from here inspired a classic 19th-century painting, John Constable's *Salisbury Cathedral,* now hung in the Constable Room of London's National Gallery. Continue farther along the town path in the same direction until you come to the **Old Mill,** dating from the 12th century. It is now a restaurant and coffee shop under the same management as the Old Mill Hotel next door.

Numbers in the margin correspond to points of interest on the South map.

Salisbury stands close to the confluence of five rivers (the Avon, the Bourne, the Nadder, the Wylye, and the Ebble), each of which winds slowly through its own wooded valley into the heart of Wiltshire.

Following the valley of the Nadder west about 5 miles along A30 will lead you to the ancient town of **Wilton,** from which the county takes its name. A traditional market is held here every Thursday. But the main attraction is **Wilton House and Gardens,** home of the earl of Pembroke. The original Tudor house burned down in 1647, but the present mansion replacing it was designed by Inigo Jones, Ben Jonson's stage designer and the architect of London's Banqueting House. It contains a superb collection of paintings by Rubens, Breughel, and Rembrandt, among others, as well as family treasures such as Napoleon's pearl-inlaid dispatch box and a lock of Queen Elizabeth I's hair. The main focus of interest, however, is the house itself. There's a "single cube room" (designed as an exact 30-foot cube) and a "double cube room" (twice as long), both elaborately decorated with gilded moldings of fruit and flowers and sumptuously furnished with 18th-century sofas and chairs upholstered in red velvet. It was in the double cube room that Eisenhower planned the Normandy invasion. The gardens have a number of magnificent old cedars and an imposing Palladian bridge, built in 1737. *Tel. 0722/ 743115. Admission: Inclusive ticket, £5.50 adults, £3.50 children, £4.50 senior citizens, £14.50 family ticket. Open Easter–mid-Oct., daily 11–4:45; grounds only: £2 adults, £1.50 children. Restaurant opens at 11.*

Continuing west on A30 for about 13 miles will bring you into Dorset and the charming village of **Shaftesbury.** When you reach the village, head for **Gold Hill,** a steep, cobbled street lined with cottages. From the top you can catch a sweeping view of the surrounding countryside. Though Gold Hill itself is something of a tourist cliché (it has even appeared in TV commercials), it is still well worth visiting.

Nine miles northwest of Shaftesbury (follow B3081 to B3092), close to the village of **Stourton,** lies another of Wiltshire's many country-house-and-garden combinations. Most of **Stourhead House** was built between 1721 and 1725 by a wealthy banker named Henry Hoare.

The pavilions (containing the library and picture gallery) were added by his grandson about 70 years later. The library (which escaped the fire that gutted the central block in 1902) has a stepladder, a writing desk, and book tables made by Thomas Chippendale, as well as a beautiful carved wood chimneypiece. Many of the rooms contain Chinese and French porcelain and other objets d'art. The most famous is a 17th-century Italian cabinet inlaid with marble and semiprecious stones, which was brought from Rome in 1742.

The house is set in extensive grounds, and just over the hill is a celebrated landscaped garden, in which temples, grottoes, and bridges have been skillfully placed among colorful shrubs, trees, and flowers. A walk around the lake (1 mi) reveals a series of ever-changing vistas. The best time to visit is early summer, when the massive banks of rhododendrons are in full bloom, but it is beautiful at any time of year. *Stourton, near Mere, tel. 0747/840348. House admission: £4.10 adults, £2.10 children. Open Apr.–Oct., Sat.–Wed. 12–5. Gardens open all year, daily 8AM–7 PM or sunset. Gardens admission: Mar.–Oct. £4.10 adults, £2.10 children, Nov.–Feb. £3.10 adults, £1.50 children. Open daily 8 AM–dusk.*

❸❹ Follow B3092 about 6 miles north from Stourhead House to yet another famous private estate—**Longleat House,** home of the marquess of Bath. The glorious Italian Renaissance building was completed in 1580 (for just over £8,000, an astronomical sum at the time), and contains outstanding tapestries, paintings, porcelain, and furniture, as well as notable period features of its own, such as the Victorian kitchens, the Elizabethan minstrels' gallery, and the great hall, with its massive wooden beams. Giant antlers of the extinct Irish elk decorate the walls. In 1966, the grounds of Longleat became Britain's first safari park. Giraffes, zebras, camels, rhinos, and lions are all on view.

Apart from the house and safari park, Longleat has dollhouses, a butterfly garden, a private railroad, the world's largest hedge maze, and an adventure castle. All of these make it extremely popular, particularly in summer and during school vacations, so don't expect to have the place to yourself! *Near Warminster, tel. 0985/844400. Admission: inclusive ticket, £10 adults, £8 children and senior citizens. House only, £4 adults, £2 children under 14, £3 senior citizens. Open Easter–Sept., 10–6; Oct.–Easter, 10–4. Closed Christmas. Longleat Safari Park, tel. 0985/844328. Admission: £5.50 adults, £3.50 children, £4.50 senior citizens. Open Easter–Oct., daily 10–6.*

❸❺ From Longleat, go north on B3092 to Frome, then take A361 to Trowbridge. Follow it through Devizes to **Avebury** (a total of 25 mi or so). As you approach Avebury, on your left you will pass **Cherhill Down,** with a vivid white horse carved into its slope. This is the first in a series of hillside carvings in Wiltshire, but, unlike the others, this one isn't an ancient symbol—it was put there in 1780 to indicate the highest point of the downs between London and Bath. (The best view of the horse is from A4, on the approach from Calne.)

Time Out   **The Waggon and Horses** (Beckhampton), just beside the traffic circle linking A4 and A361, serves an excellent sandwich lunch (it has won prizes for them) beside a blazing fire. The thatch-roofed pub is built of stones taken from the Avebury site.

❸❻ Turning right at the traffic circle onto A4, **Silbury Hill** rises up on your right. This man-made mound, 130 feet high, dates from about 2500 BC. Excavations over 200 years have provided no clue as to its original purpose, but the generally accepted notion is that it was a massive burial chamber.

Next, turn left onto B4003 and follow the **Kennett Stone Avenue,** a sort of prehistoric processional way leading to Avebury. The stones of the avenue were spaced 80 feet apart, but only the last half mile survives intact. The lost ones are marked with concrete. The **Avebury monument** at the end consists of a wide, circular ditch and bank, about 1,400 feet across and well over half a mile around. The perimeter is broken by entrances at roughly the four points of the compass, and inside stand the remains of three stone circles. The largest one originally had 98 stones, though only 27 remain. Many of the stones on the site were destroyed centuries ago, especially in the 17th century, when they were the target of religious fanaticism.

The first stones at Avebury predate those at Stonehenge by at least 200 years, but here they are much more domesticated—literally so, for many were pillaged to build the thatched cottages you see flanking the fields. Finds from the Avebury area are displayed in the **Alexander Kieller Museum,** run by English Heritage. *Tel. 06723/250. Admission: £1.35 adults, 65p children, £1 senior citizens. Open Apr.–Oct., daily 10–6; Nov.–Mar., daily 10–4.*

The entire area is crowded with relics of the prehistoric age, so be sure to stop off at the **West Kennett Long Barrow,** a chambered tomb dating from around 3250 BC, a mile east of Avebury on A4. About 7

㊲ miles east of Avebury on A4 is the attractive town of **Marlborough,** which developed as an important staging post on the old London–Bath stagecoach route. Today it is better known for its unusually wide main street, its elegant Georgian houses—these replace the medieval town center, which was destroyed in a great fire in 1653—and its celebrated public school. The grounds of the school, on the west side of town, enclose a small, man-made hill called Castle Mound, or Maerl's Barrow, which gave the town its name. This was said to be the grave of Merlin, King Arthur's court wizard, but it is clearly much older than the period when the historic Arthur may have lived. A Tourist Information Center (open in summer) is housed in the 15th-century deconsecrated church of St. Peter and St. Paul.

Time Out If you need a restorative after exploring Marlborough, relax under the traditional oak beams of the **Sun** on High Street, a handsome 16th-century inn with French landlords. The bar food is unusually good and there's a small courtyard.

Leaving Marlborough, join A345 south toward Stonehenge (about 17 mi). At Amesbury, turn west onto A344. Here, near the junction with A303, stands one of England's most visited and most puzzling monuments.

㊳ Most days, **Stonehenge** is dwarfed by its lonely isolation on the wide sweep of Salisbury Plain, the great circle of stones enclosed by barriers to keep back the relentless throngs of tourists. During the summer solstice, it becomes the target of the feeble remnants of the Alternate Society, which embarks on an annual struggle with the police to celebrate, in the monument's imposing shadow, a barely understood pagan festival. But if you visit in the early morning, when the crowds have not yet arrived, or in the evening, when the sky is heavy with scudding clouds, you can experience Stonehenge as it once was: a magical, mystical, awe-inspiring place.

Stonehenge was begun around 2800 BC, enlarged between 2100 and 1900 BC, and altered yet again by 150 BC. It has been excavated and rearranged several times over the centuries. The medieval phrase "Stonehenge" means "hanging stones." (Interestingly enough, the use of "henge" to denote a circular arrangement of stone or wooden elements seems to have come from Stonehenge itself—an example of what wordsmiths call back-formation.) The monument, however, did not start out with great stones at all, but with the ditch and bank that still encircle the site. The first stone to be added was probably the Heel Stone, outside the circle, near the main road.

Many of the huge stones that ringed the center were brought here from great distances. The original 80 bluestones (dolerite), which made up the two internal circles, were transported from the Preseli mountains, near Fishguard on the Atlantic coast of Wales, presumably by raft on sea and river. Next they were dragged on rollers across country—a total journey of 130 miles as the crow flies, but closer to 240 by the easiest route. Later, great blocks of sarsen stone were quarried in north Wiltshire, dressed, and fitted together with primitive joints. The labor involved in quarrying, transporting, and carving these stones was astonishing, all the more so when you remember that it was accomplished before the major Pyramids of Egypt were built.

We still do not know why the great project at Stonehenge was undertaken in the first place. It is fairly certain that it was a religious site, and that worship here involved the cycles of the sun; the alignment of the stones to point to sunrise at midsummer and sunset in midwinter makes this clear. One thing is certain: The Druids had nothing to do with the construction. The monument had already been in existence for nearly 2,000 years by the time they appeared. There has been speculation that Stonehenge may have been a kind of neolithic computer, with a sophisticated astronomical purpose. One of the latest of the hundreds of books on the subject is *Stonehenge*, by Julian Richards, in the English Heritage series (*Batsford, £13.95*). It is a manageable survey of all the evidence by a freelance archaeologist who lives and works in Wessex.

As you can't get very close to the monoliths, and then only along one section of the site, it's a good idea to take a pair of binoculars along to make out the details more clearly. The visitors' amenities at Stonehenge are rather squalid, but there are plans to improve them. *Near Amesbury. Admission: £2.85 adults, £1.40 children, £2.15 senior citizens. Open Apr.–Oct., daily 10–6; Nov.–Mar., daily 10–4.*

39 Leaving Stonehenge, head south along A360 to Salisbury, then follow A36 and local roads another 15 miles or so to **Lyndhurst,** known as the "capital of the New Forest." Alice Hargreaves (*née* Liddell), Lewis Carroll's Alice, is buried in the churchyard here. The town provides an excellent base for travelers wishing to explore this beautiful wooded region. This is also a good, easy area for hiking. Ask the **Tourist Information Center** (tel. 0703/282269) in the main parking lot for details of local walks.

You have a choice of routes now. To explore the depths of the New Forest, take A35 out of Lyndhurst (the road continues southwest to Bournemouth). **The New Forest** consists of 145 square miles of mainly open, unfenced countryside interspersed with dense woodland, a natural haven for herds of free-roaming deer, cattle, and hardy New Forest ponies. The forest was "new" in 1079, when William the Conqueror cleared the area of farms and villages and turned it into his private hunting forest. He left it unfenced so as not to hinder the free run of deer, the main quarry of the royal hunting parties. Three centuries ago, large numbers of oaks were cut down to build houses and ships, but otherwise the landscape has not changed much over the last 1,000 years. Although some favorite spots can get crowded in summer, there are ample parking lots, picnic grounds, and campgrounds. Miles of walking trails crisscross the region and the best way to explore is on foot.

40 If you want to see more of the southern coast, leave Lyndhurst by B3056 for the 6 miles or so to **Beaulieu** (pronounced "Bewley"), which offers three major attractions.

Beaulieu Abbey was established by King John in 1204 for the Cistercian monks, who gave their new home its name, which means "beautiful place" in French. It was badly damaged during the reign of Henry VIII, leaving only the cloister, the doorway, the gatehouse, and two buildings, one of which today contains a well-planned exhibition re-creating daily life in the monastery. The gatehouse has been incorporated into **Palace House,** home of the Montagu family since 1538. In this stately home you can see drawing rooms, dining halls, and a number of very fine family portraits. The present Lord Montagu is noted for his work in establishing the **National Motor Museum,** which traces the development of motor transport from 1895 to the present, with over 200 classic cars, buses, and motorcycles. Museum attractions include a monorail, audiovisual presentations, and a trip in a 1912 London bus. *Tel. 0590/612345. Admission to Palace House, Abbey, and Motor Museum: £7 adults, £5 children, £5.50 senior citizens, £23 family ticket. Open Easter–Sept., 10–6; Oct.–Easter, 10–5.*

41 Among local places of interest is **Buckler's Hard,** an almost perfectly restored 18th-century hamlet of 24 brick cottages, leading down to an old shipyard on the River Beaulieu. Nelson's favorite ship, HMS *Agamemnon,* was built here of New Forest oak, as recalled in the fascinating **Maritime Museum.** *Tel. 0590/616203. Admission: £2.50 adults, £1.70 children, £2.05 senior citizens, £7 family ticket. Open Easter–May, daily 10–6; Jun.–Sept., daily 10–9; Oct.–Easter, daily 10–4:30.*

From Beaulieu, take any of the minor roads leading west through Lymington and pick up A337 for the popular seaside resort of Bournemouth, a journey of about 18 miles.

Tour 3: Southern Literary Landscapes: Bournemouth to Lyme Regis

42 **Bournemouth** was founded in 1810 by Lewis Tregonwell, an ex-army officer who had taken a liking to the area when stationed there some years before. He settled near what is now **The Square** and planted the first pine trees in the steep little valleys—or chines—cutting through the cliffs to the famous Bournemouth sands. The scent of fir trees was said to be good for "consumption" (tuberculosis) sufferers, and the town grew steadily as more and more people came for prolonged rest cures.

The Square and the beach are linked by gardens laid out with flowering trees and lawns. This is an excellent spot to relax and listen to stirring music wafting from the **Pine Walk bandstand.** Regular musical programs take place at the **Pavilion** and at the **Winter Gardens** (home of the Bournemouth Symphony Orchestra) nearby. There are also regular shows at the **Bournemouth International Centre** in

Exeter Road (tel. 0202/297297), which includes a selection of restaurants, bars, and a swimming pool.

Time Out Stop at **The Coriander** (14 Richmond Hill), just up the road from the Pine Walk bandstand, for an inexpensive lunch with a Mexican flavor (closed for Sunday lunch).

On the corner of Hilton Road stands **St. Peter's** parish church, easily recognizable by its 200-foot-high tower and spire. Lewis Tregonwell is buried in the churchyard. Here, too, you will notice the elaborate tombstone of Mary Shelley, author of *Frankenstein* and wife of the great Romantic poet, whose heart is buried with her. Admirers of Shelley will want to visit the **Casa Magni Shelley Museum** in **Boscombe** (on the west side of Bournemouth), with its touching collection of Shelley memorabilia. *Boscombe Manor, Beechwood Ave., tel. 0202/551009. Small admission fee. Open June–Sept., Mon.–Sat. 10:30–5; Oct.–May, Thurs.–Sat. 10:30–5.*

In Bournemouth itself you will find the interesting **Russell-Coates Art Gallery and Museum.** This late-Victorian mansion, perched on top of East Cliff, overflows with Victorian paintings and miniatures, cases of butterflies, and treasures from the Far East, including an exquisite suit of Japanese armor. *Tel. 0202/551009. Admission: £1 adults, 50p children and senior citizens, free on Sat. and Sun. Open Tues.–Sun. 10–5.*

Time Out For an old-fashioned tea, try the **Cumberland Hotel** (East Overcliffe Drive), which serves out of doors in summer.

Leaving Bournemouth, follow the signs northwest (A341) to the quiet market town of **Wimbourne Minster,** 10 miles away. Its impressive twin-towered minster makes it seem like a miniature cathedral city. **The Priest's House Museum** in a Tudor building with a garden, features Roman and Iron-Age exhibits, including a cryptic, three-faced Celtic stone head. *23 High St., tel. 0202/882533. Admission: £1.50 adults, 50p children, £1 senior citizens. Open Apr.–Oct., Mon.–Sat. 10:30–4:30, Sun. 2–4:30; Nov.–Christmas, weekends only; closed July 29.*

Time Out At 26 Westborough you'll find **Quinneys,** a bakery and eating house run by the Skidmore family for nearly 30 years. They sell delicious pastries and cakes, and have a daily-changing blackboard selection of such lunch specialties as grilled trout.

Turning south now, follow A349 about 6 miles to the fast-growing modern town of **Poole,** which has a huge natural harbor, with more than 90 miles of serrated coastline and myriad bays, inlets, and islands. Ferries make regular trips to **Brownsea Island,** which belongs to the National Trust and is open to visitors who enjoy roaming the woods, relaxing on the beach, and observing rare waterfowl. *Boats from Poole Quay (tel. 0202/680580 or 0202/666226) leave about every 30 minutes. Round-trip: £3.15 adults, £2.15 children, £2.90 senior citizens. Landing charge: £2.10 adults, £1 children, £5.20 family ticket. Operates Apr.–Sept., daily 10–8 (or dusk).*

From Poole, follow A351 southwest to Wareham, then southeast about 12 miles to **Corfe Castle,** whose spectacular ruins overlook the pretty village of Corfe. The castle site guards a gap in the surrounding range of hills, and has been fortified from very early times. The present ruins are of the castle built between 1105, when the great central keep was erected, and the 1270s, when the outer walls and towers were built. It owes its ramshackle state to Cromwell's soldiers, who blew it up in 1646 during the Civil War. This is one of the most impressive ruins in Britain, and will stir the imagination of all history buffs. It is looked after by the National Trust, which also runs a coffee shop at the entrance. *Tel. 0929/481294. Admission: £2.90 adults, £1.40 children under 16. Open early Feb.–Oct., daily 10–5:30; Nov.–early Feb., weekends noon–3:30.*

Time Out **The Fox** in Corfe (West St.) is an age-old pub with a fine view of the castle from its flowery garden and an ancient well in the lounge bar. The bar food is excellent for a pleasant lunch.

From Corfe Castle, take A351 and A352 west for 21 miles to **㊼ Dorchester,** which is in many ways a traditional southern country town. To appreciate its character, visit the local Wednesday market in the **Market Square,** where you can find Dorset delicacies, such as Blue Vinney cheese (which some connoisseurs prefer to Blue Stilton), and various handcrafted items.

Dorchester owes much of its fame to its connection with Thomas Hardy, whose bronze statue looks westward from a bank on **Colliton Walk.** Born in a cottage (now preserved by the National Trust) in the hamlet of Higher Brockhampton, about 3 miles northeast of Dorchester, Hardy attended school in the town and was apprentice to an architect here. Later he had a house, Max Gate (not open to the public), built to his own design on the edge of Dorchester. Hardy's study there has been reconstructed in the **Dorset County Museum,** which houses a diverse and fascinating collection. Exhibits range from ancient Celtic and Roman remains to a vicious, 19th-century mantrap, used to snare poachers. It was this very trap that Hardy had in mind when writing the mantrap episode in *The Woodlanders. High West St., tel. 0305/262735. Admission: £1.95 adults, 95p children and senior citizens. Open Mon.–Sat. 10–5.*

Time Out Try lunch at **The Royal Oak** (20 High West St.), whose first license to sell liquor was granted in 1697.

Roman history and artifacts abound in Dorchester. The town was laid out by the Romans around AD 70, and if you walk along **Bowling Alley Walk, West Walk,** and **Colliton Walk,** you will have followed the approximate line of the original Roman town walls. On the north side of Colliton Park lies an excavated **Roman villa** with a marvelously preserved mosaic floor. Possibly even more interesting is **Maumbury Rings,** the remains of a Roman amphitheater on the edge of town. The site was later used as a place of execution. (Hardy's *Mayor of Casterbridge* contains a vivid evocation of the Rings.) As late as 1706, a girl was burned at the stake here.

The town is also associated with Monmouth's Rebellion of 1685, when Charles II's illegitimate son, the duke of Monmouth, led a rising against his unpopular uncle, James II. The rising was ruthlessly put down, and the chief justice, Lord Jeffreys, conducted the Bloody Assizes to try rebels and sympathizers, many of whom were from Dorset and Hampshire (*see* Winchester in Tour 1 *above*). A swearing, bullying drunkard, Jeffreys was the prototypical hanging judge, and memories of his mass executions lingered for centuries throughout the South. His courtroom in Dorchester was located in what is now the Antelope Hotel on South Street.

Time Out Try **The Potter Inn** (19 Durngate St.) for deliciously fattening cakes
and pastries. It is on two floors of an attractive little 17th-century
house, where local crafts are also sold.

Excursions to the north of Dorchester will quickly bring you onto
the downs, the chalky hills that curve across the northern half of the
county, sheltering quiet villages and remote farms linked by narrow, winding roads. Take time to explore one of the last undeveloped
areas of southern England; there are no major highways or railroads
here, and it still retains much of the strongly agricultural atmosphere of the 19th century.

48 North, 3 miles on A352, is the village of **Cerne Abbas,** worth a short
exploration on foot. Some appealing Tudor houses line the road beside the church. Nearby you can also see the original village stocks.
If you pass through the graveyard, you will arrive at a shallow pool
known as **St. Augustine's Well.** Legend holds that the saint created it
by striking the ground with his staff, thereby ensuring a regular
supply of baptismal water. Tenth-century **Cerne Abbey** itself is now
a ruin, with little left to see except its old gateway, though the nearby Abbey House is still in use. Cerne Abbas's main claim to fame is
the colossal **figure of a giant,** cut in chalk on a hillside overlooking the
village. The 180-foot-long giant with a huge club bears a striking resemblance to Hercules, although he probably originated as a tribal
fertility symbol long before the Romans. His outlines are formed by
2-foot-wide trenches. The present giant is thought to have been
carved in the chalk around AD 1200, but he could well be based on a
very much older figure.

49 Return to the outskirts of Dorchester on A352 or any one of a number of scenic minor roads. Here, stop first at **Maiden Castle** (2 mi
southwest, on A354), which is, after Stonehenge, the most extraordinary pre-Roman archaeological site in England. It is not a castle at
all, but an enormous, complex hill fort of stone and earth, built, like
Stonehenge, by England's mysterious prehistoric inhabitants.
Many centuries later it was a Celtic stronghold. In AD 43, the invading Romans, under the general (later emperor) Vespasian, stormed
it. One of the grimmest exhibits now on display in the Dorset County
Museum in Dorchester was excavated here: the skeleton of a Celtic
warrior transfixed by a Roman arrow. To experience an uncanny silence and sense of mystery, climb Maiden Castle early in the day (access to it is unrestricted), when other tourists are unlikely to be
stirring.

Any road leading south from Dorchester will bring you to the characteristic quiet bays, shingle beaches, and low chalk cliffs of the
Dorset coast. The well-marked **Dorset Coast Path** enables you to
walk along some or all of the shoreline, or you can drive the narrow,
country lanes hugging the coast.

50 About 8 miles south of Dorchester on A354 is **Weymouth,** Dorset's
main coastal resort, known both for its wide, safe, sandy beaches
and its royal connections. King George III took up sea bathing here
for his health in 1789, setting a trend among the wealthy and fashionable people of his day. They left Weymouth with many fine period
buildings, including the Georgian row houses lining the esplanade.
Historical details clamor for your attention. A wall in **Maiden Street,**
for example, still holds a cannonball that was embedded in it during
the Civil War. Nearby, a **column** commemorates the launching of the
American forces from Weymouth on D-Day, June 6, 1944.

Time Out Try the **Old Rooms** (Trinity Rd.) for a fisherman's pub full of character and low beams. The lunchtime sandwiches are particularly good, and the pub has great views over the harbor.

A 5-mile-long peninsula jutting south from Weymouth leads to the **⑤** **Isle of Portland,** the eastern end of the unique geological curiosity **㉜** known as **Chesil Beach**—a 200-yard-wide, 30-foot-high bank of pebbles that decrease in size from east to west. The beach extends for 18 miles. A powerful undertow makes swimming dangerous, and tombstones in local churchyards attest to the many shipwrecks the beach has caused.

㉝ At the western end of Chesil Beach lies the village of **Abbotsbury.** A lagoon here is a famous breeding place for swans, first introduced by Benedictine monks as a source of meat in winter. The swans have remained for centuries, building new nests every year in the soft, moist pampas grass. **The Swannery's** 600th anniversary in 1993 was commemorated with a specially designed set of stamps. *Abbotsbury Swannery, New Barn Rd., tel. 0305/871684. Admission: £2.90 adults, £1 children under 16, £2.30 senior citizens. Open Apr.–Oct., daily 9:30–5.*

On the hills above Abbotsbury stands **Hardy's Monument**—dedicated not to the novelist, as many suppose, but to Sir Thomas Masterman Hardy, Nelson's flag captain at Trafalgar, to whom Nelson's dying words, "Kiss me, Hardy" (or was it, "Kismet, Hardy"?) were addressed. The monument itself is without much charm, but the surrounding view more than makes up for it. In clear weather you can scan the whole coastline between the Isle of Wight and Start Point in Devon.

Time Out The rambling, thatched **Ilchester Arms,** near the Swannery, is an ideal spot for a good hot lunch in a conservatory.

Two more places of interest in southwest Dorset are the so-called **㉞** **Fossil Coast** and the ancient town of **Lyme Regis.** The cliffs in this area are especially fossil-rich. In 1810, a local child named Mary Anning dug out a complete ichthyosaurus here (it is on display in London's Natural History Museum). You may prefer to browse in the **Fossil Shop** in Lyme Regis. The town itself is famous for its curving stone breakwater, **The Cobb,** built by King Edward I in the 13th century to improve the harbor. It was here that the duke of Monmouth landed in 1685 in his ill-fated attempt to overthrow his uncle, James II. The Cobb figures prominently in the movie *The French Lieutenant's Woman,* based on John Fowles's novel. Fowles himself is currently Lyme's most famous resident.

What to See and Do with Children

Blackgang Chine is a theme park built on top of a cliff overlooking a former smugglers' landing place. It features Dinosaur-Land, Smugglers-Land, Jungle-Land, and other attractions for ages 3–12. *Ventnor, Isle of Wight, tel. 0983/730330. Admission: £4.99 adults, £3.99 children. Open Apr.–Oct., daily 10–5; late May–late Sept., daily 10–10.*

Paulton's Park is a large theme park with a Gypsy Museum, Rio Grande Train, Magic Forest, and over 40 other attractions. There's enough to occupy a full day, and refreshments are also available. *Just off exit 2 of M27, near Southampton, tel. 0703/814442. Admis-*

sion: £6.50 adults, £5.50 children and senior citizens, £22.50 family ticket. Open Apr.–Oct., daily 10–6:30.

Dorchester's popular **Dinosaur Museum** has life-size models and interactive displays. *Icen Way, off High East St., tel. 0305/269880. Admission: £2.95 adults, £1.95 children, £2.50 senior citizens, £8.95 family ticket. Open daily 9:30–5:30.*

An amusement park, also open daily, is located beside the long, safe beach of **Hayling Island,** a family-vacation resort close to Portsmouth and joined to the mainland by a bridge.

Both adults and children will love **Natural World** in Poole, a superb aquarium and "seaquarium" featuring sharks, piranhas, crocodiles, and rarer creatures. *Poole Quay, tel. 0202/686712. Admission: £2.95 adults, £2.50 children, £2.75 senior citizens, £8.90 family ticket. Open daily 10–6.*

Off the Beaten Track

Close to Stockbridge (10 mi northwest of Winchester by A272) is **Danebury Hill,** a fascinating Iron Age hill fort, where careful excavations have revealed the structure of complex earthworks surrounding a complete town. Danebury Hill can be visited any time without charge, and it lies in a good area for hiking.

An important slice of English history, not without contemporary significance, can be found in the Dorset village of **Tolpuddle,** about 7 miles east of Dorchester on A35. A small museum here commemorates six 19th-century farm laborers who were transported to hard labor in the Australian convict colony for resisting exploitation by their employer, and who thus won fame as early martyrs in the labor union movement.

From east to west between Salisbury Plain and the Marlborough Downs lies the beautiful **Vale of Pewsey.** It is especially famous for its splendid, though relatively modern **White Horse** cut into the hillside.

Shopping

Poole **Poole Pottery** (The Quay, tel. 0202/666200) has a shop where you can buy the popular creamy ware, as well as watch demonstrations of potting and decorating.

Salisbury **Watsons** (8–9 Queen St., tel. 0722/320311) is worth visiting for its circa-1306 building, which has some original windows, a carved oak mantelpiece, and other period features. The company specializes in Aynsley and Wedgwood bone china, Waterford and Dartington glass, Royal Doulton, and a wide range of fine ornaments.

Winchester The **Antiques Market** (King's Walk, tel. 0962/862277) sells crafts and gift items, as well as antiques. A complete list of local antiques stores is available from Winchester Tourist Information Center (tel. 0962/840222, ext. 2361).
H. M. Gilbert, an antiquarian bookseller, is located (19 The Square, tel. 0962/852832) in a network of ancient streets. The shop is housed in five medieval cottages.

Markets Open-air markets are almost daily events (a complete list is available from the Southern Tourist Board). Among the best are Salisbury's traditional city market (Tues. and Sat.), Kingsland Market in Southampton for bric-a-brac (Thurs.), and a general country market

(Wed.) at Ringwood, near Bournemouth. New Forest ponies are rounded up Wild West style and auctioned to dealers at the pony market, held six times a year beside B3506 (Lyndhurst to Beaulieu road) near the Beaulieu Station Hotel. Check dates with the Lyndhurst TIC (tel. 0703/282269).

Sports and the Outdoors

Bicycling Try **Peter Hansford** (Bridge Rd., Park Gate, Southampton, tel. 0489/573249; £12 a day, £35 a week, deposit £100) or **Weymouth Cycles** (6C King St., Weymouth, tel. 0305/787677; £1.50 an hour, £5 a day, £20 a week, deposit £10 with an ID, more for mountain bikes).

Golf **New Forest Golf Course** (Southampton Rd., Lyndhurst, tel. 0703/282450); **Shanklin and Sandown** (The Fairway, Sandown, Isle of Wight, tel 0983/403170); **Salisbury and South Wiltshire Golf Club,** Netherhampton, Salisbury, tel. 0722/742131); **Dunwood Manor Country Club** (Shootash Hill, nr. Romsey, tel. 0794/40549); **Marlborough Golf Club** (The Common, Marlborough, tel. 0672/512147); **Lyme Regis Golf Club** (Timber Hill, Lyme Regis, tel. 0297/442043).

Horseback Riding The New Forest was custom-built for riding and there's no better way to enjoy it than on horseback. **The New Park Stables Equestrian Centre** (Lyndhurst Rd., Brockenhurst, tel. 05902/3467) gives full instruction. Try also **Russell Equestrian Centre** (Black Farm, Gaters Hill, West End, Southampton, tel. 0703/473693).

Walking The **Dorset Coast Path** runs from Lyme Regis to Poole, bypassing Weymouth, 72 miles in all. Some highlights along the way are Golden Cap, the highest point on the South Coast; the Swannery at Abbotsbury; Lulworth Cove (between Corfe Castle and Weymouth); and Chesil Bank. As with most walks in Britain, the route is dotted with villages and isolated pubs for meals; there are also a lot of rural B&Bs, and many isolated farmhouses take guests.

The **New Forest** is more domesticated than, for example, the Forest of Dean, and the walks it provides are not much more than easy strolls. For one such walk (about 4 miles), start from Lyndhurst, and head for Brockenhurst, a commuter village. You will pass through woods, pastureland, and leafy river valleys—you may even see some New Forest ponies. (New Forest Museum and Visitors Centre, Main Car Park, Lyndhurst, Hampshire S043 7NY, tel. 0703/282269.)

There is a 15-mile walk through Hardy country, the **Tess of the D'Urbervilles Tour,** following in the sad steps of Hardy's heroine on her Sunday mission to her father-in-law, Parson Clare of Beaminster, in an attempt to rescue her failed marriage. (Tour No. 2 from the Thomas Hardy Society, Box 1438, Dorchester, Dorset DT1 1HY, tel. 0305/251501.)

Dining and Lodging

Dining Fertile soil, well-stocked rivers, and a long coastline ensure excellent farm produce and a plentiful stock of fish throughout the South. Try fresh-grilled river trout or sea bass poached in brine, or dine like a king on the New Forest's famous venison.

Highly recommended restaurants are indicated by a star ★.

Category	Cost*
$$$$	over £50
$$$	£40–£50
$$	£20–£40
$	under £20

per person including first course, main course, dessert, and VAT; excluding drinks

Lodging Modern hotel chains are well represented , and in rural areas there are elegant country-house hotels, traditional coaching inns, and modest guest houses. Note that some seaside hotels won't accept one-night bookings in the busy season.

Highly recommended hotels are indicated by a star ★.

Category	Cost*
$$$$	over £150
$$$	£90–£150
$$	£50–£90
$	under £50

All prices are for two people sharing a double room, including service, breakfast, and VAT.

Abbotsbury
Dining and
Lodging

Manor Hotel. This comfortable hotel/restaurant's pedigree goes back over 700 years—note its flagstone floors, oak paneling, and beamed ceilings. Among the English and French dishes in which the Manor specializes are scallops and guinea fowl. It also has 13 pine-furnished bedrooms. *Beach Rd., West Bexington DT2 9DF (3 mi west of Abbotsbury), tel. 0308/897785, fax 0308/897035. 13 rooms with bath. Facilities: garden, sea fishing. Restaurant: Reservations advised; dress: casual. AE, DC, MC, V. $$*

Blandford
Forum
Dining and
Lodging

La Belle Alliance. There are constantly changing set menus (bistro and gourmet) in this attractive, small, country restaurant. The relaxed decor and the friendly owners make for an enjoyable meal (try the pigeon breasts). This is one of the increasing number of British restaurants that bans smoking. There are also six bedrooms with canopied beds. *Portnam Lodge, Whitecliffe Mill St., tel. 0258/452842, fax 0258/480053. 6 rooms. Reservations advised. Jacket and tie required. AE, MC, V. Open Tues.–Sat. dinner. Closed Jan. $$*

Bournemouth
Dining

Langtry Manor Hotel. The French cuisine here is served on lacy tablecloths, with real silver cutlery and other details in keeping with the restaurant's Edwardian atmosphere (Lillie Langtry was the mistress of Edward VII and he built her this house in 1877). The dishes include Lillie's Special—meringue in the shape of a swan. There's an Edwardian banquet every Saturday. *26 Derby Rd., East Cliff, tel. 0202/553887. Reservations advised. Dress: casual. AE, DC, MC, V. $$$*

Sophisticats. As the name suggests, there's a lot of felinity in the decor here. This useful restaurant, hidden in a shopping mall, just outside the center of town, is especially adept with seafood, though there's Javanese fillet steak on the menu, too. It's quite small (seating just 34), so a reservation's a good idea. *43 Charminster Rd., tel. 0202/291019. Jacket and tie required. No credit cards. Open Tues.–Sat., dinner only. Closed 2 weeks Feb. and Nov., 1 week July. $$*

Dining and
Lodging
★
Carlton Hotel. Formerly a private mansion, built in 1900, this gracious cliff-top hotel has large rooms, some with balconies overlooking the sea. The hotel's restaurant, **Fredericks,** has a set dinner menu, but the setting is sumptuous and the food excellent. *Meyrick Rd., East Overcliff BH1 3DN, tel. 0202/552011, fax 0202/299573. 71 rooms with bath. Facilities: restaurant, swimming pool, sauna, solarium, gym, games room, hairdresser, spa. AE, DC, MC, V. $$$$*

Lodging
Swallow-Highcliff Hotel. This large Victorian hotel has some of its rooms in converted coast-guard cottages. The bedrooms are full of period atmosphere, with mahogany wardrobes. There is a funicular that takes you down to the promenade. *105 St. Michael's Rd., West Cliff BH2 5DU, tel. 0202/557702, fax 0202/292734. 157 rooms with bath. Facilities: restaurant, garden, pool, solarium, disco. AE, DC, MC, V. $$$*

San Remo. This well-built Victorian hotel is near the sea and the town center. The whole lodging has been refurbished, with cheerful flower-patterned wallpapers in the bedrooms, all of which have TVs. Dinner is available at 6 PM (bring your own wine). *7 Durley Rd., BH2 5JQ, tel. 0202/290558. 18 rooms, 13 with bath or shower. No credit cards. Closed Dec.–Easter. $*

Dorchester
Dining and
Lodging
★
Yalbury Cottage. A thatch roof and inglenook fireplaces enhance the traditional ambience here, just 2½ miles east of Dorchester, close to Hardy's cottage. The four-course fixed-price menu, changed daily and featuring English and Continental dishes, might include lamb Fenchurch (with port and red-currant sauce), and beef fillets in puff pastry. There are also eight comfortable bedrooms available in a discreet extension. *Lower Bockhampton, DT2 8PZ, tel. 0305/262382, fax 0305/266412. Reservations advised. Dress: casual. AE, MC, V. Closed Jan. and 2 weeks mid-winter. $$*

Lodging
★
Casterbridge Hotel. This Georgian building (1790) reflects its age, with period furniture and Old World elegance—it's small but full of character. *49 High East St., DT1 1HU, tel. 0305/264043, fax 0305/260884. 15 rooms with bath. Facilities: bar, conservatory, courtyard garden, no restaurant. AE, DC, MC, V. Closed Dec. 25–26. $$*

Lamperts Cottage. Here's an idyllic little B&B about 3 miles from Dorchester. It has a thatched roof and a stream in front and back so you have to cross a little bridge to reach it; in summer, it is covered with roses. The house, dating from the 16th century is very comfortable though small; the interior has exposed beams and fireplaces. You can be sure of a warm welcome. *Dorchester Rd., Sydling St. Nicholas, Cerne Abbas, DT2 9NU, tel. 0300/341659. 3 rooms. 2 bathrooms, but not en-suite. No credit cards. $*

Isle of Wight
Dining
Dean House (Ryde). In this comfortable, stylish restaurant on a hill overlooking the seafront, the talented chef specializes in traditional English dishes, such as smoked fish and pepper steak. *2 Dover St., The Esplanade, tel. 0983/562535. Reservations required. Dress: casual. AE, DC, MC, V. $$*

Lodging
Winterbourne Hotel (Bonchurch). This manor house was one of Charles Dickens's many homes. The bedrooms are named after characters in *David Copperfield*, part of which he wrote here. The furnishings are, of course, Victorian, and the gardens, with waterfalls, are beautifully kept. *Near Ventnor, PO38 1RQ, tel. 0983/852535, fax 0983/853056. 19 rooms, 17 with bath. Facilities: restaurant, outdoor pool, garden. AE, DC, MC, V. Closed Nov.–Feb. $$$*

Farringford Hotel (Freshwater). This was once the splendid home of the Victorian poet laureate Alfred, Lord Tennyson, but it is now an unpretentious hotel. The 18th-century house is set in 33 acres of grounds and has outbuildings that contain 24 self-catering suites and cottages, as well as normal bedrooms. *Bedbury La., PO40 9PE, tel. 0983/752500. 68 rooms with bath. Facilities: restaurant, 9-hole golf course, outdoor pool, tennis. AE, DC, MC, V. $$*

The Ryde Castle. Ivy-clad walls, battlements, and commanding views of the sea set the scene at this first-class hotel with many period features. It was built in 1540 by Henry VIII to defend The Solent. The current refurbishment has revealed some fine plaster moldings. Standards of service and comfort are high. The best rooms have a sea view. *The Esplanade, PO33 1JA, tel. 0983/563755, fax 0983/ 568925. 17 rooms with bath. Facilities: 2 restaurants, 3 bars, lounge, in-house movies. AE, DC, MC, V. $$*

Marlborough
Lodging

Ivy House. This Georgian house right on the attractive, colonnaded High Street makes an excellent touring base. The bedrooms are comfortably furnished, with small modern bathrooms attached. There is a courtyard bistro for relaxed meals. *43 High St., SN8 1HJ, tel. 0672/515333, fax 0672/515338. 34 rooms with bath. Facilities: restaurant. AE, MC, V. $$*

New Milton
Dining and Lodging
★

Chewton Glen. Once the home of Captain Frederick Marryat, author of *The Children, of the New Forest* and many naval adventure novels, this 18th-century country house is now a deluxe hotel, among the most expensive in Britain, set in extensive grounds. All the rooms are sumptuously furnished with an eye to the minutest detail. Gourmets consider its restaurant, the **Marryat Room,** and the cooking of its chef, Pierre Chevillard, worthy of a pilgrimage. With a genuinely helpful and friendly staff, Chewton Glen deserves its fine reputation. *Christchurch Rd., New Milton BH25 6QS, tel. 0425/ 275341, fax 0425/272310. 58 rooms with bath. Facilities: indoor pool, tennis, golf course, helipad, in-house movies. Restaurant reservations required. Jacket and tie required. AE, DC, MC, V. $$$$*

Poole
Lodging

Antelope Hotel. This historic coaching inn lies near the quay. It is partly 15th, partly 18th century, and has been well modernized. The bedrooms at the back are the quietest, but those in front have more character. *8 Old High St., BH15 1BP, tel. 0202/672029, fax 0202/ 678286. 21 rooms with bath. Facilities: restaurant. AE, DC, MC, V. $$*

Sheldon Lodge. Set in the Branksome Park area of Poole, this guest house is surrounded by trees and features many amenities, including billiards, a bar, and a solarium. The sunny bedrooms, all with private bathrooms, have TVs and appliances for making tea and coffee. *22 Forest Rd., Branksome Park, BH13 6DA, tel. 0202/761186. 14 rooms with bath or shower. MC, V. $$*

Portsmouth
Dining

Bistro Montparnasse. Candles, prints, and pink tablecloths help foster the intimate atmosphere of a traditional French restaurant. Among the dishes featured are turbot with a basil and champagne sauce, and a refreshingly sharp lemon soufflé. *103 Palmerston Rd., Southsea, tel. 0705/816754. Reservations advised. Dress: casual. AE, MC, V. Closed Sun. and Mon., and 3 weeks in Jan. $$*

Lodging
★

Westfield Hall. Portsmouth is well supplied with Hiltons, Fortes, and Holiday Inns, but here's a pleasant smaller establishment with personal service and character. Westfield Hall is in a converted turn-of-the-century house with big bay windows, close to the water in Southsea, the quieter, southern part of Portsmouth. It has satellite TV and a video channel in all rooms, five of which are on the ground floor. Dinner is available. *65 Festing Rd., PO4 0NQ, tel. 0705/826971, fax 0205/870200. 17 rooms, 14 with bath or shower. Facilities: dining room. AE, MC, V. $$*

Romsey
Dining

Old Manor House. This is one of those restaurants that is inseparable from its owner/chef, in this case Mauro Bregoli. The decor is typical of the area, with oak beams and huge fireplaces, and the Italian-influenced food is rich and flavorsome. Specialties include quenelle of pike, duck breast with apples, hare, suckling pig, and venison. The wine list is exceptionally good. There are worthwhile set menus, especially at lunch. *21 Palmerston St., tel. 0794/517353. Reservations required. Jacket and tie required. AE, MC, V. Closed Sun. evening, Mon., 3 weeks Aug., Christmas. $$$$*

Lodging
★

Potters Heron Hotel. An ideal place to stay if you're visiting Broadlands, this hotel has been renovated, adding a modern extension to the original thatched building. Choose an old or new room to suit your taste; many have balconies. Dine in the English restaurant with its table d'hôte and à la carte menus. *Ampfield (3 mi east of Romsey) SO51 9ZF, tel. 0703/266611, fax 0703/251359. 54 rooms with bath. Facilities: sauna, game rooms, fitness equipment. AE, DC, MC, V. Closed Christmas. $$$*

Salisbury
Dining
★

Crustaceans. Here, the serene blue-and-pink decor makes for a stylish, contemporary setting. This restaurant offers traditional fish dishes, including Dover sole, bass, turbot, and John Dory, as well as the more exotic bouillabaisse and crayfish. During the winter season you can sample local game, too. *2–4 Ivy St., tel. 0722/333948. Reservations advised. Jacket and tie required. MC, V. Closed Sat. lunch and Sun. $$*

Harper's. This is a spacious, airy, second-floor restaurant overlooking the market place. Its cuisine mingles English and French dishes and its specialties include chicken with ginger and fillet of salmon. There is a good-value Shopper's Special lunch. Friendly service makes dining here a pleasure. *7 Ox Row, Market Pl., tel. 0722/333118. Reservations advised. Dress: casual. AE, DC, MC, V. Closed Sun. in winter. $$*

Dining and Lodging

Red Lion Hotel. A former coaching inn—parts of the building date from 1320—this hotel is now in the Best Western chain. There's a choice of comfortable rooms in either modern or antique style. It's centrally located and an ideal base for exploring the city. *Milford St., SP1 2AN, tel. 0722/323334, fax 0722/325756. 56 rooms with bath. Facilities: restaurant, bistro. AE, DC, MC, V. $$$*

★ **Byways House.** Friendly service, good value for money, and a quiet location are some of the reasons this double-fronted Victorian house is popular with visitors. It was recently redecorated, and an extension was added. The hotel offers large traditional English breakfasts. Ask for a room with a view of the cathedral. *31 Fowlers Rd., SP1 2QP, tel. 0722/328364, fax 0722/322146. 23 rooms, 19 with bath. Facilities: large garden. MC, V. $$*

Grasmere House. Another large late-Victorian edifice (1896), this redbrick lodging covered with creeper, has fine views over the river to the cathedral. The comfortable bedrooms are named after local worthies (a saint, a canon, and so on). The restaurant, located in a conservatory, also provides peaceful country views. Its menu features fresh local ingredients. *70 Harnham Rd., SP2 8JN, tel. 0722/338388. 5 rooms, all with bath. MC, V. $$*

Southampton
Dining

La Brasserie. This is a busy spot at lunchtime, popular with the business community, though it quiets down in the evening. The decor is straightforward and ungimmicky, while the atmosphere is as traditionally French as the menu. *33–34 Oxford St., tel. 0703/635043. Reservations advised at lunch. Dress: casual. AE, MC, V. Closed Sat. lunch and Sun. $$*

Lodging **The Dolphin Hotel.** Originally a Georgian coaching inn—though there's been an inn of some sort on this site for seven centuries—the Dolphin offers stylish accommodations in large, comfortable rooms. The service is excellent—discreet but attentive. *35 High St., SO9 2DS, tel. 0703/339955, fax 0703/333650. 71 rooms with bath. Facilities: restaurant, garden. AE, DC, MC, V. $$$*

Warminster **Bishopstrow House.** It's not often that you'll find a Georgian house
Dining and converted into a luxurious hotel that combines Jacuzzis with an-
Lodging tiques and fine carpets. There's an airy conservatory, attractive
★ public areas, and peaceful rooms overlooking the grounds (25 acres) or an interior courtyard. The restaurant offers imaginatively prepared meals, appealing views of the gardens, and a menu which is regularly changed. Bishopstrow House is 1½ miles out of town. *Boreham Rd., BA12 9HH, tel. 0985/212312, fax 0985/216769. 32 rooms with bath. Facilities: indoor and outdoor pools, indoor and outdoor tennis, fishing and golf available, helipad. AE, DC, MC, V. $$$$*

West Lulworth **Castle Inn.** This charming, thatched hotel, just five minutes' walk
Lodging from the sea, has a flagstone bar and other 15th-century features. There's a good restaurant with an à la carte menu for evening meals and Sunday lunch. The bedrooms are plain but comfortable, and there is a lovely rose garden to sit in and satisfying walks to take nearby. *Main St., BH20 5RN, tel. 092941/311, fax 092941/415. 14 rooms, 10 with bath. Facilities: bar, garden. AE, DC, MC, V. $*

Weymouth **Perry's.** A fairly basic restaurant, right by the harbor, with simple
Dining dishes of the best local seafood. Try skate with capers and black butter—a fish hard to find these days. The meat dishes, such as venison with cassis, or rack of lamb, are tasty, too. *The Harbourside, 4 Trinity Rd., tel. 0305/785799. Reservations advised. Dress: casual. MC, V. Closed Mon. and Sat. lunch, and Sun. dinner in winter. $$*

Dining and **Streamside Hotel.** Quiet and cozy, this hotel/restaurant on the out-
Lodging skirts of town always graces its tables with fresh flowers and can-
★ dles. The cuisine is English, with specialties such as smoked salmon with melon, and steak in cream and brandy sauce. There are 15 comfortable rooms available, and the hotel, with award-winning gardens, is only 200 yards from the beach. *29 Preston Rd., Overcombe DT3 6PX, tel. 0305/833121, fax 0305/832043. Reservations advised. Dress: casual. AE, DC, MC, V. $$*

Winchester **Brann's Wine Bar and Restaurant.** You can have low-priced food at
Dining the wine bar, or select from the set menu in the quieter restaurant. In both areas, there's a fine selection of wines, some by the glass. While you're eating, you can feast your eyes on the cathedral that towers outside. *9 Great Minster St., The Square, tel. 0962/864004. Reservations needed. Dress: casual. AE, MC, V. $–$$*

Dining and **Royal.** At this classy hotel, you'll find an attractive walled garden
Lodging and some very comfortable bedrooms. It's within easy reach of the cathedral, but lies on a quiet side street. You can have an excellent lunch in the bar, or a fuller meal in the moderately priced restaurant. This is a Best Western hotel, and one of the swankier links in the chain. Some of the rooms are in a recent extension, but the older rooms have more atmosphere. *St. Peter St., SO22 8BS, tel. 0962/840840, fax 0962/841582. 75 rooms with bath. Facilities: restaurant, garden. Reservations advised for the restaurant. Jacket and tie required. AE, DC, MC, V. $$*

Wykeham Arms. This old inn is centrally located, close to the cathedral and the college. The four popular bars are happily cluttered with everything from old sports equipment to pewter mugs. The seven bedrooms are comfortably furnished in pine. The restaurant is very popular with the locals, so call ahead. *75 Kingsgate St., SO23 9PE, tel. 0962/053834, fax 0962/854411. 7 rooms with bath. Restaurant: Reservations advised; dress: casual. Facilities: restaurant, garden, sauna. AE, DC, MC, V. $$*

Lodging **Lainston House.** Dating from 1668, this elegant country-house hotel has wood paneling and other restored 17th-century features. All rooms are attractively decorated and comfortably furnished, but do try for the Garden Suite, which has access to the grounds. The hotel recently opened an attractive annex in a converted stable. *Sparsholt (3½ mi northwest of Winchester) SO21 2LJ, tel. 0962/863588, fax 0962/776672. 38 rooms with bath. Facilities: tennis, 63 acres parkland, helipad. AE, DC, MC, V. $$$$*

The Arts

Festivals The **Salisbury Festival** (tel. 0722/323883), in September, features excellent classical concerts, recitals, and plays. **Bournemouth** holds a **Music Festival** (tel. 0202/291718) June–July, with choirs, brass bands, and orchestras, some from overseas. The **Gold Hill Fair** (tel. 0747/51881), a traditional street fair held in **Shaftesbury** in July, features music and crafts.

Theaters The refurbished **Mayflower Theatre** (Commercial Rd., tel. 0703/330083) in Southampton, among the larger theaters outside London, has a full program of popular plays and concerts.

The **Nuffield Theatre** (tel. 0703/581576), on Southampton University campus, has its own repertory company and also hosts national touring groups, which perform some of the leading West End productions.

The **Salisbury Playhouse** (Malthouse La., tel. 0722/320333) presents high-caliber drama all year, and is the focus for the Salisbury Festival.

6 The Southwest

Somerset, Devon, Cornwall

The Southwest of England, the peninsula known as the West Country, comprises three counties—Somerset, Devon, and Cornwall—each with its own distinct character. Long one of Britain's favorite vacation areas, it encompasses an endless variety of natural and historic attractions, and despite a continuous influx of visitors, has managed to retain its rugged, magical beauty. In addition to its pleasant villages and popular beaches, it has vast tracts of moorland and unspoiled wooded stretches, ideal for walking.

Although King Arthur's name is linked with more than 150 places in Britain, no area can claim stronger ties than the West Country. According to tradition, Arthur was born at Tintagel Castle in Cornwall and later lived at Camelot, in the kingdom of Avalon (said to be Glastonbury, in Somerset).

Somerset, the region's tranquil northernmost county, is characterized by miles and miles of rolling green countryside. Along the north coast stand the Quantock and Mendip hills, and at their feet the stark, heather-covered expanse of Exmoor, setting for R. D. Blackmore's historical romance, *Lorna Doone*. Below this lies the county's boggy "Sedgemoor" region, known as the Levels. Central Somerset boasts some of England's richest agricultural land.

Devon, farther south, is famed for its wild moorland—especially Dartmoor, home to wild ponies and an assortment of strange "tors," rock outcrops sometimes eroded into weird shapes, sometimes covered in smooth turf. Devon also has soft, green hills, quiet villages with thatched cottages, and rocky beaches. Its large coastal towns are as interesting for their cultural and historical appeal—many were smugglers' havens—as for their scenic beauty. The best time to visit Devon is late summer and early fall, during the end-of-summer festivals, especially in the small towns of eastern Dartmoor.

Cornwall, England's southernmost county, has a mild climate, and nowhere are you more than 20 miles from the sea. This is a land of Celtic legend, where the ancient Cornish language survived until the 18th century. Until relatively recently, the county regarded itself as separate from the rest of Britain. Its Atlantic coast is punctuated with high jagged cliffs that look dangerous and dramatic and are a menace to passing ships, while the south coast relaxes with sunny beaches, delightful coves, and popular resorts.

Essential Information

Important Addresses and Numbers

Tourist Information **The West Country Tourist Board,** 60 St. David's Hill, Exeter, Devon EX4 4SY, tel. 0392/76351, fax 0703/420891. Open weekdays 9:30–5. **The Cornwall Tourist Board,** 59 Lemon St., Truro, Cornwall TR1 2SY, tel. 0872/74057, fax 0872/40423. **Devon Tourism,** Exeter Services, Sandygate (M5), Exeter, Devon EX2 7NJ, tel. 0392/437581. **Somerset Tourism,** County Hall, Taunton, Somerset TA1 4DY, tel. 0823/255010, fax 0823/255036.

Local TICs are usually open Mon.–Sat. 9:30–5:30.

Exeter: Civic Centre, Paris St., tel. 0392/265700.
Penzance: Station Rd., tel. 0736/62207.
Plymouth: Civic Centre, Royal Parade, tel. 0752/264849.
St. Ives: The Guildhall, Street-an-Pol, tel. 0736/796297.
Truro: City Hall, Boscawen St., tel. 0872/74555.

Wells: Town Hall, Market Pl., tel. 0749/672552.

Travel Agencies	**American Express:** 139 Armada Way, Plymouth, tel. 0752/228708. **Thomas Cook:** 177 Sidwell St., Exeter, tel. 0392/54971; 9 Old Town St., Plymouth, tel. 0752/667245.
Car-Rental Agencies	**Exeter: Avis,** Speedway Garage, Cowick St., tel. 0392/59713; **Plymouth: Avis,** Airport, tel. 0752/221550; **Europcar Ltd.,** Grevan Cars Ltd., 19 Union St., tel. 0752/669859; **Hertz,** Scot Hire, Walkham Business Park, tel. 0752/705819. **Truro: Avis,** Tregolls Rd., tel. 0872/262226.

Arriving and Departing

By Plane Plymouth has a small airport (tel 0752/705151) 3 miles from town.

By Car The fastest way from London to the Southwest is via the M4 and M5 motorways, bypassing Bristol (115 mi) and heading south to Exeter, in Devon (172 mi).

By Train **British Rail** serves the region from London's Paddington Station (tel. 071/262–6767). Average travel time to Exeter, 2¼ hours; to Plymouth, 3¾ hours; and to Penzance, about 5 hours.

By Bus **National Express** (tel. 071/730–0202) buses leave London's Victoria Coach Station for Bristol (2½ hrs.), Exeter (3¾ hrs.), Plymouth (4½ hrs.), and Penzance (about 8 hrs.).

Getting Around

By Car Driving can be tricky, especially in the western parts. Most of the small roads are twisting country lanes flanked by high stone walls and thick hedges, which severely restrict visibility. The main roads heading west are A30, which leads all the way to Land's End, at the tip of Cornwall, A39 (to the north) and A38 (to the south).

By Train Regional **Rail Rover** tickets are available for seven days' unlimited travel throughout the Southwest, and there are localized **Rovers** covering Devon or Cornwall.

By Bus **Western National Ltd.** (tel. 0752/664011) operates a regular service in Plymouth and throughout Cornwall, and also offers one-day **Explorer** and seven-day **Key West** tickets.

Guided Tours

The **West Country Tourist Board** (tel. 0392/76351) and local TICs have lists of qualified guides.
Designer Touring (28 Peasland Rd., Torquay TQ2 8PA, tel. 0803/326832) offers guided tours by bus or car.

Exploring the Southwest

Our circular tour of the Southwest covers a lot of territory, from the gentle hills of Somerset, two hours outside London, to the remote and rocky headlands of Devon and Cornwall. The first leg starts in the cathedral city of Wells and continues via Glastonbury, possibly the Avalon of Arthurian legend, south to Taunton, then west along the Somerset coast into Devon. Tour 1 ends at the cliff-top ruins of Tintagel Castle in Cornwall, legendary birthplace of Arthur.

Our second tour travels southwest from Tintagel along the north Cornish coast to Land's End, the westernmost tip of Britain, known for its savage land and seascapes and panoramic views. From Land's End we turn northeast, stopping in the popular seaside resort of Penzance, the harbor city of Falmouth, and a string of pretty Cornish fishing villages. Next we set off across the boggy, heath-covered expanse of Bodmin Moor, and then turn south to Plymouth, Devon's largest city.

For the final tour from Plymouth back to Wells, you have a choice of heading north to explore the vast, boggy reaches of Dartmoor Forest (setting for the Sherlock Holmes classic *The Hound of the Baskervilles*), or continuing east along Start Bay to Torbay, known as the English Riviera. Both routes end in the ancient Roman capital of Exeter, Devon's county seat. From Exeter we meander south to Exmouth, then turn northeast to Yeovil in Somerset, re-entering King Arthur country at Cadbury Castle, the legendary Camelot.

Highlights for First-time Visitors

Buckland Abbey: Tour 2
Glastonbury Tor: Tour 1
Land's End: Tour 2
The Lizard Peninsula: Tour 2
Lydford Gorge: Tour 2
Mayflower Steps, Plymouth: Tour 2
Montacute House: Tour 3
St. Michael's Mount: Tour 2
Tintagel: Tour 1
Wells Cathedral: Tour 1
Wookey Hole and the Cheddar Caves: Off the Beaten Track

Tour 1: King Arthur Country — From Wells to Tintagel

Numbers in the margin correspond to points of interest on the Southwest map.

❶ **Wells,** England's smallest cathedral city, lies at the foot of the Mendip Hills, about 132 miles southwest of London. While it feels more like a quiet country town than a city, Wells is home to one of the great masterpieces of Gothic architecture. The city's name refers to the underground streams that bubble up into St. Andrew's Well within the grounds of the Bishop's Palace. Spring water has run through the High Street since the 15th century.

The ancient **Market Place** in the city center is surrounded by 17th-century buildings. William Penn was arrested here in 1695 for preaching without a license at the Crown Hotel (*see* Dining and Lodging, *below*). Though the elaborate fountain at the entrance to the square is only 200 years old, it's on the same spot as the lead conduit that brought fresh spring water to the market in medieval times.

The great west towers of the famous **Cathedral Church of St. Andrew** are visible for miles. To appreciate the elaborate west front facade, approach the building on foot from the cathedral green, accessible from Market Place through a great medieval gate called "penniless porch" (named after the beggars who once waited here to collect alms from worshipers). The cathedral's west front is twice as wide as it is high and is adorned with some 300 statues. This is the oldest surviving English Gothic church, begun in the 12th century. Vast inverted arches were added in 1338 to stop the central tower from sinking to one side. Present erosion is causing a great deal of anxie-

The Southwest

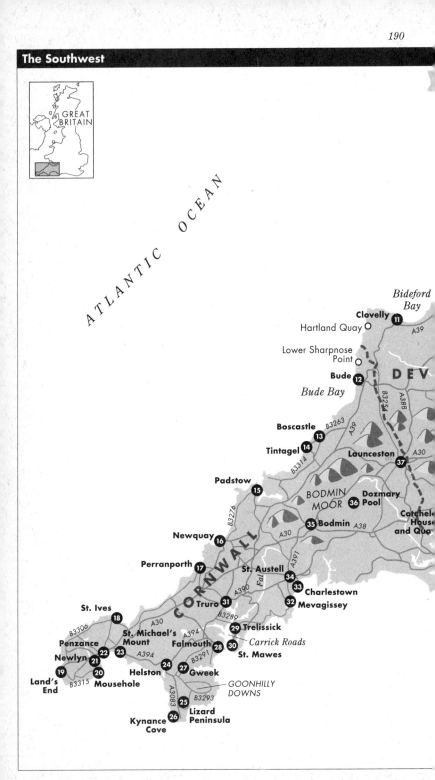

GREAT BRITAIN

ATLANTIC OCEAN

Bideford Bay

Clovelly **11**
Hartland Quay ○
A39

Lower Sharpnose Point ○

Bude **12**
DEV
B3254
A388

Bude Bay

Boscastle **13**
B3263
A39

Tintagel **14**
B3314

Launceston **37**
A30

Padstow **15**
B3276

BODMIN MOOR

Dozmary Pool **36**

Cotehele House and Qua...

Newquay **16**
Bodmin **35**
A30
A38

Perranporth **17**

St. Austell **34**
A391
Charlestown **33**

Truro **31**
A390
Fal
Mevagissey **32**

B3289

St. Ives **18**
A30
B3306

Trelissick **29**

St. Michael's Mount
A394
Falmouth **28**
Carrick Roads

Penzance
30
St. Mawes

Newlyn **22** **23**
A394

21
20
Helston **24** **27**
Gweek

Land's End **19**
B3315
Mousehole
GOONHILLY DOWNS

25
A3083
B3293

Kynance Cove **26**
Lizard Peninsula

CORNWALL

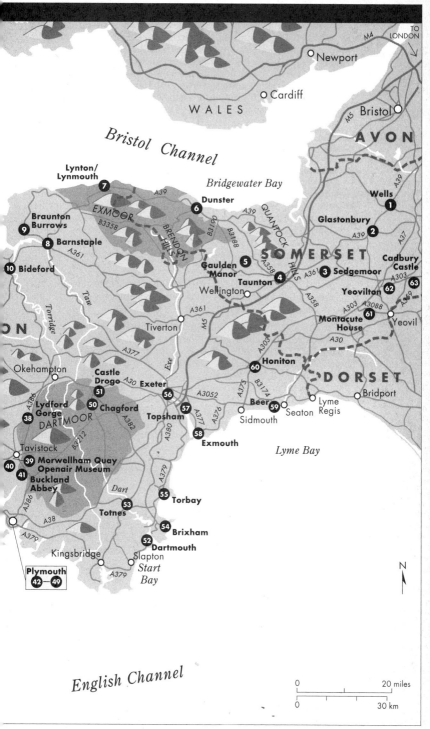

ty, and a restoration program is under way. The cathedral also boasts a rare, medieval clock, consisting of the seated figure of a man called Jack Blandiver, who strikes a bell on the quarter hour while mounted knights circle in mock battle. Near the clock you will find the entrance to the chapter house—a small, wooden door opening onto a great sweep of stairs worn down on one side by the tread of pilgrims over the centuries. Every capital and pillar in the church has a carving; look for the one of a man with a toothache and another with a thorn in his foot.

Time Out The **Cathedral Cloisters Café,** inside the cathedral, serves scones, cake, sandwiches, soup, and a hot dish at lunchtime.

The second great gate leading from Market Place, the Bishop's Eye, takes you to the **Bishop's Palace.** Most of its original 12th- and 13th-century residences remain, and you can also see the ruins of a late-13th-century great hall, which lost its roof in the 16th century because Edward VI needed the lead! The palace is surrounded by a moat that's home to a variety of waterfowl, including swans. *Market Pl., tel. 0749/678691. Admission: £2 adults, children under 16 free. Open Apr.–Oct., Tues., Thurs. 10–6, Sun. 2–6; Aug., national holidays, daily 10–6.*

North of the cathedral, **Vicar's Close,** Europe's oldest street, has terraces of handsome 14th-century houses with strange, tall chimneys, and a tiny medieval chapel that's still in use.

❷ Five miles southwest of Wells, just off A39, is **Glastonbury,** steeped in history, myth, and legend. The town lies at the foot of **Glastonbury Tor,** a grassy hill rising 520 feet. In legend, Glastonbury is identified with Avalon, the paradise into which King Arthur was born after his death. It is also said to be the burial place of Arthur and Guinevere, his queen. And according to Christian tradition, it was to Glastonbury, the first Christian settlement in England, that Joseph of Arimathea brought the Holy Grail, the chalice used by Christ at the Last Supper. At the foot of the tor is **Chalice Well,** the legendary burial place of the Grail. It's a stiff climb up the tor, but you'll be rewarded by the view across the Vale of Avalon. At the top stands a ruined tower, all that's left of **St. Michael's Church,** which collapsed after a landslide in 1271. The tor is now owned by the National Trust, and is open free to the public.

In the town below lie the ruins of the great **Abbey of Glastonbury.** According to legend, this is the site where Joseph of Arimathea built a church in the 1st century; a monastery had certainly been erected here by the 9th century. The ruins are those of the abbey completed in 1524 and destroyed in 1539, during Henry VIII's dissolution of the monasteries. *Tel. 0458/832267. Admission: £2 adults, £1 children, £1.50 senior citizens. Open June–Aug., daily 9–6; Sept.–May, daily 9:30–dusk.*

While you are in Glastonbury, visit the Abbey Barn, which now houses the **Somerset Rural Life Museum.** This 14th-century tithe barn stored the one-tenth portion of the town's produce due the church, and it is more than 90 feet long. *Chilkwell St., tel. 0458/831197. Admission: £1.20 adults, 30p children, 80p senior citizens. Open Easter–Oct., weekdays 10–5, weekends 2–6:30; Nov.–Easter, weekdays 10–5, weekends 2:30–5.*

From Glastonbury take A39 and A361 to Taunton, 22 miles away. The road crosses the Somerset Levels, marshes that have been drained by open ditches (known as rhines), where peat is dug.

❸ **Sedgemoor** is where, in 1685, the duke of Monmouth's troops were routed by those of his uncle James II in the last battle fought on English soil. R. D. Blackmore's novel, *Lorna Doone*, is set during Monmouth's Rebellion.

❹ **Taunton,** Somerset's principal town, lies in the heart of the cider-making country. In these parts, cider rather than beer is the traditional beverage. Fermented and alcoholic, it can be a lot more potent than English beer. In the fall, some cider mills open their doors to visitors. If you're interested, visit **Sheppys,** a local farm, shop, and cider museum. *Three Bridges, Bradford-on-Tone (on A38 west of Taunton), tel. 0823/461233. Admission: £1.50 adults, £1 children, £1.25 senior citizens; guided tour (2 hours) £3 adults, £2 children, £2.75 senior citizens. Open Oct.–Mar., Mon.–Sat. 8:30–6; May.–Sept., Mon.–Sat. 8:30–6:30; Easter–Christmas, Sun. noon–2.*

Time Out | **Porters Wine Bar** (49 E. Reach) in Taunton serves both light lunches and more substantial meals at very reasonable prices.

North of Taunton you will see the outlines of the **Quantock** and **Brendon hills.** The eastern Quantocks are covered with beech trees and are home to herds of handsome red deer. Climb to the top of the hills for a spectacular view of the Vale of Taunton Deane and to the north the Bristol Channel. Nearby, in a quiet valley between these ❺ two lines of hills, is **Gaulden Manor,** a small 12th-century manor, whose house is built of red sandstone. Its elegant grounds include an Elizabethan herb garden. Henry Wolcott, who lived here in the 17th century, was an ancestor of Oliver Wolcott, a signer of the U.S. Declaration of Independence. It was also the home of the Turberville family, a name familiar to readers of *Tess of the d'Urbervilles*, by Thomas Hardy. *Tolland (9 mi northwest of Taunton), tel. 09847/213. Admission: £2.80 adults, £1.25 children; garden only, £1.25. Open 1st Sun. in May–1st Sun. in Sept., Sun. and Thurs. and national holidays 2–5:30.*

From Tolland, follow B3188, B3190, and A39 about 12 miles north-❻ west to the village of **Dunster,** which lies between the Somerset coast and the edge of Exmoor National Park. Dunster is a picture-book village with a broad main street. Look for the eight-sided **yarn market building** dating from 1589. The village is dominated by its 13th-century fortress, **Dunster Castle,** a National Trust property boasting fine plaster ceilings and a magnificent 17th-century staircase. Note that there is a steep climb up to the castle from the parking lot. *Tel. 0643/821314. Admission: £4.60 adults, £2.30 children; gardens only: £2.50 adults, £1.20 children, £6.50 inclusive family ticket. Open Apr.–Sept., Sat.–Wed. 11–5; Oct., Sat.–Wed. 11–4. Gardens open Feb.–mid-Dec., daily 11–4.*

Heading west, the coast road A39 mounts **Porlock Hill,** an incline so steep that signs are posted to encourage drivers to "Keep Going." The views across Exmoor and north to the Bristol Channel and ❼ Wales are worth it. Nineteen miles west of Dunster lie **Lynton** and **Lynmouth,** a pretty pair of Devonshire villages separated by a hugely steep hill. Lynmouth, a fishing village, is at the bottom, crouching below 1,000-foot cliffs at the mouths of the Rivers East and West Lynne.

❽ **Barnstaple,** 21 miles southwest on A39, on the banks of the river Taw, is northern Devon's largest city. It's a bustling market town surrounded by modern developments, though the center retains its traditional look. Try to visit on Friday, market day, to see the colorful scene in Butchers' Row and Pannier Market. West of Barnstaple, along the Taw estuary, lie desolate stretches of sand dunes offering

(9) long vistas of marram grass and sea. **Braunton Burrows,** 10 miles west on the north side of the estuary, is a National Nature Reserve, with miles of trails running through the dunes. This is a first-class bird-watching spot, especially in winter.

Broad Bideford Bay is fed by the confluence of the Taw and Torridge

(10) rivers. **Bideford** lies on the Torridge estuary, about 8 miles west of Barnstaple by A39. Cross the river either by the 14th-century, 24-arch bridge or by the more modern structure to reach the scenic hillside sheltering the town's elegant houses. At one time they were all painted white, and Bideford is still sometimes called the "little white town." The area was a mainstay of 16th-century shipbuilding; the trusty vessels of Sir Francis Drake among others were built here.

(11) Next, continue west around the bay to picturesque **Clovelly,** perched precariously among cliffs, a steep, cobbled road leading down to the tiny harbor. This road isn't open to private cars, but a Land Rover service (in summer) will take you to and from the parking lot at the top.

(12) Fifteen miles south, just across the Cornish border, is **Bude,** a popular Victorian seaside town known for its long sandy beaches. But beware: in summer, the town and beaches are overrun with tourists.

(13) **Boscastle,** another 15 miles farther on, is a somewhat more tranquil spot. Some of the stone and slate cottages at the foot of the steep valley here date from the 1300s.

Five miles farther along the coast is the ruined clifftop castle of

(14) **Tintagel,** said to have been the birthplace of King Arthur. Archaeological evidence, however, suggests that the castle dates from much later, about 1150, when it was the stronghold of the earls of Cornwall, and the site may have been occupied by the Romans. The earliest identified remains at the castle are of Celtic (5th-century) origin, and these may have some connection with the legendary Arthur. But legends aside, nothing can detract from the stunning castle ruins, dramatically set on the wild, windswept Cornish coast, part on the mainland, part on an island connected by a narrow isthmus. (There are also traces of a Celtic monastery on the island.) You can still see the ruins of the Great Hall, some walls, and the outlines of various buildings. Paths lead down to the pebble beach, to a cavern known as **Merlin's Cave.** Exploring Tintagel Castle involves some arduous climbing up and down steep steps. *Tel. 0840/770328. Admission: £2.10 adults, £1.05 children, £1.55 senior citizens. Open Apr.–Oct., daily 10–6; Nov.–Mar., daily 10–4.*

In the town of Tintagel, which has more than its share of tourist junk—including Excaliburgers!—stop in at the **Old Post Office,** situated in a 15th-century stone manor house with smoke-blackened beams. *Tel. 0840/770024. Admission: £1.90 adults, 95p children. Open Apr.–Oct., daily 11–5.*

Tour 2: The Devon and Cornwall Coasts— From Tintagel to Plymouth

(15) Continue on A39 and A389 15 miles to **Padstow,** an important port until a treacherous sand bar formed here. According to legend, this "Doom Bar" appeared when a fisherman shot at a mermaid; in retaliation she flung sand across the estuary mouth. Though modern development has crowded the town's Tudor and medieval buildings—a few survive, such as the Elizabethan facade of Prideaux Place—the sand dunes remain unspoiled and are popular bird-watching points.

⑯ About 14 miles southwest of Padstow by B3276 is **Newquay,** a largish town that's the principal resort on the north Cornwall coast. Established in 1439, the town was once the center of the trade in pilchards (a small herring-like fish). On the headland sits a little white hut, where a lookout known as a "huer" watched for pilchard schools and directed the boats to the fishing grounds. Eight miles south of Newquay lies **Perranporth,** past the sandy shores of Perran Bay. This 3-mile stretch of beach, one of Cornwall's most popular seaside spots, is extremely crowded in high season. The swell here attracts swarms of surfers, too. The best times to visit are the beginning and end of the summer. There are enchanting coastal walks along the dunes and cliffs.

⑰ Leaving Perranporth, continue south about 20 miles along A30 to the fishing village of **St. Ives,** named after St. Ia, a 5th-century female Irish missionary said to have arrived on a floating leaf. The town has attracted artists and tourists for more than 100 years, and is now a well-established artists' colony. Dame Barbara Hepworth, who pioneered abstract sculpture in England, lived here for 26 years. She died tragically in a fire in her studio in 1975. The house and garden, now the **Barbara Hepworth Museum and Sculpture Garden,** is run by the Tate and is fascinating to anyone interested in sculpture. It is best to park outside the town. *Trewyn Studio, Barnoon Hill, tel. 0736/796226. Entrance is included in Tate Gallery admission (see below). Open June–Aug., Mon. 11–7, Tues. and Thurs. 11–9, Sun. 1–7; Sept.–May., Tues.–Sat. 11–5, Sun. 1–5.*

The new **Tate Gallery St. Ives** opened in spring 1993. The four-story gallery, set on a cliff with dramatic sea views, houses the work of artists who lived and worked in St. Ives, mostly from 1925 to 1975, drawn from the rich collection of the Tate Gallery in London. This is the latest move in the Tate's plan to spread its artistic wealth outside the capital. It may be the only art gallery in the world with a special storage space for visitors' surfboards. *Porthmeor Beach, tel. 0736/ 796226. Admission: £2.50 adults, £1.50 senior citizens, £10 family tickets (price includes Hepworth Museum). Open Sept.–May, Tues. 11–9, Wed.–Sat. 11–5, Sun. 1–5; June–Aug., Mon.–Sat. 11–7, Tues. and Thurs. 11–9, Sun. 1–7.*

Examples of current artists' work can be found for sale at the St. Ives Society of Artists in the **Old Mariner's Church** (tel. 0736/ 795582) in Norway Square. Admission: 25p.

Time Out Built in 1312, the **Sloop Inn** beside St. Ives harbor is one of England's oldest pubs. Pub lunches are available in the handsome, wood-beamed rooms every day except Sunday.

The B3306 coastal road south from St. Ives is a winding route passing through some of Cornwall's most beautiful countryside. Stark hills crisscrossed by low stone walls drop abruptly to rocky cliffs and wide bays. Evidence of the ancient tinmining industry—the remains of smokestacks and pumping houses—is everywhere. In some places the workings extended beneath the sea, forcing miners to toil away with the noise of waves crashing over their heads. Be careful if you decide to explore: many of the old shafts are open and unprotected.

B3306 ends at the western tip of Britain at what is, quite literally,
⓳ **Land's End.** Although the point draws tourists from all over the
world, and a multimillion-dollar glitzy theme park has been added,
its savage grandeur remains undiminished. The sea crashes against
its rocks and lashes ships battling their way around it. Approach it
from one of the coastal footpaths for the best panoramic view. Over
the years, sightseers have caused some erosion of the paths, but new
ones have recently been built, and Cornish "hedges" (granite walls
covered with turf) planted to prevent future erosion.

Leaving Land's End, start your journey northeast along B3315,
⓴ stopping in at **Mousehole** (pronounced "Mowzel"), an archetypal
Cornish fishing village of tiny stone cottages. It was the home of
Dolly Pentreath, supposedly the last native Cornish speaker, who
died in 1777.

㉑ A stone's throw north of Mousehole along the coast is **Newlyn,** the
most important fishing port in the county and also a popular artists'
colony at the end of the 19th century. A few of the appealing
fishermen's cottages that first attracted artists here remain. The
Penzance and District Museum and Art Gallery in Penzance exhibits
paintings by members of the so-called Newlyn School. *Penlee Park,*
tel. 0736/63625. Admission: 75p adults, 50p senior citizens, children
free. Open weekdays 10:30–12:30 and 2:30–4:30, Sat. 10:30–12:30.

From Newlyn, it's only 1½ miles to the popular seaside resort of
㉒ **Penzance,** with its spectacular views over Mount's Bay. Because of
the town's isolated position, it has always been open to attack from
the sea. During the 16th century, Spanish raiders destroyed most of
the original town, and the majority of old buildings you see date
from as late as the 18th century. The main street is called Market
Jew Street, a folk mistranslation of the Cornish expression
"Marghas Yow," which actually means "Thursday Market." Look for
Market House, constructed in 1837, an impressive, domed granite
building that is now a bank.

One of the prettiest streets in Penzance is **Chapel Street,** formerly
the main street. It winds down from Market House to the harbor,
where typical Georgian and Regency houses suddenly give way to
the extraordinary **Egyptian House,** whose facade is an evocation of
ancient Egypt. Built around 1830 as a geological museum, today it
houses a National Trust shop. A little farther down the street is the
17th-century **Union Hotel,** where in 1805 the death of Lord Nelson
and the victory of Trafalgar were first announced from the minstrels' gallery in the assembly rooms. Nearby is one of the few remnants of old Penzance, the **Turk's Head,** an inn said to date from the
13th century.

Time Out Another Penzance inn, the 15th-century **Admiral Benbow** (Chapel
St.), was once a smugglers' pub and is full of seafaring memorabilia,
a brass cannon, model ships, ropes, and figureheads. It's a popular
pub, serving good, solid food. Try the steak and Guinness pie.

The town's **Nautical Museum,** also on Chapel Street, simulates the
lower decks of a four-deck man-of-war, and exhibits items salvaged
from shipwrecks off the Cornish coast. *19 Chapel St., tel. 0736/*
68890. Admission: £1.50 adults, 75p children, £4 family ticket.
Open Easter–Oct., Mon.–Sat. 10–5.

About 3 miles east of Penzance on A394 is one of Cornwall's great-
㉓ est natural attractions, **St. Michael's Mount,** a spectacular granite
and slate island rising out of Mount's Bay just off the coast. A 14th-

century castle perched at the highest point, 200 feet above the sea, was built on the site of a Benedictine chapel founded by Edward the Confessor. In its time, it has been a church, a fortress, and a private residence. The buildings around the base of the rock range from medieval to Victorian, but appear harmonious. The Mount is surrounded by fascinating gardens, where a great variety of plants flourish in micro-climates—snow can lie briefly on one part, while it can be 70° in another. To get there, follow the causeway or, when the tide is in in the summer, take the ferry. If you have to wait for the ferry, there is a handy restaurant at the harbor. *Marazion, tel. 0736/710507. Admission: £3.20 adults, £1.60 children, £8 family ticket. Open Apr.–Oct., weekdays 10:30–4:45; Nov.–Mar., Mon., Wed., Fri. by guided tour only.*

㉔ Take the coastal road 13 miles east to **Helston.** This attractive Georgian town is most famous for its annual "Furry Dance," which takes place on Floral Day, May 8 (unless the date is a Sunday or Monday, when it takes place on the nearest Saturday). The whole town is decked with flowers for the occasion, while dancers weave their way in and out of the houses following a 3-mile route. To explore more of

㉕ the coastline, follow A3083 from Helston down the **Lizard Peninsula,** the southernmost point in mainland Britain, and an officially designated Area of Outstanding Natural Beauty. The huge, eerily rotating dish antennae of the **Goonhilly Satellite Communications Earth Station** are visible from the road as it crosses Goonhilly Downs, the backbone of the peninsula. The National Trust owns much of the Lizard coastline, so this spectacular area is protected from development. One path here, close to the tip, plunges down 200-foot cliffs to

㉖ tiny **Kynance Cove,** with its handful of pint-sized islands. The sands here are reachable only in the 2½ hours before and after low tide. The Lizard's cliffs are made of greenish, serpentine rock, interspersed with granite; local souvenirs are carved out of the stone.

㉗ Head back north to the fishing village of **Gweek,** 2 miles east of Helston at the head of the Helford River. Gweek is known for its **Seal Sanctuary,** which shelters sick and injured seals brought in from all over the country. Try to be there for feeding time, 11 AM and 4 PM. *Tel. 0326/221361. Admission: £4.50 adults, £2.95 children, £3.50 senior citizens. Open summer, daily 9–6; winter 10–5; the seals are fed twice a day at 11 (all year), and 3 (summer), 4 (winter).*

㉘ Take B3291 northeast 7 miles to **Falmouth,** which has one of the finest natural harbors in the country. The bustling confusion of this busy resort town's fishing harbor, yachting center, and commercial port only adds to its charm. The oldest section is on the northern side of the Pendennis Peninsula, while the seaward side is lined with modern hotels. In the 18th century, Falmouth was a mailboat port, and in Flushing, a village across the inlet, are the slate-covered houses built by prosperous mailboat captains. A ferry service now links the two towns. On Falmouth's quay, near the **Customs House,** is the **King's Pipe,** an oven in which seized contraband was burned.

At the end of the Peninsula stands formidable **Pendennis Castle,** built by Henry VIII in the 1540s and later improved by his daughter Elizabeth I. From here there are sweeping views over the English Channel and across the water known as Carrick Roads, to St. Mawes Castle on the Roseland Peninsula (*see below*), designed as a companion fortress to guard the roads. *Pendennis Head, tel. 0326/316594. Admission: £2.10 adults, £1.05 children, £1.55 senior citizens. Open Apr.–Oct., daily 10–6; Nov.–Mar., daily 10–4.*

From Falmouth, circle around the Carrick Roads estuary, stopping off at **Trelissick** on B3289, where the **King Harry Ferry,** a chain-drawn car ferry, runs to the Roseland Peninsula at regular intervals daily, except Sundays during the winter. From its decks you can see all the way up and down the Fal, a deep, narrow river with steep, wooded banks. The river's great depth provides ideal mooring for old ships waiting to be sold; these mammoth shapes lend a surreal touch to the riverscape.

If you go over on the ferry, make your way south down the Roseland Peninsula to **St. Mawes.** At the tip of the peninsula stands the Tudor-era **St. Mawes Castle.** Its cloverleaf shape makes it seemingly impregnable, yet during the Civil War, its royalist commander surrendered without firing a shot. (In contrast, Pendennis Castle held out at the time for 23 weeks before submitting to the siege.) *St. Mawes, tel. 0326/270526. Admission: £1.35 adults, 65p children, £1 senior citizens. Open Apr.–Oct., daily 10–6; Nov.–Mar., daily 10–4.*

The shortest route from St. Mawes to Truro is via the ferry. The longer way swings in a circle on A3078 for 19 miles through attractive countryside, where subtropical shrubs and flowers thrive in the gardens along the way, past the town of Portloe (and its cozy hotel) and the 123-foot church tower in the village of **Probus,** flaunting its gargoyles and pierced stonework.

Truro is a compact, elegant Georgian city, nestled in a crook at the head of the river Truro. Though Bodmin is the county seat of Cornwall, Truro is Cornwall's only real city. The **Cathedral Church of St. Mary**—the first cathedral built in England since the completion of St. Paul's in London in the early 1700s—dominates the city; although comparatively modern (built 1880–1910), it evokes the feeling of a medieval church, with an impressive exterior in early English Gothic style. The inside is not so interesting, apart from a side chapel, all that remains of the original 16th-century parish church. In front of the west porch there is an open, cobbled area called High Cross, and the city's main shopping streets fan out from here.

Time Out   The **Globe** (Frances St.) is a thoroughly comfortable pub, with paneling, oak beams, and relaxing chairs. The self-service lunchtime bar food is homemade and a great value.

For an overview of Truro's Georgian housefronts, take a stroll down **Lemon Street.** The 18th-century facades along this steep, broad street are of mellow-colored stone, unusual for Cornwall, where granite predominates. Another typical Georgian street is **Walsingham Place,** a curving, flower-lined, pedestrian oasis. Near here is the **Royal Cornwall Museum,** which offers a sampling of Cornish art, archaeology, an extensive collection of minerals and a new café and shop. *River St., tel. 0872/72205. Admission: £1.20 adults, 60p children and senior citizens; children accompanied by adults free. Open Mon.–Sat. 9–5.*

Just east of the cathedral, near the Quay, the rivers Allen and Kenwyn merge into the River Truro, which then becomes the River Fal. Truro's days as an important port for tin and copper export were over by the early 18th century, but there is still some commercial traffic here, and pleasure boats ply the river in summer. In winter, when the water is low, boat trips begin and end at **Malpas,** just south of Truro. *Enterprise Boats, 66 Trefusis Rd., Flushing (north of Falmouth), tel. 0326/374241. Boats travel each way 4 times a day during the summer. The 1-way trip takes about 1 hour.*

32 From Truro, continue eastward on A390, turn right at Sticker, and follow signs to the busy fishing town of **Mevagissey** (about 15 miles). (Like most Cornish coastal villages, it is not suitable for cars, so if you stop to visit, use the large parking lot on the outskirts.) About 4

33 miles north is **Charlestown,** a harbor town built in 1791. It is still active in china-clay export, which explains the strange white dust coating the 18th-century houses along the port. It was also one of the ports from which 19th-century emigrants left for America. Its period look has made it a popular film location. The center of the chi-

34 na-clay industry is **St. Austell,** just inland of Charlestown. The hinterland here, with its brilliantly white heaps of clay waste visible for miles around (*see* Off the Beaten Track, *below*), is known as the White Alps of Cornwall.

35 From St. Austell, follow A391 13 miles north to **Bodmin.** This was the only Cornish town recorded in the 11th-century *Domesday Book*, William the Conqueror's census of English towns and holdings. During World War I, both the *Domesday Book* and the Crown Jewels were sent to Bodmin Prison for safekeeping. From the **Gilbert Memorial** on the Beacon Hill you can see both of Cornwall's coasts.

For another taste of Arthurian legend, follow A30 northeast out of Bodmin across the boggy, heather-clad granite plateau of Bodmin

36 Moor, and turn right at Bolventor to get to **Dozmary Pool.** A considerable lake rather than a pool, it was here that King Arthur's magic sword Excalibur was supposedly returned to the Lady of the Lake after Arthur's last battle.

Time Out At Bolventor, in the center of Bodmin Moor, just off A30, look for **Jamaica Inn,** made famous by Daphne du Maurier's novel of the same name. Originally a farmstead, it is now Cornwall's best-known pub and a good spot to try a Cornish pasty.

After crossing Bodmin Moor, the first large town you come to is

37 **Launceston** (pronounced "Lanston"), Cornwall's ancient capital. Parts of its medieval walls survive, including the South Gate. For a full view of the surrounding countryside, climb up to the ruins of 14th-century **Launceston Castle.** *Tel. 0566/772365. Admission: £1.25 adults, 65p children, 95p senior citizens. Open Apr.–Oct., daily 10–6.*

Leaving Launceston, continue east along A30, following the signs to

38 **Lydford Gorge,** 9 miles away, where the River Lyd has carved a spectacular chasm through the rock. Two paths follow the gorge past gurgling whirlpools and waterfalls with names such as the Devil's Cauldron and the White Lady. *Lydford, tel. 082282/441 or 082282/320. Admission: £2.80 adults, £1.40 children. Open Apr.– Oct., daily 10:30–5:30; in winter, walk restricted to main waterfall.*

East of Lydford, pick up A386 south via Tavistock, then A390. Be-

39 fore reaching Gunnislake on this road, you'll find the **Morwellham Quay Openair Museum.** This was England's main copper-exporting port in the 19th century, and it has been restored as a working museum, with quay workers and coachmen in costume, and a copper mine open to visitors. *Tel. 0822/832766 or 0822/833808 (recorded information). Admission: £6.75 adults, £4.60 children, £6 senior citizens. Open Apr.–Oct., daily 10–5:30 (last admission at 4); Nov.–Mar., daily 10–4 (last admission 2:30).*

40 At Albaston, turn left off A390 for **Cotehele House and Quay.** Formerly a busy port, Cotehele now offers a late-medieval manor house complete with original furniture, armor, and needlework; gardens; a restored mill; and a quay museum, the whole complex now run by the National Trust. *St. Dominick (north of Saltash), tel. 0579/ 50434. Admission: £5 adults, £2.50 children; gardens and mill only £2.50 adults, £1.25 children. Open Apr.–Oct., Sat.–Thurs., 12– 5:30; gardens all year, daily during daylight hours.*

(41) Return via A390 to Tavistock, and take A386 south to Crapstone, then west to **Buckland Abbey,** a 13th-century Cistercian monastery which became the home of Sir Francis Drake in 1581. Today it is full of mementos of Drake and the Spanish Armada. The abbey has a licensed restaurant. *Yelverton, tel. 0822/853607. Admission: £4 adults, £2 children; gardens only, £2 adults, £1 children. Open Easter–Oct., Fri.–Wed. 10:30–5:30; church only Nov.–Mar., Wed., Sat., and Sun. 2–5.*

Less than a mile from Buckland Abbey in Buckland Monachorum is **The Garden House,** an incredibly rich garden, not to be missed. Terraced around the remains of a 16th-century vicarage and incorporating its walled garden, this superb spot is vivid with wisterias rioting over ancient brick walls, azaleas, roses, and innumerable other flowering plants, many of them rare. It is seen at its best in spring and early summer. Light lunches and teas are served in the main house, and you can buy specimen plants. *Buckland Monachorum, near Yelverton, tel. 0822/854769. Admission: £2.50 adults, 50p children, £2.25 senior citizens. Open Apr.–Sept., daily 10:30–5; Oct., Nov., and Feb., weekdays 2–5.*

(42) Next, follow A386 about 9 miles south to **Plymouth.**

Numbers in the margin correspond to points of interest on the Plymouth map.

(43) Devon's largest city has long been linked with England's commercial and maritime history. From the **Hoe,** a wide, grassy esplanade with crisscrossing walkways high above the city—and especially from **(44)** **Smeaton's Tower**—you can get a magnificent view of the many inlets, bays, and harbors that make up Plymouth Sound. At the end of **(45)** the Hoe stands the huge **Royal Citadel,** built by Charles II in 1666. A new visitors center displays exhibits on both old and new Plymouth.

(46) The **Barbican,** which lies east of the Royal Citadel, is the oldest surviving section of Plymouth (much of the city center was destroyed by air raids in World War II). Here, Tudor houses and warehouses rise from a maze of narrow streets leading down to the fishing docks and harbor. Many of these buildings have become antiques shops, art shops, and bookstores. By the harbor you can visit the **Mayflower** **(47)** **Steps,** where the Pilgrims embarked in 1620; the **Mayflower Stone** marks the exact spot. Nearby, on St. Andrew's Street, the largely **(48)** 18th-century **Merchant's House** has a museum of local history. *33 St. Andrew's St., tel. 0752/668000, ext. 4383. Small admission charge. Open weekdays 10–1 and 2–5:30, Sat. 10–1 and 2–5.*

(49) The **Royal Naval Dockyard,** on the west side of town, was begun in the late 17th century by William III. It is still a navy base and much is hidden behind the high dock walls, but parts of the 2-mile-long frontage can be seen from pleasure boats that travel up the River Tamar. *Plymouth Boat Cruises Ltd., Millpool House Head, Millbrook, Torpoint, Cornwall, tel. 0752/822797; also Tamar Cruising, Penhellis, Maker La., Millbrook, Torpoint, Cornwall, tel. 0752/822105. Both companies run 1-hr boat trips around the sound and the dockyard, leaving every 40 minutes from Phoenix Wharf*

and the Mayflower Steps, Easter–Oct., daily 10–4. Cost: £3 adults,
£1.50 children.

Three and a half miles east of Plymouth city center lies **Saltram
House,** a lovely 18th-century house built around the remains of a
late-Tudor mansion. It has two fine rooms designed by Robert
Adam and paintings by Sir Joshua Reynolds, first president of the
Royal Academy of Arts, who was born nearby in 1723. The house is
set in a beautiful garden, with rare trees and shrubs. There is a restaurant in the house and a cafeteria in the Coach House. *Plympton,
tel. 0752/336546. Admission: £5 adults, £2.50 children; garden only,
£2.20 adults, £1.10 children. Open Apr.–Oct., Sun.–Thurs. 12:30–
5:30 (Oct. to 5); garden only, same as house, but open from 10:30.*

Tour 3: From Plymouth to Wells

*Numbers in the margin correspond to points of interest on the
Southwest map.*

From Plymouth, you have a choice of routes north to Exeter. If rugged, desolate, moorland scenery appeals to you, take A386 and
B3212 northeast across Dartmoor Forest. Even on a summer's day,
the scarred and brooding hills of this sprawling national park appear
a likely haunt for such monsters as the Hound of the Baskervilles.
Sir Arthur Conan Doyle set his Sherlock Holmes thriller in this
landscape. Sometimes the wet, peaty wasteland vanishes in rain and
mist, while in very clear weather you can see as far north as Exmoor.
Much of northern Dartmoor consists of open heath and moorland,
uninvaded by roads—wonderful walking territory, but an easy
place to lose your bearings. A large area is used as an army range
(clearly marked when firing is in progress). Dartmoor's earliest inhabitants left behind stone monuments, burial mounds, and hut circles, which make it easy to imagine prehistoric man roaming the
bogs and pastures here.

50 If you have crossed the moor by B3212, turn left to Chagford 3 miles
before Moretonhampstead. **Chagford** was once a tin-weighing station and an area of fierce fighting between the Roundheads and the
Cavaliers in the Civil War. A Roundhead was hanged in front of one
of the pubs on the village square.

51 An intriguing house near Chagford is **Castle Drogo,** at Drew-
steignton across A382. Though designed by Sir Edwin Lutyens and
built between 1910 and 1930, it is an extraordinary interpretation of
a medieval castle, complete with battlements. Unfortunately, the
rich grocer who commissioned it ran out of cash, so only half of the
castle plans were built. *Tel. 0647/433306. Admission: £4.60 adults,
£2.30 children; grounds only, £2 adult, £1 children. Open Apr.–
Oct., Sat.–Thurs. 11–5:30.*

The coastal route from Plymouth follows A379 east for 21 miles to
Kingsbridge and on to Start Bay, where the sea is on one side and
Slapton Ley, a lake and a haven for wildfowl, on the other. A Sher-
man tank remains as a memorial to 700 U.S. soldiers killed here during a rehearsal for the D-Day landings—a disaster kept secret until
52 very recently. A379 continues north along the coast to **Dartmouth,**
an important port in the Middle Ages and now a favorite haunt of
yacht owners. Traces of its past include the old houses in **Bayard's
Cove** near Lower Ferry, the 16th-century covered **Butterwalk,** and
the two castles guarding the entrance to the River Dart. But the
town is dominated by the **Royal Naval College,** built in 1905. Two fer-

Barbican, **46**
The Hoe, **43**
Mayflower Stone, **47**
Merchant's House, **48**
Royal Citadel, **45**
Royal Naval Dockyard, **49**
Smeaton's Tower, **44**

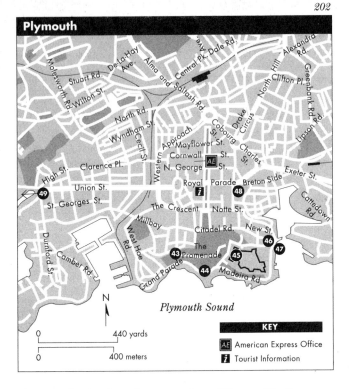

ries cross the river here; in summer, to avoid long waiting lines, you may want to try the inland route via Totnes (A3122 and A381).

Time Out The **Cherub** (Higher St.), built around 1380, once a wool merchant's house, is now a popular pub with a wide range, appetizing and reasonable, of lunchtime food.

---

53 **Totnes,** about 9 miles north of Dartmouth, is a busy market town which preserves an atmosphere of the past, particularly on summer Tuesdays and Saturdays, when most of the shopkeepers dress in Elizabethan costume. If you climb up to the ruins of Totnes's **Norman castle,** you can get a wonderful view of the town and the river. *Tel. 0803/864406. Admission: £1.35 adults, 65p children, £1 senior citizens. Open Apr.–Oct., daily 10–6; Nov.–Mar., Tues.–Sun. 10–4.*

54 **Brixham,** at the southern point of Tor Bay (10 mi from Totnes by A385 and AS3022), has kept much of its original charm, partly be-
55 cause it is still an active fishing village. **Torbay** (5 mi north via A3022) describes itself as the "English Riviera." Since 1968, the towns of Paignton and Torquay (pronounced "Torkee") have been amalgamated with the town of Torbay to form the Southwest's most important resort. Torquay is the supposed site of the hotel in the popular British television show *Fawlty Towers.*

56 Leaving the Torbay area, follow one of the coast roads north to Exeter. Devon's county seat, **Exeter,** has been the capital of the region since the Romans established a fortress here 2,000 years ago. Little evidence of the Roman occupation exists, apart from the great city walls. Despite being badly bombed in 1942, Exeter retains much of its medieval character, as well as the gracious architecture of the 18th and 19th centuries.

At the heart of Exeter is the great Gothic **Cathedral of St. Peter,** begun in 1275 and completed almost a century later. The twin towers are even older survivors of an earlier Norman cathedral. The 300-foot stretch of unbroken Gothic vaulting, rising from a forest of ribbed columns, is the longest in the world. Myriad statues, tombs, and memorial plaques adorn the interior. In the minstrels' gallery, high up on the left of the nave, stands a group of carved figures singing and playing musical instruments, including bagpipes. The cathedral is surrounded by a charming **Close,** a pleasant green space for relaxing on a sunny day. The buildings along the east side date from the 15th century, though many facades are of a later date. Don't miss the 400-year-old door to No. 10, the bishop of Crediton's house, which is ornately carved with angels' and lions' heads.

In one corner of the Close is **Mol's Coffee House** (now a store), with its black-and-white, half-timbered facade bearing the coat of arms of Elizabeth I. It is said that Sir Francis Drake met his admirals here to plan strategy against the Spanish Armada in 1588. Near Mol's stands the **Royal Clarence Hotel** (*see* Dining and Lodging, *below*). Built in 1769, it was the first inn in England to be described as a "hotel"—a designation applied by an enterprising French manager. It is named after the duchess of Clarence, who stayed here in 1827 on her way to visit her husband, the future William IV.

Time Out   While you're exploring the Close, stop in at **Tinley's,** ideal for lunch, coffee, snacks, or one of Devon's famous cream teas (served with jam, scones, and cream). Baking is done on the premises. Remains of the original city wall, against which the house was built, can be seen on the first floor.

On High Street, just behind the Close, stands the **Guildhall,** the oldest municipal building in the country. Town council meetings are still held here. The present hall dates from 1330, although a guildhall has been on this site since at least 1160. Its timber-braced roof is one of the earliest in England, dating from about 1460. *Tel. 0392/72979. Admission free. Open Mon.–Sat. 10–5:30, unless in use for a civic function.*

Behind the Guildhall lie Exeter's main shopping areas, Harlequins Arcade and the Guildhall Shopping Centre. In their midst stands the tiny, 11th-century Norman **Church of St. Pancras,** a survivor not only of the 1942 Blitz, but of the dramatic urban-renewal efforts of the 1950s and '60s.

On the far side of these two shopping areas is Queen Street, home of the **Royal Albert Memorial Museum,** where natural-history displays, a superb collection of Exeter silverware (*see* Shopping, *below*), and the works of some West Country artists are housed. There is also a fine archaeological section. *Tel. 0392/265858. Admission free. Open Tues.–Sat. 10–5:30.*

Off Queen Street, behind the museum, is **Rougemont Gardens,** which was first laid out at the end of the 18th century. The land was once part of the defensive ditch of **Rougemont Castle,** built in 1068 by decree of William the Conqueror. Here you will find the original Norman gatehouse and the remains of the Roman city wall, the latter forming part of the ancient castle's outer wall; nothing else is left. The spot offers a panoramic view of the countryside and the Haldon Hills rising up in the west.

Return to the cathedral and make your way down to the river and historic waterfront. This now tranquil spot was once the center of Exeter's medieval wool industry. The **Customs House,** built in 1682, is the earliest surviving brick building in the city; it is flanked by Victorian warehouses. There is also a Heritage Centre in **Quay House** (a stone warehouse contemporary with the Customs House) which documents the maritime history of the city and offers an audiovisual display. *The Quay, tel. 0392/265213. Admission free. Open Sept.–June, daily 10–5; July–Aug., daily 10–6.*

Close to the Customs House, in the canal basin, is the **Exeter Maritime Museum,** comprising the largest collection of historic, working ships in the country. The more than 140 vessels on exhibit include a dhow (used for pearl diving in the Persian Gulf), a Chinese junk, a Danish steam tug, and a swan-shaped rowboat. This is a hands-on museum; you can board nearly all the boats, as well as try your hand at winding a winch or turning a capstan. *Haven Banks, tel. 0392/58075. Admission: £3.75 adults, £2.25 children, £2.95 senior citizens. Open Sept.–June, daily 10–5; July–Aug., daily 10–6; closed Dec. 25–26.*

57 Five miles south of Exeter on A376 is the town of **Topsham,** full of narrow streets and hidden courtyards. Once a bustling port, it is rich in 18th-century houses and inns. **Topsham Museum** occupies a 17th-century Dutch-style merchant's house, which has recently been refurbished, beside the river. *25 the Strand, tel. 0392/873244. Admission: £1 adults, 25p children, 75p senior citizens. Open Mar.–Nov., Mon., Wed., Sat. 2–5; also July—Sept., Sun. 2–5.*

Time Out   Topsham boasts several fine pubs including **The Bridge,** a 16th-century inn by the river, which offers a choice of traditional ales, and the **Steam Packet,** next to the quay—all flagstones, scrubbed boards, brick, and stripped stonework.

Leaving Topsham, continue south on A376 toward Exmouth, stopping off near Lympstone at **A la Ronde,** an extraordinary 16-sided circular house built in 1798 and inspired by the Church of San Vitale in Ravenna, Italy. Among the 18th- and 19th-century curiosities here is an elaborate display of feathers and shells. The property has recently been acquired by the National Trust. *Summer La., on A376 near Exmouth, tel. 0395/265514. Admission: £3 adults, £1.50 children. Open Apr.–Oct., Sun.–Thurs. 11–5:30.*

58 **Exmouth** is now a large, sprawling town and a popular seaside resort, but its 19th-century elegance lives on in the houses on the **Beacon,** the swanky part of town. Both Lady Byron and Lady Nelson, the respective widows of the poet and the admiral, ended their days here. The Devon coast from Exmouth to the Dorset border 26 miles to the east has been designated an Area of Outstanding Natural Beauty. The reddish, grass-topped cliffs of the region are punctuated by quiet, seaside resorts such as **Budleigh Salterton, Sidmouth,** and **Seaton.**

59 **Beer,** just outside Seaton, was once a favorite smugglers' haunt. It was also the source of the white stone used to build Exeter Cathedral. Some of the old quarries can still be visited. *Beer Quarry Caves, Quarry La., tel. 029780/282. Admission: £2.50 adults, £1.85 children and senior citizens, £8 family ticket. Open Apr.–Sept., daily 9–5.*

60 Ten miles inland from Beer on A3052/A375 is the town of **Honiton,** whose long High Street is lined with handsome Georgian houses.

Modern storefronts have intruded, but the original facades have been preserved at second-floor level. For three centuries the town was known for lacemaking, and the Honiton lace industry was revived when Queen Victoria selected the fabric for her wedding veil in 1840. The town has a **lace museum,** as well as stores where both old and new lace are sold. *All Hallows Museum, High St., tel. 0404/ 87397. Admission: 80p adults, 30p children. Open mid-May–Sept., Mon.–Sat. 10–5; Oct., Mon.–Sat. 10–4.*

Time Out   For a satisfying lunch, try **Dominoes** winebar (178 High St.), where you can get everything from crispy Szechuan duck to steak and oyster pie.

Leaving Honiton, take A30 and A303 east toward Yeovil, about 30 miles away. This part of Somerset is famous for its golden limestone, used in the construction of local villages and mansions. A fine exam-

61 ple is **Montacute House** on A3088 (turn right off A303 at Stoke sub Hamdon), built in the late 16th century. This Renaissance house has a 189-foot gallery brimming with Elizabethan and Jacobean portraits, most on loan from the National Portrait Gallery. *Tel. 0935/ 823289. Admission: £4.70 adults, £2.40 children; garden and park only, Mar.–Oct., £2.60 adults, £1.20 children; Nov.–Apr. £1.20 adults, 60p children. Open Apr.–Oct., Wed.–Mon. 12:30–5:30. Garden and park open daily 11:30–5:30 or dusk.*

62 About 7 miles northeast, in **Yeovilton,** the 20th century reasserts itself with the **Fleet Air Arm Museum.** Here, more than 50 historic aircraft are on show, including the Concorde 002. The museum opened a spectacular new exhibition in 1994—a "Carrier" display, costing £2 million. It includes a simulated helicopter ride over the ocean to an aircraft carrier; a unique re-creation of the flight deck of a working carrier, complete with 12 real planes from the 1960s and 1970s; and an "experience" chamber simulation of the launch and recovery of the carrier's aircraft. *Royal Naval Air Station, tel. 0935/840565. Admission: £5.50 adults, £3 children, £4.50 senior citizens, £14 family ticket. Open Mar.–Oct., daily 10–5:30; Nov.–Feb., daily 10– 4:30.*

63 **Cadbury Castle,** 7 miles northeast, off A359, is said to be the site of Camelot—one among several contenders for the honor. Glastonbury Tor, rising dramatically in the distance across the plain, adds to the atmosphere of Arthurian romance. There is even a legend that every seven years the hillside opens and Arthur and his followers ride forth to water their horses at close-by Sutton Montis. Cadbury Castle is, in fact, an Iron Age fort (c. 650 BC), with grass-covered, earthen ramparts forming a green wall 300 feet above the surrounding fields. From here it's about 17 miles to Wells, our original starting point. Or the A303/M3 will take you back to London.

What to See and Do with Children

Buckfast Butterfly Farm and Dartmoor Otter Sanctuary's colorful inhabitants come from around the world. The farm is on A38, halfway between Exeter and Plymouth. *Buckfastleigh, tel. 0364/ 642916. Admission: £4.25 adult, £3.75 senior citizens, £2.75 children, £10.95 family ticket. Otters open Mar.–Nov., daily 10–5:30 or dusk; butterflies Apr.–Oct., daily 10–5:30 or dusk.*

Cheddar Caves and **Wookey Hole** (*see* Off the Beaten Track, *below*).

Dart Valley Steam Railway runs through 7 wooded miles of the Dart valley to Kingswear, across from Dartmouth. *Buckfastleigh, tel. 0364/42338. Easter and daily in summer.*

Flambards Theme Park has an aircraft collection, a re-creation of a wartime street during the Blitz, and a reconstructed Victorian village. *Near Helston, tel. 0326/574549 or 0326/573404. Admission: £7.95 adults, £6.95 children, £25, £30, £35 family tickets. Open Easter–Nov., daily 10–5.*

The National Shire Horse Centre offers three daily parades of shire horses (the largest breed of draft horse, originally bred to carry knights in armor), flying displays at the falconry center, and an adventure playground. *Yealmpton (on A379 east of Plymouth), tel. 0752/880268. Admission: £5.50 adults, £3.50 children, £4.95 senior citizens, £15.50 family ticket. Mid-Mar.–Oct. flying displays daily 1 and 3:30; parades daily 11:30, 2:30, 4:15; Nov.–mid-March no parades or flying displays; closed Christmas.*

Off the Beaten Track

Signs in Wells town center will direct you 2 miles north to **Wookey Hole,** a fascinating complex of limestone caves in the Mendip Hills that may have been the home of Iron Age people. In addition to a museum, there is an underground lake and several newly opened chambers to explore, plus a working papermill and a display of Madame Tussaud's early waxwork collection dating from the 1830s. *Tel. 0749/672243. Admission: £5.40 adults, £3.40 children, £4.70 senior citizens. Open Mar.–Oct., daily 9:30–5:30; Nov.–Feb., daily 10:30–4:30. Closed one week before Christmas.*

Six miles farther north by A371 lie the **Cheddar Caves.** This beautiful, subterranean world of stalactites, stalagmites, and naturally colored stone is enhanced by holograms and stunning man-made optical effects. *Cheddar, tel. 0934/742343. Admission: £5 adults, £3 children, £15 family ticket. Open summer, daily 10–5:30; winter, daily 10:30–4:30.*

At **Chewton Cheese Dairy** north of Cheddar Gorge, you can see how Cheddar cheese is made in the traditional truckles, and watch butter being churned by hand. *Priory Farm, Chewton Mendip (north of Wells), tel. 076121/666. Shop and restaurant open Mon.–Sat. 8:30–5, Sun. 10–4:30; cheesemaking Mon.–Wed., Fri., and Sat., best time to view noon–2:30.*

Winegrowers in Somerset are reviving a British tradition that goes back to the 10th century. At **Pilton Manor,** 6 miles southeast of Wells, you can wander in the vineyard, taste English wines, and have lunch in the wine bar; stuffed vine leaves are a specialty. *The Manor House, Pilton, Shepton Mallet, tel. 074989/325. Admission: free. Open for exploration May–Sept., Wed.–Sun. 11–5. Open for bottle sales daily 8:30–5 all year.*

The wool trade was the mainstay of Devon's wealth for centuries, and at Uffculme, 6 miles east of Tiverton by A373, **Coldharbour Mill** has been restored as a working museum where you can see the stages in the transformation of fleece into cloth. The Mill now displays a New World Tapestry, depicting the story of colonization between 1583 and 1642. *Uffculme, Cullompton, tel. 0884/840960. Admission: £3.50 adults, £1.75 children, £9.25 family ticket. Open Easter–Oct., daily 11–5; Nov.–Easter, weekdays 11–5.*

The 11-mile-long **Grand Union Canal,** opened in 1814, runs past Tiverton, and in the summer you can travel up part of it by horse-drawn barge. *Grand Western Houseboat Co., The Wharf, Canal Hill, Tiverton, tel. 0884/253345. Call for sailing times and ticket prices.*

China clay has been St. Austell's main industry for 200 years. **Wheal Martyn,** an old mine 2 miles north of St. Austell on A391, offers an audio-visual presentation on the history and processes of the china-clay industry, a history trail through the mine, and several other exhibits, including two waterwheels. *Carthewm, tel. 0726/850362. Admission: £3.90 adults, £1.95 children, £3.10 senior citizens. Open Apr.–Oct., daily 10–6.*

Shopping

Whole groups of artists and craftspeople have settled in Devon and Cornwall. Ancient crafts, too, are still carried on, such as the making of baskets and shoes.

Bideford   The **Dartington Glass** factory (Linden Close, Great Torrington, near Bideford, tel. 0237/471011) has tours of the works weekdays 9:30–10:30 and noon–3:30, every 15 minutes. There are also a "seconds" shop and café on the premises.

Dartington   Near Dartington Hall (2 mi north of Totnes) is a collection of stores selling world-famous Dartington lead crystal as well as shoes, woolens, farm foods, kitchenware, pottery, and many other Devon wares. **Dartington Trading Centre** (Shinners Bridge, 2 mi west of Totnes, tel. 0803/864171), a collection of shops and two restaurants, housed inside the old Dartington Cider Press, sells handmade crafts from Devon, including clothes, glassware, and kitchenware.

Exeter   Until 1882 Exeter was the silver-assay office for the entire West Country, and it is still possible to find **Exeter silver,** particularly spoons, in some antiques and silverware stores. The earliest example of Exeter silver dates from 1218 (a museum piece), but Victorian pieces are still sold—the Exeter assay mark is three castles. Try **William Bruford** (1 Bedford St., tel. 0392/54901) for interesting antique jewelry and silver.

Glastonbury   Somerset is sheep country, and one of several good outlets for sheepskin products is **Morlands Factory Shop** (2 mi southwest on A39, tel. 0458/835042), which sells coats, slippers, and rugs; there is also a history center.

Plymouth   **Dolls and Miniatures** (54 Southside St., The Barbican, tel. 0752/663676) is an attractive store, selling antique and reproduction dolls, dollhouses, and kits. Also by mail order.

Markets   Market days in Barnstaple are Tuesday and Friday. In Exeter there is a daily market on Sidwell Street. Glastonbury has a market every Tuesday, and Wells has a market on Wednesday and Saturday.

Sports and the Outdoors

Horseback Riding   The Southwest is ideal for cross-country **pony riding,** and it is often possible to ride the Dartmoor and Exmoor breeds of ponies. Centers include **Lydford House Riding Stables** (Lydford House Hotel, Lydford, tel. 082282/347) and **Skaigh Stables Farm** (Skaigh La., near Okehampton, tel. 0837/840429).

Walking A wonderful 10-mile walk is a clifftop hike along the coast from Hartland Quay down to Lower Sharpnose Point. The coast below Bude is also ideal for walking, especially the section around Tintagel. Experienced hikers may find many Dartmoor walks of great interest. The areas around Widgery Cross, Becky Falls, and the Bovey Valley, and—for the really energetic and adventuresome—Highest Dartmoor, south of Okehampton, are all worth considering. A much shorter walk, but no less spectacular, is along the Lydford Gorge (*see* Tour 2, *above*). Long walks on Dartmoor, which is a lonely region, are only for the most experienced walkers. (Contact: National Parks Authority, Parke, Haytor Rd., Bovey Tracey, Newton Abbot, Devon TQ13 9JQ, tel. 0626/832093.)

For those interested in "theme" walks, there is the **Saints Way.** This 25-mile Cornish walk is between Padstow and the Camel Estuary on the north coast to Fowey on the south coast. The path follows a Bronze Age trading route, later used by Celtic saints to reach scattered farms and moor communities, and several relics of such times can be seen along the way. (Contact: The Cornwall Tourist Board, 59 Lemon St., Truro, Cornwall TR1 2SY, tel. 0872/74057.)

Water Sports Looe, on the south coast of Cornwall, is known for shark **fishing,** and boats can be rented for mackerel fishing from most harbors on the south coast. This is also a good **sailing** area, with plenty of safe harbors, new marinas, and deepwater channels, mainly at Falmouth, Plymouth Sound, and Torbay.

Its beaches have long made the Southwest one of Britain's main family-vacation areas. Be aware of the tides if you want to explore around an adjoining headland; otherwise you may find yourself cut off. At many of the major resorts, flags show the limits of safe **swimming,** as there can be strong undertows, especially on the northern coast.

Dining and Lodging

Dining Somerset is the home of Britain's most famous cheese, the ubiquitous Cheddar, from the Mendip Hills village. If you are lucky enough to taste real farmhouse Cheddar, made in the traditional "truckle" (*see* Off the Beaten Track, *above*), you may find it hard to return to processed cheese. The calorie-conscious should beware of Devon's cream teas, which traditionally consist of a pot of tea, homemade scones, and lots of thickened "clotted" cream and strawberry jam.

Cornwall's specialty is the "pasty," a pastry shell filled with chopped meat, onions, and potatoes. The pasty was originally devised as a handy way for miners to carry their dinner to work.

"Scrumpy," a homemade dry cider, is refreshing but carries a kick. English wine, which is similar to German wine, is made in Somerset (*see* Off the Beaten Track, *above*), while in Cornwall you can get mead made from local honey.

Highly recommended restaurants are indicated by a star ★.

Category	Cost*
$$$$	over £50
$$$	£40–£50

$$	£20–£40
$	under £20

per person, including first course, main course, dessert, and VAT; excluding drinks

Lodging Accommodations in the Southwest range from national hotel chains that extend as far west as Plymouth, to bed-and-breakfast places. With the growth of the tourist industry, many farmhouses in rural areas have begun renting out rooms.

Highly recommended lodgings are indicated by a star ★.

Category	Cost*
$$$$	over £150
$$$	£95–£150
$$	£50–£95
$	under £50

All prices are for two people sharing a double room, including service, breakfast, and VAT.

Barnstaple
Dining and Lodging

Lynwood House. The emphasis at this family-run hotel/restaurant is on fresh local fish, including salmon from the River Taw. Be sure to try the fish soup. Lynwood House, located on A377 between Barnstaple and Exeter, also has five bedrooms, all comfortably furnished, with two for nonsmokers. *Bishop's Tawton Rd., EX32 9DZ, tel. 0271/43695, fax 0271/79340. Reservations advised. Dress: casual. AE, MC, V. Closed Sun. $$*

The Royal and Fortescue Hotel. Edward VII, who stayed here when he was Prince of Wales, gave this Victorian hotel the royal part of its name. It's in the center of town and has recently been refurbished. All rooms are furnished to a high standard and there's a choice of à la carte or table d'hôte menu in the restaurant. *Boutport St., EX31 1HG, tel. 0271/42289, fax 0271/78558 (refer to hotel No. 7). 62 rooms, 33 with bath. Facilities: live music and dances weekly. AE, DC, MC, V. $$*

Dartmouth
Dining
★

The Carved Angel. Situated on the quay with views of the harbor, its offerings include Provençal cuisine and fresh local products, such as Dart River salmon and samphire, a seashore plant used in fish dishes. The restaurant enjoys a long-standing reputation as one of Britain's finest eateries. *2 S. Embankment, tel. 0803/832465. Reservations required. Jacket and tie required. No credit cards. Closed Sun. dinner, Mon., Jan., 2 weeks Feb., and 1st week Oct. $$$$*

Billy Budd's. This is a very friendly bistro, candlelit for evening dinners. The seafood dishes take the prize here; the fish pie is especially good. You might also try the noisettes of lamb. To finish your meal indulge in one of the scrumptious homemade ice creams. *7 Foss St., tel. 0803/834842. Reservations advised. Jacket advised for dinner. MC, V. Closed Sun. and Mon., 1 month in winter. $$*

Lodging

Royal Castle Hotel. Here's a hotel that really earned the name "Royal"—several monarchs have slept here. Part of Dartmouth's historic waterfront, it was built in the 17th century, reputedly of timber from wrecks of the Spanish Armada. There are traditional fireplaces and beamed ceilings, and six rooms have four-poster beds. *11 The Quay, TQ6 9PS, tel. 0803/833033, fax 0803/835445. 25 rooms* *with bath or shower. Facilities: live music and dancing Sun., nonsmoking library lounge. AE, DC, MC, V. $$*

Stoke Lodge Hotel. Three miles southwest of Dartmouth by A379, this establishment was once a 17th-century family house, and is now a family-run hotel surrounded by 4 acres of gardens. It is equipped for year-round vacations—and children—with indoor and outdoor swimming pools. *Cinders La., Stoke Fleming TQ6 0RA, tel. 0803/770523, fax 0803/770851. 24 rooms with bath. Facilities: restaurant, sauna, Jacuzzi, indoor and outdoor pools, sun terrace. MC, V. $$*

Exeter
Dining
Golsworthy's. Part of St. Olaves Court Hotel, set in a Georgian house with a walled garden, this restaurant offers both set and à la carte menus. Try the rack of lamb with port, or the hazelnut *galette* with pear. *Mary Arches St., tel. 0392/217736. Weekend reservations required. Jacket and tie required. AE, DC, MC, V. $$*

Lodging
The Royal Clarence Hotel. This historic hotel *(see* Tour 3, *above)* is located within the cathedral Close. It boasts a good restaurant and has been made a great deal more attractive by recent redecoration. The most expensive rooms are those with a view of the cathedral. Many rooms feature oak paneling. *Cathedral Yard, EX1 1HD, tel. 0392/58464, fax 0392/439423. 56 rooms with bath. Facilities: restaurant, carvery, 2 bars. AE, DC, MC, V. $$$*

Rougemont Hotel. Large, rambling, and Victorian—complete with chandeliers, molded ceilings, and pillars—this hotel is ideal for those who want comfortable accommodations downtown. Most of the rooms have recently been refurbished. *Queen St., EX4 3SP, tel. 0392/54982, fax 0392/420928. 90 rooms with bath. Facilities: restaurant. AE, DC, MC, V. $$*

The White Hart. It is said that Oliver Cromwell stabled his horses here; in any event, guests have been welcomed since the 15th century. The main building has all the trappings of a period inn—beams, stone walls, a central courtyard, and warm hospitality—but there are also fully modern bedrooms in a new wing. *65 South St., EX1 1EE, tel. 0392/79897, fax 0392/50159. 61 rooms with bath or shower. Facilities: restaurant, bar, garden. AE, DC, MC, V. $$*

Exmouth
Dining
River House. The ambience here is wonderful, with the Exe estuary flowing right under the windows, waterfowl nearby, and a great view of Powderham Castle. The food isn't bad either! Try the fresh salmon or brill—the meat is delicious, too. There is a less expensive set menu. The husband-and-wife team are friendly and welcoming. There are also two bedrooms. *The Strand, Lympstone (3 mi north on A376), tel. 0395/265147. Reservations required. Dress: casual. AE, MC, V. Closed Sun. evening and Mon. $$$*

Lodging
Royal Beacon Hotel. Overlooking the sea with views across the estuary to Torquay in the distance, this gracious, relaxed Georgian hotel was once a posting house where coaches changed their horses. *The Beacon, EX8 2AF, tel. 0395/264886, fax 0395/268890. 30 rooms with bath. Facilities: 2 restaurants, horseback riding, sauna, sunbed. AE, DC, MC, V. $$*

Fairy Cross
Lodging
★
The Portledge Hotel. More peaceful, rural surroundings than these would be hard to imagine. The house is a 17th-century mansion, with family portraits, lovely paneling, antiques, and attractive fabrics everywhere. It's set in 60 acres of parkland on the edge of Bideford Bay. *Near Bideford, EX39 5BX, tel. 0237/451262, fax 0237/451717. 35 rooms with bath. Facilities: restaurant, coffee shop, garden, tennis, croquet, swimming pool, fishing. MC, V. $$*

Falmouth
Dining
Pandora Inn. This thatched pub, with both a patio and a moored pontoon for summer dining, is a great discovery. The ambience derives

from maritime memorabilia and fresh flowers, and you can eat either in the bars or in the candlelit restaurant. The backbone of the menu is fresh seafood—try the seafood stroganoff or crab thermidor. The menu depends on the catch of the day. *Restronguet Creek, Mylor Bridge, tel. 0326/372678. Reservations advised. Dress: casual. Dinner only. MC, V. Closed Sun. in winter. $$*

★ **The Seafood Bar.** The window of this restaurant on the quay is a fish tank, and beyond it is the very best seafood. Try the thick crab soup; the turbot cooked with cider, apples, and cream; or the locally caught lemon sole. *Lower Quay Hill, tel. 0326/315129. Reservations advised. Dress: casual. MC, V. Open for dinner only Tues.–Sat. $$*

Lodging **Greenbank Hotel.** Mailboat captains used to stay at this harborside hotel. Although it has been well modernized, it hasn't lost its maritime atmosphere; watch the yachts sail past the windows. There is a new wing with 17 bedrooms. *Harbourside, TR11 2SR, tel. 0326/312440, fax 0326/211362. 61 rooms with bath. Facilities: restaurant, garden, solarium, sea fishing. AE, DC, MC, V. Closed Christmas–early Jan. $$$*

Royal Duchy. This late-Victorian, cliff-top hotel is in an imposing position with wide sea views. The comfortable rooms are furnished with Regency-style pieces and have functional bathrooms. Dinner is included in the room price. *Cliff Rd., TR11 4NX, tel. 0326/313042, fax 0326/319420. 47 rooms with bath. Facilities: restaurant, garden, indoor pool, childrens' pool, sauna. AE, DC, MC, V. $$$*

St. Michael's Hotel. At this seaside hotel in a long, low white building overlooking Falmouth Bay, there are beautiful gardens sweeping down to the sea. St. Michael's is constantly being updated—the bedrooms have all just had a face-lift. Recommended especially for families. *Stracey Rd., TR11 4NB, tel. 0326/312707, fax 0326/211772. 75 rooms with bath. Facilities: indoor pool, sauna, Jacuzzi, babysitters. AE, DC, MC, V. $$$*

Gyllyngvase House Hotel. This hotel is centrally located, near the seafront. The bedrooms are a bit small but pleasantly furnished. There is a garden at the back. *Gyllyngvase Rd., TR11 4DJ, tel. 0326/312956. 15 rooms, 12 with bath or shower. No credit cards. Closed Nov.–Mar. $*

Gittisham **Combe House Hotel.** Rolling parkland, 3,000 acres in all, surrounds
Lodging this Elizabethan manor house. From the imposing entrance hall with its huge, open fireplace, to the individually decorated bedrooms—all of them large and two with four-posters—the emphasis is on style and comfort. *Near Honiton, EX14 0AD, tel. 0404/42756, fax 0404/46004. 15 rooms with bath. Facilities: restaurant, 1½-mile river for fly-fishing. AE, DC, MC, V. Closed Jan.–mid-Feb. $$$*

Glastonbury **No. 3.** This small, French-style restaurant is elegant yet relaxed; it's
Dining in a Georgian house next to the abbey ruins. There are log fires in
★ the winter and a terrace for summer evenings. The fixed, four-course menu features mainly seafood; try the Cornish lobster in season, and any of the superb ice creams. There are also six attractive bedrooms available. *3 Magdalene St., tel. 0458/832129. Reservations required. Jacket and tie required. MC, V. Closed lunch (except Sun.), Sun. and Mon. dinner. $$*

Lodging **George and Pilgrims Hotel.** Pilgrims en route to Glastonbury Abbey stayed here in the 15th century. Today, all the modern comforts are here, but you can enjoy them in rooms with flagstone floors, wooden beams, and antique furniture; ask for a room with a four-poster bed or, if it appeals to you, the one room that is supposed to be haunted. *1 High St., BA6 9DP, tel. 0458/831146, fax 0458/832252. 14 rooms, 12* *with bath, 3 with four-posters. Facilities: restaurant, Pilgrims Bar. AE, DC, MC, V. $$*

Helston **Nansloe Manor.** Although near Helston's center, this peaceful man-
Dining and or house gives the impression of being deep in the country, with its
Lodging rhododendron-lined driveway and 5 acres of grounds. The à la carte
menu at the restaurant is short but changes frequently. *Meneage
Rd., TR13 0SB, tel. 0326/574691, fax 0326/564680. 7 rooms with
bath. MC, V. $$*

Honiton **New Dolphin Hotel.** The age of this former coaching inn shows in the
Lodging sloping floors, but every room has modern comforts. It's located in
the town center. *High St., EX14 8LS, tel. 0404/42377, fax 0404/
47662. 15 rooms with bath. MC, V. $$*

Lewdon **Lewtrenchard Manor.** This spacious 1620 manor house, on the north-
Dining and ern edge of Dartmoor (off A30), is full of paneled rooms, stone fire-
Lodging places, and ornate leaded windows. Some bedrooms have antique
four-posters. The restaurant, with its big log fire and family portraits, serves good fresh fish, caught an hour away. *Lewdon, between Launceston and Okehampton, EX20 4PN, tel. 056683/256,
fax 056683/332. 8 rooms, 7 with bath. Facilities: restaurant, garden,
fishing, helipad. Restaurant: jacket and tie required. AE, DC, MC,
V. Closed last 3 weeks in Jan. $$$*

Lynmouth **Rising Sun.** A recent conversion from a 14th-century inn and a row of
Lodging thatched cottages has created this intriguing hotel. It has great
★ views over Lynmouth, especially from the terraced garden out back.
The rooms are furnished either in pine or older pieces, and the whole
effect is comfortable and welcoming. The poet Shelley spent his
honeymoon in a cottage in the garden. *Harbourside, EX35 6EQ, tel.
0598/53223, fax 0598/53480. 16 rooms with bath. Facilities: restau-
rant, garden. AE, DC, MC, V. Closed Jan.–mid-Feb. $$*

Montacute **The King's Arms.** Built of the same warm, golden stone as nearby
Dining and Montacute House (*see* Tour 3, *above*), this 16th-century inn features
Lodging charming interior decor; one room has a four-poster bed. Meals
★ available range from bar snacks to a full à la carte menu in the Abbey
Room Restaurant. *Bishopston, TA15 6UU, tel. 0935/822513, fax
0935/826549. 11 rooms with bath. AE, DC, MC, V. Closed Christ-
mas. $$*

Penzance **Berkeley.** Atypical for its after-dinner dancing (until 1 AM) and 1930s
Dining decor, Berkeley serves homemade pasta in such dishes as tortellini
with crab or mushrooms. You can also try its fresh scallops or lemon
sole. Berkeley is the restaurant in the **Club Zero** nightclub. *Abbey St.,
tel. 0736/62541. Reservations essential. Dress: casual. AE, MC, V.
Closed lunch in winter, Sun. and Mon. dinner in summer. $$*

Lodging **Abbey Hotel.** Staying in this small, privately run 17th-century hotel
★ is like visiting someone's home; the drawing room is filled with
books and many of the rooms are furnished with antiques. The attractive restaurant has a short but intriguing menu, with seafood
gratin, rack of lamb, and homemade ice cream. Dining privileges are
normally reserved for residents, but you may be able to get a table.
*Abbey St., TR18 4AR, tel. 0736/66906, fax 0736/51163. 7 rooms with
bath. AE, DC, MC, V. Closed 2 weeks in Jan. $$*
Camilla House. The Camilla stands on a parallel road to the Prome-
nade. It is comfortably furnished, and the front rooms have sea
views. The Camilla is close to the harbor and, as the owners are
agents for the ferry line, they can help with trips to the Scilly Isles.
The restaurant specializes in fresh fish from Newlyn harbor. *Regent*

Terr., TR18 4DW, tel. 0736/63771. 9 rooms, 3 with bath. AE, MC, V. $

Plymouth
Dining
★

Chez Nous. This French—*very* French—restaurant is worth searching for among the rows of stores in the shopping precinct. Fresh local fish is served, and the atmosphere is pleasant and relaxed. Chez Nous is at the top of the expensive range. *13 Frankfort Gate, tel. 0752/266793. Reservations advised. Dress: casual chic. AE, DC, MC, V. Closed Sun., Mon., national holidays, and first 3 weeks in Feb. and Sept. $$$*

Piermaster's. Fresh fish landed at nearby piers is served here. Located in the Barbican, the Piermaster has "basic seafront" decor, with a tiled floor and wooden tables. *33 Southside St., Barbican, tel. 0752/229345. Reservations advised. Dress: casual. AE, DC, MC, V. Closed Sun. $$*

Lodging

Copthorne Hotel. Situated downtown, this large, efficient, modern hotel offers the expected comforts. Its Burlington Restaurant has been given an Edwardian look. *Armada Centre, Armada Way, PL1 1AR, tel. 0752/224161, fax 0752/670688. 135 rooms with bath. Facilities: restaurant, bar, swimming pool, sauna, solarium. AE, DC, MC, V. $$$*

Bowling Green. This reconditioned Victorian house overlooks Sir Francis Drake's bowling green on Plymouth Hoe. It's in a central location for shopping and sightseeing. *9–10 Osborne Pl., Lockyer St., PL1 2PU, tel. 0752/667485, fax 0752/255150. 12 rooms with bath or shower. MC, V. $*

Portloe
Lodging
★

The Lugger. This small hotel on the edge of a tiny cove is made up of several 17th-century cottages. Many of the snug cottage bedrooms look out to sea, while in the beamed bar the world of the smugglers doesn't seem so far away. It's definitely worth the drive through the narrow, banked roads 12 miles southeast from Truro to get here. *TR2 5RD, tel. 0872/501322, fax 0872/501691. 20 rooms with bath. Facilities: restaurant, sauna, solarium. AE, DC, MC, V. Closed Dec. and Jan. $$$*

St. Ives
Dining

Pig 'n' Fish. Concentrate on the "fish" here, because it's a great spot for seafood. This simple, small restaurant has worthwhile pictures on display—after all this is St. Ives. Try the oysters (less pricey than elsewhere), or the salmon with fennel and basil vinegar. The desserts are scrumptious. *Norway La., tel. 0736/794204. Reservations advised. Dress: casual. MC, V. Dinner only. Closed Sun. and Christmas–mid-Feb. $$*

Lodging

Garrack Hotel. A family-run, ivy-clad hotel overlooking the beach, the Garrack offers a relaxed, undemanding atmosphere. There are traditional rooms in the main house and more modern ones in the annex. *Burthallan La., TR26 3AA, tel. 0736/796199, fax 0736/798955. 21 rooms, 16 with bath. Facilities: garden, indoor pool, sauna, restaurant, coffee shop. AE, DC, MC, V. $$*

Taunton
Dining and
Lodging
★

The Castle. The battlements and towers of this 300-year-old building will leave you in no doubt as to why this hotel, reputed to be among England's finest, has the name it does. The facade is covered by a huge, 350-year-old wisteria, magnificent when in flower. Bedrooms are individually decorated, and garden suites have separate dressing rooms. In the hotel's restaurant, with its daily-changing, fixed-price menus, the *haute cuisine* ranges from classic roasts to elaborate seafood dishes such as poached scallops with mussels, tomatoes, garlic, and ginger. The cheese selection includes many English cheeses and is served with homemade walnut bread. *Castle Green, TA1 1NF, tel. 0823/272671, fax 0823/336066. 35 rooms with bath. Fa-*

cilities: garden. Reservations advised. Jacket and tie required in restaurant. AE, DC, MC, V. $$$

Tavistock **The Horn of Plenty.** A "restaurant with rooms" is the way this estab-
Dining and lishment describes itself. From the restaurant in a Victorian house
Lodging there are magnificent views across the wooded, rhododendron-filled
★ Tamar Valley. The set menu is changed monthly, and the cooking is
mainly classic French with some traditional English recipes (try the
terrine of rabbit with apricot chutney). There are excellent-value
set menus. A converted barn next to the house offers six modern
guest rooms. It is 3 miles west of Tavistock on A390. *Gulworthy,
PL19 8JD, tel. and fax 0822/832528. 7 rooms with bath. Reserva-
tions required. Dress: casual. AE, MC, V. Closed lunch Mon. and
Christmas. $$$$*

Torquay **Capers.** This small, select restaurant goes in for serious cooking, and
Dining it is a spot for anyone who likes enthusiasm along with the food. Lo-
★ cal fish ranks high on the menu, with vegetables and herbs grown by
the chef. Try the turbot with lime and ginger and the duck with wal-
nut salad, or the salmon in pastry with sorrel. *7 Lisburne Sq., tel.
0803/291177. Reservations essential. Dress: casual. MC, V. Dinner
only Tues.–Sat. $$$*
Remy's. Come here for delightful, straightforward French country
cooking. Lamb with basil and tomato, sweetbreads with a Calvados
sauce, and above all fish freshly caught by local boats are among the
specialties. The wine list has a selection of good Alsatian vintages. *3
Croft Rd., tel. 0803/292359. Reservations advised. Dress: casual.
AE, MC, V. Closed Sun., Mon. and lunch. $$*

Lodging **The Imperial.** This is arguably Devon's most luxurious hotel, per-
★ ched high above the sea, overlooking Torbay. The gardens sur-
rounding the hotel are magnificent, and the interior . . . well,
imperial, with chandeliers, marble floors, and the general air of a
bygone world. Most bedrooms are large and very comfortable, some
with seaward balconies. The staff is attentive. *Park Hill Rd., TQ1
2DG, tel. 0803/294301, fax 0803/298293. 166 rooms with bath. Facili-
ties: restaurant, beauty parlor, health center, tennis, squash, sau-
na, indoor and outdoor pools. AE, DC, MC, V. $$$$*
Fairmount House Hotel. Near the village of Cockington, on the edge
of Torquay, this Victorian hotel has a pretty garden and a restau-
rant that favors fresh local produce. *Herbert Rd., Chelston, TQ2
6RW, tel. and fax 0803/605446. 8 rooms with bath or shower. Facili-
ties: restaurant. AE, MC, V. Closed Oct.–Feb. $*

Totnes **The Cott.** The exterior of this inn has remained almost completely
Lodging unchanged since 1320. It is a long, low, thatched building with flag-
stone floors, thick ceiling beams, and open fireplaces. Bar snacks
and more elaborate meals are available from the restaurant.
*Shinner's Bridge, Dartington (2 mi west of Totnes on A385) TQ9
6HE, tel. 0803/863777, fax 0803/866629. 6 rooms. AE, DC, MC, V.
$$*

Truro **Alverton Manor.** This was once a bishop's house, then a convent, and
Dining and is now an up-to-date hotel/restaurant, both efficient and atmospher-
Lodging ic. The former chapel is used as an unusual conference room. The
rooms are large, with French cherrywood furniture. Talented chefs
come and go in the Terrace Restaurant, but the standard of cooking
stays high with the help of the best local produce. *Tregolls Rd., TR1
1XQ, tel. 0872/76633, fax 0872/222989. 25 rooms with bath or shower. Facilities: garden. Reservations required for restaurant. Jacket
and tie required. AE, DC, MC, V. $$*

Wells **Ancient Gate House.** Traditional Italian dishes made largely from lo-
Dining cal produce are the specialty here. There is also an English menu. *20 Sadler St., tel. 0749/72029. Reservations advised. Dress: casual. AE, DC, MC, V. $$*

Ritcher's. This is a combination eatery—bistro downstairs, restaurant upstairs, in a loft filled with plants. There you can get a fixed-price lunch and dinner and many interesting à la carte dishes, too. Try the steak and mushroom pie, pork with stilton, or the guinea fowl en croûte. *5 Sadler St., tel. 0749/679085. Reservations advised for restaurant. Dress: casual. MC, V. Upstairs closed Sun. and Mon. $$*

Dining and **Swan Hotel.** Built in the 15th century, this former coaching inn faces
Lodging the cathedral. Nine of the rooms have four-poster beds, and on cold days you can relax in front of a log fire in one of the lounges. The restaurant displays costumes owned by the great Victorian actor, Sir Henry Irving. Its menus change daily. *11 Sadler St., BA5 2RX, tel. 0749/678877, fax 0749/677647. 38 rooms with bath. Facilities: restaurant. AE, DC, MC, V. $$–$$$*

The Crown. This hotel has been a landmark in Wells since the Middle Ages; William Penn was arrested here in 1695 for illegal preaching. There is a period atmosphere to the place, enhanced by the fact that four of the rooms have four-poster beds. There's also a particularly helpful staff. The Penn Bar and Eating House serves salads and such hot dishes as steak-and-kidney pie. *Market Pl., BA5 2RP, tel. 0749/673457, fax 0749/67983. 21 rooms with bath. AE, DC, MC, V. $$*

The Arts

Festivals Among the best known is the **Exeter Festival** (tel. 0392/265095), a mixture of musical and theater events held in late May and early June. The **Three Spires Festival** (tel. 0872/863346), based in Truro Cathedral, takes place in June. At **St. Endellion,** near Wadebridge in Cornwall, a music festival is regularly held at Easter. Local **country festivals** abound in late August and early September. Keep an eye out for posters, or consult local TICs. The villages of northern and eastern Dartmoor have some particularly colorful celebrations; try Moretonhampstead's.

Theaters At the **Northcott Theatre** (tel. 0392/54853) in Exeter, and the **Theatre Royal** (tel. 0752/669595) in Plymouth, you can often see plays by one of the best London companies.

At the open-air **Minack Theatre** (tel. 0736/810694) in Porthcurno, near Penzance, begun in the early 1930s, the natural slope of the cliff forms an amphitheater, with terraces and bench seats and the sea as a backdrop. Plays are performed here throughout the summer, ranging from classical dramas to modern comedies.

7 The Channel Islands

Guernsey, Jersey

The Channel Islands became part of the British Isles when their ruler, Duke William of Normandy, or William the Conqueror, seized the English throne in 1066. The connection with the British royal house has lasted ever since, with only very few breaks. One result of this link was that the Norman code of law formed the foundation of the present Common Law practiced in the Islands, which differs from the legal system followed in the rest of Britain. This is only one of the many ways in which the Channel Islands are set apart from the rest of the kingdom; they do not impose VAT (which means that shopping is 17.5% cheaper), and they also issue their own currency and stamps.

The islands served as the background for struggles between Royalists and Roundheads in the 17th-century Civil War. In 1781, just after the French Revolution, the French made an unsuccessful attempt to invade. Since 1066, the islands have only been seriously invaded once. The Germans occupied them from 1940 to 1945, incorporating them into their great Western defense system, the "Atlantic Wall." All over the islands there is still evidence of the German fortifications, which were built by thousands of slaves who used 613,000 cubic meters of reinforced concrete. The coasts bristled with gun emplacements, and the rocky landscape was honeycombed with tunnels to provide hospitals and ammunition magazines. In fact, the islands became total fortresses. When the Allies overran Europe in 1944, they circumvented the Islands, leaving their elaborate defenses untouched.

Though part of Britain since 1066, the Channel Islands have a self-ruling system, and thus have no allegiance to the Parliament in Westminster, just to the monarch. For governmental purposes, the archipelago is divided into two sections, called bailiwicks. There is the Bailiwick of Jersey, consisting solely of that island, and the Bailiwick of Guernsey, which includes Guernsey and the smaller islands of Alderney, Sark, Herm, and Jethou. Each of the bailiwicks has its own government, called states, headed by a bailiff and a lieutenant-governor, who is the queen's representative and the states' contact person with Westminster. Alderney, though part of the Bailiwick of Guernsey, also has its own states. Tiny Sark is a feudal island, ruled over by a hereditary seigneur. Jethou is privately owned.

The most popular island is Jersey (44½ sq. mi), because of its mild climate, magnificent beaches, and well-run hotels and restaurants, all promoted by a strong department of tourism. Second to Jersey, both in size and popularity, is Guernsey (24½ sq. mi), which has 2,000 hours of sunshine a year and runs at a more relaxed pace.

All the islands are bordered by magnificent cliffs that provide superb walking trails—very tough on the leg muscles—with great views both seawards and inland. The landscapes of both Jersey and Guernsey are crowded with prosperous, neat houses, all threaded together by an interminable network of winding lanes. For this reason the islands are very difficult to explore by car, even for a visitor who is extremely adept at map reading. But both islands have excellent bus services, which provide a cheap, worry-free means of sightseeing.

Essential Information

Important Addresses and Numbers

Tourist Information In London, **Jersey Tourism Office,** 38 Dover St., London W1X 3RB, tel. 071/493–5278. On the islands the offices are:

Jersey Tourism Department, Liberation Sq., St. Helier JE1 1BB, tel. 0534/500700; for accommodations tel. 0534/500777, fax 0534/500899. **Guernsey Tourist Board,** Crown Pier, St. Peter Port tel. 0481/726611, fax 0481/721246. Guernsey also handles information for Alderney, Herm, and Sark. **Alderney States Tourist Office,** Queen Elizabeth II St., tel. 048182/2811. **Sark Tourism Committee,** Information Centre, tel. 048183/2345.

Travel Agencies *Jersey and Guernsey* **Bellingham Travel,** 33 Queen St., St. Helier, Jersey, tel. 0534/27575; 41 Commercial Arcade, St. Peter Port, Guernsey, tel. 0481/726333. **Marshall's Travel,** 1 Quennevais Precinct, St. Brelade, Jersey, tel. 0534/41278.
OSL Channel Islands Travel Service Ltd., Guernsey Airport, Forest, Guernsey, tel. 0481/35471.
Thomas Cook, 14 Charing Cross, St. Helier, Jersey, tel. 0534/77955; 22 Le Pollet, St. Peter Port, Guernsey, tel. 0481/724111.

Alderney **Raymond Travel Bureau,** Box 12, Albert Mews, Alderney, tel. 048182/2881.

Car-Rental Agencies *Jersey* **Avis,** St. Peter's Garage, St. Peter, tel. 0534/483288; **Budget Rent a Car,** Airport Rd., St. Brelade, tel. 0534/46191; **Europcar,** Arrivals Hall, Jersey Airport, St. Peter, tel. 0534/43156; **Hertz,** Arrivals Hall, Jersey Airport, tel. 0534/45621.

Guernsey **Avis,** Airport, tel. 0481/35266; **Budget Rent a Car,** Lande du Marche Garage, tel. 0481/56555; **Hertz,** Airport Forecourt; tel. 0481/37638; **Rent a Car Guernsey,** Forest Rd., St. Martin, tel. 0481/38786.

Currency Although the islands use pounds and pence, both of the bailiwicks have their own version of them, with specially printed bills. This currency is *not* legal tender elsewhere in the United Kingdom, though you will be able to use U.K. currency on the islands. Financial wheeling and dealing is big business here, and you'll find bureaus de change at banks, travel agencies, the main post offices, airports, and the main harbors.

Arriving and Departing

By Plane **Jersey** is well served by flights from both mainland Britain and the Continent. There are direct flights from Heathrow (British Airways), Gatwick (Jersey European), Plymouth (Brymon), Southampton (Air UK, Jersey European, Channel Island Travel Service), Manchester (Air Europe Express, BA, Loganair), and Glasgow (British Midland, Channel Island Travel Service, Loganair). Flying time from London is 1 hour, from Manchester 1 hour 20 minutes, from Plymouth 45 minutes. The London/Jersey round-trip fare is £79 (£99 in summer).

Guernsey Airport is served by Air UK, British Midland, Brymon, Jersey European, and Loganair.

For further flight information contact: British Airways (tel. 081/897–4000); Brymon (tel. 0752/707023); Loganair (tel. 061/889–3181); Jersey European (tel. 0345/676676); Channel Island Travel Service (tel. 0534/46181); Air UK (tel. 0345/666777); British Midland (tel. 0332/854854); Guernsey Airlines (tel. 0293/546571).

By Boat   You can sail to Jersey or Guernsey from Weymouth. **Condor Ltd.** (tel. 0305/761551) has daily sailings from Weymouth from April to November. Most boats call at Guernsey first. The average time from Weymouth by the night ferry is 8¼ hours to Guernsey, 2¼ hours more to Jersey. By day, ferry time is 5½ hours and 3½. An average fare runs from £60 for a 5-day Saver return for a foot passenger to £210 and up for a car with two passengers.

Getting Around

By Car   You can ship your car by ferry from mainland Britain at fairly low rates or rent a car (*see above*), but the islands are small and can easily be explored by local bus. The traffic, especially on Jersey, can be regularly snarled up, especially in high season. Driving is on the left, and the speed limit is 40 mph on Jersey; 35 on Guernsey and Alderney; cars are not permitted on Sark.

By Bus   There are buses only in summer on Alderney, but Jersey and Guernsey have excellent services, including regular buses to and from both airports, and all over both islands. The services are **Jersey Motor Transport Co.** (Central Bus Station, Weighbridge, St. Helier, tel. 0534/21201) and **Guernseybus** (Picquet House, St. Peter Port, tel. 0481/724677). They both have reasonably priced Rover tickets, which provide unlimited travel over a short period of time.

Between the Islands   Island hopping by sea or air will add fun to your archipelago vacation. There are regular daily flights all summer between Jersey, Guernsey, and Alderney, fewer flights in winter. You can also fly to the islands from France for a quick visit. Alderney can be reached by **Aurigny Air Services** (tel. 0481/723474), who also have interisland service.

Larger ferries travel between Jersey and Guernsey; those from the British mainland call at both islands going and returning. Fast hydrofoils skim around all the islands. Sark can be reached from Guernsey in around 45 minutes by **Sark Shipping** (tel. 0481/724059); Herm can be reached from Guernsey in 15 minutes by **Herm Seaways** (tel. 0481/724677); **Condor** (tel. 0481/726121) has a twice-weekly service from both Jersey and Guernsey to Alderney in summer and hydrofoil service to St. Malo.

Exploring the Channel Islands

The tours of Jersey and Guernsey begin in the capital cities of St. Helier and St. Peter Port, respectively; most attractions are here or close by. Alderney and Sark—though well preserved and scenic—offer few tourist attractions. A visit to these islands is suggested as a jaunt to break up the time in the larger resort areas (*see* Getting around, *above*).

Highlights for First-time Visitors

Castle Cornet: Guernsey
Eric Young Orchid Foundation: Jersey
Glass Church: Jersey
Gorey Castle: Jersey

Hautville House: Guernsey
Jersey Wildlife Trust: Jersey
Sark
Sausmarez Manor: Guernsey

Jersey

Numbers in the margin correspond to points of interest on the St. Helier map.

1 Begin your island tour at **Fort Regent** in St. Helier—the panoramic view will give you an idea of the town's layout. The fort was built between 1806 and 1811, high on a rock, as a defense against Napoleon's army (although the measure was never tested). In World War II, German anti-aircraft guns were sited in the fort. In 1958, the British government sold the fortification to the State of Jersey, which in 1967 turned it into a vast leisure complex, with a terraced swimming pool, concert hall, squash courts, World of Sea Aquarium, a good-sized amusement park, restaurants, bars, and cafés. During peak season there are guided tours with two audiovisual presentations. *Tel. 0534/73000. Admission: £3.50 adults, £2.50 children, £3 senior citizens; after 5 PM £1.50 adults, £1 children, £1.25 senior citizens. Extra fees for the amusements.*

2 Leave Fort Regent by cable car and turn left onto Hill Street to reach **Royal Square.** Now shaded by chestnut trees, the square used to be the site of executions and the town pillory. Among those put to death were four alleged witches who were hanged and then burned in 1611. Witchcraft and its punishment were constant elements in Jersey life for most of the 16th and 17th centuries, with endless trials all over the island.

3 At present, the States offices, the **Royal Court,** and the **States Chamber** (Jersey's parliament) surround the square. On the west side is the **parish church** of St. Helier, or "Town Church," the latest in the 900-year-old series of churches that have stood here. The 12th- to 14th-century structure currently houses two gifts from the diocese of New Jersey, the processional cross and the chair in which the bailiff sits when he attends service.

4 Leaving the parish church, turn south onto Pier Road to reach the **Jersey Museum.** The museum is run jointly by the Jersey Heritage Trust and the Société Jersiaise, which was founded in 1873 to preserve Jersey's traditions. The museum, in a lovely building completed in 1817 for the merchant and shipbuilder Philippe Nicolle, contains some fascinating collections that shed light on Jersey's past: works by local artists; re-creations of Victorian rooms; and memorabilia of Lillie Langtry, the beautiful mistress of Edward VII. "The Jersey Lily" was born on the island and is buried in St. Saviour's churchyard. *9 Pier Rd., tel. 0534/75940. Admission: £2.50 adults, £1.25 children and senior citizens. Open summer Mon.–Sat. 10–5, Sun. 1–5, winter Mon.–Sat. 10–4, Sun. 1–4.*

5 From the museum, walk west past the bus station to **Weighbridge,** the busy center of St. Helier's harbor life. Follow the Esplanade west again to reach **The Island Fortress–Occupation Museum,** which has an extensive display of World War II propaganda relating to Germany's presence on the island. Videos describing the event are screened. *9 Esplanade, tel. 0534/34306. Admission: £2.50 adults, £1.50 children, £2 senior citizens. Open Mar.–Nov., daily 9:30 AM–10 PM; Nov.–Mar., daily 10–4.*

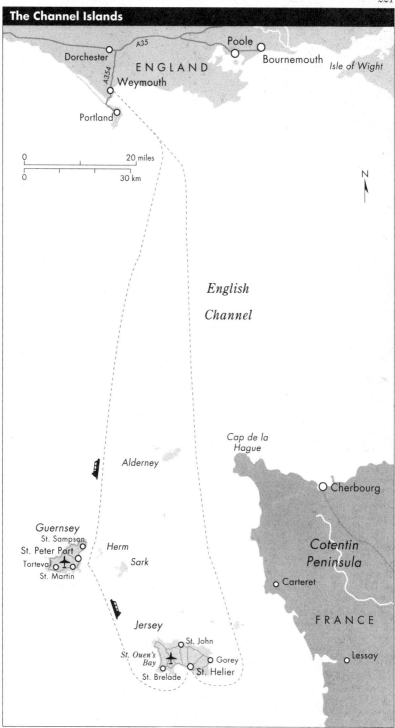

The Channel Islands

Dorchester

A35

ENGLAND

Poole

Bournemouth

Isle of Wight

Weymouth

Portland

0   20 miles

0   30 km

N

English

Channel

Cap de la Hague

Cherbourg

Alderney

Guernsey

St. Sampson

St. Peter Port

Torteval

St. Martin

Herm

Sark

Cotentin Peninsula

Carteret

Jersey

St. John

St. Ouen's Bay

St. Brelade

Gorey

St. Helier

FRANCE

Lessay

Elizabeth Castle, **6**

Fort Regent, **1**

Jersey Museum, **4**

The Island Fortress-Occupation Museum, **5**

Parish Church, **3**

People's Park, **7**

Royal Square, **2**

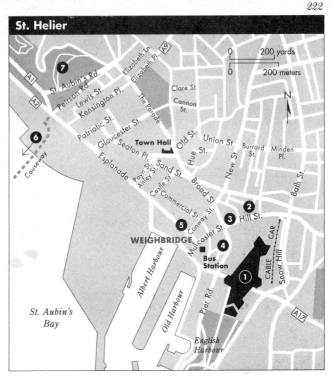

St. Helier

As you follow the Esplanade west, you will pass on the left the Albert Harbour Marina, where yachts from all over the world berth. You can take short or long cruises from here, including an evening cocktail trip down the coast or a weekend jaunt to Brittany. Across

6 the main harbor is **Elizabeth Castle,** on an island joined to the Esplanade by a causeway that begins opposite the Grand Hotel, by

7 **People's Park.** You can cross the causeway between high tides but keep an ear open for the bell which is rung from the castle's gatehouse half an hour before the sea covers the stones; the water can get up to 15 feet deep. When the causeway is not usable, an amphibious craft takes visitors across.

The little island was a holy isle beginning in the 6th century with the arrival of Helier, the missionary son of a Belgian aristocrat. Legend places his cell on the headland beyond the castle, still called **Hermitage Rock.** Close to the castle's entrance is a military museum, in former barracks, housing an exhibition that tells the building's story. In the granite-built Governor's House in the heart of the complex there are waxwork tableaux of events in the castle's long history, notably the meeting of Sir Philippe de Carteret and Charles II, who took refuge here in 1646. Carteret had been born on Jersey, at St. Ouen in 1610, and while he was bailiff the island was a haven for Royalists on the run from Cromwell's troops. For his sterling service, after the Restoration Carteret was one of the eight men to whom Charles entrusted the territory between the Hudson and the Delaware. The region was called New Jersey in Carteret's honor. *St. Aubin's Bay, tel. 0534/23971. Admission: £2.50 adults, £1.25 children and senior citizens. Open Apr.–Oct., daily 9:30–5:30.*

The following Jersey highlights are arranged clockwise, starting just west of the capital. About 1½ miles from Elizabeth Castle is St. Matthew's Church, the **"Glass Church"** in Millbrook, a Victorian chapel restored in 1934 as a memorial to Sir Jesse Boot, a millionaire pharmacist known throughout Britain for his drugstore chain, Boots. The fashionable Parisian glass sculptor, René Lalique (1860–1945), transformed the interior with glass. Inside, the church is embellished with fluid Art Deco glass forms—the front seems to be supported by a cluster of icicles; the glass cross, pillars, and altar rail all glitter with refracted light. *Millbrook, St. Aubin's Rd., St. Lawrence, tel. 0534/20934. Admission free. Open weekdays 9–6 (or dusk), Sat. 9–1, Sun. for worship only.*

From Millbrook, A1 and A12 (Grand Route de St. Ouen) will take you to the northwest corner of the island, where you will find the **Battle of Flowers Museum.** The parade of flowers has been held annually (except during wartime) since 1902. Originally, the decorated floats were torn to pieces for ammunition in the battle, but now they survive longer, some to become exhibits in this museum (with materials like dyed hare's tail and marram grass instead of flowers). There is a lakeside tearoom beside the museum that's open from May to September. *La Robeline, Mont des Corvées, St. Ouen, tel. 0534/482408. Admission: £1.75 adults, 70p children, £1.50 senior citizens. Open Easter–Dec., daily 10–5. Battle of Flowers information tel. 0534/30178.*

Half a mile inland from Bouley Bay is the zoo of the **Jersey Wildlife Trust.** The trust was started in 1963 by wildlife writer Gerald Durrell, who chose the 25 acres of Augres Manor as a center for breeding and conserving endangered species, including gorillas, orangutans, lemurs, snow leopards, and marmosets, together with many kinds of birds and reptiles. This is a great place for a family outing, as well as for anyone interested in conservation. There's also the Café Dodo, named after a bird Durrell was too late in saving. *Les Augres Manor, Trinity, tel. 0534/864666. Admission: £4.60 adults, £2.60 children, £3.10 senior citizens. Open daily 10–6 (or dusk).*

Just over a mile south of the zoo you will find the **Eric Young Orchid Foundation,** where the viewing area is landscaped with small waterfalls, rocks, and trees, and vivid cascades of showy orchids. Five big greenhouses re-create the particular environments needed for certain orchids. *Victoria Village, Trinity, tel. 0534/861963. Admission: £2 adults, £1 children, £1.50 senior citizens. Open Thurs–Sat. 10–4.*

East of Victoria Village for 3½ miles of winding road stands **Gorey Castle,** otherwise named **Mont Orgueil** (Mount Pride). For centuries Jersey's chief fortress, the castle rises square-cut on its granite rock above the busy harbor. Built mainly in the 14th century as a series of concentric defenses, it is pierced by five gateways. At its heart is the great Somerset Tower, and around it are grouped the Guard House, the Great Hall, the Kitchen, and St. Mary's Chapel (12th century), probably the oldest part of the castle. There are also waxwork tableaux of historic events. *Tel. 0534/53292. Admission: £2.50 adults, £1.25 children and senior citizens. Open Apr.–Oct., daily 9:30–5.*

Guernsey

About 16,000 people, just over one third of the population of Guernsey, live in **St. Peter Port,** which has prospered over the centuries from the harbor around which it climbs. Guernsey is well placed for trade—legal or illegal—between France and England. In the 18th and 19th centuries, St. Peter Port was a haven for privateers who preyed on merchantmen; the operations were licensed by the British who skimmed off part of the considerable profits. Victor Hugo furnished his house (*see below*) with some of the looted pieces flooding the Guernsey market. In a modern version of its privateering past, St. Peter Port is now home to many tax exiles, who have luxurious houses on the town's outskirts.

Numbers in the margin correspond to points of interest on the St. Peter Port map.

❶ The heart of the old town, around the harbor, is usually jammed with traffic. The **parish church of St. Peter,** right beside The Quay, dates back at least to the days of William the Conqueror, though the oldest part of the present building is from the 12th century. Events through the centuries have played havoc with it, not least an air raid in 1944. Walking along the quaint streets in the old quarter will provide at least a morning's entertainment. You might start at Trinity Church Square and continue on Mansell Street.

❷ The southern arm of the harbor, Castle Emplacement, leads out to **Castle Cornet,** where you can get a bird's-eye view of St. Peter Port and an 8-miles-away glimpse of France. The castle was built early in the 13th century to guard the fledgling town, and was badly damaged in an explosion in 1672, when the powder magazine was struck by lightning. Today the castle contains three museums, the **Royal Guernsey Militia Museum,** the **Armoury,** and the **Main Guard Museum,** whose collection ranges from model ships to relics from the German occupation, to island art. There's a cafeteria. *Tel. 0481/726518. Admission: £4 adults, £1.50 children, £2 senior citizens, £9 family ticket. Open Apr.–Oct., daily 10:30–5:30.*

❸ You will have to climb up from Castle Pier to Hauteville (High Town) in order to reach **Hauteville House,** once the home of writer Victor Hugo (1802–85). For 18 years he was a voluntary political exile on Guernsey; in 1856 he bought this house. It is now owned by the City of Paris, and is a completely French enclave, filled with lovely old furniture and tapestries. From the top floor he could see across to his beloved France, and also into the house of his mistress, Juliette Drouet, who lived across the street. *Tel. 0481/721911. Admission: £3 adults, £1.50 children and senior citizens. Open Apr.–Sept., Mon.–Sat. 10–11:30, 2–4:30. Guided tours only, limited to 15 people.*

❹ Just north of the town center, inland from the North Beach Marina, is the **Beau Sejour Centre,** a multipurpose sports and entertainment complex built 15 years ago. Equipped with an indoor heated pool, squash, badminton, and tennis courts, a "trim trail," a cinema/theater, a cafeteria, and a bar, this is the perfect place to come on a rainy day. *Amherst, tel. 0481/728555. Admission: holiday membership £3. Open: 9 AM–11 PM, but check for pool schedule and other activities.*

❺ **Sausmarez Manor** (not to be confused with Saumarez Park, northwest of St. Peter Port), about 2 miles to the south of downtown St. Peter Port, is Guernsey's only stately home open to the public. Although there was a Norman house on the site, the present building, a solid, plain structure, dates to the 18th century. It is set among lovely gardens, the most important of which is the Woodland Garden, full of tropical plants. Inside, tapestries, family portraits, and James II's wedding attire are on display. Sir Edmund Andros, whose family lived in the house from 1557 to 1749, was Bailiff of Guernsey, as well as Governor of New York, North Carolina, Virginia, and Massachusetts. *Tel. 0481/35571. Admission: £3 adults, £1*

Beau Sejour
Centre, **4**

Castle Cornet, **2**

German Military
Underground
Hospital, **6**

Hauteville
House, **3**

Parish Church of
St. Peter, **1**

Sausmarez
Manor, **5**

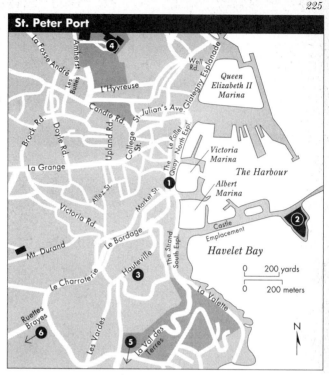

children, extra for additional attractions (see What to See and Do With Children, below). Open for guided tours only late May–Sept., Tues.–Thurs. 10:30–12 and 2:30–4:30.

6 The **German Military Underground Hospital,** 2½ miles southwest of St. Peter Port, is the main relic attesting to the German occupation here. These grim catacombs were built by slave labor, and many of the workers died on the job and are entombed in the concrete. There is also an underground network at **La Vallette** (tel. 0481/22300) that has been converted into a military museum; another, also a museum, near the **German Occupation Museum** (tel. 0481/38205); and a third in **St. Saviour's Tunnel** (tel. 0481/64679). *Underground Hospital, La Vassalerie Rd., St. Andrew's, tel. 0481/39100. Admission: £2 adults, 60p children and senior citizens. Open Nov. and Mar., Sun. and Thurs. 2–3; Apr. and Oct., daily 2–4; May–Sept., daily 10–noon and 2–5.*

Alderney and Sark

Alderney (6 sq. mi) and **Sark** (3.5 × 1.5 mi) are the "other islands"—much smaller and less visited by tourists. Their landscapes can be seen by touring the craggy coastlines, where cliffs and rocks teem with seabirds and other wildlife. **Alderney** is so close to France it has been looked upon throughout history as a fortress island. In the 1800s, a chain of 12 forts was built around the coast; today some of those are attractive private homes. Under the German occupation the island's population was evacuated and three concentration camps set up. The **Alderney Society's Museum** (High St., tel. 0481/823222) has exhibits on this horrible event.

Sark, the odd-man-out of the Channel Islands, has turned its back on the 20th century and banned the automobile, allowing only horse- or tractor-drawn carriages. Even planes are prohibited from flying overhead unless special permission has been granted. The tranquil island is in two sections, the smaller part, Little Sark, joined to the main island by a narrow neck of land whose vertiginous drop is 260 feet.

Off the Beaten Track

Jersey At **La Hogue Bie,** Grouville, halfway between St. Helier and Mont Orgueil castle, there's one of the finest neolithic tombs in Western Europe. It lies in a mound topped by two medieval chapels, and was excavated in 1924. The museum here has archaeological, farming, and old Jersey Railway exhibits. There is also a German bunker with an extensive occupation display. *Tel. 0534/53823. Admission: £2 adults, £1 children and senior citizens. Open mid-Mar.–Oct., Sun.– Thurs. 10–4:30.*

The **Carnation Nursery and Butterfly Farm** in the north of the island (off B23) has magnificent displays of carnations grown under glass in the grounds of an old farmhouse. Visitors can wander among hundreds of rare and exotic butterflies, living and breeding in their natural habitat. *Retreat Farm, St. Lawrence, tel. 0534/65665. Admission free. Open summer, daily 9–5; winter, weekdays 9–5:30, Sat. 9–1.*

Guernsey Here too you can get away from castles and fortresses with a visit to the **Friquet Flower and Butterfly Centre** (Le Friquet, Castel, tel. 0481/54378). Walk among thousands of free-flying butterflies, and, later, take in an evening barbecue or dinner at the restaurant. The **Tropical Vinery and Gardens** (St. Saviour's, tel. 0481/63566) has glass houses crowded with hibiscus, lemons, limes, bougainvillea, and bananas. Also, for 100 years of tomato-growing history, see the **Tomato Centre** (King's Mills, Castel, tel. 0481/54389), and taste the tomato wine!

What to See and Do with Children

In Jersey, **Fort Regent** has year-round attractions and activities, and one of its features, Humfrey's Playground, is for kids up to age 14. The **Jersey Zoo** at the Jersey Wildlife Trust is a fascinating spot for all the family. **Guernsey Toys** (25–27 Victoria Rd., St. Peter Port, tel. 0481/723871) produces cuddly soft toys, and children can see how they are made. There is a notable collection of dollhouses at **Sausmarez Manor** on Guernsey, as well as two model railways. *Admission: £3 adults, £1 children. Extra fees for railway and dollhouses.*

Shopping

It's a pleasant surprise that the Channel Islands don't add the usual 17.5% VAT to prices. **St. Helier** and **St. Peter Port** are full of shops selling everything from cosmetics to liquor, and the towns have branches of all the major chain stores.

Jersey In St. Helier pedestrian malls on **Queen Street** and **King Street** have classic shops selling international brands, while smaller boutiques line roads like **Bath Street, New Street,** and **Halkett Place.** Two major markets are the **Central Market** and **Indoor Market,** also in this area. For crafts, visit the **Oatlands Craft Centre** (St. Sampson's, tel. 0481/

49478), where glassblowers, silversmiths, potters, and quilters demonstrate and sell their works. Also visit the **Bee Centre** (in the complex), for beeswax candles.

Guernsey   The main shopping district in St. Peter Port, not as glitzy as St. Helier, begins in **Le Pollet,** near Queen Elizabeth marina. The mostly pedestrian area is a network of lanes with specialty shops—particularly jewelers. This is a great place to buy a watch. For antiques and women's fashions head for the old quarter and **Mill Street, Mansell Square,** and **Trinity Square.** Pottery mavens should visit the **Moulin Houet Pottery** (Moulin Houet Bay, tel. 0481/37201), which is located at the head of a lush valley, running down to the sea. The goods here are sturdy and attractive.

Sports and the Outdoors

Bicycling   While in St. Helier, Jersey, rent from **Doubleday Garage** (19 Stopford Rd., tel. 0534/31505); **Lawrence de Gruchy** (46 Don St., tel. 0534/30090); and the **Hire Shop** (St. Albin's Rd., Milbrook, tel. 0534/73699). On Guernsey, you can rent bikes from **The Cycle Shop** (The Bridge, St. Sampson's, tel. 0481/49311); **Moullins Cycle Shop** (St. George's Esplanade, St. Peter Port, tel. 0481/721581); and **West Coast Cycles** (Les Tamaris, Portinfer La., Vale, tel. 0481/53654). On Sark, **Jackson's Cycle Hire** (tel. 0481/832161) and **Isle of Sark Carriage and Cycle Hire** (tel. 0481/832262) rent bikes.

Golf   Jersey has two 18-hole courses, both of which can be used by any visitor who is affiliated with a golf club back home. These are **La Moye** (St. Brelade, tel. 0534/42701) and **Royal Jersey Golf Club** (Grouville, tel. 0534/51042).

The 18-hole **Royal Guernsey** (L'Ancresse, Vale, tel. 0481/47022) has wonderful views of the beach and sea. To play here visitors must produce handicap certificates, and they can't play Sundays, Thursdays, and Saturday afternoons. On Alderney there is a **9-hole course** (Route des Carriers, tel. 0481/822835), which welcomes players any time except on competition days.

Walking   On all the islands the best routes for walking are along the well-marked coast trails. On Jersey's north coast, walk from **Grosnez** in the west to **Rozel** in the east. Part of this route will take you along 300-foot cliffs. On Guernsey, the coastal trail runs for almost 30 miles, with views as sensational as those in Jersey.

If you are feeling particularly healthy, you can do the full length of these paths all at once, or, if you just want a comfortable stroll, any section of them that takes your fancy. The best time is in spring and early summer, when the wildflowers are at their riotous best. Be careful in fall, though; the paths can get very muddy and treacherous. You should also be warned that the walks often involve some very steep climbing, when the cliffs are interrupted by deep valleys, where inland streams flow into the sea. There are cafés open all along the coasts in the tourist season, so having a coffee break is no problem. As the bus services on Jersey and Guernsey are so good, you can take a bus to any point that you want to start your walk, and pick up one whenever you feel like giving up. Maps and guides to the cliff walks are available at the islands' Tourist Offices—**Jersey:** Liberation Sq., St. Helier, tel. 0534/500700; **Guernsey:** Crown Pier, St. Peter Port, tel. 0481/726611.

Water Sports   To dive in Jersey, contact **Watersports** (First Tower, tel. 0534/32813)
Diving   or the **Diving Centre** (Bouley Bay, tel. 0534/861817). In Guernsey

contact the **Blue Dolphin Sun Aqua Club** (Rue des Cottes, St. Sampson's, tel. 0481/53878).

Sail-Boarding and Surfing At St. Ouen Bay, in Jersey, there's great surfing. Windsurfing is popular at St. Aubin and St. Brelade's Bay. Rent equipment from **Watersplash** (St. Ouen's Bay, tel. 0534/482885) or the **Gorey Watersports Centre** (Grouville Bay, tel. 0534/522033). In Guernsey try the surf at Vazon Bay. The island's windsurfing authority is **Windsurfing International** (Cobô, tel. 0481/53313).

Swimming The unpolluted water and magnificent beaches are a major attraction of these islands. Although the tides can be fierce, most popular beaches have guards on duty. On Jersey, **St. Clement's Bay** and **Royal Bay** of Grouville have excellent sand and safe water. On Guernsey, try **Vazon Bay,** which has one section reserved for surfers; **Petit Pot Bay,** especially for sunbathing; and **L'Ancresse Bay,** where the water is shallow.

Dining and Lodging

Dining The specialty of the Channel Islands is seafood in all its delectable glory. Crab and lobster dishes are on many menus, but don't overlook the daily catch from the tiny harbors or the mollusk called Jersey Ormer or sea ear—appropriately named. When you tire of seafood, the locally bred lamb is superb, and thick cream slathers the desserts.

Highly recommended restaurants are indicated by a star ★.

Category	Cost*
$$$$	over £40
$$$	£30–£40
$$	£20–£30
$	under £20

per person, including first course, main course, and dessert; excluding drinks

Lodging Jersey is chockablock with hotels, guest houses, and bed-and-breakfasts, all organized and well regulated by the **Jersey Hotel and Guest House Assoc.** (60 Stopford Rd., St. Helier, Jersey JE2 4LB, tel. 0534/21421). You can also get a comprehensive listing from the Jersey tourist board or the Guernsey tourist board. Many places offer half-board (MAP), at a savings. Outlying parts of Jersey are more low-key than the comparative razzmatazz of St. Helier. Guernsey is Jersey writ small, more relaxed, with hotels to match. If you want to stay on Alderney or Sark, plan well ahead.

Highly recommended lodgings are indicated by a star ★.

Category	Cost*
$$$$	over £130
$$$	£90–£130

$$	£50–£90
$	under £50

All prices are for two people sharing a double room, including service and breakfast.

Alderney
Dining

Nellie Gray's. One of the few places to dine on Alderney, Nellie Gray's is reliable and has a homey atmosphere. Like most of the restaurants on the islands, the menu here relies on the day's catch and local produce. You can eat in the garden or indoors. *Victoria St., St. Anne, tel. 0481/823333. Reservations required. Dress: casual. AE, DC, MC, V. Closed Nov.–Apr., and Sun. $$*

Dining and Lodging

Georgian House. You get a choice of great bar food—steak and mushroom pie, or fresh fish—in this friendly, whitewashed town house, or you can have a full meal in the dining room. During summer enjoy barbecue in the garden, or, on Wednesday and Saturday evenings (year-round), there's a carvery buffet. For overnighters, there are four bedrooms. *Victoria St., St. Anne, tel. 0481/822471. Reservations advised for the restaurant. Dress: casual. AE, DC, MC, V. Bar $; Restaurant $$*

Inchalla Hotel. Even for relaxed Alderney, this is a peaceful place. It is set in lovely grounds on the edge of St. Anne, looking out over the sea. The bedrooms are simple and comfortable and the restaurant has wonderfully fresh fish—try the squid Provençal. *The Val, St. Anne, tel. 0481/823220, fax 0481/823551. 10 rooms with bath. Facilities: restaurant, garden, sauna, solarium, outdoor pool. AE, MC, V. $$*

Guernsey
Dining

The Absolute End. This quietly elegant little restaurant in a neat, white building facing the sea is about a mile north along the coast from the center of St. Peter Port. The emphasis here is, of course, on seafood dishes, with home-smoked fish and shellfish as a very tasty starter. Try the salmon coubiliac. There is a good-value set menu at lunch for £10. The Absolute End won the best island restaurant award in 1993. *Longstore, St. George's Esplanade, St. Peter Port, tel. 0481/723822. Reservations advised. Dress: casual but neat. AE, DC, MC, V. $$*

★ **Café du Moulin.** This restaurant is in a converted watermill in a peaceful valley on the east of the island, close to the Longfree nature reserve. Naturally, fish comes first. Try the crêpinette of seafood, or a casserole of sole. It's all ultrafresh and tasty, with a touch of East Asia in many of the dishes. The bar is one of the best-stocked on the island. *Route du Quanteraine, St. Peters, tel. 0481/65944. Reservations advised. Dress: casual. MC, V. Closed Mon. and Tues., 2 weeks Feb., 2 weeks Nov. $$*

La Nautique. As with all the best restaurants in the Channel Islands, fish is the order of the day here. In this old-established eatery it comes with every sauce imaginable—lobster flambéed with whisky, sole *duglère*, turbot *hollandaise*. The cooking is French, and the service stylish, which is not the case with many Guernsey restaurants. *The Quay Steps, St. Peter Port, tel. 0481/721714. Reservations essential. Dress: jacket and tie. AE, DC, MC, V. Closed Sun., 2 weeks Jan. $$*

Dining and Lodging

La Frégate. This small 17th-century manor house has been carefully converted into a hotel. Its setting in colorful gardens on a quiet hillside that overlooks the harbor and islands makes it an excellent choice for a restful vacation. The bedrooms are all comfortable and sizable, some have balconies, and the staff is attentive. The restaurant, with big windows overlooking the town, serves topnotch cuisine, especially seafood dishes. Try the *timbale de crustacés*, or the home-marinated salmon with dill. *Les Côtils, St. Peter Port, tel. 0481/724624, fax 0481/720443. 13 rooms with bath. AE, DC, MC, V. $$$*

Lodging **Imperial Hotel.** Here is a simple hotel that's very popular for family vacations. The bedrooms, decorated with sturdy furnishings, are uncluttered, and some offer views of the sandy beaches of Rocquaine Bay. There are two bars reserved for residents, and another, the Portlet Bar, is the haunt of locals. *Torteval, tel. 0481/64044, fax 0481/66139. 16 bedrooms, 14 with bath. MC, V. $$*

Jersey **Granite Corner.** Set in an attractive little cottage, tucked away be-
Dining side Rozel Bay, this is one of the few truly French restaurants on the island. The *patron*/chef, Jean-Luc Robin, comes from Périgord, and his specialties reflect his home region, often featuring truffles from the area. He is also a whiz with fish caught fresh from Rozel Bay. If you prefer meat, try the classic tournedos Rossini. *Rozel Harbour, Trinity, tel. 0534/863590. Reservations essential. Dress: casual chic. MC, V. Closed Sun. evening, Mon. lunch, and 2 weeks Jan. $$$$*

Victoria's. The Grand Hotel's restaurant is *the* place to go for dinner and dancing. The decor is firmly Victorian. There's a long menu, but the critics' choice is the lemon sole or the medallions of lamb. *Grand Hotel, Pierson Rd., St. Helier, tel. 0534/22301. Reservations required. Jacket and tie required. AE, DC, MC, V. $$$*

Jersey Pottery. This restaurant is part of the Jersey Pottery complex and boasts that Queen Elizabeth lunched here when visiting her dukedom. The restaurant, in an attractive conservatory, offers great seafood, but as it's very popular and often full, the cafeteria is an alternative. *Gorey Village, Grouville, tel. 0534/851119. Reservations advised. Dress: casual. AE, DC, MC, V. Open for lunch only, Mon.–Fri. $$*

Dining and **Hotel l'Horizon.** L'Horizon is one of Jersey's luxury hotels, with
Lodging wonderful views over St. Brelade's Bay. Though the hotel is big, it manages to maintain a bright, upbeat feeling, with large, comfortable bedrooms, and plenty of places to relax in comfort. There are two restaurants—the **Crystal Room** and the **Star Grill.** The food is the same in both, but the atmosphere differs; the Crystal Room is traditionally elegant, while the Grill is more relaxed. Try the quail salad, roast saddle of lamb, or any of the wonderful seafood dishes, especially the scampi in mouthwatering ginger, honey, and lemon sauce. If you want to drop by for a special tea, try the **Beach Lounge.** *St. Brelade's Bay, St. Brelade, tel. 0534/43101, fax 0534/46269. 107 rooms with bath. Facilities: 2 restaurants, garden, indoor pool, sauna, solarium, in-house movies. Reservations and jacket and tie required for the restaurants. AE, DC, MC, V. $$$$*

★ **Longueville Manor.** The Manor is one of Britain's few members of the Relais and Châteaux group. It's set in lovely grounds and has the look of polished age, elegance, and comfort, derived from long-established, caring proprietors. Antiques abound, the bedrooms are supremely comfortable, and the bathrooms luxurious. The food in the paneled dining room is essentially traditional English, but venison pâté with onion marmalade, grilled salmon with béarnaise sauce, liver with sausage, and black pudding are all standouts. Try a selection of specialties in the eight-course *menu dégustation.* There's passion-fruit sorbet or the Eton Mess, an unbelievable creation with crushed meringue and strawberries, with Jersey cream topping it off. *Longueville, St. Saviour, tel. 0534/25501, fax 0534/31613. 33 rooms with bath. Facilities: restaurant, gardens, outdoor* *pool, in-house movies. Reservations and jacket and tie required for the restaurant. AE, DC, MC, V. $$$$*

Château la Chaire. This dignified, mock-French château is hidden on a cul-de-sac just above Rozel Harbour. The building is large but offers only 14 bedrooms, though all are luxurious and sunny; some of the bathrooms have Jacuzzis. The property is opulent, and the restaurant is no exception. This is the place to try Jersey's excellent fresh fish in a variety of elegant preparations. *Rozel Valley, tel. 0534/863354, fax 0534/865137. 14 rooms with bath. Facilities: restaurant, garden, in-house movies. Reservations and jacket and tie required for the restaurant. AE, DC, MC, V. $$$*

Moorings Hotel. Although this seaside hotel is not one of Jersey's fanciest, it does offer attractively decorated, very cozy bedrooms (13 of them with harbor views), and friendly, helpful service. The restaurant, too, is on the simple side, but the lamb carved from the trolley and the superbly fresh seafood dishes are well above average. *Gorey Pier, tel. 0534/853633, fax 0534/857618. 16 rooms with bath. Facilities: restaurant, patio. Reservations required for the restaurant. Dress: casual. AE, MC, V. $$$*

The Old Court House Inn. This is an ancient inn—the core of the building is around 500 years old—with a few rooms, two atmospheric lunchtime bars, and a fine restaurant. Grilled oysters, crab Creole, Jersey plaice—all feature on the big menu. The busy inn overlooks the harbor; the best view, though, is from the penthouse. *The Bulwarks, St. Aubin's Harbour, tel. 0534/46433, fax 0534/45103. 9 rooms with bath. Facilities: restaurant, 2 bars, patio. Reservations advised for the restaurant. Dress: casual. AE, DC, MC, V. $$*

Sark Dining and Lodging
Stock's Hotel. For a relaxed lunch—and what else would you expect on Sark?—try the restaurant here. Lunchtime fare in the Courtyard Bistro might be quiche, or the local lobster and crab. The seafood Provençal is memorable. If you feel like staying over, there are 24 bedrooms. The **Cider Press Restaurant** also serves more formal meals. For a light snack, Stock's cakes and pastries rank high on the menu. *Tel. 0481/832001, fax 0481/832130. 25 rooms, 20 with bath. No reservations. Dress: casual. DC, MC, V. Closed Oct.–Easter. Hotel $$$; Restaurant $$; Bistro $*

The Arts

Festivals
Jersey has an international **Jazz Festival** in April in St. Helier (tel. 0534/24779). The **Battle of Flowers** is held in August (*see* Exploring, above), and a **Folk and Blues Festival** is held in September, in St. Helier. Films, theater, and celebrity concerts are put on all year in Fort Regent (*see* Exploring, *above*).

Guernsey has an **Eisteddfod** at the end of February, an **International Dance Festival** in June, and a **Battle of Flowers** in August. Contact the tourist board for the latest dates.

Performing Arts
During the summer months there are concerts by visiting bands in the Howard Davis Park, St. Helier. The **Jersey Arts Centre** (Phillips St., St. Helier, tel. 0534/73767) has regular exhibitions of art, as well as drama, films, and music.

8 The Thames Valley

Windsor, Henley-on-Thames, Oxford

Like many another great river, the Thames creates the illusion that it flows not only through the prosperous countryside of Berkshire and Oxfordshire, but through long centuries of history, too. The magic of past times seems to rise from its swiftly moving waters like an intangible mist. In London, where it is a broad, oily stream, it speeds almost silently past great buildings, menacingly impressive. Higher upstream it is a busy part of the living landscape, flooding meadows in spring and fall, linking a chain of great houses created by power brokers who needed to be near the capital, and rippling past places of significance not just to England but to the world. Runnymede is one of these. Here, on a riverside greensward, the Magna Carta was signed, that first crucial step in the Western world's progress toward democracy.

Nearby rises the medieval bulk of Windsor Castle, home to eight successive royal houses. Anyone who wants to understand the mystique of the British monarchy should visit Windsor, where a fraction of the present queen's vast wealth is on display in surroundings of pomp, power, and solid magnificence. Farther upstream lies Oxford, where generations of the ruling elite have been educated. In the bustling modern city, with industrial development on its outskirts, the colleges maintain their scholarly calm amid the traffic's clamorous rush.

Scattered throughout the spreading landscape of trees, meadows, and rolling hills, are endless small villages and larger towns, some totally spoiled by ill-considered modern building, some still sleepily preserving their ancient charm. Reading is a sad example of the former, Ewelme the epitome of the latter. Apart from the meandering thread of the river, which ties the area together, the Thames Valley is crisscrossed by superhighways carrying heavy traffic between London, the West Country, and the Midlands. These highways and the railroad have made much of this area into commuter territory, but you can easily leave these beaten tracks, and head down leafy lanes to discover timeless villages in a landscape kept green by the river and its wandering tributaries.

Essential Information

Important Addresses and Numbers

Tourist Information	**Henley:** Town Hall, tel. 0491/578034. **Marlow:** c/o Court Garden Leisure Complex, Pound La., tel. 0628/483597. **Oxford:** St. Aldate's, tel. 0865/726871. **Windsor:** Central Station, Thames St., tel. 0753/852010. **Woodstock:** Hensington Rd., tel. 0993/811038.
Travel Agencies	**Thomas Cook,** 5 Queen St., Oxford, tel. 0865/240441. **Windsor Travel House,** 1 Bolton Rd., Windsor, tel. 0753/857117.
Car-Rental Agencies	**Oxford: Europcar Interrent,** Hartford Motors, Seacourt Tower, Botley, tel. 0865/246373; **Hertz,** City Motors Ltd., The Roundabout, Woodstock Rd., tel. 0865/57291. **Windsor: Ford Rent a Car,** A. A. Clark, 72–74 Arthur Rd., tel. 0753/856419.

Arriving and Departing

By Car	M4 and M40 radiate west from London, bringing Oxford (57 mi) and Reading (42 mi) within an hour's drive except in rush hour.

By Train **British Rail** serves the region from London's Paddington Station (tel. 071/262–6767) with fast trains to the main towns, and a reliable commuter service. There's also hourly service to Oxford (travel time is one hour).

By Bus **City Link** (tel. 0865/711312) runs a regular London–Oxford service (1 hr. 40 min.), with departures every 20 minutes from London's Victoria Coach Station. **London Link** (tel. 0734/581358) has a regular London–Reading shuttle, and service from Heathrow and Gatwick airports to Oxford. The Reading-based **Bee Line** (tel. 0734/581358) serves the smaller towns of Berkshire.

Getting Around

By Car Although the roads are good, this wealthy section of the commuter belt has surprisingly heavy traffic, even on the smaller roads. Parking in towns can be a problem, too, so allow plenty of time.

By Train For local timetables, phone 0865/722333 (Oxford area), 0734/595911 (Reading area), or 0753/38621 (Windsor area).

By Bus The **Oxford Bus Company** (tel. 0865/711312) offers a one-day "Compass" ticket and a seven-day "Freedom" ticket, for unlimited bus travel within Oxford. Local bus services link the towns between Oxford and Windsor—for example **Thames Transit** (tel. 0865/778849).

Guided Tours

Orientation **Guide Friday** (Windsor tel. 0753/855755, Oxford tel. 0865/790522) runs guided tours of Windsor (£7 adults, £2 children, £4 senior citizens) and Oxford (£5 adults, £1.50 children, £4 senior citizens).

Aficionados of the British television detective Morse have a wide choice of tours which visit the locations of his cases. **British Heritage Tours of Chester** (Richmond Pl., 125 Boughton, Chester CH3 5BJ, tel. 0244/342222) have "Morse Tours of Oxford" guided by an ex-policeman who spent 15 years as Marshal of the University. They also run Morse weekends and coach trips. **Spires and Shires** (4 Walton Well Rd., Oxford OX2 6ED, tel. 0865/513998) have tours of the Morse locations, which, because they are student-led, give a real insight into university life. Spires and Shires also have tours to the Cotswolds, Blenheim Palace, Stratford, and Stonehenge.

River Tours The best way to see the Thames region is from the water; summertime trips range from 30 minutes to all day. **Hobbs and Sons** (tel. 0491/572035) covers the Henley Reach and also rents boats from Station Road, Henley-on-Thames. **Salter Brothers** (Folly Bridge, Oxford, tel. 0865/243421) runs daily steamer cruises, mid-May to mid-September from Windsor, Oxford, Abingdon, Henley, Marlow, and Reading. **Thames River Cruises** (tel. 0734/481088) conducts outings from Caversham Bridge, Reading, Easter–September. **Windsor Boat Company** (tel. 0753/862933) operates 35-minute and two-hour river trips from The Promenade, Windsor.

Exploring the Thames Valley

We begin exploring the Thames Valley in the lively tourist town of Windsor, favorite home-away-from-home of Britain's royal family. From there we follow the river to Henley, site of the famous regatta, and then follow a counterclockwise sweep as far east as Marlow and west to Wallingford—the countryside immortalized by *The Wind in the Willows*—stopping in the busy town of Reading, Berkshire's county seat. Finally we go to Oxford, and end with a visit to some of the region's stately homes and palaces.

Highlights for First-time Visitors

Blenheim Palace: Tour 3
Eton College: Tour 1
Ewelme: Tour 2
Magdalen College, Oxford: Tour 3
Runnymede: Tour 1
Vale of the White Horse, Uffington: Tour 3
Windsor Castle: Tour 1

Tour 1: Royal Berkshire—Windsor and Environs

Numbers in the margin correspond to points of interest on the Thames Valley map.

① **Windsor,** just 21 miles west of London and easily accessible, makes a rewarding day trip. The town's principal attraction is the castle, rising majestically on its bluff above the Thames, visible for miles around. But the city itself, with its narrow streets brimming with shops and ancient buildings, is well worth a visit.

The most impressive view of Windsor Castle is from the A332 road, on the southern approach to the town. Although there have been settlements here from time immemorial, including a Roman villa, the present castle was begun by William the Conqueror in the 11th century, and modified and extended by Edward III in the mid-1300s. One of his largest contributions was the enormous and distinctive **round tower.** Finally, between 1824 and 1837, George IV transformed what was essentially still a medieval castle into the fortified royal palace you see today. In all, work on the castle was spread over more than eight centuries, with most of the kings and queens of England demonstrating their undying attachment to it. In fact, Windsor is the only royal residence that has been in continuous use by the royal family since the Middle Ages.

As you enter the castle, **Henry VIII's gateway** leads uphill into the wide castle precincts, where visitors are free to wander. Directly opposite the entrance is **St. George's Chapel,** where the queen invests new knights at the colorful Order of the Garter ceremonies in June, and where several of her predecessors are buried, including her father, George VI. One of England's finest churches, the chapel was built in the 15th- and 16th-century Perpendicular style and features elegant stained-glass windows, a high, vaulted ceiling, and intricately carved choir stalls. The heraldic banners of the Knights of the Garter hang in the choir, giving it a richly medieval look. The ceremony in which the knights are installed as members of the order has been held here with much pageantry since 1348. Senior mem-

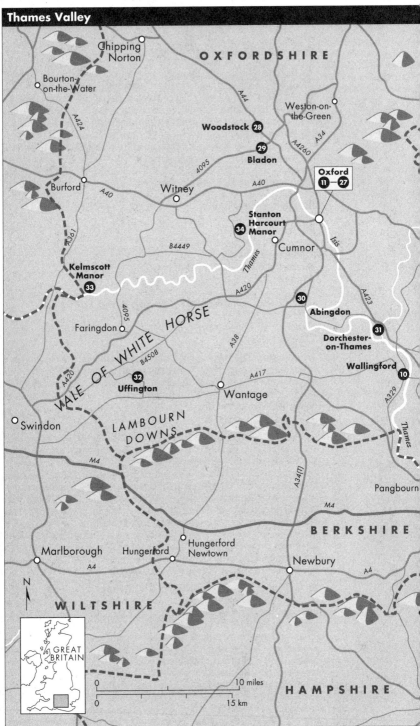

Thames Valley

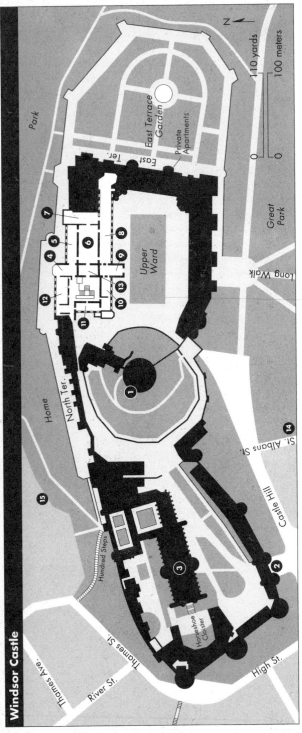

Windsor Castle

238

N

110 yards
100 meters

Park

East Terrace Garden

East Ter.

Private Apartments

Upper Ward

Great Park

Long Walk

Home

North Ter.

Hundred Steps

Thames St.

River St.

High St.

Horseshoe Cloister

Castle Hill

St. Albans St.

Round Tower, **1**
Henry VIII's Gateway, **2**
St. George's Chapel, **3**
State Apartments/ Queen Mary's Doll's House, **4**

Throne Room, **5**
Waterloo Chamber, **6**
Grand Reception Room, **7**
St. George's Hall, **8**
Queen's Grand Chamber, **9**

Queen's Presence Chamber, **10**
Queen's Ballroom, **11**
State Bedchamber, **12**
Grand Vestibule, **13**
Royal Mews, **14**
Choir School, **15**

bers of the choir of St. George's Chapel live close by in the 15th-century timbered buildings of the Horseshoe Cloister. The choir school is just outside the castle, below the North Terrace.

The **North Terrace** provides especially good views across the Thames to Eton College (*see below*), perhaps the most famous of Britain's exclusive "public" boys' schools. From the terrace, you enter the **State Apartments,** a series of splendid rooms containing priceless furniture, including a magnificent Louis XVI bed; Gobelin tapestries and paintings by Canaletto, Rubens, Van Dyck, Holbein, Dürer, and del Sarto. The high points of the tour are the **Throne Room** and the **Waterloo Chamber,** where Sir Thomas Lawrence's portraits of Napoleon's victorious foes line the walls. You can also see a collection of arms and armor, much of it exotic, and an exhibition of items from the **Queen's Collection of Master Drawings:** works by Leonardo da Vinci, plus 87 Holbein portraits, and many others. (We are obviously unable to say which art treasures will be on view at any time.)

The terrible fire of November 1992, which started in the Queen's private chapel, totally gutted some of the State Apartments. A swift rescue effort meant that, miraculously, hardly any works of art were lost. The repairs will take years to complete—probably until well into the next century. It is now hoped that most of the restoration work will be completed by 1998. If you visit at this time, you will be able to watch some of the expert restoration work in progress.

Queen Mary's Doll's House, on display to the left of the entrance to the State Apartments, is a perfect palace-within-a-palace, with functioning lights, running water, and even a library of Lilliputian-size books especially written by famous authors of the 1920s. Just outside the castle, on St. Albans Street, is the **Royal Mews,** where the royal horses are kept, with carriages, coaches, and splendid red and gold harness. The highlight is the Scottish State Coach. *Tel. 0753/831118 (recording). Admission: £8 adults, £4 children, £5.50 senior citizens (these fees cover the Precincts, the State Apartments, the Gallery, St. George's Chapel, and the Albert Memorial Chapel). Doll's House or Royal Mews, £1.60 adults, 80p children, £1.40 senior citizens. Check in advance for opening times as they vary considerably.*

Only a small part of old Windsor—the settlement that grew up around the castle in the Middle Ages—has survived. Opposite the castle entrance you can explore tiny Church Lane and Queen Charlotte Street, both narrow and cobbled. The old buildings now house antiques shops or restaurants. Around the corner, on High Street, stands the colonnaded **Guildhall** built in the 1680s by Sir Christopher Wren, who designed London's St. Paul's Cathedral (his father was dean of Windsor). Wren also built himself a fine house overlooking the river in Thames Street, now a hotel.

Time Out The **Dôme** (5 Thames St.) will provide a good lunch with a French accent: pâté, charcuterie, and interesting salads.

❷ A footbridge across the Thames links Windsor with its almost equally historic neighbor, **Eton.** With its single main street leading from the river to the famous school, Eton is a much quieter town than Windsor and retains an old-fashioned charm. The splendid redbrick, Tudor-style buildings of **Eton College,** founded in 1440 by King Henry VI, border the north end of High Street; drivers are warned of "Boys Crossing." During the college semesters, the schoolboys are a distinctive sight, dressed in their pinstripe trousers, swallow-tailed coats, top hats, and white collars. The oldest buildings, grouped around a quadrangle called School Yard, include the **Lower School,** which is one of the oldest schoolrooms in use in Britain. The Gothic **Chapel** rivals St. George's at Windsor in both size and magnificence. Beyond the cloisters are the school's famous playing fields where, according to the duke of Wellington, the Battle of Waterloo was won, since so many of his officers had learned discipline in their schooldays there. The **Museum of Eton Life** has displays on the school's history, and there are guided tours of the Lower School and chapel. *Brewhouse Yard, tel. 0753/671000. Admission: £2.20 adults, £1.50 children; £3 or £4.50 adults, £2.50 or £4.50 children, depending on length of tour. Open Apr.–Sept., daily 2–4:30; out-of-term, daily 10:30–4:30.*

Just south of Windsor Castle, stretching for some 8 miles (about 5,000 acres), is **Windsor Great Park,** the remains of an ancient royal hunting forest. Much of it is open to the public and can be explored by car or on foot. Focal points include the 3-mile **Long Walk,** the **Royal Mausoleum** at Frogmore, where Queen Victoria and her husband, Prince Albert, are buried (open only two days a year, in May); **Virginia Water,** a 2-mile-long lake; and the **Savill Garden,** which offers a huge variety of trees and shrubs. *Wick La., Englefield Green, Egham, tel. 0753/860222. Admission (garden): £3.20 adults, children under 16 free, £2.70 senior citizens. Open weekdays 10–6, weekends 10–7 or sunset.*

❸ Directly southeast of Windsor on the A308 is **Runnymede,** a tiny island in the middle of the Thames where King John, under his barons' compulsion, signed the Magna Carta in 1215, affirming the individual's right to justice and liberty. On the wooded hillside, in a meadow given to the United States by Queen Elizabeth in 1965, stands a **memorial to President John F. Kennedy.** Nearby is another memorial, in the style of a classical temple, erected by the American Bar Association to commemorate the 750th anniversary of the signing.

❹ In woods high above the River Thames, north of Windsor, stands **Cliveden,** the imposing country mansion made famous by the Astors, who had it rebuilt in the 1860s. For 250 years, Cliveden was one of the most important houses in England. Set in glorious rural river scenery, yet easily accessible from London, it attracted generations of eminent politicians and writers as house guests. In the 1920s and '30s it was the setting for the Cliveden Set, the strongly political *salon* presided over by Nancy Astor, who was the first woman to sit in Parliament, though she was an American, born in Danville, Virginia, in 1879. The house now belongs to the National Trust, which has leased it for use as a *very* exclusive hotel. The public can visit the lovely grounds and formal gardens with their fine views over the Thames, as well as three rooms in the west wing of the house. Among the attractions in the grounds is a small amphitheater in which "Rule Britannia" was first sung in 1739. There is a convenient restaurant for lunch (*see* Dining and Lodging, *below*). *Grounds— admission: £3.80 adults, £1.90 children, £9.50 family ticket; house £1 extra. Open Mar.–Oct., daily 11–6. House open Apr.–Oct., Thurs. and Sun. 3–6. Restaurant in the Orangery open Apr.–Oct., Wed.–Sun. 11–5.*

In prettier, more rural surroundings is the village of **Cookham.** This area was the subject of the paintings of Sir Stanley Spencer (1891–1959), some of which are on display at the **Stanley Spencer Gallery.** *King's Hall, Cookham, tel. 06285/20890. Admission: 50p adults,*

10p children, 25p senior citizens. Open Easter–Oct., daily 10:30–5:30; Nov.–Easter, weekends and national holidays, 11–5.

To the east of Cookham you will find **Burnham Beeches,** a 600-acre tract of beeches, great oaks, birches, and other majestic trees that's a beautiful spot for walks throughout the year. The area has been forested since the Ice Age, and some of the beech trees are as much as 500 years old. This is a wonderful area for a relaxed walk. Not only are the trees interesting, but the wildlife here is particularly rich.

Tour 2: From Marlow to Wallingford— "Wind in the Willows" Country

❺ Follow A4155 northwest to **Marlow,** and take particular note of its unusual suspension bridge, which William Tierney Clark built in the 1830s. (He also built the bridge over the Danube linking Buda with Pest.) Marlow has a number of striking old buildings, particularly the stylish, privately owned Georgian houses along Peter and West streets. In 1817, the Romantic poet Percy Bysshe Shelley stayed with friends at 67 West Street and then bought **Albion House** on the same street. His second wife, Mary, completed her Gothic novel *Frankenstein* here. Marlow Place, in Station Road, dates from 1721, and has been lived in by several princes of Wales.

Time Out One of the town's fine old pubs is the 400-year-old **Ship Inn** (on West St.), whose beams were once ship timbers.

❻ Continue on A4155 for 7 miles to **Henley.** Mention Henley to Britons, and even those who have scarcely seen a boat will conjure up idyllic scenes of summer rowing. Indeed, Henley Royal Regatta, held in early July each year on a long, straight stretch of the River Thames, has made the charming little riverside town famous throughout the world.

Henley-on-Thames, set in a broad valley between gentle hillsides just off A423, about 8 miles from Reading and 36 miles from central London, has been an important river crossing since the 12th century. The handsome Henley Bridge, its keystones carved with personifications of the Thames and Isis rivers, is more than 200 years old. Now, unfortunately, the bridge is a serious traffic bottleneck, especially on weekends.

Henley's many historic buildings, including one of Britain's oldest theaters, are all within a few minutes' walk. Half-timbered Georgian cottages and inns abound. Many have courtyards that once witnessed the brutal sport of bear-baiting, where tethered bears were tormented to death by hungry dogs. There is also an interesting selection of small antiques and gift shops, and several historic pubs. The mellow brick **Red Lion Hotel,** beside the bridge (*see* Dining and Lodging, *below*), has been the town's focal point for nearly 500 years. Kings, dukes, and writers have stayed here, including Charles I and James Boswell. The duke of Marlborough, who used the hotel as a base during the building of Blenheim Palace, even arranged to have a room in the hotel furnished to his specifications.

Overlooking the bridge is the 16th-century "checkerboard" tower of **St. Mary's Church** on Hart Street. The building is made of alternating squares of local flint and white stone. If the church's rector is about, you can ask permission to climb to the top for the superb views up and down the river. The **Chantry House,** connected to the church by a gallery, was built as a school for poor boys in 1420. It is an unspoiled example of the rare timber-frame design, with upper floors jutting out. *Hart St., tel. 0491/577340. Admission free. Open Thurs. and Sat. 10–noon.*

Townspeople launched the Henley Regatta in 1839, initiating the Grand Challenge Cup, the most famous of its many trophies. After 1851, when Prince Albert, Queen Victoria's consort, became its patron, it was known as the Royal Regatta. Oarsmen compete in crews of eight, four, or two, or as single scullers. For many of the spectators, however, the social side of the event is far more important. Elderly oarsmen wear brightly colored blazers and tiny caps; businesspeople entertain wealthy clients, and everyone admires the ladies' fashions.

Another traditional event in the third week of July is Swan-Upping, which dates back 800 years. Most of the swans on the Thames are owned by the Queen, though a few belong to two City of London companies, the Dyers and the Vintners, descendants of the medieval crafts guilds. Swan markers in Thames skiffs start from Sunbury-on-Thames, catching the new cygnets and marking their beaks in order to establish ownership. The Queen's Swan Keeper, dressed in scarlet livery, presides over this colorful ceremony, complete with festive banners.

Time Out You are never far from a pub in Henley, a town where beer has been brewed for over 200 years. One of the most popular inns is the **Three Tuns** (5 Market Pl.), which has a buttery with massive beams and a small summer terrace. The bar food is reasonable and filling—hot salt beef, vegetarian lasagna, mixed seafood—and should be washed down with good local beer.

Across the river, on the eastern side, follow the towpath north along the pleasant, shady banks to **Temple Island,** a tiny, privately owned island with trailing willows and a solitary house. This is where the regatta races start. On the south side of the town bridge, a riverside promenade passes **Mill Meadows,** where there are gardens and a pleasant picnic area. Along both stretches, the river is alive with boats of every shape and size, from luxury "gin palace" cabin cruisers to tiny rowboats.

Edged by the gently sloping Chiltern Hills and in a wide horseshoe-shaped valley, the Thames meanders from Henley through a cluster of small country towns and villages. Main roads follow the river on both sides, but it is along the narrow lanes that the villages and wooded countryside—generally prettiest north of the river—are best explored. Plan to enjoy the area at a leisurely pace, stopping for morning coffee, a pub lunch, or a cream tea at one of the ancient inns overlooking the river, and then visit shops or stroll along the river towpath to visit a lock. For more serious sightseers, the region offers a wide range of earthworks, churches, and stately homes.

About 5 miles southwest of Henley, via Sonning Common, is **Mapledurham House,** a redbrick Elizabethan mansion with tall chimneys, mullioned windows, and battlements. Its 15th-century water mill is the last working grain mill on the Thames. The house is still the home of the Eyston family, and so has kept a warm, friendly atmosphere along with pictures, family portraits, magnificent oak staircases, and Tudor plasterwork ceilings. Mapledurham can also be reached by boat from Caversham Promenade in Reading. (The boat leaves at 2 PM, and travel time is about 40 minutes.) *Mapledurham, near Reading, tel. 0734/723350. Admission: house and mill £4 adults; house only £3; grounds and mill £2.50; children half price. Open Easter–Sept., weekends only 2:30–5. The house also has 11* *self-catering cottages available for rent, some of them over 300 years old, for between £155 and £475 a week.*

This section of the river, from Caversham to Mapledurham, inspired Kenneth Grahame's classic children's book, *The Wind in the Willows*, which began as a bedtime story for Grahame's son Alastair while the Grahames were living at Pangbourne. E. F. Shepherd's charming illustrations are of specific sites along the river. Return to Henley, and continue northwest on A423/B480. There, lost in the network of leafy country lanes, is **Stonor Park,** the home of the Catholic Stonor family for more than 800 years. A medieval mansion with a Georgian facade, it stands in a wooded deer park. Mass has been celebrated in its tiny chapel since the Middle Ages, and there is an exhibition of the life and work of the Jesuit Edmund Campion, who took shelter here in 1581 before his martyrdom. *Stonor, tel. 0491/ 638587. Admission: £3.50 adults, children under 14 free. Opening times are very restricted and changeable, so check locally.*

West again, just beyond the towns of Pishill and Cookley Green, lies **Ewelme,** one of England's prettiest and most unspoiled villages. Its picture-book almshouses, church, and school—one of the oldest in Britain—huddle close together, all built more than 500 years ago. The church shelters the carved alabaster tomb of Alice, duchess of Suffolk, the granddaughter of England's greatest medieval poet, Geoffrey Chaucer. Jerome K. Jerome, author of the humorous book *Three Men in a Boat*, describing a Thameside vacation, is also buried here. He came to live in the village in 1887.

Two miles west of Ewelme is **Wallingford,** a typical riverside market town. Its busy marketplace is bordered by a town hall, built in 1670, and an Italianate corn exchange now a theater and cinema. Market day is Friday. Thirteen miles northwest on A329/423 will bring you into Oxford.

Tour 3: Oxford and Surroundings

The most picturesque approach to **Oxford** is from the east, over Magdalen (pronounced "Maudlin") Bridge. Among the ancient honey-colored buildings and elegant spires, you will see the 15th-century tower of Magdalen College, famous for its May Day carol service. Magdalen Bridge leads you directly into the broad, gently curving High Street, flanked by ancient colleges.

In Oxford the rarefied air of academia and the bustle of modern life compete with one another. In addition to its historic university, Oxford is home to two major industrial complexes: the Rover car factory and the Pressed Steel works. In the city center, "town and gown" merge, as modern stores sit side by side with centuries-old colleges and their peaceful quadrangles. With its tremendous historical and architectural wealth—no fewer than 653 buildings are designated as being of "architectural or historical merit"—Oxford deserves a serious visit. Keep in mind, however, that congested sidewalks jammed with students, townspeople, tourist groups, and legions of foreign schoolchildren can be hell to negotiate.

Newcomers are surprised to learn that the University of Oxford is not one unified campus, but a collection of many colleges and buildings, new as well as old, scattered across the city. All together there are 40 different colleges where undergraduates live and study. Most of the college grounds are open to tourists, including the magnificent dining halls and chapels, though the opening times (displayed at the entrance lodges) vary greatly. Some colleges are open only in

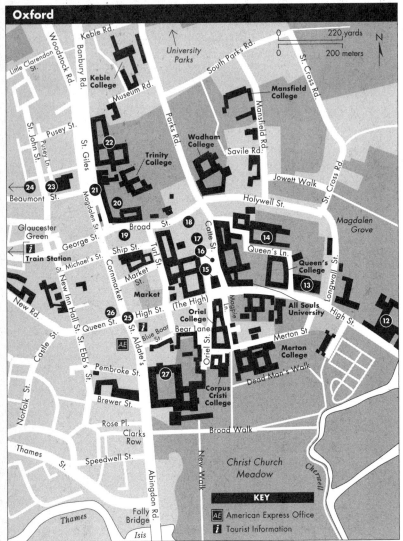

Oxford

Ashmolean, **23**

Balliol College, **20**

Bodleian Library, **17**

Carfax, **25**

Christ Church College, **27**

Magdalen College, **12**

Martyrs' Memorial, **21**

New College, **14**

Oxford Story Exhibition, **19**

Radcliffe Camera, **16**

St. Edmund Hall, **13**

St. John's College, **22**

St. Martin's Church, **26**

Sheldonian Theatre, **18**

University Church, **15**

Worcester College, **24**

the afternoons during university semesters, when the undergraduates are in residence.

Numbers in the margin correspond to points of interest on the Oxford map.

⓬ Let's begin with **Magdalen College,** one of the largest and most impressive of Oxford's colleges, founded in 1458. Its ancient vaulted cloisters, overhung with wisteria, enclose a serene quadrangle. Beyond this, a narrow stone passage leads through to a large, open park with grazing deer and a cluster of imposing classical buildings; farther on lies the sleepy Cherwell River. At the foot of Magdalen Bridge you can rent (for £5 an hour) a punt, a shallow-bottomed boat that is poled slowly up the river. Students punting on summer afternoons sprawl on cushions, dangling champagne bottles in the water to cool.

⓭ Farther along the High Street is **St. Edmund Hall,** one of the smallest and oldest colleges (founded c. 1220). Its tiny quadrangle, entered through a narrow archway off Queen's Lane, has an ancient
⓮ well in the center. Along Queen's Lane you come to **New College** (founded in 1379), with its extensive gardens overlooking part of the medieval city wall. This was the home of the celebrated Dr. Spooner, father of "spoonerisms." He is reputed to have told a wayward student, "You have hissed your mystery lectures and tasted a whole worm."

⓯ The 14th-century tower of the **University Church** (St. Mary the Virgin), a few yards farther on, provides a splendid panoramic view of the city's famous skyline—the pinnacles, towers, domes, and spires spanning every architectural style since the 11th century. The interior is crowded with 700 years' worth of funeral monuments, including one belonging to Amy Robsart, the wife of Dudley, Elizabeth I's favorite. *Tel. 0865/243806. Admission to tower: £1 adults, 50p children. Tower open daily 9:15–7, 9:15–4:30 in winter.*

Immediately opposite the church is one of the largest domes in Brit-
⓰ ain, that of the **Radcliffe Camera.** This building contains part of the
⓱ **Bodleian Library's** collection, which was begun in 1602 and has grown to more than 2 million volumes. The library is one of the six British copyright libraries, all of which receive a copy of every book published in Britain. The general public can visit only the former Divinity School, a superbly vaulted room with constantly changing exhibitions of manuscripts and rare books.

⓲ The university's ornate **Sheldonian Theatre** is where the impressive graduation ceremonies are held, conducted entirely in Latin. Built in 1663, it was the first building designed by Sir Christopher Wren. Semicircular like a Roman amphitheater, it has pillars, balconies, and an elaborately painted ceiling. Outside, beige stone pillars are topped by the massive stone heads of 18 Roman emperors, sculpted in the 1970s to replace the originals that had been rendered faceless by air pollution. *Tel. 0865/277299. Admission: 50p adults, 25p children. Open Mon.–Sat. 10–12:45 and 2–4:45; Dec.–Feb., closes 3:45.*

Broad Street, known to undergraduates as "the Broad," is a wide, straight thoroughfare lined with colleges and bow-fronted, half-timbered shops. Among them is **Blackwell's,** a family-run bookstore offering one of the largest selections of books in the world. It has been in business since 1879.

⓳ While you are in Broad Street, stop in at the **Oxford Story Exhibition,** situated in a converted warehouse. The imaginative presentation makes 800 years of Oxford life come alive with models, sounds, and smells. Visitors ride through the exhibition in small cars shaped like medieval students' desks. *Tel. 0865/728822. Admission: £4.50 adults, £3.25 children, £3.95 senior citizens, £14 family ticket. Open daily 10–4 with seasonal variations.*

Broad Street leads westward to **St. Giles,** reputed to be the widest
⑳ street in Europe. At the corner is prestigious **Balliol College** (1263). The wooden doors between Balliol's inner and outer quadrangles still bear scorch marks from 1555 and 1556, during the reign of Mary I ("Bloody Mary"), when Bishops Latimer and Ridley and Archbishop Cranmer were burned on huge pyres in Broad Street for their Protestant beliefs. A small cross on the roadway marks the actual
㉑ spot. The three men are also commemorated by the tall **Martyrs' Me-**
㉒ **morial** in St. Giles. A little farther up St. Giles, step inside **St. John's College** (1555), whose huge gardens are among the city's loveliest.

Time Out Stop in for lunch at the **Eagle and Child** pub, with its narrow interior leading to a conservatory and small terrace. This was the meeting place of J. R. R. Tolkien and his friends, the "Inklings." It gets crowded on weekends.

Beaumont Street, running west from St. Giles, is the site of the
㉓ **Ashmolean,** Britain's oldest public museum. Among its priceless collections (all university owned) are many Egyptian, Greek, and Roman artifacts uncovered during archaeological expeditions conducted by the university. Michelangelo drawings, antique silver, and a wealth of important paintings are also on display. *Beaumont St., tel. 0865/278000. Admission free. Open Tues.–Sat. 10–4, Sun. 2–4.*

㉔ Beaumont Street leads on to **Worcester College** (1714), noted for its wide lawns, colorful cottage garden, and large lake. It was built on the site of a former college, founded in 1283.

A side trip into the southern part of town should begin in **Cornmar-**
㉕ **ket,** Oxford's main shopping street. As you pass through **Carfax,**
㉖ where four roads meet, you will see the tower of **St. Martin's Church,** where Shakespeare once stood as godfather for William Davenant, who himself became a playwright. Continue south on St. Aldate's to
㉗ reach **Christ Church College** (1546), referred to by its members as "The House." Christ Church boasts Oxford's largest quadrangle, "Tom Quad," named after the huge bell (6¼ tons) that hangs in the gate tower. Its clock is stubbornly set to its own time, calculated by its distance from the Greenwich Meridian. The vaulted, 800-year-old chapel in one corner has been Oxford's cathedral since the time of Henry VIII. The college's medieval dining hall contains portraits of many famous alumni, including John Wesley, William Penn, and 14 of Britain's prime ministers. The **Canterbury Quadrangle** offers a fine picture gallery exhibiting works by Leonardo, Michelangelo, Rubens, Dürer, and other old masters. *Deanery Gardens, tel. 0865/ 276172. Admission: £1 adults, 50p children and senior citizens. Open Mon.–Sat. 10:30–1 and 2–4:30, Sun. 2–4:30 (later in summer).*

Beyond the quadrangle lies the extensive **Christ Church Meadow**, where the wide, tree-lined paths are as quiet and green as the depths of the countryside. On its journey through here, the Thames takes on a new name—the Isis. During the university terms it is always busy as college eights (teams of oarsmen) practice their rowing.

Time Out The **Perch** at Binsey and the **Trout** at Godstow are two excellent Thameside pubs on the northern edge of Oxford. Connoisseurs go to the thatched Perch at lunchtime to enjoy its wide lawn, unusual sandwiches, and cooing doves. In the evening they go to the creeper-covered Trout for a meal or a drink and to watch its peacocks strutting back and forth beside the weir.

Numbers in the margin correspond to points of interest on the Thames Valley map.

Leaving Oxford, follow A34/A44 north about 8 miles to **㉘** **Woodstock**—site of **Blenheim Palace,** Britain's largest stately home and the birthplace of Winston Churchill. During the summer you can catch an open-top bus from the Oxford train station.

A classical-style mansion built by Sir John Vanbrugh in the early 1700s, Blenheim Palace stands in 2,000 acres of parkland and gardens landscaped by Capability Brown. Queen Anne gave the palace to General John Churchill, first duke of Marlborough, and it is now the home of the 11th duke. Winston Churchill (his father was the younger brother of the then-duke), wrote that the unique beauty of Blenheim lay in its perfect adaptation of an English parkland to an Italian palace. In addition to paintings, tapestries, and furniture, it houses an exhibition devoted to Winston Churchill, including some of his own paintings. The palace has a restaurant and a cafeteria. *Woodstock, tel. 0993/811325. Palace—admission: £6.90 adults, £3.70 children, £4.90 senior citizens. Open mid-Mar.–Oct., daily 10:30–5:30. Park admission free. Open daily 9–4:45.*

㉙ Sir Winston Churchill is buried in the village of **Bladon,** about 2 miles south on A4095. His grave in the small, tree-lined churchyard is all the more impressive for its total simplicity.

Eight miles south of Oxford along A34 is the market town of **㉚** **Abingdon.** The town's origins can be traced to AD 675, when its abbey was founded. St. Ethelwold, the 10th-century abbot, diverted water from the Thames to create a millstream here. Today the Upper Reaches Hotel (*see* Dining and Lodging, *below*) stands on the tiny island that Ethelwold's millstream formed. *Abbey Buildings, Thames St., tel. 0235/847401. Admission: small charge. Open daily 2–6.*

Continuing 7 miles southeast from Abingdon you come to **㉛** **Dorchester-on-Thames,** with another ancient abbey. In addition to secluded cloisters and gardens, this one has a spacious church (1170), with interesting medieval windows. The east window was restored in 1966 by the American Friends of the Abbey in memory of Sir Winston Churchill. One of the abbey's corbels (projecting stone supports) shows the sculpted head of Mrs. Edith Stedman of Cambridge, Massachusetts, who founded the association to raise money for its restoration and sponsored the construction of the museum in the old guest house. *Tel. 0865/340056. Admission free. Open May–Sept., Tues.–Sat. 10:30–12:30 and 2–6, Sun. 2–6.*

Dorchester itself, founded by the Romans, is a charming village with timbered houses, thatched cottages, and ancient inns. Crossing the Thames at Day's Lock and turning left at Little Wittenham takes you on a pleasant walk past the intriguing remains of the village's Iron Age settlements.

Southwest of Oxford, stretching up into the foothills of the Berkshire Downs, is a wide, fertile plain known as the **Vale of the White Horse.** To reach it, follow A420, then B4508 to the village of

32 Uffington. Here, cut into the chalk hillside, is the huge figure of a white horse. No one really knows when it was done. Some historians suggest that it may have been carved to commemorate King Alfred's victory over the Danes in 871, while others think it dates back to the Iron Age, around 750 BC. **Dragon Hill,** below, is equally mysterious. An unlikely legend suggests that St. George slew his dragon there. Uffington was the home of Tom Brown, fictional hero of the Victorian classic *Tom Brown's Schooldays.* The novel's author, Thomas Hughes, was born in Uffington in 1822.

Oxford has been a major focus for Britain's writers and artists for centuries, so the area's estates and country villages are alive with **33** literary associations. About 7 miles north of Uffington is **Kelmscott Manor,** home of the Victorian artist, writer, and socialist William Morris (1834–96), who had a great effect on English design, and is buried in the local churchyard. The handsome, 400-year-old gabled stone house contains many examples of Morris's work. *Tel. 0367/ 252486. Admission: £5 adults, £2.50 children. Open Apr.–Sept., Wed. 11–1 and 2–5; Thur. and Fri. prebooked guided tours.*

Back toward Oxford—about 12 miles east, through twisting lanes— **34** lies **Stanton Harcourt Manor,** nestled among streams, small lakes, and woods. It was here, in 1718, that Alexander Pope translated Homer's *Iliad.* But the manor is worth a visit apart from this association; it has 12 acres of gardens and boasts an interesting medieval tower and a fine collection of silver, pictures, and antique furniture. *Stanton Harcourt, tel. 0865/881928. Admission: House and garden, £3 adults, £2 children and senior citizens; garden only, £1.50 adults, £1 children and senior citizens. Open Apr.–Sept., certain Sun. and Thurs. 2–6. Check locally.*

What to See and Do with Children

Oxford Story Exhibition in Oxford (*see* Tour 3, *above*).

Queen Mary's Doll's House at Windsor (*see* Tour 1, *above*).

If children have read (or been read) *The Wind in the Willows,* they'll like a boat trip on the Thames from Caversham to Mapledurham. They'll also enjoy exploring the extensive grounds of Mapledurham House (*see* Tour 2, *above*).

Punting on the River Cherwell, a favorite pastime at Oxford, will appeal to most children (*see* Tour 3, *above*).

At the **Shire Horse Center,** on A4 just 2½ miles west of Maidenhead, children can watch the world's largest draft horses being groomed and harnessed and can also see blacksmiths at work. *Littlewick Green, tel. 0628/824848. Admission: £3 adults, £2 children and senior citizens. Open Mar.–Oct., daily 11–5.*

Off the Beaten Track

The Thames area abounds with tiny villages hidden from the major highways. While you are driving along the main roads, it's worth turning off from time to time to see if that tiny hamlet, deep in the trees, is as attractive as its name sounds.

Basildon Park, a huge, 18th-century house near **Pangbourne,** 7 miles northwest of Reading on A329, boasts some exceptionally fine plasterwork, and the windows of its unusual **Octagon Room** provide magnificent views over the Thames Valley. The gardens are handsomely laid out, and the surrounding woods are ideal for walks. A tearoom serves teas and light lunches. *Tel. 0734/843040. Admission: House and grounds, £3.50 adults, £1.75 children, £9 family ticket; grounds only, £2.50 adults, £1.25 children, £6 family ticket. Open Apr.–Oct., Wed.–Sat. 2–6, Sun. noon–6.*

In the tiny village of **Nuffield,** half a mile south of A423 between Wallingford and Henley, a simple lettered slab beside the 13th-century flint church marks the **grave of William Morris**—not the writer who lived at Kelmscott, but the man who built an automobile factory at Cowley, on the edge of Oxford—who began his career repairing undergraduates' bicycles. His immense success—he was England's version of Henry Ford—led to his being granted the title first viscount of Nuffield. He later founded Oxford's Nuffield College, and he is still celebrated in the names of two classic autos: the MG, whose initials stand for "Morris Garages," and the Morris Minor.

Great Milton, just south of M40 about 7 miles east of Oxford, has attractive thatched cottages built of local stone, and a single street around a mile long with wide grass verges. This is another stop on the literary pilgrim's route, for the poet John Milton, author of *Paradise Lost* (1667), was married in the church here. The church also has an unusual collection of old musical instruments.

On the edge of **Witney,** 14 miles west of Oxford by A40, is the **Cogges Farm Museum,** a working farm which operates just as it did some 80 years ago. The animals are descendants of those which were bred then, the interior is furnished as it would have been in Edwardian days. *Tel. 0993/72602 in the summer, 0993/811456 in winter. Admission free. Open May–Oct., Tues.–Sun. 10:30–5:30.*

Shopping

Antiques are worth looking for in most towns—particularly Eton, Windsor, and Dorchester-on-Thames—but will be pricey.

Oxford Oxford now has several malls within easy walking distance of Carfax. Cornmarket and Queen streets are lined with small shops, while the Clarendon and Westgate centers which lead off them have branches of several nationally known stores. Along High Street there are traditional tailors like **Shepherd & Woodward** (No. 109, tel. 0865/249491) and specialists in Scottish woolens and tweeds. The **Oxford Gallery** (No. 23, tel. 0865/242731) carries prints in limited editions, as well as a wide stock of crafts. It holds monthly art exhibitions.

Specialty stores are gathered around Golden Cross, a cobbled courtyard with pretty window boxes, between Cornmarket and the excellent covered food market. They include the **Oxford Collection** (tel. 0865/247414), with stylish glassware and table mats; and the **Tea House** (tel. 0865/728838), specializing in teapots and tea. Broad Street is famous for bookstores, including **Blackwell's** (tel. 0865/792792). **Culpepers** (7 New Inn Hall St., tel. 0865/249754) sells natural toiletries and soaps.

Windsor and Eton Many Windsor stores are open on Sunday, particularly those selling antiques. Try Peascod Street, High Street, and King Edward Court, a new precinct.

The **Edinburgh Woollen Mill** (10 Castle Hill, tel. 0753/855151) has a large range of Scottish knitwear, tartans and tweeds, particularly for women. **Best of British** (44 King Edward Ct., tel. 0753/859929) has handmade items that are good for gifts.

Eton has a reputation for excellent, if pricey, antiques shops, most of them along the High Street. **Turk's Head Antiques** (No. 98, tel. 0753/863939) has jewelry, silver, and lace.

Sports and the Outdoors

Bicycling Bikes can be rented in Oxford at Dentons (294 Banbury Rd., tel. 0865/53859) and **Pennyfarthing** (15 George St., tel. 0865/249368).

Golf **Southfield** (tel. 0865/242158) is a parkland 18-hole course close to Oxford, where visiting players are welcome on weekdays. **Huntercombe,** Nuffield (tel. 0491/641207), is a wooded, heathland 18-hole course, and rather formal, with jacket and tie required in the clubhouse. At **Badgemore Park,** Henley-on-Thames (tel. 0491/573667), a parkland, 18-hole course, visitors are welcome on weekdays, and on weekends by arrangement.

Walking For long-distance walkers, the **Oxfordshire Way** runs 65 miles from Henley-on-Thames to Bourton-on-the-Water, on the eastern edge of the Cotswolds. A 13-mile ramble starts in Henley, runs north through the **Hambleden Valley,** takes in Stonor Park, and returns to Henley via the Assendons, Lower and Middle. For a less arduous walk, try the trails through the beechwoods at **Burnham Beeches** (*see* Tour 1, *above*).

All the Thames Valley walks include busy traffic areas. There are, of course, always the **riverside paths** from town to town, which are mostly quiet and scenic. The Countryside Commission (John Dower House, Crescent Pl., Cheltenham, Gloucestershire GL50 3RA, tel. 0424/521381) has been working for years on the Thames paths from the outskirts of London, through Windsor, to Oxford and Lechlade. Most of them are open to the public, and the Commission offers publications about them. (Contact: Countryside Commission Publications, Printworks La., Levenshulme, Manchester M19 3JP, tel. 061/224–627.) The Rambler's Association also publish an excellent book on the subject, *The Thames Walk*, by David Sharp (£3.65 from the Rambler's Association, 1/5 Wandsworth Rd., London SW8 2XX, tel. 071/582–6878), a guide to the whole length of the river, from Greenwich to Gloucestershire, with detailed maps. This is a good area for gentle walking, not too hilly, with handy eateries, especially pubs— many of them beside the river—and plenty of easily accessible, civilized lodgings. There is also good public transportation in the region, so you can easily start and stop anywhere along the route you fancy.

Spectator **Henley Royal Regatta,** one of the highlights of Britain's sporting and **Sports** social calendar, takes place over four days at the beginning of July each year. A vast community of large tents goes up, especially along both sides of the unique stretch of straight river here (1 mi, 550 yd), and every surrounding field becomes a parking lot. The most prestigious place for spectators is the stewards' enclosure, but admission is by invitation only and, however hot, men must wear jackets and ties—and ladies in trousers are refused entry. Fortunately, there is plenty of space on the public towpath to see the early stages of the races.

Oxford's Eights Week at the end of May is much more informal. From mid-afternoon to early evening, Wednesday to Saturday, men and women from the university's colleges compete to be "Head of the River." Because the river is too narrow and twisting for eights to race side-by-side, they set off, 13 at a time, one behind another. Each boat tries to catch and bump the one in front. Spectators can watch all the way.

Oxford University Cricket Club competes against leading county teams and also has a game each summer against the major foreign team visiting Britain. The massive trees surrounding the club's grounds in the University Parks make it one of the loveliest in England.

Dining and Lodging

Dining Simple pub food, as well as classic French cuisine, can be enjoyed in waterside settings at many restaurants beside the Thames. Even in towns away from the river, well-heeled commuters support top-flight establishments. At weekends it is advisable to make reservations.

Category	Cost*
$$$$	over £50
$$$	£40–£50
$$	£20–£40
$	under £20

per person, including first course, main course, dessert, and VAT; excluding drinks

Lodging Many hotels in the area started out centuries ago as coaching inns. Others have been converted more recently from country mansions. Both types usually have plenty of character, with antiques and attractive decor—and often, well-kept gardens.

Category	Cost*
$$$$	over £150
$$$	£90–£150
$$	£50–£90
$	under £50

All prices are for two people sharing a double room, including service, breakfast, and VAT.

Abingdon
Lodging

The Upper Reaches. This Forte hotel has a spectacular setting overlooking the Thames. Surrounded by a millstream, it was once a grain mill and has been cleverly converted. *Thames St., OX14 3TA, tel. 0235/522311, fax 0235/555182. 26 rooms with bath, 6 in annex. Facilities: restaurant, terrace garden, river mooring. AE, DC, MC, V. $$$*

Burnham
Lodging

Burnham Beeches Moat House. In 1742, Thomas Gray wrote the famous elegy inspired by Stoke Poges churchyard while staying in this secluded country house with large grounds. Its room capacity has been greatly increased by a modern extension. *Grove Rd., SL1 8DP, tel. 0628/603333, fax 0628/603994. 75 rooms with bath. Facilities: restaurant, indoor pool, sauna, games room, in-house movies, tennis, croquet lawn. AE, DC, MC, V. $$$*

Cumnor
Dining
★

The Bear and Ragged Staff. This excellent spot, close to Oxford (4½ miles southwest via A420), is a 17th-century inn—the name comes from the medieval insignia of the Warwick family—and has long been a popular haunt of Oxford town and gown. The food is traditional British, with such fare as roast duck and venison with a wine sauce. *19 Appleton Rd., tel. 0865/862329. Reservations advised. Jacket and tie required. AE, DC, MC, V. $$*

Dorchester-on-Thames
Lodging

George Hotel. Overlooking Dorchester Abbey, this 500-year-old hotel was built as a coaching inn—there's still an old coach parked outside—and it retains whitewashed walls, exposed beams, and log fires. Each room has an individual style and two have four-poster beds. *23 High St., OX10 7HH, tel. 0865/340404, fax 0865/341620. 17 rooms with bath. Facilities: restaurant, garden. AE, DC, MC, V. $$$*

Eton
Dining

The Cockpit. Cockfighting once took place in the courtyard of this 500-year-old inn with oak beams. Specialties include guinea fowl, and bacon casserole in mushroom sauce. *47–49 High St., tel. 0753/860944. Reservations advised. Jacket and tie required. AE, DC, MC, V. Closed Mon. $$$*

Great Milton
Dining and Lodging
★

Le Manoir aux Quat' Saisons. Although this 15th/16th-century manor house is also a hotel—with sumptuously luxurious rooms—it has held its position as one of Britain's leading restaurants for years. The owner/chef, Raymond Blanc, exercises his award-winning French culinary skills in a captivating setting. Aux Quat' Saisons is both very popular and *very* expensive (well above our normal range), though the set menus can make it almost reasonable. *Church Rd., OX44 7PD, tel. 0844/278881 or 800/845–4274, fax 0844/278847. 19 rooms with bath. Facilities: heated pool, tennis, gardens. Reservations essential. Jacket and tie required. AE, DC, MC, V. Restaurant closed 4 weeks at Christmas. $$$$*

Henley
Dining

Little Angel Inn. Housed in a quaint building over 500 years old, this is an associate of the French Routier chain of restaurants, which are known for their good value and no-nonsense food. Specialties include fish and duck. Less expensive meals are served in the bar, which is open even when the restaurant is closed. *Remenham (¼ mi from Henley on A423), tel. 0491/574165. Reservations advised. Dress: casual. AE, DC, MC, V. Closed Sun. eve., Mon. $$$*

Stonor Arms. Four miles north of Henley lies this 18th-century restaurant, once a pub. There is a simple brasserie in an old conservatory and two dining rooms—one formal, the other bright and summery. The food is as good to eat as it is to look at—local game, poached turbot, fried mussels and scallops—and there's a comprehensive wine list. *Stonor, tel. 0491/638345, fax 0491/638863. Reservations advised. Dress: casual. AE, MC, V. Dinner only Mon.–Sat. $$$*

Dining and Lodging

The Red Lion. This historic hotel overlooks the river and the town bridge. During its 400-year history, guests have included King Charles I and Dr. Samuel Johnson, the 18th-century critic, poet, and lexicographer. The hotel has recently been refurbished. *Hart St., RG9 2AR, tel. 0491/572161, fax 0491/410039. 26 rooms, 21 with bath. Facilities: restaurant, four-poster beds, garage. AE, MC, V. $$–$$$*

Flohr's. Just a short walk from the town center, this small, elegant Georgian hotel has an expensive *cordon bleu* restaurant supervised by the owner, Gerd Flohr. *15 Northfield End, RG9 2JG, tel. 0491/573412, fax 0491/579721. 9 rooms, 3 with bath. AE, DC, MC, V. $$*

Hurley
Lodging

Ye Olde Bell. This is reputed to be the oldest inn in England, having been built in 1135 as a guest house for the Benedictine monastery nearby. Some rooms are attractively modern, others are elegantly furnished in traditional style; the few overlooking the pretty courtyard gardens have been refurbished recently. *High St., SL6 5LX,* *tel. 0628/825881, fax 0628/825939. 36 rooms with bath. Facilities: restaurant, four-poster beds, garden, garage. AE, DC, MC, V. $$$*

Oxford **Restaurant Elizabeth.** These small, elegant dining rooms in a 16th-
Dining century bishop's palace have wonderful views overlooking Christ Church College. Salmon rolls, roast lamb, duck à l'orange, and crème brûlée are among the Spanish chef's specialties. *84 St. Aldate's, tel. 0865/242230. Reservations advised. Dress: casual. AE, DC, MC, V. Closed Mon. $$$*

★ **Gee's.** This brasserie in a conservatory, formerly a florist's shop, is located just north of the town center. The food is Italian-based, with a large menu, and is very popular with both town and gown. *61 Banbury Rd., tel. 0865/53540. Reservations essential. Dress: casual. AE, MC, V. $$–$$$*

Cherwell Boathouse. About a mile north of town, this is an ideal spot for a meal in a riverside setting. The menus change weekly, but may include mussels in white wine and cream, breast of pigeon, or hare with a vinegar and pepper sauce. It's a very friendly spot so be prepared to linger. There are good set menus available. *Bardwell Rd. (off Banbury Rd.), tel. 0865/52746. Reservations advised. Dress: casual. AE, MC, V. Closed Mon. and Tues. lunch, and Sun. dinner. $$*

Fifteen North Parade. Just outside the city center, this intimate restaurant is decorated with attractive cane furniture and plants. Try such specialties as pot-roast pheasant, medallions of lamb with garlic, Mediterranean fish soup, and venison with Madeira. There are good value fixed-price menus as well. *15 North Parade Ave., tel. 0865/513773. Reservations advised. Dress: casual. MC, V. Closed Sun. dinner and 2 weeks Aug. $$*

Browns. So popular is this restaurant with both undergraduates and local people that you may have to wait for a table. The wide choice of informal dishes includes steak, mushroom and Guinness pie, and hot chicken salad. Potted palms and mirrors give the otherwise plain rooms a cheery atmosphere. *5–11 Woodstock Rd., tel. 0865/511995. No reservations. Dress: casual. MC, V. $*

Lodging **The Randolph.** Oxford's only large, central hotel is just across from the Ashmolean; in neo-Gothic style, and elegantly traditional, its grand Victorian interior has recently been extensively restored. There is a spaciously handsome restaurant, **Spires.** *Beaumont St., OX1 2LN, tel. 0865/247481, fax 0865/791678. 109 rooms with bath. Facilities: coffee shop, garage. AE, DC, MC, V. $$$$*

★ **The Old Parsonage.** This is a discovery. It's rare to find an attractive country-house hotel, with stone gables and mullioned windows, in the middle of a city. The Old Parsonage was established in 1660, but completely restored and refurbished in 1991. Open fires, fascinating pictures, comfortable rooms, and immaculate service make this a hotel to remember—and return to. The **Parsonage Bar** serves excellent simple food. *1 Banbury Rd., OX2 6NN, tel. 0865/310210, fax 0865/311262. 30 rooms with bath. Facilities: restaurant, garden. AE, DC, MC, V. $$$*

The Eastgate Hotel. Retaining the style of a traditional inn, this hotel on High Street is flanked by ancient university buildings and colleges. Its bar is a favorite of undergraduates, so this is a good place to get an insight into university life. There is no smoking in public rooms. *High St., OX1 4BE, tel. 0865/248244, fax 0865/791681. 42 rooms with bath. Facilities: carvery restaurant, four-poster beds. AE, DC, MC, V. $$$*

Cotswold House. This small, modern guest house, about 2 miles north, on the Banbury Road (A4260), is pleasantly furnished with modern pieces. The bedrooms are comfortable and of a good size, all with TV and fridges. The owners are ever ready to help with sight-seeing problems. *363 Banbury Rd., tel. 0865/310558. 7 rooms with shower. No credit cards. $$*

Shinfield
Dining
★

L'Ortolan. This elegant country restaurant lies just over 4 miles south of Reading, on A327. It's an attractive spot, with an airy, light feel to the dining room. The nouvelle dishes are the imaginative work of the owner/chef, John Burton-Race, and are every bit as interesting as the setting. Try the *mousseline loup de mer et de homard* (seafood and lobster mousse). The fixed-price menus allow for a serious tasting session. There are two menus, expensive and very expensive, so choose carefully. *The Old Vicarage, Church La., tel. 0734/883783. Reservations required. Jacket and tie required. AE, DC, MC, V. Closed Sun. dinner, Mon. $$$$*

Sonning-on-Thames
Lodging

The Great House. A former 16th-century inn, this hotel commands superb views over the river and has extensive gardens—the roses are lovely—leading to a half-mile of moorings. There is a choice of period or modern rooms, some in cottage annexes. *Thames St., RG4 0UT, tel. 0734/692277, fax 0734/441296. 34 rooms with bath. Facilities: restaurant, gardens, moorings. AE, DC, MC, V. $$-$$$*

Taplow
Dining and Lodging
★

Cliveden. Cliveden has to be one of the grandest hotels in Britain—and one of the most expensive. This is sophisticated luxury at its very best. There are 376 acres of magnificently tended gardens and parkland with wonderful river views. The interior is opulent in the extreme: the Orkney Tapestries in the Great Hall were commissioned by the duke of Marlborough; there are suits of armor; a library; a richly panelled staircase; endless paintings, mostly fine historic portraits; and room after room with beautifully molded plaster ceilings. The ultracomfortable bedrooms are named after the famous people who once stayed here—including Lady Astor herself (which costs £495 a night); a basic double costs £215 a night. There is every kind of activity available; you can venture onto the Thames on an Edwardian boat or tour the area in the hotel's Daimler. There are two main restaurants: The Terrace, with Rococo decorations, fine garden views, Spode china, and French cuisine, and Waldo's, panelled and more intimate. Or you can have smorgasbord or salads in the Pavilion. *Taplow, near Maidenhead SL6 0JF, tel. 0628/668561, fax 0628/661837. 31 rooms with bath. Facilities: garden and park, 3 restaurants, health center, indoor and outdoor pools, tennis, squash, riding, fishing, 3 boats. AE, DC, MC, V. $$$$*

Weston-on-the-Green
Lodging

Weston Manor Hotel. Eight miles northeast of Oxford, this hotel is one for the history buffs. Once a monastery, it's set in 13 acres of grounds. The oak-paneled restaurant has a minstrels' gallery, and one of the bedrooms claims a ghost. It is part of the Hidden Hotel chain. *OX6 8QL, tel. 0869/50621, fax 0869/50901. 37 rooms, 36 with bath. Facilities: outdoor heated pool, garden, squash, fishing, croquet. AE, DC, MC, V. $$$*

Windsor
Dining and Lodging

Oakley Court. This ornate hotel stands in large grounds beside the river, 3 miles west of Windsor. It was originally a Victorian mansion, but half the rooms are in a modern annex. All the bedrooms have been redone. There is an excellent restaurant, the **Oak Leaf Room,** which serves essentially English fare, such as fillet of beef with Stilton mousse, and has a good wine list. *Windsor Rd., Water Oakley, SL4 5UR, tel. 0628/74141, fax 0628/37011. 91 rooms with bath. Restaurant: Reservations required; jacket and tie required. Facilities: gardens, croquet, fishing, putting green, pocket billiards, helipad. AE, DC, MC, V. $$$$*

Sir Christopher Wren's House Hotel. This was a private mansion built by the famous architect in 1676, but modern additions have converted it into a hotel. Restoration of antique features complements the fine design, and its restaurant overlooks the river. It is renowned, too, for its cream teas on the terrace. *Thames St., SL4 1PX, tel. 0753/861354, fax 0753/860172. 41 rooms with bath. Facilities: four-poster beds, air-conditioning, terrace garden. AE, DC, MC, V. $$$*

Woodstock
Dining and
Lodging
★

The Feathers. The hotel here is small but very comfortable, and expertly staffed. It's a 17th-century building which has been thoughtfully restored. In the restaurant's luxurious, wood-paneled rooms, you can enjoy a set-price, five-course gourmet menu. Among the specialties are tartlet of quails' eggs and leeks, a three-way salmon dish (marinated, smoked, and tartare), roast duck with orange and cointreau sauce, and a selection of rich desserts. *Market St., OX7 1SX, tel. 0993/812291, fax 0993/8131158. 17 rooms with bath. Restaurant: Reservations required; jacket and tie required. AE, DC, MC, V. $$$*

The Arts

Festivals and
Music

Henley Festival takes place during the week following the regatta each year. All kinds of open-air concerts and events are staged at this popular summer occasion. *Henley Festival, Festival Yard, 42 Bell St., Henley, tel. 0491/410414.*

Oxford Pro Musica, the city orchestra, performs concerts throughout the year in the Oxford area and abroad. In July and August, the orchestra gives concerts twice a week, in a "Beautiful Music in Beautiful Places" series, in some of the city's most historic buildings, and in Christ Church Meadow. *The Old Rectory, Paradise Sq., OX1 1TW, tel. 0865/252365.*

Music at Oxford is a highly acclaimed series of weekend chamber concerts performed from late June to mid-September in such illustrious surroundings as Christ Church Cathedral and Sir Christopher Wren's Sheldonian Theatre, or outdoors on the grounds of stately homes in the area. The music is mainly early Baroque and is performed by chamber ensembles and choirs from all over the world, as well as from both Oxford and Cambridge. Information and tickets are available from *Music at Oxford, 6A Cumnor Hill, Oxford OX2 9HA, tel. 0865/864056.*

The **Windsor Festival** is usually held in early fall, September or October, with occasional events taking place in the castle itself.

Theaters

Windsor's **Theatre Royal** (Thames St., tel. 0753/853888), where productions have been staged for nearly 200 years, is one of Britain's leading provincial theaters. It puts on a range of plays and musicals throughout the year (often with starring players), including pantomime for six weeks after Christmas.

The Apollo (George St., tel. 0865/244544) is Oxford's main theater. It stages a varied program of plays, opera, ballet, pantomime, and concerts, and is the recognized second home of the Welsh National Opera and the Glyndebourne Touring Opera.

The Oxford Playhouse (Beaumont St., tel. 0865/247134) is an altogether more serious theater, presenting classical and modern drama productions appropriate for a university city.

During university terms, many undergraduate productions are held in the colleges or local halls. In the summer, there are usually some outdoor performances in ancient quadrangles or college gardens. Look for announcement posters.

9 The Heart of England

Stratford-upon-Avon, the Cotswolds, the Forest of Dean, Bath, Bristol, Birmingham

The Heart of England is a name we have borrowed from the tourist powers-that-be—and by which is meant the heart of *tourist* England, so immensely popular are its attractions. Here it means the three counties of west-central England, Warwickshire (pronounced "Worrick"), Gloucestershire (pronounced "Gloster"), and Avon. Together they make up a sweep of land stretching from Shakespeare country in the north down through Bath to the Bristol Channel in the south.

The Forest of Arden, immortalized in Shakespeare's *As You Like It*, once overspread the county of Warwickshire; only a few small pockets of actual forest are left now, but the whole area is still shaded by ancient trees, scattered through rich farmlands. Timber was always readily available here for building, and the Tudor houses of Stratford-upon-Avon and its surrounding villages are typically half-timbered, with wattle-and-daub sections (plaster over woven sticks) between the beams. The grandest houses here were built of brick, mellowed now to a rich, velvety red.

Stratford is the key town for the visitor. It is a small market town, like dozens of others across the land, but set apart from them by being the birthplace of Shakespeare. It is that rare thing, a living shrine—living because it contains, apart from the houses connected with Shakespeare, a theater which performs his works, and, for the most part, performs them to the highest international standard. The town can be vulgar—it is full to overflowing with souvenir shops—but it also has a lot of quiet charm. To wander along the riverbank from the theater to the parish church on a spring day can be a gently fulfilling experience. Only a few miles away, Warwick, with its magnificent castle and picturesque houses, provides yet another "Heart of England" thrill, while Birmingham continues to rise above its reputation as one of the ugliest cities in Britain. Its active artistic life is drawing people who have now begun to appreciate its civic architecture, some of the most fascinating to be found anywhere.

Gloucestershire is dominated by the Cotswolds, high, treeless hills crisscrossed by dry-stone (unmortared) walls to control the sheep which have grazed here for centuries. This is another area of England to which sheep brought great prosperity in the Middle Ages, and the legacy of those times can be seen in the substantial buildings of the idyllic little towns and villages nestling in the valleys. Local stone was easy to quarry, and the houses built from it have now seasoned to a glorious golden-gray. The churches, manor houses, and cottages still stand as solidly as the day they were built, up to five centuries ago. This is an area for walking, for getting to know the countryside intimately. Here you will see hovering kestrels; wild flowers from February to late fall; newborn lambs and "boxing" hares in March, and tiny, wild blueberries in August. All the year round the remnants of ancient woods and the long rolling vistas over the hills will delight you.

To the south of this region is the city of Bath—like Stratford, one of the tourist meccas of Britain. Although it was originally founded by the Romans when they discovered here the only true hot springs in England, the town's popularity during the 17th and 18th centuries ensured its immortality. Bath's fashionable period luckily coincided with one of Britain's most elegant architectural eras, producing quite a remarkable urban phenomenon—money available to create virtually a whole town of stylish buildings. Today's city fathers have been wise enough to make sure that Bath is kept spruce and welcoming; its present prosperity keeps the streets overflowing with flowers in the summer and is channeled into cleaning and painting the city center, making it a joy to explore.

Essential Information

Important Addresses and Numbers

Tourist Information
The West Country Tourist Board, 60 St. David's Hill, Exeter, Devon EX4 4SY, tel. 0392/76351, fax 0932/420891. Information on Bath/Avon.
Local tourist information centers are normally open Mon.–Sat. 9:30–5:30, but times vary according to season. Centers include:
Bath: 27 The Colonnades, 11–13 Bath St., tel. 0225/462831.
Birmingham: Convention and Visitor Bureau, 2 City Arcade, tel. 021/643–2514.
Bristol: 14 Narrow Quay, tel. 0272/260767.
Cheltenham: 77 Promenade, tel. 0242/522878.
Gloucester: St. Michael's Tower, The Cross, tel. 0452/421188.
Stow-on-the-Wold: Hollis House, The Square, tel. 0451/831082.
Stratford-upon-Avon: Bridgefoot, tel. 0789/293127.

Travel Agencies
American Express, 5 Bridge St., Bath, tel. 0225/444747.
Thomas Cook, 20 New Bond St., Bath, tel. 0225/463191; 32 Upper Precinct, Coventry, tel. 0203/229233; and 24 Eastgate St., Gloucester, tel. 0452/529511.

Car-Rental Agencies
Bath: Avis, Unit 4B, Bath Riverside Business Park, Riverside Rd., tel. 0225/446680.
Birmingham: Avis, 7–9 Park St., tel. 021/632–4361; **EuroDollar Rent-a-Car,** Snow Hill Service Station, St. Chads, tel. 021/200–3010.
Cheltenham: Budget Rent-a-Car, Haines & Strange Ltd., 53 Albion St., tel. 0242/235222; **Hertz,** Pike House Service Station, Tewkesbury Rd., tel. 0242/242547.
Gloucester: Avis, Cotswold Service Station, 122 London Rd., tel. 0452/380356.
Stratford-upon-Avon: Hertz, Rail Station, tel. 0789/298827.

Getting Around

By Car
M4 is the principal route west from London to Gloucestershire and Avon. From exit 18, take A46 south to Bath. From exit 20, take M5 north to Gloucester (25 mi), Cheltenham, and Tewkesbury; and from exit 15 take A361 to A419 north to the Cotswolds. From London take M40 for Stratford-upon-Avon (97 mi) and for Birmingham (122 mi) take M1, then M6.

By Train
British Rail serves the western part of the region from London's Paddington Station (tel. 071/262–6767). Travel time to Bath: 1 hour and 55 minutes (though there are trains which take just over an hour); to Birmingham: 1 hour 45 minutes from London's Euston Station (tel. 071/387–7070); and 2 hours 25 minutes to Stratford-upon-Avon, with changes at Oxford and Leamington Spa (the Stratford station is closed Sunday in winter). A seven-day "Heart of England Rover" ticket is valid for unlimited travel within the region.

By Bus
National Express (tel. 071/730–0202) serves the region from London's Victoria Coach Station.
Flights Coach Travel Ltd. of Birmingham (tel. 021/554–5232) operates "Flightlink" services from London's Heathrow and Gatwick airports to Coventry and Warwick.

Cheltenham & Gloucester Omnibus Co. Ltd. (tel. 0242/511655) serves Gloucestershire.
Midland Red (South) Ltd. (tel. 0789/204181) serves the Stratford-upon-Avon, Birmingham, and Coventry areas.

Guided Tours

The Heart of England Tourist Board (tel. 0905/763436) and the **West Country Tourist Board** (tel. 0392/76351) can arrange a variety of tours.
Historic Gloucester Guided Walks (tel. 0452/501666) organizes tours of the city and docks by appointment.
Guide Friday (tel. 0789/294466 Stratford and 0225/444102 Bath) does guided tours of Stratford and Bath in open-top single- and double-decker buses (Stratford: £7 adults, £2 children, £4 senior citizens; Bath: £5.50 adults, £2 children, £4 senior citizens).

Exploring the Heart of England

The four tours in this chapter have been organized around the region's three major points of interest for the visitor—Stratford-upon-Avon, the Cotswold Hills, and Bath.

Stratford is well suited as an exploring base for a limited area containing tiny villages, several with legends connected with Shakespeare (dubious for the most part), some beautiful architecture dating from his time, and one magnificent castle, Warwick. We finish up this tour with a visit to Birmingham, now one of the best places in England for the performing arts and rapidly redeeming itself from its reputation as a badly built city.

The Cotswolds are peppered with pretty villages, built of the golden Cotswold stone. Our circular swing around this area, using Bourton-on-the-Water as a base, goes to: Chipping Campden; the oversold village of Broadway, which has many rivals for beauty hereabouts; Winchcombe and Sudeley Castle; Northleach; Burford; and back to Bourton. This is definitely a region where it pays to wander off the beaten track to take a look at that village hidden in the trees.

To the west of this tour lie Gloucester and Cheltenham, almost twin towns, and beyond them, between the Severn River and the border of Wales, the mysterious Forest of Dean. The road from Gloucester to Bath takes you through Roman territory at Cirencester, and by the evocative castle at Berkeley. Bath, which can also be easily visited on a day out from London, makes an elegant center from which to travel westward to Bristol, the Severn Estuary, and prehistoric sites, this time in the Chew Valley.

Highlights for First-time Visitors

Bath: Tour 4
Berkeley Castle: Tour 3
Birmingham Symphony Hall: Tour 1
Chedworth Roman Villa: Tour 2
Corinium Museum, Cirencester: Off the Beaten Track
Forest of Dean: Tour 3
Gloucester Cathedral: Tour 3

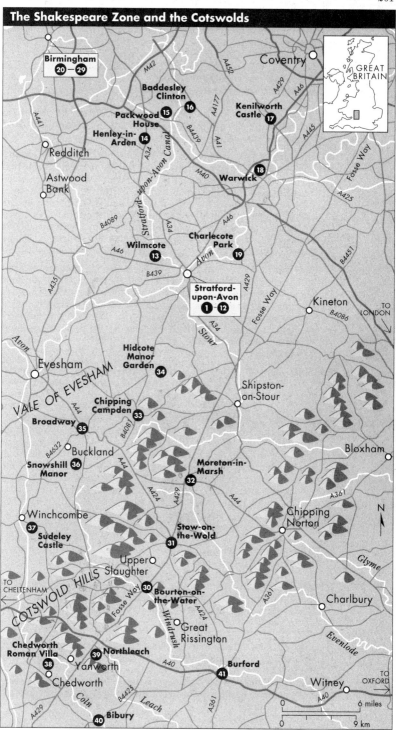

The Shakespeare Zone and the Cotswolds

GREAT BRITAIN

Coventry

Birmingham
20 — 29

Baddesley Clinton

Packwood House 15 16

Henley-in-Arden 14

Kenilworth Castle 17

Redditch

Astwood Bank

Warwick 18

Wilmcote 13

Charlecote Park 19

Kineton

TO LONDON

Stratford-upon-Avon 1 12

Evesham

Hidcote Manor Garden 34

VALE OF EVESHAM

Shipston-on-Stour

Chipping Campden 33

Bloxham

Broadway 35

Buckland

Moreton-in-Marsh 32

Snowshill Manor 36

Chipping Norton

Winchcombe

Stow-on-the-Wold 31

37

Sudeley Castle

Upper Slaughter

N

Charlbury

TO CHELTENHAM

Bourton-on-the-Water 30

COTSWOLD HILLS

Great Rissington

Chedworth Roman Villa 38

Northleach 39

Yanworth

Burford 41

Chedworth

Witney

TO OXFORD

Bibury 40

0   6 miles
0   9 km

Hidcote Manor Garden: Tour 2
Stratford-upon-Avon Shakespeare Trust Properties: Tour 1
Sudeley Castle: Tour 2
Warwick Castle: Tour 1

Tour 1: Stratford-upon-Avon and the Shakespeare Zone

Numbers in the margin correspond to points of interest on the Shakespeare Zone and the Cotswolds and the Stratford-upon-Avon maps.

 Its connections with Shakespeare have made **Stratford-upon-Avon** a mecca for tourists from all over the world. But it is conceivable that the town would have attracted a fair number of tourists even without its famous son. By Elizabethan times (16th century), this was a prosperous market town with thriving guilds and industries. Its characteristic, half-timbered houses from this era have been preserved over the centuries, and they are set off by the charm of later architecture, such as the elegant Georgian storefronts on Bridge Street, with their 18th-century porticoes and arched doorways.

Yet Stratford is far from being a museum piece; it has adapted itself well to the rising tide of visitors. Though the town is full of souvenir shops—every back lane seems to have been converted into a shopping mall, with boutiques selling everything from sweaters to china models of Anne Hathaway's Cottage—Stratford isn't particularly strident in its search for the quick buck. If you prefer to seek out traces of its history in peace, try to visit the place out of season, or at a time of day before the bus tours arrive, or after they leave.

 Start your tour at the **Shakespeare Centre** on Henley Street, home of the Shakespeare Birthplace Trust. This modern building was erected in 1964 as a 400th-anniversary tribute to the playwright; it contains a small BBC Television **Shakespeare Costume Exhibition.** Next door, and reached from the centre, is **Shakespeare's Birthplace,** a half-timbered house typical of its time, although much altered and restored since Shakespeare lived here. Half the house has been furnished to reflect Elizabethan domestic life, the other half contains an exhibition illustrating Shakespeare's professional life and work. The Birthplace is one of five Shakespeare Trust properties in the area. *Henley St., tel. 0789/204016. Admission: Shakespeare's Birthplace only, £2.60 adults, £1.20 children; Town Heritage Trail (3 town properties), £5 adults, £2.30 children, £4.50 senior citizens; joint ticket for all 5 Shakespeare Trust properties, £7.50 adults, £3.50 children, £7 senior citizens. Open Mar.–Oct., Mon.–Sat. 9–5:30, Sun. 10–5:30; Nov.–Feb., Mon.–Sat. 9:30–4, Sun. 10:30–4; Jan. 11:30–4:30; closed Good Friday and Dec. 24–26.*

Time Out   **Mistress Quickly** (named after Falstaff's long-suffering hostess in Shakespeare's *Henry IV Parts 1* and *2*) at 59–60 Henley Street serves meals and snacks throughout the day. Look for its jigsaw tree sculpture as you climb the stairs.

If you go down Henley Street, then Bridge Street toward the river, you will find the **tourist office** at the bottom, at Bridgefoot. From here return to the High Street, turn left and walk along it to **Harvard House,** next to the Garrick Inn, a half-timbered, 16th-century home of Catherine Rogers, mother of the John Harvard who founded Harvard University in 1636. There is little to see here, as

Anne
Hathaway's
Cottage, **12**

Guildhall/
Grammar
School, **5**

Hall's Croft, **6**

Harvard
House, **3**

Holy Trinity
Church, **7**

Nash's House
and New Place, **4**

Royal
Shakespeare
Theatre, **9**

Shakespeare
Centre and
Birthplace, **2**

Swan
Theatre, **10**

The Other
Place, **8**

World of
Shakespeare, **11**

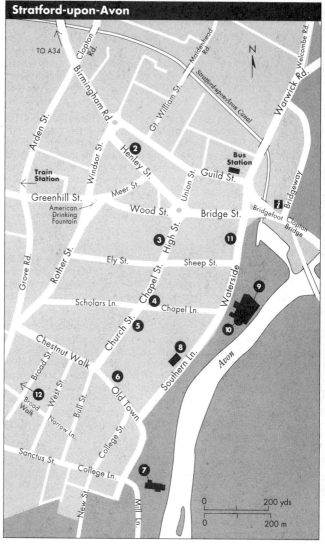

Stratford-upon-Avon

the house is virtually unfurnished. *Open May–Sept. Contact the
Shakespeare Centre for hours.*

❹ Across the street is **Nash's House,** home of the Thomas Nash who
married Shakespeare's granddaughter, Elizabeth Hall. The heavily
restored house has been furnished in 17th-century style, and it also
contains a local museum. In the gardens, (where there's an intricately laid out Elizabethan knot garden), are the foundations of **New
Place,** the house in which Shakespeare died in 1616. Built in 1483 for
a Lord Mayor of London, it was Stratford's grandest piece of real
estate when Shakespeare bought it in 1597 for £60, but sadly, it was
torn down in 1759. *Chapel St., tel. 0789/293455. Admission: £1.80
adults, 80p children. Open Mar.–Oct., Mon.–Sat. 9:30–5, Sun.*

10:30–5; Nov.–Feb., Mon.–Sat. 10–4, Sun. 1:30–4; closed Dec. 24–26 and Good Friday; Jan. 1 open 1:30–4:30.

Continue into Church Street. On your left are poorhouses built by the Guild of the Holy Cross in the early 15th century. On the second floor of the adjoining **Guildhall** is the **Grammar School,** which Shakespeare probably attended as a boy and which is still used as a school. *Tel. 0789/293351. Open Easter and summer school vacations, daily 10–6.*

Turn left at the end of Church Street into Old Town (a street) and you will see **Hall's Croft,** one of the finest surviving Tudor town houses, with a walled garden behind. This was the home of Shakespeare's elder daughter Susanna and her husband, Dr. John Hall, whose dispensary is on view along with the other rooms, all containing heavy oak Jacobean (early-17th-century) furniture. *Tel. 0789/292107. Admission: £1.80 adults, 80p children. Open Mar.–Oct., Mon.–Sat. 9:30–5, Sun. 10:30–5; Nov.–Feb., Mon.–Sat. 10–4, Sun. 1:30–4; closed Dec. 24–26 and Good Friday; Jan. 1 open 1:30–4:30.*

At the end of Old Town is the 13th-century **Holy Trinity Church,** in which are buried William Shakespeare, his wife, Anne, his daughter Susanna, his son-in-law John Hall, and his granddaughter's husband, Thomas Nash. The bust of Shakespeare is thought to be an authentic likeness, executed a few years after his death. *Small fee for chancel.*

From the church, walk north along Southern Lane or through the gardens along the River Avon, and you'll come to **The Other Place,** a new auditorium for experimental production. Nearby is the **Royal Shakespeare Theatre,** where the Royal Shakespeare Company (RSC) stages plays from late March to late January (*see* The Arts, *below*). At the rear is the **Swan Theatre,** created in the only part of the Victorian theater to survive a fire in the 1930s. It was built with the financial backing of an Anglophile American philanthropist, Frederick Koch. The theater follows the lines of Shakespeare's original Globe and is one of the most exciting acting spaces in Britain. Beside the Swan is an art gallery, where you can see the RSC's exhibition of costumes and props, and book tours of the theater, preferably well in advance. *Southern La., tel. 0789/296655, ext. 421. Tours weekdays except Thurs. and Sat. (matinee days) at 1:30, 5:30; 4 tours Sun. Cost (tours): £3.50 adults, £2.50 students and senior citizens, £10 family ticket (Sun. only). Exhibition open Mon.–Sat. 9:15–evening intermission and Sun. afternoon (hours vary). Admission: £1.50 adults, £1 students and senior citizens.*

Time Out | The **Black Swan,** locally called the Dirty Duck, has a little veranda overlooking the theaters and the river. It serves draft beer and bar meals on Southern Lane.

Across the small park in front of the theater is the Heritage Theatre's **World of Shakespeare,** a glorified waxworks show, using recorded dialogue and dramatic lighting to re-create the "royal progress" of Queen Elizabeth I from London to Kenilworth, where she was lavishly entertained by her favorite, the earl of Leicester (pronounced "Lester"), in 1575. Some will consider it a mite pricey for just under half an hour's show. *13 Waterside, tel. 0789/269190. Admission: £3.50 adults, £2.50 children, senior citizens, and students; £8 family ticket. Open daily 9:30–5 (9 in summer); performances every half-hour. Closed Dec. 25.*

⑫ The most picturesque of the Shakespeare Trust properties is **Anne Hathaway's Cottage,** family home of the woman Shakespeare married in 1582, in what was evidently a shotgun wedding. The Hathaway "cottage," actually a beautiful and substantial farmhouse, with a thatch roof and large garden, is in the village of Shottery, now a western suburb of Stratford. The best way to get there is to walk, especially in late spring when the hawthorns and apple trees are in blossom. *Tel. 0789/292100. Admission: £3 adults, £1 children. Open Mar.–Oct., Mon.–Sat. 9–5:30, Sun. 10–5:30; Nov.–Feb., Mon.–Sat. 9:30–4, Sun. 10:30–4; closed Dec. 24–26 and Good Friday; Jan. 1 open 1:30–4:30.*

Numbers in the margin correspond to points of interest on the Shakespeare Zone and the Cotswolds map.

⑬ Three miles northwest of Stratford, at **Wilmcote,** off A3400, is the fifth Shakespeare Birthplace Trust Property, **Mary Arden's House,** a Tudor farmhouse, the family home of Shakespeare's mother. Combined with the adjoining glebe (church-owned farm) it forms the **Shakespeare Countryside Museum,** with crafts exhibits, falconry demonstrations, a café, a 16th-century dovecote, and a garden of trees mentioned in the plays. *Tel. 0789/293455. Admission: £3 adults, £1.30 children, £7.50 family ticket. Open Mar.–Oct., Mon.–Sat. 9:30–5, Sun. 10:30–5; Nov.–Feb., Mon.–Sat. 10–4, Sun. 1:30–4; Jan. 1, 1:30–4:30; closed Good Friday and Dec. 24–26.*

⑭ Continue north on A3400, passing under the Stratford-upon-Avon Canal aqueduct and through **Henley-in-Arden,** whose wide main street is an architectural pageant, presenting attractive buildings of various periods. You are now in the area of what was once the Forest of Arden, where Shakespeare set one of his greatest comedies, *As You Like It.*

⑮ Follow A3400 north another 4 or 5 miles, turn right, just before Hockley Heath, onto B4439, and follow the signs to **Packwood House,** which is 2 miles farther on a back road. This house combines red brick and half-timbering, while its tall chimneys are another distinctive Tudor characteristic. The grounds include a formal 17th-century garden, as well as a remarkable topiary garden of that period, in which yew trees depict Christ's Sermon on the Mount. *Near Hockley Heath, tel. 0564/782024. Admission: £3.20 adults, £1.60 children, £8.80 family ticket (gardens only £2 adults, £1 children). Open Apr.–Sept., Wed.–Sun. and national holiday Mon. 2–6; Oct., Wed.–Sun. 12:30–4:30; closed Good Friday.*

⑯ Just 2 miles from Packwood House, on a winding back road off A4141, is **Baddesley Clinton,** a moated, medieval manor house which still has its great fireplaces, 17th-century paneling, and priest holes (secret chambers for Roman Catholic priests, who were persecuted at various times throughout the 16th and 17th centuries). *Near Chadwick End, 6 mi northwest of Warwick, tel. 0564/783294. Admission: £4 adults, £2 children, £11 family ticket (grounds only £2 adults, £1 children). Open Mar.–Sept., Wed.–Sun. and national holiday Mon. 2–6; Oct., Wed.–Sun. 12:30–4:30; closed Good Friday. Restaurant, National Trust store, and grounds open at 12:30.*

⑰ In Baddesley Clinton village, turn right onto A4141; then left, northeast, onto A4177; and finally right again, onto A452, toward **Kenilworth Castle.** Soon the great, red ruins loom ahead. Founded in 1120, this castle remained one of the most formidable fortresses in England until it was finally dismantled by Oliver Cromwell after the Civil War in the mid-17th century. Its keep (central tower), with 20-foot-thick walls; its great hall; and its curtain walls (low outer walls forming the castle's first line of defense) are largely intact. Here the earl of Leicester, one of Queen Elizabeth I's favorites, entertained her four times, most notably in 1575 with 19 days of sumptuous feasting and revelry. *Kenilworth, tel. 0926/52078. Admission: £1.80 adults, 90p children, £1.35 senior citizens. Open Apr.–Oct., daily 10–6; Nov.–Mar., daily 10–4; closed Dec. 24–26.*

Time Out Have a substantial bar meal in the **Clarendon Arms** (Castle Green, Kenilworth), a cozy, flagstone-floored pub.

⓲ Four miles south on A46 is **Warwick,** the county seat of Warwick-shire, an interesting architectural mixture of Georgian red brick and Elizabethan half-timbering. Much of the town center has been spoiled by unattractive postwar development, but look for the 15th-century **Lord Leycester Hospital,** which has been a home for old sol-diers since the earl of Leicester dedicated it to that purpose in 1571. *High St., tel. 0926/492797. Admission: £2.25 adults, £1 children, £1.50 senior citizens. Open Apr.–Sept., Tues.–Sun. 10–5; Oct.–Mar., Tues.–Sun. 10–4; closed Good Friday and Dec. 25.*

Well worth visiting, too, is the **Collegiate Church of St. Mary,** on Church Street, especially for the florid Beauchamp (pronounced Beecham) Chapel, burial chapel of the earls of Warwick. Its gilded, carved, and painted tombs are the very essence of late medieval and Tudor chivalry.

The city's chief attraction is **Warwick Castle,** the finest medieval cas-tle in England, which is built on a cliff overlooking the Avon. Its most powerful commander was the 15th-century earl of Warwick, known during the Wars of the Roses as "the Kingmaker." He was killed in battle near London in 1471 by Edward IV, whom he had just deposed in favor of Henry VI. Warwick Castle's monumental walls now enclose one of the best collections of medieval armor and weapons in Europe, as well as historic furnishings and paintings by Rubens, Van Dyck, and other old masters. Twelve rooms are de-voted to an imaginative Madame Tussaud's wax exhibition, "A Royal Weekend Party—1898." A new exhibit opened in 1994, displaying the sights and sounds of a great medieval household as it prepares for an important battle. The year chosen is 1471, when the powerful Earl of Warwick, the Kingmaker, was killed by Edward IV at the Battle of Barnet. Below the castle, along the Avon, strutting pea-cocks patrol 60 acres of grounds landscaped by Capability Brown in the 18th century. There is a restaurant in the cellars, for lunch dur-ing your visit. *Tel. 0926/495421. Admission: £7.75 adults, £4.75 chil-dren, £5.50 senior citizens, £5.95 students; £19.95 family ticket. Open Mar.–Oct., daily 10–5:30; Nov.–Feb., daily 10–4:30; closed Dec. 25.*

⓳ To continue the circular tour back to Stratford, go on to **Charlecote Park** by taking A429 south from Warwick 4 or 5 miles, and then turn-ing right onto B4088. Queen Elizabeth I is known to have stayed at Charlecote Park, the Tudor manor house of the Lucy family, which was extensively renovated in neo-Elizabethan style in the 19th cen-tury. According to tradition, soon after his marriage Shakespeare was caught poaching deer here and was forced to flee to London. Years later he is supposed to have retaliated by portraying Charlecote's owner, Sir Thomas Lucy, as the foolish Justice Shallow in *Henry IV Part 2. Charlecote, tel. 0789/470277. Admission: £4 adults, £2 children (under 5 free), £11 family ticket. Open Mar.–Sept., Wed.–Sun. and national holiday Mon. 2–6; Oct., Wed.–Sun. 12:30–4:30; closed Good Friday.*

20 The A3400 or an hourly train will take you the 25 miles north from Stratford to **Birmingham,** England's second largest city, which was grossly disfigured by injudicious planning and building in the post–World War II period. Mercifully, the city fathers have adopted a new policy in the last few years of humanizing the areas which their immediate predecessors did so much to ruin.

The city flourished in the boom years of the 19th century's Industrial Revolution. Iron and steel industries grew and the city became a major center of arms manufacture in both world wars. Birmingham's inventive, hard-working citizens accumulated great wealth, and at one time the city had some of the finest Victorian buildings in the country. But 20th-century civic "planning" managed to destroy many of them. There are still architectural treasures to be found, but it means a dedicated search, carefully negotiating the city's impossible road network. While most communities manage to keep their manic motorways on the edge of town, Birmingham's inner ring road twists right through the city center. But this is all changing: city planners are making Birmingham pedestrian-friendly by replacing the ring road with a network of local access roads and by turning the downtown shopping area into pedestrian arcades and buses-only streets.

Birmingham is at the center of a system of restored waterways built during the Industrial Revolution to connect inland factories to rivers and seaports—by 1840 the canals extended more than 4,000 miles throughout the British Isles. Contact the Convention and Visitor Bureau for maps of walks along the towpaths and for details on canal barge cruises.

Numbers in the margin correspond to points of interest on the Birmingham map.

21 Start your visit in the heart of the city at the **International Convention Centre,** which was opened in June 1991 by the queen. Inside there is a good tourist desk to help you with further information. The main atrium of this high-tech building is dominated by a network of blue struts and gleaming air ducts, somewhat softened by banks of indoor plants.

22 Connected to the Convention Centre is the **Symphony Hall**—a significant addition to English musical life. This auditorium has been hailed as an acoustical triumph: Hearing a concert in it is a good reason to visit Birmingham. The internationally recognized City of Birmingham Symphony Orchestra, which has won awards for its recordings under its young conductor Simon Rattle, has found a very welcome home here (*see* The Arts, *below*).

23 Once outside the Convention Centre, you are in **Centenary Square,** a sort of miniature complex for the performing arts. It is paved with a pattern of bricks of various shades, like a Persian carpet, designed by artist Tess Jaray. She was also responsible for the square's landscaping, designing the benches, bins, and planted areas, as well as the unusual paving, which echoes the fancy brickwork that Victori-
24 an architects were so fond of. To one side stands the **Birmingham Repertory Theatre,** which houses one of England's oldest and most esteemed theater companies (*see* The Arts, *below*).

Time Out The Birmingham Rep. (as it's always called) has an excellent cafeteria/restaurant in its foyer, behind sweeping windows that allow for a great view over the square.

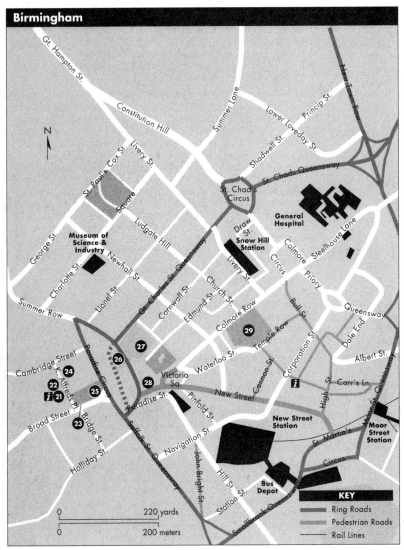

Birmingham

Birmingham Cathedral (St. Philip's), **29**

Birmingham Repertory Theatre, **24**

Centenary Square, **23**

Central Library, **26**

City Museum and Art Gallery, **27**

Hall of Memory, **25**

International Convention Centre, **21**

Symphony Hall, **22**

Town Hall, **28**

In the middle of the square is a group sculpture by a Birmingham artist, Raymond Mason, called *Crowd Scene*. It celebrates Birmingham's past with a thrusting crowd of people, backed by factories belching smoke. Behind the sculpture is a small modern bronze fountain, embodying the civic virtues of Enterprise, Industry, and Learning.

㉕ Across the square from the Convention Centre you will find the **Hall of Memory**, an octagonal war memorial built in the 1920s in remembrance of those who fell during World War I. Inside, there is a book containing their names: The pages are turned regularly. *Admission free. Open Mon.–Sat., 10–4 all year.*

Leave the Hall of Memory, and pass over the road on a footbridge,
㉖ through Paradise Forum mall, and on the left is the **Central Library**. Prince Charles said it "looks like a place where books are incinerated." It used to be bare, brutal concrete, but now dons boxes of flowers and plants in an attempt to soften its facade. In any case, the treasures are inside the building. In the **Shakespeare Memorial Room**, on the sixth floor, there are around 50,000 books in the Shakespeare collection and thousands of illustrations. Also in this complex of buildings are the Adrian Boult Concert Hall and the Birmingham School of Music. *Library: Open Mon.–Fri. 9–8, Sat. 9–5; closed Sun.*

Go beyond the library, and you will find yourself in **Chamberlain Square,** which used to be the city's central square and now makes a linked complex with Centenary Square. The square was named for the Chamberlain family, civic leaders of Birmingham, one of whose members was Neville Chamberlain, the prime minister when war with Germany broke out in 1939.

In the middle of the square is the ornate, Victorian **Chamberlain Memorial Fountain** (1881), which looks rather forlorn and is dwarfed by the modern architecture behind it. Across the square from the li-
㉗ brary is the **City Museum and Art Gallery,** a huge place containing a magnificent collection of Victorian art, featuring works by the Pre-Raphaelites. All the big names are here—Ford Madox Brown, Holman Hunt, Edward Burne-Jones (who was born in Birmingham), Dante Gabriel Rossetti, and many more. One room houses the Arthurian *Holy Grail* tapestries, designed by Burne-Jones and executed by the William Morris Arts Workers' Guild. The collection reflects the enormous wealth of 19th-century Birmingham and the taste of its industrialists. In addition, there are natural-history and tribal-art collections, and imaginative displays tracing the history of the city. There is an excellent crafts shop, a museum shop, and a café. *Chamberlain Sq., tel. 021/235–2834. Admission free. Open Mon.–Sat. 9:30–5, Sun. 2–5.*

㉘ Turn right when you leave the gallery, and the **Town Hall,** surrounded by classical columns, will be on your right. It is a copy of the Temple of Castor and Pollux in Rome and took two decades to build. It used to be the home of the symphony orchestra—it heard the first performances of Mendelssohn's *Elijah* and Elgar's *Dream of Gerontius*—and now is host to concerts and exhibitions. *Victoria Sq., tel. 021/235–3942.*

Now turn left through the newly renovated Victoria Square, and walk down Colmore Row. Three blocks farther will bring you to
㉙ **Birmingham Cathedral** (St. Philip's) on your right. The paths around the cathedral are edged with the actual square cobblestones which used to cover the roads of the city. The early-18th-century building is undergoing a major restoration and preservation pro-

gram at the moment, so it is shrouded in scaffolding. The gilded Georgian interior is elegant and has some lovely plasterwork. You will immediately be struck by the windows behind the altar, which seem to glow with a garnet light. They were designed by Burne-Jones and made by William Morris. At the end of the south aisle is a vivid modern tapestry.

Tour 2: The Cotswold Hills

30 **Bourton-on-the-Water,** off A429 on the eastern edge of the Cotswold Hills, is deservedly famous as a classic Cotswold village. The little River Windrush runs through Bourton, crossed by low stone bridges. This village makes a good touring base, but in summer, like Stratford and Broadway, it's overcrowded with tourists. Then, you will find a quieter, more typical Cotswold atmosphere in nearby villages with such evocative names as Upper Slaughter, Lower Slaughter, Upper and Lower Swell.

A stroll through Bourton takes you past Cotswold cottages, many now converted to little stores and coffee shops. Follow the rushing stream and its ducks to the end of the village and the old mill, now the **Cotswold Motor Museum and Exhibition of Village Life.** In addition to 30 vintage motor vehicles and a collection of old advertising signs, this museum offers an Edwardian store, a blacksmith's forge, a wheelwright's shop, a country kitchen, and a huge trove of children's toys. *The Old Mill, tel. 0451/821255. Admission: £1.40 adults, 70p children, £4.20 family ticket. Open Feb.–Nov., daily 10–6.*

31 **Stow-on-the-Wold,** 3 miles north, is another exemplary Cotswold town, its imposing golden stone houses built around a wide square. Many of these have now been discreetly converted into quality antiques stores. Look for the Kings Arms Old Posting House, its wide entrance still seeming to wait for the stagecoaches that once stopped here on their way to Cheltenham. At 800 feet elevation, Stow is the highest, as well as the largest, town in the Cotswolds. It's also an antiques hunter's paradise, and, like Bourton, a convenient base.

Time Out The **Queen's Head** (The Square) is an excellent stopping-off spot for a pub lunch. In summer, the courtyard out back or the bench in front, under a climbing rose, makes for relaxed outdoor drinking.

32 From Stow, take A429 5 miles north to **Moreton-in-Marsh** for the fine views across the hills. In Moreton the houses have been built not around a central square but along a street wide enough to accommodate a market every Tuesday.

33 West of Moreton-in-Marsh, off A44, B4081 swings north to **Chipping Campden,** a lovely Cotswold market town. Its broad High Street, lined with houses in an attractive variety of styles, represents the wealth acquired in the medieval wool trade. In the center is the **Market Hall,** a gabled Jacobean structure built by Sir Baptiste Hycks in 1627 "for the sale of local produce." *High St. Admission free. Always open.*

One of the oldest buildings in Chipping Campden, built in the 14th century, is **Woolstaplers Hall.** It houses the local TIC, as well as the museum, a 1920s movie theater, and collections of medical equipment. *High St., tel. 0386/840289. Admission: £2 adults, £1 children. Open Apr.–Oct., daily 10–5.*

Time Out **Greenstocks** (Cotswold House Hotel, The Square) is just the place for a delicious lunch or a coffee break.

---

34 Three miles north of Chipping Camden—the route is clearly marked —is **Hidcote Manor Garden**, laid out around a Cotswold manor house (not open to the public), and is arguably the most interesting and attractive large garden in Britain. An American horticulturalist Major Lawrence Johnstone, was given the manor in 1907 by his mother, who had inherited her wealth from her two husbands, a Baltimore banker and a New York lawyer. Johnstone was not just an imaginative gardener, but a widely traveled plantsman as well, who brought back specimens from all over the world. Hidcote now belongs to the National Trust. The garden is divided into formal and informal sections. The formal part is arranged in "rooms" without roofs, separated by hedges, often with fine topiary work and walls. These divisions all have suggestive names—the Stilt Garden, the Pillar Garden, the Fuschia Garden, the Poppy Garden, and so on. Shakespearean plays are performed in summer on the Theatre Lawn. The White Garden was probably the forerunner of the popular white gardens at Sissinghurst and Glyndebourne. The larger, informal section is a controlled profusion of trees, bushes, and wildflowers—many from distant lands such as China and Japan. Here the juxtaposition of colors is masterly, especially in spring and fall. Several popular strains of garden plants have originated here— Hidcote lavender and the red verbena "Lawrence Johnstone" among them. *Hidcote Bartrim, tel. 0386/438333. Admission: £4.80 adults, £2.40 children, £13.20 family ticket. Open Apr.–Oct., Mon., Wed., Thurs., and weekends 11–7; last admissions at 6 or 1 hour before sunset.*

35 Take B4081 and then A44 southwest to **Broadway;** on the way you can glimpse the distant Malvern Hills to the west in Worcestershire. Named for its wide main street, Broadway offers many shops and a renowned hotel, the **Lygon Arms** (*see* Dining and Lodging, *below*). Its striking facade dates from 1620, but the restored building has several modern extensions. Sophisticated travelers tend to avoid Broadway in the summer, when it is clogged with cars and buses.

On the outskirts of Broadway, off A44, is **Broadway Tower Country Park.** From the top of the tower, an 18th-century "folly" built by the sixth earl of Coventry, you can see over 12 counties. Nature trails, picnic grounds with barbecue grills, an adventure playground, and rare animals and birds are surrounded by peaceful countryside. *Tel. 0386/852390. Admission: £2.75 adults, £1.75 children and senior citizens; £7.50 family ticket. Open Apr.–Oct., daily 10–6.*

36 Two miles south is **Snowshill Manor,** whose 17th-century facade hides its Tudor origins. It contains a delightful clutter of musical instruments, clocks, toys, bicycles, weavers' and spinners' tools, and more. Children love it. *Snowshill, tel. 0386/852410. Admission: £4.20 adults, £2.10 children, £11.60 family ticket. Open Apr. and Oct. weekends only 1–5; May–Sept., Wed.–Mon. 1–6.*

37 Follow B4632 southwest to Winchcombe and **Sudeley Castle,** the home and burial place of Catherine Parr (1512–48), Henry VIII's sixth and last wife, who outlived him by one year. Today the castle's peaceful air belies its turbulent history; its magnificent grounds are the setting for outdoor theater, concerts, and other events in summer. *Winchcombe, tel. 0242/602308. Admission: £4.90 adults, £2.75 children, £4.50 senior citizens, £13 family ticket. Grounds open Apr.–Oct., daily 11–5:30; castle open noon–5.*

Just west of Winchcombe, turn left (south) and follow the back roads, many of which are single-track, passing through Brockhampton and across A40 to Compton Abdale and on to
38 Yanworth and Chedworth, to pick up the signs to **Chedworth Roman Villa,** the best-preserved Roman villa in England. Surrounded by woodland, the site overlooks the Cotswold Hills. Thirty-two rooms, including two complete bath suites, have been identified. The visitor center and museum give a picture of Roman life in Britain. *Yanworth, tel. 0242/890256. Admission: £2.60 adults, £1.30 children, £7.15 family ticket. Open Mar.–Oct., Tues.–Sun. and national holiday 10–5:30; Nov., Wed.–Sun. 11–4; closed Good Friday.*

39 From the Roman Villa follow the signs east to **Northleach** for a look
40 at the magnificent church, then take B4425 to **Bibury,** in its idyllic setting beside the little river Coln. Bibury's huge, 17th-century water mill, on a site recorded in the *Domesday Book*, is now the **Arlington Mill Museum.** Its 16 rooms contain examples of the work of William Morris (*see* the Thames Valley, Tour 3) and the late-19th-century Arts and Crafts Movement, as well as many agricultural and country exhibits. *The museum was changing hands at press time: check locally for details. Tel. 0285/740368.*

41 From Bibury, take B4425/A40 east to **Burford,** whose broad main street leads steeply down to a narrow bridge across the River Windrush. Burford boasts many historic inns, having been a stagecoach stop for centuries.

Time Out At **The Golden Pheasant Hotel** (High St., Burford), have afternoon tea in the lounge while relaxing in a deep, velvet armchair. In winter you can sit by a log fire, but afternoon tea is served only on weekends.

Tour 3: Cheltenham, Gloucester, and the Forest of Dean

Numbers in the margin correspond to points of interest on the Forest of Dean and Bath Environs map.

West of the Cotswolds there's a rather urbanized axis connecting Gloucester with Cheltenham; and along the Welsh border, the low-lying Forest of Dean. This once private hunting ground of kings is now a recreation area for the general public, with some of the most extensive and beautiful woodlands in the country, rich with conifers and broad-leaved trees and an ideal spot for either a quiet stroll or a more serious hike.

42 We begin our tour with **Cheltenham** in the north. If you visit this historic health resort in the spring or summer, you'll see its stunning architecture enhanced by a profusion of flower gardens. The flowers cover even traffic circles, while the elegantly laid-out avenues, crescents, and terraces, with their characteristic row houses, balconies, and iron railings, make Cheltenham an outstanding example of the Regency style.

Although it can't compare either in fame, history, or scale with Bath, Cheltenham has been popular since the visit of George III and Queen Charlotte in 1788. During the Regency period Cheltenham's status was ensured by the visits of the duke of Wellington, the national hero of Waterloo. The **Rotunda** building on Montpellier (street)—now a bank—contains the spa's original "pump room," i.e., the room in which the mineral waters were on draft; such rooms, as in Bath, often evolved into public drawing rooms of polite society. Parallel to Montpellier Street is Montpellier Walk, where more than 30 statues, like the caryatids in Athens, adorn the storefronts. Wander past **Imperial Square,** with its intricate ironwork balconies, past the ornate Neptune's Fountain and along the elegant Promenade.

A 20-minute walk from the town center brings you to the **Pittville Pump Room,** built in the late 1820s, where the mineral waters can still be tasted. The pump room now houses the **Gallery of Fashion,** which tells the history of the town through an extensive costume collection. *Pittville, tel. 0242/512740. Admission: £1 adults, 50p children and senior citizens, £2.25 family ticket. Open Apr.–Sept., Tues.–Sun. 10:30–5.*

Time Out The **Old Swan** (37 High St.), a large, comfortable old pub, serves homemade lunches and has tea and coffee on tap.

---

❹❸ Nine miles west is **Gloucester,** the county seat. Much of this city's ancient heritage has been lost to nondescript modern stores and offices, but the **Gloucester Folk Museum** is housed in a row of fine Tudor and Jacobean half-timbered houses. *99–103 Westgate St., tel. 0452/526467. Admission free. Open Oct.–June, Mon.–Sat. 10–5; July–Sept., Mon.–Sat. 10–5, Sun. 10–4.*

Across Westgate Street is the magnificient **Gloucester Cathedral,** originally a Norman abbey church, consecrated in 1100. The exterior soars in elegant lines, and the interior has largely been spared the sterilizing attentions of modern architects who like to strip cathedrals down to their original bare bones. The place is a mishmash of periods, and the clutter of centuries mirrors perfectly the slow growth of ecclesiastical taste, good, bad, and indifferent. The interior is almost completely Norman, with the massive pillars of the nave left untouched since their completion. The fan-vaulted roof of the cloisters is the finest in Europe. The cloisters enclose a peaceful garden, where one can easily imagine medieval monks at prayer. Look for the tomb of Edward II, who was imprisoned and murdered in Berkeley Castle in 1327 (*see below*). *Westgate St., tel. 0452/28095. Admission free, but a donation of at least £2 per adult requested. Open daily 8–6, except during services and special events.*

Time Out The **Dick Whittington** (100 Westgate St.), a large, wooden-floored pub serving beer and wine from the barrel, commemorates a famous native son, who was three times Lord Mayor of London in the Middle Ages. Its lunches and snacks are excellent, and in summer there are barbecues in the garden.

A short walk from the Cathedral, at the end of Westgate Street, along the canal, are the historic **Gloucester Docks.** The docks still function, though now on a much reduced scale. The vast Victorian warehouses are being restored, and new shops and cafés added to bring the area back to life. Tours, starting at the **Mariner's Chapel** by the Southgate Street entrance to the docks, are conducted every Friday in July and August at 2:30. One of the warehouses is now the **Antique Centre** (*see* Shopping, *below*). Another holds **The National Waterways Museum,** with examples of canal houseboats and barges. *Llanthony Warehouse, Gloucester Docks, tel. 0452/307009. Admission: £3.95 adults, £2.95 children and senior citizens; £9.95 family ticket. Open Apr.–Sept., daily 10–6; Oct.–Mar., daily 10–5.*

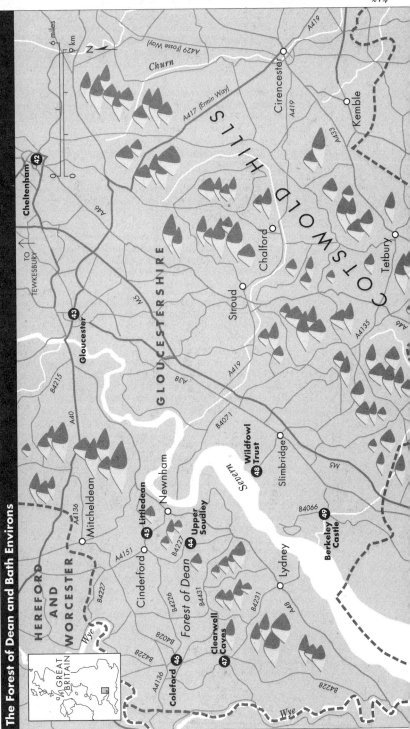

The Forest of Dean and Bath Environs

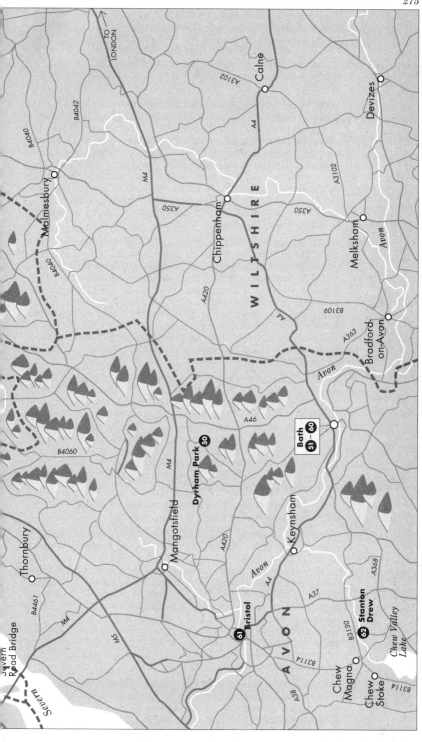

Take A40 and A4136 west past Mitcheldean, and continue on to the **Forest of Dean.** This mysterious forest covers much of the valley between the Rivers Severn and Wye. Although the primordial forest has long since been cut down and replanted, the landscape here remains one of strange beauty, hiding in its folds and under its hills deposits of iron, silver, and coal that have been mined for thousands of years.

㊹ When you see A4151, take it south to Cinderford and then turn right for **Upper Soudley,** where you'll find the **Dean Heritage Centre.** Based in a restored mill building in a wooded valley, the center tells the history of the forest, with reconstructions of a mine and a miner's cottage, a water wheel, and a "beam engine" (a primitive steam engine used to pump water from flooded coal mines). Outside the center is a tiny farm with a pig and poultry, as well as natural-history exhibitions. Watch craftspeople at work in the outbuildings. *On B4227, tel. 0594/822170. Admission: £2.60 adults, £1.60 children, £2.10 senior citizens. Open Feb.–Oct., daily; Nov.–Jan., weekends; hours: summer, 10–6, winter, 10–5.*

㊺ Backtrack north on B4227, turn east on A4151, to **Littledean.** From here "Scenic Drive" signs direct you through the best of the forest. Of the original royal forest established in 1016 by King Canute, 27,000 acres are preserved by the Forestry Commission. It's still an important source of timber, but parking lots and picnic grounds have been created and eight nature trails marked. One trail links sculptures, commissioned by the Forestry Commission, around **Speech House,** the medieval verderer's court in the forest's center. The verderer was responsible for the enforcement of the forest laws. It was usually a capital offense to kill game or cut wood without authorization.

㊻ Drive west on A4151, and then west again on B4226 and B4028 to reach **Coleford.** The TIC (tel. 0594/836307) has details of picnic grounds, nature trails, and tours of the forest. The area is a maze of weathered and moss-covered rocks, huge ferns, and ancient yew trees—a shady haven on a summer's day. Underground iron mines, worked continuously from Roman times to 1945, can be visited at **㊼** **Clearwell Caves.** *Off B4228 south of Coleford, tel. 0594/832535. Admission: £2.70 adults, £1.70 children, £2.20 senior citizens. Open Mar.–Oct. daily 10–5; Dec., Christmas workshops, weekdays 2–6, weekends 10–5; admission £3.*

B4231 heads southeast through the forest toward the River Severn. At Lydney take A48 northeast back to Gloucester.

㊽ Travel now southwest along A433. After 2 miles you will pass the source of the River Thames off to your left. At Tetbury turn west onto A4135 for 12 miles through an arm of the Cotswolds toward the fertile, flat Severn valley. Cross the M5 motorway to Slimbridge; head west and across the little swing bridge over the Sharpness Canal to the **Wildfowl Trust** on the banks of the Severn. Its 73 acres of rich marshland harbor Britain's largest collection of wildfowl. Thousands of swans, ducks, and geese come to winter here; in spring and early summer, you will be delighted by cygnets, ducklings, and goslings. *Tel. 0453/890333. Admission: £4.50 adults, £2.25 children, £3.40 senior citizens, £11.25 family ticket. Open daily 9:30–5 or dusk; closed Dec. 24–25.*

㊾ **Berkeley Castle** in the sleepy little village of **Berkeley** (pronounced "Barkley"), 4 miles south of Slimbridge, is perfectly preserved, everyone's ideal castle. It was the setting for the gruesome murder of King Edward II in 1327—the cell can still be seen. He was deposed by his French consort, Queen Isabella, and her paramour, the earl of Mortimer. They then connived at his imprisonment and subsequent death. The castle was begun in 1153 by Roger De Berkeley, a Norman knight, and has remained in the family ever since. The state apartments here are full of magnificent furniture, tapestries, and pictures. The surrounding meadows, now the setting for pleasant Elizabethan gardens, were once flooded to make a formidable moat. *Berkeley, tel. 0453/810332. Admission: £3.80 adults, £1.90 children, £3 senior citizens and students, £10 family ticket. Open May–Sept., Tues.–Sat. and national holidays 11–5, Sun. 2–5; Apr., Tues.–Sun. 2–5; Oct., Sun. only 2–4:30.*

From Berkeley you can take A38/M5 to Bristol (17 mi), or cross back over the M5 and head southeast toward Bath (30 mi via A4135 and A46), both on the River Avon. Our tour goes first to Bath. Eight
50 miles north of Bath lies **Dyrham Park**, a late-17th-century country house with paneled interiors and a deer park, which is the setting for occasional open-air concerts in the summer. *Dyrham, tel. 0272/ 372501. Admission: £4.70 adults, £2.35 children; park only: £1.50 adults, 75p children. House and garden open Apr.–Oct., Sat.–Wed. 12–5:30; park open daily all year noon–5:30 or dusk, if earlier; closed Dec. 25.*

Tour 4: Bath and Beyond

Numbers in the margin correspond to points of interest on the Bath map.

51 One of the delights of staying in **Bath** is being surrounded by the magnificent 18th-century architecture, a lasting reminder of the elegant world described by Jane Austen. Bath suffered slightly from World War II bombing and even more from urban renewal, but the damage was halted before it could ruin the center of the city. This doesn't mean that Bath is a museum. It is lively and interesting, offering dining and entertainment, excellent art galleries, and theater, music, and other performances throughout the year. It is also a city with plenty of civic pride, and the streets are filled with flowers in summer.

The Romans first put Bath on the map in the first century, when they built a temple here in honor of the goddess Minerva, and a sophisticated network of baths to make full use of the mineral springs, which gush from the earth at a constant temperature of 116°F. Much later, 18th-century society took the city to its heart, and Bath became the most fashionable spa in Britain. The architect John Wood (1704–54) created a harmonious city, building beautiful terraces, crescents, and Palladian villas of the same local stone used by the Romans.

52 The **Pump Room** is Bath's primary "watering hole." People still gather here to drink the mineral waters—which taste revolting—and to socialize. The baths as such are no longer in use, and this magnificent Georgian building now houses a tourist information desk, a souvenir store, and a restaurant. Almost the entire Roman bath complex has been excavated, and you can see the remains of swimming pools, saunas, and Turkish baths, as well as part of the temple of Minerva, with the bronze head of the goddess and votive offerings left by worshipers nearly 2,000 years ago. *Abbey Churchyard, tel. 0225/461111, ext. 2783. Admission: Pump Room free; Roman Baths £5 adults, £3 children, £13 family ticket; combined ticket with Costume Museum, £6.60 adults, £3.50 children, £16 family ticket. Open*

Abbey, **53**
Assembly Rooms, **57**
The Circus, **56**
Claverton Manor, **60**
Holburne Museum and Crafts Study Centre, **59**
Number 1, Royal Crescent, **58**
Pulteney Bridge, **54**
Pump Room, **52**
Theatre Royal, **55**

Bath

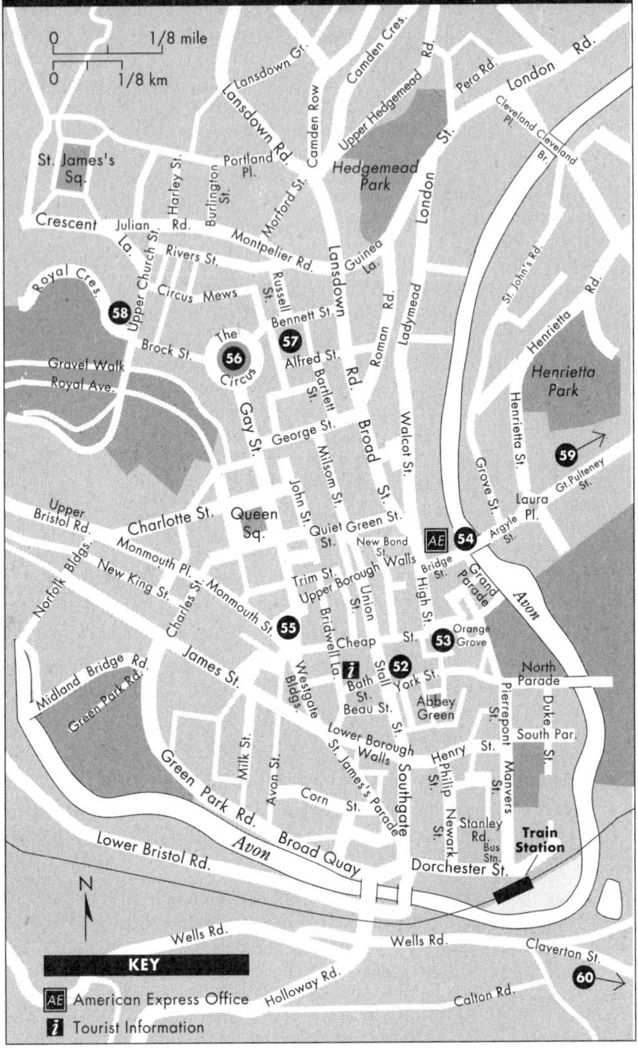

Mar.–Oct. daily 9–6 (and Aug. 8 PM–10 PM), Nov.–Feb., Mon.–Sat. 9–5, Sun. 10–5.

Time Out The **Pump Room** serves morning coffee and afternoon tea, often to music by a string trio. Nearby **Sally Lunn's** (North Parade Passage), the oldest house in Bath, still serves the famous Sally Lunn bun invented here.

---

(53) Next to the Pump Room is the **Abbey,** dating from the 15th century. It was built in the Perpendicular (English Gothic) style on the site of a Saxon abbey, and has superb, fan-vaulted ceilings in the nave. *Abbey Churchyard. Admission: £1. Open most times, though visitors are asked not to enter during services.*

Off Abbey Churchyard, where buskers (strolling musicians) of all kinds perform, are tiny alleys leading to little squares of stores, galleries, and eating places. Walk up Stall and Union streets toward Milsom Street, and you'll find numerous alleyways with fascinating small stores (*see* Shopping, *below*). Work your way east to Bridge
54 Street and **Pulteney Bridge,** an 18th-century span lined with little
55 shops. Head back along Upper Borough Walls to find the **Theatre Royal,** which opened in 1805 and was restored in 1982. Next door, the former home of Richard "Beau" Nash—the dictator of fashion for mid-18th-century society in Bath—and his mistress Juliana Popjoy, is now a restaurant called Popjoy's (*see* Dining, *below*).

Turn north, and admire the Georgian houses along Queen Square,
56 Gay Street, and **The Circus,** where three perfectly proportioned Georgian terraces outline the round garden in the center. Turn east
57 from The Circus to the **Assembly Rooms,** which figure in Jane Austen's novel *Persuasion*. This classical-style building, once a social center like the Pump Room, now houses the completely redesigned **Museum of Costume.** It displays costumes from Beau Nash's day up to the present, in lavish settings. *Bennett St., tel. 0225/ 461111. Admission: £3.20 adults, £2 children, £9 family ticket. Open Mar.–Oct., Mon.–Sat. 9:30–6, Sun. 10–6; Nov.–Feb., Mon.– Sat. 10–5, Sun. 11–5.*

Turn west from The Circus and you'll arrive at Royal Crescent, the crowning glory of architecture in Bath, and much used as a location for period films. A house at the center is now Bath's most elegant hotel, the Royal Crescent (*see* Dining and Lodging, *below*). On the
58 corner, **Number 1, Royal Crescent,** has been turned into a museum and furnished as it might have been at the turn of the 19th century. The museum crystallizes a view of the English class system: Upstairs all is gentility and elegance; downstairs is a fascinating kitchen museum. *Tel. 0225/428126. Admission: £3 adults, £2.50 children, senior citizens, and students. Open Mar.–Oct., Tues.–Sun. 10:30– 5; Nov.–mid-Dec., Tues.–Sun. 11–4.*

Across the Avon, in an elegant 18th-century building, is the
59 **Holburne Museum and Crafts Study Centre,** which houses a small but superb collection of 17th- and 18th-century fine and decorative arts. There are also some 20th-century crafts. *Great Pulteney St., tel. 0225/466669. Admission: £3.50 adults, £1.50 children, £3 senior citizens, £7 family ticket. Open Easter–Oct., Mon.–Sat. 11–5, Sun. 2:30–6; Nov.–mid-Dec. and mid-Feb.–Easter, Tues.–Sat. 11–5, Sun. 2:30–6.*

High above the city—2½ miles southeast on the Warminster road,
60 A36—is **Claverton Manor,** a Greek revival (19th-century) mansion housing the first museum of Americana to be established outside the United States, quietly sponsored by an American millionaire, Dallas Pratt. A series of furnished rooms portrays American domestic life from the 17th to the 19th centuries. The fine parkland includes a replica of George Washington's garden and an arboretum. You can even have tea with American cookies. *Claverton Down, tel. 0225/ 460503. Admission: £5 adults, £2.50 children, £4.50 senior citizens and students. Open Easter–Oct., Tues.–Sun. 2–5, national holidays and preceding Sun. 11–5; closed Mon.*

Numbers in the margin correspond to points of interest on the Forest of Dean and Bath Environs map.

61 Leave Bath by A4 to travel the 13 miles northwest to **Bristol,** which has been a major city since medieval times. In the 17th and 18th centuries, it was an important port for the North American trade, but now that the city's industries no longer rely on the docks, the historic harbor has been largely given over to pleasure craft. The quayside offers an arts center, movie theaters, museums, stores, pubs, and restaurants; carnivals, speedboat races, and regattas are held regularly.

On view in the harbor is the **S.S. *Great Britain,*** the first iron ship to cross the Atlantic. Built by the great English engineer Isambard Kingdom Brunel in 1843, it remained in service until the end of the century, first on the North American route and then on the Australian. *Great Western Dock, off Cumberland Rd., tel. 0272/260680. Admission: £2.50 adults, £1.70 children and senior citizens (children under 5 free). Open Apr.–Sept., daily 10–6; Oct.–Mar., 10–5; closed Dec. 24–25.*

Bristol is also the home of the **Church of St. Mary Redcliffe,** called "the fairest in England" by Queen Elizabeth I. It features rib-vaulting and dates from the 1300s, built by Bristol merchants who wanted a place in which to pray for the safe (and profitable) voyages of their ships. *Redcliffe Way, a 5-minute walk from Temple Meads train station toward the docks.*

Dissenters from the Church of England also found a home in Bristol; John Wesley built the first **Methodist church** here in 1739. Its austerity contrasts sharply with the Anglican churches. *Broadmead. Open Mon.–Sat. 10–4; closed Wed. in winter.*

Time Out | The Scottish mailboat ***Lochiel*** is now a floating pub and restaurant moored on St. Augustin's Reach, behind the Watershed Exhibition Centre.

If you cross the Avon Gorge via Clifton Suspension Bridge, built in 1828 (also by Brunel), you will reach the **Bristol Zoo,** where more than 1,000 species of animals live in 12 acres of landscaped gardens. *Clifton, tel. 0272/738951. Admission: £5.50 adults, £2.50 children (children under 3 free), £4 senior citizens. Open Apr.–Sept., daily 10–6; Oct.–Mar. 9–5; closed Dec. 25.*

The area south of Bristol is notable for its scenery and walks, its photogenic villages, and the ancient stone circles. Take A38 (follow signs for airport), then B3130 and B3114 to the villages of **Chew Magna** and **Chew Stoke,** and on to **Chew Valley Lake,** a reservoir in a drowned valley surrounded by woods, which shelters 240 species of birds. At Chew Magna—note the gargoyles on the ancient church— **62** turn east on B3130 to **Stanton Drew.** Beyond Stanton Drew are the neolithic **Stanton Drew Circles,** where three rings, two avenues of standing stones, and a burial chamber make up one of the grandest and most mysterious monuments in the country. The site lies in a field reached through a farmyard—you'll need suitable shoes to visit it. *Stanton Drew. The stones stand on private land, but are supervised by English Heritage. The landowner charges a small admission fee. Open any reasonable time (not Sun.).*

What to See and Do with Children

At the Royal Shakespeare Theatre in Stratford-upon-Avon, children can play with the props in the adjoining gallery.

In Warwick, **St. John's House** (tel. 0926/412021) exhibits a Victorian schoolroom, costumes, and scenes of domestic life. May–Sept. only. The **Warwickshire Doll Museum** (Oken's House, Castle St., tel. 0926/

412500. Open Easter–Sept.) houses a large collection of dolls, toys, and games.

At the **Birmingham Museum of Science and Industry** (Newhall St., tel. 021/235–1661) there are aircraft, vintage cars, traction engines, and an ancient working steam engine. Some of the machines can be switched on so you can see how they work.

The **Cotswold Motor Museum** (*see* Tour 2).

In Bourton-on-the-Water the **Model Railway Exhibition** is in itself interesting and it has some toys on sale. *Box Bush, High St., tel. 0451/820686.* **The Model Village** (The Old New Inn, tel. 0451/820467) is an outdoor working replica of Bourton village, built in 1937 to a scale of one-ninth.

The **Dean Heritage Centre** at Soudley (*see* Tour 3).

Broadway Tower Country Park, Broadway (*see* Tour 2).

Just south of Newent (8 mi northwest of Gloucester on B4215, then south to Clifford's Mesne) is a **Falconry Centre** (tel. 0531/820286) that holds daily demonstrations with the largest collection of birds of prey in Europe. *Closed Dec.–Jan.*

Weston-super-Mare, on the Severn Estuary, 20 miles west on A370 or M5 from Bristol, is a brash and lively town with a wide, sandy beach, where there are Punch and Judy puppet shows and donkey rides on the sands and a miniature railroad along the seafront.

Off the Beaten Track

From Stratford, take A46 north about 20 miles to **Coventry** to visit the **cathedral.** As a testament to history, the 1,000-year-old building, destroyed by air raids in 1940 and 1941, has been left as a bombed-out shell next to the magnificent new cathedral. The new one contains the best of modern religious art in Britain of the time (1954–62), including an engraved glass screen by John Hutton; a tapestry by Graham Sutherland; stained-glass windows by John Piper; and various pieces by Sir Jacob Epstein, the New York–born sculptor. The visitors center beneath the cathedral uses audio, video, and holograms to show the history of Coventry and its cathedrals. About the rest of the city, which contains some of the worst postwar rebuilding to be seen in Britain, the less said the better. *Priory Row, tel. 0203/227597. Admission free; tower, £1 adults, 50p children; visitors center, £1.25 adults, 75p children and senior citizens, £3 family ticket. Open Apr.–Sept., daily 9–7:30; Oct.–Mar., 9–5:30; closed during services.*

At **The Barber Institute of Fine Arts,** in the University of Birmingham, there's a superb small art collection, including works by Bellini, Canaletto, Guardi, Poussin, Murillo, Gainsborough, Turner, Whistler, Renoir, Gauguin, and van Gogh. The Barber also owns collections of miniatures, watercolors, and sculptures (notably by Roubiliac, Degas, and Rodin) and some works by Redon, Magritte, and other painters of the early 20th century. Art lovers look on it as paradise. *Take the Cross City Line train from New Street Station south to University Station or Bus 61, 62, or 63 from the city center. The Barber Institute is off Edgbaston Park Rd., near the East Gate. Tel. 021/472–0962. Admission free. Open Mon.–Fri. 10–5, Sat. 10–1.*

From Gloucester head southeast on A417, which follows the Roman Ermin Way for 11 miles, and should get you in the mood for the Roman experience you are about to have. **Cirencester** (sometimes pronounced "Cīcester") has been the hub of the Cotswolds since Roman times when it was called Corinium and lay at the intersection of the Fosse Way and the Ermin Way. Cirencester is a lovely old market town, full of mellow stone buildings—take a stroll down Dollar Street to see the bow-fronted stores—and with a magnificent parish church, St. John the Baptist. The **Corinium Museum** has an excellent collection of Roman artifacts, as well as full-scale reconstructions of local Roman interiors. *Park St., tel. 0285/655611. Admission: £1.25 adults, 75p children, £1 senior citizens and students. Open Mon.–Sat. 10–5, Sun. 2–5; Nov.–Mar. closed Mon.; closed last 2 weeks of Dec.*

From Gloucester, take A38 north 10 miles to **Tewkesbury,** an ancient town of black-and-white, half-timbered buildings on the River Avon, from which you can enjoy a cruise up the river in the *Avon Belle.* The stonework in the Norman **Tewkesbury Abbey** bears the same mason's marks as that of Gloucester Cathedral, but the abbey has been built in the Romanesque (12th-century) and Decorated Gothic (14th-century) styles. It is a beautifully kept church, often with massive flower displays along the nave. *Church St., tel. 0684/850959. Open daily.*

Shopping

Marketing antiques has reached the level of a major industry in the Cotswolds, so don't expect to find many bargains. Markets are held in **Moreton-in-Marsh** on Tuesday and **Chipping Norton** on Wednesday. Ask about others.

Bath Bath's excellent shopping district centers on Stall and Union streets (modern stores) and Milsom Street (traditional stores). Leading off these main streets are fascinating alleyways and passages lined with galleries and a wealth of antiques shops. The **Bath Antiques Market** (Guinea La.) is a wonderful place to browse. Ninety dealers have stalls here. There is also a restaurant. *Open Wed. only 6:30 AM to 2:30 PM.* **Great Western Antique Centre** (Bartlett St.) delights antiques lovers with over 100 stalls selling every kind of antique imaginable, including clothing, linens, and furniture. **Beaux Arts Ceramics** (York St., tel. 0225/464850) carries the work of prominent potters, and holds six solo exhibitions a year. Book lovers should visit **Margaret's Buildings,** (halfway between The Circus and Royal Crescent), a lane mostly of secondhand and antiquarian bookshops.

Birmingham Ten minutes' walk northward from the city center is the **Jewellery Quarter,** with over 200 manufacturing jewelers and 50 silversmiths. Work with precious metals was first recorded here in 1460, and there are still more than 100 shops that sell and repair gold and silver handcrafted jewelry, clocks, and watches. The city has its own Assay Office with an anchor as its silver mark. The history of the neighborhood and the craft of the jeweler are explained at the **Discovery Centre** (77–79 Vyse St., tel. 021/554–3598). *Admission: £2 adults, £1.50 children and senior citizens, £5 family ticket. Open Mon.–Sat. 10–5.*

Bourton-on-the-Water The **Cotswold Perfumery** (Victoria St., tel. 0451/820698) has a wide range of perfumes, which are manufactured here. While deciding what to buy, visit the **Exhibition of Perfumery** and the **Perfumed Garden** (admission to exhibition: £1.50 adults, £1.30 children and senior citizens). Perfume bottles, jewelry, and porcelain dolls are also on sale.

Cheltenham A walk along elegant Montpellier Walk and then along the flower-bedecked Promenade will take you past boutiques like **Liberty** and **Hoopers.** Both **Martin** and **Scott Cooper** on the Promenade are worth visiting for jewelry and silver. Behind the Promenade is the Regent Arcade, a modern shopping area with a wide variety of stores. A market is held every Sunday at the racecourse, a produce market every Thursday morning on Market Street, and undercover stalls Tuesday through Saturday on Winchcombe Street.

Gloucester The locals say it's best to look in Cheltenham and buy in Gloucester, where prices are lower. Gloucester offers neither the variety nor the sophistication of Cheltenham stores, but you might find a bargain or two at the **Antique Centre** (tel. 0452/529716), in a restored Victorian warehouse at Gloucester Docks. Next to the Cathedral Gate is the house of Beatrix Potter's tailor in her story *The Tailor of Gloucester.* It is now the **Beatrix Potter Gift Shop** (College Ct., tel. 0452/422856).

Stratford-upon-Avon Stratford-upon-Avon's bustling shopping district has **Jaeger** (tel. 0789/292818), for excellent clothes, and **Waterstone** (tel. 0789/414418), for books, as well as antiques and specialty shops. There is an open market every Friday in the Market Square. **Antique Arcade** (Sheep St.) has 14 dealers selling china, jewelry, and art deco. At the **Antique Market** (Ely St.), you will find 50 stalls of jewelry, silver, linens, porcelain, and memorabilia. **Jean A. Bateman** (Sheep St., tel. 0789/298494) specializes in antique jewelry. **Robert Vaughan** (20 Chapel St., tel. 0789/205312) is the best of Stratford's many second-hand bookshops. **Once a Tree** (8 Bard's Walk, tel. 0789/297790) is thoroughly "green," selling items crafted from sustainable wood sources—animals, bowls, and dozens of imaginative articles, ideal for presents. **B & W Thornton** (23 Henley St., tel. 0789/269405), just above Shakespeare's birthplace, has an extensive range of fine china for sale. Many of the pieces are unique works by leading potters. Thornton also stocks a range of exclusive Moorcroft ware.

Sports and the Outdoors

Bicycling The Gloucester Tourist office (tel. 0452/421188) has a full range of "go as you please" cycle touring route packs (£2).

Horse Racing Important steeplechase races take place at **Cheltenham;** the National Hunt Festival in mid-March is crowned by the Gold Cup awards on the last day. *Tel. 0242/513014.*

Show Jumping The Badminton Horse Trials are held annually in May at the duke of Beaufort's estate in **Badminton.** *Tel. 0454/218272.*

Walking This part of England offers glorious, gentle countryside, with many short walks in the areas round the historic towns of the region, such as Stratford. The local Tourist Information Centers often have route maps for themed walks available. If you want to branch out on your own and not get lost, one way is to track the rivers on which most of these towns are built. They usually have tow paths running alongside them which are easy to follow and scenically very attractive. The only thing is that they wind a lot, and you may find yourself walking for much longer than you had intended.

The **Forest of Dean** is quite special for walking. It is densely wooded, with interesting villages, and monastic ruins to view. Many of its public footpaths are way-marked, as are most of the Forestry Commission trails. You'll find easy walks out of Newland, around New Fancy (great view) and Mallards Pike Lake, and a slightly longer one (3 hrs.) which takes in Wench Ford, Danby Lodge, and Blackpool

Bridge. There are picnic grounds, good car parking, and hidden old pubs where you can wet your thirst. (Contact: Forestry Commission, 231 Corstophine Rd., Edinburgh EH12 7AT, tel. 031/334–0303.)

Dining and Lodging

Dining The steady flow of tourism has brought good restaurants to this area. Chefs have no problem here with a supply of excellent produce, and there are salmon from the Rivers Severn and Wye, local lamb, and venison from the Forest of Dean. Pheasant, partridge, quail, and grouse are also abundant in season.

Highly recommended restaurants are indicated by a star ★.

Category	Cost*
$$$$	over £50
$$$	£40–£50
$$	£20–£40
$	under £20

per person, including first course, main course, dessert, and VAT; excluding drinks

Lodging You'll find all kinds of accommodations, from bed-and-breakfasts in village homes and farmhouses, to ultimate luxury in country-house hotels—formerly private mansions that have been converted for paying guests. Most hotels offer two- and three-day packages.

In Birmingham, all the best moderately priced lodging is well out of the city center. There are fairly good suburban bus and train services.

Highly recommended lodgings are indicated by a star ★.

Category	Cost*
$$$$	over £150
$$$	£90–£150
$$	£50–£90
$	under £50

All prices are for two people sharing a double room, including service, breakfast, and VAT.

Bath **Popjoy's Restaurant.** Named for the mistress of Beau Nash, the res-
Dining taurant provides an elegant setting for a fine, English-style, after-
★ theater dinner. Coffee and *petits fours* are served upstairs in a lovely Georgian drawing room. *Beau Nash House, Sawclose, tel. 0225/ 460494. Reservations advised, required after theater and weekends. Dress: casual. AE, MC, V. Closed Sat. lunch, Sun. dinner, and Mon. $$*

Tarts. This is a good spot, close to the abbey, for a meal on a sightseeing day. In a network of small and snug cellar rooms, you can choose Michel Lemoin's set menu or the daily specials. The dishes change regularly—try the sushi starter or the poached veal with lentils and capers—and then there's the chocolate truffle cake. There's a very good wine list. *8 Pierrepont Pl., tel. 0225/330280. Reservations advised. Dress: casual. AE, MC, V. Closed Sun. $$*

Number Five. Just over the Pulteney Bridge from the center of town, this airy bistro, with its plants, framed posters, and cane-backed chairs, is an ideal spot for a light lunch on a sightseeing day. The regularly changing menu includes tasty homemade soups, and such dishes as seafood terrine. *5 Argyle St., tel. 0225/444499. Reservations not needed. MC, V. Closed Mon. lunch and Sun. $*

Lodging **Royal Crescent Hotel.** This lavishly converted house, part of the

★ Royal Crescent, is an architectural treasure. The decor has been carefully designed to preserve the building's period elegance, and if some of the bedrooms are on the small side, there are ample luxuries to compensate. The Palladian villa in the garden provides extra rooms. *16 Royal Crescent, BA1 2LS, tel. 0225/319090, fax 0225/ 339401. 42 rooms with bath, including 13 suites. Facilities: restaurant. AE, DC, MC, V. $$$$*

Bath Hotel. Just a couple of minutes from the station, this very attractive modern hotel is delightfully sited beside the confluence of the River Avon and the Kennett and Avon Canal. The refurbished interior is light and cheerful with lots of plants, cane furniture, cool colors, and big windows. *Widcombe Basin, BA2 4JP, tel. 0225/ 338855, fax 0225/428941. 94 rooms with bath. Facilities: restaurant, terrace, fishing. AE, DC, MC, V. $$$*

Francis Hotel. Another successful conversion, this one from six Georgian houses, fronts a leafy square. You have a choice of period furnishings in the old part of the hotel, or more functional ones in the newer part. All the bedrooms are quite large. *Queen Sq., BA1 2HH, tel. 0225/424257, fax 0225/319715. 93 rooms with bath. Facilities: restaurant. AE, DC, MC, V. $$$*

Priory Hotel. Out beyond the Royal Crescent, the Priory is an early-19th-century Gothic building, standing in attractive grounds. Guest rooms are spacious and comfortable, the public areas elegant with fine old furniture, and big windows look out on the 2 acres of gardens. Three dining rooms serve solid, old-fashioned English fare. *Weston Rd., BA1 2XT, tel. 0225/331922, fax 0225/448276. 21 rooms with bath. Facilities: restaurant, garden, outdoor pool. AE, DC, MC, V. $$$*

★ **Queensberry Hotel.** This intimate, elegant hotel, in a quiet residential street near The Circus, is in a 1772 town house built by the architect John Wood for the Marquis of Queensberry. The hotel was completely renovated in 1988, preserving the Regency stucco ceilings and cornices and original marble tiling on the fireplaces. Each room is uniquely decorated in pastels and flower prints. Below stairs, The Olive Tree bistro serves English and Mediterranean dishes; chef Stephen Ross is one of the owners of the hotel. *Russell St., BA1 2QF, tel. 0225/447928, fax 0225/446065. 22 rooms with bath. Facilities: restaurant, bar, terrace. AE, MC, V. Closed Dec. 23– Jan. 5. $$$*

Tasburgh Hotel. This refurbished Victorian mansion, a mile from the city center, boasts views over the valley and a canal at the bottom of the 2-acre garden. The owner/managers see to it that service is attentive. *Warminster Rd., tel. 0225/425096, fax 0225/425096. 14 rooms, 10 with bath. AE, DC, MC, V. $$*

Cranleigh. Standing on the hill high above the city, Cranleigh offers wonderful views over Bath from some of the back rooms. All the comfortable bedrooms have TVs, and one has a four-poster. The excellent breakfasts are served in the dining room which looks out on the garden, but there are no evening meals. *159 Newbridge Hill,*

BA1 3PX, tel. 0225/310197. 8 rooms, 3 with bath or shower. MC, V.
$

Berkeley **Greenacres Farm.** Inglenook fireplaces and pretty bedrooms with
Lodging sweeping views are some of the features of this 300-year-old farmhouse; it is located on a horse and cattle farm. *A38 north from Bris-*
tol, then B4509. Breadstone, near Berkeley, GL13 9HF, tel. 0453/
810348. 4 rooms with bath. No credit cards. Closed Dec. $

Birmingham **Henry's.** One of a pair of Cantonese restaurants, this is located in the
Dining jewelry district, so it is a haven for lunch during a shopping spree.
The other one, Henry Wong, is 2 miles from the city center. The
menu offers more than 100 dishes, and vegetarians have plenty of
choice. *27 St. Paul's Sq., tel. 021/200–1136. Reservations advised.*
Dress: casual. AE, DC, MC, V. Closed Sun. $$

★ **Sloans.** This restaurant in the southeast shopping district comes as a
pleasant surprise (most of the best things in Birmingham are hidden
in the outskirts). The menu is fairly large, with an interesting
range—try the veal and mushrooms with a leek and truffle sauce, or
lamb with soubise sauce, and finish with a mouth-watering lime
soufflé. *27–29 Chad Sq., Hawthorne Rd., tel. 021/455–6697. Reser-*
vations advised. Dress: casual. AE, MC, V. Closed Sat. lunch and
Sun. $$

Dining and **New Hall.** The lush tree-lined drive that leads through 26 acres of
Lodging gardens and open land to this moated 13th-century manor house-
★ turned-country hotel merely hints of the luxury inside. The guest
rooms are decorated in English country style; they all (with marble-
tiled, en suite baths) have expansive views overlooking the grounds.
Some rooms of the original house have 17th-century, leaded-glass
windows that open to the garden courtyard—a popular place for
small business meetings. The public rooms feature 16th-century
oak-paneled walls and Flemish glass, 18th-century chandeliers, and
a molded stone fireplace from the 17th century. The formal restaurant is an elegant setting in which to indulge in Chef Glenn Purcell's
award-winning cuisine. *Walmley Rd., Sutton Coldfield, Birming-*
ham B76 8QX, tel. 021/378–2442 or 800/847–4358, fax 021/378–4637.
60 rooms. Restaurant: Reservations required; jacket and tie sug-
gested. Facilities: 3 meeting rooms, croquet, access to golf, squash,
badminton, and horseback riding. AE, MC, V. $$$

Swallow Hotel. Once a group of offices, this very elegant turn-of-
the-century building is now a luxuriously renovated hotel. The
building has an interior rich with dark wood and chandeliers; the
spacious bedrooms offer air-conditioning and all the latest comforts.
The **Sir Edward Elgar** formal restaurant has a fixed-price menu that
changes daily, and **Langtry's Brasserie** serves traditional British
dishes in a more casual surrounding. *12 Hagley Rd., Five Ways, B16*
8SJ, tel. 021/452–1144, fax 021/456–3442. 98 rooms with bath. Facil-
ities: 2 restaurants, indoor pool, health club. Reservations advised
for restaurant. Dress: restaurant, jacket and tie; brasserie, casual.
AE, DC, MC, V. Hotel and restaurant $$$; Brasserie $$

Lodging **Hyatt Regency.** The Hyatt Regency occupies a sheer glass tower,
right beside the Convention Centre, adding a futuristic touch to the
Birmingham skyline. The inside is as smooth as the outside—a
glass-roofed, marble-floored atrium is filled with the obligatory
plants and trees; floor-to-ceiling windows in the luxury bedrooms
give stunning views over the city. The **Number 282** restaurant, on
the ground floor, is tops for seafood. *2 Bridge St., B1 2JZ, tel. 021/*
643–1234, fax 021/616–2323. 319 rooms. Facilities: restaurant, fit-
ness center. AE, DC, MC, V. $$$$

Beech House. Beech House is outside the city center on the A5127, close to exit 6 of the M6 motorway. It is a large, comfortable Edwardian house, mock-Tudor in design. The bedrooms are comfortably furnished, and there are two lounges, one for nonsmokers. The dining room has a fine Art Nouveau stained-glass window. *21 Gravelly Hill N, Erdington B23 6BT, tel. 021/373–0620. 9 rooms, 4 with bath. No children under 5. MC, V. $*

Bourton-on-the-Water
Lodging

Coombe House. At this neat guest house you'll find an attractive garden with some unusual and interesting plants. The comfortable bedrooms have TVs and appliances for making tea or coffee. This is a no-smoking establishment. There's ample parking. *Rissington Rd., GL54 2DT, tel. 0451/821966. 7 rooms with bath. AE, MC, V. $$*

Bristol
Dining

L' Hermitage. Yet another restaurant in a converted building, this time a library. It's been elegantly redone with chandeliers and polished stairs, and the French cuisine matches the suave surroundings. The regularly changing menu features the finest local fish and meat. *30 King St., tel. 0272/226161. Reservations required. Jacket and tie required. AE, DC, MC, V. Closed Sat. lunch, Sun. $$$*

Bell's Diner. Though it's a Bristol institution, this bistro is rather hidden—take the A38 (Stokes Croft) north, then turn right into Picton Street, which will lead you to York Road. Bell's is in a converted corner shop, with Bristol prints on its pale gray walls, polished wooden floors, and open fires. The inventive menu changes regularly, with light dishes and toothsome desserts. *1 York Rd., Montpelier, tel. 0272/240357. Reservations advised. Dress: casual. MC, V. Closed Tues.–Sat. lunch. $$*

Marwick's. This restaurant, in busy downtown Bristol, is in a basement that was once a safety deposit. Black-and-white marble floors and iron grille doors retain the vault-like atmosphere, but the food is excellent. Try the fish soup, or the local turbot and sea bass. The set menus are good value. *43 Corn St., tel. 0272/262658. Reservations advised. Dress: casual. AE, MC, V. Closed Sat. lunch and Sun. $$*

Lodging

Bristol Marriott. If you'd like the amenities of an international chain hotel try the Bristol Marriott. Opened in 1992 after extensive renovations, the hotel is near the city center, where its front rooms overlook Castle Park. A traditional French menu is offered in Le Chateau restaurant, and there's also a coffee shop. *Lower Castle St., Old Market, BS1 3AD, tel. 0272/294281, fax 0272/225838. 290 rooms with bath. Facilities: 2 restaurants, bar, fitness center, indoor pool, satellite TV. AE, DC, MC, V. $$$–$$$$*

Redwood Lodge Hotel. This is a handy stopover for anyone touring by car as it is located just off A4 close to the Clifton Suspension Bridge. Modern and attractively furnished, it has a number of amenities, including pleasant woodland surroundings. *Beggar Bush La., Failand, BS8 3TG, tel. 0275/393901, fax 0275/392104. 108 rooms with bath. Facilities: restaurant, coffee shop, tennis, gym, squash, indoor and outdoor pools, in-house movies. AE, DC, MC, V. $$–$$$*

Broadway
Dining and Lodging

The Lygon Arms. Here you'll find luxury combined with Old World charm (at least in the older sections)—the Lygon has been in business since 1532 and is now part of the Savoy Hotels group. Although on the main street, it has 3 acres of formal gardens for guests to enjoy. But be warned that it is *very* popular, and can be crowded and correspondingly noisy. *High St., WR12 7DU, tel. 0386/852255, fax 0386/858611. 65 rooms with bath. Facilities: restaurant, garden, indoor pool, golf, tennis, helipad. AE, DC, MC, V. $$$$*

★ **Dormy House Hotel.** Guest rooms here overlook the Vale of Evesham from high on the Cotswold ridge. This luxurious country-house hotel has been converted from a 17th-century Cotswold farmhouse.

Bedrooms are individually and beautifully furnished, some with four-poster beds. *Willersey Hill (2 mi north from Broadway), WR12 7LF, tel. 0386/852711, fax 0386/858636. 50 rooms with bath. Facilities: restaurant, garden. AE, DC, MC, V. Closed Christmas period. $$$*

Buckland
Dining and
Lodging
★
Buckland Manor. As an alternative to the razzmatazz of Broadway, try this exceptional hotel 2 miles away, just off B4632. Parts of the building date back to Jacobean times and there are pleasant old pictures and fine antiques everywhere. The garden is lovely, and the place is so peaceful you can hear a swan's feather drop. *Near Broadway, WR12 7LY, tel. 0386/852626, fax 0386/853557. 11 rooms with bath. Facilities: restaurant, garden, outdoor pool, tennis, riding, croquet. AE, MC, V. Closed mid-Jan.–early Feb. $$$$*

Burford
Dining and
Lodging
Bay Tree. Quietly located away from Burford's bustle, the atmospheric Bay Tree is in a 16th-century stone house, visited in its prime by both Elizabeth I and James I. It recently had a face-lift and has emerged more comfortable than ever. Try for a room in the main house. The restaurant, looking out into the garden, serves a three-course set menu of mainly English dishes. The stress is on healthy eating. *Sheep St., OX18 4LW, tel. 0993382/2791, fax 099382/3008. 22 rooms with bath. Facilities: no-smoking restaurant, garden. AE, DC, MC, V. $$$*

Charingworth
Dining and
Lodging
Castle Coombe Manor House. This lodging is partly 14th-century, though as a manor it dates back to the Normans. Just 10 miles northeast of Bath, it stands in a large park that is ideal for exploring, and on the edge of a pretty village. The bedrooms are very comfortably furnished, with lavish bathrooms attached; some are in separate cottages. There are log fires in the public rooms, and antiques everywhere. The restaurant serves imaginative cuisine—try the fish casserole with water chestnuts, or the French-inspired soufflé specialties. *Castle Coombe SN14 7HR, tel. 0249/782206, fax 0249/782159. 36 rooms with bath. Dress in dining room: jacket and tie. Facilities: tennis, swimming pool, helipad. AE, DC, MC, V. $$$–$$$$*

Charingworth Manor. Views of the Cotswold countryside are limitless from this 14th-century manor-house hotel. A new section in light golden stone was added in 1988. Each room is named after a previous owner, and is individually done in English floral fabrics, with antique and period furniture. Rooms in the old manor have the best views and original oak beams. *Charingworth, 3 mi east of Chipping Campden, GL55 6NS, tel. 0386/78555, fax 0386/78353. 27 rooms with bath, including 3 suites. Facilities: restaurant, health club, indoor pool, tennis, sauna, solarium. AE, DC, MC, V. $$$*

Charlecote
Lodging
The Charlecote Pheasant. Farm buildings have been converted into a pleasant, country-house hotel across from Charlecote Park (follow B4086 northeast out of Stratford). The fine, 17th-century redbrick has been matched in the new wing, and the bedrooms—some with four-poster beds—in both the old and the new buildings are prettily decorated and have ceiling beams. *CV35 9EW, tel. 0789/470333, fax 0789/470222. 67 rooms with bath. Facilities: restaurant, bar, pool, tennis court, solarium, Turkish baths, sauna, exercise room, pool tables. AE, DC, MC, V. $$–$$$*

Cheltenham
Dining
Le Champignon Sauvage. Everything is made on the premises here, including bread and vinegar! Relaxing music—classical at lunch, soft jazz in the evening—accompanies French dishes like wild rabbit stuffed with coriander in light shrimp and Madeira sauce. There is an excellent "Tasting Menu" until 8:30 PM. *24 Suffolk Rd., tel. 0242/*

573449. Reservations advised. Dress: casual. AE, MC, V. Closed Sat. lunch and Sun. $$$

Redmond's. Views of the Malvern Hills from Cleeve Hill outside Cheltenham enhance the atmosphere of this Continental-style restaurant. The tables are decked with fine linen, crystal, and silver, and specialties include fresh salmon and sweetbreads. *On A46, 4 mi north of Cheltenham, Cleeve Hill, tel. 0242/672017. Reservations required. Jacket and tie suggested. AE, MC, V. Closed lunch Mon. and Sat., dinner Sun. $$$*

Bonnets Bistro. This is a busy, colorful, but still elegant bistro, run with ebullience by the owner/chef, Paul Lucas. Favorite dishes include the Scottish salmon with a grapefruit sauce, the ragout of lamb, or the baked Alaska. *12 Suffolk Rd., tel. 0242/260666. Reservations advised. Dress: casual chic. AE, DC, MC, V. Closed Sat. lunch, all day Sun., 3 weeks June. $$*

Lodging **Queens Hotel.** Overlooking Imperial Gardens from the center of The Promenade, this classic Regency building has welcomed visitors to Cheltenham since 1838. The hotel's decor is very British, and every bedroom is individually designed. It has a garden. *The Promenade, GL50 1NN, tel. 0242/514724, fax 0242/224145. 74 rooms with bath. Facilities: restaurant. AE, DC, MC, V. $$$$*

★ **Lypiatt House.** This splendid Victorian house is an award-winning bed-and-breakfast—only a short walk from central Cheltenham. The bedrooms are a comfortable size, with modern bathrooms. There's a small dining room and attentive service from the two young owners. *Lypiatt Rd., GL50 2QW, tel. 0242/224994. 10 rooms with bath or shower. MC, V. $$*

Stretton Lodge Guest House. Bedrooms here are decorated with color-coordinated curtains and quilt covers, and comfortably furnished. Although set in a quiet Regency street, the lodge is only 10 minutes' walk from Cheltenham's busy center. *Western Rd., GL50 3RN, tel. 0242/528724. 9 rooms with bath. AE, MC, V. $$*

★ **Regency House.** This attractive guest house is quite exceptional—it's beautifully furnished with antiques and period-style wallpaper. The front rooms have views of trees in the square, and the back ones look out at a garden. All rooms have TVs, tea and coffee making appliances, and hair dryers. *50 Clarence Sq., Pittville, GL050 4JR, tel. 0242/582718, fax 0242/262697. 10 rooms with bath. MC, V. $–$$*

Chipping **Cotswold House Hotel.** Though it is in the center of a small country
Campden town, the Cotswold House has an acre of stone-walled garden at the
Dining and back and a flair for dramatic design inside. The bedrooms here are
Lodging small masterpieces of theme decor. There's an Indian room, a French room, and, for homesick travelers, a Colonial Room. The restaurant is also striking, with windows onto the garden. The game and fish dishes are always interestingly presented. *The Square, GL55 6AN, tel. 0386/840330, fax 0386/840310. 15 rooms with bath. Facilities: restaurant, garden, coffee shop. Restaurant: jacket and tie suggested. AE, DC, MC, V. Lunch Sun. only. $$$*

Lodging **Noel Arms Hotel.** In the heart of Chipping Campden, this inn was built for foreign wool traders in the 14th century and is the oldest inn in the town. It retains its period atmosphere with exposed beams and stonework, even though it has been recently enlarged. Its individually decorated bedrooms—some with four-posters—offer every modern comfort. *High St., GL55 6AT, tel. 0386/840317, fax 0386/841136. 26 rooms with bath. Facilities: restaurant. AE, MC, V. $$*

Clearwell
Dining
★
Wyndham Arms. This may be a modest, Old World village inn, but its restaurant offers sophisticated cuisine. Try the local salmon or one of the excellent steaks, followed by *zuppa inglese*—a mouth-watering chocolate, rum, and meringue concoction. *Near Coleford, tel. 0594/833666. Reservations required. Dress: casual. AE, DC, MC, V. $$*

Lodging
Clearwell Castle. Peacocks strut around this recently refurbished neo-Gothic castle built in 1727 and restored in 1929. Lounges are large and imposing; the gatehouse bedrooms are decorated like country cottages, while those in the castle have four-poster beds and are individually furnished. There are plenty of antiques scattered about. *GL16 8LG, tel. 0594/832320, fax 0594/835523. 15 rooms with bath. Facilities: restaurant, gardens. AE, DC, MC, V. $$$*

Easton Grey
Dining and Lodging
Whatley Manor. This was once a manor/farmhouse, built of warm Cotswold stone, and is now thickly covered with creeping vines. Guest rooms are large, furnished in appropriate period style, with great views over the River Avon. The restaurant serves interesting set menus with local produce well to the fore. *Near Malmesbury SN16 0RB, tel. 0666/822888, fax 0666/826120. 29 rooms with bath. Facilities: garden, outdoor pool, tennis, sauna, solarium, croquet. AE, DC, MC, V. $$$*

Gloucester
Dining
College Green. With a keen notion of the right meal in the right place, this upstairs restaurant, with views out over the cathedral, serves classic English cooking—beef casserole, duck with apricot sauce—and provides a respectable wine list. *9 College St., tel. 0452/520739. Reservations advised. Dress: casual. AE, MC, V. Closed Sun. $$*

Lodging
Hatherley Manor. Because the manor stands on 37 acres of grounds 2 miles north of Gloucester, it is fairly quiet unless one of the frequent conferences is going on. It is a 17th-century house, recently renovated, and there's a four-poster honeymoon suite. *Down Hatherley La., GL2 9QA, tel. 0452/730217, fax 0452/731032. 56 rooms with bath. Facilities: restaurant, garden, croquet, helipad. AE, DC, MC, V. $$$*

Hunstrete
Dining and Lodging
★
Hunstrete House Hotel. In 90 acres of parkland, with its own deer park, this hotel seems more like a friendly, though luxurious, country house. Fresh flowers and log fires mark the passing seasons, and discreet, efficient service adds to the cossetting effect. Hunstrete is north of A368 just past Marksbury, 8½ miles west from Bath. *Near Chelwood, BS18 4NS, tel. 0761/490578, fax 0761/490732. 24 rooms with bath, 1 cottage suite. Facilities: restaurant, outdoor pool, tennis court, croquet lawn. MC, V. $$$$*

Kenilworth
Dining
Restaurant Bosquet. This attractive, small restaurant serves set menus cooked by the French *patron*, with regularly changing à la carte selections. Try the veal with wild mushrooms, or breast of duck with cherry sauce. The desserts are mouth-watering. It is mainly a dinner spot, though lunch is available on request. *97A Warwick Rd., tel. 0926/52463. Reservations advised. Dress: casual. AE, MC, V. Closed dinner Mon. $$*

Lower Slaughter
Dining and Lodging
Washbourne Court. This fine 17th-century building stands amid 4 acres of ground beside the River Eye. The interior has stone-flagged floors, beams, and open fires. The bedrooms in the main building have a deliberately country feel to them, while they are more modern in the converted barn and cottages. The food in the restaurant is appropriately traditional English. *Lower Slaughter, GL54 2HS, tel.*

0451/822143, fax 0451/821045. 15 rooms and suites, all with bath or shower. AE, MC, V. $$–$$$

Stow-on-the-Wold
Lodging

Fosse Manor. This lovely manor-house hotel, just out of town (1¼ mi south on A429), has a long-standing reputation for solid comfort and service. It has recently been refurbished. There are golf, hunting, and riding available nearby. *Fosse Way, GL54 1JX, tel. 0451/830354, fax 0451/832486. 20 rooms, 18 with bath. Facilities: restaurant, garden. AE, DC, MC, V. $$$*

Stow Lodge Hotel. Set well back from the main square of Stow-on-the-Wold in its own quiet gardens, the lodge is a typical Cotswold manor house; its large, open fireplaces provide added warmth in the winter. *The Square, GL54 1AB, tel. 0451/830485. 20 rooms with bath. Facilities: restaurant. AE, DC. Closed Dec. 25–Jan. 31. $$*

Stratford-upon-Avon
Dining

★ **Box Tree Restaurant.** This attractive dining spot in the Royal Shakespeare Theatre overlooks the River Avon, and has some of the best food in town. It's worth eating here, either before or after a play. Specialties include *noisettes* of lamb, and poached fillet of Scottish beef. *Waterside, tel. 0789/293226. Reservations required. Jacket and tie required. AE, MC, V. Closed when theater is closed. $$$*

★ **The Opposition.** Just up from the theater, this restaurant, set in a converted 16th-century building, offers pre- and post-theater dining. The American and Continental dishes on the menu are popular with the locals. Try the Cajun chicken and the aubergine pie. *13 Sheep St., tel. 0789/269980. Reservations advised. Dress: casual. MC, V. $$*

River Terrace. At this informal cafeteria in the theater, the meals and snacks are crowd-pleasers. They include lasagna, shepherd's pie, salads, sandwiches, and cakes, with wine and beer available. *Royal Shakespeare Theatre, Waterside, tel. 0789/293226. No reservations. Dress: casual. No credit cards. Closed when theater is closed. $*

Lodging

Alveston Manor. Across the river from the Royal Shakespeare Theatre, this redbrick Elizabethan manor house has a modern extension. In the old manor house, rooms have individual, Old World style. Decor is modern in the extension, but all rooms have up-to-date bathrooms. *Clopton Bridge, CV37 7HP, tel. 0789/204581, fax 0789/414095. 108 rooms with bath. Facilities: restaurant. AE, DC, MC, V. $$$$*

★ **Ettington Park Hotel.** This marvelously restored, huge Victorian house makes an ideal spot to stay if you want to see the plays at Stratford but don't want to cope with the crowds. It stands in its own grounds—which contain a ruined church—and looks across tranquil river meadows haunted by herons. The bedroom decor complements Victorian Gothic furniture. The restaurant has extremely good food, imaginatively cooked. *6 mi from Stratford southeast on A34. Alderminster, CV37 8BS, tel. 0789/450123, fax 0789/450472. 48 rooms with bath. Facilities: restaurant, health club with pool, tennis, fishing. AE, DC, MC, V. $$$$*

Shakespeare Hotel. Minutes from the theater and right in the heart of Stratford, this half-timbered Elizabethan town house is also close to most of the Shakespeare Trust properties. Inside, it has been comfortably modernized. *Chapel St., CV37 6ER, tel. 0789/294771, fax 0789/415111. 63 rooms with bath. Facilities: restaurant. AE, DC, MC, V. $$$$*

Falcon Hotel. Founded as a tavern in 1640, the hotel still has the atmosphere of a friendly inn. The heavily beamed rooms in the oldest part of the building are small and quaint; the modern extension has international-standard bedrooms. *Chapel St., CV37 6HA, tel. 0789/*

205777, fax 0789/414260. 73 rooms with bath. Facilities: restaurant. AE, DC, MC, V. $$$

★ **Caterham House.** Built in 1830, this comfortable, old building is in the center of town, within an easy walk of the theater. You may spot an actor or two among the guests. Its bedrooms are individually decorated in early 19th-century style, featuring brass beds and antique furniture. *58 Rother St., CV37 6LT, tel. 0789/267309. 14 rooms, 2 with bath. Facilities: restaurant. MC, V. $*

Thornbury **Thornbury Castle.** This is the kind of baronial surroundings where
Dining and Douglas Fairbanks might come sliding down a velvet drape.
Lodging Thornbury has everything a genuine 16th-century castle needs:
★ huge fireplaces, antiques, paintings, and mullioned windows, to say nothing of an extensive garden. The standards of comfort and luxury are legendary, and people come from all over to eat in the restaurant. *12 mi north of Bristol, off A38. Castle St., BS12 1HH, tel. 0454/281182, fax 0454/416188. 18 rooms with bath. Reservations required for the restaurant. AE, DC, MC, V. Closed first week of Jan. $$$$*

Upper **Lords of the Manor Hotel.** A characteristic 16th-century Cotswold
Slaughter manor house, "the Lords" also has its own fishing stream. It offers
Dining and comfort and a warm welcome, and its location, Upper Slaughter, is a
Lodging quintessential Cotswold village. (The name has nothing to do with mass murder. It comes from the Saxon word *sloh* which means a marshy place.) Extensive refurbishment has meant additional bedrooms available in converted outbuildings, now more modern than those in the main house. *GL54 2JD, tel. 0451/820243, fax 0451/820696. 29 rooms, all with bath. Facilities: fishing, restaurant. AE, DC, MC, V. $$$$*

Warwick **Fanshawe's.** Fanshawe's is centrally located on the market square in
Dining Warwick and carries a wide-ranging menu. The restaurant is friendly with cheerful prints and vases of flowers. You can have simple open sandwiches if you just want a light lunch, or try the saddle of lamb with tomato or the cod with chervil butter. Game also served in season. *22 Market Pl., tel. 0926/410590. Reservations advised. Dress: casual. AE, MC, V. Open Tues.–Sat. $-$$*

Dining and **Tudor House Inn.** Here is a simple hotel and restaurant of genuine
Lodging character. The Tudor House dates from 1472, having survived the great Warwick fire of 1694 by being situated on the road to Stratford, beyond the West Gate, outside the devastated medieval town center. The rooms are beamed and basic, and the floors creak satisfactorily. The great hall, with its cavernous fireplace and gallery, acts as the bar and restaurant, and the inexpensive food served here is hearty and plentiful. This inn is a must for collectors of historic atmosphere. *90–92 West St., CV34 6AW, tel. 0926/495447, fax 0926/492948. 11 rooms, 6 with bath. AE, DC, MC, V. $$*

The Arts

Festivals The **Bath International Festival** is 46 years old in 1995 (May 6–June 11). Concerts, dance, and exhibitions will be held in and around Bath. Some take place in the Assembly Rooms and the Abbey, and opening night festivities are held in the Royal Crescent. *Bath Festival Office, Linley House, 1 Pierrepont Pl., Bath BA1 1JY, tel. 0225/462231.*

Cheltenham's annual **International Festival of Music** (July) highlights new compositions, often conducted by the composer, together with classical repertory pieces. The town's **Festival of Literature**

(October) brings together world-renowned authors, actors, and critics. *Contact Festival Office, Town Hall, Imperial Sq., Cheltenham GL50 1QA, tel. 0242/521621.*

The **Stratford-upon-Avon Shakespeare Birthday Celebrations** take place on the weekend nearest to April 23, with colorful receptions, processions, a special performance of one of the plays, and other events. *Details from Shakespeare Center, Henley St., Stratford-upon-Avon CV37 6QW, tel. 0789/204016.*

Theater The **Royal Shakespeare Theatre** (Stratford-upon-Avon CV37 6BB, tel. 0789/205301) usually puts on five of Shakespeare's plays in a season lasting from March to January each year. In the **Swan Theatre** at the rear, plays by Christopher Marlowe and Ben Jonson are staged. In **The Other Place,** some of the RSC's most advanced work is done. Seats go fast, but "day of performance" and returned tickets are often available.

The **Theatre Royal** in Bath, a superb example of a Regency playhouse, restored in 1982, has a year-round program that often includes pre- or post-London tours. You have to reserve the best seats well in advance, but you can line up for same-day standby seats or standing room. Check the location of your seats—sightlines can be poor. *Box Office, Sawclose, Bath BA1 1ET, tel. 0225/448844.*

The **Birmingham Repertory Theatre,** founded in 1913, is equally at home in modern or classical work. There is a restaurant on the ground floor. *Centenary Square, Broad St., tel. 021/236-6771.*

The **Alexandra Theatre** in Birmingham welcomes touring companies on their way to or from London's West End. It is also home to the **D'Oyly Carte Opera Company,** world-renowned for Gilbert and Sullivan operas. *Station St., tel. 021/633-3325.*

Ballet The second company of the Royal Ballet, which used to be based at Sadler's Wells in London, has become the **Birmingham Royal Ballet.** It is based at the **Hippodrome Theatre,** which also hosts visiting companies like the Welsh National Opera. *Hurst St., tel. 021/622-7486.*

Concerts The **City of Birmingham Symphony Orchestra** performs regularly in **Symphony Hall,** also the venue for visiting artists. *International Convention Centre, tel. 021/212-3333.*

10 East Anglia

Bury St. Edmunds,
Cambridge, Norwich, Lincoln

Occupying an area of southeastern England that juts out, knoblike, into the North Sea, East Anglia comprises the counties of Essex, Norfolk, Suffolk, and Cambridgeshire.

Despite its easy access from London, East Anglia (with the notable exception of Cambridge) is relatively unfamiliar to tourists. It was a region of major importance in ancient times—as evidenced by the Roman settlements at Colchester and Lincoln—while in medieval times, trade in wool with the Netherlands saw the East Anglian towns become strong and independent. But the region was bypassed by the Industrial Revolution and has remained somewhat of a backwater ever since. The deflection of industrialization preserved much of the special cultural character and the stunning landscape—which inspired two of the greatest English painters in that genre, Thomas Gainsborough, who was born in Sudbury, Suffolk, and John Constable, also born and bred in Suffolk. The cities and villages of East Anglia have kept intact their ancient architecture, much of it financed with the wealth from medieval wool, once prized across Europe. Few parts of Britain can boast so many stately churches and half-timbered houses. The towns are more like large villages; even the largest city, Norwich, still only has a population of around 120,000.

The fens in Norfolk are unforgettable; the water in the marshes and dikes reflects the arching sky that stretches to seemingly infinite horizons, a sky deeply blue and with ever-changing cloudscapes. The sunsets here are to be treasured. The fens resemble areas of Holland directly across the North Sea, and, indeed, much of the drainage work here was carried out by Dutch engineers. In both Norfolk and Suffolk, the reed-bordered Broads make a gentler landscape of canals and lakes that are ideal for boating and alive with birds and animals. Along the coast, stretches of sand dunes alternate with low cliffs and with areas—in some cases whole communities—lost to the encroaching sea.

Northwest of East Anglia, the marshes continue, across the Wash and into Lincolnshire, whose historic towns of Lincoln and Boston in particular are worth visiting. Here, you're very much off the main routes—a worthy detour if you'd like to see more of hidden England.

Essential Information

Important Addresses and Numbers

Tourist Information
East Anglia Tourist Board, Toppesfield Hall, Hadleigh, Suffolk IP7 7DN, tel. 0473/822922.
Boston: Blackfriars Arts Centre, Spain La., tel. 0205/356656.
Bury St. Edmunds: 6 Angel Hill, tel. 0284/764667.
Cambridge: Wheeler St., tel. 0223/322640.
Colchester: 1 Queen St., tel. 0206/712920.
Ely: Oliver Cromwell's House, 29 St. Mary's St., tel. 0353/662062.
Great Yarmouth: Town Hall, Hall Quay, tel. 0493/846345.
Ipswich: Town Hall, Princes St., tel. 0473/258070.
King's Lynn: Old Gaol House, Saturday Market Pl., tel. 0553/763044.
Lincoln: 9 Castle Hill, tel. 0522/529828.
Norwich: Guildhall, Gaol Hill, tel. 0603/666071.

Travel Agencies
American Express: 25 Sidney St., Cambridge, tel. 0223/351636.
Thomas Cook: 18 Market St., Cambridge, tel. 0223/67724; Grafton Centre, Cambridge, tel. 0223/322611; 4 Cornhill Pavement, Lincoln, tel. 0522/510070; 15 St. Stephens St., Norwich, tel. 0603/621547.

Car-Rental Agencies **Cambridge: Avis,** 245 Mill Rd., tel. 0223/212551; **Budget Rent-a-Car,** 303–305 Newmarket Rd., tel. 0223/323838; **Hertz,** Willhire Ltd., Barnwell Rd., tel. 0223/414600.

Colchester: Avis, 213 Shrub End Rd., tel. 0206/41133; **Hertz,** Willhire Ltd., Rota House, Cowdray Ave., tel. 0206/866559.

Lincoln: Europcar Ltd., Hartford Motors, 186 Wragby Rd., tel. 0522/531947.

Norwich: Avis, Norwich Airport, Cromer Rd., tel. 0603/416719; **Budget Rent-a-Car,** Denmark Opening, Sprowston Rd., tel. 0603/484004; **Hertz,** Norwich Airport, Cromer Rd., tel. 0603/404010.

Arriving and Departing by Car, Train, and Bus

By Car From London, Cambridge (54 mi) is just off M11. At exit 9, M11 connects with A11 to Norwich (114 mi); A45, off A11, goes to Bury St. Edmunds. A12 from London goes through east Suffolk via Colchester, Ipswich, and Great Yarmouth. For Lincoln (131 mi), take A1 via Huntingdon, Peterborough, and Grantham to A46 at Newark-on-Trent. A more scenic alternative is to leave A1 at Grantham and take A607 to Lincoln.

By Train **British Rail** serves the entire region from London's Liverpool Street Station (tel. 071/928–5100); in addition, there are trains to Cambridge and Lincoln from King's Cross Station (tel. 071/278–2477), as well as from Liverpool Street. Average travel times are 60 minutes to Colchester, 60–90 minutes to Cambridge, 1 hour 50 minutes to Norwich, and 2 hours to Lincoln.

By Bus **National Express** (tel. 071/730–0202) serves the region from London's Victoria Coach Station. Average travel times: 2½ hours to Bury St. Edmunds, 2 hours to Cambridge, 2 hours to Colchester, 4 hours to Lincoln, and 3 hours to Norwich.

Getting Around

By Car East Anglia has few fast main roads. The principal routes are those covered above (*see* Arriving and Departing By Car), but once off the A roads, traveling within the region often means taking country lanes with many twists and turns. These are also used by slow-moving farm vehicles, but as the countryside is mainly flat, open land, visibility is excellent.

By Train You can get a one-day, round-trip ticket for the East Suffolk line from Ipswich to Lowestoft (50 mi), which lets you disembark to explore any of the little towns en route. A seven-day Regional Rover ticket for unlimited travel in East Anglia is also available for £35 from major regional train stations. For local travel information, call the stations at Cambridge (tel. 0223/311999), Colchester (tel. 0206/564777), Ipswich (tel. 0473/693396), Lincoln (tel. 0302/340222), and Norwich (tel. 0603/632055).

By Bus **Eastern Counties** (tel. 0603/613613) provides local bus services for Norfolk and parts of the surrounding counties. An **Eastern Counties Explorer ticket** (available on board the bus) gives a day's unlimited travel on the whole network for £4.20 adults, £2.70 children, £3.45 senior citizens. Cambridgeshire's largest bus company is **Cambus** (tel. 0223/423554), which also sells daily and weekly tickets valid for unlimited travel within the city of Cambridge and the county.

Guided Tours

Qualified guides for walking tours of the five touring bases—Bury St. Edmunds, Cambridge, Colchester, Lincoln, and Norwich—can be booked through the respective TICs.

Guide Friday (tel. 0223/62444) operates a city tour of Cambridge every 30 minutes on weekends and every hour during the week. The tour takes in the Backs, the colleges, and the American war cemetery.

Vaudrey Catering (tel. 0728/628226) offers a tour of rural Suffolk by horse and carriage, followed by lunch or dinner.

Byways Bicycles (tel. 0728/668764) has a choice of bicycles for hire, with planned routes to choose from in Suffolk.

Ely Tourist Information Guide Service (tel. 0353/662062) offers guided walks through the cathedral city; it's essential to book in advance.

Exploring East Anglia

The first of East Anglia's four tours starts in the ancient university city of Cambridge, detours to the cathedral town of Ely to the north, then moves south and east to the attractive small towns whose prosperity was built on the medieval wool trade. They have lovely buildings and disproportionately large churches. The second tour starts in Norwich, East Anglia's regional capital and a town with atmosphere to spare, then visits the lake-strewn Broads and the beaches and salt marshes of the North Sea coast. The third tour begins in Colchester, in the south of East Anglia, and takes in the sweep of the Suffolk Heritage Coast, which runs northeast through Southwold. A final jump takes you away to Lincoln in the north, with its tall, fluted cathedral towers rising above the rolling hills, then around the Lincolnshire Wolds to Boston, from where the Pilgrims tried, without success, to sail to the New World.

Highlights for First-time Visitors

Audley End House: Tour 1
Blickling Hall: Tour 2
Bury St. Edmunds: Tour 1
Cambridge—Queen's College and King's College Chapel: Tour 1
Colchester Castle: Tour 3
Ely Cathedral: Tour 1
Holkham Hall: Tour 2
Lincoln Cathedral: Tour 4
Norwich Cathedral: Tour 2
Suffolk Heritage Coast: Tour 3

Tour 1: Cambridge and the Suffolk Wool Churches

Numbers in the margin correspond to points of interest on the East Anglia and Cambridge maps.

With the spires of its university buildings framed by towering trees and expansive meadows, its medieval streets and passages enhanced by gardens and riverbanks, the city of **Cambridge** is among the loveliest in England. Situated on a bend of the River Cam, on the edge of the once uninhabited and inhospitable Great Fen, the city has been settled since prehistoric times. It was a Roman town, and later the

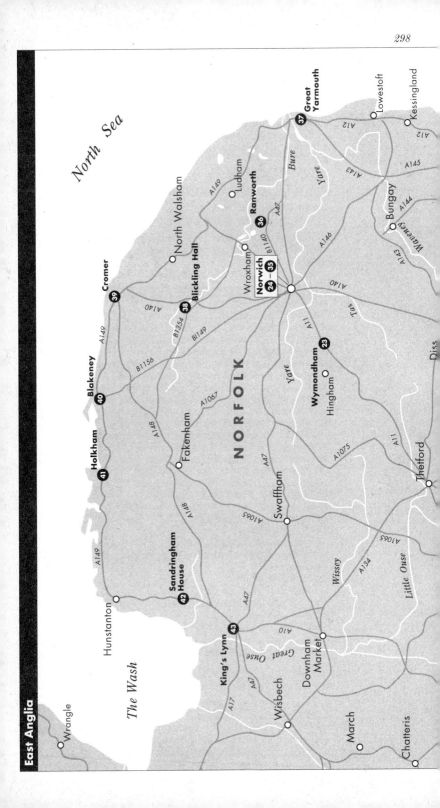

East Anglia

North Sea

The Wash

NORFOLK

Great Yarmouth **37**

Lowestoft

Kessingland

A12

A145

A12

A143

Bungay

A144

Waveney

A143

Ludham

Ranworth **36**

North Walsham

Bure

Yare

A47

A146

B1140

Blickling Hall **38**

Wroxham

Norwich
24 – 35

A140

Cromer **39**

A140

B1354

B1149

A11

Tas

A1151

Blakeney **40**

B1156

A1067

Yare

Wymondham **23**

Hingham

Diss

Holkham **41**

A148

Fakenham

A47

A1075

A11

Thetford

A148

Swaffham

A1065

Wissey

A134

A1065

Little Ouse

Sandringham House **42**

A149

Hunstanton

King's Lynn **43**

A47

A10

Great Ouse

Downham Market

Wrangle

A17

A47

Wisbech

March

Chatteris

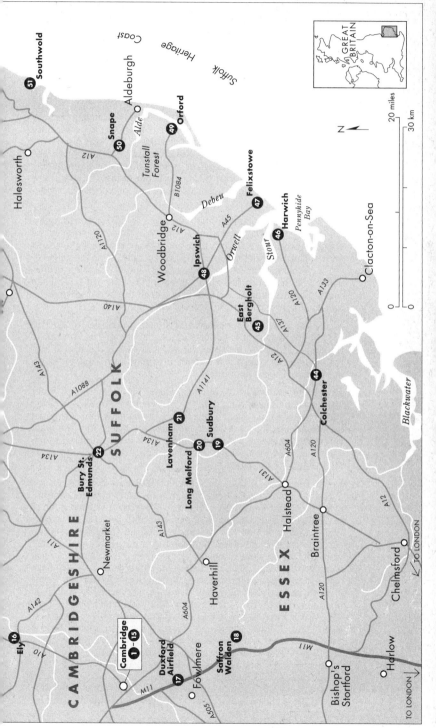

GREAT BRITAIN

N

20 miles
30 km

CAMBRIDGESHIRE

Ely 16

Newmarket

Cambridge 1 15

Duxford Airfield 17

Fowlmere

Saffron Walden 18

TO LONDON

Bishop's Stortford

Harlow

TO LONDON

ESSEX

Chelmsford

Braintree

Halstead

Haverhill

SUFFOLK

Bury St. Edmunds 22

Lavenham 21

Long Melford 20

Sudbury 19

Colchester 14

East Bergholt 45

Clacton-on-Sea

Blackwater

Harwich 46

Felixstowe 47

Pennyhide Bay

Stour

Orwell

Ipswich 48

Woodbridge

Deben

Orford 49

Aldeburgh

Snape 50

Southwold 51

Halesworth

Tunstall Forest

Suffolk Heritage Coast

Alde

A12
A1120
A143
A1088
A140
A134
A1141
A131
A604
A120
A133
A137
A12
A45
B1084
A11
A142
A10
M11
A505
A12
A130

Cam helped to protect it from Danish raiders. During the Middle Ages, Cambridge gained its real importance with the founding of the university, which is still the heart of the city. Several college buildings survive from the medieval period, and most generations since have added buildings. These were often designed by the best architects of their respective periods and financed by royal or aristocratic foundations, with the result that today the city and university provide an illustrated history of the best of English architecture.

For centuries the University of Cambridge has been among the very greatest universities, rivaled in Britain only by Oxford, and, since the time of its most famous scientific alumnus, Sir Isaac Newton, it has outshone Oxford in the natural sciences. In recent years, the university has taken advantage of its scientific prestige, pooling its research facilities with various hightech industries. The city is now surrounded by space-age factories, and a new prosperity has enlivened the city center.

The 25 colleges are built around a series of courts, or quadrangles, whose velvety lawns are the envy of many an amateur gardener. As students and fellows (faculty) live and work in these courts, access for tourists is restricted, especially in term time (when the university is in session). Tourists are not normally allowed into college buildings other than chapels and dining halls. The peace of the college courts is quite remarkable, and just to stroll through them gives an immediate sense of over 700 years of scholastic calm.

❷ The oldest college is **Peterhouse,** on Trumpington Street, founded in 1281 by the Bishop of Ely. Parts of the dining hall date from 1290; the chapel, in late Gothic style, dates from 1632. On the river side of the buildings is a large and tranquil deer park—without any deer, but with some good apple trees.

❸ Across the road stands **Pembroke College** (1347), whose first court has some buildings dating from the 14th century. On the south side Christopher Wren's chapel—his first major commission, completed in 1665—looks like a distinctly modern intrusion. You can walk through the college, around a delightful garden, and past the fellows' bowling green. The British Poet Laureate, Ted Hughes, attended Pembroke College.

Down Pembroke Street and Downing Street, on St. Andrew's
❹ Street, is **Emmanuel College** (1584), whose chapel and colonnade are again by Christopher Wren. Among the portraits of famous members of the college hanging in Emmanuel Hall is one of John Harvard, founder of Harvard University. Indeed, the college was an early center of Puritan learning; a number of the Pilgrim Fathers were Emmanuel alumni, and they remembered their alma mater in
❺ naming Cambridge, Massachusetts. The gateway of **Christ's College** (1505), also on St. Andrew's Street, bears the enormous coat of arms of its patroness, Lady Margaret Beaufort, mother of Henry VII. In the dining hall there are portraits of John Milton and Charles Dar-
❻ win, two of the college's more famous students. **Sidney Sussex College** (1436), located where St. Andrew's Street becomes Sidney Street, is a smaller foundation with many 17th- and 18th-century buildings. Oliver Cromwell was a student here in 1616; the Hall contains his portrait, and his head has been buried here since 1960.

Time Out Walk across Jesus Green to the **Fort St. George,** a riverside pub overlooking the college boathouses, with plenty of outdoor space for summer drinking.

Cambridge

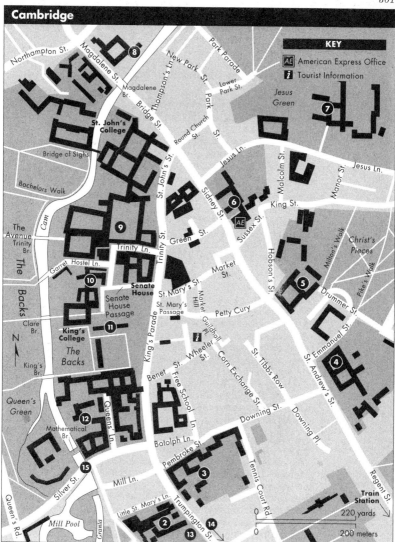

Christ's College, **5**

Emmanuel College, **4**

Fitzwilliam Museum, **13**

Jesus College, **7**

King's College Chapel, **11**

Magdalene College, **8**

Pembroke College, **3**

Peterhouse, **2**

Queens' College, **12**

Sidney Sussex College, **6**

Silver Street Bridge, **15**

Trinity College, **9**

Trinity Hall, **10**

University Botanic Garden, **14**

In contrast to the compact Sidney Sussex College is its spacious
❼ neighbor, **Jesus College** (1496). Parts of the chapel here were built in
the Middle Ages for the nunnery of St. Radegund, which existed on
the site before the college. Victorian restoration of the building includes some Pre-Raphaelite stained-glass windows. Unique in Cambridge, this college incorporates cloisters, also a remnant of the
nunnery.

Across Magdalene (pronounced "maudlin") Bridge, a cast-iron 1820
❽ structure, is **Magdalene College,** distinguished by pretty redbrick
courts. It was a hostel for Benedictine monks for over 100 years before the college was founded in 1542. The college's Pepys Library
contains the books and desk of the 17th-century diarist, Samuel
Pepys. *Admission free. Open Apr.–Sept., daily 11:30–12:30, 2:30–
3:30.*

Back over the bridge, on St. John's Street, **St. John's** is Cambridge's
second-largest college, founded in 1511 by Henry VII's mother,
Lady Margaret Beaufort. Its structures lie on two sites: from the
original buildings, a copy of the Bridge of Sighs in Venice reaches
across the Cam to the mock-Gothic New Court (1825), whose white
crenellations have earned it the nickname "the wedding cake."

❾ Farther south, **Trinity College**—founded in 1546 by Henry VIII (replacing a 14th-century educational foundation)—is the largest
college in either Cambridge or Oxford, with nearly 700 undergraduates. It, too, straddles the river and can sometimes be approached
by a bridge that joins it with neighboring St. John's College. This
approach gives a fine view of Christopher Wren's magnificent library, colonnaded and seemingly constructed as much of light as of
stone. Many of Trinity's features match its size, not least its 17th-
century "great court" and the massive and detailed gatehouse that
houses Great Tom, a giant clock that strikes each hour with high and
low notes. Past alumni include Sir Isaac Newton; Lords Byron, Tennyson, and Macauley; and William Thackeray; more recently, Prince
Charles was an undergraduate here in the late 1960s.

Cambridge's celebrated **"Backs"** are gardens and meadows running
down to the River Cam's banks; some colleges back onto them. A
good vantage point from which to appreciate the Backs is Trinity's
❿ neighbor, **Trinity Hall** (1350), where you can sit on a wall by the river
and watch students in punts manipulate their poles under the ancient bridges of Clare and King's. Between the bridges is one of the
few strictly university buildings (i.e., not part of a particular college), the **Senate House,** a classical structure of the 1720s used for
graduation ceremonies and other university events.

Across Trinity Street from the Senate House, the church of **St. Mary
the Great** is known as the "university church," and has its origins in
the 11th century, though the present building dates from 1478.
Cranmer, Ridley, and Latimer all preached here; the main reason to
visit today is for the view from the tower, which—at 113 feet high—
offers a superb view over central Cambridge. *Market Hill. Admission: £1 adults, 20p children. Open daily 10–6.*

Time Out   **The Copper Kettle** is a strategically placed coffee shop, on King's Parade, and a traditional students' hangout, with a view of King's College.

⓫ **King's College Chapel** is for most people the high point of a visit to
Cambridge. It is one of the most beautiful buildings in England. Begun in the mid-15th century by Henry VI, it was not completed for

100 years, mainly through lack of funds. Built in the late-Gothic, English style known as Perpendicular, its great fan-vaulted roof is supported only by a tracery of soaring side columns, and it seems to float over a huge space, lit by ever-changing light from the vast and ancient stained-glass windows. Rubens's *Adoration of the Magi* hangs behind the altar. Every Christmas Eve, a festival of carols is broadcast from the chapel to the world.

⑫ Tucked away on Queens Lane, next to the wide lawns that lead down from King's to the Backs, is **Queens' College** (1446), named after the respective consorts of Henry VI and Edward IV. The secluded "cloister court" looks untouched since its completion in the 1540s. Queens' boasts a very different kind of masterpiece from King's College Chapel in the **Mathematical Bridge** (best seen from the Silver Street road bridge), an arched wooden structure that was originally held together without fastenings. The present bridge, dating from 1902, is securely bolted.

⑬ Walk south down Trumpington Street, past elegant 18th-century houses, to the **Fitzwilliam Museum,** a classical building with an outstanding collection of art (including paintings by John Constable, Gainsborough, and the French Impressionists) and antiquities. The opulent interior displays its treasures to marvelous effect, with the Egyptian section in the lower gallery particularly outstanding. Exhibits here range from inch-high figurines and burial goods to mummies, painted coffins, and stone inscriptions. In addition to its archaeological collections, the Fitzwilliam contains a large display of English Staffordshire and other pottery, as well as a fascinating room full of armor and muskets. The upstairs gallery is devoted to paintings and sculpture. The museum has a coffee bar and restaurant. *Trumpington St., tel. 0223/332900. Admission free but £2 donation preferred. Open Tues.–Sat., lower galleries 10–2, upper galleries 2–5; Sun. all galleries 2:15–5. Guided tours every Sun. at 2:30 PM.*

⑭ Five minutes' beyond, past lovely Brookside whose houses overlook a small stream, is the **University Botanic Garden,** in Bateman Street, off Trumpington Road. It was laid out in 1846 and contains, among its rare specimens, a limestone rock garden. *Cory Lodge, Bateman St., tel. 0223/336265. Admission free Mon.–Sat., Sun. £1 adults, 50p children. Open May–Sept., Mon.–Sat. 8–6, Sun. 10–6; Nov.–Jan., Mon.–Sat. 8–4, Sun. 10–4; Feb.–Apr., Oct., Mon.–Sat. 8–5, Sun. 10–5.*

⑮ The **Silver Street Bridge** and **Mill Lane** are good places to rent punts on the river. You can either punt along the Backs to Magdalene Bridge and beyond or punt upstream to **Grantchester,** a village celebrated by Rupert Brooke, one of a generation of poets lost in World War I. Grantchester is a long way for the inexperienced punter, so you may prefer to make the scenic 2-mile trip on foot. The path roughly follows the river, going through college playing fields and the Grantchester Meadows.

Time Out Walkers (or punters) to Grantchester can reward themselves with a pint and lunchtime food at the **Red Lion** or the **Green Man** pubs. Both are centrally located by the river.

Numbers in the margin correspond to points of interest on the East Anglia map.

About 4 miles west of Cambridge (by A1303 and A45), you can visit the **American Military Cemetery** at Madingley, now more or less a suburb of Cambridge. It contains the graves of 3,811 U.S. service-men who lost their lives during World War II.

16 From Cambridge, make a single foray north to **Ely,** 15 miles on A10. Ely is the Fenland's "capital," the center of what used to be a sepa-rate county called, appropriately, the Isle of Ely. It is a small, dense town dominated by its cathedral. The shopping area and little mar-ket square lie to the north and lead down to the attractive riverside, while the well-preserved medieval buildings of the cathedral grounds and the King's School (which trains cathedral choristers) spread out to the south and west.

Ely Cathedral, on one of the few ridges in the whole of the Fens, can be seen for miles. Known affectionately as the Ship of the Fens, the cathedral was begun by the Normans in 1083, on the site of a Bene-dictine monastery founded by the Anglo-Saxon Queen Etheldreda in the year 673. In the center can be seen one of the marvels of medie-val architecture, the octagonal lantern—a sort of stained-glass sky-light of vast proportions. Much of the decorative carving of the 14th-century Lady Chapel was defaced during the Reformation (mostly by knocking off the heads of the statuary), but enough of the delicate tracery-work remains to show its original beauty. The fan-vaulted, carved ceiling remains intact, as it was too high for the iconoclasts to reach.

A major program of restoration is being undertaken on the cathe-dral's main fabric. The diocese of Ely was one of the first to charge admission to a cathedral, not only to help with the restoration but to cover the enormous maintenance costs of a building this size, which run to £1,000 per day. The cathedral also includes a stained-glass museum, up a flight of 41 steps. *Chapter Office, The College, tel. 0353/667735. Cathedral admission: £2.80 adults, £2.10 children un-der 16 and senior citizens (up to two accompanied children free); free on Sun. Open Apr.–Oct., daily 7–7; Nov.–Mar., daily 7:30–5. Stained-Glass Museum, tel. 0353/778645. Admission: £1.50 adults, 70p children and senior citizens. Open Mar.–Oct., Mon.–Sat. 10:30–4, Sun. noon–3; Nov.–Feb., Sat. and Sun. noon–3.*

Time Out **The Steeplegate Tearooms and Gallery** (Steeplegate St.), on the 16th-century street that originally led to the churchyard of St. Cross but now connects the cathedral grounds with High Street, offers light food as well as high-quality local crafts, especially wood carv-ings.

A short walk from the cathedral, across the green and along St. Mary's Street, lies a half-timbered medieval house, which for 10 years from 1636 was the home of Oliver Cromwell and his family. **Oli-ver Cromwell's House** now contains an exhibit on its most famous oc-cupant and audiovisual presentations both about Cromwell and about the draining of the local fens. The house is also the site of Ely's tourist information center. *29 St. Mary's St., tel. 0353/662062. Ad-mission: £1.50 adults, £1 children and senior citizens. Open May–Sept., daily 10–6; Oct.–Apr., Mon.–Sat. 10–5:15. Closed Dec. 25–26 and Jan. 1.*

From Ely, return to Cambridge to begin a swing round the wool churches southeast of the city.

17 Eleven miles south of Cambridge, at junction 10 of M11, is **Duxford Airfield.** This former Royal Air Force base, used in the Battle of Britain and assigned to the U.S. Air Force in the latter years of World War II, is now the Imperial War Museum's aviation branch, set up in the 1970s to house an extensive collection of fighters, bombers, and ancillary equipment. By skillful use of the original hangars, control tower, and other structures, the whole place powerfully evokes a World War II air base in action. In addition, there are historic examples of civil aircraft, including a prototype Concorde, and occasional demonstration flights. *Duxford, tel. 0223/835000. Admission: £5.95 adults, £2.95 children under 16, £3.95 senior citizens, £16.25 family ticket; children under 5 free. Open Mar.–Oct., daily 10–6; Nov.–Mar., Sat. and Sun. 10–4 (Mon.–Fri. limited viewing only by appointment). Closed Dec. 24–26, Jan. 1.*

Time Out It is a short drive from Duxford to the **Chequers** (High St.) at Fowlmere (off A505), an elegant 16th-century coaching inn visited by Samuel Pepys in 1660. The Chequers has excellent bar food and outdoor tables in a pretty garden.

A few miles south, just to the east of M11 (junction 9), is the town of ⑱ **Saffron Walden,** which owes its name to its saffron fields. It has many typical East Anglian, timber-frame buildings, some with elaborate pargeting (decorative plasterwork), especially on the walls of the former Sun Inn, which was used by Cromwell during his campaigns. In a similar military vein, the old **Grammar School** here was the World War II headquarters of the U.S. Air Force's 65th Fighter Wing.

A mile or so west of Saffron Walden is palatial **Audley End House,** a famous example of Jacobean (early 17th-century) architecture. Remodeled in the 18th and 19th centuries, it shows the architectural skill of Sir John Vanbrugh, Robert Adam, and Biagio Rebecca as well as original Jacobean work in the magnificent Great Hall. You can also enjoy a leisurely walk around the park, which was landscaped by Capability Brown in the 18th century. *Tel. 0799/522399. Admission: house and park, £5.20 adults, £2.60 children under 16, £3.90 senior citizens; park only, £2.85 adults, £1.40 children, £2.15 senior citizens. Open Apr.–Sept., Wed.–Sun. and national holidays; park noon–5, house 1–5.*

⑲ **Sudbury,** 15 miles east of Saffron Walden, has more impressive, half-timbered East Anglian houses, as well as three fine local churches, all financed from the profits of an early silk-weaving industry. The town is also known as the fictionally famed "Eatanswill" of Dickens's *Pickwick Papers.* In real life, Thomas Gainsborough, one of the greatest English portrait and landscape painters, was born here in 1727; a statue of the artist holding his palette stands on Market Hill. His family's home is now a museum, containing paintings by the artist and his contemporaries, as well as an arts center. Although **Gainsborough's House** presents an elegant Georgian facade, with touches of the 18th-century neo-Gothic style, the building is essentially Tudor. In the walled garden behind the house, a mulberry tree planted in 1620 is still growing. *46 Gainsborough St., tel. 0787/ 372958. Admission: £2 adults, £1 children, £1.50 senior citizens, free in Dec. Open Apr.–Oct., Tues.–Sat. 10–5, Sun. and national holidays 2–5; Nov.–Mar., Tues.–Sat. 10–4, Sun. 2–4.*

⑳ **Long Melford,** one of the great wool towns of the area, lies just 2 miles north of Sudbury on A134. By approaching it from this direction, you will appreciate the effect of the 2-mile-long main street as it broadens to include green squares and trees and finally opens out into the large triangular green on the hill. The town's buildings are an attractive mixture—mostly 15th-century half-timbered or Georgian—and many house antiques shops. Telegraph poles are banned from both Long Melford and Lavenham, to preserve the towns' ancient look. On the hill, the **Church** is unfortunately obscured by Trinity Hospital, thoughtlessly built there in 1573. But close up, the delicate, flint flushwork and huge, 16th-century Perpendicular windows that take up most of the church's walls have great impact, especially as the nave is 150 feet long. Much of the original stained glass remains, notably the Lily Crucifix window. The Lady Chapel has an unusual interior cloister.

Now a National Trust property, **Melford Hall,** distinguished from the outside by its turrets and topiaries (trees trimmed into decorative shapes), is a mid-16th-century house with a fair number of 18th-century additions. Much of the porcelain and other fine pieces in the house come from the *Santissima Trinidad*, a ship captured by one of the house's owners in the 18th century, when she was sailing back to Spain full of gifts from the emperor of China. The hall is set in parkland leading down to a walk by Chad Brook. *Tel. 0787/880286. Admission: £2.60 adults, £1.30 children; tours £2 adults, £1 children. Open Apr., Sat. and Sun. 2–5:30; May–Sept., Wed., Thurs., Sat., Sun. 2–5:30; Oct., Sat. and Sun. 2–5:30; tours May–Sept., Wed., Thurs.*

Time Out **The Bull** (Hall St.), a black-and-white, timber-framed, medieval inn with antique furniture and an open fire, serves good bar lunches and real ale in Long Melford.

Half a mile north of Long Melford Green is **Kentwell Hall,** a redbrick Tudor manor house, surrounded by a wide moat. It was built at much the same time as Melford Hall and has a similar interior design, though it was heavily restored inside after a fire in the early 19th century. Today, a restoration program is again under way, and the original gardens are being re-created. Two or three weekends a year (from late June to late July), a reenactment of Tudor life is performed here by costumed "servants" and "farmworkers," with great panache and detail. Other theatrical and crafts events also take place here. *Tel. 0787/310207. Admission: house and gardens £4 adults, £2.50 children, £3.40 senior citizens; increased fees for special events. Open Apr.–June, Sun. noon–5; late July–Sept., daily noon–5.*

㉑ Continue north from Kentwell Hall up A134 for a mile and a half, then turn right onto a side road leading to **Lavenham,** a town virtually unchanged since the height of its wealth in the 15th and 16th centuries. The weavers' and wool merchants' houses occupy not just one show street but most of the town. These are timber-framed in black oak, the main posts looking as if they could last for another 400 years. The grandest building of them all, the **Guildhall** (1529), is owned by the National Trust and is open to visitors. *Market Pl., tel. 0787/247646. Admission: £2.40 adults, 60p children. Open Apr.–Oct., daily 11–5.*

The **Wool Hall** was torn down in 1913, but it was reassembled immediately at the request of Princess Louise, sister of the then-reigning king, George V. In 1962, it was joined to the neighboring **Swan Hotel** (*see* Dining and Lodging, *below*), a splendid Elizabethan building in its own right. The Swan Inn had a long history as a coaching inn, and in World War II served as the special pub for the U.S. Air Force's 48th Bomber Group.

Lavenham Church is set apart from the village. The church was built with wool money by local cloth merchant Thomas Spring between 1480 and 1520. The height of its tower (141 feet) was meant to surpass those of the neighboring churches. In this it succeeded, though the rest of the church is of perfect proportions, with a spacious design similar to that of Long Melford. A long nave and attractive exterior flush work are its most obvious features, while the southern porch is particularly decorative.

Time Out Have lunch or tea at **The Priory,** a timber-framed building on Water Street with a garden growing over 100 varieties of herbs, or at the **Great House** (Market Pl.), where you can dine on fine, French-inspired food in the garden.

㉒ From Lavenham take A1141 and A134 north for 12 miles to **Bury St. Edmunds,** which rises from the pleasant valley of the Rivers Lark and Linnet. The town owes its unusual name and its initial prosperity to the martyrdom of Edmund, last king of the Anglo-Saxon kingdom of East Anglia, who was hacked to death by the pagan Danes in 869. He was subsequently canonized and his shrine attracted pilgrims, settlement, and commerce. In the 11th century the building of a great Norman abbey confirmed the town's importance as a religious center. Today only the Norman Gate Tower, the fortified Abbot's Bridge over the Lark, and a few picturesque ruins remain, for the abbey was yet another that fell during Henry VIII's dissolution of the monasteries. You can get some idea of the abbey's enormous scale, however, from the surviving gate tower on Angel Hill. The ruins are now the site of the **Abbey Botanical Gardens,** with rare trees, including a Chinese tree of heaven originally planted in the 1830s. The abbey walls enclose separate, specialized gardens. One of these, the yew-hedged **Appleby Rose Garden,** was founded with the royalties from *Suffolk Summer,* a memoir by a U.S. serviceman, John Appleby, who had been stationed at nearby Rougham during World War II.

Originally there were three churches within the abbey walls, which gives some idea of the extent of the grounds, but only two have survived. **St. Mary's,** built in the 15th century, is the finer, with a blue-and-gold embossed "wagon" (i.e., barrel-shaped) roof over the choir. Mary Tudor, Henry VIII's sister and queen of France, is buried here. **St. James's** also dates from the 15th century; the brilliant paintwork of its ceiling and the stained-glass windows gleaming like jewels are the result of restoration in the 19th century by the architect Sir Gilbert Scott. Don't miss the memorial (by the altar) to an event in 1214, when the barons of England gathered here to take a solemn oath to force King John to grant the Magna Carta. The cathedral's original **Abbey Gate** was destroyed in a riot, and it was rebuilt in the 14th century on clearly defensive lines—you can see the arrow slits. *Tel. 0284/757490. Admission free. Open weekdays 7:30 AM–½ hr. before dusk, weekends 9 AM–dusk.*

A walk along **Angel Hill** is a journey through the history of Bury St. Edmunds. Along one side, the Abbey Gate, cathedral, Norman Gate Tower, and St. Mary's Church make up a continuous display of medieval architecture. On the other side, the elegant Georgian houses include the **Athenaeum,** an 18th-century social and cultural meeting place, still the site of concerts and recitals, and the splendid **Angel Hotel** (*see* Dining and Lodging, *below*), the scene of Sam Weller's meeting with Job Trotter in Dickens's *Pickwick Papers.* Dickens stayed here while he was giving readings at the Athenaeum.

Farther along Angel Hill, the road becomes Crown Street, and off to the left, down Honey Hill, the **Manor House Museum** faces the abbey's grounds. The Georgian mansion contains excellent art and horological collections: paintings, clocks, watches, furniture, costumes, and ceramics from the 17th to the 20th centuries. The clocks and watches in particular are extraordinarily beautiful, and there's a café and gift shop, too. *Honey Hill, tel. 0284/757072. Admission: £2.50 adults, £1.50 children. Open Mon.–Sat. 10–5, Sun. 2–5.*

Time Out Opposite the Greene King brewery, on Crown Street at the end of Angel Hill, try Greene King draft ale and local sausages in the lofty back room of the **Dog and Partridge,** where the rough brick walls are hung with dray horse mementos.

The shopping streets of Bury St. Edmunds follow an ancient grid pattern from Abbey Gate to Cornhill, with Abbeygate Street in the center. The public buildings within this area have a varied grandeur; there is, first, the medieval **Guildhall;** next, 18th-century classicism as interpreted by Robert Adam in the **Art Gallery**, and then Victorian classicism in the **Corn Exchange.**

The Art Gallery has no permanent collections; instead there are changing exhibits of paintings, sculpture, and crafts, as well as frequent concerts. *Market Cross, Cornhill, tel. 0284/762081. Admission: 50p adults, 30p children and senior citizens. Open Tues.–Sat. 10:30–4:30, Sun. by appointment.*

Walk down to the end of Cornhill and turn right for the 12th-century **Moyse's Hall,** probably the oldest building in East Anglia, which houses in the original tiny rooms local archaeological collections. It also has a macabre display relating to the Red Barn murder, a case that gained notoriety in an early 19th-century blood-and-thunder play, *Maria Marten, or the Murder in the Red Barn;* Maria Marten's murderer was executed in Bury St. Edmunds in 1828. *Buttermarket, tel. 0284/757072. Admission free. Open Mon.–Sat. 10–5, Sun. 2–5.*

To travel from Bury St. Edmunds to Norwich, first take A134/A11 north and east for 30 miles to Wymondham (pronounced Windham). The road passes through **Thetford Forest,** the largest forest in the country, covering almost 150 square miles. The principal landowners now are the Ministry of Defence and the Forestry Commission. Much of the northern part is reserved for military exercises and is clearly marked "Battle Area." In King's Forest and **West Stow Country Park,** however, it is possible to wander freely along paths among oak, beech, and mature pine. If you are lucky you will see wild deer. Look for the reconstructed Saxon village in a forest clearing; there's a visitor center and a shop here, where you can obtain more information about local nature trails through the woodlands. *West Stow Country Park, between West Stow and Icklingham, tel. 0284/ 728718. Admission: park free; Saxon village £2.50 adults, £1.20 children, £1.50 senior citizens, £7 family ticket. Park open summer, daily 8–8, winter, daily 8–5; Saxon village open daily 10–5.*

㉓ Wymondham is an ancient market town with timber-framed houses overhanging the sidewalks, steep streets lined with a variety of fascinating architecture, and a magnificent 14th-century abbey church that seems far too grand not to be a cathedral. The soaring roof has great hammerbeams decorated with flying angels, while the altar screen gleams with golden figures. The remaining structure is only a part of the original building, but it gives a good idea of just how huge Wymondham abbey must have been.

Another 9 miles along A11 will bring you to Norwich.

Tour 2: Norwich and the Broads

Numbers in the margin correspond to points of interest on the East Anglia and Norwich maps.

 Established by the Saxons because of its fine trading position on the Rivers Yare and Wensum, **Norwich,** now a modern county town, still has its heart in the triangle between the two waterways, dominated by the castle and cathedral. The inner beltway follows the line of the old city wall, much of which is still visible, and it is worth driving around after dark to see the older buildings, thanks to skillful flood-lighting, uncluttered by their much newer neighbors.

By the time of the Norman Conquest, Norwich was one of the largest towns in England, though much was destroyed by the Normans to create a new town endowed with grand buildings. Grandest of these is **Norwich Cathedral,** whose spire, at 315 feet, is visible everywhere. You cannot see the building itself until you go through St. Ethelbert's Gate. The cathedral was begun in 1096 by Herbert de Losinga, who had come from Normandy in 1091 to be its first bishop. His splendid tomb is by the high altar. The plain west front and dramatic crossing tower, with its austere, geometrical decoration, are distinctively Norman. The remarkable length of the nave is immediately impressive; unfortunately, the similarly striking height of the vaulted ceiling makes it a strain to study the delightful colored bosses (ornamental knobs at junction points), where Bible stories are illustrated with great vigor and detail—look for the Pharaoh and his cohorts drowning in a vivid Red Sea. Note also the wood carving on the choir-stall misericords (semi-seats), a wonderful revelation of medieval skill and religious beliefs. The stalls were originally intended for the Benedictine monks who ran the cathedral, and the beautifully preserved cloister is part of what remains of their great priory. *62 The Close, tel. 0603/764385. Admission free but donation requested. Open mid-May–mid-Sept., daily 7:30–7; mid-Sept.–mid-May, daily 7:30–6; free guided tours June–Sept., Mon.–Fri. 11 AM and 2:15 PM, Sat. 11 AM.*

Past the buildings of various periods on the cathedral grounds, a path leads down to the ancient water gate, **Pulls Ferry.** The grave of Norfolk-born nurse Edith Cavell, the British World War I heroine shot by the Germans in 1915, is outside the cathedral.

From Pulls Ferry retrace your steps to St. Ethelbert's Gate, proceed to the traffic lights, and turn left. The **castle,** on the hill to your right, is also Norman, but the wooden bailey (wall) on the castle mound was later replaced with a stone keep (tower). The thick walls and other defense works attest to the castle's military function, but the unique, decorated stone facing of the walls makes the castle seem like a child's illustration. For most of its history the castle has been a prison, and executions took place here well into the 19th century. There are daily guided tours of the battlements and dungeons. An excellent museum here features displays of different facets of Norfolk's history, including a gallery devoted to the Norwich School of painters who, like the Suffolk artist John Constable, devoted their work to the everyday Norfolk landscape and seascape as revealed in the East Anglian light. *Norwich Castle, tel. 0603/223624. Admission: £2 adults, £1 children, £1.20 senior citizens. Open Mon.–Sat. 10–5, Sun. 2–5.*

At the castle, turn right at the traffic lights on the right, cross over, and go down the steps to the market. Behind the market, the early 20th-century **City Hall** has one of the best views in Norwich from its

Castle, **27**

City Hall, **28**

Elm Hill, **31**

Norwich
Cathedral, **25**

Pulls Ferry, **26**

Sainsbury
Centre for the
Visual Arts, **35**

St. Peter
Hungate, **32**

St. Peter
Mancroft, **29**

Strangers
Hall, **33**

Tombland, **30**

University of
East Anglia, **34**

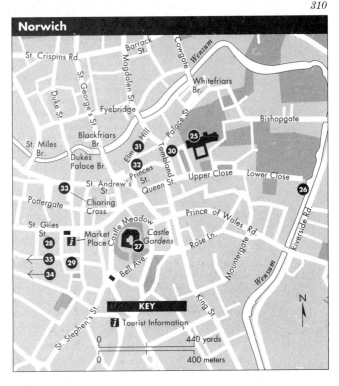

Norwich

KEY

i Tourist Information

0 ————————— 440 yards

0 ————————— 400 meters

㉙ steps, between the bronze Norwich lions. On your right rises the elaborate church tower of **St. Peter Mancroft,** below are the brightly colored awnings of the market stalls, and opposite looms the castle. Narrow lanes that used to be the main streets of medieval Norwich **㉚** lead away from the market and end at **Tombland** by the cathedral. Neither a graveyard nor a plague pit, Tombland was the site of the Anglo-Saxon trading place, now a busy thoroughfare. In Tombland **㉛** turn left and take the second turning on the left to **Elm Hill,** a cobbled and pleasing mixture of Tudor and Georgian houses, now mostly given over to gift shops and tearooms.

㉜ At the southern end of Elm Hill, **St. Peter Hungate,** a 15th-century former church, displays church art and furnishings; here you can try your hand at brass rubbing. *Princes St., tel. 0603/667231. Admission free; brass rubbing £1–£5. Open Mon.–Sat. 10–5.*

From Princes Street, follow St. Andrew's Street to Charing Cross, **㉝** where you'll find **Strangers Hall,** a good example of a medieval merchant's house. Built originally in 1320, it went on growing until the mid-18th century and is now a museum of domestic life, each room appropriately furnished with pieces from various periods, from Tudor to Victorian. *Charing Cross, tel. 0603/667229. Admission: £1 adults, 50p children, 70p senior citizens. Open Mon.–Sat. 10–5.*

The River Yare was once a busy commercial waterway; now most of the traffic is for pleasure. During the summer months, a boat trip starting from Roaches Court at Elm Hill will give you a fresh perspective on Norwich; longer trips are available down the Rivers Wensum and Yare to the nearer Broads. A marked riverside walk follows the Wensum from St. George's Bridge to the city wall at Carrow Bridge.

Time Out **The Adam and Eve** is said to be Norwich's oldest pub, dating back to 1249, convenient from both the river and the cathedral on Bishopsgate. The pub's terrace, set up for outdoor dining, and its generous servings of bar food, make it popular with the lunchtime crowd.

In complete contrast to Norwich's historical composition is the mod-
❸❹ ern **University of East Anglia** (UEA), built during the great expansion of higher education in the 1960s. Its site on the slopes of the River Yare, 1½ miles west of the town center, was used by architect Denys Lasdun to give a dramatic, stepped-pyramid effect. The campus is linked by walkways that open out at different levels and center on a fountain courtyard.

❸❺ Close by, the award-winning **Sainsbury Centre for the Visual Arts,** which was opened in 1972, holds the remarkable private art collection of the Sainsbury family, owners of a huge supermarket chain. The collection includes a remarkable quantity of tribal art and 20th-century works, especially Art Nouveau. There is a coffee bar and restaurant on the premises. Bus Nos. 12, 14, 23, 26, 27, 33, and 34 run from Norwich Castle Meadow to UEA, providing access to both the university and the Sainsbury Centre. *Earlham Rd., tel. 0603/56060. Admission: £1 adults, 50p children and senior citizens. Open Tues.–Sun. noon–5.*

Numbers in the margin correspond to points of interest on the East Anglia map.

For an excellent example of what the Broads have to offer, take B1140 east out of Norwich, and turn left at Panxworth (about 7 miles) for **Ranworth Broad.** A 450-yard nature trail leads through oak woods, swamp, and reed beds to the center, where the moored floating Broadland Conservation Center has an exhibition on the ecology of the Broads. *Ranworth, tel. 060549/479. Admission: £1 adults, 75p students, children, and senior citizens. Open Apr.–Oct., Sun., Tues.–Thurs. 10–5, Sat. 2–5.*

❸❻ The view from the church tower at **Ranworth** is well worth the climb. It provides a special perspective on the Broads, the horizons vanishing away to infinity. Inside the church are 12 beautiful screen paintings of saints from the early 15th century, all painstakingly restored in the 1960s. Look for St. Michael's dragon with seven heads.

Until recently, rivers were the main routes of trade for the Broads—much more important than roads. Traditional Norfolk sailing barges, known as wherries, plied their trade all over the area from their main port at Great Yarmouth, 20 miles east of Norwich on A47. In the late 19th and early 20th century, the leisure potential of these fine boats was first realized, and some were built as wherry yachts for luxurious vacations afloat. The *Albion*, based at Ludham, is the only working wherry left, maintained by the Norfolk Trust, while the *Norada* and the *Olive* are historic wherry yachts based at Wroxham. All may be chartered for cruises of up to 12 people. Alternatively, there are one- to three-hour summer riverbus tours from the bridge at Wroxham along the River Bure; call Broads Tours (tel. 0603/782207) for information. *The Albion, Norfolk Wherry Trust, tel. 0603/413720. The Olive and the Norada, tel. 0603/782470.*

❸❼ **Great Yarmouth** itself is now the busiest seaside resort on the Norfolk coast, with a long (if undistinguished) seafront promenade backed by cafés, guest houses, and amusement arcades. The sands here are usually fairly clean, though the water can be bitingly cold and the offshore oil and gas exploration platforms do little to encourage a dip. Dickens stayed at a hotel on the waterfront here in 1848. Unless you book well in advance in summer, you're unlikely to be able to emulate him.

38 Directly north of Norwich (14 mi), A140 leads to **Blickling Hall** (turn left onto B1354, then right, down a little lane). Now a National Trust property, it belonged to a succession of historical figures, including Sir John Fastolf, the model for Shakespeare's Falstaff; Anne Boleyn's family, who owned it until Anne was executed by her husband, Henry VIII; and finally Lord Lothian, an ambassador to the United States. This redbrick Jacobean house is framed by a mighty yew hedge, and the grounds include a formal flower garden and parkland whose woods conceal a temple, an orangery, a pyramid, and a secret garden. Blickling Hall houses a National Trust's textile conservation workshop, fine tapestries, and a long gallery (127 ft.) with an intricate plasterwork ceiling decorated with Jacobean emblems. The superb 17th-century staircase is also worth examining. *Blickling, tel. 0263/733084. Admission: house and garden £4.90 adults, £2.40 children; garden only £2.50 adults, £1.25 children. House open Apr.–Oct., Tues., Wed., Fri.–Sun., and national holidays 1–5; gardens open July and Aug., daily noon–5.*

39 Return to A140 and go 13 miles north to the coast at **Cromer,** one of the prettiest seaside villages in this area. (From Great Yarmouth, take the largely coastal B1159 north, a journey of around 40 mi; the road cuts slightly inland at times but offers a fine series of marine and rural views.) The town sits high above a fine beach and features an attractive 15th-century church. Plenty of hotels and pubs offer good views of the sea below, while in the back streets you should be able to find locally caught crabs—a delicacy.

West of Cromer is a string of villages along the A149 coast road, with harbors used for small fishing boats and yachts. You can take a boat **40** trip from **Blakeney,** 20 miles from Cromer, one of the most attractive of the coastal villages, past Blakeney Point, a National Trust nature reserve, to see the seals on the sandbanks and the birds on the dunes.

Time Out **The Crown** (The Buttlands), at Wells-next-the-Sea, 8 miles west of Blakeney, is a comfortable old inn facing a square of attractive Georgian houses. In one of the various rooms, or the conservatory overlooking the garden, you can have lunch: well-cooked, generously portioned pub food accompanied by hand-pumped real ale.

---

41 At **Holkham,** 10 miles farther along A149 from Blakeney, is **Holkham Hall,** amid a huge expanse of sandy beaches, dunes, and salt marsh backed by pine woods. The estate is the seat of the Coke (pronounced "Cook") family, the earls of Leicester. In the late 18th century, Thomas Coke went on the fashionable "grand tour" of the Continent, returning with art treasures and determined to build a house according to the new Italian ideas; the result was this Palladian palace, one of the most splendid in Britain. The magnificence of the Marble Hall pales in comparison to the great hall, which is 60 feet high and brilliant with gold and alabaster. Twelve stately rooms follow, each filled with Coke's collection of masterpieces, including paintings by Gainsborough, Van Dyck, Rubens, Raphael, and other old masters. This transplant from neoclassical Italy is set in extensive parkland landscaped by Capability Brown in 1762. *Near Wells-*

next-the-Sea, tel. 0328/710227. Admission: £3 adults, £1.50 children. Open Easter–Sept., Sun.–Thurs. 1:30–5.

Fifteen miles west of Holkham, the coast road turns sharply south at the coastal resort of **Hunstanton.** Nine miles south and just off this road is **Sandringham House,** one of the queen's country residences, used for royal family vacations. This huge, redbrick Victorian mansion was clearly designed for enormous country-house parties, with a ballroom, billiard room, and bowling alley, as well as a shooting lodge on the grounds. The house and gardens are closed when the queen is in residence, but the woodlands, nature walks, and museums (the latter housed in the old stables) remain open, as does the church, medieval but in heavy Victorian disguise. *Sandringham, tel. 0553/772675. Admission: house and gardens £3 adults, £1.50 children, £2 senior citizens; grounds and museum £2 adults, £1 children, £1.50 senior citizens. Open Apr.–Sept., Mon.–Thurs. 11–5, Sun. noon–5.*

Time Out Five miles north of Sandringham, at Caley Mill, homemade teas (light meals) are served at **The Old Miller's Cottage** in the middle of Norfolk's lavender fields.

The tour finishes in **King's Lynn,** 8 miles south of Sandringham, close to the mouth of the Great Ouse on the Wash. Now an important container and fishing port, King's Lynn gained importance in the 15th century, especially for trade with northern Europe. **Trinity Guildhall,** with its striking checkered stone front, is now the Civic Hall of the Borough Council and is not generally open to the public, although you can visit it during the King's Lynn Festival (*see* The Arts, *below*) and on occasional guided tours in the summer; inquire at the tourist information center. However, the **Regalia Rooms,** housed in the Guildhall Undercroft and entered through the Old Gaol (jail) House (now the tourist information center), exhibit charters dating from the time of King John (reigned 1199–1216), as well as the 14th-century chalice known as King John's Cup. *Saturday Market Pl., tel. 0553/763044. Admission: £1 adults, 50p children and senior citizens. Open Easter–Oct., Mon.–Sat. 10–5.*

Another early 15th-century guildhall, St. George's, forms part of the **King's Lynn Arts Centre,** now a thriving arts and theater complex administered by the National Trust, and the focal point for the annual King's Lynn Festival. There is also an art gallery, and a crafts fair every September. The center's coffee bar serves snacks all day. St. George's Guildhall is the largest surviving English medieval guildhall, and it adjoins a Tudor house and a warehouse used during the Middle Ages. *27 King St., tel. 0553/774725. Admission free. Open weekdays 10:30–5, Sat. 10–12:30.*

Tour 3: Colchester and the Aldeburgh Coast

Less than an hour's journey from London is **Colchester,** England's oldest recorded town. Recent archaelogical research indicates a settlement at the head of the Colne estuary at least as early as 1100 BC. At the time of Christ it was the center of the domain of Cunobelin (Shakespeare's Cymbeline), who was king of the Catuvellauni. On Cunobelin's death, the Romans invaded in AD 43 and the Emperor Claudius—who was supposed to have entered Colchester on an elephant—built his first stronghold here and made it the first Roman colony in Britain, appropriately renaming the town *Colonia Victricensis* ("Colony of Victory"). Colchester received its royal charter in

1189 from King Richard the Lionheart; throughout 1989, the 800th-year anniversary, special celebrations were held.

Evidence of Colchester's four centuries of Roman history is visible everywhere. Although the Romans prudently relocated their administrative center to London after the Celtic Queen Boudicca burned the place in AD 60, Colchester was important enough for them to build massive fortifications around the town. The **Roman Walls**—dating largely from the reign of Emperor Vespasian (AD 69–79)—can still be seen, especially along Balkerne Hill (to the west of the town center), with its splendid Balkerne Gate, and along Priory and Vineyard streets, where there is now a Roman drain exposed halfway along. In Maidenburgh Street, near the castle, the remains of a Roman amphitheater have been discovered—the curve of the foundations is outlined in the paving stones of the roadway, and part of the walls and floor have been exposed and preserved in a modern building, where they can be viewed through a window.

Colchester has always had a strategic importance and there is still a military garrison here; a tattoo (military spectacle) is held in even-numbered years. The **castle** was built by William the Conqueror in about 1076, one of the earliest to be built of stone (largely taken from the Roman ruins), and although all that remains is the keep (main tower), it is the largest in Europe. The castle was actually built over the foundations of the huge Roman Temple of Claudius, and in the vaults you can descend through 1,000 years of history. A superb museum inside contains an ever-growing collection of prehistoric and Roman remains, mostly from Colchester itself. Spread across two floors of the castle vaults, highly engaging displays chart the original Celtic inhabitation of the region before recording in detail the Roman invasion and subsequent occupation. One of the finest of all Roman Britain's bronze statues—of Mercury, messenger of the gods—stands right by the reception desk, while other exhibits tell of everyday Roman life. Magnifying glasses are available for a closer examination of Roman coins. Children, especially, will appreciate being able to try on a toga, a slave's neck chain, or an actor's mask. To really make your visit come alive, take a guided tour of the Roman vaults and castle dungeons (daily in July and August, weekends in April–June and September). *Tel. 0206/712931 or 712932 (information about all Colchester's museums is available at these numbers). Admission £2 adults, £1 children and senior citizens. Open Apr.–Oct., Mon.–Sat. 10–5, Sun. 2–5; Nov.–Mar., Mon.–Sat. 10–5; closed Good Friday and Christmas week.*

Next door to the castle, at the edge of the castle park, is **Hollytrees,** a pleasing early-18th-century brick house with a collection of costumes, dolls, and toys. It's currently closed for reorganization; consult the tourist office for the latest information. *High St. Admission free. Open Tues.–Sat. 10–noon and 1–5.*

Opposite Hollytrees is a group of graceful 18th-century townhouses, two of which have been turned into an art gallery known as **The Minories.** Recently taken over by the Colchester and District Visual Arts Trust (CADVAT), this gallery displays intriguing changing exhibitions of art and applied art; call ahead for a current program of events. The restaurant provides light meals and drinks. *74 High St., tel. 0206/577067. Admission free. Open Tues.–Sat. 10–5, Sun. 2–4; closed Christmas week.*

Also close to the castle, just up from the tourist office on High Street, All Saints Church has been turned into the county **Natural History Museum** (Admission free. Open Tues.–Sat. 10–1 and 2–5), whose exhibits cover the local environment from the Ice Age to the present day. A second church to be converted in this way is Holy Trinity Church, a few minutes' signposted walk away on Trinity Street. Begun in around AD 1000, and incorporating visible Roman materials, the church now houses the **Social History Museum,** covering town and country life in Colchester over the past three centuries. *Admission free. Open Apr.–Oct., Tues.–Sat. 10–noon and 1–5.*

Continuing west, toward Balkerne Hill, the church of **St. Mary-at-the-Wall** is now an arts center, offering a varied program throughout the year, while across the way is Colchester's **Mercury Theatre** (*see* The Arts, *below*). This stands in the shadow of the town's enormous late-19th-century redbrick water tower (known locally as "Jumbo"). A few steps beyond is the impressive Roman **Balkerne Gate;** most of its foundations lie beneath the neighboring Hole-in-the-Wall pub. Back at the theater turn right and walk down Balkerne Passage, which leads to the top of North Hill; there, turn right again into High Street, which follows the line of the main Roman road. Along High Street you will pass the Victorian **Town Hall,** standing on the site of the original Moot (assembly) Hall. The narrow, medieval streets behind the town hall are called the **Dutch Quarter** because weavers from the Low Countries settled here in the 16th century, when Colchester was the center of a thriving cloth trade. Across the High Street and beyond the modern Culver Square pedestrian mall lie the medieval streets of Long Wyre Street, Short Wyre Street, and Sir Isaac's Walk, where there are many small antiques stores and crafts and gift shops.

Off Culver Street West, on Trinity Street, **Tymperley's Clock Museum** displays a unique collection of Colchester-made clocks in the surviving wing of an Elizabethan house. *Trinity St., tel. 0206/712943. Admission free. Open Apr.–Oct., Mon.–Sat. and national holidays, 10–1 and 2–5.*

Colchester is the traditional base for exploring **Constable Country,** that quintessentially English rural landscape on the borders of Suffolk and Essex made famous by the early 19th-century painter, John Constable. This area runs north and west of Colchester along the **45** valley of the River Stour and includes his birthplace at **East Bergholt** (5 mi north of Colchester, off A12); **Dedham** (2 mi south), where he went to school and whose church and other town features served as inspiration for his works; and the peaceful village of **Flatford,** a mile east, where those familiar with Constable's *The Hay Wain* will recognize the Mill and **The Thatched Bridge Cottage.** The latter is a National Trust property open to the public, featuring a display about the artist's life. *Near East Bergholt, tel. 0206/298260. Admission free. Open Apr.–May, Wed.–Sun. 11–5:30; June–Sept., daily 10–5:30; Oct., Wed.–Sun. 11–5:30; Nov., Wed.–Sun. 11–3:30.*

Time Out The **Marlborough Head** (Mill La.), in Dedham, is an early 18th-century pub opposite Constable's school, serving fine lunches from quiche to steak. It gets very busy during the summer, so get there early to ensure a table.

46 From Colchester, A137 and A120 run the 20 miles northeast to **Harwich,** a port town on the estuary of the Stour and Orwell rivers. (The latter, incidentally, provided one Eric Blair with a pseudonym in 1932, when *Down and Out in Paris and London* was first published; George Orwell's parents lived in Southwold—*see below*—just 35 mi to the north.) Harwich is an important ferry port, providing year-round service to the Netherlands, Germany, Denmark,

Sweden, and Norway, though there is no other reason to include it on your itinerary.

④⑦ Just across the estuary lies larger **Felixstowe,** a fairly attractive seaside resort, also with ferry service to the Netherlands. **Landguard Fort,** a mile south of town, dates from the 18th century, though built on a site originally fortified by Henry VIII, and remained in use until after World War II. There's a museum inside the fort; try to attend one of the guided tours to make the most of your visit. *Tel. 0394/ 286403. Museum admission: 50p adults, 25p children and senior citizens; tours at 2:45 PM and 4 PM: £1.20 adults, 60p children and senior citizens, includes entry to the museum. Open June–Sept., Wed., Sun. 2:30–5.*

④⑧ You reach Felixstowe via the town of **Ipswich,** 14 miles north of Colchester on A12; at Ipswich, take A45 southeast to Felixstowe. You may well want to stop briefly in Ipswich on your way farther north, since the center of this busy town has a glut of medieval parish churches and several buildings dating from its period of greatest prosperity, the 17th and 18th centuries. The tourist office can assist with walking tours.

From Felixstowe northward to Kessingland lies the **Suffolk Heritage Coast,** a beautiful 40-mile stretch including many sections designated by an Act of Parliament as "Areas of Special Scientific Interest." You can only reach them on minor roads running east off A12 north of Ipswich. One of the most interesting areas is found at **④⑨** **Orford,** 15 miles north; take B1084 east from Woodbridge. Here, **Orford Castle** retains a splendid triple-towered keep, built in 1160 as a coastal defense. *Tel. 03944/50472. Admission: £1.70 adults, 85p children, £1.30 senior citizens. Open Easter–Sept., daily 10–6; Oct.–Easter, Tues.–Sun. 10–4.*

Head northwest along B1078 through **Tunstall Forest,** and turn right **⑤⓪** at Tunstall on B1069 for **Snape.** Its disused Victorian malt works was converted in 1969 into **the Maltings,** an opera house and general arts center hosting the Aldeburgh Festival (*see* The Arts, *below*), founded by the composer, Lord Benjamin Britten. *Tel. 0728/452935. Admission free. Open daily 10–5.*

Aldeburgh itself, 5 miles east on A1094, is a quiet seaside resort and was Britten's home for some time, though he was actually born in the busy seaside resort of Lowestoft, some 30 miles to the north. For a more tranquil end to your tour, drive instead only as far as **⑤①** **Southwold,** 15 miles north, a very attractive seaside town of old houses set among seven greens. Orwell's parents lived at 36 High Street during the 1930s, though for a house more typical of the town visit the **Southwold Museum,** which is in a Dutch-gabled cottage. *Victoria St., no phone. Admission free. Open late May–Sept., daily 2:30–4:30.*

Tour 4: Lincoln and Boston

Numbers in the margin correspond to points of interest on the Lincoln Region map.

⑤② Northwest of the area already covered in this section lies **Lincoln,** an old settlement going back to Roman times and beyond; its crowning glory is the great Cathedral of St. Mary (which you should try to see at night, when it is floodlit). Commanding views from the top of the steep limestone escarpment above the River Witham reveal the strategic advantages of the city's site from earliest times. Weapons from the pre-Roman, tribal era have been found in the river; later, the Ro-

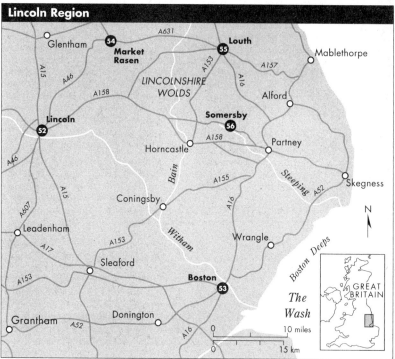

Lincoln Region

Glentham • 54 Market Rasen • A631 • Louth 55 • Mablethorpe
A15 A46 LINCOLNSHIRE WOLDS A157
A153 A16 Alford
A158 Somersby 56
Lincoln 52 Horncastle A158 Partney
A46 Bain A155 Steeping A52 Skegness
A607 A15 Coningsby A16
Leadenham Witham Wrangle
A17 A153 Boston Deeps
Sleaford A153 Boston 53 The Wash
A153 Donington A16 GREAT BRITAIN
Grantham A52
0 10 miles
0 15 km
N

mans (always quick to see the potential of a site) left their usual permanent underpinning; and a wealth of medieval buildings—quite apart from the cathedral and castle—seem to tumble together down the steep hillside lanes leading to the river.

The **cathedral** is the most obvious starting point for any visitor to Lincoln. For hundreds of years, it was the tallest building in Europe, but this magnificent medieval building is now among the least known of the European cathedrals. It was begun in 1072 by the Norman bishop Remigius; the Romanesque church he built was irremediably damaged, first by fire, then by earthquake (in 1185), but you can still see parts of the ancient structure at the west front. The next great phase of building, initiated by Bishop Hugh of Avalon, is mainly 13th century in character. The west front, topped by the two west towers, is a unique structure, giving tremendous breadth to the entrance. It is best seen from the 14th-century Exchequer Gate arch in front of the cathedral, or from the castle battlements beyond.

Inside, a breathtaking impression of space and unity belie the many centuries of building and rebuilding. The stained-glass window at the north end of the transept, known as the Dean's Eye, is one of the earliest (13th-century) traceried windows, while its opposite number at the south end shows a 14th-century sophistication in its tracery (i.e., interlaced designs). St. Hugh's Choir in front of the altar and the Angel Choir at the east end behind it have remarkable vaulted ceilings and intricate carvings. Look for the famous Lincoln Imp upon the pillar nearest to St. Hugh's shrine, and even farther up (binoculars or a telephoto lens will help) to see the 30 angels who are playing musical instruments, and who give this part of the cathedral its name.

Among the many chapels is one commemorating Lincolnshire's connections with North America and Australia. Through a side door on the north side lies the chapter house, a 10-sided building that sometimes housed the medieval Parliament of England during the reigns of Edward I and Edward II. The chapter house is connected to the 13th-century cloisters, notable for its grotesquely amusing ceiling bosses. The cathedral library, a restrained building by Christopher Wren, was built onto the north side of the cloisters after the original library collapsed. *Tel. 0522/544544. Admission free but £2.50 donation requested. Open May–Aug., Mon.–Sat. 7:15 AM–9 PM, Sun. 7:15–6; Sept.–Apr., Mon.–Sat. 7:15–6, Sun. 7:15–5.*

In the **Minster Yard,** which surrounds the cathedral on three sides, are buildings of various periods, including graceful examples of Georgian architecture. A statue of Alfred, Lord Tennyson, who was born in Lincolnshire, stands on the green near the chapter house exterior, and the medieval **Bishop's Palace,** on the south side, is open to the public. *Tel. 0522/527468. Admission: 75p adults, 40p children, 55p senior citizens. Open Apr.–Sept., daily 10–6.*

Time Out There is a pleasant coffee shop serving light meals just off the cathedral cloisters. It can also be reached from the Tennyson statue green.

Lincoln Castle, facing the cathedral across Exchequer Gate, was originally built on two great mounds by William the Conqueror in 1068, incorporating part of the remains of the Roman garrison walls. The castle was a military base until the 17th century, after which it was used primarily as a prison. In the extraordinary prison chapel you can see the cage-like stalls in which Victorian convicts were compelled to listen to sermons. *Castle Hill, tel. 0522/511068. Admission: £2 adults, £1.20 children and senior citizens. Open Apr.–Oct., Mon.–Sat. 9:30–5:30, Sun. 11:30–5:30; Nov.–Mar., Mon.–Sat. 9:30–4, Sun. 11:30–4.*

The Roman presence in Lincoln is particularly evident near the cathedral. At the end of Bailgate, traffic still passes under the **Newport Arch,** once the north gate of the Roman city, *Lindum Colonia.* Ermine Street, stretching north from the arch to the River Humber, replaced an important Roman road lying 8 feet below the surface. The foundations of the east gate have been excavated and permanently exposed in the forecourt of the Forte Crest Hotel, and the columns of a 175-foot Roman colonnade are marked along the roadway in Bailgate.

South of the cathedral the ground slopes away sharply down to the river. Here narrow medieval streets cling to the hillside, with the aptly named **Steep Hill** at their center. Well-preserved domestic buildings, such as the early-12th-century Jew's House, and 14th- and 15th-century timbered buildings, such as Harding House and the Harlequin and Dernstall House (at the end of High St.), now contain bookstores, antiques shops, boutiques, and restaurants. These hillside streets lead into Lincoln's shopping district (mainly pedestrianized).

Through the busy shopping district, where you can walk under the 15th-century **Stonebow arch** with the **Guildhall** above it, the River Witham flows unobtrusively, crossed by the incongruously named **High Bridge**—a low, vaulted Norman bridge topped by 16th-century, timber-framed houses. West of High Bridge the river opens out into **Brayford Pool,** still busy with river traffic (and, unfortunately, road traffic, as a large, unsightly, multistoried parking lot has been built on one side). Here you can rent various kinds of boats. In addition, from April to September small cruisers tour the River Witham, showing you the city from the water. *Contact Cathedral City Cruises at Brayford Wharf East, tel. 0522/546853.*

Time Out Have a pub lunch with a view of Brayford Pool at **The Royal William IV** on Brayford Wharf East.

The countryside around Lincoln, especially the Lincolnshire Wolds (chalk hills) to the northeast, consists of rolling hills and copses, with dry-stone (unmortared) walls dividing well-tended fields. The unspoiled rural area of the Wolds, strikingly evoked in Tennyson's poetry, is particularly worth a visit, while the long coastline with its miles of sandy beaches and its North Sea air offers all the usual, if occasionally tacky, seaside facilities for the family.

The River Witham flows right through the Lincolnshire Fens, from **53** Lincoln to the port of **Boston,** whose 14th-century **Church of St. Botolph** has a lantern tower (288 ft.) known affectionately as Boston Stump. It can be seen for 20 miles from both land and sea and serves as a directional beacon for aircraft as well. The Pilgrims, who were finally to reach Massachusetts in 1620, originally tried to sail from Boston to Holland in their search for religious freedom but were captured and imprisoned here in 1607. The 15th-century guildhall, now the **Boston Borough Museum,** contains the cells where they were held. *St. Mary's Guildhall, South St., tel. 0205/365954. Admission: 80p adults, 60p senior citizens, accompanied children free. Admission includes a 45-minute personal audio guided tour. Open Mon.–Sat. 10–5, Sun. (Apr.–Sept. only) 1:30–5.*

There are other reminders of Boston's transatlantic links, especially the early 18th-century **Fydell House,** next to the guildhall, now a school, where a room is set aside for visitors from Boston, Massachusetts. *South St., tel. 0205/351520. Admission free. Open weekdays 9:30–12:30, 1:30–4:30.*

After Lincoln and Boston, Lincolnshire itself has few major attractions to delay you, though there are several towns with varying, often off-beat, reasons for a visit. If you're curious, **Grantham** (30 mi west of Boston on A52) is the hometown of former British Prime Minister Margaret Thatcher, whose father was a grocer there. Six-**54** teen miles northeast of Lincoln, **Market Rasen** (on A46) is one of the major centers of horse racing in England. Between Market Rasen and Louth lie the **Lincolnshire Wolds,** designated an Area of Out-**55** standing Natural Beauty. **Louth,** 14 miles east of Market Rasen on A631, is most famous for its splendid parish church of St. James, which boasts the tallest parish church spire in England. Tennyson **56** was born at **Somersby,** south of Louth.

Time Out On your way back south, stop at **The Beehive** pub, on Castlegate in Grantham. It is famous for its beehive (full of bees) in a tree outside, which has been there since the beginning of the 19th century. Ploughman's lunches (bread, cheese, onions, and pickles) are served, as well as other bar snacks and soups.

What to See and Do with Children

Almost all the seaside resorts have something to offer children in the way of amusement parks, shows, and sports. Clacton-on-Sea (Essex), Lowestoft (Suffolk), Great Yarmouth and Hunstanton

(Norfolk), and Mablethorpe and Skegness (Lincolnshire) have some of the best children's attractions.

Inland, **Colchester Zoo** (tel. 0206/330253) offers 40 acres of parkland exhibiting a worldwide collection of mammals, birds, fish, and reptiles, as well as a miniature railroad. The **Banham Zoo and Monkey Park** (tel. 095387/771) has a children's play area, and **Pensthorpe Waterfowl Park** (tel. 0328/851465), 1 mile southeast of Fakenham, has one of the world's largest collections of exotic waterbirds as well as nature trails in a 200-acre park. A more unusual wildlife attraction is the **Otter Trust** (tel. 0986/893470) near Bungay, Suffolk, where otters can be observed in near-natural conditions; there are also attractive river walks.

In Essex, the **Colne Valley Railway** (tel. 0787/61174) runs steam trains through the Colne Valley, from Castle Hedingham Station (near Halstead on A604). There are dining and buffet cars on the train. A permanent display of vintage steam and diesel locomotives is open daily except Monday, from 10 to 5, and there are "steam days" from Easter to October on most Sundays, at Christmas, and on national holiday weekends. The narrow-gauge railroad in Suffolk at the **Bressingham Live Steam Museum** (tel. 0379/88386) offers a 6-mile ride on a small steam train through internationally famous gardens. In northern Norfolk, the **Wells and Walsingham Light Railway** (contact Wells-next-the-Sea tourist office, tel. 0328/710885) is the longest 10¼-gauge railroad in Britain—8 miles round-trip. It runs daily from Easter to October, the first train leaving Wells at 10 AM.

Off the Beaten Track

Those who enjoy solitary outdoor walks should try the embankments of the Ouse inlets (called "washes") or the Fenland drainage canals. For bird-watchers, the **Wildfowl and Wetlands Trust Centre** (tel. 0353/860711) at Welney, 12 miles north of Ely, has rare Bewick and Whooper swans in winter (open daily 10–5). Alternatively, drive to **Sutton Gault** off B1381 at Sutton (16 mi north of Cambridge), where the washes are at their narrowest point and the causeway floods so regularly there is a footbridge to the other side.

Southwest of King's Lynn lies **Peterborough** (34 mi on A47). This ancient city was an important Roman settlement on the road north from London and has been recently largely developed. But the city's heart is the **cathedral,** whose history traces back to its original 7th-century Ango-Saxon foundation. Originally a monastery church, the building is basically Norman, but one gets a sense of light inside, partly because the original 12th-century Norman windows were replaced by larger ones in the 13th and 15th centuries, and also because Cromwell's troops smashed all the stained glass during the Civil War. The painted wooden nave ceiling, dating from the 13th century, is one of only three surviving in Europe. From the gallery that runs around the inside of the central tower you can see across the fens to Ely. Two queens were buried here. Katherine of Aragon, Henry VIII's first wife, lies under a plain, gray stone in the north choir aisle under the 16th-century standards of England and Spain. Mary, Queen of Scots, was buried in the south aisle after her execution in 1587, although her son James I later had her body moved to Westminster Abbey in London. *Chapter Office, 12 Minster Precincts, tel. 0733/343342. Admission free. Open Mon.–Fri. 7–6:30, Sat. and Sun. 7–5:30.*

Near the beautiful town of **Stamford** (35 miles southwest of Boston on A16) is **Burghley House,** the splendid mansion built in 1587 by

William Cecil, first Baron Burghley, when he was Elizabeth I's high treasurer. Set in fine parkland, it has 18 staterooms, with carvings by Grinling Gibbons and ceiling paintings by Verrio, as well as a priceless art collection. *Tel. 0780/52451. Admission: £4.10 adults, £2.50 children, £3.80 senior citizens, £11 family ticket. Open Apr.– Sept., daily 11–5.*

East Anglia has many connections with America. From **Hingham,** 4 miles west of Wymondham on B1108, nearly 200 inhabitants left between 1633 and 1638 to start a new life in America, including, in 1637, a young apprentice named Samuel Lincoln, paternal ancestor of Abraham Lincoln. A bust of the great president stands in the **church,** which is amazingly large, with a 120-foot tower. It is not especially beautiful as Norfolk churches go, but impressive all the same.

Shopping

Bury St. Edmunds The area around Abbeygate Street contains the best stores in town. The **Parsley Pot** (17 Abbeygate St., tel. 0284/760289) has a good selection of local crafts, and **Thurlow Champness** (14 Abbeygate St., tel. 0284/754747) has above-average silver, jewelry, and Copenhagen porcelain. The **Silk House** (14 Hatter St., tel. 0284/767138) concentrates on Macclesfield silk goods and men's neckties (Macclesfield has been the center of England's silk production for centuries).

Cambridge Cambridge is a main shopping area for a wide region, and it has all the usual chain stores, many situated in the **Grafton Centre Shopping Precinct.** More interesting are the small specialty stores found among the colleges in the center of Cambridge, especially in and around Trinity Street, King's Parade, Rose Crescent, and Market Hill.

Bookshops are Cambridge's pride and joy. The **Cambridge University Press** bookshop (1 Trinity St., tel. 0223/351688) stands on the oldest bookstore site in Britain, with books sold here since the 16th century. **Heffer's** is one of the world's biggest bookstores, with an enormous stock of books, many rare or imported. The main bookstore (20 Trinity St., tel. 0223/358351) is spacious, with a galleried upper floor. There is also a charming children's branch (30 Trinity St., tel. 0223/356200). Cambridge is also known for its secondhand bookshops. Antiquarian books can be found at **G. David** (3 and 16 St. Edward's Passage, tel. 0223/354619), which is tucked away near the Arts Theatre. A few doors away, **The Haunted Bookshop** (9 St. Edward's Passage, tel. 0223/312913) offers a great selection of old, illustrated books and British classics. Across the bridge, **The Bookshop** (24 Magdalene St., tel. 0223/62457) is the best of Cambridge's secondhand bookshops, with a wide variety of books to offer.

Handcrafted jewelry and leather goods, much of it made on the premises, can be found at **Workshop Designs** (31 Magdalene St., tel. 0223/354326). **Primavera** (10 King's Parade, tel. 0223/357708) is an excellent gallery, where top-class craftspeople exhibit in a small but lively ground floor and basement. Ceramics, glass, paintings, jewelry and sculpture are all for sale at reasonable prices, often less than £50. Also on King's Parade is the **Benet Gallery** (19 King's Parade, tel. 0223/353784), which specializes in antique prints and lithographs. **CCA Galleries** (6 Trinity St., tel. 0223/324222), exhibits sculpture and local art, and also frames prints.

Colchester Colchester's most interesting stores are in the medieval streets between High Street and St. John's Street, some of which are pedestrianized or have restricted traffic. **Gunton's Food Shop** (81 Crouch St.) is an old family business, considered a local version of London's Harrods' food hall. **Cants of Colchester** (Nayland Rd., Mile End) are rose specialists who cultivate new varieties, with rose fields on view from July to September, and **Berrimans** (68 Culver St. E, tel. 0206/575650) sells china, glass, porcelain, novelties, and collectibles. Among the many antiques stores in the town, the **Trinity Antiques Centre** (7A Trinity St., tel. 0206/577775) has the widest selection.

Ely Ely has handmade wooden crafts at the **Steeplegate Tearoom and Gallery** (16 High St., tel. 0353/664731) and affordable paintings and prints by local Fenland artists at **The Old Fire Engine House Restaurant** (*see* Dining and Lodging, *below*). The real treasure trove, however, is **Waterside Antiques** (The Wharf, tel. 0353/667066), where a wealth of antiques at very competitive prices are sold in an authentic river warehouse.

King's Lynn In addition to its well-established open markets, King's Lynn is home to the **Caithness** factory, producers of fine crystal, which welcomes visitors on weekdays throughout the year.

Lincoln Lincoln's main shopping area, mostly pedestrianized, is at the bottom of the hill below the cathedral, around the Stonebow gateway and Guildhall, and along High Street. However, the best stores are on Bailgate, Steep Hill, and the medieval streets leading directly down from the cathedral and castle. Steep Hill has several good bookstores, antiques shops, and crafts and art galleries, such as **Harding House, Steep Hill Galleries,** and **The Long Gallery** (the top of High St.). **David Hansord** (32 Steep Hill, tel. 0522/530044) specializes in antiques, especially antique scientific instruments.

Norwich The medieval lanes of Norwich, around Elm Hill and Tombland, contain the best stores. Antiquarian books can be found at **Peter Crowe** (75 Upper St. Giles St., tel. 0603/624800). For new books, guides, and maps, visit the **Black Horse Bookshop** (8–10 Wensum St., tel. 0603/626871). Antiques shops abound in this area: **James and Ann Tillett** (12–13 Tombland, tel. 0603/624914) specialize in antique jewelry and silver, and **St. Michael-at-Plea** (Bank Plain, tel. 0603/619129) is a church converted into an antiques market. The **Elm Hill Craft Shop** (12 Elm Hill, tel. 0603/621076) has interesting stationery and dollhouses, while **Hovell's** (Bedford St., tel. 0603/626676) is a basketware specialist, among other things.

Sports and the Outdoors

Bicycling Cambridge is the perfect city in which to rent a bike. **Geoff's Bike Hire** (65 Devonshire Rd., tel. 0223/65629) is a short walk from the railroad station and charges from £6 per day, £15 per week. Advance reservations are essential in July and August. In addition, the city operates a **Community Bike Scheme**, which allows you to pick up a bike for free at various central points and drop it off later for others to use. The bikes in the program are painted green, and there's a pick-up point outside the train station.

Fishing Keen British anglers know all about **Rutland, Grafham and Pitsford Waters,** and **Ravensthorpe Reservoir,** which are trout fisheries of the highest standard. Fishing season is from April to December, and fishing lodges at each place sell day permits and offer boat rental and weekend courses. For more information contact the lodges at

Grafham (tel. 0480/810531); Pitsford (tel. 0604/781350); and Rutland (tel. 0780/86770).

Horse Racing The center of British horse racing lies at **Newmarket,** where there are meets on weekdays and Saturdays (no Sunday racing in Britain), depending on the season. For information, call 0638/664151. Tours can also be made of the **National Stud,** one of Britain's principal racing stables, where you can see the horses being trained, and if you're sufficiently interested be sure to take in the **National Horseracing Museum,** which traces the history of the sport and has a fine collection of paintings. *National Stud, tel. 0638/663464. Tours offered from the end of Apr. to Sept., weekdays at 11:15 AM and 2:30 PM and sometimes Sat. in summer at 11:15 AM and Sun. at 2:30 PM. Admission: £3.50 adults, £2 children, students, and senior citizens. Advance booking essential. National Horseracing Museum, 99 High St., tel. 0638/667333. Admission charges and opening hours were unavailable at press time; call for the latest information.*

Swimming Quite apart from the coastline, where the swimming can be extremely cold, there are heated indoor pools at various local leisure centers. Two of the best, with good facilities for children, are **Broadland Aquapark** (Drayton High Rd., Hellesdon, Norwich, tel. 0603/788912) and **Bury St. Edmunds Leisure Centre** (Beetons Way, Bury St. Edmunds, tel. 0284/753496).

Walking The AD 1st-century Roman road which originally ran from Colchester to Lincolnshire today provides some of the finest walking in England. Much of the road is incorporated within a long-distance footpath known as **Peddar's Way,** of which the best part is perhaps the route from Castle Acre, just north of Swaffham, to Holme-next-the-Sea, close to Hunstanton, a distance of around 20 miles. For this route, the best starting point is King's Lynn, whose tourist information center (*see* Tourist Information, *above*) can advise about local B&B establishments and hotels. It also sells a comprehensive booklet called *Walking the Peddar's Way,* which gives much more detail about the route. Several other footpaths link with Peddar's Way to provide short or long hikes throughout different parts of Norfolk. Most attractive is **Weaver's Way,** a 56-mile-long footpath between Cromer—also on Peddar's Way—and Great Yarmouth, which follows several lengths of disused railway line, as well as regular footpaths and minor roads. To walk the entire route would take at least three days, and there are overnight facilities (inns, pubs, and B&Bs) in most of the towns and villages en route as well as camping at Manor Farm (tel. 0493/700279), in Tunstall, near Halvergate Marshes, west of Great Yarmouth. For more information, and a walking brochure, contact either Norwich or Great Yarmouth tourist information centers (*see* Tourist Information, *above*).

Dining and Lodging

Dining East Anglia is a rich agricultural region with excellent produce. Traditional favorites like Norfolk Black turkeys and a variety of game are frequently available. The long coastline also provides a wide selection of fish year-round—Cromer crabs and Yarmouth bloaters (a kind of smoked herring) are notable—and the Essex coast near Colchester has been producing oysters since Roman times. There's an equally long East Anglian tradition in wine-making. The Romans first introduced vines to Britain, and they took especially well to this region. Today there are more than 40 vineyards in East Anglia, most of which offer tours and tastings to visitors. If you want to try a bottle (dry whites are best), check wine lists in local restaurants.

Among the touring bases, Lincoln and Colchester are particularly well served with downtown restaurants. Cambridge, which was once a gastronomic desert, has seen a renaissance, and now harbors two of the region's best restaurants.

Highly recommended restaurants are indicated by a star ★.

Category	Cost*
$$$$	over £40
$$$	£30–£40
$$	£15–£30
$	under £15

per person, including first course, main course, dessert, and VAT; excluding drinks

Lodging The intimate nature of even East Anglia's larger towns has meant that there are few hotels with more than 100 rooms. As a result, even the biggest have a friendly atmosphere and offer personal service. Cambridge has relatively few hotels downtown, and these tend to be rather overpriced: There simply isn't room for hotels among the historic buildings crowded together, although there are many guest houses in the suburbs. The town fills up in the summer months, and you may have to look farther afield for accommodation.

Highly recommended hotels are indicated by a star ★.

Category	Cost*
$$$$	over £150
$$$	£90–£150
$$	£55–£90
$	under £55

All prices are for two people sharing a double room, including service, breakfast, and VAT.

Bury St.
Edmunds
Dining

Mortimer's Seafood Restaurant. Mortimer's gets its name from the original watercolors by a Victorian artist, Thomas Mortimer, which are displayed on the walls of the dining room. The seafood menu varies with the season's catch, but there are generally grilled fillets of local trout and Scottish salmon as well as mussels and oysters. Cheaper counter lunches are offered in addition to the cheery, full service in the two main dining rooms. *30 Churchgate St., tel. 0284/ 760623. Weekend reservations (at least a week in advance) required. Dress: casual. AE, DC, MC, V. Closed Sat. lunch, Sun., Dec. 24– Jan 6, last week in Aug., and first week in Sept.* $$

Dining and
Lodging
★

Angel Hotel. This is the quintessential ivy-clad, historic, market-town hotel. A former coaching inn, its rooms are spacious and well furnished, with the best ones overlooking the Abbey ruins. Several have four-poster beds, and one, the Charles Dickens Room, is where the man himself stayed. The bed is fairly small, but the rest of the room is in perfect 19th-century English style. Morning coffee and afternoon tea are served in the cozy lobby, complete with open fireplace, while elegant dining is to be found in the **Regency Restaurant.**

TAKE THE TRIP THAT RANKS
RIGHT UP THERE WITH KITTY HAWK, APOLLO 11
AND THE INAUGURAL CONCORDE FLIGHT.

*Rail Europe invites you to be among
the first to ride the Eurostar train through the Channel Tunnel.*

Be one of the first to take the trip that will change the history of travel. Rail Europe and

the high-speed, high-tech passenger train, Eurostar, can take you through the Channel

Tunnel from the center of London to the

center of Paris in three short hours. All

you do is relax, enjoy a drink or a meal and become part of history in the making.

For information on a variety of affordable Eurostar tickets call your travel

agent or Rail Europe.

Rail Europe

EUROPE. TO THE TRAINED EYE.

All the Best Trips Start with Fodor's

COMPASS AMERICAN GUIDES
Titles in the series: Arizona, Canada, Chicago, Colorado, Hawai'i, Hollywood, Las Vegas, Maine, Manhattan, New Mexico, New Orleans, Oregon, San Francisco, South Carolina, South Dakota, Utah, Virginia, Wisconsin, Wyoming.

"A literary, historical, and near-sensory excursion."—*Denver Post*

"Tackles the 'why' of travel...as well as the nitty-gritty details."—*Travel Weekly*

FODOR'S BED & BREAKFASTS AND COUNTRY INN GUIDES
Titles in the series: California, Canada, England & Wales, Mid-Atlantic, New England, The Pacific Northwest, The South, The Upper Great Lakes Region.

"In addition to information on each establishment, the books add notes on things to see and do in the vicinity."
— *San Diego Union-Tribune*

THE BERKELEY GUIDES
Titles in the series: California, Central America, Eastern Europe, Europe, France, Germany, Great Britain & Ireland, Italy, London, Mexico, The Pacific Northwest & Alaska, Paris, San Francisco.

The best choice for budget travelers, from the Associated Students at the University of California at Berkeley.

"Berkeley's scribes put the funk back in travel." — *Time*

"Fresh, funny and funky as well as useful." — *The Boston Globe*

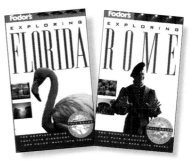

EXPLORING GUIDES
Titles in the series: Australia, Britain, California, Caribbean, Florida, France, Germany, Ireland, Italy, London, New York City, Paris, Rome, Singapore & Malaysia, Spain, Thailand.

"Authoritatively written and superbly presented, they make worthy reading before, during or after a trip. "
— *The Philadelphia Inquirer*

"A handsome new series of guides, complete with lots of color photos, geared to the independent traveler."
— *The Boston Globe*

Visit your local bookstore, or call 24 hours a day 1-800-533-6478
Fodor's The name that means smart travel.

Here, overlooking the abbey's main gate, a classic English menu is offered and impeccably served, including dishes like grilled lemon sole or roast duck with port sauce. *3 Angel Hill, IP33 1LT, tel. 0284/ 753926, fax 0284/750092. 40 rooms with bath. Facilities: 2 restaurants, bar. Restaurant: reservations required; jacket and tie preferred. AE, DC, MC, V. $$$*

Lodging **Chantry Hotel.** This pretty, 18th-century town house has a traditionally furnished older part and a modern new extension. Rooms are not particularly large, but they are very cozy, and you have the advantage of being extremely central, close to the abbey and Manor House Museum, off Honey Hill. *8 Sparhawk St., IP33 1RY, tel. 0284/ 767427. 17 rooms with bath. Facilities: evening meals for residents, bar. MC, V. $$*

Suffolk Hotel. This reliable Georgian hotel has nicely proportioned and pleasantly furnished rooms overlooking the busy and historic downtown area. *38 Buttermarket, IP33 1DL, tel. 0284/753995, fax 0284/750973. 33 rooms with bath. Facilities: restaurant, bar. AE, DC, MC, V. $$*

Cambridge **Midsummer House.** A classy restaurant set beside the River Cam,
Dining across Midsummer Common, the gray-brick Midsummer House is
★ particularly lovely in summer; it has a comfortable conservatory. Set menus for lunch and dinner parade a selection of gourmet haute cuisine inspired by the various places in which chef Hans Schweitzer has cooked. Mussel and rockfish soup with saffron, and pesto-filled supreme of chicken on black olive sauce are favorite entrées, though the menu changes throughout the year. Some find the cooking too fussy, though most applaud the stunning array of pastries and other sweets to end the meal. *Midsummer Common, tel. 0223/69299. Reservations necessary. Jacket and tie preferred. AE, DC, MC, V. Closed Sat. lunch, Sun. evening, Mon. $$$*

Three Horseshoes. This is an early 19th-century thatched cottage that includes a recently added conservatory. A pub restaurant serves beautifully prepared grilled fish, and the conservatory menu offers traditional English fare and seafood, also beautifully presented. There are homemade sorbets and ice creams for dessert. *Madingley (3 mi outside Cambridge, 10-minute taxi ride), tel. 0954/ 210221. Reservations advised. Dress: casual. AE, DC, MC, V. $$*

★ **Twenty-Two.** An intimate dining room in a modest, semidetached house half a mile from the center of Cambridge, the restaurant offers an extremely good-value fixed-price dinner. The modern British specialties include fish and game; baked salmon with herb crust, or roast lamb on a bed or ratatouille, are typical dishes. *22 Chesterton Rd., tel. 0223/351880. Reservations advised. Dress: casual. MC, V. Open evenings only. Closed Sun., Mon., and Christmas week. $$*

Brown's. This huge, airy, French-American-style brasserie-diner was converted from the outpatient department of the old Addenbrooke's Hospital, directly opposite the Fitzwilliam Museum. Large fans still keep things cool in the pale yellow dining room, while willing staff usher people from bar to table. The bountiful menu ranges from toasted tuna sandwiches to steak and Guinness pie, house hamburgers, spaghetti, and salads; check the daily specials, too—there's usually fresh fish. It's very busy on weekends, when you may have to wait in line. *23 Trumpington St., tel. 0223/ 461655. No reservations. Dress: casual. No credit cards. Closed Dec. 25–26. $$*

Hobbs Pavilion. Housed in an old cricket pavilion on the western edge of Parker's Piece, this is a cheery place for pancakes, both sweet and savory. The ice cream is also recommended, homemade from free-range eggs, double cream, and honey. Three-course fixed-price menus are a special bargain. *Park Terr., tel. 0223/67480. Reservations not necessary. No credit cards. Closed Sun. and Mon. $*

Lodging **Garden House Hotel.** Set among the colleges, this fairly luxurious, modern hotel makes the most of its riverside location. Its gardens, lounge, bar, and conservatories all have river views, as do most of the rooms—if you want one, make it clear when you make your reservation because some of the rooms at the rear of the L-shaped hotel have less desirable views. The brightly furnished guest rooms are comfortable, with minibar and TV, and fine bathrooms, and the staff is extremely helpful. *Granta Pl., CB2 1RT, tel. 0223/63421, fax 0223/316605. 118 rooms with bath. Facilities: restaurant, bar, garden, in-house movies, punt rental, 24-hr. room service. AE, DC, MC, V. $$$–$$$$*

University Arms Hotel. There has been ongoing refurbishment of the public areas and bedrooms in this city-center De Vere hotel; most rooms have now been attractively upgraded without impairing the hotel's original 19th-century elegance. Space is at a premium in central Cambridge, and it shows here: Guest rooms are comfortable and well-appointed without being overly large, though views of Parker's Piece, the green backing the hotel, from many rooms compensate. The central lounge provides a cozy, comfortable place for afternoon tea, where you can sit by the fire enjoying a pot of Darjeeling and smoked salmon sandwiches. If you don't have a room with a view, then Parker's Bar also overlooks Parker's Piece. *Regent St., CB2 1AD, tel. 0223/351241, fax 0223/315256. 117 rooms with bath. Facilities: restaurant, 3 bars, TV, 24-hr. room service. AE, DC, MC, V. $$$*

Arundel House Hotel. This is an elegantly proportioned Victorian row hotel that overlooks the River Cam, with Jesus Green in the background. The bedrooms are all furnished very comfortably with locally made mahogany furniture, and come equipped with TV and tea- and coffee-making appliances. A novel idea for first-time visitors to Cambridge is a videotaped tour of the city, which can be viewed on the hotel's TV information channel. Ask about the hotel's special weekend rates, which are an excellent value. *53 Chesterton Rd., CB4 3AN, tel. 0223/67701, fax 0223/67721. 88 rooms with bath or shower. Facilities: restaurant, bar, TV with video of guided tour of Cambridge. AE, DC, MC, V. Closed Dec. 25–26. $$*

Colchester **Pasquale.** This cheerful and friendly Italian restaurant serves well-cooked pastas and other classic Italian dishes in a light, simple, Italian-style dining room near the Roman Balkerne Gate and the Mercury Theatre. *2–4 Balkerne Passage, tel. 0206/549080. Weekend reservations advised. Dress: casual. AE, DC, MC, V. Closed Sun. $$*
Dining

Warehouse Brasserie. Colchester's most popular eating place has a fairly anonymous exterior and location: It's tucked away in a converted warehouse, down a cul-de-sac off St. John's Street. Inside, though, all is cheerful, with a charming pastel green and rich red split-level dining room, wooden tables, and large wall mirrors. The menu mixes brasserie favorites—fish soup, Caesar's salad, and steaks—with classic English dishes like Lancashire hot pot and more daring Asian ones, such as crispy won ton. Service is brisk, if occasionally offhand, but the large servings more than compensate, and there's an above-average selection of wines by the glass as well as a decent range of specialty teas. *Chapel St. N, tel. 0206/765656. Reservations advised on weekends. Dress: casual. MC, V. Closed Sun. evening. $$*

Dining and
Lodging

George Hotel. In downtown Colchester, this 500-year-old hotel—
once a coaching inn—has been renovated to include a modern extension but has lost none of its age-old charm. Many rooms incorporate
original oak beams and are comfortably furnished. The George Bar
also retains its historic beams, while in the cellar there's a section of
Roman pavement and a 16th-century wall painting on display. The
Carver's Room restaurant fits in with the style of the rest of the hotel. The split-level dining room has wood paneling and a rustic brick
canopy, and dishes include fine roasts as well as grilled fish and
steaks. *116 High St., CO1 1TD, tel. 0206/578494, fax 0206/761732. 47
rooms with bath. Facilities: Carver's Room restaurant and grill,
bar, sauna, minigym, solarium. AE, DC, MC, V. $$*

King's Ford Park Hotel. This large, 18th-century country-house ho-
tel about 2 miles from the center of Colchester boasts individually
decorated rooms and antique furniture; some rooms have four-post-
er or oval beds. *Layer Rd., CO2 0HS, tel. 0206/734301, fax 0206/
734512. 10 rooms with bath. Facilities: restaurant, bar, 18 acres of
gardens and woodlands. AE, DC, MC, V. $$*

The Maltings. This very friendly bed-and-breakfast establishment
is about 4 miles from the center of Colchester. The house dates back
to the 15th century, which means a preponderance of oak beams and
rooms that are homey and cottage style. Guests have their own dining room and lounge with an open fire; there's also a lovely walled
garden and swimming pool. *Mersea Rd., Abberton CO5 7HR, tel.
0206/735780. 3 rooms, 1 family room with bath. Facilities: light suppers on request, open-air swimming pool in garden. No credit cards.
Closed Christmas week. $*

Dedham
Dining

Le Talbooth. In a Tudor house idyllically situated beside the River
Stour, the restaurant has a floodlit terrace where drinks are served
in the summer. Inside, original beams, black-lead windows, and a
brick fireplace add to the historic atmosphere. A four-course, gourmet fixed-price menu is offered, perhaps including chicken served
with various light sauces or fresh fish. After 40 years, the cooking is
as accomplished as you would expect. *Gun Hill, tel. 0206/323150.
Reservations advised, especially weekends. Jacket and tie required.
AE, MC, V. $$$*

Dining and
Lodging
★

The Dedham Vale Hotel. Part of the Talbooth Group, and just a short
walk from Le Talbooth restaurant, this small, friendly hotel in a
converted Edwardian house offers tastefully decorated bedrooms,
full of light and with garden views. There's a pleasant lounge and
bar—the latter with *trompe l'oeil* wall decoration—and 3 acres of
terraced gardens, though the main attraction for guests is the con-
servatory-style Terrace Restaurant, full of plants. At lunch, choose
from a fine smorgasbord; the renowned dinners revolve around se-
lections from the rotisserie. *Stratford Rd., CO7 6HW, tel. 0206/
322273, fax 0206/322752. 6 rooms with bath. Facilities: restaurant
(reservations advised; dress: casual), bar, gardens. AE, MC, V. $$*

Duxford
Lodging

The Duxford Lodge Hotel. This Georgian country house, set in its
own grounds in Duxford village, was the operations headquarters
for Duxford Airfield during World War II. Extensively renovated,
the rooms are comfortably furnished and individually decorated in
traditional style, although those in the modern annex are more basic. It's worth asking if one of the good-value suites are available:
Two of them have four-poster beds. Elsewhere, the hotel is rich in
burnished wood, while the garden features a lovely little terrace for
relaxing. *Ickleton Rd., CB2 4RU, tel. 0223/836444, fax 0223/832271.
15 rooms with bath. Facilities: restaurant, bar. AE, DC, MC, V.
Closed 5 days between Christmas and New Year's. $$$*

Ely   **The Old Fire Engine House.** This restaurant near the cathedral has
Dining   two dining rooms: The main one, with scrubbed pine tables, opens
★   into the garden; the other, with an open fireplace and a polished
wood floor, is also an art gallery. Among the English dishes are traditional Fenland recipes, like pike baked in white wine, as well as eel
pie and game in season. Local artists exhibit here, and all their work
is for sale. *25 St. Mary's St., tel. 0353/662582. Reservations required
at least 24 hrs. in advance in summer and on weekends. Dress: casu-
al. MC, V. Closed Sun. evening, 2 weeks at Christmas. $$*

Dominique's. Not far from the cathedral, this delightful little res-
taurant with stripped pine floors serves brunch, lunch, and dinner.
There are good-value set meals, or choose from the blackboard list of
daily specials, which includes vegetarian dishes and a good range of
hearty English desserts. There's an outdoor patio in summer. *8 St.
Mary's St., tel. 0353/665011. Reservations advised for dinner
(served Fri. and Sat. only). No credit cards. Closed Mon. $–$$*

Lodging   **The Black Hostelry.** This bed-and-breakfast has enormous rooms
★   and is situated right in the cathedral grounds, in one of the finest
medieval domestic buildings still in use. It's adjacent to the Chapter
House, at the end of Firmary Lane. Extremely comfortable, with
antiques and old-fashioned English furnishings, this medieval hostel offers a high degree of privacy. It's so popular that you'll need to
reserve a room well in advance. *Cathedral Close, The College, CB7
4DL, tel. 0353/662612. 4 rooms with bath or shower. Facilities: full
English breakfast in the Undercroft. No credit cards. Closed Dec.
24–26. $*

Old Egremont House. Just five minutes' walk from the town center,
this wonderful 17th-century house has beautiful views of the cathedral from its two largest rooms. Inside the oak-beamed house,
everything is immaculate—the family still lives here—and there are
books and antiques all around. There's a lovely private garden, a delight to sit in during the summer, and the English breakfast includes
homemade bread and marmalade. *31 Egremont St., tel. 0353/
663118. 3 rooms, 1 with bath. Facilities: garden. No credit cards.
Closed Christmas week. $*

Great   **Seafood Restaurant.** A short walk from the center of town, the res-
Yarmouth   taurant features an extensive menu entirely devoted to fresh fish
Dining   and shellfish. Many dishes are Mediterranean in character and very
rich. The food is all very competently cooked, and there's a decent
wine list, too. The restaurant is comfortable enough to linger in, and
service is attentive. *85 North Quay, tel. 0493/856009. Reservations
advised, especially weekends. Dress: casual. AE, DC, MC, V.
Closed Sat. lunch, Sun. $$$*

Ipswich   **Hintlesham Hall.** This is a luxurious Georgian-style manor house
Dining and   hiding a basically Tudor building; the rear view of redbrick chim-
Lodging   neys, overlooking fine gardens, shows visitors the real age of the
★   hall. There are grand public rooms with antique furniture, but the
house has been completely renovated and guest rooms are equally
impressive—comfortable but not showy and retaining original
beams and woodwork in some of the rooms. The restaurant is excel-
lent and features a set weekday lunch that allows you to sample a
good cross-section of the talented chef's offerings. The standard
room rate includes a very good English breakfast and dinner.
*Hintlesham IP8 3NS, tel. 0473/652334, fax 0473/652463. 33 rooms
with bath. Facilities: restaurant, pool, tennis, billiards, trout fish-
ing, 18-hole championship golf course, clay pigeon shooting, cro-
quet, 9 acres of gardens and parkland. Restaurant: reservations es-*

sential; jacket and tie required. AE, DC, MC, V. Closed Sat. lunch. $$$–$$$$

Ixworth
Dining
★

Theobalds. This is a small, well-established restaurant with a good, varied menu that attracts a regular local clientele. The influences at work are mainly French, though modern British cooking rears its head here, too; hare served with a sauce derived from local berries is a typical entrée. There are excellent desserts, cheeses, and a large wine list with some splendid French names. *68 High St., tel. 0359/ 31707. Reservations required. Dress: casual. MC, V. Closed Sat. lunch, Sun. evening, Mon. $$*

King's Lynn
Dining

Riverside Rooms. Part of the Arts Centre, the building housing this restaurant reflects the style of the original 15th-century ware-house. There are some tables outside, overlooking the river. The English cuisine emphasizes locally caught fish and Cromer crabs. There is also an inexpensive coffee shop in the historic undercroft that serves homemade snacks and pastries. *27 King St., tel. 0553/ 773134. Reservations not necessary. Jacket preferred. MC, V. Closed Sun. $$*

Lavenham
Lodging
★

The Swan Hotel. Now a Forte Heritage hotel, the Swan is a glorious-ly atmospheric 14th- to 15th-century lodging, with oak beams, ram-bling public rooms, and antique furniture. The bedrooms are all individually decorated, and some have four-poster beds; many of them have lovely oak cabinets and original wood paneling. The res-taurant even retains its minstrel's gallery. *High St., CO10 9QA, tel. 0787/247477, fax 0787/248286. 47 rooms with bath, 3 suites. Facili-ties: restaurant, 2 bars, 5 lounges, garden, baby-sitting. AE, DC, MC, V. $$$–$$$$*

Lincoln
Dining
★

Jew's House. Situated in one of Lincoln's oldest buildings (12th-cen-tury), the restaurant has an intimate atmosphere enhanced by an-tique tables and oil paintings. The cosmopolitan menu, featuring Continental specialties, changes daily, and the restaurant is re-nowned for its fresh fish and rich desserts, all homemade. *15 The Strait, tel. 0522/524851. Reservations advised. Dress: casual. AE, DC, MC, V. Closed Sun. and Mon. lunch and 2–4 weeks in Feb. each year for redecoration. $$*

Wig and Mitre. This interesting downtown pub/café/restaurant stays open all day until 11 PM, offering an extremely wide range of food from breakfast to full evening meals. Produce comes from the local markets, and dishes may include fresh fish, warming seasonal soups, European specialties, or classic English pies and roasts. *29 Steep Hill, tel. 0522/535190. Reservations for dinner advised. Dress: casual. AE, DC, MC, V. Closed Christmas. $–$$*

Lodging
★

The White Hart. Lincoln's most elegant hotel (another Forte Heri-tage property) is luxuriously furnished with a wealth of antiques, including some fine clocks and china. The establishment has been a hotel for 600 years, reflecting a volume of experience that makes the service personal and extremely friendly. Guest rooms are tradition-ally decorated, paneled with walnut in the bathrooms, while the bedrooms retain solid English furniture and are painted in subdued colors. The hotel abuts the cathedral grounds, although cathedral views are somewhat obscured by the surrounding buildings. *Bailgate, LN1 3AR, tel. 0522/526222, fax 0622/531798. 50 rooms with bath, 3 full suites. Facilities: Georgian restaurant, Orangery coffee shop, lounge bar. AE, DC, MC, V. $$$–$$$$*

Hillcrest Hotel. A small, unpretentious hotel, formerly a Victorian rectory, Hillcrest is in a very quiet area about five minutes' walk from the cathedral. The interior features simple but pleasing modern furnishings, and service is friendly and relaxed. Rooms at the back look out over the garden and arboretum. *15 Lindum Terr., LN2 5RT, tel. and fax 0522/510182. 17 rooms with bath. Facilities: restaurant, bar. AE, MC, V. Closed 2 weeks at Christmas. $$*

Norwich **Adlard's.** This is a very comfortable restaurant, mainly decorated in
Dining green, that offers highly accomplished cooking. The specialties
★ change regularly, but you might be lucky and find lamb with Jerusalem artichokes or Dover sole with all kinds of fish sauces. The cheese board has lots of English and French cheeses, and the wine list has delicious selections from all over the world. *79 Upper St. Giles St., tel. 0603/633522. Reservations required. Jacket and tie required. AE, DC, MC, V. Closed Sat. lunch, Sun., Mon. $$$*

Brasted's. Tucked away down one of Norwich's medieval lanes, this restaurant has a plain outside that gives nothing away. Inside, excellent, carefully prepared meals are served in elegant surroundings, and the menu shows a mix of modern and traditional cooking styles: There might be salads of asparagus and leeks as well as lamb or oxtail. *8–10 St. Andrews Hill, tel. 0603/625949. Reservations advised. Dress: casual. AE, DC, MC, V. Closed Sat. lunch, Sun., last 2 weeks Aug. $$$*

Green's Seafood Restaurant. Seafood is served here, and fresh linen and live piano music contribute to the pleasant ambience. Specialties include turbot with prawns and herb butter as well as poached salmon, or ask about the daily specials. There are some meat dishes, too, and an oyster bar serves seafood in a less formal atmosphere. *82 Upper St. Giles St., tel. 0603/623733. Reservations required. Dress: casual. MC, V. Closed Sat. lunch, Sun., Mon. lunch. $$*

★ **Marco's.** The Georgian architecture of this building is complemented inside by paneled walls, open fires, and pictures, all contributing to a warm, friendly, private atmosphere. Specialties of the Italian cuisine include *salmone al cartoccio* and *gnocchi alla Marco;* game and local crab are served when available. *17 Pottergate, tel. 0603/624044. Reservations advised. Dress: casual. AE, DC, MC, V. Closed Sun., Mon., and mid-Sept.–mid-Oct. $$*

Lodging **The Hotel Nelson.** This new hotel by the river is brightly decorated, with good modern furniture, especially in the executive wing. Many of the rooms have balconies overlooking the water. They're a little more pricey than the standard rooms but are worth it. *Prince of Wales Rd., NR1 1DX, tel. 0603/760260, fax 0603/620008. 121 rooms with bath. Facilities: 2 restaurants, 2 bars, riverside lounge, gardens. AE, DC, MC, V. $$$*

Sprowston Manor. This inviting Victorian country house—recently renovated—is set in 8 acres of gardens next to a golf course, a relaxing base from which to tour the city. It lies 3¼ miles northeast of Norwich on A1151. Rooms, decorated in a modern style, are a generous size and the facilities are particularly good; the lounge bar serves food all day to weary sightseers. *Wroxham Rd., NR7 8RP, tel. 0603/410871, fax 0603/423911. 103 rooms with bath. Facilities: restaurant, lounge bar, sauna, solarium, fitness center, gardens. AE, DC, MC, V. $$$*

The Georgian House Hotel. This hotel offers comfortable accommodations in two converted, elegant 18th-century houses. It's the best choice in the city center if you want something a little more traditional, though the older buildings by necessity mean smaller guest rooms than elsewhere. *32–34 Unthank Rd., NR2 2RB, tel. 0603/615655, fax 0603/765689. 26 rooms with bath or shower. Facilities: restaurant, bar. AE, DC, MC, V. Closed Christmas. $$*

Orford **Butley-Orford Oysterage.** What started as a little café that sold oys-
Dining ters and cups of tea has become a large, bustling, no-nonsense restaurant. It still specializes in oysters and smoked salmon, as well as
other seafood in season; smoking still takes place in the adjacent
smokehouse. *Market Hill, tel. 0394/450277. Reservations advised,
especially weekends. Dress: casual. No credit cards. Closed Sun.–
Thurs. evenings in winter. $$*

Lodging **The Crown and Castle.** Near Orford Castle is this small, well-estab-
lished hotel in an 18th-century building thought to have had smug-
gling connections. The tone is set by the timbered facade, and inside
the rooms are small, cozy, and very quiet. A four-poster bed is there
for the taking in some rooms if you want to take traditional English
life even more seriously. *Market Hill, IP12 2LJ, tel. 0394/450205,
fax 0394/450176. 20 rooms, 16 with bath. Facilities: restaurant, bar,
lounge, secluded garden, baby-listening service. AE, DC, MC, V.
$$*

Saffron **Saffron Hotel.** This conversion of three houses into one has resulted
Walden in a comfortable, modern hotel inside a 16th-century building. Re-
Dining and cent renovations have increased the number of guest rooms, and
Lodging three now feature splendid bathrooms and four-poster beds. The
Saffron Restaurant has straightforward food, with plenty of local
specialties, such as a delicious lamb dish. A recently opened conservatory restaurant is already winning local plaudits, as much for its
light and airy setting as for its adventurous menu choices. A roast
lunch is served on Sunday, and bar meals are served when the restaurants are closed. *10–18 High St., CB10 2AY, tel. 0799/522676, fax
0799/513979. 24 rooms with bath. Facilities: 2 restaurants, bar,
lounge. Restaurant (reservations advised; dress: casual; closed
Sat. lunch, Sun. evening). AE, DC, MC, V. $$*

Shipdam **Shipdam Place.** This former rectory near Thetford maintains the air
Dining and of a private country house in its beautifully furnished rooms. Parts
Lodging of the house date back 300 years, while later additions include a fine
Regency structure at the front and a 19th-century flint-clad exten-
sion. Furniture, too, is antique, while log fires and original wooden
window shutters help keep things cozy in winter. The excellent res-
taurant serves English dishes, accompanied by a good wine list. In
summer, some of the produce is taken from the old rectory's kitchen
garden. *Church Close, IP25 7LX, tel. 0362/820303. 8 rooms with
bath. Facilities: restaurant (reservations advised; jacket recom-
mended), 2 lounges, gardens. MC, V. $$*

Southwold **Crown Hotel.** Since Adnams Brewery took it over, the restaurant at
Dining and the Crown has vastly improved. It specializes in locally caught fish
Lodging and has one of the best wine lists in England. The set dinner, served
★ in the simple, but tastefully decorated, yellow-and-green dining
room by friendly and informed staff, is an amazingly good value; you
can eat at even more reasonable prices by choosing from the adventurous bar menu. The building itself is 17th century, so though public rooms are spacious enough, you might find some of the guest
rooms on the small side. Antique furniture and a pleasing decorative
eye by the management more than compensate, however. *90 High
St., 0502/722275, fax 0502/724805. 12 rooms, 9 with bath or shower.
Facilities: restaurant, bar. Restaurant (reservations advised;
dress: jacket and tie preferred; closed 1 week in Jan.) AE, MC, V. $$*
The Swan Hotel. Southwold's other top choice, this lovely, 17th-cen-
tury inn near the beach (scenes from *David Copperfield* were filmed
here) features spacious public rooms and decent-size bedrooms dec-
orated in traditional English country style. There are 18 secluded

and quiet garden rooms around the old bowling green. The hotel staff prides itself on personal service. The restaurant's bay windows overlook the street; dishes are mainly traditional English, accompanied by a similarly excellent wine list. *Market Pl., IP18 6EG, tel. 0502/722186, fax 0502/724800. 45 rooms with bath. Facilities: restaurant, bar. Restaurant: reservations advised; jacket and tie preferred. AE, DC, MC, V. $$*

Sudbury **Mabey's Brasserie.** Chef Robert Mabey has created a simple
Dining brasserie with a touch of excitement. Dishes are prepared at the
★ front of the house, and the atmosphere benefits accordingly. This isn't pretentious food but excellently prepared local produce, with the specialties always changing depending on the market. This is haute cuisine at middling prices. *47 Gainsborough St., tel. 0787/374298. Reservations required. Dress: casual. AE, MC, V. Closed Sun., Mon. $$*

Lodging **Old Bull and Trivets.** This 16th-century inn is furnished with leather chairs and antiques. Some bedrooms have beams and galleries, and one room has a four-poster bed. The excellent informal restaurant (dinner only) serves French dishes. It is 10 minutes' walk from the town center. *Church St., Ballingdon, CO10 6BL, tel. 0787/374120, fax 0787/379044. 9 rooms with bath or shower. Facilities: restaurant, lounge, bar, patio garden. AE, DC, MC, V. $–$$*

The Arts

Festivals The most important arts festival in East Anglia, and one of the best known in Great Britain, is the **Aldeburgh Festival,** held for two weeks in June every year in Snape, at the **Maltings Concert Hall** (tel. 0728/453543), which also offers a year-round program of events. Founded by the composer Benjamin Britten, the festival naturally concentrates on music, but there are also related exhibitions, poetry readings, and even walks. *Program published in Mar. by Aldeburgh Foundation, High St., Aldeburgh IP15 5AX, tel. 0728/452935.*

Only slightly less notable than Aldeburgh are the festivals in Cambridge (last two weeks of July) and King's Lynn (roughly the same time as Cambridge's, although for a slightly shorter period). The **Cambridge Festival** is mainly music, performed by international orchestras and artists in some of the most beautiful venues in England, including King's College Chapel and Ely Cathedral. However, it's currently unclear if the festival will continue in its present format; direct inquiries to the tourist office for the latest information.

Much of the **King's Lynn Festival** is based at the Arts Centre and encompasses concerts, exhibitions, theater, dance, films, literary events, and children's programs. *King's Lynn Festival Office, 27 King St., King's Lynn PE30 1HA, tel. 0553/773578. Festival program available in Apr. or May.*

Smaller festivals are held in Lincoln, Bury St. Edmunds, and Ely during the summer. Check with these tourist information centers for details.

Music Both Cambridge and Lincoln support symphony orchestras, and regular musical events are held in many of the colleges, especially those with large chapels. Evensong at King's College Chapel is held Tues.–Sat. at 5:30 PM, Sunday at 3:30 PM; call tel. 0223/350411 for more information. Concerts are also held in Cambridge's **Corn Exchange** (Wheeler St., tel. 0223/357851).

Cambridge's largest musical event is the long-established, annual **Cambridge Folk Festival** in July, spread over two days at Cherry Hinton Hall; the event attracts major international folk singers and groups. Details are available from the City Council Amenities and Recreation Department (tel. 0223/358977), or look in the local press.

Norwich's **Theatre Royal** (tel. 0603/630000) hosts musical performances of all kinds, and you can also listen to music in **St. Andrews Hall** (Blackfriars, tel. 0603/628477), or hear organ recitals in **St. Peter Mancroft.** The cathedrals of Ely, Norwich, Peterborough, and Lincoln serve as uplifting settings for orchestral and choral performances.

In a country-house setting, **Wingfield College** (Wingfield, near Diss, tel. 0379/384505) has an annual season of concerts, talks, and recitals by artists of international standing.

Theater In Cambridge, **The Arts Theatre** (Peas Hill, tel. 0223/352001) puts on major touring productions, a Christmas pantomime every year, and one of the classical Greek dramas every three years. It also hosts the annual Cambridge Footlights Review, training ground for much comic talent in the past 30 years. The **Arts Cinema** (8 Market Passage, tel. 0223/352001) is an important venue for art films and the annual Cambridge Animated Film Festival. Cambridge's other theater, the **ADC Theatre** (Park St., tel. 0223/352000), is the headquarters of the University Amateur Dramatics Club. Anything but amateur, the club stages productions comparable to those of the best professional theater, with performances held during the university term and at Christmas.

Bury St. Edmunds's splendid **Theatre Royal** (Westgate St.) is run by the National Trust. A working theater offering a wide variety of touring shows, it was built in 1819 and is a perfect example of Regency theater design, a delightfully intimate place to watch a performance. It may be closed altogether during parts of the summer, so telephone first to avoid disappointment. *Westgate St., tel. 0284/ 769505. Open Mon.–Sat. 10 AM–8 PM, and for performances; closed Good Friday and national holiday Mon.*

In Norwich, the **Maddermarket Theatre** (Maddermarket, tel. 0603/ 620917), patterned after Elizabethan theater design, was founded in 1911 by an amateur repertory company and now performs all sorts of plays, including Shakespeare, to a high standard. The theater is closed for performances in August. Norwich has a small **Puppet Theatre** (St. James, Whitefriars, tel. 0603/629921), housed in a former church. Not just for children, this theater has a national reputation.

Colchester's **Mercury Theatre** (Balkerne Gate, tel. 0206/573948) stages a wide variety of plays, including tour productions, pre– West End runs, and local productions. It's in a modern building not far from the **Colchester Arts Centre** (St. Mary-at-the-Wall, Church St., tel. 0206/577301), which hosts theater, exhibitions, and workshop events. Jazz is featured every other Thursday, with top names from Britain, the Continent, and America.

The **Theatre Royal** in Lincoln (Clasketgate, tel. 0522/525555) is a fine Victorian theater previewing shows before their London runs and offering tour productions. There are also occasionally concerts on Sundays.

11 The Welsh Borders

Worcester, Hereford,
Shrewsbury, Chester

England's border with the principality of Wales stretches from the town of Chepstow on the Severn estuary in the south to the city of Chester in the north. Along this border, in the counties of Herefordshire, Shropshire, and southern Cheshire, lies some of England's loveliest countryside, remote and tranquil. But today's rural peace belies a turbulent past. Relations between the English and the Welsh have seldom been easy, and from the earliest times the English have felt it necessary to keep the "troublesome" Welsh firmly on the other side of the border. A string of medieval castles bears witness to this history. Many are romantic ruins; some are dark and brooding fortresses. Built to control the countryside and repel invaders, they still radiate a sense of mystery and menace.

For the last 500 years or so, the people of this border country have enjoyed more peaceful lives, with little to disturb the traditional patterns of country life. In the 18th century, however, one small corner of Shropshire heralded the birth of the Industrial Revolution, for here, in a wooded stretch of the Severn Gorge, the first coke blast furnace was invented and the first iron bridge was erected (1774).

Herefordshire, in the south, is a county of rich, rolling countryside and river valleys, gradually opening out in the high hills and plateaus of Shropshire. North of the Shropshire hills, the gentler Cheshire plain stretches toward the great industrial cities of Liverpool and Manchester (*see* Chapter 13). This is dairy country, dotted with small villages and market towns, many rich in the 13th- and 14th-century black-and-white, half-timbered buildings so typical of northwestern England. These are the legacy of a forested countryside, where wood was easier to come by than stone. In the market towns of Chester and Shrewsbury, the more elaborately decorated half-timbered buildings are monuments to wealth, dating mostly from the early Jacobean period at the beginning of the 17th century.

Essential Information

Important Addresses and Numbers

Tourist Information
The Heart of England Tourist Board, Woodside, Larkhill, Worcester WR5 2EF, tel. 0905/763436, fax 0905/763450, open Mon.–Thurs. 9–5:30, Fri. 9–5. Local tourist information centers, normally open Mon.–Sat. 9:30–5:30, include:
Chester: Town Hall, Northgate St., tel. 0244/317962.
Hereford: Town Hall Annexe, St. Owens St., tel. 0432/268430.
Ludlow: Castle St., tel. 0584/875053.
Ross-on-Wye: 20 Broad St., tel. 0989/62768.
Shrewsbury: The Music Hall, The Square, tel. 0743/350761.
Worcester: The Guildhall, High St., tel. 0905/726311.

Travel Agencies
Thomas Cook: 10 Bridge St., Chester, tel. 0244/323045; 4 St. Peter's St., Hereford, tel. 0432/356461; 36–37 Pride Hill, Shrewsbury, tel. 0743/231144; and 26 High St., Worcester, tel. 0905/28228.
American Express: 27 Claremont St., Shrewsbury, tel. 0743/236387.

Car-Rental Agencies
Chester: Avis, 128 Brook St., tel. 0244/311463; **Hertz,** Auto Travel Agency, Abley House, Trafford, tel. 0244/374705.
Hereford: Practical Car and Van Rental, Puremass Ltd., Coningsby St., tel. 0432/278989.
Worcester: Europcar Interrent, Peter Cooper, Redhill Filling Station, London Rd., tel. 0905/354096.

Arriving and Departing

By Car M4/M5 from London takes you to Worcester in just under three hours. The prettier, more direct route (120 mi) on M40 via Oxford to A40 across the Cotswolds, is actually slower because it is only partly motorway. For Shrewsbury (150 mi) and Chester (180 mi), take M1/M6.

By Train British Rail serves the region from **London's Paddington** (tel. 071/262-6767) and **Euston** (tel. 071/387-7070) stations. Average travel times include: Paddington to Hereford, 3 hours; to Worcester, 2½ hours; Euston to Shrewsbury and Chester, 3 hours.

By Bus National Express (tel. 071/730–0202) serves the region from London's Victoria Coach Station. Average travel time to Chester is 4¼ hours; to Hereford, 4 hours; to Shrewsbury, 3 hours; and to Worcester, 3 hours.

Getting Around

By Car Driving can be difficult in the western reaches of this region—especially in the hills and valleys west of Hereford, where steep, twisting roads often narrow into mere trackways. Winter travel here can be particularly grueling.

By Train A direct local service links Hereford, Shrewsbury, and Chester. **Midland Day Ranger** tickets and seven-day **Heart of England Regional Rover** tickets allow unlimited travel.

By Bus For information about local services and Rover tickets, contact **Crosville Bus Station** in Chester (tel. 0244/381461) and **Midland Red (West) Travel** in Worcester (tel. 0905/359393).

Guided Tours Local tourist offices can recommend day or half-day tours of the region and will have the names of registered Blue Badge guides. **Yeomans Travel** (Coach Station, Commercial Rd., Hereford, tel. 0432/56201) conducts tours of the Wye Valley.

Exploring the Welsh Borders

We begin our first tour in the city of Worcester, renowned for its proud cathedral and fine bone china. From there we work our way south and west, along the lovely Malvern Hills, taking in the peaceful spa town of Great Malvern and others before stopping in the prosperous agricultural city of Hereford. Then we head north to Bewdley, terminus of the Severn Valley Railway, and continue into the West Midlands—birthplace of modern British industry.

Tour 2 begins in the handsome medieval city of Shrewsbury, moves on to the wooded banks of the River Severn to visit the cluster of Ironbridge museums, and ends in Ludlow, an architectural jewel of a town. Tour 3 takes in the ancient city of Chester, then wanders northeast via Nantwich, the Jodrell Bank Observatory, Knutsford, and the stately home at Tatton Park.

Highlights for First-time Visitors

The Black Country Museum—Dudley: Tour 1
The Rows—Chester: Tour 3
Hereford Cathedral: Tour 1
Ironbridge Gorge Museum: Tour 2
Jodrell Bank Science Centre: Tour 3

Knutsford: Tour 3
Ludlow: Tour 2
Worcester Cathedral: Tour 1

Tour 1: From Worcester to Shrewsbury

Numbers in the margin correspond to points of interest on the Welsh Borders map.

❶ **Worcester** (pronounced as in Wooster, Ohio) sits on the Severn River in the center of Worcestershire, 118 miles northwest of London. It is an ancient city proud of its history, and in particular, its nickname, "The Faithful City," bestowed on it for its steadfast allegiance to the crown during the English Civil War. In this conflict between king and Parliament two major battles were waged here. The second one, the decisive Battle of Worcester in 1651, resulted in the exile of Charles II. More recently the town's name has become synonymous with the fine bone china produced here.

Despite "modernization" during the 1960s, some of medieval Worcester remains. This ancient section forms a convenient and pleasant walking route around the great cathedral.

There are few more quintessentially English sights than that of **Worcester Cathedral,** its towers overlooking the green expanse of the county cricket ground, its majestic image reflected in the swift-flowing—and frequently flooding—waters of the River Severn. There has been a cathedral here since the year 680, and much of what remains dates from the 13th and 14th centuries. Notable exceptions are the Norman crypt (built in the 1080s), the largest in England, and the ambulatory, a cloister built around the east end. The most important tomb in the cathedral is that of King John (1167–1216), one of the country's least admired monarchs, who alienated his barons and subjects through bad administration and heavy taxation and in 1215 was forced to sign the Magna Carta, the great charter of liberty. The cathedral's most beautiful decoration is in the vaulted **chantry chapel of Prince Arthur,** Henry VII's elder son, whose body was brought to Worcester after his death at Ludlow in 1502. (Chantry chapels were endowed by the wealthy to enable priests to celebrate masses there for the souls of the deceased.) *Tel. 0905/28854. Open daily 8:30–6.*

South of the cathedral (follow Severn St.) is the **Royal Worcester Porcelain Factory.** Here you can browse in the showrooms or rummage in the "seconds" stores; especially good bargains can be had in the January and July sales. Tours of the factory take you through the processes of porcelain-making. The **Dyson Perrins Museum,** in another part of the factory, houses a comprehensive collection of rare Worcester porcelain, from the start of manufacturing in 1751 to the present. *Severn St., tel. 0905/23221. Admission free; prebooked tours of factory, weekdays, ¾ hr., £3.25 adults, £2 children; Connoisseur Tours, 2 hrs, £10 adults, £8 children. Open weekdays 9:30–5, Sat. 10–5.*

Across the road from the porcelain factory is **The Commandery,** a cluster of 15th-century half-timbered buildings built as a poorhouse and later the headquarters of the Royalist troops during the Battle of Worcester. Now a museum, it presents a colorful audiovisual presentation about the Civil War in the magnificent, oak-beamed **great hall.** *Sidbury, tel. 0905/355071. Admission: £3 adults, £2 children and senior citizens, £8 family ticket. Open Mon.–Sat. 10–5, Sun. 1:30–5:30.*

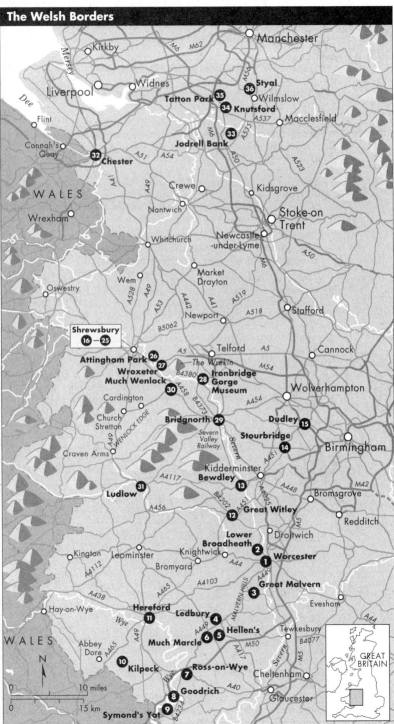

The Welsh Borders

Time Out **The Commandery** has a small tearoom, where you can eat on a terrace and watch houseboats bobbing on the canal.

Between The Commandery and the cathedral lies medieval **Friar Street.** As you walk toward the Cornmarket there are several buildings of particular interest, among them the **Tudor House,** a museum of domestic and social history, and **King Charles's House,** now a restaurant, where the beleaguered Charles II hid before his escape from the city (*see* Dining and Lodging, *below*). *Tudor House, tel. 0905/725371. Admission free. Open Mon.–Wed., Fri., and Sat. 10:30–5.*

Follow High Street, which is closed to traffic, back toward the cathedral. To your right you will see the **Guildhall** set back behind ornate iron railings. The hall's 18th-century facade features gilded statues of Queen Anne, Charles I, and Charles II, and a carving of Cromwell's head pinned up by the ears, a savage addition by the royalist citizens of Worcester.

At the end of High Street stands a **statue of Sir Edward Elgar** (1857–1934), one of Britain's best-known composers, who spent his early childhood in his parents' music store just a few yards from the cathedral. If you walk down Deansway, you can turn left into the riverside gardens and work your way back along the river below the cathedral and porcelain factory.

Southwest of Worcester lie the **Malvern Hills,** their long, low, purple profile rising starkly from the surrounding plain. These were the hills that inspired much of Elgar's oh-so-English music, as well as his remark that "there is music in the air, music all around us." Stop in
❷ and visit the **Elgar Birthplace Museum** at **Lower Broadheath** (follow B4204) before exploring the hills. Set in a peaceful little garden, the tiny brick cottage in which the composer was born now exhibits photographs, musical scores, letters, and such. *Crown East La., Lower Broadheath, tel. 0905/333224. Admission: £3 adults, 50p children, £2 senior citizens. Open mid-Feb.–Apr. and Oct.–mid-Jan., Thurs.–Tues. 1:30–4:30; May–Sept., Thurs.–Tues. 10:30–6.*

The Malverns shelter a string of communities whose main town is
❸ **Great Malvern,** off A449 about 7 miles south of Worcester. A Victorian spa town, its architecture has changed little since the mid-1800s. Exceptionally pure spring water is still bottled here and exported all over the world—the queen never travels without a supply. Some of the large hotels built in the spa days have been converted into "public" schools. Great Malvern is known today both as an educational center and as a great place for old folks' homes. The town also has a **Winter Gardens complex** with a theater, movie theater, and gardens, but it is the **Priory** that dominates the steep streets downtown. This is an early Norman Benedictine abbey in Perpendicular style, decorated with vertical lines of airy tracery and fine 15th-century glass. *Entrance opposite the church. Admission free. Open 8AM–dusk.*

Follow A449 southwest about 10 miles through Malvern Wells and
❹ Little Malvern to the market town of **Ledbury.** Here among black-and-white half-timbered buildings, take special note of two late-16th-century ones: the **Feathers Hotel** and the **Talbot Inn.** At the 17th-century **market hall,** perched on 16 chestnut columns, you can still buy produce on Saturdays. Look for the cheesemaker, and be sure to sample his very rare Single Gloucester, less rich and oily than the traditional orange-red Double Gloucester.

Time Out Right beside the market hall stands **The Market Place,** which is open all day for vegetarian lunches and teas.

Almost hidden behind the market hall is a cobbled lane leading to the church, crowded with medieval, half-timbered buildings. The **Old Grammar School** is now a Heritage Center tracing the town's history from Anglo-Saxon times. *Admission free. Open June–Sept., daily 11–5; Oct.–May, weekends 11–5.*

❺ Rejoin A449 and continue about 4 miles to **Hellen's** in Much Marcle. This is a beautiful mansion (part of it from the 13th century) in singularly authentic and pristine condition. The gloom and dust are part of the atmosphere; the house is still lit by candles, and central heating has been scorned. *Tel. 0531/84668. Admission: £2.50 adults, £1 children by guided tour only. Open Easter–Sept., Wed. and weekends 2–6.*

❻ **Much Marcle** is one English village that still holds an ancient annual ceremony. On Twelfth Night, January 6, the villagers go "wassailing," beating the apple trees to make them fruitful in the coming year. If you have a detailed map and plenty of time to spare, this is an area to wander around and discover tiny villages down sleepy lanes overhung by high hedges.

❼ Six miles southwest of Much Marcle by A449 lies **Ross-on-Wye,** a small market town with steep streets, perched high above the River Wye. It comes alive on Thursdays and Saturdays—market days—but is always a happy hunting ground for antiques.

❽ From here take B4234 for 3 miles to **Goodrich.** The ruins of **Goodrich Castle,** the English equivalent of a Rhine castle, loom dramatically over the Wye River crossing at Kerne Bridge. From the south it looks picturesque in its setting of green fields, but standing on its battlements on the north side, you quickly see its grimmer face. Dating from the late 12th century, the castle is surrounded by a deep moat carved out of solid rock, from which its walls appear to soar upward. Built to repel Welsh raiders, Goodrich was destroyed in the 17th century during the Civil War. *Tel. 0600/890538. Admission: £1.80 adults, 90p children, £1.35 senior citizens. Open Apr.–Oct., daily 10–6; Nov.–Mar., daily 10–4.*

❾ Continue south out of Goodrich on B4432 to the village of **Symond's Yat** ("gate"), where the 473-foot-high Yat Rock commands superb views of the River Wye as it winds through a narrow gorge and swings around in a great 5-mile loop.

❿ Turning toward Hereford, drive 11 miles northwest on small side roads to **Kilpeck,** a tiny hamlet blessed with one of the best-preserved Norman churches in Britain. It is lavishly decorated inside and out, with exceptional carving for a country church. The carvings depict all manner of subjects, from rabbits to scenes so lewd that they were removed by high-minded Victorians. (One or two ribald ones remain, however, so look carefully.) Don't miss the gargoyle rainwater spouts, either. From Kilpeck, A465 will lead you the 7 miles into Hereford.

⓫ **Hereford** is a busy country town, the center of a wealthy agricultural area known for its cider, fruit, and cattle—the white-faced Hereford breed has spread across the world. It is also an important cathedral city, its massive Norman cathedral towering proudly over the River Wye. Before 1066, Hereford was the capital of the Anglo-Saxon kingdom of Mercia and, earlier still, the site of Roman, Celtic, and Iron Age settlements. Today, tourists come primarily to see the cathedral, but quickly discover the charms of a town that has changed slowly but fairly unobtrusively with the passing centuries.

The town center is small. Attractive old buildings of various periods remain, but the stores are generally unremarkable. **Buttermarket,** in High Town, is a good place for local produce, while the **cattle market** provides an unmistakable glimpse of English country life. Livestock auctions are held every Wednesday.

Hereford Cathedral, built of local red sandstone with a massive central tower, has some fine 11th-century Norman carvings but suffered considerable "restoration" in the 19th century. Inside, the greatest glories include the 14th-century **bishop's throne;** some fine **misericords** (the elaborately carved undersides of choristers' seats); and the extraordinary **Mappa Mundi,** Hereford's own picture of the medieval world. This great map shows the Earth as flat, with Jerusalem at its center. It is now thought that the Mappa Mundi was the center section of an altarpiece, dating from 1290. The dean of the cathedral caused a furor in 1988 when he began negotiations with Sotheby's to put the piece on the market, to raise funds for the cathedral. Britain suddenly realized that the rich heritage of art treasures held mostly in cathedrals, might be under threat. The map was withdrawn from sale and is now on view in the crypt temporarily.

Best of all the cathedral's attractions is the library, containing some 1,500 chained books. Among the most valuable volumes is an 8th-century copy of the Four Gospels. Chained libraries are extremely rare: They date from medieval times, when books were as precious as gold. A gallery is being specially built for Mappa Mundi and the chained library. The expected opening will be in mid-1995. *Tel. 0432/ 359880. Cathedral admission free. Open Mon.–Sat. 8:30–5:30, Sun. 12:30–3:30. Mappa Mundi admission (includes audiovisual display): £2.60 adults, £1.60 children and senior citizens. Chained library: 40p adults, 10p children. Open Apr.–Oct., Mon.–Sat. 10:30– 12:30 and 2–4; Nov.–Mar., weekdays 11–11:30, Sat. 11–11:30 and 3–3:30.*

Leaving the cathedral by the north door, walk down Church Street to find the town's more unusual stores: jewelers, bookstores, and crafts and antiques shops.

Time Out The **Lichfield Vaults** (Church St.) is an attractive half-timbered pub on a pedestrians-only street near the cathedral. There's good bar food and space for outdoor eating and drinking.

From Church Street, cross East Street and follow the passageway into **High Town,** a large pedestrian square, and **The Old House,** a fine example of domestic Jacobean architecture, furnished in 17th-century style on three floors. *Tel. 0432/268121, ext. 207. Admission: £1 adults, 50p children and senior citizens. Open Apr.–Sept., Mon.– Sat. 10–1 and 2–5:30; Oct.–Mar., Mon.–Sat. 10–1.*

On the west side of High Town is the 13th-century **All Saints Church,** which contains an additional 300 chained books, as well as canopied stalls and fine misericords. From All Saints, walk down the pedestrian Eign Gate, through the pedestrian underpass, and down Eign Street, which continues as Whitecross Road. At the traffic lights turn left into Grimmer Road and bear right for the **Cider Museum.** A farm cider-house and a cooper's workshop have been re-created here, and you can tour ancient cider cellars, complete with huge oak vats. Apple brandy (applejack) has recently been made here for the first time in hundreds of years, and the museum has its own brand for sale. *Pomona Pl., off Whitecross Rd., tel. 0432/354207. Admission: £2 adults, £1.50 children and senior citizens. Open Apr.–Oct., daily 10–5:30; Nov.–Mar., weekdays 1–5.*

⑫ Now take A465 northeast toward Bromyard (14 mi), turn east onto A44 to Knightsford Bridge, turn north on B4197 to **Great Witley.** Pause to see the shell of **Witley Court,** whose remains will conjure up a haunting vision of its Edwardian heyday. The tiny Baroque parish church escaped the fire. Note its balustraded parapet, a small golden dome over its cupola, and, inside, a painted ceiling by Bellucci, 10 colored windows, and the ornate case of an organ once used by Handel. *Witley Ct., tel. 0299/896341. Admission: £1.25 adults, 60p children, 95p senior citizens. Open Apr.–Oct., daily 10–6; Nov.–Mar., Wed.–Sun. 10–4.*

⑬ About 8 miles north is **Bewdley,** an exceptionally attractive Severn Valley town, with many tall, narrow-fronted Georgian buildings clustered around the river bridge. In what was the 18th-century butchers' market, the **Shambles,** there is now an imaginative museum of local crafts. Workshops occupy either side of the old cobbled yard, and there are exhibitions and practical demonstrations of rope-making, charcoal-burning, clay-pipe-making, and glassblowing; there is also a working brass foundry. *Load St., tel. 0299/403573. Admission: £1 adults, children free, 60p senior citizens. Open Mar.–Nov., Mon.–Sat. 10–5:30, Sun. 2–5:30.*

Bewdley is the southern terminus of the **Severn Valley Railway,** a restored steam railroad running 16 miles north along the river to Bridgnorth (*see* Tour 2, *below*). It stops at a handful of sleepy stations where time has apparently stood still since the age of steam. You can get off at any of these little stations, enjoy a picnic by the river, and walk to the next station to get a train back. *Severn Valley Railway Co., Railway Station, Bewdley, Worcestershire DY12 1BG, tel. 0299/403816. May–Sept., trains run daily; check for irregular winter hours (weekends mostly).*

⑭ Eight miles northeast of Bewdley via A451 lies **Stourbridge,** home of Britain's crystal-glass industry. You can find bargains at "factory seconds" stores and tour the factories, too. *Stuart Crystal, Redhouse Glassworks, Vine St., Wordsley, tel. 0384/71161. Admission free. Tours weekdays 10–3. Royal Brierley Crystal, North St., Brierley Hill, tel. 0384/70161. Admission free. Tours Mon.–Thurs. 11, noon, and 1; Fri. 11. Royal Doulton Crystal, Webb-Corbett Glassworks, High St., Amblecote, tel 0384/440442. Admission free. Guided tours weekdays 10 and 11:15. Reservations required.*

⑮ Northeast of Stourbridge, on the edge of Birmingham, is **Dudley,** where the **Black Country Museum** was established to ensure that the area's industrial heritage is not forgotten. An entire industrial village has been constructed with disused buildings from around the region. There is a chain-maker's house and workshop, with demonstrations of chain-making; a druggist and general store, where costumed women describe life in a poor industrial community in the last century; a Methodist chapel; the Bottle & Glass pub, serving local ales and the traditional fagots and peas (a fried pork liver dish); and a coal mine and wharf. You can also ride on a canal houseboat through a tunnel, where an audiovisual show portrays canal travel of yesteryear. *Tipton Rd., tel. 021/557–9643. Admission: £4.95 adults, £3.40 children, £4.45 senior citizens, £14 family ticket. Open Mar.–Oct., daily 10–5; Nov.–Feb., Wed.–Sun. 10–4.*

Tour 2: Skirting the "Black Country"— Shrewsbury to the Cheshire Plain

Numbers in the margin correspond to points of interest on the Shrewsbury map.

⓰ Shrewsbury (pronounced "Shrose-bury"), the county seat of Shropshire, is within a great horseshoe loop of the Severn. One of England's most important medieval towns, it has a wealth of 16th-century half-timbered buildings and elegant ones from later periods. The market square forms the natural center of the town; leading off it are narrow alleys overhung with timbered gables. These alleys, called "shuts," were designed to be closed off at night to afford their residents greater protection. The town is especially proud of its flower displays, for which it has won many national awards. In the summer, window boxes and hanging baskets are a vivid contrast to the stark black-and-white buildings.

Shrewsbury is an ideal town to see on foot, and indeed, traffic has been banned in some of the most historic streets. A good starting point for a walking tour is the small square between **Fish Street** and **Butchers Row.** These streets are little changed since medieval times, when some of them took their names from the principal trades carried on there, but Peacock Alley, Gullet Passage, and Grope Lane clearly got their names from somewhere else. Nearby

⓱ are **St. Alkmund's** (the only church in England to be named after a

⓲ Saxon saint) and **St. Mary's churches,** both worth a visit for their iron-framed stained glass (an indication of the proximity of the Ironbridge Gorge). Below is **Bear Steps,** a cluster of restored half-timbered buildings which link Fish Street with Market Square.

⓳ Here the most notable building is **Ireland's Mansion,** a massive house with elaborate Jacobean timbering, richly decorated with quatrefoils.

⓴ Princess Street leads from the square to College Hill and **Clive House,** the home of Sir Robert Clive when he was Shrewsbury's member of Parliament in the mid-18th century. Better known as "Clive of India," this soldier-statesman was especially famous for winning the Battle of Plassey in 1757, thereby avenging the atrocity of the Black Hole of Calcutta. The house contains rooms furnished in Clive's period, and striking displays of fragile Staffordshire wares, particularly pieces from the Caughley and Coalport factories. *College Hill, tel. 0743/354811. Admission: £1 adults, 50p children, 80p senior citizens. Open Mon.–Sat. 10–5.*

Time Out **Poppies** (Princess St.) serves home-baked snacks—or try the **Golden Cross,** next door, for something stronger.

Below Swan Hill (turn left out of Clive House, then left again) you
㉑ will see the manicured lawn of **Quarry Park** sloping down to the river. In a sheltered corner is the Dingle, a colorful garden offering changing floral displays throughout the year. St. John's Hill in the Mardol, another of Shrewsbury's strangely named streets, will take
㉒ you back into town, or you can head for **Welsh Bridge** and stroll along
㉓ the riverbank. As the river loops away, the **castle** rises up on the right. Originally Norman, it was dismantled during the Civil War and later rebuilt by Thomas Telford, the distinguished Scottish engineer who designed a host of notable buildings and bridges at the beginning of the 19th century. The castle now houses the **Shropshire Regimental Museum,** providing an interesting reflection on 200 years of the county's past; you need not be a military-history buff to

Castle/
Shropshire
Regimental
Museum, **23**

Clive House, **20**

English
Bridge, **24**

Ireland's
Mansion, **19**

Quarry Park, **21**

St.
Alkmund's, **17**

St. Mary's, **18**

Shrewsbury
Abbey
Church, **25**

Welsh Bridge, **22**

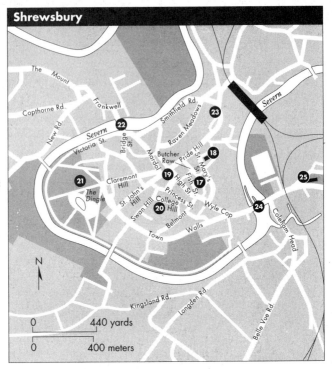

appreciate it. It was this regiment that was responsible for burning down the White House in Washington in 1814. The museum suffered from an IRA bomb in 1992; at press time, the repairs were scheduled for completion in 1994. *Tel. 0743/354811.*

24 25 If you cross the river by the **English Bridge** you'll reach **Shrewsbury Abbey Church,** almost all that remains of the monastery that stood here from 1083. The abbey figures in a series of popular medieval whodunits by Ellis Peters, which feature the detective Brother Cadfael and provide an excellent idea of life in this area during the Middle Ages. The Abbey Restoration Project has developed intriguing medieval walking tours. (Details from Restoration Project Office, 1 Holy Cross Houses, Abbey Foregate, Shrewsbury SY2 6BS, tel. 0743/232723.)

Numbers in the margin correspond with points of interest on the Welsh Borders map.

The rural scenery around Shrewsbury is among England's loveliest, with small towns, stately homes, and evocative museums scattered across the wide, open landscape. Four miles southeast of Shrews-
26 bury, just off A5, is **Attingham Park,** a mansion built in 1785 by George Steuart, who designed the round church of St. Chad's in Shrewsbury. It has an impressive three-story portico, with a pediment carried on four tall columns, dominating a wide sweep of parkland. Inside are painted ceilings, delicate plasterwork, and a collection of 19th-century Neapolitan furniture. *Tel. 0743/709203. Admission: £3.30 adults, £1.75 children, £8.25 family ticket. Open Apr.–Sept., Sat.–Wed. 1:30–5, Sun. 11–5; Oct., weekends 1:30–5.*

㉗ A mile farther east is **Wroxeter,** originally Viroconium, which flourished around AD 150 and was the fourth largest city in Roman Britain. Excavations beginning in 1863 revealed the foundations of the shattered pillars of the forum and fragments of the town walls. A complex of buildings around the forum has now been unearthed, providing a clear impression of the original town plan. Your imagination is helped along by an artist's reconstructions placed around the site. The small museum houses the Roman artifacts found in the last 100 years. *Tel. 0743/761330. Admission: £1.80 adults, 90p children, £1.35 senior citizens. Open Apr.–Oct., daily 10–6; Nov.–Mar., Wed.–Sun. 10–4.*

Continuing southeast on B4380, you will see, rising on the left, the **Wrekin,** a strange, conical extinct volcano. A few miles farther on you enter the wooded gorge of the Severn River. Here you can see the world's earliest iron bridge (1774), a monument to the discovery of how to smelt iron ore using coke (a coal residue), rather than char-

㉘ coal. The **Ironbridge Gorge Museum,** spread over 6 square miles, has six component sections. A good half-day will let you take in the major sites and stroll around the famous bridge, perhaps hunting for Coalport china in the stores clustered near it.

The best starting point is the **Severn Warehouse,** which has a good selection of literature and an audiovisual show on the gorge's history. From here you can drive (or in summer, take the museum's "park and ride" service) to Coalbrookdale and the **Museum of Iron,** which explains the production of iron and steel. You can see the original blast furnace built by Abraham Darby, who developed the coke process in 1709. Retrace your steps along the river until the graceful arches of the **Iron Bridge** come into view. You can still stroll across it to enjoy the sight of the river snaking through the gorge. The tollhouse on the far side houses an exhibition on the bridge's history and restoration.

A mile farther along the river is the old factory and the **Coalport China Museum** (the china is now made in Stoke-on-Trent). There are exhibits of some of the factory's most beautiful wares, and craftsmen give demonstrations. Above Coalport is **Blists Hill Open-Air Museum,** where you can see old mines, furnaces, and a wrought-iron works. But the main draw is the re-creation of a Victorian town, with the doctor's office, the sweet-smelling bakery, the candlemaker's, the sawmill, the printing shop, and the candy store.

Other attractions are the **Jackfield Tile Museum;** the **Tar Tunnel,** still oozing natural bitumen; **Rosehill House,** home of the Darby family of ironmasters; and **Rose Cottages.** *Ironbridge Gorge Museum Trust, Ironbridge, Telford, Shropshire TF8 7AW, tel. 0952/433522. Admission ticket to all sites: £8 adults, £5 children, £7 senior citizens, £25 family ticket. Open June–Aug., daily 10–6; Sept.–May, daily 10–5.*

Time Out **The New Inn** (Blists Hill Museum), a Victorian building, was moved to Blists Hill from Walsall, 22 miles away, so that it could be part of the open-air museum. It is a fully functioning pub, with gas lamps, sawdust on the floor, and traditional ales served from the cask. For an inexpensive meal, you can try a ploughman's lunch, a pastry from the antique-style bakery, or a pork pie from the butcher's store next door.

㉙ From Ironbridge the Severn turns south to **Bridgnorth** (take B4373), a pretty market town perching perilously close to the river. Built on a high sandstone ridge, Bridgnorth has two distinct parts, High Town and Low Town, connected by a winding road, flights of steep steps, and—best of all—a cliff railroad. Even the tower of the Norman castle seems to suffer from vertigo, having a 17-degree list (three times the angle of the Leaning Tower of Pisa). The Severn Valley Railway terminates here.

㉚ Take A458 northwest for just over 7 miles to **Much Wenlock,** a town full of half-timbered buildings, including a 16th-century guildhall, and the romantic ruins of the Norman **Wenlock Priory,** set in an attractive garden full of topiary. *High St., tel. 0952/727466. Admission: £1.80 adults, 90p children, £1.35 senior citizens. Open Apr.– Oct., daily 10–6; Nov.–Mar., Wed.–Sun. 10–4.*

Running southwest from Much Wenlock is the high scarp of **Wenlock Edge,** which provides a splendid view. This is hiking country, and if a healthy walk sounds inviting, turn off the Edge down through Cardington, and drive through Church Stretton into Cardingmill Valley, or to the wide, heather uplands on top of Long Mynd. In one of these inviting places, leave your car and set off on foot.

㉛ Take A49 a few miles south to **Ludlow,** which has often been described as the most beautiful small town in England, with medieval, Georgian, and Victorian buildings, centered on the great **Church of St. Lawrence.** Look for the **Feathers Hotel,** to admire its extravagantly decorated half-timbered facade. Cross the river and climb **Whitcliff** for the most spectacular view. The town is dwarfed by the massive, ruined, red sandstone **castle,** which dates from 1085 and was a vital stronghold for centuries. It was the seat of the Marcher Lords who ruled "the Marches," the local name for the border region. It is still privately owned by the earl of Powys. Follow the terraced walk around the castle for a lovely view. *Tel. 0584/873947. Admission: £2 adults, £1 children, £1.50 senior citizens, £6 family ticket. Open Feb.–Apr. and Oct.–Nov., daily 10:30–4; May–Sept., daily 10:30–5.*

Tour 3: Chester to Knutsford and Thereabouts

㉜ **Chester,** 35 miles due north of Shrewsbury, is in some ways similar to it, though it has many more "magpie" (black-and-white) half-timbered buildings, and its medieval walls are still standing. Chester has been a prominent city since the late 1st century AD, when the Roman Empire expanded northward and a fortress called Deva was established here, on the banks of the River Dee. The original Roman town plan is still evident: The principal streets, Eastgate, Northgate, Watergate, and Bridge Street, lead out from the Cross—the site of the central area of the Roman fortress—to the four city gates.

Since Roman times, seagoing vessels have sailed up the estuary of the Dee and anchored under the walls of Chester. The port enjoyed its most prosperous period during the 12th and 13th centuries. This was also the time when Chester's unique **Rows** originated. Essentially, they are double rows of stores, one at street level (or sometimes sunken just below), and the other on the second floor with galleries overlooking the street. The Rows line the junction of the four streets in the old town. They have medieval crypts below them, and some reveal Roman foundations.

History seems more tangible in Chester than in many other ancient cities. So much medieval architecture remains that the town center is quite compact, and modern buildings have not been allowed to intrude. A negative result of this perfection is that Chester has become a favorite bus-tour destination, with gift shops and casual restaurants, noise, and crowds.

Better to take to the **walls,** which are accessible from various points and provide splendid views of the city and its surroundings. The whole circuit is 2 miles, but if your time is short, climb the steps at Newgate and walk along toward Eastgate to see the great ornamental clock, erected to commemorate Queen Victoria's Diamond Jubilee in 1897. Here you will get a good aerial view of the street and a much better impression of the architectural detail than would be possible at ground level. Lots of small shops by this part of the walls sell old books, old postcards, antiques, and jewelry. Where the **Bridge of Sighs**—named after the enclosed bridge in Venice it closely resembles—crosses the canal, descend to street level and walk up Northgate Street into Market Square.

The **cathedral** is on St. Werburgh Street just off the square. Tradition has it that a church of some sort stood on this site in Roman times, but the earliest records indicate construction around AD 900. The earliest work traceable today, mainly in the north transept, is that of the 11th-century Benedictine abbey. Only a little later in date are the undercroft, the nave, and the chapter house. After Henry VIII dissolved the monasteries in the 16th century, the abbey-church became the cathedral-church of the new diocese of Chester. It was extensively restored in the 19th century by Sir Gilbert Scott.

In Eastgate Street you will see the impressive frontage of the Grosvenor Hotel (*see* Dining and Lodging, *below*), surrounded by the best of the city's boutiques. Over the Cross in Watergate Street, the stores specialize in antiques and arts and crafts.

Time Out   The **Falcon** (Lower Bridge St.) is a typical old pub that serves a wide range of lunch food. The **Witches Kitchen** (19 Frodsham St.), near the cathedral, is in a supposedly haunted building. It is good for pizzas and teas.

Bridge Street continues down toward the **castle** and the river. The castle's moats, and battlements were largely done away with at the end of the 18th century to make way for the classical-style civil and criminal courts, jail, and barracks. The castle now houses the **Cheshire Military Museum,** exhibiting uniforms, memorabilia, and some fine silver. *Tel. 0244/347617. Small admission fee. Open daily 9–noon and 1–5.*

From here you can follow the riverbank past the old bridge to the site of the **Roman amphitheater** beside Newgate, now a simple, grassy spot with an information board. The plain surrounding Chester is rich dairy land, famous for Cheshire cheese. To the west lies the coast road to northern Wales. To the southeast the countryside is gentle and wooded, dotted with the characteristic "magpie" villages.

From Chester, take A54 east for 23 miles to Holmes Chapel, then turn northeast on A535 for about 5 miles. Here you will see the giant ❸ radiotelescope of **Jodrell Bank.** Its 250-foot-wide reflector, weighing 2,000 tons, receives radio impulses from a host of distant stars. The planetarium offers a three-dimensional voyage into outer space; you can see an exhibition of radioastronomy, watch closed-circuit television demonstrations, and operate a model radiotelescope. *Lower*

Withington, Macclesfield, tel. 0477/71339. Admission: £3.50 adults,
£1.90 children, £2.50 senior citizens, £10.50 family ticket. Open
Easter–Oct., daily 10:30–5:30; Nov.–Easter, weekends 11–4:30.

㉞ Knutsford, 6 miles northwest on A50 or A535 and A537, retains a
distinctive air of 19th-century gentility. The Victorian novelist
Elizabeth Gaskell took Knutsford and its strong sense of local community as the inspiration for *Cranford,* her best-known novel. The
town seems little changed. There is an unhurried atmosphere here,
and the narrow streets are lined with fine stores. Walk along Princess Street, down the little cobbled lane beside the church, and onto
King Street, noting the Art Nouveau decoration—the elaborate
Belle Époque restaurant is a good example (*see* Dining and Lodging,
below).

㉟ Just north of Knutsford, 3½ miles off M6 via exit 19, is **Tatton Park,** a
fine stately home offering a wide variety of attractions. The mansion, built in the early 19th century for the Egerton family, is sumptuously decorated and furnished. In contrast, the family's previous
home, the 15th-century Old Hall also on the site, is austerely furnished in the style of its time. But the 1,000 acres of parkland and the
Japanese and Italian gardens at Tatton are the prize-winning features: deer graze and rhododendrons and azaleas flourish. The
grand vistas planned 200 years ago are best seen from the south terrace, across the formal gardens to the distances beyond. Tatton's
home farm has also been preserved and is now run as it would have
been half a century ago. There are marked trails throughout the
park, as well as two boating lakes. *Tel. 0565/654882. Admission (in-*
clusive ticket for mansion, gardens, Old Hall, and farm): £6 adults,
£4.20 children; separate fees for individual sights. Open daily year-
round. Telephone for exact times.

Time Out   There is a cafeteria-style restaurant in the stableblock of Tatton
Park. To book a table, call 0565/632914.

㊱ A few miles east is **Quarry Bank Mill** at **Styal,** a water-powered cotton mill. The massive buildings, dating from 1784, have been restored as a living museum of the cotton industry. Fibers and fabrics,
as well as spinning and weaving, are illustrated, and there are frequent live demonstrations. The old village re-creates the Quarry
Bank community of the 19th century, contrasting the hardships endured by the millworkers with the affluent lives of their masters,
the Greg family, who owned this factory right up until 1959, when it
finally ceased production. The 250 acres of woodland and riverside
are now a country park. *Styal, Wilmslow, tel. 0625/527468. Admis-*
sion: Mill: £3.30 adults, £2.40 children and senior citizens, £9.50
family ticket. Apprentice House and Garden: £2.50 adults, £2 chil-
dren and senior citizens, £8 family ticket; combined tickets £4.25
adults, £3 children and senior citizens, £12.50 family ticket. Open:
Mill, Oct.–Mar., Tues.–Sun. 11–4; Apr.–Sept., daily 11–5; Ap-
prentice House times differ, so check locally.

From Styal, which is close to Manchester Airport, you can return to
London or go on to visit the Northwest and the Lake District (*see*
Chapter 13).

What to See and Do with Children

The **Black Country Museum** in Dudley (*see* Tour 1).

The **Ironbridge museum complex** (*see* Tour 2).

The **Jodrell Bank Science Centre** (*see* Tour 3).

The **Severn Valley Railway** (*see* Tour 1).

Off the Beaten Track

The area known as **the Potteries,** less than an hour's drive from Shrewsbury northeast on A53, is the center of Britain's ceramic industry, immortalized in Arnold Bennett's novels, for example *Anna of the Five Towns.* There are, in fact, six towns—all now administered as "the City of **Stoke-on-Trent,**" where three award-winning museums evocatively portray the industrial and social history of this area:

The Gladstone Pottery Museum, a preserved Victorian potbank (pottery factory), has two of the old bottle-ovens, which stand in a cobbled yard surrounded by old workshops now used for exhibitions—including a gallery of chamber pots and wonderful colorful tiles. There are also displays on the history of Staffordshire's potters, and demonstrations by local craftsmen. *Uttoxeter Rd., Longton, tel. 0782/319232. Admission: £3 adults, £1.50 children, £2.30 senior citizens. Open Nov.–Feb., Mon.–Sat. 10–5; Mar.–Oct., Mon.–Sat. 10–5, Sun. 2–5.*

The Stoke-on-Trent City Museum and Art Gallery has a ceramic gallery of international standing, and is a particularly well-designed modern museum. Its extensive collection of Staffordshire wares is unique; there are also excellent galleries devoted to the fine arts. *Bethesda St., Hanley, tel. 0782/202173. Admission free. Open Mon.–Sat. 10–5, Sun. 2–5.*

Stop in at **Wedgwood's Visitor Centre and Museum** to learn about the pottery industry and look at Wedgwood wares. The craft area shows every stage of production, and you can chat with the craftspeople. There is an art gallery, and, of course, "firsts" and "seconds" stores. *Barlaston, tel. 0782/204218. Admission: £2.95 adults, £1.50 children and senior citizens, £6.95 family ticket. Open Apr.–Oct., weekdays 9–5, weekends 10–5; Nov.–Mar., weekdays 9–5, Sat. 10–4.*

South of the Potteries is **Shugborough,** an 18th-century mansion that is the ancestral home of Lord Lichfield, the queen's cousin and a well-known photographer. The **Staffordshire County Museum,** in what was the servants' quarters, re-creates 19th-century life with beautifully restored kitchens, laundry, and brewhouse. There is also a farm with rare breeds of livestock, and extensive parkland with formal gardens. *Milford, on A513, east of Stafford, tel. 0889/881388. Admission (to each site): £3.50 adults, £2 children; all-inclusive ticket: £7.50 adults, £5 children; family tickets: £10 (2 sites), £15 (3 sites). Open Easter–Oct., daily 11–5.*

Not far from Shugborough (17 mi southeast on A51), **Lichfield Cathedral** is worth a detour. The only English cathedral with three spires, the present building dates mainly from the 12th and 13th centuries, and has some fine 16th-century stained glass from the Cistercian Abbey of Herkenrode, near Liège, in Belgium. It stands in peaceful grounds surrounded by half-timbered houses. *Open daily 7:30–6:15.*

On the Wirral Peninsula, north of Chester, the **Boat Museum** at Ellesmere Port traces the history of Britain's inland waterways. Over 50 boats are on display, many still under restoration. You can board a 19th-century canal houseboat to find out how people managed to raise families on boats no wider than a modern hallway.

Dockyard Rd., tel. 051/355–5017. Admission: £4.50 adults, £3 chil-
dren, £3.50 senior citizens, £14 family ticket. Open Apr.–Oct., daily
10–5; Nov.–Mar., daily 11–4, closed Fri. Boat trips: £1.50 adults,
£1 children.

Shopping

Chester In an old Georgian building, 16 dealers fill two floors of the **Melodies Galleries** (32 City Rd., tel. 0244/328968) with a wide mix of fine furniture, porcelain, brass and copper, linen, books, and bric-a-brac—there's even a section selling old radios, called "On the Air." Export can be arranged.

Bookland (12 Bridge St., tel. 0244/347323), in an ancient building with a converted 14th-century crypt, has a wealth of travel and general-interest books, technical maps, sheet music, and plenty of tourist information.

Hereford **The Hereford Book Shop** (Church St., tel. 0432/357617) has new and secondhand books, guidebooks, maps, and greeting cards.

At the **Hereford Society of Craftsmen** in cobbled Capuchin Yard, off Church Street (tel. 0432/266049), you can see a violin-maker and a potter at work. Aside from the usual crafts, knitwear, posters, and watercolors are for sale.

Shrewsbury **Manser & Son** (53–54 Wyle Cop, tel. 0743/351120), close to the English Bridge, displays quality antiques, and has stores within stores of furniture, silver, lighting, pictures, and jewelry of the 17th to 20th centuries—from £2 to £10,000.

The Parade, just behind St. Mary's Church, is a shopping mall created from the former Royal Salop Infirmary, built in 1830. It's one of the most appealing malls you'll ever see, with attractive boutiques, posh apartments upstairs, a restaurant, and a terrace overlooking the river and the abbey.

St. Julian's Crafts Centre (High St., tel. 0743/353516) is worth visiting for gifts of pottery, wood, or jewelry. Housed in a deconsecrated church, it is quite unlike any craft center you have seen before. Open Mon.–Sat. 10–5 (closed most Thurs.).

Worcester **Framed** (46 Friar St., tel. 0905/28836), a contemporary art gallery in a half-timbered building, displays an extensive collection of original paintings, pastels, drawings, sculptures, and prints. Both gallery owners exhibit their own work.

Don't forget the shop at the **Royal Worcester Porcelain** factory (*see* Tour 1), where, among other items, you can buy "seconds."

Bygones has two stores in Worcester, one at 32 College Street (tel. 0905/25388), beside the cathedral, and the other not far away at 55 Sidbury, near the Commandery. Both have antiques, items of fine craftsmanship, and a selection of small gifts in silver, glass, and porcelain.

Markets Chester has a market every day except Wednesday. Hereford has a different market each day—food, clothing, livestock—on New Market Street. In Shrewsbury, there is a market on Tuesday, Wednesday, Friday, and Saturday; Worcester holds a market every Friday and Saturday at the Corn Market.

Sports and the Outdoors

Bicycling Bikes can be rented from **Little and Hall** (48 Broad St., Ross-on-Wye, tel. 0989/62639) and from the Foregate Street station in **Worcester** (tel. 0905/613501).

Boating This is an area crisscrossed with rivers and canals. **Severn Bank Centre** (Minsterworth, tel. 045275/357) organizes weekly courses on canoeing.

Golf Visitors are welcome at **Belmont** (tel. 0432/352666), 2 miles south of Hereford at an 18-hole course set amid rolling meadowland. The 18-hole course at **Cirencester** (tel. 0285/653939) is run by a club almost 100 years old. The **Tewkesbury Park Hotel** (*see* Dining and Lodging, *below*) has an 18-hole course, and visitors are welcome with a handicap certificate.

Walking The **Malvern Hills** make for climbs and walks of varying length and difficulty. The best places to start are Great Malvern and Ledbury. The route has been designated the "Elgar Way," and extends for 45 miles, but you don't need to do the whole thing. The views across the countryside from the top of the hills are spectacular. The hills are isolated, rising up from the fairly flat plain rather like Ayers Rock does in Australia, and providing vistas for many miles around. The area around **Ross-on-Wye** offers ideal walks with scenic river views. (Contact: Malvern Tourist Office, Winter Gardens Complex, Grange Rd., Worcs. WR14 3HB, tel. 0684/892289; Ross-on-Wye Tourist Office, 20 Broad St., Herefordshire, HR9 7EA, tel. 0989/62768.)

One of Britain's major long-distance hikes lies mostly within this area: the **Offa's Dyke Path,** named after the earthwork built by an 8th-century king to mark the boundary with Wales. The whole route is 168 miles, but only about 60 miles is along the actual dike. The Offa's Dyke Association (Offa's Dyke Centre, West St., Knighton, Powys LD7 1EW, tel. 0547/528753) promotes the conservation and understanding of the Welsh border region, including the Dyke itself. It publishes guides, along with other materials. This is an area of lush woods and swift rivers, with hidden villages and spectacular views; you'll find it very rewarding walking country. Lodging and dining are easily found. Local TICs and bookstores have details, books, and maps.

Dining and Lodging

Highly recommended hotels and restaurants are indicated by a star ★.

Dining Formal restaurants are few and far between in this rural area, and those that exist are mostly small. In many the owners do the cooking, concentrating on English country fare and using local produce whenever possible.

Category	Cost*
$$$$	over £50
$$$	£40–£50

$$	£20–£40
$	under £20

*per person, including first course, main course, dessert, and VAT; excluding drinks

Lodging You won't find many large, international-style hotels in the Welsh borders. Our selection aims to present a mix of larger hotels, often with considerable local historical significance, and smaller, family-owned establishments that form the bulk of the accommodations available. The latter are homier, friendlier, and invariably cheaper.

Category	Cost*
$$$$	over £150
$$$	£90–£150
$$	£50–£90
$	under £50

*All prices are for two people sharing a double room, including service, breakfast, and VAT.

Abberley
Dining and Lodging

The Elms Hotel. This traditional country-house hotel, in an ivy-clad Queen Anne building surrounded by formal gardens, is 16 miles northeast of Worcester and near Great Witley. All the rooms are individually and comfortably decorated in this former mansion. The restaurant, with its imaginative cooking and pleasant, family-dining-room ambience, is worth a visit on its own. *Stockton Rd., WR6 6AT, tel. 0299/896666, fax 0299/896804. 25 rooms with bath. Facilities: restaurant, garden, tennis, helipad. Restaurant reservations required. Jacket and tie required. AE, DC, MC, V. $$$*

Chester
Dining

Abbey Green and Garden House. This two-section restaurant in downtown Chester serves award-winning vegetarian cuisine in one part, and meat and fish in the other. Specialties include *parmigiana*, a dish composed of cashew and cream cheese balls on a bed of red-wine ratatouille; and a Szechuan dish of eggplant and tofu parcels, with stir-fried vegetables in wheatflour pancake on a bed of couscous. *1 Rufus Ct., off Northgate St., tel. 0244/313251. Reservations advised. Dress: casual. MC, V. Closed Sun., dinner Mon. $$*

Dining and Lodging

Chester Grosvenor Hotel. This is a traditional deluxe hotel in a Tudor-style, downtown building; it's remarkable to find such quiet luxury and sumptuous comfort in a small country town. The **Arkle Restaurant** is just as splendid as the rest of the hotel, with marble and stone walls, solid mahogany tables, candlelight, and gleaming silver. The style here is *cuisine légère*, using little cream or butter, only natural ingredients, and sauces made by reduction rather than thickening. There's an excellent choice of English and French cheeses and well-priced set menus. *Eastgate St., CH1 1LT, tel. 0244/324024, fax 0244/313246. 86 rooms with bath. Facilities: brasserie, sauna, solarium, gym. Restaurant reservations required. Jacket and tie required. AE, DC, MC, V. Restaurant closed Sun. and Mon. lunch. $$$$*

★ **Crabwall Manor.** This dramatic, castellated, part-Tudor, part-neo-Gothic mansion is set on 11 acres of farm and parkland (2¼ mi northwest on A540). It has elegant, subtle furnishings in floral chintzes, a wonderful stone staircase, and extremely comfortable bedrooms. The spacious restaurant boasts *cordon bleu* cooking and is worth visiting—say, for lunch, while exploring the neighborhood. *Parkgate Rd., Mollington CH1 6NE, tel. 0244/851666, fax 0244/851400. 48 rooms with bath. Restaurant reservations required. Dress: casual. AE, DC, MC, V. $$$$*

Green Bough Hotel. The Green Bough is in a large Edwardian house, with a variety of antiques and bric-a-brac. Rooms in the annex are modern. One of the comfortable bedrooms has a four-poster. There's a handy dining room with a sensible, home-cooked menu. *60 Hoole Rd., CH2 3NL, tel. 0244/326241, fax 0244/326265. 19 rooms with bath or shower. MC, V. $$*

Fownhope **Green Man Inn.** In this friendly 15th-century half-timbered inn, lo-
Dining and cated in a quiet village (on B4224) midway between Hereford and
Lodging Ross-on-Wye, the rooms are a mix of modern and traditional. The bar food is generous; there are two restaurant rooms. *Near Hereford, HR1 4PE, tel. 0432/860243, fax 0432/860207. 15 rooms with bath. MC, V. $$*

Hereford **The Orange Tree.** This is a refurbished, wood-paneled pub conve-
Dining niently located on King Street where it joins Bridge Street, near the
★ cathedral. It is a comfortable stopping place on a sightseeing day, with good, solid bar food at lunchtime. *16 King St., tel. 0432/267698. No credit cards. $*

Lodging **Castle Pool.** All that's left of Hereford Castle is the moat, home to a family of ducks. Next to the moat, this 1850 building, dubbed Castle Pool, now features blandly furnished but comfortable and quiet bedrooms. The restaurant has some Middle Eastern dishes on its menu. *Castle St., HR1 2NR, tel. 0432/356321. 27 rooms with bath. Facilities: restaurant, garden. AE, DC, MC, V. $$*

Ferncroft Hotel. This small, family-run hotel is decorated in Victorian style, with some antique furniture. The restaurant serves local produce, thoughtfully prepared. *144 Ledbury Rd., HR1 2TB, tel. 0432/265538. 12 rooms, 4 with bath. MC, V. Closed 2 weeks at Christmas. $*

Hopbine Hotel. The Hopbine is a mile from the center of town in the direction of Leominster, but it's worth the jaunt. This Victorian guest house stands amid 2 acres of grounds. The very comfortable, quiet rooms come equipped with a television and appliances for making tea and coffee. Evening meals are available. You'll appreciate the friendliness of this simple place. *Roman Rd., HR1 1LE, tel. 0432/268722. 12 rooms, 5 with bath. No credit cards. $*

Ironbridge **The Library House.** Nestled into the hillside near the Ironbridge
Lodging museums, this small hotel was redone in 1992 to lighten its look yet keep its attractive Victorian style. *11 Severn Bank, TF8 7AN, tel. 0952/432299. 3 rooms with bath. No credit cards. $*

Kington **Penrhos Court.** This fascinating hotel/restaurant virtually on the
Dining and Welsh border is in the 13th-century cruck hall (a room with a curved
Lodging timber roof) of an Elizabethan manor house. The bedrooms all have
★ bird names and are attractively decorated. The food is the work of chef/proprietor Daphne Lambert, and is very inventive. Specialties change regularly, but might include breast of chicken with langoustine sauce, or a splendid fish ragout. There are tables outside in summer. *Kington (15 mi west of Leominster on A44), tel. 0544/230720, fax 0544/230754. 19 rooms with bath or shower. Reservations required. Dress: neat but casual. AE, DC, MC, V. Closed lunches except Sun. $$$*

Knutsford **La Belle Époque.** The restaurant contrasts its unusual, somewhat
Dining theatrical art nouveau decor with a lighter style of French cooking, typified in such dishes as boned local quail with chicken-liver and

pine-nut filling, and saddle of local venison with three-fruit sauce. In summer you can dine in the roof garden. *60 King St., tel. 0565/ 633060. Reservations advised; required weekends. Dress: casual. AE, DC, MC, V. Dinner only Mon.–Sat., closed Sun. and national holidays. $$$*

Lodging **Royal George Hotel.** A coaching inn dating back in part to the 14th century, it is located in the center of this quiet town. Comfortable rooms are furnished in traditional style. *King St., WA16 6EE, tel. 0565/634151, fax 0565/634955. 31 rooms, all with bath. AE, DC, MC, V. $$*

Ledbury **Hope End Country House Hotel.** An 18th-century house well off the *Dining and* beaten track (2 mi north on B4214), with Oriental embellishments *Lodging* and period decorations, this hotel is set in 40 acres of wooded park- ★ land. It was the childhood home of the poet Elizabeth Barrett Browning. Much of it burned in 1910, but what's left is architectural- ly interesting. The restaurant, which uses vegetables and herbs from its own kitchen garden, has won awards. *Hope End, HR8 1SQ, tel. 0531/633613, fax 0531/636366. 9 rooms with bath. Facilities: gar- den. MC, V. Restaurant closed Mon., Tues., and Dec.–Feb. Hotel closed mid-Dec.–mid-Feb. $$$*

Leominster **The Marsh.** This is a new country-house hotel at Eyton, 2½ miles *Dining and* northwest of Leominster off B4361. It is a partly 14th-century house *Lodging* with a timbered medieval hall in an idyllic setting teeming with wildlife. The cooking is mainly French provincial, using fresh herbs from the garden. *Eyton, HR6 0AG, tel. 0568/613952. 5 rooms with bath. Facilities: restaurant, garden. AE, MC, V. $$$*

Ludlow **Dinham Hall.** Dinham Hall is a converted merchant's 1792 town *Dining and* house near Ludlow Castle. The owners have managed to combine *Lodging* the original historic elements in the house with modern comforts. The dining room serves imaginative dishes such as salmon with wild mushrooms and venison with noodles. This is a good base for explor- ing the region. *Off Market Sq., SY8 1EJ, tel. 0584/876464, fax 0584/ 876019. 14 rooms with bath. Facilities: restaurant, garden, sauna. Restaurant: Reservations advised; jacket and tie required. AE, MC, V. Restaurant $$; Hotel $$$*

Malvern **The Cottage in the Wood.** This hotel sits in its shady grounds high up *Dining and* on the side of the Malvern Hills with splendid views of the country- *Lodging* side. The furnishings are country-house comfortable; the rooms vary in size. The restaurant has the best of the panorama through its tall windows. Food is English, with enough international influences to make the menu interesting, and there is a wide selection of En- glish wines. *Holywell Rd., WR14 4LG, tel. 0684/573487, fax 0684/ 560662. 20 rooms with bath. Facilities: restaurant, garden. Reser- vations required for restaurant. Jacket and tie required. AE, MC, V. $$$*

Sidney House. In addition to its great views, this dignified Georgian hotel, run by a friendly husband-and-wife team, is also near the town center. The adequately sized bedrooms with television make this lodging a good bet for people traveling on a budget. Dinner is available for about £16 a person. *40 Worcester Rd., WR14 4AA, tel. 0684/574994. 8 rooms, 5 with bath or shower. AE, MC, V. $$*

Malvern Wells **Croque en Bouche.** In this traditional French restaurant, the food is *Dining* the very best bourgeois cuisine, with superb handling of excellent ★ local ingredients. Japanese dishes are also on the menu. The chef/ proprietor, Marion Jones, has earned a considerable reputation. Specialties include skate with pesto sauce, ragout of venison, sushi, and roast guinea fowl with coriander. There is a very special wine list. *221 Wells Rd., tel. 0684/565612. Reservations required. Jacket and tie required. MC, V. Dinner only. Wed.–Sat. $$$*

Nantwich
Dining and Lodging

Rookery Hall Hotel. This large, elegant restaurant (one of two in the hotel) boasts mahogany- and walnut-paneled walls and an ornate plasterwork ceiling. (The other restaurant is more restrained. Both have great views of the gardens.) Cheshire sausages on a bed of leeks, and rack of Welsh lamb with a sauce made from home-grown mustard seed, are typical old English dishes. It is also an excellent place to sample English cheeses, and there's a first-rate international wine list. The hotel in which these excellent restaurants are located is a lovely old house, surrounded by wide grounds with lakes. The service is friendly and personal, the bedrooms luxurious with old furniture and modern plumbing. *Worleston CW5 6DQ, tel. 0270/ 610016, fax 0270/626027. 45 rooms with bath. Facilities: restaurant, gardens, tennis, helipad. Restaurant reservations required. Jacket and tie required. AE, DC, MC, V. $$$*

Ross-on-Wye
Lodging

The Chase Hotel. This well-renovated Georgian-style country-house hotel is set in 11 acres. Rooms are simply and comfortably furnished in the main house, and more modern in the newer wing. Bowls of fresh fruit and decanters of sherry welcome you. *Gloucester Rd., HR9 5LH, tel. 0989/763161, fax 0989/768330. 40 rooms with bath. Facilities: restaurant, garden. AE, MC, V. $$*

Shrewsbury
Dining

Country Friends. An attractive, imitation black-and-white building, 5 miles south of Shrewsbury by the A49, houses this light and airy restaurant overlooking a garden and pool. There are log fires in winter. Specialties include halibut with wild mushrooms and smoked oysters, venison with black currant sauce, and lamb noisettes roasted in mustard crust with mint hollandaise. There are also three simple bedrooms available. *Dorrington, tel. 0743/718707. Reservations required. Dress: casual. AE, DC, MC, V. Closed Sun.–Mon., 2 weeks end July, and middle week in Oct. $$*

Traitors Gate. Installed in a series of 13th-century, vaulted, brick cellars, this atmospheric restaurant serves freshly prepared, reasonably priced meals that make for a perfect break in a day's sightseeing. The restaurant is located close to the local castle, and gains its name from an incident in the Civil War, when a young Roundhead lieutenant ransacked the Cavalier-held fortress. He was later executed as a traitor. The service is very friendly. *St. Mary's Water La., tel. 0743/249152. Reservations not necessary. Dress: casual. MC, V. $*

Lodging

Prince Rupert Hotel. This black-and-white, half-timbered inn in the historic city center was the headquarters of Prince Rupert, the most famous Royalist general (he was also the nephew of Charles I) during the Civil War. It is now furnished in modern style, although four rooms have four-poster beds. *Butcher Row, SY1 1UQ, tel. 0743/ 236000, fax 0743/357306. 66 rooms with bath. Facilities: restaurant, recreation room, in-house movies. AE, DC, MC, V. $$–$$$*

Sandford House. This late-Georgian B&B, close to the river and the town center, is run by the hospitable Jones family. The bedrooms are clean and functional, but well furnished. There is a spacious blue-and-white breakfast room, and an attractive rear garden. *St. Julian Friars, SY1 1XL, tel. 0743/343829. 10 rooms, 8 with bath or shower. MC, V. $$*

Tewkesbury
Lodging

The Royal Hop Pole. This is one of the most famous old English inns and is now a part of the Trusthouse Forte chain. The rooms at the rear have wood beams and views of the pretty gardens running down to the river. One of the front rooms has a four-poster. *Church St.,*

GL20 5RT, tel. 0684/293236, fax 0684/296680. 29 rooms with bath. Facilities: restaurant, garden. AE, DC, MC, V. $$$
Tewkesbury Park Hotel, Golf and Country Club. Just outside town (1¼ mi south on A38), this former 18th-century mansion is the ideal stopover point for the athletically inclined. There's almost every sports facility anyone could want, plus the wonderful countryside. The Park also caters to a flourishing conference trade. *Lincoln Green La., GL20 7DN, tel. 0684/295405, fax 0684/292386. 78 rooms with bath. Facilities: restaurant, coffee shop, garden, indoor pool, sauna, gym, tennis, squash, golf course, in-house movies. AE, DC, MC, V. $$$*

Worcester
Dining
★

Brown's. A former grain mill houses this light and airy riverside restaurant. The fixed-price menu and daily specialties include warm salad with breast of duck and croutons, and crayfish-and-bacon kebabs. *24 Quay St., tel. 0905/26263. Reservations advised. Dress: casual. AE, DC, MC, V. Closed Sat. lunch and Sun. dinner. $$$*
King Charles II Restaurant. Here you can enjoy dining in the black-and-white, half-timbered house in which Charles II hid after the Battle of Worcester. It is now an oak-paneled, silver-service restaurant with a very friendly atmosphere. Cuisine is mainly French and Italian, but there are also traditional English selections, such as beef Wellington, and such fresh fish dishes as Dover sole meunière. *29 New St., tel. 0905/22449. Reservations advised. Dress: casual. AE, DC, MC, V. Closed Sun. $$*
Tilley's Brasserie. The deluxe Fownes Hotel, a converted Victorian glove factory, now houses this French café named for the raunchy 19th-century burlesque artist, Vesta Tilley, who was born in Worcester in 1864. You can eat the nouvelle fare for a fairly reasonable cost. Come here for afternoon tea and Friday evening jazz performances. *Fownes Hotel, City Walls Rd., tel. 0905/613151. Reservations advised. Dress: casual. AE, DC, MC, V. $$*

Lodging
Ye Old Talbot Hotel. The Old Talbot was originally a courtroom belonging to the cathedral, which stands close by. The hotel has been refurbished, and there are modern extensions to the 16th-century core of the building. *Friar St., WR1 2NA, tel. 0905/23573, fax 0905/612760. 29 rooms with bath. Facilities: restaurant. AE, DC, MC, V. $$*
49 Britannia Square. This attractive guest house in a quiet, elegant, Georgian square is half a mile from downtown. *49 Britannia Sq., WR1 3HP, tel. 0905/22756. 3 rooms, 1 with bath. No credit cards. Closed Dec. 25–Jan. 1. $*

The Arts

Festivals
The **Three Choirs' Festival** has been held on a three-year rotation between the cathedral cities of Gloucester, Worcester, and Hereford since about 1717. In 1995 it will be held in Gloucester (August 19–26). The festival celebrates the English choral tradition, often with specially commissioned works. The program appears in March. *Details from The Festival Secretary, Three Choirs Festival, Community House, College Green, Gloucester GL1 2LZ, tel. 0452/529819.*

Malvern has historical connections with Sir Edward Elgar as well as with George Bernard Shaw, who premiered many of his plays there. The **Malvern Festival** was originally devoted to their works, although now it also offers a wide variety of new music and new drama. The **Malvern Fringe Festival** has an exceptional program of alternative events. Both festivals run for two or three weeks from the end of May to early June. *Details from Malvern TIC, Winter*

So, you're getting away from it all.

Just make sure you can get back.

Here's a travel tip that will make it easy to call back to the States. Dial the access number for the country you're visiting and connect right to AT&T. It's the quick way to get English-speaking AT&T operators and can minimize hotel telephone surcharges.

If all the countries you're visiting aren't listed above, call **1 800 241-5555** for a free wallet card with all AT&T access numbers. Easy international calling from AT&T. **TrueWorld Connections.**

AT&T

American Express offers Travelers Cheques built for two.

Cheques *for Two*™ from American Express are the Travelers Cheques that allow either of you to use them because both of you have signed them. And only one of you needs to be present to purchase them.

Cheques *for Two* are accepted anywhere regular American Express Travelers Cheques are, which is just about everywhere. So stop by your bank, AAA* or any American Express Travel Service Office and ask for Cheques *for Two*.

Garden Complex, Grange Rd., Hereford & Worcs WR14 3HB, tel. 0684/892289.

In Shropshire, the **Ludlow Festival,** starting at the end of June, sums up all that is English: Shakespeare is performed in the open air against the romantic backdrop of the ruined castle to an audience armed with cushions, raincoats, lap robes, and picnic baskets, as well as hip flasks. Reservations are accepted starting in early May. *Details from The Festival Box Office, Castle Sq., Ludlow, Shropshire SY8 1AY, tel. 0584/872150.*

During the **Shrewsbury International Music Festival,** in June and July, the town vibrates to traditional and not-so-traditional music by groups from America, western Europe, and sometimes eastern Europe. *Details from Concertworld (UK) Ltd., 150 Waterloo Rd., London SE1 8BD, tel. 071/401–9941.*

12 Wales

Wales, apart from being called the Land of Song, is also a land of mountain and flood, where wild peaks challenge the sky and waterfalls thunder down steep, tree-clad chasms. It is a land of gray-stoned medieval castles, ruined abbeys, little steam trains chugging through dramatic scenery, male-voice choirs, and a handful of cities. Small pockets of the south and northeast have been heavily industrialized—largely with mining and steelmaking—since the 19th century, but long stretches of the coast and the mountainous interior remain areas of unmarred beauty. Fewer than 5 percent of American visitors to Britain go to Wales, and many of those are heading for the Irish ferries, yet to miss out on Wales is to miss one of Britain's great scenic experiences.

Wales was finally united with England in 1536, under the Tudor King Henry VIII (the Tudors came originally from the Isle of Anglesey off the Welsh coast), but it has nonetheless retained an identity and character quite separate from that of the rest of Britain; the Welsh will not thank you if you confuse their country with England.

The Welsh are a Celtic race. Although the Romans made sporadic attempts to subdue Wales, the people were never Romanized as, later, they were never Anglicized. When, toward the middle of the first millennium AD, the Anglo-Saxons spread through Britain, they pushed the indigenous Celts farther back into their Welsh mountain strongholds. (In fact, "Wales" comes from the Saxon word "Weallas," which means "strangers," the impertinent name given by the new arrivals to the natives. The Welsh, however, have always called themselves "Y Cymry," "the companions.") The Normans made attempts to extend their influence over Wales in the 11th century, but it was not until the fearsome English king, Edward I (1272–1307), waged a brutal and determined campaign to conquer Wales that English supremacy was established. Welsh hopes were finally crushed with the death in battle of Llywelyn ap Gruffudd, the last native Prince of Wales, in 1282. Dreams of nationhood were revived under the brilliant and popular leadership of Owain Glyndwr between 1400 and 1410. He ruled virtually the whole of Wales at one point, but English might prevailed again.

In the 15th and 16th centuries, the Tudor kings Henry VII and Henry VIII continued England's ruthless domination of the Welsh, principally by attempting to abolish their language. Ironically it was another Tudor monarch, Elizabeth I, who ensured its survival by authorizing a Welsh translation of the Bible in 1588. Today, many people still say they owe their knowledge of Welsh to the Bible. The language is spoken by only a fifth of the population, but it still flourishes. Signs are bilingual, but don't worry; everyone speaks English, too.

Pronouncing Welsh correctly can be tongue-twisting, even for English visitors who live nearby, so there's no need to feel self-conscious when you try. The best way to learn is to ask a friendly local—who will appreciate your interest. Welsh is not as difficult as it looks, for it is almost entirely phonetic. And place names helpfully tell you a great deal about their surroundings and sometimes their historical associations.

Aber, for example, means "river mouth or confluence"; thus Aberystwyth means mouth of the river Ystwyth. And the common place-name component *llan* means "church or enclosure," so Llandudno means "the church of St. Tudno." Other terms that crop up frequently are *bach* or *fach* (small), *blaen* (head, end, source), *bryn* (hill), *bwlch* (pass), *cefn* (ridge), *craig* or *graig* (rock), *cwm* (valley), *cymer* (meeting of rivers), *dyffryn* (valley), *eglwys* (church), *glyn* (glen), *llyn* (lake), *llys* (court, hall), *maen* (stone), *mawr* or *fawr* (great, big), *merthyr* (church, burial place), *moel* or *foel* (bare hill), *mynydd* or *fynydd* (mountain, moorland), *pen* (head, top, end), *pentre* (village, homestead), *plas* (hall, mansion), *pont* or *bont* (bridge), *sarn* (causeway, old road), *ystrad* (valley floor).

The language is just one key to Wales's distinctiveness. English-speaking Welsh—the vast majority of the country's 2.75 million inhabitants—regard themselves as being just as Welsh as anyone else, which sometimes leads to differences of opinion, mainly about cultural affairs. But everyone feels a deep-rooted attachment to the country, and there's a strong sense of Welsh identity.

A love of landscape and sense of place are recurring themes in Welsh literature. Despite its small size, Wales has three National Parks (Snowdonia, the Brecon Beacons, and the Pembrokeshire Coast) and five "Areas of Outstanding Natural Beauty" (the Wye Valley, Gower Peninsula, Llŷn Peninsula, Isle of Anglesey, and Clwydian Range), as well as large tracts of unspoilt moor and mountain in mid-Wales, the least traveled part of the country.

Essential Information

Important Addresses and Numbers

Tourist Information
The Wales Bureau, The British Travel Centre, 12 Lower Regent St., London SW1Y 4PQ, tel. 071/409-0969. Open weekdays 9–6:30, weekends 10–4.
The Wales Tourist Board, Brunel House, 12th Floor, 2 Fitzalan Rd., Cardiff, S. Glamorgan CF2 1UY, tel. 0222/499909. Visitors should go to the Cardiff tourist information center (*see below*).
Cadw: Welsh Historic Monuments, Brunel House, 2 Fitzalan Rd., Cardiff CF2 1UY, tel. 0222/465511.
Tourist information centers, normally open Mon.–Sat. 9:30–5:30, but varying according to the season, include:
Aberystwyth: Terrace Rd., tel. 0970/612125.
Betws-y-Coed: Royal Oak Stables, tel. 0690/710426.
Caernarfon: Oriel Pendeitsh (opposite castle entrance), tel. 0286/672232.
Cardiff: Central Station, tel. 0222/227281.
Llandrindod Wells: Old Town Hall, tel. 0597/822600.
Llandudno: Chapel St., tel. 0492/876413.
Llanfair P.G.: Station Site, Isle of Anglesey, tel. 0248/713177.
Llangollen: Town Hall, tel. 0978/860828.
Machynlleth: Owain Glyndwr Centre, tel. 0654/702401.
Ruthin: Craft Centre, tel. 0824/703992.
Swansea: Singleton St., tel. 0792/468321.
Tenby: The Croft, tel. 0834/842402.
Welshpool: Flash Leisure Centre, tel. 0938/552043.

Travel Agencies
American Express: 3 Queen St., Cardiff, tel. 0222/668858.
Thomas Cook: 16 Queen St., Cardiff, tel. 0222/224886; and 3 Union St., Swansea, tel. 0792/464311.

Car-Rental Agencies
Cardiff: Avis, 14–22 Tudor St., tel. 0222/342111; **Eurodollar,** 10 Dominions Way Industrial Estate, Newport Rd., tel. 0222/496256; **Europcar,** 1–11 Byron St., tel. 0222/497110; **Hertz,** 9 Central Sq., tel. 0222/224548.

Arriving and Departing

By Car From London, M1/M6 is the most direct route to north Wales. A55, the coast road from Chester on the English side of the north Wales border, goes through Bangor. For Cardiff (157 mi), Swansea (196 mi), and South Wales, take M4. Aberystwyth (211 mi) and Llandrindod in mid-Wales are well-served by major roads. The A40 is also an important route through central and South Wales.

By Train **British Rail** serves Wales from London Euston (tel. 071/387–7070) and London Paddington (tel. 071/262–6767) stations. Average travel times include: from Euston, 3¾ hours to Llandudno in North Wales (some direct trains, otherwise change at Crewe) and around five hours to Aberystwyth in mid-Wales (changing at Birmingham). From Paddington, it is less than two hours to Cardiff and less than three to Swansea in South Wales. The trains into Wales operate under the InterCity banner.

By Bus **National Express** (tel. 071/730–0202) serves Wales from London's Victoria Coach Station and also direct from London's Heathrow and Gatwick Airports. Average travel times from London are: 3½ hours to Cardiff; four hours to Swansea; 5½ hours to Aberystwyth; and 4½ hours to Llandudno.

Getting Around

By Car Distances in miles may not be great in Wales, but getting from place to place takes time because there are few major highways. The mountains mean that there is no single fast route from north to south, although A470 is good—and scenic—and A487 does run along or near most of the coastline. The mountains also mean that many of the smaller roads are winding and difficult to maneuver, but they do reveal magnificent views of the surrounding landscape.

By Train British Rail's **Regional Railways** service (tel. 0222/228000) covers the valleys of South Wales, western Wales, central Wales, the Conwy Valley and the North Wales coast on many highly scenic routes: the **Cambrian Coast Railway,** for example, running 70 miles between Aberystwyth and Pwllheli; the **Heart of Wales** line, linking Swansea and Craven Arms, near Shrewsbury, 95 miles away. You can buy economical unlimited-travel Rail Rover tickets. All-Wales and North and mid-Wales tickets for three and seven days also include travel on certain bus services and the Ffestiniog Railway, as well as discounts for travel on some of Wales's other famous "Little Trains" (*see below*).

Wales is undoubtedly the best place in Britain for narrow-gauge steam railways. The *Great Little Trains of Wales*—narrow gauge—operate during the summer months through the mountains of Snowdonia and central Wales. Many of these lines wind through landscapes of extraordinary grandeur; for example, the **Ffestiniog Railway,** which links two British Rail lines at the old slate town of Blaenau Ffestiniog and Porthmadog, climbs the mountainside around an ascending loop more reminiscent of the Andes than rural Britain. Tiny, copper-knobbed engines, panting fiercely, haul narrow carriages packed with tourists through deep cuttings and along rocky shelves above ancient oak woods through the heart of the Snowdonia National Park. Other lines include: the **Talyllyn,** following a deep valley from the coastal resort of Tywyn; the **Vale of Rheidol Railway,** from Aberystwyth to Devil's Bridge; the **Welshpool and Llanfair Light Railway,** between Welshpool and Llanfair Caereinion; the **Welsh Highland Railway** from Porthmadog;

the **Brecon Mountain Railway** from Merthyr Tydfil; and the **Llanberis Lake Railway.** Wanderer tickets are available for unlimited travel on the "Great Little Trains of Wales": four days £20, eight days £27, children half-price. Concessions are available for groups. Full details, including summary timetables, are available from **Great Little Trains of Wales** (c/o The Station, Llanfair Caereinion, Powys SY21 0SF, tel. 0938/810441).

Snowdonia also has Britain's only Alpine-style steam rack railway, the **Snowdon Mountain Railway,** where little sloping boilered engines on rack-and-pinion track push their trains 3,000 feet up from Llanberis to the summit of Snowdon, Wales's highest mountain. Details of services from **Snowdon Mountain Railway** (Llanberis, Caernarfon, Gwynedd, tel. 0286/870223).

By Bus Although the overall pattern is a little fragmented, most parts of Wales are accessible by bus. The main operators are: **Cardiff Bus** (tel. 0222/396521), **Newport Transport** (tel. 0633/262914), **South Wales Transport** (tel. 0792/475511), and **Red and White** (tel. 0633/265100) for South Wales; **Crosville Wales** (tel. 0492/592111) for mid- and North Wales. Crosville offers unlimited-travel Day Rover and Weekly Rover tickets. It also has long-distance routes: the daily TrawsCambria cross-country service between Cardiff and Bangor (calling at Swansea, Carmarthen, Aberystwyth, Dolgellau, and Caernarfon) and another less frequent service between Cardiff and Mold (through central Wales and the border country, calling at Chester).

Although primarily a carrier into Wales, **National Express** (*see* Arriving and Departing, *above*) also has routes through Wales (from Cardiff farther west, for example, or along the North Wales coast).

Guided Tours

If you are interested in having a personal guide, then contact the **Wales Official Tourist Guide Association** through Margaret Butler, 210 Cyncoed Rd., Cardiff, S. Glamorgan CF2 6RS, tel. 0222/752679. WOTGA only uses guides recognized by the Wales Tourist Board. It will put together tailor-made tours for you and, if you wish, have your guide meet you at the airport. You can book either a driver/guide or someone to accompany you as you drive.

Another good way of seeing Wales is by local tour bus; in summer there's a large choice of day and half-day excursions to most parts of the country. In major resorts and cities you should ask at a tourist information center or bus station for details.

Exploring Wales

We have chosen to concentrate our five tours of Wales along its coasts and among its soaring mountains. Tour 1 begins off the northwest coast, on the island of Anglesey at Beaumaris, where you'll visit the first of many castles. From there the tour goes via Caernarfon and Llanberis into the mountains of Snowdonia, crossing to Betws-y-Coed and up to the seaside resort of Llandudno and Conwy Castle, taking in the glorious garden at Bodnant en route. The road then turns southeast from the coast, visiting Denbigh and Ruthin, crossing the spectacular Horseshoe Pass to reach Llangollen, and Wales's "Little Switzerland," the Ceiriog Valley.

Our second tour heads westward, through the magnificent mountain scenery around Lakes Vyrnwy and Bala, to visit the slate caverns at Blaenau Ffestiniog, and proceeds from there to the coast and then south to Aberystwyth.

From Aberystwyth, Tour 3 hugs the coastline southward on route A487, with some magnificent sea views, toward the Pembrokeshire Coast National Park and the spiritual heart of Wales, St. David's. There the road turns southeast to end at the resort town of Tenby.

The fourth tour visits Swansea, on the south coast, and the beautiful Gower Peninsula, then turns north through sheep-farming country and mountains, takes a detour to the Welsh lake district, ending at splendid Powis Castle in Welshpool. Tour 5 turns south again through charming upland villages, visits the Victorian spa town of Llandrindod Wells and the bookselling center of Hay-on-Wye, wanders through the Black Mountains, hits the market towns of Abergavenny and Brecon, and ends in the capital of Cardiff.

Highlights for First-time Visitors

Beaumaris Castle: Tour 1
Bodnant Garden: Tour 1
Bwlch y Groes (Pass of the Cross): Tour 2
Caernarfon Castle: Tour 1
Carreg Cennen Castle: Tour 4
Harlech Castle: Tour 2
Llechwedd Slate Caverns: Tour 2
Powis Castle: Tour 4
St. David's Cathedral: Tour 3
Tretower Court: Tour 5
Welsh Folk Museum: Tour 5

Tour 1: Beaumaris to Llangollen—Castles and Waterfalls

Numbers in the margin correspond to points of interest on the Wales map.

 Beaumaris, which means "beautiful marsh," is on Anglesey, the largest island off the shore of either Wales or England. It is linked to the mainland by the Britannia road and rail bridge and by Thomas Telford's remarkable chain suspension bridge built in 1826 over the dividing Menai Strait. Bangor, 10 minutes away on the mainland, has the nearest mainline train station; a regular bus service operates between it and Beaumaris.

An elegant town of simple cottages, Georgian terraces, and bright shops, Beaumaris looks across the strait to the magnificence of Snowdonia, the dramatic range of North Wales mountains. The town dates from 1295, when Edward I, the English invader, commenced work on the **castle** that guards the entrance to the Menai Strait, the last and largest link in an "iron ring" of fortifications around North Wales built to contain the Welsh. Standing at the far end of the town, the castle is solid and symmetrical, with arrow slits and a moat: a fine example of medieval defensive planning. Look for the mooring rings on the southern side, a reminder that the sea once slapped against the castle walls. *Tel. 0248/810361. Admission: £1.50 adults, 90p children and senior citizens. Open mid-Mar.–mid-Oct., daily 9:30–6:30; mid-Oct.–mid-Mar., Mon.–Sat. 9:30–4, Sun. 2–4.*

Opposite the castle is the **courthouse,** built in 1614, which houses one of the oldest courts in Britain still hearing cases. A plaque depicts one view of the legal profession: Two farmers pull a cow, one by the

Wales

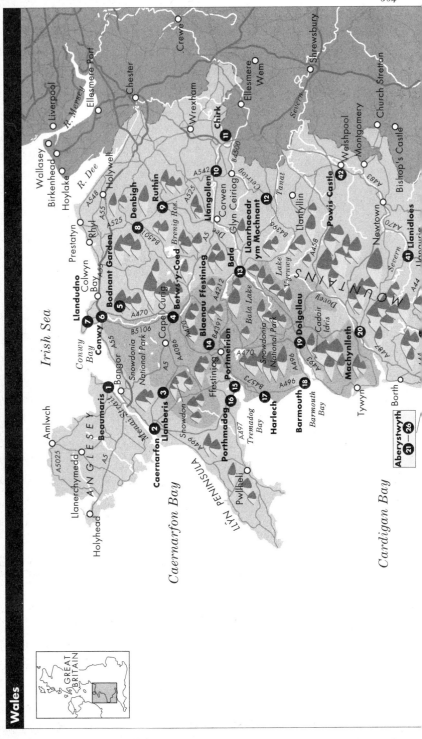

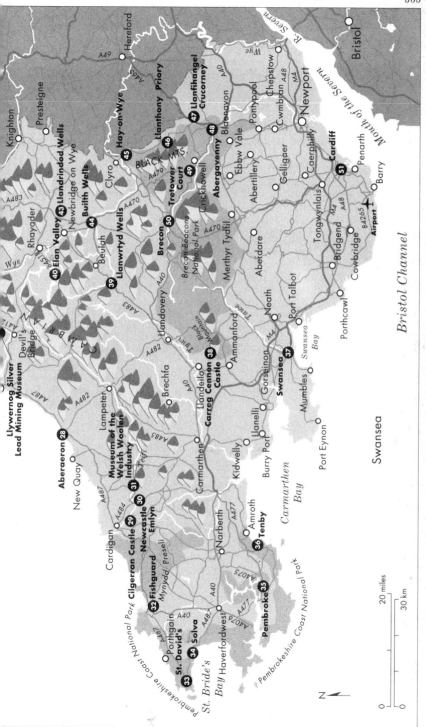

Bristol

R. Severn

Mouth of the Severn

Hereford

A49

A465

Presteigne

Knighton

Newbridge on Wye

Hay-on-Wye

45

Clyro

A438

Llanfihangel
Crucorney 47

Llanthony Priory
46

BLACK MTS.

A40

Chepstow

Cwmbran A48

Pontypool

Newport

M4

48 Abergavenny

Blaenavon

43 Llandrindod Wells

A483

Rhayader

A470

A479

Crickhowell

Bristol Channel

Ebbw Vale

Gelligaer

Caerphilly

Cardiff

51

Penarth

Barry

Builth Wells 44

49 Tretower
Court

Abertillery

Elan Valley 40

A45

Beulah

50 Brecon

Brecon Beacons
National Park

Merthyr Tydfil

Aberdare

Airport

B4265

Bridgend M4

Cowbridge

Porthcawl

Llanwrtyd Wells 39

A483

Llandovery

A40

A470

Mynydd Ddu

A48

Tongwynlais

Llywernog Silver
Lead Mining Museum

Devil's
Bridge

C A M B R I A N

A44

A487

Brechfa

A482

A482

Lampeter

Museum of the
Welsh Woollen
Industry

Teifi

A485

Neath

Port Talbot

Swansea
Bay

Port Eynon

Swansea

Carreg Cennen
Castle 38

Llandeilo

Ammanford

M4

Gorseinon

Swansea

37

Mumbles

A40

Tywi

Neath

28 Aberaeron

New Quay

A487

Cardigan

Pembrokeshire Coast National Park

A484

Newcastle
Emlyn

29

Cilgerran Castle

30

31

Carmarthen

Narberth

A477

Kidwelly

Llanelli

Burry Port

Carmarthen
Bay

A40

A477

Amroth

Tenby

36

Fishguard 32

Mynydd Preseli

A487

Porthgain

A40

A478

A478

Haverfordwest

Solva 34

St. David's

33

St. Bride's
Bay

Pembrokeshire Coast National Park

A4075

A4075

A40

A477

Pembroke

35

Pembrokeshire Coast National Park

Swansea

N

0   20 miles

0   30 km

horns, one by the tail, while a lawyer sits in the middle milking. Many people were transported from here to convict colonies in Australia—one woman, in 1773, for stealing goods worth less than a shilling. *Tel. 0286/679098. Joint admission ticket for court and gaol (see below): £2.80 adults, £2.10 children and senior citizens, £6.75 family ticket. Open Easter, weekends in May, and end May–end Sept., Mon.–Fri. 11–5; weekends 2–5; except when court is in session.*

Just beyond is the **Museum of Childhood,** an Aladdin's cave of music boxes, magic lanterns, trains, cars, toy soldiers, rocking horses, and mechanical savings banks. *1 Castle St., tel. 0248/712498. Admission: £2.50 adults, £1.25 children, £1.50 senior citizens. Open Mar.–Jan., Mon.–Sat. 10–5:30, Sun. 12–5.*

Nearby, in Castle Street, is **The Tudor Rose,** a house dating back to 1400, and an excellent example of Tudor timberwork.

Time Out At the other end of Castle Street from the castle, the **Liverpool Arms** pub, with its nautical bar, specializes in inexpensive seafood—try the crab sandwiches.

Turning right up Steeple Lane brings you to the old **gaol,** built in 1829 by Joseph Hansom, who was also the designer of the hansom cab. It was considered a model prison, the best in Britain at the time, but an exhibition shows what life there was really like. You can wander the corridors, be locked in the soundproof punishment cell or the condemned cell, and see the country's only working treadwheel, where prisoners trudged hopelessly around like hamsters in a cage. *Tel. 0286/679098. Joint admission with Beaumaris Courthouse (see above).*

Opposite the gaol is the 14th-century **parish church.** In 1862 an innocent man was hanged on the gibbet outside the prison wall—to give the crowd a good view—and he cursed the clock on the church tower. Locals say that from that day the clock never kept good time until it was overhauled in 1980.

❷ The town of **Caernarfon,** across the Menai Strait, 13 miles to the southwest, is dominated by **Caernarfon Castle,** begun in 1283. Its towers, unlike those of Edward I's other castles, are polygonal and patterned with bands of different colored stone. According to tradition, it was here, in 1301, that the first English Prince of Wales was presented to the Welsh people. Their conqueror, Edward I, had promised them a prince who did not speak English—and duly offered his baby son, later Edward II. The tradition that the first-born son of the monarch shall become Prince of Wales continues, and in July 1969, Caernarfon glowed with pageantry when Elizabeth II presented her eldest son, Prince Charles, to the people of Wales as their prince. This was the first time the ceremony had been held since 1911, when Prince Edward, the late duke of Windsor, was presented by his father, George V. In the Queen's Tower, an intriguing museum charts the history of the local regiment, The Royal Welch Fusiliers. *Tel. 0286/677617. Admission to castle: £3.50 adults, £2.50 children and senior citizens, £10 family ticket. Museum free. Open mid-Mar.–mid-Oct., daily 9:30–6:30; mid-Oct.–mid-Mar., Mon.–Sat. 9:30–4, Sun. 2–4.*

A wander through Caernarfon takes you back centuries. Even the new administrative complex is built in a moderately convincing medieval style. Don't miss the garrison church of **St. Mary,** built into the city walls. Outside the town is the extensive excavation site of the **Roman Fortress of Segontium** and the **Museum of the Legions,** a branch of the National Museum of Wales. It contains material found on the site, one of Britain's most famous Roman forts. *Tel. 0286/ 675625. Admission free. Open Mar.–Oct., Mon.–Sat. 9:30–5:30 (until 6 May–Sept.), Sun. 2–5; Nov.–Feb., Mon.–Sat. 9:30–4, Sun. 2–5.*

Time Out **Bakestone,** on Hole in the Wall Street, near the castle entrance, has been voted the best bistro in Britain, and the food here really is delicious. Try the crêpes.

Caernarfon Airport (at the end of Dinas Dinlle beach road) operates **Pleasure Flights** in light aircraft (including a vintage Rapide) over Snowdon, Anglesey, and Caernarfon. The airport also contains the **Caernarfon Air World** museum. *Tel. 0286/830800. From £15 per seat; flights daily, all year round.*

❸ The village of **Llanberis,** seven miles southeast on A4086, is the starting point for the steep **Snowdon Mountain Railway**—some of its track at a gradient of 1 in 5—which terminates within 70 feet of the 3,560-foot summit. **Snowdon,** Yr Wyddfa in Welsh, is the highest peak south of Scotland and is set in more than 800 square miles of national park. From the summit on a clear day you can see as far as the Irish Wicklow Mountains, about 90 miles away. *Tel. 0286/ 870223. Maximum round-trip fare, £12.80 adults, £9.30 children. Open (weather permitting) Mar.–Oct., daily from 9AM.*

Also in Llanberis is the **Museum of the North,** another branch of the National Museum of Wales, which sets out to interpret the history, geology, and sociology of the Snowdonia area. The museum also conducts guided tours of the awesome underground hydro-electric plant that has been built in the mountainsides. *Tel. 0286/870636. Admission: £3.50 adults, £1.75 children, £2.60 senior citizens (power station, £1.50, 75p, and £1.15). Open June–mid-Sept., daily 9:30–6; Mar.–May and mid-Sept.–Oct., daily 10–5; Feb. and Nov., daily 10:30–4.*

Across the lake, the workshops of the old Dinorwig slate quarry now contain the **Welsh Slate Museum.** *Dinorwig Quarry, Llanberis, tel. 0286/870630. Admission: £1.50 adults, 80p children, £1.20 senior citizens, £3.80 family ticket. Open Easter–Sept., daily 9:30–5:30.*

Try a lakeside ride on the **Llanberis Lake Railway,** which once transported the slate (tel. 0286/870549).

A4086 will carry you across the northern flanks of Snowdon, through the **Pass of Llanberis,** nearly 1,200 feet up. There are hiking tracks up from this point, but the going can be rough for the inexperienced; ask local advice before starting on even the briefest ramble. At the **Pen-y-Gwryd Hotel,** to the left of the road, Lord Hunt and his team planned their successful ascent of Everest in 1953.

Turn off A4086 onto A5 at Capel Curig. From here it is six miles into Betws-y-Coed, past the **Swallow Falls** (small admission charge), ❹ which tumble down through a wooded chasm. **Betws-y-Coed** lies among tree-clad cliffs, where the rivers Llugwy and Conwy meet. This is a striking village, with an ornate iron bridge (1815) over the Conwy, designed by Telford.

Turn due north from here and follow A470 to Conwy, on the River Conwy's east bank. (B5106, on the west bank from Llanrwst, will take longer, but leads through some lovely scenery.) Beautiful ❺ **Bodnant Garden,** off A470, features terraces, lawns, thickets of magnolias, and Himalayan rhododendrons, while the mountains of Snowdonia form a complementary backdrop. *Tal-y-Cafn, tel. 0492/ 650460. Admission: £3.60 adults, £1.80 children. Open daily mid-Mar.–Oct., 10–5.*

6 **Conwy** is the site of another of Edward I's castles, approached on foot by a dramatic suspension bridge, and on the Quay, what is said to be the smallest house in Britain, furnished in mid-Victorian Welsh style—it can hold only a few people at a time. Two miles north
7 of Conwy is **Llandudno,** a charmingly old-fashioned North Wales seaside resort with a wealth of well-preserved Victorian architecture and an ornate pier.

8 Head southeast 20 miles for **Denbigh,** served by A55 and A525 and accessible by bus from Llandudno. This market town (Wednesdays) was much admired by Dr. Samuel Johnson, who stayed on Pentrefoelas Road at Gwaenynog Hall, where he designed two rooms. A walk along the river bank at nearby Lawnt, a spot he loved, brings you to a monumental urn placed in his honor. Not that it pleased him: "It looks like an intention to bury me alive," thundered the great lexicographer.

Denbigh Castle is known as "the hollow crown" because it is not much more than a shell set on high ground, dominating the town. A tiny museum inside is devoted to Denbigh native son H. M. Stanley, the 19th-century journalist and explorer who found Dr. Livingstone in Africa. *Tel. 0745/813979. Admission: £1.50 adults, 90p children and senior citizens. Open mid-Mar.–mid-Oct., daily 9:30–6:30; mid-Oct.–mid-Mar., Mon.–Sat. 9:30–4, Sun. 2–4.*

9 From Denbigh it is just 8 miles (A525) southeast to **Ruthin,** the capital of Glyndwr country, where the 15th-century Welsh hero Owain Glyndwr lived and ruled. Its well-preserved buildings date from the 16th to the 19th centuries. Ruthin also has elegant shops, good inns, and an interesting crafts complex which displays the work of different craftspeople. Since the 11th century, they have been ringing the curfew here each evening at 8.

The spectacular **Horseshoe Pass** (on A525, then A542), 14 miles southeast of Ruthin, leads past the substantial ruins of the Cister-
10 cian **Abbey of Valle Crucis** to **Llangollen,** birthplace of the International Musical Eisteddfod. The tradition of the *eisteddfod,* held throughout Wales, goes back to the 12th century. Originally gatherings of bards, the *eisteddfodau* of today are more like competitions or festivals. The Llangollen event was started as a gesture of friendship after World War II by a newspaperman who wanted, in effect, to have a concert and invite the whole world to join in. Amazingly, it worked, and now choirs and dancers from all over the world make for an unusual arts festival. The six-day event takes place each year in early July.

While you are in Llangollen, visit **Plas Newydd,** home from 1778 to 1828 of the eccentric Ladies of Llangollen, who set up a scandalous single-sex household, collected curios and magnificent wood carvings, and entertained celebrated guests, among them William Wordsworth, Sir Walter Scott, and the Duke of Wellington. The Ladies had a servant with the delightful name of "Mollie the Basher." *Hill St., tel. 0978/861523. Admission: £1.70 adults, 75p children. Open April–end Oct., daily 10–5.*

From the **Canal Museum** on the wharf, you can take a horse-drawn boat along the Shropshire Union Canal. *Tel. 0978/860702. Museum*

admission: £1 adults, 70p children, 80p senior citizens. Open Eas-
ter–Oct., daily 10–5:30; 45-min boat trip: £2 adults, £1.30 children.

Llangollen's bridge, over the River Dee, a 14th-century stone structure, is named in a traditional Welsh folk song as one of the "Seven
Wonders of Wales." Near the bridge is the terminus of the
Llangollen Railway, a restored standard-gauge, steam-powered
line. It runs for a few miles along the scenic Dee Valley. *Tel. 0978/*
860979 and 0978/860951 (24-hr. recorded information). Round-trip
fare: £4.80 adults, £2.40 children. Open Mar.–Nov., daily 10–5.

There are easy walks along the banks of the River Dee or along part
of **Offa's Dyke Path.** The 167-mile-long dyke, a defensive wall whose
earthen foundations still stand, was built along the border with England in the 8th century by King Offa of Mercia to keep out Welsh
raiders.

Time Out By the old Dee bridge, **Bishop Trevor Tearooms** are cheerful and traditional.

⓫ For a scenic loop drive, head via **Chirk** (8 mi east on A5), site of an
imposing 13th-century castle, just across the border to England and
the **Ceiriog Valley,** nicknamed Little Switzerland. Take B4500 west 6
miles through the picturesque valley back into Wales and the town of
Glyn Ceiriog, where the **Chwarel Wynne** slate mine gives another
fascinating glimpse into Britain's industrial past. Ask the guide
about the ghost and the Women's Institute outing. *Tel. 0691/718343.*
Admission: £2.50 adults, £1 children, £2 senior citizens. Open Eas-
ter–Oct., daily 10–5 (last entrance 4:30).

Tour 2: Llangollen to Aberystwyth—Through Mountain and Mine

Take B4500 southwest from Glyn Ceiriog, and then its unnumbered
⓬ continuation, to reach **Llanrhaeadr ym Mochnant,** in the peaceful
Tanat Valley. Here, in 1588, the Bible was translated into Welsh,
thus ensuring the survival of the language. Turn northwest and go 4
miles up the road to **Pistyll Rhaeadr,** the highest waterfall in Wales,
with its peat-brown water thundering down a 290-foot double cascade.

Time Out **Tanypistyll,** at the foot of the waterfall, specializes in steak pies,
scones, and *bara brith* (Welsh currant bread).

Return to Llanrhaeadr ym Mochnant and turn right to take B4396
5 miles west to the little village of Penybontfawr. From here another
5 miles on B4396 will bring you to mysterious and romantic **Lake**
Vyrnwy (in Welsh "Efyrnwy"—neither easy to pronounce!), man-
made to supply water to Liverpool, 75 miles (as the aqueduct flows)
to the north. The damming of the small River Vyrnwy and the creation of the lake between 1880 and 1890 drowned the little village of
Llanwddyn, whose story is told in the visitor center. *Tel. 069173/*
246. Admission free. Open Easter–May, weekends 11–6; June–
Sept., weekdays noon–6, weekends 11–6.

This is an area of dense woods and sweeping hillsides, with the waters of the lake still and dark. From Vyrnwy, two vertiginous mountain roads lead west and north to **Bala Lake.** The more direct
northern route is perhaps the less challenging, but if you want to experience Wales at its wildest, follow the narrow road westward to

Bwlch y Groes (Pass of the Cross), the highest road in Wales, whose sweeping panoramas are literally breathtaking.

Bala, the largest natural lake in Wales, 4 miles long, has a narrow-gauge railway (tel. 06784/666), one of the Great Little Trains of Wales, running along its southern shore. The town of **Bala** is at the northern end of the lake.

From Lake Bala take A4212 to its junction with B4391, passing the **Llyn Celyn** reservoir, only 30 years old, but already an integral part of this dramatic landscape. B4391 will bring you to **Ffestiniog** and **Blaenau Ffestiniog.** At Blaenau, the **Llechwedd Slate Caverns** offer two trips: a tram ride through floodlit tunnels where Victorian working conditions are re-created, or a ride on Britain's deepest underground railway to a mine where you can walk by an eerie underground lake. Aboveground are exhibitions and audiovisual shows, house names carved to order in slate, and a restaurant/Victorian-style pub, The Miner's Arms. *Tel. 0766/830306. Admission: surface free; (for 1 of the 2 underground tours) £4.75 adults, £3.25 children, £4.25 senior citizens; for both tours: £7.25 adults, £5 children, £6 senior citizens. Open Mar.–Sept., daily 10–5:15; Oct.–Feb., daily 10–4:15.*

A mile farther up the road is **Gloddfa Ganol Slate Mine,** the world's largest. Tour the tunnels, try your hand at splitting slate, enjoy the museum, restaurant, and shop. Visit both the caverns and the mine and there won't be much you don't know about Welsh slate. *Tel. 0766/830664. Admission: £3.75 adults £2 children. Open Easter–Sept., weekdays 10–5:30 and Sun. from end of July to Aug.*

It is now time to turn toward the coast. From Ffestiniog, take A496 and then A487 toward Porthmadog. Just before you reach it you'll come to **Portmeirion,** a tiny fantasy Italianate village built in 1926 by architect Clough Williams-Ellis, complete with hotel, restaurant, and town hall. He called it his "light opera approach to architecture" and the result is pretty, though distinctly unWelsh. The cult '60s TV series "The Prisoner" was filmed here (*see* Dining and Lodging, *below*). *Tel. 0766/770228. Admission: £3 adults, £1.35 children, £2.40 senior citizens. Open daily 9:30–5:30.*

Beyond Portmeirion, you have to cross a mile-long embankment known as The Cob (the small toll charge goes to charity) to get to the little seaside town of **Porthmadog** at the gateway to Llŷn, an unspoiled peninsula of beaches, wildflowers, and country lanes. The **Ffestiniog Railway,** oldest of the Welsh narrow-gauge lines, was built in the mid-19th century to bring slate from the Blaenau Ffestiniog quarries down to the harbor at Porthmadog. *Tel. 0766/ 512340. Open Mar.–Nov., plus limited winter service.*

Near Porthmadog is **Tremadog,** a handsome village that was the birthplace of T. E. Lawrence, better known as Lawrence of Arabia. A few miles west lies **Criccieth,** a charming Victorian seaside resort whose headland is crowned by a medieval castle.

Retrace your steps through Porthmadog and then take A496 or B4573 south for 6 miles to **Harlech.** Dominating the town from a craggy hilltop are the ruins of 13th-century **Harlech Castle.** Its ominous presence, visible for miles and commanding wide views, is as dramatic as its history. At the beginning of the 15th century Owain Glyndwr held out here for five years against the English, and later in the same century the Lancastrians survived an eight-year siege during the Wars of the Roses. It was the last Welsh stronghold to fall in the 17th-century Civil War. *Tel. 0766/780552. Admission: £2.90* *adults, £1.50 children and senior citizens, £8 family ticket. Open mid-Mar.–mid-Oct., daily 9:30–6:30; mid-Oct.–mid-Mar., Mon.–Sat. 9:30–4, Sun. 2–4.*

Time Out **Plas Café** on High Street, with a crafts shop and a summer terrace overlooking the golf course, serves excellent snacks.

From Harlech follow the coast, lined with sandy beaches, wooded estuaries, and green headlands southwards to Aberystwyth. A496 ⑱ will lead you 11 miles south to the seaside resort of **Barmouth** (**Abermaw** in Welsh). There are not many full-fledged seaside resorts in Wales, but Barmouth is one of them. Ideally situated on the northern side of the picturesque estuary of the Mawddach, it boasts a 2-mile-long promenade, wide expanses of golden beach, and facilities for sea, river, and mountain lake fishing. Its splendid setting is best appreciated from the footpath beside the railway bridge across the mouth of the estuary. Even 100 years ago Barmouth was a popular holiday resort. Tennyson wrote part of *In Memoriam* there, and was inspired to write *Crossing the Bar* by the spectacle of the Mawddach rushing to meet the sea. Percy Bysshe and Mary Shelley stayed there in 1812; Darwin worked on *The Origin of Species* and *The Descent of Man* in a house by the shore. Essayist and art critic John Ruskin was a constant visitor and was trustee of the St. George's cottages built there by the Guild of St. George in 1871.

From Barmouth, you can strike inland along the Mawddach estuary ⑲ to **Dolgellau** (pronounced Dolgethlee), a solidly Welsh town with attractive dark buildings and handsome old coaching inns. It was the center of the Welsh gold trade in the 19th century, when high quality gold was discovered locally; you can still try your luck and pan for gold in the Mawddach. A nugget of Dolgellau gold is still used to make royal wedding rings. From Dolgellau, you can visit an authentic gold mine hidden deep in the forests to the north. The round-trip takes three hours and includes a guided underground tour of the Gwynfynydd Gold Mine. *Tel. 0341/423332. Tour price: £9.50 adults, £5 children, £7.50 senior citizens. A courtesy bus leaves from the Welsh Gold Visitor Centre in Dolgellau Apr.–Oct., daily 9:30–4 (please call ahead in winter)*

The Dolgellau area has strong links with the Quaker movement and the Quakers' emigration to America. To commemorate these historic associations, a **Museum of the Quakers** (tel. 0341/422341) has recently been opened in the town square.

To the south rises the menacing bulk of Cadair Idris (2,927 feet); the name means "the Chair of Idris," though no one is completely sure just who Idris was—probably a warrior bard. It is said that anyone sleeping for a night in a certain part of the mountain will awaken either a poet or a madman. The **Talyllyn narrow-gauge railway** (tel. 0654/710472) runs from Tywyn on the coast to the foothills of Cadair Idris. There are several routes up Cadair Idris.

Take A493 west on the south side of the estuary, and 24 miles south ⑳ make another inland detour, via **Machynlleth,** to negotiate the estuary of the river Dovey. At Machynlleth, take a short detour north on A487 to the fascinating **Centre for Alternative Technology.** Founded in the 1970s long before energy conservation and proper use of the earth's resources became fashionable, this "village of the future" has gradually built up an international reputation for its environment-friendly aerogenerators, solar panels, organic gardens, waterwheels, and waste recycling. Visitors follow self-guided trails through the centre. *Tel. 0654/702400. Admission: £4.50 adults,*

£2.50 children. £3.50 senior citizens, £12.50 family ticket. Open daily 10–5.

From Machynlleth, follow A487 southwest for 18 miles to Aberystwyth.

Tour 3: Aberystwyth to Tenby—A Spectacular Coast

Numbers in the margin correspond to points of interest on the Aberystwyth map.

㉑ The seaside resort of **Aberystwyth** on hill-sheltered Cardigan Bay is an ideal vacation center for exploring mid-Wales. It has plenty of hotels and guest houses, good bus and rail service, a once-elegant seafront promenade with a bandstand, and the King's Hall for summer shows. Aberystwyth, which came to prominence as a Victorian "watering hole," is also a university town and a major shopping center. A fine, curving beach edges the bay, with the university's old campus at the southern end and Constitution Hill on the northern. The

㉒ modern **university campus,** on the hill above town, includes the National Library of Wales, an arts center with galleries, a theater, concert hall, and crafts shop—all open to visitors. The original university, founded in the 19th century, stands on the seafront. *The Library, tel. 0970/623816. Admission free. Open weekdays 9:30–6, Sat. 9:30–5.*

㉓ The **castle,** at the southern end of the bay, was built in 1277 and rebuilt in 1282 by Edward I. It was one of several strongholds to fall, in 1404, to the Welsh leader Owain Glyndwr. Recaptured by the English, it became a mint in the 17th century, using silver from the Welsh hills. Today it is a romantic ruin on a headland separating the north shore from the harbor shore.

㉔ At the end of the promenade, **Constitution Hill** offers the energetic a zigzag cliff path/nature trail to the view from the top. But it's more fun to travel up by the **Aberystwyth Cliff Railway,** the longest electric cliff railway in Britain. Opened in 1896, to great excitement, it has been refurbished without diminishing its Victorian look. It takes you up 430 feet to the **Great Aberystwyth Camera Obscura,** a modern version of a Victorian amusement: A massive 14-inch lens gives a bird's-eye view of more than 1,000 square miles of sea and scenery, including the whole of Cardigan Bay and 26 Welsh mountain peaks, Snowdon among them. *Tel. 0970/617642. Admission to Camera Obscura free; railway £1.85 adults, £1 children, £1.60 senior citizens. Open Easter–Oct., daily 10–6; mid-July–Aug., daily 10–9.*

㉕ The excellent **Ceredigion Museum** in an old theater on Terrace Road displays coins minted at the castle, and many items of folk history. There is also a fascinating **Aberystwyth Yesterday** private collection in the town (housed above the British Rail station), which shows 19th-century fashions, furniture, toys, and photographs. Contact the Tourist Information Center for current information. *Ceredigion Museum, Terrace Rd., tel. 0970/634212. Admission free. Open Mon.–Sat. 10–5.*

㉖ At Aberystwyth Station you can hop on the narrow-gauge steam-operated **Vale of Rheidol Railway** (tel. 0970/625819 or 0970/615993). The terminus, an hour's ride away, is **Devil's Bridge,** where the Rivers Rheidol and Mynach meet in a series of spectacular falls. The walk down to the lowest bridge, "the devil's," is magnificent but strictly for the sure-footed!

Castle, **23**

Ceredigion Museum, **25**

Constitution Hill, **24**

University campus sites (old and new), **22**

Vale of Rheidol Railway, **26**

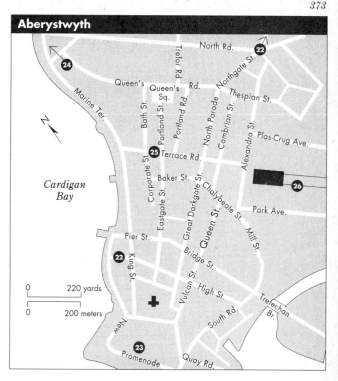

Numbers in the margin correspond to points of interest on the Wales map.

Three miles north of Devil's Bridge on A4120, the award-winning **㉗ Llywernog Silver Lead Mining Museum** lies near Ponterwyd, 13 miles east of Aberystwyth on A44. Silver and lead were produced in this area from 1740 to 1910; restoration work and an imaginative exhibition, "The California of Wales," have turned the clock back to the mining boom of the 1870s. *Tel. 0970/85620. Admission (including underground tour): £3.50 adults, £2 children, £3 senior citizens. Open Easter–Oct., daily 10–6.*

A scenic drive leads along the coast from Aberystwyth down to Cardigan, and then circles around the Pembrokeshire Coast National Park to Tenby on Carmarthen Bay. This is one of the most spectacular coastal stretches in Britain—150 miles or so, allowing for the broken coastline. As far as Cardigan the ruggedness of the north is still apparent, but the county of Pembrokeshire, now part of Dyfed, manifests a gentler mood, with tiny coves and sheltered beaches.

㉘ Aberaeron, 16 miles south of Aberystwyth on A487, was nearly all built in Georgian style in the early 19th century, which gives the town a pleasing sense of harmony and coherence. The **Aerial Ferry,** a form of cable car, can carry you across the harbor in a gondola, which, like Aberystwyth's Camera Obscura, is a Victorian replica. *Tel. 0970/617642. Standard fare: 90p (round-trip), 50p (one-way). Open Easter–Sept., daily 10–6.*

About 2 miles south of Cardigan, 26 miles from Aberaeron by A487/ **㉙** A478, the dramatic ruins of 13th-century **Cilgerran Castle** stand above a deep wooded gorge through which flows the River Teifi. *Tel.*

0239/615136 or 0239/615007. Admission: £1.50 adults, 90p children and senior citizens. Open mid-Mar.–mid-Oct., daily 9:30–6:30; mid-Oct.–mid-Mar., Mon.–Sat. 9:30–4, Sun. 2–4.

Every August the village of Cilgerran holds a festival week culminating in coracle races. A coracle is a tiny, light, one-man boat, built on a frame of hazel and willow laths in a style which has scarcely changed since the Iron Age—and it's extremely tricky to handle. To appreciate this sport's original context, visit the **National Coracle Centre and Flour Mill** beside the beautiful **Cenarth Falls** about 5 miles east of the castle on A484. *Tel. 0239/710980. Admission: £1 adults, 50p children. Open Easter–Oct., Sun.–Fri. 10:30–5:30.*

For still another glimpse of the past, continue a few miles farther on **30** A484 to **Newcastle Emlyn** to visit the nearby **Felin Geri Mill.** Here flour is ground, as it has been for 350 years, by a water-powered mill. A bakery, using the mill's fresh-ground flour, supplies a restaurant serving traditional farmhouse lunches and cream teas. A rare waterwheel-powered sawmill, craft workshops, and a fishing museum complete the picture. *Tel. 0239/710810. Admission: £2.50 adults, £1.50 children, £2 senior citizens. Open Easter–Oct., daily 10–6.*

A few miles east of Newcastle Emlyn, off A484, in what was once the most important wool-producing area in Wales, is the fascinating **31** **Museum of the Welsh Woolen Industry** at **Drefach Felindre.** It has working exhibits and displays that trace the evolution of the industry, with regular demonstrations. As a bonus there are other craft workshops and a working woolen mill beside the museum site. *Tel. 0559/370929. Admission: £1 adults, 50p children, 75p senior citizens. Open Apr.–Sept., Mon.–Sat. 10–5; Oct.–Mar., Mon–Fri. 10–5.*

From Cardigan A487 skirts the **Preseli Hills,** from which the bluestone used for the monoliths at Stonehenge was mined. Before you get to Newport, turn inland off the main road and follow signs through the lanes to **Pentre Ifan Cromlech,** one of Wales's finest prehistoric burial chambers, built of Preseli bluestones around 3000– **32** 4000 BC. In **Fishguard,** 17 miles down the coast from Cardigan, the harbor in the lower town was the film location for Dylan Thomas's *Under Milk Wood,* starring Richard Burton. At Carreg Wastad Point, near Fishguard, the last invading foreign army landed in Britain: a French force, in 1797, commanded by an American, Colonel Tate. Legend holds that the invaders surrendered after being frightened by a group of women in red shawls and tall black hats whom they mistook for Guardsmen.

Half an hour's drive away (16 mi west on A487) is the smallest city in **33** Britain, **St. David's,** where the patron saint of Wales established a monastery in the 6th century; Christian tradition has continued unbroken here ever since. St. David's, actually a large, friendly village, is legally a city because it has a **cathedral.** Unlike other British cathedrals, this one nestles in a valley and, indeed, was probably built there to hide it from Viking raiders. The exterior is simple, but inside treasures include the fragile fan vaulting in Bishop Vaughan's Chapel, the intricate carving on the choir stalls, and the substantial oaken roof over the nave. Across the brook are the ruins of the 14th-century **Bishop's Palace.**

A spectacular cliff walk of about an hour takes you to **St. Non's Bay.** St. Non was St. David's mother, and the path leads between tall hydrangea bushes to her well, reputed to have the power to heal eye diseases. Beyond is her ruined chapel, possibly the oldest religious building still standing in Wales, where St. David is said to have been born in AD 530.

The entire area around St. David's, steeped in sanctity and history, was a place of pilgrimage for many centuries—two journeys to St. David's equalling one to Rome. The savagely beautiful coastline— Pembrokeshire at its unspoilt best—also gives St. David's a special atmosphere. You can walk sections of the coastal footpath or take one of the boat trips available locally (some of which go to Ramsey Island).

③ Three miles east on A487 toward Haverfordwest lies **Solva,** on the coast, a village of white, typically Welsh cottages clustering at the foot of the hillside. Its harbor, on a long inlet of the sea, is the most sheltered haven along this stretch of the coast. In times gone by, it was a busy seafaring port and a place from which Welsh emigrants sailed to America, paying just over £3 for their passage. The little town has a number of fine craft shops.

Continue 13 miles southeast to Haverfordwest, then turn south for **③** another 9 on A4076/A477 to the town of **Pembroke,** where there's a magnificent **castle** dating from 1190. Its walls remain stout, its gatehouse mighty, and the enormous cylindrical keep proved so impregnable to cannon fire in the Civil War that Cromwell's men had to starve out its Royalist defenders. It was the birthplace, in 1457, of Henry VII, the Tudor king who seized the throne of Britain in 1485, and whose son Henry VIII united Wales and England. *Tel. 0646/ 681510. Admission: £2 adults, £1.20 children and senior citizens, £6 family ticket. Open summer, daily 9:30–6; winter, daily 10–4.*

About 10 miles east of Pembroke is the picturesque seaside resort of **③** **Tenby,** where pastel-colored Georgian houses cluster around a harbor, and below the hotel-lined clifftop stretch two golden sandy beaches. Medieval Tenby's ancient **town walls** still stand, enclosing narrow streets and passageways full of shops, inns, and places to eat. The ruins of a **castle** stand on a headland overlooking the sea, close to the excellent **Tenby Museum** (tel. 0834/842809), which recalls the town's maritime history and growth as a fashionable resort. The **Tudor Merchant's House** (tel. 0834/842279), in town, shows how a prosperous trader would have lived in the Tenby of old. From the harbor, you can take a boat trip to **Caldey Island** and visit the famous monastery, whose monks make perfume.

Tour 4: Swansea to Welshpool

Driving east from Tenby, follow A478/A477 and A40 to Carmarthen (22 miles), where you take A48 to M4 (junction 49), which leads to **③** **Swansea,** Wales's second city and birthplace of poet Dylan Thomas (1914–53). Go first to Swansea's splendid **Maritime Quarter.** The city was extensively bombed during World War II, and its old dockland has been transformed into a modern marina with attractive housing and shops and a seafront that commands wonderful views across the sweep of Swansea Bay. The **Swansea Maritime and Industrial Museum,** beside the marina, tells the story of the city's growth and houses a fully operational woolen mill. *Tel. 0792/650351 or 0792/470371. Admission free. Open Tues.–Sun. 10:30–5:30.*

Within a short walk of the marina is Swansea's modern shopping center. Despite the city's typically postwar, rather utilitarian and undistinguished architecture, the **covered market** here is not to be missed. It's the best fresh-foods market in Wales, where you can buy cockles from the Penclawdd beds on the nearby **Gower Peninsula** and laverbread, that unique Welsh delicacy made from seaweed, which is normally eaten with bacon and eggs. Gower is also worth exploring. The 14-mile-long peninsula, the first part of Britain to be declared an Area of Outstanding Natural Beauty, has a spectacular southern shore with sandy coves, cliffs, and windy headlands.

From Swansea, drive north along A483 to Ammanford and on to Llandeilo, a pleasant country town set on a ridge above the Towy **38** Valley. In the hills a few miles southeast stands the dramatic **Carreg Cennen Castle** at Trapp, perched on a sheer cliff overlooking the empty expanses of Black Mountain (not to be confused with the Black Mountains in Tour 5). This gnarled, weatherbeaten medieval fortress powerfully evokes the troubled times of old. It's a stiff climb, but worth every step; the views from the ruined ramparts are magnificent, and you can follow a passageway to an underground chamber deep below the castle's foundations. *Tel. 0558/822291. Admission: £1.80 adults, £1 children and senior citizens. Open mid-Mar.–mid-Oct., daily 9:30–6:30; mid-Oct.–mid-Mar., Mon.–Sat. 9:30–4, Sun. 2–4.*

From Llandeilo, follow A40, a route once used by stagecoaches, northeast to Llandovery, another authentic, appealing old market town, which has changed little over the years. Continue northeast on A483, a scenic road that winds through tranquil sheep-farming **39** country to sleepy **Llanwrtyd Wells,** its gabled Victorian and Edwardian villas a reminder of busier times when people came to "take the waters" at the once-popular spa. On its eastern outskirts you can visit the **Cambrian Woolen Mill** (tel. 05913/211), a working mill with an imaginative woolen museum and its own shop selling Welsh flannels.

At Beulah, continue northeast on B4358 to Newbridge on Wye, then follow A470 north to Rhayader (a good center for pony trekking), **40** where a southwest turn on B4518 brings you to the **Elan Valley,** Wales's Lake District. This 7-mile chain of lakes, winding between gray-green hills, was created in the 1890s by a system of dams to supply water to the city of Birmingham, 73 miles to the east. The giant dam holding back the **Claerwen reservoir** to the west was built in 1952 to supplement it. The area is one of Britain's foremost ornithological sites, still home to the red kite, peregrine, merlin, and buzzard. You can see and hear all about it at the **Elan Valley Visitor Centre** by Caban Coch reservoir. *Tel. 0597/810880. Admission free. Open Easter–Oct., daily 10–6.*

Return to Rhayader and take A470 northwest about 9 miles to Llangurig.

Time Out   The **Glansevern Arms,** Pant Mawr, 4½ miles northwest of Llangurig, is a snug roadside inn serving lunchtime snacks and evening meals, including seasonal specialties, at its reliable restaurant. There's no evening meal on Sunday.

---

41 Five miles northeast (still on A470) is **Llanidloes,** remarkable for its half-timbered market house, standing on sturdy timber legs, the only one of its kind left in Wales; it now contains the **Museum of Local History and Industry.** *Market Hall. Admission free. Open Easter–Sept., Mon.–Sat. 11–1 and 2–5.*

Hamer's, the butcher shop on the main street, bears the Royal Arms, having served eight royal families. The lamb sold here, from the nearby Plynlimon mountains, is exceptionally sweet and succulent. Follow A470/A489 northeast 14 miles to Newtown and then

about 14 miles more by A483 to the outskirts of **Welshpool**
("Trallwng" in Welsh), where you will see **Powis Castle,** one of mid-
Wales's greatest treasures.

In continuous occupation since the 13th century, and now a National
Trust property, Powis in one of the most opulent residential castles
in Britain. Its battlements rearing high on a hilltop, the castle is surrounded by splendid grounds and terraced gardens, bounded by gi-
gantic yew hedges, which fall steeply down to wide lawns and neat
Elizabethan gardens. It contains many treasures: Greek vases;
magnificent paintings by Gainsborough, Reynolds, and Romney,
among others; superb furniture, including a 16th-century Italian table inlaid with marble; and, since 1987, the **Clive of India Museum,**
with a fine collection of Indian art. The tearoom here is excellent.
*Tel. 0938/554336. Admission: £5.80 adults, £2.90 children; gardens
only: £3.80 adults, £1.90 children, £9.50 family ticket. Open Apr.–
June, Sept. and Oct., Wed.–Sun.; July and Aug. Tues.–Sun. Castle
and museum noon–5, gardens 11–6. Last admission ½ hr. before
closing.*

Tour 5: Welshpool to Cardiff

Return to Newtown, then take A483 south. This is a snaking road
that curves and climbs through glorious uplands with a scattering of
small villages. Stop at Llananno to admire the exquisite rood screen
in the local church. This elaborately carved wood screen, full of fine
detail and dating from the 15th century, displays amazingly delicate
workmanship.

Llandrindod Wells, known locally as Llandod, is an old spa town
which will impress lovers of Victorian architecture, for it preserves
its original layout and look. Though not to everyone's tastes, it is architecturally fascinating, with an array of fussy turrets, cupolas,
loggias, and balustrades, and greenery everywhere. The climate—
it is 700 feet above sea level—is said to be exceptionally healthy, and
it is well situated for exploring the region. On a main line rail route,
it also enjoys good bus service.

Llandrindod emerged as a spa in 1670 but did not reach its heyday
until the second half of the 19th century when the railway came and
most of the town was built. The **Museum,** in Memorial Gardens, details the development of the spa from Roman times and explains
some of the Victorian "cures" in gruesome detail. *Tel. 0597/824513.
Admission free. Open Mon., Tues., Thurs., and Fri. 10–12:30, 2–
4:30.*

Llandrindod is easily explored on foot. Cross over to South Crescent, passing the Glen Usk Hotel with its wrought-iron balustrade
and the Victorian bandstand in the gardens opposite, and you soon
reach Middleton Street, another Victorian thoroughfare. From
there head to Rock Park and the path that leads down through
wooded glades to the handsomely restored **Pump Room** where visitors would "take the waters" (Llandrindod has now been forced to
stop serving its own water because of heavy-handed bureaucratic
rules and regulations applied by the European Union). But the
Pump Room is still thankfully allowed to serve tea and refreshments, and it plays a part during the town's Victorian Festival (*see*
Arts, *below*).

On the other side of town, the lake with its boathouse, café, and gift
shop is in a lovely setting: wooded hills on one side, a broad common
on the other, flooded in spring by golden daffodils. Interesting spe-

cies of waterfowl, including grebe, live on the lake, and in early spring thousands of toads arrive to spawn, giving Llandrindod the nickname of Toad Town.

Time Out Drop in at **Spencer's Bar,** Hotel Metropole (Temple St.), where inexpensive snacks are served in the height of Victorian luxury.

❹❹ Only a short drive south from Llandrindod is **Builth Wells,** a traditional farming town on the banks of the River Wye that's the site of the Royal Welsh Agricultural Show, usually held in July. The countryside around Llandrindod and Builth varies considerably. Some of the land that lies along the border with England is soft and rich, with rolling green hills and lush valleys. The Black Mountains, a formidable upland chain to the southeast, where the scenery is much wilder and more dramatic, form a stark contrast. On the doorstep of **❹❺** the Black Mountains lies **Hay-on-Wye,** about 28 miles southeast of Llandrindod, a border town dominated by its mostly ruined castle. In 1961 Richard Booth established a small secondhand and antiquarian bookshop here; other booksellers soon got in on the act, and bookshops now fill several houses, a movie theater, shops, and a pub. The town is now the largest secondhand bookselling center in the world, where priceless 14th-century manuscripts rub spines with "job lots" selling for a few pounds. Hay now hosts an important Festival of Literature in early summer, which attracts famous writers from all over the world.

One mile west across the River Wye is **Clyro,** the village made famous by the Rev. Francis Kilvert, whose 1870–72 diary gives a charming and evocative picture of his simple world and the people in it. As you enter the village, don't miss Adam Dworski's **Wye Pottery,** with its powerful, swirling sculptures and gentle Madonnas. Southeast from Hay you can take a narrow road (unnumbered) 10 miles over the Black Mountains through the high Gospel Pass and Capel-y-**❹❻** ffin to **Llanthony Priory,** founded in 1108 and now a romantic ruin in the remote, breathtakingly beautiful **Vale of Ewyas.** Keep going an-**❹❼** other 5 miles to **Llanfihangel Crucorney,** where the minor road meets A465. Here you'll discover the Skirrid Inn, mentioned in 1110 and possibly the oldest inn in Britain, certainly in Wales. In 1685 it was used as one of the courts of the so-called "Bloody Assize" by the notorious Judge Jeffreys. Some of the accused, who supported the duke of Monmouth's rebellion against the monarchy, are said to have been hanged from a beam in the inn, which, as you'd expect, has the reputation of being haunted.

❹❽ Six miles south, the market town of **Abergavenny** has a **castle** founded early in the 11th century. At Christmas in 1176 the Norman knight William de Braose invited the neighboring Welsh chieftains to a feast—and, in a crude attempt to gain control of the area, had them all slaughtered as they sat, unarmed, at dinner. Afterward, the Welsh attacked and virtually demolished the castle. Little remains of the building now, but you can visit the **museum,** with exhibits ranging from the Iron Age to the early part of this century. The Welsh Kitchen is particularly appealing, with its old utensils, pans, and butter molds. There is also a delightful **Museum of Childhood and Home** (tel. 0873/856014) in the town. *Castle Museum, Castle St., tel. 0873/854282. Admission: £1 adults, 50p senior citizens, children free if accompanied by adult. Open Mar.–Oct., daily 11–1, 2–5; Nov.–Feb., Mon.–Sat. 11–1, 2–4.*

Taking A40 northwest out of Abergavenny, you pass the **Sugar Loaf** mountain and **Crickhowell,** a pretty town on the banks of the River

Usk with attractive little shops, an ancient bridge, and ruined cas-
49 tle. Two miles farther (by A479) is **Tretower Court,** a splendid example of a fortified medieval manor house, with gatehouse, galleried
courtyard, and banquet hall, furnished in appropriate period style
by local craftsmen. Nearby is a ruined Norman castle. *Tel. 0874/
730279. Admission: £1.80 adults, £1 children and senior citizens, £5
family ticket. Open mid-Mar.–mid-Oct., Mon.–Sat. 9:30–6:30,
Sun. 2–6:30; mid-Oct.–mid-Mar., Mon.–Sat. 9:30–4, Sun. 2–4.*

50 Stay on A40 for **Brecon,** a historic market town of narrow passageways, handsome Georgian buildings and pleasant riverside walks.
There are a number of sights worth seeing here, including the cavernous **cathedral** on the hill above the center, and two good museums—the **Brecknock Museum** (tel. 0874/624121), with its superb
collection of carved love spoons, and the **South Wales Borderers' Museum** (tel. 0874/623111), a military museum whose exhibits span centuries of conflict. For the best atmosphere, time your visit to Brecon
to coincide with market day (Tuesday and Friday). South of Brecon,
follow the signs for the **Brecon Beacons Mountain Centre,** on
Mynydd Illtyd, a high, grassy stretch of upland west of A470. The
center, run by the Brecon Beacons National Park, is an excellent
source of information for park attractions and activities, and gives
wonderful panoramic views across to Pen-y-fan, at 2,906 feet the
highest peak in South Wales. *Tel. 0874/623366. Admission free.
Open daily 9:30–5 (until 4:30 in winter).*

The A470 cuts through the Brecon Beacons, running beside a string
of scenic reservoirs to Merthyr Tydfil and the start of industrial
south Wales. From Merthyr, in the 19th century called the "iron capital of the world," a fast divided highway (still A470) makes short
51 work of the 25 miles to **Cardiff,** Wales's capital city since 1956. Although the city was settled by the Romans and used by the Normans
as a strategic fortress, it wasn't until the Industrial Revolution and
the arrival of the railroad in the 19th century that it suddenly began
to expand. As heavy industry declined in this century, Cardiff diver-
sified as an administrative and commercial center. It is now a city of
office blocks, not bustling dockyards, though the old waterfront is
being redeveloped on an ambitious scale.

Begin your exploration at Cardiff's **castle,** in Bute Park—one section of Cardiff's hundreds of acres of parkland. The castle is a mishmash of periods: Parts of the walls are Roman, the solid keep is Norman, and the whole complex was restored a hundred years ago by
the 3rd Marquess of Bute. He employed William Burges (1827–81),
an architect obsessed by the Gothic period, and Burges transformed
the castle inside and out into an extravaganza of medieval color and
detailed craftsmanship. It's well worth a visit. *Tel. 0222/822083. Admission: Guided tour of the castle, £3.30 adults, £1.70 children and
senior citizens, £6.60 family ticket (off-season only); grounds only:
£2.20 adults, £1.10 children and senior citizens, £4.40 family ticket
(off-season only). Open May–Sept., daily 10–6, Mar., Apr., Oct.,
daily 10–5; Nov.–Feb., daily 10–4:30.*

Two blocks east of the castle is Cardiff's **Civic Centre,** a well-designed complex of tree-lined avenues and civic buildings with Portland stone facades. City Hall, the National Museum of Wales, the
Law Courts, the Welsh Office (seat of government), and the University campus are all here.

The **National Museum** could take several hours to explore properly.
It sets out to tell the story of Wales through its plants, rocks, archaeology, art, and industry. It also has a fine collection of modern Euro-

pean art, especially Postimpressionist works—don't miss *La Parisienne* by Renoir. The museum has a convenient cafeteria on the top floor. *Main Building, Cathays Park, tel. 0222/397951. Admission: £2 adults, £1 children, £1.50 senior citizens. Open Tues.–Sat. 10–5, Sun. 2:30–5.*

South of the Civic Centre are the shopping and business areas of Cardiff. Here in a large, modern shopping mall is **St. David's Hall,** one of Europe's best new concert halls, with outstanding acoustics, where people come for classical music, jazz, rock, ballet—even snooker championships. This hall has recently been joined by the **Cardiff International Arena,** a £23 million multipurpose center for exhibitions, concerts, and conferences.

Time Out   At the bottom of Queen's Street is the **Capitol shopping mall,** with a number of fast-food outlets, ranging from salad bars to Continental food bars—an ideal spot for morning coffee or a light lunch.

The **Welsh Industrial and Maritime Museum** (tel. 0222/481919) is in the old dockland 2 miles south of the city center. There is also an interesting "hands-on" science and technology center here, known as **Techniquest** (tel. 0222/460211).

Cross the River Taff and follow Cathedral Road for about 2 miles, to reach **Llandaff,** a suburb of Cardiff that retains its village atmosphere, and **Llandaff Cathedral,** which was completely renovated after serious bomb damage in World War II. Inside you will immediately be drawn to the overwhelming statue by Jacob Epstein (1880–1959) of *Christ in Majesty.*

Four miles west of Llandaff is the open-air **Welsh Folk Museum** at St. Fagans. In 100 acres of parkland and gardens lie farmhouses, cottages, and terraced houses that show the evolution of Welsh building styles, and an Elizabethan mansion built within the walls of a Norman castle. There are craft workshops, a saddler, cooper, blacksmith, and woodturner; demonstrations of these country skills are given in summer. Special events highlight ancient rural festivals—May Day, Harvest, and Christmas among them. There is a cafeteria, a coffee tavern, restaurants, and a museum shop. *Tel. 0222/ 569441. Admission: £3.50 adults, £1.75 children, £2.60 senior citizens. Open Apr.–Oct., daily 10–5; Nov.–Mar., Mon.–Sat. 10–5.*

North of Cardiff, 4 miles via A470, beside the village of Tongwynlais, is **Castell Coch,** the Red Castle. It was built (on the site of a medieval castle) in the 1870s around the time that Ludwig of Bavaria was creating his fantastic dream castles, and it might almost be one of them. Instead, the castle was another collaboration of the 3rd Marquess of Bute and William Burges, whose work you will already have seen in Cardiff Castle. Here Burges recreated everything—architecture, furnishings, carvings, murals—in a remarkable exercise in Victorian-Gothic whimsy. *Tel. 0222/810101. Admission: £2 adults, £1.30 children and senior citizens, £6 family ticket. Open mid-Mar.–mid-Oct., daily 9:30–6:30; mid-Oct.–mid-Mar., Mon.–Sat. 9:30–4, Sun. 2–4.*

What to See and Do with Children

The **Museum of Childhood** in Beaumaris (*see* Tour 1).

Twelve miles southwest of Beaumaris along the Menai Strait at Brynsiencyn is the **Anglesey Sea Zoo,** where you can see almost every form of marine life found in the surrounding waters, including a

9-foot conger eel. There's a mysterious wreck, a "touch tank," and a "tide tank" which simulates conditions on the nearby beach. There's a tearoom, a gift shop, and miniature radio-controlled motor boats, also indoors. *Brynsiencyn, tel. 0248/430411. Admission: £3.95 adults, £2.75 children, £3.50 senior citizens. Open Mar.–Oct., daily 10–5; Nov.–Feb., daily 11–3.*

The **Welsh Mountain Zoo** at Colwyn Bay near Llandudno is in a beautiful setting, just right for the free-flying displays of hawks, falcons, and eagles that take place daily. The **Jungle Adventureland** and **Chimpanzee World** are also fun. *Colwyn Bay, tel. 0492/532938. Admission: £4.95 adults, £2.95 children, £3.95 senior citizens, £14.30 family ticket. Open mid-Mar.–Oct., daily 9:30–5; Nov.–mid-Mar., daily 9:30–4.*

Rhyl Sun Centre is an enclosed "tropical island" on the northern coast, with surfing, a splash pool, and a roof-top monorail. *East Parade, Rhyl, tel. 0745/344433. Admission: £3.75 for everyone. Open Apr.–Sept., daily 10–8:30; also open weekends in Oct. 11:30–6.*

At the **Alice in Wonderland Visitor Centre** in Llandudno, Alice's adventures are colorfully brought to life in enchanting tableaux of the best-known scenes from the book. *Trinity Sq., Llandudno, tel. 0492/860082. Admission: £2.50 adults, £1.95 children, £2.20 senior citizens, £8.50 family ticket. Open daily 10–5 except closed Sun. Nov.–Easter.*

Off the Beaten Track

Plas Newydd is an 18th-century mansion on the Menai Strait close to the Menai Bridge (not to be confused with the Plas Newydd in Tour 1, at Llangollen). In 1936–40 the society artist Rex Whistler painted the mural in the dining room here, his largest work. A military museum commemorates the Battle of Waterloo, where the first marquess of Anglesey, Wellington's cavalry commander, lost his leg. The interior has some fine 18th-century Gothic-revival decorations, and the gardens have been restored to their original design. There are magnificent views across the Strait from here. *Llanfairpwll, Anglesey, tel. 0248/714795. Admission: £3.80 adults, £1.90 children, £9.50 family ticket. Open Apr.–Sept., Sun.–Fri. noon–5; Oct., Fri. and Sun. noon–5. Last admission ½ hr. before closing.*

Bodelwyddan Castle (near the north coast, off A55, between Abergele and St. Asaph), is a restored Victorian castle in spacious formal gardens, surrounded by lovely countryside. As an offshoot of the National Portrait Gallery in London, it exhibits Regency and Victorian portraits by the likes of Sargent, Lawrence, G. F. Watts, and Landseer. *Tel. 0745/584060. Admission: £4 adults, £2.50 children and senior citizens, £10 family ticket. Grounds only: £2.50 adults, £1.50 children and senior citizens, £5 family ticket. Open Apr.–June, Sept.–Oct., Sat.–Thurs.; July–Aug., daily; Nov.–Feb., Tues.–Thurs., Sat. and Sun. Times: 10:30–5 (summer), 11–4 (winter).*

Dolaucothi Gold Mines (8 mi southeast of Lampeter), a source of gold for almost 2,000 years, has a museum of working machinery and a visitor center, but the best part is the guided tour underground—helmet with lamp provided. *Pumsaint, near Lampeter, tel. 05585/359. Admission (late May–late Sept. inclusive of underground guided tour): £4.80 adults, £2.40 children. Admission (Apr.–late May and late Sept–Oct.): £3 adults, £1.50 children. Open daily 10–6 (high season), 11–5 (low season).*

At **Big Pit Mining Museum,** in Blaenavon, southwest of Abergavenny, ex-miners take you underground on a conducted tour of an authentic coalmine, for a look at the life of the South Wales miner. You will also see the pithead baths and workshops. *Tel. 0495/ 790311. Surface admission: £1.75 adults, £1 children, £1.50 senior citizens. Combined tour: £4.95 adults, £3.50 children, £4.50 senior citizens, £15 family ticket. Open Mar.–Nov., daily 9:30–5 (underground tours 10–3:30).*

Shopping

Wales is particularly noted for its crafts—tweeds woven at local mills, pottery, slate sculpture, knitwear, and hand-carved wooden "love spoons"—and you'll find crafts stores throughout the principality. Look for the Daffodil label of the Wales Crafts Council, which is a guarantee of quality.

Abergavenny: The Welsh Doll's House Shop, on Brecon Road, sells beautiful Georgian and Victorian dollhouses.

Betws-y-Coed is one of several towns with a branch of the **Craftcentre Cymru,** a chain that markets craft goods. At the **Penmachno Woolen Mill,** just outside town on B4406, fabric is woven for exclusively designed clothing.

Cardiff: Cardiff is one of Wales's major shopping centers, with branches of the big stores. Among the smaller, more unusual places to shop is the **Old Library Craft Centre** (in The Hayes), which sells high quality items. The city's covered Victorian arcades also contain many interesting small stores.

Harlech: At **The Old Pottery** just off Harlech's High Street you'll discover attractive handmade pots and other craft items.

Hay-on-Wye: Book lovers are unlikely to do better anywhere in Britain—or, arguably, the world—than here. Bookshops jostle each other on the main street and on many side streets. Give yourself several happy hours of exploring.

Llanfairpwllgwyngyllgogerychwyrndrobwllllantysiligogogoch: This really is the name of a town on Anglesey. The **James Pringle Woolen Mill** here, a large crafts shop next to the station, markets good, if expensive, clothing. By the way, unless you can get the name down pat, just say "Llanfair P. G.," like everyone else.

Portmeirion: With its distinctive design, **Portmeirion pottery** is almost as famous as the town's hotel. You can buy firsts in nearby Porthmadog at 9 High Street, while the Seconds Shop in Portmeirion village sells pottery with tiny, often invisible flaws.

Ruthin: Those who brake for antiques shops should stop in at **Castle Antiques** (Castle St.), where the stock ranges from 17th-century oak tables to Victorian plates. **The Craft Centre** (Park Rd.), on the traffic circle, has craft workshops, a gallery, restaurant, and tourist information center. It's a good all-around place for Welsh crafts. **The Bookshop** (Upper Clwyd St.) is a bookworm's haven.

Sports and the Outdoors

Golf Welsh golf courses tend to the spectacular. **Llandrindod Wells,** at 1,000 feet above sea level, is one of the highest in Britain (tel. 0597/ 822010); at **Llangollen,** the ninth, with its dog-leg left and two-tier green, is said to be the most challenging in North Wales (tel. 0978/ 860040); **Llanymynech,** near Oswestry, has 15 holes in Wales and three across the border in England (tel. 0691/830542). **Royal Porthcawl** in South Wales (tel. 0656/782251) is host to many championship events, some international; **Royal St. David's** at Harlech (tel. 0766/780361) is also a championship links.

Horseback Riding
Even beginners can go pony trekking on amiable Welsh cobs; the more experienced can try trail riding and even show jumping. The **Ponies Association UK** (Chesham House, 56 Green End Rd., Sawtry, Huntingdon, Cambridgeshire PE17 5UY, tel. 0487/830278) will supply a full list of approved centers, many of which offer accommodation as well.

Some riding centers near our tours are: **Gromlech Riding Centre,** Tyn-y-Gongl, Anglesey, tel. 0248/853489; **Lion Royal Hotel Pony Trekking Centre,** Weir St., Rhayader, tel. 0597/810202; and **Pinewood Riding Stables,** Sychnant Pass Rd., Conwy, tel. 0492/592256.

Walking
The **Ramblers Association** (Pantwood, Pant La., Marford, Wrexham, Clwyd LL12 8SG, tel. 0978/855148) can supply you with information on walking in Wales. Local tourist offices have details on guided walks; those in **Snowdonia National Park** (National Park Office, Penrhyndeudraeth, Gwynedd LL48 6LS, tel. 0766/770274) are among the most spectacular. Snowdonia contains some of the most rugged, rocky mountains in England and Wales, and although there are many paths to follow, walkers should be experienced and well equipped for sudden changes in weather. Good bases for exploring the park are Beddgelert, Betws-y-Coed, and Llanberis. One of the longest (and hardest) official trails in Wales is **Glyndwr's Way,** 121 miles from Knighton to Welshpool, with some spectacular panoramic views along the route.

The **Pembrokeshire Coast Path** (National Park Office, County Offices, Haverfordwest, Dyfed SA61 1QZ, tel. 0437/764591) starts 2 miles northwest of St. Dogmael's and stretches 180 miles around the coast to Amroth, near Saundersfoot. You can join or leave the path at several points, mostly near inns for overnight stops; and a special bus service links the particularly interesting stretches. Good centers for path walkers are Broad Haven, Fishguard, St. David's, and Tenby. Another challenging walk, the **Offa's Dyke Path,** follows the line of the 8th-century border between Wales and England for 167 miles (details from Offa's Dyke Association, The Old School, West St., Knighton, Powys LD7 1EW, tel. 0547/528753). Some of the best-preserved sections of King Offa of Mercia's ancient earthwork border are found in the unexplored hills around Knighton.

Rolling hills and open moorlands await walkers in the 519-square-mile **Brecon Beacons National Park,** with some of the most beautiful scenery in southeast Wales. The **Brecon Beacons Mountain Centre** (near Libanus, Brecon, Powys LD3 8ER, tel. 0874/623366) can suggest routes and give further information. The variety of walking terrain in the Beacons is tremendous. You can follow mountain paths along the smooth, grassy flanks of the Beacons, or enjoy gentler riverside and forest trails. As with Snowdonia, walkers who want to explore the high country should always be well equipped, for mist and rain can quickly descend, and the Beacons' summits can become very exposed to high winds. Brecon and Crickhowell are good walking centers. **Crickhowell Adventure Gear,** on the corner of Ship Street in Brecon (with a smaller shop in Crickhowell itself), rents canoes and mountain bikes and sells climbing gear to people who want to explore the park.

Water Sports Aberaeron, Aberdovey, Aberystwyth, and Barmouth are sailing centers, and Aberdovey and Barmouth are particularly good for waterskiing. But there are water sports facilities and sailing clubs around most of the Welsh coast. Check at tourist centers for the local possibilities.

Dining and Lodging

Dining Look for the sign "Blas Ar Gymru" ("A Taste of Wales"), which means that Welsh specialties are on the menu.

Highly recommended restaurants are indicated by a star ★.

Category	Cost*
$$$$	over £30
$$$	£25–£30
$$	£12–£25
$	under £12

per person, including first course, main course, dessert, and VAT; excluding drinks

Lodging A 19th-century dictum, "I sleeps where I dines" still holds true in Wales. Good hotels and good restaurants mostly go together, and since conversion is the rage, that means castles, country mansions, farmhouses, smithies, even workhouses and small railroad stations are being transformed into hotels and restaurants. Traditional inns, many with four-poster beds, remain the country's pride.

Highly recommended lodgings are indicated by a star ★.

Category	Cost*
$$$$	over £110
$$$	£80–£110
$$	£40–£80
$	under £40

All prices are for two people sharing a double room, including service, breakfast, and VAT.

Aberdovey
Dining and Lodging

Penhelig Arms. Robert and Sally Hughes run a hotel and restaurant noted for excellence and exceptional value for money. Their immaculate, friendly inn is on the water's edge at the pretty sailing center of Aberdovey. Most of the rooms have wonderful sea views. You can meet the locals in the wood-paneled Fisherman's Bar, and dine in style at the Penhelig Arms' fine restaurant. *Gwynedd LL35 0LT, tel. 0654/767215, fax 0654/767690. 11 rooms with bath. Facilities: restaurant, bar. Dress in restaurant: casual. MC, V. Hotel $$; Restaurant $$*

Aberystwyth
Dining

Gannets. A simple bistro, Gannets specializes in locally supplied meat, fish, and game, which are transformed into hearty roasts and pies. Organically grown vegetables and a good French house wine are further draws for a university crowd. *7 St. James' Sq., tel. 0970/617164. Reservations advised. Dress: casual. MC, V. Closed Sun. $–$$*

Dining and Lodging **Conrah Country Hotel.** This is an unusual and distinguished country-house hotel. Part of its appeal is that it feels quite secluded, but it is only minutes from town and from the beautiful Cambrian coast. The owners have decorated the house with traditional country furnishings and antiques, and fresh flowers fill each room. The restaurant is known for its good food and wines, with imaginative modern and traditional British cuisine making use of local game, fish, and meat. *Chancery, Aberystwyth, Dyfed SY23 4DF, tel. 0970/617941, fax 0970/624546. 20 rooms with bath. Facilities: sauna, indoor pool, croquet. AE, DC, MC, V. $$$*

Lodging **The Four Seasons.** Located in Aberystwyth's town center, this family-run hotel and restaurant has a relaxed atmosphere and friendly staff. The spacious rooms are simply and attractively decorated, while the restaurant serves excellent meals at reasonable prices. *50–54 Portland St., Dyfed SY23 2DX, tel. 0970/612120, fax 0970/627458. 14 rooms, 11 with bath. AE, MC, V. $$*

Bala **Tyddyn Llan Country House.** Gray-stone Tyddyn Llan stands in the peaceful Vale of Edeyrnion, midway between Bala and Corwen, a **Dining and Lodging** convivial and hospitable place to stay. The luxurious little hotel, reflecting the interests of owner-hosts Peter and Bridget Kindred, is ★ full of antiques, paintings, and period furniture. Bridget prepares interesting meals based on fresh local ingredients in season and herbs from the hotel's kitchen garden. *Llandrillo, near Corwen, Clwyd LL21 0ST, tel. 049084/264, fax 049084/414. 10 rooms with bath. Facilities: private fishing on stretch of River Dee. MC, V. $$$*

Beaumaris **Ye Olde Bull's Head.** Originally a coaching inn built in 1472, this **Dining and** place is small and charming. The oak-beamed dining room, dating **Lodging** from 1617, serves French specialties, including warm salad of pigeon breast with hazelnut oil, as well as local widgeon (wild duck), and is also noted for its seafood. *Castle St., Anglesey, Gwynedd LL58 8AP, tel. 0248/810329, fax 0248/811294. 11 rooms with bath. Restaurant reservations advised. Jacket and tie required. Restaurant closed Sun. dinner. MC, V. $$*

Betws-y-Coed **The Ty Gwyn.** After a browse through the small antiques shop next **Dining** door, stop for a bite at the restaurant, which is under the same management. Inside the 17th-century building it's all prints and chintz, old beams and copper pans, and there's a nice view of the nearby Waterloo bridge. Homemade pâté is a specialty. *Gwynedd LL24 0SG, tel. 0690/710383. Reservations advised. Dress: casual. MC, V. $$*

Brechfa **Ty Mawr Country Hotel.** This little jewel, deep in the heart of the **Lodging** country northeast of Carmarthen, is well worth seeking out. Dick ★ and Beryl Tudhope are charming hosts. They run an immaculate hotel, steeped in character and history, based on the philosophy of offering "simplicity with style." The pink-washed building, many hundreds of years old, has exposed stone walls, old beams, and cozy, neat bedrooms. *Near Carmarthen, Dyfed SA32 7RA, tel. 0267/202332, fax 0267/202437. 5 rooms with bath. AE, MC, V. $$*

Brecon **Llangoed Hall.** This hotel, the brainchild of Sir Bernard Ashley, **Dining and** widower of Laura Ashley, opened in May 1990 and has already made **Lodging** a name for itself. An early guest was Arthur Miller. The Hall is set in ★ the spectacular valley of the Wye, about 8 miles from Hay-on-Wye and Brecon, with views over the Black Mountains. Inside there are Laura Ashley fabrics everywhere, of course, complementing the antiques and paintings. The restaurant serves a six-course, set-price menu using mostly local produce. *Llyswen, near Brecon, Powys LD3 0YP, tel. 0874/754525, fax 0874/754545. 23 rooms with bath. Facili-*

ties: restaurant, garden, tennis, helipad. Restaurant reservations advised. Jacket and tie preferred. AE, DC, MC, V. $$$$

Griffin Inn. Halfway between Brecon and Hay-on-Wye, in the village of Llyswen, stands one of the oldest inns in the upper Wye Valley (said to date from 1467). There is easy access to river and lake fishing, shooting, walking, and pony trekking in the Brecon Beacons. A former winner of Britain's "Pub of the Year," the Griffin's traditional cuisine takes advantage of local produce, such as salmon and beef. The bedrooms are comfortably furnished, and the exposed stonework and old beams contribute to the historic character of the building. *Llyswen, near Brecon, Powys LD3 0UR, tel. 0874/754241, fax 0874/754592. 8 rooms with bath. AE, DC, MC, V. $$*

Caernarfon **Ty'n Rhos.** This is an immaculate farmhouse with a difference: It of-
Lodging fers the highest standard of accommodation. It has a beautifully furnished lounge and dining room, with views across the fields to the Isle of Anglesey. The cooking is exceptional, and there are homemade cheeses and yogurt. The bedrooms are comfortable and nicely decorated. This is an ideal touring base, because it stands between Snowdonia and the sea close to Caernarfon and Anglesey. *Llanddeiniolen, near Caernarfon, Gwynedd LL55 3AE, tel. 0248/670489, fax 0248/670079. 10 rooms with bath. MC, V. $$*

Cardiff **Armless Dragon.** A window-front full of plants enlivens this bright,
Dining friendly restaurant out beyond the Cathays stadium, which is popular with the university crowd. Seafood dishes are always a good bet here; much of the fish comes from local waters. For even more uniquely Welsh flavor, try the laverballs, made out of seaweed. *97 Wyeverne Rd., Cathays, tel. 0222/382357. Reservations advised. Dress: casual. AE, DC, MC, V. Closed Sat. lunch, Sun., and Mon. $$*

Le Cassoulet. A genuinely French restaurant, decorated with touches of red and black, in the maze of Victorian streets west of Cathedral Road. Try the namesake dish for a filling meal. The *patron/*chef also creates a very tasty fish soup. *5 Romilly Crescent, tel. 0222/221905. Reservations advised. Dress: casual. AE, MC, V. Closed Sat. lunch, Sun., and Mon. $$*

Quayles. Formerly Gibson's, this neighborhood brasserie is close to Sohpia Gardens. The modern cuisine is reasonably priced, with a more elaborate Sunday lunch and brunch. A good-value, inexpensive fixed-price menu is available before 8 PM. *6 Romilly Crescent, Canton, tel. 0222/341264. Reservations unnecessary. AE, DC, MC, V. $-$$*

Lodging **Cardiff Marriott.** The high-rise Marriott (formerly the Holiday Inn) is a fair representative of Cardiff's new breed of hotels. It is central—close to St. David's Hall and the shopping center—practical, and has plenty of facilities. *Mill La., CF1 1EZ, tel. 0222/399944, fax 0222/395578. 182 rooms with bath. Facilities: restaurant, coffee shop, indoor pool, sauna, squash. AE, DC, MC, V. $$$-$$$$*

Egerton Grey Country House. Although not in Cardiff itself (the hotel is located near Barry about 8 miles west of the city), Egerton Grey is a convenient and comfortable base for visiting Wales's capital and the Vale of Glamorgan. The fine old house—a rectory in Victorian times—has all the trappings of luxurious country living: restored Edwardian bathrooms, open fireplaces, antiques, wood paneling, and peaceful, secluded grounds. *Porthkerry, Barry, South Glamorgan CF6 9BZ, tel. 0446/711666, fax 0446/711690. 9 rooms with bath. AE, MC, V. $$$*

The Town House. A gregarious American couple, Bart and Iris Zuzik, run this immaculate guest house, the best B&B in Cardiff, located along Cathedral Road and near the city center. You stay in a tall Victorian building that has been tastefully converted. The bedrooms are neat and well equipped, and guests can enjoy traditional British or American breakfasts in the beautifully appointed dining room. No evening meals are served. *70 Cathedral Rd., Cardiff, South Glamorgan CF1 9LL, tel. 0222/239399, fax 0222/223214. 6 rooms with bath. No credit cards. $$*

Cardigan
Lodging

Penbontbren Farm Hotel. You won't find a more traditionally Welsh hotel than this friendly one in peaceful countryside off A487 east of Cardigan. Welsh-speakers Barrie and Nan Humphreys have created an unusual hotel at a farm that's been in Nan's family for centuries. Barns have been tastefully converted into comfortable bedrooms, a restaurant is just across the courtyard, and the hotel has its own little Countryside Museum. *Glynarthen, near Cardigan, Dyfed SA44 6PE, tel. 0239/810248, fax 0239/811129. 10 rooms with bath. MC, V. $$*

Ceiriog Valley
Dining and
Lodging

The Golden Pheasant. Jenny Gibourg searched the country to furnish the 200-year-old hotel with antiques and Victorian-style fabrics, and the result is chinoiserie in the bar, horse prints and aspidistras in the lounge, draped curtains and parlor palms in the dining room, and no two bedrooms alike. Specialties include Ceiriog trout, pheasant, and game pie. *Glyn Ceiriog, near Chirk, Clwyd LL20 7BB, tel. 0691/718281. 18 rooms with bath. Facilities: shooting, riding center. Restaurant reservations advised. AE, DC, MC, V. $$*

The West Arms. Located in wonderful walking country, this 16th-century inn offers both modern and more traditional rooms. Traditional Welsh cuisine is a specialty, including leg of lamb. *Llanarmon Dyffryn Ceiriog, near Llangollen, Clwyd LL20 7LD, tel. 069176/ 665, fax 069176/662. 14 rooms with bath. Facilities: tennis, private fishing, restaurant (reservations advised, dress: casual). AE, DC, MC, V. $$$*

Crickhowell
Lodging

Ty Croeso Hotel. On a hillside overlooking the Usk Valley, this charming little hotel was once a Victorian workhouse. Its bedrooms are comfortable, though the main attractions here are the warm, relaxing atmosphere (the hotel's name means "House of Welcome") and the creative food, which represents excellent value. Try the "Taste of Wales" menu. *Llangattock, near Crickhowell, Powys NP8 1PU, tel. and fax 0873/810573. 8 rooms with bath. AE, MC, V. $$*

Fishguard
Dining and
Lodging

Tregynon Country Farmhouse Hotel. This 16th-century farmhouse, overlooking the Gwaun Valley, is ideal for a quiet, reasonably priced stay in the country. The cooking concentrates on whole-food dishes and vegetarian fare, though Tregynon easily satisfies all tastes, serving everything from vegetarian pancakes to oak-smoked bacon. *Pontfaen, Gwaun Valley, near Fishguard, Dyfed SA65 9TU, tel. 0239/820531, fax 0239/820808. 8 rooms with bath. MC, V. $$*

Harlech
Dining and
Lodging
★

Hotel Maes-y-Neuadd. Set in 8 acres of its own glorious gardens and parkland (3½ miles northeast of Harlech by B4573), this hotel dates from the 14th century. Purportedly favored once by Jackie Onassis, it has walls of local granite, oak-beamed ceilings, an inglenook fireplace, and a menu that features Welsh, English, and French specialties. *Talsarnau, near Harlech, Gwynedd LL47 6YA, tel. 0766/ 780200, fax 0766/780211, U.S. 800/635–3602. 16 rooms with bath. AE, DC, MC, V. Closed mid-Jan.–early Feb. $$$*

Castle Cottage. Close to Harlech's mighty castle, this cozy, friendly hotel is a charming "restaurant with rooms." The emphasis here is on the exceptional cuisine served by chef/proprietor Glyn Roberts, who makes the best possible use of fresh ingredients to create imaginative, beautifully presented dishes. The rooms, though small, are attractively appointed and decorated. Guests should find this lodging an excellent all-round value. *Harlech, Gwynedd LL46 2YL, tel. 0766/780479. 6 rooms. AE, MC, V. $$*

Hay-on-Wye
Dining and
Lodging

Old Black Lion. This 17th-century coaching inn is close to the center of Hay, ideal for lunch while ransacking the bookshops, or for an overnight stay. The low-beamed, atmospheric bar serves its own food—with tables outside in summer—and the breakfasts are especially good. Its "sophisticated country cooking with an international twist" has been praised by food guides. *Lion St., Powys HR3 5AD, tel. 0497/820841. 10 rooms with bath. AE, MC, V. $-$$*

Lake Vyrnwy
Lodging

Lake Vyrnwy Hotel. This country mansion on 27 acres of lakeside grounds overlooking superb scenery offers the ultimate sporting holiday: Guests can fish, shoot (over 16,000 acres), bird-watch, play tennis, or take long walks around the estate. Bicycles and sailboats are also available. Rooms are quite comfortable and the restaurant is excellent. The menu centers around trout, pheasant, and duck from the estate and vegetables and fruit from the garden. *Llanwddyn, via Oswestry, Shropshire SY10 0LY, tel. 069173/692, fax 069173/259. 30 rooms with bath. Facilities: restaurant, tennis, nature trails. AE, DC, MC, V. $$$*

Llandrindod
Wells
Dining and
Lodging

The Bell Country Inn. A few miles from town, this extended village inn has a well-earned reputation for its food. The accommodation, in modernized rooms with up-to-date amenities, is unimaginative but light and airy. *Llanyre, near Llandrindod Wells, Powys LD1 6DY, tel. 0597/823959, fax 0597/825899. 9 rooms with bath. Facilities: 2 restaurants, bar. MC, V. $$*

Llandudno
Dining and
Lodging
★

Bodysgallen Hall. Set in wide, walled gardens 2 miles out of town, the Hall is part 17th-, part 18th-century, full of antiques, comfortable chairs by cheery fires, pictures, and polished wood. The bedrooms (a few suites are available) combine elegance and practicality, and from some of them you'll see the mountains. The restaurant serves fine traditional meals, with an emphasis on such local fare as lamb and smoked salmon; its prices are relatively low for the standard it offers. *Gwynedd LL30 1RS, tel. 0492/584466, fax 0492/ 582519. 28 rooms with bath. Facilities: croquet, tennis. Restaurant reservations advised. Dress: neat but casual. AE, DC, MC, V. $$$$*

Lodging

Bryn Derwen Hotel. British seaside resort hotels do not enjoy the best reputation; many hoteliers have not moved with the times to upgrade their accommodations and food. If only they were all like Stuart and Val Langfield, whose immaculate Victorian hotel exemplifies how it should be done. Fresh flowers and attractive furnishings set the tone, and the food, prepared by Stuart, an award-winning chef, lives up to the surroundings. *Abbey Rd., Llandudno, Gwynedd LL30 2EE, tel. 0492/876804. 9 rooms with bath. MC, V. $$*

Llangammarch
Wells
Lodging

The Lake Hotel. This is the place to go for total Victorian country elegance. Its 50 acres of sloping lawns and lush rhododendrons contain a trout-filled lake which attracts keen anglers. The Lake Hotel is comfortable and quiet; the service is first class, and the cuisine excellent. The rooms are large and tastefully furnished, and some have four-poster beds. *Powys LD4 4BS, tel. 05912/202, fax 05912/ 457. 19 rooms with bath. Facilities: fishing, shooting, golf nearby. AE, MC, V. Closed first 2 weeks in Jan. $$$-$$$$*

Llanerchymedd
Lodging
★

Llwydiarth Fawr. In the north central part of Anglesey, this exceptional farmhouse accommodation offers a convenient touring base for the island. It's a spacious, elegant Georgian house on an 850-acre cattle and sheep farm, whose deluxe rooms are superior to those in many hotels. Owner Margaret Hughes welcomes guests warmly, serves good country cooking, and in a nutshell, offers country living in style. *Anglesey, Gwynedd LL71 8DF, tel. 0248/470321. 3 rooms with bath. No credit cards. $$*

Llanrhaeadr ym Mochnant
Lodging
★

Bron Heulog. This guest house north of Welshpool has lovely antique furniture and paintings and serves magnificent dinners for less than £10. *Waterfall Rd., near Oswestry, Shropshire SY10 0JX, tel. 0691/780521. 3 rooms, none en-suite but with guest bathroom and, on request, private shower room. No credit cards. $*

Machynlleth
Lodging
★

Ynyshir Hall. This supremely comfortable country-house hotel is in a beautiful Georgian house in idyllic private grounds near a wildlife reserve. The artistic talents of its owners, Joan and Rob Reen, are evident in the wealth of Rob's paintings (he's an established artist) and in the taste of the decoration and furnishings. Personal service is paramount here, and the hotel is noted for its food. *Eglwysfach, near Machynlleth, Powys SY20 8TA, tel. 0654/781209, fax 0654/781366, U.S. 800/777-6536. 9 rooms with bath. AE, MC, V. $$$-$$$$*

New Quay
Lodging

Park Hall. Standing on a grassy rise above secluded Cwmtydu Cove on the Cardigan Bay coast, Park Hall is Victoriana personified. The term "guest house" doesn't really do justice to the place: Owners Chris and Peter McDonnell have emphasized the character of their gabled house and given it a strong period atmosphere with ornate furnishings, rich colors, and creative decorative touches. Each bedroom is different, and downstairs there's an airy conservatory where the food is served. *Cwmtydu, near New Quay, Dyfed SA44 6LG, tel. 0545/560306. 5 rooms with bath. AE, DC, MC, V. $$*

Porthgain
Dining

Harbour Lights. Tucked away on an attractive stretch of coast about 7 miles northeast of St. David's, this family-run shore restaurant prides itself on serving everything homemade, right down to the cheese and biscuits. Try the fresh local seafood dishes. The walls are hung with pictures by local artists, all for sale. *Croesgoch, Dyfed SA62 5BW, tel. 0348/831549. Reservations advised. Dress: casual. MC, V. Closed Jan. and Feb. $$*

Portmeirion
Dining and Lodging
★

Hotel Portmeirion. This is one of the most elegant—and unusual—places to stay in Wales. The mansion house that is now its main building was already here when Clough Williams-Ellis began to build his Italianate fantasy-village around it; he restored its original Victorian splendor, preserved the library and the Mirror Room, and created the curved, colonnaded dining room. Accommodation has been increased by 20 fully serviced rooms in cottages around the village, none more than a few minutes' walk from the main building. *Gwynedd LL48 6ET, tel. 0766/770228, fax 0766/771331. 19 rooms with bath in main hotel, 20 rooms with bath in village. Facilities: pool, tennis, free golf at Porthmadog Golf Club. AE, DC, MC, V. $$$-$$$$*

Pwllheli
Dining and Lodging
★

Plas Bodegroes. Chef Chris Chown has won many awards for his modern, innovative cuisine at what is probably the finest restaurant in Wales. Accommodation at this "restaurant with rooms" is also of a high order. Many diners choose to make a night of it and stay in the attractive late 18th-century house set in its own grounds. *Nefyn Rd., Pwllheli, Gwynedd LL53 5TH, tel. 0758/612363, fax 0758/*

701247. 8 rooms with bath. Reservations advised. Dress: casual. AE, MC, V. Restaurant $$$; Hotel $$$

Rhayader
Dining and Lodging

Brynafon Country House. This hotel is a converted Victorian workhouse; and though its exterior might be still a bit forbidding, it is completely up to date. Apart from its attractions as a hotel, it also has a notable restaurant—**The Workhouse**, once the kitchen, with white-painted stone walls and a flagstone floor. Here you can put visions of *Oliver Twist* behind you and enjoy good-value bar food and fixed-price menus. "Food, glorious food!" *South St., Rhayader, Powys LD6 5BL, tel. 0597/810735 or 0597/810111, fax 0597/811497. 21 rooms, 10 with bath (2 suites). Facilities: pool, table tennis. Reservations advised. Dress: casual. MC, V. Restaurant closed Sun. evening and Mon. Hotel $; Restaurant $$*

Ruthin
Lodging
★

Eyarth Old Railway Station. This Victorian railway station was closed for 17 years before being converted in 1981 to an award-winning bed-and-breakfast. (In 1988 it was voted "Best Bed-and-Breakfast Establishment in the World" by the Worldwide B&B Association.) The bedrooms are spacious, with large windows looking out onto breathtaking rural scenery. *Llanfair Dyffryn Clwyd, near Ruthin, Clwyd LL15 2EE, tel. 0824/703643. 6 rooms with bath. Facilities: pool. MC, V. $–$$*

Swansea
Dining and Lodging

Fairyhill. Situated on the west of the Gower Peninsula, about 11 miles from Swansea, Fairyhill is an 18th-century country house, with a restful atmosphere, luxuriously furnished public rooms, spacious bedrooms, and extensive wooded grounds. The hotel is known in the area for its accomplished cuisine and well-chosen wine list. *Reynoldston, near Swansea, West Glamorgan SA3 1BS, tel. 0792/ 390139, fax 0792/391358. 11 rooms with bath or shower. AE, MC, V. $$–$$$*

Number One. This excellent regional restaurant serves dishes such as Penclawdd cockles with laverbread and bacon; fresh sea bass, wild salmon, and monkfish are regularly featured. The atmosphere is friendly and seating is limited, so reservations are advised. *1 Wind St., Swansea, West Glamorgan SA1 1DE, tel. 0792/456996. Dress: casual. AE, MC, V. Closed Sun., dinner Mon. and Tues. $$*

Tenby
Lodging

Penally Abbey Hotel. Penally Abbey, overlooking the sea close to town, is a convenient and comfortable base for exploring Pembrokeshire. The dignified old house is full of character, and most bedrooms have four-posters. Hosts Steve and Elleen Warren's lack of formality brings to their hotel a relaxed atmosphere with first-class service. Everything is tuned to the guests' needs, even if that means serving breakfast at 11 AM. The hotel is also noted for its fine food. *Penally, near Tenby, Dyfed SA70 7PY, tel. 0834/843033, fax 0834/ 844714. 11 rooms with bath. Facilities: pool. MC, V. $$$*

The Arts

Festivals

The **Beaumaris Festival** (tel. 0248/810930) is held annually late May–early June. The whole town is used as a site, from the 14th-century parish church to the concert hall. The festival offers an eclectic mix of concerts, recitals, jazz, madrigals, art, sculpture, poetry, folk singing and dancing, a regatta on the strait, and medieval and Civil War battles in the castle. There's a similar festival at **Criccieth** (tel. 0766/810584) later in June.

The **Llangollen International Musical Eisteddfod** (tel. 0978/860236), held in early July, attracts singers and dancers from all over the world. Just wandering around the field is fun. The evening concerts are of international standard. Later in July there's the **Royal Welsh Agricultural Show** (tel. 0982/553683), held at Builth Wells. It has a much wider appeal than its title suggests: the Royal Welsh is not only Wales's prime gathering of farming folk, but also a colorful countryside jamboree that attracts huge crowds.

Late July to early August is the time for Wales's greatest cultural festival, the **Royal National Eisteddfod** (tel. 0222/763777). 1995's event takes place at Colwyn Bay. It is a totally Welsh festival (with translation facilities) of music, poetry, dance, art, and crafts. The pseudo-historic ceremonies are fascinating.

Brecon is at its liveliest in mid-August when the internationally re-nowned **Brecon Jazz Festival** is on (tel. 0874/625557). Later in August, Llandrindod Wells has a **Victorian Festival** (tel. 0597/823441). Shop assistants, hotel staff, and postmen wear costume, and every-one is encouraged to follow suit, so to speak. The **North Wales Music Festival** (tel. 0745/584508) takes place at the end of September at the Cathedral of St. Asaph in Clwyd, which is noted for its almost per-fect acoustics.

Cardiff and Swansea and many other towns put on major arts festi-vals in September and October. Call in at tourist offices for full de-tails, or contact the Wales Tourist Board.

Opera Wales, as might be expected in a country where singing is a way of life, has one of Britain's four major opera companies, the **Welsh Na-tional.** Its home base is at the **New Theatre** in Cardiff, but it spends most of its time touring Wales and England. Its performances, even in a small Welsh town, are of an international standard, and its pro-ductions often among the most exciting in Britain. For details of per-formances contact *Welsh National Opera, John St., Cardiff CF1 4SP, tel. 0222/464666.*

Theater **Theatr Clwyd** in Mold has two theaters within the same arts com-plex. It has its own professional company, with an international rep-utation. *Tel. 0352/55114.*

13 The Northwest and Lake District

Manchester, Liverpool, Blackpool, and Lake District National Park

The Northwest—comprising the counties of Greater Manchester, Merseyside, Lancashire, and Cumbria—is perhaps England's most contrary region, sporting a diversity of scenery and surroundings that's hard to beat. In less than 100 miles, you move from the industrial cities of Manchester and Liverpool—driving forces of the Industrial Revolution—through the country's largest seaside resort at Blackpool and on to the Lake District, an area brimming with beautiful alpine and lake scenery.

Although most visitors to the region are in a hurry to reach the Lake District, the cities should not be missed, certainly not by anyone with an interest in England's unique industrial history. By the mid-18th century, the Lancashire cotton industry was firmly established in Manchester and enjoyed a special relationship with the port of Liverpool, to the west. Here, at the massive docks, cotton was imported from America and sent to the Lancashire mills; the finished cotton goods later returned to Liverpool for export to the rest of the world. Both cities suffered a marked decline during this century, though the downtown areas are currently undergoing a remarkable architectural and cultural revitalization. Nevertheless, they remain best known the world over for their musical and sporting prowess: The Beatles launched the Merseysound of the '60s, while contemporary Manchester groups dominate British and American airwaves, and in the 25 years after 1968, Manchester United and Liverpool soccer clubs won everything worth winning in Britain and Europe.

Farther north, along the Lancashire coast, lie a series of vacation resorts that flourished during the first half of this century. Several lost their business to European resorts in the '70s and '80s, but Blackpool is still very much worth a detour, attracting millions each year to its miles of beaches, acres of gardens, and 19th-century architectural charms.

Lancashire gives way to the county of Cumbria, and here the Lake District begins, measuring roughly 35 miles square; it can be crossed by car in around an hour. Yet within this compact area is a landscape of extraordinary beauty and variety, changing with every valley, lake, and mountain. Rugged peaks and cliffs give way to deep blue lakes, rolling green pastures, isolated farms and villages, and beyond these to the south, the waters of Solway Firth, Morecambe Bay, and the Irish Sea.

The mountains here are not high by international standards—Scafell Pike, England's highest peak, is only 3,210 feet above sea level—but they can be as steep and craggy as the Alps. In the spring, many of the higher summits remain snowcapped long after the weather below has turned mild. The valleys between them cradle famous lakes, more than 100 altogether, ranging in size from tiny mountain pools to 11-mile-long Windermere, the largest lake in England.

As with many regions of England, the Lake District has its own language variations. For instance a lake is a mere, as in Buttermere, or water, as in Ullswater; a smaller lake is a tarn; mountains are frequently referred to as fells; a waterfall is a force; a small stream is a beck; and the addition of "thwaite," of Scandinavian origin, to place names implies a clearing.

The Lake District is probably best known for its associations with the English Romantic poets, especially William Wordsworth, whose vivid descriptions brought the first tourists here in the early 19th century. Wordsworth was born in the area, and lived in Grasmere, on the banks of Rydal Water. Other literary figures who made their homes in the region include Samuel Taylor Coleridge, Thomas De

Quincey, Robert Southey, John Ruskin, Matthew Arnold, and later, Hugh Walpole, children's writer Beatrix Potter, and the poet Norman Nicholson.

The whole area of the Lake District is a national park, the largest and most popular in Britain. Many thousands of acres of land here—about one quarter of the entire park—have been given to or purchased by the National Trust, and the area observes rigid controls on growth and pays strict attention to conservation. But that doesn't mean visitors are not welcome; indeed, the Lake District is one of Britain's most popular vacation spots—perhaps too popular in summer.

Essential Information

Important Addresses and Numbers

Tourist Information
The North West Tourist Board, Swan House, Swan Meadow Rd., Wigan Pier, Wigan WN3 5BB, tel. 0942/821222. Open weekdays 9–5.
The Cumbria Tourist Board, Ashleigh, Holly Rd., Windermere, Cumbria LA23 2AQ, tel. 05394/44444. Open Mon.–Thurs. 9:30–5:30, Fri. 9:30–5.
Ambleside: The Old Courthouse, Church St., tel. 05394/32582.
Blackpool: 1 Clifton St., tel. 0253/21623; Pleasure Beach, 11 Ocean Blvd., South Promenade, tel. 0253/403223.
Cockermouth: Riverside Car Park, Market St., tel. 0900/822634.
Grasmere: Redbank Rd., tel. 05394/35245.
Kendal: Town Hall, Highgate, tel. 0539/725758.
Keswick: Moot Hall, Market Sq., tel. 07687/72645.
Liverpool: Merseyside Welcome Centre, Clayton Square Shopping Centre, tel. 051/709–3631; Atlantic Pavilion, Albert Dock, tel. 051/708–8854.
Manchester: Town Hall Extension, Lloyd St., tel. 061/234–3157; International Arrivals Hall, Manchester Airport, tel. 061/436–3344.
Windermere: The Gateway Centre, Victoria St., tel. 05394/46499.

Travel Agencies
American Express: 54 Lord St., Liverpool, tel. 051/708–9202; 10–12 St. Mary's Gate, Manchester, tel. 061/833–0121.
Thomas Cook: 49 Stricklandgate, Kendal, tel. 0539/724258; 55 Lord St., Liverpool, tel. 051/236–1951; 23 Market St., Manchester, tel. 061/833–1110.

Car-Rental Agencies
Kendal: Avis, Station Rd., tel. 0539/733582.
Keswick: Keswick Motor Company, Lake Rd., tel. 07687/72064.
Manchester: Avis, Gateway Garage, Piccadilly Station Approach, tel. 061/236–6716, and airport, tel. 061/436–2020; **Budget Rent-a-Car,** Crown St., tel. 061/839–6626, and airport, tel. 061/436–1317; **Europcar Ltd.,** York St., tel. 061/832–4114, and airport, tel. 061/436–2200; **Hertz,** 31 Aytoun St., tel. 061/236–2747, and airport, tel. 061/437–8208.

Arriving and Departing by Plane

Manchester International Airport (tel. 061/489–3000) is about 10 miles south of the city. It's northern England's main airport and serves European and other international cities as well as domestic flights from all over Britain. To reach the city center, take the train which runs from the airport direct to Picadilly Station (24-hour service; departures every 15 minutes). Travel time is 20 minutes and the cost is £2 (£3.85 in peak hours, before 9 AM). There is also a bus service (No. 44), which leaves every 30 minutes (6 AM–10:30 PM) and also costs £2, but it takes almost an hour to reach Picadilly Gardens. For more information about either service, contact the Manchester Airport Tourist Center.

Arriving and Departing by Car, Train, and Bus

By Car To reach Manchester from London, take M1 north to M6, leaving M6 at exit 21a and joining M62 east, which becomes M602 as it enters Greater Manchester. Liverpool is reached by leaving M6 at the same junction, exit 21a, and following M62 west into the city. For Blackpool, continue north on M6, and take exit 32 for M55 into town. To get to the Lake District, stay on M6, getting off either at exit 36 and joining A590/A591 west (around the Kendal bypass to Windermere) or at exit 40, joining A66 direct to Keswick and the northern lakes region. Travel time to Manchester or Liverpool is about 3–3½ hours; to Kendal, about 4 hours; and to Keswick, 5–6 hours.

By Train **British Rail** serves the region from London's Euston Station (tel. 071/387–7070). Direct service to Manchester and Liverpool takes approximately 2½ hours. For Blackpool and the Lake District, take an InterCity train bound for Carlisle, Edinburgh, or Glasgow. For Blackpool, change at Preston; for the Lake District, change at Oxenholme for branch line service to Kendal and Windermere. Average travel time to Windermere (including the change) is 4½ hours. If you're heading for Keswick, you can either take the train to Windermere and continue from there by Cumberland bus (70 minutes) or stay on the main London–Carlisle train to Penrith station (4 hrs.), from which Cumberland buses also run to Keswick (45 minutes).

By Bus **National Express** (tel. 071/730–0202) serves the region from London's Victoria Coach Station. Average travel time to Manchester or Liverpool is 4 hours; to Kendal just over 7 hours; to Windermere, 7½ hours; and to Keswick, 8¼ hours.

Getting Around

By Car Roads within the region are generally very good, although many of the Lake District's minor routes and mountain passes can be both steep and narrow. Warning signs are normally posted if snow has made a road impassable. In July and August and during the long public holiday weekends, expect heavy traffic; construction on M6 can also delay journeys. The Lake District has plenty of parking lots, which should be used to avoid blocking narrow lanes or gateways.

By Train There are trains between Manchester's Piccadilly Station (tel. 061/832–8353) and Liverpool Lime Street every half-hour during the day; the trip takes approximately 50 minutes. A similar service operates from Manchester Piccadilly to Blackpool North, taking just over an hour. Train connections are good around the edges of the Lake District, especially on the Oxenholme–Kendal–Windermere line and the Furness and West Cumbria branch lines from Lancaster to Grange-over-Sands, Ulverston, Barrow, and Ravenglass.

Seven-day regional **North West Rover** tickets (£42) are good for unlimited travel within the area (including trips on the scenic Carlisle-Settle line running just east of the Lake District).

The **Lakeside & Haverthwaite Railway Co.** (tel. 05395/31594) runs vintage steam trains in summer on the branch line between Lakeside and Haverthwaite along Lake Windermere's southern tip.

Ravenglass & Eskdale Railway (tel. 0229/717171) offers a steam train service covering the 7 miles of glorious countryside between Ravenglass and Dalegarth. There is daily service from April to October and reduced service in winter.

By Bus Manchester's Chorlton Street Bus Station (tel. 061/228–3881) is the departure point for regional and long-distance **National Express** coaches. For information on Greater Manchester buses, call 061/273–5341; for city buses, call 061/228–7811. There's also a new tram system—**the Metrolink** (tel. 061/205–2000)—running through Manchester and its surroundings. It's mostly of use to commuters from the outlying suburbs, but you might want to ride the tram from its terminus at Picadilly Station: either north up High Street, past the Arndale Shopping Centre to Victoria Station; or south, down Mosley Street, past the Crowne Plaza Midland Hotel, to the G-Mex Centre.

In summer, **Mountain Goat** (Victoria St., Windermere, tel. 05394/45161) runs a local Lake District minibus service linking Keswick, Grasmere, Ambleside, Windermere, and Kendal.

Cumberland Motor Services (tel. 0946/63222) operates year-round throughout the Lake District and into north Lancashire.

By Boat **Bowness Bay Boating Co.** (tel. 05394/43360) runs small vessels around Lake Windermere, particularly to Ambleside and Brockhole National Park Centre.

Keswick-on-Derwentwater Launch Co. (tel. 07687/72263) conducts cruises on vintage motor launches around Derwentwater, leaving from Keswick.

Steam Yacht Gondola (tel. 05394/41288) runs the National Trust's luxurious Victorian steam yacht *Gondola* between Coniston and Park-a-Moor at the south end of Coniston Water, daily from late March through October.

Ullswater Navigation & Transit Co. (tel. 0539/721626 or 07684/82229) sends its oil-burning 19th-century steamers the length of Lake Ullswater between Glenridding and Pooley Bridge. Service operates April through October.

Windermere Iron Steamboat Co. (tel. 05395/31188) employs its handsome fleet of vintage cruisers—the largest ships on the lake—in a regular service between Ambleside, Bowness, and Lakeside on Lake Windermere.

By Bicycle **Keswick Mountain Bikes** (tel. 07687/73717) rents reliable mountain bikes, an ideal—if energetic—way to see the Lake District countryside. Guided bike tours are available, too (*see also* Guided Tours, *below*).

Guided Tours

The **National Park Authority** (tel. 05394/46601) at Brockhole, near Windermere, has an advisory service that puts you in touch with members of the Blue Badge Guides, who are experts on the area. From Easter until October, they will take you on half-day or full-day walks and introduce you to the history and natural beauties of the Lake District. The Authority has nine information offices throughout the district. *See* Sports, *below*, for more information.

English Lakeland Ramblers (tel. 0229/587382) organize single-base and inn-to-inn tours of the Lake District from May to October. All meals and inn accommodations are included in packages, and Blue Badge guides lead you on informative walks, hikes, and sightseeing around a variety of areas. A lake steamer cruise and a ride on a narrow-gauge steam railroad line are all part of the adventure.

Mountain Goat Holidays (tel. 05394/45161) provides special minibus sightseeing tours with skilled local guides. These are half- and full-day tours, which really get off the beaten track, departing from Bowness, Windermere, Ambleside, and Grasmere.

Tracks North (1 Railway Terr., Lowgill, Kendal LA8 0BN, tel. 0539/824666) conducts escorted railroad tours on vintage steam trains. These run mainly on the Seattle and Carlisle line but also use other scenic rail routes. The package includes hotel accommodations.

Lakes Supertours (1 High St., Windermere, tel. 05394/42751) offers full-day tours by coach and boat, with plenty of opportunities for getting out and strolling around.

Trackers Leisure Bikes (66 Main St., Keswick, tel. 07687/71372) provides guided mountain bike tours, catering to all ability levels and lasting from three to eight hours.

The **Liverpool Heritage Walk** is a self-guided 7.4-mi walk through Liverpool city center, following 75 metal markers which point out sights of historic and cultural interest. An accompanying guidebook (£1.50) is available from either of the Liverpool Tourist Information centers.

Cavern City Tours (051/236–9091) offers a Beatles Magical Mystery Tour, departing from Clayton Square daily at 2:30 PM. The two-hour bus tour runs past John Lennon's childhood home, local schools attended by the Beatles, and other significant mop-top landmarks.

Exploring the Northwest and Lake District

The first tour begins in Manchester. From there it's a quick side trip west to Liverpool, but it's better to take the train rather than combat local traffic. Both city centers are easy to walk around. From Liverpool, head north and west to the Lancashire coast and Blackpool, where the tour finishes.

It's an easy drive north to Windermere, on the wooded shores of the Lake District's largest lake. From here the second tour explores the southern lakes, stopping in Grasmere, a town closely associated with the poet William Wordsworth, then swings south to the Lakeland fells and on to Barrow-in-Furness and the bayside resort of Grange-over-Sands, before turning north to Kendal.

The third tour ventures north from Kendal through the wondrously desolate countryside at the foot of Shap Fells to the attractive market town of Penrith. Next it makes a sharp detour to Helvellyn, one of the Lake District's most celebrated mountains. On the way west to Keswick and Cockermouth, Wordsworth's birthplace, you'll pass under the imposing shadow of Blencathra and Skiddaw, drive along Derwentwater, through the Borrowdale Valley, by Buttermere and Crummoch Water. Then you'll swing east again, to Windermere, the starting point.

Highlights for First-time Visitors

Aira Force Waterfalls: Tour 3
Albert Dock, Liverpool: Tour 1
Blackpool Tower: Tour 1
Boat Trip on Windermere: Tour 2
Brantwood—Ruskin's Home: Tour 2
Derwentwater: Tour 3
Dove Cottage—Wordsworth's Home: Tour 2
Helvellyn: Tour 3
Holker Hall: Tour 2
Levens Hall Garden: Tour 2
Lodore Falls: Tour 3
Museum of Science and Industry, Manchester: Tour 1

Tour 1: Manchester, Liverpool, and Blackpool

Numbers in the margin correspond to points of interest on the Northwest and Manchester maps.

The mechanization of the cotton industry—the first cotton mill powered by steam opened in 1783—caused the rapid growth of Manchester; then, in 1894, the opening of the Manchester Ship Canal turned the world's cotton capital into a major inland port. Until only a few years ago, Manchester was a blackened, forbidding city, unlovely and unloved. But now it has been spruced up, and the once-begrimed buildings in the center of town, masterpieces of sturdy Victorian architecture, have been cleaned. Severe damage caused by World War II bombing has been remedied by modern development, not all of it attractive, and visitors now see an expansive center city, which has managed to keep much of its architectural heritage safe.

In recent years, Manchester has undergone a remarkable transformation, with heavy investment in a new transportation system and impressive sporting and leisure facilities. In part, this was due to successive attempts to bring the Olympic Games to the city: Manchester bid unsuccessfully for the 1996 and, most recently, the 2000 Games (losing out to Sydney). But despite the great local disappointment at not securing the games for Britain, the bequest to the people of Manchester has been a fine set of civic and sporting amenities.

Within just a few blocks you can visit most of the important sights. Start at the **City Art Gallery,** a strikingly neoclassical building housing a fine collection. Many Manchester industrial barons of the 19th century spent some of their vast wealth on paintings, and their interests are reflected in the art on display here. The ground- and first-floor galleries have recently been much renovated, allowing the permanent collection to be re-hung with improved effect. Apart from a large collection of Pre-Raphaelites, there are works by Gainsborough, Samuel Palmer, Turner, Claude Lorrain, and Bellotto. A re-creation of the living room and studio of L. S. Lowry—the popular Manchester artist who died in 1976—adds a touch of local interest. *Mosley St., tel. 061/236–5244. Admission free. Open Mon.–Sat. 10–5:45, Sun. 2–5:45. Free guided tours, Sat. and Sun. at 2:30 PM.*

The City Art Gallery also manages several other outlets in Manchester, including the **Atheneum Gallery,** next door, a showcase for changing contemporary shows, and the **Gallery of English Costume,** south of the center at Platt Hall in Rusholme. *Details of events and exhibitions are available from the City Art Gallery, see above.*

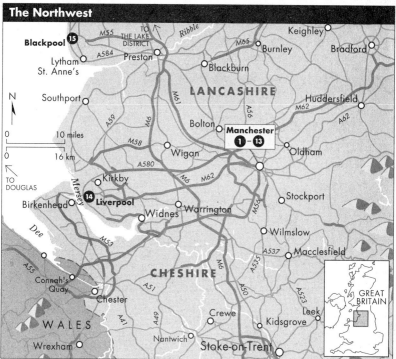

The Northwest

3 Two blocks northwest of the Art Gallery is the **Town Hall,** a magnificent Victorian Gothic building (1867–76), with extensions added just before World War II. The Great Hall, with its soaring hammerbeam roof, is decorated with proud murals of the city's history, painted by the Pre-Raphaelites' contemporary, Ford Madox Brown, between 1852 and 1865. As the Town Hall is used for meetings a great deal, the murals are sometimes covered up for their own protection. *Free guided tours Mon., Wed., Thurs. 10 AM; Wed. 2:30 if there are no meetings in progress.*

4 To one side of the Town Hall is the **Central Library;** the Library Theatre is part of the complex (*see* The Arts, *below*). Turn right at the library onto Peter Street and two blocks down you will find the Italianate **Free Trade Hall,** restored after World War II damage; it has been the home of the Hallé Orchestra for more than a century. The orchestra will have a custom-built auditorium of its own soon (*see* The Arts, *below*). The Free Trade Hall itself stands on the site of Peter's Field, where, in 1819, one of the most infamous episodes in British history occurred. Sixty thousand workers attending a meeting on the reform of Parliament were fired upon by the local guard, killing 11 in what became known as the "Peterloo Massacre."

6 South of the Free Trade Hall is the **G-Mex Centre,** formerly Manchester's central railroad station, now housing the city's biggest and brightest exhibitions and events (*see* The Arts, *below*).

To the west, following Great Bridgewater Street and Liverpool Road, you enter the district of **Castlefield,** site of an early Roman fort and later the center of Manchester's first canal and railroad developments. The district has since been restored as an urban heri-

Cathedral, **12**

Central
Library, **4**

City Art Gallery/
Atheneum
Gallery, **2**

Free Trade
Hall, **5**

G-Mex Centre, **6**

John Rylands
Library, **9**

Museum of
Science and
Industry, **7**

Opera House, **8**

Royal
Exchange, **11**

St. Ann's
Church, **10**

Town Hall, **3**

Whitworth Art
Gallery, **13**

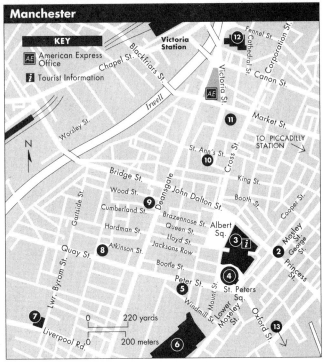

Manchester

tage park. In addition to the reconstructed gate to the Roman fort, the 7-acre site contains the various buildings of the excellent **Museum of Science and Industry.** Separate buildings, including the world's oldest surviving train station, show marvelous collections relating to the city's industrial past and present. You can walk through a reconstructed Victorian sewer and examine a huge collection of working steam mill engines. *Castlefield, tel. 061/832–1830. Admission: £3.50 adults, £1.50 children and senior citizens. Open daily 10–5.*

Walk back down Liverpool Road to Deansgate and head north; the **Opera House** lies one block west. It is on Quay Street, an ornate refurbished building that hosts major dance and opera groups (*see* The Arts, *below*).

Four blocks north on Deansgate is the **John Rylands Library,** named after a rich weaver whose widow spent his money founding the library. It became part of the University of Manchester in 1972. Built in a late-Gothic style in the 1890s, the library houses one of Britain's most important collections—priceless historical documents and charters, Bibles in over 300 languages, manuscripts dating from the dawn of Christianity, and fine bindings. There are always exhibitions from the library's treasures, including one of the possible accurate likenesses of Shakespeare, the Grafton portrait. *150 Deansgate, tel. 061/834–5343. Admission free. Open weekdays 10–5:15, Sat. 10–1.*

Up Deansgate toward the River Irwell and on the right, down St. Ann's Street, you will come upon **St. Ann's Church,** a handsome 1712 building, which contains *The Descent from the Cross,* a painting by

⑪ Annibale Carracci (1561–1609). Outside, to the right side of the square, is the **Royal Exchange,** once the cotton market; it was built with impressive panache and could accommodate 7,000 traders. Its echoing bulk now houses one of the most imaginative theaters in Britain (*see* The Arts, *below*).

Time Out Close to the Royal Exchange, in Shambles Square in the modern Arndale Centre, **Sinclairs Oyster Bar** is an atmospheric 18th-century pub serving excellent lunches (including, naturally, oysters) and good northern beer. In summer, you can sit outside in the pedestrianized square.

⑫ To complete this stroll around downtown Manchester, continue north up Victoria Street to the **cathedral,** beside the river. It was originally the medieval parish church of the city but gradually went up in the world to finally become a cathedral in 1847. It's a strange shape, very broad for its length; indeed, it's recognized as having the widest medieval nave in Britain. Inside is a wealth of attractive items: early 16th-century choir stalls, with intriguing misericord seats; paintings of the Beatitudes by Carel Weight (1908–89); a sculpture by Eric Gill (1882–1919), famed for the typeface that he designed and which bears his name; a fine tomb brass of Warden Huntingdon, who died in 1458; and an octagonal chapter house from 1485. *Admission free. Open daily 8–6.*

⑬ One of the most interesting places to visit outside the center of Manchester is the university-run **Whitworth Art Gallery,** southeast of town in an area called Moss Side. At the Piccadilly bus depot ask for a bus to the Manchester Royal Infirmary, which is just across the road from the Whitworth. The collections in the gallery are especially strong in British watercolors, old master drawings, and Postimpressionism. And its captivating rooms full of textiles—Coptic and Peruvian cloths, Spanish and Italian vestments, tribal rugs, and contemporary fabrics—are just what you might expect in a city built on textile manufacture. There's a gallery bistro for light meals and a good gallery shop. *Oxford Rd., tel. 061/273–4865. Admission free. Open Mon.–Wed., Fri.–Sat. 10–5, Thurs. 10–9.*

Numbers in the margin correspond to points of interest on the Northwest map.

⑭ From Manchester it's under an hour by train or car to **Liverpool.** As part of the 18th-century slave trade triangle, between Africa, America, and Britain, Liverpool quickly grew into the country's largest port, a position it retained even after abolition of the slave trade. The Industrial Revolution placed it firmly at the center of Britain's burgeoning economy, connected to the rest of the country by train and to the rest of the world by cargo ships and, later, transatlantic passenger ships. The city has suffered severe decline since World War II, and despite a certain amount of regeneration, there isn't the same feeling of growth and opportunity as there is in neighboring Manchester.

Still, there are compelling reasons to visit, not least the surviving, proud 19th-century buildings opposite the downtown **Lime Street Station.** These include **St. George's Hall,** built in 1839–47 and considered one of the country's finest Greek Revival buildings. Just to the north, the **Walker Art Gallery** maintains its position as one of the best art collections outside London with a fine display of British art (some of the best on show in its newly refurbished Victorian Gallery) and some superb Italian and Flemish works. In particular, you'll find paintings by Turner, Constable, Stubbs, and Landseer, as well as representative work by the Pre-Raphaelites. *William Brown St., tel. 051/207–0001. Admission free. Open Mon.–Sat. 10–5, Sun. noon–5.*

On the southern side of Lime Street Station, follow Mount Pleasant for the 10-minute walk up to the modern Roman Catholic **Metropolitan Cathedral of Christ the King.** Built in 1962, it's a striking—some say overbearing—funnel-like structure of concrete, stone, and mosaic, topped with a glass lantern. *Mount Pleasant, tel. 051/709–9222. Admission free but donation welcome. Open Mon.–Sat. 8–6, Sun. 8–5.*

By way of contrast, be sure to walk farther south, along Hope Street, to the **Anglican Cathedral,** the largest church in Britain, overlooking the city and the River Mersey. Built from local sandstone, the Gothic-style cathedral took 75 years to complete. It was begun in 1903 by architect Giles Gilbert Scott (who died in 1960), and work finally finished in 1978. *St. James' Rd., tel. 051/709–6271. Admission free but donation welcome. Open daily 9–6.*

Liverpool's other main area of interest is to the west, down at **Albert Dock** on the waterfront. Built in the mid-19th century, Albert Dock was recently rescued from neglect and its fine colonnaded, brick warehouse buildings converted to new museums, shops, offices, and restaurants. It's a stunning achievement and there's enough here to occupy you for a whole day. And since every attraction is indoors, within the old warehouse buildings, it's an obvious choice if your visit coincides with one of the Northwest's rainy spells. There is free parking at the dock, but if you've come by train from Manchester, a bus runs here every 30 minutes (Mon.–Sat. only) from Lime Street Station.

Of the museums at the dock, the **Merseyside Maritime Museum** is the most relevant to the area and the most interesting, telling the story of the port of Liverpool by way of models, paintings, and original boats and equipment. *Albert Dock, tel. 051/207–0001. Admission: £2.50 adults, £1.30 children and senior citizens, £7 family ticket.*

Also at the dock, the **Tate Gallery**—an offshoot of the London gallery of the same name—exhibits constantly changing displays of challenging modern art. It has an excellent shop selling prints and posters. *Tel. 051/709–3223. Admission free. Open Tues.–Sun. 10–6.*

New features of the dock include a **Museum of Liverpool Life,** housed in a former Boat Hall opposite the Maritime Museum, and for nostalgic visitors, **The Beatles Story,** where you can follow in the footsteps of the Fab Four in a series of entertaining re-created scenes from their career. *The Beatles Story, Britannia Vaults, Albert Dock, tel. 051/709–1963. Admission: £3.95 adults, £2.45 children and senior citizens, £8.95 family ticket. Open daily 10–6.*

Just to the north, you can finish your tour of the city by taking a **ferry** from Pier Head across the River Mersey to Birkenhead and back. Ferries leave regularly throughout the day and offer fine views of the city. *Mersey Ferries, tel. 051/630–1030. Ferries every 30–60 minutes throughout the day; 80p adults, 50p children; cruises £2.75 adults, £1.40 children.*

The quickest way to Blackpool is, unfortunately, by motorway, but you can follow a slower, more scenic route, taking A59 from Liverpool to Preston (31 mi) and then A583 and A584, which run along the Fylde coast to the west.

Twelve miles west of Preston, you pass through genteel **Lytham St. Anne's,** a retirement area rich in golf courses and large residential homes, before entering the resort of **Blackpool** at the southern end of its 7-mile promenade. The largest vacation resort in Europe, Blackpool attracts more than 16 million visitors a year to its sands, piers, parks, and Pleasure Beach—a Coney Island–style amusement park covering over 40 acres south of the town center. To the British, Blackpool is something of an old joke; the pier and promenade stalls sell sickly Day-Glo candy and plastic hats emblazoned with "Kiss Me Quick" slogans. July and, to a lesser extent, August are the peak months, when accommodations are at a premium and the myriad bars, discos, cafés, and restaurants are stuffed to the gills. The beaches, too, are covered with bodies, though be wary of swimming. The local waters don't qualify for the EEC clean water standard, and you'd do best to amuse children with a donkey ride up and down the sands instead.

Better yet, visit outside the peak summer season, when there's space to explore properly what's left of 19th-century Blackpool. It was one of the earliest British seaside resorts, and the fixtures and fittings still reflect that era. Trams run up and down the promenade, saving your legs a long walk, and pass the town's three 19th-century piers and the central **Blackpool Tower,** built in 1894 and inspired by the Eiffel Tower. The views from the top of the tower are magnificent, while inside are seven floors of amusements and rides. Take a look, too, at the superbly restored gilt ballroom, where there are daily tea dances. *Tower World, tel. 0253/22242. Admission: £6.95 adults, £5.95 children; £4.95 in winter. Open Apr.–Oct., daily 10AM– 11PM; Nov.–Mar., Sat. 10 AM–11 PM, Sun. 10 AM–6 PM; daily 10–6 during Christmas week except Christmas Day.*

Time Out Robert's Oyster Rooms (92 North Shore), close to the tower, is an anachronistic survival amid all the fast-food outlets. Stop in at the snug wood-paneled café for fresh oysters on the half shell, accompanied by bread and butter and hot tea, or try one of the other traditional British shellfish snacks: cockles, whelks, winkles, or prawns.

If you are in Blackpool in September or October, you'll coincide with the **Illuminations,** a spectacular light display that runs the length of the promenade. Each year, the switching-on ceremony is performed by a famous personality; one year this duty fell to the horse Red Rum, a British Grand National winner.

From Blackpool, head north for the 70 miles or so to Windermere and the start of Tour 2.

Tour 2: From Windermere to Kendal— The Southern Lakes

Numbers in the margin correspond to points of interest on the Lake District Map.

⑯ Windermere is a natural touring base for the southern half of the Lake District, with its wealth of tourist facilities and good transportation links. The name "Windermere" applies both to the lake and to the main town nearby. The town of Windermere was a hamlet originally called Birthwaite, but when the railroad was extended here from Kendal in 1847, local officials named the new station Windermere in order to cash in on the lake's reputation, already well established thanks to Wordsworth and the Romantic poets. Later, **⑰** another village by the lake, **Bowness-on-Windermere,** was swal-

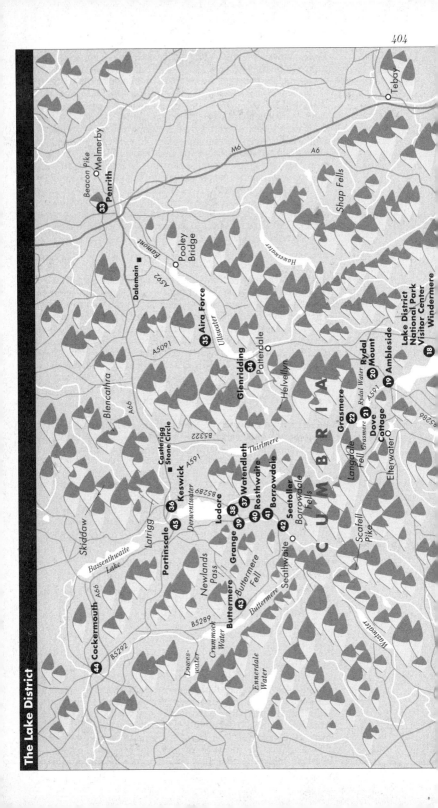

The Lake District

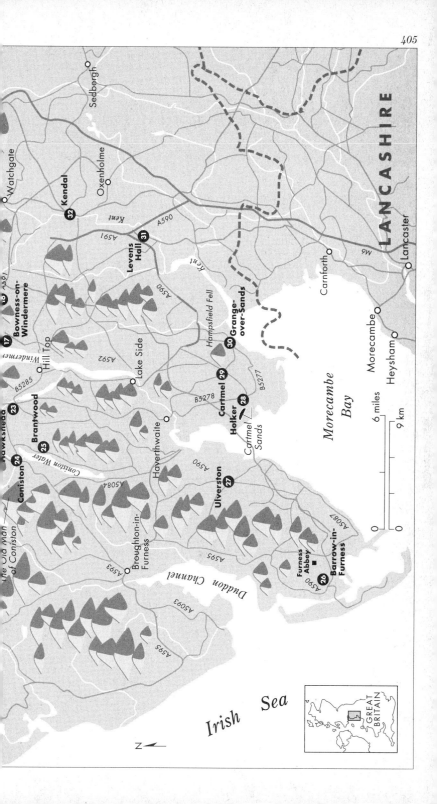

Sedbergh

Watchgate

Kendal **32**

Oxenholme

Bowness-on-
Windermere **47**

Hill Top

Windermere

B5285

Brantwood **23**

Hawkshead

Coniston **24**

Levens
Hall **31**

A591

A590

Kent

A592

Lake Side

Hampsfield Fell

Grange-
over-Sands **30**

Kent

Carmel **29**

B5278

Holker **28**

B5277

Carnforth

LANCASTER *(LANCASHIRE)*

M6

Lancaster

Morecambe

Heysham

*Morecambe
Bay*

Carmel
Sands

Haverthwaite

A590

Ulverston **27**

A5084

Coniston Water

*The Old Man
of Coniston*

A593

Broughton-in-
Furness

A595

A590

A5087

Furness
Abbey ■

Barrow-in-
Furness **26**

Duddon Channel

A5093

A595

Irish Sea

N

0 — 6 miles
0 — 9 km

**GREAT
BRITAIN**

lowed by the new town. Today the part of town around the station is known as Windermere, while the lakeside area 1½ miles away is still called Bowness. A minibus, leaving from outside Windermere train station, links the two.

Bowness is definitely more attractive than Windermere. Of special interest is the **New Hall Inn,** dating from 1612 and best known as the **Hole in t'Wall,** just behind the village center. Its most famous landlord was Thomas Longmire, a 19th-century Cumbrian wrestler who won no fewer than 174 championship belts. Charles Dickens stayed at the inn in 1857 and described Longmire as a "quiet-looking giant."

Time Out At the **Hole in t'Wall** (Fallbarrow Rd.), sample traditional Cumbrian ales and tasty pub lunches in authentic 19th-century surroundings, with slate floors and a flagstoned courtyard. There's a spitting log fire in winter.

In Bowness, also visit the 15th-century parish church of **St. Martins,** which has an Anglo-Saxon font, chained Bibles, original stained-glass windows, and an unusual wooden sculpture of St. Martin. One of the stained-glass windows shows the striped coat-of-arms of John Washington, ancestor of George; the design is said to have been the original source of the stripes in the American flag.

Although Windermere's marinas and piers have some charm, you can bypass the busier stretches of shoreline (and in summer they can be packed solid) by walking beyond the boathouses. Here, from among the pine trees, is a fine view across the lake. The car ferry (which also carries pedestrians) crosses the water at this point to reach Far Sawrey and the road to Hawkshead; the crossing takes just a few minutes. Ferry information available from Windermere tourist information center (*see* Essential Information, *above*). *Ferries run continuously throughout the day and evening, with crossings every 20 minutes. Cars £1.50, foot passengers 20p.*

On the other side of the promenade, beyond the main cluster of hotels in Bowness, is the **Windermere Steamboat Museum,** which exhibits a remarkable collection of steam- and motor-powered yachts and launches. The *Dolly,* built around 1850, is one of the two oldest mechanically powered boats in the world. She was raised from the bottom of Ullswater in 1962, having lain there for 70 years. *Rayrigg Rd., tel. 05394/45565. Admission: £2.50 adults, £1.40 children, £1.80 senior citizens, £5.80 family ticket. Open Easter–Oct., daily 10–5.*

The lake itself, which is 11 miles long, 1½ miles wide, and 200 feet deep, fills a rocky gorge between steep, thickly wooded hills. Its waters make for superb fishing, especially for char, a rare kind of reddish lake trout prized by gourmets.

During the summer, Lake Windermere is alive with all kinds of boats. Waterskiing is a favorite pastime here, and the area can become extremely noisy, so if you're seeking peace and tranquility, you might be happier on any other of the dozens of lakes in the region (waterskiing is not permitted anywhere else). Nevertheless, a boat trip on Windermere, particularly the round trip from Bowness to Ambleside and down to Lake Side (*see* Getting Around, *above*), remains a wonderful way of spending a few summer hours.

For a memorable view of Lake Windermere—at the cost of a rigorous climb—follow signs near the Windermere Hotel (across from the station) to **Orrest Head.** These will guide you to a rough, uphill track (*see* What to See and Do with Children, *below*). Eventually you will see a stile on your right; climb over it and continue up the path to a rocky little summit where you can sit on a bench and enjoy a breathtaking panorama of the mountains and lake. The walk back is only a mile but takes most people at least an hour.

Time Out **The Queen's Head** (at Troutbeck, on A592, just north of Windermere) has lost none of its 17th-century character, despite a recent face-lift. The small, snug rooms are lovely to lounge in, and there's a fine array of adventurous bar food.

From Windermere, it's easy to reach most of the Lake District's attractions, especially the southern part of the national park and the Furness area. **Brockhole National Park Centre,** 3 miles northwest from Windermere station on A591, makes a good starting point; it's easily accessible by bus and boat. A magnificent lakeside mansion with terraced gardens sloping down to the water houses the official 🔞 **Lake District National Park Visitor Center.** In addition to tourist information, the center offers a fine range of exhibitions about the Lake District, including geological, agricultural, industrial, wildlife, and literary displays. The gardens are at their best in the spring, when floods of daffodils cover the lawns and the azaleas burst into bloom. Park activities include lectures, guided walks, and demonstrations of such Lakeland crafts as dry-stone-wall building. There's also a bookstore. *Ambleside Rd., near Windermere, tel. 05394/46601. Admission free (£2 parking fee each car). Open Easter–late Oct., daily 10–4.*

Time Out The **Terrace Cafeteria Restaurant** at Brockhole specializes in local delicacies such as Cumbrian courting cake, Helvellyn tarts, rum butter, and tempting salads. It's an ideal place for morning coffee, lunch, or afternoon tea.

Four miles north of Brockhole along A591 at the head of the lake is 🔞 the town of **Ambleside,** a popular center for Lake District excursions. It lies in the green valley of the River Rothay, which empties into Windermere, and is certainly handsomely sited, but—as with much of this southern region—it suffers terribly from tourist overcrowding in high season. One of the town's most unusual features is **Bridge House,** a tiny 17th-century cottage perched on an arched stone bridge spanning Stock Beck. The building now houses a National Trust shop and information center, open daily from Easter through November.

If you fancy stretching your legs, it's easy enough to escape the crowds at Ambleside. Follow A593 west out of the village and take the turning at Skelwith Bridge for the delightful little village of **Elterwater,** a popular stop for hikers. The B5343 continues west from here for another couple of miles to **Langdale Fell,** where you can park and attempt one of several excellent walks: there are information boards at the various parking places. Either stroll up the river valley, or embark on much more energetic hikes to Stickle Tarn or to one of the peaks of the so-called Langdale Pikes. When you're ready to return to the main route, it's just a 7-mile drive back to Ambleside.

North of Ambleside, the road winds around the lakeside edges of Rydal Water and Grasmere, through a delicate landscape of birch and oak woods, carpeted with wild daffodils in the spring. Here, the craggy mountain summits form a dramatic backdrop, at their most impressive when cloaked in the golden-brown colors of fall.

Continuing north along A591 from Ambleside toward Grasmere (a journey of around 3 miles), you'll pass two places closely associated with William Wordsworth. First you'll come to **Rydal Mount,** where he lived from 1813 until his death 37 years later. Wordsworth and his family moved to these grand surroundings when he was nearing the height of his career, and his descendants still live here, surrounded by his furniture, portraits, and the 4½-acre garden laid out by the poet himself. *Rydal, Ambleside, tel. 05394/33002. Admission: £2 adults, 80p children. Open Mar.–Oct., daily 9:30–5; Nov.–Feb., Wed.–Mon. 10–4; closed Jan. 10–Feb. 1.*

You will reach Wordsworth's earlier home, **Dove Cottage,** just before coming to Grasmere. A much humbler place than Rydal Mount, it was the poet's home from 1799 (he moved here when he was 19) until 1808. First opened to the public in 1891, this tiny house, formerly an inn, still contains much of his furniture and many personal belongings. There's also a coffee shop and restaurant.

Dove Cottage is also the headquarters of the **Centre for British Romanticism,** which documents the contributions Wordsworth and his remarkable associates (sometimes called the Lake Poets) made to world literature. Among these were his sister Dorothy, Samuel Taylor Coleridge, Thomas De Quincey, and Robert Southey, the last of whom Wordsworth succeeded as poet laureate in 1843. The museum places this outburst of creative genius in its historic, social, and regional context, exhibiting portraits, watercolors, letters, and memorabilia. Poems can be heard on headphone sets in front of display cases of the poets' original manuscripts. The center holds residential summer study conferences on Wordsworth and the Romantics, as well as winter study schools. *The Wordsworth Trust, Dove Cottage, Grasmere LA22 9SH, tel. 05394/35544. Admission to Dove Cottage: £3.90 adults, £1.95 children. Open mid-Feb.–mid-Jan., daily 9:30–5.*

Although Wordsworth was born in Cockermouth, northwest of Keswick, it is the town of **Grasmere,** with its tiny, wood-fringed lake, that is most closely associated with him. Among his American guests here were the authors Ralph Waldo Emerson and Nathaniel Hawthorne. Grasmere, too, is overwhelmed in summer by tourists and cars, but it is worth braving the crowds to explore the crooked lanes, whose charming slate-built cottages house interesting shops, cafés, and galleries. Wordsworth, his wife, Mary, his sister Dorothy, and his daughter Dora are buried in Grasmere churchyard.

Take the minor road out of Grasmere, skirting Rydal Water, and follow the signs south about 8 miles to **Hawkshead.** Just outside of town, on B5286, you'll see the **Hawkshead Courthouse,** built by the monks of nearby Furness Abbey in the 15th century. If you're driving, you'll have to leave your car outside the village; it's closed to traffic. Walk in and enjoy its narrow, cobbled streets and little bow-fronted stores. You can see Wordsworth's name carved on a desk at the **Hawkshead Grammar School,** where the poet was a pupil from 1779 to 1787. He later boarded at Ann Tyson's cottage, half a mile north of the village on B5286. *The Courthouse, tel. 05394/35599. Admission free. Open Apr.–Nov., daily 10–5. If you find it locked, ask for the key at the Hawkshead information center.*

From Hawkshead, continue west along B5285 for about 3 miles until you come to **Coniston.** Formerly a copper-mining village, Coniston is now a small lake resort and boating center, wonderfully sited at the foot of the **Old Man of Coniston** (2,635 feet). Tracks lead up from the village past an old mine to the peak, which you can reach in about two hours. Coniston's lake, **Coniston Water,** is about 5 miles long, and many world speedboat records have been set here. Donald Campbell set a water speed record of 260 miles per hour in 1959 but was killed when trying to beat it in 1967. His body was never recovered after his boat crashed, and a stone seat in the village commemorates him.

㉕ Just outside Coniston is **Brantwood,** the home of Victorian artist, critic, and social reformer John Ruskin (1819–1900). Drive along the eastern lake shore from Coniston (about 2½ mi), or go by boat, either taking the *Ruskin Ferry* (Apr.–Jan., hourly service from Coniston Pier or Waterhead), or the steam yacht *Gondola* (4–5 trips daily) from Coniston Pier (*see* Getting Around, *above*). Brantwood is a rambling white 18th-century house (with Victorian alterations) set in a 250-acre estate. Here you'll find a collection of Ruskin's own paintings, drawings, and books, as well as much of the art he collected in his long life, not least a superb group of drawings by Turner. Ruskin's coach and private boat are still here, too. The extensive grounds, complete with woodland walks, were laid out by Ruskin himself. *Tel. 05394/41396. Admission: £3 adults, £1.50 students. Open mid-Mar.–mid-Nov., daily 11–5:30; mid-Nov.–mid-Mar., Wed.–Sun. 11–4.*

Time Out | Brantwood's **Jumping Jenny's** (tel. 05394/41715) brasserie and tearoom offers Pre-Raphaelite decor, an open log fire, and mountain views as the setting for morning coffee, lunch, or afternoon tea.

Leaving Coniston, continue southwest on A593 to A595, passing through **Broughton-in-Furness,** a peaceful little town that seems to have been built with hardly a level space anywhere, until you come
㉖ to the port of **Barrow-in-Furness,** a trip of about 27 miles. Although Barrow itself is a rather gloomy iron- and steel-producing town, you can visit the ruins of **Furness Abbey,** once one of the wealthiest monasteries in Britain, in the darkly named Vale of Deadly Nightshade, 1½ miles north of town. Founded in 1124, this Cistercian abbey once owned large tracts of land all over the Lake District. The red sandstone ruins are extensive; what remains intact are a series of graceful arches overlooking the cloisters and some magnificent canopied seats in the presbytery (the part of the church reserved for the officiating priest). A small visitor center and museum outline the abbey's history. *Tel. 0229/823420. Admission: £2 adults, £1 children, £1.50 senior citizens. Open Apr.–Sept., daily 10–6; Oct.–Mar., Tues.–Sun. 10–1 and 2–4.*

About 9 miles northeast of Furness Abbey by A590 is the typically
㉗ Cumbrian market town of **Ulverston,** whose sole claim to fame is that it is the birthplace of the comedian Stan Laurel, born here on June 16, 1890. The **Laurel and Hardy Museum** traces Stan's childhood in the town and exhibits films, tapes, props, and personal items of the famous comedy team. The museum is the work of owner and curator Bill Cubin, who is on hand to answer questions; you can buy any number of items here relating to Stan and Ollie, from buttons to statues. There's a snack bar here, too. *4C Upper Brook St., tel. 0229/ 52292. Admission: £2 adults, £1 children and senior citizens, £4 family ticket. Open daily 10–5.*

From Ulverston, follow A590 to Haverthwaite, then turn right onto
㉘ B5278 for the village of **Holker** (pronounced "Hooker"), and watch for signs to **Holker Hall.** This mainly 17th-century country house (not to be confused with Holkham Hall in East Anglia), surrounded by a splendid 122-acre deer park, is still owned by the Cavendish

family, relatives of the duke of Devonshire. The gardens are not to be missed. There are 25 acres of magnificent displays and an impressive array of fountains, waterfalls, and ponds. A Victorian wing is filled with richly carved woodwork, fine furniture, porcelain, and paintings. There's also a museum of vintage cars, a Victorian and Edwardian kitchen exhibition, an exhibition of patchwork and quilting, an adventure playground, and a cafeteria—enough to occupy the entire family for hours. *Cark-in-Cartmel, Grange-over-Sands, tel. 05395/58328. Admission: £5.25 adults, £3 children, £14.50 family ticket; gardens, grounds, and exhibition only £2.75 adults, £1.55 children, £8 family ticket. Open Easter–Oct., Sun.–Fri. 10:30–4:30 (park until 6).*

㉙ When you are at Holker Hall, look for signs to the nearby village of **Cartmel.** This is a charming place, one of southern Lakeland's oldest villages, and has a particularly pretty market square, off which radiate ancient streets leading to old bridges, inns, gift shops, and galleries. Its noble **church,** the surviving portion of an Augustinian priory dating from the 12th century, is built on the scale of a cathedral. It has some fine carved choir stalls, impressive memorials, and an unusual, "skewed" central tower. In the churchyard are the graves of local citizens who drowned crossing the sands of the nearby Kent and Leven estuaries. Until the coming of the railroad, these treacherous sand bars provided the only practical route across the area.

㉚ From Cartmel, continue east along the minor roads to **Grange-over-Sands,** an unspoiled 19th-century seaside resort about 3 miles away. Its sheltered cove overlooks the broad sands of Morecambe Bay. The gardens, quiet promenades, hotels, and shops here offer an atmosphere very different from that of central Lakeland. You can enjoy magnificent views of the Lakeland mountains to the north from the top of **Hampsfield Fell** (727 feet) behind the town.

㉛ Leaving Grange-over-Sands, pick up A590 toward Kendal, stopping off after 8 miles at **Levens Hall.** This 16th-century house is famous for its rare topiary garden laid out in 1692, with yew and box hedges cut into curious and elaborate shapes. The hall is also notable for its ornate plasterwork, oak paneling, and leather-covered walls. It has a spacious deer park, a fascinating steam engine collection, a store, and a cafeteria. (Buses from Kendal stop here.) *Levens Park, Levens, tel. 05395/60321. Admission: house and gardens £3.50 adults, £1.90 children, £3 senior citizens; gardens only £2.20 adults, £1.10 children, £2 senior citizens. Open Easter–Sept., Sun.–Thurs. 11–5.*

㉜ Next, continue north 5 miles to the ancient town of **Kendal,** one of the most important textile centers in northern England before the Industrial Revolution. It's an attractive town, cut through by a bubbling river and with stone houses framed by the hills behind. So close are these, that with the aid of a walking guide picked up from the tourist information center, you can be astride the tops within an hour. In Kendal itself, once you're away from the busy main road, you'll discover quiet, narrow, winding streets and charming courtyards, many dating from medieval times. Off Stricklandgate, in Market Place, there's been a market held since 1189. The old market hall has now been converted into an indoor shopping center, though outdoor stalls still do business here every Saturday.

Time Out   Just around the corner from the market, **Farrers** (13 Stricklandgate) is a 19th-century building which houses a fine tea and coffee shop, where you can enjoy excellent freshly brewed coffee and specialty teas—and even buy packets of both to take home.

Take a pleasant stroll along the River Kent, where—close to the Parish Church—you can visit the 18th-century **Abbott Hall.** Here the **Museum of Lakeland Life and Industry,** housed in the former stable block, offers interesting exhibits on blacksmithing, wheelwrighting, farming, weaving, printing, local architecture and interiors, and regional customs. In the main building is the **Art Gallery,** featuring works by Ruskin and 18th-century portrait painter George Romney, who worked (and died) in Kendal. *Kirkland, tel. 0539/722464. Admission to both museum and gallery: £4 adults, £2 children and students, £10 family ticket; one museum £3 adults, £1.50 children and students, £6 family ticket. Open Apr.–Oct., Mon.–Sat. 10–5, Sun. 2–5; Nov.–Mar., Mon.–Fri. 11–4, Sat. and Sun. 2–5.*

At the northern end of town, close to the train station, the **Kendal Museum** was first founded in 1796, moving into a former wool warehouse in 1913. Its dominant collections are of natural history and archaeology. It details splendidly the flora and fauna of the Lake District, and also contains displays on Alfred Wainwright, the region's most avid chronicler of countryside matters, who died in 1991. His multivolume Lake District walking guides are famous the world over; you'll see them in every local book and gift shop. *Station Rd., tel. 0539/721374. Admission: £1.50 adults, 80p children. Open Mon.–Sat. 10:30–5, Sun. 2–5.*

Tour 3: From Kendal to Keswick

The journey north from Kendal is the longest and bleakest leg of the Lake District tours. This 32-mile drive on A6 will take you through the wild and desolate **Shap Fells,** which rise to a height of 1,304 feet. Even in the summer it's a lonely place to be, and in the winter snows, the road can be dangerous.

33 The town of **Penrith** was the capital of the semi-independent kingdom of Cumbria in the 9th and 10th centuries. Later, Cumbria was part of the Scottish kingdom of Strathclyde; in the year 1070, it was incorporated into England. Even at this time, Penrith was a thriving market town and an important staging post on the road to Scotland. The warning beacon on the hill above the town (**Beacon Pike,** where a stone tower still stands) was lit to alert townsfolk to approaching enemies, usually Scots. The last invasion from Scotland was that of the Jacobites in 1745, who followed Bonnie Prince Charlie in his romantic but ill-fated attempt to restore the Stuart dynasty to the British throne.

To find out more about Penrith's history, stop in at the **Penrith Museum** on Middlegate. Built in the 16th century, the building served as a school from 1670 to the 1970s; it now contains a fascinating exhibit of local historical artifacts. Ask at the museum about the historic "town trail" route. It takes you through narrow byways to the plague stone on King Street, where food was left for the plague-stricken; to a churchyard with 1,000-year-old "hog-back" tombstones (i.e., stones carved as stylized "houses of the dead"); and finally to the ruins of the 15th-century red sandstone castle. *Robinson's School, Middlegate, tel. 0768/64671, ext. 228. Admission free. Open Easter–June and Oct., Mon.–Sat. 10–5, Sun. 1–5; June–Sept., Mon.–Sat. 10–7, Sun. 1–6; Nov.–Easter, Mon.–Sat. 10–5.*

Time Out Five miles northeast of Penrith by A686, in Melmerby, is **The Village Bakery** (tel. 0768/881515). It's well worth the detour, as the baking is done in a wood-fired brick oven and the result is bread, cakes, and sponges that are sensational. Try the Celebration Fruit Cake. The Calthwaite Jersey cream that accompanies the scones and homemade jam is a weight-watcher's idea of hell. The bakery also serves a delicious lunch. Closed Sun. at Christmas and New Year.

Three miles southwest of Penrith, just off A592, is **Dalemain**, a country house with a 12th-century peel (tower) built to protect the occupants from raiding Scots. A medieval hall was added, as well as a number of extensions from the 16th to the 18th centuries, culminating in an imposing Georgian facade of local pink sandstone. The result is a delightful hodgepodge of architectural styles. Inside you can see a magnificent oak staircase, furniture dating from the mid-17th century (including Cumbrian "courting" chairs), a Chinese drawing room adorned with hand-painted wallpaper, a 16th-century "fretwork room" with intricate plasterwork, a nursery complete with an elaborate 18th-century dollhouse, and many fine paintings, including masterpieces by Van Dyck. The tower houses a small military museum with mementos from local army regiments. There's also a coffee shop, a picnic area, and sweeping gardens, which include an intriguing Tudor grotto. *Tel. 07684/86450. Admission: house, garden, and museum £3.80 adults, £2.80 children, £10.40 family ticket, free to visitors in wheelchairs; garden only £2.50 adults. Open Easter–Sept., Sun.–Thurs. 11:15–5.*

Follow A592 southwest along the River Eamont to Ullswater, the region's second-largest lake. Hemmed in by towering hills, the lake is a spectacular setting, and some of the finest views are from A592 as

❹ it sticks to the lake's western shore, through **Glenridding** to Patterdale at the southern end. Here, you're at the foot of **Helvellyn** (3,118 feet), which lies to the west. It is an arduous climb to the top and shouldn't be attempted in poor weather or by inexperienced hikers. Paths run from the road between Glenridding and Patterdale and pass by **Red Tarn**, at 2,356 feet the highest Lake District tarn. For those who'd rather see Ullswater from a less exalted level, steamers leave Glenridding's pier for Pooley Bridge, offering a pleasant tour along the lake.

Next, backtrack a bit along A592 and make a detour north on A5091

❺ to **Aira Force**, 5 miles from Patterdale, a spectacular series of waterfalls pounding through a wooded ravine to feed into Ullswater. Just above Aira Force in the woods of Gowbarrow Park, William Wordsworth and his sister Dorothy were walking on April 15, 1802. Dorothy remarked that she had never seen "daffodils so beautiful . . . they tossed and reeled and danced and seemed as if they verily laughed with the wind that blew upon them." Two years later Wordsworth transformed his sister's words into one of the best-known lyric poems in English, "I Wandered Lonely as a Cloud."

Leaving Aira Force, continue to follow A5091 north through the tiny villages of Dockray and Matterdale End. When you hit A66, 5 miles farther on, follow the signs west to Keswick, a distance of about 12 miles. Before you enter the town, you might stop off at **Castlerigg Stone Circle.** A clearly marked route leads to a 200-foot-long path running through a pasture; beyond this, set in a great natural hollow called St. John's Vale, stands an intriguing circle of neolithic or Bronze Age stones, none of them tall, but nonetheless impressive in this awesome setting ringed with mountains. The circle can be visited during daylight hours, and there is no admission charge.

36 The great Lakeland mountains of Skiddaw and Blencathra brood over the gray slate houses of **Keswick** (pronounced "Kezzick"), on the scenic shores of Derwentwater. An old market and mining center, Keswick was transformed by the arrival of the railroad. Since many of the best hiking routes radiate from here, it is more of a touring base than a tourist destination. People stroll the congested, narrow streets in boots and corduroy hiking trousers, and there are plenty of mountaineering shops in addition to hotels, guest houses, pubs, and restaurants.

With a population of only 6,000, Keswick is a compact town, and all the interesting sights lie within easy walking distance of the central streets: Market Place, Main Street, and Lake Road. The town received its market charter in the 13th century, and its Saturday market is still going strong. Later centuries brought a wealth of industries, especially textile manufacturing, which was dependent on power from the area's fast-flowing streams. The introduction of lead and copper mining in the 16th century brought scores of skilled German laborers here.

Time Out **Bryson's Tearoom** (38–42 Main St.) is a comfortable eatery over a family bakery, with home-cooked lunches and freshly made cakes. You can have a Lakeland cream tea here with rum butter. Closed Sunday.

The handsome 19th-century **Moot Hall** (assembly hall) on Market Place has served as both the Keswick town hall and the local prison. Now it houses the main **tourist information center** for the region.

Keswick offers a number of outdoor attractions, among them **Hope Park** (Lake Rd., open Easter–Oct.), just beside the lake, with a putting green and an aviary. **Fitz Park,** a garden area bordering the River Greta (just behind the town center), is pleasant for picnics and leisurely strolls. Here you will also find the **Keswick Museum and Art Gallery.** Exhibits include manuscripts by Wordsworth and other Lakeland writers, a diorama of the Lake District, a local geological and natural-history collection, some unusual "musical" stones, and an assortment of watercolor paintings. *Station Rd., tel. 07687/ 73263. Admission: £1 adults, 50p children. Open Easter–Oct., Sun.–Fri. 10–noon, 1–4.*

Another aspect of Keswick's history comes into sharp focus at the **Cumberland Pencil Museum.** Keswick was the first place in the world to manufacture pencils, as graphite (the material from which pencil lead is made) was discovered in neighboring Borrowdale in the 16th century. Pencils are still produced here, and the museum, housed in the factory just off Main Street, outlines their history—in a more entertaining fashion than you would expect from the subject—from early times to the present. *Southey Works, Greta Bridge, tel. 07687/73626. Admission: £2 adults, £1 children and senior citizens, £4.50 family ticket. Open daily 9:30–4.*

Hill walks originating in Keswick include routes across the **Latrigg** and **Skiddaw** mountains and the great ridge of **Blencathra.** You can reach Latrigg (1,203 ft.), the nearest of the three, from Station Road: Pass the Keswick Hotel, then follow the road under the old railroad bridge, keeping left, toward Briar Rigg. After about 100 yards, a sign on the right indicates the trail to Latrigg—a two-hour round-trip from Keswick.

To understand why **Derwentwater** is considered one of England's finest lakes, take a short walk from Keswick's town center to the lake shore, and follow the **Friar's Crag** path—about 15 minutes' level walk from the center. This pine-tree-fringed peninsula is a favorite vantage point, with its view over the lake, the surrounding ring of mountains, and many tiny wooded islands. Ahead you will see the crags that line the **Jaws of Borrowdale** and overhang a dramatic mountain ravine—the perfect setting for a Romantic painting or poem.

Another essential excursion is a wooden-launch cruise around Derwentwater. Between late March and November, cruises set off every hour in each direction from a wooden dock at the lake shore. You can also rent a rowboat here. Landing stages around the lake provide access to some spectacular hiking trails in the nearby hills.

Walking is perhaps the best way to discover the delights of this area. Don't worry if you don't have all the equipment; you can buy all the relevant maps and provisions in Keswick and even rent a pair of hiking boots. You may want to leave your car behind, as parking is difficult in the higher valleys, and both the Derwentwater launches and the Borrowdale bus service between Keswick and Seatoller run frequently. A number of pleasant country hotels, guest houses, and bed-and-breakfasts, both on the lake and in the interior valley, can provide a base for your walking excursions. For more information, contact Keswick's Lake District National Park information center (Lake Rd., tel. 07687/72803).

If you do decide to explore the area by car, follow B5289 from Keswick along the eastern edge of Derwentwater and turn left when **37** you see the sign for **Watendlath.** Follow either the country lane or the adjacent National Trust path past an old, hump-backed bridge at **Ashness.** Here you will be rewarded with a panoramic view of the lake. Next you will come to an isolated farm beside a small mountain tarn, where one-day fishing licenses are available.

Time Out Daily from April to October, **Watendlath Farm** serves old-fashioned farmhouse teas in its parlors or, in warm weather, on scrubbed tables outside.

38 Next rejoin B5289 and turn left. **Lodore's** waterfall, behind the Lodore Swiss Hotel (*see* Dining and Lodging, *below*), is worth another slight detour from the main road, though it's only really at its best after a day of rain. Then follow B5289 about a mile south to the **39** village of **Grange,** at the head of the Borrowdale valley. This is a popular center for walkers, particularly in the summer. An assortment of cafés allows you to fuel up before beginning your vigorous walk across the fells.

40 From Grange, drive south about 2 miles to **Rosthwaite,** a tranquil farming village with an ample supply of bed-and-breakfasts and **41** guest houses. Here, you're in the **Borrowdale** valley, whose varied landscape of green valley floor and surrounding crags has long been considered one of the region's most magnificent spots.

42 Two miles farther south along the main road lies **Seatoller,** the southernmost settlement in the Borrowdale valley, little more than a cluster of buildings and one excellent restaurant, the Yew Tree (*see* Dining and Lodging, *below*). At 1,176 feet, Seatoller is the terminus for buses to and from Keswick as well as the location of a Lake District National Park information center (Dalehead Base, Seatoller Barn, tel. 07687/77294). Behind Seatoller, the vaultingly steep

Borrowdale Fells rise up dramatically. Get out and walk wherever inspiration strikes, and in the spring, keep an eye open and your camera ready for newborn lambs roaming the hillsides. From here, to the south, you can also see England's highest mountain, **Scafell** (pronounced "Scarfell") **Pike** (3,210 ft.). The most usual route up the mountain, for experienced walkers, is from the hamlet of Seathwaite, just a mile or so south of Seatoller.

Beyond Seatoller, B5289 turns westward through Honister Pass (1,176 feet) and Buttermere Fell. It's a superb drive along one of the most dramatic of the region's roads, which is lined with huge boulders and at times channels through soaring rock canyons. The road sweeps down from the pass to the appealing Lakeland village of **Buttermere,** sandwiched between two lakes—the small, narrow **Buttermere** and the much larger **Crummock Water**—at the foot of high, craggy fells. From here, you can return to Keswick by a scenic minor road through **Newlands Pass** (once a silver mining center). The first Lake District guidebook, published in 1778, described the area as having "Alpine views and pastoral scenes in a sublime style."

If you wish to explore further, continue north along B5289 about 13 miles, skirting the east shore of **Crummock Water** and driving through the charming flat-land countryside of Lorton Vale, to **Cockermouth,** an attractive little town at the confluence of the Derwent and Cocker rivers. Slightly larger than Keswick, Cockermouth has a maze of narrow streets, a delight to wander. There's no public access to the ruined 14th-century castle, but there's plenty of enjoyment to be derived from the brisk market-town atmosphere here. The outdoor market, held each Monday, still retains its traditions; an old bell is rung at the start of trading. There's an indoor livestock market, too, which every month, on Sunday, is turned over to a vast junk and bric-a-brac garage sale.

Cockermouth was the birthplace of William Wordsworth (and his sister Dorothy), whose childhood home, **Wordsworth House,** is a typical 18th-century north-country gentleman's home, now owned by the National Trust. Some of the poet's furniture and personal items are on display here, and you can explore the garden he played in as a child. *Main St., tel. 0900/824805. Admission: £2.40 adults, £1.20 children. Open Apr.–Oct., weekdays 11–5.*

Wordsworth's father is buried in the churchyard nearby, and in the church itself is a stained-glass window in memory of the poet. Outside is the site of the old grammar school Wordsworth attended, now covered with other buildings. Another pupil here was Fletcher Christian, ringleader of the notorious mutiny on HMS *Bounty,* who was born nearby in 1764.

Leaving Cockermouth, start making your way back to Keswick along A66, which hugs the western shore of pretty Bassenthwaite Lake. Stop off at **Lingholm Gardens** in **Portinscale,** just outside of Keswick; it's best in the spring or fall, when the rhododendrons, azaleas, gentians, and begonias are in bloom. *Tel. 07687/72003. Admission: £2.50 adults, accompanied children free. Open Apr.–Oct., daily 10–5; tearoom open Mon.–Sat. 11–5, Sun. 1–5.*

If you want to return to Windermere, where Tour 2 began, rejoin A591 on the east side of Keswick and follow it due south for 26 miles, along the shores of Thirlmere, in the imposing shadow of Helvellyn.

What to See and Do with Children

The **Granada Studios Tour,** in the center of Manchester, has a lot to offer imaginative children. A very British version of the popular Hollywood studio tours, here you can see firsthand the work that goes on behind TV programs. There are backstage tours, 3D film shows, and other special events. It's from here that Britain's longest-running soap opera, "Coronation Street," is broadcast. *Water St., tel. 061/833–0880. Admission: £9.99 adults, £6.99 children. Open mid-Apr.–Sept., daily 9:45–7, last admission at 4; Oct.–mid-Apr., weekdays 9:45–5:30, weekends 9:45–6:30, last admission at 3.*

The Lake District is an ideal place to introduce children to hiking, providing you start with a modest itinerary. The scenery is wonderful, and you can often plan a walk to an easily reached summit such as **Orrest Head** or **Cat Bells.** The latter was the imaginary home of Beatrix Potter's Mrs. Tiggy-Winkle (*see below*). **Loughrigg,** near Grasmere, provides another good, gentle climb for young hikers, ending on a dramatic mountaintop.

Boat trips on **Windermere, Coniston, Ullswater,** or **Derwentwater** are popular with children of all ages (*see* Getting Around, *above*).

A trip on the **Lakeside & Haverthwaite** steam train (*see* Getting Around, *above*) from Lakeside, Windermere, can be easily combined with a Windermere boat trip. One train journey will provide almost a full day of entertainment. "Little Ratty," the 7½-mile narrow-gauge **Ravenglass & Eskdale Railway**, has small steam locomotives made precisely to scale, hauling a string of miniature cars through glorious scenery (*see* Getting Around, *above*). Either drive to Ravenglass or drive to Grange-over-Sands and then catch the British Rail Cumbrian coast line from Grange to Ravenglass. This line, too, offers a spectacular trip across an undulating landscape of mountains and estuaries. Train schedules are available at tourist information centers.

Of the indoor amusements, many children will appreciate **The World of Beatrix Potter,** a three-dimensional presentation of some of her most famous characters, alongside videos and films of her stories. There are good Beatrix Potter souvenirs here, and a tea room. *The Old Laundry, Crag Brow, Bowness-on-Windermere, tel. 05394/88444. Admission: £2.75 adults, £1.50 children. Open Easter–Sept., daily 10–7; Oct.–Easter, daily 10–4.*

The Northwest has many museums, many of which are of enormous interest to children. Of those covered in our tours, the museums at **Castlefield** in Manchester and **Albert Dock** in Liverpool (*see* Tour 1, *above*) are by far the most popular. Otherwise, a good choice is the **Cumberland Toy and Model Museum** which has exhibits of mainly British toys from 1900 to the present. Two buildings contain particularly good model train collections, the re-creation of a 1930s toy shop, and large collections of dolls and dollhouses. There's a play area for younger children, a quiz to take, and special exhibits throughout the year. *Banks Ct., Market Pl., Cockermouth, tel. 0900/827606. Admission: £1.40 adults, 70p children. Open Feb.–Nov., daily 10–5.*

Off the Beaten Track

Superb areas of scenic desolation are never far away in the Lake District. One such area lies to the east, toward the hills of the North Pennines. To get there, take A591 from Windermere directly to

Kendal, then follow the signs on A684 to **Sedbergh,** 9 miles east. This small, quiet town sits on the edge of the **Howgill Fells,** a cluster of domelike, green hills offering marvelous hiking territory.

It was in this quiet setting that the Friends (Quaker) sect was founded. In 1642, on a hillside here called **Firbank Knots** (about 4 miles from Sedbergh), George Fox preached to a thousand "seek-ers," who were later to become the founding members of the inter-national Quaker movement. At **Brigflatts,** just off A683, a mile west of Sedbergh, you can visit one of the world's first Quaker meetinghouses, virtually unchanged since it was built in the 1670s.

To complete a circular tour of the Howgills, follow scenic A683 north about 12 miles to the little-known town of **Kirkby Stephen,** with its ancient church and attractive old marketplace. From here you can return to Kendal (via Tebay) along A685. On the way you'll pass the dramatic scenery of **Lune Gorge,** where highway, motorway, and railroad squeeze through a narrow pass between the mountains. From Windermere, the round-trip to the Howgills is about 60 miles.

There is some lovely, tranquil countryside northeast of Keswick. Silloth, for example, is an old seaside resort on the Solway Firth (the body of water tucked between north Cumbria and southwest Scotland), famous for its beautiful sunsets. To get there, follow A591 north past Lake Bassenthwaite to Bothel, turn southwest onto A595, and then travel 3 miles before picking up B5301 to Silloth, via Aspatria. You can return by taking the coastal road B5300 to Maryport, then A594 to Cockermouth. In Cockermouth, pick up A66 southeast to Keswick.

It is difficult to escape literary associations in the Lake District, as so many writers have been inspired by its landscape or have sought a quiet refuge here. If you travel to the village of Hawkshead via the Windermere ferry, you'll pass **Hill Top,** home of children's author and illustrator Beatrix Potter, most famous for her *Peter Rabbit* stories. Now run by the National Trust, Hill Top is a popular—and often crowded—spot, even though it is definitely off the beaten track. The house is so tiny that admission has to be strictly con-trolled. Try to avoid visiting on summer weekends and during school vacations. You can also get to Hill Top by car. It's 2 miles south of Hawkshead on B5285. *Near Sawrey, Ambleside, tel. 05394/36269. Admission: £3.20 adults, £1.60 children. Open Apr.–Oct., Sat.–Wed. 11–4:30.*

It's surprisingly easy to get off the beaten track in the cities of the Northwest, too. Both **Manchester** and **Liverpool** boast a series of walking trails that take enquiring visitors through the less-fre-quented parts of the cities to see remnants of their fascinating in-dustrial heritage. The tourist information centers can offer advice about specific routes. Be sure, too, to ask about Manchester's less-er-known museums—such as the Jewish Museum or the National Museum of Labour History—which deal with thought-provoking ta-les of ethnic and urban life that aren't covered in the mainstream city museums.

Shopping

Grasmere **Craglands, The Weaving Mill Shop,** and **Jumpers** (all on Stock La.) sell high-quality woolens, including cashmeres, mohairs, and Arran sweaters.

For something a little different try **The English Lakes Perfumery** (College St., tel. 05394/35444), which offers locally produced perfumes, floral scents, lotions, soaps, and creams; you can sample the perfumes at a test bar before buying.

Kendal An excellent place for serious shopping, Kendal has its more interesting stores tucked away in the quiet lanes and courtyards around Market Place, Finkle Street, and Stramongate.

Henry Roberts Bookshop (7 Stramongate, tel. 0539/720425), in Kendal's oldest house (a 16th-century cottage), has a superb selection of Lakeland books.

The main road through town, although busy, has some good antiques shops and galleries, but for high-quality Lake District crafts, you might want to concentrate your efforts on the store in **Abbot Hall** (tel. 0539/722464) in Kirkland, where you can buy woven goods, tiles, ceramics, and glass, all of exceptional quality.

The **Kentdale Rambler** (34 Market Pl., tel. 0539/729188) is the best local store for walking boots and equipment, maps, and guides (including Wainwright's illustrated guides).

Four miles north of town along A591, **Peter Hall & Son** (Danes Rd., Staveley, tel. 0539/821633) is a woodcraft workshop selling ornamental bowls and other attractive gifts, all made from local woods.

Keswick Thanks to its size, Keswick is probably the most sophisticated shopping area in the Lake District. You will find a good choice of bookstores, crafts shops, and wool clothing stores. **Mayson's** (Lake Rd., tel. 07687/74107) sells Art Nouveau objects d'art, rugs and cushions, leather, and glass goods.

George Fisher (2 Borrowdale Rd., tel. 07687/72178) is famous for outdoor clothing: parkas, boots, skiwear, and many other kinds of sportswear. It also sells maps, and daily weather information is posted in the window.

There are a few boutiques, too, such as **Laura Hardy** (19 Bank St., tel. 07687/72774), which sells classic tweeds, knitwear, gloves, and hats; this store also has a mailing service for sending purchases anywhere in the world.

Liverpool The new shop at the **Walker Art Gallery** (William Brown St., tel. 051/207–0001) contains a high-quality selection of glassware, ceramics, and jewelry by local designers. The annual Merseycraft exhibition winners are on exclusive display in the shop every December.

Manchester The **Royal Exchange Crafts Centre** (St. Ann's Sq., tel. 061/833–9333) is an unusual glass structure, in the foyer of the Royal Exchange theater, and specializes in jewelry, ceramics, glassware, and textiles produced throughout the country. Next door, the **Royal Exchange Shopping Centre** houses, on its first floor, **The Design Centre,** a series of stores featuring the creations of young fashion designers.

The **Manchester Crafts Centre** (17 Oak St., tel. 061/832–4274) is made up of 18 workshops-cum-retail outlets. You can see potters, jewelers, hatters, theatrical costumers, and metal enamelers at work and can buy the fruits of their labors.

The **Whitworth Art Gallery** (Oxford Rd., tel. 061/273–4865) has a fine shop that specializes in handmade cards, postcards, and prints. It also sells stationery, art books, jewelry, and ceramics; from time to time there is a potter on the premises. Along the same lines, the **University of Manchester Museum** shop (Oxford Rd., tel. 061/275–

2000) offers a similar selection but specializes in books and imaginative toys for children.

Windermere You'll find the best selection at the Bowness end of town on Lake Road and around Queen's Square: clothing stores, crafts shops, and souvenir stores of all kinds.

Mansion House (Queen's Sq., tel. 05394/42568) has an outstanding range of English cut glass and fine bone china, including Royal Brierly, Wedgwood, Royal Doulton, and Crown Derby.

Abbey Horn of Kendal (Crag Brow, tel. 05394/44519) is one of the last British firms to practice the craft of horn-carving; its craftsmen make a remarkable variety of goods, including jewelry, utensils, mugs, and walking sticks with elaborately carved handles.

At **Lakeland Jewellers** (Crag Brow, tel. 05394/42992), the local experts set semiprecious stones in necklaces, pendants, rings, bracelets, earrings, and brooches.

The Lakeland Sheepskin Centre (Lake Rd., tel. 05394/44466), which also has branches in Ambleside and Keswick, offers moderately priced leather and sheepskin goods, as well as woolens and knitting wool.

Lake District Markets Kendal's market is on Wednesdays and Saturdays; Keswick's is on Saturdays, too. Cockermouth has a market on Mondays, Penrith on Tuesdays, and Ambleside on Wednesdays.

Sports and the Outdoors

Participant Sports

Fishing If you are tempted by the thought of landing the elusive char, or even the common perch, pike, and eel, you can buy an NRA Rod License (£12.50), valid for one year, for fishing in Windermere, Derwentwater, or the River Greta. Licenses are available at the **Windermere Tourist Information Center** or at **Field & Stream** (79 Main St., Keswick, tel. 07687/74396).

Golf **Blackpool** has an 18-hole and nine-hole course, plus a driving range. There's also a new 18-hole course under construction, adjacent to Blackpool Zoo Park. Information can be obtained from the local tourist office.

If you are a member of another golf club and call well in advance, you will probably be welcome at **Windermere** (tel. 05394/43123), **Kendal** (tel. 0539/724079), and **Grange-over-Sands** (tel. 05395/33180) golf courses. **The Derwentwater Hotel** in Portinscale (*see* Dining and Lodging, *below*) will arrange special golf vacations.

Horseback Riding Blackpool beach has horseback and donkey riding for children and adults throughout the summer.

In the Lake District, both **Keswick Riding Centre** (Swan Hill Stables, tel. 07687/73804) and **Rookin House Farm** (tel. 07684/83561), 3½ miles from Ullswater, offer riding lessons, including jumping, as well as trail rides.

Swimming **Blackpool's** 7 miles of beaches offer safe swimming, but the water quality isn't everything it should be. Instead, it's wiser to rely on one of the town's indoor pools. **Blackpool Sandcastle** (South Promenade, tel. 0253/343602) is a complete entertainment complex with pools, slides, and chutes, open daily from May to October.

You can swim in many of the **Lake District's** waters, but they can be bitterly cold, even in summer. It's better to stay on the water (*see below*), rather than in it.

Walking   The Lake District is undeniably beautiful, and to see it at its best, it's necessary to get out of the car and walk through at least part of the region. There's enough variation in the area to suit all tastes, from gentle rambles in the vicinity of the most popular towns and villages to full-scale hikes and climbs up some of England's most impressive peaks. Anyone can undertake a local ramble, and information boards are posted at car parks throughout the region pointing out the possibilities. The famous **Old Man of Coniston,** the **Langdale Pikes, Scafell Pike,** and **Helvellyn** are also all accessible, though for these you'll need a certain amount of walking experience and a great deal of energy.

For all walks, it's essential that you are dressed correctly and have the right equipment. Good walking shoes or boots are the first requirement, followed by several layers of warm clothing (even in summer, since the weather can be unpredictable), waterproof jacket and trousers, a good map, food, and water. Depending on the route you're tackling, you may also need a compass. Stores in Kendal and Keswick (*see* Shopping, *above*), and throughout the region, stock the right equipment, books, and maps; always check on weather conditions before setting out on anything more than just a local stroll, since mist, rain, or worse can roll in without warning.

For short, local walks it's always best in the first instance to consult the relevant tourist information centers: those at Ambleside, Cockermouth, Grasmere, Kendal, Keswick, or Windermere (*see* Tourist Information, *above*) are experienced in gauging visitor's requirements and can provide maps and guides. The other main source of information are the various **Lake District National Park information centers,** whose head office is at Brockhole, near Windermere (*see* Guided Tours, *above*); there are useful local offices at Bowness (tel. 05394/42895), Coniston (tel. 05394/41533), Grasmere (tel. 05394/35245), Hawkshead (tel. 05394/36525), Keswick (tel. 07687/72803), Pooley Bridge (tel. 07684/86530), Seatoller (tel. 07687/77294), Ullswater (tel. 07684/82414), and Waterhead (tel. 05394/32729). All these offices can help you plan your own itinerary. Since almost every hamlet, village, and town can provide scores of local walking opportunities, there really is no limit to the number of hikes you can undertake—the doyen of Lake District walking, Alfred Wainwright, spent 70 years tramping the hills and valleys.

If you're sufficiently experienced, and want to climb the higher and harder peaks, then you'll require the services of a specialist organization: **Mountain Adventure Guides** (Eel Crag, Melbecks, Braithwaite, west of Keswick, CA12 5TL, tel. 07687/78517) and **Summitreks** (14 Yewdale Rd., Coniston LA 21 8DU, tel. 05394/41212) coordinate climbing trips for individuals or groups on a daily or weekly basis, and accommodations are arranged when needed.

Water Sports   Water sports thrive on the lakes, especially Windermere. At **Windermere Lake Holidays Afloat** (Gilly's Landing, Glebe Rd., Windermere LA23 3HE, tel. 05394/43415) you can rent every kind of boat, from small sailboats to large cabin cruisers.

Derwentwater Marina (Portinscale, Keswick CA12 5RF, tel. 07687/72912) offers boat rental and instruction in canoeing, sailing, windsurfing, and rowing.

Coniston Boating Centre (tel. 05394/41366) rents out launches, canoes, or traditional wooden rowboats—and there's a picnic area near the center, too.

Spectator Sports

Horse Racing Britain's most famous horse race, the **Grand National** steeplechase, has been run at Liverpool's **Aintree Race Course** (Ormskirk Rd., tel. 051/523–2600) almost every year since 1839. The race is held every March/April, and even if you don't attend, you'll be able to see the race on every TV in the country.

Soccer The main spectator sport in the Northwest is soccer. Greater Manchester, Merseyside, and Lancashire have some of the most successful teams in Britain. Matches are played on Saturdays (and, increasingly, Sundays and Mondays). Admission prices vary, but the cheapest seats start at about £10–£15. The best matches to catch are the local "derby" games between each city's two major teams: Liverpool's teams are called **Liverpool** (which plays at Anfield) and **Everton** (Goodison Park); Manchester's are **Manchester United** (Old Trafford) and **Manchester City** (Maine Road). Local tourist offices have match schedules and directions to the grounds.

Wrestling and Fell Running Folk sports in the Lake District include Cumberland and Westmorland wrestling, a variety of traditional English wrestling in which the opponents must maintain a grip around each other's body. Fell (cross-country) running is also popular in these parts. Not surprisingly, local shepherds dominate the latter sport. These sports are often the highlights at local shows and meets like the Grasmere sports event in August. A calendar of events is available at tourist information centers.

Dining and Lodging

Dining The cities of Manchester and Liverpool, not surprisingly, have a huge number of restaurants, serving modern British, Continental, and various ethnic cuisines. Manchester has one of Britain's most vibrant Chinatowns, featuring excellent Cantonese cuisine, and locals set great store in the 20-odd Asian restaurants along Wilmslow Road, in the suburb of Rusholme, a few miles south of the city center. Here you can enjoy Bangladeshi, Pakistani, and Indian food in places ranging from simple cafés where no alcohol is served (though often BYOB) to smart designer restaurants serving rich curries and tandoor-baked breads.

Cumbria is noted for its good country food. Dishes center on the abundant local supply of lamb, beef, game, and fish, especially salmon and river and lake trout hooked from the district's network of freshwater streams and lakes. Cumberland sausage, a thick, meaty pork sausage that is a meal in itself, is another regional specialty. You may also enjoy the baked goodies here: bread, cake, pastries, gingerbread, and scones.

Apart from local traditional fare, Cumbria offers health-food and vegetarian restaurants, as well as some excellent Continental ones. Standards vary, so it's worth doing a little research. Pubs often give the best value at lunchtime, offering appetizing bar lunches at prices beginning at around £3.50.

Highly recommended restaurants are indicated by a star ★.

Category	Cost*
$$$$	over £40
$$$	£30–£40
$$	£15–£30
$	under £15

per person, including first course, main course, dessert, and VAT; excluding drinks

Lodging It's easy to locate reasonably priced, central accommodations in the cities of the Northwest, and facilities tend to be fairly standard. The larger hotels in Manchester and Liverpool, which rely on the business trade during the week, often offer reduced rates on weekends.

The Lake District has been attracting tourists for over 200 years and has built up a reputation for taking good care of them. You'll find everything from small country inns to grand lakeside hotels, most with a charm befitting their rich past. There are more modern hotels and motels as well, but these tend to lack the rural ambience most visitors expect from the Lake District. Medium-size, family-run hotels can offer the best value and plenty of comfort and hospitality. Don't overlook the bed-and-breakfasts (B&Bs), however: They provide the cheapest, simplest accommodations and come in every shape and size, from the house on Main Street renting out one room to farmhouses with an entire wing to spare. On average, you can expect to pay around £15–£20 per person at a B&B. Standards are high, and many places have rooms with TV.

Most country hotels gladly cater to keen hikers and climbers and can provide you with on-the-spot information and advice for these pursuits. Their lounges and bars are filled with photographs, route maps, and newspaper clippings recording the derring-do of Lake District climbers past and present. There's also a great cameraderie among walkers in the Lake District's network of youth hostels, which are in fact open to anyone with a membership card from their home country's hostel association. Some hostels are located on specific hiking routes, or in strategic walking areas, and though they can be fairly basic, keen walkers will find them an invaluable option. They are extremely inexpensive, but you must book well in advance in summer; local tourist information centers have all the relevant information.

Summer is the busiest season in the Northwest—and that means *very* busy indeed. Finding a room in Blackpool in July can be one of life's more frustrating experiences. At other times of the year, you can travel easily without advance reservations, choosing your accommodations once you're actually in the region.

Highly recommended lodgings are indicated by a star ★.

Category	Cost*
$$$$	over £150
$$$	£90–£150
$$	£55–£90
$	under £55

All prices are for two people sharing a double room, including service, breakfast, and VAT.

Askham **Queen's Head Inn.** The Queen's Head is a very friendly 17th-century
Lodging inn, just 5 miles south of Penrith. Big open fires, plenty of shining
copper and brass, pleasant old furniture, and simple, comfortable
bedrooms make this a good budget selection. *Near Penrith, CA10
2PF, tel. 0931/712225. 7 rooms without bath. Facilities: restaurant.
No credit cards. $*

Blackpool **Harry Ramsden's.** Fish-and-chips are the traditional British seaside
Dining food, and there's no better place to eat them than at the Blackpool
branch of Harry Ramsden's, a famous Yorkshire company. The
smart restaurant is competently run, and service is brisk and
friendly. Helpings of cod and chips are large, crispy, and the tastiest
in Britain; wine and beer are served, but the best accompaniments
are hot tea and bread and butter. *60–63 The Promenade, tel. 0253/
294386. Reservations not required, but expect a wait at lunch.
Dress: casual. MC, V. $*

Dining and **The Imperial.** Flushed with Victorian splendor, this Forte Grand ho-
Lodging tel sits on the North Promenade, overlooking the sea. It's the favor-
ite choice of Britain's political leaders, who regularly stay during
the annual party conferences; the comfortable No. 10 Bar (as in
Downing Street) is festooned with mementos and photographs.
Guest rooms are furnished in turn-of-the-century style, with long
drapes and period reproduction paintings. The celebrated **Palm
Court Restaurant** features local specialties, especially fish and shellfish, and has a good carvery, for roast meats. *North Promenade,
FY1 2HB, tel. 0253/23971, fax 0253/751784. 183 rooms with bath. Facilities: restaurant (reservations advised; jacket and tie preferred),
2 bars, heated pool, gym, solarium, sauna, steam room. AE, DC,
MC, V. $$$*

Braithwaite **Coledale Inn.** This early 19th-century inn (once a woolen mill) and
Lodging adjacent guest house in the quiet village of Braithwaite (about 3 mi
west of Keswick on A66) offers good food, real ale, and comfortable
rooms with great hillside views. Superb mountain hiking, guided
walks, and minitours can be arranged here, and if you make the inn
your base for longer than one night, discounts are offered. *CA12
5TN, tel. 07687/78272. 12 rooms with shower. Facilities: restaurant.
MC, V. $–$$*

Cartmel **Cavendish Arms.** The village's oldest inn is the place for filling,
Dining home-cooked meals, served either in the bar or dining room. Specialties include good steak; accompany it with the local real ale. *Under
the Arch, tel. 05395/36240. Reservations not required. Dress: casual. No credit cards. $*

Elterwater **The Britannia Inn.** You'll sleep peacefully at the Britannia, a friend-
Dining and ly, family-owned inn in the heart of some of the best of the Lake Dis-
Lodging trict's walking country. The inn itself has a fine, welcoming
★ atmosphere, with quaint little rooms and outdoor seating, quickly
taken up by resting ramblers. In summer, Morris dancing on the village green opposite keeps the drinkers amused. The hearty homemade English food is excellent—pies are always good—and the local
beer the best accompaniment, though wine is available, too. Guest
rooms, modern in style but comfortable, are a little larger than is
usual in countryside inns. All in all a splendid choice. *Elterwater, on
B5343, 4 mi west of Ambleside, tel. 05394/37210. 13 rooms, 7 with
bath. Facilities: restaurant (reservations advised; dress casual),
bar. MC, V. Hotel $–$$; Restaurant $*

Kendal **The Moon.** A bistro ambience prevails in this small, centrally located
Dining restaurant, with cream and burgundy decor. Its good reputation
★ has been won with quality homemade dishes on a menu that changes

at least monthly. There's always a strong selection of vegetarian dishes, and the cooking can be adventurous, using Mediterranean and Asian flourishes at times. The service is extremely friendly and there's a short, but good and reasonably priced wine list, too. *129 Highgate, tel. 0539/729254. Reservations advised. Dress: casual. MC, V. Open evenings only; closed Christmas, New Year's Day, and mid-Jan.–mid-Feb. $–$$*

Lodging **The Woolpack.** The town's best hotel is ideally placed, right on the main street. Formerly a coaching inn, the building dates back to the 17th century, its ground floor once Kendal's wool auction room, which explains the hotel's name. The public rooms—bar, restaurant, and carvery—retain a whiff of bygone days, with their oak beams and stone walls. Guest rooms are decorated in a modern style, but are no worse for that: pleasant and well-equipped, and attended to by courteous staff. *Stricklandgate, tel. 0539/723852, fax 0539/728608. 54 rooms with bath. Facilities: restaurant, carvery, 2 bars. AE, MC, V. $$*

Keswick **La Primavera.** The River Greta runs below this stylish restaurant,
Dining which is somewhat isolated at the north end of town. Here you have a choice of English or Italian dishes—the grilled steaks are particularly good—and a good wine list. The daily specials are always worth inquiring about. *Greta Bridge, High Hill, tel. 07687/74621. Reservations advised. Dress: casual. MC, V. Closed Mon. and Jan. $$*

★ **The Four in Hand.** This is a typical Cumbrian pub—once a stagecoach inn on the route between Keswick and Borrowdale—with a 19th-century paneled bar decorated with horse brasses and banknotes. The imaginative touches in its menu include hot asparagus rolled in ham and pâté with red-currant jelly; traditional dishes are steaks, meat pies, and Cumberland sausage. All orders are taken at the bar. *Lake Rd., tel. 07687/72069. Reservations not required. Dress: casual. No credit cards. $*

Lodging **Keswick Hotel.** Turrets and balconies are the most noticeable architectural characteristics of this Victorian hotel. Built to serve railroad travelers in the 19th century, it has all the grandeur and style of that age, although it has been modernized. The most recent renovations have been accomplished in 22 of the guest rooms, now decorated and equipped to the highest standard. It sits in 4½ acres of private gardens in the center of Keswick. There is a large conservatory where tea is served. The room rate includes dinner, as well as breakfast, though you can opt for a stay without dinner if you wish. *Station Rd., CA12 4NQ, tel. 07687/72020, fax 07687/71300. 66 rooms with bath. Facilities: restaurant, putting green, croquet lawn. AE, DC, MC, V. $$$*

Lyzzick Hall Hotel. Set in 2 acres on the lower slopes of Skiddaw (2 mi northwest of Keswick on A591), this converted Victorian country house boasts superb views across Derwentwater. It makes a relaxed base, set in large gardens; Two lounges with log fires keep things cozy in winter, while the food in the restaurant is also commendable. *Under Skiddaw, near Keswick, CA12 4PY, tel. 07687/72277, fax 07687/72278. 24 rooms with bath. Facilities: restaurant, bar, heated pool. AE, DC, MC, V. Closed Feb. $$*

Skiddaw Hotel. Recently renovated, this is a modern hotel at the edge of Market Square, with fine interior decor and good facilities. Guest rooms are colorfully decorated and comfortable. The hotel can arrange pony trekking and offers boot and wet-weather-clothing rental for walkers. *Market Sq., CA12 5BN, tel. 07687/72071, fax*

07687/74850. 40 rooms with bath. Facilities: restaurant, gym, sauna, solarium, free golf (weekdays), squash. AE, MC, V. $$

Highfield Hotel. Overlooking the lawns of Hope Park between Keswick and Derwentwater, this small, green slate hotel is comfortable and serves good, home-cooked food. Some of the rooms are a bit smaller than others, but they're all well-appointed and cheerfully decorated. Family run, it's just a few minutes' walk from lake or town and offers super views of the local valley surroundings. *The Heads, CA12 5ER, tel. 07687/72508. 19 rooms, 15 with bath. Facilities: restaurant, bar. No credit cards. Closed Nov.–Easter. $–$$*

Liverpool
Dining
★

Armadillo. This downtown restaurant—Liverpool's finest—lies on the ground floor of a converted redbrick warehouse, its lofty windows overlooking Matthew Street. These are unsophisticated surroundings, but the fine Mediterranean cooking more than compensates. Classic dishes appear alongside current trendy favorites; starters may include lentil salad or eggplant and mozzarella combinations, and there's always plenty for vegetarians to enjoy. Desserts are a highlight, and the wine list carries some strong French names. Lunches and early suppers (Tues.–Fri. 5–6:45 PM) offer the chance to choose from a less expensive menu of bistro favorites. Service is informal. *20–22 Matthew St., tel. 051/236–4123. Reservations advised. Dress: casual. MC, V. Closed Sun., Mon., and Christmas week. $$*

Est Est Est. This is the top choice in the Albert Dock complex, a lively spot for lunch. The restaurant makes good use of the old warehouse brickwork, though tables are a bit cramped. Still, the Italian menu is strong on appetizers—including a feast of antipasto—and includes excellent crisp pizzas. If you're still hungry, the dessert trolley trundles reassuringly round the restaurant. Service is brisk, the atmosphere bubbling, the coffee good. *Unit 6, Edward Pavilion, Albert Dock, tel. 051/708–6969. Reservations advised on weekends. Dress: casual. AE, MC, V. $*

Lodore
Dining and
Lodging
★

Stakis Lodore Swiss Hotel. Opened by a Swiss family, this famous hotel is now run by a Greek hotelier. Near the great waterfall at Lodore on Derwentwater, this large, comfortable, world-class country lodge, with its plethora of facilities, is about 3 miles south of Keswick on B5289 in the Borrowdale Valley. Built of Lakeland slate, it's a handsome building, set amid 40 acres of land. Inside, the en-suite rooms are very comfortable, with little extras like a trouser press and hair dryer as standard provisions. Service throughout is as slick as you would expect. The restaurant offers superb Anglo-Swiss cuisine in elegant surroundings. *Borrowdale, CA12 5UX, tel. 07687/77285, fax 07687/77343. 70 rooms with bath. Facilities: restaurant, bar, 24-hour room service, swimming pool, squash, tennis, solarium, sun terrace, gym. Restaurant: reservations advised; jacket and tie required. AE, DC, MC, V. Closed Nov.–Feb. $$$*

Loweswater
Dining and
Lodging
★

Kirkstile Inn. This 16th-century inn stands just 7 miles south of Cockermouth in lovely, quiet surroundings, overlooking the gushing river that runs between tiny Loweswater and larger Crummock Water. Low, white, and slate-roofed, this lodging has been welcoming travelers for almost 400 years. There's a cozy pub downstairs, with a roaring fire in winter, around which sit weary hikers, and 10 rooms upstairs, arranged along a long, oak-beamed corridor. The rooms are all simple, with rather garish floral carpets, but they're cool in summer, and well-heated in winter, while the beds are supremely comfortable—just the thing after a day's walking. There's perfectly reasonable food available in the bar, but much more adventurous and locally renowned five-course dinners are served in the small, traditionally furnished, restaurant—you must make it clear when you book that you want dinner, since there's very limited room. The inn is quite tricky to find, and you'd do best to phone for directions before setting off. *Loweswater, Cockermouth, CA13 ORU, tel. 0900/85219. 10 rooms with bath. Facilities: restaurant, bar, packed lunches available. Restaurant ($$): reservations essential; dress: casual. MC, V. $$*

Manchester
Dining
★

Market Restaurant. This is an unpretentious, dinner-only spot that is serious about its cooking. It is the place to taste some very original British recipes, culled from famous cooks all over the island, as well as other interesting in-house creations. Its menu changes monthly with an emphasis on vegetarian dishes; desserts are always inventive. The proprietor, a beer enthusiast, maintains an excellent selection of international bottled beers, as well as an interesting wine list. *104 High St., tel. 061/834-3743. Reservations advised. Dress: casual. Open Wed.–Sat., evenings only; closed 1 week at Christmas, at Easter, and throughout Aug. AE, DC, MC, V. $$*

Yang Sing. One of Manchester's good Chinese restaurants, it's popular with Chinese families, always a good sign, but *so* popular that you must reserve ahead. The cooking is Cantonese, and there's a huge range to choose from. The *dim sum* is always a good bet, and don't forget to ask about the daily specials—they're often only listed in Chinese on the menu. There is also a slightly cheaper offshoot, **Little Yang Sing** (17 George St., tel. 061/228-7722). This was Manchester's original Yang Sing restaurant; it has a rather cramped basement setting but still serves fine Cantonese food. *34 Princess St., tel. 061/236-2200. Reservations required. Dress: casual. AE, MC, V. $$*

Indian Cottage. While most of Rusholme's many Asian eateries pack diners in for quick (though admittedly excellent) meals, this more upscale, first-floor restaurant allows you plenty of time to explore a menu strong on tandoor-baked dishes and breads. A central rock pool and lavish decoration add some spice, but it's the food, among the best in town, that makes the difference. The restaurant is a couple of miles south of the city center; take a taxi. *501 Claremont Rd., tel. 061/224-0446. Reservations advised. Dress: casual. MC, V. $–$$*

Café Istanbul. This is an authentic Turkish place, where you can find Turkish coffee, Turkish pastries, even Turkish wine. It is always popular and has recently expanded its premises. The *meze* are inexpensive and there's a special *meze* menu for those who like to fill up on the multitude of little dishes—*hummus*, stuffed grape leaves, cheese-filled pastries, *taramasalata*, and other treats. *79 Bridge St., tel. 061/833-9942. Reservations advised. Dress: casual. MC, V. Closed Sun. $*

Dining and
Lodging
★

Victoria & Albert Hotel. Manchester's most exciting new hotel development in years, the Victoria & Albert recently won *Executive Travel Magazine*'s Best New Hotel in the World award. Formerly a warehouse, built in 1843, and situated just out of the city center opposite the Granada Studios Tour, the hotel is an object lesson in how to handle renovation without destroying the historic kernel of a building. Exposed brickwork and cast-iron pillars throughout make for highly individualized accommodations—no two rooms are the same. All guest rooms are named after Granada TV programs; four suites have thematic decor (the Sherlock Holmes suite recreates a slice of Victorian London); and there's a separate "Ladies Wing" designed for solo women travelers, with panic alarms, closed circuit TV, and individual toiletries in the very comfortable bathrooms. Elsewhere, facilities are top-class. The bar has urban river views from its conservatory, while the highly rated **Sherlock Holmes Restaurant** features special gourmet dinners as well as an à la carte menu of classic English food with a Continental (and occasional Asian) twist. *Water St., tel. 061/832–1188, fax 061/834–2484. 132 rooms with bath. Facilities: restaurant, bar, coffee shop, gym, sauna, business center, 24-hr. room service. Restaurant: reservations advised; jacket and tie preferred. AE, DC, MC, V. $$$*

Lodging **Holiday Inn Crowne Plaza Midland.** The name is a real mouthful these days since Holiday Inn took over the management, but the Midland remains the city's finest downtown hotel. The Edwardian splendor of the public rooms—including a truly fine lobby and bar—still evokes the turn-of-the-century days when the Midland was Manchester's railroad hotel. Guest rooms are comfortable, while never quite living up to the standards of the rest of the hotel, but the other facilities are as up-to-the-minute as you'd expect: bar and grill, restaurant, health club, swimming pool, and squash court. And to cap it all, the city's theaters, restaurants, and pubs are all within easy walking distance. *Peter St., tel. 061/236–3333, fax 061/228–2241. 303 rooms with bath. Facilities: restaurant, bar and grill, swimming pool, sauna, squash court, gym. AE, DC, MC, V. $$$*

Penrith **Passepartout.** Continental, Italian, and unusually good English cui-
Dining sines are offered here, with the emphasis on local specialties like wild boar, venison, Dumfries (Scottish) salmon, and lobster. There is also an international wine list. *51 Castlegate, tel. 0768/65852. Reservations advised. Dress: casual. MC, V. Open Tues.–Sat. evenings only. $$*

Pooley Bridge **Sharrow Bay.** Set between the lush green fields near Pooley Bridge
Dining and and the increasingly rugged crags around Howtown, the hotel com-
Lodging mands a view of exceptional and varied beauty. Its luxurious ap-
★ pointments complement its stunning surroundings; the bedrooms are extremely comfortable, though the rooms in the two annexes are somewhat more simple, especially those in Bank House, about 1½ miles away. The cuisine has been renowned for many years, and it's almost impossible to find fault, though some think both food and rooms could be a little more restrained. That said, you'll find little to complain about in the food itself: classic British and Continental dishes cooked with panache. Those who can't fit in the Sharrow Bay as an overnight stop should certainly stop by for the splendid afternoon tea, a gargantuan affair that will leave you feeling weak at the knees. *Howtown Rd., Pooley Bridge, Ullswater CA10 2LZ, tel. 07684/86301, fax 07684/86349. 28 rooms, 24 with bath. Room charges include dinner. Facilities: restaurant. Restaurant: reservations required; jacket and tie required. AE, DC, MC, V. Closed Dec.–Feb. $$$$*

Portinscale **Derwentwater Hotel.** Named after the lake it is set on, this handsome
Dining and hotel west of Keswick has 16 acres of gardens and specializes in ac-
Lodging tivity vacations for those interested in windsurfing, fishing, hiking, mountaineering, and golf. Equipment loans and instruction are offered at the hotel. It's worth paying extra for the deluxe rooms here, which are more spacious and have unrivaled views of the lake. Take your aperitif in the lakeside gardens in good weather—or in the splendid conservatory—and look forward to dinner in the recently refurbished restaurant. Roast meats are a specialty, and other dishes include local fish. Elsewhere, the interior is enlivened by log fires in the winter. *Portinscale, off A66, CA12 5RE, tel. 07687/72538, fax 07687/71002. 52 rooms with bath. Facilities: restaurant, bar, coffee shop, 9-hole putting green, tennis, lawn bowling. AE, DC, MC, V. $$*

Seatoller
Dining
★

Yew Tree Restaurant. One of the best of the Lakes' hidden restaurants, the Yew Tree, at the foot of Honister Pass, has been converted from two 17th-century cottages. The atmosphere here is intimate and gracious, and the inventive menu is based largely on local produce. Specialties include pan-fried trout and, as an appetizer, marinated and smoked fish. Other English country dishes, including venison, hare, eel, and salmon, are seasonally available. The low-beamed ceiling, long open fireplace, and excellent bar add to the pleasure of eating here, and you'll not be hurried—service is friendly and relaxed. *Seatoller, Borrowdale, tel. 07687/77634. Reservations advised. Dress: casual. MC, V. Closed Mon., Fri. lunch, and Jan.–mid-Feb. $$*

Ulverston
Dining and
Lodging

Bay Horse Inn. This restaurant, 1¼ miles east of Ulverston, is a pub and bistro combined, with the bistro situated in a veranda over the water. The cooking here is thoroughly imaginative and unexpected, due to the influence of coproprietor John Tovey, who is also in charge of Miller Howe (*see below*). There may be cheese and fennel soup, pork cutlet with sage and apple purée, *moules marinière,* or sweetbreads with tongue and mushrooms in marsala listed on one of the ever-changing menus. There's a great view over the Morecambe estuary to enjoy while you eat and similar views from the half dozen comfortable rooms, added recently, which may well tempt you to stay overnight. *Canal Foot, LA12 9EL, tel. 0229/583972, fax 0229/ 580502. 6 rooms with bath. Room charges include dinner. Facilities: restaurant, pub. Restaurant: reservations required; jacket and tie preferred. MC, V. Closed Sun., Mon. lunch, and Jan.–Feb. $$$*

Windermere
Dining
★

Porthole Eating House. Located in an intimate 18th-century house in the center of Bowness, the small restaurant has a French and Italian menu featuring homemade pasta and excellent meat and fish dishes, including stuffed duck, fresh salmon, and (when available) Windermere char. Other nice touches include opera recordings played as you eat, good homemade bread and petits fours served with coffee. In winter, a large open fire adds to the ambience, and the friendly staff is knowledgeable about the massive wine list, which includes some excellent German wines and a whole range of French, Italian, and New World options. *3 Ash St., Bowness-on-Windermere, tel. 05394/42793. Reservations advised. Dress: casual. AE, DC, MC, V. Open evenings only. Closed Tues. and mid-Dec.–late Feb. $$*

Roger's. This is a centrally located restaurant, small and darkly decorated, but with a menu that contains the best French food in the region. There may be suckling pig with apricot sauce or fillet of salmon with sorrel sauce. There's a good selection of cheeses, some very rich desserts, and a short but interesting wine list that covers the New World as well as France. *4 High St., tel. 05394/44954. Reservations required. Dress: casual. AE, DC, MC, V. Open Mon.–Sat. evenings only. $$*

Dining and
Lodging
★

Miller Howe. This small, white Edwardian hotel with an international reputation for comfort and cuisine, is beautifully situated, with views across Windermere to the Langdale Pikes. Every attention has been given to the interior decor, which includes fine antiques and paintings. The lounge has especially comfy chairs and a conservatory, where afternoon tea is served, overlooks the lake. The bedrooms, too, have exceptional individual style, and fresh and dried flowers are everywhere. The outstanding restaurant serves an imaginative set menu that has been masterminded by John Tovey, renowned for his experimental British cuisine (and for dishes that often utilize alcohol or cream to what might seem, to a curmudgeon, excess). This award-winning restaurant also has an excellent wine list, while testimonials to the success of the establishment are posted in impressive numbers around the entrance. *Rayrigg Rd., Bowness-on-Windermere LA23 1EY, tel. 05394/42536, fax 05394/ 45664. 13 rooms with bath. Room rate includes dinner. Facilities: restaurant. Restaurant: reservations required; jacket and tie required. AE, DC, MC, V. Closed Dec.–mid-Mar. $$$$*

Gilpin Lodge. Gilpin Lodge is a peaceful spot, hidden in 20 acres of grounds, 2½ miles out of town on the B5284 Kendal road. It's an away-from-the-crowds place, its public rooms furnished with comfortable sofas, warmed by log fires, brightened by flowers, and scattered with books and magazines. Guest rooms are in the same welcoming style, with four-poster beds and smart bathrooms. The food is especially good, with a chef with French experience offering a five-course, fixed-price menu of changing dishes that always delights. Sunday lunch is £12.75, dinner £24. *Crook Rd., LA23 3NE, tel. 05394/88818, fax 05394/88058. 9 rooms with bath. Facilities: restaurant (reservations advised; jacket and tie required). AE, DC, MC, V. Open dinner and Sun. lunch. $$$*

Lodging **The Langdale Chase.** This hotel's 5 acres of landscaped gardens overlook Windermere, and it has its own dock. Built in the 19th century and tastefully refurbished, it has an atmosphere of grandeur evoked by the baronial entrance hall and oak-paneled lounge. The hotel is just off A591, halfway between Windermere and Ambleside, and makes an excellent, relaxed base for local touring. *LA23 1LW, tel. 05394/32201, fax 05394/32604. 35 rooms, some in separate lodges, 33 with bath or shower. Facilities: restaurant, lake swimming, boating, tennis, miniature golf. AE, DC, MC, V. $$$*

Hideaway Hotel. Ivy-covered Lakeland-stone walls and a large garden surround this hotel, a tranquil setting for its comfortable rooms and good service. Much of the interior has been refurbished recently: There are fireplaces in the bar and lounge, and the restaurant's Swiss-trained chef prepares English and Continental dishes. *Phoenix Way, LA23 1DB, tel. 05394/43070. 15 rooms with bath. Facilities: restaurant, bar, lounge, garden. No credit cards. $$*

The Mortal Man. This converted 17th-century Lakeland inn is in a valley about 3 miles north of Windermere, well away from the bustle of the town; there are magnificent views all around. It wouldn't be a Lakeland inn without its log fire, which crackles away in winter. Guest rooms are fairly simple, but pleasantly decorated, and there's a relaxing atmosphere to the place that's hard to beat, helped along by the welcoming staff. Both lunch and dinner are served. *Troutbeck LA23 1PL, tel. 05394/33193, fax 05394/31261. 12 rooms with bath. Facilities: restaurant, bar. No credit cards. Closed mid-Nov.–mid-Feb. $$*

Oakbank Hotel. Recently renovated and in the center of Bowness, the very friendly hillside Oakbank provides smart, well-equipped rooms, some with fine views over the lake, and all tastefully decorated in pale colors. The breakfast room overlooks town and lake; and you're very near Bowness's restaurants. *Helm Rd., Bowness-on-Windermere, tel. 05394/43386. 11 rooms with bath. MC, V. $–$$*

The Arts

Festivals The Lake District hosts some of Britain's most unusual country festivals, featuring traditional music, sports, and entertainment. Major festivals include **Cockermouth** and **Keswick carnivals** (June), **Ambleside Rushbearing and Sports** (July), and **Grasmere Rush-**

bearing and Sports and **Kendal Folk Festival** (August). Full details can be obtained from local tourist offices.

Music Manchester's Hallé Orchestra currently performs at the **Free Trade Hall** (Peter St.), though it will eventually have its own auditorium; for now, the box office is in Albert Square (tel. 061/834–1712). For rock, reggae, jazz, R&B, and many other kinds of music, the best venue is **Band on the Wall** (25 Swan St., tel. 061/832–6625), which has live music six nights a week. Other concerts are held at the university and at the **Royal Northern College of Music** (124 Oxford Rd., tel. 061/273–4504). For musical events at **G-Mex,** call the box office at 061/832–9000.

The **Keswick Jazz Festival** (tel. 0900/602122 or 07687/75383) is held each May; it consists of four days of music and events. In November, there's the annual **Kendal Jazz and Blues Festival,** based at the Brewery Arts Centre (*see* Theater and Performing Arts, *below*), which can provide program details.

Theater and Manchester has an enviable reputation in the arts, especially in the
Performing performing arts. There are three main theaters in town: the **Opera**
Arts **House** (Quay St., tel. 061/831–7766), which hosts touring companies, both British and international, as well as a wide spectrum of entertainment; the **Library Theatre** (tel. 061/236–7110), which stages mostly classic and serious drama; and the **Royal Exchange Theatre** (St. Ann's Sq., tel. 061/833–9333), an extremely inventive acting space with a sky-high reputation for daring productions. It is a very modern, airy, tubular steel-and-glass structure, set down in the middle of the vast echoing spaces of this Victorian building, like a space ship delicately parked in a great cathedral. For more offbeat productions, **The Green Room** (54–56 Whitworth St. W, tel. 061/236–1677) puts on a full program of theater, poetry, dance, and performance art.

The **Brewery Arts Centre** in Kendal is a converted brewery that now holds an **art gallery,** a **theater,** a **theater workshop,** and a **cinema.** One of the most active centers of creative performance in the southern part of the Lake District, it offers special events, festivals, and art exhibitions throughout the year. It also has an excellent coffee bar, a real-ale bar, and a health-food café open for lunch. *Highgate, tel. 0539/725133. Open Mon.–Sat. 9 AM–11 PM. Free parking.*

The Lake District has a history of little theaters that come and go, providing excellent entertainment during the summer season. **The-atre-in-the-Forest** in Grizedale offers daytime exhibitions and evening plays, folk concerts, special events, and guest appearances. *Near Hawkshead, tel. 0229/860291. Open Tues.–Sat. 10–5.*

The **Old Laundry** *(Crag Brow, Bowness-on-Windermere, tel. 05394/88444)* provides an intriguing mixture of theater, exhibitions, and events throughout the year.

14 The Peaks and Yorkshire Moors

Buxton, Bradford, Haworth, York, Scarborough, and Leeds

If you imagine England as a small, cozy country of cottages and gently flowing streams, the Peak District of Derbyshire (pronounced "Darbyshire") and the Yorkshire Moors might come as a bit of a surprise. For this is a wilder, grander part of England, a region of open spaces, wide horizons, and hills that seem to rear violently out of the plain. On a stormy day on the Moors, it's not hard to imagine Emily Brontë's Heathcliff from *Wuthering Heights* galloping on horseback over their cloud-swept ridges.

The Pennines, a line of hills that begins in the Peak District and runs as far north as Scotland, is sometimes called the "backbone of England," and it's a fitting description. This is a landscape of rocky outcrops and vaulting meadowland, where you'll see nothing for miles but sheep, dry-stone (unmortared) walls, and farms, interrupted only occasionally by villages made of the local dark gray stone.

To the east, the bleak areas of moorland that characterize Yorkshire are linked by lush, green valleys. Here, the high rainfall produces luxuriant vegetation, swift rivers, sparkling streams, and waterfalls that contrast with the dark, heather-covered Moors. Its villages are among the most utterly peaceful in England. Three of Britain's 10 national parks are in this region: the Peak District itself; the Yorkshire dales; and across the fertile Vale of York, the great, flat hills and spectacular coastline of the North York moors.

In the center of the fertile plain that separates the Pennines from the Moors lies York, dominated by the towers of its great minster. Once England's second most important city, this ancient town has survived the ravages of time, war, and industrialization; its medieval walled city is one of the best-preserved in Europe (and an eager-beaver tourist office makes the most of it).

Buxton, Haworth, and Scarborough on the east coast are three very different, rather provincial, towns, yet each provides a peaceful place to stay or use as a base for forays into the deeper countryside.

Essential Information

Important Addresses and Numbers

Tourist Information
The Yorkshire and Humberside Tourist Board, 312 Tadcaster Rd., York, North Yorkshire YO2 2HF, tel. 0904/707961. Open Mon.–Thurs. 9–5:30, Fri. 9–5.
East Midlands Tourist Board, Exchequergate, Lincoln LN2 1PZ, tel. 0522/531521. Open weekdays 9–5:30.

Tourist information centers, normally open Mon.–Sat. 9:30–5:30, but varying according to season, include the following:

Bakewell: Old Market Hall, Bridge St., Derbyshire DE4 1DS, tel. 0629/813227.
Bradford: National Museum of Photography, Film and TV, Prince's View, West Yorkshire BD5 0TR, tel. 0274/753678.
Buxton: The Crescent, Derbyshire SK17 6BQ, tel. 0298/25106.
Harrogate: Royal Baths Assembly Rooms, Crescent Rd., North Yorkshire HG1 2RR, tel. 0423/525666.
Haworth: 2–4 West La., West Yorkshire BD22 8EF, tel. 0535/6432329.
Leeds: The Basement, 19 Wellington St., West Yorkshire LS1 4DG, tel. 0532/478301.
Richmond: Friary Gardens, Queen's Rd., North Yorkshire DL10 4AJ, tel. 0748/850252.

Scarborough: St. Nicholas Cliff, North Yorkshire YO11 2EP, tel. 0723/373333.
Whitby: New Quay Rd., North Yorkshire YO21 1YN, tel. 0947/602674.
York: De Grey Rooms, Lendel Bridge, Exhibition Sq., North Yorkshire YO1 2HB, tel. 0904/621756; York Railway Station, Outer Concourse, North Yorkshire YO2 2AY, tel. 0904/643700, and Rougier St., tel. 0904/620557.

Travel Agencies **Thomas Cook:** Ivebridge House, 67 Market St., Bradford, tel. 0274/732411; 51 Boar La., Leeds, tel. 0532/432922; 47 Westborough, Scarborough, tel. 0723/364444; and 4 Nessgate, York, tel. 0904/653626.

Car-Rental Agencies **Bradford: Avis,** Bowling Bridge Service Station, Wakefield Rd., tel. 0274/370727; **Europcar,** 172 Thornton Rd., tel. 0274/733048; **Eurodollar-Rent-a-Car,** Nelson St., tel. 0274/722155. **York: Budget Rent-a-Car,** Station House, Foss Island Goods Yard, Foss Islands Rd., tel. 0904/644919 and **Hertz,** York Rail Station, Station Rd., tel. 0904/612586.

Arriving and Departing

By Car M1, the principal route north from London, gets you to the region in about two hours, with longer travel times up into north Yorkshire. For the Peak District, leave M1 at exit 29, then head via A617/A619/A6 to Buxton.

For York (193 mi) and the Scarborough areas, stay on M1 to Leeds (189 mi), then take A64. For the Yorkshire dales, take M1 to Leeds, then A660 to A65 north and west to Skipton.

By Train **British Rail** serves the region from London's King's Cross (tel. 071/278–2477) and London's Euston (tel. 071/387–7070) stations. Average travel times from King's Cross: 2½ hours to Leeds and two hours to York.

By Bus **National Express** (tel. 071/730–0202) serves the region from London's Victoria Coach Station. Average travel times include 4½ hours to York and 6½ hours to Scarborough. To reach Buxton, change to the **Trans-Peak** bus service at Derby.

Getting Around

By Car The trans-Pennine route, M62, between Liverpool and Hull, crosses the region. (From Buxton, the A515 south, a former Roman road, is a good route through the dales.)

Some of the steep, narrow roads in the countryside off the main routes are difficult drives and can be particularly perilous in winter, but the landscape is simply beautiful.

By Train There are local services from Leeds to Skipton, from York to Knaresborough and Harrogate, and to Scarborough (which has connections on to the seaside towns of Filey and Bridlington), and from Manchester to Buxton. To reach Buxton from London take the Manchester train and switch at Stockport. England's most scenic railway, the **Settle–Carlisle** line, can be reached from Leeds, where daily trains travel via Shipley, Keighley, and Skipton to the start of the line at Settle. For train times, call Leeds station (*see below*).

Two **Regional Rover** tickets for seven days' unlimited travel are available: **North East** and **Coast and Peaks.**

For local travel information, call the following stations: Bradford and Leeds (tel. 0532/448133); Scarborough (tel. 0723/373486); York (tel. 0904/642155).

By Bus There are local buses from Leeds and Bradford (tel. 0274/732237) into the more remote parts of the Yorkshire dales. In York, the transportation center for reaching the moors, the main local bus operator is **Rider York** (tel. 0904/624161); for East Yorkshire call 0482/27146. Many local districts have Rover tickets; local tourist offices have more details.

Guided Tours

Guide Friday (tel. 0904/640896) operates frequent city tours of York, including visits to the York Minster, the Castle Museum, the Shambles, and the Jorvik Viking Centre. The tour lasts about an hour, but you can leave and rejoin the bus at will. Tickets cost £5.50 adults, £1.50 children, £3.50 senior citizens.

The Yorkshire Guild of Guide Lecturers (tel. 0904/641952) can arrange fully qualified Blue Badge guides for customized tours according to your interests.

The York Association of Voluntary Guides (tel. 0904/640780, Mon.–Fri. 9:30 AM–11:30 AM) runs short free walking tours daily around the city of York, leaving from Exhibition Square. Tours leave daily at 10:15 AM, with extra tours from April to October at 2:15 PM and from June to August at 7 PM.

Yorktour (tel. 0904/641737) offers open-top bus, riverboat, and walking tours of the city of York and area attractions.

Exploring the Peaks and Yorkshire Moors

Our exploration of the Peak District and Yorkshire is broken into four distinct areas. The first tour starts in Buxton, a gracious spa town, and then swings through the Peak District, calling at Bakewell, Matlock, the stately home of Chatsworth House, the Peak Cavern, and, finally, Edale.

Tour 2 explores the Yorkshire dales: Wharfedale; the Yorkshire Dales National Park; Bradford, Haworth, the home of the Brontës; Bolton Abbey, the ruins of a great monastery; Wensleydale and Swaledale, stomping grounds of James Herriot, the celebrated vet; and, finally, the lovely little town of Richmond.

Tour 3 starts in the city of York, whose medieval attractions alone merit a visit. From York we go to Marston Moor, site of a fierce battle; to Leeds; to Harrogate, another of the area's fine spa towns; the magnificent Fountains Abbey; and, finally, Newby Hall.

The last tour explores the coast around Scarborough, then strikes inland to the North Moors National Park, and visits Rievaulx Abbey and splendidly elegant Castle Howard.

Highlights for First-time Visitors

Bolton Abbey: Tour 2
Brontë Parsonage Museum: Tour 2
Castle Howard: Tour 4

Chatsworth House: Tour 1
Fountains Abbey: Tour 3
North Moors National Park: Tour 4
Rievaulx Abbey: Tour 4
York: Tour 3

Tour 1: Buxton and the Peak District

Numbers in the margin correspond to points of interest on the Buxton and Peak District map.

❶ If you approach **Buxton** from the north, south, or west, you'll traverse wild, mountainous roads over the last great contortions of the Pennine Hills before they level out into the gentler country of the English Midlands. From the east, however, it's a gradual ascent through a series of limestone valleys. Buxton's sheltered position in a great natural bowl of hills gives it a surprisingly mild climate, considering its altitude: at over 1,000 feet, it's the second-highest town in England.

The Romans arrived in AD 79 and named Buxton *Aquae Arnemetiae*—loosely translated as "The Waters of the Goddess of the Grove"—suggesting they considered this Derbyshire hill town to be special. The mineral springs, which emerge from 3,500 to 5,000 feet below ground at a constant 82°F, were believed to cure a variety of ailments, and in the 18th century established the town as a popular spa, a minor rival to Bath. You can still drink water from the ancient St. Anne's Well (across from The Crescent), and it's also bottled and sold throughout Britain; it's excellent with a good malt whiskey.

Buxton's spa days have left a legacy of 18th- and 19th-century buildings, parks, and open spaces that now give the town an air of faded grandeur. A good place to start exploring is **The Crescent** on the northwest side of The Slopes park (the town hall is on the opposite side); almost all out-of-town roads lead toward this central green. The three former hotels that comprise the Georgian-era Crescent, with its arches, Doric colonnades, and 378 windows, were built in 1780 by John Carr for the fifth duke of Devonshire (of nearby Chatsworth House). The splendid ceiling of the former assembly room now looks down on the town's public library, and the thermal baths at the end of The Crescent house look out on a shopping center.

The Devonshire Royal Hospital, behind The Crescent, also by Carr, was originally a stable with room for 110 of the hotel guests' horses; it was converted into a hospital in 1859. The circular area for exercising horses was covered with a massive 156-foot-wide slate-colored dome and incorporated into the hospital.

The Buxton Museum, on the eastern side of The Slopes, has a collection of Blue John stone, a semiprecious mineral found only in the Peak District, while in The Crescent, **The Buxton Micrarium** features microscopic displays of insects, plants, and other specimens. *Museum: Terrace Rd., tel. 0298/24658. Admission: £1 adults, 50p children and senior citizens. Open Tues.–Fri. 9:30–5:30; Sat. 9:30–5. Micrarium, The Crescent, tel. 0298/78662. Admission: £2.50 adults, £1.50 children, £2 senior citizens. Open late Mar.–late Oct., daily 10–5.*

Just adjacent to The Crescent and The Slopes on the west, the **Octagon**—part of the Pavilion—with its ornate iron-and-glass roof, was originally a concert hall and ballroom. Erected in the 1870s, it is still

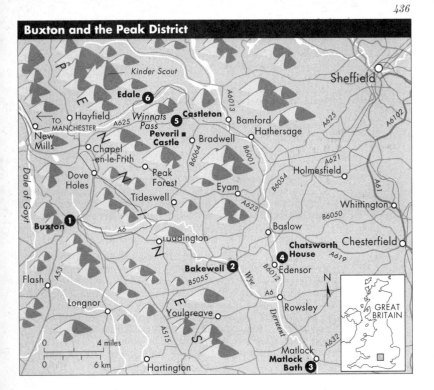

Buxton and the Peak District

a lively place, with a conservatory, several bars, a restaurant, and a cafeteria, set in 25 acres of well-kept Pavilion gardens. Bordering the gardens on the north, the **Parish Church of St. John the Baptist** on St. John's Road is in a handsome, Regency-Tuscan-style building dating from 1811, with some extremely fine mosaic and stained glass. A good deal more architecturally exuberant is the **Opera House** built in 1903, a massive marble structure bedecked with carved cupids.

If you follow the Broad Walk through the Pavilion gardens and continue southwest along Temple Road for about half an hour, you'll come to **Poole's Cavern,** a large limestone cave far beneath the 100 wooded acres of Buxton County Park. Named after a legendary 15th-century robber, the cave was inhabited in prehistoric times and contains, in addition to the standard stalactites and stalagmites, the source of the River Wye, which flows through Buxton. Poole's Cavern was also known to the Romans, who built baths nearby; a display of Roman archaeology, as well as a nature trail, and visitors center are outside. *Green La., tel. 0298/26978. Admission (including tour): £2.50 adults, £1.25 children, £2.20 senior citizens. County Park and visitors center free. Open Easter–Nov., daily 10–5; closed Wed. in Apr., May, and Oct.*

Buxton is a convenient base for exploring the 540 square miles of the Peak District, Britain's oldest national park, internationally recognized for its conservation activities. "Peak" is perhaps misleading here; although this is a hilly area, it contains only long, flat-topped rises that don't reach much higher than 2,000 feet. Yet the views are enchanting, and the inclines can be fairly steep.

❷ Make the quiet market town of **Bakewell,** 12 miles southeast of Buxton on A6, your first stop. On the way, you'll pass through the spectacular valleys of Ashwood Dale, Wyedale, and Monsal Dale. Bakewell, set on the winding River Wye, is appealing with its narrow streets and houses built out of the local gray-brown stone; a medieval bridge crosses the river in five graceful arches. Market day (Monday), attended by local farmers, is an event not to be missed, and an interesting agricultural show is held in the first week of August. Bakewell is also the source of the renowned Bakewell Tart, said to have been created by accident when, sometime last century, a cook at the town's Rutland Arms Hotel spilled a rich cake mixture over some jam tarts.

As in other parts of the Peak District, the inhabitants of Bakewell still practice the early-summer custom of "well-dressing," during which certain wells or springs are elaborately decorated or "dressed" with flowers. Although the floral designs usually incorporate biblical themes, they are just a Christian veneer over an ancient pagan celebration of the water's life-giving powers. In Bakewell, the lively ceremony is the focus of several days of festivities in June.

❸ **Matlock** and its neighbor **Matlock Bath,** both about 10 miles southeast of Bakewell on A6, are former spa towns compressed into a narrow gorge on the River Derwent. The **Matlock River Illuminations,** a flotilla of beautifully lit boats shimmering after dark along the still waters of the river, take place on weekends from mid-August through mid-October. From just west of Matlock Bath, one of the British Isles' rare cable cars takes visitors to the **Heights of Abraham,** a cave with a visitor center on the crags above.

Back on A6, head north for 5 miles and turn off at Rowsley onto B6012, which will take you another 4 miles through glorious park-
❹ land to **Chatsworth House,** ancestral home of the dukes of Devonshire and one of England's greatest country houses. As you approach, the great expanse of parkland, grazed by deer and sheep, opens before you to set off the Palladian-style elegance of "the Palace of the Peak." Built by various dukes over several generations starting in 1686, Chatsworth was conceived on a grand, even monumental, scale. It is surrounded by woods, elaborate colorful gardens, greenhouses, rock gardens, cascading water, and terraces—all designed by two great landscape artists, Capability Brown and, later, Joseph Paxton, an engineer as well as a brilliant gardener. He was responsible for most of the eye-catching waterworks. There's also a farmyard area and an adventure playground that are both perennially popular with children. Plan on at least half a day to explore the grounds properly, and avoid going on Sunday, when the place is very crowded.

Inside, the 175 rooms are filled with treasures: intricate carvings, Van Dyck portraits, Rembrandt's *Portrait of an Oriental*, sculptures, tapestries, superb furniture and china. The magnificent condition of much of the furnishings and decorations is largely because the dowager duchess supervises an ongoing program of in-house repair and restoration. *Bakewell, tel. 0246/582204. Admission: house and gardens: £5.50 adults, £2.75 children, £4.75 senior citizens, £14 family ticket; gardens only: £3 adults, £1.50 children, £2.50 senior citizens; £8 family ticket; farmyard area £5 for adults, children, and senior citizens. Open late Mar.–early Nov., daily, house 11–4:30; garden 11–5.*

❺ **Castleton** (take A623, then B6049 north from Chatsworth), a town in the Hope Valley, which also tends to be crowded in the peak season, is somewhat commercialized, but is worth a visit to see the ruins of **Peveril Castle,** built in the 12th century on a crag south of town. There are superb views of the Peak District from here. *Tel. 0433/20613. Admission: £1.10 adults, 55p children, 85p senior citizens. Open Apr.–Oct., daily 10–6; Nov.–Mar., Tues.–Sun. 10–4.*

Also interesting is the massive **Peak Cavern,** under the castle, where rope has been made on a great ropewalk for over 400 years: A prehistoric village has been excavated here as well. *Tel. 0433/620285. Admission: £2.50 adults, £1.50 children and senior citizens. Open Apr.–Oct., daily 10–5; Nov.–Mar., Tues.–Sun. 10–5.*

Castleton has a number of other caves and mines open to the public, including some former lead mines and Blue John mines. (Blue John is amethystine spar; the unusual name is a local corruption of the French *bleu-jaune.*) Try to visit the **Speedwell Cavern** at the bottom of Winnats Pass, 2 miles west of Castleton, the only mine in England you can tour by boat, traveling through great illuminated caverns 840 feet below ground to reach the "Bottomless Pit." There is also an exhibition and a store selling Blue John jewelry. *Tel. 0433/620512. Admission: £4.50 adults, £2.75 children under 14, £3.50 senior citizens. Open daily 9:30–5:30 (Nov.–Mar. to 4:30); closed Christmas.*

6 If you're interested in hiking, take the signposted road to **Edale,** 5 miles northwest of Hope. It's a sleepy village in the shadow of Mam Tor and Lose Hill, and the moorlands of Kinder Scout (2,088 feet), set among some of the most breathtaking scenery in Derbyshire. This extremely popular walking center is the starting point of the 250-mile Pennine Way and several much shorter routes into the Edale valley. The Edale information center has maps, guides, and information on walks in the area. *Tel. 0433/670207. Open Easter–Oct., daily 9–5:30; Nov.–Mar., daily 9–5.*

Tour 2: Brontë Country and the Yorkshire Dales

Numbers in the margin correspond to points of interest on the Yorkshire and the Dales map.

7 This tour begins in **Bradford,** a little less than 50 miles north of Buxton. There are several possible routes through the hills and valleys skirting Manchester, before you join the M62 east, turning off for Bradford at junction 26. A major wool town since the 16th century, Bradford today is a likeable northern city, its center adorned with Victorian buildings from its period of greatest prosperity: St. George's Hall on Bridge Street (1851) and the Wool Exchange on Market Street (1864) are two fine examples.

Pleasing though the buildings are, tourists come to Bradford for the exciting museums, particularly the **National Museum of Photography, Film, and Television,** which opened in 1983. This remarkable museum traces the history of the photographic media with participatory displays, educational programs, and excellent graphics. Make sure to allow time for a screening at the museum's IMAX movie screen—the biggest in Britain. *Pictureville, Prince's View, tel. 0274/727488. Admission: museum free; IMAX cinema £3.65 adults, £2.50 children and senior citizens. Open Tues.–Sun. and national holidays 10:30–6.*

Bradford's history as a wool-producing town and the growth of the textile industry are outlined at the **Industrial Museum,** housed in a former spinning mill northeast of the town center. Exhibits include workers' dwellings dating from the 1870s to the 1950s and a mill owner's house from the 19th century, while five- to 10-minute demonstrations of the mighty machinery that once powered the mill take place every hour on the hour. *Moorside Rd., tel. 0274/631756. Admission: free. Open Tues.–Sun. 10–5.*

Bradford's work opportunities attracted many thousands of Asian immigrants here after World War II, which has made Bradford a cosmopolitan city. Consequently, there are scores of Asian restaurants serving excellent, inexpensive food.

North and west of Bradford the Yorkshire Moors begin, where many are drawn by the tragic story of the Brontë sisters. They lived in **⑧ Haworth,** a straggling stone village on the edge of the moors, and wrote at least two immortal novels, *Jane Eyre* and *Wuthering Heights.*

Haworth's steep, cobbled Main Street has changed little since the days of the famous sisters, and it is now largely free of traffic. At the end is the **Black Bull** pub, where Branwell, the Brontës' only brother, drank himself into an early grave, and which is still, despite the crowds, an atmospheric place to stop off. Here also are the post office from which Charlotte, Emily, and Anne sent their manuscripts to their London publishers; an information center with guides and maps; the church, with its gloomy graveyard (Charlotte and Emily are buried inside the church); and the **Brontë Parsonage Museum,** in the somber Georgian house in which the sisters grew up. The museum has some enchanting mementos, including the sisters' spidery, youthful graffiti on the nursery wall, and Charlotte's tiny wedding shoes. *Tel. 0535/642323. Admission: £3.50 adults, £1 children 16 and under, £2.50 senior citizens, £8 family ticket. Open daily 11–5; closed mid-Jan.–early Feb. and Dec. 24–27.*

If you know and love the Brontës' works, you'll also probably want to walk (an hour or so along a field path, a lane, and a moorland track) to the **Brontë Waterfall,** described in Emily's and Charlotte's poems and letters. Farther into the austere moor is **Top Withins** (3 miles), the remains of a bleak hilltop farm, which, although often taken to be the main inspiration for Heathcliff's gloomy mansion, Wuthering Heights, probably isn't, as a plaque nearby baldly states. Wear sturdy shoes and protective clothing: If you've read *Wuthering Heights*, you'll have a fairly good idea of what weather can be like on the Yorkshire moors!

It's only 12 miles north from Haworth through Airedale on A629 to **⑨ Skipton,** a typical Dales market town (markets every day except Tuesday and Sunday), with as many farmers as tourists milling in the streets. At the top of busy High Street is **Skipton Castle,** built by the Normans and unaltered since the Civil War (17th century). In the central courtyard, a yew tree, planted 300 years ago by feminist and philanthropist Lady Anne Clifford, still flourishes. Lady Anne was the last of the Cliffords, one of England's most famous baronial families; you can see the striking heraldry on the tombs of her ancestors, the earls of Cumberland, inside Skipton Church, just by the castle. *Skipton Castle, tel. 0756/792442. Admission: £2.40 adults, £1.20 children under 18. Open Mon.–Sat. 10–6, Sun. 2–6; closed Christmas.*

From Skipton, strike east into **Wharfedale,** one of the longest of the Yorkshire Dales; most, but not all, take their names from the rivers **⑩** that run through them. About 5 miles along A59, **Bolton Abbey,** the ruins of an Augustinian priory, sits on a grassy embankment inside a great curve of the River Wharfe. You can wander through the 13th-century ruins or visit the priory church, which is still the local parish church; it's open daily, with free access in the daytime. Among

Yorkshire and the Dales

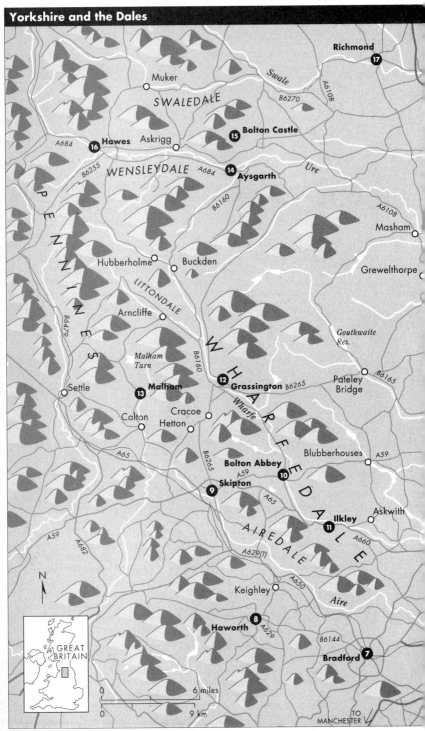

Richmond 17

Muker

SWALEDALE

Swale

A6108

B6270

A684 16 Hawes

Askrigg

15 Bolton Castle

WENSLEYDALE A684 14 Aysgarth

Ure

A6108

Masham

B6255

P E N N I N E S

B6160

Grewelthorpe

Hubberholme

Buckden

B6479

LITTONDALE

Arncliffe

Gouthwaite
Res.

Malham
Tarn

B6160

W H A R F E

12 Grassington B6265

Pateley
Bridge

B6165

13 Malham

Settle

Calton

Cracoe
Hetton

Wharfe

A65

B6265

Bolton Abbey

Blubberhouses

A59

A59

A682

Bolton Abbey
A59
10

Skipton 9

A65

A I R E D A L E

11 Ilkley

Askwith

A629(T)

A660

A59

Keighley

A650

Aire

8

Haworth

A629

B6144

Bradford 7

N

GREAT
BRITAIN

0   6 miles
0   9 km

TO
MANCHESTER

Catterick

A1(T)

Leeming

Swale

Northallerton

Rievaulx

A170

Helmsley

Thirsk

A170

A61

North Stainley

Hovingham

A6108

35 Ripon

B6265

Easingwold

34 A61

Studley Royal/
Fountains
Abbey

36 Newby Hall

Ure

A61

A6055

B1363

A1(T)

A19(T)

A64

B6165

A1(T)

Nidd

33 Knaresborough

B6265

32 Harrogate

A59

A661

MARSTON
MOOR

A64

A166

York

A1079

18 — **29**

A658

A61

B1224

Wetherby

A19

Pool

30 A659

Harewood
House

A64

Ouse

A61

A659

Tadcaster

Wharfe

A64

A1

A162

Leeds **31**

Selby

M1

A63

Aire

TO
LONDON

Ouse

M62

TO
SHEFFIELD

the famous visitors enchanted by Bolton Abbey were William Wordsworth (who described "Bolton's mouldering Priory" in his poem "The White Doe of Rylstone"); J. M. W. Turner, the 19th-century painter; and John Ruskin, the Victorian art critic. The abbey is surrounded by some of the most romantic woodland scenery in England, and nearby the river plunges between a narrow chasm in the rocks (a dangerous stretch of white water known as "the Strid") before reaching a medieval hunting lodge, **Barden Tower.** Barden Tower is now a ruin and can be visited just as easily as Bolton Abbey, in whose grounds it stands.

⑪ Take a detour 6 miles south of Bolton Abbey, to the former spa town of **Ilkley,** from which it's easy to stroll up onto **Ilkley Moor.** Footpaths run right across the top, south to Keighley. A famous, and rather grisly, Yorkshire song with dialect words tells the tale of a man who went courting on the moor "baht 'at" (without a hat); he catches cold, dies, and is buried; his body eaten by worms, the worms eaten by ducks, the ducks eaten by people until "we shall all have etten thee."

The **White Wells Museum,** about a 20-minute walk from the town center on the northern slopes of the moor, contains an 18th-century natural spring bath, and the tearoom serves tea made with the local spring water. *Wells Rd., no phone. Admission free. Open Tues., Wed., and Fri.–Sun. 10–6.*

⑫ Returning to Bolton Abbey, follow the river north through Wharfedale (via B6160) for 7 miles until you get to **Grassington.** A stone village, built around an ancient cobbled marketplace, it's well situated for exploring Upper Wharfedale. The National Park Centre (near the bus station) has information on a wide choice of village and country tours. In Grassington itself, you'll find a small museum and a surprisingly good range of stores, pubs, and cafés. *National Park Centre, tel. 0756/752748. Open Apr.–Oct., daily 10–5; Nov.–Mar., weekends 10–4.*

⑬ From Grassington take B6265 south 2 miles through Cracoe, then branch west onto the minor road past Hetton and Calton to reach **Malham,** a village surrounded by some of Britain's most remarkable limestone formations. **Malham Cove,** a huge natural rock amphitheater, is a short walk from the National Park Centre. Also nearby is **Gordale Scar,** a deep natural chasm between overhanging limestone cliffs, through which the white waters of a moorland stream plunge 300 feet. This is an area of international importance in the fields of natural history and Roman archaeology, and maps at the National Park Centre will give you some idea of what there is to do and see. *Tel. 0729/830363. Open Easter–June, Sept.–Oct., daily 9:30–5; July–Aug., daily 9–5:30; Nov.–Easter, weekends 10–4.*

⑭ Continuing this dramatic moorland drive, take the road north (skirting Malham Tarn), to Arncliffe in Littondale. Follow the signs for B6160 and go north to **Buckden,** the last village in Wharfedale. From here you can go directly through Kidstone Pass (still on B6160) to **Aysgarth** in Wensleydale (don't forget to sample the local crumbly white cheese). Here you can view the **Aysgarth Force,** a se-
⑮ ries of waterfalls on the River Ure, and **Bolton Castle,** where Mary, Queen of Scots, was imprisoned in the 16th century—the tower in which she was held still stands.

⑯ From Aysgarth, follow A684 10 miles west to the market town of **Hawes,** which serves the two main northern dales, **Wensleydale** and **Swaledale.** This is where the James Herriot TV series was filmed;

you might recognize the village of Askrigg, east of Hawes, which was dubbed "Darrowby" in the program.

Hawes's National Park Information Centre in the old train station contains the **Dales Countryside Museum,** which helps give a picture of Dales life in past centuries; a traditional ropewalk (rope-making shop) here also welcomes visitors. There's a good range of pubs and cafés in the area. *National Park Centre, tel. 0969/667450. Open Apr.–June and Sept.–Oct., daily 10–4; July and Aug., daily 9:30–4:30. The Dales Countryside Museum, tel. 0969/667494. Admission: £1.40 adults, 80p children 5–15 and senior citizens. Open Apr.–Oct., daily 10–5; some winter weekends, phone for details.*

Many people regard **Swaledale,** the next dale north, as the finest of all the Yorkshire dales. Awesomely crooked and steep, its narrow valley road twists over the Buttertubs Pass the 7 miles between Hawes and **Muker.**

From here, the B6270 follows the course of Swaledale east before joining the A6108 on to **Richmond.** This is a jewel of a town, tucked into a curve in the River Swale, with a network of narrow Georgian streets and terraces opening into the largest cobbled marketplace in the country. The immense keep of a Norman **castle** towers above the River Swale. Dating from the 11th century, it's one of the best-preserved monuments of this era, retaining its curtain wall, chapel, and great hall. *Castle, tel. 0748/822493. Admission: £1.50 adults, 75p children, £1.10 senior citizens. Open Apr.–Sept., daily 10–6; Oct.–Mar., Tues.–Sun. 10–4; closed Dec. 24–26 and Jan. 1.*

On Friars Wynd, in Richmond, you'll discover the tiny 18th-century **Georgian Theatre Royal,** the oldest theater in England still in use, and unchanged since the days of the 18th-century Shakespearean actor David Garrick; you can watch performances from either smart gallery boxes or old wooden seats. It's an intimate theater, remarkable for its authentic detail (except that it uses electric lights instead of candles). Try to reserve tickets well in advance. Also, outside performance times, the theater has a small museum featuring unique painted scenery dating from 1836. *Tel. 0748/823021. Museum admission: £1 adults, 70p children. Open late Mar.–Oct., Mon.–Sat. 11–4:45, Sun. 2:30–4:45.*

From Richmond take the fast, though largely unattractive, A1 and A59 roads south to York.

Tour 3: York and Leeds to Harrogate and Fountains Abbey

Numbers in the margin correspond to points of interest on the York map.

Spend as much time as you can in **York;** the layers of history within its walls cannot be explored quickly. Named "Eboracum" in Latin, York was the military capital of Roman Britain, and traces of Roman garrison buildings still survive in the Museum gardens, among other places. The base of the medieval Multangular Tower was also part of the garrison, and the foundations of York Minster itself rise from remains of the *principia*, or garrison headquarters. If you ask the landlord at the Roman Bath Inn (St. Sampson's Sq.), he might show you part of a Roman hot-air bath below his pub.

Following the fall of the Roman Empire in the 5th century, a Saxon town grew up over the ruins of the Roman fort. On Christmas Eve, AD 627, the Northumbrian King Edwin introduced Christianity to

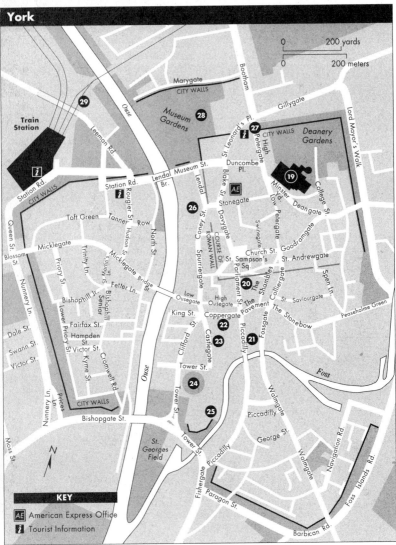

York

0 _____ 200 yards
0 _____ 200 meters

Marygate
CITY WALLS

Museum Gardens

Bootham

Gillygate

Lord Mayor's Walk

29

Train Station

Leeman Rd.

Ouse

28

St. Leonard's Pl.

27

CITY WALLS

Deanery Gardens

High Petergate

Duncombe Pl.

AE

19

Minster Yd.

College St.

Station Rd.

CITY WALLS

Station Rd.

Lendal Br.

Museum St.

Lendal

Blake St.

Stonegate

Low Petergate

Deangate

Goodramgate

Toft Green

Tanner Row

Rougier St.

Hudson St.

North St.

26

Coney St.

Davygate

Swinegate

Church St.

St. Andrewgate

Micklegate

Blossom St.

Trinity Ln.

Priory St.

Bishophill Jr.

Queen St.

Nunnery Ln.

Dale St.

Swann St.

Victor St.

Bishophill Senior

Fetter Ln.

Micklegate Bridge St.

Kilnery St.

Fairfax St.

Hampden St.

Victor St.

Kyme St.

Cromwell Rd.

Spurriergate

ROMAN WALL

COURSE OF

Low Ousegate

King St.

Clifford St.

High Ousegate

Coppergate

St. Sampson's Sq.

Parliament St.

20

The Shambles

The Pavement

Collergate

St. Saviourgate

Spen Ln.

Peaseholme Green

The Stonebow

Lower Priory St.

22

23

Castlegate

21

Piccadilly

Fossgate

Foss

Tower St.

24

Nunnery Ln.

Prices Ln.

CITY WALLS

Bishopgate St.

Moss St.

Ouse

Tower St.

25

Walmgate

Piccadilly

George St.

Walmgate

Navigation Rd.

St. Georges Field

Tower St.

Fishergate

Piccadilly

Paragon St.

Barbican Rd.

Foss Islands Rd.

N

KEY

AE American Express Office

i Tourist Information

Bootham Bar, **27**
Castle Museum, **25**
Clifford's Tower, **24**
Jorvik Viking Centre, **22**
Mansion House/ Guildhall, **26**
Merchant Adventurers' Hall, **21**

National Railway Museum, **29**
St. Mary's/Heritage Centre, **23**
The Shambles, **20**
York Minster, **19**
Yorkshire Museum, **28**

the area by being baptized in a little wooden church in York. The city grew in importance in the 9th century, after the Viking conquerors of northern and eastern England made York—which they called "Jorvik"—their English capital. You'll notice that many of the city's street names are suffixed with the word "-gate" (Goodramgate, Micklegate, for example)—"gate" was the Viking word for "street."

One memorable way to see the city is by taking a stroll along the **city walls.** Originally earth ramparts erected by York's Viking kings to repel raiders, the present stone structure (probably replacing a stockade) dates from the 14th century and has been extensively restored. A narrow paved walk runs along the top (originally 3 miles in circumference), passing over York's distinctive fortified gates or "bars."

Because of its strategic position on the River Ouse, York developed throughout Norman and Plantagenet times (11th–14th century) into an important trade center and inland port, particularly for the export of wool to the Continent. Wealthy guilds of craftsmen and merchants flourished, and it became a favored royal destination. Henry II and Edward II held parliaments here and Richard II gave the city its first Sword of State. The great York Minster, officially the Cathedral of St. Peter, was founded in Norman times, and its size and beauty reflect medieval York's wealth and importance. Today the archbishop of York is still second only to the archbishop of Canterbury in the hierarchy of the Church of England.

The old city center of York is a compact, dense web of narrow streets and tiny alleys—"snickleways"—and not a good place for driving. Congestion is so bad that traffic has been banned around the minster. It's easy to lose your sense of direction in the crooked streets, so have a street map handy. Bus tours of the city leave from outside the train station, but you'll probably get a better sense of York by simply wandering around. It's a popular place; try to avoid July and August when crowds choke the narrow streets and cause long lines at the popular museums. April, May, and October are far better; April is also the time to see the embankments beneath the city walls filled with the pale gold ripple of daffodils.

⑲ Start your tour in the north of the city, at the largest Gothic church in England, **York Minster:** It is 534 feet long, 249 feet across its transepts, and 90 feet from floor to roof; the central towers are 184 feet high. Mere statistics, however, cannot convey the scale and beauty of the building. Its soaring columns; the ornamentation of its 14th-century nave; the great east window, one of the greatest pieces of medieval glazing in the world; the enormous choir screen portraying every king of England from William the Conqueror (reigned 1066–1087) to Henry VI (reigned 1422–1461); the imposing tracery of the splendid Rose Window (just one of the minster's 128 stained-glass windows) commemorating the marriage of Henry VII and Elizabeth of York in 1486 (the event that ended the Wars of the Roses and began the Tudor dynasty)—all contribute to its magnificence. The minster also contains a rich array of chapels, monuments, and tombs, and don't miss the exquisite 13th-century **Chapter House.** The **Undercroft Museum and Treasury,** with Saxon and Roman remains, houses among other treasures the ancient Horn of Ulf given to the minster by a relative of the Danish king Canute, who ruled England from 1016 to 1035. The **Crypt** is also unmissable, holding some of the minster's oldest and most valuable treasures, among them the 12th-century statue of a heavy-footed Virgin Mary. The gift shop sells a good range of informative books on the minster, York, and area walks.

After exploring the interior, you might take the 275 winding steps to the roof of the great **Central Tower** (strictly for those with a head for heights), not only for the close-up view of the cathedral's detailed carving but also for a magnificent panorama of York and the surrounding Pennines and Yorkshire moors. *York Minster Undercroft Museum and Treasury, Chapter House, Crypt, and Central Tower, tel. 0904/624426. Admission: Minster free, although £1.50 donation appreciated; Undercroft £1.80 adults, 50p children and senior citizens; Chapter House 60p adults, 30p children and senior citizens; Crypt 60p adults, 30p children and senior citizens; Central Tower £2 adults, £1 children and senior citizens. Minster open summer, daily 7 AM–8:30 PM, winter 7–5; Undercroft, Chapter House, Crypt, and Central Tower open Mon.–Sat. 10–6:30, Sun. 1–6:30; gift shop open daily 9:30–4:30.*

After leaving the minster, walk down Low Petergate to Colliergate. The town center's mixed architectural heritage ranges over many periods, although in some places nondescript modern development has taken its toll. **The Shambles** (right off Colliergate), however, is a perfectly preserved medieval street with half-timbered stores and houses whose overhangs are so massive you could almost reach across the street from one second-floor window to another.

Walk the length of the Shambles, taking time to browse in the crafts and souvenir shops along the way, and into The Pavement. From here turn right into Fossgate where you'll find the **Merchant Adventurers' Hall** on the right. This former guildhall, dating from the mid-14th century, is the largest half-timbered hall in York, with a pretty garden in the back. *Tel. 0904/654818. Admission: £1.80 adults, 50p children, £1.50 senior citizens. Open Mar.–Nov., daily 8:30–5; Dec.–Feb., Mon.–Sat. 8:30–3.*

From the Merchant Adventurers' Hall you can walk along the river a little way before turning right into an area containing two interesting museums: In the **Jorvik Viking Centre,** on an authentic Viking site, archaeologists have re-created a Viking street with astonishing attention to detail. Its "time-cars" whisk visitors through the streets to experience the sights, sounds, and smells (!) of Viking England, while excellent displays show visitors the extraordinary breadth of the Viking culture and social system. *Coppergate, tel. 0904/643211. Admission: £3.80 adults, £1.90 children, £2.85 senior citizens. Open Apr.–Oct., daily 9–7; Nov.–Mar., daily 9–5:30.*

York's 20 or so surviving medieval churches—almost any of which could stand alone as an architectural showpiece—tend to be largely ignored by tourists and are therefore good places to explore without the crowds. **St. Mary's** now houses **The York Story,** an exhibit devoted to the history of the city. *Castlegate, tel. 0904/628632. Admission: £1.40 adults, 90p children and senior citizens. There is a joint ticket with the Castle Museum, £4.70 adults, £2.70 children, £10.50 family ticket. Open Mon.–Sat. 10–5, Sun. 1–5.*

Continue down Castlegate and turn right into Tower Street. On your left you'll see **Clifford's Tower,** which dates from the early 14th century. It stands on the mound originally erected for the keep of York Castle, long since gone (the site now occupied by the Assize Courts and the Castle Museum). In 1190 this was the scene of one of the worst outbreaks of antisemitism in medieval Europe, when 150 Jews who had sought sanctuary in the castle were massacred. *Tower St., tel. 0904/646940. Admission: £1.20 adults, 60p children, 90p senior citizens. Open Apr.–Sept., daily 10–6; Oct.–Mar., daily 10–4.*

② The **Castle Museum,** a former 18th-century debtor's prison, offers a number of detailed exhibitions and re-creations, including a cobblestoned Victorian street complete with crafts shops; a working water mill; domestic and military displays; and, most important, the Coppergate Helmet, a 1,200-year-old Anglo-Saxon helmet (one of only three ever found) discovered during recent excavations of the city. You can also visit the cell where Dick Turpin, the 18th-century highwayman and folk hero spent the night before his execution. He once rode nonstop from London to York on his horse, Black Bess. *Clifford St., tel. 0904/653612. Admission: £3.80 adults, £2.70 children and senior citizens. Joint ticket with York Story, £4.70 adults, £2.70 children, £10.50 family ticket. Open Apr.–Oct., Mon.–Sat. 9:30–5:30, Sun. 10–5:30; Nov.–Mar., Mon.–Sat. 9:30–4, Sun. 10–4.*

A walk up Castlegate to Spurriergate into Coney Street brings you
② to the 18th-century **Mansion House** and the earlier **Guildhall,** right on the river. Although damaged by World War II bombing, the Guildhall has been faithfully restored to its mid-15th-century glory. *St. Helen's Sq., tel. 0904/613161. Admission free. Open May–Oct., Mon.–Thurs. 9–5, Fri. 9–4, Sat. 10–5, Sun. 2–5; Nov.–Apr., Mon.–Thurs. 9–5, Fri. 9–4.*

From the Guildhall, make your way across into pedestrianized **Stonegate,** a narrow street of Tudor and 18th-century storefronts and courtyards with considerable charm. A passage just off Stonegate, at 52A, leads to a 12th-century Norman stone house, one of the very few to have survived in England.

Time Out In St. Helen's Square, on the opposite end of Stonegate to the Minster, **Betty's,** ranged elegantly across two large floors in a beautiful Art Nouveau building, has been a York institution since 1912. Best-known for its teas, served with mouth-watering cakes and desserts (try the "fat rascal," a plump bun bursting with cherries and nuts), Betty's also offers light meals, and a splendid selection of exotic coffees, all served with old-fashioned style and refinement. Get a table on the upper floor if you can, next to the ceiling-to-floor windows, etched with decorative stained glass.

Back on Stonegate, continue toward the minster and turn left onto
② High Petergate. Walk out of the walled city through **Bootham Bar,** one of its old gates, which retains its Norman archway. To your left are the gardens and ruins of St. Mary's Abbey, founded in 1089,
② which now houses the **Yorkshire Museum.** In these gardens (or at the Theatre Royal) the city's cycle of mystery plays is performed every four years (*see* The Arts, *below*); the next performance is in 1996. The museum itself covers the natural and archaeological history of the whole county, including a great deal of material on the Roman, Anglo-Saxon, and Viking aspects of York. Here you can also see the 15th-century Middleham Jewel, a pendant resplendent with a large sapphire and the best piece of Gothic jewelry found in England in this century. *Museum Gardens, tel. 0904/629745. Admission: £2.50 adults, £1.25 children and senior citizens, £6 family ticket. Open Nov.–Mar., Mon.–Sat. 10–5, Sun. 1–5; Apr.–Oct., daily 10–5.*

Enjoy a stroll through the atmospheric gardens with their crumbling medieval columns and blaze of summer flowers, and then make your way to Lendal Bridge and cross the river onto Station Road.
② Take a right onto Leeman Road and follow the signs to the **National Railway Museum,** which houses Britain's national collection of locomotives and is perhaps the world's best train museum. Among the

exhibits are gleaming giants of the steam era, including *Mallard*, holder of the world speed record for a steam engine (126 mph). You can clamber aboard some of the trains. Passenger cars used by Queen Victoria are also on display. *Tel. 0904/621261. Admission: £3.95 adults, £2 children, £2.60 senior citizens, £11 family ticket. Open Mon.–Sat. 10–6, Sun. 11–6.*

Numbers in the margin correspond to points of interest on the Yorkshire and the Dales map.

From York make your way west along B1224 across Marston Moor where in 1644 Oliver Cromwell won a decisive victory over the royalists during the Civil War. At Wetherby, 10 miles away, continue another 6 miles westward along A659 to **Harewood House** (pronounced "Harwood"), home of the earl of Harewood, a cousin of the queen. This neoclassical mansion, built in 1759 by John Carr of York (who designed the best of Buxton's buildings, too), is known for its Robert Adam interiors, important paintings and ceramics, and Chippendale furniture (Chippendale himself was born in nearby Otley). Within the grounds are gardens, woods, a lake, a bird garden, an adventure playground, and a butterfly house. *Harewood, tel. 0532/ 886225. Admission: £5.75 adults, £3 children, £4.50 senior citizens, £15 family ticket. Open Apr.–Nov., daily 11–5.*

Follow A61 to detour south 6 miles into the congested traffic and tangle of main routes that lead to and through the industrial city of **Leeds.** It's difficult for visitors to believe that the area surrounding the core makes it one of the greenest cities in Europe. In addition to the parks, long green routes radiate from the **City Centre.** You can walk from Golden Acre Park along the Meanwood Valley Trail—the green route to the city—or follow the canal along the Aire Valley.

Leeds is well known for its superb **Victorian Arcades,** but the Georgian squares and streets of the West End are just as notable. Tucked away among the streets you'll find old pubs and yards that were laid out in the 14th century. The **Art Gallery,** with its fine collection of 20th-century work, and **Henry Moore Study Centre, City Museum,** and **Craft Design Centre** are all adjacent to the **Town Hall.** Different kinds of crafts from all over the world can be found at **Granary Wharf** in the Canal Basin, which is reached via the **Dark Arches,** where the River Aire flows under the City Station. This is one of the many projects that are reviving the Leeds riverside.

From Leeds, take A64/A1/A661 north about 18 miles to **Harrogate**, an elegant town which flourished during Regency and early Victorian periods, when its mineral springs began to attract the noble and wealthy. You can still drink the evil-smelling (and -tasting) spa waters at the newly restored **Royal Pump Room Museum,** which charts the story of Harrogate from its modest 17th-century beginnings. *Opposite Valley Gardens. Tel. 0423/503340. Admission: £1 adults, 60p children and senior citizens, £2.75 family ticket. Open Tues.– Sat. 10–5, Sun. 2–5.*

Numerous coffee shops and wine bars line the town's graceful esplanades, and tea and toasted teacakes are served in the pump room in the **Royal Baths** (1897). You can still take a Turkish bath or a sauna in its exotic, tiled rooms. When the spas no longer drew crowds, Harrogate shed its old image to become a modern business center, and built a huge complex that attracts international conventions. It has been tactfully located so as not to spoil the town's landscape of poised Regency row houses, pleasant walkways, and sweeping green spaces (the one in the town center is known as The Stray).

③③ Just 2 miles northeast of Harrogate on A6055, the photogenic old town of **Knaresborough** is built in a steep, rocky gorge along the River Nidd. Attractions include its river, lively with pleasure boats, a little marketplace, a medieval castle where Richard II was once imprisoned, a house carved out of the cliff face, and a "petrifying well," which will cover anything placed in it with a thin layer of limestone in a matter of weeks.

③④ From Knaresborough take B6165 west 5 miles, then A61 north another 4 miles until you reach the back road leading to Fountains Abbey and Studley Royal. The 18th-century water garden and deer park, **Studley Royal**, together with the ruins of **Fountains Abbey**, blends the glories of English Gothic architecture with a neoclassical vision of an ordered universe. The gardens include lakes, ponds, and even a diverted river, while waterfalls splash around classical temples, statues, and a grotto; the surrounding woods offer long vistas toward the great tower of Ripon Cathedral, some 3 miles north. The majestic ruins of Fountains Abbey, with its own high tower and soaring 13th-century arches, make a striking picture on the banks of the River Skell. Founded in 1132, but not completed until the early 1500s, the abbey still possesses many of its original buildings, and it's one of the best places in England to learn about medieval monastic life. The whole of this complex is now owned by the National Trust. There's a small restaurant (lunch only) and two stores, as well as an exhibition and video display in the 17th-century **Fountains Hall**, one of the earliest neoclassical buildings in northern England. *Tel. 0765/608888. Admission: £3.80 adults, £1.60 children, £9 family ticket (reduced rates in winter). Hall open daily Apr.–Sept., 11–6; Oct.–Mar., 11–4; Gardens and Abbey open daily Apr.–Sept., 10–7; Oct.–Mar., 10–5.*

③⑤ **Ripon,** just northeast of Fountains Abbey, was thriving as early as the 9th century. Successive churches here were destroyed by the Vikings and the Normans, and the present structure, dating from the 12th and 13th centuries, is particularly noted for its finely carved choir stalls and Saxon crypt. Despite its small size, the church has been designated a cathedral since the mid-19th century, which makes Ripon (only 15,000 or so inhabitants) technically a city. Market day here is Thursday, probably the best day to stop by.

③⑥ Southeast of Ripon is **Newby Hall,** an early-18th-century house that was redecorated later in the same century by Robert Adam for his patron William Weddell; it contains some of the finest interior decorative art of its period in Western Europe. One room has been designed around a set of priceless Gobelin tapestries, and another was created to show off Roman sculpture. The famous grounds, which extend down to the River Ure, include a collection of old species roses, rare shrubs, and delightful sunken gardens. The children's adventure playground, narrow-gauge steam railroad, river steamers, and garden restaurant make a visit to Newby a full day's outing. *Tel. 0423/322583. Admission: house and gardens, £4.80 adults, £2.70 children, £3.80 senior citizens. Open Easter–Oct., Tues.–Sun. 11–5.*

The return to York, 21 miles due southeast, can be along B6265/A59, part of which is the old Roman Dere Street.

Tour 4: Scarborough and the North York Moors

Numbers in the margin correspond to points of interest on the Scarborough and North York Moors map.

A great sweep of cliffs above its sandy bay, a rocky promontory capped by a ruined castle, and a harbor with a lighthouse make **Scarborough** on the northeast Yorkshire coast the classic picture of an English seaside resort. In fact, the city claims to be the earliest one in Britain, dating from the chance discovery in the early 17th century of a mineral spring on the foreshore. Not unexpectedly, this led to the establishment of a spa, whose users were encouraged not merely to soak themselves in seawater but even to drink it. By the late 18th century, when sea bathing was firmly in vogue, no beaches were busier than Scarborough's with "bathing machines," cumbersome wheeled cabins drawn by donkeys or horses into the surf and anchored there. These contraptions afforded modest swimmers relative privacy, as the cabin door faced seaward.

Scarborough's initial prosperity dates from this period, as evidenced in the handsome Regency and early Victorian residences and hotels in the city. The advent of train travel further popularized seaside vacations in Britain, and the extension of the railroad from York to Scarborough in the mid-19th century made it easily accessible for larger numbers of people. Smaller hotels and boarding houses sprang up for the industrial workers from around the region, and an atmosphere of cheerful brashness soon became as characteristic of Scarborough as of the other British seaside resorts.

Yet Scarborough has kept its two distinct faces. The contrast between the two makes Scarborough all the more appealing. Its older, more genteel side in the southern half of town consists of carefully laid out crescents and squares, and cliff-top walks and gardens with spectacular views across Cayton Bay. The northern side is a riot of ice-cream stands, cafés, stores selling "rock" (no British seaside vacation is complete without this impossibly sweet hard candy), crab hawkers, bingo halls, and candyfloss (cotton candy). In addition, enough survives of the tight huddle of streets, alleyways, and red-roofed cottages around the harbor to give an idea of what the city was like before the resort days. One revealing relic is a tall, 15th-century stone house, now a restaurant, which is said to have been owned by Richard III.

Scarborough harbor is busy with coastal fishing and shipping, as well as pleasure cruisers. Stop in at the old harbor lighthouse, which doubles as a deep-sea fishing museum. Paths link the harbor with the ruins of **Scarborough Castle** on the promontory; dating from Norman times, it is built on the site of a Roman signal station and near a former Viking settlement. From the castle there are spectacular views across the North Bay, the beaches, and the shore gardens. *Tel. 0723/372451. Admission: £1.70 adults, 85p children, £1.30 students and senior citizens. Open Apr.–Sept., daily 10–6; Oct.–Mar., Tues.–Sun. 10–4.*

At the little medieval church of **St. Mary,** near the castle on the way into town, you'll find the grave of Anne, the youngest Brontë sister, who died in 1849; she was taken to Scarborough from Haworth in a final desperate effort to save her life in the sea air. Happier literary associations are to be found at **Wood End** on the Crescent, vacation home of 20th-century writers Edith, Osbert, and Sacheverell Sitwell, a sister and two brothers. The early Victorian house, in delightful grounds, is now the **Woodend Museum of Natural History;** the adjoining house is the **Art Gallery.** *Tel. 0723/367326. Admission free. Open May–Sept., Tues.–Sat. 10–1 and 2–5, Sun. 2–5; Oct.–Apr., Tues.–Sat. 10–1 and 2–5.*

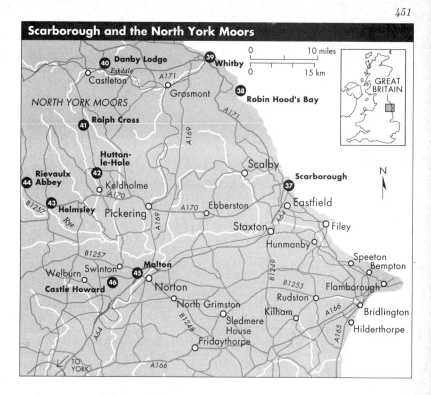

Scarborough and the North York Moors

A short walk below Wood End leads to the **Rotunda Museum,** an extraordinary circular building housing important archaeological and local history collections. Constructed in 1829 for the Scarborough Philosophical Society, it was one of the first public buildings in the country to be erected as a museum. *Vernon Rd., tel. 0723/374839. Admission and opening times same as Woodend Museum.*

Except for the hottest summers, England's northeastern seaboard isn't the warmest place for a beach vacation, though there are good sandy beaches at **Filey** (7 mi) and **Bridlington** (18 mi). Scarborough's own beaches are a mixture of sand and rock. However, not the least of Scarborough's attractions is its proximity to outstanding countryside. The 55-mile stretch of coast from **Saltburn-by-the-Sea** north of Whitby down to Bridlington has wonderful, sheer sea cliffs, and the unspoiled inland towns and villages are fun to poke around in.

 Begin by making your way north, either on A171 or by the more interesting minor roads, and take time to stop off at **Robin Hood's Bay** (20 mi), a tiny fishing village squeezed into a narrow ravine near where a stream courses over the cliffs. Perilously steep, narrow roads are fringed with tiny, crazily scattered houses, and space is so tight you are not allowed to drive into the village center. The tiny beach was once a notorious smugglers' landing; contraband was passed up the streambed beneath the cottages, often with customs officers in hot pursuit. Today, the tide rushes in very quickly, so do take care.

 Another 5 miles north brings you to **Whitby.** Now a small laid-back resort, Whitby was once a great whaling port, and it was here that Captain James Cook (1728–79), explorer, navigator, and discoverer of Australia, served his apprenticeship. Visit the **Captain Cook Memorial Museum** in the 18th-century house where Cook lived as an apprentice from 1746 to 1749, and see mementos of his epic expeditions, including maps, diaries, and drawings. *Grape La., tel. 0947/601900. Admission: £1.50 adults, £1 children and senior citizens. Open Easter–Oct., daily 9:45–5; Mar. and Nov., weekends 11–3.*

Climb the 199 steps from Whitby harbor and you are at the romantic ruins of **Whitby Abbey,** set high on the cliffs. St. Hilda founded the abbey in AD 657, and Caedmon (died c. 670), the first identifiable poet of the English language, was a monk here. In 664 the abbey was the site of the Synod of Whitby, where the Roman and Celtic churches met for the first time to discuss their respective religions. *Tel. 0947/603568. Admission: £1.50 adults, 75p children, £1.10 senior citizens. Open Apr.–Sept., daily 10–6; Oct.–Mar., daily 10–4.*

The nearby Mariners' Church of **St. Mary** is designed in the style of an 18th-century ship's deck. Don't miss the spooky, weather-beaten churchyard, filled with the crooked old gravestones of ancient mariners and affording superb views of the sea and the town itself. It was here that Bram Stoker's Dracula claimed Lucy as his victim.

From Whitby, follow the minor roads west through sleepy moorland villages across the top of the dramatic north York moors. The area set off by the **North Moors National Park** is dominated by rolling heather-covered hills which, in late summer and early fall, are a rich blaze of crimson and purple. Other parts of the park are densely wooded, and between the woods and moorland lie the grassy valleys that shelter Yorkshire's charming older villages and hamlets. Unlike the Pennine dales to the west, where everything is built of gray stone, the natural building material here is a mellower brown stone.

⑩ Take time if you can to visit the National Park's **Moor's Centre** at **Danby Lodge,** Eskdale (about 15 mi from Whitby and not far from Danby Station). Here, in a converted country house, you'll find exhibitions, displays, and a wide range of pamphlets and books about the area, as well as a varied program of lectures, guided walks, and national park events. *Danby, tel. 0287/660654. Admission free. Open Apr.–Oct., daily 10–5; Nov.–Mar., Sat. and Sun. 11–4.*

From Danby take the road due west 1½ miles to Castleton, then south over the top of the moors—where it is called Blakely Ridge Road. The road offers magnificent views over the park, especially at
⑪ **Ralph Cross,** the highest point.

⑫ Fourteen miles south, you'll come to **Hutton-le-Hole,** a tiny hamlet based around a pretty village green with sheep wandering contentedly about. Visit the 2-acre **Ryedale Folk Museum,** which records life in the dales from prehistory, and features a series of 16th-century cottages and a 19th-century blacksmith's shop. *Tel. 0751/417367. Admission: £2.50 adults, £1.25 children, £2 senior citizens. Open Apr.–Oct., daily 10:30–5:30.*

⑬ Head 6 miles west from Keldholme on A170 to **Helmsley,** a town with a castle and a traditional country marketplace surrounded by fine old inns, cafés, and stores. It's just over 2 miles from here by road
⑭ (B1257) or hiking path to the ruins of **Rievaulx Abbey** (pronounced "Reevoh"), once a great Cistercian center of learning, whose graceful Gothic arches are superbly set off by its dramatic setting on the River Rye. The best view of the ruins is from **Rievaulx Terrace,** a long, grassy walkway on the hillside above, flanked by Tuscan- and Ionic-style temples. The abbey is now in the hands of English Heri-

tage and the terraces in those of the National Trust. *Rievaulx Abbey, tel. 04396/228. Admission: £2 adults, £1 children, £1.50 senior citizens. Open Apr.–Sept., daily 10–6; Oct.–Mar., 10–4. Rievaulx Terrace, tel. 04396/340. Admission: £2.10 adults, 90p children. Open Apr.–Oct., 10:30–6.*

45 Continuing southeast on B1257 for 16 miles, you come to **Malton,** a pleasant market town and once an important Roman post. One of
46 Yorkshire's most famous houses, **Castle Howard,** lies in the Howardian Hills to the west of Malton. Perhaps best known these days as the setting for the TV series "Brideshead Revisited," it was designed by Sir John Vanbrugh, who also designed Blenheim, Winston Churchill's birthplace. Castle Howard took 60 years to build (1699–1759), and the baroque grandeur of its conception inside and out is without equal in northern England. A magnificent central hallway spanned by a hand-painted ceiling leads to a series of staterooms and galleries packed with furniture and works of fine art, while outside, a neoclassical landscape was created for the house. Carefully arranged woods, lakes, bridges, obelisks, temples, pyramids, and a mausoleum compose a scene far more like a painting than a natural English landscape. *Coneysthorpe, tel. 065384/333. Admission: £5.50 adults, £3 children, £5 senior citizens. Open mid-Mar.– late Oct., daily, grounds 10–4:30, house 11–4:30.*

What to See and Do with Children

Scarborough is full of cheerful attractions that appeal to kids, among them an activity center in North Bay known as **Kinderland,** designed to keep children (and their parents) entertained whatever the weather. *Burniston Rd. (North Bay) tel. 0723/354555. Admission: £2.95 and £3.50 (depending on season). Open Easter, then weekends until May Day Monday, then May–mid-Sept.; opening times vary widely; check locally.*

The **Scarborough Sea Life Centre** presents marine life and environmental matters in an entertaining way, with various different marine habitats combined under one roof. *Scalby Mills, near Scarborough, tel. 0723/376125. Admission: £4.25 adults, £2.95 children, £3.25 senior citizens. Open fall–spring, daily 10–6; summer, daily 10–9.*

Flamingo Land, between Malton and Pickering, combines a traditional zoo with an amusement park complete with white-knuckle rides and dolphin shows. *Flamingo Land Fun Park and Zoo, Kirkby Misperton, tel. 0653/86287. Admission: £7 (all rides included). Open Easter–Oct., daily 10–6.*

Farther inland, **Lightwater Valley Theme Park** features buggy rides, a miniature Wild West railroad, waterslides, an old-time fair, and pony rides. *North Stainley, near Ripon, tel. 0765/635321. Admission: £7.99 adult, £6.99 children (all rides included). Open Apr.– Sept.; phone to check opening times.*

Older children will enjoy a ride behind a real steam locomotive, an experience you can have either at the **North York Moors Railway** (tel. 0751/473535) between Pickering (tel. 0751/472508) and Grosmont (tel. 0947/85359) or on the **Keighley and Worth Valley Railway** (Keighley Station, 8 mi north of Haworth on A629; tel. 0535/645214), which runs between Keighley and Oxenhope. The **National Railway Museum** at York (*see* Tour 3, *above*) and the **National Museum of Photography, Film, and Television** at Bradford (*see* Tour 2, *above*) are additional attractions.

Off the Beaten Track

Outside the main towns and sites, there are dozens of quiet roads and isolated villages that time has little disturbed. A trip into the **Yorkshire wolds**—a range of low chalk hills and valleys east of York—is an ideal change from crowded cities. Such tranquil hamlets as **Bishop Burton, Fridaythorpe,** and **Londesborough** have appealing narrow lanes, old churches, and country pubs. Take A166 east from York to Fridaythorpe and then the scenic B1251 along the crest of the wolds (via Sledmere House and Rudston, with its prehistoric megaliths) toward Bridlington, a little fishing port and resort with an ancient harbor. Continue northward to **Flamborough** and **Flamborough Head,** where a huge bank of chalk cliffs juts out into the North Sea; from there, a coastal path over the cliff tops ends at **Bempton Cliffs,** one of the finest seabird sanctuaries on the east coast. Scarborough is just as convenient for a trip into the wolds. Take A64 south as far as Staxton, where B1249 will take you along the wolds escarpment; once there, you have your choice of back roads and trails to follow.

If you drive from Ilkley (9 mi east of Skipton on A65) across the River Wharfe, then along back roads to Askwith, you can pick up a moorland road that climbs the Washburn Valley to **Blubberhouses.** Many quiet routes lead north from here to **Pateley Bridge, Grewelthorpe, Masham,** and the gentle, unchanging, eastern Dales country.

From Buxton it's a little harder to find the quiet spots, particularly on weekends, but the smaller roads from the western edge of the national park down into the **Goyt Valley** and through **Macclesfield Forest** provide a restful, scenic drive.

East of Leeds (4 mi on A63) stands **Temple Newsam,** a huge Elizabethan and Jacobean building, which was altered in the 18th century. It was the birthplace in 1545 of Darnley, the doomed husband of Mary, Queen of Scots. Surrounded by one of the largest public parks in Western Europe, the house now belongs to Leeds City Council, which uses it to display its rich collections of furniture, paintings, and ceramics. There is a restored Georgian long gallery, now often used for recitals and concerts, and a Chinese drawing room. The vast park, with its walled rose gardens, greenhouses, and miles of woodland walks, was originally laid out by Capability Brown in 1762. *Leeds LS15 0AE, tel. 0532/647321. Admission: £1.30 adults, 65p children and senior citizens. Open Tues.–Sun. 10:30–5:30 (or dusk in winter).*

Shopping

Buxton   You'll find a wide variety of stores in Buxton, especially around Spring Gardens, the main shopping street. Near the **Old Court House** complex there is a pleasant arcade of small stores, while on The Crescent, try the new **Cavendish Arcade** built on the site of the old thermal baths. Both offer a pleasing range of fashion, cosmetic, and leather stores in stylish surroundings. Buxton is also well stocked with antiques shops and jewelers. **Ratcliffe's** (7 Cavendish Circus, tel. 0298/23993) specializes, among other things, in fine silver cutlery and items made out of the rare Blue John stone, mined only in the Peak District.

Haworth   West Yorkshire is synonymous with wool production, and the region has a large number of "mill shops" where high-quality knitting wool, sweaters, and woven wool for skirts or suits can be bought at factory prices; the tourist information center in Bradford will supply a full list of mill shops in the area. In Haworth, at the **Brontë Weaving Shed and Edinburgh Woollen Mill** (Townend Mill, tel. 0535/646217), you can, on Sunday and Wednesday afternoons, see handloom weavers making tweed the traditional way; an attached store sells the finished product including kilts and other clothing.

Scarborough Scarborough's most fashionable stores are on or near Bar Street (off Newborough), the main shopping street. On this quiet, pedestrian street near the sea, you'll find **Premier Engraving**, for jewelry; and the **Potter's Wheel** (Huntriss Row, tel. 0723/360630), offering pottery including Royal Doulton and Crown Derby. Newborough and Eastborough comprise the rest of the main shopping area, with department stores like **Debenham's.** There is also a large, indoor market near the harbor, selling fresh produce and fish.

Whitby For something special from the Yorkshire coast, when in Whitby select some jet jewelry, which was very popular in Victorian times as mourning decoration. You can choose from earrings, brooches, signet rings, and handsome strings of beads in local antiques shops. For more jewelry and secondhand goods, try **Jowsey and Row** (7 Sandgate, tel. 0947/602252).

York You are not likely to find any bargains in York, but the new and secondhand bookstores around Petergate, Stonegate, and the Shambles are excellent. **Blackwell's** (tel. 0904/624531), at Stonegate 32, has a large stock of new titles, and a convenient mail-order service. For secondhand books, head for the Minster and the **Minster Gate Bookshop** (tel. 0904/621812). For something high in quality and typically English, **Mulberry Hall** (tel. 0904/620736) on Stonegate, a large, half-timbered house dating from the 15th century, is a sales center for all the famous names in fine bone china: Wedgwood, Royal Worcester, Spode, Minton, Royal Doulton, and Royal Crown Derby. You'll also find outstanding cut glass and crystal, like Waterford, Stuart, Baccarat, and Lalique. Mulberry Hall has a reliable mailing service, and the staff can advise you on duties and tax rebates. **Robert Smart Menswear** (tel. 0904/652718) on Low Petergate is a comfortingly old-fashioned clothes store selling stylish, very English tweeds and woolens.

Markets Colorful local markets are held on the following days—Bakewell, Monday; Buxton, Tuesday and Saturday; Hawes, Tuesday; Ripon, Thursday; York, street markets on Newgate every weekday.

Sports and the Outdoors

Bicycling Strenuous or gentle routes are equally accessible, and it's easy and inexpensive to rent bikes; try **Bob Trotter** (13–15 Lord Mayor's Walk, tel. 0904/622868). National parks information centers have information on rentals, roads, and traffic-free routes (such as the High Peak and Tissington Trails).

Caving Caving (or "potholing"), which entails underground exploration, is popular here, especially as a family activity. Contact national park information centers.

Fishing Yorkshire is famous for its salt and freshwater fishing, and the dales rivers are excellent for trout. For a license, inquire at your hotel or at an information center. Sea angling is a busy trade in Scarborough; scheduled fishing trips are much cheaper than individually chartered ones—look for ads in the town, or, again, check at the information center.

Horse Racing Horse racing is quite popular in Yorkshire. The main racetrack is Knavesmire near York (tel. 0904/620911), but there are also tracks at Wetherby (tel. 0937/62035), Thirsk (tel. 0845/22276), and Doncaster (tel. 0302/20066).

Swimming The east coast beaches are usually fine for swimming, though you'll find the water cold. Beaches at Scarborough, Whitby, and Filey have patrolled bathing areas: swim between the red-and-yellow flags; and don't swim when a red flag is flying. Major towns also have indoor swimming pools; there's a particularly good one at Scarborough (tel. 0723/367137).

Walking Walking and hiking are natural activities in this area, and no equipment should be necessary except for all-weather clothing and waterproof shoes. One of the major trails is the **High Peak Trail,** which runs for 17 miles from Cromford (south of Matlock Bath) to Dowlow, following the route of an old railway. It has some fine scenery along the way. The national parks offices all have guidebooks, guide services, and maps. Each park's head office can supply you with information about the whole area: Peak District (tel. 0629/814321); the North Yorkshire Moors (tel. 0756/752748); the Yorkshire Dales (tel. 0969/650456).

Dining and Lodging

Dining This part of the country, with its fresh air and exhilarating hilltop walks, positively encourages hearty appetites. Locally produced meat and vegetables are excellent. One not-to-be-missed specialty is Yorkshire pudding, a popover-like pastry cooked in meat juices and served with gravy. Fresh fish from Whitby or Scarborough is a real treat with freshly fried chips (thick french fries); don't bother asking for a fish-and-chip shop—just follow your nose! The cheese from Wensleydale has a subtle, delicate flavor with a slightly honeyed aftertaste. Bakewell Tart, made from the traditional recipe and sold in many local Bakewell bakeries, is a good, sticky snack. Wherever you are, go for the freshly baked bread and homemade cakes.

Highly recommended restaurants are indicated by a star ★ .

Category	Cost*
$$$$	over £40
$$$	£30–£40
$$	£15–£30
$	under £15

per person, including first course, main course, dessert, and VAT; excluding drinks

Lodging Accommodations to suit all tastes and pocketbooks are available—look for farmhouse bed-and-breakfasts as you're traveling around the countryside, and when you want to be in the center of things, try town inns and hotels, which usually have more in the way of creature comforts and sophisticated facilities. Combine hotel stays with a couple of nights in countryside bed-and-breakfasts to get a real flavor of northern hospitality and cuisine. In seaside resorts rooms fill very quickly in July and August.

Highly recommended lodgings are indicated by a star ★ .

Category	Cost*
$$$$	over £150
$$$	£90–£150
$$	£55–£90
$	under £55

*All prices are for two people sharing a double room, including service, breakfast, and VAT.

Baslow
Dining and Lodging

Fischer's. The menu at this award-winning establishment, which calls itself a "restaurant with rooms," run by the friendly Fischer family, represents a range of Continental cuisines, with some fine local produce. Try the venison or one of the especially good fish dishes. One of the dining rooms has recently been converted into a café (closed Sun.), which serves food of the same high quality, at slightly lower prices. The six rooms are pretty and cozy, with en-suite facilities. *Baslow Hall, Calver Rd., Baslow (near Chatsworth), DE45 1RR, tel. 0246/583259, fax 0246/583818. Reservations advised. Dress: casual. AE, MC, V. Closed to nonresidents Sun. dinner. Hotel $$$; Restaurant $$*

Bolton Abbey
Lodging
★

Devonshire Arms. Originally an 18th-century coaching inn, and still belonging to the dukes of Devonshire, this hotel is in a superb setting on the River Wharfe, within easy walking distance of Bolton Abbey. Portraits of various dukes hang on the walls, and bedrooms in the original building are tastefully decorated by the Duchess of Devonshire; all have four-poster beds. There's even the feminine "Mitford Room" for lady executives traveling alone. *Bolton Abbey, Skipton, North Yorkshire, BD23 6AJ, tel. 0756/710441, fax 0756/710564. 40 rooms with bath. Facilities: restaurant, bar, fishing, croquet lawn, putting green. AE, DC, MC, V. $$$*

Buxton
Dining

Nathaniel's. Decorated with Victoriana, Nathaniel's offers a choice of English and French cuisine. The à la carte menu changes regularly; dishes may include Barbary duck breast with a raspberry or cassis sauce. *35 High St., tel. 0298/78388. Reservations advised. Dress: casual. AE, DC, MC, V. Closed Sun. dinner and Mon. $$*

Lodging
★

The Palace. A hotel on a grand scale from the halcyon days of the spa, it's set on 5 acres overlooking the town center and surrounding hills. All rooms have been totally refurbished and updated. *Palace Rd., SK17 6AG, tel. 0298/22001, fax 0298/72131. 122 rooms with bath. Facilities: heated pool, sauna, gym. Jacket and tie suggested. AE, DC, MC, V. $$$*

The Old Hall. Mary, Queen of Scots, stayed here sometime between 1573 and 1582, a unique distinction. This friendly, centrally located hotel overlooking the Opera House has a restaurant, wine bar, and in some rooms, four-poster beds. *The Square, SK17 6BD, tel. 0298/22841, fax 0298/72437. 37 rooms, 35 with bath. AE, MC, V. $$*

★ **Lakenham Guest House.** This large Victorian house with a sweeping garden has been converted into a comfortable guest house, with some attractive antique furniture and ample parking for guests. The totally refurbished and redecorated bedrooms all have excellent views. *11 Burlington Rd., SK17 9AL, tel. 0298/79209. 6 rooms, 5 with bath. MC, V. $*

Haworth
Dining

Weavers. Traditional Yorkshire cuisine, including Yorkshire pudding and local stews, is served in this restaurant, which has been created by converting old cottages. There are more elaborate dishes, too, including a daily fish special, and there's a specially priced set dinner for early arrivals; get there before 7. *15 West La., tel. 0535/643822. Reservations advised. Dress: casual. AE, DC, MC, V. Open Tues.–Sat. dinner only and Sun. lunch. $$*

Matlock
Dining and
Lodging
★

Riber Hall. This partly Elizabethan, partly Jacobean manor-house hotel—also a restaurant—has half-timbered bedrooms decorated with antiques, flowers, oak beams, and four-poster beds, in keeping with the inn's style. Chef Jeremy Brazelle prepares imaginative dishes with superbly fresh ingredients, many locally produced. There's even a daily vegetarian menu. *Riber Hall, Matlock, DE4 5JU, tel. 0629/582795, fax 0629/580475. 11 rooms with bath, 5 of them with Jacuzzi. Reservations required in the restaurant. Jacket and tie required. AE, DC, MC, V. $$$–$$$$*

Pool-in-
Wharfedale
Dining

Pool Court. On the northern edge of Leeds, Pool Court is very popular with the local food fanciers. Modern English food, with Mediterranean influences, are served in this distinctly elegant, professional place, with a highly experienced chef, David Watson, at the helm. Fish is always a good choice, while duck and game are expertly cooked, too. Try the salad of wood pigeon with wild duck, mushroom ravioli, and crispy fried vegetables. There's a variously priced wine list. *Pool, near Otley, tel. 0532/842288. Reservations advised. Dress: casual. AE, DC, MC, V. Closed Sun. and Mon; lunch on request for 10 or more. $$$*

Scarborough
Dining
★

Lanterna Restaurant. An intimate atmosphere and a high standard of cuisine make this Italian restaurant a good choice. The classic dishes are all represented, among them chicken cooked with brandy and cream, but more unusual seasonal specials are worth investigating, too, using fresh vegetables and fish unavailable at other times of the year. It's also noted for the quality of its service and its wine cellar. *33 Queen St., tel. 0723/363616. Reservations advised. Dress: casual. MC, V. Closed Sun., Mon., and lunch. $$*

Lodging

The Crown. The centerpiece of Scarborough's Regency Esplanade, this period hotel overlooks South Bay and the castle headland. Originally built to accommodate fashionable 19th-century visitors to Scarborough Spa, it has been considerably refurbished. *The Esplanade, YO11 2AG, tel. 0723/373491, fax 0723/362271. 83 rooms with bath. Facilities: restaurant, cocktail bar, games room, solarium, hair salon, baby-listening service. AE, DC, MC, V. $$$*

Whitby
Dining

Magpie Café. This excellent fish-and-chip restaurant is a real bargain. With the fishing quay within a stone's throw, everything is ultrafresh. Go for the set lunch, with Whitby crab if you're lucky, and sole, haddock, plaice, or even lobster to follow. The Mackenzie family has been running the Magpie for upwards of 40 years, and what they don't know about fish isn't worth knowing. *14 Pier Rd., tel. 0947/602058. Reservations not necessary. Dress: casual. Open daily 11:30–6:30 (last orders). MC, V. Closed end-Nov.–early Mar. $–$$*

Lodging

York House. Set in windswept moorland halfway between Whitby and Robin Hood's Bay, this charming, small redbrick countryside hotel stands in its own grounds. It's a no-smoking hotel, and the bedrooms are of a decent size, complete with TV. There's a dining room, too, if you want to take dinner at the hotel. *High Hawkser, YO22 4LW, near Whitby, tel. 0947/880314. 4 rooms with bath. Facilities: dining room, bar, lounge, parking. No credit cards. $*

York
Dining
★

19 Grape Lane. A narrow, slightly cramped restaurant in a typically leaning timbered York building in the heart of town, this place is hugely popular, serving modern English food from a blackboard of specials. Try the pan-fried wild salmon on a bed of pasta in a red wine sauce. It also serves a moderately priced light lunch menu until 1:45 PM. *19 Grape La., tel. 0904/636366. Reservations advised. Dress: casual. MC, V. Closed Sun. and Mon., 2 weeks in Feb., 2 weeks in Sept. $$$*

Melton's. Just 10 minutes from the Minster, this unfussy restaurant has local art on the walls and an open kitchen. The excellent seasonal menu, cooked up by chef Michael Hjort, an alumnus of the Roux empire, caters to everyone, with modern English, Continental, and fish dishes. Tuesday the menu focuses on fish, Wednesday on desserts, and Thursday on vegetarian dishes. *7 Scarcroft Rd., tel. 0904/634341. Reservations advised. Dress: casual. MC, V. Closed Sun. dinner and Mon. lunch, 3 weeks at Christmas, 1 week in Sept. $$–$$$*

Partners. The owner here is Polish, so you'll find the occasional Eastern European dish among the modern English cuisine in this simple, elegant restaurant, tucked well off the road and surrounding a pretty paved courtyard. Mushrooms are also a specialty, served in a variety of delicious guises; try the Kulebiake Russian fish pie with oyster mushrooms in olive oil with spring onions and olives. *13a High Ousegate, tel. 0904/627929. Reservations advised. Dress: casual. AE, MC, V. Closed Sun. $$–$$$*

Hudson's Below Stairs. Eat traditional roast beef and Yorkshire pudding in this atmospheric Victorian hotel restaurant five minutes' walk from the Minster. Morning coffee, lunch, and afternoon teas are also served. *60 Bootham, tel. 0904/621267. Reservations advised. Dress: casual. AE, DC, MC, V. $$*

Kites. Climb a steep narrow staircase to find an innovative restaurant serving offbeat, health-conscious food, using herbs from the owner's garden. Recommended dishes include the goat's cheese and hazelnut soufflé and the rose-petal ice-cream. *13 Grape La., tel. 0904/640750. Reservations advised. Dress: casual. MC, V. Closed lunch Mon.–Sat. $$*

Four Seasons. This cheery restaurant in the heart of York's medieval center serves homemade pies and traditional English meat dishes in a 16th-century beamed hall with a stone floor. *45 Goodramgate, tel. 0904/633787. Reservations advised. Dress: casual. AE, DC, MC, V. $–$$*

Dining and Lodging
★
Middlethorpe Hall. This handsome, superbly restored 18th-century mansion is located on the edge of the city beside the racetrack. The rooms are filled with antiques, paintings, and fresh flowers, and the extensive grounds boast a lake, a 17th-century dovecote, and "ha-has"—drops in the garden level that create cunning views. The large kitchen garden grows fresh vegetables for the hotel's award-winning Anglo-French restaurant, where you can eat in the original dining room by candlelight. *Bishopthorpe Rd., YO2 1QB, tel. 0904/641241, fax 0904/620176. 30 rooms with bath. Reservations essential for restaurant. Jacket and tie required for dinner. Facilities: large garden, croquet. AE, DC, MC, V. $$$–$$$$*

Lodging **Dean Court.** Directly opposite the Minster, this family-run establishment in a Victorian house has comfortably furnished rooms with plump sofas, TVs, and great views overlooking the Minster. Parking is a few minutes from the hotel, but there is a valet parking service. The restaurant serves good English cuisine. *Duncombe Place, YO1 2EF, tel. 0904/625082, fax 0904/620305. 40 rooms with bath. Facilities: coffee shop, bar, lounge, in-house movies. AE, DC, MC, V. $$$*

Mount Royale Hotel. Two elegant town houses, dating from the 1830s, have been furnished in a traditional English country-cottage style to make a comfortable hotel about 15 minutes from the town center. The open-plan "garden rooms" are decorated with real tropical plants, such as oranges, figs, and bougainvillea; they extend onto the hotel's lovely grounds. The fine Anglo-French restaurant serves dishes based on local produce. *119 The Mount, YO2 2DA, tel. 0904/ 628856, fax 0904/611171. 23 rooms with bath. Facilities: garden, health center, open-air pool, cable TV. AE, DC, MC, V. Closed Christmas Eve to New Year's Eve. $$–$$$*

Grasmead House. The large, comfortable bedrooms in this small family-run hotel all have four-poster beds, as well as tea- and coffee-making appliances. The friendly owners are more than willing to share their local knowledge with guests. It's an easy walk from the lodging to the city center. *1 Scarcroft Hill, YO2 1DF, tel. 0904/ 629996. 6 rooms with bath or shower (3 are nonsmoking rooms). Facilities: bar, lounge, parking. MC, V. $$*

Savages. Despite its name, this pleasant small hotel on a leafy road near the town center is eminently refined, with a reputation for attentive service. Once a Victorian home, the interior is stylish and welcoming, and there's a bar in which to relax. *15 St. Peter's Grove, YO3 6AQ, tel. 0904/610818, fax 0904/627729. 18 rooms with bath. Facilities: bar, restaurant, garden. AE, DC, MC, V. $$*

Abbey Guest House. This quaint, pretty guest house, a 10-minute walk from the train station and town center, enjoys a lovely riverside location, with a peaceful garden right on the river. *14 Earlsborough Terr., Marygate, YO3 7BQ, tel. 0904/627782. 7 rooms with basins. Facilities: lounge, baby-sitting service, parking, picnic lunches and evening meal on request. AE, DC, MC, V. $*

The Arts

Festivals   **Buxton Opera House** (Water St., Buxton, tel. 0298/72190) is the focal point of the town's renowned **Festival of Music and the Arts** (Festival Office, 1 Crescent View, Hall Bank, tel. 0298/70395), held during the second half of July and the beginning of August each year. It includes opera, drama, classical concerts, jazz, recitals, and lectures. An amateur drama festival also takes place at the opera house during the summer and you can see excellent theater, ballet, and jazz performances here all year.

Playing on its Viking past, York hosts the annual **Viking Festival** in February. The celebrations end with the Jorvik Viking Combat, when ravaging Northmen confront their Anglo-Saxon enemies. *Jorvik Viking Festival Office, Clifford Chamber, 4 Clifford St., tel. 0904/611944.*

The quadrennial performance of the medieval **York Mystery Plays** will take place in 1996, but an **Early Music Festival** is held each summer (except in Mystery Play years). *For details of the York Festival, call 0904/613161, ext. 1823.*

In York, the annual English **Bonfire Night** celebrations on November 5 have added piquancy, since the notorious 16th-century conspirator Guy Fawkes was a native of the city. They commemorate Fawkes's failure to blow up the Houses of Parliament, and his effigy is burned atop every fire. Ask at the tourist office for the locations of the best fires and fireworks displays.

Music   The **Huddersfield Contemporary Music Festival** is an annual, award-winning celebration with concerts at several venues throughout this West Yorkshire woolen town south of Bradford. It takes place in November. *For details contact the Festival Box Office, Albion St., Huddersfield, tel. 0484/430808.*

Opera **Opera North,** England's first major provincial opera company, has its home in Leeds at the **Grand Theatre** (tel. 0532/459351 or 0532/440971). The Grand has an opulent, gold-and-plush auditorium, modeled on Milan's La Scala, and it's worth getting a seat to see both the excellent company and its ornate home.

Theater Scarborough has an internationally known artistic native son in Alan Ayckbourn, a widely popular contemporary playwright. The **Stephen Joseph Theatre in the Round** at Valley Bridge near the train station (tel. 0723/370541) stages many of his plays before they head for London or Broadway. You might be lucky enough to catch an Ayckbourn premiere, directed by the master himself, at this small theater.

York's **Theatre Royal** (St. Leonard's Place, tel. 0904/623568) is a lively professional theater in a lovely old building, with many other events besides plays: string quartets, choral music, poetry reading, and art exhibitions.

Richmond's lovely **Georgian Theatre Royal** (Victoria Rd., tel. 0748/832021), the oldest and smallest playhouse in the country, also has a full program of theatrical and musical events.

The ultramodern **West Yorkshire Playhouse** in Leeds, costing £13.5 million, was opened in March 1990. It is on the slope of an old quarry (where a notorious slum once stood), and its interior is designed to be completely adaptable to all kinds of staging. Anyone interested in modern theater design should make the trip to Leeds. *Information and box office tel. 0532/442111.*

15 The Northeast

Durham, Hexham,
Berwick-upon-Tweed

England's northeast corner is relatively unexplored by tourists. Although one of its villages (Allendale Town, southwest of Hexham) lays claim to being the geographical center of the British Isles, there is a decided air of remoteness to much of the region. Consequently, visitors are often impressed by the wide-open spaces and empty country roads; they also like the value for money in shopping and accommodations, the unspoiled villages and uncrowded beaches, and the warmth and friendliness of the people.

Mainly composed of the two large counties of Durham and Northumberland (in ancient times known as Northumbria), the Northeast includes among its attractions the English side of the Scottish Border area, renowned in ballads and romantic literature for feuds, raids, and battles. Hadrian's Wall, much of it still intact, runs through this region, marking the northern limit of the Roman Empire. There was another Roman wall farther north, the Antonine, which was built around AD 145, but it was abandoned as unworkable within about 50 years. Also in this area are Kielder Forest, the largest planted forest in Europe; Kielder Water, the largest man-made lake in northern Europe; and some of the most interesting parts of Northumberland National Park.

The western side of the region is dominated by the range of hills known as the Pennines. The north Pennines, officially designated an Area of Outstanding Natural Beauty, feature some of England's wildest and least populated countryside. Farther north the Pennine hills merge almost imperceptibly with the rolling, sheep-cropped Cheviot (pronounced "Cheeviot") hills, which stretch along the border with Scotland.

On the region's eastern side is a 100-mile line of largely undeveloped coast, including quiet stone-built villages, empty beaches with the occasional outcrop of high cliff or offshore rocks, and islands populated by multitudes of seabirds. Several outstanding castles perch on headlands and promontories along here. For 1,000 years, the great cathedral of Durham was the seat of bishops who had their own armies and ruled the turbulent northern diocese as prince bishops with quasi-royal authority.

In more recent times, industrialization left its mark. Steel, coal, railroads, shipbuilding, and chemicals made prosperous such towns as Newcastle upon Tyne, Darlington, Sunderland, Hartlepool, and Middlesbrough in the 19th and early 20th centuries. Attractions that reflect the area's industrial history are the open-air museum at Beamish (northwest of Durham), voted "Best Museum in Europe"; the Railway Museum at Darlington, on the site of the world's first passenger railroad line; and a tiny cottage at Wylam (west of Newcastle) devoted to George Stephenson, who invented the steam locomotive (*see* Off the Beaten Track, *below*).

Essential Information

Important Addresses and Numbers

Tourist Information | **Northumbria Regional Tourist Board,** Aykley Heads, Durham DH1 5UX, tel. 091/384–6905. Open weekdays 9–5.

Tourist information centers, normally open Mon.–Sat. 9:30–5:30, but varying according to the season, include:

Alnwick: The Shambles, Northumberland NE66 1TN, tel. 0665/510665.

Berwick-upon-Tweed: Castlegate Car Park, Northumberland TD15 1JS, tel. 0289/330733.
Darlington: 4 West Row, Co. Durham DL1 5PL, tel. 0325/382698.
Durham: Market Pl., Co. Durham DH1 3NJ, tel. 091/384–3720.
Hexham: Manor Office, Hallgate, Northumberland NE46 1XD, tel. 0434/605225.
Middlesbrough: 51 Corporation Rd., Cleveland TS1 1LT, tel. 0642/243425.
Newcastle upon Tyne: Central Library, Princess Sq., Tyne and Wear NE99 1DX, tel. 091/261–0691, and an office in the train station (open during the summer), tel. 091/230–0030.

Travel Agencies **Thomas Cook:** 24–25 Market Pl., Durham, tel. 091/384–8569; 6 Northumberland St., Newcastle, tel. 091/261–2163.

Car-Rental Agencies **Durham: Ford Rent-a-Car,** Durham City Ford, A1 (M) Carrville, tel. 091/386–1155.
Hexham: Abbey Cars, County Buildings, tel. 0434/602022; **Tyne Mills Motor Company,** Tyne Mills Industrial Estate, tel. 0434/607091.
Newcastle upon Tyne: Avis, 1 George St., tel. 091/232–5283; **Hertz,** Central Station, Neville St., tel. 091/261–1052.

Arriving and Departing

By Car The most direct north–south route is A1, linking London and Edinburgh via Newcastle upon Tyne (274 mi from London; 5–6 hrs) and Berwick-upon-Tweed (338 mi from London; 2 hrs. past Newcastle).

A697, which branches west off A1 north of Morpeth, is a more attractive road north. It leads the motorist right past the 16th-century battlefield of Flodden. A696/A68 northwest out of Newcastle is also a more attractive alternative to A1, but it is an increasingly busy road.

By Train **British Rail** serves the region from London's King's Cross Station (tel. 071/278–2477). Average travel times include 2¾ hours to Darlington, 3 hours to Durham, 3¼ hours to Newcastle, and 3¾ hours to Berwick-upon-Tweed.

By Bus **National Express** (tel. 071/730–0202) serves the region from London's Victoria Coach Station. Average travel times include 4¾ hours to Durham, 5¼ hours to Newcastle, and 8¼ hours to Berwick-upon-Tweed. Connecting services to other parts of the region leave from Newcastle.

Getting Around

By Car A66 and A69 run east–west, providing cross-country access. Many traffic-free country roads provide quiet and scenic, if slower, alternatives to the main routes.

Part of the Cheviot hills, which run along the Northumbrian side of the Scottish border, is now a military firing range. Don't drive here when the warning flags are flying. The military, though, has restored the Roman road, Dere Street, which crosses this region. Try also B6318, which is a well-maintained road that runs alongside Hadrian's Wall on the south side.

By Train From Newcastle, there is local service north to Alnmouth (for Alnwick) and to Corbridge and Hexham on the east–west line to Carlisle. A seven-day "Northeast Regional Rover" ticket (£56) is available for unlimited travel in the area, which includes the scenic Carlisle–Settle line. The one-day "Tees Ranger" ticket (£9) allows unlimited travel in the Teesside area, including the "heritage line" from the town of Bishop Auckland, and the handsome Esk Valley.

For information, call Berwick-upon-Tweed (tel. 0289/306771), Darlington (tel. 091/232–6262), Hexham (tel. 091/232–6262), and Newcastle upon Tyne (tel. 091/232–6262).

By Bus **The United Bus Company** (tel. 0325/465252) in Darlington and **Northumbria Motor Services** (tel. 091/232–4211) in Newcastle offer reasonable one-day "Explorer" tickets for unlimited local travel. For information on the area's fairly limited bus service, pick up a Northumberland public transport guide (£1) from a local tourist office.

Guided Tours **The Northumbria Regional Tourist Board** (tel. 091/384–6905) has a register of professional guides.

Escorted Tours Ltd. (tel. 091/536–3493) runs day and half-day tours of Northumbria by luxury minibus; itineraries vary. Based near Sunderland, the company picks you up at your hotel in Durham or Newcastle.

Further Afield (tel. 06977/47358) offers group walking tours of Northumbria.

Holiday with a Knight (tel. 0287/632510) is run by Shirley Knight, a guide specializing in general tours of northern England, as well as theme tours based on history, literature, and ghosts and legends.

Northumbria Experience (tel. 091/374–3454) has specialized in Northeast tours for 25 years.

Exploring the Northeast

This exploration of the Northeast begins in the cathedral city of Durham, which has dominated the region for centuries. From Durham, Tour 1 continues along Weardale to a lead-mining center, a folk museum, and a massive waterfall at High Force. The ruins of Barnard Castle and the riches of the Bowes Museum come next, followed by Raby Castle and the large industrial towns of Darlington and Middlesbrough. The tour then takes in the Beamish Open-Air Museum before finishing at Newcastle upon Tyne, the region's main city.

Tour 2 opens in Hexham, with its medieval abbey, then explores the fascinating archaeology of Hadrian's Wall. The huge lake at Kielder Water and the vast man-made Forest of Kielder nearby, along with surrounding areas, close this tour.

The coast, from ancient Alnwick north to Berwick-upon-Tweed, is explored in Tour 3, which includes a series of stunning castles and offshore islands, especially the Farne Islands and Holy Island, also known as Lindisfarne.

Highlights for First-time Visitors

Alnwick Castle: Tour 3
Beamish Open-Air Museum: Tour 1
Bowes Museum: Tour 1
Darlington Railway Centre and Museum: Tour 1
Durham Cathedral: Tour 1
Hexham Abbey: Tour 2

High Force Waterfall: Tour 1
Housesteads Roman Fort: Tour 2
Lindisfarne: Tour 3
Washington Old Hall: Tour 1

Tour 1: Durham to Newcastle

Numbers in the margin correspond to points of interest on the Northeast and Durham maps.

① The cathedral and castle of the city of **Durham,** seat of Durham County, stand high on a wooded peninsula almost entirely encircled by the River Wear (rhymes with "beer"). For centuries these two ancient structures have dominated the city—now a thriving university town, the northeast's equivalent to Oxford or Cambridge—and the surrounding countryside. Durham was once the capital of the Anglo-Saxon kingdom of Northumbria (i.e., the land north of the River Humber, the 40-mile-long estuary that flows into the North Sea) and for a millennium the seat of the powerful prince bishops. The city's glorious past is proudly preserved and protected. Ingenious street plans keep pedestrians and traffic separate, and older buildings have been carefully restored. Recently, the castle and cathedral were jointly designated a World Heritage Site.

② Centrally located on the neat Palace Green, the **Cathedral** is an ideal starting point for a walking tour of Durham. Architectural historians come from all over the world to admire and study the great church's important Norman features, such as the relief work on its massive pillars and the rib vaulting in the roof.

The origins of the cathedral go back to the 10th century. Monks fleeing a devastating Viking raid in the year 875 on Lindisfarne Abbey (on Holy Island) brought the body of St. Cuthbert to this site in 995, and soon the wealth attracted by Cuthbert's shrine paid for the construction of a cathedral. The prestige of the area grew until the Bishop of Durham acquired his title of "prince bishop" and the power to rule in both a political and a religious sense—even to raise armies, mint coins, and appoint judges. The **bishop's throne** in the cathedral is still the loftiest in all medieval Christendom; his miter is the only one to be encircled by a coronet; and his coat of arms is the only one to be crossed with a sword as well as a crosier.

Many visitors take a snapshot of the 12th-century bronze **Sanctuary Knocker,** shaped like the head of a ferocious mythological beast, on the massive northwestern entrance door. By grasping the ring clenched in the animal's mouth, medieval felons could claim sanctuary; cathedral records show that 331 criminals (especially murderers) sought this protection between 1464 and 1524. But the knocker now in place is, in fact, a replica; the original is kept for security in the cathedral **treasury,** along with ancient illuminated manuscripts, St. Cuthbert's coffin, and more church treasure.

The power and the glory of the prince bishop, as manifested in the richly decorated alabaster **tomb of Bishop Hatfield** and the lofty episcopal throne described above, are a marked contrast to the delicately intricate stonework of the **shrine of St. Cuthbert** (behind the high altar) and the simple tomb (in the Galilee Chapel) of the Venerable Bede, the scholar and saint whose body was brought here in 1020.

Many more ornate features would have survived had not the cathedral been used to imprison 4,000 Scottish soldiers after the Battle of Dunbar in 1650. These fierce Protestants went on a rampage,

Cathedral, **2**

Durham Castle, **3**

Durham Light Infantry Museum, **6**

Durham University Oriental Museum, **7**

Framwelgate Bridge, **5**

Prebends Footbridge, **4**

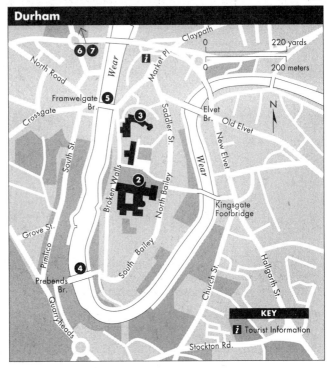

smashing effigies and burning woodwork, although they spared the cathedral's elaborate clock because the thistle emblem of Scotland figures in its design.

The **Chapel of the Nine Altars** has soaring, polished pillars made from a local limestone known as Frosterley marble. Polishing this stone was a painstaking and time-consuming task, so perhaps it is not surprising to find that only the visible surfaces were polished (probe behind the pillars and you can feel the rough, unfinished parts). There is also a restaurant in the undercroft that is open seven days a week. *Tel. 091/386–2367. Admission: cathedral free but donation welcome; treasury £1 adults, 40p children. Cathedral open May–Sept., daily 7:15 AM–8 PM; Oct.–Apr. 7:15–6; treasury open Mon.–Sat. 10–4:30, Sun. 2–4:30; choral evensong service weekdays 5:15, Sun. 3:30.*

❸ On the opposite side of Palace Green is **Durham Castle,** which commands a strategic position overlooking the River Wear. For over 750 years the castle was the home of successive warlike prince bishops. Today the castle houses University College, one of several colleges of the University of Durham, the oldest university in England after Oxford and Cambridge. You can tour the castle at certain times, and, during college vacations, tourist accommodations are available. The great hall, dating from 1284, is still in use, as are the 15th-century kitchens and buttery; the castle crypt serves as a student lounge, while the old servants' hall is now the college library. *Palace Green, tel. 091/374–3800. Admission: £1.50 adults, 90p children. Open July–Sept., daily 10–noon, 2–4:30; Oct.–June (tours only), Mon., Wed., Sat. 2–4:30.*

Time Out **Almshouse Café** serves light lunches and afternoon meals in a historic almshouse on Palace Green, between the cathedral and castle.

❹ From the southern end of Palace Green, a path to **Prebends Footbridge** (which bears an inscription of several lines by Sir Walter Scott) leads across the river and north along South Street. Recross **❺** the River Wear at **Framwelgate Bridge,** and go into Market Place. From here, Saddler Street and South Bailey lead back to the cathedral by Dun Cow Lane. Many of the elegant town houses on these streets are now departments of the university. At every turn there are glimpses of river, castle, cathedral, and town. Durham Regatta, held on the river every year in mid-June, is the oldest rowing event in Britain and attracts teams in all classes from the entire country.

Time Out **Shakespeare Inn** (Saddler St.) is a traditional half-timbered pub serving bar meals in the historic quarter.

❻ The **Durham Light Infantry Museum** at Aykley Heads (½ mi northwest of the city center on A691) is devoted to the history of the county regiment, exhibiting uniforms, weapons, and regalia alongside mementos of British campaigns in India, Iran, the Crimea, and Africa. On the second floor the arts center offers a changing program of events throughout the year. Outdoor events, such as brass-band concerts and military vehicle rallies, take place in the landscaped grounds. *Tel. 091/384–2214. Admission: 75p adults, 35p children and senior citizens, free on Fri. Open Tues.–Sat. 10–4:30, Sun. 2–4:30.*

❼ The **Durham University Oriental Museum** is devoted solely to Oriental art and crafts. Collections cover all parts of the East, showing everything from tiny, meticulously carved jade and ivory ornaments to full-size representations of Buddha, a Chinese portable bedroom, and an Egyptian mummy. *Elvet Hill, off South Rd. (A1050), tel. 091/374–2911. Admission: £1 adults, 50p children and senior citizens. Open weekdays 9:30–1, 2–5, weekends 2–5; closed 10 days at Christmas.*

Take A690 southwest about 4 miles through the village of **❽** **Brancepeth,** which boasts a flamboyantly restored castle (not open to the public), rows of well-preserved cottages, and a church containing tombs of the Nevilles, one of the most powerful northern families in feudal times. Ten miles farther at Wolsingham, take A689, which follows the river west through Upper Weardale (the **❾** valley of the River Wear). Near the hamlet of **Frosterley,** 3 miles away, the limestone known as Frosterley marble was once quarried; this beautifully etched marble with fossil patterns is shown to particularly good effect in Durham cathedral.

Another 10 miles west, at the head of the dale, a wild, high, remote **❿** place, is the open-air **Killhope Lead Mining Centre,** where a restored 34-foot-high waterwheel looms over the site. The visitor center incorporates working models, push-button audiovisual shows, and displays of minerals in portraying the story of the local lead mines and the harsh lives of the miners and millworkers. You can pan for lead in the stream and operate the primitive machinery once used to separate valuable ore from gravel. *2 mi northwest of Cowshill on A689, tel. 0388/537505. Admission: £2 adults, £1 children and senior citizens. Open Apr.–Oct., daily 10:30–5; Nov., Sun. 10:30–5.*

Retrace your route 3 miles southeast on A689 to the village of **⓫** **Ireshopeburn;** the **Weardale Folk Museum** has been established here in a former parsonage close to a chapel where John Wesley, the founder of Methodism, often preached. One room is set out as an 1870 cottage would have looked, and a collection of crystallized minerals is included in a display on local life and landscape. The caretaker can show you around the adjoining chapel. *Tel. 0388/537417. Admission: 80p adults, 30p children. Open May–July and Sept., Wed., Thurs., Sat 1–5, Sun 1–4; Aug., daily 1–5.*

From the village of St. John's Chapel, about a mile southeast of Ireshopeburn, a moorland road provides an exhilarating drive "over the tops" into the valley of Teesdale, where England's highest wa-

⑫ terfall (72 ft.) can be viewed at **High Force,** just south of B6277. This road leads downstream through the quiet Dales town of Middleton-

⑬ in-Teesdale (3½ mi) to the village of **Romaldkirk** (7½ mi), whose extravagantly proportioned church is known as "the Cathedral of the Dale," and where the stocks for punishing wrongdoers are still on the village green. Two miles farther on, at Cotherstone, a soft, crumbly cheese is made and sold at the village store.

⑭ Continue 3 more miles on your southeast route to **Barnard Castle,** where the substantial ruins of the fortress that gave this market town its name cling to an aerie on a cliff overlooking the river. Inside, you can see parts of the 14th-century Great Hall and the cylindrical, 13th-century tower, built by the castle's original owners, the Anglo-Scottish Balliol family. *Tel. 0833/38212. Admission: £1.10 adults, 55p children, 85p senior citizens. Open Apr.–Sept., daily 10–6; Oct.–Mar., Tues.–Sun. 10–1 and 2–4.*

In the little town, the unusual butter-market hall, surmounted by a fire alarm bell, marks the junction of the streets Thorngate, Newgate, and Market Place, which are lined with stores, pubs, and cafés. In 1838 Charles Dickens stayed at the **King's Head Inn** here while researching his novel *Nicholas Nickleby,* which dealt with the abuse of children in local boarding schools. The local tourist office has a *Dickens Drive* leaflet of the places he visited in the area. The main attraction is **Bowes Museum,** a vast French-inspired chateau built between 1869 and 1885 to house an art collection that includes paintings by Canaletto and Boucher; Meissen figurines; furnished period rooms; and Britain's largest collection of Spanish paintings, among them some fine works by El Greco. There's also a splendid clock in the form of a celestial globe, but most unusual of all, perhaps, is the 18th-century silver swan that Mark Twain described in *Innocents Abroad.* Once every day an attendant ceremoniously activates the mechanism that enables the swan to gracefully catch and swallow a fish to the accompaniment of a haunting tune. *Follow signs from Barnard Castle town center, tel. 0833/690606. Admission: £2.30 adults, £1.30 children and senior citizens. Open Mon.– Sat. 10–5:30, Sun. 2–5; closed Christmas week, New Year's.*

Time Out The **Market Place Teashop** (29 Market Pl.) is an early 18th-century house, with low beams and flagstone floors. It serves excellent hot lunches, the emphasis very much on no-nonsense English fare, with steak and kidney pudding or leek au gratin, as well as cakes and scones at teatime.

⑮ In the village of **Bowes,** 4 miles southwest of Barnard Castle on A67, the house on which Dickens modeled *Nicholas Nickleby*'s Dotheboys Hall can still be seen, although it's not open to the public. A notoriously cruel boarding school once occupied the last building in the main street, west of the village. The courtyard pump described in the novel is still there.

From Barnard Castle, A688 leads 6 miles northeast to Staindrop and **Raby Castle,** home of the 11th Baron Barnard. Set in 200 acres of landscaped deer park, this castle displays luxuriously furnished rooms crammed with treasures, in addition to well-preserved medieval kitchens, with original Victorian copperware and other domestic equipment. The chapel was built in the 1360s and is still consecrated. Stone arcades display five full-length portraits of Raby personages, including Richard III's mother, who died here. One of the castle estate surveyors was Jeremiah Dixon, who in the 1760s helped survey the Mason-Dixon line marking the boundary between Maryland and Pennsylvania. *1 mi north of Staindrop, tel. 0833/ 60202. Admission: £3 adults, £1.30 children, £2.25 senior citizens; park, gardens, and carriage collection only £1 adults, 75p children and senior citizens. Open Apr.–June, Wed., Sun. 1–5 (castle), 11– 5:30 (park and gardens); July–Sept., Sun.–Fri. 1–5 (castle), 11– 5:30 (park and gardens).*

From Raby Castle, continue about 7 miles northeast on A688 to the town of **Bishop Auckland,** where the prince bishops of Durham had their official residence in **Auckland Castle.** This grand episcopal palace dates mainly from the 16th century, though the limestone and marble chapel, with its dazzling stained-glass windows, was built in 1665 from the ruins of a 12th-century banqueting hall. The unusual 18th-century "deerhouse" of adjoining Bishops Park testifies to at least one of the bishops' extracurricular interests. The castle itself offers architectural styles ranging from the medieval to the neo-Gothic. *Off Market Pl., tel. 0388/601627. Admission: £1.50 adults, 65p children and senior citizens. Open mid-May–Sept., Tues. 10– 12:30, Wed., Thurs., Sun. 2–5; also Sat. in Aug. 2–5; chapel only Thurs. 10–noon.*

To travel southeast from Bishop Auckland on A6072 is to move from the medieval world into the 19th-century industrial world. Ten miles away the town of **Darlington** (on A68 east of A1[M]) expanded quickly with the success of the railroads in the 1830s. That expansion brought not only prosperity but fame, for here, on the Stockton–Darlington route, the world's first steam passenger railroad (the trains traveled at 15 mph) was established by George Stephenson in 1825. The **Darlington Railway Centre and Museum** is housed in one of his original railroad stations, built in 1842. You can inspect historic engines, including Stephenson's *Locomotion I,* as well as photographs, documents, and models. *North Road Station, tel. 0325/ 460532. Admission: £1.60 adults, 75p children, £1.10 senior citizens. Open daily 9:30–5; closed Christmas, New Year's.*

About 12 miles farther east, toward the mouth of the River Tees, lies the industrial town of **Middlesbrough.** In 1802, a mere dozen people lived here, but the discovery of iron ore spawned a boom town, with steel mills and later, chemical industries. The town's unusual Transporter Bridge built in 1911 is the largest of its kind in the world, a vast structure like a giant's Erector-set model, whose gantry system still takes 12 cable cars, holding 200 passengers each, across the river every 20 minutes. A special viewing platform stands on the south bank. Upstream you'll find Newport Bridge, the world's largest lift span bridge, another remarkable sight. *Tel. 0642/247563. Crossing time, 2 minutes. Fare: 25p pedestrians, 57p cars. Open Mon.–Sat. 5 AM–11 PM, Sun. 2–11.*

Middlesbrough's more conventional attraction is the **Captain Cook Birthplace Museum** in the leafy suburb of Marton. Here the life and times of the 18th-century circumnavigator and explorer are vividly depicted, including his remarkable voyages to Australia, New Zealand, Canada, Antarctica, and Hawaii, where he was murdered. A conservatory near the museum houses many of the exotic plants Cook discovered during his travels. *Stewart Park, Marton, off A174, south of city center, tel. 0642/311211. Admission: £1.20 adults, 60p children and senior citizens. Open Oct.–Apr., Tues.– Sun. 9–3:30; May–Sept., Tues.–Sun. 10–4:45.*

㉟ From Middlesbrough, it's less than 20 miles on A177 back to Durham. About 12 miles north of the city, near the town of **Washington,** careful navigation will take you to **Washington Old Hall,** the ancestral home of the first U.S. president. His direct forebears lived here between 1183 and 1288; other members of the family continued to live in the house until 1613, when the present property was rebuilt. Now owned by the National Trust, the mansion retains a decidedly Jacobean (17th-century) appearance. There are special celebrations on the Fourth of July. *From A1(M), 5 mi west of Sunderland, follow signs to Washington New Town, District 4, and then on to Washington Village. Tel. 091/416–6879. Admission: £2 adults, 90p children. Open Apr.–Oct., Sat.–Thurs. and Good Friday 11–5 (last admission 4:30).*

㉑ A few miles southwest of Washington in the town of **Beamish** is the **Beamish Open-Air Museum.** Set aside at least half a day to fully enjoy all the facilities on the 260-acre site. A streetcar will take you across a reconstructed 1920s High Street, including a dentist's operating room, a pub, and a grocery. In the coal miner's cottage, you will be offered "stotty cake" (unleavened bread) hot from the oven and thickly buttered. A stableman will talk to you about the Clydesdale workhorses in his care, once used to draw brewery wagons. On the farm you can see such local breeds as Durham Shorthorn cattle and Cheviot sheep. Other attractions include a railroad station, a coal mine, and a transportation collection. The large gift store specializes in period souvenirs and locally made crafts. *Off A693, between Chester-le-Street and Stanley, tel. 0207/231811. Admission: £7 adults, mid-July–Sept., £6 in winter; £4 children and senior citizens, mid.-July–Sept., £2.50 in winter. Open Nov.–mid-Mar., Tues.–Sun. 10–5; Easter–Oct., daily 10–5.*

Time Out At the entrance to the museum a traditional-style inn, **The Shepherd and Shepherdess,** serves hot and cold bar meals and afternoon teas (light meals). Stop at least to admire the inn sign. It's a good idea to grab refreshments here and avoid the lines inside the museum.

㉒ From Beamish, head east along A693 and then north on A167 for the short run into **Newcastle upon Tyne,** where this tour ends. The main city of the Northeast, Newcastle (as it's more commonly known) still manages to impress with its sweeping, central neoclassical streets, despite the decay wrought by economic decline—a common late-20th-century problem in this part of the country. Overlooking the Tyne river, the remains of the **Norman castle** remind visitors of the city's earlier status as a defensive stronghold. This was the "new castle," originally built in 1080, that gave the city its name. *St. Nicholas St., tel. 091/232–7938. Admission: £1. Open Apr.–Sept., daily 9:30–5:30; Oct.–Mar., 9:30–4:30.*

To the north of the city center, the university buildings house Newcastle's best museums. Here you'll find a **Museum of Antiquities,** showing finds from Hadrian's Wall—a useful stop before undertaking Tour 2—as well as the **Hatton Gallery** of contemporary European art and the interesting **Greek Museum,** containing ancient arms, ceramics, and terra-cotta pieces. *The University, tel. 091/*

222–7844 or 091/222–6000. Admission free. Museum of Antiquities open Mon.–Sat. 10–5; Hatton Gallery open Mon.–Fri. 10–5:30; Greek Museum open Mon.–Fri. 9:30–4:30.

Tour 2: Hexham and Hadrian's Wall

㉓ Best-known as the gateway to Hadrian's Wall country, the historic market town of **Hexham,** on A69 about 21 miles west of Newcastle, is well worth a visit for its own sake.

The best day to visit is Tuesday, when the weekly market, dating back to 1239, is held in Market Place. In 1761, the marketplace was the site of a massacre of protesting lead miners by the North Yorkshire Militia, henceforth known as the Hexham Butchers. The town's livestock market, the third largest in the country, is also held on Tuesday when the air is thick with the noise of the animals and the buyers and sellers.

From Market Place, you can enter ancient **Hexham Abbey,** which forms one side of the square. Inside, climb the 35 worn stone "night stairs," which once led from the main part of the abbey to the canon's dormitory, to overlook this tranquil, peaceful place of Christian worship for over 1,300 years. Most of the present building dates from the 12th century, and much of the stone was taken from the Roman fort at Corstopitum a few miles northeast. Near the foot of the stairs, a Roman tombstone set into the wall records the death of one Flavinus, a 25-year-old standardbearer, shown on horseback above a crouched Briton armed with a dagger. Death is also starkly depicted on the unusual 15th-century altar screen, which is ornamented with skeletons. Fugitives could claim sanctuary by sitting on the 8th-century stone throne called both the Frith Stool and St. Wilfrid's Chair, after the abbey's founder. *Beaumont St., tel. 0434/ 602031. Admission free. Open May–Sept., daily 9–7; Oct.–Apr., daily 9–5. No tours during services.*

Upon leaving the abbey, you can either stroll through the gardens and parkland opposite or explore the shops around Market Place. From the bowling green there is a particularly fine view of the abbey. Paths lead to the cheerful-looking bandstand and on to **Queens Hall,** built in the style of a French chateau and now incorporating a library, a 400-seat theater, an arts center, and exhibition galleries. On display is the Tynedale Tapestry (8 by 14 ft.), made in the early 1980s by more than 300 people working from a loom on a scaffold. The tapestry illustrates the theme of "theater," with the bright, traditional figures of Harlequin, Columbine, and Pantaloon. *Beaumont St., tel. 0434/607272. Admission free. Open Mon.–Sat. 9 AM– 11 PM.*

Continuing away from the abbey and past Queens Hall, turn left down Battle Hill to Priestpopple, and turn down Fore Street, a thronged, traffic-free shopping area that leads back into Market Place. On the side of Market Place opposite the abbey an exhibition gallery now occupies the ground floor of the Moot Hall in which the archbishop's court was held. A little way beyond, toward the main parking lot, the Manor Office, built as a jail in 1330, now houses the Information Center.

Manor Office also hosts the **Border History Museum.** Photographs, models, drawings, a reconstructed blacksmith's shop, a Border house interior, armor, and weapons help tell the story of the "Middle March"—the medieval administrative area governed by a warden and centered on Hexham. *The Old Gaol, Hallgate, tel. 0434/604011,*

ext. 235. Admission: £1 adults, 50p children and senior citizens.
Open late Mar.–Oct., daily 10–4.

Time Out **Mrs. Miggin's Coffee Shop** (St. Mary's Wynd, off Beaumont St.)
serves light refreshments and homemade cakes on pine tables, or at
a sofa where you can read magazines and newspapers.

Hexham is the best base from which to explore **Hadrian's Wall,** recently designated a World Heritage Site. Begun after the Roman
emperor Hadrian's visit in AD 121 following repeated barbarian in-
vasions from Scotland, the wall spanned 73 miles from Wallsend
("Wall's End") just north of Newcastle, in the east, to Bowness-on-
Solway beyond Carlisle, in the west. Each mile was reinforced by a
"milecastle," or small fort, and each third of a mile by a turret. In
addition, at strategic points, large garrison forts were built behind
the wall. This formidable line of fortifications marked the northern
border of the Roman Empire, which stretched eastward for 2,500
miles to what is now Iraq.

Although a path can be followed along the entire wall, this is rugged
country, unsuited to the inexperienced hiker. Most trekkers here
organize their routes around the various excellent visitor centers,
which are near the best-preserved sections of the wall or in the area
of milecastles, turrets, or excavations. Ten miles of wall altogether
are standing today.

One of the best ways to approach Hadrian's Wall is to begin with the
Roman Army Museum at the garrison fort of Carvoran, near the village of **Greenhead** (at the junction of A69 and B6318, about 18 mi
west of Hexham) and work your way east. At the museum, full-size
models and excavations bring to life this remote outpost of empire;
you can even inspect authentic Roman graffiti on the walls of an excavated barracks. The gift store stocks, among other unusual items,
Roman rulers (1 foot = 11.6 inches) and Roman cookbooks. Opposite
the museum, at Walltown Crags on the Pennine Way (a long-distance
hiking route), are 400 yards of the best-preserved section of the
wall. *Tel. 06977/47485. Admission: £2.10 adults, £1.10 children,*
£1.60 senior citizens. Open Feb., Nov., weekends 10–4; Mar., daily
10–4:30; Oct., daily 10–5; Apr., Sept., daily 10–5:30; May–June,
daily 10–6; July–Aug., daily 10–6:30.

Time Out On B6318, 3½ miles east of Greenhead, the **Milecastle Inn** serves excellent lunches in either the bar or the attached restaurant. It's a
stone inn on a windswept stretch of road, and specialties include
homemade beef and venison or wild boar and duckling pies.

From the museum, take B6318 toward Hexham; it follows much of
the length of the wall, with roadside signs indicating paths to reach
major sites. About 8 miles to the east, you'll pass the great garrison
fort of **Vindolanda,** where there are the remains of eight successive
Roman forts and civilian settlements. Excavations are always going
on here, and a section of the wall has been reconstructed. Recorded
information interprets the site, while the museum contains leather,
wood, glass, and pottery exhibits. There's even a reconstructed Roman kitchen. *Near Bardon Mill, tel. 0434/344277. Admission:*
grounds only, £1.50 adults, 90p children, £1.15 senior citizens;
grounds and museum, £3 adults, £1.75 children, £2.25 senior citi-
zens. Grounds open daily except Christmas. Museum open mid-
Feb.–Oct. 10–5; Apr.–Sept. 10–5:30; May–June 10–6; July–Aug.
10–6:30; Nov. and early Feb., Sat. and Sun. 10–4 (last admission ½
hr. before closing).

26 If you have time to visit only one Hadrian's Wall site, **Housesteads Roman Fort,** just a few miles farther east along B6318, is your best bet. It offers an interpretive center, views of long sections of the wall, the excavated 5-acre fort itself, and a museum. It's a steep, 10-minute walk up from the parking lot by B6318 to the site, but it's worth the effort, especially for the view of the wall disappearing over hills and crags into the distance. The excavations reveal granaries, gateways, barracks, and the commandant's house. There are also altars, inscribed stones, and models. *3 mi northeast of Bardon Mill, tel. 0434/344363. Admission: £2 adults, £1 children, £1.50 senior citizens. Open Apr.–Sept., daily 10–6; Oct.–Mar., Tues.–Sun. 10–4.*

For a garrison fort with equal, if different, appeal, continue east along B6318 toward Hexham; just southwest of Chollerford is **27** **Chesters Roman Fort,** in a wooded valley on the banks of the North Tyne River. This fort ("Cilurnum") protected the point where the wall crossed the river; you approach it directly from the parking lot, and, while the site cannot compete with Housesteads in terms of setting, there is a fascinating collection here of Roman artifacts, including statues of river and water gods, altars, milestones, iron tools, weapons, and handcuffs. The military bathhouse near the river is the best-preserved example in Britain. Drawings and diagrams provide an idea of what the fort looked like originally; its present, mellowed appearance gives little sense of the Romans' brightly painted pillars, walls, and altars. *½ mi southwest of Chollerford (on B6318), tel. 0434/681379. Admission same as for Housesteads. Open Apr.–Sept., daily 10–6; Oct–Mar., daily 10–4.*

Take A6079 southeast from Chesters Fort and head 7 miles toward Corbridge for the remains of **Corstopitum,** a Roman fort occupied **28** longer than any other on the wall; in fact, it predates the wall by 40 years. Strategically positioned at the junction of the east/west and north/south Roman routes—Stanegate ran west to Carlisle, Dere Street led north to Scotland and south to London—the fort now contains a museum rich in artifacts. The Corbridge Lion sculpture probably decorated an important tomb at one time; it later graced a fountain. A temple frieze depicts Castor and Pollux, the god Jupiter's twin sons, and there is an altar dedicated to their father as well. *On a back road ½ mi northwest of Corbridge, tel. 0434/632349. Admission and hours same as for Chesters Fort.*

29 **Corbridge** itself is a small town of honey-colored stone houses and riverside walks, a prosperous-looking place with an abundance of welcoming pubs and attractive shops. In the churchyard of St. Andrew's Church by Market Place is the Vicar's Pele. Nearly 700 years old, this fortified tower was a refuge from Scottish raiders and was built from stones taken from Corstopitum.

Time Out The **Wheatsheaf** (Watling St.), once a farmhouse, is a friendly pub, with stone figures, possibly Roman, in the stable yard. Its great bar food is reasonably priced.

After exploring Hadrian's Wall, you can drive into the rugged hills to the north, which the Romans must have scanned anxiously from their watchtowers (from Corbridge, take A68 and B6318 back to Chollerford; from there, drive 10 miles on B6320 to a minor road picked up at Bellingham, and drive another 10 miles west). On the western edge of Northumberland National Park, only 3 miles from **30** the Scottish border, lies **Kielder Water,** northern Europe's largest man-made lake, surrounded by Europe's largest planted forest.

This modern reservoir has become an established attraction since it was completed in 1982, and it actually encourages visitors, offering facilities for such aquatic sports as waterskiing. A cruise service (tel. 0434/240436 or 0434/220423) operates from May to September from Tower Knowe Visitor Centre. Fishing is popular, and the upper part of the lake, designated a conservation area, attracts many bird-watchers.

The **Tower Knowe Visitor Centre** (tel. 0434/240398), at the southeast corner of the lake (approaching it from Bellingham), is a spring-board from which to enjoy and explore not only the lake area but also the vast **Forest of Kielder.** Exhibitions and films illustrate the region's wildlife and natural history, and guided forest walks are offered in the summer. A 12-mile toll road heads north of the lake
31 through the forest, starting at **Kielder Castle** at the lake's northwest corner, formerly a shooting lodge belonging to the duke of Northumberland and now a Forestry Commission visitor center. After about 10 miles, the toll road rejoins A68 south of Carter Bar close to the Scottish border.

32 **Wallington House,** a striking 17th-century mansion with Victorian decoration, can be visited at Cambo, 15 miles northeast of Hexham. Take A6079 north from Hexham through Chollerford, cross A68, and follow B6342 and the highway signs marked Wallington. This cross-country approach shows Wallington House, in the midst of an extensive, sparsely populated agricultural region, to its best advantage. Stone heads of beasts glare at passing drivers from the grounds in front of the hall. In addition to the house, with its fine plasterwork, furniture, porcelain, and dollhouse collection, the walled, terraced garden is a major attraction. Striking murals depict scenes from Northumbria's history, including the death of the Venerable Bede (AD 673–735), England's scholar-saint; incidents from the life of St. Cuthbert; and the building of Hadrian's Wall. During the summer, open-air events are held in the gardens and grounds (there are 100 acres of woodlands and lakes), including recitals, productions of Shakespeare, and concerts. *Tel. 067074/283. Admission: £4.40 adults, £2.20 children; walled garden only £2.20 adults, £1.10 children. Hall open Apr.–Oct., Wed.–Mon. 1–5:30; walled garden open Apr.–Sept., daily 10:30–7; Oct., daily 10–6; Nov.–Mar., daily 10:30–4.*

Tour 3: The Coast from Alnwick to Berwick

33 **Alnwick** (pronounced "Ann-ick"), 30 miles north of Newcastle on route A1 to Berwick, is a good base from which to explore the dramatic coast and countryside of northern Northumberland. Once a county seat, the town is dominated by its vast castle, but there is plenty more to see. Start at the cobbled Market Place, where a weekly open-air market (every Saturday) has been held for over 800 years (*see* Shopping, *below*); beginning on the last Sunday in June, this site is also host to the annual week-long Alnwick Fair, a festival noteworthy for the enthusiastic participation of a colorfully decked-out local populace in medieval costume. On Shrove Tuesday (Mardi Gras), a traditionally boisterous game of soccer is played in the streets. Note the market cross, built on the base of an older cross; the town crier once made his proclamations from here. Along the unusually named Bondgate Within Street, the White Swan Hotel has a unique claim to fame: Its large, paneled lounge on the ground floor was removed intact from the *Olympic*, sister ship of the *Titanic*. Here you can dine in an alcove and imagine you are at sea in a pre-World War I liner (*see* Dining and Lodging, *below*).

Another town curiosity is the window of **Olde Cross Inn** on Narrowgate Street, at the opposite end of Bondgate Within. The grimy bottles in the window have been left untouched for over 150 years. Why? A 19th-century proprietor fell down dead while arranging the window display, and all subsequent proprietors have refused to touch the bottles, believing them to carry a curse. Not surprisingly, the pub has been nicknamed "The Dirty Bottles."

Alnwick Castle, on the edge of the town center just above the junction of Narrowgate and Bailiffgate, is still the home of the dukes of Northumberland, whose family (the Percys) dominated the northeast for centuries. Everything about this castle is on a grand scale, earning it the well-justified epithet "the Windsor of the North." The entrance, at the side of the barbican (gate tower) doorway, is surmounted by a lion rampant (rearing on hind legs), the heraldic emblem of the dukes of Northumberland; on the dizzy heights of the battlements, remarkably realistic life-size statues stand guard. In contrast with the cold, formidable exterior, the inside of the building has all the opulence of the palatial home it still is: although you are only permitted to see six of more than 150 rooms, among the treasures on show are a galleried library, Meissen dinner services, ebony cabinets mounted on gilded wood, tables inlaid with intricate patterns, niches with larger-than-life-size marble statues, and Venetian-mosaic floors. The terrace overlooks the river and the parkland laid out by Capability Brown (an 18th-century, Northumberland-born landscape architect)—disappointingly, vast tracts of the gardens are closed to the public. *Tel. 0665/510777. Admission: £3 adults, £2 children, £2.60 senior citizens. Open Apr. 28–Oct. 4, daily 11–5; closed Sat. in May and Sept.*

34 About 2½ miles north on B1340, take a side road east to the tiny fishing village of **Craster,** whose harbor smokehouses are known for that great English breakfast delicacy, kippers: herring salted and smoked over smoldering oak shavings. You can visit the tar-blackened smokehouses, eat your fill of fresh and traditionally smoked fish, and even have smoked salmon mailed home to your friends.

Time Out Opposite the smokehouse near the harbor, you can savor Craster kippers for lunch or afternoon tea at **Craster Fish Restaurant** (open Easter–Sept.). Or stop in at the **Jolly Fisherman** pub, opposite, where you can feast on its famous fresh crab sandwiches while enjoying the views of crashing waves from the pub's splendid picture window.

35 Just north of Craster, the romantic ruins of **Dunstanburgh Castle** stand on a cliff 100 feet above the shore. Built in 1316 by the earl of Lancaster as a defense against the Scots, and later enlarged by John of Gaunt (the powerful duke of Lancaster who virtually ruled England in the late 14th century), the castle is known to many from the popular paintings by 19th-century artist J.M.W. Turner, and more recently from scenes in the 1990 film version of *Hamlet* with Mel Gibson. You can approach it by a bracingly windy, mile-long path along the coast from Craster village. *Tel. 0665/576231. Admission: £1.20 adults, 60p children, 90p senior citizens. Open Apr.–Sept., daily 10–6; Oct.–Mar., Tues.–Sun. 10–4; closed Christmas.*

Farther north are several sandy bays, such as those at **High Newton-by-the-Sea** (3 mi from the castle) and **Beadnell** (4 mi), good for swimming and other water sports. From **Seahouses** (6 mi), boat trips visit **36** the **Farne Islands** (owned by the National Trust), which host impressive colonies of seabirds and gray seals; you can land on two of the islands, Inner Farne and Staple Island. Inner Farne, where St. Cuthbert, the great abbot of Lindisfarne, died in AD 687, features a tiny chapel dedicated to his memory. *2½-hr. boat trips to the islands sail from Seahouses 7 days a week, Apr.–Sept. weather permitting; tel. 0665/720308, 720388, 721144, 720825. Fares: £4 adults, £3 children. Landing fees vary and are payable to the wardens. Access is restricted during the seal breeding season (May 15–July 15). Information Easter–Oct. from Seahouses Tourist Information Centre, tel. 0665/720884.*

㊲ On a great crag north of Seahouses is **Bamburgh Castle,** whose ramparts offer sweeping views of Lindisfarne (Holy Island), the Farne Islands, the stormy coastline, and the Cheviot hills inland. Much of the castle has been restored—although the great Norman keep (central tower) remains intact—and the present Lady Armstrong lives there now. Exhibits include collections of armor, porcelain, jade, furniture, and paintings. There are apartments for rent inside the castle, one of the most romantic addresses in the world for those who can afford it. The castle is especially stunning when floodlit at night, dominating the view for miles. *Bamburgh, 3 mi north of Seahouses, tel. 0668/214208. Admission: £2.50 adults, £1.20 children, £2.10 senior citizens. Open Apr.–June, Sept., daily 1–5; July, Aug., daily noon–6; Oct., daily 1–4:30.*

Take a walk along the beach below the castle, a magnificent sweep of sand backed by high dunes. Then stroll into the village of Bamburgh, behind the castle, where the **Grace Darling Museum** commemorates a local heroine as well as the Royal National Lifeboat Institute, an organization of unpaid volunteers who keep watch at the rescue stations on Britain's coasts. Grace Darling became a folk heroine in 1838, when she and her father rowed out to save the lives of nine shipwrecked sailors from the SS *Forfarshire*. The museum displays the rowboat (a Northumbrian fishing "coble") Darling used in the rescue, as well as letters and contemporary accounts of her life. In the wind-battered churchyard opposite you can see her tomb, covered by a resplendent Gothic canopy. *Radcliffe Rd., opposite church near village center. Admission: 50p. Open Apr.–Oct., Mon.–Sat. 11–7, Sun., 2–6.*

㊳ Continue northward around 8 miles along the coast to **Holy Island** (or **Lindisfarne**), which is reached from the mainland by a long drive along a causeway. As the causeway is flooded at high tide, you *must* check locally to find out when crossing is safe. The times, which change every day, are displayed at the causeway, and printed in local newspapers. As traffic can be heavy, allow at least a half hour for your return trip.

The religious history of the island dates from the very origins of Christianity in England, for St. Aidan established a monastery here in AD 635. Under its greatest abbot, the sainted Cuthbert, Lindisfarne became one of the foremost centers of learning in Christendom. But in the year 875, Vikings destroyed the Lindisfarne community; only a few monks managed to escape, carrying with them Cuthbert's bones, which they finally reburied in Durham (*see* Tour 1, *above*). It was reestablished in the 11th century by monks from Durham, and today the Norman ruins of the **Lindisfarne Priory** remain both impressive and beautiful. *Tel. 0289/89200. Admission: £2.20 adults, £1.10 children, £1.65 senior citizens. Open Apr.–Sept., daily 10–6; Oct.–Mar. 10–4; closed Christmas, New Year's.*

From the small village that abuts the priory, a pretty walk leads around the curving rocky coast to **Lindisfarne Castle,** which, seen from a distance, appears to grow out of the rocky pinnacle on which it was built 400 years ago. In 1903, architect Sir Edwin Lutyens sensitively converted the castle into a private home that retains the original's ancient features. Across several fields from the castle is a walled garden, surprisingly sheltered from the storms and winds; its 16th-century plan was discovered in, of all places, California, and the garden has since been replanted, providing again a colorful summer display. *Holy Island, 6 mi east of A1, north of Bamburgh, tel. 0289/89244. Admission: £3.20 adults, £1.60 children. Open Easter–Sept., Sat.–Thurs. 1–5:30; Oct., Wed. and weekends 1–5:30.*

39 **Berwick-upon-Tweed** lies 10 miles farther up the coast, just within England's border, although historians estimate that it has changed hands between the Scots and the English 14 times. The market on Wednesday and Saturday draws plenty of customers from both sides of the border. The town's 16th-century walls are among the best-preserved in Europe (a path follows the ramparts). The parish church, Holy Trinity, was built during Cromwell's Puritan Commonwealth with stone from the castle.

In Berwick's **Military Barracks,** built between 1717 and 1721, three accommodation wings surround a square, with the decorated gatehouse forming the fourth side. An exhibition called "By Beat of Drum" depicts the life of the common soldier from the 1660s to the 1880s. *The Parade, off Church St. in town center, tel. 0289/304493. Admission: £2.20 adults, £1.10 children, £1.60 senior citizens. Open Apr.–Sept., daily 10–6; Oct.–Mar., Wed.–Sun. 10–4; closed Christmas, New Year's.*

Time Out **The Town House** (Marygate) serves a delicious variety of fresh quiches, pastries, and other snacks. It's a bit tricky to find: Cross Buttermarket under the Guildhall and go through the old jail. The café's proprietors say, "Please persevere to find your way in—it's easy when you know how!"

What to See and Do with Children

Pan for minerals at the **Killhope Lead Mining Centre** (*see* Tour 1, *above*). At **Bowes Museum** you'll find, in addition to the mechanical swan, a collection of 19th-century games, toys, models, dollhouses, etc. Next to the **Captain Cook Birthplace Museum** in Middlesbrough (*see* Tour 1, *above*) is a small children's zoo.

At **Washington Waterfowl Park** 100 acres of ponds, woods, and riverside are home to ducks, geese, swans, and other birds, including such exotic creatures as the Chilean flamingo. *District 15, east of Washington, tel. 091/416–5454. Admission: £3.40 adults, £1.70 children, £2.55 senior citizens. Open Apr.–Oct., daily 9:30–5:30; Nov.–Mar., daily 9:30–4:30; closed Christmas.*

Visit **Hadrian's Wall,** particularly the **Roman Army Museum** and the line of wall and path at **Housesteads** (*see* Tour 2, *above*).

Take a boat trip to the **Farne Islands** (*see* Tour 3, *above*).

Off the Beaten Track

Venerable Bede Monastery Museum and **St. Paul's Church,** in the town of Jarrow, on the River Tyne east of Newcastle, offer substantial monastic ruins, a visitor center-cum-museum, and the church of St. Paul, all reflecting the long tradition of religion and learning that began here in AD 681. A model of the monastery in its days of glory is on display, and the excellent audiovisual program tells its history, quoting an early monk: "Here at Jarrow we are lighting a candle which will spread the light of Christ throughout Northumbria." Still used for regular worship, St. Paul's contains some of the oldest stained glass in Europe and the oldest dedicatory church inscription in Britain (a carved stone inscribed in AD 685). *Church Bank, tel. 091/489–2106. From southern exit traffic circle at South Tyne tunnel, take A185 to South Shields; then follow signs to "St. Paul's Church and Jarrow Hall." Admission: £1 adults, 50p children and senior citizens. Open Apr.–Oct., Tues.–Sat. 10–5:30, Sun. 2–5:30; Nov.–Mar., Tues.–Sat. 11–4:30, Sun. 2:30–5:30. Coffee shop open same times.*

George Stephenson's Birthplace is a tiny, red-roofed stone cottage in Wylam, now a wooded suburb of Newcastle upon Tyne. Here, in 1781, the "Father of the Railroads" was born. One room of the house is open to the public—a modest tribute to an engineer whose invention of the steam locomotive touched every corner of the world. You can park your car in the village by the war memorial, 10 minutes' walk away. *Wylam (8 mi west of Newcastle; 1½ mi south of A69), tel. 0661/853457. Admission: £1 adults, 50p children. Open Apr.–Oct., Thurs., weekends 1–5:30; other times by appointment.*

Chillingham Park (16 mi northwest of Alnwick on B6346, with a right turn just before New Berwick) is famous for its wild cattle. Ruled by a bull "king," they are thought to be descendants of the extinct European bison, a herd of which may have been enclosed when the 600-acre Chillingham estate was walled in over 700 years ago. Remember that these creamy-white cattle with curved, black-tipped horns are dangerous; approach them only under the supervision of an experienced guide. *Estate House, tel. 06685/250. Admission: £2.50 adults, 50p children, £1.50 senior citizens. Open Apr.–Oct., Mon., Wed.–Sat. 10–noon, 2–5, Sun. 2–5.*

Eight miles southwest of Alnwick on B6341 (a mile north of Rothbury) is the National Trust's Victorian mansion of **Cragside,** built between 1864 and 1895 by the first Lord Armstrong, an early electrical engineer. The house was the first to be lit by hydroelectricity, generated by the ingenious Lord Armstrong's system of artificial lakes and underground piping. In the library you can see antique vases adapted for use as electric lamps; staircase banisters are topped with specially designed lights. An energy center, with restored mid-Victorian machinery, including a hydraulic pump and a water turbine, is being established on the grounds; this project has won a Ford European Conservation Award. In June, rhododendrons bloom in the 660-acre park surrounding the mansion; 30 rooms of the house, some with Pre-Raphaelite paintings, are open to the public. *Tel. 0669/20333. Admission: £5.50 adults, £2.75 children; country park only £3.40 adults, £1.70 children. House open Apr.–Oct., Tues.–Sun. 1–5:30; country park and energy center open Easter–Oct., daily 10:30–7 or dusk, whichever is earlier, Nov.–Dec., Tues., weekends 10:30–4.*

Shopping

Some of the local crafts centers act as cooperatives for groups of craftspeople. Two are the **Northumbrian Crafts Centre** (The Chantry, Bridge St., Morpeth, tel. 0670/511217), which also has artists in residence.

Alnwick **Northumbria** (35 Fenkle St.) is chock-full of collectors' items on three floors, including paintings, pottery, ceramics, and figurines.

Narrowgate Pottery (22 Back Narrowgate, tel. 0665/604744) is a small workshop specializing in domestic stoneware pottery, including the distinctive Alnwick "pierced ware."

The **House of Hardy** (tel. 0665/602771), just outside Alnwick (from downtown, take A1 south to just beyond traffic circle on left, clearly marked), is one of Britain's finest stores for country sports, especially fishing. It has a worldwide reputation for handcrafted tackle.

Durham The **University Bookshop** (55 Saddler St., tel. 091/384–2095) offers both general and academic books, with over 25,000 volumes in stock, including secondhand and antiquarian books.

Bramwells Jewellers (24 Elvet Bridge, tel. 091/386–8006) sells jewelry, watches, clocks, silverware, crystal, and enamel boxes. The specialty of the store is a pendant replica of the gold-and-silver cross of St. Cuthbert.

Hexham The **Abbey Gift Shop** (Beaumont St., tel. 0434/603057) provides a good selection of moderately priced gifts, such as commemorative plates and tapes of choir and music recitals.

Abbey Prints (22 Hallgate, tel. 0434/602244) sells a collection of paintings and prints by local artists. It's a good place to look for images of Hadrian's Wall and the surrounding countryside.

The **Northumbrian Country Clothing Design Studio** (Monks House, Woodlands, tel. 0434/604790) produces designer jackets for women from natural tweed, as well as hand-printed jersey cotton clothing with Celtic designs by Sorcha. Call in advance, Monday–Saturday.

Ireshopeburn **Michael and Mary Crompton, Weavers** (Forge Cottage, tel. 0388/537346), create striking tapestries inspired by the changing seasons of Weardale. Also on sale are smaller spun and handwoven fabrics, including rugs, shawls, bags, belts, and made-to-order items.

Markets In Alnwick, the open-air market takes place every Saturday on the cobbled main street. Tuesday market in Hexham's Market Place means crowded stalls set out under the long slate roof of the Shambles; other stalls take their chances with the weather, protected only by their bright awnings.

Sports and the Outdoors

Bicycling This is an area to gladden the heart of any cyclist, offering wide vistas, quiet roads, and magnificently fresh air. Rent bikes from **Weardale Mountain Bikes** (39 Front St., Frosterley, Weardale, Co. Durham DL13 2QP, tel. 0388/528129). Mountain bikes can also be rented from **Kielder Bikes** (Hawkhope Car Park, tel. 0434/220392) at Kielder Water.

Boating In Durham, **Brown's Boat House** (Elvet Bridge, tel. 091/386–3779) rents rowboats and offers short cruises from April to early November.

Fishing The rivers and lakes in the Hadrian's Wall region have brown and rainbow trout, salmon, and other game fish. You'll need an NRA rod licence (£13.25), which is good from January until December and is available from the Hexham tourist information office. The best fishing spots are **Kielder Water,** with 27 miles of shoreline and boat-fishing available (*see* Tour 2, *above*); **Derwent Reservoir** (tel. 0207/55250), 10 miles southeast of Hexham; and **Langley Dam** (tel. 0434/688846), 8 miles west of Hexham. The fishing season at all these places runs from around March to October, and advance booking is advised.

Golf The northeast has a wide range of nine- and 18-hole courses to choose from. One 18-holer is the **Gosforth Park Golf Centre** (Wideopen, Newcastle upon Tyne, tel. 091/236–4480), which also boasts a floodlit, 30-bay driving range and a pitch-and-putt course. There's another at **Hexham Golf Club** (Spital Park, Hexham, tel. 0434/603072), 1 mile west of town on B6531.

Horseback Riding There are several riding schools in the region offering hour-long rides to full-day treks on horseback. For a full list, contact the Hexham tourist information office; advance booking in summer is essential. There's also a 10-mile riding trail at Kielder Water (tel. 0434/220242).

Walking Although all this wide open region offers good walking opportunities, **Northumberland National Park,** in the northwest corner of the area, is probably the best place for serious walkers. The **Pennine Way** (250 mi) begins at Hadrian's Wall and crosses the Cheviots, finishing over the border in Scotland; alternatively experienced hikers might like to follow the long-distance path along **Hadrian's Wall** (73 mi). The **Heritage Way** winds some 69 miles, beginning at Gateshead near Newcastle upon Tyne. For those in search of less strenuous walks, the wide, firm sands of the coast are ideal; try the splendid 3-mile walk from Bamburgh to Seahouses, giving good views over to the Farne Islands.

Water Sports Many quiet, unspoiled beaches may be found on the coast north of Amble (8 mi south of Alnwick); you can swim there in summer. **Northumbria Waters** offers a wide range of water-sports facilities at Kielder Water and 16 other regional reservoirs. *Details from Regent Center, Gosforth, tel. 091/284–3151.*

Dining and Lodging

Dining The Northeast is one of the best areas in England for fresh local produce. Keep an eye out for restaurants that serve game from the Kielder Forest, local lamb from the hillsides, and fish both from the streams threading through the wild valleys and from the fishing fleets along the coast. Don't miss out on the simple fresh seafood sandwiches served in many of the region's local pubs. You might also wish to sample Alnwick Vatted Rum, a blend of Guyanese and Jamaican rum, or Lindisfarne mead, a traditional, highly potent spirit produced on Holy Island, and made of honey vatted with grape juice and mineral water.

Highly recommended restaurants are indicated by a star ★.

Category	Cost*
$$$	over £30
$$	£15–30
$	under £15

per person, including first course, main course, dessert, and VAT; excluding drinks

Lodging The northeast is not an area where the large hotel chains have much of a presence outside the few large cities. Rather, this is a region where you can expect to find country houses converted into welcoming hotels, old coaching inns that still greet guests after 300 years, and cozy bed-and-breakfasts conveniently located near hiking trails. Visitors are often pleasantly surprised at the low prices of accommodations, even at the very top end of the scale.

Highly recommended lodgings are indicated by a star ★.

Category	Cost*
$$$	over £90
$$	£55–£90
$	under £55

All prices are for two people sharing a double room, including service, breakfast, and VAT.

Alnwick
Dining

John Blackmore's. A stone town house, close to the castle, is the place to try some imaginative modern British cooking by owner and chef John Blackmore. Mousses are a house specialty—vegetarians like the fennel mousse with mushrooms and Stilton sauce—while fresh fish and seafood are always popular. *1 Dorothy Foster Ct., Narrowgate, tel. 0665/604465. Reservations advised. Jacket and tie preferred. AE, DC, MC, V. Open Tues.–Sat. evenings only; closed Jan. $$*

Dining and Lodging ★

White Swan Hotel. Standing on the site of the Old Swan Inn on the stagecoach route between Newcastle and Edinburgh, this building was restored by a Victorian architect, Salvin, who also worked on Alnwick Castle. The main lounge, reconstructed from the paneling and furnishings of an ocean liner, is memorable. One of the hotel's assets is its refurbished **Bondgate Restaurant.** The modern but romantic blue-and-pink decor is a relaxing background for a menu largely drawn from classic Northumbrian cooking. Specialties include Kielder game pie, cooked in rich Guinness sauce, and cranachan, a thick cream dessert made with Alnwick rum, raspberries, and oatmeal. *Bondgate Within, NE66 1TD, tel. 0665/602109, fax 0665/510400. 50 rooms with bath. Facilities: restaurant, use of local recreation center and squash club. Restaurant reservations advised, especially in summer; dress: casual. AE, MC, V. $$*

Lodging

Bondgate House Hotel. This is a small, family-run hotel, close to the medieval town gateway. Housed in a 250-year-old building, it's a reasonably priced base for touring the area, and it has parking space for eight cars. *20 Bondgate Without, NE66 1PN, tel. 0665/602025. 8 rooms, 3 with bath. Facilities: restaurant. No credit cards. $*

Bamburgh
Dining and Lodging

Waren House Hotel. Set in 6 acres of woodland situated off the road on a quiet bay between Bamburgh and Holy Island, this Georgian house hotel has tastefully decorated bedrooms each with different styles of decor, from Victorian to Oriental. There are romantic views of Holy Island from the restaurant, which serves fresh local produce—the fish is highly recommended, and there are good vegetarian choices. Although guests are permitted to smoke in the plush, welcoming library, all the bedrooms are nonsmoking, and children are not allowed. *Waren Mill, Belford, NE70 7EE, tel. 0668/ 214581, fax 0668/214484. 7 rooms with bath. Facilities: restaurant, bar, library, tea- and coffee-making appliances. AE, MC, V. $$$*

Lord Crewe Arms. This is a cozy stone-walled inn with oak beams and open fires, in the heart of the village close to Bamburgh Castle, an ideal spot to have lunch while touring the area and its wild coast. The bedrooms are fairly simple, but the food, especially the local seafood, is excellent. *Front St., NE69 7BL, tel. 06684/243. 25 rooms, 21 with bath. Restaurant reservations advised; dress: casual. MC, V. Closed late Oct.–Mar. $–$$*

Berwick-upon-Tweed
Dining

Funnywayt'Mekalivin. This is an idiosyncratic eatery, and with a name like that who could resist? It's in a cottage that was once a craft shop, and the place is still full of interesting bits and pieces. It is not large, and the chef/owner, Elizabeth Middlemiss, produces imaginative dishes like venison casserole, seafood crumble, or carrot and apple soup. *53 West St., tel. 0289/308827. Reservations required. Dress: casual. MC, V. Open Mon.–Fri. lunch and Wed.–Sat. evenings. $$*

Lodging

Turret House. Just outside Berwick, this privately owned guest house stands in 2 acres of grounds. It would make an excellent stopover either on the way to or from Scotland. This is a quiet, elegant hotel, with open-plan bar/dining room/lounge and comfortable bedrooms. *Etal Rd., Tweedmouth TD15 2EG, tel. 0289/330808, fax 0289/330467. 13 rooms, 8 with bath. Facilities: restaurant. AE, DC, MC, V. $$*

Blanchland
Dining and Lodging

Lord Crewe Arms Hotel. A historic hotel that once provided guest accommodations for Blanchland Abbey, this unusual place in the tiny stone village of Blanchland has lots of intriguing medieval and Gothic corners, including a priest's hideout and a vault-roofed crypt with its own bar. One of the bedrooms is said to be haunted by the ghost of a local girl, while the restaurant's decor reinforces an atmosphere of cloistered calm. Specialties drawn from traditional cuisine include game in season (venison, grouse, pheasant). *Off B6306, about 8 mi south of Hexham, DH8 95P, tel. 0434/675251, fax 0434/ 675337. 18 rooms with bath. Facilities: restaurant, bar. Restaurant reservations advised. Dress: casual. AE, DC, MC, V. $$*

Chester-le-Street
Dining and Lodging

Lumley Castle Hotel. This is a real castle, right down to the dungeons, and a hotel experience not to be missed. Superb bedrooms in all sizes (some with four-poster beds and/or Jacuzzis) are combined with up-to-date facilities. There's plenty of space to wander and an appealing library-bar, with over 3,000 books and a log fire, for before-dinner drinks. The **Black Knight Restaurant** features English specialties such as *filet de boeuf* (prime roast beef with Stilton cheese, wrapped in bacon) and Landes duck (duck caramelized and served with pâté de foie gras, mango, and piquant ginger sauce); the restaurant occasionally hosts Elizabethan banquets with traditional food and entertainment. *1 mi east of Chester-le-Street by B1284, DH3 4NX, tel. 091/389–1111, fax 091/387–1437. 66 rooms with bath. Restaurant reservations advised; dress: casual, but no jeans. AE, DC, MC, V. Closed Christmas, New Year's. $$$*

Durham **Royal County Hotel.** This comfortable, attractively redecorated
Dining and Georgian hotel retains many of its historic details. It's the city's top
Lodging establishment, with a convenient downtown location and spacious
rooms, some with four-poster beds. The oak staircase comes from
Loch Leven castle in Scotland, where Mary, Queen of Scots was imprisoned. There is also the luxurious **County Restaurant**, whose specialties include wild boar steaks and seafood paella. *Old Elvet, DH1*
3JN, tel. 091/386–6821, fax 091/386–0704; toll-free reservations in
U.S., tel. 800/444–1545. 150 rooms with bath, 1 room for people with
disabilities. Facilities: restaurant, coffee shop, satellite TV, leisure
center. Restaurant reservations advised; jacket and tie required.
AE, DC, MC, V. Hotel $$$; Restaurant $$

Lodging **The Georgian Town House.** Exactly as the name suggests, this well-
sited hotel, overlooking cathedral and castle, makes the best of its
Georgian exterior and fittings. Some rooms have views of the cathedral; all are comfortable and make a good base for city walks. *10*
Crossgate, DH1 4PS, tel. 091/386–8070. 6 rooms with bath. No cred-
it cards. $

Greenhead **Holmhead Guest House.** This former farmhouse is not only built *on*
Lodging Hadrian's Wall but also *of* it. It has stone arches, exposed beams,
and antique furnishings; there's open countryside in front and a ruined castle almost in the backyard. In addition to "the longest breakfast menu in the world," a set dinner is served (for guests only) at the
farmhouse table in the stone-arched dining room, and ingredients
for all three courses are likely to have been growing in the kitchen
garden only hours before. Specialties include homemade soup,
steak-and-kidney pie, and roast rack of lamb with fresh herbs, and
organic wines are also served. Local guidebooks are on hand, and
Mrs. Pauline Staff is a qualified guide who can give talks and slide
shows on Hadrian's Wall and the area. *Off A69, about 18 mi west of*
Hexham, CA6 7HY, tel. 06977/47402. 4 double rooms with shower.
No smoking in bedrooms or dining rooms. AE, MC, V. Closed
Christmas, New Year's. $

Hexham **The Black House.** This restaurant is housed in converted farm build-
Dining ings, fitted with lots of old furniture and attractive china. The tradi-
★ tional English menu is changed monthly and is always refreshingly
imaginative and wisely limited; puddings are a strong point. *Dipton*
Mill Rd., tel. 0434/604744. Reservations advised. Dress: casual.
MC, V. Open Tues.–Sat. evenings only. $$
Harlequin's Restaurant. Occupying the ground floor of the Queen's
Hall Arts Centre, this light and airy place overlooks the park and
abbey. The dining room is decorated with original modern paint-
ings, and the cheerful staff is busy at lunchtime serving neighbor-
hood workers and shoppers. Local game and fish are the specialties,
but there are also vegetarian and fresh pasta dishes. *Beaumont St.,*
tel. 0434/607230. Dinner reservations advised. Dress: casual. AE,
DC, MC, V. Closed Sun., national holidays. $

Dining and **Langley Castle Hotel.** A genuine 14th-century castle was rescued by
Lodging its American owner and converted into a luxury hotel and restau-
★ rant. Its 7-foot-thick walls are complete with turrets and battle-
ments. All public rooms are grandly furnished, and the bedrooms
have luxurious appointments. The restaurant has an unusual atmos-
phere—although perhaps not for a castle—with exposed beams,
wall tapestries, and a welcoming fire. Specialties include a casserole
of local pheasant with shallots and sultanas, flavored with Bordeaux
and game gravy; and beef Cadwallader, which consists of strips of
beef tossed with shallots and mushrooms in oyster sauce with red

wine and cream. *Langley-on-Tyne (6 mi west of Hexham), NE47 5LU, tel. 0434/688888, fax 0434/684019. 8 rooms with bath. Restaurant reservations required; dress: casual. AE, DC, MC, V. $$–$$$*

County Hotel. The friendly proprietor here is proud of the old-fashioned, homey feel of his establishment, known to local people, who frequent the hotel bar, simply as "the County." Reminders of his former occupation as a pheasant breeder decorate the walls of the public rooms, which are usually crowded with farmers on auction days. Food is served all day in the paneled dining room and in the more informal lounge. High teas (late-afternoon meals) are a specialty (5:30–6:30), and homemade meat pies, pastries, and Northumbrian lamb are often featured on the menu, along with international dishes. *Priestpopple, NE46 1PS, tel. 0434/602030. 10 rooms, 4 with bath. Facilities: restaurant, bar, lounge. Restaurant reservations advised; dress: casual. AE, MC, V. $$*

Longframlington
Dining and Lodging
★

Embleton Hall. The 5 acres of beautiful grounds are reason enough to stay in this stone country mansion, parts of which date back to 1675; its individually furnished rooms are decorated with lovely antiques and original paintings. Another reason to visit is the restaurant, its chintz draperies and cut-glass chandeliers perfect accompaniments to the traditional English dishes, served here. Entrées include braised rabbit in an apricot and port sauce and roast Northumbrian pheasant in rich gravy. *On A697, 10 mi southwest of Alnwick, NE65 8DT, tel. 0665/570249. 10 rooms with bath. Restaurant reservations required; jacket and tie suggested. AE, DC, MC, V. $$–$$$*

Besom Barn. The comfortable bedrooms in this converted farmhouse, all on the ground floor, have direct access to a patio where breakfast is served in good weather. There are moorland views from the picture windows. The **Besom Barn Restaurant** features a woodburning stove in the center of the dining room. Specialties include Besom Pie (pork, venison, and rabbit with Scottish ale). *On A697, ½ mi north of the village, NE65 8EN, tel. 0665/570627. 4 rooms with bath. Restaurant reservations required; dress: casual. AE, DC, MC, V. $$*

Granby Inn. This is a regular pub, with excellent bar food and a restaurant serving great fresh fish dishes and homemade soups. It was a stopping place for 17th-century coaches along Weardale. All the rooms are comfortably furnished and have TV and tea/coffee-making appliances. *High St., NE65 8DP, tel. 0665/570228. 6 rooms, 5 with bath. Facilities: restaurant, bar. MC, V. $$*

Newcastle Upon Tyne
Dining

Courtney's. This converted quayside building offers a popular brasserie menu; standard dishes like Caesar salad are supplemented by daily specials, including seafood and game. It's a relaxed place for lunch, with slick service and an interesting, if brief, wine list. *5–7 The Side, tel. 091/232–5537. Reservations advised. Dress: casual. AE, MC, V. Closed Sat. lunch, Sun., national holidays. $$*

Rothbury
Dining and Lodging

Queen's Head Hotel. The beautifully situated village of Rothbury is a handy base for visiting the extraordinary Cragside mansion. This cheery inn is just 1½ miles away. It offers pleasant, straightforward rooms and a first-floor dining room with a carvery and a vegetarian menu. *Rothbury, Morpeth NE65 7SR, tel. 0669/20470, fax 0830/520530. 9 rooms, 5 with bath. Facilities: restaurant, bar. Restaurant reservations not required; dress: casual. MC, V. $*

South Shields
Dining

Marsden Grotto. Built into a cliff from which there are spectacular views of the sea and the Marsden Rock Bird Sanctuary, this unusually sited restaurant is entered from the clifftop promenade via an elevator that descends into the rock. Lobster and steak are the staples here. *Coast Rd., Marsden, tel. 091/455–2043. Reservations advised. Dress: casual. MC, V. $$*

Wylam
Dining and
Lodging

Laburnum House. This friendly restaurant in a 1716 building has simple decor and a copious blackboard menu. Try the seafood—always a good bet in this area—which comes in many guises, all tasty, or the duck or pheasant. There are also four en-suite bedrooms available. *Main St., tel. 0661/852185. Reservations required. Dress: casual. AE, MC, V. Closed lunch, Sun., Dec. 26, Jan. 1. Restaurant $$–$$$; Hotel $*

The Arts

Northern Arts is the official body that promotes the arts in the Northeast. *9–10 Osborne Terr., Jesmond, Newcastle upon Tyne NE2 1NZ, tel. 091/281–6334.*

Festivals The **Alnwick Fair,** held in June/July, features a costumed re-enactment of a medieval fair, processions, a market, and concerts. *Alnwick Fair, Box 2, Alnwick NE66 1AA, tel. 0665/605004 or 0665/602234.*

Billingham International Folklore Festival is held each year in the third week of August. *Festival Office, Municipal Buildings, Town Center, Billingham (north of Middlesbrough), Cleveland TS23 2LW, tel. 0642/552663.*

Theater The region has several excellent theaters that put on plays and other entertainment throughout the year. Newcastle's **Theatre Royal** (Grey St., tel. 091/232–2061) is the most established, with a variety of high-quality productions. In Hexham, the **Queen's Hall Arts Centre** (Beaumont St., tel. 0434/606787) is the most adventurous venue, offering drama, dance, and exhibition space for local artists. Berwick-upon-Tweed has **The Maltings** (Eastern La., tel. 0289/330661), and check to see what's on at Alnwick's **Playhouse** (Bondgate Without, tel. 0665/510785).

16 Scotland: Edinburgh and the Borders

Edinburgh (pronounced "-boro," not "-burg") almost seems to have been deliberately designed as a tourist attraction. A variety of factors make this city so appealing: its outstanding geography—like Rome, it is built on seven hills—the Old Town district, with all the evidence of its colorful history, and the large number of elegant, classical buildings conceived in the surge of artistic creativity of the second half of the 18th century.

In a skyline of sheer drama, Edinburgh Castle watches over the city, frowning down on Princes Street as if disapproving of its modern razzmatazz. Its ramparts still echo with gunfire when the one o'clock gun booms out each day, startling unwary tourists. The top of Calton hill, to the east, is cluttered with sturdy neoclassical monuments, like the abandoned set for a Greek tragedy. Also conspicuous from Princes Street is Arthur's Seat, a backdrop of bright green and yellow furze springing up behind the spires of the Old Town. This child-size mountain jutting 800 feet above its surroundings has steep slopes and little crags, like a miniature Highlands in the middle of the busy city.

There is no escaping the very literal sense of theater if you visit the city from August to early September. The Edinburgh International Festival has attracted all sorts of international performers since its inception in 1947. Even more obvious to the casual stroller during this time is the refreshingly irreverent Edinburgh Festival Fringe, unruly child of the official festival, which spills out of halls and theaters all over town.

These theatrical elements give a unique identity to downtown, but turn a corner, say, off George Street (parallel to Princes Street), and you will see, not an endless cityscape, but blue sea and a patchwork of fields. This is the county of Fife, beyond the inlet of the North Sea called the Firth of Forth; a reminder, like the Highlands to the northwest glimpsed from Edinburgh's highest points, that the rest of Scotland lies within easy reach.

The Borders area comprises the great rolling hills, moors, wooded river valleys, and farmland that stretch south from Lothian, the region crowned by Edinburgh, to England. All the distinctive features of Scotland—paper currency, architecture, opening hours of pubs and stores, food and drink, and accent—start right at the border; you won't find the Borders a diluted version of England.

Essential Information

Important Addresses and Numbers

Tourist Information The **Edinburgh and Scotland Information Centre** is adjacent to Edinburgh Waverley railway station, above Waverley Market. Here, visitors arriving in Edinburgh can get expert advice on what to see and do in the city and throughout Scotland. In addition to free information and literature, services include accommodation reservations, route-planning, coach tour tickets, theater reservations, a Scottish bookshop, and currency exchange. Visitors can also buy National Trust, Historic Scotland, and Great Britain Heritage passes. *3 Princes St., tel. 031/557–1700; 24-hr. Talking Tourist Guide, tel. 0891/775700 (36p/minute cheap rate, 48p at all other times). Open May, June, Sept., Mon.–Sat. 9–7, Sun. 11–7; July, Aug., Mon.–Sat. 9–8, Sun. 11–8; Nov.–Mar., Mon.–Sat. 9–6, closed Sun.; Oct. and Apr., Mon.–Sat. 9–6, Sun. 11–6.*

East Lothian Tourist Board: 31 Court St., Haddington, tel. 0620/827422, fax 0620/827291.

Forth Valley Tourist Board: Annet House, High St., Linlithgow, tel. 0506/844600, fax 0506/670427.

Midlothian Tourism Bureau: 2 Clerk St., Loanhead, tel. 031/440–2210.

Scottish Borders Tourist Board: 70 High St., Selkirk, tel. 0835/863435, fax 0835/864099.

Travel Agencies **American Express:** 139 Princes St., Edinburgh EH2 4BR, tel. 031/225–7881.

Thomas Cook: 79A Princes St., Edinburgh EH2 2ER, tel. 031/220–4039.

Car-Rental Agencies **Edinburgh: Avis,** 100 Dalry Rd., tel. 031/337–6363, also at the airport; **Budget Rent-a-Car,** Royal Scot Hotel, 111 Glasgow Rd., tel. 031/334–7739; **Europcar,** 24 E. London St., tel. 031/661–1252, also at the airport; **Hertz U.K. Ltd.,** 10 Picardy Pl., tel. 031/556–8311, also at the airport and Edinburgh Waverley railway station.

Arriving and Departing by Plane

Edinburgh Airport has air links with all the major airports in Britain and many in Europe. The **Airport Information Centre** (tel. 031/333–1000) answers questions regarding schedules, tickets, and reservations.

From the Airport to Downtown Buses run at 15-minute intervals during peak times from the Edinburgh Airport main terminal building to Waverley Bridge downtown; they are less frequent after rush hours and on weekends. The roughly 25-minute trip costs £3 one-way; the 20-minute trip by taxi costs roughly £12. By car, the airport is about 7 miles west of Princes Street downtown, and is clearly marked from A8. The usual route to downtown is via Corstorphine.

Glasgow Airport to Edinburgh. Glasgow Airport is 8 miles from Glasgow city center, and regular bus and train services link them. (Trains leave from Paisley Gilmour Street Station, 2 mi from the airport; take a taxi or bus—service every 30 minutes from the main entrance.) From Queen Street Station you can get a train to Waverley Station in Edinburgh (departures every half hour). Adjacent to Queen Street Station is the Buchanan Street Bus Station, with connections to Edinburgh and other areas.

Arriving and Departing by Car, Train, and Bus

By Car Downtown Edinburgh usually means Princes Street, which runs east–west. Entering from the east coast, drivers will come in on A1, Meadowbank Stadium serving as a good landmark. The highway bypasses the suburbs of Musselburgh and Tranent; therefore, any bottlenecks will occur close to downtown. From the Borders, the approach to Princes Street is by A7/A68 through Newington, an area offering a wide choice of budget accommodations. Approaching from the southwest, drivers will join the west end of Princes Street, via A701 and A702, while those coming east from Glasgow or Stirling will meet Princes Street from A8 on the approach via M90/A90—from Forth Road Bridge/Perth/east coast—the key road for getting downtown is Queensferry Road.

By Train Edinburgh's main train station, Waverley, is downtown, below Waverley Bridge. The station has recorded summaries of services to King's Cross Station in London—telephone for weekday information (tel. 031/557–3000), Saturday service (tel. 031/557–2737), and Sunday service (tel. 031/557–1616). For information on all other destinations, or other inquiries, telephone 031/556–2451. King's Cross Station can be reached on 071/278–2477. Travel time from Edinburgh to London by train is as little as four hours.

By Bus Several companies provide bus service to and from London, including **Scottish Citylink Coaches** (Bus Station, St. Andrew Sq., tel. 031/ 556–8464. Recorded timetable: tel. 031/556–8414). Edinburgh is approximately eight hours by bus from London.

Getting Around

By Car Edinburgh can be explored easily on foot, so a car is hardly needed.

By Bus **Lothian Region Transport,** operating dark red-and-white buses, is the main operator within Edinburgh. The **Edinburgh Freedom** ticket, allowing unlimited one-day travel on the city's buses, can be purchased in advance. More expensive is the **Tourist Card,** available in units of from two to 13 days, which gives unlimited access to buses (except Airlink) and includes vouchers for savings on tours. *Waverley Bridge, tel. 031/220–4111. Open Mar.–Oct., Mon.–Sat. 8–7, Sun. 9–4:15; Nov.–Feb., Mon.–Sat. 8–6, closed Sun.; also 14 Queen St., tel. 031/554–4494. Open weekdays 9–5.* **S.M.T.** (Bus Station, St. Andrew Sq., tel. 031/556–8464), operating green buses, provides much of the service into Edinburgh, and also offers day tours around and beyond the city.

Guided Tours

Bus Tours **Lothian Region Transport** and **S.M.T.** both offer tours in and around the city (*see* Getting Around, *above*).

Chauffeured Tours **Ghillie Personal Travel** (64 Silverknowes Rd. E, tel. 031/336–3120) and **Little's Chauffeur Drive** (33 Corstorphine High St., tel. 031/334–2177) both offer flexible, customized tours in all sizes of cars and buses, especially suitable for groups.

Walking Tours **The Cadies and Witchery Tours** (tel. 031/225–6745) organizes historic Old Town walks, Ghost Hunt, pub, and Murder and Mystery tours of Edinburgh throughout the year.

Exploring Edinburgh and the Borders

We have divided our coverage of Edinburgh (Tour 1) into two sections, but only the Old Town and Royal Mile area is really an organized route. The New Town, north of the castle, is ideal for unstructured wandering, drinking in the classical elegance of the squares and terraced houses, exploring the antiques shops, and dropping into pubs and wine bars.

Tour 2 surveys Sir Walter Scott territory south of Edinburgh among the ruined Border abbeys. This tour can be done in one long day, or better still, taken in two bites, returning to Edinburgh overnight.

Highlights for First-time Visitors

Abbotsford: Tour 2
Edinburgh Castle: Tour 1
Melrose Abbey: Tour 2

National Gallery of Scotland: Tour 1
Palace of Holyroodhouse: Tour 1
Royal Museum of Scotland: Tour 1
Traquair House: Tour 2
The view from Calton Hill: Tour 1

Tour 1: Edinburgh

Numbers in the margin correspond to points of interest on the Edinburgh map.

1 The dark, brooding presence of the castle dominates **Edinburgh,** the very essence of Scotland's martial past. The castle is built on a crag of hard, black volcanic rock formed during the Ice Age when an eastward-moving glacier scoured around this resistant core, forming steep cliffs on three sides. On the fourth side, a "tail" of rock was left, a ramp from the top that gradually runs away eastward. This became the street known as the Royal Mile, the backbone of the Old Town.

Time and redevelopment have swept away some of the narrow closes (alleyways) and tall tenements of the Old Town, but enough survive for you to be able to imagine the original shape of Scotland's capital, straggling between the guardian fortress on its crag at one end of the Royal Mile, and the royal residence, the Palace of Holyroodhouse, at the other. It was not until the Scottish Enlightenment, a civilizing time of expansion in the 1700s, that the city fathers decided to break away from the Royal Mile's rocky slope and build another Edinburgh, a little to the north, below the castle. This is the New Town, with elegant squares, classical facades, wide streets, and harmonious proportions. The main street, Princes Street, was conceived as an exclusive residential address with an open vista south and up at the castle. It has since been completely altered by the demands of business and shopping.

Victorian expansion and urban sprawl have hugely increased the city's size; though the Old and New Towns are separated by Princes Street Gardens (and the railroad), their contrasting identities are still the key to understanding Edinburgh.

2 Probably every visitor to the city tours **Edinburgh Castle**—which is more than can be said for many residents. Its popularity as an attraction is due not only to the castle's symbolic value as the center of Scotland but to the outstanding views offered from its battlements.

Recent archaeological discoveries have established that the rock was inhabited as far back as 1000 BC, in the later part of the Bronze Age. There have been fortifications here since the mysterious people called Picts first used it as a stronghold in the 3rd and 4th centuries AD. They were dislodged by Saxon invaders from northern England in AD 452, and for the next 1,300 years the site saw countless battles and skirmishes.

The castle has been held by Scots and Englishmen, Catholics and Protestants, soldiers and royalty; during the Napoleonic Wars, it even contained French prisoners of war, whose carvings can still be seen on the vaults under the great hall. In the 16th century Mary, Queen of Scots, chose to give birth there to the future James VI of Scotland, who was also to rule England as James I. In 1573, it was the last fortress to hold out for Mary as rightful Catholic queen of Britain, only to be virtually destroyed by English artillery.

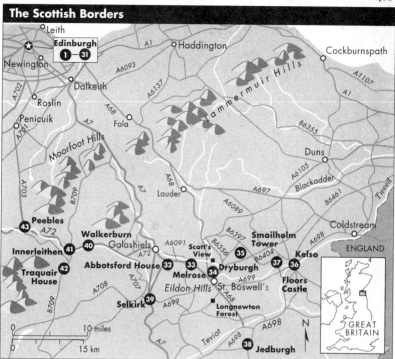

The Scottish Borders

The oldest surviving building in the complex is the tiny 11th-century **St. Margaret's Chapel,** the only building spared when the castle was razed in 1313 by the Scots, having won it back from their English foes. Also worth seeing are the **crown room,** which contains the **regalia of Scotland**—the crown, scepter, and sword that once graced the Scottish monarch; the **old parliament hall;** and **Queen Mary's apartments,** where she gave birth to James. The **great hall** features an extensive collection of arms and armor, and has an impressive vaulted, beamed ceiling.

There are several military features of interest, including the **Scottish National War Memorial,** the **Scottish United Services Museum,** and the famous 15th-century cannon *Mons Meg,* which is so huge that 100 men, five carpenters, and a large number of oxen were needed to heave it into position. The **Esplanade,** the huge forecourt of the castle, was built in the 18th century as a parade ground and now serves as the castle parking lot. It comes alive with color each year when it is used during the Festival for the Tattoo, a magnificent military display and pageant. *Tel. 031/244–3101. Admission: £5 adults, £3 senior citizens and unemployed, £1 children under 16. Open Apr.–Sept., daily 9:30–5:15; Oct.–Mar., daily 9:30–4:15.*

Time Out **Mills Mount Restaurant** (at the castle) offers morning coffee, light lunches, and afternoon teas in bright premises with panoramic views over the city.

❸ The **Royal Mile** starts immediately below the Esplanade. It runs roughly west to east, from the castle to the Palace of Holyroodhouse (*see below*), and progressively changes its name from Castlehill to

494

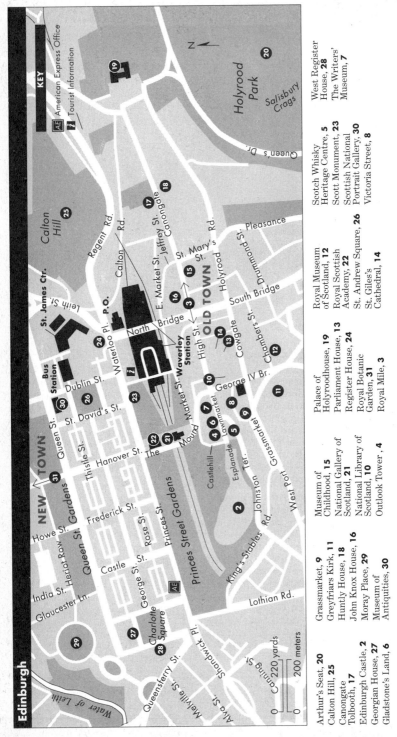

Edinburgh

KEY

AE American Express Office

7 Tourist Information

Arthur's Seat, **20**
Calton Hill, **25**
Canongate
Tolbooth, **17**
Edinburgh Castle, **2**
Georgian House, **27**
Gladstone's Land, **6**

Grassmarket, **9**
Greyfriars Kirk, **11**
Huntly House, **18**
John Knox House, **16**
Moray Place, **29**
Museum of
Antiquities, **30**

Museum of
Childhood, **15**
National Gallery of
Scotland, **21**
National Library of
Scotland, **10**
Outlook Tower, **4**

Palace of
Holyroodhouse, **19**
Parliament House, **13**
Register House, **24**
Royal Botanic
Garden, **31**
Royal Mile, **3**

Royal Museum
of Scotland, **12**
Royal Scottish
Academy, **22**
St. Andrew Square, **26**
St. Giles's
Cathedral, **14**

Scotch Whisky
Heritage Centre, **5**
Scott Monument, **23**
Scottish National
Portrait Gallery, **30**
Victoria Street, **8**

West Register
House, **28**
The Writers'
Museum, **7**

Lawnmarket, High Street, and Canongate. On your stroll downhill from the castle, you will need imagination, to re-create the former life of the city; and sharp eyes, to spot such details as the historic plaques and ornamentation that make the excursion interesting. On Castlehill, for example, note the bronze plaque recalling the burning of witches here in the late 16th century. Notice also the cannonball embedded in the wall of Cannonball House. Legend says it was fired from the castle during the Jacobite rebellion in 1745 led by Bonnie Prince Charlie; it is probably a height mark to do with the city's water supply.

❹ On the left of Castlehill, the **Outlook Tower** offers armchair views of the city with its **Camera Obscura** which, on a clear day, projects an image of the city onto a white, concave table. The building was constructed in the 17th century, but was significantly altered in the 1840s and 1850s with the installation of the optical instrument. *Tel. 031/226–3709. Admission: £2.90 adults, £1.50 children, £2.30 students, £1.85 senior citizens, £7.90 family ticket. Open Apr.–Oct., weekdays 9:30–6, weekends 10–6; Nov.–Mar., weekdays 10–5, weekends 10–3:30 (shop 5 PM).*

❺ Opposite, the **Scotch Whisky Heritage Centre** reveals the mysterious process that turns malted barley and spring water into one of Scotland's most important exports. *358 Castlehill, tel. 031/220–0441. Admission: £3.80 adults, £2 children, £2.30 senior citizens, £3.20 students, £10.60 family ticket. Open daily 10–5 (extended hours in summer); closed Christmas and New Year's.*

Farther down on the left, the **Tolbooth Kirk,** built in 1842–44 for the General Assembly of the Church of Scotland ("kirk" means church), boasts the tallest spire in the city—240 feet. From Lawnmarket you can start your discovery of the **Old Town closes,** the alleyways that are like ribs leading off the Royal Mile backbone.

❻ The six-story tenement known as **Gladstone's Land,** just beside the Assembly Hall, is a survivor from the 17th century, demonstrating typical architectural features, including an arcaded ground floor and an entrance at second-floor level. It is furnished in the style of a 17th-century merchant's house. *Tel. 031/226–5856. Admission: £2.50 adults, £1.30 children, students, and senior citizens. Open Apr.–Oct., Mon.–Sat. 10–5, Sun. 2–5 (last admission 4:30).*

❼ Close by Gladstone's Land, down yet another close, is **The Writers' Museum,** housed in a good example of 17th-century urban architecture known as Lady Stair's House. Built in 1622, it evokes Scotland's literary past with exhibits on Sir Walter Scott, Robert Louis Stevenson, and Robert Burns. *Off Lawnmarket, tel. 031/225–2424, ext. 4901. Admission free. Open June–Sept., Mon.–Sat. 10–6, Sun. during festival 2–5; Oct.–May, Mon.–Sat. 10–5.*

For a worthwhile shopping diversion, turn right down George IV
❽ Bridge, then down **Victoria Street** to the right, a 19th-century improvement—or intrusion—on the shape of the Old Town. Its shops offer antiques, old prints, clothing, and quality giftware. Down in
❾ the **Grassmarket,** which for centuries was, as its name suggests, an agricultural market, the shopping continues.

To visit another of Edinburgh's historic churches, walk from the Grassmarket back up Victoria Street to George IV Bridge, where
❿ you'll see the **National Library of Scotland** straight ahead (free exhibitions; open Mon., Tues., Thurs., Fri. 9:30–8:30; Wed. 10–8:30; Sat. 9:30–1). Farther down George IV Bridge, to the right, is the
⓫ **Greyfriars Kirk,** built on the site of a medieval monastery. Here, in

1638, the National Covenant was signed, declaring the independence of the Presbyterian Church in Scotland from government control. The covenant plunged Scotland into decades of civil war. *Greyfriars Pl., tel. 031/225–1900. Admission free. Open Easter–Sept., weekdays 10:30–4:30, Sat. 10:30–2: Oct.–Easter, Thurs. 1:30–3:30.*

Before returning to Lawnmarket, you might detour down Chambers Street, which leads off from George IV Bridge. Here, in a lavish ⑫ Victorian building, the **Royal Museum of Scotland** displays a wide-ranging collection drawn from natural history, archaeology, scientific and industrial history, and the history of mankind and civilization. The great Main Hall, with its soaring roof, is architecturally interesting in its own right. *Chambers St., tel. 031/225–7534. Admission free. Open Mon.–Sat. 10–5, Sun. 12–5.*

Return to High Street and, near Parliament Square, look on the right for a heart set in the cobbles. It marks the site of the vanished Tolbooth, the center of city life from the 15th century until its demolition in 1817. This ancient civic building, formerly housing the Scottish Parliament, then used as a prison from 1640 onward, inspired Scott's novel *The Heart of Midlothian*. Nearly every city and town in Scotland once had a Tolbooth—originally a customs house where tolls were gathered, the name came to mean the town hall and later a prison, since the detention cells were located in the basement of the ⑬ town hall. **Parliament House**—the seat of government until 1707, when the crowns of Scotland and England were united—is partially hidden by the bulk of St. Giles's Cathedral. *Parliament Sq., tel. 031/225–2595. Admission free. Open weekdays 9:30–4:30.*

⑭ **St. Giles's Cathedral,** originally the city's parish church, called the High Kirk of St. Giles, became a cathedral in 1633. There has been a church on the site since AD 854, although most of the present structure dates from 1829. The spire, however, was completed in 1495, the choir is mostly 15th-century, and four of the interior columns date from the early 12th century. The **Chapel of the Order of the Thistle,** bearing the belligerent national motto "Nemo Me Impune Lacessit" ("No one assails me with impunity"), was added in 1911. *High St., tel. 031/225–4363. Admission free. (Thistle Chapel: 50p.) Open Mon.–Sat. 9–5 (7 in summer), Sun. 2–5 (services 8 AM, 10 AM, 11:30 AM, 8 PM).*

Another landmark of Old Town life can be seen just east of St. Giles's. The **Mercat Cross** ("mercat" means "market"), a focus of public attention for centuries, is still the site of royal proclamations.

On High Street, a short walk east of the North Bridge–South ⑮ Bridge junction, is the **Museum of Childhood,** a celebration of toys that even adults may well enjoy. *42 High St., tel. 031/225–2424. Admission free. Open June–Sept., Mon.–Sat. 10–6, Sun. during festival 2–5; Oct.–May, Mon.–Sat. 10–5.*

⑯ Across High Street is **John Knox House,** a 16th-century dwelling. It is not absolutely certain that Knox, Scotland's severe religious reformer (1514–72), lived here, but mementos of his life are on view inside. *45 High St., tel. 031/556–2647. Admission: £1.25 adults, £1 senior citizens, 75p children. Open Mon.–Sat. 10–4:30.*

Beyond this point, you would once have passed out of the safety of the town walls. A plaque outside the **Netherbow Arts Centre** depicts the **Netherbow Port** (gate), which once stood at this point. Below is the **Canongate** area, named for the canons who once ran the abbey at Holyrood, now the site of Holyroodhouse. Canongate originally was an independent "burgh," a Scottish term meaning, essentially, a community with trading rights granted by the monarch. This explains the presence of the handsome **Canongate Tolbooth,** on the left, where the town council once met. It's now the setting for "The People's Story" exhibition which tells the history of the people of Edinburgh. *Canongate, tel. 031/225–2424, ext. 4057. Admission free. Open June–Sept., Mon.–Sat. 10–6 (Sun. during the festival 2–5); Oct.–May, Mon.–Sat. 10–5.*

Almost next door, in the graveyard of **Canongate Kirk,** are buried some notable Scots, including Adam Smith, author of *The Wealth of Nations* (1776). Opposite is timber-fronted **Huntly House,** a museum of local history. *142 Canongate, tel. 031/225–2424, ext. 4143. Admission free. Open June–Sept., 10–6, Sun. during festival 2–5; Oct.–May, Mon.–Sat. 10–5.*

Time Out You can get a good cup of tea and a sweet bun (a quintessentially Scottish indulgence) from **Clarinda's** (69 Canongate) or the **Abbey Strand Tearoom** (The Sanctuary, Abbey Strand) near the palace gates.

Facing you at the end of Canongate are the elaborate wrought-iron gates of the **Palace of Holyroodhouse,** official residence of the queen when she is in Scotland.

Holyrood Palace came into existence originally as a guest house for the medieval abbey founded in 1128 by Scottish king David I, after a vision of the cross ("rood" means "cross") saved his life on a hunting trip. David gave the land for the abbey to Augustinian friars in gratitude to God, and commanded them to build the Abbey of Holyrood—the Church of the Holy Cross. Since then, the palace has been the setting for high drama, including at least one notorious murder, a spectacular funeral, several major fires, and centuries of the colorful lifestyles of larger-than-life, power-hungry personalities. The murder occurred in 1566 when Mary, Queen of Scots, was dining with her favorite, David Rizzio, who was hated at court for his social climbing. Mary's second husband, Lord Darnley, burst into the chamber with his henchmen, dragged Rizzio into an antechamber, and stabbed him over 50 times. (Darnley himself was murdered in Edinburgh the next year, to make way for the queen's marriage to her lover, Bothwell.) Only 22 years before these shocking events, the palace had been severely damaged by an invading English army, which set fire to it; only the great tower (on the left as you look at the front facade) survived. In 1650, this time by accident, the palace burned again, and the great tower's massive walls again resisted the flames. Oliver Cromwell, the Protestant lord protector of England, who had conquered Scotland, ordered the palace rebuilt after the 1650 fire, but the restorations were poorly carried out, and lasted only until the restoration of the monarchy after Cromwell's death. When Charles II assumed the British throne in 1660, he ordered Holyrood rebuilt in the architectural style of the French "Sun King," Louis XIV, and that is the palace that visitors see today.

When the royal family is not in residence, you can walk freely around the palace and go inside for a conducted tour. *Tel. 031/556–7371; recorded message with visitor information, tel. 031/556–1096. Admission: £3 adults, £1.50 children, £2.50 senior citizens, £7.50 family ticket. Open Apr.–Oct., Mon.–Sat. 9:30–5:15, Sun. 10:30–4:30; Nov.–Mar., Mon.–Sat. 9:30–3:45; closed during royal and state visits.*

Behind the palace lie the open grounds of **Holyrood Park,** which en-
㉟ close Edinburgh's own mini-mountain, **Arthur's Seat.** The park was
the hunting ground of early Scottish kings.

In 1767, a civic competition to design a new district for Edinburgh
was won by an unknown young architect, James Craig. His plan was
for a grid of three main east–west streets, balanced at either end by
two grand squares. These streets survive today, though some of the
buildings that line them were altered by later development. Princes
Street is the southernmost, with Queen Street to the north and
George Street as the axis, punctuated by St. Andrew and Charlotte
squares. A look at the map will show you its geometric symmetry,
unusual in Britain. Even Princes Street Gardens are balanced by
Queen Street Gardens to the north.

Start your walk on **The Mound,** the sloping street that joins Old and
New Towns. Two galleries tucked immediately east of this great
linking ramp are both the work of W. H. Playfair (1789–1857), an
architect whose neoclassical buildings contributed greatly to
㉑ Edinburgh's earning the title, the "Athens of the North." **The National Gallery of Scotland** has a wide-ranging selection of paintings,
from the Renaissance to Postimpressionism, with works by Velás-
quez, El Greco, Rembrandt, Turner, Degas, Monet, and van Gogh,
among many others, as well as a fine collection of Scottish art. The
rooms of the gallery are attractively decorated, making it a pleasure
to browse. *Tel. 031/556–8921. Admission free. Open Mon.–Sat.
10–5 (extended during festival), Sun. 2–5. Print Room, weekdays
10–12 and 2–4, by appointment.*

㉒ The other gallery, **The Royal Scottish Academy,** with its imposing
columned facade overlooking Princes Street, holds an annual exhibition of students' work. *Princes St., tel. 031/225–6671. Admission
charges vary—depending on exhibition. Open late Apr.–July,
Mon.–Sat. 10–5, Sun. 2–5, and during the festival.*

The north side of **Princes Street** is now one long sequence of chain
stores whose unappealing modern storefronts can be seen in almost
any large British town. Luckily, the well-kept gardens on the other
side of the street act as a wide green moat to the castle on its rock.
Walk east until you reach the unmistakable soaring Gothic spire of
㉓ the 200-foot-high **Scott Monument,** built in 1844 in honor of
Scotland's most famous author, Sir Walter Scott (1771–1832), author of *Ivanhoe, Waverley,* and many other novels and poems. Note
the marble statue of Scott and his favorite dog. *Princes St., tel. 031/
225–2424. Admission: £1. Open Apr.–Sept., Mon.–Sat. 9–6 (last
admission 5:45); Oct.–Mar., Mon.–Sat. 9–3.*

㉔ **Register House,** on the left opposite the main post office, marks the
end of Princes Street. This was Scotland's first custom-built archives depository, partly funded by the sale of estates forfeited by
Jacobites after their last rebellion in Britain (1745–46). Work on the
building, designed by Robert Adam, Scotland's most famous neoclassical architect, started in 1774. The statue in front is of the duke
of Wellington. *Tel. 031/556–6585. Admission free. Open weekdays,
legal collection 9:30–4:30, historical collection 9–4:30.*

Time Out   Immediately west of Register House is the **Café Royal** (17 W. Register St.), one of the city's most interesting pubs. It has good beer and
lots of character, with ornate tiles and stained glass contributing to
the atmosphere.

㉕ The monuments on **Calton Hill,** growing ever more noticeable ahead as you walk east along Princes Street, can be reached by continuing along Waterloo Place, and either climbing steps to the hilltop or taking the road farther on that loops up at a more leisurely pace. Beyond the photogenic collection of columns and temples, the views from Calton Hill range over the Lomond Hills of Fife in the north, to the Pentland Hills southwest, behind the spire of St. Giles. The incomplete Parthenon look-alike is known as Edinburgh's Disgrace— it was intended as a National War Memorial in 1822 but contributions did not come in. On the opposite side of the road, in the Calton Old Burying Ground, is a monument to Abraham Lincoln and the Scottish-American dead of the Civil War. (An impressive American monument to the Scottish soldiers of World War I stands in West Princes Street Gardens, among various memorials of Scottish and foreign alliances.) The tallest monument on Calton Hill is the 100-foot-high **Nelson Monument,** completed in 1816 in honor of Britain's naval hero. *Tel. 031/556–2716. Admission: £1. Open Apr.–Sept., Mon. 1–6, Tues.–Sat. 10–6; Oct.–Mar., Mon.–Sat. 10–3.*

㉖ Make your way to **St. Andrew Square** by cutting through the **St. James Centre** shopping mall and the bus station.

On St. Andrew Square, next to the bus station, is the headquarters of the **Royal Bank of Scotland;** take a look inside at the lavish decor of the central banking hall. In the distance, at the other end of George Street, on Charlotte Square, you can see the copper dome of the former St. George's Church. In Craig's symmetrical plan for the New Town, a matching church was intended for the bank's site, but Sir Lawrence Dundas, a wealthy and influential baronet, somehow managed to acquire the space for his town house—string-pulling at city hall is nothing new. The grand mansion was later converted into the bank. The church originally intended for the site, St. Andrew's, is a little way down George Street.

Walk west along George Street, with its variety of shops, to Charlotte Square. Note particularly the palatial facade of the square's north side, designed by Robert Adam—it's considered one of Europe's finest pieces of civic architecture. Here you will find the
㉗ **Georgian House,** which the National Trust for Scotland has furnished in period style to show the elegant domestic arrangements of an affluent family of the late 18th century. Note, for instance, how the hallway was designed to take sedan chairs, in which the well-to-do of the 18th century were carried through the streets. *7 Charlotte Sq., tel. 031/225–2160. Admission: £3 adults, £1.50 senior citizens and children. Open Apr.–Oct., Mon.–Sat. 10–5, Sun. 2–5 (last admission 4:30).*

Also in the square, the former St. George's Church now fulfills a dif-
㉘ ferent role as **West Register House,** an extension of the original Register House. *Tel. 031/556–6585. Admission free. Open weekdays, exhibitions 10–4, research room 9–4:45.*

To explore further in the New Town, choose your own route north-
㉙ ward, down the wide and elegant streets centering on **Moray Place,** a fine example of an 1820s development, with imposing porticoes and a central, secluded garden. The area remains primarily residential, in contrast to the area around Princes Street. The Moray Place gardens are still for residents only.

㉚ A neo-Gothic building on Queen Street houses the **Scottish National Portrait Gallery** and the **Museum of Antiquities.** The gallery contains a magnificent Gainsborough and portraits by the Scottish artists Ramsay and Raeburn. In the museum, don't miss the 16th-century

Celtic harps and the Lewis chessmen—mysterious, grim-faced chess pieces carved from walrus ivory in the Middle Ages. *Tel. 031/ 225-7534. Admission free to both. Both open Mon.-Sat. 10-5, Sun. 2-5.*

31 Another attraction within reach of the New Town is the **Royal Botanic Garden.** Walk down Dundas Street, the continuation of Hanover Street, and turn left across the bridge over the Water of Leith, Edinburgh's small-scale river. These 70-acre gardens offer the largest rhododendron and azalea collection in Britain; peat, rock, and woodland gardens; a magnificent herbaceous border; an arboretum, and capacious greenhouses. There is also a convenient café and shop. *Inverleith Row, tel. 031/552-7171. Admission free (voluntary donation for greenhouses). Open Mar., Apr., Sept., and Oct., daily 10-6; May-Aug., daily 10-8; Nov.-Feb., daily 10-4. Café, shop, and exhibition areas, open daily Mar.-Oct. 10-5, Nov.-Feb. 10-3:30. Closed Christmas and New Year's Day.*

The **Scottish National Gallery of Modern Art,** in a former school building close to the New Town, features paintings and sculpture, including works by Picasso, Braque, Matisse, and Derain. *Belford Rd., tel. 031/556-8921. Admission free. Open Mon.-Sat. 10-5, Sun. 2-5 (extended during the festival).*

Tour 2: The Borders— In the Footsteps of Scott

Numbers in the margin correspond to points of interest on the Scottish Borders map.

One of the best ways to approach the Borders region is to take as the theme of your tour the life and works of the man who focused world attention on this part of Scotland and is largely responsible for its romantic image—Sir Walter Scott. Route A7, to Galashiels, 27 miles southeast of Edinburgh, then a mile farther on A6091, will take you
32 through the Moorfoot Hills to **Abbotsford House,** the small, castellated mansion which Scott built for himself between 1818 and 1823. He took a rather damp farmhouse on the banks of the River Tweed and transformed it into a pseudo-monastic, pseudo-baronial hall. Ruskin called the result "the most incongruous pile that gentlemanly modernism ever devised." Here Scott entertained such visitors as Wordsworth and Washington Irving. Abbotsford is still owned by Scott's descendants; his library, as well as a large collection of weapons, armor, and Scottish artifacts, are on display. *Tel. 0896/2043. Admission: £2.60 adults, £1.30 children. Open late Mar.-Oct., Mon.-Sat. 10-5, Sun. 2-5.*

33 In the peaceful little town of **Melrose,** 3 miles east on A6091, you'll find the ruins of a Cistercian abbey that was the most famous of the great Borders abbeys. All the abbeys were burned in the 1540s in a calculated act of destruction by English invaders acting on the orders of Henry VIII; Scott himself supervised the partial reconstruction of **Melrose Abbey,** one of the most beautiful ruins in Britain. *Tel. 089/682-2562. Admission: £2.30 adults, £1.20 children and senior citizens, £5.50 family ticket. Open Apr.-Sept., Mon.-Sat. 9:30-6, Sun. 2-6; Oct.-Mar., Mon.-Sat. 9:30-4, Sun. 2-4.*

At the Ormiston Institute in the Square at Melrose you will find the **Trimontium Trust,** an exhibit of Roman artifacts found during excavations at the Roman fort nearby at Newstead. Tools and weapons, a blacksmith's shop, pottery, and scale models of the fort are included in the display. *The Square, Melrose, tel. 089/682–2463. Admission: £1 adults, 50p children. Open Easter–Oct., daily 10:30–4:30.*

㉞ Five miles southeast of Melrose, still on A6091, is Scott's burial place at **Dryburgh,** another of the ruined Borders abbeys, set in a bend of the Tweed among strikingly shaped trees. Combine a visit here with a stop at **Scott's View,** 3 miles north on B6356, which provides a good view of the Tweed valley and the Eildon Hills. It is said that the horses pulling Scott's hearse paused automatically at Scott's View, because their master had so often halted them there. *Dryburgh, near St. Boswells, tel. 089/682–0835. Admission and opening hours same as Melrose Abbey.*

㉟ Another famous Borders lookout point is **Smailholm Tower,** a 16th-century watchtower that now houses a museum displaying costumed figures and tapestries relating to Scott's Border folk ballads (5 mi east of St. Boswells, off B6404). Scott spent his childhood on a nearby farm, where he imbibed his love of Border traditions and romances. *Smailholm, tel. 05736/332. Admission: £1.50 adults, £1 senior citizens, 75p children. Open Apr.–Sept., Mon.–Sat. 9:30–6, Sun. 2–6.*

㊱ From Smailholm, take B6397 and then A6089 east to **Kelso,** where Scott attended the grammar school. Kelso has an unusual Continental air, with fine Georgian and early Victorian buildings surrounding a spacious, cobbled marketplace. Its abbey is a magnificent ruin.

㊲ Rennie's Bridge on the edge of town provides good views of **Floors Castle.** Designed by Adam in 1721 and later altered by Playfair, this is the largest inhabited house in Scotland, an architectural extravagance of pepper-mill turrets and towers. *Tel. 0573/223333. Admission: £3.40 adults, £1.70 children over 8, £2.60 senior citizens, £8.50 family ticket; £1.50 grounds only. Open Easter, and May–Sept., Sun.–Thurs. 10:30–5:30 (also Fri. and Sat., July–Aug.); Oct., Sun. and Wed. 10:30–4. Check locally for variations.*

Time Out Try the 18th-century coaching inn, the **Queen's Head** (Bridge St.), for ample helpings of home-cooked food and a selection of cool draft ales.

㊳ To round out your tour of the Borders abbeys, take A68 12 miles southwest to **Jedburgh,** a little town just 13 miles north of the border, which lay in the path of marauding armies for centuries. **Jedburgh Abbey** is the most intact of the Borders abbeys and has an informative visitor center that explains the role of the abbeys in the life of the Borders until their destruction around 1545. *High St., tel. 0835/63925. Admission and opening hours same as Melrose Abbey.*

㊴ From Jedburgh, take A68 7 miles north to the A699 junction, turn left, and follow A699 7 miles through attractive river-valley scenery to reach the ancient hilltop town of **Selkirk.** Scott was sheriff (county judge) of Selkirkshire from 1800 until his death in 1832, and his statue stands in Market Place, outside the courthouse where he presided. *Sir Walter Scott's Courtroom, tel. 0750/20096. Admission free. Open July–Aug., daily 2–4, other times by appointment.*

㊵ Take A707 north from Selkirk and turn west onto A72. At **Walkerburn** is the **Scottish Museum of Woollen Textiles,** with the entrance through a tempting tweeds and woolens store. *Tel. 089687/ 281. Admission free. Open all year Mon.–Sat. 9–5:30, and from Easter–Christmas, Sun. 11–5.*

A few miles west of Walkerburn on A72, pass through the old spa of
⑪ Innerleithen (setting of Scott's novel *St. Ronan's Well*). Here you'll
find **Robert Smail's Printing Works,** a fully restored Victorian print
shop with its original machinery in working order and a printer in
residence. *7/9 High St., tel. 0896/830206. Admission: £2 adults, £1
children. Open Apr.–Oct., Mon.–Sat. 10–1 and 2–5, Sun. 2–5.*

⑫ Turn south on B709 to reach **Traquair House.** This is said to be the
oldest continually occupied house in Scotland, and is probably the
friendliest and most cheerful of the Borders' grand houses. Its laird
(or "lord") supported Stuart aspirations to the British throne in the
Jacobite uprisings, closing the gates at the end of the driveway after
the departing Bonnie Prince Charlie and swearing never to open
them until he returned as king. They remain closed to this day.
Traquair House Ale is still brewed in the 18th-century brewhouse.
*Near Innerleithen, tel. 0896/830323. Admission: £3.50 adults, £1.50
children, £3 senior citizens, £8 family ticket. Open Easter; May,
June, and Sept., daily 1:30–5:30; July and Aug., daily 10:30–5:30
(last admission 5 PM).*

From Traquair, return to A72 and continue west to the pleasant
⑬ town of **Peebles,** on the banks of the Tweed. Walk a mile upstream
until **Neidpath Castle** comes into view through the tall trees, perched
artistically above a bend in the river. The castle is a medieval structure remodeled in the 17th century, with dungeons hewn from solid
rock. You can return on the opposite riverbank after crossing an old,
finely skewed railroad viaduct. *Near Peebles, tel. 0721/720333. Admission: £1.50 adults, 75p children, £1 senior citizens and students.
Open Easter–Sept., Mon.–Sat. 11–5, Sun. 1–5.*

What to See and Do with Children

Edinburgh Butterfly and Insect World is a warm and humid indoor
experience of breathtaking color, with butterflies in profusion,
along with other insect life. *Melville Nurseries, near Dalkeith, tel.
031/663–4932. Admission: £3.25 adults, £1.90 children, £2.55 senior
citizens and students, £9.30 family ticket. Open Mar.–Dec., daily
10–5 (last entry 4:30).*

The **Museum of Childhood** (*see* Tour 1, *above*).

Edinburgh Zoo now offers areas for children to approach or handle
animals. Noted for its penguins, the zoo puts them on a delightful
parade every day during the summer. *Corstorphine Rd., tel. 031/
334–9171. Admission: £4.80 adults, £3 senior citizens, £2.50 children, £13 family ticket. Open Apr.–Sept., Mon.–Sat. 9–6; Mar. and
Oct., 9–5; Nov.–Feb., 9–4:30; Sun. opening time 9:30, closing times
as above.*

Edinburgh Brass Rubbing Centre offers a varied selection of replica
brasses and inscribed stones, with full instructions and materials
supplied. *Trinity Apse, Chalmers Close, Royal Mile, tel. 031/225–
2424, ext. 4143. Admission: free, but a charge (40p–£10.50) is made
for every rubbing. Open June–Sept., Mon.–Sat. 10–6; during festival, Sun. 2–5; Oct.–May, Mon.–Sat. 10–5.*

Deep Sea World. This recently opened aquarium across the Firth of
Forth, 20 minutes from Edinburgh, offers a fascinating diver's-eye
view of underwater life, with up to 5,000 fish. There is also a shop
and a café. *North Queensferry, tel. 0383/411411. Admission: £4.50
adults, £3 children (and senior citizens Mon.–Fri.), £13.50 family
ticket. Open daily 9–6 (shorter hours in winter), closed Christmas
and New Year's.*

Off the Beaten Track

Tucked behind Arthur's Seat, **Duddingston** village is a brisk walk from Princes Street via Holyrood Park. This little community—formerly of butchers and weavers—has an interesting church with a Norman doorway and a watchtower in its graveyard to guard against body snatchers, who sold corpses for dissection. The church overlooks **Duddingston Loch,** popular with bird-watchers.

Edinburgh's ancient seaport, **Leith,** has been revitalized in recent years, with the restoration of the remaining fine commercial buildings which survived an earlier and insensitive redevelopment phase. It is worth exploring the lowest reaches of the Water of Leith and especially the proliferating pubs and restaurants. *Buses 7, 10, 11, 16; 10–15 min. from Princes St.*

Near A701, 7 miles south of Edinburgh, **Rosslyn Chapel** is located on a pleasantly wooded site near the village of Roslin. This 15th-century chapel houses some of Scotland's finest examples of stone carving, including the ornate **Prentice Pillar,** said to have been carved by a medieval apprentice while his master was absent. When the master returned, he killed the boy in a fit of jealousy. According to another legend, a red glare over the chapel portends disaster to the Sinclair family, who were buried there in their armor instead of coffins. *Tel. 031/440–2159. Admission: £2 adults, 75p children, £1.50 senior citizens. Open Apr.–Oct., Mon.–Sat. 10–5, Sun. 12–4:45.*

About 10 miles west of Edinburgh, overlooking the Firth of Forth, is **Hopetoun House,** designed by the great Robert Adam, the most spectacular stately home in the area, with an especially grand approach. Inside, you'll find the usual stately home panoply of fine furniture, paintings, tapestries, and carpets. Outside there are gardens, a deer park, and a nature trail. *South Queensferry, off A904, tel. 031/331–2451. Admission: £3.80 adults, £1.90 children, £3.10 senior citizens and students, £10.50 family ticket. Open Apr.–Sept., daily 10–5:30 (last admission 4:45).*

Near the coast, east of Edinburgh, is **Paxton House,** also of Adam design, which is now an out-station of the National Gallery of Scotland, with some of the country's finest paintings. The grounds include extensive woodlands along the River Tweed. *Berwick-on-Tweed, tel. 0289/386291. Admission: £3.50 adults, £1.75 children, £3 senior citizens. Open Easter–Oct., daily noon–5 (grounds open 10–sunset).*

Shopping

Edinburgh features a cross section of Scottish specialties, such as tartans and tweeds, rather than products peculiar to the area. If you are interested in learning the background of your tartan purchases, try **Scotland's Clan Tartan Centre** (James Pringle Ltd., Bangor Rd., Leith), where extensive displays on various aspects of tartanry will keep you informed.

For some ideas on exactly what Scotland has to offer in the way of crafts, visit the **Royal Mile Living Craft Centre** (12 High St.), where you can chat to and buy from craftspeople as they work. Also along the Royal Mile, you will find several shops selling high-quality tartans and woollen goods. **Judith Glue** (64 High St.) carries brilliantly patterned Orkney knitwear and a wide selection of crafts, cards, wrapping paper, jewelry, toiletries, and candles. **Aika** (60 High St.)

also stocks its own label knitwear in angora, cashmere, silk, and lambswool; pottery; and greeting cards.

A popular gift selection comes from **Edinburgh Crystal,** just a few miles from the city, in Penicuik (Eastfield, tel. 0968/75128).

The antiques business is suffering from the economic recession and shops open and close with great rapidity, so it's smart to concentrate on areas with a number of stores close together, for instance, **Bruntsfield Place, Causewayside,** or **St. Stephen Street.**

Princes Street   **Jenners,** opposite the Scott Monument, is Edinburgh's last independent department store, specializing in upscale tweeds and tartans. The **Edinburgh Woollen Mill** (No. 62), popular with overseas visitors, also sells top-quality items. **Gleneagles of Scotland,** nearby in Waverley Market, is not quite so upscale.

George Street   George Street features a few London names, such as **Laura Ashley, Liberty,** and **Waterstones** bookstore. Do not confuse the last-mentioned with **Waterston's** (No. 35), which carries stationery and a range of Scottish gifts. Farther along, there is a good selection of Scottish titles in the **Edinburgh Bookshop** (No. 57).

Rose Street   Try **Alistir Tait** (No. 116A) for silver and jewelry, or **Tiso** (Nos. 115–123) for outdoor gear, among Rose Street's interesting shops.

Victoria Street/ West Bow/ Grassmarket   Where these three streets run together, there's a number of specialty stores in a small area. **Ampersand** (18 Victoria St.) is an interior designer's that also stocks a large selection of small collectibles and unusual fabrics by the yard. **Robert Cresser's** brush store (No. 40) features, not surprisingly, brushes of all kinds, each one handmade, while on the same side and a little farther down **Pine & Old Lace** (No. 46) has a carefully-chosen selection of antique textiles and small pieces of furniture. **Iain Mellis Cheesemonger** (No. 30A) has around 30 varieties of British cheese; the shop's brochure is an education in itself. **Kinnells House Tea and Coffee Emporium** (Nos. 36–38) serves morning coffee, lunches, and teas, and sells nearly 100 different types of freshly roasted coffees and specialty teas to take out and try at home. **Le Magasin** (No. 14) stocks every imaginable edible item from France for homesick Francophiles: groceries, cheese, charcuterie, wine.

At **Mr. Wood's Fossils,** down in the Grassmarket, an unusual item, such as a small shark encased in rock, may solve your gift-buying problems. **Bill Baber** (No. 68) is another long-established, enterprising and original Scottish knitwear designer.

Stockbridge   This northern suburb is an oddball shopping area of some charm, particularly on St. Stephen Street. Look for **Hand in Hand** (3 NW Circus Pl.) for beautiful antique textiles. There are also several antiques shops and yet more knitwear.

William Street/ Stafford Street   This is a small, upscale shopping area in a Georgian setting. **Sprogs** (45 William St.) sells end-of-season children's designer clothes in modern, not traditional styles, at 50%–70% off. **Something Simple** (10 William St.) offers a pleasing selection of women's classic clothing. **Studio One** (10–14 Stafford St.), is well established and wide-ranging in its inventory of gift articles.

Flea Markets   Edinburgh is far too self-conscious to do this sort of thing really well. **Byzantium** (9A Victoria St.), with its antiques, crafts, paintings, books, and jewelry comes the closest, though perhaps it's too tasteful, clean, and restrained.

Peebles While on your tour of the Borders abbeys, visit Peebles for its old-fashioned shopping in locally owned specialty shops with time to serve their customers well. Try **Keith Walter** (28 High St.) for silver and jewelry.

Sports and the Outdoors

Golf Edinburgh is well endowed with **golf courses,** with 20 or so near downtown (even before the nearby East Lothian courses are considered). **Braids United** course, south of the city center, welcomes visitors (tel. 031/447–6666); **Bruntsfield Links** (tel. 031/336–1479) and **Duddingston** (tel. 031/661–7688) permit visitors to play on weekdays by appointment; all have 18 holes. Here are three courses in the Borders, to go with the abbeys we list—**Jedburgh** (tel. 0835/863587) and **Melrose** (tel. 0896/822855), nine holes, and **St. Boswells** (tel. 0835/22359), 18 holes.

A quite exceptional destination is **Gullane** (tel. 0620/842255), about 20 miles east of Edinburgh on A198, with three courses, all 18-hole, and several others nearby, **Luffness New** (tel. 0620/843336, fax 0620/842933) among them.

Jogging The most convenient spot downtown for joggers is **West Princes Street Gardens,** which is separated from traffic by a 30-foot embankment, with a half-mile loop on asphalt paths. In **Holyrood Park,** stick to the road around the volcanic mountain for a 2¼-mile trip. For a real challenge, charge up to the summit of Arthur's Seat, or to the halfway point, the Cat's Nick.

Walking Walks in this area range from city walkways—along **the banks of the Water of Leith,** for example—to fairly demanding excursions on Scotland's only east–west official footpath, the **Southern Upland Way.** This is a signposted 212-mile route, from Cockburnspath on the east coast to Portpatrick in the far southwest of Galloway, which takes in some high and exposed ground on the way, as well as some fine, lower-level river valleys and woods. An official guide to the walk is published by Her Majesty's Stationery Office and is available at most booksellers and tourist information centers.

One place of recreation for the locals is the **Pentland Hills,** with their breezy but not over-demanding slopes especially popular on weekends; there's easy access to the Hills at Hillend, by the artificial ski slope, or in Bonaly Country Park. Alternatively, there is also good **East Lothian coastal walking** at many points from Aberlady, eastwards.

As the Borders are essentially rural and hilly, there are a number of walking options, of which **Loch Skeen** above the Grey Mare's Tail Waterfall, northwest of Moffat, is just one example; the walk here is not too demanding, but strong footwear is advised. **Peebles,** within easy reach of Edinburgh, offers excellent level walking along the banks of the River Tweed, while a visit to **Melrose,** with its Abbey, can be further enjoyed by a climb to the top of the Eildon Hills with wonderful views, though you should allow a couple of hours. Again, strong shoes or boots (and lungs!) are advised. In all cases, local tourist information centers carry full information on local walks and trails.

Dining and Lodging

Dining Edinburgh is a diverse, sophisticated city, which its cuisine reflects with an interesting mix of traditional and exotic food, from Scottish dishes to infinite ethnic variety. Make reservations well in advance, particularly at festival time.

Look for the "Taste of Scotland" sign in restaurant windows, indicating the use of the best Scottish game, cheese, fruit, vegetables, and seafood. The sign usually attests to high standards of preparation as well. However, the fact that a menu is written in creaking, mockantique Scots does not guarantee that it is adventurous. For instance, "tassie o' bean bree"—"tassie" being an uncommon word for "cup," and "bree" usually meaning "soup" or "brine"—translates as a plain cup of coffee.

Highly recommended restaurants are indicated by a star ★.

Category	Cost*
$$$$	over £40
$$$	£30–£40
$$	£15–£30
$	under £15

per person, including first course, main course, dessert, and VAT; excluding drinks

Lodging Edinburgh has many accommodations in lovely traditional Georgian properties, some even in the New Town, a few minutes from downtown. There are also upscale hotels downtown, each with an international flavor. You must book months in advance, however, for the festival. **Dial-a-Bed**, a new free central reservations service (tel. toll-free in the U.K. 0800/616947; from the U.S. 31/556–3955 or fax 31/557–4365) can book rooms in more than 70 Edinburgh hotels and guest houses.

Highly recommended lodgings are indicated by a star ★.

Category	Cost*
$$$$	over £110
$$$	£75–£110
$$	£40–£75
$	under £40

All prices are for two people sharing a double room, including service, breakfast, and VAT.

Edinburgh Dining **Pompadour.** The decor here, with its elegant plasterwork and rich murals, is inspired by the France of Louis XV, as may be expected in a restaurant named after the king's mistress, Madame de Pompadour. The cuisine is also classic French, with top-quality Scottish produce, such as sea bass, lobster, and venison, featured on the menu. The well-chosen wine list is extensive. Lunchtime here tends to be more relaxed and informal. *Caledonian Hotel, Princes St., tel. 031/225–2433. Reservations advised. Jacket and tie required. AE, DC, MC, V. $$$*

L'Auberg. A number of Edinburgh restaurants take the best Scottish food and prepare it French style, but L'Auberge is actually French through and through. The menu is all in French, with only a cursory translation. The owner-manager enjoys explaining the recipes to you in detail, so you must ask. The menu changes frequently, but you may be able to choose a seafood terrine, guinea fowl with mushrooms and claret sauce, or venison with Armagnac. The impressive wine list includes excellent dessert wines. There are excellent three-course fixed-price menus available. *56–58 St. Mary's St., tel. 031/556–5888. Reservations advised. Dress: casual. AE, DC, MC, V. $$–$$$*

★ **Martins.** Don't be put off by the look of this restaurant on the outside. It's tucked away in a little back street, and has a typically forbidding northern facade. All's well inside, though, and the food is tops. The specialties are all light and extremely tasty, with fish and game in the lead. Try the halibut with leeks and carrot and basil coulis, or the breasts of mallard and pigeon with red cabbage and raisins, plus gorgeous homemade sorbets. *70 Rose St. North Lane (between Castle and Frederick Sts.), tel. 031/225–3106. Reservations required. Jacket and tie preferred. AE, DC, MC, V. Closed Sat. lunch, Sun. and Mon. $$–$$$*

Indian Cavalry Club. The menu of this cool and sophisticated restaurant reflects a confident, up-to-date approach—with its steamed specialties it's almost an Indian *nouvelle cuisine*. The **Club Tent** in the basement serves light meals. *3 Atholl Pl., tel. 031/228–3282, fax 031/225–1911. Reservations advised. Jacket and tie suggested. AE, DC, MC, V. $$*

Jackson's. Intimate and candlelit in an historic Old Town close, Jackson's offers good Scots fare. Aberdeen Angus steaks and Border lamb are excellent, and there are also seafood and vegetarian specialties. The decor is rustic, with lots of greenery, stone walls, pine farmhouse-style tables and chairs, and fresh flowers. The wine list includes 60 malt whiskies and some Scottish country wines to complete the Scottish experience. *2 Jackson Close, 209–213 High St., Royal Mile, tel. 031/225–7793. Reservations advised. Dress: casual. AE, MC, V. Closed for lunch Sat. and Sun. $$*

Kweilin. This excellent, very popular Chinese restaurant specializes in Cantonese cuisine made from very fresh ingredients. The waterchestnut pudding is recommended. Service is particularly speedy and efficient. *19–21 Dundas St., tel. 031/557–1875. Reservations advised. AE, MC, V. $$*

★ **The Vintner's Room.** In the Leith section of Edinburgh, this restaurant is a pleasant escape from the bustle of downtown. Tasteful decor, including fine plasterwork and a relaxed atmosphere, combine with dishes such as sautéed scallops, smoked salmon, and grilled oysters with bacon and hollandaise sauce, to make any meal here a treat. *The Vaults, 87 Giles St., Leith, tel. 031/554–6767. Reservations advised. Dress: casual. AE, DC, MC, V. Closed Sun. and 2 weeks at Christmas. $$*

Henderson's. This was Edinburgh's original vegetarian restaurant, long before that cuisine became fashionable. Try the vegetarian haggis. *94 Hanover St., tel. 031/225–2131. Reservations not required. Dress: casual. AE, MC, V. Closed Sun. except during festival. $*

Howie's. Here's a simple neighborhood bistro with a lively clientele; it's unlicensed, so you have to bring your own bottle. The steaks are tender Aberdeen beef, the Loch Fyne herring are sweet-cured to Howie's own recipe. *75 St. Leonard's St., tel. 031/668–2917 (also at 63 Dalry Rd., tel. 031/313–3334). Reservations advised. Dress: casual. MC, V. Open lunch Tues.–Sun., dinner daily. $*

★ **Kalpna.** This eatery has a reputation for outstanding value. Indian art adorns the walls, enhancing your enjoyment of the exotic specialties like *shahi sabzi* (spinach and nuts in cream sauce), and mushroom curry. All dishes are vegetarian and are skillfully and deliciously prepared. *2–3 St. Patrick's Sq., tel. 031/667–9890. Reservations advised. Dress: casual. MC, V. Closed Sun. $*

Pierre Victoire. There are four branches of this very popular bistro chain in Edinburgh. They are fairly chaotic, friendly, enjoyable eateries serving healthy portions at low prices. The fish is fresh and especially good; try the baked oysters with bacon and hollandaise. *38 Grassmarket, tel. 031/226–2442 (open daily); 10 Victoria St., tel. 031/225–1721 (closed Sun.); 8 Union St., tel. 031/557–8451 (closed Mon.); and 5 Dock Pl., Leith, tel. 031/556–6178 (closed Sun.). Reservations not necessary. Dress: casual. MC, V. $*

Dining and Lodging **Balmoral Hotel.** The attention to detail in the elegant rooms and the sheer élan that has re-created the Edwardian splendor of this former grand railroad hotel make staying at the Balmoral a very special way to see Edinburgh. Here, below the impressive clocktower marking the east end of Princes Street, you get a strong sense of being at the center of Edinburgh life. The main restaurant is the plush and stylish Grill Room, serving delicacies such as beef carpaccio with warm mushroom salad and grilled salmon steak with hollandaise sauce. *Princes St. EH2 2EQ, tel. 031/556–2414, fax 031/557–8740. 167 bedrooms, 22 suites. Facilities: 2 restaurants, bar, wine bar, patisserie, health club. Main restaurant reservations advised. Jacket and tie required in Grill Room. AE, DC, MC, V. $$$$*

★ **Caledonian Hotel.** "The Caley" recalls the days of the great railroad hotels, although its nearby station has long gone. Recently modernized and refurbished at vast expense, its imposing Victorian decor has been faithfully preserved and has lost none of its original dignity and elegance. In addition to the **Pompadour** (*see* Dining, *above*), the less formal **Carriages** restaurant supplies traditional Scottish roasts, fish, and game. *Princes St., EH1 2AB, tel. 031/225–2433, fax 031/225–6632. 239 rooms with bath. Facilities: 2 restaurants, in-house movies. Restaurant: reservations advised; jacket and tie required. AE, DC, MC, V. Hotel $$$$; Restaurant $$$*

Lodging **George Intercontinental Hotel.** This imposing and extensively refurbished 18th-century building in the heart of the New Town retains some elegant Georgian features in its public areas, while the bedrooms are up-to-date and moderately luxurious. Although busy keeping this large hotel running smoothly, the courteous staff will always take the time to be helpful. *19 George St., EH2 2PB, tel. 031/225–1251, fax 031/226–5644. 195 rooms with bath. Facilities: 2 restaurants, bar. AE, DC, MC, V. $$$$*

Howard Hotel. The Howard, close to Drummond Place, is a good example of a New Town building, elegant and superbly proportioned. It is small enough to continue to offer personal attention. All bedrooms and suites are spacious and well equipped, some looking out onto the garden. *32 Great King St., EH3 6QH, tel. 031/557–3500, fax 031/557–6515. 16 rooms with bath. Facilities: restaurant. AE, DC, MC, V. $$$$*

Mount Royal Hotel. The front bedrooms at this modern hotel have views of the Edinburgh Castle and Princes Street Gardens. With a friendly staff, the Mount Royal is conveniently located near major sights and shopping. *53 Princes St., EH2 2DQ, tel. 031/225–7161, fax 031/220–4671. 160 rooms with bath. Facilities: restaurant. AE, DC, MC, V. $$$$*

Scandic Crown. This modern hotel has been designed to blend into the surrounding ancient buildings on the Royal Mile, and its location is the main reason to stay here. The spacious bedrooms with bland decor lack personality. The hotel serves Scandinavian-inspired cuisine, with *smörgåsbord* a feature. *80 High St., Royal Mile EH1 1TH, tel. 031/557–9797, fax 031/557–9789. 238 rooms with bath. Facilities: restaurant. AE, DC, MC, V. $$$–$$$$*

Channings. Five Edwardian terraced houses have become an elegant hotel in an upscale neighborhood minutes from Princes Street. Restrained colors, antiques, quiet rooms, and great views toward Fife (from the north-facing rooms) set the tone. The Brasserie offers excellent value, especially at lunchtime; try the crabcakes with crayfish bisque. *South Learmonth Gardens, EH4 1EZ, tel. 031/315–2226; fax 031/332–9631. 48 rooms with bath. Facilities: restaurant. AE, DC, MC, V. $$$*

Albany. Three fine Georgian houses with many of their original features have been carefully converted into a comfortable city-center hotel. There's a good restaurant in the basement, and a friendly bar with piano. *39 Albany St., EH1 3Q4, tel. 031/556–0397, fax 031/557–6633. 20 rooms with bath. MC, V. $$*

Brunswick Hotel. This bed-and-breakfast, close to the city center, is in a lovely Georgian building with parking. All rooms have tea- and coffee-making appliances and TVs; two rooms have four-posters. *7 Brunswick St., EH7 5JB, tel. and fax 031/556–1238. 10 rooms with shower. AE, MC, V. $$*

Dorstan Private Hotel. A villa dating from the Victorian era, this hotel is in a quiet neighborhood a fair way from the city center. Bedrooms have been modernized to offer both the charm of the old and ease of the new. Peaceful pastel colors predominate in the decor, adding to this hotel's restfulness. *7 Priestfield Rd., EH16 5HJ, tel. 031/667–6721, fax 031/668–4644. 14 rooms, 9 with bath or shower. MC, V. Closed Dec. 24–Jan. 2. $$*

★ **Salisbury Guest House.** This guest house in a Georgian building is located in a peaceful conservation area. It is also convenient for city touring, and offers excellent value for the money. *45 Salisbury Rd., EH16 5AA, tel. and fax 031/667–1264. 12 rooms, 9 with bath or shower. No credit cards. Closed Christmas and Jan. 1. $*

Galashiels **Woodlands House Hotel.** This Gothic Revival–style hotel has stun-
Dining and ning views over Tweeddale. The main restaurant specializes in fresh
Lodging seafood and hearty Scottish cuisine, while **Sanderson's Steakhouse** is named after a former owner of the house, whose portrait gazes down on diners. *Windyknowe Rd., TD1 1RG, tel. and fax 0896/4722. 9 rooms with bath. Facilities: 2 restaurants, garden, golfing, fishing, horseback riding. MC, V. $$*

Gullane **Greywalls.** Gullane, on the Firth of Forth, is 19 miles northeast of
Lodging Edinburgh by A198 and totally surrounded by golf links. It is, in fact, the ideal hotel to choose for a golfing vacation, comfortable, with excellent food and attentive service. The house itself is an architectural treasure. Edward VII used to stay here, as have Nicklaus, Trevino, Palmer, and a host of other golfing greats. *Muirfield, Gullane EH31 2EG, tel. 0620/842144, fax 0620/842241. 22 rooms with bath. Facilities: restaurant, garden, tennis, croquet, golf. AE, DC, MC, V. Open Apr.–Nov. $$$$*

Innerleithen **Traquair Arms.** Near Innerleithen, famous for its medicinal springs
Lodging and for Traquair House, this family-run hotel is a fine traditional inn offering a warm welcome, simple, clean rooms, and very good food. *Traquair Rd., EH44 6PD, tel. 0896/830229, fax 0896/830260. 10 rooms (8 with shower, 2 with bath). Facilities: restaurant, bar, garden, private fishing. MC, V. $$*

Jedburgh **Spinney Guest House.** Made up of unpretentiously converted and
Lodging modernized farm cottages, this is a bed-and-breakfast offering the
★ very highest standards for the price. *Langlee, TD8 6PB, tel. and fax
0835/863525. 3 rooms, 1 with bath, 2 with shower. No credit cards.
Closed Nov.–Feb. $*

Kelso **Sunlaws House Hotel.** Owned by the duke of Roxburghe, this large,
Dining and restful country house has a library that doubles as the bar, a plant-
Lodging filled conservatory, spacious bedrooms, and all the other facets of
gracious living intact. The restaurant is excellent; the menu changes
daily and the chef is outstanding. The food is archetypically Scottish—with local salmon prominent on the menu—and the wine comes from the grand cellars of nearby Floors Castle, where the duke
lives and which guests can visit free. *Heiton, Kelso, Roxburghshire
TD5 8JZ, tel. 0573/450331, fax 0573/450611. 22 rooms with bath. Facilities: restaurant, bar, fishing, tennis, helipad, trapshooting
school. AE, DC, MC, V. $$$$*

Lodging **Ednam House Hotel.** This large, attractive hotel is right on the
★ banks of the River Tweed, close to Kelso's grand abbey and the old
Market Square. Ninety percent of the guests are return visitors,
and the open fire in the hall, sporting paintings, and cozy armchairs
give the place a homey feel. *Bridge St., TD5 7HT, tel. 0573/224168,
fax 0573/226319. 32 rooms with bath or shower. Facilities: restaurant, garden, fishing, golf, horseback riding. MC, V. Closed Christmas–early Jan. $$–$$$*

Melrose **Marmion's Brasserie.** Outstanding country-style cuisine is the at-
Dining traction at this cozy restaurant; it's a great place to stop for lunch
★ after visiting Abbotsford. *Buccleuch St., tel. 089682/2245. Reservations advised. Dress: casual. MC, V. Closed Sun. $*

Dining and **Burts Hotel.** This distinctive black-and-white traditional town hos-
Lodging telry dating from the early 18th century offers up-to-date comfort.
The elegant dining room features dishes such as pheasant terrine,
and venison with a whisky-and-cranberry sauce. *Market Sq., TD6
9PN, tel. 089682/2285, fax 089682/2870. 21 rooms, 14 with bath, 7
with shower. Facilities: restaurant; fishing and shooting arranged.
Restaurant: reservations advised; jacket and tie preferred. AE,
DC, MC, V. $$*

Peebles **Cringletie House Hotel.** A Scottish baronial mansion set in 28 acres
Dining and of gardens and woodland, Cringletie is run by a family who believe in
Lodging spoiling their guests with friendly, personalized service. They
make you feel as if you're their houseguest. Much of the fruit and
vegetables served in the restaurant comes from the hotel's own gar-
den. *Peebles, EH45 8PL, tel. 0721/730233, fax 0721/730244. 13
rooms with bath. Facilities: restaurant, gardens, croquet, putting
green, tennis. Restaurant: reservations advised. MC, V. $$–$$$*

Quothquan **Shieldhill.** This foursquare Norman manor has been standing here
Lodging since 1199 (though greatly enlarged in 1560). It is ideally placed for
touring the Borders—just 27 miles from Edinburgh and 31 from
Glasgow. The rooms are named after great Scottish battles—
Culloden, Glencoe, Bannockburn, etc.—and are furnished with
great comfort (miles of Laura Ashley fabrics and wallpapers).
*Quothquan, near Biggar, ML12 6NA, tel. 0899/20035, fax 0899/
21092. 11 rooms with bath. Facilities: restaurant, garden. AE, DC,
MC, V. $$$–$$$$*

St. Boswells **Dryburgh Abbey Hotel.** Right next to the abbey ruins, this civilized
Dining and hotel is surrounded by beautiful scenery and features a restaurant
Lodging specializing in Scottish fare. Bar snacks are also available. *St.*

Boswells TD6 ORQ, tel. 0835/22261, fax 0835/23945. 26 rooms with bath. Facilities: restaurant, golfing. Restaurant: reservations advised; jacket and tie required. Restaurant is no-smoking. MC, V. $$–$$$

Selkirk **Philipburn House Hotel.** This Georgian-style country house stands
Lodging on 4 acres of gardens and woodland. The house has recently been ex-
★ tended and the bedrooms updated; they and the dining room have a
Scandinavian feel, all pine and florals. The owners are attentive and
helpful. *Linglie Rd., TD7 5LS, tel. 0750/20747, fax 0750/21690. 16
rooms with bath or shower. Facilities: restaurant, outdoor heated
pool. DC, MC, V. $$$*

The Arts

The flagship of arts events in the city is the **Edinburgh International
Festival** (1995 dates: Aug. 13–Sept. 2), which for 45 years has at-
tracted performing artists of international caliber in a great cele-
bration of music, dance, and drama. *Advance information,
programs, tickets, and reservations during the festival: Edinburgh
Festival Office, 21 Market St., Edinburgh EH1 1BW, tel. 031/226–
4001.*

The **Edinburgh Festival Fringe** offers a huge range of theatrical and
musical events, some by amateur groups (you have been warned),
and is much more of a grab bag than the official festival. The fringe
offers a vast choice (a condition of Edinburgh's artistic life found
only during the three- or four-week festival season). During festival
time, it's possible to arrange your own entertainment program from
morning to midnight and beyond. *Information, programs, and tick-
ets: Edinburgh Festival Fringe, 180 High St., Edinburgh EH1 1QS,
tel. 031/226–5257 or 5259.*

The **Edinburgh Film Festival** (held in Aug.) is yet another aspect of
this summer festival logjam. *Advance information, tickets, and
programs: The Filmhouse, 88 Lothian Rd., Edinburgh EH3 9BZ,
tel. 031/228–4051.*

The **Edinburgh Military Tattoo** might not be art, but it is certainly
entertainment. It is sometimes confused with the festival itself,
partly because the dates overlap (1995 dates: Aug. 4–26). This great
celebration of martial music and skills is set on the castle esplanade,
and the dramatic backdrop augments the spectacle. Dress warmly
for the late-evening performances. Even if it rains, the show most
definitely goes on. *Tickets and information: Edinburgh Military
Tattoo, 22 Market St., tel. 031/225–1188.*

Away from the August–September festival overkill, the **Edinburgh
Folk Festival** usually takes place around Easter each year. The 10-
day event presents performances by Scottish and international folk
artists of the very highest caliber.

Theater Edinburgh's main theaters are the **Royal Lyceum** (Grindlay St., tel.
031/229–9697), which offers contemporary and traditional drama;
the **King's** (Leven St., tel. 031/229–1201), for such "heavyweight"
material as ballet, and light entertainment, like Christmas panto-
mime; the **Traverse** (Cambridge St., tel. 031/228–1404), housed in
specially designed flexible space that's ideal for its avant-garde
plays; and the new **Edinburgh Festival Theatre** (Nicolson St.), which
stages theatrical and musical entertainment.

Concert Halls **Usher Hall** (Lothian Rd., tel. 031/228–1155) is Edinburgh's grand-
est, and the venue for the Royal Scottish Orchestra in season; the

Queen's Hall (Clerk St., tel. 031/668–3456) is more intimate in scale and hosts smaller recitals. The **Playhouse** (Greenside Pl., tel. 031/557–2692) leans toward popular artists.

Nightlife

Edinburgh's nightlife is quite varied, with discos, casinos, and "ceilidhs" (pronounced "kay-lees"), or Scottish musical evenings, for the older set. The Edinburgh and Scottish Information Centre above Waverley Market (*see* Important Addresses, *above*) can supply up-to-date information on various categories of nightlife, including places offering dinner-dances.

Discos/   **Buster Browns** (25–27 Market St., tel. 031/226–4224) offers main-
Nightclubs   stream sounds Fri.–Sun. 10:30 PM–2 AM.

The Cavendish (W. Tollcross, tel. 031/228–3252) has a variety of different clubs and types of music. Open Thurs.–Sat. 9 PM–3 AM.

The Lanes (South Charlotte La., tel. 031/226–6828) is a basement bar with a dance floor, popular with the 20s–30s crowd. Open Mon.–Thur. 9 PM–3 AM, Fri. 5 PM–3 AM, Sat. and Sun. 7 PM–3 AM.

Minus One (Carlton Highland Hotel, North Bridge, tel. 031/556–7277) has live music and a DJ on Fri. and Sat., DJ only on Thurs., playing mainstream sounds; the place is not for teeny boppers or old fogies. Open Thurs.–Sat. 10 PM–3 AM.

Red Hot Pepper Club (3 Semple St., tel. 031/229–7733) plays mainstream music Fri.–Sat. 10 PM–4 AM.

Casinos   **Berkeley Casino Club** (2 Rutland Pl., tel. 031/228–4446) is a private club that offers free membership on 48 hours' notice, as do **Casino Martell** (7 Newington Rd., tel. 031/667–7763) and **Stanleys** (5B York Pl., tel. 031/556–1055). **Stakis Regency Casino** (14 Picardy Pl., tel. 031/557–3585) also makes membership available after a 48-hour waiting period. Its restaurant is highly rated.

Folk Clubs   Various pubs throughout the city regularly feature folk performers. At the **Edinburgh Folk Club** (Cafe Royal, 17 W. Register St., tel. 031/339–4083) there's folk music every Wed. at 8 PM.

Scottish   Several hotels present traditional Scottish music evenings in the
Entertainments   summer season, including the **Carlton Highland Hotel** (North
and Ceilidhs   Bridge, tel. 031/556–7277) and **George Hotel** (George St., tel. 031/225–1251).

Another well-established Scottish entertainment includes **Jamie's Scottish Evening** (King James Hotel, Leith St., tel. 031/556–0111).

The **Scottish Experience and Living Craft Centre** (12 High St., tel. 031/557–9350) puts on Scottish evenings, offering traditional food, song, and dance.

Cocktail Bars   **Harry's Bar** (7B Randolph Pl., tel. 031/539–8100) is an Americana-decorated basement bar with disco music that is hugely popular with locals. Open daily noon–1 AM.

L'Attache (beneath the Rutland Hotel, 1 Rutland Pl., tel. 031/229–3402) is another basement bar with live folk/rock music nightly. Open Sun.–Thurs. 8 PM–1:30 AM, Fri. and Sat. 8 PM–2 AM.

Madogs (38A George St., tel. 031/225–4308) was one of Edinburgh's first all-American cocktail bar/restaurants; it remains popular with professionals after work, with live music most weeknights. Open Sun. 6:30 PM–2 AM, Mon.–Wed. noon–2 AM, Thurs.–Sat. noon–3 AM. No sneakers.

17 Scotland: Southwest and Highlands

Glasgow, Scotland's largest city, suffered gravely from the industrial decline of the 1960s and '70s, but recent efforts at commercial and cultural renewal have restored much of the style and grandeur it had in the 19th century at the height of its economic power. Now it is again a vibrant metropolitan center with a thriving artistic life—so much so that it was selected as Europe's Cultural Capital for 1990. Glasgow is a very convenient touring center, too, in easy reach of the Clyde coast to the south and with excellent transportation links to the rest of Scotland.

The Dumfries and Galloway region south of Glasgow is a hilly and sparsely populated area, divided from England by the Solway Firth; it's a region of somber forests and radiant gardens, where the palm, in places, is as much at home as the pine. The county seat is Dumfries, associated with Robert Burns (1759–96) in much the same way as the Borders are with Sir Walter Scott.

Stirling, once the capital, commanded the strategic route linking north and south Scotland. Its castle is second only to Edinburgh's in grandeur. Other ancient towns that have contributed much to Scotland's colorful past include St. Andrews, on the windswept coast, and Perth, former seat of Scottish kings. Not far from Stirling lie the Trossachs with their woodlands and lochs, the Highlands in miniature.

Ben Nevis, Britain's highest peak, rises from magnificent scenery in the west, while, sweeping southward, the long Kintyre peninsula is a wonderland of sea views, spectacular sunsets, and prehistoric monuments.

West and north lie the Highlands. The great surprise to unprepared visitors is the changing scenery and the stunning effects of light and shade, cloud, sunshine, and rainbows. In a couple of hours you may pass from heather, bracken, and springy turf to granite rock and bog, to serrated peak and snow-water lake, to the red Torridon sandstone of Wester Ross, and the flowery banks of Loch Ewe and Loch Maree. Sea inlets are deep and fjordlike. The black shapes of the isles cluster like basking whales on the skyline. Cliffs where quartzite gleams above crescents of hard sand lead around a northern shore that looks from the air as though it had been trimmed by an axe. Westward, the next stop is North America.

Essential Information

Important Addresses and Numbers

Tourist Information **The Greater Glasgow Tourist Board,** 35–39 St. Vincent Pl., Glasgow, tel. 041/204–4400. Open Mon.–Sat. 9–6 (extended hours in summer).

Aviemore and Spey Valley Tourist Board, Grampian Rd., Aviemore, tel. 0479/810363, fax 0479/811063.

Ayrshire Tourist Board, Suite 1005, Prestwick Airport, Prestwick, tel. 0292/79000, fax 0292/78874.

City of Dundee Tourist Board, 4 City Sq., Dundee, tel. 0382/27723, fax 0382/26353.

Clyde Valley Tourist Board, Horsemarket, Ladyacre Rd., Lanark, tel. 0555/662544, fax 0555/666143.

Dumfries and Galloway Tourist Board, Campbell House, Bankend Rd., Dumfries, tel. 0387/50434, fax 0387/50462.

Fort William and Lochaber Tourism Ltd., Cameron Centre, Cameron Sq., Fort William, tel. 0397/703781, fax 0397/705184.

Isle of Arran Tourist Board, Information Centre, The Pier, Brodick, tel. 0770/302140, fax 0770/302395.

Inverness, Loch Ness and Nairn Tourist Board, Castle Wynd, Inverness, tel. 0463/234353, fax 0463/710609.

Isle of Skye and South West Ross Tourist Board, Information Centre, Portree, Skye, tel. 0478/612137, fax 0478/612141.

Loch Lomond, Stirling and Trossachs Tourist Board, 41 Dumbarton Rd., Stirling, tel. 0786/475019, fax 0786/471301.

Perthshire Tourist Board, Lower City Mills, West Mill St., Perth, tel. 0738/27958, fax 0738/30416.

Shetland Isles Tourism, Market Cross, Lerwick, tel. 0595/3434, fax 0595/5807.

St. Andrews and North East Fife Tourist Board, 70 Market St., St. Andrews, tel. 0334/72021, fax 0334/78422.

Western Isles Tourist Board, 26 Cromwell St., Stornoway, Lewis, tel. 0851/703088, fax 0851/705244.

West Highlands and Islands of Argyll Tourist Board, Albany St., Oban, tel. 0631/63122, fax 0631/64273.

Travel Agencies

American Express: 115 Hope St., Glasgow, tel. 041/221–4366. **Thomas Cook:** 22 City Sq., Dundee, tel. 0382/200201; 15–17 Gordon St., Glasgow, tel. 041/221–6611; 65 High St., Perth, tel. 0738/35279; 11–13 Murray Pl., Stirling, tel. 0786/451466.

Car-Rental Agencies

Aberdeen: Avis, 16 Broomhill Rd., tel. 0224/574252, and at the airport, tel. 0224/722282; **Europcar,** 121 Causewayend, tel. 0224/631199, and at the airport, tel. 0224/770770; **Hertz,** Railway Station, tel. 0224/210748, and at the airport, tel. 0224/722373.

Dundee: Budget Rent-a-Car, Tayford Motor Co. Ltd., Balfield Rd., tel. 0382/644664; **Hertz,** 18 Marketgait, tel. 0382/23711.

Glasgow: Avis, 161 North St., tel. 041/221–2827; **Budget Rent-a-Car,** The Moat House Hotel, Congress Rd., tel. 041/226–4141; **Hertz,** 106 Waterloo St., tel. 041/248–7736.

Inverness: Europcar Ltd., The Highlander Service Station, Millburn Rd., tel. 0463/235337; **Hertz,** Mercury Motor Inn, Junction A9/A96, Millburn Rd., tel. 0463/224475.

Perth: Europcar, 26 Glasgow Rd., tel. 0738/36888; **Hertz,** 405 High St., tel. 0738/24108.

Stirling: Europcar Ltd., Mogil Motors Ltd., Drip Rd., tel. 0786/472164.

Arriving and Departing by Plane

Glasgow Airport (tel. 041/887–1111) is 8 miles from town, with a motorway link, buses, and trains. It is currently undergoing major expansion, and a new international terminal is due for completion in summer 1995. British Airways, Northwest, American, Air Canada, British Midland, and Air UK serve Glasgow, as well as United Airlines, Loganair, Air France, Lufthansa, SAS, Sabena, Aer Lingus, and Iceland Air.

Aberdeen Airport (tel. 0224/722331), as the central airport for the North Sea oil fields, handles a wide range of international routes. **British Airways** (tel. 081/897–4000) and **Air UK** (tel. 0224/722331) have direct flights between London and Aberdeen and from Aberdeen to other Scottish destinations. BusinessAir, SAS, Brymon, and Gill Air also serve Aberdeen. There are direct flights to Aberdeen from Amsterdam, Stavanger, and Bergen, and also flights from Paris and Frankfurt.

Arriving and Departing by Car, Train, and Bus

By Car The quickest route from London into southern Scotland and on to Glasgow is M1/M6/A74 (397 mi). A more visually pleasing route is via A68 over Carter Bar, and the quietest is A697 via Coldstream.

By Train **British Rail** serves western Scotland from London's Euston Station (tel. 071/387–7070). Average travel time from Euston to Carlisle is four hours and to Glasgow, 5½ hours.

By Bus **Scottish Citylink** (tel. 041/332–9191) serves Scotland from London's King's Cross and Victoria Coach Station. Average travel time to Glasgow is 7–7½ hours.

Getting Around

By Plane **Inverness Airport** (tel. 0463/232471) is central for a wide range of internal flights covering the Highlands and islands region. British Airways serves Inverness from Glasgow, Kirkwall, Stornoway, and the Shetlands. **Loganair** (tel. 0667/62332) has direct Glasgow–Inverness flights and includes Kirkwall, in the Orkneys, among its routes.

By Car Great improvements have been made on Highland roads in recent years. A9 now has some stretches of divided highway, and A835 puts the northwest touring base of Ullapool little more than an hour beyond Inverness. Ballachulish Bridge, on the Oban–Fort William road, and Kylesku Bridge, north of Lochinver, have replaced ferries and reduced crossing times. If you are coming from eastern Scotland, allow a comfortable three hours from Edinburgh to such Highland destinations as Oban, Fort William, or Inverness.

By Train Two notably scenic branches are the **Kyle Line,** from Inverness west to Kyle of Lochalsh (the ferry port for Skye), and the **Fort William to Mallaig** section of the West Highland line (a continuation of services from Glasgow). The attractions of both lines are further enhanced by the option, in summer months, of vintage carriages to Kyle or steam locomotive to Mallaig. "ScotRail Rover" tickets cover almost the entire Scot-Rail network, and "West Highland" and "North Highland" local Rovers are also available.

By Bus The **Scottish Citylink** office in Glasgow (tel. 041/332–9191) provides full information on Lowland and Highland bus services and sells network "Explorer" tickets.

By Ferry **Caledonian MacBrayne** (tel. 0475/650100, fax 0475/637607) runs a useful ferry service between the Clyde coast and the southwest Highlands: Wemyss Bay–Rothesay (Bute), Gourock–Dunoon, and Ardrossan–Brodick (Arran); and operates ferries to the Western Isles from various west coast ports such as Oban. Inter-island ferries make island-hopping an attractive option.

ScotRail Travelpass The "ScotRail Travelpass" is a comprehensive pass covering nearly all train and ferry transport, and giving discounts on buses, in the Highlands and islands for either eight or 15 days. It is available at any main train station in Scotland.

Guided Tours

Orientation Tours The following companies run regular bus tours around the region: **Clydeside 2000 plc,** Paisley, tel. 041/889–3191; **Scott Guide Coaches,** Glasgow, tel. 041/942–6453; and **Scottish Citylink,** Glasgow, tel. 041/332–9191.

Special-
Interest Tours

The Scottish Tourist Guides Association (tel. and fax 041/776–1052) can recommend fully qualified guides who will arrange walking or driving excursions of varying lengths to suit your interests.

The following also offer car-and-driver tours tailored to your personal interests and needs: **Little's Chauffeur Drive,** Glasgow, tel. 041/883–2111, and **Man Friday Services,** Greenock, tel. 0475/633151 or 0475/632378.

Exploring Southwest and Highlands

These explorations begin in central and southwest Scotland, covering a handful of major cities and a host of scenic lake and coastal areas. Tour 1 starts in Glasgow, then travels to Loch Lomond and the Clyde coast, to the Isle of Arran and on to Ayrshire; some gardens farther south are also included.

The second tour starts in Stirling, then moves northwest to the Trossach lochs. An alternative excursion leads east to St. Andrews, then returns west via the cities of Dundee and Perth.

Tour 3 explores the western Highlands. From a base in Oban, excursions head south to Kintyre, east to Loch Fyne and Loch Awe and on through Inveraray and Glencoe, and north to Fort William, Glenfinnan, and Mallaig.

The final tour takes in the northern Highlands. Two separate journeys based from Inverness travel east to Culloden Moor, then south to Aviemore, and southwest to Loch Ness.

Highlights for First-time Visitors

Cawdor Castle: Tour 4
Culzean Castle and Country Park: Tour 1
Inverary Castle: Tour 3
Loch Lomond: Tour 1
Loch Ness: Tour 4
Pulpit Hill, Oban: Tour 3
Scone Palace, Perth: Tour 2
Stirling Castle: Tour 2
Victorian Glasgow: Tour 1

Tour 1: Glasgow, the Clyde Valley, and the Southwestern Coast

Numbers in the margin correspond to points of interest on the Southwest Scotland and the Western Highlands and the Glasgow maps.

❶ Until fairly recently, **Glasgow** was a depressed city infamous for its slums. Today, its renewal shows itself in the trendy downtown stores, a booming and diverse cultural life, stylish restaurants, and above all, a general air of confidence.

Glasgow's development over the years has been unashamedly commercial, tied up with the wealth of its manufacturers and merchants, who constructed a vast number of civic buildings throughout the 19th century. Many of these have been preserved, and Glasgow claims, with some justification, to be Britain's greatest Victorian city.

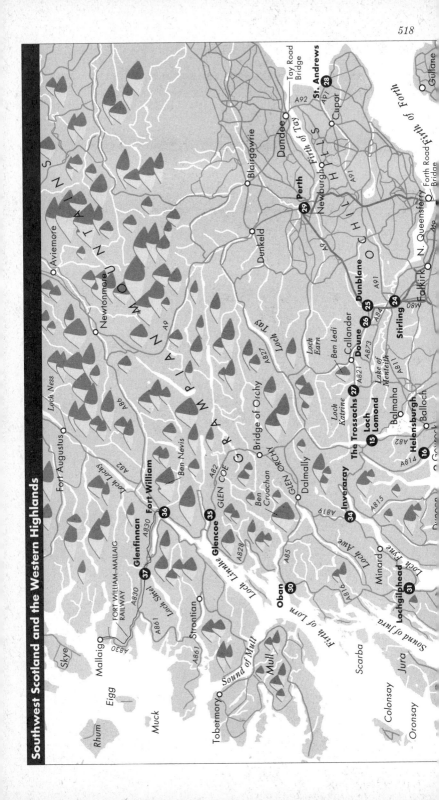

Southwest Scotland and the Western Highlands

George Square, the focal point of Glasgow's business district, is the natural starting point for any walking tour. The magnificent Italian Renaissance–style **City Chambers** on the east side of the square were opened by Queen Victoria in 1888. *Tel. 041/227–4017. Free guided tours Mon.–Fri., 10:30, 2:30 (may be closed for occasional civic functions).*

Leave the square by Queen Street to the south, and note the fine neo-classical facade of the Royal Exchange of 1827, now **Stirling's Library.** Pass through Royal Exchange Square and under the arch to the pedestrian section of Buchanan Street; the elegant **Princes Square** shopping mall is here (*see* Shopping, *below*). Next, turn east into Argyle Street. Like Buchanan Street, it is an important shopping district where you can wander without the threat of traffic. Head toward the River Clyde, via Stockwell Street, to discover the new face of Glasgow shopping at the **St. Enoch Centre** (*see* Shopping, *below*).

In the nearby park, Glasgow Green, is the **People's Palace.** Opened in 1898 and recently refurbished, it has extensive exhibits on Glasgow's social history. The rear half of the premises is a Victorian greenhouse called the Winter Gardens. *Tel. 041/554–0223. Admission free. Open Mon.–Sat. 10–5, Sun. 11–5.*

Make your way next up High Street, which was the center of the downtown area before Glasgow expanded westward in the 18th century. These days, High Street seems unimpressive, but keep a lookout for **Provand's Lordship,** the oldest building in Glasgow. This 15th-century town house, said to have been the lodgings of three Scottish monarchs, overflows with portraits, stained glass, and tapestries. *Castle St., tel. 041/552–8819. Admission free. Open Mon.– Sat. 10–5, Sun. 11–5.*

Glasgow Cathedral, on a site sacred since St. Mungo founded a church there in the late 6th century, is an unusual double church, one above the other. Its 13th-century crypt was built to hold the relics of St. Kentigern. *Cathedral St., tel. 031/244–3101. Admission free. Open Apr.–Sept., Mon.–Sat. 9:30–6, Sun. 2–5; Oct.–Mar., Mon.–Sat. 9:30–4, Sun. 2–4 and for services.*

Nearby is the newly opened **St. Mungo Museum of Religious Life and Art,** which houses an outstanding collection of artifacts. *2 Castle St., tel. 041/357–3929. Admission free. Open Mon.–Sat. 10–5, Sun. 11–5; closed Christmas, New Year's.*

On your return to George Square you can enjoy the architecture of this area, known as "the Merchant City." Just south of the square, look for **Hutcheson's Hall,** a visitor center, shop, and regional office for the National Trust for Scotland. The elegant, neoclassical building was designed by David Hamilton in 1802. *158 Ingram St., tel. 041/552–8391. Admission free. Open weekdays 9–5, Sat. 10–4. Shop open Mon.–Sat. 10–4.*

Nearby, just south of Ingram Street, the buildings on Virginia Street recall the days of the rich "tobacco barons" who traded with the Americas. At No. 33, a former tobacco exchange survives. Nearby **Virginia Court,** somewhat faded now, also echoes those far-off days. (Peer through the bars of the gates and note the wagon-wheel ruts still visible in the roadway.) If you want to see today's commercial life, visit the **Scottish Stock Exchange** on West George Street, which is worthwhile for the exterior alone: It was built in 1877 in an ornate "French Venetian" style.

521

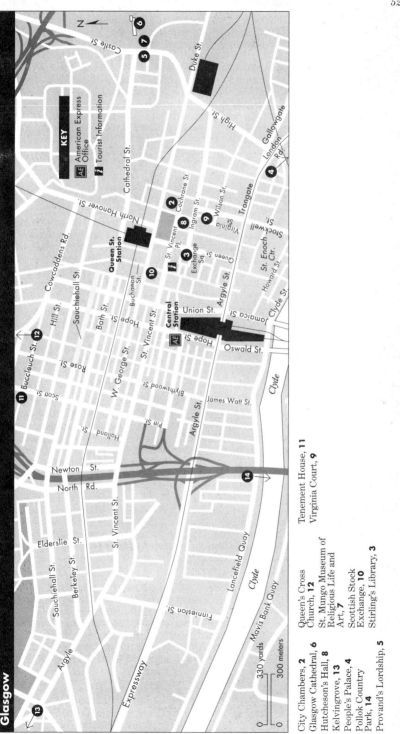

Glasgow

KEY

AE American Express Office

ℹ️ Tourist Information

0   330 yards
0   300 meters

City Chambers, **2**
Glasgow Cathedral, **6**
Hutcheson's Hall, **8**
Kelvingrove, **13**
People's Palace, **4**
Pollok Country Park, **14**
Provand's Lordship, **5**

Queen's Cross Church, **12**
St. Mungo Museum of Religious Life and Art, **7**
Scottish Stock Exchange, **10**
Stirling's Library, **3**

Tenement House, **11**
Virginia Court, **9**

⑪ Just beyond the downtown area, the **Tenement House,** in the Garnethill area north of Charing Cross Station, is a fascinating time capsule, painstakingly preserved with the everyday furniture and belongings of half a century of occupation by the same owner. The building dates from 1892. *145 Buccleuch St., tel. 041/333–0183. Admission: £2 adults, £1 senior citizens and children. Open Mar.– Oct., daily 1:30–5 (other times by appointment).*

Time Out The **Willow Tearoom** (217 Sauchiehall St.) is restored to its original archetypal Art Deco design, by Charles Rennie Mackintosh, right down to the decorated tables and chairs. The tree motifs are echoed in the street address, as "sauchie" is an old Scots word for "willow."

To learn more about the Glasgow-born designer Mackintosh, head **⑫** for **Queen's Cross Church,** now the Charles Rennie Mackintosh Society Headquarters. Although one of the leading lights in the turn-of-the-century Art Nouveau movement, Mackintosh died in 1928 with his name scarcely known, least of all in his native city. Now he is confirmed as an innovator. This center provides a further insight into Glasgow's other Mackintosh-designed buildings, which include the Scotland Street School, the Glasgow School of Art, and the reconstructed interiors of the Hunterian Art Gallery. *870 Garscube Rd., tel. 041/946–6600. Admission free. Open Tues., Thurs., Fri. noon–5, Sun. 2:30–5 (or by arrangement).*

In **Kelvingrove Park,** west of the M8 beltway, is the city's main art **⑬** gallery and museum, **Kelvingrove.** Looking like a combination of cathedral and castle, it houses a fine collection of British and Continental paintings, 17th-century Dutch art, a selection from the French Barbizon school, French Impressionists, Scottish art from the 17th century to the present, silver, ceramics, European armor, and even Egyptian archaeological finds. *Tel. 041/357–3929. Admission free. Open Mon.–Sat. 10–5, Sun. 11–5.*

Across Kelvingrove Park are two other important galleries, both maintained by Glasgow University. They house the collections of William Hunter, an 18th-century Glasgow doctor who assembled a staggering quantity of extremely valuable material. The **Hunterian Museum,** the city's oldest (1807), displays Hunter's hoards of coins, manuscripts, and archaeological artifacts in a striking Victorian Gothic building. Even more interesting is the **Hunterian Art Gallery,** which has the doctor's pictures plus other collections bequeathed to the university—works by Reynolds, Rodin, Rembrandt, Tintoretto, Whistler, and a large section devoted to the work of Charles Rennie Mackintosh, including reconstructed interiors of his house. *Museum: tel. 041/330–4221. Admission free. Open Mon.–Sat. 9:30–5. Gallery: tel. 041/330–5431. Admission free. Open Mon.–Sat. 9:30–5.*

⑭ **Pollok Country Park** provides a peaceful green oasis off Paisley Road, just 3 miles southwest of the city center. The key attraction here is the **Burrell Collection,** Scotland's finest art collection. A modern, custom-built, airy, and elegant building houses treasures of all descriptions, from Chinese ceramics, bronzes, and jade to medieval tapestries, stained glass, and 19th-century French paintings—the magpie collection of an eccentric millionaire. *Tel. 041/ 649–7151. Admission free. Open Mon.–Sat. 10–5, Sun. 11–5.*

Also located in Pollok Country Park is **Pollok House,** which dates from the mid-1700s and contains the Stirling Maxwell Collection of paintings, including works by El Greco, Murillo, Goya, Signorelli, and William Blake. Fine 18th- and early 19th-century furniture, silver, glass, and porcelain are also on display. *Tel. 041/632–0274. Admission free. Open Mon.–Sat. 10–5, Sun. 11–5.*

Numbers in the margin correspond to points of interest on the Southwest Scotland and the Western Highlands map.

15 Leaving Glasgow, follow A82 northwest toward **Loch Lomond,** at 23 miles long the largest and most famous of Scotland's lochs. The southern end is less than 20 miles (only about 30 minutes) from downtown Glasgow. The town of **Balloch** is the southern gateway to the loch, but it is not especially attractive. The very best view of Loch Lomond is from **Duncryne Hill,** farther east. The loch, dotted with tiny islands, spreads out beyond the fields and lush Lowland hedgerows, then narrows and extends northward into the Highlands. Scenic cruises leave from both Balloch and Balmaha, about 6 miles north on the eastern shore.

The Clyde coast was once the playground for Glasgow's prosperous merchants, who built their splendid Victorian country homes here. These mansions line the shores of the Gare Loch (note that this one is spelled differently from the Gairloch that appears later in this **16** chapter) and fill the resort town of **Helensburgh** (5 mi west of Loch Lomond on B832), where you can embark on a Clyde estuary cruise. The Mackintosh-designed **Hill House,** complete with his custom-designed furniture, is here, in calm, leafy surroundings on the hill just behind the promenade. It was originally built for Glasgow publisher William Blackie in 1902–04. *Upper Colquhoun St., tel. 0436/73900. Admission: £3 adults, £1.50 children and senior citizens. Open Apr.–Dec., daily 1:30–5:30.*

Three Clyde ferry ports—Gourock, Wemyss Bay, and Ardrossan—all lie within easy touring distance of Glasgow on A78. You can catch a car ferry from Gourock across the Firth of Clyde to **Dunoon,** a traditional coastal resort, or take the ferry from Wemyss Bay (5 mi south of Gourock on A770/A78) to **Rothesay,** a faded but appealing resort on the **Isle of Bute.** The island offers a host of relaxing walks and scenic vistas. Fifteen miles farther down the coast at **Ardrossan,** ferries leave regularly for the island of **Arran,** whose rugged scenery is reminiscent of that of the Scottish Highlands. **Brodick Castle, 17** dating from the 13th century, and an ancient seat of the dukes of Hamilton, is the island's most famous attraction. It offers lavish interiors and gardens where early rhododendrons enjoy shelter from the frost. The gardens are a country park. *Brodick, tel. 0770/302202. Admission: £4 adults, £2 children and senior citizens. Open early Apr. and May–Sept., daily 1–5; late Apr. and early Oct., Sat., Sun. 1–5. Grounds and country park open daily 9:30–sunset.*

Time Out In the **Servant's Hall** at Brodick Castle, an award-winning restaurant serves morning coffee (with six different types of hot scones—try the date and walnut!), a full lunch menu that changes daily (venison casserole or salmon steaks might be available), and afternoon teas with home-baked goods, including the bread. Eat out on the terrace on a fine day, with chaffinches clamoring for crumbs.

From Ardrossan, follow A78/A77 south about 15 miles to the popu-**18** lar commercial and tourist city of **Ayr,** a good place to begin a tour of the western coast and the county of Ayrshire. The region combines abandoned industries, old mines, and forgotten railroads with vivid green pastures that are home to the celebrated Ayrshire breed of dairy cattle, small seaside ports, and high moors. The county is also known for its associations with Robert Burns, Scotland's national poet, and for its fine coastal golf resorts, such as **Troon,** near Prestwick.

The port of Ayr is Ayrshire's chief town, but if you're on the Burns **⑲** trail, head for **Alloway,** on B7024 in Ayr's southern suburbs. Here, among the many middle-class residences, you'll find the one-room thatched **Burns Cottage,** where the poet was born in 1759. *Tel. 0292/ 441215. Admission: £2.20 adults, £1.10 children and senior citizens, £5.25 family ticket (includes admission to Burns Monument). Open June–Aug., Mon.–Sat. 9–6, Sun. 10–6; Apr., May, Sept., Oct., Mon.–Sat. 10–5, Sun. 1–5; Nov.–Mar., Mon.–Sat. 10–4.*

Near the Burns Cottage, opposite Alloway's ruined church, is the **Land o' Burns Centre,** offering exhibitions and audiovisual presentations on the life of Burns. *Tel. 0292/443700. Admission free (small charge for presentations). Open Sept.–June, daily 10–5; July, Aug., daily 10–5:30.*

Auld (old) **Alloway Kirk** (church), across the road, is where Tam o' Shanter, hero of Burns's well-known poem of the same name, un- luckily passed a witches' revel—with Old Nick himself playing the bagpipes—on his way home from a night of drinking. Close by is the **Brig o' Doon** ("brig" is Scots for "bridge"), which Tam, in flight from the witches, managed to cross just in time. His gray mare, Meg, lost her tail to the closest witch. (Any resident of Ayr will tell you that witches cannot cross running water.) The **Burns Monument** (en- trance fee included in charge for Burns Cottage) overlooks the Brig o' Doon.

For a different perspective on Ayrshire's history, take A719 12 miles **⑳** southwest from Ayr to **Culzean** (pronounced "Ku*lain*") **Castle and Country Park,** the National Trust for Scotland's most popular prop- erty. The castle, complete with walled garden, is a superb neoclassi- cal mansion designed by Robert Adam in 1777. The country park welcomes 300,000 visitors a year, yet remains unspoiled. In addition to its marvelous interiors, the castle contains the National Guest Flat, given by the people of Scotland in appreciation of General Eisenhower's services during World War II. As president he stayed once or twice at Culzean and his relations still do occasionally. Be- tween visits it is used by the N.T.S. for official entertaining. Ap- proach is by way of rooms evoking the atmosphere of World War II: Mementos of Glenn Miller, Winston Churchill, Vera Lynn, and other personalities of the epoch all help create a suitably 1940s mood. *Tel. 06556/269. Admission: country park and castle £5.50 adults, £3 children and senior citizens; country park £3 adults, £1.50 senior citizens and children. Castle open Apr.–Oct., daily 10:30–5:30; country park open all year, daily 9:30–sunset.*

Time Out At **Culzean Country Park Visitor Centre,** housed in converted farm buildings close to the castle, there is a licensed restaurant (open 10:30–5:30) which serves snacks and a full lunch menu in attractive surroundings of sandstone walls and country-style, heavy wooden tables and chairs.

Ayrshire gradually merges with Galloway among the dark, domed hills and forested strips of the southwest. Galloway catches the best of the mild, southwesterly winds and has a south-facing coastline— not very common in Scotland. As a result, there is a superb range of gardens here as well as the sprawling and impressive **Galloway For- est Park,** 25 miles south of Ayr on A713. The park comprises several separate forests—Glentrool, Carrick, and so on—grouped around a circle of mountains and lakes.

㉑ Among the gardens to look for here are **Threave Garden** (tel. 0556/
502575), the National Trust for Scotland's School of Gardening near
㉒ **Castle Douglas,** at the southern end of A713; **Castle Kennedy** (tel.
㉓ 0776/702024), just before **Stranraer** off A75; and the **Logan Botanic
Garden** (tel. 0776/860321) at **Port Logan** on the Rinns peninsula, 10
miles south of Stranraer. The best time to see these gardens is early
in the season, when the rhododendrons, azaleas, and magnolias are
at their brilliant best, although there's plenty to see all summer and
well into the fall. *Admission: Threave £3 adults, £1.50 children and
senior citizens; Castle Kennedy £2 adults, £1.50 senior citizens, £1
children; Logan Botanic £1.50 adults, £1 senior citizens, 50p children. Threave open daily 9:30–sunset; Castle Kennedy open Easter–Sept., daily 10–5; Logan Botanic open mid-Mar.–Oct., daily
10–6.*

Tour 2: Stirling and the Lowland Lochs to St. Andrews and Perth

㉔ **Stirling,** about 23 miles northeast of Glasgow, is another of Britain's
great historic towns. A simple way to enjoy an aerial view of the
Highlands is to head for **Stirling Castle;** its esplanade, which is open
even when the castle is not, commands superb, sweeping views. The
castle, built in the 15th and 16th centuries, was a royal residence of
the Stuart kings, who were—in every sense of the word—monarchs
of all they surveyed! Take time to inspect this lovely Renaissance citadel of crow-stepped gables, stone carvings, and twisted chimneys.
The hammer-beamed Parliament Hall still whispers of dark 16th-
century deeds, and across the courtyard, the fine regimental museum of the Argyll & Sutherland Highlanders houses more recent battle memories. Several kings and queens were born or crowned in
these buildings. Mary, Queen of Scots, lived there in her infancy before she was sent to France. An embrasure on the battlements with
the inscription "MR 1561" is still called Queen Mary's Lookout. *Tel.
031/244–3101. Admission: £3.50 adults, £2 senior citizens, £1 children. Open Apr.–Sept., daily 9:30–5:15; Oct.–Mar., daily 9:30–
4:15.*

You will have already met the **Royal Burgh of Stirling Visitor Centre**
on the way into the castle. On the esplanade, it houses a shop and
exhibition hall with an audiovisual production on the town and surrounding area. *Tel. 0786/462517. Admission free. Open same hours
as the castle.*

On the right as you go down into the town is **Mar's Wark,** the roofless
ruin of a mansion that the earl of Mar, premier earl of Scotland, put
up in 1570. The building of slightly later date on the left, the **Argyll
Ludging** ("ludging" was "lodging," a nobleman's town house), was
for many years a military hospital and is now a youth hostel.

Time Out The building where Lord Darnley (Mary, Queen of Scots' second
husband) stayed when she was in residence at Stirling Castle is now
the **Darnley Coffee House** (16–18 Bow St.). Try the fresh coffee and
homemade cakes.

Before you descend to modern Stirling's shopping streets you pass
the old **Town House** (City Hall); the **Mercat Cross,** where proclamations were made; and the parish church of the **Holy Rude** ("rood,"
meaning "cross"), a fine Gothic building dated 1414. Here King
James VI was crowned at the age of one year; the presiding clergyman was John Knox, the Scottish religious reformer.

Close by in Back Walk stands the quaint 17th-century **Cowane's Hospital,** built as a refuge for the old. You can walk from here along the south side of the castle hill to the **Smith Art Gallery and Museum.** As you start, note the square patch of ground beside Dumbarton Road (A811) called the **King's Knot.** It was once a garden of intricately intersecting paths and borders and dates from around 1628. *Dumbarton Rd., tel. 0786/471917. Admission free. Open Apr.–Sept., Tues.–Sat. 10:30–5, Sun. 2–5; Oct.–Mar., Tues.–Fri. 12–5, Sat. 10:30–5, Sun. 2–5.*

Stirling Castle at one time commanded the only overland route between the Highlands and Lowlands, at the River Forth's lowest bridging point. Many decisive battles were fought near here. The story of the great battle of **Bannockburn** in 1314, which regained 400 years' independence for Scotland, is told at the National Trust for Scotland's **Bannockburn Heritage Centre,** 2 miles south of Stirling on A91. *Glasgow Rd., tel. 0786/812664. Admission: £1.80 adults, 90p senior citizens and children. Open Apr.–Oct., daily 10–5:30.*

Just north of Stirling, high on the Abbey Craig, the **Wallace Monument** commemorates Scotland's earliest freedom fighter, William Wallace, who lived at the end of the 13th century. Recently refurbished, it offers an exhibit, audiovisual presentation, and the chance to climb to the top of the 200-foot tower. *Abbey Craig, tel. 0786/472140. Admission: £2.35 adults, £1.20 senior citizens and children. Open Apr.–Oct., daily 10–5; Nov.–Mar., Sat and Sun. 11–3.*

㉕ To explore northwestward into the hills, take M9 up to **Dunblane,** 7 miles north of Stirling. In the middle of town, standing in a sleepy square, are the partly restored ruins of a large cathedral. King David built the existing structure in the 13th century on the site of St. Blane's little 8th-century cell. **Dunblane Cathedral** is contemporary with the Border abbeys (*see* Chapter 16), but more mixed in its architecture—part Early English and part Norman. Dunblane ceased to be a cathedral, as did most others in Scotland, at the time of the Reformation in the mid-16th century. *Tel. 031/244–3101. Admission free. Open Apr.–Sept., Mon.–Sat. 9:30–6, Sun. 2–6; Oct.–Mar., Mon.–Sat. 9:30–4, Sun. 2–4; and for services.*

Just under 4 miles due west of Dunblane on A820 is the little town of **㉖** **Doune. Doune Castle,** in its impressive setting by the River Teith, is one of the best-preserved of Scotland's medieval fortifications. (Optimum photo vantage point is upstream from the A84 bridge.) *Tel. 031/244–3101. Admission: £2 adults, £1.25 senior citizens, 75p children. Open Apr.–Sept., Mon.–Sat. 9:30–6, Sun. 2–6; Oct.–Mar., Mon.–Wed., Sat. 9:30–4, Thurs. 9:30–noon, Sun. 2–4.*

From Doune, take A84 northwest to **Callander,** where the peak of **Ben Ledi** (2,882 ft.) looms impressively at the end of the main street. The town itself is unashamedly tourist-oriented—an accommodation and refreshment stop on the route west—but worth exploring nonetheless. If you tire of shopping, explore the **Callander Crags** or the less steep **Bracklinn Falls** (both behind the town) for a sample of Highland scenery.

Time Out Just off the main street, right in the center, is **Pip's Coffee House** (tel. 0877/330470), a cheerful little eating place that offers light meals, soups, and salads, as well as Scottish home-baking and more substantial three-course meals in the evenings (between April and October). There is also a little picture gallery with plenty of Scottish material to browse through.

㉗ From Callander, take A84, then A821, west to **the Trossachs** lochs, beginning at **Loch Venachar.** The Trossachs have been a tourist mecca since the late 18th century. They combine the wildness of the Highlands with the prolific vegetation of an old Lowland forest. Their open ground is a dense mat of bracken and heather; their woodland is of silver birch, dwarf oak, and hazel that fasten their roots into every crevice of the rocks and stop short on the very brink of the lochs.

Though there is a range of forest tracks and trails, for many people the easiest way to enjoy the Trossachs' splendor is to walk from the main parking lot along the north bank of **Loch Katrine** (pronounced "*Ka*-trin"). This is on a well-surfaced road owned by the Strathclyde Water Board and open only to pedestrians and cyclists.

The steamer *Sir Walter Scott* leaves from a nearby pier on its Loch Katrine cruise. Take the cruise if time permits, as the shores of Katrine remain undeveloped and impressive. This loch is the setting of Scott's narrative poem "The Lady of the Lake," and Ellen's Isle is named after his heroine. It was Scott's influence that led to the Trossachs becoming a major tourist attraction. *Trossachs Pier, tel. 041/ 355–5333. Cost: £3.25 adults, £1.90 children and senior citizens, £8.50 family ticket (morning cruises are cheaper). Cruises early Apr.–late Sept., Sun.–Fri. 11, 1:45, 3:15, Sat. 2, 3:30.*

An alternative exploration from Stirling will take you east following A91 along the southern edge of the Ochil Hills, through the communities known as the Hillfoots towns. Here, the streams tumbling off the steep pastures provided water power and grazing for livestock—two factors that combined to create a booming textile industry, second only to that of the Borders. The main road continues, via the market town of Cupar in Fife, all the way to the ancient port town of St. Andrews on the North Sea coast.

㉘ **St. Andrews** is world famous as the birthplace of golf, originally played with a piece of driftwood, a shore pebble, and a convenient rabbit hole on the sandy, coastal turf. However, the town also offers a wide range of attractions for nongolfers. The cathedral, its ancient university (founded in 1411), and castle are poignant reminders that the town was once the ecclesiastical capital of Scotland. The now largely ruined **cathedral** was one of the largest churches ever built in Scotland. The **castle** is now approached via a visitor center with audiovisual presentation and shop. *Admission: cathedral museum and St. Rule's Tower £1.50 adults, £1 senior citizens, 75p children; castle £2 adults, £1.25 senior citizens, 75p children; to all £3 adults, £1.75 senior citizens, £1 children. Grounds, museum, and tower open Apr.–Sept., Mon.–Sat. 9:30–6, Sun. 2–6; Oct.–Mar., Mon.– Sat. 9:30–4, Sun. 2–4.*

Time Out **Ma Brown's** (24 North St., tel. 0334/73997) is close to the castle; it serves coffee, light lunches, and teas in premises that used to be a grocer's and wine store. The handsome old shop counter and shelving still remain, adding to the old-world atmosphere.

From St. Andrews, drive back west to Cupar on A91 and then take A913 northwest to Newburgh on the Firth of Tay. Continue following A913 until it joins A912 and turns up to Perth.

㉙ **Perth** does not give the impression of being an ancient historic site, yet this old town was the Scottish capital from the 12th century until the King of Scotland, James I, was assassinated here in 1437. His successor, James II, moved the court to the better-fortified castle at

Stirling. Today Perth is a bustling place, where the country folk, in from the prosperous hinterland of Lowland farms and Highland estates, mix with strolling tourists on the busy shopping streets.

At the Round House, the **Fergusson Gallery** displays a selection of 6,000 works by the Scottish artist J. D. Fergusson. *Marshall Pl., tel. 0738/441944. Admission free. Open Mon.–Sat. 10–5.*

Perth's main historical interest lies in nearby **Scone Palace** (2 miles north by A93, Braemar Road). This grandly embellished, castellated mansion stands on the site of earlier royal palaces. While still the home of the earl of Mansfield, it is well equipped to deal with visitors who flock to view its vast collections of 16th-century needlework, china, furniture, vases, and other objets d'art. Within its grounds is **Moot Hill,** the ancient coronation place of the Scottish kings. To be crowned, they sat upon the Stone of Scone, which was seized in 1296 by Edward I of England, Scotland's greatest enemy, and placed in the coronation chair at Westminster Abbey in London, where it is still on view. Some Scots hint darkly that Edward was fooled by a substitution, and that the real stone is hidden north of the border, waiting for Scotland to regain its independence. *Tel. 0738/52300. Admission: £4.20 adults, £2.30 children, £3.40 senior citizens, £12.50 family ticket. Open Easter–Oct., Mon.–Sat. 9:30–5, Sun. 1:30–5 (July and Aug. 10–5).*

Tour 3: Oban and the Western Highlands

In the mountainous west, the county of Argyll offers some of Scotland's finest scenery. Here, where the west winds bring mild rain, you will find a highly photogenic harmony of hill, loch, and lush woodland.

㉚ Oban, the most lively of the west Highland mainland resorts, faces a bewildering tangle of isles in the Firth of Lorn. It is a great yachting center—for the experienced!—as well as a ferry port for the islands and a collection point for cargoes of shellfish. With its russet-stone, white-painted houses, it has a venerable air, but most buildings were the result of an influx of early 20th-century vacationers.

Time Out **MacTavish's Kitchen** (High St., tel. 0631/63064) serves morning coffee and traditional lunches of hearty stews and roast beef with vegetables.

Romantic views from this great crossroads of the Highlands are also to be had from **Pulpit Hill** at the south end of Oban; from **MacCaig's Tower,** a Victorian architectural extravagance just behind Pulpit Hill (panorama boards help identify landscape features); and from the high ground beyond **Dunnollie Sands**—simply follow the promenade northward until it ends.

One possible trip out of Oban follows A816 onto the long arm of the peninsula that runs due south of town to the Mull of Kintyre, around 70 miles. All the way down this route, intrusive sea lochs cut almost through the peninsula. The 9-mile-wide neck of land at **Loch-㉛ gilphead** was severed by the picturesque Crinan Canal, surveyed by James Watt around 1793, built by John Rennie, and in use by 1801. The Crinan area is famous also for its wealth of prehistoric monuments, cairns, standing stones, medieval carved grave-slabs, and, on a high, bare rock overlooking the Crinan levels, **Dunadd Fort,** the ancient capital of Dalriada, an early kingdom from which Celtic Scotland sprang.

The main A83, south from Lochgilphead, is a fast road down the west side of Kintyre, giving superb sea-glittering views of the silhouetted hills of the island of Jura, and also little Gigha, closer to the coast. The east-side road is the narrower and winding B842, with a summer-only ferry connection to Arran at Claonaig. Either way, you reach **Campbeltown,** a well-stocked town, complete with palm trees by the harbor and famed for its whisky and its local cheeses.

Minor roads from the B842 south of Campbeltown lead down to the **Mull of Kintyre.** Sunsets are spectacular here. Park well above the lighthouse and stroll on to the moorland nearby.

A second excursion from Oban will lead you into the real heartlands of Argyll, around the sea inlet of **Loch Fyne** and **Loch Awe,** slightly to the north. Visit Loch Awe by driving eastward from Oban along A85, via the Pass of Brander with its tree-strewn crags. The scale of the lake and mountains, particularly the spiky dragon-back of **Ben Cruachan** (3,695 feet), can best be seen by following signs from Dalmally to Monument Hill.

Turn south on A819 just before Dalmally, and drive through Glen Aray 15 miles to **Inveraray.** The duke of Argyll is the chieftain of the Campbell clan, and you can visit **Inveraray Castle,** the duke's seat and headquarters of the clan since the 15th century. The present castle was rebuilt in the 18th century. It's an elegant place with a self-satisfied air, dominating a well-ordered town. Here Dr. Johnson was entertained in 1773, and here, as Boswell tells, the celebrated lexicographer first tasted Scotch whisky. At the castle you can inspect items that successive dukes of Argyll have salvaged from the Tobermory galleon, a vessel from the Spanish Armada that sank (legend says it was blown up by a daring Scot) in the Sound of Mull near Tobermory. *Tel. 0499/2203. Admission: £3.50 adults, £1.75 children, £2.50 senior citizens, £9 family ticket. Open Apr.– June, Sept.–mid-Oct., Mon.–Thurs., Sat. 10–1, 2–5:30, Sun. 1–5:30; July–Aug., Mon.–Sat. 10–5:30, Sun. 1–5:30.*

Return north on A819 to Dalmally and turn east for 3 miles to where narrow B8074 leads off to the left (north). You will now enter **Glen Orchy,** a scenic glen with particularly fine riverscapes and waterfalls. It is virtually empty of settlement since it was ruthlessly cleared of its farming population in the last century to make way for the sheep of the local landowner, the marquis of Breadalbane. B8074 joins A82 just before **Bridge of Orchy,** the only village for miles around, and a small one at that. A82 continues north over Rannoch Moor and then turns west to enter the portals of **Glencoe,** where great craggy buttresses loom darkly over the road. The National Trust for Scotland's **visitor center** at Glencoe (at the western end of the glen) offers excellent displays on local geology and history, especially the infamous massacre here in 1692—still remembered in the Highlands for the treachery with which soldiers of the Campbell clan treated their hosts, the MacDonalds. According to Highland code, in his own home a clansman should give shelter even to his sworn enemy. In the face of bitter weather, the Campbells were accepted as guests by the MacDonalds. Apparently acting on orders from the British government, the Campbells subsequently turned on their hosts, committing murder "under trust." *Tel. 08552/307. Admission: 50p adults, 25p children. Open Apr.–May, early Sept.– late Oct., daily 10–5; June–early Sept., 9:30–6.*

You can return to Oban by way of A828, southward along the Firth of Lorn (36 mi). Alternatively, you can take A82 northward over the elegant bridge across the Ballachulish narrows to reach **Fort Wil-**

liam (15 mi). As its name suggests, this town originated as a military outpost, first established by Cromwell's General Monk in 1655 and refortified in stone by George I in 1715 to help combat an outbreak by the turbulent Jacobite clans. It remains the southern gateway to the Great Glen—Glen Mor, the 60-mile-long valley (and geological fault) that crosses northern Scotland—and to the far west. Scotland's (and Britain's) highest mountain, the 4,406-foot **Ben Nevis,** looms over Fort William less than 4 miles from the sea. The mountain is a challenge to climb: Only fit and well-equipped walkers should make the hike to its summit.

Nearby, in a converted church at Corpach on A830, **Treasures of the Earth** displays a huge collection of gemstones, crystals, and fossils, including a 26-pound uncut emerald. *Tel. 0397/772283. Admission: £2.50 adults, £1.50 children. Open July, Aug., Sept., daily 9:30–7; Oct.–Dec., Feb.–June, daily 10–5; Jan. by appointment.*

This area is strongly associated with the Jacobite hero Prince Charles Edward Stuart ("Bonnie Prince Charlie"). The tale of his doomed struggle to restore the Stuart monarchy is told at the visitor center of the National Trust for Scotland's **Glenfinnan Monument** at **Glenfinnan,** about 19 miles west of Fort William on A830. Here, at the head of Loch Shiel, Charles raised his standard in 1745 and succeeded in rousing various clans to follow him, especially the Camerons. *Tel. 039783/250. Admission: £1 adults, 50p children. Open Apr.–May, early Sept.–late Oct., Mon.–Sat. 10–1, 2–5; Sun. 10:30–1, 2–5; June–early Sept., Mon.–Sat. 9:30–6, Sun. 10:30–6.*

Railroad buffs will want to inspect the nearby **Glenfinnan railroad viaduct,** one of the very earliest examples of mass concrete construction. Built at the turn of the century, and 100 feet high, it carries the tracks 1,248 feet across the valley. In summer, you can tell when a steam train is due on this structure by the sudden sprouting of camera tripods on every heathery knoll in the vicinity.

A830 continues west to the port of **Mallaig** and the southernmost of the ferry connections to the Isle of Skye, the largest of the Inner Hebrides. The most relaxing way to take in the birch- and bracken-covered wild slopes, however, is on the **Fort William–Mallaig Railway** (tel. 0397/703791), especially by steam locomotive in the summer.

Tour 4: The Inverness Area

Numbers in the margin correspond to points of interest on the Inverness Area map.

The northern Highlands are often described as one of Europe's last wilderness areas. Certainly the landscapes of the northwest have no equal anywhere else in Britain. This stark, uncompromising landscape, glittering with lochans (small lakes), will either cast a lifetime spell on you or make you long for the safe, effete pastures of the south.

Inverness is a logical touring base, with excellent roads radiating out to serve an extensive area. Known for centuries as the Capital of the Highlands, Inverness is not exclusively Highland in flavor, however. Part of its hinterland includes the farmlands of the Moray Firth coastal strip, as well as of the Black Isle. It is open to the sea winds off the Moray Firth, while the high hills, although close at hand, are mainly hidden. Few of Inverness's buildings are of great antiquity—thanks to the Highland clans' careless habit of burning the town to the ground. Even its castle is a Victorian replacement on the site of a

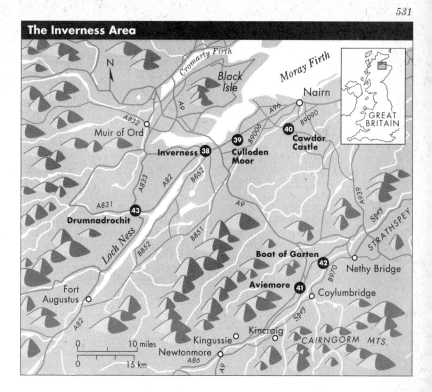

The Inverness Area

fort blown up by Bonnie Prince Charlie. Now bypassed by A9, still the town in summer does not simply bustle, it positively roars. Be careful in its one-way traffic system, whether walking or driving.

The cemetery here is something of a tourist attraction. Spreading over the wooded slopes of Tomnahurich (Hill of the Fairies), about a mile west of the town, it overlooks a panorama of firth, river, canal, and loch. At about the same distance from the town center, following the Ness River upstream toward its loch, you come to the Ness Islands. Footbridges neatly connect them to each other and to either side of the river. Among them are bandstands and an open-air theater with regular programs of summer entertainment—nothing very sophisticated, but convincing demonstrations of the Highland capital's love and respect for the old piping and dancing traditions.

Two separate excursions through the country about Inverness are suggested. The first sallies out 5 miles east on B9006 to visit **❸❾ Culloden Moor,** scene of the last battle fought on British soil. Here, on a cold April day in 1746, the outnumbered Jacobite forces of Bonnie Prince Charlie, exhausted by a night march, ill-fed and badly led, were decimated by the superior firepower of George II's army, which included the Campbells among other Highlanders, as well as Lowland Scottish regiments. (This was not, in any sense, a Scotland-versus-England confrontation.) The victorious commander, the duke of Cumberland (George II's son), earned the name of "Butcher" Cumberland for the bloody reprisals carried out by his men on Highland families, Jacobite or not, who were caught in the vicinity. The National Trust for Scotland has, slightly eerily, re-created the battlefield as it looked in 1746. The uneasy silence of the open moor almost drowns out the merry clatter from the visitor center's coffee shop and the tinkle of the cash registers. *Tel. 0463/ 790607. Admission (visitor center and audiovisual display): £1.80 adults, 90p children, senior citizens, and students. Open Apr.– Oct., daily 9–6; Feb., Mar., Nov., Dec., daily 10–4 (closed December 25–26).*

From Culloden Moor, continue on B9006, then turn right on B9090 (around 10 mi) to reach **Cawdor Castle,** near Nairn. This cheerfully idiosyncratic, mellowed, and mossy family seat has a 15th-century central tower. The castle is associated with Shakespeare's *Macbeth* as the home of the thanes (clan chiefs) of Cawdor. *Tel. 06677/615. Admission: £4 adults, £2.20 children, £3.10 senior citizens, £12 family ticket; garden and grounds only £2. Open May–Sept., daily 10–5:30.*

If you continue eastward along the Moray Firth from Nairn, just north of Cawdor, you'll pass miles of inviting sandy beaches and a string of fishing communities. From Nairn to Fraserburgh at the extreme eastern end of the coast is around 70 miles. Alternatively, from Cawdor you can take the smaller roads B9090, B9006, and B851 southwest to reach A9, which will lead you for 25 miles across the empty moors on the northern edge of the Grampian Mountains to the valley of Strathspey (in Gaelic, "strath" means "broad valley"), where the river Spey links a number of communities. These include **Aviemore**—a 1960s attempt to create a classy, St. Moritz–type Highland playground and ski resort—as well as the more appealing villages of Newtonmore, Kingussie, Kincraig, Coylumbridge, Boat of Garten, and Nethybridge. For a fine view of the great **Cairngorm massif,** increasingly nibbled at and disfigured by resort developers, the **Strathspey Railway** will take you round-trip from Aviemore to **Boat of Garten,** through fine scenery of moor and birch, with the Cairngorm Mountains as a backdrop to the east. You can board the train at Aviemore or Boat of Garten. *Tel. 0479/810725. Round-trip fares (3rd class): £4 adults, £2 children (1st class £6 adult), £10 family ticket. Operates late May, July, Aug., daily; June, Sept., Sun.– Fri.; Apr., May, Oct., Sun. and Wed.; additional service Easter, Christmas, New Year's; occasional theme weekends (e.g., Thomas the Tank Engine). Timetable changes according to season.*

Time Out | If you enjoy restored steam locomotives, try a pub lunch at the **Boat Hotel** (Boat of Garten), a former station hotel, where whistles and clanking are suitable accompaniments to simple home cooking.

Inverness is also the northern gateway to the Great Glen, the result of an ancient earth movement that dislocated the entire top half of Scotland. The main road south from Inverness is the busy A82 route along the west bank of **Loch Ness,** though leisurely drivers may prefer the east bank road, B862 and B852, to Fort Augustus, at the lake's southern end (32 miles). Monster watchers should visit the "official" **Loch Ness Monster Exhibition** at **Drumnadrochit** on A82, midway on the west bank. Loch Ness's huge volume of water has a locally warming effect on the weather, making the lake conducive to mirages in still, warm conditions. These are often the circumstances in which the "monster" appears, and you may draw your own conclusions. *Tel. 0456/450573 and 0456/450218. Admission: £4 adults, £2.50 children, £3 senior citizens and students, £10.50 family ticket. Open July–mid-Sept., daily 9–9:30. Off-season opening times vary; please phone to check.*

What to See and Do with Children

Haggs Castle in Glasgow is a museum with exhibits aimed exclusively at younger children. Workshops and children's activities abound; there's everything from face painting to doll making. *100 St. Andrew's Dr., tel. 041/427–2725. Admission free. Open Mon.–Sat. 10–5, Sun. 11–5.*

The **Scottish Wool Centre,** at Aberfoyle, tells the story of Scottish wool "from the sheep's back to your back." Live specimens of the main breeds are on show in the Sheep Amphitheatre, while the Textile Display Area gives the opportunity to try spinning and weaving. There is also a Kids' Farm (with lambs and kids) and Sheepdog Training School. The shop stocks a huge selection of woolen garments and knitwear. *Tel. 0877/382850. Admission: £2.50 adults, £1.50 children, £5 family ticket; Kids' Farm 50p. Open Apr.–Sept., daily 9:30–6; Oct.–Mar., daily 10–5 (live sheep shows only in summer).*

With plenty of beaches on the west, north, and east coasts— Dornoch, Gairloch, and Nairn among them—you'll have no problem arranging a traditional sun-and-sandcastle vacation. All along the coasts, children's fair-weather entertainment is of the outdoor variety: fishing, hiking, seal watching, boat trips, cross-country pony riding, and so on.

Other outstanding places for children are the **Sea-Life Centres** at **Barcaldine** (Barcaldine, Connel, Argyll, tel. 0631/72386) and **St. Andrews** (St. Andrews, Fife, tel. 0334/74786). Both offer a fascinating display of marine life. The restaurant at Barcaldine (midway between Fort William and Oban on the west coast and easy to reach from either town) is particularly recommended.

Off the Beaten Track

Five miles east of Dumfries by B724 is the **Ruthwell Cross,** one of the most important monuments surviving from the Dark Ages. Carved in the 8th century, it stands 18 feet high in an apse of the Ruthwell Church. *Admission free.*

The villages of **Leadhills** and **Wanlockhead,** perched more than 1,300 feet above sea level in the Lowther hills of Galloway, are the highest in Scotland. Once lead was mined from the domed, heather-covered uplands nearby. The **Museum of the Scottish Lead Mining Industry** tells the story and offers subterranean tours. *Goldscaur Rd., Wanlockhead, on B797, northeast of Sanquhar, 27 mi northwest of Dumfries, tel. 0659/74387. Admission: £2.99 adults, £1.25 children, £2.50 senior citizens, £7.50 family ticket; includes visit to mine. Open Apr.–Oct., daily 11–4:30, last tour at 4; winter by appointment.*

Nine miles northeast of Moffat, itself about 35 miles southeast of Glasgow, the spectacular waterfall known as the **Grey Mare's Tail** can be seen from A708. Now in the care of the National Trust for Scotland, the waterfall is in an area that offers plenty of hiking routes for the adventurous. There are also interesting botanical specimens on the hills above, especially on White Coomb Mountain (2,695 ft.).

The little Wester Ross village of **Shieldaig,** curved around a sheltered bay, offers breathtaking views of the Torridon hills—if you can find the lookout point. The main road from Torridon, A896, enters the village and swings south and left along the seafront. From the point where the main road reaches the shore, another dead-end road goes right and uphill. Walk up the latter road. At its end, a path heads north over the heathery headland. Walk as far as you like—the view gets better with every step.

Balquhidder Glen is about 1½ hours' drive from Glasgow via A81 and A84 north. Green hills and silver water, the scent of new birch leaves in spring: This is a breath of the Highlands just minutes from A84, between Callander and Lochearnhead.

Loch Lomond may be serenely beautiful, but try one of its islands for real tranquillity. You can reach **Inchcailloch** from the boatyard at Balmaha, where a little boat will take you over. This small island has ancient oak woods ringing with birdsong, blankets of bluebells underfoot, and a nature trail.

In a sense, all of the Highlands lies off the beaten track, which explains why much of the landscape remains comparatively unspoiled. North of Lochinver, off A837, in Sutherland, B869 runs in a spectacular loop to the Kylesku bridge and some breathtaking views in the area. Beyond the village of **Stoer,** a narrow road heads west to the outlying houses and the lighthouse (Cluas Deas). Park at the lighthouse and stroll northward over the moorland. Away from the cliff edge, rising ground gives a spectacular, arm's-length view of the northwest mountains rising starkly on the horizon. Only the energetic will reach the rock stack called the **Old Man of Stoer.**

Cape Wrath is the tip of northwest Scotland. "Wrath" has nothing to do with anger: The headland got its name from a Norse word meaning "turning point." You can reach the tip only by minibus along the lighthouse road, after a short ferry crossing of the Kyle of Durness.

On the shore of **Bo'ness,** 15 miles southeast of Stirling by A905, on the Firth of Forth, a typical branch-line railroad station has been reconstructed by the **Scottish Railway Preservation Society.** Its line will eventually join the main Glasgow–Edinburgh line at Linlithgow. Steam trains usually run on weekends and in the summer. Distance, frequency, and fares are subject to change as the line is extended (for full details tel. 0506/822298 or 0506/822446).

Shopping

Glasgow is rapidly challenging Edinburgh as a shopping center, as it does in many other fields, and is a lot more fun than its staid rival. Elsewhere in the region you will find excellent woolens and tweeds. Keep an eye out for unusual designs in Scottish jewelry, especially when they employ local stones. Scotland has always been a very bookish country, priding itself on the high rate of literacy, and you will often find a surprisingly well-stocked secondhand bookshop in a fairly remote town.

Aberlour In this pretty little town on the banks of the River Spey, **Country Cousins** (126 High St.) sells an unusual and interesting range of ladies' clothing, knitwear, and leather and tapestry bags. It's worth a browse if you're a "fishing widow."

Corpach The shop at **Treasures of the Earth** (*see* Tour 3, *above*) stocks an Aladdin's Cave assortment of gemstone jewelry, crystal ornaments, mineral specimens, polished stones, and books on related subjects. It's a real treasure trove of unusual holiday gifts.

Glasgow Glasgow's main shopping districts occupy the southeastern part of town, in a square grid that runs south to Clyde Street on the banks of the river, north to St. Vincent Street, and east–west from City Chambers to the Central Station. From George Square to Argyle Street the area is called Merchant City—and you'll see why, as you pass the many designer boutiques and great shopping "precincts" (malls), complete with fountains and glass-walled elevators, on Buchanan and Glassford streets. **Ichi Ni San** (123 Candleriggs) is a glitzy fashion shrine, all beaten metal and distressed plaster. **Princes Square,** off Buchanan Street, is a chic and modern mall, with specialty shops on three levels and a café complex above, all under a glittering dome. You'll find **Katharine Hamnett** here, or try the **Scottish Craft Centre** for unusual, high-quality items—no tartan dolls. **Stockwell China Bazaar** (67–77 Glassford St.) specializes in fine china and giftware. **The Warehouse** (61–65 Glassford St.) has designer clothes (Rifat Ozbek, Jean Paul Gaultier, and Jasper Conran) and shoes—floor after floor of them.

Just off Buchanan Street you'll find **William Porteous & Co. Ltd.** (9 Royal Exchange Pl.), which features maps, souvenir books and prints, and Scottish-made crafts and gifts. The **Italian Centre** (John St.), a reminder of Glasgow's cosmopolitan image, has the only British **Emporio Armani** outside London, as well as **Gianni Versace** and a choice of Italian restaurants.

At the southern end of this area you'll find the **St. Enoch Centre,** the latest of Glasgow's new generation of shopping malls. The **Argyll Arcade** (corner of Buchanan and Argyle sts.) is a handsome 19th-century shopping mall preserved in its original form with a wide selection of jewelers' shops displaying their wares. On Howard Street is another row of shopping outlets including **Slater Menswear,** where you'll find high-quality tweeds, woolens, and sportswear for men.

Sauchiehall Street has a good selection of shopping, but perhaps its highlight is above **Hendersons the Jewellers** (No. 217), where you will find the **Willow Tearoom** (*see* Time Out, Tour 1, *above*) for afternoon tea and a snack.

Uptown Glasgow, in the Kelvingrove/University section, has shopping areas centering on Hillhead and Kelvinbridge, including a selection of small commercial art galleries. **DeCourcy's Arcade,** off Byre's Road, features a number of lovely little antiques shops.

Glasgow's weekend market, the **Barras,** is just north of Glasgow Green. "Barras" means "barrows" (pushcarts), but all of the market stalls are covered. You can find just about anything here, in any condition, from very old model railroads to almost new cheese rolls. Antiques hunters might strike pay dirt, but don't be surprised if you come away empty-handed. *Tel. 041/552–7258. Admission free. Open weekends 9–5.*

Inverness   As you would expect, Inverness features a number of shops with a distinct Highland flavor. At **Pringle's Woollen Mill** (Dores Rd.) you can take a free guided tour of the mill; a fine shop on the premises sells lovely tweeds, tartans, and, of course, wool clothing. **The Kilt Maker** (4–9 Huntly St.) has a huge selection of kilts, or will run one up for you made to measure. **Duncan Chisholm & Sons** (47–51 Castle St.) is another fine shop specializing in Highland tartans, woolens, and crafts. A variety of both specialty shops and larger department stores can be found at the **Eastgate Shopping Centre** (11 Eastgate).

In addition to these traditional stores, more unusual crafts shops are nearby. **Highland Aromatics Ltd.** (Drumchardine, 7 mi west on A862) sells perfumed toilet soap made with Scottish ingredients and all manner of perfumes, colognes, bath salts, and toiletries. **High-**

land Wineries Ltd. (Kirkhill, 2 mi farther on B9164) makes wine from local products, including sap from silver birch trees.

Lanark This town offers an interesting selection of shops within walking distance of each other. **McKellar's the Jewellers** (41 High St.) has a good range of Charles Rennie Mackintosh–inspired designs in gold and silver. **Strands** (2 Broomgate) carries a wide variety of yarns and knitwear, including Aran designs and one-of-a-kind creations by Scottish designers. **Hop Skip n'Jump** (8 Broomgate) is an excellent children's clothes boutique, stocking British and Continental items. **The Lanark Gallery** (116–118 North Vennel) displays paintings, pottery and ceramics, and sculptures all by Scottish artists.

Lochinver About 3 miles south of Lochinver (in the far northwest), the back road to the town (B869) drops steeply downhill, crosses the little River Kirkaig, and turns toward the shore. Immediately beyond the bridge, beside a parking lot, a sign points to a path that goes far into the loch-mirrored interior, toward the rocky flanks of the mountain Suilven. But much closer, in fact, about two minutes from the parking lot, is **Achins Book and Craft Shop** (Inverkirkaig) which also has a café serving light lunches and home-baked goods. You should easily be able to stock up on all your vacation reading and gift-book shopping here.

Luss In this town, 34 miles west of Stirling and 40 miles north of Glasgow, the **Thistle Bagpipe Works** (tel. 043686/250) will let you commission your own made-to-order bagpipe. You can also order a complete Highland outfit: kilt, jacket, etc.

Oban Oban is the home of one of Scotland's best glassworks. **Oban Glassworks** (Heritage Wharf, tel. 0631/63386) makes Caithness Glass, and here you can see the manufacturing process and buy a memento of Scotland to treasure. Especially lovely are the paperweights with swirling colored patterns.

Perth Perth has upscale shopping aspirations. Native freshwater pearls feature in the superb gold designs of **Cairncross Ltd., Goldsmiths** (18 St. John's St.). **Timothy Hardie** (25 St. John's St.) sells fine jewelry and antique silver. **The Perthshire Shop** (Lower City Mills, West Mill St.) sells a variety of giftware, including items in Perthshire's own tartan: rugs, scarves, handbags, mugs, and more. **William Watson & Sons** (163–167 High St.) specializes in quality china and glassware.

Stirling Stirling offers a range of shops, from down-to-earth to positively eccentric. **R. R. Henderson Ltd.** (6–8 Friars St.) calls itself "Highland outfitters," selling tartans, woolens, and accessories. **Ezhe Hirsh** (10 Friars St.) specializes in jewelry design. **Whinwell Crafts** (22 Broad St.) weaves its own unique designs on silk, woolens, and fine knits.

Sports and the Outdoors

Golf It has been argued that golf came to Scotland from Holland, but the historical evidence points to Scotland being the cradle, if not the birthplace, of the game. Citizens of St. Andrews were playing golf on the town links (public land) as far back as the 15th century. Rich golfers, instead of gathering on the common links, formed themselves into clubs by the 18th century. The Royal Burgess in Edinburgh is both early and exclusive, though, arguably, the world's first golf club was the Honourable Company of Edinburgh Golfers (Leith, 1744) now at Muirfield, East Lothian. The Society of

St. Andrews Golfers (1754) became the Royal and Ancient Golf Club of St. Andrews in 1834.

Scotland is now packed with golf courses: The Gleneagles Hotel boasts four courses of its own, including the new Monarch's Course, opened in early 1993 and designed by Jack Nicklaus. Every town and village has its course and its club. Celebrated courses—Carnoustie, Muirfield, Royal Troon, Turnberry, and others—attract international championships in their turn.

Golf in Scotland is quite a plebeian game, whereas in England it is a distinctly middle-class pastime. A round on a Scottish municipal course costs very little, and the Scottish clubs, apart from a few pretentious places modeled on the English fashion, demand only modest entrance fees.

Here are the names and descriptions of a few Scottish courses that welcome visitors:

Gleneagles Hotel (Auchterarder, near Perth, tel. 0764/663453) has four courses on undulating moorland. Visitors must write in advance. The club was founded in 1908; the King's, Queen's, and Monarch's courses have 18 holes, while the Wee Course has nine.

St. Andrews Links (St. Andrews, tel. 0334/73393). These six seaside courses all welcome visitors; five have 18 holes—the Old Course, New Course, Jubilee, Eden, and Strathtyrum—while the Balgrove Course has nine holes.

Royal Troon (Troon, Ayrshire, tel. 0292/311555). Two 18-hole courses (Old, 6,649 yds.; and Portland, 6,274 yds.) make up this club, founded in 1878. (Access for visitors is limited—ring for details.)

Skiing   Scotland entered the winter-sports arena late, although within a couple of decades Aviemore has blossomed into a major winter-sports center, along with other villages at the foot of the Cairngorms. Other popular ski centers have arisen at Glenshee and Glencoe, but accommodations are limited and likely to remain so. Up-and-coming winter-sports developments include the Lecht, near Aviemore, and Nevis Range, near Fort William.

Compared with the well-known Swiss and Austrian centers, the ski resorts of Scotland suffer from cloudy weather, high winds, and difficulty in keeping access roads snow-free; but when conditions are right the skiing in Scotland can be first-class. The season varies in length because the climate is unpredictable. It can begin as early as November, but the experts prefer February and March.

Walking   Well below the "Highland line," the **Galloway Forest Park** offers a good range of not overly demanding woodland trails, as well as some excursions into the higher hills. However, it is the north which makes real walking demands. The Scots themselves invented the term "the Munros"—a Munro is any Scottish hill over 3,000 feet—and there are 279 of them, though this figure varies a little, depending on the map. With many Scots outdoor enthusiasts these hills are a passion. They range from the very popular Ben Lomond overlooking Loch Lomond near Glasgow to the remote Ben Hope far to the north in Sutherland.

Official footpaths in the Highlands include the **West Highland Way,** running 98 miles from the outskirts of Glasgow to Fort William, by Loch Lomond, Rannoch Moor, and Glen Coe. The track here is well used (some might say loved to death) and moderately demanding in places. Slightly gentler is the **Speyside Way,** taking its name from one of Scotland's premier salmon rivers, which runs down to the sea via Moray's malt whisky country. The Speyside Way offers excellent river valley and some moorland walking for 47 miles, right from the Moray Firth coast up to the foothills of the Cairngorms. Both footpaths are covered in official guides available from bookshops and tourist information centers.

However, if this still sounds too energetic, then inquire at local tourist information centers. They carry details of local Ranger Services who lead guided walks of varying lengths. There are guided walks for such popular areas as the Trossachs and Loch Lomond, as well as wilder areas such as Glen Coe and Kintail. Look out, too, for signposted trails on property controlled by the Forestry Commission (the government forest agency) as well as Highland beauty spots such as the Hermitage, near Dunkeld, or the Bruar Falls above Blair Atholl. Both make pleasant interludes to driving the main A9 to Inverness.

Cawdor Castle Nature Trails provides a choice of four hikes through some of the most beautiful and varied woodlands in Britain. You will pass ancient oaks and beeches, magnificent waterfalls, and deep river gorges. *Cawdor Castle (Tourism) Ltd., Cawdor Castle, Nairn, near Inverness, IV12 5RD, tel. 06677/615. Open May–Sept.*

Highland Edge Walk runs along the Highland boundary fault edge, offering superb views of both the Highlands and Lowlands, 6 miles south of the Trossachs on A821. *Forestry Commission, Aberfoyle, Stirlingshire FK8 3UX, tel. 0877/382383.*

The Highland Games Caber-tossing (the "caber" is a long, heavy pole) and other traditional events figure in the **Highland Games**, staged throughout the Highlands during summer. All Scottish tourist information centers have full details. It is said that these games, a unique combination of music, dancing, and athletic prowess, grew out of the contests held by clan chiefs to find the strongest men for bodyguards, the fastest runners for messengers, and the best musicians and dancers to entertain guests and increase the chief's prestige.

Dining and Lodging

Dining Never assume that because a restaurant is a little off the beaten track its cuisine lacks sophistication. In the Highlands, the reverse is often true. Local game and seafood are often presented with great flair, while oatmeal, local cheeses, and even malt whisky (turning up in any course) amplify the Scottish dimension.

As for fish, many restaurants deal directly with local boats, so freshness is guaranteed. The quality and range of fish is such that local residents can afford curious prejudices; mackerel, for instance, no matter how tasty, is considered second-class fare. With rich pastures supporting the famous Aberdeen Angus beef cattle, good meat is also guaranteed.

Highly recommended restaurants are indicated by a star ★.

Category	Cost*
$$$$	over £40
$$$	£30–£40

$$	£15–£30
$	under £15

per person, including first course, main course, dessert, and VAT; excluding drinks

Lodging In large cities, many hotels are as efficiently faceless and blandly international as you will find anywhere; in general, you must get out of the major population centers if you're looking for real Scottish hospitality. Try Galloway or Argyll, for example, as just two areas with a good choice of smaller, family-run hotels.

Since the removal of much of its indigenous population by forced emigration, many parts of the Highlands have been playgrounds for estate owners or Lowland industrialists, who built themselves shooting lodges, grand mansions, and country estates. Many of these are now fine hotels. Do not, however, expect your hosts always to be Scots—many experienced hoteliers from the wealthy south of England fulfill their ambitions by opening a Highland hotel, where real estate is cheaper, the scenery beautiful, and the pace of life relaxed.

Highly recommended lodgings are indicated by a star ★.

Category	Cost*
$$$$	over £110
$$$	£75–£110
$$	£40–£75
$	under £40

All prices are for two people sharing a double room, including service, breakfast, and VAT.

Arisaig
Dining and Lodging

Arisaig House Hotel. This secluded and grand Victorian mansion offers tranquillity and some marvelous scenery, including views of the Inner Hebrides. The bedrooms are plush and restful, with soft pastel colors, original moldings, and antique furniture. The cuisine at the restaurant showcases fresh local produce. *Beasdale (6 mi south of Mallaig on A830), Arisaig PH39 4NR, tel. 06875/622, fax 06875/626. 2 suites, 12 rooms with bath. Facilities: restaurant, croquet, sailing, fishing, island trips, library, billiards, golfing at Trigh. No children under 10. MC, V. Closed Nov.–Easter. $$$–$$$$*

Auchterarder
Dining and Lodging
★

Auchterarder House Hotel. Secluded and superbly atmospheric, here is a wood-paneled, richly furnished, Victorian country mansion. The staff is particularly friendly, and guests will enjoy the personal attention in this family home. The plush, exuberantly styled dining room, filled with glittering glassware, is an appropriate setting for an unusual and creative use of many locally produced foods: Typical dishes include lamb with a Dubonnet and red wine sauce or poached langoustines with rhubarb. *On B8062, 15 mi southwest of Perth, PH3 1DZ, tel. 0764/663646, fax 0764/662939. 15 rooms with bath. Facilities: restaurant, golf, swimming, tennis, squash, croquet. Restaurant: reservations required; jacket and tie required. AE, DC, MC, V. $$$$*

Gleneagles Hotel. One of Britain's most famous hotels, Gleneagles is the very image of modern grandeur. Like a vast, secret palace, it stands hidden in breathtaking countryside amid world-famous golf courses, including the Monarch's, designed by Jack Nicklaus and opened last year. Recreation facilities are nearly endless, and there are three restaurants: the **Strathearn,** for à la carte and table d'hôte; the **Dormy Grill** (at the 18th hole of the King's Course), for à la carte; and the **Country Club Brasserie,** by the swimming pool. All this plus a shopping arcade, Champneys Health Spa, the Gleneagles Mark Phillips Equestrian Centre, the British School of Falconry, and Gleneagles Jackie Stewart Shooting School make a stay here a luxurious and unforgettable experience. *PH3 1NF, tel. 0764/662231, fax 0764/662134. 236 rooms with bath. Facilities: 3 restaurants, 4 golf courses, tennis, swimming, saunas, gym. Restaurant: reservations essential; jacket and tie required in formal areas of the hotel after 7 PM; dress casual otherwise. AE, DC, MC, V. $$$$*

Auchterless   **Towie Tavern.** On the main Aberdeen–Turriff road, with Fyvie Cas-
Dining   tle nearby as a good reason for exploring the rural hinterland of Aberdeenshire, the Towie Tavern is a friendly and informal traditional eating place. Food is straightforward local fare; check the blackboard for the "Towie Treats"—changing selections of (for example) fresh seafood. The good nature of the staff and the air of coziness more than make up for unsophisticated desserts. *Near Turriff, tel. 08884/201. Reservations advised. Dress: casual. MC, V. $$*

Aviemore   **The Winking Owl.** Freshly decorated and popular with locals as well
Dining   as visitors, this "aprés-ski" resort restaurant serves a blend of traditional English and Scottish dishes. *Grampian Rd., tel. 0479/810646. Reservations advised. Dress: casual. MC, V. $–$$*

Balloch   **Cameron House.** This luxury hotel offers a mix of top-quality hotel
Dining and   and country-club facilities (included in price), set on the shores of
Lodging   Loch Lomond. Award-winning chef Jef Bland (ex-Caledonian Hotel, Edinburgh) oversees cuisine of the highest order, with a Scottish-French slant, in rich Victorian surroundings. Bedrooms are decorated in modern pastel shades with high-quality reproduction antique furniture. The keynote throughout is lavish. *Loch Lomond, Alexandria, Dunbartonshire G83 8QZ, tel. 0389/55565, fax 0389/ 59522. 68 rooms with bath. Facilities: restaurant, pools, gymnasium, squash, golf, tennis, fishing, sailing. Restaurant: reservations required; dress: smart. AE, DC, MC, V. $$$–$$$$*

Banff   **Eden House.** Surrounded by woodland, this Georgian mansion house
Lodging   set high above the River Deveron has magnificent views and makes an elegant but comfortable base from which to explore the northeast. Since it is also the home of the proprietors, you are likely to feel like a houseguest rather than a room number. Tennis, billiards, fishing, and shooting can all be arranged, while numerous golf courses are within easy reach. Relax in the evening surrounded by carefully chosen antiques. Dinner (guests only) might include local seafood, Deveron salmon, game, or Scottish beef. *AB45 3NT, tel. 02616/282. 5 rooms, 2 with bath, 1 with shower. Dress: casual. No credit cards. Closed Christmas, New Year's. $$*

Braemar   **Invercauld Arms.** This handsome stone-built Victorian hotel in the
Dining and   center of Braemar makes a good base for exploring Royal Deeside
Lodging   (Balmoral Castle is just down the road). Interiors are traditional in style and recently refurbished, with plenty of interesting prints decorating the walls. *Braemar AB35 5YR, tel. 03397/41605, fax 03397/41428. 68 rooms with bath and shower. Facilities: restaurant, cocktail bar, fishing and shooting arranged. Restaurant: reservations advised; dress: smart casual. AE, DC, MC, V. $$$*

Crinan
Dining and
Lodging
★

Crinan Hotel. This turn-of-the-century property overlooking the picturesque Crinan Canal and the Sound of Jura has been extensively refurbished. Friendly and helpful, the present owner is an interior decorator on the side, hence the very high standard of the decor in each room. Two restaurants offer both Scottish cuisine and the freshest local seafood: **The Westward Room** serves dinner in a luxurious, country-mansion setting, where you are surrounded by antiques and floral arrangements; the rooftop **Lock 16** has a nautical theme, and superb sunsets accompany the award-winning fresh seafood. *Near Lochgilphead (20 mi south of Oban on A816) PA31 8SR, tel. 054683/261, fax 054683/292. 22 rooms with bath. Facilities: 2 restaurants, coffee shop, sea fishing, boat trips. Restaurant: reservations essential; jacket and tie required in Lock 16. AE, DC, MC, V. Lock 16 closed Sun., Mon. Hotel $$$–$$$$; Restaurants $$$*

Drybridge
Dining
★

Old Monastery. Sitting high on a hillside, with fabulous views, this restaurant is in a building that was formerly a priory. It boasts pine ceilings and walls stenciled by monks 100 years ago. The chef's imaginative recipes make use of very fresh seafood (some of Scotland's largest fishing ports are nearby) and local game. The desserts are also especially good. *Near Buckie (35 mi east of Inverness off A98), tel. 0542/832660. Reservations advised. Dress: casual. AE, MC, V. Closed Sun., Mon., 2 weeks in Nov., 3 weeks in Jan. $$*

Dunblane
Dining and
Lodging

Cromlix House Hotel. This Victorian hunting lodge's period atmosphere is enhanced by cherished furniture and paintings, the original conservatory, and the library. The restaurant offers country-house decor and a choice of two elegant dining rooms. Specialties include game and lamb from the hotel estate. Try the delicious cheese and potato terrine as a starter, followed by beef with pickled walnuts. *Kinbuck (on B8033, 3 mi northeast of Dunblane) FK15 9JT, tel. 0786/822125, fax 0786/825450. 14 rooms with bath. Facilities: restaurant, tennis, trout fishing, grouse and pheasant shooting. Restaurant: reservations advised; dress: smart casual—no jeans. AE, DC, MC, V. Closed Christmas and late Jan.–early Feb. $$$$*

Dunoon
Dining and
Lodging
★

Ardfillayne Hotel. Sixteen acres of wooded garden surround this 150-year-old mansion. The decor is Victorian in inspiration, in keeping with the antique furniture, and the owners clearly enjoy looking after their guests. The food is French, with a Taste of Scotland mixed in. *West Bay (3 mi west of Gourock across the Firth of Clyde) PA23 7QJ, tel. 0369/2267, fax 0369/2501. 7 rooms with bath. Facilities: restaurant. Reservations advised; dress: smart casual. AE, DC, MC, V. $$–$$$*

Elgin
Dining and
Lodging

Mansion House Hotel. This Scots-baronial mansion complete with tower, 38 miles east of Inverness on A96, is set on the River Lossie. The rooms are individually decorated; all provide comfort and pleasant surroundings. The restaurant serves elaborately presented, above-average meals. *The Haugh, IV30 1AW, tel. 0343/548811, fax 0343/547916. 23 rooms with bath. Facilities: restaurant, gardens, bistro bar, indoor pool, sauna, gymnasium, solarium, beauty salon, in-house movies. Restaurant: reservations advised; dress: casual chic—no jeans. AE, DC, MC, V. $$$–$$$$*

Fort William
Dining and
Lodging

Inverlochy Castle. A red-granite Victorian castle, Inverlochy stands in 50 acres of woodlands in the shadow of Ben Nevis, with striking Highland landscape on every side. Queen Victoria stayed here and wrote, "I never saw a lovelier or more romantic spot." Dating from 1863, the hotel retains all the splendor of its period, with a fine frescoed ceiling, crystal chandeliers, handsome staircase in the Great Hall, paintings and hunting trophies everywhere, and plush, comfortable bedrooms. The restaurant is exceptional—a lovely room with wonderful cuisine. Many of the specialties use local produce, such as roast saddle of roe deer or wood pigeon consommé, with orange soufflé as the final touch. *Torlundy (3 mi northeast of Fort William on A82) PH33 6SN, tel. 0397/702177, fax 0397/702953. 16 rooms with bath. Facilities: restaurant, billiards, tennis, croquet, fishing. AE, MC, V. Closed Dec.–mid-Mar. Restaurant: reservations essential; jacket and tie preferred. $$$$*

Glasgow **Buttery.** This restaurant's exquisite Victorian/Edwardian sur-
Dining roundings are echoed by the staff's period uniforms. Food includes
★ the best of Scottish fish, beef, and game as well as an excellent vegetarian menu. Service is friendly and the ambience relaxed. *652 Argyle St., tel. 041/221–8188. Reservations advised. Dress: smart casual. AE, DC, MC, V. Closed Sat. lunch, Sun. $$$*

★ **Rogano.** The striking art deco design of this restaurant is enough to recommend it—the bonus is that the food, at the lively **Café Rogano**, at the main restaurant on the ground floor, and at the oyster bar near the entrance, is excellent. Specialties include game terrine and fresh seafood superbly prepared. Vegetarians are also catered for. Café Rogano is much cheaper and more informal than the main restaurant, but the quality of food is the same. *11 Exchange Sq., tel. 041/248–4055. Reservations advised. Dress: smart casual. AE, DC, MC, V. Closed Sun. lunch, national holidays. $$–$$$*

The Drum and Monkey. This is a spectacular bar/restaurant in relaxed Victorian surroundings and is a popular lunch and evening meeting place for businessmen and businesswomen. Snacks and bar meals are appetizing, and the bistro serves exceptional Scottish-French cuisine. *93–95 St. Vincent St., tel. 041/221–6636. Reservations advised. Dress: casual. MC, V. $$*

★ **The Ubiquitous Chip.** Much loved locally, this restaurant has a glass-covered courtyard with lush greenery and a dining room with exposed ceiling beams. Specialties depend on what is available fresh at top quality but will usually include fish and seafood, venison, haggis, and lamb. The wine list is outstanding. *12 Ashton La., tel. 041/334–5007. Reservations advised. Dress: casual. AE, DC, MC, V. $$*

Cafe Gandolfi. In the heart of the Merchant City, this restaurant has a wealth of carved wood paneling to admire. The food is interesting, innovative, and reasonably priced; the cold smoked venison with red-currant sauce is memorable. *64 Albion St., tel. 041/552–6813. Reservations advised. Dress: casual. MC, V. $–$$*

Harry Ramsden's. There is now a branch of this world-famous fish-and-chips restaurant and carryout in Glasgow. Maybe it's not quite as cheap as your average "chippie," but the quality gives a benchmark against which all others must be judged. *251 Paisley Rd., tel. 041/429–3700. Reservations not required. Dress: casual. MC, V. Closed Christmas, New Year's. $*

Dining and **One Devonshire Gardens.** This fine town mansion offers luxury ac-
Lodging commodations. Elegance is the theme, from the sophisticated drawing room to the sumptuous bedrooms with their rich drapery and traditional furnishings, including four-poster beds (in three bedrooms). The restaurant is equally stylish, with a new menu for each meal. Specialties include salmon with orange and ginger sauce, chicken livers with almonds, and magnificent fillet steaks. *1 Devonshire Gardens, G12 0UX, tel. 041/339–2001, fax 041/337–1663. 27 rooms, 24 with bath, 3 with shower. Facilities: restaurant. Restaurant: reservations advised. Dress: smart casual. AE, DC, MC, V. $$$$*

★ **Glasgow Hilton.** This is a typical international hotel on first impression but breathtakingly professional. Glasgow friendliness permeates its very upscale image. Two themed restaurants, **Cameron's** (a Highland shooting lodge) and **Minsky's** (a colonial/Singapore bar, complete with waiters in safari suits), serve superb food. *1 William St. G3 8HT, tel. 041/204–5555, fax 041/204–5004. 321 rooms with bath. Facilities: 2 restaurants (reservations advised: jacket and tie essential in Cameron's), 2 bars, conference facilities, health and leisure club. AE, DC, MC, V. Hotel $$$$; Restaurant $$$–$$$$*

Central Hotel. The thick carpets, mobcapped chambermaids, and ample rooms here are typical of a railroad hotel of the Victorian era. Public areas feature brass chandeliers and plenty of greenery. The **Entresol** restaurant serves breakfast, lunch, and dinner. *Gordon St., G1 3SF, tel. 041/221–9680, fax 041/226–3948. 221 rooms with bath. Facilities: restaurant, pool, leisure center, bar, in-house movies. AE, DC, MC, V. $$–$$$*

Cathedral House. In the heart of old Glasgow, near the cathedral, this small, friendly, freshly decorated hotel is convenient for sightseeing. The café bar offers a fixed-price lunch, a good value, and there is also a restaurant with an à la carte menu. *28–32 Cathedral Sq. G4 0XA, tel. 041/552–3519, fax 041/552–2444. 7 rooms with bath. Facilities: restaurant, bar. Restaurant reservations advised; dress: casual chic. AE, DC, MC, V. $$*

Babbity Bowster. This wonderful old pub, restaurant, and lodging house in the heart of the Merchant City is an atmospheric hangout for musicians and artists. The public café bar and the restaurant both serve a mixture of traditional Scottish and French food, ranging from filled baked potatoes in the bar to venison or salmon with sophisticated sauces in the restaurant. This is the place to experience "Glasgow Alive," though don't expect peace and quiet late at night; the bar stays open. Bedrooms are basic—pine furnished but adequate. *16–18 Blackfriars St. G1 1PE, tel. 041/552–5055, fax 041/552–5215. 6 rooms with shower. Facilities: restaurant, bar. Restaurant: reservations advised; dress: casual chic. AE, MC, V. $–$$*

Lodging
★
Kirklee Hotel. Located in a quiet district of Glasgow near the university, this bed-and-breakfast hotel is small and cozy. (No evening meals are available, but Glasgow is awash with good restaurants.) The owners take pride in being friendly and helpful and in keeping the hotel spotless and comfortable. *11 Kensington Gate, G12 9LG, tel. 041/334–5555, fax 041/339–3828. 9 rooms with bath. MC, V. $$*

Glenfarg
Dining and Lodging
Bein Inn. Tucked away in a wooded valley just south of Perth, this former cattle drovers' inn makes an excellent base for touring. (M90 is only minutes away but out of hearing.) Furnishings in the lounge, bar, and dining room have an old-fashioned mix of styles, untouched by the uniformity of the interior decorator. Bedrooms, four of which are in an annex, are plainly but comfortably furnished. *PH2 9PY, tel. 0577/830216. 13 rooms with bath. Facilities: restaurant, 2 bars, lounge. Restaurant: reservations advised; dress: smart casual. MC, V. $$*

Inverness
Dining
Culloden House. Although this is a hotel, and was Bonnie Prince Charlie's headquarters during the Battle of Culloden, it is listed here for its restaurant. The food, under the eye of the chef, Michael Simpson, is magnificent. Try the wild salmon in a lobster sauce or venison in Madeira for a taste of the region's delicious produce. *Near Culloden, 6 mi east of Inverness by A9 and B9006, tel. 0463/790461, fax 0463/792181. Reservations advised. Jacket and tie required. AE, DC, MC, V. $$$*

Dining and
Lodging
★

Dunain Park Hotel. Guests receive individual attention in a "private house" atmosphere in this 18th-century mansion 2½ miles southwest on A82. A log fire awaits you in the living room, where you can sip a drink and browse through books and magazines. Antiques and traditional decor make the bedrooms equally cozy and attractive. You can enjoy French-influenced Scottish dishes in the restaurant, where candlelight gleams off bone china and crystal. Saddle of venison in port sauce and boned quail stuffed with pistachios are two of the specialties. *Dunain IV3 6JN, tel. 0463/230512, fax 0463/224532. 14 rooms with bath. Facilities: restaurant, indoor heated pool, sauna, 14 acres of wooded gardens. Restaurant: reservations advised; dress: smart casual. AE, DC, MC, V. Closed 2 weeks in Feb. Restaurant $$; Hotel $$$$*

Lodging

Ballifeary House Hotel. A Victorian property redecorated and well maintained, this one serves good home cooking and offers especially high standards of comfort and service. The hotel is within easy reach of downtown Inverness. *10 Ballifeary Rd., IV3 5PJ, tel. and fax 0463/235572. 8 rooms with bath. MC, V. No smoking in hotel. Closed Nov.–Feb. $$*

Atholdene House. This family-run, late-19th-century stone villa offers a friendly welcome and modernized accommodations. Evening meals can be provided, on request. The bus and railway stations are a short walk away. *20 Southside Rd., 1V2 3BG, tel. 0463/233565. 9 rooms, 7 with shower. No credit cards. $–$$*

Daviot Mains Farm. A 19th-century farmhouse 5 miles south of Inverness on A9 provides the perfect setting for home comforts and traditional Scottish cooking for guests only; lucky guests may find wild salmon on the menu. *Daviot Mains, tel. 0463/772215. 3 rooms, 1 with bath, 1 with shower. MC, V. $*

Kentallen
Dining and
Lodging

Holly Tree Hotel. Housed in a former railway station, this hotel offers views of Loch Linnhe and superb sunsets. The emphasis in the restaurant is on fresh local produce—pigeon, venison, lamb, halibut, and salmon—in modern British cuisine. (Dinner is included in the room rate.) Bedrooms are modern in style and well equipped, if on the small side. *On A828, 17 mi south of Fort William, tel. 063174/292, fax 063174/345. 12 rooms with bath or shower. Facilities: restaurant. Restaurant: reservations required; dress: casual. MC, V. Restaurant $$; Hotel $$–$$$*

Kilmore
Lodging

Glenfeochan House. This family-run Victorian mansion, 5 miles south of Oban on A816, stands in 350-acre grounds and offers tastefully decorated rooms with antique furniture and original plasterwork. *PA34 4QR, tel. 063177/273, fax 063177/624. 3 rooms with bath. Facilities: garden, fishing. MC, V. Closed Nov.–Mar. $$$$*

Langbank
Dining and
Lodging

Gleddoch House Hotel. Originally the home of a shipbuilding magnate, this white-painted hotel was constructed in the 1920s. Spacious, attractive bedrooms are decorated in floral motifs and either period furnishings or more modern style. Specialties such as venison on creamed celeriac and scallops with artichokes in pink pepper sauce with pâté de foie gras are served in the traditional dining room. *Langbank, Renfrew PA14 6YE (17 mi northwest of Glasgow city center), tel. 0475/540711, fax 0475/540201. 33 rooms with bath. Facilities: restaurant, garden, sauna, squash, golf, horseback riding. Restaurant: reservations essential; jacket and tie required. AE, DC, MC, V. Restaurant $$$; Hotel $$$$*

Mull
Lodging
★

Tiroran House Hotel. Family silver and glassware attest to the fact that this enchanting country house is more a family home than a hotel. Its tranquil island setting adds to the peace and homeyness of the place. Candlelit dinners are served in the intimate dining room. *Tiroran PA69 6ES, tel. and fax 06815/232. 9 rooms with bath. Facilities: dining room, recreation room, croquet lawn. No credit cards. Closed Nov.–Apr. $$$$*

Tobermory Hotel. This 18th-century building by the quay on the northeastern tip of the island commands superb views. The ambience is crisp and bright; fresh flowers bedeck every windowsill, and the rooms are spacious and sunny (weather permitting, of course!). *Tobermory PA75 6NT, tel. 0688/2091, fax 0688/2140. 17 rooms, 9 with bath or shower. MC, V. $$*

Nairn **Clifton House.** The Clifton is a very attractive, creeper-clad Victori-
Dining and an villa, full of antiques, flower arrangements, and fires, and offers
Lodging great views over the Moray Firth. You may just want to drop by for a meal while touring eastward; there are two excellent dining rooms to choose from. The seafood is especially good. Nairn lies 16 miles northeast of Inverness via A96. *Viewfield St., IV12 4HW, tel. 0667/53119, fax 0667/52836. 16 rooms with bath. Facilities: 2 restaurants, garden. AE, DC, MC, V. Closed Dec.–Jan. $$$*

Oban **Columba Hotel.** Situated between the quayside and the town, this
Lodging hotel offers modern, elegant public areas and attractive bedrooms. *North Pier, Corran Esplanade, PA34 5QD, tel. 0631/62183, fax 0631/64683. 49 rooms with bath. Facilities: 2 bars. AE, MC, V. $$*

Perth **Timothy's.** This restaurant is more Scandinavian than Scottish, as
Dining the menu is built on a kind of *smørrebrød* system, with all kinds of
★ surprising elements making up the small dishes. There are some major offerings, though, such as fondue bourguignonne. *24 St. John St., tel. 0738/26641. Reservations advised. Dress: casual. MC, V. Closed Sun., Mon. $*

Lodging **Sunbank House Hotel.** You'll find this early Victorian graystone mansion in a fine residential area near Perth's Branklyn Gardens. Recently redecorated in traditional style, it offers solid, unpretentious comforts along with great views over the River Tay and the city. *50 Dundee Rd., PH2 7BA, tel. and fax 0738/24882. 10 rooms with bath or shower. MC, V. $$*

Port Appin **Airds Hotel.** At this hotel, you have some of the finest views in Scot-
Dining and land. Located in a peaceful little village 24 miles north of Oban via
Lodging A85 and A828, this former ferry inn, dating back to the 17th centu-
★ ry, is a long white building backed by trees. It is furnished in a friendly, homey way, with touches of family history, right down to the quilted bedspreads. The restaurant serves fine Scottish cuisine with the help of prime local produce. *Port Appin, Argyll PA38 4DF, tel. 063173/236, fax 063173/535. 12 rooms with bath. Facilities: restaurant, shooting and fishing can be arranged. Restaurant: reservations advised; jacket and tie preferred. AE, MC, V. Closed Jan., Feb. $$$$*

St. Andrews **Grange Inn.** This old farmhouse-type building houses a simple, tra-
Dining ditional restaurant where excellent bar lunches are individually prepared. Dinner is a candlelit affair, with fine food—try the gravlax with sweet dill mustard—and a good selection of malt whiskies. *Grange Rd., tel. 0334/72670, fax 0334/78703. Reservations advised. Dress: casual. AE, DC, MC, V. $*

Lodging **Rusack's Hotel.** Right beside the Old Course, this is clearly a hotel for the well-heeled golfer. It has plenty of opulent Victorian elements in the decor—fake marble and crystal chandeliers. Some of the bedrooms have stunning views. Dinner is included. *Pilmour Links KY16 9JQ, tel. 0334/74321, fax 0334/77896. 50 rooms with* *bath. Facilities: restaurant, golf shop, sauna, solarium. AE, DC, MC, V. $$$$*

Skye **Kinloch Lodge.** Providing elegant comfort on the edge of the world,
Lodging the lodge is run by Lord and Lady MacDonald with flair and considerable professionalism. It is a supremely comfortable country house, with very snug bedrooms and imaginative cuisine in the handsome dining room. *Sleat IV43 8QY, tel. 04713/333, fax 04713/ 277. 10 rooms with bath. Facilities: restaurant, garden, fishing. MC, V. Closed Dec.–early Mar. $$$–$$$$*

Stewarton **Chapeltoun House Hotel.** Real log fires and oak paneling are just two
Lodging of the lovely features of this turn-of-the-century mansion. A feeling
★ of timelessness is enhanced by the seclusion offered on its 20 acres of surrounding private grounds. The rooms are spacious; the restaurant cuisine superb. *On A735 (15 mi southeast of Glasgow), KA3 3ED, tel. 0560/482696, fax 0560/485100. 8 rooms with bath. Facilities: restaurant, gardens. AE, MC, V. $$$$*

Stirling **Heritage.** This elegant 18th-century establishment is run by a
Dining French family. The decor is all fanlights and candles; the menu features French and Scottish classics. *16 Allan Park, tel. 0786/473660. Reservations advised. Dress: casual. MC, V. Closed Christmas, New Year's. $$*

Cross Keys Inn. A quaint, stone-walled dining room adds atmosphere to this restaurant's varied, traditionally Scottish menu. *Main St., Kippen (A811, west of Stirling), tel. 0786/870293. Reservations advised. Dress: casual. MC, V. $$*

Lodging **Stirling Highland Hotel.** The handsome and historic building that this hotel occupies was once the Old High School. Many original architectural features were retained and add to the historic atmosphere. Furnishings are old-fashioned, with solid wood, tartan, florals, and low-key, neutral color schemes. *Spittal St., FK8 1DU, tel. 0786/475444, fax 0786/462929. 76 rooms with bath, 4 suites. Facilities: 2 restaurants, piano bar, sport and leisure club. AE, DC, MC, V. $$$$*

Terraces Hotel. This is a centrally located hotel, useful for exploring Stirling, and as there is plenty of parking space, it makes a good base for touring the region, too. It's a comfortable Georgian town house that has been converted, and since it's comparatively small, the service is attentive. *4 Melville Terr., FK8 2ND, tel. 0786/472268, fax 0786/450314. 18 rooms with bath or shower. Facilities: restaurant. AE, MC, V. $$*

Troon **Piersland House Hotel.** This is located in a late-Victorian mansion,
Dining and formerly the home of a whisky magnate. Oak paneling and log fires
Lodging are the backdrop for specialties such as beef medallions in pickled walnut sauce. *15 Craigend Rd., tel. 0292/314747, fax 0292/315613. 19 rooms with bath or shower. Facilities: restaurant, garden. Restaurant: reservations required; dress: casual. AE, DC, MC, V. Restaurant $$; Hotel $$$*

Ullapool **Altnaharrie Inn.** Be prepared for a real treat. Follow A9/A832 to
Lodging A835 for 60 miles from Inverness to Ullapool, where a private launch
★ takes you to Dundonnell, some 5 miles south, on the banks of Loch Broom. The restaurant is superb, and dinner is included in the room rate. A set menu of local specialties is skillfully prepared, including scallops in white burgundy and bitter cress sauce or medallions of roe deer with leek, grape juniper, and dill sauce, with wild raspberry ice cream and a good selection of cheeses to finish. Bedrooms are comfortable if a little compact. You will need to book far in advance

for this popular inn. *IV26 2SS, tel. 085483/230. 8 rooms, 7 with bath, 1 with shower. Facilities: restaurant. No credit cards. Closed late Oct.–Easter. $$$$*

Whitebridge **Knockie Lodge Hotel.** Part 18th-century hunting lodge, with tra-
Lodging ditional and antique furniture, this hotel offers very peaceful surroundings, though with easy access to Inverness, 20 miles northeast. Dinner is included. The dining room seats 18; nonguests are welcome if there's space. *IV1 2UP, tel. 0456/486276, fax 0456/486389. 10 rooms with bath. Facilities: fishing, deer hunting, sailing. AE, DC, MC, V. Closed Nov.–Apr. $$$$*

The Arts

Festivals The second largest arts festival in Scotland is now Glasgow's **Mayfest,** held in the city during virtually all of May.

Theater Glasgow is better endowed with functioning theaters than Edinburgh. One of the most exciting in Britain is the **Citizen's Theatre** (119 Gorbals St., tel. 041/429–0022), where productions of often hair-raising originality are the order of the day. The **King's Theatre** (Bath St., tel. 041/227–5511) stages light entertainment and musicals. The **Theatre Royal** (Hope St., tel. 041/332–9000) is the enchanting home of the Scottish Opera.

A thinly scattered population makes life difficult for theater operations, but there are repertory companies at Perth (**Perth Theatre,** High St., tel. 0738/21031) and Dundee (**Dundee Repertory,** Lochree Rd., tel. 0382/23530).

Inverness's theater, the **Eden Court** (tel. 0463/221718), is a reminder that just because a town is in northern Scotland, it need not be an artistic wasteland. This multipurpose 800-seat theater and its art gallery offer a varied program year-round.

Both Stirling and St. Andrews universities have dynamic arts centers, while the smallest theater in Britain is on the island of Mull. Its small size—just 36 seats—has earned the **Mull Little Theatre** (Dervaig, tel. 06884/267) a place in *The Guinness Book of World Records.*

Index

Abberley, *352*
Abbey (Bath), *278*
Abbey Botanical Gardens, *307*
Abbey of Glastonbury, *192*
Abbey of Valle Crucis, *368*
Abbotsbury, *177, 180*
Abbotsford House, *500*
Abbott Hall, *411*
Aberaeron, *373*
Aberdovey, *384*
Abergavenny, *378, 382*
Aberlour, *534*
Abermaw, *371*
Aberystwyth, *360, 372, 384–385*
Aberystwyth Cliff Railway, *372*
Abingdon, *247, 251*
Admiralty Arch, *65*
Aerial Ferry, *373*
Aira Force, *412*
A la Ronde, *204*
Albert Memorial, *76*
Albion House, *241*
Aldeburgh, *316*
Aldeburgh Festival, *332*
Alderney, *225, 229*
Alexander Kieller Museum, *171*
Alice in Wonderland Visitor Centre, *381*
Alloway, *524*
All Saints Church (Hereford), *341*
Alnwick, *464, 476–477, 481, 483, 487*
Alnwick Castle, *477*
Alum Bay Glass Company, *167*
Ambleside, *394, 407, 429*
American Chapel, *78*
American Military Cemetery, *303–304*
Angel Hill, *307*
Anglesey Sea Zoo, *380–381*
Anglican Cathedral, *402*

Anne Hathaway's Cottage, *265*
Apartment rentals, *37*
Appleby Rose Garden, *307*
Apsley House, *75*
Aquariums, *145, 178, 502*
Architectural styles, *52–56*
Ardrossan, *523*
Argyll Ludging, *525*
Arisaig, *539*
Arlington Mill Museum, *272*
Arran Island, *523*
Arreton, *166*
Art Gallery (Bury St. Edmunds), *308*
Art Gallery (Kendal), *411*
Art Gallery (Leeds), *448*
Art Gallery (Scarborough), *450*
Arthur, King, *163, 187, 192, 194, 199*
Arundel, *125, 138–139, 148*
Arundel Castle, *138–139*
Ashmolean, *246*
Ashness, *414*
Askham, *423*
Assembly Rooms, *279*
Athenaeum, the, *307*
Atheneum Gallery, *398*
ATMs, *9–10*
Attingham Park, *344*
Auchterarder, *539–540*
Auchterless, *540*
Auckland Castle, *471*
Audley End House, *305*
Auld Alloway Kirk, *524*
Austen, Jane, *41–42, 164*
Avebury, *170–171*
Avebury monument, *171*
Aviemore, *514, 532, 540*

Ayr, *514, 523–524*
Aysgarth, *442*

Baby-sitting services, *19*
Baddesley Clinton, *265*
Bakewell, *432, 437*
Bala, *370, 385*
Bala Lake, *369*
Ballet, *40, 122, 293*
Balliol College, *246*
Balloch, *523, 540*
Balquhidder Glen, *534*
Bamburgh, *483–484*
Bamburgh Castle, *478*
Banff, *540*
Banham Zoo and Monkey Park, *320*
Bank hours, *31*
Bank of England, *80*
Bannockburn Heritage Centre, *526*
Banqueting House, *69*
Barbara Hepworth Museum and Sculpture Garden, *195*
Barber Institute of Fine Arts, *281*
Barbican (London), *79*
Barbican (Plymouth), *200*
Barcaldine, *533*
Barden Tower, *442*
Barge House, *87*
Barge tours, *4*
Barmouth, *371*
Barnard Castle, *470*
Barnstaple, *193, 209*
Baron's Hall, *142*
Barrow-in-Furness, *409*
Basildon Park, *248–249*
Baslow, *457*
Batemans, *144*
Bath, *41–42, 43, 277–279, 282, 284–286, 292–293*
Bath House Arms, *137*
Battle, *135, 148*
Battle Abbey, *135*

Battle of Britain Museum, *90*
Battle of Flowers Museum, *223*
Beaches, *177, 208, 228, 403, 419–420, 456, 482*
Beacon Pike, *411*
Beadnell, *477*
Beamish, *472*
Beamish Open-Air Museum, *472*
Beauchamp Tower, *81*
Beaulieu, *173*
Beaumaris, *363, 366, 385, 390*
Beau Sejour Centre, *224*
Becket, Thomas à, *127*
Bed-and-breakfasts, *36*
Beer (town), *204*
Bempton Cliffs, *454*
Ben Cruachan, *529*
Ben Ledi, *526*
Ben Nevis, *530*
Berkeley, *276–277, 286*
Berkeley Castle, *276–277*
Berwick-upon-Tweed, *464, 479, 484, 487*
Bethnal Green Museum of Children, *89*
Betws-y-Coed, *360, 367, 382, 385*
Bewdley, *342*
Bibury, *272*
Bicycling, *34*
Channel Islands, *227*
East Anglia, *322*
Heart of England, *283*
the Northeast, *481*
the South, *179*
Thames Valley, *250*
tours, *4*
Welsh Borders, *351*
Yorkshire Moors, *455*
Bideford, *194, 207*
Big Ben, *70*
Big Pit Mining Museum, *382*

Billingham, *487*
Birdcage Walk, *68*
Birmingham,
*267–270, 282,
286–287, 303*
Birmingham
Cathedral, *269–270*
Birmingham Museum
of Science and
Industry, *281*
Bishop Auckland, *471*
Bishop's Palace
(Lincoln), *318*
Bishop's Palace (St.
David's), *374*
Bishop's Palace
(Wells), *192*
Black Country
Museum, *342*
Blackfriars Bridge, *84*
Blackgang, *166–167*
Blackgang Chine, *177*
Blackpool, *394, 403,
419, 423*
Blackpool Tower, *403*
Blackwell's, *245*
Bladon, *247*
Blaenau Ffestiniog,
370
Blakeney, *312*
Blanchland, *484*
Blandford Forum, *180*
Blenheim Palace, *247*
Blickling Hall, *312*
Blists Hill Open-Air
Museum, *345*
Bloody Tower, *81*
Blubberhouses, *454*
Bluebell Railway, *146*
Boat and waterbus
systems, *29–30*
Boating, *34, 100, 351,
481*
Boat Museum,
349–350
Boat of Garten, *532*
Boat Race, the, *100*
Bodelwyddan Castle,
381
Bodiam Castle, *144*
Bodleian Library, *245*
Bodmin, *199*
Bodnant Garden,
367–368
Bolton Abbey, *439,
442, 457*
Bolton Castle, *442*
Bo'Ness, *534*
Books on Britain,
22–23

Bootham Bar
(Norman gate), *447*
Border History
Museum, *473–474*
Borrowdale, *414*
Borrowdale Fells, *415*
Boscastle, *194*
Boscombe, *174*
Boston, *295, 319*
Boston Bureau
Museum, *319*
Botanic Gardens
(Ventnor), *166*
Bournemouth, *157,
173–174, 180–181*
Bourton-on-the-Water,
270, 282, 287
Bowes, *470*
Bowes Museum, *470*
Bowness-on-
Windermere, *403,
406*
Bowyer Tower, *81*
Box Hill, *141*
Bracklinn Falls, *526*
Bradford, *432,
438–439*
Brading, *166*
Brading Roman Villa,
166
Braemar, *540*
Braithwaite, *423*
Brancepeth, *469*
Brantwood, *409*
Brass Rubbing
Centre, *70*
Braunton Burrows,
194
Brechfa, *385*
Brecknock Museum,
379
Brecon, *379, 385–386*
Brecon Beacons
Mountain Centre,
379, 383
Brecon Beacons
National Park, *383*
Bressingham Live
Steam Museum, *320*
Bridge House, *407*
Bridge of Orchy, *529*
Bridge of Sighs, *347*
Bridgnorth, *346*
Bridlington, *451*
Brigflatts, *417*
Brighton, *125, 136,
146, 148–150, 155*
Brighton Museum
and Art Gallery, *137*
Brig o' Doon, *524*

Bristol, *279–280, 287*
Bristol Zoo, *280*
British Library, *74*
British Museum, *44,
74*
British Tourist
Authority (BTA), *2*
Brixham, *202*
Broadlands, *165*
Broadstairs, *133*
Broadway, *271,
287–288*
Broadway Tower
Country Park, *271*
Brockhole National
Park, *407*
Brodick Castle, *523*
Brompton Oratory, *76*
Brontë Parsonage
Museum, *439*
Brontë Waterfall, *439*
Broughton-in-Furness,
409
Brownsea Island, *174*
Buckden, *442*
Buckfast Butterfly
Farm, *205*
Buckingham Palace,
68
Buckland, *288*
Buckland Abbey, *200*
Buckler's Hard, *173*
Bude, *194*
Builth Wells, *378*
Burford, *272, 288*
Burghley House,
321–322
Burnham, *251*
Burnham Beeches,
241
Burns, Robert, *524*
Burrell Collection,
522
Burwash, *144*
Bury St. Edmunds,
*295, 307–308, 321,
324–325, 333*
Business hours, *31–32*
Bus travel, *27–28. See
also* transportation
under specific areas
Butler's Wharf, *82*
Buttermere, *415*
Buxton, *432,
435–436, 454, 457,
460*
Buxton Micrarium,
435
Buxton Museum, *435*
Bwlch y Groes, *370*

Cabinet War Rooms,
68–69
Cadbury Castle, *205*
Caernarfon, *360,
366–367, 386*
Caernarfon Air World
museum, *367*
Caernarfon Castle,
366
Cairngorm massif,
532
Caldey Island, *375*
Callander, *526*
Cambridge, *295, 297,
300–304, 321,
325–326, 332, 333*
Camden Lock, *89*
Campbeltown, *529*
Camping, *34*
Canal Museum,
368–369
Canary Wharf, *90*
Canongate Kirk, *497*
Canongate Tolbooth,
497
Canterbury, *125, 127,
130–132, 146, 150,
155*
Canterbury Heritage
Museum, *132*
Canterbury Tales
exhibition, *131*
Cape Wrath, *534*
Captain Cook
Birthplace Museum,
471–472
Captain Cook
Memorial Museum,
452
Cardhu distillery, *43*
Cardiff, *360, 379–380,
382, 386–387*
Cardigan, *387*
Carfax, *246*
Carisbrooke Castle,
167
Carlton House
Terrace, *65*
Carnation Nursery
and Butterfly Farm,
226
Carreg Cennen
Castle, *376*
Car renting and
leasing, *15–16, 29.
See also under
specific areas*
Carroll, Lewis, *141*
Cartmel, *410, 423*
Car travel, *28–29.*

Car travel
(continued)
See also
transportation *under*
specific areas
**Casa Magni Shelley
Museum,** *174*
Cash machines, *9–10*
Casinos, *123, 512*
Castell Coch, *380*
Castle Cornet, *224*
Castle Douglas, *525*
Castle Drogo, *201*
Castle Howard, *453*
Castle Kennedy, *525*
Castle Museum, *447*
**Castlerigg Stone
Circle,** *412–413*
Castles, *32*
Channel Islands, *222,
223, 224*
East Anglia, *309,
314, 316, 318*
Edinburgh, *492–493*
Heart of England,
*265–266, 271,
276–277*
the Northeast, *468,
470, 471, 476, 477,
478, 479*
Scottish Borders,
501, 502
Scottish southwest
and highlands, *523,
524, 525, 526, 527,
529, 532, 533*
the South, *164, 167,
174–175, 176*
the Southeast, *133,
134, 135, 138–139,
141, 142–143, 145*
the Southwest, *193,
197, 198, 199, 201,
202, 203, 205*
Thames Valley, *235,
239*
tours of, *44*
Wales, *363, 366, 368,
370, 372, 373–374,
375, 377, 378, 379,
380, 381*
Welsh Borders, *340,
343, 346, 347*
Yorkshire Moors,
*438, 439, 442, 443,
450, 453*
Castleton, *437–438*
Cat Bells, *416*
**Cathedral Church of
St. Andrew,** *189, 192*

**Cathedral Church of
St. Mary,** *198*
**Cathedral of St.
Peter,** *203*
Caverns, *134, 194,
206, 276, 370, 436,
438*
Caving, *455*
Cawdor Castle, *532*
Ceiriog Valley, *368,
387*
Cenarth Falls, *374*
Cenotaph, the, *69*
Central Library, *269,
399*
**Centre for Alternative
Technology,** *371–372*
**Centre for British
Romanticism,** *408*
Ceredigion Museum,
372
Cerne Abbas, *176*
Cerne Abbey, *176*
Chagford, *201*
Chalice Well, *192*
**Changing of the
Guard ceremony,** *68*
Channel Islands,
217–231
the arts, *231*
car rentals, *218*
children, *226*
currency, *218*
hotels, *228–231*
restaurants, *228–231*
shopping, *226–227*
sightseeing, *219–226*
sports, *227–228*
tourist and travel
information, *218*
transportation,
218–219
Channel Tunnel, *30*
Chantry House,
241–242
**Chapel of Edward the
Confessor,** *70*
Chapel of St. John, *81*
**Chapel of the Nine
Altars,** *468*
**Chapel of the Order
of the Thistle,** *496*
Chapel Royal, *65*
**Chapter House
(London),** *70–71*
**Chapter House
(Salisbury),** *167–168*
**Chapter House
(York),** *445*
Charingworth, *288*

Charlecote, *288*
Charlecote Park, *266*
**Charles Dickens
Centre,** *145*
Charles I, statue of,
64
Charlestown, *199*
Chartwell, *143*
Chatham, *145*
Chatsworth House,
42, 437
Chawton, *164*
Cheddar Caves, *42,
206*
**Chedworth Roman
Villa,** *43, 272*
Cheltenham, *272–273,
283, 288–289,
292–293*
**Cheltenham Festival
of Literature,**
292–293
Cherhill Down, *170*
**Cheshire Military
Museum,** *347*
Chesil Beach, *177*
Chester, *346–347,
350, 352–353*
Chester Cathedral,
347
Chester-le-Street, *484*
Chesters Roman Fort,
475
Chew Magna, *280*
Chew Stoke, *280*
**Chewton Cheese
Dairy,** *206*
Chew Valley Lake,
280
Chichester, *125,
139–140, 150–151*
**Children, attractions
for.** *See under
specific areas*
traveling with, *18–19*
Children's Farm, *145*
Chilham, *132*
**Chilham Castle
Gardens,** *132*
Chillingham Park,
480
Chipping Campden,
270, 289
Chirk, *369*
**Christchurch
Cathedral,** *130–131*
**Christ Church
College,** *246*
Christ's College, *300*
Churches

Channel Islands, *220,
223, 224*
East Anglia, *302,
304, 306, 307, 309,
310, 315, 317–318,
319, 320, 321*
Edinburgh, *493, 495,
496*
Heart of England,
*264, 266, 269–270,
273, 278, 280, 281,
282*
London, *64, 68, 70,
71, 72, 73, 77, 78,
79, 80, 81, 83–84,
85, 86, 90–91, 93*
the Northeast, *466,
468, 473, 478,
479–480*
the Northwest,
*400–401, 402, 406,
410*
Scottish Borders,
500, 501, 503
Scottish southwest
and highlands, *520,
522, 524, 527*
the South, *159, 162,
167–168, 174*
the Southeast, *127,
130–131, 132, 138,
139, 140–141, 142,
145*
the Southwest, *189,
192, 195, 198, 203*
Thames Valley, *235,
239, 241–242, 245,
246, 247*
Wales, *366, 368, 374,
379, 380*
Welsh Borders, *337,
341, 342, 343, 344,
346, 347, 349*
Yorkshire Moors,
*436, 439, 442, 445,
446, 449, 450, 452*
Churchill, Winston,
70, 143, 247
**Church of King
Charles the Martyr,**
142
**Church of St.
Botolph,** *319*
**Church of St.
Lawrence,** *346*
**Church of St. Mary
Redcliffe,** *280*
**Church of St.
Pancras,** *203*
Chwarel Wynne, *369*

Cider Museum, 341–342

Cilgerran Castle, 373–374

Cinque Ports, 133

Circus, the (Bath), 279

Cirencester, 43, 282

City Art Gallery, 398

City Chambers, 520

City Mill, 163

City Museum, 163

City Museum (Leeds), 448

City Museum and Art Gallery (Birmingham), 269

City Museum and Art Gallery (London), 91

Claerwen reservoir, 376

Clandon Park, 141

Clarence House, 65

Claverton Manor, 279

Clearwell, 290

Clearwell Caves, 276

Clifford's Tower, 446

Climate, 5–6

Cliveden, 240

Clive House, 343

Clive of India Museum, 377

Clock Tower, 91

Cloisters, the (Canterbury), 130–131

Cloisters, the (London), 70

Clovelly, 194

Clwyd, 391

Clyro, 378

Coalport China Museum, 345

Cockermouth, 394, 415

Cogges Farm Museum, 249

Colchester, 295, 313–315, 320, 322, 326–327, 332

Colchester Zoo, 320

Coldharbour Mill, 206

Coleford, 276

College Chapel, 86

Collegiate Church of St. Mary, 266

Colne Valley Railway, 320

Commandery, the, 337

Commonwealth

Institute, 77

Computers, traveling with, 13

Coniston, 394, 408–409

Coniston Water, 409

Constable, John, 315

Constitution Hill, 372

Conwy, 368

Cook, James, 452

Cookham, 240–241

Corbridge, 475

Corfe Castle, 174–175

Corinium Museum, 282

Corn Exchange, 308

Corpach, 534

Corstopitum, 475

Cost of traveling, 10

Cotehele House and Quay, 199–200

Cotswold Motor Museum, 270

Cottages, 36

Country Crafts Village, 166

County Hall, 85

Courtauld Institute Galleries, 74

Court Dress Collection, 77

Courthouse (Beaumaris), 363, 366

Coventry Cathedral, 281

Cowane's Hospital, 526

Cowes, 166

Craft Design Centre, 448

Cragside, 480

Cranbrook, 151

Craster, 477

Criccieth, 370

Crickhowell, 378, 387

Crinan, 541

Cromer, 312

Cromwell, Oliver, 304

Crown Jewels, 81–82

Crummock Water, 415

Culloden Moor, 531–532

Culture tours, 4

Culzean Castle and Country Park, 524

Cumberland Pencil Museum, 413

Cumberland Toy and Model Museum, 416

Cumnor, 251–252

Currency of Britain, 9, 10, 218

Customs, 11–13

Customs House, 197, 204

Cutty Sark, 86

Dalemain, 412

Dales Countryside Museum, 443

Danby Lodge, 452

Danebury Hill, 178

Dane John Mound, 132

Dark Arches, 448

Darlington, 464, 471

Darlington Railway Centre and Museum, 471

Dartington, 207

Dartmoor Otter Sanctuary, 205

Dartmouth, 187, 201, 209–210

Dart Valley Steam Railway, 206

D-Day Museum, 165

Deal, 133

Deal Castle, 44, 133

Dean Heritage Centre, 276

Dedham, 315, 327

Deep Sea World, 502

Denbigh, 368

Denbigh Castle, 368

Derbyshire, 42

Derwentwater, 414

Design Museum, 82–83

Devil's Bridge, 372

Devonshire Royal Hospital, 435

Dickens, Charles, 75, 145, 155, 470

Dickens House, 75

Dinosaur Museum, 178

Disabilities, hints for travelers with, 19–20

Distilleries, 42–43

Diving, 227–228

Dr. Johnson's House, 71

Dog-collar museum, 143

Dolaucothi Gold Mines, 381

Dolgellau, 360, 371

Dorchester, 157, 175, 181

Dorchester-on-Thames, 247, 252

Dorking, 151

Dorset County Museum, 175

Doune Castle, 526

Dove Cottage, 408

Dover, 125, 133–134, 151

Dover Castle, 44, 134

Dozmary Pool, 199

Dragon Hill, 248

Drake, Francis, 200

Drefach Felindre, 374

Driver's licenses, 15

Drumnadrochit, 532

Drusilla's Zoo Park, 145

Drybridge, 541

Dryburgh, 501

Duddingston, 503

Dudley, 342

Dulwich College Picture Gallery, 90

Dunadd Fort, 528

Dunblane, 526, 541

Dunblane Cathedral, 526

Duncryne Hill, 523

Dunoon, 523, 541

Dunstanburgh Castle, 477

Dunster, 193

Durham, 464, 466, 468–469, 481, 485

Durham Castle, 468

Durham Cathedral, 466, 468

Durham Light Infantry Museum, 469

Durham University Oriental Museum, 469

Duties, 11–13

Duxford, 327

Duxford Airfield, 304–305

Dyrham Park, 277

Dyson Perrins Museum, 337

East Anglia, 295–333
the arts, 332–333
car rentals, 296
children, 319–320
guided tours, 297
hotels, 323–332
restaurants, 300, 302, 303, 304, 305, 306, 307, 308, 311, 312,

East Anglia
(continued)
313, 315, 318, 319,
323–332
shopping, 321–322
sightseeing, 297–321
sports, 322–323
tourist and travel
information, 295
transportation, 296
East Bergholt, 315
Eastbourne, 125
Eastbridge Hospital,
132
Easton Grey, 290
Edale, 438
Edinburgh, 489–512
the arts, 510–511
car rentals, 490
children, 502
climate, 6
festival, 7
guided tours, 491
hotels, 506–511
nightlife, 512
restaurants, 497, 498,
501, 506–511
shopping, 503–505
sightseeing, 491–503
sports, 505
tourist and travel
information, 489–490
transportation,
490–491
**Edinburgh Brass
Rubbing Centre**, 502
**Edinburgh Butterfly
and Insect World**,
502
Edinburgh Castle,
492–493
**Edinburgh Festival
Fringe**, 511
**Edinburgh
International
Festival**, 7, 511
Edinburgh Zoo, 502
**Edwardian
architecture**, 55
Egyptian House, 196
Elan Valley, 376
Electricity, 8
Elgar, Edward, 339
Elgin, 541
Elizabeth Castle, 222
**Elizabethan
architecture**, 53
Elterwater, 407, 423
Ely, 295, 304, 322,
328

Ely Cathedral, 304
Embassies, 62
Emergencies
London, 62
Emmanuel College,
300
English Bridge, 344
English homes tours,
4
Epsom, 7
**Eric Young Orchid
Foundation**, 223
Eton, 239–240,
249–250, 252
Eton College,
239–240
**Eurotunnel Exhibi-
tion Centre**, 145–146
Ewelme, 243
Exeter, 187, 202–204,
207, 210, 215
**Exeter Maritime
Museum**, 204
Exmouth, 204, 210

FA Cup Final, 100
Fairy Cross, 210
Falconry Centre, 281
Falmouth, 197,
210–211
**Farmhouse
accommodations**, 36
Farne Islands,
477–478
Faversham, 133,
151–152
Felin Geri Mill, 374
Felixstowe, 316
Fell running, 421
Fergusson Gallery,
528
Ferries, 158, 176, 198,
219, 516, 523
**Festivals and seasonal
events**, 6–7, 40, 155,
185, 215, 231, 255,
292–293, 356–357,
390–391, 429–430,
460, 487, 511, 547
Ffestiniog, 370
Ffestiniog Railway,
370
Figure of a Giant, 176
Filey, 451
Finchcocks, 144
Firbank Knots, 417
**Fishbourne Roman
Palace**, 140
Fishguard, 374, 387
Fishing, 208,

322–323, 419, 455,
482
Fitness centers, 100
Fitz Park, 413
Fitzwilliam Museum,
303
**Flambards Theme
Park**, 206
Flamborough, 454
Flamingo Land, 453
Flamingo Park, 166
Flatford, 315
**Fleet Air Arm
Museum**, 205
Floors Castle, 501
**Florence Nightingale
Museum**, 85
Folkestone, 134
Fordwich, 132
Forest of Dean, 276
Forest of Kielder, 476
Fort Regent, 220, 226
Fort William,
529–530, 541–542
**Fort William-Mallaig
Railway**, 530
Fossil Coast, 177
Fountains Abbey, 449
Fountains Hall, 449
Fowles, John, 177
Fownhope, 353
Framwelgate Bridge,
469
Free Trade Hall, 399
**Friquet Flower and
Butterfly Centre**, 226
Frosterley, 469
Furness Abbey, 409
Fydell House, 319

Gabriel's Wharf, 84
**Gainsborough's
House**, 305
Galashiels, 509
Gallery of Fashion,
273
Galloway Forest Park,
524
Garden House, 200
Gardens
Channel Islands, 223,
226
East Anglia, 303, 308
Edinburgh, 500
Heart of England,
271
London, 75, 76, 77,
87–88, 89, 90, 93
museum on, 85
the Northwest, 413,

415
Scottish southwest
and highlands, 525
the South, 166, 169
the Southeast, 132,
146
the Southwest, 195,
200, 203
Thames Valley, 240,
242
tours, 4
Wales, 367–368
Yorkshire Moors, 449
**Gardens of the
Zoological Society of
London**, 89
Garrick Club, 73
Gasoline, 29
Gatwick Airport, 59,
126
Gaulden Manor, 193
**Gay and lesbian
travelers, hints for**,
21–22
**Geffrye Museum of
Furniture**, 92
**George Stephenson's
Birthplace**, 480
Georgian House, 499
**Georgian Theatre
Royal**, 443
**German Military
Underground
Hospital**, 225
**German Occupation
Museum**, 225
Gilbert Memorial, 199
Gipsy Moth IV, 86
Gittisham, 211
**Gladstone Pottery
Museum**, 349
**Gladstone's Land
(building)**, 495
Glasgow, 7, 517, 520,
522–523, 534–535,
542–543, 547
Glasgow Cathedral,
520
Glass Church, 223
Glasshouse, 73
Glastonbury, 192,
207, 211–212
Glencoe, 529
Glenfarg, 543
Glenfiddich distillery,
43
Glenfinnan, 530
Glen Grant distillery,
43
Glenlivet distillery, 43

Glen Orchy, *529*

Glenridding, *412*

Gloddfa Ganol Slate Mine, *370*

Gloucester, *43, 273, 283, 290*

Gloucester Cathedral, *273*

Gloucester Docks, *273*

Gloucester Folk Museum, *273*

Glyndebourne Opera House, *155*

G-Mex Centre, *399*

God's House Tower, *165*

Golf, *34*
Channel Islands, *227*
Edinburgh, *505*
London area, *100*
the Northeast, *482*
the Northwest, *419*
Scottish southwest and highlands, *536–537*
the South, *179*
the Southeast, *147*
Thames Valley, *250*
tours, *5*
Wales, *382–383*
Welsh Borders, *351*

Goodrich Castle, *340*

Goonhilly Satellite Communications Earth Station, *197*

Gordale Scar (chasm), *442*

Gorey Castle, *223*

Gothic architecture, *52–53*

Government tourist offices, *2*

Gower Peninsula, *375–376*

Grace Darling Museum, *478*

Grahame, Kenneth, *243*

Granada Studios' Tour, *416*

Granary Wharf, *448*

Grand Union Canal, *207*

Grange, *414*

Grange-over-Sands, *410*

Grantchester, *303*

Grantham, *319*

Grasmere, *394, 408, 417–418*

Grassington, *442*

Great Aberystwyth Camera Obscura, *372*

Great Bookham, *141*

Great Hall, *163*

Great Malvern, *339*

Great Milton, *249, 252*

Great Witley, *342*

Great Yarmouth, *295, 311–312, 328*

Greek Museum, *472–473*

Greenhead, *474, 485*

Greenwich Park, *86–87*

Grewelthorpe, *454*

Greyfriar's Kirk, *495–496*

Grey Mare's Tail (waterfall), *533*

Guards Chapel, *68*

Guards Museum, *68*

Guernsey, *218, 223–226, 227, 229–230, 231*

Guildford, *125, 140–141, 152*

Guildford Castle, *141*

Guildford Cathedral, *141*

Guildford Museum, *141*

Guildhall (Bury St. Edmunds), *308*

Guildhall (Exeter), *203*

Guildhall (Guildford), *140*

Guildhall (Lavenham), *306*

Guildhall (Lincoln), *318*

Guildhall (London), *80*

Guildhall (Sandwich), *133*

Guildhall (Stratford-upon-Avon), *264*

Guildhall (Windsor), *239*

Guildhall (Worcester), *339*

Guildhall (York), *447*

Guinness World of Records, *89*

Gullane, *509*

Gweek, *197*

Haddon Hall, *42*

Hadrian's Wall, *44, 474*

Haggs Castle, *533*

Hall of Memory, *269*

Hall's Croft, *264*

Ham House, *87*

Hampsfield Fell, *410*

Hampton Court Palace, *87*

Harbledown, *132*

Hardwick Hall, *42*

Hardy, Thomas, *41, 175, 177*

Hardy's Monument, *177*

Harewood House, *42, 448*

Harlech, *370–371, 382, 387–388*

Harlech Castle, *370–371*

Harrods, *75, 99*

Harrogate, *432, 448–449*

Harvard House, *262–263*

Harwich, *315–316*

Haslemere, *152*

Hastings, *125, 135, 152–153*

Hastings Castle, *135*

Hatton Gallery, *472–473*

Hauteville House, *224*

Hawes, *442–443*

Hawkhurst, *144*

Hawkshead, *408*

Haworth, *432, 439, 454–455, 457*

Hayling Island, *178*

Hay-on-Wye, *378, 382, 388*

Hay's Galleria, *83*

Hayward Gallery, *85*

Heart of England, *258–293*
the arts, *292–293*
car rentals, *259*
children, *280–281*
guided tours, *260*
hotels, *284–292*
restaurants, *262, 264, 266, 267, 270, 272, 273, 278, 280, 284–292*
shopping, *282–283*
sightseeing, *260–283*
sports, *283–284*
tourist and travel

information, *259*
transportation, *259–260*

Heathrow Airport, *59*

Heights of Abraham, *437*

Helensburgh, *523*

Hellen's House, *340*

Hellfire Caves, *134*

Helmsley, *452*

Helston, *197, 212*

Helvellyn, *412*

Henley, *233, 241–242, 250, 252, 255*

Henley-in-Arden, *265*

Henley Royal Regatta, *242, 250*

Henry VII Chapel, *70*

Henry Moore Study Centre, *448*

Hereford, *340–342, 350, 353*

Hereford Cathedral, *341*

Hermitage Rock, *222*

Herne Bay, *133*

Herstmonceux, *153*

Hever Castle, *142–143*

Hexham, *464, 473–474, 481, 485–486, 487*

Hexham Abbey, *473*

Hidcote Manor Garden, *271*

High Force, *470*

Highland Games, *538*

High Newton-by-the-Sea, *477*

Hiking, *34–35*
Channel Islands, *227*
East Anglia, *323*
Edinburgh, *505*
Heart of England, *283–284*
the Northeast, *482*
the Northwest, *420*
Scottish southwest and highlands, *537–538*
the South, *179*
the Southeast, *147*
the Southwest, *208*
Thames Valley, *250*
Wales, *383*
Welsh Borders, *351*
Yorkshire Moors, *456*

Hill House, *523*

Hill Top, *417*

Hingham, *321*

History of Britain, 46–49

H.M.S. *Belfast,* 83

H.M.S. *Victory,* 164

H.M.S. *Warrior,* 164

Holburne Museum and Crafts Study Centre, 279

Hole in t'Wall, 406

Holidays, 32

Holker, 409

Holker Hall, 409

Holkham Hall, 312–313

Hollytrees, 314

Holy Island, 478

Holyrood Palace, 497

Holyrood Park, 498

Holy Rude, 525

Holy Trinity Church (Colchester), 326

Holy Trinity Church (Stratford), 264

Home exchanges, 37

Honiton, 204–205, 212

Hope Park, 413

Hopetoun House, 503

Horniman Museum, 89

Horseback riding, 179, 207, 383, 419, 482

Horse Guards Parade, 69

Horse racing, 283, 323, 421, 456

Horseshoe Pass, 368

Hospital of the Blessed Trinity, 140

Hotels, 36–37. *See also under specific areas*

Housesteads Roman Fort, 475

Howgill Fells, 417

Howlett's Zoo Park, 145

Huddersfield, 460–461

Hunstanton, 313

Hunstrete, 290

Hunterian Art Gallery, 522

Hunterian Museum, 522

Huntly House, 497

Hurley, 252–253

Hutcheson's Hall, 520

Hutton-le-Hole, 452

Hyde Park, 75

Ightham Mote, 143

Ilkley Moor, 442

Illuminations, 403

Imperial War Museum, 85–86

Inchcailloch, 534

Industrial Museum, 438–439

Innerleithen, 502, 509–510

Inns of Court, 71–72

Insurance, 14–15, 16

International Convention Center, 267

Inveraray Castle, 529

Inverness, 515, 530–531, 535–536, 543–544, 547

Ipswich, 295, 316, 328–329

Ireland's Mansion, 343

Ireshopeburn, 469–470, 481

Iron Bridge, 345

Ironbridge, 353

Ironbridge Gorge Museum, 345

Island Fortress-Occupation Museum, 220

Isle of Portland, 177

Isle of Wight, 165–167, 181–182

Iveagh Bequest, 90

Ixworth, 329

Jackfield Tile Museum, 345

Jacobean architecture, 53–54

James, Henry, 134

Jaws of Borrowdale, 414

Jedburgh, 501, 510

Jedburgh Abbey, 501

Jersey, 218, 220, 222–223, 226, 230–231

Jersey Museum, 220

Jersey Wildlife Trust, 223

Jersey Zoo, 226

Jesus College, 302

Jewish Museum, 92

Jodrell Bank, 347–348

Jogging, 100–101, 505

John Knox House, 497

John Rylands Library, 400

Johnson, Samuel, 71

Jorvik Viking Centre, 446

Jubilee open-air market, 73

Jungle Adventureland, 381

Kedleston Hall, 42

Keighley and Worth Valley Railway, 453

Kelmscott Manor, 248

Kelso, 501, 510

Kelvingrove, 522

Kendal, 394, 410–411, 418, 423–424, 430

Kendal Museum, 411

Kenilworth, 265–266, 290

Kenilworth Castle, 265–266

Kennett Stone Avenue, 171

Kensington Gardens, 75, 76

Kensington Palace, 76–77

Kensington Palace Gardens, 77

Kentallen, 544

Kent and East Sussex Railway, 146

Kentwell Hall, 306

Kenwood House, 90

Keswick, 394, 413–414, 418, 424–425, 430

Keswick Museum, 413

Kew Palace, 88

Kielder Castle, 476

Kielder Water, 475–476

Killhope Wheel Lead Mining Centre, 469

Kilmore, 544

Kilpeck, 340

Kinderland, 453

King Charles's House, 339

King Harry Ferry, 198

Kings and queens, 50–51

Kingsbridge, 201

King's College Chapel, 302–303

King's Head Inn, 470

King's Knot, 526

King's Lynn, 295, 313, 322, 329, 332

King's Lynn Art Centre, 313

King's Pipe, 197

Kington, 353

Kipling, Rudyard, 144

Kirkby Stephen, 417

Knaresborough, 449

Knole, 143

Knutsford, 348, 353–354

Kynance Cove, 197

Lace museum, 205

La Hogue Bie (neolithic tombs), 226

Lake District. *See* the Northwest and Lake District

Lake District National Park, 407

Lakeside & Haverthwaite steam train, 416

Lake Vyrnwy, 369, 388

Lamb and Flag pub, 73

Lamberhurst Vineyard, 144

Lambeth Palace, 85

Lamb House, 134

Lanark, 536

Lancaster House, 65

Landgate, 134

Landguard Fort, 316

Land o' Burns Centre, 524

Land's End, 196

Langbank, 544

Langdale Fell, 407

Launceston, 199

Laurel and Hardy Museum, 409

La Vallette, 225

Lavenham, 306, 329

Lavenham Church, 306–307

Leadenhall Market, 80

Leadhills, 533

Ledbury, 339–340, 354

Leeds, 432, 448, 461

Leeds Castle, 44, 143

Leighton House, 77–78

Leith, 503

Leominster, 354

Leonardslee Gardens,

146
Levens Hall, *410*
Lewdon, *212*
Lewes, *125, 135–136,
146–147, 153*
Libraries
Edinburgh, *495–496*
Heart of England,
269
London, *74*
Northwest, *399, 400*
Oxford, *245*
Scottish southwest
and highlands, *520*
the Southeast, *140*
Welsh Borders, *341*
Lichfield Cathedral,
349
Lightwater Valley
Theme Park, *453*
Lincoln, *295,
316–318, 322,
329–330, 332*
Lincoln Castle, *318*
Lincoln Cathedral,
317–318
Lincolnshire Wolds,
319
Lincoln's Inn, *72*
Lindisfarne Castle
and Priory, *478–479*
Lingholm Gardens,
415
Linley Sambourne
House, *77*
Littledean, *276*
Little Venice, *89–90*
Liverpool, *394,
401–402, 417, 418,
425*
Lizard Peninsula, *197*
Llanberis, *367*
Llanberis Lake
Railway, *367*
Llandaff Cathedral,
380
Llandrindod Wells,
360, 377, 388
Llandudno, *360, 368,
388*
Llanerchymedd, *389*
Llanfair P.G., *360,
382*
Llanfihangel
Crucorney, *378*
Llangammarch Wells,
388
Llangollen, *7, 360,
369, 390–391*
Llangollen Railway,

369
Llanidloes, *376*
Llanrhaeadr ym
Mochnant, *369, 389*
Llanthony Priory, *378*
Llanwrtyd Wells, *376*
Llechwedd Slate
Caverns, *370*
Lloyd's of London, *80*
Llyn Celyn Reservoir,
370
Llywernog Silver
Lead Mining
Museum, *373*
Loch Awe, *529*
Loch Fyne, *529*
Lochgilphead, *528*
Lochinver, *536*
Loch Katrine, *527*
Loch Lomond, *523*
Loch Ness, *532*
Loch Venachar, *527*
Lodore, *414, 425*
Logan Botanic
Garden, *525*
London, *58–123*
airports, *59*
the arts, *120–122*
Bayswater, *119–120*
Belgravia, *117–119*
Bloomsbury, *74–75,
110, 120*
buses, *59, 61*
Cheapside, *80*
Chelsea, *94, 107,
117–119*
children, *88–89*
the City, *78–82,
110–111*
climate, *6*
Covent Garden, *73,
94, 108–110, 120*
Docklands, *90*
Downing Street, *69*
Dulwich Village, *90*
embassies, *62*
emergencies, *62*
festivals, *6–8*
Fleet Street, *71*
free attractions, *88*
Greenwich, *86–87*
guided tours, *62–63*
Hampstead, *90*
hotels, *112–120*
Kensington, *75–77,
94, 103, 106–107,
117*
Kew, *87–88*
Knightsbridge,
75–77, 94, 103,

117–119
Legal London, *71–73*
Mall, the, *65*
Mayfair, *94, 102–103,
113, 116–117*
nightlife, *122–123*
Notting Hill,
106–107, 119–120
Oxford Street, *94*
parks, *65, 75–77,
86–87, 88, 90, 94*
Parliament Square,
69
pharmacies, *62*
Piccadilly, *94*
pubs, *73, 84, 87, 111*
Regent Street, *94*
restaurants, *65, 71,
76, 77, 79, 80, 84,
85, 101–112*
Richmond, *87*
shopping, *75, 83,
94–100*
sightseeing, *63–94*
Soho, *107–108, 120*
South Bank, *82–86*
sports, *100–101*
St. James, *94,
101–102, 113,
116–117*
street markets,
99–100
taxis, *61*
Thames Barrier, *87*
tourist and travel
information, *62*
Trafalgar Square, *64*
transportation, *59–61*
Underground, *61*
walking tours, *69*
Westminster, *64–65,
68–71*
wine bars, *79, 80, 83,
112*
London Bridge, *83*
London Dungeon, *83*
**London International
Financial Futures
Exchange**, *80*
London Planetarium,
93
**London Toy and
Model Museum**, *89*
**London Transport
Museum**, *73*
London Wall, *79*
Longframlington, *486*
Longleat House, *170*
**Long Man of
Wilmington**, *135*

Long Melford,
305–306
**Lord Leycester
Hospital**, *266*
Lotherton Hall, *42*
Louth, *319*
Lower Broadheath,
339
Lower Slaughter,
290–291
Loweswater, *425–426*
Ludlow, *346, 354, 357*
Luggage, *8–9, 14*
Lune Gorge, *417*
Luss, *536*
Lydford Gorge, *199*
Lygon Arms, *271*
Lyme Regis, *177*
Lympne Castle, *44*
Lyndhurst, *172*
Lynmouth, *193, 212*
Lynton, *193*
Lytham St. Anne's,
403

MacCaig's Tower, *528*
Machynlleth, *360,
371, 389*
Madame Tussaud's,
93–94
**Magdalene College
(Oxford)**, *245*
**Magdalene College
(Cambridge)**, *302*
Magistrates Court, *74*
Magna Carta,
167–168
Maiden Castle, *176*
Maidstone, *125, 143*
Mail, *31*
Maison Dieu Hall, *134*
Malham, *442*
Mallaig, *530*
Malpas, *198*
Maltings, *316*
Malton, *453*
Malvern, *354*
Malvern Festival, *356*
Malvern Hills, *339,
351*
Malvern Wells,
354–355
Manchester, *394,
398–401, 417,
418–419, 426–427,
430*
**Manor House
Museum**, *307–308*
Manor houses, *32*
accommodations in,

Manor houses *265*
(continued)
36
Channel Islands,
224–225
East Anglia, *305,*
306, 307–308, 312,
313
Edinburgh, *498*
Heart of England,
265, 271, 277, 279
London, *65, 68, 69,*
77–78, 80, 87, 90
the Northeast, *476,*
480
the Northwest, *409,*
410, 412
Peak District, *437*
Scottish Borders,
500, 502, 503
Scottish southwest
and highlands, *523,*
528
the South, *165, 169,*
170, 173
the Southeast, *137,*
138, 139, 142, 143,
144
the Southwest, *192,*
193, 199–200, 201,
205
Thames Valley, *240,*
242–243, 247, 248
tours of, *42*
Wales, *379*
Welsh Borders, *340,*
343, 344, 348
Yorkshire Moors,
437, 448
Mansion House, *80*
Mansion House,
(York), *447*
Mapledurham House,
242–243
Mappa Mundi, *341*
Marathon, *100*
Margate, *133*
Mariner's Chapel, *273*
Maritime Museums,
173, 402
Market Building, *73*
Market Hall, *270*
Market House, *196*
Market Rasen, *319*
Marlborough, *171*
Marlow, *241*
Mar's Walk, *525*
Martyrs' Memorial,
246
Mary Arden's House,

265
Mary Rose, *164*
Masham, *454*
Mathematical Bridge,
303
Matlock, *437, 458*
Matlock Bath, *437*
Matlock River
Illuminations, *437*
Maumbury Rings, *175*
Mayflower Park, *165*
Mayflower Stone, *200*
Mealtimes, *35–36*
Melbourne Hall, *42*
Melford Hall, *306*
Melrose, *500, 510*
Melrose Abbey, *500*
Mercat Cross, *496,*
525
Merchant Adventurers
Hall, *446*
Merchant's House
(museum), *200*
Mercury Theatre, *315*
Merlin, *194*
Merlin's Cave, *194*
Merseyside Maritime
Museum, *402*
Metropolitan
Cathedral of Christ
the King, *402*
Mevagissey, *199*
Middlesbrough, *464,*
472
Midhurst, *139*
Military Barracks,
479
Mill Meadows, *242*
Minories, The, *314*
Model Railway
Exhibition, *281*
Model Village, *281*
Modern architecture,
55–56
Mold, *391*
Mol's Coffee House,
203
Mompesson House,
168
Money, *9–10*
Montacute, *212*
Montacute House, *205*
Mont Orgueil, *223*
Monument, the, *81*
Moor's Centre, *452*
Moot Hall, *413*
Moot Hill, *528*
Moreton-in-Marsh,
270
Morris, William

(author), *248*
Morris, William
(automaker), *249*
Morwellham Quay
Openair Museum,
199
Mountbatten, Lord,
165
Mousehole, *196*
Movies, *84–85, 122*
Moyses Hall, *308*
Much Marcle, *340*
Much Wenlock, *346*
Muker, *443*
Mull of Kintyre, *529,*
544–545, 547
Museum of Antiqui-
ties (Edinburgh),
499–500
Museum of Antiqui-
ties (Newcastle-
upon-Tyne), *472–473*
Museum of Childhood
(Beaumaris), *366*
Museum of Childhood
(Edinburgh), *496*
Museum of Childhood
and Home, *378*
Museum of Costume,
279
Museum of Eton Life,
240
Museum of Garden
History, *85*
Museum of Iron, *345*
Museum of Lakeland
Life, *411*
Museum of Liverpool
Life, *402*
Museum of Local
History and
Industry, *376*
Museum of London,
79
Museum of Science
and Industry, *400*
Museum of the
Legions, *367*
Museum of the
Moving Image, *84–85*
Museum of the North,
367
Museum of the
Quakers, *371*
Museum of the
Scottish Lead
Mining Industry, *533*
Museum of the Welsh
Woolen Industry, *374*
Museums, *32*

Channel Islands, *220,*
223, 224, 225, 226
East Anglia, *303,*
307–308, 311, 314,
315, 316, 319, 320
Edinburgh, *493, 495,*
496, 497, 498, 499,
500
Heart of England,
265, 270, 272, 273,
279, 280, 281, 282
London, *64, 68, 71,*
72, 73, 74, 75, 76,
79, 82–83, 84, 85,
86, 88, 89, 90, 91,
92–93
the Northeast, *469,*
470, 471, 472, 473,
474, 478, 479–480
the Northwest and
Lake District, *398,*
400, 401, 402, 406,
413, 416
Scottish Borders, *501*
Scottish southwest
and highlands, *520,*
522, 526, 533
the South, *163,*
164–165, 171, 173,
174, 175, 178
the Southeast, *132,*
137, 139, 141, 142,
143, 144
the Southwest, *192,*
195, 196, 198, 199,
200, 203, 204, 205
Thames Valley, *240,*
246, 249
Wales, *366, 367,*
368–369, 371, 372,
373, 374, 375, 376,
377, 379, 380, 382
Welsh Borders, *337,*
341, 342, 343–344,
345, 347, 349
Yorkshire Moors,
435, 438, 439, 442,
443, 445, 447, 448,
450, 451, 452, 454
Music, *41*
Channel Islands, *231*
East Anglia, *332–333*
Edinburgh, *511*
Heart of England,
267, 303
London, *88, 121,*
122–123
Northwest and Lake
District, *430*
Thames Valley, *240,*

255
tours, *5*
Yorkshire Moors, *461*

Nairn, *545*
Nantwich, *355*
Nash's House,
  263–264
National Coracle
  Centre and Flour
  Mill, *374*
National Film
  Theatre, *84–85*
National Gallery, *64*
National Gallery of
  Scotland, *498*
National Library of
  Scotland, *495*
National Maritime
  Museum, *86*
National Motor
  Museum, *173*
National Museum
  (Cardiff), *379–380*
National Museum of
  Photography, Film
  and Television, *438*
National Portrait
  Gallery, *64*
National Postal
  Museum, *79*
National Railway
  Museum, *447–448*
National Shire Horse
  Centre, *206*
National Trust
  properties and
  historic houses. *See*
  Manor houses
National Waterways
  Museum, *273*
Natural History
  Museum
  (Colchester),
  314–315
Natural History
  Museum (London),
  76
Natural World, *178*
Nautical Museum, *196*
Needles, the, *167*
Neidpath Castle, *502*
Nelson, Horatio, *164*
Nelson Monument,
  499
Nelson's Column, *64*
Netherbow Arts
  Centre, *496*
New Armouries, *81*
Newby Hall, *449*

Newcastle Emlyn, *374*
Newcastle upon Tyne,
  464, 472–473, 486
New College, *245*
New Forest, *172–173*
New Hall Inn, *406*
Newlands Pass, *415*
Newlyn, *196*
New Milton, *182*
Newport, *167*
New Quay (Wales),
  389
Newquay, *195*
Nightlife. *See under
  specific areas*
Norman architecture,
  52
Norman castles, *202,
  472*
the Northeast,
  463–487
the arts, *487*
car rentals, *464*
children, *479*
guided tours, *465*
hotels, *482–487*
restaurants, *469, 470,
  472, 474, 475, 477,
  479, 482–487*
shopping, *481*
sightseeing, *465–480*
sports, *481–482*
tourist and travel
  information, *463–464*
transportation,
  464–466
Northleach, *272*
North Leigh, *43*
North Moors National
  Park, *452*
The Northwest and
  Lake District,
  393–430
the arts, *437*
car rentals, *394*
children, *416*
guided tours,
  396–397
hotels, *421–429*
restaurants, *421–429*
shopping, *417–419*
sightseeing, *398–417*
sports, *419–421*
tourist and travel
  information, *394*
transportation,
  395–396
North York Moors
  Railway, *453*
Norwich, *295,*

*309–311, 322, 330,
  333*
Norwich Cathedral,
  309
Nuffield, *249*

Oakwell Hall, *42*
Oban, *528, 536, 545*
Offa's Dyke path,
  351, 369
Old Alresford, *163*
Olde Cross Inn, *477*
Older travelers, hints
  for, *20–21*
Old Grammar School,
  340
Old House, *341*
Old Man of Coniston,
  408
Old Mariner's
  Church, *195*
Old Royal
  Observatory, *86–87*
Old St. Thomas's
  Hospital, *83*
Oliver Cromwell's
  House, *304*
Opera, *39–40,
  121–122, 155, 391,
  461*
Opera House
  (Buxton), *436*
Opera House
  (Manchester), *400*
Orford, *316, 331*
Orford Castle, *316*
Oriental Armoury, *81*
Orrest Head, *406, 416*
Osborne House, *166*
Other Place, the, *264*
Otter Trust, *320*
Outlook Tower, *495*
Overlord Embroidery,
  165
Oxford, *233, 243, 249,
  250–251, 253–254,
  255*
Oxford Story
  Exhibition, *245–246*
Oxo Tower, *84*

Package deals, *3–5*
Packing, *8–9*
Packwood House, *265*
Padstow, *194–195*
Painted Hall, *86*
Palace House, *173*
Palace of
  Westminster, *69*
Palace Pier, *137*

Palladian
  architecture, *54*
Pallant House,
  139–140
Palm House, *88*
Pangbourne, *248*
Parish Church of St.
  John the Baptist, *436*
Parliament House
  (Edinburgh), *496*
Pass of Llanberis,
  367
Passports, *11*
Pateley Bridge, *454*
Patterdale, *412*
Paulton's Park,
  177–178
Paxton House, *503*
Peak Cavern, *438*
Peak District,
  432–461
the arts, *460–461*
car rentals, *433*
children, *453*
guided tours, *434*
hotels, *456–460*
restaurants, *456–460*
shopping, *454–455*
sightseeing, *434–454*
sports, *455–456*
tourist and travel
  information, *432–433*
transportation,
  433–434
Peebles, *502, 505, 510*
Pembroke, *375*
Pembroke College,
  300
Pembrokeshire Coast
  Path, *383*
Pendennis Castle, *197*
Penrith, *411, 427*
Penrith Museum, *411*
Penshurst Place, *142*
Pensthorpe Waterfowl
  Park, *320*
Pentre Ifan Cromlech,
  374
Pen-y-Gwryd Hotel,
  367
Penzance, *187, 196,
  212–213*
Penzance and District
  Museum and Art
  Gallery, *196*
People's Palace, *520*
People's Park, *222*
Percival David
  Foundation of
  Chinese Art, *74*

Performing arts, 37–41

Perranporth, 195

Perth, 527–528, 536, 545, 547

Peterborough, 320

Peterhouse College, 300

Petersfield, 164

Pets, 12

Petworth House, 139

Pevensey, 135

Pevensey Castle, 135

Peveril Castle, 438

Photographers, tips for, 13

Pilgrim Fathers' Memorial, 165

Pilton Manor, 206

Pistyll Rhaeadr, 369

Pittville Pump Room, 273

Planetariums, 93, 347–348

Plane travel, 23–25, 26

Channel Islands, 218–219

Edinburgh, 490

London, 59

the Northwest, 394–395

Scottish southwest and highlands, 515

the South, 158

Plas Newydd (Llangollen), 368

Plas Newydd (Menai), 381

Plymouth, 187, 200–201, 207, 213

Polesden Lacey, 141

Pollock's Toy Museum, 89

Pollok Country Park, 522

Pollok House, 522–523

Poole, 174, 178, 182

Poole's Cavern, 436

Pooley Bridge, 427

Pool-in-Wharfedale, 458

Poor Priests' Hospital, 132

Porchester Castle, 164

Porlock Hill, 193

Port Appin, 545

Porthgain, 389

Porthmadog, 370

Portinscale, 427

Portloe, 213

Portmeirion, 370, 382, 389

Portsmouth, 157, 164, 182

Potter, Beatrix, 416

Potteries, the, 349

Poultry Cross, 168

Powis Castle, 377

Prebends Footbridge, 469

Prentice Pillar, 503

Preseli Hills, 374

President Kennedy Memorial, 240

Preston Manor, 138

Priest's House Museum, 174

Prince Henry's Room, 72

Priory, the, 339

Probus, 198

Provand's Lordship, 520

Public Record Office, 72

Pull's Ferry, 309

Pulteney Bridge, 279

Pump House, 137

Pump Rooms, 277–278, 377

Purcell Room, 85

Pwllheli, 389–390

Pyx Chamber, 70

Quantock and Brendon hills, 193

Quarry Bank Mill, 348

Quarry Park, 343

Quay House, 204

Queen Anne's Gate, 68

Queen Elizabeth Country Park, 164

Queen Elizabeth Hall, 85

Queen Mary's Doll's House, 239

Queen's Chapel, 65

Queen's Collection of Master Drawings, 239

Queen's College, 303

Queen's Cross Church, 522

Queen's Gallery, 68

Queens Hall, 473

Quothquan, 510

Raby Castle, 471

Radcliffe Camera (building), 245

Rail passes, 16–17

Railroads
East Anglia, 320
the Northeast, 471
the Northwest, 416
Scottish southwest and highlands, 530, 532, 534
the South, 163
the Southeast, 146
the Southwest, 206
tours of, 5
Wales, 367, 369, 370, 371
Welsh Borders, 342
Yorkshire Moors, 447–448, 453

Ralph Cross, 452

Ramsgate, 133

Ranworth, 311

Ravenglass & Eskdale Railway, 416

Red Lion Hotel, 241

Red Tarn, 412

Regent's Canal, 89–90

Register House, 498

Restaurants, 35–36. See also under specific areas

Rhayader, 390

Rhyl Sun Centre, 381

Richborough Castle, 44

Richmond, 432, 443, 461

Richmond Park, 87

Rievaulx Abbey, 452–453

Ripon, 449

Robert Smail's Printing Works, 502

Robin Hood's Bay, 451

Rochester, 145

Rochester Castle, 145

Rochester Cathedral, 145

Rock Circus, 89

Romaldkirk, 470

Roman Army Museum, 474

Roman artifacts, 91, 127, 130, 140, 164, 175, 272, 281–282, 314, 315, 320, 345, 347, 367, 400, 443, 473, 474, 475,

500–501
tours of, 43–44

Roman Pavement, 127

Roman Walls, 314

Romney, Hythe, and Dymchurch Railway, 146

Romney Marsh, 134

Romsey, 183

Rose Cottages, 345

Rosehill House, 345

Rosslyn Chapel, 503

Ross-on-Wye, 340, 351, 355

Rosthwaite, 414

Rothbury, 486

Rothesay, 523

Rotten Row, 75

Rotunda, the, 272–273

Rotunda Museum, 451

Rougemont Castle and Gardens, 203

Round Pond, 76

Royal Academy of Arts, 92–93

Royal Air Force Museum, 90

Royal Albert Hall, 76

Royal Albert Memorial Museum, 203

Royal Armouries, 81

Royal Bank of Scotland, 499

Royal Baths, 448

Royal Botanic Garden, 500

Royal Botanic Gardens at Kew, 87–88

Royal Burgh of Stirling Visitors Centre, 525

Royal Citadel, 200

Royal Clarence Hotel, 203

Royal Cornwall Museum, 198

Royal Courts of Justice, 72

Royal Exchange (London), 80

Royal Exchange (Manchester), 401

Royal Festival Hall, 85

Royal Guernsey Militia Museum, 224

Royal Mausoleum, 240
Royal Mews (London), 68
Royal Mews (Windsor), 239
Royal Mile, 493, 495
Royal Museum of Scotland, 496
Royal National Theatre, 84
Royal Naval College (Dartmouth), 201–202
Royal Naval College (London), 86
Royal Naval Dockyard, 200
Royal Navy Museum, 164–165
Royal Opera House, 73–74
Royal Pavilion, 137
Royal Pump Room Museum, 448
Royal Scottish Academy, 498
Royal Shakespeare Company, 264
Royal Shakespeare Theatre, 264, 293
Royal Tunbridge Wells. See Tunbridge Wells
Royal Worcester Porcelain Factory, 337
Runnymede, 240
Ruskin, John, 409
Russell-Coates Art Gallery and Museum, 174
Ruthin, 360, 368, 382, 390
Ruthwell Cross, 533
Rydal Mount, 408
Ryde, 157, 166
Rye, 125, 134, 153

Saffron Walden, 305, 331
Sail-boarding, 228
Sainsbury Centre, 311
St. Albans, 43, 90–91
St. Alkmund's (church), 343
St. Andrews, 7, 515, 527, 533, 545–546
St. Ann's Church, 401–402

St. Augustine's Abbey, 132
St. Augustine's Well, 176
St. Austell, 199
St. Boswells, 510–511
St. Bride's Church, 71
St. David's, 374
St. Edmund Hall, 245
St. Endellion, 215
St. George's Chapel, 235
St. George's Church, 127
St. George's Hall, 401
St. Giles Cathedral, 496
St. Giles's Hill, 173
St. Giles without Cripplegate, 79
St. Helier, 220
St. Ives, 187, 195
St. James's Church, 307
St. James's Palace, 65
St. James's Park, 65
St. John's Church, 71
St. John's College (Cambridge), 302
St. John's College (Oxford), 246
St. John's House, 280
St. Margaret's Chapel, 493
St. Martin-in-the-Fields, 64
St. Martins, 406
St. Martin's Church, 246
St. Mary (Caernarfon), 366
St. Mary (Scarborough), 450
St. Mary (Whitby), 452
St. Mary Abbotts Church, 77
St. Mary-at-the-Wall, 315
St. Mary-le-Bow, 80
St. Mary's Church (Bury St. Edmunds), 307
St. Mary's Church (Guildford), 141–142
St. Mary's Church (Henley), 241–242
St. Mary's Church (London), 85

St. Mary's Church (Shrewsbury), 343
St. Mary's Church (York), 446
St. Mary the Great (Cambridge), 302
St. Matthew's Church, 223
St. Mawes Castle, 198
St. Michael's Church, 192
St. Michael's Mount (island), 196–197
St. Murgo Museum of Religious Life and Art, 520
St. Non's Bay, 374–375
St. Paul's Cathedral, 78–79
St. Paul's Church (Jarrow), 479–480
St. Paul's Church (London), 73
St. Peter Church, 224
St. Peter Hungate, 310
St. Peter Mancroft, 310
St. Peter Port, 223–224
St. Peter's Church (Bournemouth), 174
St. Peter's Church (London), 90–91
St. Stephen's Tower, 70
St. Swithin's Church, 162
St. Thomas's Hospital, 85
Sales tax, 10, 33–34
Salisbury, 157, 167–169, 178, 183, 185
Salisbury Cathedral, 167–168
Saltburn-by-the-Sea, 451
Saltram House, 200
Sandown, 166
Sandringham House, 313
Sandwich, 133
Sark, 226, 231
Sausmarez Manor, 224–225, 226
Savill Garden, 240
Scafell Pike, 415
Scarborough, 433,

450–451, 453, 455, 458, 461
Scarborough Castle, 450
Scarborough Sea Life Centre, 453
Science Museum, 76
Scone Palace, 528
Scotch Whiskey Heritage Centre, 495
Scotland, 489–547
Scott, Sir Walter, 498, 500, 501
Scottish Borders, 489–512. See also Edinburgh
guided tours, 491
hotels, 506–511
restaurants, 506–511
sightseeing, 500–503
sports, 505
tourist information, 489–490
Scottish Museum of Woollen Textiles, 501
Scottish National Gallery of Modern Art, 500
Scottish National Portrait Gallery, 499–500
Scottish National War Memorial, 493
Scottish Railway Preservation Society, 534
Scottish southwest and highlands, 514–547
the arts, 547
car rentals, 515
children, 533
guided tours, 516–517
hotels, 538–547
restaurants, 522, 523, 524, 525, 526, 527, 528, 532, 538–547
shopping, 534–536
sightseeing, 517–534
sports, 536–538
tourist and travel information, 514–515
transportation, 515–516
Scottish Stock Exchange, 520
Scottish United Services Museum, 493

Scottish Wood Centre, 533

Scott Monument, 498

Scott's View, 501

Seahouses, 477

Sea Life Centre (Brighton), 145

Sea Life Centres (Barcaldine and St. Andrews), 533

Seal Sanctuary, 197

Seatoller, 414–415, 427

Sedbergh, 417

Sedgemoor, 193

Segontium fortress, 366

Selkirk, 501, 511

Senate House (Cambridge), 302

Senate House (London), 74

Sevenoaks, 143

Severn Valley Railway, 342

Severn Warehouse, 345

Shaftesbury, 169

Shakespeare, William, 262–265, 266, 269, 293

Shakespeare Centre, 262

Shakespeare Costume Exhibition, 262

Shakespeare Countryside Museum, 265

Shakespeare Globe Museum, 84

Shambles (museum), 342

Shambles (York), 446

Shanklin, 166

Shap Fells, 411

Sheldonian Theatre, 245

Shelley, Mary, 174, 241

Sheppys, 193

Shieldaig, 533–534

Shinfield, 254

Shipdam, 331

Ships, historic, 83, 86, 164

Ship travel, 25–26, 396

Shire Horse Center, 248

Shopping, 33–34. See

also under specific areas

Show jumping, 283

Shrewsbury, 343–344, 350, 355, 357

Shrewsbury Abbey Church, 344

Shropshire Regimental Museum, 343

Shugborough, 349

Sidney Sussex College, 300

Silbury Hill, 170–171

Singleton, 139

Sir John Soane's Museum, 72–73

Sissinghurst Castle, 144

Skiing, 537

Skipton, 439

Skipton Castle, 439

Skye, 546

Slapton Ley, 201

Smailholm Tower, 501

Smeaton's Tower, 200

Smith Art Gallery and Museum, 526

Snape, 316

Snowdon Mountain Railway, 367

Snowshill Manor, 271

Soccer, 100, 421

Social History Museum, 315

Solva, 375

Somersby, 319

Somerset Rural Life Museum, 192

Sonning-on-Thames, 254

the South, 157–185

the arts, 185

car rentals, 157

children, 177–178

guided tours, 158–159

hotels, 179–185

restaurants, 163, 164, 165, 166, 167, 168–169, 170, 171, 174, 175–176, 177, 179–185

shopping, 178–179

sightseeing, 159–178

sports, 179

tourist and travel information, 157

transportation, 158

Southampton, 165, 183–184

South Bank Arts Complex, 84–85

the Southeast, 125–155

the arts, 155

car rentals, 126

children, 145

guided tours, 126–127

hotels, 147–154

restaurants, 131, 133, 134, 135, 137, 139, 140, 142, 144, 147–154

shopping, 146–147

sightseeing, 127–146

sports, 147

tourist and travel information, 125–126

transportation, 126

South Shields, 486–487

South Wales Borderers' Museum, 379

Southwark Cathedral, 83–84

the Southwest, 187–215

the arts, 215

car rentals, 188

children, 205–206

guided tours, 188

hotels, 208–215

restaurants, 192, 193, 195, 196, 198, 199, 202, 203, 204, 205, 208–215

shopping, 207

sightseeing, 41–42, 189–207

sports, 207–208

tourist and travel information, 187–188

transportation, 188

Southwold, 316, 331–332

Southwold Museum, 316

Speech House, 276

Speedwell Cavern, 438

Sports, 5, 34–35. See also under specific areas

S.S. *Great Britain*, 280

Staffordshire County Museum, 349

Stamford, 320–321

Stanley Spencer Gallery, 240–241

Stanton Drew, 280

Stanton Harcourt Manor, 248

Stewarton, 546

Stirling, 515, 525–526, 536, 546

Stirling Castle, 525

Stirling's Library, 520

Stoer, 534

Stoke-on-Trent 349

Stoke-on-Trent City Museum and Art Gallery, 350

Stonehenge, 171–172

Stonor Park, 243

Stourbridge, 342

Stourhead House, 169–170

Stourton, 169–170

Stow-on-the-Wold, 270, 291

Strangers Hall, 310

Stranraer, 525

Stratford-upon-Avon, 6–7, 262–265, 283, 291–292, 293

Strathspey Railway, 532

Stuart, Prince Charles, 530

Student and youth travel, 17–18

Studley Royal, 449

Styal, 348

Sudbury, 305, 332

Sudeley Castle, 271

Suffolk Heritage Coast, 316

Sugar Loaf, 378

Surfing, 228

Sutton Gault, 320

Swaledale, 442, 443

Swallow Falls, 367

Swan Hotel, 306

Swannery, 177

Swansea, 360, 375–376, 390

Swansea Maritime and Industrial Museum, 375

Swan Theatre, 264

Swan-upping, 242

Swimming, 35, 208, 228, 323, 419–420, 456

Symond's Yat, 340

Symphony Hall, 267, 293

Tamdhu distillery, *43*
Tamnavulin distillery, *43*
Taplow, *254*
Tar Tunnel, *345*
Tate Gallery, *71*
Tate Gallery (Liverpool), *402*
Tate Gallery (St. Ives), *195*
Tatton Park, *348*
Taunton, *193, 213–214*
Tavistock, *214*
Techniquest, *380*
Telephones, *11, 30–31*
Temperate House, *88*
Temple Church, *72*
Temple Island, *242*
Temple Newsam, *454*
Tenby, *375, 390*
Tenby Museum, *375*
Tenement House, *522*
Tennis, *34, 100*
Tewkesbury, *282, 355–356*
Thames Barrier, *87*
Thames River, *86–88*
Thames Valley, *233–256*
the arts, *255–256*
car rentals, *233*
children, *248*
guided tours, *234*
hotels, *251–255*
restaurants, *239, 241, 242, 246, 251–255*
shopping, *249–250*
sightseeing, *235–249*
sports, *250*
tourist and travel information, *233*
transportation, *233–234*
Thatched Bridge Cottage, *315*
Theater, *38–39*
East Anglia, *333*
Edinburgh, *511*
Heart of England, *264, 267, 293*
London, *121*
the Northeast, *487*
the Northwest, *430*
Scottish southwest and highlands, *547*
South, *185*
the Southeast, *155*
the Southwest, *215*
Thames Valley,

255–256
Wales, *391*
Yorkshire Moors, *443, 461*
Theatre Museum, *73*
Theatre Royal, *279, 293*
Thetford Forest, *308*
Thornbury, *292*
Threave Garden, *525*
Tintagel, *194*
Tipping, *31*
Tolbooth Kirk, *495*
Tolpuddle, *178*
Tomato Centre, *226*
Tombland, *310*
Tomb of the Unknown Warrior, *70*
Tonbridge, *153–154*
Topsham, *204*
Top Withins, *439*
Torbay, *202*
Torquay, *214*
Totnes, *202, 214*
Tours and Packages, *2–5, 18, 20, 21*
Tower Bridge, *82*
Tower Hill Pageant, *82*
Tower of London, *81–82*
Town Hall (Birmingham), *269*
Town Hall (Colchester), *315*
Town Hall (Manchester), *399*
Town Model and Living History Center (Lewes), *136*
Train travel, *26–27, 30. See also* Railroads; transportation *under specific areas*
Traquair House, *502*
Traveler's checks, *9*
Treasures of the Earth, *530*
Trelissick, *198*
Tremadog, *370*
Tretower Court, *379*
Trimontium Trust, *500–501*
Trinity Chapel, *130*
Trinity College, *302*
Trinity Guildhall, *313*
Trinity Hall, *302*
Troon, *546*
Trooping the Color

ceremony, *69*
Tropical Vinery and Gardens, *226*
Trossachs lochs, *527*
Truro, *187, 198, 214*
Tudor architecture, *53*
Tudor House, *339*
Tudor House Museum, *165*
Tudor Merchant's House, *375*
Tudor Rose, *366*
Tunbridge Wells, *125, 142, 154*
Tunbridge Wells Museum and Art Gallery, *142*
Tunstall Forest, *316*
Turk's Head, *196*
Tymperley's Clock Museum, *315*

Uckfield, *154*
Uffington, *248*
Ullapool, *546–547*
Ulverston, *409, 428*
Undercroft, *70*
Undercroft Museum and Treasury, *445*
Union Hotel, *196*
University Botanic Garden, *303*
University Church, *245*
University College, *74*
University housing, *37*
University of East Anglia, *311*
Upper Slaughter, *292*
Upper Soudley, *276*

Vale of Ewyas, *378*
Vale of Pewsey, *178*
Vale of Rheidol Railway, *372*
Vale of the White Horse, *247*
Value added tax (VAT), *10, 33–34*
Venerable Bede Monastery Museum, *479–480*
Ventnor, *166*
Verulamium Museum, *91*
Victoria, Queen, *165, 240*
Victoria and Albert Museum, *76*
Victorian

architecture, *54*
Victoria Tower, *70*
Villa rentals, *37*
Vindolanda, *474*
Virginia Court, *520*
Virginia Water, *240*
Visas, *11*
Volk's Electric Railway, *138*

Wadhurst, *154*
Wakefield Tower, *81*
Wales, *359–391*
the arts, *390–391*
car rentals, *360*
children, *380–381*
guided tours, *362*
hotels, *384–390*
language, *359–360*
restaurants, *366, 367, 369, 371, 376, 380, 384–390*
shopping, *382*
sightseeing, *363–382*
sports, *382–384*
tourist and travel information, *360*
transportation, *361–362*
Walker Art Gallery, *401–402*
Walkerburn, *501*
Walking tours, *5*
Wallace Collection, *93*
Wallace Monument, *526*
Wallingford, *243*
Wallington House, *476*
Walmer Castle, *44, 133*
Wanlockhead, *533*
Warminster, *184*
Warwick, *266, 280–281, 292*
Warwick Castle, *266*
Warwickshire Doll Museum, *280–281*
Washington, *472*
Washington Old Hall, *472*
Washington Waterfowl Park, *479*
Watendlath, *414*
Waterfalls, *369, 372, 412, 414, 439, 470, 526, 533*
Waterloo Barracks, *81*
Water sports, *35, 147, 208, 227–228, 384,*

Water sports
(continued)
420–421, 482
Waxhouse Gate, *91*
Wax museums, *93–94*
**Weald and Downland
Open Air Museum,**
139
**Weardale Folk
Museum,** *469–470*
Weather, *5–6*
Weavers' Houses,
131–132
**Wedgwood's Visitor
Centre and Museum,**
349
Wellington Arch, *75*
Wellington Barracks,
68
Wellington Museum,
75
Wells, *188, 189, 215*
**Wells and
Walsingham Light
Railway,** *320*
Welsh Borders,
335–357
the arts, *356–357*
car rentals, *335*
children, *348–349*
guided tours, *336*
hotels, *351–356*
restaurants, *339, 340,
341, 343, 345, 347,
348, 351–356*
shopping, *350*
sightseeing, *336–350*
sports, *351*
tourist and travel
information, *335*
transportation, *336*
Welsh Folk Museum,
380
**Welsh Industrial and
Maritime Museum,**
380
Welsh Mountain Zoo,
381
Welshpool, *360, 377*
Welsh Slate Museum,
367
Wenlock Edge, *346*
Wenlock Priory, *346*

Wensleydale, *442*
West Clandon, *141*
**Westgate Museum of
Militaria,** *132*
**West Kennett Long
Barrow,** *171*
West Lulworth, *184*
Westminster Abbey,
70–71
Westminster Bridge,
85
Westminster Hall, *69*
Westminster School,
71
Weston-on-the-Green,
254
Weston-super-Mare,
281
West Register House,
499
**West Stow Country
Park,** *308*
Weymouth, *176, 184*
Wharfedale, *439*
Wheal Martyn, *207*
Whitby, *433,
451–452, 455, 458*
Whitby Abbey, *452*
Whitebridge, *547*
**White Horse
(carving),** *178*
White Tower, *81*
White Wells Museum,
442
Whitstable, *133*
**Whitworth Art
Gallery,** *401*
Wildfowl Trust, *146,
276, 320*
Wildlife reserves, *146,
166, 172–173, 194,
223, 276, 311, 320,
480*
**William the
Conqueror,** *135*
Wilmcote, *265*
Wilmington, *135*
**Wilton House and
Gardens,** *169*
**Wimbledon tennis
championships,** *7,
100*
Wimbourne Minster,

174
Winchelsea, *135–136*
Winchester, *42, 157,
159, 162–163, 178,
184–185*
Winchester Cathedral,
159, 162
Winchester College,
163
Windermere, *394,
403, 406, 419,
428–429*
**Windermere
Steamboat Museum,**
406
Windsor, *235, 239,
249, 250, 254–255*
Windsor Castle, *235,
239*
Windsor Great Park,
240
Wingfield College,
333
Winter Gardens, *339*
Wiring money, *10*
Witley Court, *342*
Witney, *249*
Wood End, *450*
**Woodend Museum of
Natural History,** *450*
Woodstock, *247, 255*
Wookey Hole, *206*
Woolstaplers Hall, *270*
Worcester, *337, 339,
350, 356*
Worcester Cathedral,
337
Worcester College,
246
Wordsworth, William,
408, 415
Wordsworth House,
415
**World of Beatrix
Potter,** *416*
**World of Shakespeare
(waxworks),** *264*
Wrekin, *345*
**Wren, Sir
Christopher,** *54,
78–79, 239*
Wrestling, *421*
"Writers at home"

tour, *41–42*
Wroxeter, *345*
Wye Pottery, *378*
Wylam, *487*
Wymondham, *308*

**Ye Olde Cheshire
Cheese** (pub), *71*
**Ye Olde Fighting
Cocks** (inn), *91*
Yeovilton, *205*
York, *433, 443,
445–448, 455,
458–460, 461*
York House, *65*
York Minster,
445–446
Yorkshire Moors,
432–461
the arts, *460–461*
car rentals, *433*
children, *453*
guided tours, *434*
hotels, *456–460*
restaurants,
456–460
shopping, *454–455*
sightseeing, *434–454*
sports, *455–456*
tourist and travel
information,
432–433
transportation,
433–434
Yorkshire Museum,
447
Yorkshire wolds, *454*
York Story, *446*
Youth hostels, *18, 37*
Ypres Tower, *134*

Zoos
Channel Islands, *223,
226*
East Anglia, *320*
Edinburgh, *502*
Heart of England,
280
London, *89*
the South, *170*
the Southeast, *145*
Wales, *380–381*

Personal Itinerary

Departure *Date*

Time

Transportation

Arrival *Date*   *Time*

Departure *Date*   *Time*

Transportation

Accommodations

Arrival *Date*   *Time*

Departure *Date*   *Time*

Transportation

Accommodations

Arrival *Date*   *Time*

Departure *Date*   *Time*

Transportation

Accommodations

Personal Itinerary

Arrival *Date*   *Time*

Departure *Date*   *Time*

Transportation

Accommodations

Arrival *Date*   *Time*

Departure *Date*   *Time*

Transportation

Accommodations

Arrival *Date*   *Time*

Departure *Date*   *Time*

Transportation

Accommodations

Arrival *Date*   *Time*

Departure *Date*   *Time*

Transportation

Accommodations

Personal Itinerary

Arrival *Date*   *Time*

Departure *Date*   *Time*

Transportation

Accommodations

Arrival *Date*   *Time*

Departure *Date*   *Time*

Transportation

Accommodations

Arrival *Date*   *Time*

Departure *Date*   *Time*

Transportation

Accommodations

Arrival *Date*   *Time*

Departure *Date*   *Time*

Transportation

Accommodations

Personal Itinerary

Arrival *Date*   *Time*

Departure *Date*   *Time*

Transportation

Accommodations

Arrival *Date*   *Time*

Departure *Date*   *Time*

Transportation

Accommodations

Arrival *Date*   *Time*

Departure *Date*   *Time*

Transportation

Accommodations

Arrival *Date*   *Time*

Departure *Date*   *Time*

Transportation

Accommodations

Personal Itinerary

Arrival *Date*   *Time*

Departure *Date*   *Time*

Transportation

Accommodations

Arrival *Date*   *Time*

Departure *Date*   *Time*

Transportation

Accommodations

Arrival *Date*   *Time*

Departure *Date*   *Time*

Transportation

Accommodations

Arrival *Date*   *Time*

Departure *Date*   *Time*

Transportation

Accommodations

Personal Itinerary

Arrival *Date*   *Time*

Departure *Date*   *Time*

Transportation

Accommodations

Arrival *Date*   *Time*

Departure *Date*   *Time*

Transportation

Accommodations

Arrival *Date*   *Time*

Departure *Date*   *Time*

Transportation

Accommodations

Arrival *Date*   *Time*

Departure *Date*   *Time*

Transportation

Accommodations

Personal Itinerary

Arrival *Date*   *Time*

Departure *Date*   *Time*

Transportation

Accommodations

Arrival *Date*   *Time*

Departure *Date*   *Time*

Transportation

Accommodations

Arrival *Date*   *Time*

Departure *Date*   *Time*

Transportation

Accommodations

Arrival *Date*   *Time*

Departure *Date*   *Time*

Transportation

Accommodations

Addresses

Name	*Name*
Address	*Address*
Telephone	*Telephone*
Name	*Name*
Address	*Address*
Telephone	*Telephone*
Name	*Name*
Address	*Address*
Telephone	*Telephone*
Name	*Name*
Address	*Address*
Telephone	*Telephone*
Name	*Name*
Address	*Address*
Telephone	*Telephone*
Name	*Name*
Address	*Address*
Telephone	*Telephone*
Name	*Name*
Address	*Address*
Telephone	*Telephone*
Name	*Name*
Address	*Address*
Telephone	*Telephone*

Addresses

Name	*Name*
Address	*Address*
Telephone	*Telephone*
Name	*Name*
Address	*Address*
Telephone	*Telephone*
Name	*Name*
Address	*Address*
Telephone	*Telephone*
Name	*Name*
Address	*Address*
Telephone	*Telephone*
Name	*Name*
Address	*Address*
Telephone	*Telephone*
Name	*Name*
Address	*Address*
Telephone	*Telephone*
Name	*Name*
Address	*Address*
Telephone	*Telephone*
Name	*Name*
Address	*Address*
Telephone	*Telephone*

Addresses

Name

Address

Telephone

Name

Address

Telephone

Name

Address

Telephone

Name

Address

Telephone

Name

Address

Telephone

Name

Address

Telephone

Name

Address

Telephone

Name

Address

Telephone

Name

Address

Telephone

Name

Address

Telephone

Name

Address

Telephone

Name

Address

Telephone

Name

Address

Telephone

Name

Address

Telephone

Name

Address

Telephone

Name

Address

Telephone

Notes

Notes

Notes

The only guide to explore a Disney World® you've never seen before:

The one for grown-ups.

0-679-02490-5 $14.00 ($18.50 Can)

This is the only guide written specifically for the millions of adults who visit Walt Disney World® each year <u>without</u> kids. Upscale, sophisticated, packed full of facts and maps, *Walt Disney World® for Adults* provides up-to-date information on hotels, restaurants, sports facilities, and health clubs, as well as unique itineraries for adults. With *Walt Disney World® for Adults* in hand, you'll get the most out of one of the world's most fascinating, most complex playgrounds.

At bookstores everywhere, or call **1-800-533-6478**.

Fodor's Travel Guides

Available at bookstores everywhere, or call 1–800–533–6478, 24 hours a day.

U.S. Guides

Alaska

Arizona

Boston

California

Cape Cod, Martha's Vineyard, Nantucket

The Carolinas & the Georgia Coast

Chicago

Colorado

Florida

Hawaii

Las Vegas, Reno, Tahoe

Los Angeles

Maine, Vermont, New Hampshire

Maui

Miami & the Keys

New England

New Orleans

New York City

Pacific North Coast

Philadelphia & the Pennsylvania Dutch Country

The Rockies

San Diego

San Francisco

Santa Fe, Taos, Albuquerque

Seattle & Vancouver

The South

The U.S. & British Virgin Islands

USA

The Upper Great Lakes Region

Virginia & Maryland

Waikiki

Walt Disney World and the Orlando Area

Washington, D.C.

Foreign Guides

Acapulco, Ixtapa, Zihuatanejo

Australia & New Zealand

Austria

The Bahamas

Baja & Mexico's Pacific Coast Resorts

Barbados

Berlin

Bermuda

Brittany & Normandy

Budapest

Canada

Cancún, Cozumel, Yucatán Peninsula

Caribbean

China

Costa Rica, Belize, Guatemala

The Czech Republic & Slovakia

Eastern Europe

Egypt

Euro Disney

Europe

Florence, Tuscany & Umbria

France

Germany

Great Britain

Greece

Hong Kong

India

Ireland

Israel

Italy

Japan

Kenya & Tanzania

Korea

London

Madrid & Barcelona

Mexico

Montréal & Québec City

Morocco

Moscow & St. Petersburg

The Netherlands, Belgium & Luxembourg

New Zealand

Norway

Nova Scotia, Prince Edward Island & New Brunswick

Paris

Portugal

Provence & the Riviera

Rome

Russia & the Baltic Countries

Scandinavia

Scotland

Singapore

South America

Southeast Asia

Spain

Sweden

Switzerland

Thailand

Tokyo

Toronto

Turkey

Vienna & the Danube Valley

Special Series

Fodor's Affordables

Caribbean

Europe

Florida

France

Germany

Great Britain

Italy

London

Paris

Fodor's Bed & Breakfast and Country Inns Guides

America's Best B&Bs

California

Canada's Great Country Inns

Cottages, B&Bs and Country Inns of England and Wales

Mid-Atlantic Region

New England

The Pacific Northwest

The South

The Southwest

The Upper Great Lakes Region

The Berkeley Guides

California

Central America

Eastern Europe

Europe

France

Germany & Austria

Great Britain & Ireland

Italy

London

Mexico

Pacific Northwest & Alaska

Paris

San Francisco

Fodor's Exploring Guides

Australia

Boston & New England

Britain

California

The Caribbean

Florence & Tuscany

Florida

France

Germany

Ireland

Italy

London

Mexico

New York City

Paris

Prague

Rome

Scotland

Singapore & Malaysia

Spain

Thailand

Turkey

Fodor's Flashmaps

Boston

New York

Washington, D.C.

Fodor's Pocket Guides

Acapulco

Bahamas

Barbados

Jamaica

London

New York City

Paris

Puerto Rico

San Francisco

Washington, D.C.

Fodor's Sports

Cycling

Golf Digest's Best Places to Play

Hiking

The Insider's Guide to the Best Canadian Skiing

Running

Sailing

Skiing in the USA & Canada

USA Today's Complete Four Sports Stadium Guide

Fodor's Three-In-Ones (guidebook, language cassette, and phrase book)

France

Germany

Italy

Mexico

Spain

Fodor's Special-Interest Guides

Complete Guide to America's National Parks

Condé Nast Traveler Caribbean Resort and Cruise Ship Finder

Cruises and Ports of Call

Euro Disney

France by Train

Halliday's New England Food Explorer

Healthy Escapes

Italy by Train

London Companion

Shadow Traffic's New York Shortcuts and Traffic Tips

Sunday in New York

Sunday in San Francisco

Touring Europe

Touring USA: Eastern Edition

Walt Disney World and the Orlando Area

Walt Disney World for Adults

Fodor's Vacation Planners

Great American Learning Vacations

Great American Sports & Adventure Vacations

Great American Vacations

Great American Vacations for Travelers with Disabilities

National Parks and Seashores of the East

National Parks of the West

The Wall Street Journal Guides to Business Travel

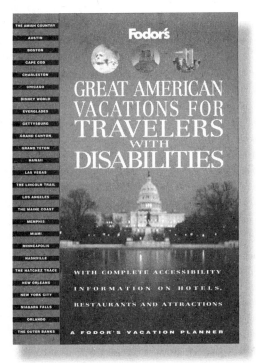

AT LAST

YOUR OWN PERSONALIZED LIST
OF WHAT'S GOING ON IN THE
CITIES YOU'RE VISITING.

KEYED TO THE DAYS WHEN
YOU'LL BE THERE, CUSTOMIZED
FOR YOUR INTERESTS,
AND SENT TO YOU BEFORE YOU
LEAVE HOME.

GET THE INSIDER'S
PERSPECTIVE. . .

UP-TO-THE-MINUTE
ACCURATE
EASY TO ORDER
DELIVERED WHEN YOU NEED IT

Fodor's WORLDVIEW
TRAVEL UPDATE

Now there is a revolutionary way to get customized, time-sensitive travel information just before your trip.

Now you can obtain detailed information about what's going on in each city you'll be visiting <u>before</u> you leave home—up-to-the-minute, objective information about the events and activities that interest you most.

Travel Updates contain the kind of time-sensitive insider information you can get only from local contacts – or from city magazines and newspapers once you arrive. But now you can have the same information before you leave for your trip.

The choice is yours: current art exhibits, theater, music festivals and special concerts, sporting events, antiques and flower shows, shopping, fitness, and more.

The information comes from hundreds of correspondents and thousands of sources worldwide. Updated continuously, it's like having your own personal concierge or friend in the city.

You specify the cities and when you'll be there. We'll do the rest — personalizing the information for you the way no guidebook can.

It's the perfect extension to your Fodor's guide and the best way to make the most of your valuable travel time.

**Use Order Form on back
or call 1-800-799-9609**

Your Itinerary:
Customized reports available for 160 destinations

a
to
990.
Regent
The an
in this a
domain of
tion as Joe
worthwhile.
the perfomanc
Tickets are usual.
venue. Alternate
mances are cancelle
given. For more infor
Open-Air Theatre, Inner
NW1 4NP Open Air Th
Tel: 935-5756. Ends: 9-11-9
International Air Tattoo
Held biennially, the worl
military air display
demostra
tions, mi
ban

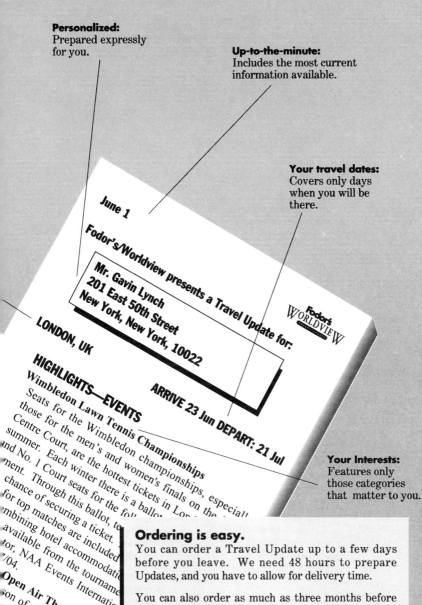

Personalized:
Prepared expressly
for you.

Up-to-the-minute:
Includes the most current
information available.

Your travel dates:
Covers only days
when you will be
there.

June 1

Fodor's/Worldview presents a Travel Update for:

Mr. Gavin Lynch
201 East 50th Street
New York, New York, 10022

Fodor's
WORLDVIEW

LONDON, UK

ARRIVE 23 Jun DEPART: 21 Jul

HIGHLIGHTS—EVENTS

Wimbledon Lawn Tennis Championships

Seats for the Wimbledon championships, especiall
those for the men's and women's finals in the
Centre Court, are the hottest tickets in Lon
summer. Each winter there is a ballot
nd No. 1 Court seats for the foll
ment. Through this ballot, te
chance of securing a ticket.
for top matches are included
mbining hotel accommodatio
available from the tournam
or, NAA Events Internation
/04.

Open Air Theatre Season
son of open-air theater produ
nd lovely park, once the
y dandies, is as much of an
Broadway in the Park and e
to bring your largest umbre
ften interrupted by showe
ble for the almost 1,200-seat
are offered when perfor-
rain, but refunds are not
contact Sheila Benjamir
Regent's Park, I
Regent's P

Your Interests:
Features only
those categories
that matter to you.

Ordering is easy.
You can order a Travel Update up to a few days
before you leave. We need 48 hours to prepare
Updates, and you have to allow for delivery time.

You can also order as much as three months before
you leave. We can send your Travel Update
immediately, or if you prefer, we can hold your
order until just before you leave so that the
information is as current as possible.

There's an order form at the end of this special
section. Choose your destinations and interests; mail
or fax the completed form to us. Or if you prefer, you
can call us toll-free. We'll send out your personalized
Update within 48 hours.

**Special concerts—
who's performing
what and where**

**One-of-a-kind,
one-time-only events**

**Special interest,
in-depth listings**

Children — Events

Angel Canal Festival

The festivities include a children's funfair, entertainers, a boat rally and displays on the water. Regent's Canal. Islington. N1. Tube: Angel. Tel: 267 9100. 11:30am-5:30pm. 7/04.

Blackheath Summer Kite Festival

Stunt kite displays with parachuting teddy bears and trade stands. Free admission. SE3. BR: Blackheath. 10am. 6/27.

Megabugs

Children will delight in this infestation of giant robotic insects, including a praying mantis 60 times life size. Mon-Sat 10am-6pm; Sun 11am-6pm. Admission 4.50 pounds. Natural History Museum, Cromwell Road. SW7. Tube: South Kensington. Tel: 938 9123. Ends 10/01.

Childminders

This establishment employs only women, providing nurses and qualified nannies to

Music — Jazz & Blues

Tito Puente's Golden Men of Latin Jazz

The father of mambo and Cuban rumba king comes to town. Royal Festival Hall. South Bank. SE1. Tube: Waterloo. Tel: 928 8800. 8pm. 7/15.

Georgie Fame and The New York Band

Riding a popular tide with his latest album, the smoky-voiced Fame and his keyboard are on a tour yet again. The Grand. Clapham Junction. SW11. BR: Clapham Junction. Tel: 738 9000. 7:30pm. 7/07.

Jacques Loussier Play Bach Trio

The French jazz classicist and colleagues. Kenwood Lakeside. Hampstead Lane. Kenwood. NW3. Tube: Golders Green, then bus 210. Tel: 413 1443. 7pm. 7/10.

Tony Bennett and Ronnie Scott

Royal Festival Hall. South Bank. SE1. Tube: Waterloo. Tel: 928 8800. 8pm. 7/11.

Santana

Royal Festival Hall. South Bank. SE1. Tube: Waterloo. Tel: 928 8800. 8pm. 7/12.

Count Basie Orchestra and Nancy Wilson Trio

Royal Festival Hall. South Bank. SE1. Tube: Waterloo. Tel: 928 8800. 8pm. 7/14.

King Pleasure and the Biscuit Boys

Royal Festival Hall. South Bank. SE1. Tube: Waterloo. Tel: 928 8800. 6:30 and 9pm. 7/16.

Al Green and the London Community Gospel Choir

Royal Festival Hall. South Bank. SE1. Tube: Waterloo. Tel: 928 8800. 8pm. 7/13.

BB King and Linda Hopkins

Mother of the blues and successor to Bessie Smith, Hopkins meets up with "Blues Boy" King. Royal Festival Hall. South Bank. SE1. 928 8800. 6:30 and 9pm

Music — Classical

Marylebone Sinfonia

Kenneth Gowen conducts music by Puccini and Rossini. Queen Elizabeth Hall. South Bank. SE1. Tube: Waterloo. Tel: 928 8800. 7:45pm. 7/16.

London Philharmonic

Franz Welser-Moest and George Benjamin conduct selections by Alexander Goehr, Messiaen, and some of Benjamin's own compositions. Queen Elizabeth Hall. South Bank. SE1. Tube: Waterloo. Tel: 928 8800. 8pm.

London Pro Arte Orchestra and Forest Choir

Murray Stewart conducts selections by Rossini, Haydn and Jonathan Willcocks. Queen Elizabeth Hall. South Bank. SE1. Tube: Waterloo. Tel: 928 8800. 7:45pm.

Kensington Symphony Orchestra

Russell Keable conducts Dvorak's Elizabeth Hall. South Bank.

Here's what you get . . .

Detailed information about what's going on — precisely when you'll be there.

Reviews by local critics

Show openings during your visit

Handy pocket-size booklet

Exhibitions & Shows—Antique & Flower

Westminster Antiques Fair
Over 50 stands with pre-1830 furniture and other Victorian and earlier items. Thu-Fri 11am-8pm; Sat-Sun 11am-6pm. Admission 4 pounds, children free. Old Royal Horticultural Hall. Vincent Square. SW1. Tel: 0444/48 25 14. 6-24 thru 6/27.

Royal Horticultural Society Flower Show
The show includes displays of carnations, summer fruit and vegetables. Tue 11am-7pm; Wed 10am-5pm. Admission Tue 4 pounds, Wed 2 pounds. Royal Horticultural Halls. Greycoat Street and Vincent Square. SW1. Tube: Victoria. 7/20 thru 7/21.

Hampton Court Palace International Flower Show
Major international garden and flower show taking place in conjunction with

Theater — Musical

Sunset Boulevard
In June, the four Andrew Lloyd Webber musicals which dominated London's stages in the 1980s (Cats, Starlight Express, Phantom of the Opera and Aspects of Love) are joined by the composer's latest work, a show rumored to have his best music to date. The 1950 Billy Wilder film about a helpless young writer who is drawn into the world of a possessive, aging silent screen star offers rich opportunities for Webber's evolving style. Soaring, aching melodies, lush technical effects and psychological thrills are all expected. Patti Lupone stars. Mon-Sat at 8pm; matinee Thu-Sat at 3pm. In-person sales only at the box office; credit card bookings, Tel: 344 0055. Admission 15-32.50 pounds. Adelphi Theatre. The Strand. WC2. Tube: Charing Cross. Tel: 836 7611. Starts: 6/21.

Leonardo A Portrait of Love
A new musical about the great Renaissance artist and inventor comes in for a London premiere tested by a brief run at Oxford's Old . . . The work explores

Spectator Sports — Other Sports

Greyhound Racing: Wembley Stadium
This dog track offers good views of greyhound racing held on Mon, Wed and Fri. No credit cards. Stadium Way. Wembley. HA9. Tube: Wembley Park. Tel: 902 8833.

Benson & Hedges Cricket Cup Final
Lord's Cricket Ground. St. John's Wood Road. NW8. Tube: St. John's Wood. Tel: 289 1611. 11am. 7/10.

Business-Fax & Overnight Mail

Post Office, Trafalgar Square Branch
Offers a network of fax services, the Intelpost system, throughout the country and abroad. Mon-Sat 8am-8pm, Sun 9am-5pm. William IV Street. WC2. Tube: Charing Cross. Tel: 930 9580.

Fodor's WORLDVIEW
TRAVEL UPDATE

London, England
Arriving: June 23
Departing: July 21

Interest Categories

For **your** personalized Travel Update, choose the categories
you're most interested in from this list. Every Travel Update
automatically provides you with *Event Highlights* - the best of
what's happening during the dates of your trip.

1.	**Business Services**	Fax & Overnight Mail, Computer Rentals, Photocopying, Protocol, Secretarial, Messenger, Translation Services
	Dining	
2.	**All Day Dining**	Breakfast & Brunch, Cafes & Tea Rooms, Late-Night Dining
3.	**Local Cuisine**	In Every Price Range—from Budget Restaurants to the Special Splurge
4.	**European Cuisine**	Continental, French, Italian
5.	**Asian Cuisine**	Chinese, Far Eastern, Japanese, Other
6.	**Americas Cuisine**	American, Mexican & Latin
7.	**Nightlife**	Bars, Dance Clubs, Casinos, Comedy Clubs, Ethnic, Pubs & Beer Halls
8.	**Entertainment**	Theater—Comedy, Drama, English Language, Musicals, Dance, Ticket Agencies
9.	**Music**	Country/Western/Folk, Classical, Traditional & Ethnic, Opera, Jazz & Blues, Pop, Rock
10.	**Children's Activities**	Events, Attractions
11.	**Tours**	Local Tours, Day Trips, Overnight Excursions, Cruises
12.	**Exhibitions, Festivals & Shows**	Antiques & Flower, History & Cultural, Art Exhibitions, Fairs & Craft Shows, Music & Art Festivals
13.	**Shopping**	Districts & Malls, Markets, Regional Specialities
14.	**Fitness**	Bicycling, Health Clubs, Hiking, Jogging
15.	**Recreational Sports**	Boating/Sailing, Fishing, Golf, Ice Skating, Skiing, Snorkeling/Scuba, Swimming, Tennis & Racquet
16.	**Spectator Sports**	Auto Racing, Baseball, Basketball, Boating & Sailing, Football, Golf, Horse Racing, Ice Hockey, Rugby, Soccer, Tennis, Track & Field, Other Sports

Please note that interest category content will vary by season, destination,
and length of stay.

Destinations

The Fodor's/Worldview Travel Update covers more than 160 destinations world-wide. Choose the destinations that match your itinerary from this list. (Choose bulleted destinations only.)

Europe
- Amsterdam
- Athens
- Barcelona
- Berlin
- Brussels
- Budapest
- Copenhagen
- Dublin
- Edinburgh
- Florence
- Frankfurt
- French Riviera
- Geneva
- Glasgow
- Istanbul
- Lausanne
- Lisbon
- London
- Madrid
- Milan
- Moscow
- Munich
- Oslo
- Paris
- Prague
- Provence
- Rome
- Salzburg
- * Seville
- St. Petersburg
- Stockholm
- Venice
- Vienna
- Zurich

United States (Mainland)
- Albuquerque
- Atlanta
- Atlantic City
- Baltimore
- Boston
- * Branson, MO
- * Charleston, SC
- Chicago
- Cincinnati
- Cleveland
- Dallas/Ft. Worth
- Denver
- Detroit
- Houston
- * Indianapolis
- Kansas City
- Las Vegas
- Los Angeles
- Memphis
- Miami
- Milwaukee
- Minneapolis/ St. Paul
- * Nashville
- New Orleans
- New York City
- Orlando
- Palm Springs
- Philadelphia
- Phoenix
- Pittsburgh
- Portland
- * Reno/ Lake Tahoe
- St. Louis
- Salt Lake City
- San Antonio
- San Diego
- San Francisco
- * Santa Fe
- Seattle
- Tampa
- Washington, DC

Alaska
- Alaskan Destinations

Hawaii
- Honolulu
- Island of Hawaii
- Kauai
- Maui

Canada
- Quebec City
- Montreal
- Ottawa
- Toronto
- Vancouver

Bahamas
- Abaco
- Eleuthera/ Harbour Island
- Exuma
- Freeport
- Nassau & Paradise Island

Bermuda
- Bermuda Countryside
- Hamilton

British Leeward Islands
- Anguilla
- Antigua & Barbuda
- St. Kitts & Nevis

British Virgin Islands
- Tortola & Virgin Gorda

British Windward Islands
- Barbados
- Dominica
- Grenada
- St. Lucia
- St. Vincent
- Trinidad & Tobago

Cayman Islands
- The Caymans

Dominican Republic
- Santo Domingo

Dutch Leeward Islands
- Aruba
- Bonaire
- Curacao

Dutch Windward Island
- St. Maarten/ St. Martin

French West Indies
- Guadeloupe
- Martinique
- St. Barthelemy

Jamaica
- Kingston
- Montego Bay
- Negril
- Ocho Rios

Puerto Rico
- Ponce
- San Juan

Turks & Caicos
- Grand Turk/ Providenciales

U.S. Virgin Islands
- St. Croix
- St. John
- St. Thomas

Mexico
- Acapulco
- Cancun & Isla Mujeres
- Cozumel
- Guadalajara
- Ixtapa & Zihuatanejo
- Los Cabos
- Mazatlan
- Mexico City
- Monterrey
- Oaxaca
- Puerto Vallarta

South/Central America
- * Buenos Aires
- * Caracas
- * Rio de Janeiro
- * San Jose, Costa Rica
- * Sao Paulo

Middle East
- * Jerusalem

Australia & New Zealand
- Auckland
- Melbourne
- * South Island
- Sydney

China
- Beijing
- Guangzhou
- Shanghai

Japan
- Kyoto
- Nagoya
- Osaka
- Tokyo
- Yokohama

Pacific Rim/Other
- * Bali
- Bangkok
- Hong Kong & Macau
- Manila
- Seoul
- Singapore
- Taipei

* Destinations available by 1/1/95

Fodor's WORLDVIEW Order Form

THIS TRAVEL UPDATE IS FOR (Please print):

Name

Address

City	State	Country	ZIP

Tel # (   )   -   Fax # (   )   -

Title of this Fodor's guide:

Store and location where guide was purchased:

INDICATE YOUR DESTINATIONS/DATES: You can order up to three (3) destinations from the previous page. Fill in your arrival and departure dates for each destination. **Your Travel Update itinerary (all destinations selected) cannot exceed 30 days from beginning to end.**

		Month	Day		Month	Day
(Sample) LONDON	From:	6 /	21	To:	6 /	30
1	From:	/		To:	/	
2	From:	/		To:	/	
3	From:	/		To:	/	

CHOOSE YOUR INTERESTS: Select up to eight (8) categories from the list of interest categories shown on the previous page and circle the numbers below:

1   2   3   4   5   6   7   8   9   10   11   12   13   14   15   16

CHOOSE WHEN YOU WANT YOUR TRAVEL UPDATE DELIVERED (Check one):

❑ Please send my Travel Update immediately.

❑ Please hold my order until a few weeks before my trip to include the most up-to-date information.
Completed orders will be sent within 48 hours. Allow 7-10 days for U.S. mail delivery.

ADD UP YOUR ORDER HERE. *SPECIAL OFFER FOR FODOR'S PURCHASERS ONLY!*

	Suggested Retail Price	Your Price	This Order
First destination ordered	$ 9.95	$ 7.95	$ 7.95
Second destination (if applicable)	$ 6.95	$ 4.95	+
Third destination (if applicable)	$ 6.95	$ 4.95	+

DELIVERY CHARGE (Check one and enter amount below)

	Within U.S. & Canada	Outside U.S. & Canada
First Class Mail	❑ $2.50	❑ $5.00
FAX	❑ $5.00	❑ $10.00
Priority Delivery	❑ $15.00	❑ $27.00

ENTER DELIVERY CHARGE FROM ABOVE: +

TOTAL: $

METHOD OF PAYMENT IN U.S. FUNDS ONLY (Check one):

❑ AmEx   ❑ MC   ❑ Visa   ❑ Discover   ❑ Personal Check (U. S. & Canada only)
❑ Money Order/ International Money Order
Make check or money order payable to: Fodor's Worldview Travel Update

Credit Card —/—/—/—/—/—/—/—/—/—/—/—/—/—/—/—/ **Expiration Date:___/___**

Authorized Signature

SEND THIS COMPLETED FORM WITH PAYMENT TO:
Fodor's Worldview Travel Update, 114 Sansome Street, Suite 700, San Francisco, CA 94104

OR CALL OR FAX US 24-HOURS A DAY
Telephone **1-800-799-9609** • Fax **1-800-799-9619** (From within the U.S. & Canada)
(Outside the U.S. & Canada: Telephone 415-616-9988 • Fax 415-616-9989)

(Please have this guide in front of you when you call so we can verify purchase.)
Code: FTG   Offer valid until 12/31/95.